CITY LIGHTS

CITY LIGHTS

URBAN-SUBURBAN LIFE IN THE GLOBAL SOCIETY

THIRD EDITION

E. Barbara Phillips
SAN FRANCISCO STATE UNIVERSITY

NEW YORK   OXFORD
OXFORD UNIVERSITY PRESS
2010

Oxford University Press, Inc., publishes works that further Oxford University's
objective of excellence in research, scholarship, and education.

Oxford   New York
Auckland   Cape Town   Dar es Salaam   Hong Kong   Karachi
Kuala Lumpur   Madrid   Melbourne   Mexico City   Nairobi
New Delhi   Shanghai   Taipei   Toronto

With offices in
Argentina   Austria   Brazil   Chile   Czech Republic   France   Greece
Guatemala   Hungary   Italy   Japan   Poland   Portugal   Singapore
South Korea   Switzerland   Thailand   Turkey   Ukraine   Vietnam

Published by Oxford University Press, Inc.
198 Madison Avenue, New York, New York 10016
http://www.oup.com

Oxford is a registered trademark of Oxford University Press

Library of Congress Cataloging-in-Publication Data

ISBN 978-0-19-532503-4

Printing number: 9 8 7 6 5 4 3 2 1

Printed in the United States of America
on acid-free paper

Defenceless under the night
Our world in stupor lies;
Yet dotted everywhere,
Ironic points of light
Flash out wherever the just
Exchange their messages:
May I composed like them
Of Eros and of dust,
Beleaguered by the same
Negation and despair,
Show an affirming flame.

W.H. Auden, excerpted from
"September 1, 1939"

CONTENTS

ACKNOWLEDGMENTS

Luckily for me, social science can be a social endeavor. I want to thank colleagues and friends, often one and the same, for sharing their ideas, memories, neighborhoods, and cities with me: Christine and Hugues DaBlanc, Wendy Eloit, José Correa, Martin Gorosh, Mike and Françoise Griffin, Anna and Alan Kolata, Pierre-Yves Maillard, Domnica Melone, Hermine and Antoine Mercadié, Kee Peung, Pamela Radcliff, and Carol Watson. I would also like to thank the reviewers who provided feedback on the second edition:

- Stella M. Čapek, Hendrix College
- Edward J. Jepson, Jr., University of Tennessee
- Michael Innis-Jimenez, William Paterson University
- Elvin Wyly, University of British Columbia
- Harvey K. Newman, Georgia State University
- James Bohland, Virginia Tech University
- Kent Robertson, St. Cloud State University
- Anthony Filopovitch, Minnesota State University-Mankato
- Leonard Ruchelman, Old Dominion University
- Alfreda McCollough, College of Charleston
- Mark Bouman, Chicago State University

Chief among those who have inspired me: Taylor Branch, historian of the U.S. civil rights movement; sociologists of knowledge, Peter Berger and Thomas Luckmann; Gerry Gray, founder of Survivors International and the Center for Justice and Accountability. In a category all by himself is the late Scotty Campbell, once Dean of the Maxwell School at Syracuse University. Scotty, my first professor of matters urban, was a man of action as well as theory. Together, these people exemplify the impact, through theory and/or action, that a few dedicated, savvy people can make to so many.

The late Peter Knauss, Bloke Modisane, Lena, and Martha Levitan influenced my feelings as well as my intellect. The late Theo Steele showed me parts of Paris and San Francisco I had never seen before; that was only one small contribution she made to my appreciation of life in general and Big City Life in particular. My late, dear friend, political sparring partner, and standardbearer for standards, Boston-born Mary Lou FitzGerald, Ph.D. in education and psychoanalysis, reminded me of the strength of urban villages: "I come from a tribal society where autonomy is considered ingratitude." The late Barbara Green Cohen, who called 'em as she saw 'em, was a force of honesty who greatly influenced how I viewed events.

Special thanks to communards at 1043 who cooked, laughed, and talked about ideas at all hours of the day or night. Most especially, I wish to thank Rahsaan Maxwell. For years, he buoyed my spirits, introduced me to hip-hop, great vegetarian cooking, and biodynamic wine. He made me howl at his stories and marvel at his facility for a well-turned phrase. Over a span of six years, Rahsaan earned a doctorate in Political Science from UC Berkeley and became like family.

Were he equipped, Jack la Lang-ue would probably give thanks too—for many a pat while I worked on this book.

Justine Kolata provided a youthful, fresh perspective on things urban and beyond. Her creativity, enthusiasm, and activism to make a better world give me great hope for the future. Likewise, young adult Matthew Spellberg, impassioned by things urban, reminds me that the torch of learning is being carried forth.

Leila May, professor of literature, fabulous Slow Food cook, and so much more, and Don Palmer, professor of philosophy, genial host, and again—so much more—have been a general support system, generous with their knowledge, time, and energy.

I've never met Scott Simon, Terry Gross, Harry Shearer, David Sedaris, or Ira Glass. Nonetheless, their stories on National Public Radio and their voices—full of compassion, intelligence, and wit—often inspired and informed me. They served as regular reminders of the urbane spirit. Another person whom I have never met, Steve Moore of Neilsen Claritas, graciously shared private data, reminding me that sometimes one can depend on the kindness of strangers.

What did a researcher do pre-Internet? A great debt of appreciation for modrin commune-ications, especially e-mail, Amazon.com's "Search Inside" feature, and search engines.

Andrée Abecassis shared wise counsel, wholesome meals, and a make-believe political universe centered on Bradley Whitford, Allison Janney, Janel Moloney and Richard Schiff. Political scientist Rich DeLeon gave me good leads and good advice.

Jackie Hackel and David Rubsamen regularly nourished my mind, soul, and stomach. If a medal for life support were awarded, they would surely be its recipients.

Most of all, I want to honor the memory of my parents, Elaine and Charlie Phillips. They fostered the important illusion that I could (and should) do almost anything, except play cards with strangers. Together, they gave me love, security, appreciation for learning, enthusiasm for city life, and the fearlessness to take on big projects

My greatest appreciation goes to Tim Teninty. His quirky intelligence, quarky humor, and practical skills sustained me. Not to mention that he does Windows (and VISTA). On to the next edition—can stoves be far behind?

INTRODUCTION

The late historian Arthur Schlesinger, Jr., once remarked that there are only two kinds of historians: (1) Those who admit their assumptions and (2) Those who shoot from ambush. This applies to social scientists, too, so I begin by stepping out from behind the bushes. Here are my biases and assumptions relevant to writing—and reading—this book about urban–suburban life in the global society.

WHAT YOU SEE DEPENDS ON HOW YOU LOOK AT IT...

Here is my basic assumption: Nobody has cornered the market on knowledge. No one ideology, intellectual discipline, perspective, or guru has a monopoly on truth.

Indeed, people professing *the truth* or easy answers scare me. To me, a belief in absolutes of truth and virtue is an enemy of the life of the mind.

This enemy may be stronger than ever. According to Susan Jacoby (New York: Pantheon, 2008), we in the United States are living in *The Age of American Unreason*, where anti-intellectualism and anti-rationalism reign.

In my view, the greatest and most characteristic U.S. thinkers have been skeptical, irreverent, pluralistic, and relativistic." In culinary terms, U.S. thought is like meat loaf: Its origins are humble, but it's a tasty mixture of great variability.

In my view, certainty—whether based on theology, ideology, or patriotism—is comforting but dangerous. Certainty leads to closed-mindedness and "dis-enlightenment" (to use no-relation Kevin Phillips's felicitous word).

Sixteenth-century essayist Michel de Montaigne epitomized the spirit of skepticism. For inspiration, Montaigne looked up at the beams in his chateau, where he had written the epigrams of an ancient skeptic: "I decide nothing. I understand nothing. I suspend judgment. I examine." While impossible to live without deciding or judging, these epigrams remind us to face knowledge with a modest attitude.

This book doesn't offer just one way of thinking about an issue. Instead, it aims to show *how* and *why* observers disagree on issues relevant to cities and suburbs: *what* they see, the *meaning* of what they see, and *what to do* about what they see.

...AND HOW YOU DEFINE THE PROBLEM DETERMINES ITS SOLUTION

Take the case of urban poverty. Scholars and citizens don't agree on its causes, nature, or cure. The U.S. president, the mayor of New Orleans, a Christian broadcaster, an urban planner in Bangkok, a Mexican sociologist, a London banker, auto workers in southern China, a socialist, a conservative, a homeless young woman in New York City, and an affluent retiree wherever may have different perspectives on the nature of poverty.

It follows that people of good will may not agree on how to attack poverty. If, for instance, a mayor sees the root problem as lack of money, she may fight for government funds. Or mayors may offer incentives to multinational corporations to settle in their jurisdictions, arguing that these businesses will provide jobs and a bigger tax base for the community. But if mayors define poverty as being rooted in the unequal distribution of existing resources, they will pursue very different policies—ones aimed at changing institutional structures and redistributing wealth. If citizens believe that poverty and despair are products of a government-sponsored ghetto culture, they will try to protest. In sum, there is no one right way to define an urban or suburban issue.

However, *how people define a problem determines how they try to solve it. Or ignore it.* Here is an example: climate change. According to many observers, global warming will shift the world's balance of power and money, affecting some cities more than others. Coastal cities all over the world could be abandoned. Industry could feel various impacts: wine making, for one, could be transformed—grapes might grow in now cold climates but no longer near Bordeaux, France. For some, global warming is also a human-rights issue. Inuit activist and Nobel Peace Prize nominee Sheila Watt-Cloutier, for one, says that in her own lifetime effects of climate change have threatened her community's livelihood and cultural identity. And, for Nobel Prize–winning physicist Stephen Chu (and Obama's Energy Secretary), global warming and its twin problem—the need for carbon-neutral renewable sources of energy—are science's greatest challenges today.

Opinions can change. And fast. For instance, a nationwide poll released in April 2007 showed that one-third of the people in the United States thought that global warming was the world's single largest environmental problem, *twice* the percentage polled just one year before.

Yet, there is no unanimity on the issue. Indeed, some think global warming is not a problem at all. Some contend that it is the *fear* of global warming that is dangerous. Conservative columnist George F. Will, for one, suggests (in *Newsweek*, October 22, 2007:68) that "the damage to global economic growth [that anti-warming measures] could cause in this century [might well cause] more preventable death and suffering than

was caused in the last century by Hitler, Stalin, Mao, and Pol Pot combined."

Some, including some evangelical Christians, think that global warming is either (1) a distraction from "real" issues such as abortion and same-sex marriage, (2) a sign of the coming Apocalypse, or (3) a plot by leftists to encourage world government (of which they disapprove).

In *America (The Book)*, faux newscaster-comic Jon Stewart and his fellow editors, Ben Karlin and David Javerbaum (New York: Warner Books, 2006), list various explanations for the rise of global temperature, expected to be about 1.2 degrees every 10 years. They range from "an angry sun" and "the Great Barbecue Craze of 2065" to "cow flatulence" (168).

Some warn that one aspect of global warming is scarier than potential terrorism: international insecurity. Many, including Peter Schwartz, a co-founder of the Global Business Network, point to water shortages in many nations—resulting in part from global warming—that can potentially cause uncountable deaths, widespread unrest, economic shifts, and social disaster (http://www.gbn.com/articles/pdfs/GBN%20 Bulletin_Winter%202009.pdf).

The upshot is clear. In a brief time, global warming changed from nonproblem to problem. (Indeed, some think that environmental issues such as possible climate change could serve to unite people globally—whatever their station in life.)

To conclude: In my view, defining an issue (e.g., climate change) affecting our urban world is problematic. Thus, I see my task as laying out appropriate ways of thinking about an issue, not as peddling a particular point of view. At the same time, I don't believe that all perspectives on the urban world are equally valid. For instance, I reject the idea that poor people are poor because they're lazy or stupid.

Note: Many topics discussed here, such as global warming, water availability, and food policy, are not specifically "urban" issues. But, in my view, such issues impact urban–suburban life today to an extraordinary extent: The global majority of us humans now live in urban places. As discussed in Chapter 2, I subscribe to the *urban-schmurban* stance. That is, in an interdependent world, urban–suburban life cannot be separated from national and international life.

Fig. A WHAT'S THE PROBLEM HERE? It all depends on how you see it. Chapters 2 and 3 detail how and why scholars and citizens disagree on what causes urban slums, such as these in Taichung, Taiwan. (Martin Gorosh)

USE YOUR IMAGINATION!

Focus on these real-life situations:

1. A 59-member Cultural Affairs Task Force—representing virtually every ethnic, artistic, and interest group in San Francisco—must come to some agreement on how millions of city dollars should be spent on local arts projects.
2. Sociology students complain that the person picked to teach urban-oriented courses in their department is a white, middle-class man, who is incapable of understanding poor, nonwhite minorities and, thus, incompetent to lecture on race and class in the United States. They demand that someone else be hired.

At the heart of both cases are controversial issues of politics, epistemology, and cross-cultural communication. Particularly relevant here is the challenge of understanding and fairly representing people unlike ourselves.

Is it possible? Some think not. They subscribe to the *Insider-as-Insighter* doctrine: You have to be one to understand one. That is, outsiders cannot truly understand insiders. This doctrine holds that individuals have a monopoly on knowledge or privileged access to understanding by virtue of their group membership or social position, or lack of it. In other words, the Insider doctrine holds that *only* African Americans can really understand African American history, *only* women can truly understand sexual harassment of women, *only* soldiers are capable of knowing the complex emotions of fighting a war, and so on.

But many scholars reject the notion that you have to "be one to understand one." Indeed, some denigrate writing about one's own groups as mere "mesearch."

While the principle remains controversial, many (if not most) writers and scholars believe that they *can* come to understand people unlike themselves. In this view, a Vietnamese Buddhist researcher *can* come to understand Native American history. Likewise, a 5 foot 2 inch–tall female sociologist *can* develop comprehension of male-bonding rituals among basketball players.

I agree with Henry Louis "Skip" Gates, Jr., then chair of Harvard's Afro-American Studies Department, who said years ago that being in the academy means having the freedom to examine other cultures with energy. In other words, you don't have to *be* part of what you're studying.

In my view, one strand of the Insider doctrine—the notion that race/ethnicity or religion is a person's defining characteristic—is not only wrongheaded but dangerous. First, it is rooted in the white European subjugation of colonial peoples, using their race or non-Christian beliefs as a justification for domination. For example, white Europeans claimed their mission was to "civilize" pagan or Muslim Africans. Second, it wrongly assumes homogeneity. Take, for example, the notion of *one* "African culture." British-Ghanaian-American Kwame Anthony Appiah, a philosopher and professor, reminds us that the idea of a single African culture is pure fiction—a social construction of nineteenth-century European colonialists. Africans do not share a single culture, race, religion, or color. There are hundreds of different African cultures. Indeed, African Americans do not share one culture either. When Senator Barack Obama (D-Ill.) announced his candidacy for U.S. president in 2007 (and after), he faced suspicion from some African Americans on the basis of his family and background.

The idea of race/ethnicity or religion as a defining characteristic can be seductive—but deadly. For anyone who seeks community in an uncertain world, it is a way to distinguish "us" from "them." Yet, hate and murder are the flip sides of brotherhood and sisterhood.

There seems to be no shortage of hate and loathing by insiders toward outsiders. A few place names—Darfur, Rwanda, Nazi Germany, and Baghdad—remind us of the sometimes deadly bonds of kinship.

In my own research, I polled journalists on this issue of Insiders-as-Insighters. Overwhelmingly (97 per-

cent), they rejected the Insider doctrine. My guess is that the vast majority of social scientists would also reject it. Why? (1) Social scientists would be reduced to conducting research *only* about people like themselves. This means that a male Catholic social psychologist could not conduct research concerning homeless females or the aspirations of Muslim children in Dearborn, Michigan. (2) Many social scientists argue that empathy and imagination can help outsiders in their struggle to understand insiders. This is my hope.

I think we can, to a significant degree, get inside the shoes and heads of human beings unlike ourselves. Here are a few ways. First, *doing or reading fieldwork studies* that immerse us in the culture of the insider group. The work of sociologist Löic Wacquant is exemplary. Wacquant, a white, middle-class Frenchman, came to Chicago to study the city's African American ghettos. As a grad student at the University of Chicago, Wacquant joined a (now defunct) boxing gym on the city's South Side in order to better understand the lives of those he intended to study. (*Note*: While doing his fieldwork, Wacquant, nicknamed "Busy Louie" by his boxing buddies, became good enough to compete in the Golden Gloves boxing tournament.) In *Body & Soul: Notebooks of an Apprentice Boxer* (New York: Oxford University Press, 2003), Wacquant brings to life the pain and sweat of boxing as well as the fighters' gritty camaraderie. His ethnography shows that the boxers themselves interpret what they do as both a manly craft and an escape from the harshness and temptations of the mean streets around them. Probably, most readers have never visited a boxing gym in a seamy section of a big city. Yet, via Wacquant's ethnography, they can feel what it's like to live in this subculture. (*Note*: In example 2, it was Wacquant who was the subject of grad student protests when he was being considered for employment at the University of California at Berkeley some years ago.)

Second, *taking an open heart and mind on the road.* Entering unfamiliar territory with a nonjudgmental spirit can lead to experiencing another culture or subculture from the inside out. Often, strangers or acquaintances are happy to share their stories—if only we ask them!

Third, *reading, watching, and listening to people's stories* that allow us to experience the colors and texture of a way of life or historical period. Stories, such as those on Ira Glass's National Public Radio (NPR) and TV series *This American Life*, give people a taste of what it's like to walk in the shoes of another person.

Likewise, artworks introduce us to worlds that may lie beyond our own experience. Here are just a few examples: The solo theatrical piece, *No Child...*, written and performed by Nilaja Sun (2006), portrays a multiethnic Bronx high school classroom; it brings a range of students and teachers vividly to life. The Oscar-winning film *Crash* (2005) tells complex stories of prejudice based on appearance, class, ethnicity, sexual orientation, and more. As movie critic Roger Ebert put it, anyone seeing *Crash* "is likely to leave with a little more sympathy for people not like themselves."

Asked about acting the role of a straight woman in a movie love scene, comedienne Lily Tomlin, a lesbian, expressed her rejection of the Insider-as-Insighter doctrine with these immortal words: "You don't have to be one to play one (in Jennifer Reed,2009, Lily: Sold out", Genders online, 49 http://www.genders.org/g49/g49_reed.html." Historian Taylor Branch expressed a related sentiment in *Parting the Waters* (1988: xii,New York: Touchstone), his Pulitzer Prize–winning study of the U.S. civil rights movement: "Truth requires a maximum effort to see through the eyes of strangers, foreigners, and enemies."

Indeed, some of the most thought-provoking studies of any society come from outsiders. *Democracy in America* (two volumes: 1835 and 1840) by the nineteenth-century French visitor Alexis de Tocqueville is a prime example. Another outsider, Taiwanese-born Ang Lee, is the Oscar-winning director of *Brokeback Mountain* (2005). Lee attended grad school in the United States and stayed to make films. His biculturalism, Lee says, helped him to explore American cultural icons, including cowboys. According to Lee, his vision is rooted in his outsiderness (*San Francisco Chronicle*, December 30, 2005:E8): "I didn't grow up here, so I don't know the metaphors, the subtleties. I just dive in. And that makes my perspective somewhat rare and fresh. It takes a foreign director to shoot that way, with that way of looking at things."

Why do people from other cultures such as de Tocqueville and Lee offer a fresh perspective? *Perhaps marginal people make better spies.* Outsiders (and comedians, among others, who often feel like outsiders in their own culture) often see what insiders dismiss as "natural."

Starting in Chapter 1, there are many references to fieldwork and artwork, from blogs and scholarly papers to murals. Hopefully, they will stimulate the imagination, helping you to reach beyond self and to experience a wider range of people and ways of life.

A cautionary note: Let's not confuse real experience with secondhand experience. Claude Brown's 1965 classic *Manchild in the Promised Land* ([1965]1999 New York: Touchstone) illustrates the possibility for such confusion. *Manchild* is an autobiographical novel of a Harlem, New York, childhood amid killers, drug addicts, and prostitutes. Novelist Norman Mailer praised *Manchild*'s raw narrative's ability to turn him, Mailer—an outsider—into an insider. As reported by Carlo Rotella in his 1998 book, *October Cities: The Redevelopment of Urban Literature* (Berkeley, Los Angeles, Oxford: University of California Press), Mailer said that Brown's classic book gave him an idea of what it would be like on a daily basis had he grown up in Harlem But another, less well-known reviewer, writing in the magazine *America* (1965:12), registered his fear: Readers would be mere "tourists, slummers, [and] spectators" in Harlem. The reviewer also warned that *Manchild* might be a painless substitute for "real experience": "Most of us who did not grow up in Harlem rely on novelists and journalists to have our experiences for us and pass them on, painlessly, into our lives."

Lastly, "real experience" is variable, so variable that two people witnessing the same event may experience and describe it differently. (Crime-show devotees and defense lawyers know this well: Eyewitness *misidentification* is a prime cause of wrongful incarceration.) Thus, both firsthand and secondhand experiences should be evaluated, not automatically accepted.

The following questions are often useful to ask: Does the observer or reporter have a private agenda? Who is funding the project? What are the underlying assumptions of the observer? How good an observer is the reporter? Not easy questions to answer.

BEWARE "SELF-EVIDENT TRUTHS"

Overall, the general tone of this book is tentative. As poet William Blake wrote in 1793 (in *Marriage of Heaven and Hell*), "What is now proved, was once only imagined." He might have added that *what now seems self-evident truth may be considered mere nonsense in 100 years... or maybe just 10 minutes!*

We live in a mostly changing world. And fast-changing at that! Just a few years ago, very few social scientists, politicians, or poets predicted—or imagined—the "financial tsunami" that hit the United States first, then had global repercussions in 2008. Similarly, neither the resurgence of Russia nor the political–economic influence of traffickers in a global, criminal political economy were widely predicted. In other words, much of what we think we know about reality may soon be obsolete.

Deeply-held ideas can change quickly too. Take, for instance, an idea long held by many Catholics: limbo. In 2005, the *New York Times* ran a headline summing up the change: "Church tradition of limbo heading for, well, limbo" (Ian Fisher, December 27).

Sometimes, time turns the unimaginable into the commonplace. Before the 1980s, for example, a few homeless persons camped out on U.S. city streets, but they were a rare sight. By 2005, an estimated 744,000 to 3.5 million people in the United States experienced homelessness. Estimates of homelessness differ widely—counting people without permanent addresses is an inexact process. Yet one thing is clear: In just decades and in many places, homelessness became ordinary, not extraordinary—so ordinary that it was not even mentioned by the leading candidates for U.S. president in 2007–2008.

And time often reveals new information that changes our interpretation of "facts." Here's an example close to home: In the first edition of this text, I wrote about the Tasaday, a "small Stone Age tribe living in a Philippine rain forest" who "apparently live a conflict-free existence. Some observers, particularly John Nance, portrayed the Tasaday as living in a garden of Eden." But shortly after Ferdinand Marcos was toppled from power in Manila, the "garden of Eden" was exposed as a hoax. Apparently (an important word!), Marcos's minister of culture, an American-trained anthropologist, had paid a small number of people to *act* like a Stone Age tribe. When this minister of culture left government, the Tasaday walked out of their caves because they no longer got paid! Yet, the truth remains elusive. Many respected scholars think

that the situation is much more complicated, and that the Tasaday were not paid actors.

In addition, things that seem self-evident often aren't. Take bottled water. In the United States, it is generally assumed that bottled water is more healthful than tap water. That is why many seeking to be physically fit pay for water instead of getting it from their tap. However, several brands of California bottled water were recalled a few years ago; they contained dangerous chemicals. In 2006, trace amounts of dangerous Teflon were found in Ohioans' bottled water. And it was revealed in 2007 that a best-selling bottled water is mere tap water.

Furthermore, what's obvious to one person isn't to another. Take my own case. I had assumed that violent TV shows are antisocial. Thus, it came as a shock when students in my Mass Media class found that their survey respondents who watched TV shows with multiple murders and beatings didn't see these shows as violent. Why? Because they focused on the respect and friendship between and among the police officers, that is, the shows' *non*violent aspects.

Let us remain cautious for yet another reason: *The future is unpredictable.* Natural and human-helped disasters as well as technological shifts can prove experts very wrong, very quickly.

Given this skepticism about the "obvious," as well as a commitment to tentative truths and multiple perspectives, I don't provide definitive answers to anything you may have wanted to know about cities, suburbs, or postsuburbia. Nor do I offer a checklist for measuring the quality of city life, although it would be instructive to analyze the assumptions that underlie such value-laden lists. Likewise, I do not promote one particular public policy for dealing with the use/abuse of substances defined as drugs, although I note that the definition of "drug" changes, depending upon the time, place, and usership.

My hope is that this book will help readers to choose more intelligently for themselves among competing claims and truths—and value-loaded statements—about how cities and suburbs do and should work. Alas, there are no easy routes. *We spend our entire lives sifting sense from nonsense, trying to decide which is which.*

Hopefully, we keep on questioning deeply-held opinions, constantly altering our perspective on life.

Easy to say, but harder to do for many of us with each new candle on the birthday cake. New information or experience can lead to a reexamination of our taken-for-granted notions about how the world works. But most of us have an emotional investment in continuity. This can prevent a rethink.

To encourage a re-examination of basic assumptions, here I present (1) information—ammunition for asking better questions about city life—and (2) concepts, visions, and frameworks to better understand information about cities. But note: Psychologists say that new information *alone* is not enough to jar us into rethinking what we hold as true.

THE PLACE OF URBAN "PROBLEMS"

Do urban and suburban problems really exist? A strange question? Perhaps, but nobody talked about "problems" until the twentieth century. People did speak about disagreeable, even despicable, urban conditions and conflicts, but the idea of clearly definable urban problems is recent. Such talk came into style in the early twentieth century as social scientists, eager to play the role of social doctors, began to apply medical language to the city: A city was compared to the human body. Just as people had diseases, complete with symptoms and (under a doctor's care) cures, cities had problems that could be cured.

It is now common to hear a city (or suburb) diagnosed as "healthy" or "sick." I avoid this medical terminology for several reasons.

First, talk of sick cities or suburbs masks an important idea: *There is no agreement on what constitutes an urban (or suburban) problem.* What gets defined as a metropolitan problem depends basically on two factors: (1) who's doing the talking and (2) the intellectual–political fashion of the times.

Fig. B DRUGS ARE GARBAGE. Does the La Jolla, California, sanitation company mean *legal* drugs–like alcohol and cigarettes? Presumably not. But the definition of what's legal or what's a drug can change. For example, in the 1920s alcohol was illegal in the United States. In 1994 the American Medical Association and some federal officials redefined cigarettes as addictive drugs, due to their nicotine content. *How* a substance is defined determines how public policy deals with it. Chapter 12 examines "the definition of the situation," and Chapter 19 looks at the various approaches to "solving" poverty. (Tim Teninty)

Let's take two examples. The first—San Diego wildfires—considers the disagreement on the nature of the "problem." The second, coca, shows how a nonproblem can turn into a problem.

1. When homes and wildlife habitat around San Diego, California, went up in smoke in October 2007, some blamed nature: Santa Ana winds combined with bone-dry weather. Others blamed nature plus a few arsonists. Still others blamed fire officials in part, particularly their long-standing policy not to thin forests. (Months later, a report by the California Public Utilities Commission named improperly maintained electrical lines as the cause in three of the most destructive wind-fed fires.) But a few pointed the finger at very different culprits: developers, politicians, and posh gated communities built on hilltops that cost taxpayers vast sums to protect. Iconoclast Mike Davis, for one, expressed this view. To Davis, the essential problem leading to the wildfires was land use: "the rampant, uncontrolled proliferation of firebelt suburbs." The chief architect of San Diego's land development, says Davis, was former San Diego mayor (and later California governor) Pete Wilson: as mayor, Wilson crafted "an enduring system of trade-offs, elite alliances, and sleights of hand that has simultaneously gentrified the downtown area at the expense of the poor and overrun much of San Diego's countryside with pyrophiliac gated suburbs and elite estates" (http://www.tomdispatch.com/post/174857/mike_davis_who_really_set_the_california_fires_cf).

Most observers made no such connection between the San Diego wildfires and local land-use policy. In other words, for most, land use in the San Diego area was a nonproblem.

2. Coca has long been used around the world for religious rituals and medicine. (Scholars say that coca, in the form of cocaine, was introduced to Europe in the 1500s.) In the United States there was an epidemic of cocaine and narcotics use from 1885 to 1920, but it was not defined as a "problem." So when did cocaine become a "problem" in the United States? At about the time that it spread from lower-class, ethnic neighborhoods to affluent metropolitan homes.

Furthermore, I avoid talk and pictures of urban "problems" because I have found that such talk encourages one-sided views of urban life. Indeed, my students at San Francisco State University found that the majority of grade-school students in suburban schools did not want to visit nearby San Francisco because, paraphrasing the responses, they feared crime, grime, and slime. And where did these young people get such antiurban notions? Mainly from family and the mass media.

Also, the *perception* of "problems" can change, often in a flash. Consider homelessness. Urban homelessness in the United States was a key issue in the 1988 presidential primaries. By 1992, homelessness as an issue had virtually disappeared from public debate, even as it increased dramatically. It has not returned to serious public debate since.

Furthermore, one person's "problem" can be insignificant to someone else. One issue demonstrates this truism: whether or not to add fluoride to the public drinking supply in order to prevent tooth decay. Around 1950, this was front-page news in many U.S. towns, particularly in the South. (Even today, fluoridation remains controversial in some quarters.) Some viewed fluoridation as government meddling into private decisions or, worse, a Communist plot. Others disputed the science behind its effectiveness. Meanwhile, other possible "problems," including racial segregation, racism, poverty, and hunger, were not on the public agenda; they were "nonproblems," at least on the pages of most U.S. newspapers.

The opposite can also occur. Sociologist Barry Glassner examines what he considers nonproblems hyped by the mass media, including "road rage" and "Internet addiction" (see *The Culture of Fear: Why Americans Are Afraid of the Wrong Things* [New York: Basic Books, 2000]).

No one can predict with certainty what the future holds. For example, secondhand cigarette smoke was not defined as a "problem" in the United States until the 1970s or in Europe until the 1990s.

In another redefinition, an old form of crime in the United States got a new name a generation ago: "hate crime" (the victimization of an individual based on his or her race, religion, national orientation, or disability status). As of 2006, 46 U.S. states and the District of Columbia had hate-crime laws, and anti-hate-crime ordinances at the city level have increased in recent years. (In the United States, there are more than 190,000 such incidents each year, motivated mainly by racial bias.)

In recent years, some have redefined the global food supply as problematic. The "problem" has many facets, including the price, availability, and safety of food. (*Note*: Typically, in the United States, genetically-altered foods are not defined as a problem; the opposite is true in most of Europe.)

In the United States, Alice Waters has led the charge to change diets and values about food. Waters, creator of the world-famous restaurant Chez Panisse in Berkeley, California, agrees with Anthelme Brillat-Savarin, author of *The Physiology of Taste: Or Meditations on Transcendental Gastronomy*. In 1825 Brillat-Savarin wrote in his preface translated into English in 1949 by M.F. K. Fisher, the most renowened foodie of her generation), "the destiny of nations depends on the manner in which they are fed."

Like Brillat-Savarin, Waters thinks that food is destiny. Every decision we make about food has personal and global repercussions, including individual and national health, soil depletion, water and air pollution, the loss of rural communities, and even global warming. She asks people to consider that today almost 4 billion people worldwide depend on the agricultural sector for their livelihood ("Slow Food Nation," August 24, 2006, http://www.thenation.com/doc/20060911/waters.

Scholar Raj Patel takes a related tack in *Stuffed and Starved: The Hidden Battle for the World Food System* (Brooklyn, NY: Melville Books [2007] 2008). According to Patel, one-half the world is malnourished and the other half is obese. Both, he argues, are symptoms of a global, corporate food monopoly.

Now, back to the constantly changing perceptions of "problems." What conditions are *not* defined as problems? That's harder to determine. Why? Because if a condition isn't highlighted in the media, discussed in classes, or mulled over with family and friends, it doesn't reach the public agenda of *what* to think about

or *how* to think about it. For example, those of us who are not homeless rarely (if ever) think about the less obvious downsides of life on the streets, including the lack of an address and the consequent inaccessibility to potential employers.

Thus, for all the above reasons, a number of issues affecting our urban world are discussed in this book, but the discussion is *not* organized around so-called problems—which brings us to my next assumption.

IT'S A SMALL, SMALL WORLD: URBAN-GLOBAL INTERLOCK

One word—a place name—reminds us that it's a small, small world: Chernobyl. In 1986, a nuclear reactor exploded in Chernobyl, a town in the former Soviet Union. Over 135,000 people were evacuated from their homes, but the danger of radiation did not stop at Chernobyl's city limits. Hundreds of miles away in Lapland, many reindeer had to be destroyed because their meat was contaminated. Vegetables and milk in Germany also suffered contamination.

Chernobyl reminds us that radioactive fallout does not use a passport. Neither do toxic waste and tsunamis. Or the AIDS virus, cocaine, avian bird flu, severe acute respiratory syndrome (SARS), tainted pet food, or valuable information. Earthly boundaries—city, state, region, province, or nation—can't contain environmental hazards or nuggets of knowledge.

Individual destinies have long been tied to faraway strangers. Such ties can be beneficial. Or lethal. Take the 2007 case of a poisonous, sweet solvent sold by counterfeiters, mixed into drugs, and implicated in mass poisonings around the world.

Being connected to the global economy and culture can have benefits as well as risks. For example, money in the form of remittances sent home by massive numbers of workers in the Persian Gulf from south India's Kerala is carrying the entire economy of Kerala; otherwise, an Indian demographer says, people in Kerala would have starved to death (Rajan in Jason DeParle, "Jobs Abroad Support 'Model' State in India," September 7, 2007: http://www.nytimes.com/2007/09/07/world/asia/07migrate.html?th&emc=th).

To the contrary, the city of Bissau (West Africa's capital of Guinea-Bissau) has become a valuable

Fig. C EVEN THE LONELIEST TOWN IS NOT ALONE. Far from the madding crowds, residents of tiny Eureka, Nevada, may not think about the impact of national or global policies on their daily lives. Yet their well-being may hinge on decisions made far away by corporate and government officials, including those who authorized atomic-test blasts in Nevada (affecting cancer rates), those who negotiate international-trade agreements (affecting the price of nearby metals), and those who decide where to construct theme parks (affecting land values, employment, etc.). Chapters 5, 7, and 13 detail some local–international connections in the global village. Chapter 15 discusses electronic forms of citizen input that may bring Eurekans a louder voice in decision making. Chapter 18 examines the fate of one U.S. small town that experienced technological change and why "good citizens" there suffered most. (Tim Teninty)

stopover for Colombian cocaine bound for Europe, exposing locals to new forms of addiction and mayhem. Some may prosper there, but others suffer the consequences of the globalized drug trade.

Many of us in rich, powerful countries may not appreciate the links between public policies and the fates of faraway strangers. Take, for instance, the impacts on jobs and children at U.S. military bases in the Philippines. (1) Jobs were created when a U.S. Air Force base was built in Angeles. When the base was abandoned in the early 1990s after the eruption of a nearby volcano, Angeles became a ghost town and

unemployment soared. (2) When a U.S. naval base was abandoned in 1992, so were some 10,000 Amerasian children, thrown away "like a spoiled napkin" (in the words of an Irish priest there) by their American servicemen fathers. These children lived without sanitation or running water in the filthy slums of Olongapo, a dusty town near the former naval base that existed to serve the sailors' pleasure. (Olongapo has since become a tourist mecca, with beaches and the wrecks of U.S. battleships as major attractions.)

Businesses can also impact foreigners' fates and foreign policy. Yahoo, for example, handed over

Fig. D GLOBALIZATION OF STYLES AND COMMUNICATION. A section of Cairo, Egypt, where TV satellite dishes—bringing the wider world to viewers—dot the landscape. (Susan Hoehn)

e-mails and the IP address of a Chinese dissident journalist and Yahoo user, Shi Tao, to China's secret police in 2006. On the basis of the information given by Yahoo to China, Tao was later imprisoned for 10 years.

Outsourcing, whether to Bengaluru (formerly Bangalore), India, or Mexican border towns, has also had widespread impacts on both U.S. and foreign lives. Consider many Mexican border towns, such as Ciudad Juarez, whose population exploded as a result of U.S. corporate decisions to locate *maquiladoras* (light assembly factories, often called "sweatshops") there. Even before 1994, when Canada, the United States, and Mexico launched the North American Free Trade Agreement (NAFTA), new jobs

were created in border towns. Since then, Reynosa, Matamoras, and other border towns have attracted Americans as well as Mexicans, greatly changing the local social structure: Mexicans mainly work at low-wage assembly-line jobs and live in sprawling slums. But people from north of the border work in higher-wage management and engineering jobs and live in new suburbs.

The flip side of production is consumption and the trend to internationalize markets. Zara clothing stores, owned by a Spanish firm, exemplifies this trend: Zara opened a store a day somewhere in the world during one recent year.

With the internationalization of markets, seemingly unrelated events can have serious cross-border consequences. Take the price of tortillas. In Mexico, tortilla prices rose about 60 percent in 2006, particularly hurting low-income consumers who depend on corn as their basic food. How did this happen? The exact relationship between the spike in tortilla prices in Mexico and corn prices in the United States remains murky. But a business professor at the University of California–Irvine says that "The price of oil is driving up the price of corn [due to increased ethanol production] which drives up the price of tortillas" (Peter Navarro in "Nothing Flat About Tortilla Prices," *San Francisco Chronicle*, January 13, 2007:C1).

Similarly, the perceived strength or weakness of the U.S. economy affects jobs and more—elsewhere. For example, as a *Wall Street Journal* headline put it, "Latin America Feels Pain of U.S. Housing Slump" (April 23, 2007:A2). Reporter Joel Millman wrote that the U.S. housing slump affects Mexicans in two ways: (1) less money going south in the form of remittances due to layoffs in the construction industry (Mexican workers used to send an estimated $600 million a year more back to Mexico) and (2) fewer Mexicans trying to cross the border illegally. According to Millman, "The Bush administration claims the decrease [in illegal border crossings] is because of tighter border security." But those on the Mexican side say illegal traffic has slowed for another reason: "fewer jobs waiting for those who make it across."

To conclude: More and more, there is no hiding place. Maps still divide the world by countries, but national frontiers mean fewer and fewer. First, borders are often porous and easily crossed. This applies to tourists and terrorists as well as economic refugees. Second, many nations are composed of people with separate cultural backgrounds, thus complicating the notion of a specific "national identity."

Increasingly, what happens in a distant corner of the globe has serious *local* impacts. Following are some examples. Furniture factories outside Wenzhou, China, fell victim in 2008 to a housing crisis half a world away which slowed U.S. demand for their beds and bookcases. In 2009, Tucson, Arizona, suffered kidnappings, among other things, as Mexico's drug cartels crossed the border. In other words, the whole world is becoming a single economic and ecological unit.

Many so-called local issues, in my view, are national or international in scope. *Cities and companies almost everywhere are part of a global economic system.* This global system operates via electronic communication on a 24/7 basis.

In this 24/7 borderless world, managers and owners of planetary enterprises do not put patriotism at the top of their value list. Instead, they tend to focus on the bottom line, despite the impact their policies have on nations, let alone cities.

Moving offshore exemplifies the triumph of the bottom line over flag waving. Legally, a company can move where legal liability or U.S. taxes do not apply. This is the case of once-Houston-based Halliburton, a private company and energy giant (and a controversial U.S. defense contractor). It announced in 2007 that it was moving its corporate headquarters from Texas to Dubai in the United Arab Emirates.

Offshoring, outsourcing, and worldwide competition impact workers and owners everywhere—but some more than others. Take Italy, for example. Italian mom-and-pop manufacturers, like those in the foothill town of Lumezzane, were the secret of Italy's economic success less than a generation ago. But Lumezzane's family-owned brass-valve factories can no longer compete with valves marked "Made in China." Neither can many other family-owned manufacturers throughout Italy that produce everything from brass valves to fancy buttons. Because Italy's economy depends, to a greater extent than its European neighbors, on manufacturing goods in small, family-run companies, it has been harder hit than, say, France in the global reshuffling of production.

In this global system, multinational corporations often act like private governments. Specifically, multinationals control vast resources and private communication systems, employ intelligence experts, and make decisions that affect who gets what all over the globe. Unlike most citizens everywhere, however, multinational top brass and owners salute no flag. As an executive of a multinational told a *New York Times* reporter years ago, "We at NCR think of ourselves as a globally competitive company that happens to be headquartered in the U.S. (in Louis Uchitelle, March 26, 1989 "Spread of U.S. Plants abroad Is slowing exports." (http://www.nytimes.com/1989/03/26/us/

spread-of-us-plants-abroad-is-slowing-exports.html?s
ec=&spon=&pagewanted=all).

"And for good reason too. Like many U.S.-based multinationals, the largest percentage of NCR's reported revenue at the time came from non-U.S. sources.

In other words, flag waving counts for little to global businesses. Particularly if vast riches are at stake. The tale of two cities—Washington, D.C., and Redmond, Washington—is instructive. (This tale also suggests how much clout private companies like Microsoft carry in the global economy.) When Chinese President Hu Jintao came to the United States in April 2006, he dined with President George W. Bush in Washington, D.C. The two top leaders reportedly discussed U.S. hopes for revaluing upward the Chinese yuan and liberalizing Chinese human-rights policies, but nothing concrete came out of this meeting. In contrast, Bill Gates, then-Microsoft's CEO and one of the world's richest persons, dined with the Chinese president in Redmond, Washington. Shortly after, Microsoft announced plans to spend $900 million in China, purchasing computer hardware and investing in Chinese software companies. (Earlier, Chinese computer maker Lenovo had promised it would preinstall Microsoft Windows on its new PC, a deal that could net Microsoft about $1.2 billion in sales and help curb rampant software piracy in China.)

Telecommunications, of course, is but one global industry dominated by multinationals. Another is coffee, an $80-billion industry and the world's most valuable trading commodity after oil. According to a documentary shown at the Sundance Film Festival, *Black Gold* (2006), produced by Fulcrum Productions and directed by Mark Francis and Nick Francis, the profits from espressos and cappuccinos are hardly shared with farmers who make it all possible.

Is it possible for nations—let alone citizens' groups or local governments—to reassert significant economic authority in the global system of multinationals like Microsoft and Wal-Mart and multinational criminal gangs? Most observers think not. Indeed, some claim that global markets boss nations around. That is why James Carville, a political strategist and one-time Bill Clinton advisor, once quipped that if reincarnated, he'd like to come back as the bond market because it

gets whatever it wants. That is, the bond market "can intimidate everybody." (in Niall Ferguson, *The Ascent of Money*, 2008, New York: Penguin). Years ago, a *New York Times* headline put it like this: "When Money Talks, Government Listens: Who Runs the World? In Many Ways, the Global Markets Do" (July 24, 1994, E3). More recently, both the Bush and Obama administrations decided to use billions of taxpayer dollars to bail out banks and investment firms at the heart of "the markets."

Given the importance of "the markets" and government intervention in them, how can ordinary citizens assert control over their governments and their own daily lives? This is a key question. But it is so difficult to answer that it may drive many of us to seek out easy answers!

This book offers a range of responses—*not easy answers*—from electronic participation (Chapter 15) and local ordinances (Chapter 13) to a search for community (Chapter 6). It also pays a great deal of attention to two important forces, often in conflict, that are chipping away at both the nation-state and democratic citizenship: (1) ethnic and/or religious fundamentalism and (2) global capitalism. These opposing forces, called "jihad vs. McWorld" by political scientist Benjamin R. Barber in his 1996 book of the same name(New York: Ballantine), are highlighted here in several places, including Chapter 5 (the world urban system) and Chapter 10 (global identity and cosmopolitanism versus the pull of "lesser loyalties").

"INTERMESTIC" ISSUES

I have been arguing that, in our global society, it is impossible to separate domestic from international issues. To borrow political scientist Ken Jowitt's term, we have a mesh of "intermestic" issues: issues that are simultaneously domestic and international.

This intermestic mesh was made crystal clear in fall 2008: Global markets stumbled after the United States's Dow Jones industrial average dropped more than 1,000 points. Later, stock markets from Mumbai to New York plunged as the U.S. "credit crisis" worsened. (As noted in Chapter 3, different observers point to different reasons for the economic "meltdowns.")

Of course, tax coffers are also affected by intermestic issues. For example, companies operating outside their home countries may avoid paying some taxes at home.

Here is a not-as-obvious intermestic issue: food safety. (1) In 2003, a Washington State dairy cow was found to have mad cow disease. Japan, the largest foreign consumer of U.S. beef, stopped buying U.S. beef. For two years, until the ban was lifted, the Japanese market for U.S. beef, valued at about $1.4 billion annually, dried up. (2) The U.S. Food and Drug Administration (FDA) received more than 10,000 complaints about tainted pet food in early 2007. Apparently, contaminated wheat gluten from China was found in dog and cat food sold in stores across the United States, and many pets fed the tainted food died of kidney failure. Later, the tainted food was fed to hogs in several U.S. states, and officials worried that the human food chain had been affected. This highlights the reality of a global food chain.

That crucial issues cross national boundaries has long been recognized by global leaders. Each year since 1971, for example, business, political, intellectual, and technological leaders meet in the Swiss mountains at Davos for the World Economic Forum, where they discuss intermestic issues. In 2007, the annual conference of world leaders at Davos (mainly from richer countries) considered the growing digital divide between rich and poor countries as well as the challenge of climate change, among other issues. (In 2009, by contrast, many participants focused on what they called "U.S.-style capitalism" or neoliberalism as a major cause of the global economic downturn.)

Since 2001, an alternative globalization movement—the antithesis of the Davos forum—the World Social Forum also has met regularly. "A Better World Is Possible" (via democratic, global institutions) is its mantra. Unlike the Davos leaders, participants represent the interests of citizens of poor countries and meet in poorer places, such as Porto Alegre, Brazil. Its charter states that the World Social Forum is "opposed to neoliberalism and a world dominated by capital or by any form of imperialism" (http://www.wsfindia. org/?q=node/3).

The World Economic Forum and the World Social Forum disagree on how to deal with globalization.

However, participants agree on one key issue: Crucial issues today are global in nature.

One outcome of this domestic–international mesh affects us all: *Some social groups, some cities, and some nations will be advantaged, perhaps for decades to come. Likewise, other groups and cities will be disadvantaged by forces far beyond the control of a mayor or city manager.*

THINK GLOBALLY, ACT LOCALLY—BUT HOW?

Knowing that our local environment is connected to the global environment may be intellectually satisfying. But knowledge doesn't guarantee effective action.

How can we *act* locally to have an impact on a global situation? This book notes a number of ways and examples. Here are some from the environmental field. (1) In 2001 a group of Bay Area, California, activists, with help from the cities of San Francisco, Oakland, and Berkeley, launched City CarShare. Its mission is to provide convenient and affordable access to cars in order to reduce individual car ownership and, to improve the environment and quality of life in cities. Members rent cars on a short-term basis (say, an hour or two), thus reducing traffic, parking difficulties, dependence on oil, and pollution. (2) Paris's city government provides about 20,000 bikes for subscribers. The fee-based service, Vélib (for *vélo* [bicycle] plus *liberté* [freedom]), gives riders flexibility as well as exercise; they can take a bike from any of 730 Paris stations and park it at any other. And it cuts down traffic jams.

Globally, then, jurisdictions below the nation-state level are not waiting for international agreements or national law to protect the planet. They are acting to protect the earth's ozone layer, to diminish traffic, and to improve the urban quality of life (e.g., lessen pollution, promote better health).

We could thus ask, Is there such a beast as *municipal* foreign policy? Or *municipal* national policy? Some think so. In 2007, 180 New Hampshire towns voted in their town meetings on whether or not to put climate on the agenda—the *national* agenda. In the same year, cities throughout the United States took the lead on the environment as debate stalled at the federal level; 522 mayors agreed to meet "Kyoto standards." (The Kyoto Treaty of 1997 committed industrial nations to reduce emissions of greenhouse gases, mainly carbon dioxide, by around 5.2 percent below their 1990 levels over the next decade. To come into force, the agreement needed to be ratified by the countries that were responsible for at least 55 percent of the world's carbon emissions in 1990; these included the United States, which did not sign it.)

Cities worldwide are trying to become more environmentally friendly. In New York City, cabbies are driving smaller cars. São Paulo, Brazil's largest (and, some say, the world's fourth largest) city, banned outdoor advertising as "visual pollution." In Paris, city government encourages people to abandon their cars and ride bicycles. London imposes stiff fines for driving in the city center. Almost 50 towns, including Totnes, England (where the concept was pioneered), have signed onto a "transition initiative," a movement encouraging cities, villages, and towns to prepare themselves for a carbon-free world.

Some focus on the opposite side of the spectrum: global approaches to local problems. World citizen and peace activist Garry Davis, for one, believes that global problems with local impact can best be approached via world government (see www.worldgovernment. org/gov.html).

Decades before the word "globalization" entered our everyday vocabulary, U.S.–born Davis (b. 1921), together with surrealist painter André Breton and writer Albert Camus, among others, spearheaded a movement for "mundialization" (*mundus* = "world" in Latin). To Davis, who had witnessed the carnage of World War II firsthand, mundialization means that a specific territory—say, a city or state—has rights on a world scale. Essentially, the movement seeks world peace by linking the "security and welfare of all towns and districts of the world," which, the founders felt, share a common threat: destructive war. The first "mundialized" city in the world was Cahors, a southwest French town of some 20,000 inhabitants. Voters in Cahors passed a referendum in 1949 approving the first mundialization charter, proclaiming the city to be "world territory." In part, the charter, as reapproved in 1995, declares that governing the city or at the grassroots level can more swiftly respond to natural disasters as well as threats to ecological systems and terrorism. The charter also suggests that cities and towns should lead the way to end poverty,

to care for seniors, and to promote a new sense of community.

At its height before the Korean War in the 1950s, the mundialization movement attracted over 750,000 people in 150 countries stretching from Japan and India to the United States and Canada. The movement still exists but with limited membership.

So, once again, there are a variety of approaches to urban–suburban concerns. Scattered throughout this book, I suggest some (legal) ways to act locally. In addition, I draw some connections—from North America's Main Street and Tokyo's Ginza to Trento, Italy's, Via Brennero and Brazil's rainforest—and suggest the range of urban policies dealing with global issues and vice versa.

This book brings together a wide variety of perspectives on urban–suburban–postsuburban phenomena and suggests some connections between and among phenomena. In an age of information explosion and extreme specialization, this is not easy for any of us. But let us begin by following the advice—or hope—of novelist E. M. Forster in terms of both people and ideas: "Only connect," the epigraph to his 1910 novel *Howards End*.

THINGS URBAN ARE BEST UNDERSTOOD IN A BROADER CONTEXT FROM AN INTERDISCIPLINARY PERSPECTIVE

This book puts urban–suburban–postsuburban phenomena in broader contexts. Sometimes this means putting an issue into a national or an international framework. Sometimes it means putting an issue—say, poverty—into the framework of general theory before examining its urban–suburban applications.

To better understand Los Angeles, Beijing, or Hamburg in the new millennium, I argue that their economic fates are linked to worldwide processes, national trends, and regional developments. These include the growth of the global economy; the growth of global criminal rings, including computer hackers who steal identities and credit card numbers; the internationalization of the movement of investment money; shifts in population and power; outsourcing; massive migration; and changes from industrial to postindustrial economies. For example, a generation ago, there was a common saying: When Detroit catches a cold, the U.S. economy catches pneumonia. In recent years, it's been revised, twice: (1) If the United States catches a cold, the world catches pneumonia and (2) If the *Chinese* economy catches a cold, the world catches pneumonia. (Since the financial crisis in the United States, which began in 2007 and then spread worldwide, the maxim may be revised again.)

To expand our vision of things urban and suburban, an interdisciplinary approach is essential. When discussing the economy of cities, to take one example, I blend insights from sociology, geography, history, political science, and literature as well as economic theory and data. Why? Because economic concepts don't tell the whole story. Certainly, they add nothing to our understanding of human reactions to economic change or poverty.

THE LINK BETWEEN SOCIAL ACTION AND SOCIAL THEORY

Throughout this book, I try to provide a solid theoretical base for action-oriented people. Both theory and practice are emphasized because, in my view, *there is no good social action without good social theory.*

Case studies highlight individuals and groups who have acted on their urban world. Then, their practice is linked to theories about life in the metropolis. For instance, I examine how elected officials (e.g., Richard J. Daley and his son, Richard M. Daley, both multiterm Chicago mayors) and appointed officials (e.g., New York City's master builder, Robert Moses) exercise(d) enormous influence and power. I follow the progress of lesser-known but important people such as members of Bananas, a group of California women who set out to perform a community service: providing harried parents with information about children's activities—to save them from "going bananas." Bananas learned how the political system worked and, with much persistence and hard work, got something done.

My approach—merging practice and theory—comes partly from lessons learned while trying to get things done. In West Virginia, I learned that fighting a war against poverty armed only with false hopes is a losing battle. More recently, efforts to set up a cultural center in rural France and to help famine-struck Niger reminded me that an understanding of organizational politics plus a long time line and a hearty laugh are useful for keeping one's resolve and sanity.

I hope that this book will lay the groundwork for better understanding of how cities and suburbs work and, hence, more effective metropolitan action. My aim is to make world-watching less a spectator pastime and more a contact sport.

REVELATIONS IN ORDINARY PLACES

Taking a closer look at ordinary people doing ordinary things—like riding a city bus—can reveal a great deal about metropolitan life. For instance, when we in the United States ride a crowded bus, we expect to be left alone. (This is not a universal rule as many travelers have discovered!) If, perchance, a seatmate strikes up a conversation, we note how unusual this is. The next time, we may bury our heads in a newspaper or stare out the window to avoid conversation. Chances are that no one taught us how to stave off strangers on a bus or that rules—not talking to strangers, for example—govern bus behavior. Yet, most of the time, most adults in the United States follow these implicit rules.

Unstated rules govern every culture's routine acts. Figuring them out and bringing them to consciousness is often a goal of travel writers as well as social scientists. Why? Because *by observing routine activities, we can begin to understand what rules govern social behavior and what purposes these rules serve in a particular culture or setting.* Thus, a chapter is devoted to such ordinary actions as walking down a busy street, riding a subway, and standing in an automatic teller machine (ATM) line.

NAMING AND RENAMING THE WORLD

Names count. So do name changes.

Name changes—from "Oriental" to "Asian," from "homosexual" to "gay," from "minority" to "people of color" or "unrepresented people"—count a lot. Why? Because label changes reflect shifts in the way people define themselves and one another. And the lack of an agreed-on name ("Hello, I'd like you to meet my...a hh...lover...I mean...companion or domestic partner") suggests emerging social realities.

Ordinary names can reveal much about metropolitan values. Names of streets and boulevards may be tip-offs to local heroes and heroines. Rap lyrics may reflect the singers' resistance to what they define as repression.

Urban slang often reveals different lifestyles. Take Jeffry's case. Homeless on the streets of Chicago, Jeffry told NPR's *Hidden Kitchens* program (aired December 31, 2005) that each day he goes "trailblazing"; that is, he seeks food, shelter, work, and whatever else he needs to make it through the day.

Words can also point to the trail of those who came before. In American English, that trail stretches from *adobe* to *zilch*.

Frequently, names in the news are like submerged treasures. Take, for instance, the terms "looters," "scum," and "hooligans." In fall 2005, then French Interior Minister Nicolas Sarkozy (elected president of France in May 2007) called youthful car-burners *racaille* (scum), further inflaming the passions of the dispossessed.

Who are defined as looters in the United States? Usually poor, powerless folks. For example, in summer 2005, "looters" stole relatively small-ticket items in New Orleans, devastated by Hurricane Katrina. (*Note*: The practice of naming hurricanes is at least several hundred years old. Many hurricanes in the West Indies were named for the particular saint's day on which they occurred. In 1953, the United States started naming hurricanes using female names; and in 1978, it began using both female and male names.) Despite the old saying—"Sticks and stones can break my bones but names can never hurt me"—name-calling can be hurtful.

Fig. E FROM ADOBE TO ZILCH. The language tree at the Ellis Island Immigrant Museum in New York City shows a few of the many words that U.S. English borrowed from native and immigrant cultures. Chapters 8 and 9 examine immigration, assimilation, and multiculturalism. (Roberta Tasley)

White-collar executives are rarely, if ever, termed "scum," "hooligans," or "looters." U.S. executives of WorldCom and Tyson Foods were convicted of bilking investors and/or consumers of millions of dollars but never called "scum" by the media. Similarly, Enron officials were convicted of lining their own pockets by fraud but never termed "looters." Wealthy CEOs who illegally backdated stock options, thus earning more profit, were never called "hooligans" in the early 2000s. Ditto for Bernie Madoff, convicted Ponzi schemer, and AIG traders, whose huge bonuses were called "outrageous" by President Obama.

Likewise, the terms "welfare," "government handouts," "assistance," and "subsidies" are also used selectively. In the mainstream press, a single mother in New York City or Houston gets a "government handout" or "welfare." Katrina disaster victims received government "assistance." In contrast, Boeing received about $23 billion in U.S. government "subsidies" in the period 1992–2003.

What can we conclude from these word differences? That "welfare" and "government handouts" go to the poor, "assistance" goes to the "deserving" poor (or middle class), and "subsidies" go to the powerful and/or rich.

Language is not neutral; it limits our reality. New words can refocus perception. As fund-raisers know, there is a world of difference between trying to save a "jungle" and a "rain forest."

Language can also shape memory. The late Polish author Ryszard Kapuściński described his encounter in relocating his New Delhi hotel as a young adult: "I had seen only that which I was able to name, for example, I remembered the acacia tree, but not the tree standing next to it, whose name I did not know" (*Travels with Herodotus*, 2007. New York: Knopf—:22).

Politicians especially appreciate the symbolic power of words. When the United States and Britain invaded Iraq, George W. Bush and Tony Blair defined the war as a means of self-protection against weapons of mass destruction and a means of bringing "democracy" to Iraq. By contrast, English playwright Harold Pinter defined the U.S.-led Iraq War as an "act of blatant state terrorism." Between the definitions by Pinter and U.S./British leaders lies a world of difference—and real-world consequences.

Writer Maxine Hong Kingston tries to change the world one word at a time. I try to walk in her footsteps. For instance, I avoid the word "foreign" because the concept is obsolete. We live in a timeless, borderless 24/7/365 world with a global market for ideas, information, and IOUs, all being exchanged in nanoseconds. Similarly, I avoid the term "Third World" because the so-called Second World (the Soviet Union and its satellites) no longer exists and because it is often used as a euphemism for poor countries.

INFO ALERT!

We live in the Information Age. Accurate information should be easy to get, right? Alas, it hardly ever is. Frequent Internet searchers, including myself, applaud the availability of previously buried information plus the speed with which we can find it. But we should realize that "facts" on Web sites or blogs are, or should be, suspect: Too often there are no gatekeepers to check the information's reliability.

No doubt, highly respected journalist and publisher John Seigenthaler, Sr., would agree. In 2005, Seigenthaler, a friend and colleague of the late Robert Kennedy, was shocked to read on Wikipedia, an Internet encyclopedia (written and edited by anyone—scholars, wackos, political hacks, etc.), that he had something to do with the assassinations of the Kennedy brothers and that he had lived in Russia for a number of years. In an op-ed piece in *USA Today* on November 30, 2005 (www.journalism.org), he protested the article as not only "false" but "malicious."

Yet another issue of credibility—independence—arises on blogs and vlogs; they may be influenced, even paid, to carry opinions. The case of a pro-Wal-Mart blog comment is instructive. In "Wal-Mart Enlists Bloggers in Its Public Relations Campaign" (March 7, 2006), *New York Times* reporter Michael Barbaro exposed the word-for-word source of the blog's pro-Wal-Mart comment: an e-mail press release from Wal-Mart itself.

The trustworthiness of Web sites, vlogs, and blogs is important because so many people worldwide depend on them for information. In the United States alone, according to a Pew Internet and American Life Project report released on July 19, 2006, 57 million Americans read blogs (www.pewinternet.org/~/media//Files/Reports/2006/PIP%2).

So-called citizen journalism also presents challenges. Sometimes, as in the 2008 siege in Mumbai, India, citizen journalists can provide "real-time" glimpses. (Such was the case when a professor at Harvard Medical School, visiting Mumbai, described gunfire on his Twitter feed and uploaded photos to his blog.) Opening up news production to a wider group could mean that underserved communities are better served—and heard. In practice, however, nonprofessional producers may have an ax to grind or skip fact-checking.

Data, on the Internet or elsewhere, look official—particularly when presented by official agencies in neat, tabular form. But beware! Take census data, for example. Are all the data trustworthy? The answer is unclear. First, definitions change, so making valid comparisons over time may be hard or impossible. Second, data can suffer from politicization. Third, GIGO ("garbage in, garbage out").

First, *changing definitions*. Take the case of Argentina. Blacks were brought from Africa as slaves in the 1700s. They constituted a separate category in the Buenos Aires census until 1887. Then, the category was eliminated. Currently, 97 percent of Argentina's 39 million inhabitants describe themselves as "white," but activists protest that there may be up to a million people of African ancestry, many of whom suffer racial discrimination. A civil rights group, calling itself "Afro-Argentines," claims that the Argentine government eliminated the black category in order to promote an image of homogeneity. In its place, they say, census takers introduced what Afro-Argentines call "euphemistic" race classifications.

Second, *political meddling*. This can affect when and what data are released as well as which projects are funded. U.S. census data showing increases in unemployment and decreases in income, seen as detrimental to the federal administration in power, have been revised, buried, or held back from the public, particularly near election day. Some scientists go much further, accusing political administrations of judging research proposals on their political, not scientific, merits.

Third, *GIGO*. This may apply to population counts. The U.S. Census Bureau estimates that it missed at least 6.4 million people for the 2000 Census and counted at least 3.1 million people twice (*McNeil-Lehrer Newshour*, May 25, 2001).

Aside from the challenge of collecting reliable data, there are at least two other important issues: neutrality and honesty. First, *neutrality*: In the United States and elsewhere, some social scientists work for government agencies, but they do not necessarily acknowledge their government affiliation. Their publications may appear to be neutral, but they serve political purposes more than scholarly ends. Second, *honesty*: Even highly respected scientists falsify data. Take the case of a top Chinese computer scientist, Chen Jin. He became a national hero in 2003 when he claimed he had created a sophisticated microchip capable of processing digitized data for electronic devices. But by 2006 Jin was exposed as a fraud; he had stolen his chip designs from a foreign company (news.bbc.co.uk/1/hi/business/4771583.stm). Or take the case of Dr. Hwang Woo Suk of Seoul National University. Hwang enjoyed rock-star status in South Korea before he was unmasked as a hoodwinker. In 2005, Hwang admitted to faking data for a landmark paper on therapeutic cloning in *Science*, arguably the most prestigious U.S. scientific magazine. (Hwang's lab in South Korea was the only one in the world claiming to clone human cells.) (http://seedmagazine.com/content/article/panel_declares_research_fake/)

We know that science and integrity do not always go together. Both social and physical scientists have been known to steal other people's work or words. If such unethical acts did not exist, the U.S. government would not need watchdogs such as the Office of Research Integrity, an independent entity inside the Department of Health and Human Services.

In sum, as consumers of data, we need a keen eye, critical faculties, and a cautious attitude. When evaluating research, it is wise to remain skeptical.

UNITY VERSUS DIVERSITY

Why do human beings think and feel so differently? Scholars point to many factors. Depending on their field, some name occupation, religious beliefs, educational background, and age. Some point to family upbringing, social class, unconscious premises, race/ethnicity, physical state, mental abilities, income level, and degree of power. Others say that birth order, oxytocin and other human hormones, genes, gender, stress levels, and/or environmental hazards have great impact on a person's body and mind. Still others think that the larger socioeconomic context is the key influence on an individual's personality and beliefs.

Now let's take the opposite tack. By stressing differences, we may forget that human beings share some key characteristics, particularly the capacities to think abstractly, laugh, and come to one another's aid. For example, if an elderly person—whatever his or her race, class, or gender—falls on a busy street, we are surprised if passersby do *not* help. In other words, cruelty attracts attention, but kindness goes unremarked.

A wide range of thinkers remind us that our fates are intertwined. Neither riches, skin color, beauty, power, prestige, gender, nor personal background has an impact on the direction of winds wafting radioactive air or biological toxins.

Finally, geneticists remind us how similar we all are, whatever our color, creed, nationality, or looks. Yet, a shared genetic heritage doesn't seem to bring people closer.

In dire situations, acts of kindness often do cross-cut everyday boundaries separating human beings. In Bali, London, Madrid, and New York City, color-blind bombs and/or deadly airplanes brought together survivors or victims' families to share their grief. Similarly, after a federal building was bombed in 1995, a clergyman in Oklahoma City reminded local residents that the toddlers killed in the blast were more alike than different, whatever their color or background."

Professor Kwame Antony Appiah claims, in *Cosmopolitanism: Ethics in a World of Strangers* (2006, New York: W.W.Norton), that Western intellectuals and leaders have wildly exaggerated differences among people, neglecting the "power of one": one world and one species. If true, how can we combat this emphasis on difference? How can we intensify a sense of community while, at the same time, stressing the strength of our differences? These remain questions worth thinking more about.

Here, I pay close attention to both sides of the U.S. motto: diversity (*pluribus*) and oneness (*unum*). Chapters 9 and 10 consider ethnic identity and the debate over multiculturalism, for example.

Some critics argue that unity is just a myth, built on the repression of ethnic diversity by a small white elite. In their view, assimilation (making "them" into "us") masks an underlying goal: cleansing minorities

of their own background. Others fear that diversity equals disunity.

Yet, an emphasis on cultural uniqueness can also divide people into opposing camps: "us" and "them." Such divisive, often deadly, feelings seem to be alive and well globally. Given this situation, it seems wise to recall Martin Luther King, Jr.'s, words, from April, 16, 1963 (in "Letter from a Birmingham jail): "We are caught in an inescapable network of mutuality."

ANYTHING ELSE?

Other assumptions and biases can be read between the lines of the following chapters. Choices (what issues to include? how to present them? which theorists to exclude?) are inevitable. No doubt, some choices were barely conscious, stemming from my own background, life experiences, professional training, and personal reaction to the currents of our times. Because I believe that there is an autobiographical basis—and bias—to the way authors think (myself included), I've tried to acknowledge major influences relevant to this book.

First, *academic training*. I have an undergraduate degree in history and advanced degrees in international relations, public administration, and interdisciplinary social science. With this background, I probably have a trained incapacity to stay within traditional disciplinary boundaries.

Second, *a fascination with language and maps*. On huge wall maps, Mrs. Purinton, our fifth-grade teacher, had us trace the journeys of words into English from Scandinavia, ancient Greece, the Ottoman Empire, and elsewhere. These exercises alerted me to the stewpot called "English" as well as the notion that physical space is an important factor in human relations. Several chapters reflect my continuing interest in space, both public and private.

Third, *chance*. As a child, I had flat feet. A pediatrician advised ballet lessons. I still have flat feet, but I developed a lifelong enchantment with the dance, French (the language of ballet), and the arts in general.

Growing up only an "El" ride away from Chicago's Loop (downtown) led to a special affection for music and modern architecture. I sang along at hootenannies at the Gate of Horn, attended Chicago Symphony rehearsals, listened to Ken Nordine's radio program filled with word jazz, and hung out in record stores where, by chance, I once met Thelonius Monk. Every school day, en route to high school in Oak Park, I walked by Frank Lloyd Wright's prairie houses. Regular visits to 880 Lake Shore Drive, a building designed by Mies van der Rohe where my architect uncle lived, and Chicago's Museum of Science and Industry, near my grandmother's home, were earthly delights. So there are many references and illustrations from the arts and pop culture in this book.

Fourth, *cross-cultural experience*. My views are influenced by a host of experiences both within and outside of the United States, including stints as a student in Paris, a U.S. Foreign Service officer in Africa and India, an antipoverty worker in West Virginia, and a bus traveler across the United States and southeast Asia. Starting in summer 1998, I have directed a cultural center in remote or "deep" France, way off the beaten track.

Fifth, *courses and students I've taught in the United States plus talks I've given outside the United States*. In large measure, my students' interests have shaped and reshaped this book. Some former students remain in close touch, and they continue to keep me current too.

Sixth, *my own teachers*. My teachers at Oak Park and River Forest Township High School (Illinois) encouraged me to counter received wisdom. Helen Lounsbury launched diatribes against Franklin D. Roosevelt and Andrew Carnegie ("He gave his money away toward the end of his life, hoping his philanthropy would make the fires of Hell burn less bright"). Her hope (I now believe) was to inspire her students to read more and argue back—which we did. Disputing her opinions—which she encouraged to the max—meant having information to support another point of view, not statements starting with "I think." Ellen Shuart, the high school weekly *Trapeze* newspaper's advisor when I was editor, was an inspiration; her grace under pressure did not rub off enough, alas.

The names of influential teachers remain emblazoned in my mind's eye. "Miss Rose" taught me my first words in French at age 9: *arabesque, rond de jambe*, and other ballet terms. Little could she or I have predicted how much the French language and culture would come to influence my life.

All teachers don't have classrooms. My neighbors in Oak Park, Illinois, the Stevensons, taught me to appreciate gardens as a youngster. This led to a lifelong interest in healthy, beautiful plants and vegetables.

Seventh, *generation and social background*. My formative years coincided with the heyday of U.S. economic and military power: the 1950s. After World War II, optimism was pervasive for many middle-class white teens like myself. We gyrated to Elvis, cooled out to Dave Brubeck, and laughed at Lucy. We were unaware of the dangers of X-rays at the shoe store. Cigarettes were advertised as "good for you." As singers/songwriters Simon and Garfunkel defined it, it was a time of innocence and confidence.

Many of us who grew up in the 1950s were unaware of anything outside our own little worlds. People may have been suffering in Appalachia, ghettoes, and elsewhere in the U.S., but we who lived in far different circumstances didn't know about it.

We oozed faith in the nation's future and our own ability to build a better world. Everything seemed possible! In that era, writer Albert Camus (1913–1960) captured this upbeat feeling when he called the United States a country where all is done to show that life isn't tragic.

In this postwar era, conventional behavior and male domination were rarely questioned in the middle-class United States. My parents were different: My mother encouraged my flights of fancy, and my father believed in the natural superiority of women. Never a nasty or pejorative word about any group of people was uttered in our household. I chose my historical era and my parents wisely.

Still, like people almost everywhere today, I am not immune to trepidation concerning the urban, postmodern condition. The mood, particularly in the post-9/11 United States, seems to reflect shattered confidence and fear, even paranoia. Geographer David Lowenthal, comparing 2007 to 1947, wrote that in that period, faith in the future had dwindled in the face of failed promises, such as promises to banish famine, pestilence, and ethnic and religious slaughter, as well as threats of catastrophe.

Instead of outrage or a high-flying red, white, and blue flag, there seems to be resignation and pessimism for many—perhaps most—who live in the United States. (In April 2008, a *New York Times/ CBS* poll revealed that 81 percent of respondents were dissatisfied with the nation's direction.)(See http://www.nytimes.com/2008/04/04/us/04poll. html?_r=1&hp)

Pessimism, reflected in historically high levels of conspicuous *non*consumption, gripped the United States by summer 2008.

This dark mood, reflected in the urban TV drama *The Wire* (2002–2008), is exacerbated by anti-U.S. feeling around the world. For example, a Pew Research Center poll of global attitudes in 2007 showed widespread anti-Americanism among people in the 47 nations surveyed (pewglobal.org/reports/display.php?ReportID=256).

English songwriter/singer Michael Griffin summed up his feelings about the United States in his ballad "America Come Weep," played on YouTube (http://www.michelgriffin.com/Lyric.php?Song=America,%20Come%20Weep)

> America, come weep, for what's been lost
> and what's been stolen, America, come weep, for all your
> pioneers of old; For somewhere on the way, between dream
> and realisation, I'd say you've gone and lost your soul.

Griffin sounds more disappointed than angry.

A TV character put this pessimistic mood most succinctly. Tony Soprano told his shrink in the first episode of the prize-winning HBO series *The Sopranos* (1999–2007), "Things are trending downward."

Another view focuses more on the rise of nations such as China, India, Brazil, and Russia rather than the decline of the United States. In this view, exemplified by *Newsweek*'s Fareed Zakaria in *The Post-American World* (New York: W.W. Norton, 2008), the rise of these nations will reshape the world as we know it.

Meanwhile, some global policymakers and influential voices question the United States's direction. For one, John Thornhill, a top editor at London's prestigious center-right business paper the *Financial Times*, referred to the United States in 2006 as "the national security state." (Such a critical epithet is normally used only by left-wing publications, not center-right

media.) In addition, a random-sample poll of adults in France, Germany, Spain, Italy, the United Kingdom, and the United States, taken in August 2007 showed that in every country polled—except the United States—the United States was regarded as the country that is "the greatest threat to global stability" (http://www.harrisinteractive.com/news/FTHarrisPoll/HI_FinancialTimes_HarrisPoll_Aug2007.pdf).

It is wise to remember that whatever separates us globally, we share a historical moment, perhaps a defining moment: a time of postmillenial innocence and confidence punctured by uncertainty. Indeed, some very smart people, including Benoit Mandelbrot, mathematician and coauthor of *The Misbehavior of Markets: A Fractal View of Risk, Ruin & Reward* (New York: Basic Books, 2006), and financier Nassim Nicholas Taleb, author of *The Black Swan: The Impact of the Highly Improbable* (New York: Random House, 2007), say that the 2008 financial crises are so complicated that they are barely comprehensible. Taleb thinks that the United States and the world face turbulence worse than the Great Depression (*The NewsHour*, October 21, 2008). No wonder that increasing numbers seem to be attracted to philosophies offering simple explanations for complex phenomena.

True, modern communications give us access to a wide range of opinions. But most of us rely on just a few information sources: those that mirror our own worldviews. Rarely do we seek out sources that disagree with our assumptions. Likewise, rarely do we take the opportunity to see how others see us. Even so, art forms—including commercial ones—can introduce us to alternate realities. For one, a scene in director Stephen Gaghan's movie *Syriana* (2005; Warner Bros. Pictures) portrays a religious Muslim teacher explaining to Muslim schoolboys why, from his viewpoint, Western societies are sinful and should be destroyed.

Chilling, indeed, is the violence—whether in the name of "democracy," "retribution," "nonpayment of a debt," "purity," or "righteousness"—that touches us personally or at one remove (from TV news, e.g.). Often, this violence is random. And this random violence, from stray bullets, car burnings, or global terrorism and toxins, upsets our taken-for-granted balance of power. Such random violence, whether in Sadr City,

Fig. F LEAVING HOPE BEHIND The French town of Espère (Hope) signals to visitors that they are leaving hope behind. In France, both the entrance and exit of towns are signposted. (Andrée Abecassis)

Iraq, or Aurora, Colorado, plays havoc with our sense of security.

Anyone with ears or eyes can hardly avoid bad news. In late 2008, for example, the U.S. jobless report was gloomy: Over one-half million U.S. jobs disappeared in one month, November 2008; the jobless rate soared, and this rate did not include "discouraged" workers who dropped out of the job search altogether (and thus were not counted in the jobless rate at all). Globally, significant job losses were the norm in many places.

Yet, in general, the tone in this book is not despairing. For one thing, I believe we can resist the waves of deceit, manipulation, and lies coming from officialdom, public or private.

For another, I remain skeptical but not cynical. To me, cynicism corrodes possibilities for change. To the contrary, I believe that we can act collectively with courage, will, savvy, and organization to change the direction of some contemporary trends. For me, this sense of hope is based on personal experience, the experience of friends and acquaintances, and successes in citizen-based movements (e.g., civil rights in the United States). It distinguishes me from the majority of young people in many rich nations who face the future with fear.

We are not the first, or probably the last, to experience (or to know at one remove) horrific suffering. I take heart from the words of the late comedienne, Gilda Radner (1946–1989):"I wanted a perfect ending. Now I've learned, the hard way, that some poems don't rhyme, and some stories don't have a clear beginning, middle, and end. Life is about not knowing, having to change, taking the moment and making the best of it, without knowing what's going to happen next. Delicious Ambiguity." (http://www.wisdomquotes.com/cat_confusion.html).

At least three other important biases pervade this book, and for them I am unrepentant. One concerns the role of ideas in public life. In my view, *without reasoned and lively debate over ideas, "public life" is an oxymoron.* I hope this book will stimulate debate on matters affecting our collective present and future.

The second is a preference for getting involved locally and beyond. This might mean boning up on one subject and speaking out about that issue (e.g., at meetings held by your city, say, about the placement of cell phone antennae). It could entail blogging or helping a few little kids dream big. Or starting a nonprofit. In my view, *not* getting involved—civic disengagement—threatens community life, endangers democratic institutions, and encourages alienation. I hope this book will provide some options for civic reengagement.

The third is an unabashed prourban bias. I like cities, particularly big ones. (I also like rural hamlets, particularly those with fast Internet access!) I hope my enthusiasm for cities will be apparent and even rub off a little.

Last, studying today's human settlements can seem overwhelming because the world that helps shape them is so complex. There is some help along the way: key terms in bold type, biographical sketches of theorists and practitioners, case studies of real people affecting metropolitan life or trying to change the way things are done, artworks, graphs, and boxed selections from classic essays or observations related to metropolitan life.

Most especially, you—kind reader—are invited to participate directly in discovering the metropolis.

I hope that carrying out the projects will bring the metropolis alive, encouraging serious discussion and even theory building. I would like to know what you find when doing the projects. Please write me, in care of Oxford University Press, about anything related to this book.

So, that is where the book is coming from—from a person shaped by the people, social currents, places, ideas, and media images she's known. How any of us interpret our world depends on all that we have met. That's why I've tried to reveal some of those influences instead of shooting from ambush.

Finally, I want to note how this edition differs from earlier editions. This edition reflects some ways in which the world has changed or, more precisely, my perception of these changes. In particular, since the second edition, the world's population has become majority urban, fear of nonstate actors has gripped citizens in many places (from New York City and Mumbai to Dar es Salaam and Buenos Aires), "globalization" and "green" (however interpreted) are widely used words, and the U.S. position in the world has changed. Reflecting these changes, this edition includes updates of statistical data (e.g., population changes); new topics (e.g., impacts of terrorism on cities); an emphasis on our *global* urban world (including profiles of many world cities, such as Kyoto, Mexico City, Mumbai, and Shanghai); recent developments in building "green"; new sections on comparative rules, such as office behavior in the United States and China; up-to-date looks at political, social, and economic changes that impact cities and suburbs, such as economic downturns and the Internet; and expanded discussions of U.S. politics and political theory (e.g., libertarianism).

Have a good read! And get involved!!!

Summer 2009
E. B. P.
Berkeley, California
and La Toulzanie, France

AN INVITATION TO THE CITY

Brack Brown

Oscar Graubner

CHAPTER 1
THE KNOWING EYE AND EAR

TWO PATHS TO UNDERSTANDING THE CITY
   "Acquaintance with" and "Knowledge
     about" Metropolitan Life
   Rethinking the Two Paths

**UNDERSTANDING CHICAGO IN ITS HEYDAY,
1890s–1920s**
   Using Social Science and Literature as
     Paths to Knowledge

Labor Radicalism, Industrial Progress, and
   Social Reform
Urban Researchers and Writers:
   Convergent Goals
The City Beautiful
Chicago: Microcosm of the New Industrial
   Order

Once upon a time, so the story goes, a prophet ran through the streets screaming, "We are doomed! In 24 hours our city will be flooded." Some people forgave their enemies, kissed their loved ones goodbye, and prepared to die. But others huddled together with a different idea. "Well," one woman said optimistically, "we've got 24 hours to learn how to live under water!"

This story suggests that how we respond to cities (and life in general) depends on what's *inside* our heads and hearts, as well as what's *outside* in the street. And how we judge our ability to triumph over flash floods or other urban uncertainties is probably rooted in unconscious mental habits, particularly hope or hopelessness, not logic alone.

If you close your eyes and think about the city, what do you visualize? Sleek skyscrapers? Great libraries and good food? Soul-stirring street musicians? Friends laughing over a spilled latté? A man like Joseph Charles, who every weekday morning for 30 years spread joy to strangers by waving and calling out "Keep smiling" to passing traffic on a major thoroughfare in Berkeley, California? New ideas and world-changing inventions? The birthplace of most of humankind's art, culture, and commerce? Cures for deadly diseases? Walt Whitman's Brooklyn Bridge and Gustav Eiffel's tower? Rappers rhyming? Fans cheering for the home team? Trendy fashions and diverse pleasures? The promise of personal growth—fueled by the energy and density of the city? Accidental meetings with fascinating strangers? Concerts in the park? Spring flowers popping out of sidewalk cracks? Birds that sing faster than their rural brethren?

Do you view the city as poetry? Or novelty? Or, like urban scholar Richard Florida (2004:1), do you consider cities to be "cauldrons of creativity" which mobilize and concentrate human energy?

Or do you envision airplanes crashing into New York City's modernist landmarks? Adults in Mumbai, Madrid, and Baghdad suffering from posttraumatic stress? Stressed-out drivers in suburban Los Angeles shouting in road rage? Pup tents for the poor near the Arc de Triomphe? Refrigerators floating down the streets of post-Katrina New Orleans? Luxury hotels in Siem Reap, Cambodia, ringed by dead rats? University students in a small Virginia town, hiding beneath their desks to avoid being shot? People lining up at soup kitchens? Drug dealing on dimly lit streets and crystal meth labs in dingy basements? Gunfire between gangs and police paralyzing São Paulo, Brazil, South America's largest city? Heatless rooms with roaches? Smells of Lysol and body sweat at homeless shelters? Chilling crimes and petty irritations? Triple-locked doors? Strangers lurking in alleys? Children living in tenements and dumpsters? Or estates with signs threatening "armed response"?

Perhaps your vision encompasses *both* urban glories and dilemmas. Concerning the urban condition, you may vacillate among confusion, caution, cynicism, and confidence. As a *New York Times* film critic put it, "cities have always cast their double spell" of repelling and seducing people (Scott, A.O. 2008). Or, as Swiss-

French architect Le Corbusier (1887–1965) once said about New York City, it is a "beautiful catastrophe."

One moment you may despair, thinking about dead radiators, random violence, ethnic tension, a growing gap between rich and poor, and the lack of vision for urban America—or urban anywhere. You may fear that the future holds a nightmarish cityscape in the style of *Blade Runner*'s (1982) Los Angeles. You may wonder if British writer Richard K. Morgan (2002) may be prescient; he gives readers a cyberpunk–noir vision of San Francisco (called "Bay City"), circa 2411.

a

Fig. 1.2 METROPOLITAN LIFE. Where else can you and your friends/family (*a*) go to a celebration of pastry—with free samples (like this one in Albi, southwest France, (*b*) buy sandals (or almost anything) at a street fair, (*c*) ride fun boats (in Regents Park, London), (*d*) eat at a sidewalk Brazilian restaurant (this one in Berkeley, California), (*e*) skateboard around the square (in Toledo, Spain), (*f*) shop with your dog if leashed (and in Paris), (*g*) express an opinion to your neighbors on a sidewalk blackboard (in suburban San Francisco), (*h*) watch the passing parade while playing a friendly game (in Ha Noi, Viet Nam), or (*i*) spend a lazy afternoon writing postcards at a café (this one near Budapest)? ([*a, b, d, f*] Tim Teninty, [*c*] Gesche Würfel, [*e*] Barbara Cohen, [*g*] E. Barbara Phillips, [*h*] Rahsaan Maxwell, [*i*] Susan Hoehn)

b

Fig. 1.2 (*continued*)

The next moment you may radiate joy at one of humankind's great inventions—the city. You may focus on the enriching diversity of urban life, individuals who make a difference, and institutions that fulfill the promise of urban living.

Maybe you sympathize with E. B. White's quandary:

> If the world were merely seductive, that would be easy. If it were merely challenging, that would be no problem. But I arise in the morning torn between a desire to improve the world, and a desire to enjoy the world. This makes it hard to plan the day.
>
> *(quoted in Shenker, 1969)*

You may have a very dirty face in a big city. Why? The late writer John Gunther reasoned that New York City had 22,000 soda fountains and 11 tons of soot falling per square mile every month. The combination of soot and ice cream, he thought, led to many dirty faces!

What Gunther didn't say about New York City—and other big hubs—is just as important: They are "the place to be in a globalizing world. So many functions now depend on the proximity of people" (Batty quoted in Bowley, 2007:2). Indeed, some think that the number of Web sites generated and the number of inventions produced grow exponentially as the population of any city grows.

Harvard economist Edward L. Glaeser and his coauthors think that cities are growing because so many people want to live there. That is, they are "consumer immigrants" who have a "demand for density"; big cities offer what (mainly) educated,

c

Fig. 1.2   (*continued*)

creative, and affluent people want to consume, such as sports teams, restaurants, and art museums (quoted in Bowley, 2007:2).

You may personally know neighborhoods that look and feel like war zones. Even if you have only read about such dangerous places, you may wonder, What can *I* do about it? Or, aware that crime, the economy, education, and controlling the spread of AIDS worldwide are chief public concerns, you may ask, What *should* I do about these issues?

Possibly, you focus on more abstract, theoretical questions such as these: (1) Can cities today provide personal security, an active economy based on commerce, and sights that inspire civic awe—elements that many (e.g., Kotkin, 2005) think are essential to sustain urban culture? (2) Why are today's cities throughout the world significantly different from cities of just a generation ago? (3) How have economic and demographic changes—a shift from local factories to a global assembly line, a shift from manufacturing cars to processing information, and a massive population shift out of cities to larger metropolitan regions—affected North American and European urban politics and social life? (4) What can people, working together,

d

Fig. 1.2   *(continued)*

do to make cities more humane? How can people in a U.S. **metropolitan area**—say, greater New York City—cooperate with Muscovites and Lagosians to improve their mutual well-being?

You may ask whether it is even possible to make sense out of the changing urban world. After all, the boundaries of time and space are fuzzy, thanks to computers, cell phones, and the like. The line between full-time, secure employment and temporary, insecure work is often crossed. And the once-perceived line in the United States between "safe," "pleasant" suburbs and "unsafe," "dirty" cities is shattered by grisly television images of violent crimes committed beyond

the city's limits plus suburban poverty rates that often top city poverty rates.

Perhaps, just perhaps, by studying the city, we can begin to understand the larger world. As an architectural critic of the *New York Times* remarked,

Anyone who walks down the streets of an American inner city can get a pretty good idea of the new world order. The mix of uses and populations, the porous borders surrounding neighborhoods, the interdependency of skills and service: *the city is the most accessible model we have for understanding the shape of [today's] world.* [italics mine]

(*Muschamp, 1993:30*).

e

Fig. 1.2 (*continued*)

TWO PATHS TO UNDERSTANDING THE CITY

"ACQUAINTANCE WITH" AND "KNOWLEDGE ABOUT" METROPOLITAN LIFE

Until the mid-twentieth century, it was conventional wisdom that (1) *personal experience* and (2) *abstract reflection* offer two different ways of understanding the world (including cities and suburbs). Then, as insights from physics drifted into social science, this view—of two *totally separate* paths—was shown to be misleading. However, for purposes of discussion, let's first look at each path separately.

Firsthand experience gives **acquaintance with** the city. Direct and concrete, it depends on sense experience: sight, hearing, touch, taste, smell. This mode of understanding is intuitive, nonlinear, and holistic. Psychologists associate it with right-brain thinking.

On the other hand, **knowledge about** the city comes from abstract, logical thought. This mode of understanding is analytical, linear, and rational. It may be mathematical and highly theoretical. The "knowledge about" path to understanding is sequential, ordering information by breaking it down into component parts. Psychologists associate it with left-brain thinking.

Television news, novels, and art can make us feel *as if* we have experienced something ourselves. That is, images and words may *substitute for* personal experience, giving us "unexperienced experience" (Goethals, 1982:54). Word pictures and photographic images often transmit acquaintance with an

f

g

Fig. 1.2 (*continued*)

urban scene: a sense of being there, an immediate emotional reaction. For instance, Jacob Riis's photo allows us to witness the life of poverty in New York City around 1890 (Figure 1.3). Even at one remove, the scene touches our feelings, and that was social reformer Riis's intent—to touch people's hearts, to make them understand emotionally *How the Other Half Lives* ([1890] 1971). Generations later, the bleak underside of New York City remains; only the faces have changed.

Photographic images bear witness–to joy and suffering, wealth and poverty. One photographer who captured a range of emotions and lifestyles–from Harlem's children to *Vogue* models–was Kansas-born Gordon Parks (1912–2006). As a photographer (he was also a movie producer and artist), Parks is perhaps best known for his early 1940s photo of Ella Watson in Washington, D.C.: Watson, an African American cleaning woman, was shown with her mop and broom in front an American flag. She echoes the farmer's wife in *American Gothic*, the 1930 Grant Wood painting. Parks's portraits, from New York to Rio, often capture the dignity of poor people in wretched conditions.

Similarly, portraits of poor migrants to mega-cities, taken by Brazilian-born Sebastião Salgado, bear witness to people who retain their dignity despite their deep distress. A reviewer of former economist Salgado's book *Migrations: Humanity in Transition* (2000) goes farther: "a world famous photographer said that 'you can't photograph soul'....After looking at Salgado's work I think that's definitely not true" (Neunemann, 2001).

In contrast to works of art, raw numbers don't tug at our heartstrings. Yet, they can provide a stepping stone to knowledge about cities. (*Note*: Statistics alone do not give knowledge about cities or anything else; they remain to be *interpreted within theoretical frameworks*. We merely start with numbers. Then, we look for relationships that help *explain* the numbers.)

Looking at the statistical data displayed in Tables 1.1 and 1.2, we see that in the 1990–2000 decade Phoenix was the fastest-growing of the 10 largest cities in the United States, followed by three Texas cities. In contrast, Philadelphia and Detroit lost

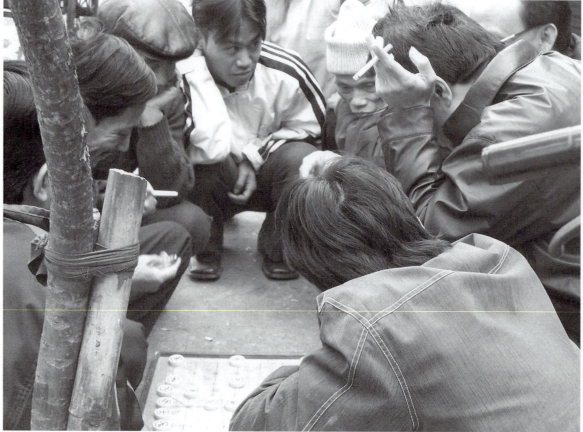

h

Fig. 1.2   (*continued*)

population during the decade. In terms of metropolitan areas, Las Vegas, Nevada, gained enormous population: over 83 percent.

Why did some U.S. cities gain or lose population? *Why* did some metropolitan areas, particularly the Las Vegas area, grow so fast? The numbers themselves do not suggest any explanation. To understand why, we must put numbers or "factoids" into larger, theoretical frameworks.

Here are some larger, theoretical frameworks that focus on large-scale (macro-level) processes that might help to explain recent U.S. population changes: (1) *a population and power shift* from industrial cities in the Northeast and Midwest (e.g.,

Hartford, Connecticut, and St. Louis, Missouri) to "suburban cities" or postsuburban places in the Sunbelt (e.g., North Las Vegas, Nevada, and Scottsdale, Arizona); (2) *an economic–technological shift* from factory to service-information jobs, often called "deindustrialization"; and (3) *a production–consumption shift* from local and national markets to a global economy.

Single concepts (often in conjunction with larger, theoretical frameworks) may be useful for a better understanding of population changes too. Take, for example, *the supply of permanent or "durable" housing*, a concept used by Harvard economist Edward L. Glaeser and his economist co-author

i

Fig. 1.2 (*continued*)

Fig. 1.3   ONE PATH OF KNOWLEDGE. A European immigrant coalheaver's windowless, cold cubicle on West 28th Street in New York City around 1890. Danish-born social reformer and *New York Tribune* police reporter Jacob Riis's photos of poverty around the turn of the twentieth century, including this one, give viewers a firsthand acquaintance with New York City's tenement life. A century later, New York City remains a leading port of entry for poor newcomers, and newer immigrants live in similar circumstances on Baxter Street. Ironically, when the *Golden Venture*, a crowded freighter carrying a smuggled cargo of undocumented Chinese immigrants, ran aground in June 1993, it was beached near a Queens, New York, park named for Jacob Riis. (Library of Congress)

Joseph Gyourko (2002) to explain why some U.S. cities, like Phoenix, grew at a very fast rate but 1950s industrial powerhouses, such as Detroit and Philadelphia, lost residents (after their heyday of being industrial powerhouses), but more slowly. In a nutshell, this is their argument: When a city's population grows quickly and significantly, housing prices tend to rise slowly. For example, the population of metro Las Vegas, Nevada, grew by leaps and bounds in the 1990s, but the average home price there did not skyrocket. To the contrary, when a city *loses* population, as Detroit and Philadelphia both did, the opposite happens: Population diminishes slowly, but housing prices tend to drop markedly. In brief, people can leave, houses cannot. If housing were not so permanent, older industrial cities might lose even more people—and very quickly. However, housing in population losers such as Detroit is relatively cheap. This attracts new homebuyers, who stem the tide of population loss a bit, thus saving older, industrial cities such as Detroit. Ditto for towns elsewhere,

TABLE 1.1　CHANGES IN POPULATION GROWTH, 1990–2000, IN THE 10 LARGEST U.S. CITIES

City and State	Population		Change, 1990–2000	
	April 1, 1990	April 1, 2000	Number	%
New York, NY	7,322,564	8,008,278	685,714	9.4
Los Angeles, CA	3,485,398	3,694,820	209,422	6
Chicago, IL	2,783,726	2,896,016	112,290	4
Houston, TX	1,630,553	1,953,631	323,078	19.8
Philadelphia, PA	1,585,577	1,517,550	-68,027	-4.3
Phoenix, AZ	983,403	1,321,045	337,642	34.3
San Diego, CA	1,110,549	1,223,400	112,851	10.2
Dallas, TX	1,006,877	1,188,580	181,703	18
San Antonio, TX	935,933	1,144,646	208,713	22.3
Detroit, MI	1,027,974	951,270	-76,704	-7.5

Source: U.S. Census Bureau, Census 2000; 1990 Census, Population and Housing Unit Counts, United States (1990 CPH-2–1).

TABLE 1.2　THE 10 FASTEST-GROWING U.S. METROPOLITAN AREAS, 1990–2000

Metropolitan Area	Population		Change, 1990–2000	
	April 1, 1990	April 1, 2000	Number	%
Las Vegas, NV	852,737	1,563,282	710,545	83.3
Naples, FL	152,099	251,377	99,278	65.3
Yuma, AZ	106,895	160,026	53,131	49.7
McAllen/Edinburg/Mission, TX	383,545	569,463	185,918	48.5
Austin/San Marcos, TX	846,227	1,249,763	403,536	47.7
Fayetteville/Springdale/Rogers, AK	210,908	311,121	100,213	47.5
Boise, ID	295,851	432,345	136,494	46.1
Phoenix/Mesa, AZ	2,238,480	3,251,876	1,013,396	45.3
Laredo, TX	133,239	193,117	59,878	44.9
Provo/Orem, UT	263,590	368,536	104,946	39.8

Source: U.S. Census Bureau, Census 2000; 1990 Census, www.census.gov.

such as Osaka, Japan, which did not become a ghost town either.

Here's another example of a single concept that can help explain city growth: "the demand for density." According to Glaeser and his coauthors (in Bowley, 2007), cities can grow because consumers want to live there. In brief, people are drawn to dense areas because they offer sought-after pleasures such as sports teams, museums, a restaurant mix, and music. In France, Glaeser and his coauthors found a correlation between the growth of particular cities and the number of restaurants in them. (*Note*: Glaeser and his coauthors conducted their study in flush economic times; the number of restaurants tends to decrease in hard economic times.)

Like higher math, shifts in consumer attitudes, population, production, housing costs, technology, and markets cannot be seen, touched, heard, or grasped concretely. Testable, abstract statements—not personal knowledge—lead to *knowledge about* such shifts. Here is one example that concerns population and investment: In 2007, Australia led all countries in buying commercial real estate in the United States (Bloomberg News, 2007:15). This kind of information cannot be grasped by sharp eyesight or other sensory input. It takes *knowledge about* cities. The same logic goes for understanding that European banks lost billions of dollars, starting in 2007, when they invested heavily in metropolitan U.S. subprime mortgages.

Knowledge about cities takes cultural knowledge too. For example, without cultural knowledge of "the hipness factor," a postmillenium observer could not understand one contemporary trend in some U.S. cities, namely, Atlanta, San Francisco, Denver, Portland, and Austin (Texas). These cities were the biggest gainers in attracting college-educated residents, called "the young and the restless" (those 25–35 years old). The biggest losers (in terms of attracting "the young and the restless") included Washington, D.C., Philadelphia, New York, and Los Angeles (Dewan, 2006).

Often, poets and other artists touch our emotions in ways that statistical tables and abstract theory cannot. (American novelist John Steinbeck noted this difference when he said that history may tell us what happened, but fiction tells us how it felt.) Such is the case with the photos of Riis and Salgado and the movies of so many splendid filmmakers, including the late cinema verité pioneer Jean Rouch (see Rouch's films, particularly *Chronique d'un été* [*Chronicle of a Summer*, in French with English subtitles, 1960–1961]), whose images give us glimpses of urban life from Paris to Niamey, Niger. Here is another: Nobel Prize winner Saul Bellow's ironic assessment of social mobility in the modern industrial city, excerpted from *The Adventures of Augie March*. It is the obituary of a real estate broker in Chicago, written by the broker's son. The son writes that his father

> found Chicago a swamp and left it a great city. He came after the Great Fire [in 1871] said to be caused

by Mrs. O'Leary's cow, in flight from the conscription of the Hapsburg tyrant, and in his life as a builder proved that great places do not have to be founded on the bones of slaves, like the pyramids of Pharaohs....The lesson of an American life like my father's...is that achievements are compatible with decency.

> *(Bellow, [1949] 1964:104)*

Literary artists like Bellow give readers a sense of the richness of life, particularly through the use of detail. Readers feel that they are personally acquainted with the characters and their settings.

Of course, great artists do more than that. They go beyond portraying particular people in specific settings. They represent typical characters in typical situations, that is, general types. As one literary critic notes,

> The goal for all great art is to provide a picture of reality in which the contradiction between appearance and reality, the particular and the general, the immediate and the conceptual, etc., is so resolved that the two converge...and provide a sense of an inseparable integrity.

> *(Lukacs, 1971:34)*

Art, then, or great art, offers both personal acquaintance with and knowledge about a subject.

RETHINKING THE TWO PATHS

Artists, philosophers, and scientists don't agree on the functions or procedures of art—or science. Yet, most now say that acquaintance with and knowledge about an object are inseparable. Some deny the existence of objective reality altogether.

In the twentieth century, artists were among the first to question the notion of scientific objectivity. For example, Pablo Picasso's influential 1907 Cubist painting *Les Demoiselles d'Avignon* (*The Young Women of Avignon*) celebrates indeterminacy and multiple points of view, not certainty or objective reality (Figure 1.4a). Television's cult classic series *Star Trek* echoes this philosophy: The Trekkian theory of life is "infinite diversity in infinite combination" (IDIC).

Even photos, often assumed to be a clear reflection of reality, are IDIC in nature. As photographer Richard Avedon once stated, "All photographs are accurate.

a

Fig. 1.4 MULTIPLE VIEWPOINTS. (*a*) In his cubist painting *Les Demoiselles d'Avignon* (1907) Pablo Picasso shows a new way of looking at "truth": from multiple points of view. Picasso's painting, called "seminal" by some and "the most important painting" of the twentieth century" by others, predated Heisenberg's uncertainty principle by nearly two decades. Even earlier, in the 1880s and 1890s, French impressionist Claude Monet showed how light and weather affect the perception of "reality." Monet painted the same scene–say, Rouen Cathedral or water lilies at his home in Giverny, France—at different times of day, offering multiple views of the same subject under different light. (*b*) In his two paintings of South San Francisco's Candlestick Park (its name has changed many times, reflecting various corporate owners, but most locals still call it "the Stick"), San Francisco painter Jack Freeman captures a related notion: that the same scene can be captured from multiple viewpoints. (*a* Museum of Modern Art, *b* Jack Freeman)

Fig. 1.4b *(continued)*

None of them is the truth (1984)." In addition, photos change their meaning with every viewer; all photos are inherently ambiguous, showing appearances without context. For example, literary critic John Berger and photographer Jean Mohr (1982) showed a photo of a grinning assembly-line worker to various viewers, and they got varied interpretations, including "He's happy the day is over" and "It makes me think of the prisoners in the German camps."

Many scholars and artists agree with Berger and Mohr's implicit point: The distinction between acquaintance with (subjective understanding) and knowledge about (so-called objective understanding) is phony. Some argue that objectivity cannot exist; all knowledge is acquaintance with knowledge because every person participates in all acts of understanding in an individual way (e.g., Polanyi, 1958). Others, notably feminist social scientists, say that the separation of subjectivity and objectivity is a "man-made" norm of mainstream/male-stream social science; they claim that a woman-centered theory of knowledge would narrow the gap between subject and object.

Deconstructionist literary critics go even further. They claim that no such thing as a "real world" exists. In their view, human beings inhabit an indeterminate universe where meaning is constantly shifting and thus unknowable. Those who identity-shift in "virtual reality" computer games, such as SecondLife, may well agree.

The late Jacques Derrida, often considered the modern founder of deconstructionism, and followers of Derrida's theory (or "dogma," as opponents call it) believe that *everything depends on interpretation*. Their conclusion is that one interpretation is no more right or wrong than any other (Derrida, 1986).

Interestingly, literary deconstructionists repeat principles associated with the quantum physicist Werner Heisenberg: indeterminism and uncertainty. Essentially, the Heisenberg **uncertainty principle** says that it is impossible to know both the location and the momentum of a subatomic particle simultaneously: "Either the energy or its location is determinable at the expense of the other" (Wolf, [1988] 1990:44).

Why is this principle of physics so important to literary critics as well as social scientists? Because it implies that (1) observers cannot eliminate themselves from what they observe and (2) people can't observe reality without changing it. Thus, people cannot study the world *except* from a point of view. If correct, this means that facts cannot be separated from values. It also means that neither scientific certainty nor objectivity is attainable. It means that there is no one way of conceptualizing reality and that scientific observations are not value-neutral. In brief, then, scientists don't tell it like "it is" but rather they tell it like they see it.

To conclude: Many thinkers now think that uncertainty characterizes *both* science and art. Einstein's theory of relativity, Picasso's cubism and collages, the blurring of "virtual" and "real" in computer games, and the new physics's quantum mechanics call into question the very ideas of a "real world" and "objectivity." In other words, human observers impose patterns and meaning onto facts.

Ironically, just as social scientists in the United States embraced precise observation and rigorous quantification (traditional research methods of the physical sciences), the physical sciences were leaving these methods behind for new ones that could deal with indeterminacy, irregularity, and unpredictability (the very qualities that many social scientists were trying to leave behind). In effect, just as the "soft" sciences tried to become "harder," the "hard" sciences were becoming "softer."

Still, many argue that the *ideal* of objective knowledge remains important. In this view, claims of objective truth are too important both politically and culturally to abandon. The question of how we know what we know has been debated by thinkers for at least 2,500 years. And like most questions worth asking, it will undoubtedly continue to be debated long past our lifetimes. Meanwhile, for **heuristic** purposes, we will draw the distinction between personal acquaintance with and knowledge about the world around us.

In light of this distinction between personal acquaintance and knowledge about, let us examine a poem: Carl Sandburg's (1878–1967) "Chicago." It may be folk art, not great art—that is a question for literary critics. But we can read it to see what and how it communicates to readers. Here is an excerpt from Sandburg's 1914 word picture of his adopted city:

> HOG Butcher for the World,
> Tool Maker, Stacker of Wheat,
> Player with Railroads and the Nation's Freight
>   Handler;
> Stormy, husky, brawling,
> City of the Big Shoulders:
> They tell me you are wicked and I believe them,
>   for I
> have seen your painted women under the gas
> lamps luring the farm boys.
> And they tell me you are crooked and I answer:
>   Yes, it
> is true I have seen the gunman kill and go free to
> kill again.
> And they tell me you are brutal and my reply is:
>   On the faces of women and children I have
>   seen the marks of wanton hunger.
> And having answered so I turn once more to
>   those who
> sneer at this my city, and I give them back the
> sneer and say to them:
> Come and show me another city with lifted head
>   singing so proud to be alive and coarse and
>   strong and cunning.
> Flinging magnetic curses amid the toil of piling
>   job on job, here is a tall bold slugger set vivid
>   against the little soft cities...
>
> *(in Williams, 1952:579)*

Sandburg's strong images paint a two-sided face of Chicago: vitality and brutality—a proud, strong, cunning and crooked, hungry, wicked city.

Aside from communicating the feel of an industrial city on the move, Sandburg's poem offers insight into the services that Chicago performs (or performed when he wrote the poem): "HOG Butcher for the World," "Tool Maker, Stacker of Wheat," and "Player with Railroads and the Nation's Freight Handler." Compare that list with the more systematic classification of city functions by Harris and Ullman (1945). According to these geographers, there are three different kinds of industrial cities, although one city may perform all three

functions: (1) *central place cities*, performing central services, such as retail trade, for their surrounding area; (2) *transport cities*, including railroad centers and ports; and (3) *specialized function cities*, performing one particular service, such as mining or meat packing. From the first three lines of Sandburg's poem, we know that Chicago is (or, rather, was) a city that performed all three functions: (1) central place, "Tool Maker, Stacker of Wheat"; (2) transport, "the Nation's Freight Handler"; and (3) specialized function, "HOG Butcher for the World." Thus, the kind of city Chicago was can be derived from Sandburg's poem, as well as from the Harris and Ullman classification scheme.

Writers, artists, and social scientists often communicate similar messages but use different methods and styles. The awareness of industrial city life is more intimate and direct in Sandburg's poetic vision than in the geographers' scheme. As a Chicagoan of Sandburg's era, sociologist Robert E. Park said in his classic essay on the city in 1916: "We are mainly indebted to writers of fiction for our more intimate knowledge of contemporary urban life" (1974:3). Park continued, however, that urban life "demands a more searching and disinterested study"—a marriage of personal acquaintance with and knowledge about the city. And that is what Park and the distinguished urban-oriented scholars at the University of Chicago proposed to do in 1916.

UNDERSTANDING CHICAGO IN ITS HEYDAY, 1890s–1920s

USING SOCIAL SCIENCE AND LITERATURE AS PATHS TO KNOWLEDGE

To novelist Nelson Algren, Chicago in the 1950s was the

> most native of American cities, where the chrome-colored convertible cuts through the traffic ahead of the Polish peddler's pushcart. And the long, low-lighted parlor-cars stroke past in a single, even yellow flow.... Big-shot town, small-shot town, jet-propelled old-fashioned town, by old-world hands with new-world tools built into a place whose heartbeat carries farther than its shout.
>
> *([1952] 1961:59–60)*

Fig. 1.5 SANDBURG'S CHICAGO. The intense energy that characterized Chicago over 100 years ago is reflected in its street life. This 1905 photo was taken at State and Madison Streets, said to be the busiest street corner in the world at the time. Note Louis Sullivan's skyscraper, later the Carson Pirie & Scott Company, at the right. Sullivan's art nouveau decoration frames the store's display windows. It has been hailed as one of the great works of modern commercial architecture. (City of Chicago Public Art Collection, Department of Cultural Affairs)

Around the time that Park and his University of Chicago colleagues were studying the city scientifically—using Chicago as their sociological laboratory—a world literature was being produced in the Windy City. From the beginning of the century until roughly 1920, Chicago produced writers the same way it had created the nation's first skyscrapers in the 1880s. Writers became so numerous in Chicago in the period 1900–1920 that some literary critics. observed that Chicago writers had nearly taken over the entire field of North American letters.

Why was Chicago like a magnet, attracting writers speaking with a new U.S. voice? Why was Chicago also an architect's dream town, with Louis Sullivan's skyscrapers and Frank Lloyd Wright's prairie houses? And why was Chicago a social scientist's town, a lab for urban research? For many of the same reasons.

Nelson Algren suggested that Chicago's great literary scene did not happen accidentally:

Chicago is the...city in which a literature bred by hard times...once became a world literature....For it was here that those arrangements more convenient to owners of property than to the propertyless were most persistently contested by the American conscience.

([1952] 1961:12–13)

"Those arrangements more convenient to owners of property" had been contested even before the turn of the century. Indeed, Chicago was a center of industry and industrial conflict by the 1870s.

The city had quickly rebounded from the Great Chicago Fire in 1871 (which wiped out the central business district and over 17,000 buildings). Ironically, the fire provided a blank slate to architects and developers to construct a new downtown with taller buildings.

LABOR RADICALISM, INDUSTRIAL PROGRESS, AND SOCIAL REFORM

Several events before 1900 give a feel for the conflicting currents in Chicago. First, there was the railroad strike in 1877, which prepared fertile ground for socialist and anarchist organizers among the workers.

Second, there was the Haymarket Square affair in 1886. This was a labor meeting which was called to protest police violence against locked-out employees at the Cyrus McCormick Harvester Works and ended in Haymarket Square. As Box 1.1 details, it ended when an unknown person or persons threw a bomb into the crowd. (Globally, except in the United States, May 1 is celebrated as international workers' day. This is ironic because May Day is celebrated in memory of Chicago's Haymarket riot.) One sociologist points out that

> On May 1, 1886, in many U.S. cities workers engaged in a general strike in support of an eight-hour day. In Chicago, 80,000 workers marched down Michigan Avenue. On the fourth day of the demonstrations, at the very end of a rally in Haymarket Square, violence broke out. Its origin is contested to this day.
>
> *(Wallerstein, 2008)*

The Haymarket Square affair, according to one urban historian, "symbolized an era in American history; it dramatized the determination of the business interests to maintain the status quo" (Spear, 1967:3). Chicago, an industrial capitalist stronghold famed for its production—from meatpacking and farm machinery to iron, steel, and men's clothing—"also became the nation's leading producer of anarchists" (Crain, 2006:84).

Third, there was the Chicago World's Fair—the Columbian Exposition—in 1893. Led by the famous architect and planner Daniel Burnham (remembered by his credo "Make no little plans. They have no magic to stir men's blood."), a group of architects, promoters, and planners constructed a "white city," part of the "City Beautiful," on Chicago's South Side. It was a monument to industrial progress, showing off the technology that was making the United States a world economic power. An estimated 27 million visitors came from all over the world to see the exposition's midway, the world's first Ferris wheel, and the Woman's Building (designed by a woman, managed by women, and featuring thousands of exhibits exclusively by women). Visitors also slurped one ancestor of fast food: ice cream. This mass-produced, affordable edible became an important treat for workers, and the World's Fair was "an ideal marketing ground" for ice cream (Binford, 1987:9).

Fourth, there was the Pullman railroad strike in 1894. The strike shut down the nation's railroads and brought federal troops to the city. Railroad magnate George Pullman had constructed a model industrial town for his workers just south of Chicago; the privately owned company town was a totally planned community, with decent housing for the workers, attractive shopping arcades, a library, and a hotel. But no matter how lovely the park-like setting and the amenities for workers in Pullman's town, it was still Pullman's town. His ownership and control carried the seeds of industrial conflict, not peace.

And, finally, there were a variety of efforts aimed at social reform. These ranged from Jane Addams's work at Hull House on the West Side to attempts to reform City Hall and improve sanitary conditions in the slums, led by local merchants and their wives.

All of this—industrial conflict, attempts at reform, monuments to "progress" and technology—was taking place in the world's fastest-growing metropolis of the era: Chicago. And all of this so shortly after Mrs. O'Leary's cow had allegedly started the 1871 fire that ravaged one-third of the city.

In its heyday, Chicago was many things to many people. It had the reputation of being the most politically radical of all American cities. Among others, it was the town of socialist Eugene V. Debs and Big Bill Haywood, leader of the Wobblies, the Industrial Workers of the World (IWW) (Box 1.1).

URBAN RESEARCHERS AND WRITERS: CONVERGENT GOALS

Chicago, "City of the Big Shoulders," was the cradle of urban research in the United States for many of the same reasons that made it the most stimulating literary scene of its day. As writer Algren put it, it was in Chicago that challenges were made to the existing economic and social arrangements by "a conscience in touch with humanity." Social scientists at the University of Chicago who pioneered urban research were an important part of that conscience.

As two University of Chicago sociologists later recalled about this period,

> By the time our studies began, the various ethnic neighborhoods were well established....By this time, too, public sentiment had crystallized into rather firm prejudice and discrimination against the new arrivals from Eastern Europe and Southern Europe....Landlords were taking advantage of the crowded housing situation....The city administration was commonly regarded as corrupt....Many families were desperately poor.
>
> *(Burgess and Bogue, 1964:5)*

BOX 1.1 CHICAGO'S "OFFICIAL HISTORY"

Haymarket Plaque, placed on a building at the corner of Desplaines and Randolph Streets in 1971. It reads as follows:

> On May 4, 1886, hundreds of workers gathered here to protest police action of the previous day against strikers engaged in a nationwide campaign for an eight-hour workday. Radicals addressed the crowd. When police attempted to disperse the rally, someone threw a bomb. The bomb and ensuing pistol shots killed seven policemen and four other persons. Although no vidence linked any radicals to the bomb, eight of them were convicted and four hanged. Three were later pardoned. The strike collapsed after the tragedy.

What Schoolchildren Learned About Their City

Analyzing history schoolbooks can be instructive for reasons other than learning history. Why? Because the writers are far from dispassionate reporters. Inevitable choices—what to include or exclude—reflect a point of view. So do names given to events, for instance, a "riot" or "civil unrest." Also, ideological assumptions creep in, masquerading as facts. Indeed, in her study of U.S. history textbooks (1980:129, 139), Pulitzer Prize–winning author Frances Fitzgerald found that most U.S. high school texts portrayed the country as a kind of "Salvation Army to the rest of the world: throughout [its] history, it had done little but dispense benefits to poor, ignorant, and diseased countries," acting in "a disinterested fashion, always from the highest of motives." That, we can assume, is the "official" version of historical reality.

Texts written for *younger* readers may be even more instructive, giving more clues to the "official" version of history at any particular time. One widely used elementary text used in Chicago about 100 years ago was Jennie Hall's *The Story of Chicago* ([1911] 1929). Interestingly—and perhaps not surprisingly—this text, distributed to schools by the Chicago Board of Education, contains no mention of certain facets of Chicago's history: political corruption, labor history, industrial conflict, or ethnic prejudice and discrimination. One does find Haymarket Square complete with a line drawing of its hustle-bustle, but the incident that immortalized it—the Haymarket Square affair in 1886—goes unmentioned. Here is what Chicago schoolchildren learned about Haymarket's function: "There is another place in Chicago besides the market on 14th Street where vegetables are sold. It is Haymarket Square on the west side....Haymarket tells you a story of the many truck gardens near this great city" (250). Yes, but Haymarket, of course, symbolizes quite another story. Haymarket, in one historian's view, was "the great social drama of the era" (Avrich, 1984).

Continued

BOX 1.1 *Continued*

Somewhat ironically, Hall (a teacher at one of Chicago's elite private schools) hoped that her book would be "a finger pointing to real material for study" (303). What is "real material," however, is usually a matter of some controversy. In the following excerpt from *The Story of Chicago*, note particularly how the text handles the problems of the city and the proposed solutions. Compare Hall's "official" version of history to one "unofficial," competing vision, that of the Industrial Workers of the World (the Wobblies, or IWW). Clearly, their views of reality are far apart.

Why did Chicago, built in a swampy wilderness, become a great city? Where will a large city grow up? There must be people living about with things to sell. Good land roads or water roads must lead to her.... [In Chicago] land travel met lake travel. That is why we are a railroad center. That is why cattle are brought here.... That is why grain comes here.... All these industries bring workers. These people need stores, theatres, churches, schools.... So the city keeps adding to itself. Soon it comes to need officers to take care of it and its people—mayor, policemen, firemen, board of health, street commissioners. Then it gets into trouble because it is so big. In some places its houses are so close together that people get no sunshine and children no place to play. Some of its tenements are too crowded. The air is smoky from factories. Many of the people are poor. The city need try no more to be large and rich. But it must try to be clean and comfortable and happy. That is the great problem now, and there is much work to be done in solving it. There are many fine public schools in Chicago.... Americanization schools help the foreigner to become a good citizen.... But there is still much to be done in making the schools as useful to all as they can be. People must be taught to make even better use of... the public libraries and the Art Institute.... (Hall, [1911] 1929:261-264, 287-288)

What Some People Were Singing About

The IWW, nicknamed the "Wobblies," were organized in Chicago in 1905. Their goal was to organize unskilled workers in the factories and fields throughout the nation. They focused their efforts on groups considered to be dispossessed and downtrodden, including textile mill workers in the Northeast, coal and iron miners in West Virginia and Minnesota, migrant workers, and Northwest lumberjacks.

"Sing and fight" was a Wobblie slogan. Many organizers shaped their protests into songs as tools for agitation. About 1909, the first edition of their *Little Red Song Book* appeared, with its cover announcing "IWW Songs—to Fan the Flames of Discontent." The most popular union song in the United States, "Solidarity Forever," was written by Wobblie organizer Ralph Chaplin after his return from a coal miners' strike near Charleston, West Virginia, in 1915. Sung to the tune of

"John Brown's Body," the song is full of revolutionary fervor. One stanza reveals the Wobblies' view of the new industrial order—class struggle—in which people are divided into two camps: "them" (owners of mines and factories, the capitalists) and "us" (the exploited workers):

> They have taken untold millions that they never toiled
> to earn,
> But without our brain and muscle not a single wheel
> could turn.
> We can break their haughty power, gain our freedom
> when we learn
> That the union makes us strong.

Wobblie organizer Joe Hill was one of the IWW's best songwriters as well as a leading agitator. In 1914, Hill was arrested in Salt Lake City on a murder charge and executed there. The day before his execution in 1915, he sent IWW head Big Bill Haywood a wire in Chicago: "Don't waste time mourning. Organize." Joe Hill's body was brought to Chicago, where a great funeral procession was held. One of the songs sung by the approximately 30,000 sympathizers was Ralph Chaplin's "The Commonwealth of Toil" (in Fowke and Glazer, [1960] 1961:14-16). Here is the first verse and the chorus:

> When each man can live his life secure and free;
> In the gloom of mighty cities,
> Midst the roar of whirling wheels,
> We are toiling on like chattel slaves of old,
> And our masters hope to keep us
> Ever thus beneath their heels,
> And to coin our very life blood into gold.

CHORUS
> But we have a glowing dream
> Of how fair the world will seem
> When each man can live his life secure and free;
> When the earth is owned by labor
> And there's joy and peace for all
> In the Commonwealth of Toil that is to be.

In 1905 former Idaho governor Frank Steunenberg was assassinated. (Six years earlier, as governor, Steunenberg had called in the U.S. military to put down a workers' strike near Coeur d'Alene's mines.) Along with other Wobblies, Big Bill Haywood stood accused of plotting the murder. In *Big Trouble: A Murder in a Small Western Town Sets Off a Struggle for the Soul of America* (New York: Touchstone, [1997] 1998), journalist J. Anthony Lukas tells this story and presents a riveting account of the ensuing trial featuring Clarence Darrow, later famous for his role in the 1925 Scopes Trial (the evolution–creationism controversy).

Sociologists tried to understand the social and economic forces at work in the slums and their effect on slum dwellers. Their objective was scientific analysis. But their hope was a moral one, and it was policy-oriented: to dispel prejudice and injustice and to help change the plight of the slum dwellers.

The numerous poets and novelists inspired or formed by the Chicago scene didn't aim for scientific analysis. Yet, they shared the social scientists' goal: to dispel prejudice and injustice. Here are a few injustices exposed by Chicago's literati. There was the injustice of grain speculators in Chicago's wheat market, exposed by Frank Norris. Norris's *The Pit* ([1903] 1970:41) paints Chicago's Board of Trade building, the global center of the wheat trade, in dark colors: "black, monolithic, crouching on its foundations like a monstrous sphinx with blind eyes, silent, grave."

There was political corruption, exposed by novelist Theodore Dreiser. The story of financier Charles T. Yerkes's buying and selling of Chicago—by corrupting city officials—is told in Dreiser's *The Financier* (1912) and *The Titan* (1914). There were the savage practices at the Union Stockyards, the place that made Chicago "HOG Butcher for the World." Socialist Upton Sinclair exposed the unsanitary conditions and adulteration of food at the nation's stockyards in the greatest muckraking novel of all, *The Jungle* (1905). This exposé had public policy impact, too, influencing

the passage of the Pure Food and Drug Act by Congress (Box 1.2).

Chicago's urban literature ranged in tone from reformist muckraking to socialist outrage. Some described what they saw as "capitalist decay" and the oppression of the many by the few. Like West Coast writer Jack London, Upton Sinclair saw the evils of capitalism in the new industrial order, represented by Chicago. Sinclair measured "what was" against "what could be" in his ideal society under socialism. By contrast, Theodore Dreiser accepted the new industrial order and its corruption as the American destiny, as natural.

There was also a bit of nostalgia for less complex times. Some novelists idealized the Jeffersonian ideal of the small town. Big-city life was sometimes viewed as destructive of human and humane values.

And there was the realization that industrial cities encouraged new standards of behavior. One new norm concerned women. Typically, nineteenth-century fictional heroines were weak and faint-hearted, dressed either in rags or in regal gowns. But some Chicago novelists (e.g., Fuller, 1895) understood that such traditional heroines had no place in the city; the new city woman was stronger and more independent, resembling social reformer Jane Addams (the founder of Chicago's Hull House) more than a shrinking violet.

In general, then, writers reacted in two different ways to Chicago and the new republic for which it

---

BOX 1.2   POLITICS AND THE NOVEL

The Impact of Upton Sinclair's *The Jungle*

In *The Jungle* (1905), Sinclair tells the tragic story of Jurgis Rudkus, a Lithuanian immigrant, and his relatives and friends who work at the Union Stockyards and live nearby, in the "back of the yards" neighborhood. There, in what Sinclair called "Packingtown," immigrants were victimized by those who had control or influence over them: landlords, real estate brokers, meatpacking bosses, supervisors, and political bosses. Sinclair paints a dreary picture of crushed lives under these conditions. In the end, Rudkus turns to socialism as the only hope for a decent life.

Ironically, very few pages of Sinclair's novel are devoted to the brutality and smell of the stockyards. But that is what

caught the public eye—and stomach. Sinclair's purpose was much broader: to expose what he considered the evils of capitalism, especially "wage slavery," and to make an appeal for socialism. But, as he said of his own work, "I aimed at the public's heart and by accident I hit it in the stomach (in Blackwell)."

The Jungle had immediate political impact but not what Sinclair had hoped for. President Theodore Roosevelt, who had seen an advance copy of the book, wired Sinclair to visit him in Washington, D.C., to talk about stockyard conditions. Six months later, over violent opposition by the meatpacking industry, the Pure Food and Drug Act and the Beef Inspection Act were passed by Congress.

stood: Some looked backward and others looked forward. Novelists of the Progressive Era (1904–1917) "based their values either on the traditional individualism and amenity of an agricultural and small owner's way of life (which was the ideal of the Progressive movement), or on...Socialism" (Kazin, [1942] 1956: 64–65).

Urban research started by the Chicago sociologists, beginning in the Progressive Era, arose from the same mix of responses to the new industrial order. Robert Park, for instance, had nostalgia for the small town in Minnesota where he grew up. At the same time, Park was deeply ambivalent about the limitations of small-town life and the sense of community it supposedly offered. Before teaching at the University of Chicago, he had been a reformist-minded news reporter in the Midwest and publicity person for Booker T. Washington's Tuskegee Institute. Park's

colleague, Ernest W. Burgess (who constructed a classic model of urban space, shown in Chapter 2), was concerned with what he assumed to be a result of urban-industrial life: social disorganization—indicated by crime, delinquency, family breakdown, and so forth.

THE CITY BEAUTIFUL

Urban research...social reform...big novels. All responses to Chicago, "the capital of the frontier world of acquisitive energy" (Kazin, [1942] 1956:94) and the pulse of the heartland. But what about other professionals and interested parties—how did they react to the expanding industrial city?

Chicago's business executives focused their energy on promoting the city's industrial development and facilitating suburbanization. City planners concentrated their efforts on making the city more beautiful, including building monumental architecture (Fig. 1.6).

Fig. 1.6   BIRD'S-EYE VIEW OF THE CHICAGO WORLD'S FAIR, 1893. The monumental neoclassical architecture of the Columbian Exposition (critics called it a "White City of wedding cake buildings") inspired the City Beautiful movement throughout the United States. (Hubert Howe Bancroft, *The Book of the Fair* [Chicago, 1893], p. 71)

It was in the Chicago Plan that the expertise and ideas of planner extraordinaire Daniel Burnham came together with the interests of Chicago's business leaders. Labeling his idea the "**City Beautiful**," Burnham persuaded the influential Chicago Commercial Club to back the Chicago Plan of 1909, a giant, even superhuman-scale, city plan. It is noteworthy that Baron Georges-Eugène Haussmann's plan for Paris in the 1860s (Chapter 17) inspired Burnham and the City Beautiful movement. For his 1909 plan of Chicago, Burnham borrowed several features from Haussmann's plan, including diagonal street layouts. Indeed, Burnham saw Chicago as "Paris on the prairie" (Thakkar, 2006). Burnham's idea was to create romantic parks and lovely waterfront landscapes by Lake Michigan with huge plazas and broad thoroughfares. This was to serve as a contrast to city life. According to Burnham:

> Natural scenery furnishes the contrasting element to the artificiality of the city. *All of us should often run away... into the wilds, where mind and body are restored to a normal condition,* and we are enabled to take up the burden of life in our crowded streets and endless stretches of buildings with renewed vigor and hopefulness.
>
> *(Burnham and Bennett in Glaab and Brown, 1983:263; italics mine)*

Clearly, Burnham thought the city was a place to escape from.

Interestingly, the Chicago Plan hardly mentioned the "burden of life" on those who carried more than their measure: the urban poor. As the University of Chicago researchers and the novelists had well noted, by 1909 parts of Chicago were one immense slum, housing new immigrants from eastern and southern Europe in crowded, overpriced, deteriorated tenements. But only two short paragraphs of Burnham's Chicago Plan are devoted to the problems of the widespread slums. And what were the suggested solutions? The plan, in familiar-sounding language, suggested two ways of dealing with what it termed the "unwholesome district": (1) cutting broad boulevards through it and (2) enforcing sanitation and cleanliness codes.

So, Chicago became a proving ground for Burnham's City Beautiful concept: that cities could be improved physically without any restructuring of economic, social, or political institutions. Most of the improvements that Burnham counseled, aside from the glorious parks for people wishing to flee the city, were meant to spur commerce and industry. For instance, Michigan Avenue and other streets were to be widened to facilitate downtown traffic. "No wonder," writes one of Chicago's biographers, "the cry went up that the Chicago Plan was in reality a scheme to tax the poor for improvements desired by the rich" (Lowe, 1978:173–174).

The Chicago Plan emphasized civic beauty, for Burnham was convinced that human nature craved beauty so much that "people will travel far to find and enjoy it." This vision of human nature and what people need to lead healthy, fulfilling urban lives was distinctly different from what Chicago's novelists and urban researchers believed.

(*Update*: One hundred years later, in 2009, Chicago celebrated Burnham's influential Chicago Plan with pavilions in Millennium Park, a park that opened a few years after the new millennium due to construction delays and cost overruns. Burnham would have no doubt liked the park, particularly a music pavilion designed by Frank Gehry. See Chapter 14 for a photo.)

The City Beautiful. The squalor of the slums. Industrial progress and poverty. Chicago was all of these. And it was a poet—Carl Sandburg—who perhaps best captured the promise and the problems of the city. In "Chicago" and other poems, Sandburg drew an image of the Windy City as a wondrous thing, a bold human enterprise. Yet Chicago, this new city, this representative of the new industrial order, corrupts what he considered human emotions. That is, in the shuffle for the almighty dollar and industrial development, Sandburg feared that friendship, mutual caring, and human dignity were lost amid the skyscrapers and the steel.

CHICAGO: MICROCOSM OF THE NEW INDUSTRIAL ORDER

Sandburg's view of Chicago—and, more broadly, urban industrial capitalist society—echoes the theories put forward by many nineteenth-century social theorists about urban life. And his views resound in the work of the Chicago school of sociology. As detailed in Chapter 6, the University of Chicago urban theorist Louis Wirth (1938) viewed "urbanism as a way of life"; several of Wirth's key ideas parallel Sandburg's poetic images.

Alienation. Rootlessness. Superficial relationships. The loss of human connections. Materialism. Money instead of personal relations as the bond of association among people. These were what poet Sandburg and theorist Wirth saw as the price to be paid for living in the modern industrial American city. At the same time, both noted the energy, the greater mobility, and the increased individual freedom that the new industrial city promised. Such were the contradictions in Chicago and in the new American industrial order that Chicago symbolized. Using ideas or images, Chicago's urbanists, poets, political organizers, and novelists alerted their different audiences to the promise and conditions of urban life.

Although beyond the scope of this chapter, it is noteworthy that many post–World War II Chicago writers bemoaned the transformation of the "City on the Make" to a postindustrial city; they viewed it as a period of literary and economic decline. For one, Mike Royko, revered Chicago newspaper columnist, rewrote Sandburg's poem in 1967 as a parody, personifying the city's change from giant of industry to "smooth salesman," from HOG Butcher for the World, Tool Maker, Stacker of Wheat" to "Hi-Rise for the World/Partygoer, stacker of stereo tapes..." (in Rotella, 1998:104).

To summarize: Chicago's writers and urbanists responded to the new industrial order that Chicago represented. Both described new phenomena, whether in the form of personal images that communicated a firsthand acquaintance with the city or in the form of abstract maps and models. Rooted in the same historical climate, their insights often ran parallel. Some theorists, like Park, had a nostalgic affection for small-town, agricultural communities; they worried about the loss of the sense of community in a big industrial city. Others, like Upton Sinclair, described similar urban conditions but saw the causes of urban problems as part of the economic and social arrangements under capitalism.

These differences in vision remain to this day. So do controversies about civic beauty and about what urbanites need to thrive. This brings us to another poem by Carl Sandburg, "Elephants Are Different to Different People" (1970:628–629):

Wilson and Pilcer and Snack stood before
the zoo elephant.
Wilson said, "What is its name? Is it from
Asia or
Africa? Is it a he or a she?
How
old is it? Do they have twins? How much does it
cost to feed? How much does it weigh? If it
dies, what will they use the bones, the fat, and
the hide for? What
use is it
besides to look at?"

Pilcer didn't have any questions; he was
murmuring
to himself, "It's a house by itself, walls and
windows,
the ears came from tall cornfields...,
I know
elephants are good to babies."
Snack looked up and down and at last said
to
himself, "He's a tough son-of-a-gun outside and
I'll bet he's got a strong heart, I'll bet he's
strong as a copper-riveted boiler inside."
They didn't put up any arguments.
They didn't throw anything in each other's
faces.
Three men saw the elephant three ways
And let it go at that.
They didn't spoil a sunny Sunday afternoon.
"Sunday comes only once a week," they
told each other.

Our aim is to see the elephant (in this case, the city) in more than three ways—and *not* let it go at that. Wide-angle vision and spirited debate, not sweeping controversy under the rug for the sake of a sunny Sunday afternoon, are essential if we want to reclaim the promise of the city and to deal effectively with urban conditions.

a

Fig. 1.7 WALLS THAT TELL STORIES. (*a*) Victor Arnautoff's *City Life* is one of the 1930s federal arts project frescoes in Coit Tower, San Francisco. (*b*) Brooke Fancher's mural, *Tuzuri Watu/We Are a Beautiful People*, also in San Francisco, celebrates African American culture, particularly female writers. ([*a*] Tim Teninty, [*b*] Deborah Mosca)

Thus, this book is not full of definitive answers or solutions. Nor is it a tract for a particular point of view. Rather, it is an invitation to open your eyes, ears, heart, and mind to experiencing and reflecting upon the city. I hope to provide tools that will assist you in deciding whether Wilson, Pilcer, or Snack sees the beast most clearly—or whether they all suffer from tunnel vision.

KEY TERMS

Acquaintance with Personal, direct, intuitive, holistic, nonlinear, concrete, subjective knowledge. Contrast: **knowledge about**.

City Beautiful A movement inspired by architect–city planner Daniel Burnham around the turn of the twentieth century. (The man responsible for the mid-nineteenth-century transformation of Paris, Baron Haussmann, was a key inspiration to Burnham; see Chapter 17.) City Beautiful planners believed that people needed to escape from the burden of city life to natural surroundings, such as large parks, and that cities could be improved physically without restructuring basic institutions.

Heuristic A model, assumption, or device that is not necessarily scientifically true but is a useful tool to aid in the discovery of new relationships. For example, classifying people as urbanites or rural dwellers is a heuristic device that assumes that urbanites share common traits in contrast to rural people.

b

Fig. 1.7 (*continued*)

Knowledge about Systematic, abstract, linear, theoretical knowledge.

Metropolitan area A concentrated, dense settlement of people in a core city together with the city's suburban population who are economically and socially interdependent The U.S. Census Bureau uses specific criteria of population size and economic interdependence to define metropolitan areas, as detailed in Chapter 7. (See also "micropolitan area" defined and discussed in Chapter 7.) Opposite: *nonmetropolitan area.*

Uncertainty principle German physicist Werner Heisenberg's principle: Observers cannot know both the position and the momentum of a moving electron with absolute certainty. Interpreted by many scholars to mean that objectivity in doing physical or social science is impossible.

PROJECTS

1. **Understanding the city through social science and art.** Compare the treatment of a city (and/or its suburbs) by artists and social scientists. Choose a city which is the backdrop or important character in at least four films. For example, greater Los Angeles. What impressions does one get of Los Angeles and its suburbs from *Punch-Drunk Love* (2002), *Magnolia* (1999), *Zoot Suit* (1981), *L.A. Story* (1991), *L.A. Confidential* (1997), *Blade Runner* (1982), *Chinatown* (1974), and *Sunset Boulevard* (1950)? Or take London or Tokyo. What impressions do viewers get about London from *My Beautiful Laundrette* (1986), *Secrets and Lies* (1996), *Love Actually* (2003), *Dirty Pretty Things* (2002), and *84 Charing Cross Road* (1986)? What feelings do you have about Tokyo from *The Fast and the Furious* (2006),

Lost in Translation (2003), *Kill Bill 1* (2003); *You Only Live Twice* (1967), *Whisper of the Heart* (1995), and *Tokyo Story* (1953)?

After screening the films (available from film libraries, rental stores, or online sources), look at statistical data and general analyses of the city or city–suburban area (data, e.g., from the U.S. Census Bureau and/or the U.K. Census 2et al). Then, choose two or three topics (e.g., the racial/ethnic makeup of the area; the "feel" of the city and its neighborhoods, including the housing stock) and write a two-page paper, comparing what you learned via "acquaintance with" and "knowledge about" the city you chose.

2. **An eye–ear tour of one city**. Walk around a city with sound equipment, such as a tape recorder, recording the city's soundscape. Are some areas noisier than others? What sounds typify different neighborhoods? (For example, are children's voices everywhere? Are street sellers or knife sharpeners calling out their services?) Also, note the landscape: What are the city's most imposing buildings, and what functions are performed in them? Are church spires, factory smokestacks, or office buildings the tallest structures? What do bulletin boards and signs advertise? If street murals exist, what do they portray?

3. **Varieties of experience**. This is a project for three to five teammates. Together, choose any two- to four-block area of a city or suburb. Then, separately, walk around the area, taking photos and/or writing down observations at different times of the day. Compare your impressions. Did you experience the area in the same way? If not, what might account for the differences?

SUGGESTIONS FOR FURTHER LEARNING

Many industrial and postindustrial cultures romanticize rural and small-town life while denigrating urban and suburban life. In the United States, this tendency is detailed in Morton White and Lucia White, *From Thomas Jefferson to Frank Lloyd Wright* (New York: Mentor, 1964).

In Europe, the pastoral life tends to be positively linked to "the good life"; the rural countryside is often represented as the antithesis of troubled cities. For example, in an article (translated as "France: Rural Roots in Peril") in *Le Monde* (February 22,

2006), author Jean-Louis Andréani cites Pascal Dibié, an ethnologist at the University of Paris-VII, who notes that the French are confronted with the "permanent contradiction between the seduction of urban culture and the attraction of a rural life that is imagined to be harmonious and familial (see http://www.lemonde.fr/web/article/0,1-0@2-3232,36-43829,0.html).

Over time—either a decade or a few centuries—rural life can become romanticized. In the United States, Grant Wood's 1930 painting *American Gothic* is exemplary of the decade-short shift. This painting depicts what may be the nation's most famous couple: a plain, stoic-looking woman and a man holding a hayfork, standing in front of a white house with a red barn in the background.

Fig. 1.8   GRANT WOOD'S *AMERICAN GOTHIC*. This "icon of Americana" and arguably the most famous painting in the United States has meant different things at different times. According to Professor Steve Biel, the painting was viewed as a satire of Iowans and farm life when painted in 1930. But in a short time, the painting came to symbolize something quite different: core U.S. values such as hard work and stability. (Art Institute of Chicago)

According to Steve Curwood, host of National Public Radio's *Living on Earth* program (November 12, 2005), *American Gothic* has become an "icon of Americana." Indeed, *American Gothic* has been reimaged many times. One redo appeared in 2007 on the cover of Robert Frank's *Richistan: A Journey Through the American Wealth Boom and the Lives of the New Rich* (New York: Crown). Here, the farmer's wife holds a toy poodle, and the couple stands in front of a big, modern home with pool.

Steve Biel, director of the history and literature program at Harvard and author of *American Gothic: The Life of America's Most Famous Painting* (Norton, 2005), notes an irony surrounding the painting: When first painted, *American Gothic* was seen as an insult to—even a satire of—Iowans, especially farm wives who saw themselves as "modern," the opposite of "folks standing around with hayforks." (In the 1930s, being "modern" was often equated with being urban in the United States.) Only later did *American Gothic* morph, in public opinion. It became part of the national mythology as a "celebratory image of wholesome American values, of stability." During the Great Depression, Biel says, "the farmer and his wife in the painting were reinterpreted—from 'repressive Puritans' to 'Jeffersonian Americans'" (Biel on *Living on Earth*, aired on KQED-radio, November 12, 2005).

For another view—that civilization in the United States survives *only* in the big cities—see H. L. Mencken, *Vintage Mencken*, ed. Alistair Cooke (New York: Vintage, 1956).

Works of art that take cities as their settings or subjects are too numerous to mention. Here is just a glimpse into the range of films over the decades, starting with the late Willard Van Dyke's early documentary film *The City* (1939), with narration by the late, great urban scholar Lewis Mumford; it romanticizes the New England small town, focuses on the lack of humanity in big industrial cities, and calls for new greenbelt communities. Fritz Lang's classic feature film *Metropolis* (1927), set in a robot-like underground city composed of workers and an affluent overground city composed of their bosses. Charlie Chaplin's *City Lights* (1931) is a tale of any city (the plot turns on a meeting between the Little Tramp and a millionaire). *Batman* (1989)

creates "Gotham City," a place of ominous opulence; a 2008 sequel, *The Dark Knight*, portrays a much more dangerous city. *Cult classic Koyaanisqatsi (1983, "Life out of Balance" in Hopi)* is a type of documentary movie with a haunting reiterative musical score by Philip Glass; director Godfrey Reggio says that his 87-minute film is "an apocalyptic vision of the collision of urban life and technology vs. the environment" (available on DVD).

The novels of small-town America include Sinclair Lewis's *Main Street* (New York: Harcourt, Brace, 1920), set in Sauk Centre, Minnesota, and Sherwood Anderson's *Winesburg, Ohio* (New York: Modern Library, 1947)—in actuality, his hometown of Clyde, Ohio, near Toledo. Both Lewis and Anderson deromanticized small-town life. iSaul Bellow's *The Adventures of Augie March* (New York: Viking, [1949] 1964), James Farrell's *Studs Lonigan* (New York: Modern Library, 1938) trilogy, and Richard Wright's *Native Son* (New York: Signet, 1940) give different views of life in Chicago after World War I. In *The Moviegoer* (New York: Popular Library, 1962), Walker Percy captures what he calls "the genie-soul" of the city:

> This is a city where no one dares dispute the claim of the wind and the skyey space to the out-of-doors. This Midwestern sky is the nakedest, loneliest sky in America. To escape it, people live inside and underground.

Novelist James Baldwin gives another view of the city—the black ghetto of New York's Harlem in *Go Tell It on the Mountain* (New York: Dell, 1952).

Chicago's urban beginnings are the subject of William Cronon's *Nature's Metropolis: Chicago and the Great West* (New York: Norton, 1991). Cronon argues that Chicago is best understood in an ecological context: the opening of the Great West from the Appalachians to the Rockies. In his view, Chicago's drive for markets and resources helped to create an integrated city–country system that transformed the U.S. landscape. Describing one environmental impact of Chicago's influence, he writes that animals' lives were "redistributed across regional space"—livestock were "born in one place, fattened in another, and killed in still a third."

English professor Carla Cappetti describes Chicago's role as a lab for both novelists and sociologists in *Writing Chicago: Modernism, Ethnography, and the Novel* (New York: Columbia University Press, 1993). Commenting on the connection between fiction and social science, she says that "James T. Farrell, Nelson Algren, and Richard Wright not only explored but kept alive the radical possibilities embedded in the discipline of sociology" (16).

Author Nelson Algren (1909–1981), winner of the first U.S. National Book Award for fiction in 1950, is considered one of Chicago's quintessential writers. (Some critics think that his prize-winning novel, *The Man with the Golden Arm*, an account of the decline of a poker-dealing heroin addict, is overwritten. Yet, they credit Algren as an authentic Chicago writer in a line from Richard Wright and James T. Farrell back to Theodore Dreiser.) Algren described the city's underside, including its corrupt politicians, crooks, addicts, and prostitutes. Jean-Paul Sartre, the life-companion of Simone de Beauvoir (also Algren's 17-year companion), translated parts of Algren's *Chicago: City of the Make* into French. This book, in English, is now available in a fiftieth anniversary edition with an introduction by one of Chicago's best-known authors, interviewers, and personalities, Studs Terkel (Chicago: University of Chicago Press, 2001).

Versions and assessments of what happened at Chicago's Haymarket Square on May 4, 1886, reflect attitudes toward many "isms," including anarchism and industrial capitalism. So do attitudes toward the hanging death of four of the accused. For one, novelist William Dean Howells (in Kazin, [1942] 1995:6) called the hanging "civic murder." Paul Avrich's *The Haymarket Tragedy* (1984) remains the definitive study, but a very readable account is by labor historian James Green, *Death in the Haymarket: A Story of Chicago, the First Labor Movement, and the Bombing that Divided Gilded Age America* (New York: Pantheon, 2006). Green details the decreasing power of craft (which was losing out to the assembly line after the Civil War) together with the growing power of corporations and the difficulties of organizing labor unions as key factors in the era's ideology of anarchism. *Haymarket* (New York: Seven Stories Press, 2005), a

novel by history professor Martin Duberman, brings the energy and turmoil of the late nineteenth-century labor movement to life as well as telling a tale of passion.

For Web discussions of the Haymarket affair, see "The Dramas of Haymarket", produced by the Chicago Historical Museum (formerly the Chicago Historical Society) and Northwestern University. Also see http://www.chicagohistory.org/dramas/overview/main.htm

The spirit of resistance lives on in the United States. Publisher Charles H. Kerr, originally inspired by the Haymarket episode, is still publishing books about labor resistance to what his press believes to be capitalist oppression, particularly the Wobblies (or the IWW). Over the decades, the Wobblies changed their organizational targets. Their original targets included miners and millworkers, but in 2007 Wobblies were trying to organize Starbucks employees into one big union. "Sing and fight" remains a Wobblie principle (hence *The Little Red Song Book*, see Box 1.1). Many IWW songs are included in Archie Green et al., eds., *The Big Red Song Book* (Chicago: Charles H. Kerr, 2007).

Some important literary figures portray post–World War II Chicago as a city transformed—and in literary decline. See Carlo Rotella, *October Cities: The Redevelopment of Urban Literature* (Berkeley: University of California Press, 1998).

Alienation and dehumanization in the modern city is a continuing theme in art. See, for example, the drawings collected in Harold Rosenberg's *Saul Steinberg* (New York: Knopf, 1978). But, to the contrary, Ralph Fasanella's paintings depict the city as a joyous place, with stickball games, as well as a place of aloneness. See Patrick Watson's *Fasanella's City* (New York: Ballantine, 1973).

An older but still useful study of a city's architecture and its relationship to the social context is David Lowe's *Lost Chicago* (Boston: Houghton Mifflin, 1978); it proceeds from the comment by the architect of the American skyscraper and inventor of art nouveau in the United States, Louis Sullivan: "Our architecture reflects us, as truly as a mirror."

A best-seller by Erik Larson, *The Devil in the White City: Murder, Magic, and Madness at the Fair that Changed*

America (New York: Vintage Paperback, 2004), reads like a novel but is an imaginative true tale. It weaves together the stories of architect Daniel H. Burnham, the key builder of the Chicago World's Fair of 1893 (called the "Columbian Exposition" in honor of the 400th anniversary of Christopher Columbus's voyage to the Americas) and a cunning serial killer who used the fair to lure his victims, mainly young, single women, to their deaths. Larson believes that the fair impacted the national psyche in lasting and powerful ways, perhaps including the later construction of Disneyland. Tantalizingly, Larson writes that Walt Disney's father, Elias, helped to construct the White City and that "Walt's Magic Kingdom may well be a descendant" (393).

For a discussion of the controversies surrounding Daniel Burnham's City Beautiful movement and many issues related to Chicago's economic and aesthetic development, see also Garry Wills's excellent, wide-ranging book review essay "Chicago Underground" (*New York Review of Books*, October 21, 1993, pp. 15–22).

One Chicago landmark, the Woman's Building at the Columbian Exposition in 1893, is the subject of Jeanne Madeline Weimann's *The Fair Women* (Chicago: Academy Chicago, 1981). Weimann honors one particular woman, Bertha Honoré Palmer, wife of Potter Palmer, for her effectiveness in bringing the building to life. (Ms. Potter Palmer was also responsible for bringing the bulk of impressionist treasures to Chicago after they were pooh-poohed in Paris in 1870. To this day, the French impressionist collection at Chicago's Art Institute is justly world-renowned.)

When visiting Chicago, take a river cruise sponsored by the Chicago Architecture Foundation. Lasting about 1.5 hours, the boat passes many landmarks, including some skyscrapers (which Chicago pioneered), art deco and modernist buildings, as well as public spaces. Well-schooled docents narrate and encourage questions (see www.architecture.org).

What is the power of a photograph? It all depends—on the skill of the photographer, the subject, and the temper of the times. Praising the emotional power of Sebastião Salgado's work, the *New York Times* once wrote that "Salgado's...photographs do not call for action so much as for a change in consciousness."

And how does Salgado feel about some of the places he photographed? Regarding mega-cities, Salgado once commented that he would forget where he was—perhaps in Cairo? Jakarta? Mexico City? They looked so similar to him. Why? Because in each city there were islands of wealth amidst the poverty, such as green areas of Manila that were private golf clubs, not public parks.

What is the power of statistics? In "America 101," his speech about urban education reprinted on TomPaine.com (November 1, 2006), veteran journalist Bill Moyers repeats the quip that "the mark of a truly educated person is to be deeply moved by statistics." Moyers continues,

> If so, America's governing class should be knocked off their feet by the fact that more than 70 percent of black children are now attending schools that are overwhelmingly non-white. In 1980 that figure was 63 percent. Latino students are even more isolated.

The upshot, says Moyers, is that the 1954 Supreme Court's decision to end segregation (*Brown v. Board of Education*) with all deliberate speed "has become slow motion in reverse."

Visual anthropologist–photographer Bill Owens gives an intimate view of *Suburbia* (San Francisco: Straight Arrow Press, 1973; republished 1999). By including the subjects' own words, Owens offers viewers/readers another layer of reality.

Of special interest are two generation-old documentaries that provide the opportunity to link personal acquaintance with knowledge about city life. In *The Writer and the City* (1970), Alfred Kazin narrates, reading the words of writers about Chicago and New York City, while powerful visual images invade the screen. In *Calcutta* (1968), a section of Louis Malle's prize-winning *Phantom India*, intellect and emotions are both stretched.

Southwestern University in Georgetown, Texas, offers a course using Chicago as a lab. The course, Chicago: Studies in Urban Sociology, an interdisciplinary study of the city in the nineteenth and twentieth centuries, gives students both a firsthand understanding of and systematic reflection about the city over time.

Countless studies and a few films raise the issues of *what* we know and *how* we know what we know. Unfortunately, few introductory social science texts (gatekeepers of a generation's knowledge) discuss the new physics, whose works reject the notions of certainty and determinacy. For a thoughtful discussion of the possibility of conducting objective, value-free social science, see Clifford Geertz, *Works and Lives: The Anthropologist as Author* (Stanford, Calif.: Stanford University Press, 1988). The racism and anti-Semitism of some historians who claim objectivity are discussed by Peter Novick in *That Noble Dream: The "Objectivity Question" and the American Historical Profession* (Cambridge: Cambridge University Press, 1988).

For examples of the ways in which scientists construct reality, see Walter Truett Anderson, *Reality Isn't What It Used to Be: Theatrical Politics, Ready-to-Wear Religion, Global Myths, Primitive Chic and Other Wonders of the Postmodern World* (New York: Harper & Row, 1990). Anderson's premise is that reality is a human construction based on the structure of language and signs.

For a readable and fascinating overview of the relation of scientific notions of objectivity to modern culture, see O. B. Hardison, Jr., *Disappearing Through the Skylight: Culture and Technology in the Twentieth Century* (New York: Viking Penguin, 1989). Hardison argues that modern and postmodern people throughout the world have grown comfortable with fragmentation and contradiction, eschewing the notion of certainty. In *Wild Knowledge: Science, Language, and Social Life in a Fragile Environment* (Minneapolis: University of Minnesota Press, 1992), sociologist Will Wright argues that the idea of knowledge is related to the structure of language and cannot be understood objectively and technically.

In *Chronique d'un été* (*Chronicle of a Summer*, in French with English subtitles, 1960–1961), ethnographer Jean Rouch and sociologist Edgar Morin present a landmark documentary of *cinema verité* (direct cinema), posing questions about the nature of reality itself. Some film buffs think it is probably the most sophisticated anthropological film ever made. (This film is often shown at film festivals and film archive centers.)

For another way of exploring the universe, see the highly readable *Parallel Worlds: A Journey Through Creation, Higher Dimensions, and the Future of the Cosmos* by Michio Kaku (New York: Anchor Books [2005] 2006). A professor of theoretical physics, Kaku guides readers through a vast amount of material, including a discussion of "objective reality."

Ethnomusicologist Alan Lomax collected global music and dance for over 60 years. In 1996, when he was 81 years old, a videotape was made of his life work: *The Global Jukebox*, a multimedia system containing sound recordings, ethnographic films, and taped performances from 400 cultures, making it possible to trace how music and dance styles migrate from one culture to another. The videotape is available from the Association for Cultural Equity at Hunter College in New York City.

REFERENCES

Algren, Nelson. [1952] 1961. *Chicago: City on the Make*. Sausalito, Calif.: Contact Editions.

Avedon, Richard. 1984. http://www.photoquotes.com/ShowQuotes.aspx?id=52&name=Avedon,Richard.

Avrich, Paul. 1984. *The Haymarket Tragedy*. Princeton, N.J.: Princeton University Press.

Bartman, Barry, and Tom Baum. 1998. "Promoting the particular as a niche cultural strategy in small jurisdictions," in W. Faulkner (ed.) *Proceedings, Progress in Tourism and Hospitality Research*. Australian Tourism and Hospitality Research Conference, Gold Coast, Australia.

Bellow, Saul. [1949] 1964. *The Adventures of Augie March*. New York: Viking.

Berger, John, and Jean Mohr. 1982. *Another Way of Telling*. New York: Pantheon.

Binford, Henry C. 1987. "I scream, you scream...the cultural significance of ice cream." *Mosaic* (Fall):6–9.

Blackwell, Jon. n.d. "1906: Rumble over 'The Jungle'." *The Trentonian*. (http://www.capitalcentury.com/1906.html)

Bloomberg News, 2007. "Australians lead in buying U.S. real estate." *International Herald Tribune* (July 12):15.

Bowley, Graham. 2007. "Letter from America: New York shows way for urban renaissance." *International Herald Tribune* (August 25–26):2.

Burgess, Ernest W., and Donald J. Bogue, eds. 1964. *Contributions to Urban Sociology*. Chicago: University of Chicago Press.

Crain, Caleb. 2006. "The terror last time: What happened at Haymarket." *New Yorker* (March 13):82–89.

Derrida, Jacques. 1986. *Philosophy Beside Itself: On Deconstruction and Modernism*. Minneapolis: University of Minnesota Press.

Dewan, Shaila. 2006 . "Cities compete in hipness battle to attract young." *New York Times* (November 25) (http://www.nytimes.com/2006/11/25/us/25young.html?ei=5090&en=48777bf4c9dfa1&ex=1322110800&pagewanted=print).

Dreiser, Theodore. 1912. *The Financier*. New York: Burt.

———. 1914. *The Titan*. New York: Boni & Liveright.

Fitzgerald, Frances. 1980. *America Revised*. New York: Vintage.

Florida, Richard. 2004. *Cities and the Creative Class*. New York: Routledge.

Fowke, Edith, and Joe Glazer, eds. [1960] 1961. *Songs of Work and Freedom*. Garden City, N.Y.: Doubleday, Dolphin.

Fuller, Henry Blake. 1895. *With the Procession*. New York: Harper.

Glaab, Charles N., and A. Theodore Brown. 1983. *A History of Urban America*. New York: Macmillan.

Glaeser, Edward L., and Joseph Gyourko. 2002. "The impact of zoning on housing affordability." Harvard Institute Of Economic Research (HIER) Discussion Paper 1948 (March).

Goethals, Gregor. 1982. *The TV Ritual*. Boston: Beacon Press.

Hall, Jennie. [1911] 1929. *The Story of Chicago*. Chicago: Rand McNally.

Harris, Chauncy D., and Edward L. Ullman. 1945. "The nature of cities." *Annals of the American Academy of Political and Social Science* 242:7–17.

Kazin, Alfred. [1942] 1956. *On Native Grounds: A Study of American Prose Literature from 1890 to the Present [1940]*. Orlando, Fla.: Harcourt Brace.

Kotkin, Joel. 2005. *The City: A Global History*. New York: Modern Library.

Le Corbusier. n.d. "Quotes on New York City."http://www.skyscrapercity.com/archive/index.php/t-122783.html

Lowe, David. 1978. *Lost Chicago*. Boston: Houghton Mifflin.

Lukacs, Georg. 1971. *Writer & Critic and Other Essays*. New York: Grosset & Dunlap.

Lukas, J. Anthony. [1997] 1998. *Big Trouble: A Murder in a Small Western Town Sets Off a Struggle for the Soul of America* (New York: Touchstone).

Morgan, Richard K. 2002. *Altered Carbon*. London: Gollancz.

Muschamp, Herbert. 1993. "Things generally wrong in the universe." *New York Times* [national edition] (April 11):sec. 2, 1+.

Neunemann, Frank. 2001. "A most touching document Review," *Human Migration*. Amazon.com (March 16):

Norris, Frank. [1903] 1970. *The Pit*. Columbus, Ohio: Merrill.

Park, Robert Ezra. [1916] 1974. "The city: Suggestions for the investigation of human behavior in the urban environment." Pp. 1–46 in Robert E. Park, Ernest W. Burgess, and Roderick D. McKenzie, eds., *The City*. Chicago: University of Chicago Press.

Polanyi, Michael. 1958. *Personal Knowledge*. Chicago: University of Chicago Press.

Riis, Jacob A. [1890] 1971. *How the Other Half Lives: Studies Among the Tenements of New York*. New York: Dover.

Roe, Colin, and Fred Koetter. n.d. *Collage City*. Cambridge, Mass.: MIT Press.

Rotella, Carlo. 1998. *October Cities: Redevelopment of Urban Literature*. Berkeley: University of California Press.

Rouch, Jean. 1960 "Chronicle of a summer" (Chronique d'un été). Film

———. 1974. "Cocorico Monsieur Poulet." Film.

Salgado, Sebastião. 2000. *Migrations: Humanity in Transition*. New York: Aperture.

Sandburg, Carl. 1970. *The Complete Poems of Carl Sandburg*. New York: Harcourt Brace Jovanovich.

Sinclair, Upton. 1905. *The Jungle*. New York: Vanguard.

Scott, A. O. 2008. "Metropolis now." *New York Times* (June 8) http://www.nytimes.com/2008/06/08/magazine/08wwin-1ede_t.html?_r=1&ref=magazine&oref=slogin.

Shenker, Israel. 1969. , "E. B. White: Notes and comment by author." *The New York Times* (July 11). http://www.nytimes.com/books/97/08/03/lifetimes/white-notes.html?_r=2

Spear, Sinclair Allan H. 1967. *Black Chicago: The Making of a Negro Ghetto, 1890–1920*. Chicago: University of Chicago Press.

Spear, Allan H. 1967. *Black Chicago: The Making of a Negro Ghetto, 1890–1920*. Chicago: University of Chicago Press

Thakkar, Jonny. 2006. "Paris on the prairie: A perfect city?" *Owl Journal* (Issue 6) http://www.theowljournal.com/article.php?issue=6&number=1&type=print&comments=1.

Wallerstein, Immanuel. 2008. "Race, gender, and class in American politics: Anything new?" Commentary 232 (May 1). Fernand Braudel Center, SUNY-Binghamton. http://www.binghamton.edu/fbc/232en.html

Williams, Oscar, ed. 1952. *A Little Treasury of Modern Poetry*. New York: Scribner.

Wirth, Louis. 1938. "Urbanism as a way of life." *American Journal of Sociology* 44:1–24.

Wolf, Fred Alan. [1988] 1990. *Parallel Universes*. New York: Simon and Schuster, Touchstone.

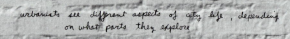

urbanists see different aspects of city life, depending
on what parts they explore

Richard Hedman

CHAPTER 2
THINKING ABOUT CITIES

WHAT YOU SEE DEPENDS ON HOW YOU LOOK AT IT

Reality lies in the eye of the beholder. This truism is whimsically illustrated in Antoine de Saint-Exupéry's tale *The Little Prince*:

> Once when I was six years old I saw a magnificent picture in a book, called *True Stories from Nature*, about the primeval forest. It was a picture of a boa constrictor in the act of swallowing an animal. Here is a copy of the drawing.

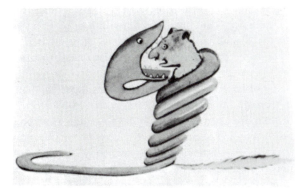

> In the book it said: "Boa constrictors swallow their prey whole, without chewing it. After that they are not able to move, and they sleep through the six months that they need for digestion."
>
> I pondered deeply, then, over the adventures of the jungle. And after some work with a colored pencil I succeeded in making my first drawing. My Drawing Number One. It looked like this:

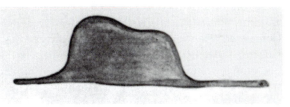

> I showed my masterpiece to the grown-ups, and asked them whether the drawing frightened them. But they answered: "Frighten? Why should anyone be frightened by a hat?"
>
> My drawing was not a picture of a hat. It was a picture of a boa constrictor digesting an elephant. But since the grown-ups were not able to understand it, I made another drawing: I drew the inside of the boa constrictor, so that the grown-ups could see it clearly. They always need to have things explained. My Drawing Number Two looked like this:

> The grown-ups' response, this time, was to advise me to lay aside my drawings of boa constrictors, whether from the inside or the outside, and devote myself instead to geography, history, arithmetic and grammar.... Grown-ups never understand anything by themselves, and it is tiresome for children to be always and forever explaining things to them.
>
> So then I chose another profession, and learned to pilot airplanes. I have flown a little over all parts of the world; and it is true that geography has been very useful to me. At a glance I can distinguish China from Arizona. If one gets lost in the night, such knowledge is valuable.
>
> In the course of this life...[whenever I met a grown-up] who seemed to me at all clear-sighted, I tried the experiment of showing him my Drawing Number One.... I would try to find out, so, if this was a person of true understanding. But, whoever it was, he, or she, would always say: "That is a hat."
>
> Then I would never talk to that person about boa constrictors, or primeval forests, or stars. I would bring myself down to his level. I would talk to him about bridge, and golf, and politics, and neckties. And the grown-up would be greatly pleased to have met such a sensible man.
>
> ([1943] 1970:3–5)

Whether we identify with the imaginative pilot or the sensible grown-ups in Antoine de Saint-Exupéry's modern fable, the point is clear: *What you see depends on how you look at it*. People can look at the same thing and see it through different lenses. Urbanists are no exception. Like other human beings, urbanists filter what they see through lenses. Whatever lens we use, our vision is necessarily limited, for some things are not focused on (like an elephant inside a boa constrictor) or are seen only partially or with distortion.

Here's a more concrete example: an urban street scene. Walking down a familiar street every day, you may not see birds overhead or hear teenagers singing. You may filter out information that seems extraneous, missing the less visible and ignoring the overall picture.

How people see and make sense out of the world depends on many factors, including their age, sex, social background, past experience, present purposes, and so on. Also, spatial perspective can be key. For example, is the person observing through a microscope, a magnifying glass, or a high-powered telescope? In a phrase, scale counts! A book by the late Massachusetts Institute of Technology (MIT) astrophysicist Philip Morrison, his wife Phyllis, and designers Charles and Ray Eames, *Powers of Ten: A Book About the Relative Size of Things in the Universe and the Effect of Adding Another Zero* (1985) (and the 1968 movie by Charles and Ray Eames, *Powers of 10*, updated/changed by others for the contemporary Internet) shows that what you see depends on the scale used. In the contemporary Internet version, we see the universe from various vantage points—at 10 to the power of 23 and 10 to the power of –16. Depending on where you focus, you see very different macro- and micro-cosmoses.

For a moment, let's concentrate on ways of seeing based on three differences. These are differences in (1) modes of understanding, (2) academic and occupational perspectives, and (3) mental maps.

DIFFERENT MODES OF UNDERSTANDING

Most schools stress reason and logic, not emotion or holistic thought. We aren't taught to see boa constrictors, primeval forests, or stars. We are taught to break down wholes into their component parts, to dissect complex phenomena logically. Of course, the sequential, analytical–rational mode is very useful, even essential, to science. After all, as Saint-Exupéry said (tongue-in-cheek), reason helped him to know whether he was flying over China or Arizona.

In his fable, Saint-Exupéry isn't saying that intuition and acquaintance with something should replace reason and systematic thought. Rather, he seems to say, isn't it a shame that sensible grown-ups have lost the childlike quality of imagining, of seeing beyond the information given? Grown-ups who don't use holistic thought and flashes of intuitive insight are robbed of an entire dimension of understanding.

This brings us to another way of ordering information: academic and occupational perspectives. While useful, they too can lead to partial or distorted vision.

ACADEMIC AND OCCUPATIONAL PERSPECTIVES

People's perception of the world is influenced by many factors—age, gender, motives, academic training, and so on. An exercise developed by Larry Susskind (1978) of the Department of Urban Studies and Planning at MIT illustrates these perceptual differences. Susskind begins by drawing a series of maps on the blackboard. Each represents a different way of seeing a city. Taking San Francisco as our example, Figure 2.5 presents several subjective or mental maps of the city—that is, **cognitive maps**. The bare outline of San Francisco (2.5a) is shared by all; the other maps are not. Figure 2.5b shows how transportation engineers might see the city. From this perspective, San Francisco is a vast array of transport networks: a ferry terminal, bus lines, cable car tracks, underground rapid transit, major arteries, and a street grid.

The environmentalist may see one city (Figure 2.5d), while others may see another. The urban designer (Figure 2.5c) may pick out the Transamerica "Pyramid," the city's most visually dominant structure. A bioregionalist may focus on native plants and ecosystems, mapping what's wild in the city. A sociologist concerned with issues of class and race may focus on neighborhoods of extreme contrast, such as white, affluent Pacific Heights and densely settled Chinatown (Figure 2.5e); other parts of the city may fade out altogether. By contrast, a bride-to-be, searching for a gown, might focus on the location of bridal shops, thrift stores, and boutiques . Finally, a poet may see an altogether different city. He or she may focus on the beauty of Golden Gate Park in springtime bloom or share the disgust of poet and long-time political dissident Ahmed Fouad Negm, who wrote (perhaps about his native Cairo) "Glory for the crazy people/In this stupid world" (in Slackman, 2006).

Is it possible that people just don't see parts of the city? Doesn't this exercise using cognitive maps grossly overstate the case? Empirical evidence suggests not.

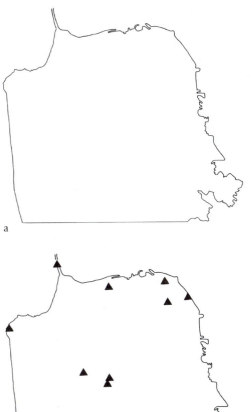

a

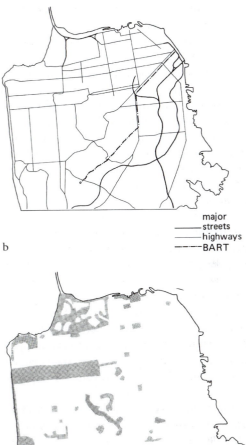

b

major
——— streets
——— highways
——·—· BART

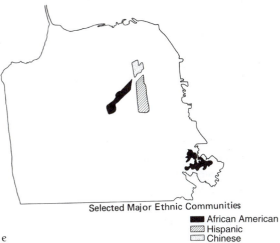

c

▲ Landmarks

d

Fig. 2.5 COGNITIVE MAPS. People with different academic training, occupations, social background, or interests often see a city through different lenses. (*a*) The bare outline of San Francisco. (*b*) How a transportation engineer might envision San Francisco—as a series of major streets, highways, and a mass-transit line. (*c*) Features of the cityscape on which an urban designer might focus, such as landmarks. (*d*) The city from the point of view of an environmentalist who wants to preserve open space. (*e*) The same city as perceived by a sociologist, showing a few of San Francisco's many ethnic communities.

Selected Major Ethnic Communities

■■■ African American
▧▧▧ Hispanic
▢▢▢ Chinese

e

When Kevin Lynch ([1960] 1974) asked Bostonians to draw maps of their city, he found that the interviewees consistently left out whole areas.

And what about unseeable parts of the city? How can we focus on some aspect of city life if it is uncharted? Take, for example, information flows. An important global market in money exchange depends on up-to-the-minute information via telecommunications (Brand, 1987:chapter 12). These information flows may be more important to a local economy than, say, feed grain or tourism. Yet the journey of information remains unmapped…and probably unnoticed.

EVEN ROAD MAPS CONTAIN A POINT OF VIEW

All maps are cognitive maps. They seem to be objective, even natural. But, as Denis Wood points out, every map contains a viewpoint because "every map shows this…but not that." The upshot: "maps construct—not reproduce—the world" (1992:17, 48).

Even an ordinary state map contains hidden messages. For example, by promoting private, car transport (over mass transportation or bike paths) state highway maps support those who profit from the highway system

To conclude: What this implies is that all of us have blind spots. The question is how to reduce them and expand our vision.

EXPANDING OUR VISION OF THE CITY

One way to reduce the blind spots is to look at urban life from many perspectives and then to combine insights. Alas, this is easier said than done. Hardly anyone today is a Renaissance person who, like Leonardo da Vinci, is a serious student of the social and physical sciences as well as a creative artist.

FRAGMENTATION OF THE SOCIAL SCIENCES

The expansion and specialization of knowledge in our high-tech society make it difficult for anyone to study systematically the many facets of any complex phenomenon, including the city. Academically speaking, this proliferation of knowledge has led to a splitting up of the world into specialist **disciplines** and professional territories such as sociology, history, and economics.

Subdisciplines (e.g., *urban* or *rural* sociology) and hybrids (e.g., economic sociology, political economy) have also developed as further responses to the knowledge explosion and to real-world concerns. This was not always the case.

In the nineteenth century (before the knowledge explosion and computerized databanks), influential social thinkers argued vigorously against carving up the world into narrow disciplines. Thinkers who agreed on little else—such as sociology's founder Auguste Comte, Karl Marx, and Cardinal John Henry Newman—agreed that social phenomena are so inextricably linked that studying one small category of the social world was fruitless. Cardinal Newman summed up this point of view in 1852. He wrote that a true university education should provide the power of viewing many things at once as "one whole, and referring them severally to their true places in the universal system, and understanding their respective values, and determining their mutual dependence" ([1852] 1919:137).

Many contemporary educators reaffirm Newman's lofty vision. A former president of Dartmouth College, for one, believes that specialization discourages students from becoming educated (Freedman, 1987:47).

Yet, despite such calls for holism, specialist disciplines continue to multiply. This fragmentation can lead to expertise in a specialized area—say, ethnic voting behavior. But scholars risk knowing more and more about less and less.

Some theorists say that there is no rational way to classify the social sciences, for distinctions among them are artificial (e.g., Duverger, 1964). Some call for new college courses, ones that do not package learning into disciplines. For example, the School of Sustainability at Arizona State University brings together professors from 35 disciplines studying urban development; the group features researchers on a variety of subjects, ranging from desert-water ecology to energy-saving building design. Nonetheless, at present, most of higher education is organized along disciplinary lines. Thus, most everywhere in the world, there are departments of sociology, history, geography, and so forth. And each discipline has developed particular perspectives on the world it tries to better understand.

What constitutes a discipline's perspective? Its substantive content, **paradigms** for doing research, and research methods. Thus, an economist and a sociologist look at the world through different lenses.

However, times are changing—and so are scholars. Increasingly, teachers, grad students, and researchers are becoming **interdisciplinary** or **multidisciplinary**. Adolph Reed, teaching at the University of Pennsylvania, exemplifies this approach. His research focuses on urban politics and twentieth-century American social thought. Reed teaches in an academic department, but his research and thought criss-cross disciplinary boundaries. (Reed also combines theory and practice; he is a founding member of the Labor Party in the United States and remains a core member.) Similarly, Texas A & M professor Joe R. Feagin draws on insights from political sociology, U.S. history, international economics, and urban geography to understand the "urban real estate game": how corporations decide where to locate, how government subsidies affect urban growth, and how citizens' movements can help control urban redevelopment (Feagin and Parker, 2002). Likewise, Rahsaan Maxwell, a 2008 Ph.D. in political science, studies the integration of Caribbeans and North Africans into French and British political life (2006); he draws on sociological insights, analyses of political institutions, and various methodologies—from statistics to interviews—to enrich his understanding and research. Increasingly, research centers and think tanks cross disciplinary boundaries. Concerning climate change, to take one example, some argue that its causes and effects can be understood *only* via an interdisciplinary approach. The director of the Center for Environmental Policy and Administration at Syracuse University (New York) put it like this: "Trying to consider the technical, economic, political, and sociological aspects all at once is the only viable way to do anything about [climate change]" (Wilcoxin in Rodgers, 2005:2).

Others, including Arizona State University, have abolished some traditional departments in favor of "transdisciplinary" institutes. Likewise, Stanford University has created many new multidisciplinary centers and programs, hoping to promote teamwork and cross-fertilization. Stanford's vice president for strategic planning says that her university's mission, in part, is to do away with "segregated academic silos" (in Theil, 2008:59): "Research in a purely academic vacuum was probably never sufficient but particularly not in this day and age."

At New York University (NYU), among others, students are being offered new international learning experiences. Students will be rotated among NYU's branches in New York City, Abu Dhabi, Florence, and other cities, including Shanghai and Buenos Aires.

Thus, this may be a time of great change in the structure of U.S. universities toward multidisciplinarity and internationalism. This shift was acknowledged by the president of Harvard University, historian Drew Faust. Shortly after being named to her post, she said she was thrilled to be at the helm of a great university at a time when the disciplines were "breaking down" (Faust, 2007). She said that she looked forward to her university's struggle to "reconfigure knowledge."

WAYS OF EXPANDING OUR VISION

This book attempts to expand our vision of things urban in several ways: (1) by encouraging both acquaintance with and knowledge about the urban world; (2) by drawing on and trying to connect insights from different disciplines, professional fields, and arts; (3) by presenting a range of ideological perspectives on urban conditions and policies; (4) by examining why honest people disagree about how cities work; (5) by reexamining what seems so obvious, such as the way people walk down busy city streets or behave on subways; and (6) by exploring the links among local, national, and international conditions. My approach will be from the point of view of urban studies. A word about this subject area is appropriate here.

URBAN STUDIES

Urban studies is a relative newcomer to academia. It developed in the 1960s as a response to the needs of academics and practitioners who sought a less piecemeal approach to urban phenomena.

It is variously called "urban studies," "urban affairs," "metropolitan studies," and "urban–suburban studies"; academics don't agree on what to call it or where to put it. It is sometimes a department, a program, or an entire school. No one label identifies its theorists and researchers. Some call themselves "urbanists" or "urbanologists"; others shrink from such labels.

Whatever it's called, urban studies is a *field of study*, not a discipline. It is often viewed as either a multi-disciplinary or an interdisciplinary field focusing on urban-related theory, issues, and policies. In academia, some see it as a promising development; others call it nothing more than "a sphere of rather disconnected interdisciplinary inquiries" (Savage and Warde, 1993:32). Popularly, it is often associated with the attempt to solve urban problems.

As a field of study, urban studies has rather ill-defined boundaries. Neither its physical nor its intellectual boundaries are well delineated. For some, urban studies means the study of cities and suburbs. For others (including myself), it encompasses global theories, data, and perspectives.

Some scholars maintain that it is no longer possible to make meaningful distinctions between things urban and nonurban. They argue, and I agree, that in an interdependent world, urban life cannot be divorced from rural, let alone national and international, life. I call this the "urban-schmurban" stance. My guess (there are no reliable data here) is that many, if not most, contemporary urbanists share this stance.

Ideally, urban studies students are encouraged to achieve interdisciplinarity. As one scholar puts it, "Almost none of the great questions of science, scholarship, or society fit in single disciplines" (Kates, 1989:B1). Brown University, for one, embraces this: Its New Curriculum, adopted in 1969 and still in place, encourages interdisciplinary courses because, today, learning requires chances to experiment and to synthesize across disciplines. synthesis. Its collage of interdisciplinary centers ranges from the Brain Science Program to the Center for the Study of Race and Ethnicity. So much for traditional disciplinary boxes!

Many scholars are trying to remake urban theory from an interdisciplinary standpoint. For one, Edward W. Soja (2000) draws on a variety of perspectives, including what he calls "geohistory," architecture, and feminism. Similarly, MacArthur fellow and self-described "Marxist-environmentalist" Mike Davis ([1992] 1995, 2006a, 2006b, [2004] 2007) has an unusual résumé for academe: truck driver, meat cutter, political activist, historian, student of economics,

and biographer of Los Angeles. His eclectic writings—whether about urban politics, the global threat of avian flu, or ethnic communities in Los Angeles—are refreshingly colorful. Another theorist, Michael Peter Smith, moves far beyond his original home base of political science to revisit *Urban Theory* (1996) and transnational urbanism (2005).

And then, in a class all by himself, is the poster child for interdisciplinarity: Manuel Castells. Castells has taught sociology, city and regional planning, the information society, communications, and technology and society. His scholarly work—over 20 books and innumerable articles—covers a broad spectrum of subjects and combines insights from a number of disciplines and fields, including history, cultural studies, law, global politics, city planning, economics, sociology, and geography. Castells, arguably the best-known contemporary urbanist in the world, speaks six languages, including his native Spanish, and has conducted research or taught on most continents. But even for Renaissance-like scholars such as Castells, synthesizing insights among disciplines is difficult, sometimes impossible. Decades ago (and it remains the case), one urbanist described the recipe for many so-called interdisciplinary studies like this: "Take a physical planner, a sociologist, an economist; beat the mixture until it blends; pour and spread" (Alonso, 1971:169). In other words, synthesizing unlike insights or data sets is like blending oil and water; it won't work.

Without basic agreement on conceptual frameworks—which does not presently exist—interdisciplinarity remains an ideal. Meanwhile, scholars often achieve some degree of integration when they work in an interdisciplinary team.

Most commonly, research team members approach the city from the perspective of their own disciplines. An example will help to clarify the various disciplinary approaches to the same phenomenon: slums.

DISCIPLINARY PERSPECTIVES: THE EXAMPLE OF SLUMS AND MEGASLUMS

According to the *Oxford English Dictionary* (1971), a slum is

> a street, alley, court, etc., situated in a crowded district of a town or city and inhabited by people of a low

Fig. 2.6 SLUM. An apartment building in the slums of Detroit, Michigan. According to the *Oxford English Dictionary* (1971), a slum may be defined as "a thickly populated neighbourhood or district where the houses and the conditions of life are of a squalid and wretched character." People living in areas called "slums" may not see it that way. (Leonard Pitt)

class or by the very poor; a number of these streets or courts forming a thickly populated neighbourhood or district where the houses and the conditions of life are of a squalid and wretched character.

(1971:2874)

People concerned with the history and use of language would be interested in the derivation of the word *slum* (British provincial slang), its first recorded usage (1825, in England), and its changing meanings over time (by the 1890s it connoted crime, viciousness, and debauchery—in other words, bad people as well as bad physical conditions).

The term **megaslum** is used by maverick urban theorist Mike Davis (2006a) to describe gargantuan

slums worldwide: huge shantytowns and squatter settlements of gut-wrenching poverty such as the world's largest—Mexico City's slum of an estimated 4 million plus inhabitants. In Davis's colorful language, megaslums are "stinking mountains of shit."

Typically, people in megaslums suffer from unspeakable poverty and live in "informal housing" on the urban periphery of so-called Third-World (read "poor," "non-North American," and "non-European") cities. These cities and their urban peripheries often house the extremely poor together (but not side-by-side) with billionaires.

Worldwide, how many people live in slums? During the last half-century, slums and megaslums

a

Fig. 2.7 MEGASLUMS. (*a*) Piles of garbage or "stinking mountains of shit," to use Mike Davis's phrase, characterize the Dharavi slum in Mumbai, India, vividly portrayed in *Slumdog Millionaire* (2008). (*b*) A squatter settlement on the outskirts of Lima, Peru. Many residents there maintain their religious faith. ([*a*] Kiran Shroff, [*b*] Andrée Abecassis)

have exploded in size. By 2005, the United Nations (UN) estimated that about 1 billion people lived in slums and put the number at double—2 billion—by 2030 (UN-HABITAT, 2003).

People living in areas called "slums" (by people who don't live there) would undoubtedly have more pressing concerns than understanding where the word *slum* came from. In other words, what is of utmost importance to one group of people may be of much less concern to another.

This observation also holds true for urbanists: What is of primary importance to people trained in one discipline or field may be peripheral to, even neglected by, those trained in another. To illustrate, we'll look at various disciplinary approaches to slums.

b

Fig. 2.7 (*continued*)

First, a word about disagreements *within* a discipline or field. Rarely, perhaps never, do urbanists, sociologists, political economists, or others in any disciplinary hybrid or field share a paradigm or research model. Historically, mainstream social science has rejected the assumptions of many contending visions, from creationism to parapsychology, but some scholars continue to work in alternative paradigms. In recent times, there seems to be an opening within mainstream social science, providing room for some of the dissenting outsiders.

ECONOMICS

"Intuition." "Whimsy." "Imagination." Economists are not normally associated with such words. One exception is Steven D. Levitt, coauthor with Stephen J. Dubner of the best-selling book *Freakonomics* (2005) and economics professor at the University of Chicago. Using research tools common to most economists (and a few uncommon ones, including personal observations), Levitt asks intriguing questions, including these: Why do drug-dealers still live with their mothers? What is the relationship between *Roe v. Wade* and the drop in U.S. crime? His counterintuitive thinking led to this research finding: "If you both own a gun and have a swimming pool in the backyard, the swimming pool is about 10 times more likely to kill a child than the gun is" (Levitt and Dubner, 2005:146).

Few economists communicate so well to non-academics as Levitt. (Having a talented journalist as his coauthor did not hurt.) Alas, many economists (and other social scientists) read like practitioners of "the dismal science," the one-time nickname of economics.

Most economists share more than a dismal writing style: Economists agree among themselves more than do members of most disciplines. Indeed, "no other social science has a single way of thinking that dominates the field to the overwhelming degree that the neoclassical model dominates economics" (Coughlin, 1993:A8). As one scholar puts it, "80 percent agree with 80 percent of it." The neoclassical model's bedrock assumptions are these: (1) people are rational calculators who act in their self-interest and (2) they operate in a free, competitive market.

Still, that leaves 20 percent. Two groups—feminist economists and radical economists—fall into that 20 percent category, questioning the basic assumptions of neoclassical economics.

What follows is a discussion from the neoclassical viewpoint. Then, a feminist view is considered. Chapter 3 includes a discussion of radical and libertarian visions.

Neoclassical or Mainstream Economics

Economics is primarily concerned with *choice*: how individuals, global corporations, or societies choose to use their scarce productive resources (land, labor, capital, know-how) to produce and distribute goods and services. Whether economists study a complex economic system, such as that of the United States or the United Kingdom, or the economic organization of child care in one city, they ask three basic and interrelated questions:

1. *What* goods and services are produced, and *how much* of alternative commodities is produced? For example, does the U.S. economy produce many weapons for national defense and few housing units? A mix of both? Or many housing units and few weapons?
2. *How* are goods produced? For instance, is high technology used? What resources are used?
3. *For whom* are the goods produced? For example, how are certain kinds of housing distributed

to the affluent and the poor or to whites and nonwhites?

These questions—*what, how,* and *for whom*—inform an economist's perspective on the issue being investigated. To answer these questions, economists use a variety of tools, mainly quantitative in nature. In an economics text, for instance, we would expect to find numbers, statistics, mathematical equations, graphs of relationships between factors involved, and econometric projections. It is the rare economist who is trained in or uses qualitative research methods common to anthropology and sociology, such as in-depth interviewing and participant-observation.

Looking at urban housing, one does not have to be a sophisticated economist to understand *what* poor people get: high-density, physically deteriorating slums (or less, a street space). Indeed, it has been said that if all of New York City were as densely populated as parts of Harlem, the entire population of the United States would fit into three of New York City's boroughs.

Why do the poor live in densely populated dwellings, usually near the center of the city, rather than on the city's fringes? The answer is not so obvious. Here, neoclassical economists' logic and models can help to explain. The key to their explanation is a heuristic device showing the way urban land prices vary in a market-based economy: the **bid rent curve**.

Figure 2.8 depicts a bid rent curve. It shows the relationship between two factors that economic analysts consider essential to explain urban land use: (1) the price of land per square foot and (2) the distance of the land from the central business district (CBD).

Important note: During recent decades in the United States, the decentralization of department stores, services, entertainment, and tourist sites, plus the rise of decentralizing information technologies, have put the logic of the bid rent curve into question. Urban economics texts (e.g., O'Flaherty, 2005), however, retain this heuristic device from the 1960s. Thus, before discussing its serious limitations (and growing irrelevance, some say) in later chapters, we will first discuss the logic behind it: Near the center of the U.S. city, land is expensive—the most expensive in the city. In Figure 2.8, it is about $235 per

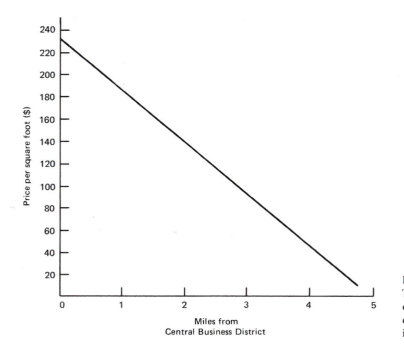

Fig. 2.8 A SIMPLE ECONOMIC MODEL. This bid rent curve shows that the price of land per square foot decreases as the distance from the central business district increases.

square foot per year. The price of land declines the farther it is located from the city center. Here, it is about $20 per square foot per year at 4.75 miles from the center of the city.

There is no norm for prices of centrally located land. The price varies widely from city to city (and from year to year, depending on the economy). For example, downtown offices in San Francisco rented for just over $33 per square foot in 2006; stores just across the Bay from San Francisco on Telegraph Avenue, the shopping street near the University of California at Berkeley's campus, rented for much less—about $1.50-$2.00 per square foot. In comparison, prices in the Mayfair district of London, the world's most expensive location to rent office space in 2006, were about $205 per square foot. (Next most expensive worldwide: Hong Kong.) Central London was also the most expensive place in the world to buy a luxury property; top-end properties sold from about $5,700 to $8,000 per square foot in 2006, while New York City's top residential properties, in comparison, rented for about $5,100 per square foot, followed by Tokyo and Hong Kong. (Parking spaces in New York City's borough of Manhattan cost about the same as an apartment per square foot!)

City land prices can and do change quickly—and dramatically. Global economic shifts, national and regional economic growth rates, housing meltdowns, and local tourism levels are important factors. In 1989, for example, Tokyo's Ginza district was the world's most expensive shopping street (in terms of rent price per square foot or square meter). By 2003 it had slipped to fifteenth most expensive, but by 2005 the Ginza moved back up to the fifth spot. (Economic crisis can change land prices very swiftly. After the Wall Street "makeover" in 2008, for example, millions of square feet of office space in U.S. financial capitals became vacant—and much cheaper. In San Francisco's Financial District, for example, class A office space dropped, on average, from $53.14 per square foot in winter 2007 to $41.34 per square foot 1 year later [Temple, 2008:C1+]. By early 2009, as companies dumped hundreds of thousands of square feet onto the market, prices nosedived.

In 2005, New York City's Fifth Avenue between 50th and 59th Streets was the most expensive shopping street in the world; its ground-floor rent averaged $1,300 per square foot. (In 1994, it was also the most expensive shopping street worldwide, but rent was much cheaper, with an average retail rent per square foot of $375.) In 2005, next came Hong Kong's Causeway Bay area, leapfrogging past Paris's Champs d'Elysées and other expensive areas. (Analysts point to a resurgent Asian economy and increases in tourism from mainland China as major factors in Hong Kong's leap to second place in 2005.)

Question: In the U.S. bid rent curve pictured in Figure 2.8, why is downtown retail and office space so expensive, relative to land farther out? *Answer*: Because centrally-located land is prime land, close to the nerve center of the city with its corporate headquarters, large department stores, banks, and so forth. At the U.S. city's edges, land is cheaper because it is not as convenient to jobs or amenities. (*Note*: "Postsuburbia," discussed in Chapter 8, plus technologies such as high-speed Internet call these assumptions into question. Yet, judging from their texts, it appears that economists retain the bid rent curve, a bedrock urban concept.)

Why urban slums in the United States are found near the center of cities rather than on the periphery, where land is cheaper, is a seeming paradox. (This is not necessarily the case outside North America. For instance, poverty-stricken suburbs ring parts of Paris, and megaslums in Latin America typically lie on cities' peripheries.)

Studying land costs in the United States, the late regional scientist William Alonso concluded that land prices are connected to *the amount* of land affordable by rich and poor. "At any given location," Alonso said, "the poor can buy less land than the rich, and since only a small quantity of land is involved [for living space], changes in its price are not as important for the poor as the costs and inconvenience of commuting" (1973:54). What Alonso claimed, then, is that the rich make a trade-off. They are willing to take more trouble and time commuting to work in exchange for living farther away from the city center (where, presumably, it is more comfortable and pleasant).

Following Alonso, the simple model in Figure 2.8 shows the value of U.S. land declining from $235 per square foot at the city's center to $20 per square foot at the city's edge. How does this relationship between the price of land and its location help us understand why the poor live in crowded settlements called "slums"? The economic analyst would point out that since centrally located land is expensive, any housing built there must try to minimize land costs: by building up or by packing people in. In the case of poor people with little money, both situations occur, resulting in slums.

To answer the *what* question, neoclassical economists frequently employ the concept of supply and demand. In a market economy (also called a "free-enterprise" or "competitive" economy), classical theory holds that goods will be supplied in the marketplace according to people's ability to pay for them. However, in the case of housing, some economists say that there is a large "noneffective" demand—that is, people want decent housing but can't afford to pay for it. The economic logic is this: The laws of the market work to give people only what they can pay for—in this case, physically deteriorating housing. (Others, particularly Harvard housing economist Edward L. Glaeser et al. [2005] are not so sure. Glaeser and his colleagues point to government regulations that slow down housing construction.)

How is slum housing provided? With the exception of a small amount of publicly assisted housing, no new housing for poor people in the United States is produced by the market. Instead, older housing units are occupied by successively lower-income groups, and this housing eventually "trickles down" to the poor. Urban economists call this the **filtering** process. Some economists argue in favor of public policies to provide more housing to upper- and middle-income people on the assumption that more and better housing will then filter down to the poor more rapidly.

However, others note than in many U.S. cities the market encourages "trickling up" (gentrification). In this process, lower-income inner-city neighborhoods are rehabilitated for upper-income housing (Palen and London, 1984). As real estate developers gentrify these neighborhoods, displaced tenants move to places they can afford—slums, in many cases. (Non-market-based [forced] gentrification occurs in many places, including Beijing, China [in the run-up to the Olympic Games in 2008], and near Phnom Penh, Cambodia, where police routinely burn poor shanty-towns to make way for new, upscale buildings.)

To conclude: Neoclassical or market economists tend to see the provision of slum housing in a market economy as an outcome of the workings of the law of supply and demand. Such factors as land costs and the journey to work determine the behavior of urbanites, whether as buyers or as renters of urban land, as owners of slum property, or as slum dwellers. Crowded, physically deteriorated slum housing, in this way of thinking, tends to trickle down to poor people or trickle up to more affluent people because of underlying market forces. In either case, in this perspective, underlying market forces are the key determinants of who lives on what land.

Feminist Economics

As a field, feminist economics emerged in 1992 with the formation of the International Association for Feminist Economics. But in the United States it dates at least to the late nineteenth century and the writings of Charlotte Perkins Gilman (e.g., [1898] 1998).

How does feminist economics differ from other forms of economic inquiry? First, it is not only a form of inquiry; it combines theory and practice. For feminist economists, academic research is not enough. They want to affect policies affecting women—and men—worldwide. Second, mainstream economic analysis is attacked for being "masculinist" or "gender-blind." On the contrary, feminist economists are not gender-blind. And they fault those who look at the economy from only the viewpoint of men's experience and who define the typical economic actor as "rational economic man." To correct this perceived bias, they apply gender-based analysis and a feminist critique of gender inequality to economic theory, economic life, and policy making.

Feminist economists try to construct alternative theoretical approaches and economic concepts which include women's experience and "feminine values" such as "caring, cooperation, and provisioning" (Matthaei, 2005). (*Note*: Calling *any* value "feminine" or "masculine" is risky. Research into the cultural and genetic characteristics of gender and their interplay is an ongoing project.)

In their research and activism, feminist economists highlight women's disadvantaged economic position in the labor market and in the household. They also examine gender differences in occupations and earnings.

Briefly, then, feminist economists reject the neoclassical model of the rational, self-interested actor. Instead, they focus on economic activities that are more cooperative and social.

Concerning slums and ghettoes, some feminist economists stress the approach they call "women in development." For example, World Bank researcher Maria Elena Ruiz Abril (2002) claims that women play key roles in "upgrading" slums (*barrios*) outside Caracas, Venezuela.

Concerning U.S. government poverty guidelines, feminist economists think they are very problematic. Why? Because dollar amounts may change each year, but the bases remain constant. Essentially, the poverty guideline in the United States is based on a family's *pretax* income, the number in a "family unit," and the ages of the members. Noncash benefits, such as food stamps, are not counted. In 2003, excluding Alaska and Hawaii but including Washington, D.C., the poverty threshold (again, pretax) for a "family unit" of one with a person under 65 was $9,573 and $14,824 for a family unit of three—an adult under 65 with two children under 18. (U.S. Census Bureau, 2004).

Feminist economists suggest that the United States needs a new definition of poverty. Their proposed redefinition of poverty is based on a *basic needs budget*, taking into account such services as child-care expenses that a poor, single, working mother must pay to continue working outside the home. In their view, the federal government's baseline for determining poverty is too low to ensure a minimally sufficient standard of living for working, single mothers. One inference of their work: Government definitions help determine who ends up in poverty—or not. Another inference: Many, especially women, might be considered poor if the U.S. poverty baseline was raised and, thus, more people (again, particularly women) would be (1) considered poor and (2) eligible for government funds to leave substandard or slum housing.

GEOGRAPHY

"Geography is fate." At least many think so. This way of thinking may have special appeal to those of us with ancestors, family, or friends caught up in war, genocide, earthquakes, floods, tsunamis, and other disasters. Often, but not always, it is the weak, the poor, the ill-housed, and the elderly who have little warning or resources to escape tragic fates.

Geographers, whether Central American specialists or urbanists, stand on common ground: space and place. Yet, like most social sciences in recent decades, geography has experienced increasing specialization and blurred boundaries (Coughlin, 1987:9). Some geographers even joke that their field is the Los Angeles of academic disciplines: It's spread over a large area, it merges with its neighbors, and it's hard to find the CBD! At the same time, scholars from neighboring disciplines, particularly those influenced by three French scholars—historian Fernand Braudel ([1986] 1990), philosopher Michel Foucault (1980), and philosopher–urbanist Henri Lefebvre ([1974] 1991)—are making geography central to their analyses of social life.

In the past generation, the geographer's central concepts of space and place have traveled to other disciplines, thereby reinvigorating urban theory. Take, for example, two important sociological studies discussed in this book: (1) *Urban Fortunes* (Logan and Molotch, 1987), which focuses on the political economy of place, and (2) *The Informational City* (Castells, 1989), which discusses urban spatial structure and the "space of flows."

Mapping is a key tool. Geographers also use mathematical and computer-assisted models, field observation, and other social science methods plus such high-tech tools as satellite observations, sometimes to do mapping. And, thanks to the Internet, millions of people not trained as geographers are doing cartography, that is, making maps. These maps are often annotated with images, video, text, and sound. Reporter Miguel Helft (2007) believes that these citizen-map-makers are "reshaping the world of mapmaking and collectively creating a new kind of atlas that is likely to be richer and messier than any other." He concludes that Internet mapmakers are also turning the Web into a medium "where maps will play a more central role in how information is organized and found." For example, there are maps of global hydrofoils, biodiesel fueling stations in the Northeast United States, and the paths of two whales that swam the wrong way, up the Sacramento River delta in 2007. The upshot, Helft predicts, is that people will "discover many layers of information" about a place of interest.

Investigating slums, a geographer might map their location and/or construct a model to predict where they will be located 50 years later. Or they might do as John Snow, a doctor–geographer, did in London during a nineteenth-century cholera pandemic. Snow and his students mapped deaths in the densely populated Soho district, pinpointing where each death occurred and where each new case was reported. Snow reasoned that it was the water pump that linked contaminated water and cholera, not bad air or physical contact, as London authorities had thought. After the pump was closed, new cholera cases dropped sharply (De Blij, 2005:42–43).

A starting point for the description of housing patterns in U.S. industrial cities, including the location of slums, is Ernest W. **Burgess's model** of urban space. This model, developed by sociologist Burgess at the University of Chicago in the 1920s, was central to urban geography for several decades and shows the interdisciplinary roots of much urban theory.

Figure 2.9 depicts the Burgess model of urban space. It suggests that U.S. **industrial cities** (i.e., cities like Chicago that developed in the era of manufacturing) expand outward from the CBD in a nonrandom way—through a series of zones or rings. One implication of this model (discussed in more detail in Chapter 16) is that poor people live in slums because they are pushed there—by changes in the city's land-use patterns.

Briefly, the logic behind the model is this: The city's changing environment leads to the sorting and sifting process that segregates individuals by social class, ethnic background and race, and family composition. As a city's population grows, demand for land in the CBD (the city's core) can be satisfied only by expanding outward. Property owners in and around the CBD will let their housing units deteriorate, for they can profit by selling their land to businesses expanding there. The result of this growth process, the Burgess model predicts, is that the poor living in slums near the CBD will be pushed out into new slums a bit farther out from the CBD.

Today, scholars doubt the relevance of Burgess's model to postindustrial cities (see Chapter 16).

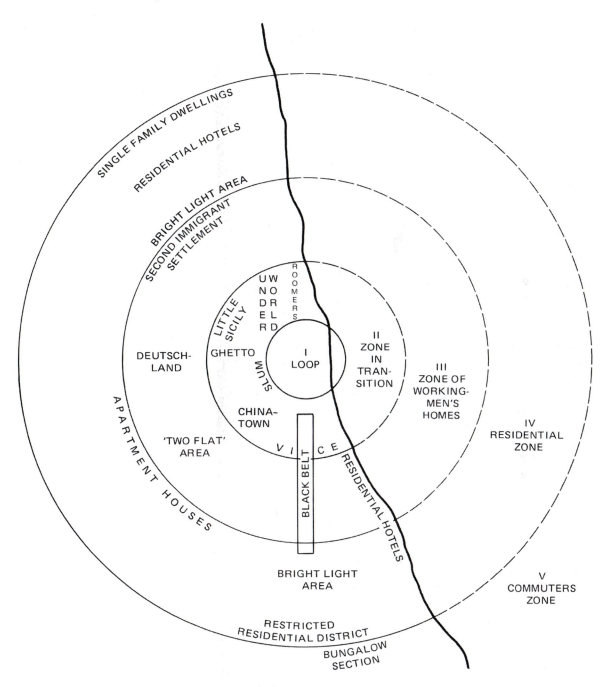

Within the diagram, the following labels appear:

SINGLE FAMILY DWELLINGS

RESIDENTIAL HOTELS

BRIGHT LIGHT AREA

SECOND IMMIGRANT SETTLEMENT

DEUTSCH-LAND

LITTLE SICILY

GHETTO

UNDERWORLD

ROOMERS

I LOOP

II ZONE IN TRAN-SITION

III ZONE OF WORKING-MEN'S HOMES

IV RESIDENTIAL ZONE

V COMMUTERS ZONE

APARTMENT HOUSES

'TWO FLAT' AREA

CHINA-TOWN

SLUM

VICE

BLACK BELT

RESIDENTIAL HOTELS

BRIGHT LIGHT AREA

RESTRICTED RESIDENTIAL DISTRICT

BUNGALOW SECTION

Fig. 2.9 BURGESS'S CONCENTRIC ZONE MODEL. Applied to Chicago, the zonal model shows that "the Loop" (Chicago's central business district) is surrounded by low-income neighborhoods in zone II. (Robert E. Park, Ernest W. Burgess, and Roderick D. McKenzie, *The City* [Chicago: University of Chicago Press, (1925) 1974], p. 55. Copyright © 1967 by the University of Chicago. Reproduced by permission of the University of Chicago Press. All rights reserved.)

Nonetheless, it is an important intellectual grandparent of land-use models.

In addition, the Burgess model is of special interest here because of its interdisciplinary nature; it combines economic assumptions about the way the world works (economic competition for urban space) with patterns of spatial and social order. For instance, it predicts that the higher people move up the socioeconomic ladder, the farther away they will live from the CBD, zone I.

Mike Davis brings Burgess's model up to date. Davis's model ([1992] 1995) of metropolitan space, also interdisciplinary, uses Burgess's "dartboard" of concentric zones where the CBD is the bull's-eye. But there are important differences between the models. First, Davis models metropolitan Los Angeles, not Chicago. Second, Davis adds what he calls a "decisive new factor" to Burgess's model: fear. Years before 9/11, Davis wrote this about reimagining Burgess's model: "My remapping of the urban structure takes Burgess back to the future. It preserves such 'ecological' determinants as income, land value, class and race, but adds a decisive new factor: fear" ([1992] 1995).

To Davis, modern Los Angeles and big cities generally are "feral" places where different social groups adopt security measures to protect themselves (e.g., gated communities, video monitoring). The upshot, Davis argues, is a militarized landscape composed of special enclaves, which he calls "social control districts." This vision of metropolitan space, clearly influenced by Burgess's model, also seems to be inspired by William Gibson's cyberpunk novel *Neuromancer* (1984) with its horrific view of urban futures.

Another type of space—and attitudes toward it—is worth noting: cyberspace. Although world-famous scholars, including the late historian Fernard Braudel ([1963] 1995), considered space to be a key to understanding civilizations, today some think that *virtual* space has caused a radical break with space as we've known it. Indeed, some consider cyberspace to be the latest U.S. frontier. And they fear it will be used for nefarious purposes, including a new kind of colonialism. For example, Florian Röetzer, a Munich-based media theorist, writes that in the United States

> The conquest of cyberspace follows the example set by the settlers, cowboys, heroes of the Wild West and soldiers who subjugated a continent that, in their eyes, didn't belong to anyone—pure colonialism.

> *(1998:131)*

Scholars are just beginning to think about the impacts of cyberspace. But many theorists who deal with space, including some geographers and architects, question the continuing relevance of any geographical boundaries in the digital, multinational age.

SOCIOLOGY

Sociologists study people: how they act, think, produce things and ideas, and live. They may study social interaction between as few as two individuals or as many as the entire world population. Their major interest lies in better understanding human action. Normally, sociologists are not concerned with one person's action.

Sociologists start with the assumption that things are not always the way they seem. For instance, universities exist, according to their high-principled mottos and public-relations brochures, to expand the frontiers of knowledge and (more recently) to provide career training. Those are their official reasons for existence, their **manifest functions**. Looking below the surface, however, sociologists may uncover some hidden or unintended purposes of universities, their **latent functions**. These include lowering the unemployment rolls by keeping people off the streets and instilling habits useful in the labor market, such as following orders from authority figures. These latent functions can't be seen with the naked eye or discovered by common sense; they emerge as one explores the connections among people, institutions, and ideas.

The sociological perspective attempts to better describe and understand the social forces that mold the lives of individuals, perhaps without their own realization. It can be applied to many events that, on the surface, seem to be purely personal experiences.

A sociologist investigating any topic, including slums, might ask the following questions:

1. *What are people doing and thinking here?* For instance, do slum dwellers vote, join church groups, or feel satisfied with their lives?
2. *What kinds of people are here?* What are their social characteristics?

3. *What rules govern behavior here?* In the case of slum dwellers, are they expected to passively accept their substandard housing?

4. *Who says so?* For example, in slum buildings, who or what group has the power to make rules and enforce them?

5. *Whose interests do these social arrangements serve?* For example, what social functions do slums serve? Do some groups in society benefit more than others from their existence?

6. *What powerful people, institutions, and structures influence these arrangements?* For example, what roles do government agencies and private developers play in creating or eradicating slums?

The work of John R. Seeley represents one approach to the study of slums. Seeley ([1959] 1970) argued that slums cannot ever be eradicated because the definition of the word "slum" is relative to how other people live. He reasoned that people at the bottom of the social ladder will still be perceived by those higher up as living in slums even if their living conditions are improved. Further, Seeley maintained that in a society where economic and social inequality exists, as in the United States, there are bound to be those who will be labeled "slum dwellers."

In his analysis of slums, Seeley employed a device common to many scientific disciplines: a **typology** or classification scheme. His typology differentiates slum dwellers on the basis of length of residence and reasons for residing in the slums. He distinguished among four major types of people who live in slums: (1) the "permanent necessitarians," who live there permanently and by necessity; (2) the "temporary necessitarians," who aspire to leave the slums but live there out of necessity; (3) the "permanent opportunists," who stay in the slums primarily because it affords them opportunities to escape the law or live the high life; and (4) the "temporary opportunists," who want to pursue dominant cultural values like success (these include recent arrivals to the city).

A now-classic study of what some (not those who lived there) called a "slum" in Boston's West End is sociologist Herbert Gans's *The Urban Villagers* (1962). In his ethnography of this working class, shabby, Italian American neighborhood—just before it was razed by urban redevelopment—Gans did not find alienation or a drive to upward social mobility among its residents. Instead, he found an "urban village." True, most residents worked at low-wage jobs and lived in tenement apartments. Yet, they lived in close proximity to family and friends and enjoyed a strong sense of community.

Writing nearly a half-century later, sociologist Sharon Zukin (2007) offers a different perspective on studying the West End—or any city neighborhood. She thinks that neighborhoods can't be studied in isolation. Instead, she advises researchers to understand a neighborhood's hierarchical relationship to other areas of a city In the case of Boston's West End, she thinks that its destruction by urban renewal cannot be understood without understanding the creation of Route 128,(Boston's Silicon Valley), the spatial domination of Boston's downtown, and other larger historical phenomena or processes. Looking backward, Zukin argues, we can now see that so-called urban renewal of U.S. cities by government-led agencies (starting with the U.S. Housing Act of 1949 and continuing until 1972 when the federal government withdrew from financing construction of public housing) "was part of the continuing drama of how to balance capital investment, social integration, and democratic state power—a crisis of modernity" (47). Thus, according to Zukin, whatever they are called—"slums" or "urban villages"—their destruction cannot be understood in just a local context.

Other sociologists explore face-to-face encounters among slum dwellers, paying special attention to how people interpret each other's actions and bring meaning to their interaction; this approach typifies the symbolic interaction school of sociology. Elijah Anderson's study *Streetwise* (1990) is exemplary. Anderson finds an influential "oppositional" youth subculture in the slum. He says this oppositional subculture is based on gangster respect and the romanticization of violence, not the values of work, love, and hope. For instance, one teenager told Anderson that he had committed murder because he was "just having a bad day." Such a study seems particularly relevant, policywise, in a time when (1) big-city violent crime increased by 40 percent from the late 1960s to the late 1990s, fear of crime increased 30 percent, and possession of firearms increased over 120 percent (Suarez, quoting a report of the Milton Eisenhower Foundation, 1999).

Sociologist Barry Glassner uses a different time line and different statistics. As a result, he ends up posing different questions about crime in *The Culture of Fear: Why Americans Are Afraid of the Wrong Things* ([1999] 2000). For example, Glassner wonders why, in the 1990s, two-thirds of Americans believed that crime rates were soaring when, actually, crime rates plunged throughout the decade. Why, Glassner asks, did 62 percent of people in the United States describe themselves as "truly desperate" about crime by 1995— almost twice as many as in the late 1980s when crime rates were higher?

Other sociologists take a more global view. Some link urban happenings to government's intervention in local affairs, the growing inability of urban politics to decide who gets what housing to live in, and the global restructuring of urban space. This approach typifies the so-called new urban sociology (Gottdiener and Feagin, 1988), an approach which was new in the late 1980s.

In a related vein, a generation ago several French sociologists studied "les grands ensembles": large, multi-unit housing developments, sponsored by the French government, located on the periphery of Paris and other big cities. These studies were concerned with possible ghettoization, exclusion, and segregation of the poor. One such study, by Kaës (1963) *Vivre dans les grands ensembles* (*Living in Large Developments*), bemoaned these postwar grands ensembles as places that promoted apathy and tedium, not democratic activity. (These 1960s studies may contain some explanations why, starting in 2005, some grands ensembles in suburban Paris—by then housing poor immigrants, mainly people of color—became hotbeds of antipolice activity, car burnings, and "acts of resistance" or "riots." "May" is the operative word here. First, observers disagree on the reasons for the events, reflected in the various terms to describe them: "resistance," "riots," and "civil disorders." Second, to claim that the buildings themselves are key to understanding human behavior is environmental determinism, discussed in Chapter 17, a much-disputed notion.)

Many sociologists combine approaches and methods. Take, for example, Löic J. D. Wacquant (1989). Wacquant combines participant-observation and an analysis of statistical data with macroeconomic theory to understand Chicago ghetto life. Wacquant says that no one factor can account for the plight of the ghetto, but "there is no denying that the accelerating decline of the inner city finds its deepest roots in the ongoing structural transformation of American capitalism" (1989:510). He adds that public policy has also played a role in perpetuating ghetto life: "the rolling back of state and federal payrolls (for example in the post office) has also reduced access to legitimate channels of upward mobility out of the ghetto" (512).

Whatever approach or method is used (ranging from mathematical models to firsthand participation and observation), sociologists focus on the social forces that shape individual lives. They look for traits that cannot be explained simply by referring to individual psychological states.

POLITICAL SCIENCE

Traditionally, political scientists have been concerned with questions of power and governance: Who governs? How do they govern? To what end? Or, as political activist Sidney Hillman (1887–1946), founder of the Amalgamated Clothing Workers of America (now UNITE!) so neatly put it, "*Who* gets *what, how,* and *why*?".

As in other disciplines, the range of topics within political science is broad. But the nature of political processes and political outcomes is central to the discipline.

The research tools of political science include mathematical models, attitude surveys, and observation of events. Most U.S. political scientists today use some form of sophisticated statistics in their work.

In the case of slums, political scientists may investigate a number of issues. Some study citizens' attitudes toward government housing policy; others explore the relations between different levels of government (federal, state, local) in establishing housing policy. Still others look at comparative political systems, exploring how different countries handle housing policy. A political scientist exploring power relationships might study conflicts of interest in which local and international decision makers stand to gain personally from land deals to raze slums. And a political philosopher might question the nature of a political system that either allows or perpetuates slums.

One classic study of slums from the perspective of political science is *Politics, Planning, and the Public Interest* (1955) by Edward Banfield and Martin Meyerson. This study centers on the decision-making process that led to the construction of low-income public-housing projects in Chicago. (These housing units, meant—at least by government definition—to provide standard housing for the poor, came to be known as "slums.")

Banfield and Meyerson found that Chicago's aldermen (city councillors) had effective veto power over public-housing construction in their wards. The proposed housing projects were going to house poor people, the majority of whom were black. Middle- and upper-class residents of predominantly white neighborhoods vigorously opposed the suggestion that such public-housing projects should be located in their neighborhoods. These affluent whites believed that if the projects came in, crime would increase, property values would decrease, and the aesthetic character of their areas would change. Their opposition to public housing was sufficient to block the original proposal: that public-housing projects be scattered throughout the city. Eventually, much less public housing than originally contemplated was built, and virtually all units were placed in a very few wards that were already nearly all African American.

Banfield and Meyerson recognize other influences but stress political factors. They focus on the politics of class and race, as well as on "clout" (influence and power), rather than on concepts central to other disciplines, such as urban growth over space.

ANTHROPOLOGY

Since the nineteenth century, anthropologists have made significant contributions to the study of urbanization and cultural change from a cross-cultural point of view. In recent years, they turned their attention away from folk or so-called primary or primitive cultures, such as that of the Trobriand Islands, focusing instead on urbanizing and urban cultures.

Wherever anthropologists work, their primary method of investigation remains fieldwork. However, many use newer tools, including DNA analysis and computer modeling. These tools have changed *what* some do and *where* they do it.

The late U.S. anthropologist Oscar Lewis used fieldwork methods to get an insider's view of family life in Mexico City. He wanted to find out what it meant to grow up in a slum tenement within a city undergoing rapid social and economic change, such as Mexico City. Using a tape recorder to take down the life histories of one Mexican family in *The Children of Sanchez* (1961), Lewis recorded their personal statements and feelings about a wide range of issues, including religion, kinship patterns, interpersonal relations, and social mobility.

But Lewis was interested in much broader issues: the effects of industrialization and urbanization on the peasant and urban masses. He sought to develop a conceptual model of what he called the "culture of poverty," that is, "a design for living which is passed down from generation to generation" among "those people who are at the very bottom of the socio-economic scale" (1961:xxiv–xxv).

A generation later, Lewis's culture of poverty model remains hotly contested. Many scholars dismiss it, arguing that chronically poor people's "ingenuity and aspirations are not different from working people's, but that their chances of success are small" (Sharff, 1987:47–48). Critic Adolph Reed, a political scientist–historian, rejects Lewis's basic assumption that poor people have different behavior or values: "Some percentage of *all* Americans take drugs, fight in families, abuse or neglect children, and have children out of wedlock. These behaviors don't cause poverty. Poor people aren't poor because they have bad values or behave improperly" (in Leopold, 1992:3–4). Reed blames public policy choices—not the victims of poverty—for ghettoization: "It's not as though jobs just up and left the cities. The shape and character of the domestic economy is guided by public policy." Citing a federal bias since the 1940s toward road construction over mass transportation, toward suburbs over cities, and toward owner-occupied housing over rental housing, Reed says, "We let government off the hook for the role it's played in increasing poverty by redistributing wealth upward."

Another critic, sociologist Ramon Grosfoguel (2003:28), argues that the culture of poverty logic has been supplanted by a "*neoculture* of poverty" argument. In his view, this newer version of the Lewis concept legitimates cultural racism. Clearly, the debate about this concept is far from settled.

In the meantime, there have been other developments in urban anthropology. For example, in recent decades, a subdiscipline of urban anthropology, urban archeology, has been tapping a rather ingenious source of information: garbage. As the head of a "dig" in Atlanta, Georgia, put it, "People's garbage never lies. It tells the truth if you know how to read it" (in Weathers et al., 1979:81). From a Newburyport, Massachusetts, garbage dig, urban archeologists discovered evidence that nineteenth-century Irish and Canadian immigrants, long presumed illiterate, could read and write. From interviewees in Tucson, students in the "Garbage Project" found that there was a wide gap between what people say they do and what they actually do. For instance, many vastly underestimated their weekly beer consumption. And according to archeologist William Rathje, head of the Garbage Project and coauthor of *Rubbish!* (Rathje and Murphy, 1992), there is a gap between good intentions and behavior: Based on their analysis of garbage, the students found that many people buy both healthy fresh vegetables and salty, cholesterol-filled microwave dinners but often throw away the veggies—untouched. (*Note:* In May 1988, the U.S. Supreme Court ruled that garbage bags outside the home and its immediate surroundings can be legally searched. The ethics of trash searching remains controversial.)

From looking at "ecofacts" (food remains, evidence of past environments) and archival records, anthropologists reconstructed one bit of African American history; they found that in Buxton, Iowa, a coal-mining town from 1900 to 1925, there had been a majority population of African Americans who prospered and interacted with local whites harmoniously (Gradwohl and Osborn, 1984).

Wherever they go to study people, anthropologists seek "to provide convincing accounts of what is happening to people in varied real life situations and to set these in a broader framework of time and space" (Southall, 1973:4). Their emphasis on the diversity of human experience, as well as the search for common or universal themes, gives anthropologists a particular perspective on the social and material world.

HISTORY

His-story and her-story—the range of humankind's experience over time—is the subject matter of historians. Some focus on a small piece or area of the whole. Others are grand (some say "grandiose") thinkers, trying to see patterns throughout human experience. Historians have contributed a variety of studies about urban life and culture, starting with the earliest known settlements in the Middle East.

They use a range of tools to investigate urban life. These include the analysis of written records, oral histories, and, more recently, quantitative techniques such as computer-aided statistical analysis.

One influential historian of urban culture is the late Lewis Mumford (1895–1990). In *The City in History: Its Origins, Its Transformations, and Its Prospects* (1961), Mumford paints a picture of the forms and functions of the city throughout the ages. He also pleads for a "new urban order" that emphasizes "local control over local needs." In his historical tour from the early origins of the city to the contemporary megalopolis, Mumford stops to comment on the development of European industrial cities between 1830 and 1910. First, he quotes his mentor, the Scots planner Patrick Geddes, who influenced a generation of U.S. city planners, and then he offers his own comments on slums:

> "Slum, semi-slum, and super-slum—to this has come the evolution of cities." Yes: these mordant words of Patrick Geddes apply inexorably to the new environment. Even the most revolutionary of contemporary critics [like Friedrich Engels] lacked genuine standards of building and living: they had no notion how far the environment of the upper classes themselves had become impoverished....[Even Engels, the revolutionary critic] was apparently unaware of the fact that the upper-class quarters were, more often than not, intolerable super-slums.
>
> (*Mumford, 1961:464–465*)

Thus, according to Mumford, the new industrial cities were not only bleak environments for the poor but also just as intolerably overcrowded, ugly, and unhygienic for the nonpoor.

A pioneering work in U.S. urban history, Arthur M. Schlesinger's *The Rise of the American City, 1878–1898* (1933), makes the claim that innovation and social change are uniquely associated with city life. Schlesinger maintains that overcrowding in slums, intense economic and social interactions in the CBD, and other aspects of urban life lead city dwellers to adopt new lifestyles in order to survive. This theme echoes the findings of theorists from other disciplines, including the Chicago school of sociology.

Other historians trace changes within one city, often using the case study approach to illuminate issues common to other cities or to generate broader theory. Sam Bass Warner, Jr.'s, "If All the World Were Philadelphia: A Scaffolding for Urban History, 1774–1930" (1968), is a case in point. In this article, Warner looks at housing patterns in Philadelphia at three points in time: 1774, 1860, and 1930. Using historical data, Warner argues that at the time of the American Revolution, poor people in Philadelphia lived around the fringes of the city, not near the city's core. He maintains that both racial segregation and the relocation of slums near the CBD in Philadelphia were nineteenth-century phenomena. What caused these changes in settlement patterns? Warner says that improvements in transportation within the city and the creation of large business organizations led to the changing residential patterns. In conclusion, Warner states that the organizing principle of the big city in the nineteenth century became "intense segregation based on income, race, foreign birth, and class" (35).

Still other historians have different takes on how poverty and inequality (and slums) work. Take, for example, Alice Kessler-Harris. This Columbia University history professor won the coveted Bancroft Prize for her book *In Pursuit of Equity* (2001). One of her aims is to show gender's key role in shaping working-class culture in the United States. Professor Kessler-Harris links the status of women in the United States to what she considers their historic restriction to economic opportunities.

PSYCHOLOGY, SOCIAL PSYCHOLOGY, AND
SOCIAL PSYCHIATRY

Is there an "urban personality" or an "urban way of life"? Do city folk suffer more mental illness than rural people? What effects do growing up poor or rich have on urbanites' beliefs about themselves and others? These are some questions explored by psychologists, social psychologists, and social psychiatrists.

A classic study in social psychology is Louis Wirth's "Urbanism as a Way of Life" (1938). This still-controversial essay, excerpted in Chapter 6, contends that city dwellers—whether slum residents or the super-rich—share certain characteristics, including indifference to others, sophistication, rationality, and calculating behavior. Presumably, urbanites develop these personality traits in order to defend themselves and preserve their sanity amid the intensity and stimulation of city life.

A generation later, Robert Coles explored the psyches of rich and poor children in both urban and rural America. In so doing, he created a new subdiscipline: social psychiatry. In his five-volume series *Children of Crisis*, Coles uses a mixture of clinical observation, oral history, narrative description, psychiatric approaches, and social comment to look at how wealth, power, cultural background, and historical influences mold the character of children and their expectations of what life can offer them. In the latter two volumes of his study, *Eskimos, Chicanos, Indians* (1977a) and *Privileged Ones: The Well Off and the Rich in America* (1977b), Coles paints a portrait of growing up poor, outside the mainstream of American culture, versus growing up wealthy. He notes striking differences. Rich children, for instance, are routinely trained to believe that their way of life is worthwhile; they grow up believing they're special. In Coles's words, the children of the wealthy have a "continuous and strong emphasis...on the 'self'" (1977b:380). In contrast, poor children, some trapped in the slums, are discouraged from being independent and assertive. They are routinely trained by parents and their environment to keep their thoughts to themselves and not to cultivate a sense of being special persons.

PUBLIC ADMINISTRATION

Historically, the professional field of public administration emerged from the discipline of political science in the United States. The field is intimately connected with the efforts to reform the U.S. city. As Dwight Waldo stated in his influential study *The Administrative State*, "Much of the impetus to public administration came from the municipal reformers [of the early 1900s], who were genuinely inspired by a City of the Future" (1948:73). Interestingly, in contrast to the intellectual bias against the city held by many social scientists in the first quarter of this century, public administration writers rejected Jefferson's idea that cities are menaces to democracy and sores on the body politic. Instead, they thought that the good life is an urban life...

It is tempting to say that what public administrators do is to manage the public business, carrying out decisions made by political leaders. But this creates a false distinction between administrators and politicians. Early theorists of public administration attempted to distinguish between administration and politics, but current thinkers reject this distinction, demonstrating that administration *is* politics. In other words, the administration of public programs, such as school busing, is a highly political process. Indeed, bureaucratic politics (e.g., the politics of constructing a city or national budget) has increasingly captured the imagination of public administration scholars.

In the case of slums, U.S. theorists and practitioners in the field have written about a number of issues, ranging from the interface between professionals and their welfare clients (e.g., Riccucci, 2005) to evaluations of government programs designed, in theory at least, to alleviate poverty and slum conditions.

CITY PLANNING AND URBAN DESIGN

Mike Davis (2006a:30), multidisciplinary theorist, estimates that there are more than 200,000 slums all over the world, including megaslums where squatter settlements and shantytowns merge in continuous belts of "informal housing and poverty, usually on the urban periphery" (2006a:26). According to Davis (2006b),

> In slums the world over, squatters trade safety and health for a few square meters of land and some security of tenure. They are pioneers of swamps, floodplains, volcano slopes, unstable hillsides, desert fringes, railroad sidings, rubbish mountains, and chemical dumps—unattractive and dangerous sites that have become poverty's niche in the ecology of the city....Today, new arrivals to the urban margin confront a condition that can only be described as marginality within marginality, or, in the more piquant phrase of a desperate Baghdad slum dweller quoted by *The New York Times*, a "semi-death."

From a global and multidisciplinary perspective, including urban planning, Davis offers this typology of slums:

A. **Metro Core**
 1. Formal
    (a) tenements (e.g., Mexico City's Casa Grande, made famous by Oscar Lewis in *The Children of Sanchez* [1961])
       (i) hand-me-downs (e.g., Harlem brownstones; the most unusual example of inherited housing is Cairo's City of the Dead, lodging one million poor people where people use Mameluke tombs as prefab housing)
       (ii) housing built for the poor (e.g., Berlin's *Mietkaserne*; Buenos Aires's wood-and-sheet metal *inquilinatos*)
    (b) public housing (the rule in Europe)
    (c) hostels, flophouses, and the like, often rooms for single males, such as those on the outskirts of Soweto, near Johannesburg
 2. Informal
    (a) Squatters—those who possess land without sale or title
       (i) authorized (settlers purchase a guarantee of tenure from powerful leaders, including gangsters or criminal cartels, such as the Triads in Hong Kong, although land is government-owned)
       (ii) unauthorized (often ingenious, such as rooftops in Phnom Penh; often located on hazardous, nearly worthless land)
    (b) pavement-dwellers (more than an estimated 100,000 homeless in Los Angeles; an estimated one million homeless in Mumbai, formerly Bombay)

B. **Periphery**
 1. Formal
    (a) private rental
    (b) public housing
 2. Informal
    (a) pirate subdivisions—"substandard [and private] commercial residential subdivisions" of squatters
       (i) owner-occupied
       (ii) rental

(b) squatters

(i) authorized (including site-and-service)

(ii) unauthorized

3. *Refugee Camps*, which hold international refugees and internally-displaced persons (IDPs), such as Gaza with 750,000 IDPs and Bogota with 400,000 IDPs (Davis, 2006a:30).

According to Davis, there has been an exponential growth of slums since the 1960s, particularly in poor countries (which he and many others often call "the South"). He argues that today's megaslums are unprecedented and not accidental. In particular, he blames the International Monetary Fund/World Bank's Structural Adjustment Program (SAP) in the mid-1970s, which he calls the equivalent of a "great natural disaster" (2006a:152). In Davis's view, SAP policies enslaved or "reenslaved" many poor people with their "devastating" consequences, including "a virtual demolition of the local state" (e.g., reduced or deteriorated urban services such as health care, sanitation, and transport in Africa), lower wages, repression, and the urbanization of poverty. (Among other culprits named by Davis: kleptocracies, charismatic churches in the Congo which promoted fears of "witch children," and neoliberal advocates of "bootstrap capitalism.") Davis claims that contemporary megaslums "pose unique problems of imperial order and social control that conventional geopolitics has barely begun to register" ([2004] 2007:131).

Davis is far from the norm. Neither his radical politics, his attention to the global *Planet of Slums* (2006a), nor his obvious outrage, made clear in his take-no-prisoners prose, about *why* much of the twenty-first-century urban world squats in squalor typifies the attitudes or scholarship of most U.S. city planners or urban designers.

Initially influenced by ideas and methods of architecture, engineering, and landscape architecture, U.S. graduate programs in city planning usually offer training in economics, information science, and policy analysis, as well as the more traditional fare. Some programs, responding to fears of natural disasters and urban terrorism, offer courses in security techniques, such as ways to protect a city's water supply.

Planning—whether for city growth or social purposes—has not had the acceptance in the United States that it enjoys in many other nations, including England and France. In France, for instance, "It is the state that embodies and guarantees the collective interests; the rest is selfish individualism" (Grunberg in Traub, 2006:40). In stark contrast, the United States, according to the late U.S. political scientist Seymour Martin Lipset, is "the most anti-statist country in the developed world" (in Burdman, 1995:A11). In large part, this reflects American individualism and nonconformity dating from frontier days, captured in this old backwoods lyric:

I'll buy my own whiskey, I'll drink my own dram,
And for them that don't like me, I don't give a
    damn!

It also reflects many Americans' long-standing preference for private enterprise and reliance on the market to regulate economic matters, including what gets built where. However, with the enlarged reach of corporate business and the expansion of federal, state, and local governments since World War II, more economic and physical (but relatively few social) planners have been added to private and public payrolls.

Wherever they work, city planners and urban designers are, of necessity, political animals. More than most urban professionals, they find themselves at the center of perpetual controversy and in a maelstrom of conflicting demands from numerous groups. They can hardly ignore the clout of private developers; citizens' preferences either for preserving the character of the community or attracting new people, business, and money; federal regulation of local programs; the political environment in which they work; and differences in aesthetics and perceived needs among local groups. Even the most functional and aesthetically pleasing (in the planners' minds, at least) design plan remains a plan until both private and public interests decide to fund it and back it.

COMMUNICATIONS AND INFORMATION TECHNOLOGY

"*Who* says *what* in *which channel* to *whom* with *what effect?*" That was the question asked by political scientist Harold Lasswell (1943), a pioneer in the

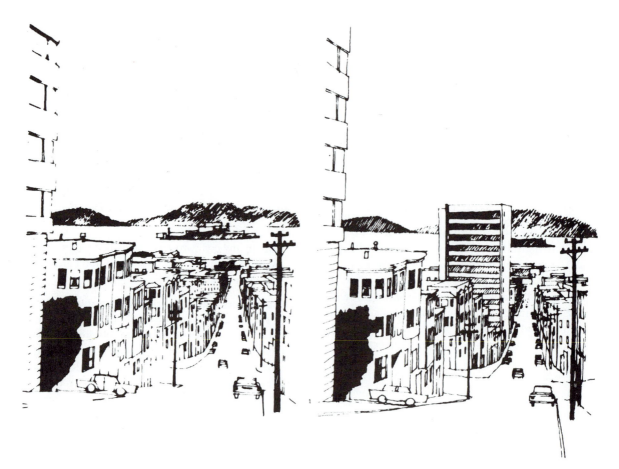

Fig. 2.10 ONCE IT LEAVES THE DRAWING BOARD....What pleases planners and urban designers may not suit various interest groups, both public and private. Drawing a plan is only the first step in the long, highly-political process of getting a plan implemented. These drawings, from *San Francisco's 1971 Urban Design Plan*, reveal the planners' preferences for long vistas of the bay, unobstructed by tall buildings. (Reprinted by permission of the San Francisco City Planning Department)

interdisciplinary field of mass communications. This question summarized the field's concerns for many decades. Usually, researchers focused on one of the five Ws: *who* (communicators), *what* (message content), *which channel* (medium of communication), *whom to* (audience analysis), and *what effect* (impact).

Since World War II, computers and other electronic media have changed how people work, where they live, how they socialize, and perhaps how they think (McLuhan, 1964; Smith, 1980; Meyrowitz, 1985; Zuboff, 1988; Castells, 1996). In the past decade or so, most scholars agree that these new communications/

information technologies have had revolutionary consequences, creating a global village, a global economy, and a global culture. Moviemaker Francis Ford Coppola summed up the changes this way: "The communications revolution makes the Industrial Revolution look like a small-time tryout out of town" (in Ganz and | Khatib,[2006] 2009).

New ways to communicate often have unforeseeable consequences. Take, for instance, the Internet, which has promoted (1) cyberbullying, (2) YouTube and similar online sites, and (3) so-called virtual reality. (1) Suburban New York teenage fighters in

February 2007 were captured on video and posted on the Internet. These teens, from Deer Park, got quick, worldwide recognition from many viewers, including local police. Since that time, at least one suicide due to cyberbullying has been recorded in the United States. (2) YouTube and similar sites may have global as well as local political consequences. As the director of a press group in Southeast Asia put it, "governments worldwide are grappling with the influence and perceived dangers of a medium that is compelling, accessible, hip and wildly popular" (Alampay, 2007). (3) Millions of Internet users now use new identities or "second lives" to communicate across the globe. Some, including those with physical issues (e.g., being confined to a wheelchair), choose to walk again in their "second life." Others, using Internet software plus an Internet-connected, global phone service spend hours online socializing rather than hanging out in clubs and other places with "real" people.

Let us not forget that "old" media can also have important impacts. For example, in 2007, the *Washington Post* ran front-page stories by their investigative reporters on the shabby conditions that greeted returning soldiers from Iraq at Washington, D.C.'s Walter Reed Army Medical Center; this series led to the "forced resignation" of several high U.S. government officials.

Computers and information technology may have profound political impacts too. One theorist even predicts the end of the nation-state because it is based on territoriality while computer-based technologies know no such geographical boundaries (Smith in Brand, 1987:239; see Chapter 6 for a fuller discussion). Others point to possible democratizing trends when, for instance, anyone with a cell phone/camera can upload a video to millions of viewers, thus bypassing traditional gatekeepers such as TV news staffs. Others are less optimistic, seeing cell phone cameras and other easy-to-use-and-carry-around electronics as promoting ever more "bubble gum for the eyes," Frank Lloyd Wright's famous putdown of TV.

How does high technology, fueling an **information economy** (Porat, 1977), affect cities and suburbs? Most scholars agree that the new "high technology is deeply modifying our cities and regions" (Castells, 1985:19). But to whose benefit and whose loss? Most probably, divisions between rich and poor cities, between cities

and suburbs, and between inner-city neighborhoods will deepen as a result of this information technology–economy gap (Castells, 1985:32). In short, at all levels—from local to international—the information-poor will probably get poorer and the information-rich richer. Why? For interconnected reasons, including the following: (1) The information economy tends to polarize the workforce into the highly-paid and well-educated versus the poorly-paid and less-educated and (2) the information economy encourages the "electronic home" and "electronic office," which in turn stimulate sprawl outside inner cities (Castells, 1985:32).

The United States, Canada, most of Western Europe, Japan, and some other countries have entered the stage of **postindustrialism** or **informationalism**—where more people manage things, serve things, think about things, and communicate about things than produce things. According to many (but not all) scholars, information processing has become the core activity of production, distribution, consumption, and management (Castells, 1989:17).

Particularly relevant to the example of slums are studies dealing with access to information in postindustrial society. Some scholars fear that the information highway is market-driven and that it "narrow casts" (instead of broadcasts) to affluent segments of the population while ignoring the poor, and thus increasing the gap between the information-rich and information-poor.

Some activists are trying to change the direction of the information highway. For one, Nicholas Negroponte (former head of MIT's innovative Media Lab) vows to bring cheap computers to the poor millions around the globe (in Israely, 2007).

From a different angle, political sociologist Claus Mueller (1973) contends that lower-class people in advanced technological societies like the United States lack both the linguistic ability and the conceptual frameworks that would allow them to gain access to necessary information to participate effectively in politics. He argues that the mass media reinforce consumerism and leisure, thus integrating the poor into the political system. Others (e.g., Phillips, 1975; Romano, 1985) maintain that local news reportage routinely ignores issues that concern the city's poor and ethnic groups; such issues become defined as non-news and don't even get debated. This suggests that even so-called objective news reports are biased in a subtle way: toward a particular view of the social world—a cosmopolitan, middle- and upper-class, educated view that reflects the news reporters' own outlook on reality. Similarly, Michael Weiss (2000:21) suggests that editorial staffs at elite U.S. newspapers, such as the *Washington Post*, are likely to live in upscale areas and, thus, may be out of touch with the communities they cover.

With newer technologies, situations can change quickly. Take one example: blogs. Whatever a person's background, opinion, or geographical home, she or he can, for an increasingly affordable sum, spread a personal point of view worldwide in a nanosecond. Millions all over the world are doing it too; numbers are unreliable, but as many as 12 million or more may be blogging.

Normally, bloggers make no claim of being objective. Au contraire. Indeed, contemporary blogs (and vlogs) resemble opinionated newspapers published in the United States before the Civil War; those newspapers made no claim to "objectivity." Nor did they avoid giving offense. (This strategy is not followed by most U.S. commercial media today because it can hurt business: Offended advertisers, subscribers, viewers, or listeners can cancel their ads or subscriptions, flip the dial, or mount campaigns to put the program or enterprise out of commission.)

At the city level, technologies can serve people who live in slums as well as those in wealthier digs. St. Cloud, Florida, for one, is using wi-fi to provide every citizen within a 15-mile radius with free network access. Other places throughout the world—from the tiny village of Cenévières in southwest France to the town of Siem Reap in Cambodia—provide either fast, reasonably priced Internet service or wi-fi access.

ENVIRONMENTAL STUDIES

Deforested jungles, ozone depletion, garbage pile-ups, hazardous waste, oil spills, nuclear accidents, and industrial smog all helped to raise global consciousness of the borderless biosphere. One response is university-based programs dedicated to the interdisciplinary field of environmental studies. Typically, these programs cover a variety of topics, from risk analysis, conflicts between job loss

and environmental destruction, and occupational health to solid waste disposal.

Environmental studies may also include the study of mass migrations and international conflict that can result from environmental degradation. Indeed, according to some, the environment is *the* national security issue of the early twenty-first century.

Environmentally speaking, some questions are long-standing. These include the following: What should be done with effluents in affluent industrial cities? What can and should be done to decrease pollutants resulting from fossil-fuel vehicles and the generation of electricity (e.g., acid rain, principally caused by sulfur and nitrogen compounds, which can be carried in the air for hundreds of miles)? How can lawmakers better deal with disasters such as Hurricane Katrina's destruction in New Orleans and beyond?

The interrelationship of socioeconomic and environmental crises, such as global warming (the existence of which is denied by some writers and politicians, mainly from the United States), has recently captured the imagination of scholars. These scholars tend to envision the world from the radical end of the political spectrum (see Chapter 3 for a discussion of ideologies). For example, in *Natural Causes*, economist–sociologist James O'Connor (1997) analyzes a wide range of environmental issues, including the Gulf War and environmental justice. He argues, provocatively, that environmental issues should be seen as social and political issues and that the global reach of present-day capitalism bears much of the responsibility for environmental degradation. Similarly, Wendell Berry ([2001] 2006), essayist and Kentucky farmer, identifies "free-market" thinking and corporations as key agents of pollution, species extinction, and loss of farmland and wilderness.

Environmental studies scholars have been asking various questions connected to slums and poverty. For example, *where* do private corporations and public governments dump toxic wastes? (Answer, according to Lee [1987]: often in poor neighborhoods of rich countries heavily populated by people of color, such as East Los Angeles, and poor countries, including West Africa's extremely poor Benin.) *Why* do poor African American urbanites have much shorter

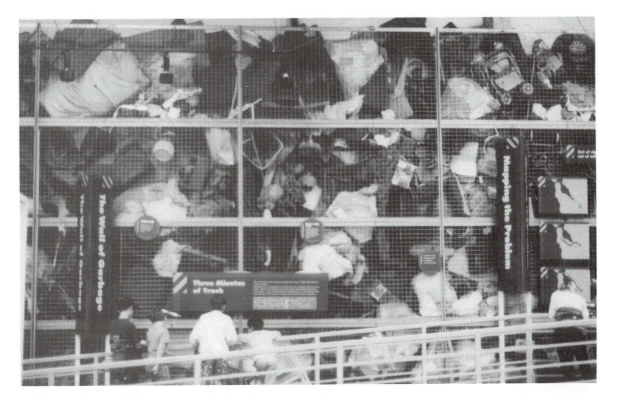

Fig. 2.11 WALL OF GARBAGE. At The Recyclery in Silicon Valley's Milpitas, California (Chapter 8) , there is a 100-foot-long, 20-foot-high "wall of garbage" representing all the junk dumped in Milpitas's county, Santa Clara, every 3 minutes, equivalent to less than 1 second for all U.S. trash. (Tim Teninty)

life expectancies than whites? (Answer, according to Weissman and Epstein [1989]: numerous factors related to poverty, such as high infant mortality rates, and some related to race, such as racial inequalities in medical care.) And *who* pays the highest price for ecological disruption? (Answer, according to sociologist–engineer–chemist Allan Schnaiberg [1980]: the urban poor. Typically, Schnaiberg argues, publicly-funded projects, such as suburban freeways, "have subsidized the material progress of affluent suburbanites at the expense of working and poverty-class urban dwellers, whose tax burdens grow and whose social services decline" [1980:337]).

LITERATURE AND THE ARTS

Often poets, songwriters, and artists speak to the soul, clarifying the human condition in ways that statistics or theoretical models cannot! Those familiar with the poor southern sharecroppers in Walker Evans's photos in James Agee's *Let Us Now Praise Famous Men* ([1939] 1960) and Dale Maharidge and Michael Williamson's *And Their Children After Them* (1989) or the Kinte clan in Alex Haley's *Roots* (1976) can feel poverty's ache. Likewise, we feel like we know the Cuban immigrants to New York City yearning for success in Oscar Hijuelos's *The Mambo Kings Play Songs of Love* (1989). And the Bangladeshi community in London's *Brick Lane* ([2003] 2008), Monica Ali's controversial novel which tells the stories of heroine Nazeen and the struggles of Islamic immigrants in pre- and post-9/11 England. All these works provide a firsthand encounter with particular people and their lives, an acquaintance with people that can touch the emotions as well as the intellect.

Poverty and slum conditions have been a theme in the arts since the Industrial Revolution, which gave us both the word "slum" and the condition called "slums." To take but one example, novelist Charles Dickens draws a portrait of Coketown, a new industrial town that could be one of many English cities in the mid-nineteenth century:

> It was a town of red brick or of brick that would have been red if the smoke and ashes had allowed it; but as matters stood it was a town of unnatural red and black like the painted face of a savage. It was a town of machinery and tall chimneys, out of which interminable serpents of smoke trailed themselves....It had a black canal in it, and a river that ran purple with ill-smelling dye, and vast piles of buildings full of windows where there was a rattling and a trembling all day long....It contained several large streets...inhabited by people equally like each other, who all went in and out at the same hours, with the same sound upon the same pavements, to do the same work, and to whom every day was the same as yesterday and tomorrow, and every year the counterpart of the last and the next.

> *([1854] 1967:17)*

No statistical table can capture the monotonous rhythm of life, the squalor and dirt, and the pervasive gloom of working conditions in nineteenth-century England as well as Dickens's word portrait.

More recently, the urban despair of poor children has been captured in their own words and images. Listen to one 12-year-old, Shemika Skipworth, speaking about what she knows firsthand—coping with a parent's drug habit:

> You smoked up your check and you can't go
>   home.
> You go to the mail pick up your check
> Go and smoke it up on the project step
> Now you're on the streets nowhere to go
> You smoked up your check and you can't go
>   home.

> *(in Williams, 1989)*

The image of poverty and slums has also been poignantly captured by the movie camera. Yet, most Hollywood movies focus on the social disorder presumed to accompany slum life. The now classic

West Side Story (1961) is a case in point. But on close inspection, the film also shows what sociologist Gerald D. Suttles calls *The Social Order of the Slum* (1968): a well-defined moral order rooted in personalistic relations and provincialism. To be sure, the rules of the gangs (the Jets and Sharks) are not those middle-class block groups. But they are widely understood by people in the neighborhood, and they serve to regulate daily life.

Other forms of popular culture and folk culture—from graffiti and street murals to bestsellers and rap music—are important sources for understanding people's responses to poverty and slum life. Consider, for instance, one American musical tradition: the blues. The blues speak of melancholy, what early American settlers from England called the "blue devils." Immigrants coming from the villages and small towns of the British Isles to the hills and hollows of the American wilderness apparently suffered from the blue devils of homesickness, and they sang about it; pioneers were often lost in the vast, raw spaces of the New World. Later, in the nineteenth century, white and black migrants from the rural countryside to the city started singing the blues. Some sang "The House of the Rising Sun Blues," the story of the poverty that forced poor country girls, perhaps as early as the 1840s, into a life of prostitution in New Orleans. Freed slaves during the Reconstruction era sang of their kinship with the boll weevil, which "was lookin' for a home, just a'lookin' for a home." And around 1900, when some African Americans left southern sharecropping and headed north, they "found the blues waiting...at every station down the line. [They had] the *Alabama Blues, The Atlanta Blues, The New Orleans Hop Scop Blues, The Fort Worth Blues and the Dallas Heart Disease, The St. Louis Blues...The Michigan Water Blues, The Wabash Blues, The State Street Blues* (in Chicago), *The Harlem Blues*" (Lomax, 1960:576). And in the textile mill towns, workers sang the "Winnsboro Cotton Mill Blues" or "Cotton Mill Colic": "I'm a-gonna starve, ev'rybody will/You can't make a livin' at a cotton mill" (Lomax, 1960:287).

By the 1920s, blues singers like Big Bill Broonzy began recording their songs for the whole world to hear. As folk song historian Alan Lomax comments:

> If all the verses of the recorded blues were laid end to end, it would make a lonesome moan that could be heard on the moon. These songs speak plainly, pithily, and powerfully about the emotional disturbances of urban society in the west. The jobless, dispossessed, unwanted predatory Negro male was the first character in our civilization to experience and express these feelings. Now we are all aware of them, and the big sad wind of the blues sings through the heart-strings from Memphis to Moscow.
>
> *(1960:576)*

More recently, African American rap artists have been singing about desperation, not melancholy. In some songs, for example, the house down the street is a prison where no one tries to save kids from their abusive parents. Neighborhoods are often described as killing fields where some residents treat an Uzi submachine gun as their best friend.

MAKING SOME CONNECTIONS

After this brief look at how various disciplines and fields of knowledge might view one urban condition through their own special lenses (and blinders), we might ask whether any common foci appear. And you might wonder, quite sensibly, whether any connections, however desirable, can be made.

Some common themes and factors do emerge from this potpourri of information about slums. For one thing, the impact of economic forces in shaping people's lives is a theme that cuts across many disciplines and fields. Economic logic underpins Burgess's model of urban growth and Alonso's model of residential bid rent. Economic forces are also emphasized in Lewis's anthropological studies of the culture of poverty, Warner's historical look at Philadelphia, Coles's social psychiatric research on children, and Mueller's analysis of communication in mass society. Other factors important to urban life that cross-cut disciplines and fields include the importance of power relations, social organization, information flows, environment, and technology in influencing individual lives.

This brief look at perspectives on slums also shows that intellectual disciplines may have unique outlooks, but scholars don't stop at disciplinary boundaries. Indeed, some scholars seem impossible to classify! For instance, Spanish-born, French-trained, U.S.-published, much-traveled scholar Manuel Castells defies national or departmental pigeonholing. Trained as a sociologist in Paris, Castells did research in the 1960s on industrial location, a concern more typical of geography and economics. By 1979, he was professor of city and regional planning at the University of California at Berkeley. Since then, he has taught at universities worldwide. Space and social structure remain key to his theory and research, which ranges widely over issues of political movements, urbanization, economic change, and comparative urban life.

Another theme emerges: People living in a certain situation—say, in Appalachian poverty or Philadelphia's slum—may understand their subjective experience differently from the way "objective" social scientists do. As I've implied by starting this book with a list of personal biases, I believe that the notion of an objective, value-free social science is a mythical ideal, not a practical possibility. Worse, in my view, it often serves as a cover, turning a professional, upper-middle-class view of what's real into the official definition of reality. This can be especially dangerous when urbanists advise policymakers. Projecting what they think is objectively good for other people (especially people who don't share the same dreams, material possessions, or values), urbanists have often imposed their values on others in the name of objectivity.

Unfortunately, no synthesis of views is on the horizon; the lack of an agreed-upon conceptual framework and the absence of meaningful consensus among urbanists prevent it. Still, we can begin the project of weaving some threads together to better understand the urban world.

As we begin that difficult, long-term project, let us recall Gertrude Stein. Her life as a writer exemplifies the quest to see beyond a mere litany of facts. On her deathbed, Stein turned to her assembled friends and asked, "What is the answer?" After a moment of stunned silence, she asked, "What, then, is the question?" Then she died (in Ozick[1945], 1996).

Chapter 3 suggests some worthwhile questions to ask. It also looks at even more reasons why urban observers disagree on answers.

KEY TERMS

Bid rent curve Description of how much a residential or retail client will bid (pay) for land or rent at varying distances from the CBD of a city. Associated with William Alonso (1933–1999)who criss-crossed disciplinary lines—from sociology and regional planning to population studies—but who is primarily remembered for this contribution to urban economics.

Burgess model Model or hypothesis constructed by sociologist Ernest W. Burgess concerning the spatial-social structure of the U.S. industrial city and its expansion over time. The hypothesis explains that a city's population is organized in a series of five concentric rings or zones, starting from the CBD.

Cognitive maps Personal, mental maps that usually bear little resemblance to official tourist maps of a city or neighborhood. Images of a city—outstanding features, landmarks, important places, and so on-differ among individuals and social groups.

Discipline A division of intellectual labor associated with higher education. As specialization increased and knowledge about the physical and social world expanded in the nineteenth century, social science split up into disciplines: economics, political science, sociology, and so forth.

Filtering The process by which housing passes or trickles down from higher-income to lower-income residents as it ages and becomes less desirable. Thus, a mansion built in 1860 for a very rich family may have filtered down to house a moderate-income family by 1920. By 1980, the same house might have filtered down still further to house four very-low-income families. Opposite: *gentrification.*

Industrial cities Cities such as Chicago and Detroit in the U.S, whose population growth and spatial pattern were influenced mainly by manufacturing and centralizing technologies. Contrasts: *Preindustrial cities* such as Paris and Tokyo; *postindustrial regions* such as Orange County, California.

Information economy A type of economy built on telecommunication highways that distribute information (which becomes a commodity, like shoes or cars) to be bought and sold. Similar terms: *information society, postindustrial society.*

Informationalism A type of social organization, evolved from industrialism, that depends on information processing as its core activity. This term is associated with sociologist-planner Manuel Castells, who argues that cities and regions of the world are being transformed by a combination of technological and economic processes.

Interdisciplinary Having a degree of integration among several disciplines. The concepts, methodology, procedures, terminology, or data may be more or less connected among two or more disciplines in an interdisciplinary study. To some, interdisciplinary connotes the attempt to bridge disciplines and apply research tools and/or perspectives from more than one discipline; to others, it is synonymous with multidisciplinary studies.

Latent function A function or purpose hidden from view and often unintended. For example, a city public-works department exists officially to build roads. Its latent function may be to provide patronage opportunities such as jobs for political supporters and ethnic voting groups.

Manifest function The officially stated, visible reason for existence. For example, building roads is one manifest function of a city's public-works department.

Megaslums Gargantuan areas, typically on the periphery of cities in poor countries. They are characterized by squalid poverty, huge populations, and "informal" housing.

Multidisciplinary Involving more than one academic discipline. In practice, multidisciplinary and interdisciplinary efforts are not always distinguishable.

Paradigm A model or patterned way of seeing the world. In the scientific disciplines, the dominant paradigm defines the problems and methods of a research field; it makes legitimate what counts as facts, what assumptions are valid, and what procedures are deemed scientific. Today there are competing paradigms in social science disciplines.

Postindustrialism As distinguished from preindustrialism and industrialism, a society and an economy characterized by high technology, which permits most people to work at jobs in the information and service sectors rather than in the agricultural and manufacturing sectors.

Typology A classification scheme composed of two or more ideal types, used to organize data and guide research--for example, four types of slum dwellers, distinguished by length of residence and reasons for being there.

Urban studies A multidisciplinary or interdisciplinary field of study whose central focus is the city and its surrounding area. Its intellectual boundaries are not well defined, and programs of urban studies vary in content from one academic institution to another.

PROJECTS

1. **What you see depends on how you look at it.** Select four individuals of differing occupations and neighborhoods (e.g., a zone II food server, a zone III shopowner, a downtown business executive, a suburban athletic coach) and ask each one to draw a simple sketch of the city you're in (or near), noting its most important places and outstanding features. Do these cognitive maps differ? If so, how?

2. **Disciplinary perspectives.** Select one issue, such as urban transportation, crime, violence, or unemployment, and examine how basic texts in at least three different disciplines or fields approach it, noting what factors they stress in their analysis. Do themes emerge?

3. **I hear the country singing.** Using the same issue selected for project 2, investigate how songwriters have approached it. For example, compare the messages in songs recorded by rap groups and pop singers. In what ways, if any, do these approaches vary from those of the three intellectual disciplines and/or professional fields?

4. **Property prices.** Why is residential and office property so expensive in London, Tokyo, New York City, and Hong Kong? Why is land so much less per square foot in Bogota, Lagos, and Phnom Penh? First, find out what property per square foot (or square meter) costs in those cities and at least 10 other cities on three continents. Then, analyze possible reasons why these differences in cost occur. Also investigate the cost of a covered parking space in various cities.

SUGGESTIONS FOR FURTHER LEARNING

For a new version of the children's literature classic, *The Little Prince*, hear and see the opera of the same name. Based on the book by Antoine de Saint-Exupéry, the opera's music was composed by Rachel Portman.

Two books about Paris illustrate the saying "What you see depends on how you look at it": Mort Rosenblum, *The Secret Life of the Seine* (Reading, Mass.: Addison-Wesley, 1994), and François Maspero, *Roissy Express: A Journey Through the Paris Suburbs* (New York: Verso, 1994). Rosenblum's romantic view of Paris comes from his life aboard a 54-foot boat. Maspero's steely-eyed perspective comes from his ride aboard the 37-mile train from Charles de Gaulle Airport to the other side of Paris, where he sees mostly dreary housing and drab, disjointed spaces when he visits each of the 38 stops.

Cognitive maps have attracted researchers from fields as diverse as psychology, geography, and urban planning for over a half-century. In *Wayfinding Behavior: Cognitive Mapping and Other Spatial Processes* (Baltimore, Md.: Johns Hopkins University Press, 1999), editor Reginald G. Golledge chooses contributors who present various perspectives, including cognitive, perceptual, neural, and animal.

For contemporary and very dissonant views on slums worldwide, see Mike Davis, *Planet of Slums* (2006) and Robert Neuwirth, *Shadow Cities: A Billion Squatters, a New Urban World* (2005). Davis paints a bleak picture of slum dwellers' future prospects. Investigative reporter Neuwirth is much more hopeful, seeing today's megaslums as gritty but vital communities, building urban communities of the future.

To better understand a social science discipline's particular perspective, look at introductory texts. Compare their key concepts, often noted in the table of contents and the index, with key concepts of other disciplines or hybrids.

The most up-to-date work in a discipline can be found online or in journals. And new journals appear regularly, reflecting the ever-increasing division of labor in scholarly thought. See, for example, a journal launched in 2008, *Journal of Global Mass Communication*, dedicated to "finding innovative ways to examine and understand mass communication in a global context." The journal's multinational editorial board reflects its stance.

For a closer look at the bid rent curve, see *Location and Land Use* (Cambridge, Mass.: Harvard University Press, 1964) by the late William Alonso. Alonso expanded a concept originated by German landowner Johann Heinrich von Thünen (1780–1850) concerning agricultural land use and urban areas.

For an example of how various perspectives can be fused to obtain a richer view, see Sharon Zukin, *The Culture of Cities* (New York: Blackwell, 1995). She draws on insights from sociology, political economy, and the analysis of visual form.

The field of mass communications and information technology has changed a great deal in past decades. For an interesting look at the history of the Internet, see Patrice Flichy, *L'Internet imaginaire* (Cambridge, Mass.: MIT Press, 2007). Media historian Flichy's study, first published in 2001 in French, explores the collective vision that underlies the Internet.

For a look at an alternative approach to a discipline, see Nancy Folbre, *Who Pays for the Kids?* (New York: Routledge, 1994). Folbre's study of child care calls into question the assumption in neoclassical economics of the so-called rational actor. Folbre wonders what a mother's self-interest is: Can she separate her self-interest from that of her own child?

British sociologists Mike Savage and Alan Warde give a history and critique of urban sociology (and the "new" urban sociology) in *Urban Sociology, Capitalism and Modernity* (New York: Continuum, 1993). They believe that "there is no solid definition of the urban" and that the label "urban sociology" is "mostly a flag of convenience." Yet, they try to "identify the common elements" explaining the persistence of their subdiscipline, urban sociology.

For a hands-on experience of how disciplines and fields work, computer software can be helpful. The most famous is a computer game designed by Will Wright, *SimCity* (now in its fourth edition with an expansion pack called *Rush Hour*, Lafayette, Calif.: Maxis Software; available from Amazon.com); it allows a player to build a city and make it work. Simulated city players fashion their own cities or play one of many disaster scenarios.

Until recently, economics was considered the "geekiest of geek subjects," according to Elise Soukup in "Sexiest Trade Alive" (*Newsweek*, Jan. 2, 2006:21). However, in 2006, economics was the hottest undergrad degree at New York University and Harvard in the United States. Perhaps one book, best-seller *Freakonomics: A Rogue Economist Explores the Hidden Side of Everything* (New York: William Morrow, 2005) by economist Steven D. Levitt and journalist Stephen J. Dubner, together with a 2005 MTV documentary film about Kenya's economy (with economist Jeffrey Sachs and actress Angelina Jolie), sparked the trend. Cornell economics and management professor Robert H. Frank's *The Economic Naturalist: In Search of Explanations for Everyday Enigmas* (New York: Basic Books, 2007) may have added some wit and whimsy to the recent trend.

For those wishing a more mathematical approach to urban economics, see, for example, the homepage of economist Thayer Watkins (http://www.sjsu.edu/faculty/watkins/alonso.htm), which features a mathematical equation expressing the bid rent curve.

Reflecting a profound change in the discipline of anthropology, urban places like Fargo, North Dakota—not the Trobriand Islands—are becoming common research sites for anthropologists. One award-winning study, Faye D. Ginsburg, *Contested Lives: The Abortion Debate in an American Community* (Berkeley: University of California Press, 1989), is based on field interviews in Fargo with middle-class women.

One work on town planning that covers its history in Europe from Hippodamus to Baron Georges-Eugène Haussmann is *Planning Europe's Capital Cities: Aspects of Nineteenth-Century Urban Development* (London: E & FN Spon [1997] 1999) by Thomas Hall, an art history professor. Among the various cities discussed in some detail are Paris, Copenhagen, Barcelona, and Rome. The book is copiously illustrated.

Too numerous to mention are the works of literary and visual art that expand our vision of the urban world. Here are a few on just one topic: the blues. In *Looking Up at Down: The Emergence of Blues Culture* (Philadelphia: Temple University Press, 1989), William B. Barlow traces the blues from its rural roots to its urbanization in Chicago, Memphis, and other regional centers. In *The History of the Blues: The Roots,* the Music, the People (Cambridge, Mass.: Da Capo [1995] 2003), Francis Davis (music critic for the *Atlantic* magazine) moves from the blues's roots in work songs, field hollers, spirituals, reels, and ballads from England and Scotland to various contemporary uses, including advertising diet soda.

For poetic commentaries on folk music and personal evocations of the communities that produced the blues, see Alan Lomax, *The Folk Songs of North America in the English Language* (Garden City, N.Y.: Doubleday, 1960) and *The Land Where the Blues Began* (New York: Pantheon, 1993). Lomax himself collected many of these songs as he traveled throughout the United States. Lomax's *Blues in the Mississippi Night* (1990, compact disc) features blues musicians reminiscing about life and music in the Deep South.

A series of eight videotapes produced by the Conference on Literature and the Urban Experience at Rutgers University shows artists, novelists, playwrights, and social scientists giving poetry readings or talking about a variety of topics, ranging from "The Language of the Streets" (James Baldwin) and "The Reinvention of Childhood" (Jonathan Kozol) to "City Limits: Village Values—Concepts of the Neighborhood in Black Fiction" (Toni Morrison).

For an excellent discussion of attitudes toward urban and rural life expressed in U.S. painting, see Sidra Stich's *Made in U.S.A.* (Berkeley: University of California Press, 1987). One section on cities, suburbs, and highways—the "New American Landscape"—argues that in the 1950s and 1960s U.S. painters called attention to "the congestion and exhilaration of the urban milieu, the comfort and conformity of suburbia, and the fascination and monotony of the highway." Such artists as Robert Bechtle and Robert Arneson "openly exposed the most banal and alienating aspects of the contemporary setting" (45).

Movies alert us to a special kind of alienation: the rage and violence of oppressive urban lives. One powerful film, Matty Rich's *Straight Out of Brooklyn* (1991), is a dynamic and tragic description of life in an African American ghetto. *River's Edge* (1987), based on a real-life event in the San Francisco Bay Area, vividly portrays the alienation of teenagers in a white working-class

suburb. *Fight Club* (1999) highlights alienation from another angle: male aggression. Based on a novel by Chuck Palahniuk, the movie is disturbing and violent, featuring antisocial behavior.

David Brodsky offers "Thirteen Ways of Looking at a Freeway" in *L.A. Freeway* (Berkeley: University of California Press, 1981); this study explores the ways in which the southern California freeway defines the way people think about the metropolitan area.

Geographer Mark Monmonier reminds us that maps may reflect unconscious bias. He notes that "a single map is but one of an indefinitely large number of maps that might be produced for the same situation or from the same data" in *How to Lie with Maps* (Chicago: University of Chicago Press, 1991).

Robert D. Kaplan infers that maps often lie. In "The Coming Anarchy" (*Atlantic Monthly*, February 1994, 44–76), Kaplan says that perhaps 15 percent of the population of the Ivory Coast's capital, Abidjan—often called the Paris of West Africa—live in shantytowns named "Chicago," "Washington," and so on; few such slums appear on maps. To Kaplan, this suggests that political maps are "products of tired conventional wisdom" and "in the Ivory Coast's case, of an elite that will ultimately be forced to relinquish power" (48). (Indeed, Kaplan's prediction about Ivory Coast has come to pass.)

In *Atlas of Cyberspace* (London: Pearson Education, 2002), information cartographers Martin Dodge and Rob Kitchin show that controversies over maps cross national borders. In this venture into virtual geography, the authors explore maps of cyberspaces—"cybermaps"—and graphic representations of new information landscapes created by "cyberexplorers" from many disciplines throughout the world.

REFERENCES

Abril, Maria Elena Ruiz. 2002. "Gender in urban infrastructure projects: The case of the Caracas Slum-Upgrading Project." http://wbln0018.worldbank.org/LAC/LACInfoClient.nsf/0/368aee02bafc888985256eb50080ac44/$FILE/CAMEBAwebversion.pdf.

Agee, James, and Walker Evans. [1939] 1960. *Let Us Now Praise Famous Men*. Boston: Houghton Mifflin.

Alampay, Roby. 2007. "You block YouTube at your peril." *International Herald Tribune* (April 12): http://www.iht.com/articles/2007/04/12/opinion/edalamp.php

Ali, Monica. [2003] 2008 *Brick Lane*. New York: Scribner.

Alonso, William. 1971. "Beyond the inter-disciplinary approach to planning." *American Institute of Planners Journal* 37:169–173.

———. 1973. "A theory of the urban land market." Pp. 45–55 in Ronald E. Grieson, ed., *Urban Economics*. Boston: Little, Brown.

Anderson, Elijah. 1990. *Streetwise: Race, Class, and Change in an Urban Community*. Chicago: University of Chicago Press.

Banfield, Edward, and Martin Meyerson. 1955. *Politics, Planning, and the Public Interest*. Glencoe, Ill.: Free Press.

Berry, Wendell. 2001. "The idea of a local economy." *Orion Magazine*, (Winter): http://www.orionmagazine.org/index.php/articles/article/299/.

Brand, Stewart. 1987. *The Media Lab: Inventing the Future at MIT*. New York: Viking.

Braudel, Fernand. [1986] 1990. *The Identity of France*. Vol. 1, *History and Environment*. Trans. Sian Reynolds. New York: Harper & Row.

———. [1963] 1995. *A History of Civilizations*. Trans. Richard Mayne. New York: Penguin.

Burdman, Pamela. 1995. "Bombings linked to social malaise." *San Francisco Chronicle* (May 1):A1+.

Castells, Manuel. 1985. "High technology, economic restructuring, and the urban–regional process in the United States." Pp. 11–40 in *High Technology, Space, and Society*. Vol. 28, *Urban Affairs Annual Reviews*. Beverly Hills, Calif.: Sage.

———. 1989. *The Informational City: Information Technology, Economic Restructuring, and the Urban–Regional Process*. Oxford: Blackwell.

———. 1996. *The Rise of the Network Society*. Oxford: Blackwell.

Coles, Robert. 1977a. *Eskimos, Chicanos, Indians*. Boston: Little, Brown.

———. 1977b. *Privileged Ones: The Well-Off and the Rich in America*. Boston: Little, Brown.

Coughlin, Ellen K. 1987. "Geographers are urged to reorient research to central concerns of place and space." *Chronicle of Higher Education* (May 13):9.

———. 1993. "Feminist economists vs. 'economic man': Questioning a field's bedrock concepts." *Chronicle of Higher Education* (June 30):A8–A9.

———. [1992] 1995. "Beyond *Blade Runner*: Urban control, the ecology of fear." Westfield, N.J.: Open Media, USA. Reprinted by Mediamatic 8#2/3, The Home Issue.

———. 2006a. *Planet of Slums*. London: Verso.

———. 2006b. "Slum ecology." *Orion Magazine* (March 6), http://www.orionmagazine.org/index.php/articles/article/167/

Davis, Mike. [2004] 2007. "The urbanization of empire." Pp. 122–131 in Mike Davis, ed., *In Praise or Barbarians*. Chicago: Haymarket.

De Blij, Harm. 2005. *Why Geography Matters: Three Challenges Facing America: Climate Change, the Rise of China, and Global Terrorism*. New York: Oxford University Press.

Dickens, Charles. [1854] 1967. *Hard Times*. New York: Dutton.

Duverger, Maurice. 1964. *An Introduction to the Social Sciences*. New York: Praeger.

Eames, Charles, and Ray Eames. 1968. The Films of Charles & Ray Eames. *The Powers of 10*, Vol. 1. DVD.

Faust, Drew. 2007. Interview with Jim Lehrer. *The Newshour with Jim Lehrer*. KQED-TV, February 12.

Feagin, Joe R., and Robert Parker. 1990. *Building American Cities: The Urban Real Estate Game*, 2nd ed. Englewood Cliffs, N.J.: Prentice Hall.

Foucault, Michel. 1980. "Questions on geography." Pp. 63–77 in C. Gordon, ed., *Power/Knowledge: Selected Interviews and Other Writings, 1972–1977*. New York: Pantheon.

Freedman, James O. 1987. "The tendency toward specialization has had fragmenting consequences." *Chronicle of Higher Education* (August 12):A47.

Gans, Herbert J. 1962. *The Urban Villagers: Group and Class in the Life of Italian-Americans*. New York: Free Press.

Gibson, William. 1984. *Neuromancer*. New York: Ace Science Fiction.

Ganz, Adam, and Lina Khatib. [2006] 2009 "Digital cinema: The transformation of film practice and aesthetics." *New Cinemas and Contemporary Film*. http://www.atypon-link.com/INT/doi/abs/10.1386/ncin.4.1.21_1

Gilman, Charlotte Perkins. [1898] 1998. *Women and Economics: A Study of the Economic Relation Between Men and Women as a Factor in Social Evolution*. Berkeley: University of California Press.

Glaeser, Edward L., Joseph Gyourko, and Raven E. Saks. 2005. "Urban growth and housing supply." (January)

http://post.economics.harvard.edu/faculty/glaeser/papers.html

Glassner, Barry. [1999] 2000. *The Culture of Fear: Why Americans Are Afraid of the Wrong Things*. New York: Basic Books.

Gottdiener, Mark, and Joe Feagin. 1988. "The paradigm shift in urban sociology." *Urban Affairs Quarterly* 24: 163–187.

Gradwohl, David M., and Nancy M. Osborn. 1984. *Exploring Buried Buxton: Archeology of an Abandoned Coal Mining Town with a Large Black Population*. Ames: Iowa State University Press.

Grosfoguel, Ramón. 2003. *Colonial Subjects: Puerto Ricans in a Global Perspective*. Berkeley: University of California Press.

Haley, Alex. 1976. *Roots*. Garden City, N.Y.: Doubleday.

Helft, Miguel. 2007. "Mapmaking for the masses, online." *International Herald Tribune* (July 27) http://www.iht.com/articles/2007/07/26/technology/maps.php

Hijuelos, Oscar. 1989. *The Mambo Kings Play Songs of Love*. New York: Farrar, Straus & Giroux.

Hillman, Sidney. n.d. http://www.brainyquote.com/quotes/quotes/s/sidneyhill170254.html

Israely, Jeff. 2007. "Bringing cheap computers to the world." (Oct. 31): http://www.time.com/time/world/article/0,8599,1678273,00.html

Kaës, R. 1963. *Vivre dans les grands ensembles* (*Living in Large Developments*. Paris: Dunod.

Kates, Robert W. 1989. "The great questions of science and society do not fit neatly into single disciplines." *Chronicle of Higher Education* (May 17):B1+.

Kessler-Harris, Alice. 2001. *In Pursuit of Equity*. New York: Oxford University Press.

Lasswell, Harold. 1943. "The structure and function of communications in society." Pp. 37–51 in Lyman Bryson, ed., *The Communication of Ideas*. New York: Institute for Religious and Social Studies.

Lee, Charles. 1987. "Waste and race report." New York: United Church of Christ.

Lefebve, Henri. [1974] 1991. *The Production of Space*. Trans. Donald Nicholson-Smith. Oxford: Blackwell.

Leopold, Wendy. 1992. "Through a glass darkly: Making sense of what happened in L.A." *Mosaic* (Summer):3–4.

Levitt, Steven D., and Stephen J. Dubner. 2005. *Freakonomics: A Rogue Economist Explores the Hidden Side of Everything*. New York: William Morrow.

Lewis, Oscar. 1961. *The Children of Sanchez*. New York: Random House.

Logan, John R., and Harvey L. Molotch. 1987. *Urban Fortunes: The Political Economy of Place*. Berkeley: University of California Press.

Lomax, Alan. 1960. *The Folk Songs of North America in the English Language*. Garden City, N.Y.: Doubleday.

Lynch, Kevin. [1960] 1974. *The Image of the City*. Cambridge, Mass.: MIT Press.

Maharidge, Dale, and Michael Williamson. 1989. *And Their Children After Them: The Legacy of* Let Us Now Praise Famous Men: *James Agee, Walker Evans, and the Rise and Fall of Cotton in the South*. New York: Pantheon.

Matthaei, Julie. 2005. Homepage: http://www.wellesley.edu/Economics/matthaei/

Maxwell, Rahsaan. 2006. "The paradoxes of political integration among Caribbeans in contemporary Britain and France." Paper presented at the Institute of European Studies, University of California at Berkeley (November 15).

McLuhan, Marshall. 1964. *Understanding Media: The Extensions of Man*. New York: McGraw-Hill.

Meyrowitz, Joshua. 1985. *No Sense of Place: The Impact of Electronic Media on Social Behavior*. New York: Oxford University Press.

Morrison, Philip, and Phyllis Morrison; and the Office of Charles and Ray Eames. 1985. *Powers of Ten: A Book About the Relative Size of Things in the Universe and the Effect of Adding Another Zero*. San Francisco: W.H. Freeman.

Mueller, Claus. 1973. *The Politics of Communication: A Study in the Political Sociology of Language, Socialization, and Legitimation*. New York: Oxford University Press.

Mumford, Lewis. 1961. *The City in History: Its Origins, Its Transformations, and Its Prospects*. New York: Harcourt, Brace & World.

Neuwirth, Robert. 2005. *Shadow Cities: A Billion Squatters, A New Urban World*. New York: Routledge.

Newman, John Henry, Cardinal. [1852] 1919. *The Idea of a University*. London: Longmans, Green.

O'Connor, James. 1997. *Natural Causes: Essays in Ecological Marxism*. New York: Guilford Press.

O'Flaherty, Brendan. 2005. *City Economics*. Cambridge, Mass.: Harvard University Press.

Oxford University Press, 1971, *The Compact Oxford Dictionary*, New York.

Ozick, Cynthia.[1946] 1996. "The saloonkeeper." http://www.nytimes.com/specials/magazine4/articles/stein.html

Palen, J. John, and Bruce London. 1984. *Gentrification, Displacement and Neighborhood Revitalization*. Albany: State University of New York Press.

Park, Robert E., Ernest W. Burgess, and Roderick D. McKenzie [1925] 1974. *The City*. Chicago: University of Chicago Press.

Phillips, E. Barbara. 1975. "The artists of everyday life: Journalists, their craft, and their consciousness." Ph.D. diss., Syracuse University.

Porat, Marc Uri. 1977. *The Information Economy: Definition and Measurement*. Washington, D.C.: Office of Telecommunications, Department of Commerce.

The Power of Maps. 1993. Washington, D.C.: Cooper-Hewitt, National Museum of Design, Smithsonian Institution.

Rathje, William L., and Cullen Murphy. 1992. *Rubbish! The Archaeology of Garbage*. New York: HarperCollins.

Riccucci, Norma M. 2005. *How Management Matters: Street-level Bureaucrats and Welfare Reform*. Washington, D.C.: Georgetown University Press.

Rodgers, Jeffrey Pepper. 2005. "Change in the weather." *Maxwell Perspective* 16(1):2–4.

Röetzer, Florian. 1998. "Outer space or virtual space? Utopias of the digital age." Pp. 120–143 in John Beckmann, ed., *The Virtual Dimension. Architecture, Representation, and Crash Culture*. New York: Princeton Architectural Press.

Romano, Carlin. 1985. "The grisly truth about bare facts." Pp. 37–78 in Robert Karl Manoff and Michael Schudson, eds., *Reading the News*. New York: Pantheon.

Saint-Exupéry, Antoine de. [1943] 1970. *The Little Prince*. Trans. Katherine Woods. New York: Harcourt Brace Jovanovich.

Savage, Mike, and Alan Warde. 1993. *Urban Sociology, Capitalism and Modernity*. New York: Continuum.

Schlesinger, Arthur M. 1933. *The Rise of the American City: 1878–1898*. New York: Macmillan.

Schnaiberg, Allan. 1980. *The Environment: From Surplus to Scarcity*. New York: Oxford University Press.

Seeley, John R. [1959] 1970. "The slum: Its nature, use and users." Pp. 285–296 in Robert Gutman and David Popenoe, eds., *Neighborhood, City, and Metropolis*. New York: Random House.

Sharff, Jagna Wojcicka. 1987. "The underground economy of a poor neighborhood." Pp. 19–50 in Leith Mulling, ed., *Cities of the United States: Studies in Urban Anthropology*. New York: Columbia University Press.

Slackman, Michael. 2006. "In Egypt, poet keeps his words sharp." *International Herald Tribune* (May 13): http://www.highbeam.com/doc/1P1–123561139.html

Smith, Anthony. 1980. *The Geopolitics of Information: How Western Culture Dominates the World*. New York: Oxford University Press.

Smith, Michael Peter. 1996. *Urban Theory*. New York: Blackwell.

———. 2005. "Transnational urbanism revisited." *Journal of Ethnic and Migration Studies* 31(2):235.

Soja, Edward W. 2000. *Postmetropolis: Critical Studies of Cities and Regions*. Malden, MA: Wiley-Blackwell.

Southall, Aidan, ed. 1973. *Urban Anthropology: Cross-Cultural Studies of Urbanization*. New York: Oxford University Press.

Suarez, Ray. 1999. *NewsHour*. PBS (December 16).

Susskind, Lawrence. 1978. Personal conversation with R. T. LeGates. Berkeley, Calif.

Suttles, Gerald D. 1968. *The Social Order of the Slum: Ethnicity and Territory in the Inner City*. Chicago: University of Chicago Press.

Taussig, Michael. 2003. *Law in a Lawless Land: Diary of a Limpreza in Columbia*. New York: New Press.

Temple, James. 2008. "Commercial renters may find bargains." *San Francisco Chronicle* (December 25):B1+.

Theil, Stefan. 2008. "The campus of the future." *Newsweek*, international edition (August 18–25):57–59.

Traub, James. 2006. "La femme." *New York Times Magazine* (May 14):36–41.

UN-HABITAT. 2003. "The challenge of slums." (January 10) http://www.unhabitat.org/content.asp?cid=3008&catid=5&typeid=6&subMenuId=0

U.S. Census Bureau. 2004. *Current Population Survey 2004 Annual Social and Economic Supplement*. www.2010census.biz/hhes/www/cpstc/nest.html

Wacquant, Löic J. D. 1989. "The ghetto, the state, and the new capitalist economy." *Dissent* (Fall):508–520.

Waldo, Dwight. 1948. *The Administrative State*. New York: Ronald Press.

Warner, Sam Bass, Jr. 1968. "If all the world were Philadelphia: A scaffolding for urban history, 1774–1930." *American Historical Review* 74:182–195.

Weathers, Diane, et al. 1979. "Urban archeology." *Newsweek* 83(April 16):81–82.

Weiss, Michael J. 2000. *The Clustered World: How We Live, What We Buy, and What It All Means About Who We Are.* Boston: Little, Brown.

Weissman, Joel, and Arnold M. Epstein. 1989. "Case mix and resource utilization by uninsured hospital patients in the Boston metropolitan area." *Journal of the American Medical Association* (June 23–30):3572–3576.

Williams, Cecil, ed. 1989. *I Have Something to Say About This Big Trouble.* San Francisco: Glide World.

Wirth, Louis. 1938. "Urbanism as a way of life." *American Journal of Sociology* 44:1–24.

Wood, Denis. 1992. *The Power of Maps.* New York: Guilford Press.

Zuboff, Shoshana. 1988. *In the Age of the Smart Machine: The Future of Work and Power.* New York: Basic Books.

Zukin, Sharon. 2007. "Reading the urban villagers as a cultural document: Ethnicity, modernity, and capital." *Cities & Community* 6(1):39–48.

Mary Swisher

CHAPTER 3

POSING THE QUESTIONS

DOING SCIENCE
  Reasoning, Deductive and Inductive
  Systematic Analysis
  Facts, Hypotheses, and Value Judgments

WHY SOCIAL SCIENTISTS DISAGREE
  Theoretical Orientations
  Disciplinary Perspectives

Research Methods
Levels of Analysis
Ideologies and Values
Subtle Influences on Researchers
Attitudes Toward Solving Social
  "Problems"

WHAT QUESTIONS TO ASK

DOING SCIENCE

At their best, urbanists make the world more understandable. In their struggle to reach this goal, they think in ways common to all intellectual disciplines. To begin with, they are skeptical. As the late astronomer Carl Sagan put it, "skeptical scrutiny is the means, in…science…by which deep insights can be winnowed from deep nonsense" (1978:xiv).

In addition, urbanists are tentative and humble about their knowledge. Many wonder if most of what we think we know about social reality is going to be soon obsolete.

Finally, more often than might be suspected, urbanists bring eagerness and passion to their work. When this happens, it results in what Sagan called the "romance of science." An ecstatic sense of discovery, of following up on hunches, and of creatively searching for meaning—these are at the heart of doing science too.

Qualities like ecstasy are best experienced first-hand or vicariously through the words and images of inspired communicators, including Sagan and writer–physician Sherwin B. Nuland (2008), a National Book Award winner who thinks that a primary aim in the training of a doctor is to become comfortable with uncertainty. But instead of dwelling on these qualities here, we'll focus on common elements of doing science that can be transmitted from generation to generation: reasoning processes, systematic analysis, and hypothesis construction.

REASONING, DEDUCTIVE AND INDUCTIVE

Deductive and inductive reasoning processes represent two ways of gaining knowledge about a subject. **Deductive reasoning** proceeds from general principles to particular examples. A model of how something works is speculatively constructed in the theorist's mind, then tested by gathering data. **Inductive reasoning** proceeds from particular instances to the general. A researcher first collects and sifts through pieces of **empirical evidence** and then derives **hypotheses** and generates **theories** about how something works.

In practice, however, the two kinds of reasoning processes are not clearly separate. None of us starts with a blank mind. We have some preconceived notions about how something might work or couldn't work; these models influence how we interpret new information. Without some assumptions or working **models**, we wouldn't even know what data to start gathering. So, most social science thinking develops as a result of both inductive and deductive reasoning.

This was the case for Ernest W. Burgess. This University of Chicago sociologist started with a hunch: that human communities are organized in ways similar to plant communities along Chicago's lakefront. Then he sent his students out to collect any data they could find—where pool hall hustlers gathered, where the rich and poor lived, what crimes were committed in which neighborhoods, and so forth. On the basis of this empirical evidence, he derived his refined concentric zone hypothesis of urban space.

SYSTEMATIC ANALYSIS

Whatever their disciplinary background, scholars are routinely taught how to use the **scientific method**. This name—"scientific method"—makes doing science sound much more methodical than is usually the case. It also masks the guesswork and creativity involved. Nonetheless, it is the model for doing science in the West, setting the step-by-step procedures for collecting, checking, classifying, and analyzing data. In theory, the scientific method proceeds as follows:

Step 1. Defining the problem and stating it in terms of existing research.

Step 2. Classifying or categorizing facts, often by constructing categories or typologies (e.g., types of slum dwellers by reasons for residence).

Step 3. Constructing hypotheses related to the problem—that is, looking for possible relationships between phenomena or factors. (For instance, in the Burgess model, it is hypothesized that an individual's social status is linked to his or her place of residence in the city: The higher the status, the farther out from the central business district the person lives.)

Step 4. Determining what methods to use for data gathering and then gathering the data.

Step 5. Analyzing the data gathered to see if hypotheses are confirmed or disconfirmed; relating findings to the existing body of theory.

Step 6. Predicting facts on the basis of findings.

In practice, scientific research doesn't usually proceed in such well-ordered, successive steps. First, the steps are often interwoven. For instance, constructing categories entails some prior observation. Second, the scientific method has no provision for intuitive flashes or acquaintance with something. It is a **positivistic** model that assumes that anything worth knowing can be known through sensory experience and verified by procedures outlined in the six steps. But we know, by Einstein's own declaration, that intuitive insight inspired his theory of relativity, a theory that forever changed our way of seeing the universe. Indeed, scientific breakthroughs often result from minds *not* hemmed in by the reigning paradigms of doing science (Kuhn, [1962] 1970).

As discussed in Chapter 1, the scientific method is now questioned by a host of scholars—philosophers of science, new physicists, phenomenological philosophers, and social scientists. Under attack are the scientific method's assumptions that there are causes and effects that can be tested, that objectivity can be achieved, and that subjective insight plays no role in actual scientific endeavors.

To conclude: Currently, the very notion of objectivity is suspect. So is the positivists' clear distinction between facts and values. Today, neither physical nor social scientists agree on what doing science really means. Nonetheless, as noted in Chapter 1, the *ideal* of scientific objectivity may be too important to discard.

FACTS, HYPOTHESES, AND VALUE JUDGMENTS

For a moment, let's play the "as if" game. Let's return to the scientific method *as if* facts can be separated from values, *as if* there are causes and effects that can be tested.

Like other scholars, urbanists are trained to use the scientific method. This method makes clear distinctions among statements of fact, statements of suggested relationships among facts, and value judgments about facts. These are called *empirical statements, hypotheses,* and *normative statements*, respectively. The ability to differentiate among these three types of statements is a prerequisite to critical analysis.

Consider the following sentences that could appear in a government report about homelessness:

1. In Our Town, 100 homeless persons (including 40 children) sleep in shelters located in "The Pits," a zone II–ish area near downtown that lacks playgrounds and schools.
2. Since no homeless shelters exist in The Heights (a high-income, high-status area), the City Council has probably vetoed the conversion of empty mansions there into homeless shelters.
3. Shelters should be scattered throughout Our Town so that homeless children will have easy access to schools and healthy places to play.

Statement 1 is presented as an empirical or factual statement. It appears to be based on scientifically gathered and accurately reported data. These facts can be checked and verified by independent researchers.

Statement 2 is disguised as a statement of fact, but it is not. Rather, it is a hypothesis—that is, a statement of relationship between two or more **variables** (factors subject to change). In this case, there are two variables: (1) spatially segregated homeless shelters and (2) the City Council's veto power. Statement 2 can be restated in the form of a hypothesis using these two variables: Our Town's clustered pattern of homeless shelters is a product of the City Council's veto power, used to prevent placing homeless shelters in affluent neighborhoods. The *independent* variable (the factor that causes or influences something—in this case, the resulting spatially segregated homeless shelters) is the City Council's veto power. The *dependent* variable (the factor determined or influenced by the independent variable) is the pattern of spatially segregated homeless shelters.

Hypotheses must satisfy two requirements: (1) *they must be testable* and (2) *they must contain a statement of relationship*. The statement that "the Devil controls the world" satisfies neither requirement. It is not testable by empirical scientific methods, nor is it a statement of relationship; it is merely an assertion. By contrast, the suggested relationship between clustered homeless shelters and the veto power of elected officials satisfies both requirements: It can be tested by the scientific method, and it contains a statement of relationship between two variables.

Statement 3 is neither a statement of fact nor a hypothesis. It is a normative statement, a value judgment about what *should* be. It is based on the researcher's own values of what is good or bad. One can agree or disagree with a normative statement, depending on one's values.

Separating empirical statements, hypotheses, and normative statements is not always easy (Box 3.1). For instance, the statement that "people on welfare don't want to work" is not factual; it is a hypothesis in disguise. It states a relationship between being poor and being lazy. In this case, the thrust of social science research (e.g., Wertheimer et al., 2001; DeParle, [2004], 2005) shows that welfare recipients prefer working to receiving government assistance and that the number of welfare mothers unwilling to work is far smaller than often believed. (And some very young, single, urban poor mothers receiving government assistance

BOX 3.1 RATIONAL ANALYSIS

Hypotheses

Distinguishing between mere assertions and hypotheses is a critical step in rational analysis. For example, the statement that "People are basically evil" (or "good") is a mere assertion. It fails to meet the two basic requirements of a hypothesis: (1) it is not testable by scientific methods and (2) it does not contain a statement of suggested relationship.

By contrast, the following is a hypothesis containing an independent and a dependent variable:

> The suicide rate among Protestants is higher than the suicide rate among Catholics and Jews.

This hypothesis suggests a relationship between religion and the suicide rate. The independent variable is religion; the dependent variable is suicide rate. It suggests that a group's religious background affects the propensity of its members to commit suicide.

The graphic model in this box (a bid rent curve) contains an implied hypothesis: a statement of relationship between two variables—cost of land and distance of land from the city center. In this model, distance determines land cost or rent: As distance from the city center increases, land cost decreases. Thus, distance is the independent variable, and cost is the dependent variable.

The following statement is a hypothesis containing several variables:

> Unemployed teenage urban males are more alienated from the political system than unemployed urban teenage females or unemployed rural teenagers.

This hypothesis suggests a relationship between place of residence (urban or rural), sex (male or female), and attitudes toward government (degree of alienation). Age and work status (unemployed) are constants—not variables—here, for all involved are unemployed teenagers. The dependent variable is attitude toward the political system; the hypothesis suggests that attitude toward the political system depends on *both* sex and place of residence.

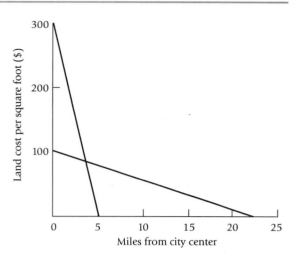

The following paragraph contains an implied hypothesis, empirical statements, and a normative statement:

> In 1990 there were 5,000 large families (with three or more children) in Our Town living below the poverty line. A child born into a large family was 3.5 times as likely to be poor as a child born into a small family (with fewer than three children). To decrease the number of people below the poverty line, governmental programs should encourage the use of contraceptives by persons who already have two children.

The implied hypothesis here is that family size is related to income level. Family size is the independent variable, and poverty status is the dependent variable. The first sentence of the paragraph is an empirical statement. The last sentence is a normative statement. An alternative normative statement, derived from the same empirical information, is this: To decrease the number of people below the poverty line, government should guarantee large families an annual income.

---

choose to be mothers for reasons connected to community standing and responsibility, not irresponsibility; see Edin and Kefalas, 2005). Thus, the hypothesis is generally invalid or null.

WHY SOCIAL SCIENTISTS DISAGREE

Ideally, social scientists seek the truth at all times and apply the scientific method to their research. Why, then, can they look at the same phenomena—say,

poverty and slums—and disagree on what they see and what should be done about it?

To explore this knotty question, let us take the example of poverty in three countries: the United States, Ecuador, and Cambodia. Suppose that the chief executive of each country declares a war on poverty. Before deciding how best to fight the war, each chief executive appoints a task force of local officials and highly respected social scientists. Each team's mission is to produce a joint report on the causes, nature, and extent of poverty in the nation's cities. Three months and $100,000 in U.S. and Ecuadorian dollars and more than 415,550 Cambodian riel later, reports are submitted for policy action. Each report contains a majority opinion and three separate minority opinions. It is clear that the researchers and the local officials disagree among themselves on basic issues. To begin with, they disagree on whether or not poverty even constitutes a problem. In addition, those who think it is a problem don't agree on whether it can be solved or on the means to solve it.

Disagreements among task force members might be based on the following kinds of differences: (1) theoretical orientations; (2) disciplinary perspectives; (3) research methods; (4) levels of analysis; (5) assumptions and values based on **ideology**, politics, and/or economics; (6) subtle influences, such as the funding source (or not so subtle influences, in the case of blatant corruption); and (7) attitudes toward social problem solving. These differences can affect what questions a researcher asks, what a researcher finds, how a researcher defines the problem and thus the solution, and/or what the researcher advises doing about it.

THEORETICAL ORIENTATIONS

First, social scientists do not share a theoretical orientation. Within any one discipline, there may be competing models or paradigms of how the world works. Taking sociology as an example, let's examine how two major theoretical orientations filter the social world through different lenses: structural–functionalism and symbolic interaction. Very briefly, *structural–functionalists* are concerned with the structures of society and their functions (purposes). They look for the connections among different parts of a social system, assuming that society, like the human body, is organized in terms of systems and subsystems. Just as each system of the body (circulation, defense against disease, etc.) serves different functions and contributes to the whole organism's welfare, so do different institutional structures in society. In this view, systems (both the human organism and the social system) seek equilibrium, balance, stability, and order. Structural–functionalists think that whatever exists—poverty, for

instance—serves a social function or it would cease to exist. Critics of structural—functionalism hold that this theoretical perspective is inherently conservative because it focuses on social order (rather than social change) and things as they are (rather than things as they might be).

Symbolic interactionists have a different focus. Instead of social systems or institutions, they focus on meaning—how people construct meanings, how they define social reality in different ways. They deal with microworlds of social behavior, such as face-to-face encounters and small-group behavior. The language people use to express themselves (both words and gestures) and the way these words and gestures are understood by others are especially interesting to symbolic interactionists. They may explore the subtle ways in which meaning is transmitted between parents and children in the slums or the interpretation of action from the actor's point of view. Researchers in this tradition are routinely trained in qualitative techniques such as participant-observation and in-depth interviewing. Herbert Gans's study of a Boston slum, *The Urban Villagers* (1962), examines the group life of Italian Americans using participant-observation. George Weissinger's 2005 study *Law Enforcement and the INS* (now called ICE, the U.S. Immigration and Customs Enforcement) also uses this method.

Each theoretical orientation looks at poverty (as a research problem) in a particular way. And, in large measure, each approach determines what questions will be asked. In turn, what questions are asked influences one's findings about the nature and causes of poverty.

It is noteworthy that scholars in one discipline may not share a theoretical orientation, but as a group they may share a vision of how the world should work. For example, a summer 2006 study by Daniel B. Klein and Charlotta Stern of the *Independent Review*, a libertarian online journal, found that sociologists answering their questionnaire overwhelmingly rejected classical liberal (as discussed later, nineteenth-century conservative) ideas.

DISCIPLINARY PERSPECTIVES

Urbanists bring their disciplinary perspectives with them when they investigate an issue. The example of

ITS AMAZING HOW MANY CONCLUSIONS YOU CAN GET FROM THE SAME FACTS

ALMOST AS IMPRESSIVE AS THE NUMBER OF FACTS YOU CAN GET FROM THE SAME CONCLUSIONS

Fig. 3.2   FACTS DON'T SPEAK FOR THEMSELVES. (© 1976 Richard Hedman)

slums in Chapter 2 illustrated how various social science disciplines, professional fields, and the humanities might see slums and poverty.

Recall that some concepts and research tools cross disciplines but each one retains its central focus. This means that scholars in the same discipline may differ in their theoretical orientations, and even in their ideologies and methods, but they still share a disciplinary perspective that sets them apart from other social scientists.

RESEARCH METHODS

Urbanists use different strategies for observing and analyzing facts. Research methods may vary among disciplines, subdisciplines, and theoretical orientations. Most economists today, for instance, use quantitative techniques (econometrics, mathematical equations and models, statistical analysis); only the very rare economist depends primarily on qualitative methods. Anthropologists, on the contrary, depend primarily on qualitative techniques—direct, intensive observation of social life through fieldwork, or what sociologists

call **participant-observation**. This entails observing people firsthand to get an intimate, personal acquaintance with their situation or way of life.

Within a single discipline, techniques vary—so much so that researchers often find it difficult to understand one other. This situation is reflected in learned journals. For example, sociologists trained mainly in qualitative methods can find it hard (or impossible) to follow current articles in the discipline's leading journals because so much research today is based on quantitative techniques.

Members of a theoretical school are routinely trained in particular methods. In sociology, for instance, symbolic interactionists are trained in the method of participant-observation. This method encourages inductive reasoning. Theory is grounded in and generated from direct observation. In contrast, structural–functionalists and neo-Marxists are more commonly trained in quantitative research methods and tend to begin with more complete models of how things work, thus applying deductive reasoning to the facts they find.

Fig. 3.3   DOING SOCIAL SCIENCE. (Richard Hedman, revised by Lisa Siegel Sullivan)

Comparison—the analysis of similarities or differences among phenomena—is considered by many theorists to be the basic method of the social sciences. But researchers use varying techniques to gather and analyze comparative data. Some study the content of written and other social documents: official statistics, diaries, graffiti, paintings, tombstones, rap lyrics, organizational records, TV soap operas, census data, and so on. Others gather information by conducting polls and interviewing random samples of the population (survey research) or setting up controlled experiments.

To express the results of these various data-gathering techniques, urbanists use a number of aids. These range from graphs, organization charts, diagrams, flowcharts, statistical tables, verbatim conversational reports, and narrative description to abstract models.

Why do the techniques used to investigate and analyze a research problem like poverty make a difference? As philosophers of science point out, the techniques used to investigate a research topic help to determine what the findings will be. Here is one

example, discussed in Chapter 15 in greater detail (where we'll see how the level of analysis, as well as methods, influences or determines research findings): Two U.S. social scientists, political scientist Robert Dahl and sociologist–anthropologist Floyd Hunter, set out to study the same questions: Who runs this town? How are political decisions made at the city level? Hunter ([1953] 1963) used a technique called the *reputational method* to explore the question, asking influential people in Atlanta, Georgia, to assess the relative power of reputed leaders in local decision making. Dahl (1961), investigating who ran New Haven, Connecticut, used another research technique, *decision analysis*. Dahl examined local decisions (e.g., urban renewal) to see who participated in making them. The two researchers found different patterns of influence and power. Hunter found a power structure that was highly centralized and monolithic. Dahl found a pluralistic structure in which various elites shared power. *To a significant degree, the research methods that Dahl and Hunter used helped to determine what kind of power structure each found.*

Each method of investigation has its own strengths and weaknesses. Participant-observation can provide direct acquaintance with poverty; no questionnaire survey can do that. But no direct observation of a few people living in poverty can yield general statements about *all* people living in poverty; the group under study may be atypical. Then again, a person constructing a questionnaire may miss salient questions without firsthand acquaintance with poverty situations. Similarly, those who depend on official statistics can be misled, even if the statistics represent the best available data. Suicide rates are illustrative. Whether a death is reported as natural or suicide is often problematic; high-status individuals may not be listed as suicides as often as low-status, low-income individuals, for family doctors can list deaths as natural to protect the high-status family from embarrassment, while the poor have fewer means to protect themselves.

To avoid some of these problems, methodologists counsel social science researchers to use a variety of techniques in their work—for example, to combine fieldwork (participant-observation and interviewing) with survey research and **unobtrusive measures** (i.e., methods that don't influence the research subjects or have reactive effects, such as analyzing the content of documents or TV shows).

LEVELS OF ANALYSIS

"Science," said the late astronomer Carl Sagan, "is a way of thinking much more than it is a body of knowledge" (1978:13). For some, doing science means reflecting on a grain of salt; for others, it means trying to understand the entire universe. And for still others, it means trying to make the connections between the grain of salt and the entire universe.

Those who study grains of salt use the micro-level approach, focusing on small-scale phenomena. *Microsociology* is the study of small groups. *Microeconomics* is the study of the economic behavior of individuals, households, and business firms.

Those who study the universe, so to speak, use the macro-level approach. (Astrophysicists and astronomers, among others, use yet another level of analysis: the cosmic perspective.) *Macrosociology* is thus the study of large-scale social systems, and

macroeconomics investigates how fiscal and monetary policies and other large-scale factors keep an economic system working.

Used in combination, the micro and macro approaches can give very different views of a phenomenon, such as poverty, than either could do alone. Elliot Liebow's classic study of black streetcorner men in Washington, D.C., *Tally's Corner* (1967, 2003), demonstrates the wisdom of using both levels of analysis to explore the same issue.

In *Tally's Corner*, Liebow gives an account, based on his participant-observation, of how this group of men spend much of their daily life hanging out on streetcorners in the nation's capital. But he didn't stop there. He related their everyday activities to larger social forces—racial discrimination, structures of economic opportunity, and other factors that shape their everyday lives (see Chapter 12).

Had he looked only at the macro level (the larger social forces that influenced the men's self-perceptions and lifestyles) or only at the micro-social structure (the streetcorner), he could not have traced the interrelationships between individual behavior and structural opportunities. Connecting micro and macro levels of analysis, Liebow finds that the behavior of Tally and his buddies is a response to their failure to reach the goals of the dominant culture—goals that the men share. Liebow concludes that it is the lack of economic opportunity and lack of skills—not distinctive cultural traits (as Oscar Lewis's "culture of poverty" thesis (1961) would have it) or laziness—that mold the lives of the 24 men who stand around the New Deal Carryout shop at Tally's corner.

IDEOLOGIES AND VALUES

Two generations ago, Harvard sociologist Daniel Bell proclaimed *The End of Ideology* (1960). Bell reasoned that in the then-emerging postindustrial society, intellectuals (including urbanists) would not have deep-seated ideological differences. Heralding the exhaustion of political ideas, Bell said that public choices in postindustrial society would be technical, not political.

Soon after Daniel Bell's pronouncements, postindustrialism arrived in the United States. Sometime later, Bell shifted ground. By the early 1990s Bell

Fig. 3.4   NEITHER CONSERVATIVE, LIBERAL, NOR RADICAL. Political ideology may help to explain some attitudes and behaviors. However, attending car worship services is not one of them. (Deborah Mosca)

thought that American intellectuals no longer agreed on the ends of public policy: "We may be at the end of old ideologies...but there are [*sic*] no unified set of beliefs to take their place" (1992:E17). Many theorists and citizens–not only in the United States—still agree with Bell.

Is there a unifying framework on the horizon? Who knows? Perhaps we are witnessing a turning point when new theories are emerging to explain socioeconomic and political organization in a global economy.

Meanwhile, many "isms" and "ocracies" compete for preeminence. The range is broad—from nationalism, occultism, tribalism, feminism, fascism, communitarianism, conservatism, religious fundamentalism,

democracy, theocracy, and technocracy to environmentalism, libertarianism, democratic socialism, neo-Nazism, and anarchism.

Here, we focus on a time-honored, tripartite division of political thought: conservative, liberal, and radical. Plus we look at libertarianism, an ideological position that shares some assumptions with conservatives, others with liberals.

First, a cautionary note: This discussion does not deal with many "theories" of politics, including so-called conspiracy theories. (Since about 2005, the dominant conspiracy theory in the United States, promoted by the ultraconservative John Birch Society, is based on the idea that U.S. sovereignty is endangered by a so-called North American union.) Let's note only that as citizens and scholars it behooves us all to try to understand which groups would benefit and which groups would lose if the alleged conspiracies actually came to pass. Now, back to three time-honored political stances.

"Conservative," "liberal," and "radical" labels are now used fairly loosely. For instance, a TV newscaster in Syracuse, New York, once described his town as "conservative." Pressed to specify what he meant by this label, he answered, "You know, Syracusans don't get married in drive-in churches or buy everything on credit." What he apparently meant was that *conservatism* refers to traditional social values. To some, a "liberal" is a person who is open-minded. To others, a conservative is "a liberal who's been mugged." "Radical" may conjure up the image of a wild-eyed, bearded bomb thrower. And to the nineteenth-century satirist Ambrose Bierce, a conservative is "a statesman who is enamored of existing evils, as distinguished from the liberal, who wishes to replace them with others."

However, these loosely applied labels do have—or have had—more precise meanings. Conservative social thinkers have had a consistent view of human nature for hundreds of years, and a rather pessimistic one at that. Radicals, on the contrary, have maintained a much rosier picture of human motivation, tending to see bad social systems, not inherently bad people. This is a more optimistic view of social change, for it follows that if a social system is altered, the personalities of the people who live under it will also change.

The "liberal" label once had a very precise denotation. To be a liberal in the nineteenth century meant holding certain ideas about how the social and economic orders did and should work. *Classical liberalism* (also called "laissez-faire economics") provides the basis for what is today called "economic conservatism." In other words, a nineteenth-century classical liberal would be called an economic conservative today in the United States.

To make things even more confusing, "liberal" is often used as a code word. As used by U.S. conservatives, it often refers to big-government, "tax-and-spend" politicians who are "soft on crime" and weak on defense and national security and who support racial "quotas" in hiring and affirmative action in general. (*Note*: These definitions do not hold in Europe for many reasons, particularly the widespread agreement that the state should take an active role in public welfare.)

It is worth mentioning that liberalism, radicalism, and conservatism—indeed, all political belief systems—share one important attribute: All ideologies pivot on a view of human nature, a view that can be neither defended nor refuted on strictly empirical grounds. Ideologies, in other words, are more faith claim than science. And powerful faith claims—people in many places and in many historical eras have sacrificed their lives in defense of their ideologies.

The Liberal and Neoliberal Perspectives

Originally, the liberal perspective saw humankind through the eyes of English philosopher Thomas Hobbes (1588–1679). According to Hobbes ([1651] 1968), the human condition is one of "the war of all against all." People are driven by personal gain, glory, and selfishness. Their lives are "solitary...nasty, brutish, and short." In order to bypass people's assumed selfishness and greed, liberal philosophers assigned all social and political decision making to a mechanism they believed to be neutral and self-regulating: the market of supply and demand.

Over the centuries, liberalism changed significantly. U.S. liberals today tend to be more optimistic about the slow but sure progress of individuals and society. They also think that the market mechanism doesn't always work to prevent major social and economic trauma, such as worldwide economic depression. Yet, through all of these changes, Hobbes's materialist conception of human nature and his atomistic individualism remain at the heart of the liberal perspective.

Before detailing the points of difference between liberals and conservatives today, let's examine their shared assumptions. These assumptions are rooted in the political economy of Adam Smith ([1776] 1970), and they can be found today between the lines in the many editions of one of liberalism's most well-read works: the best-selling introductory text *Economics* by Paul Samuelson (sixth edition, 1964) and William D. Nordhaus (fifteenth edition, 1995).

Liberals, both classical and modern, make the following assumptions:

1. *People act in their own rational self-interest.* Individuals and decision-making units (such as business firms) act in a rational way to maximize their own welfare.
2. *Consumers are sovereign in the marketplace.* Given simple constraints, individuals are free to determine how to use their scarce resources, choosing goods and services from a wide range of alternatives in the marketplace.
3. *The market is self-regulating.* The market mechanism of supply and demand still works to resolve who gets what and how.
4. *The "invisible hand" works to serve the public interest and bring about social equilibrium.* Adam Smith theorized in 1776 that each individual would act in the general interest "as if guided by an invisible hand." In other words, individual and social interests automatically harmonize; if you do well for yourself, you also benefit the entire community.
5. *A rising tide lifts all boats.* National growth and prosperity benefit all citizens.
6. *Wealth trickles down from top to bottom.* Money invested by business elites eventually filters down to those at the bottom of the social ladder, thereby benefiting everyone. Or as "Engine" Charlie Wilson, then-president of General Motors, put it in the 1950s—perhaps in a famous misquote: "What's good for GM is good for the country" (Hyde, 2008).

These key assumptions underlie classical liberalism. It is evident that the role of the free market is central to their analysis.

The major area of disagreement between U.S. liberals and conservatives today concerns the proper role of government in modern life. Liberals tend to believe that the market does not always work to provide opportunities for those at the lower end of the social ladder. In contrast, conservatives tend to think that the expansion of government regulations and programs—so-called trickle-down government—is the problem, not the solution.

(*Important note*: Rhetoric and action do not always go hand-in-hand. Under administrations considered conservative in the United States, such as the Reagan and Bush administrations, the national government—as measured in terms, of expenditures and numbers of employees, including private contractors—expanded greatly. Similarly, in 2008, it was George W. Bush's Republican administration which sponsored a federal bailout of Bear Stearns, the fifth largest U.S. securities firm. Later, it sponsored government intervention in the mortgage market and bailouts or loans to large U.S. financial institutions. Many U.S. conservatives and libertarians were unhappy about the Bush administration's foray into the marketplace, noting that the "conservatives" acted more like liberals than liberal Democrats ever did!)

Some liberals think that in the global economy "trickle down" has been replaced by "trickle out." Thus, they hold, government *should* intervene in the competitive market to affect public welfare and help individuals do better for themselves (thus benefiting the entire community). In practice, this means that liberals support the expansion of opportunities for all (through job training, education, etc.) and income redistribution (through tax policy, resource-allocation policies, etc.).

U.S. liberals today also support government intervention to promote economic stability. (In practice, not theory, so do many conservatives. For instance, Hank Paulson, former head of a U.S. securities firm and the secretary of the treasury in the George W. Bush administration, spearheaded government intervention into the financial system in 2008, attempting to stop global market panic.) They want to avoid the unemployment and instability that accompanied the Great Depression of the 1930s.

To prevent another ruinous depression and lessen the effects of massive unrest in the 1930s, Lord John Maynard Keynes advocated vast government spending to create jobs for millions of persons out of work and to intervene in the private market. Since the 1930s, Keynesian and neo-Keynesian prescriptions and economic analysis have dominated liberal economic thought. (Note, however, that it was conservatives in the U.S. government, not neo-Keynesians, who insisted on intervening in the private market, attempting to head off global financial disaster in fall 2008.) The Massachusetts Institute of Technology (MIT) is known as a bastion of neo-Keynesian thinking.

Traditionally, U.S. liberals have favored government intervention at the federal level, viewing state and local governments as incompetent, corrupt, and/or agents of the status quo. In recent years, however, some liberals have changed their tune, stressing grassroots efforts to achieve social change. Liberals were at the forefront of programs created in the 1960s such as Head Start, a federally-funded but locally-run antipoverty program.

Generally speaking, U.S. liberals view many present facts of urban life—such as poverty and homelessness—as capable of solution, or at least amelioration. Their approach to problem solving is to make incremental changes at the edges of social and economic institutions, not to restructure basic institutions. (Most radicals view this as a Band-Aid approach, and most conservatives and libertarians see such government intervention as wasteful, unworkable, and/or ill-conceived.)

In the United States, a major tool of liberal social policy is the federal income tax. Liberals view the federal income tax as a key instrument in redistributing goods and services that the market fails to provide for citizens at the bottom (and, increasingly, the middle) of the economic ladder.

Another liberal solution to U.S. urban "problems" concerns government investment in people: sponsoring programs aimed at creating conditions of supposedly equal opportunity for citizens deemed disadvantaged. Federally-sponsored Head Start, job training, and affirmative action programs are based on the liberal tenet of providing equal opportunity (not equal outcomes) for all.

Another assumption of today's liberals in the United States concerns a cast of mind: a belief in progress. Senator Ted Kennedy, arguably the iconic U.S. liberal (praised by both Democrats and Republicans in 2008 after his brain tumor was discovered) reflects his continuing belief in progress in *America Back on Track* (2006).

One key liberal assumption bears special notice. An extension of classical liberal thought, it joins liberal politics to liberal economics: pluralist democracy. Liberals assume that power is fairly widely dispersed among a multiplicity of interest groups, each representing its members' self-interest.

The liberal notion of pluralist democracy in America—where diverse interest groups bargain and negotiate in the political arena to protect their rational self-interest—helps account for their almost total inattention to or dismissal of the issue of social class. Both conservatives and radicals use the concept of social class in their analysis of society and social problems—albeit in very different ways—but liberals tend to act as if the subject did not exist. However, many liberals focus on race (instead of class) as a key factor in understanding sociopolitical life in the United States.

In recent times, liberals wrote a passel of books suggesting that liberals need *new* "new deals" (taking a page from Franklin Delano Roosevelt's New Deal), that they should not be silent about religion and moral commitments, and that they should not shrink from the notion that government can be a force for good, such as on health insurance (Krugman, Dionne, and Gitlin in Cohen, 2007).

Liberal-identified Robert Reich goes in a different direction. Clinton's secretary of labor, Reich laments that "supercapitalism" has encouraged alienation from politics and community, turning citizens into consumers and investors. (For Reich [2007], supercapitalism results from Web-based, global capitalism—where a consumer can find almost anything somewhere. This works to enlarge the piece of the economic pie for some, but it fails to be democratic.) Reich maintains that ever-bigger gaps of income and wealth, more job insecurity, and global warming are effects of such a turbo-charged system. According to Reich, traditional liberal tools to deal with social problems in the United States—such as taxation, public education, unions—are ineffective in the face of supercapitalism. Reich argues that companies, struggling to remain competitive, have become even more deeply involved in politics. And, he notes, average citizens are complicit too, for they do not risk losing money if it means speaking out against the companies in which they have invested. Reich proposes a variety of prescriptions, including some *not* in the liberal canon (e.g., abolition of the corporate income tax). In the same vein, he calls the corporate social responsibility movement counterproductive.

By and large, liberal policy proposals—more funds to cities, more social programs designed to help the poor, and so on—were rejected by U.S. presidential voters in the 1980s and early 1990s. One response: neoliberalism. Neoliberals (so-called New Democrats) see themselves as pragmatists, incorporating ideas they deem sensible from across the political spectrum. President Bill Clinton exemplified neoliberalism from 1992 to 2000. (Many "traditional" or New Deal liberals defined Clinton and some of his appointees, particularly Secretary of the Treasury Robert Rubin, as conservatives.) Great Britain's best-known neoliberal during the 1990s and early 2000s was Tony Blair.

In brief, then, U.S. liberals and neoliberals today tend to sponsor social change within prescribed limits: social change that can be managed and directed by government action, that is incremental in nature and that does not alter basic economic and social institutions. Liberals view government as the proper agent of managed social change; neoliberals see a larger role for the private sector.

The Conservative and Neoconservative Perspectives

As outlined earlier, U.S. conservatives today remain classical liberals in their economic doctrine (in theory if not always in practice). They tend to see big government as the enemy, a threat to individual freedom and prosperity. In their view, business interests—if left

Fig. 3.5 GET THE LIFE JACKETS! Liberals favor government intervention to address some failures of the "free-market" system. (© 1976 Richard Hedman)

alone and unhampered by government interference or regulations—would do a better job than government of managing the economy. This preference for the free market to determine social and political outcomes means that conservatives tend to fear big government more than big business. In contrast, contemporary U.S liberals tend to fear big business more.

Again in contrast to liberals, most U.S. conservatives today do not favor social reforms. To understand why, we must look at the conservative assumptions about human nature and the social order. Basically, conservatives are pessimistic about the human condition. In the words of a classic conservative thinker, Edmund Burke (1729–1797), people have "disorderly appetites" such as pride, avarice, lust, and ambition (Burke [1790], 1959). Or, in the words of a modern conservative, James Burnham: "man is partly corrupt as well as limited in his potential" (in Hacker, 1973:13). In other words, individuals are deeply flawed, marked with what Christian theologians call "original sin." It follows that people are *not* essentially good and that even the best-intentioned social reforms are self-defeating because people are prone to perversity. Given this view of human nature, it also follows that conservatives prize social stability, social order, and authority above all else.

So-called neoconservatives in the United States share the basic assumptions of laissez-faire economic doctrine and conservative social thought. This group of "neo-cons" emerged in the late 1960s in the wake of what they considered to be the excesses of liberalism: the Great Society programs of President Lyndon B. Johnson (including the War on Poverty), New Left politics, and countercultural lifestyles.

What makes them "neo," or "new," conservatives is not their pessimism about human nature or their distrust of the masses, for these are traditional conservative stances. Rather, it is their perception of the U.S. situation. They fear a crisis of authority, a breakdown in morality, a loss of family values, and government's inability to govern. U.S. neoconservatives fear liberal and radical solutions to poverty and social injustice more than they fear the injustices themselves.

Edward Banfield summed up the neoconservative stance toward cities in his still controversial books, *The Unheavenly City* ([1968] 1970) and *The Unheavenly City*

Revisited (1974). Banfield argued that "social problems will sometimes disappear in the normal course of events" and "government cannot solve the problems of the cities and is likely to make them worse by trying" (1970:257). Further, Banfield discussed class characteristics openly, claiming that "so long as the city contains a sizable lower class nothing basic can be done about its most serious problems" (1970:210). Banfield, together with some other urbanists, including the late Senator Daniel Patrick Moynihan (D-N.Y.) and social scientist Nathan Glazer, formed part of the neoconservative core. That was in the 1960s.

By the late 1990s, most U.S. neo-cons (called "paleocons" by their critics) had switched gears, moving their focus from the urban to the global stage. One upshot: The urbanists' influence waned. The Project for a New American Century (PNAC) is a leading example. Founded in 1997 by William Kristol of the *Weekly Standard* journal and Robert Kagan, the PNAC attracted such national figures as Dick Cheney, Donald Rumsfeld, and Paul Wolfowitz—but no urbanists. Before it shut its doors in 2006, the PNAC sought "benevolent global hegemony" by the United States. Among the PNAC's policy proposals: a war on global terrorism, headed by the United States, and a U.S.-led war in Iraq. This was a far cry from the conservative agenda of an earlier generation.

In an earlier generation, during the Reagan and George H. W. Bush administrations, conservative economics in the United States joined with neoconservative politics and moral conservatism. As the cold war of anti-Communism waned, another war galvanized moral conservatives: a cultural–religious war for what was called "the soul of America" (Buchanan, 1992). To these moral conservatives, "welfare" seemed to connote the destruction of "traditional American values," specifically hard work; individual enterprise; two-parent, heterosexual families; and productivity.

From the morally conservative standpoint, where did the United States go wrong? According to Pat Buchanan, the "problems" are pornography, public schools that expelled Christ and the Ten Commandments, rock and rap music, and a breakdown in families. His solutions follow directly from his definition of the problems: school prayer, censorship of violent movies and music, and an infusion of traditional values. To moral conservatives (dubbed "theo-conservatives" by their critics), noneconomic issues such as bans on stem cell research, abortion, and gay marriage are key. (Some conservatives concern themselves with the environment as a moral issue.)

Note, however, that some conservatives or former conservatives think the moral conservatives themselves went wrong. For one, one-time Republican strategist Kevin Phillips (no relation to the author of this book) warns that Christian evangelicals, Pentecostals, and fundamentalists are turning the United States into an *American Theocracy* (2006). In Phillips's view, Republicans have become "the first religious party in U.S. history." He claims that religious conservatives, who reject the separation of church and state and ignore the teachings of science, are ushering in an "American disenlightenment." Phillips goes further. Indeed, Phillips sees the U.S. religious right's influence on nearly every major decision that the George W. Bush administration made, including the invasion of Iraq. (Phillips claims that it was the power of millions of True Believers, a group which interprets events through the lens of prophecies in the New Testament's book of Revelation, particularly the Rapture and the Second Coming of Jesus Christ, described in the best-selling Left Behind series of novels [e.g., LaHaye and Jenkins, 2006] that influenced Bush's policies.)

Remember: Members of the U.S. "religious right" are hardly monolithic. Within the big tent of evangelicals are liberals such as Jim Wallis, founder of *Sojourners* magazine; conservatives such as Rick Warren, author of the best-seller *The Purpose Driven Life* ([2002] 2007), founder of the Saddleback megachurch in Orange County, CA, and Obama inaugural preacher, and ultraconservatives such as best-selling author Tim LaHaye and televangelist Pat Robertson, founder of the Christian Coalition.

In terms of public-policy proposals, conservatives—neo, religious, or otherwise—continue to reject government-sponsored social programs and what they consider the "liberal do-goodism" that began under Franklin D. Roosevelt. However, there is one notable exception: military spending. Conservatives urge increased U.S. military spending and military expansion. Some critics accuse the conservatives, particularly neo-cons, of pushing an agenda of U.S. imperialism and domination based on global military strength.

Concerning a long-standing and hotly debated issue in the United States (and elsewhere)—"illegal aliens" or "undocumented workers"—conservatives, neo and otherwise, are divided. Some welcome immigrants as necessary labor, mainly for dirty, low-paying jobs. Others fear economic consequences (e.g., a drain on public services, unemployment for citizens). In the same way that many white Anglo-Saxon Protestant (WASP) Americans in the 1880s and 1890s feared Catholic immigrants (see Chapter 9), some conservative voices in the United States now warn of unwanted social impacts, including cultural dispossession of big cities where citizens feel like strangers in their own nation.

What issues unify contemporary U.S. conservatives? Military spending aside, conservatives encourage the privatization of public services (e.g., turning prisons and museums over to private enterprise) and the lowering of taxes on investment. These policies are rooted in the free-market, anti-Keynesian ideology of the University of Chicago school of economics. This school of thought is associated with several Nobel Prize–winning economists, including Milton Friedman (who considered himself a libertarian near the end of his life).

Note: The fall of the Soviet Union, the increased economic role of the federal government since the global economic downturn that started in 2007, and the apparent waning of some social issues seem to have robbed U.S. conservatives of some key ideological issues. After federal electoral losses, their ability to redefine themselves for the twenty-first century remains unclear.

The Libertarian Perspective

What do libertarians stand for, and where are they located? In brief, libertarians formed a political party in the United States in 1971. Since then, several have been elected to city councils, and they have contested national elections. Today, libertarians exist mainly in rich countries.

Perhaps the best-known libertarian was the late economist Milton Friedman. A Nobel Prize winner,

Friedman was known for decades as a conservative but declared himself a libertarian in his later years.

Like Friedman, the presidential nominee on the Libertarian ticket for 2008, Bob Barr, is an ex-Republican. Barr served in Congress as a Republican, but after 9/11, he became disenchanted with his party, which he viewed as moving 180 degrees from the small-government philosophy embodied in the "Contract with America" of 1994. He registered as a Libertarian in 2006. (And, like Alan Greenspan, former head of the Federal Reserve Bank, Barr was influenced by the ideas of Ayn Rand.)

Contemporary libertarians trace their roots to multiple sources, including the minimal government ideas of Thomas Jefferson and the philosophy of classical liberals, particularly Adam Smith and John Stuart Mill. More recently, the writings of Ayn Rand and members of the Austrian school of free-market economics (e.g., 1944] 2007) have influenced libertarians. (*Sidenote*: Alan Greenspan, was once a key aide to Ayn Rand [1964].)

Their key economic assumption comes from classical liberalism: In the long run, products and services are provided more efficiently and cheaply by the private sector (the "free market") than by government or government intervention in the free market. Contributors to *Street Smart: Competition, Entrepreneurship, and the Future of Roads* (Roth, 2006), for example, suggest dealing with traffic congestion by privatizing public goods such as urban roads.

Libertarians differentiate themselves from both liberals and conservatives. They agree that classical liberalism and libertarianism shared principles in the 1800s: Both distrusted government power, promoted individualism, and advocated a free-market philosophy. But, libertarians assert, they started diverging after 1870 when European liberals began to turn statist; that is, they thought that the state could and should be used to guarantee social justice.

In the libertarians' view, liberals forgot about individual freedom, especially economic freedom. In their view and to their dismay, liberals supported higher taxes, bigger government, and more regulation.

Libertarians want to roll back the size and cost of government—including military spending—and to eliminate laws that they think stifle the economy. For example, libertarians fight government's "abusive" taking of private property for public use or public purpose via eminent domain. Indeed, some argue that eminent domain goes way beyond its intended constitutional function and is as obsolete as slavery. They also advocate moving closer to privatizing government or quasi-government agencies, particularly the U.S. postal system.

Typically, civil rights is a key area of disagreement between U.S. libertarians and conservatives, particularly moral/religious conservatives. Given their emphasis on personal freedom, combined with government mistrust, libertarians say that any lifestyle or personal preference that doesn't hurt others—be it homosexuality, gun ownership, or gambling—should be a private matter, unregulated by government. In the United States, libertarians advocate abandoning antidrug legislation and other attempts, in their view, to legislate morality. Indeed, some libertarians refer to those who wish to legislate private behavior as "self-righteous busybodies" and "neo-Puritans."

Concerning poverty, U.S. libertarians believe that government assistance to the poor has been a failure and that, even worse, it has brought more poverty. They prefer to fight poverty through a program based on opportunity, work, and individual responsibility. Many advocate replacing government welfare with private, charitable giving and slashing bureaucratic regulations in order to help small businesses succeed. Indeed, one libertarian, Peruvian-born Alvaro Vargas Llosa (2008), claims that it is a myth that "lifting the poor out of poverty requires the transfer of wealth from rich countries to poor, from the 'haves' to the 'have-nots' in poor nations." Instead, Vargas Llosa says, the real keys to economic development are individual creativity and initiative, and the sense and ability to address market needs as they arise. In one word, entrepreneurship."

According to Brink Lindsey, vice president of the Cato Institute, a leading libertarian think tank, libertarians and liberals in the United States should forge an alliance, a "liberal–libertarian entente." Why? Because, he says, today in the United States, the prevailing ideologies are "intellectually exhausted." He faults both present-day conservatism and liberalism:

> Conservatism has risen to power only to become squalid and corrupt, a Nixonian mélange of pandering

to populist prejudices and distributing patronage to well-off cronies and Red Team constituencies....The old formulation defined conservatism as the desire to protect traditional values *from* the intrusion of big government; the new one seeks to promote traditional values *through* the intrusion of big government....Liberalism, meanwhile, has never recovered from its fall from grace in the mid-'60s. Ever since, it has lacked the vitality to do more than check conservative excesses—and obstruct legitimate, conservative-led progress. As a governing philosophy, liberalism has been moribund: When Jimmy Carter and Bill Clinton managed to win the White House, they did so only by successfully avoiding the liberal stigma.

(Lindsey, 2006)

Further, Lindsey argues, both conservatives and liberals are backward-looking: "the rival ideologies of left and right are both pining for the s'50s. The only difference is that liberals want to work there, while conservatives want to go home there."

Lindsey proposes a fusion—**liberaltarianism**—combining libertarians' views on civil liberties with a new acceptance of the market and capitalism by liberals. The central challenge to bring this about, he writes, "is to elaborate a vision of economic policy, and policy reform" that both liberals and libertarians can support. This won't be easy, he says, because "Libertarians worry primarily about constraints imposed by government, while liberals worry most about constraints imposed by birth and the play of economic forces." But Lindsey proposes many areas where liberals and libertarians might work together, including tax reform and farm subsidies.

Lindsey's proposed fusion might be supported by some on the left who disapprove of government intervention to help the rich. For example, economist Dean Baker views the U.S. federal government's bailout and largesse toward Wall Street's Bear Stearns in 2008 as just "another episode of the *Conservative Nanny State* [his 2006 book], the story of how the government intervenes in the market to redistribute income from those at the middle and bottom to those at the top" (Baker, 2008).

Others have different notions. George Packer (2008) notes that the recent era of Republican conservatism in the United States, starting in 1966, was based on three pillars: military might, family values, and small government. Packer argues that this era died with George W. Bush.

A Pox on Many Houses!

James Galbraith, who teaches economics at the University of Texas (and is the son of economist John Kenneth Galbraith), urges both liberals and conservatives to abandon the so-called free market. In *The Predator State: How Conservatives Abandoned the Free Market and Why Liberals Should Too* (2008), Galbraith claims that both conservative economics and conventional liberalism are not only intellectually bankrupt but incapable of addressing the United States's urgent economic problems. At the core of this outdated thinking, he says, is policy-talk of the "free market." Tax cuts and small government, monetarism, balanced budgets, deregulation, and free trade are the core elements of this dogma, a dogma so successful that even many liberals accept it: He thinks that even liberals have bowed before the free-market altar. However, he says, conservatives in the style of George W. Bush have abandoned the market altogether. In his view, that is why principled conservatives—chief among them, the Reagan "true believers"—long ago abandoned Bush and his "corporate republic."

Galbraith challenges citizens to better understand that, instead of a free-market economy, what the United States has is a complicated combination of private and public institutions, with Medicare and housing finance plus an enormous research establishment. The nation's "real" problems and challenges, such as climate change, inequality, and the subprime mortgage crisis, he says, cannot be solved by looking to the market. He advises planning and other policies that will transform markets. (Indeed, the Bush administration—no doubt *not* on the advice of James Galbraith—struggled to curb the "economic contagion" threatening the United States and the global economy in 2008 by intervening in the market. George W. Bush's secretary of the treasury, Henry (Hank) Paulson, led the charge in order to "contain an economic contagion stemming from a disintegrating housing sector, volatile financial markets and frozen credit, skyrocketing energy and food prices, widening job losses, and a precipitous fall in the dollar" (Weisman and Anderson, 2008).

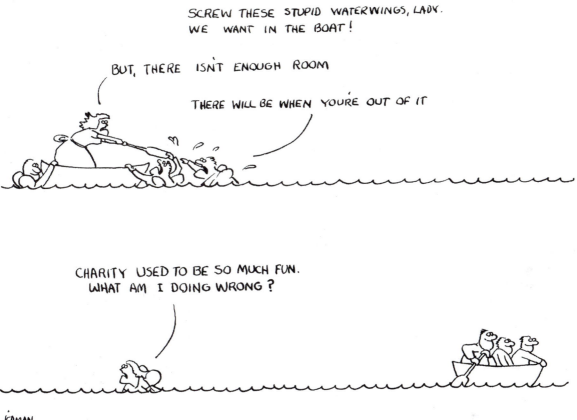

Fig. 3.6 GET SOME NEW BOATS! Radicals call for basic changes in the relationships between social classes in order to meet the problems of people and cities in distress. (© 1976 Richard Hedman)

The Radical Perspective

The radical perspective is a misnomer. Radicals range from anti-federal-government, white Christian suprem-acist revolutionaries in the United States to anticorporate rebels (e.g., activists of the Social Forum, an alternative to the Davos, Switzerland, "establishment" Economic Forum) and revolutionaries. Here, I focus on only one strand of radicalism: thought rooted in the theories of Karl Marx. Why? Because in social science, his ideas have been both influential and inescapable.

A note at the outset: When discussing Marx and his interpreters, you need a scorecard to know who thinks what. There are at least five varieties of neo-Marxists, and they disagree among themselves on (1) how to interpret what Marx originally said and (2) how best to apply Marx's notions to the contemporary world. Even so, they tend to share a basic notion: Most social problems *cannot* be solved within the context of the present institutional structure. This radical idea is in contrast to (1) conservatives and neoconservatives, who think that few social problems can be solved (especially by government programs), and (2) liberals and neoliberals, who think that government action can improve social life. Marxists reject the liberal problem-solving approach of incremental change at the edges of basic social and economic institutions. They say that only by going to the roots (*radical* means "root") of economic instability and social injustice can problems be solved.

Fiddling around with marginal changes, radicals claim, is like applying Band-Aids to social cancers; superficial responses won't cure the root problem. For Marxists, it is not possible to abolish poverty and leave the present economic system intact. In their view, capitalism and authority structures that grow out of that social–economic–political system are the roots of the problem.

Urban geographer David Harvey (1973, 1989, 2005) is a spokesperson for one branch of neo-Marxism. Harvey starts with this assumption: Poverty is a manifestation of social structural problems in monopoly capitalism, the national and international socioeconomic system. In his view, what is needed is not liberal reform or conservative benign neglect of social problems. What is needed is radical restructuring along socialist lines.

Some neo-Marxists point to such conditions as the unequal distribution of wealth and income among social classes and the capitalist state's alliance with business interests and elite groups as forces that perpetuate poverty. Since most neo-Marxists think that government is part of the problem, they don't look to government for the solution.

One Marxist analysis of society proceeds from the following assumptions:

1. *The productive forces in society determine its essential character.* The prevailing beliefs, legal system, politics, and social relationships in a society are determined by that society's mode of production (e.g., the state of technology, the ownership and management of scarce resources, and the authority relations that result from a particular productive mode, such as feudalism or capitalism).

2. *There is no such thing as "human nature."* This follows from the first assumption that the ways people think, relate to other people and their work, and even feel are linked to the prevailing mode of production. For instance, people tilling the soil in preindustrial rural societies, fashioning handicrafts in medieval towns, or attaching left-rear bumpers on an assembly line in capitalist urban-industrial societies necessarily interpret their worlds in very different ways. People are formed by the productive activities

in society. They are not basically "economic animals," as the liberal perspective maintains; rather, they are active agents who transform the material world and master nature. Marx used the term *Homo faber* ("man the maker" or "producer") to express this notion.

3. *Social conflict between classes dominates capitalist societies.* Under the capitalist mode of production, social harmony does not exist (as liberals maintain). Rather, economic and political life is primarily determined by the conflict between two great social classes: those who own or control factories, global finance, information, and other productive forces in society (the bourgeoisie, now including the upper executive and professional corporate sectors) and those who neither own nor control the society's productive forces (the have-nots, or the proletariat, now including clerical workers, the "new working class" of the service economy). Under capitalism, a few "continue to obtain enormous shares of wealth and leisure, while others continue to support themselves and others with their labor" (Gordon, 1977:7). In other words, neo-Marxists see a necessary connection between poverty and wealth under capitalism: Some are poor because others are rich.

4. *Government (the state) under capitalism is not neutral.* Whereas liberals see diverse interest groups bargaining and negotiating for scarce resources in the political arena in the context of a neutral government, some (but not all) neo-Marxists see the state as a tool of the bourgeoisie. Decision making is dominated by those who own and control society's productive forces or by civil servants who act to protect their interests. In short, public policy under capitalism is dominated by urban business and creditor classes.

5. *Under monopoly capitalism today, the self-regulating market mechanism is a fiction.* The theory of the free market as self-regulating neglects the facts of monopoly price-fixing, the creation of needs by advertising, the corporate political economy that tries to avoid competition in its own interest, and government intervention on

behalf of private enterprise (e.g., "welfare for the rich" in the form of business subsidies, tax breaks, and bailouts).

6. *The sum of the private interests does not equal the public interest.* Believing, as classical liberals (conservatives) do, that the "invisible hand" works to ensure social harmony and individual well-being is illogical; it assumes that the lead of private greed can be transmuted into the gold of public welfare.

Democratic socialist Irving Howe (1920–1993) addressed points 4 to 6 in his radical critique, saying that the dominant ethic of the Reagan–George H. W. Bush years was a heartless social Darwinism. He lamented that the era's mindless chanting for "the free market" neglected key realities: that government and the economy are intertwined, and that the rich got richer while the poor got poorer (Howe, 1993:A19). Howe thought that

> Sooner or later, the U.S. will have to address the fact that multinational corporations can carry on production anywhere in the world and can disregard governments that would set standards (minimum wages, child labor laws, Social Security). This systemic problem requires, at the least, enforcement of international labor standards.
>
> *(1993:A19)*

Like many before him, Howe suggested that the (multinational) tail may be wagging the (government) dog, not vice versa.

Radical sociologist Immanuel Wallerstein may not be a neo-Marxist, but he offers an explanation of recent economic crises with which neo-Marxists could agree. Wallerstein (2008) says that analysts must look beyond derivatives, subprime mortgages, and oil speculators and focus, instead, on medium-term and long-term structural trends of the capitalist world economy, including the so-called Kondratieff cycle. According to Wallerstein, the United States achieved "hegemonic dominance" in 1945 but this dominance has been declining since the 1970s. Now, he says, we live in a "multipolar world": The United States will remain a strong power but will "continue to decline relative to other powers" in coming decades. He concludes that "There is not much that anyone can do to change this."

Political scientist Michael Parenti (2009) holds similar views. According to Parenti, the U.S. (and then worldwide) economic crisis, starting in 2007, convinced even some prominent free marketeers that something is gravely amiss with capitalism. Why? Because, Parenti thinks, capitalism has yet to come to terms with several historical forces "that cause it endless trouble: democracy, prosperity, and capitalism itself, the very entities that capitalist rulers claim to be fostering."

In sum, neo-Marxists and democratic socialists look at structural trends in the capitalist world economy and capitalist states. They don't expect any capitalist state to change its basic institutional structure. On the contrary, they see government policies and programs—affirmative action and college loan programs, for example—as smoke screens, diverting attention from structural problems inherent in capitalism. In their view, such superficial programs give the populace a false feeling of change, ignoring the roots of unemployment, alienation, and economic meltdown. Further, in their view, liberal programs mainly substitute racial conflict for class struggle.

New Dimensions

By tradition, Marxists, socialists, and syndicalists (e.g., the Wobblies) are considered to fall on the left of the political spectrum, while liberals occupy the center and conservatives the right. Most probably, this left–center–right distinction originated in the seating arrangements of the eighteenth-century French National Assembly: Socialists and other radicals took the chamber's left wing, moderates were seated in the middle, and social conservatives of the day sat on the right.

People still identify political ideologies as left-wing, right-wing, and middle-of-the-road. Yet this one-dimensional view obscures a great deal.

First, it overlooks the centralist–decentralist dimension. Decentralists agree with the economist E. F. Schumacher (1973) that "small is beautiful." They tend to be anti-bigness and pro-self-sufficient, small community. Decentralists of the left and right come together on such concerns as ecological consciousness and the desire to meet human needs rather than to encourage economic growth. One decentralist project, eating locally produced food, is associated with such writers as Barbara Kingsolver ([2007] 2008) and Michael Pollan ([2006] 2007).

By contrast, centralists tend to be pro-bigness: either big government or big business plus big technology. Centralists of the left and right come together on such issues as the preference for large-scale organizations (assumed to be efficient and economical providers of goods and services) and economic growth as a necessary condition of human welfare.

Second, the left–right spectrum may be breaking down on other grounds. According to one-time Republican strategist Kevin Phillips (1992:38), in times of "economic trauma and disillusionment," U.S. voters ignore ideological boundaries. His logic seems to resonate more than ever since he wrote that in 1992.

Others have questioned the left–right distinction on other grounds. Helen Keller (1880–1968) was one such critic. Although Keller was blind and deaf, some say she nailed it decades ago when she commented that politics in the United States was a contest between Tweedle-Dee and Tweedle-Dum. That is, there is not much difference between the political parties claiming they represented left and right. (*Note*: Keller was not neutral. She considered herself a Socialist, and she was active in Wobblie politics, discussed in Chapter.1 See DemocraticUnderground.com,n.d.)

To conclude: Social scientists, including urbanists, disagree on fundamental issues of political ideology. Preferences (e.g., for right-wing politics) influence how they see the world. Ideological preferences also influence how they advise policymakers to cope with the world—or try to change it.

Important note: Whatever their personal politics— radical, conservative, liberal, or some fusion of these ideologies—some are predicting that the very bonfires of capitalism are burning out. For one, novelist Tom Wolfe. Wolfe's *Bonfires of the Vanities* ([1987] 2008) chronicles and satirizes the travails of a bond trader on Wall Street and "Master of the Universe." Wolfe told a reporter in 2007 that "We may be witnessing the end of capitalism as we know it" (in Sorkin, 2008:13).

Contrarian law professor Philip Bobbitt (2008) predicts a very different future. He argues that Western society (including Australia, Japan, Indonesia,

Singapore, South Korea, South Africa, and India, in his view) is now undergoing a world-historical transformation. He contends that globalization, nuclear proliferation, and telecommunications are revolutionizing the very nature of the state: to a twenty-first-century conception of a "market state." In his view, this market state will maximize the opportunity of its citizens.

Tom Wolfe and Phillip Bobbitt's predictions conflict. If either comes true, what will it mean for city life, including the future of "global cities" (Chapter 5) such as New York and Tokyo? Only the future will tell.

SUBTLE INFLUENCES ON RESEARCHERS

Disagreements among urbanists can also stem from another factor: dependence on funding sources. In an era of government- and corporate-sponsored research, it is almost impossible for researchers to be independent intellectuals.

Scholars of various ideologies decry the ever-increasing dependence on corporate and government funding sources. One fear is that "he who pays the piper calls the tune."

Still, some stand up to possible funders. Members of the American Psychological Association (APA), for example, voted in 2007 to oppose the United States's use of torture, sleep deprivation, and other practices considered inhumane on terror suspects. The APA voting majority feared the distortion of professional values in order to serve the ends of government.

ATTITUDES TOWARD SOLVING SOCIAL "PROBLEMS"

Can social scientists solve social "problems"? Should they even try? Among themselves, social scientists don't agree, and their opinions often are linked to their ideologies.

First, a note on the term "social problem." About 100 years ago, there were disagreeable social conditions, issues, and conflicts—but no social "problems" or social "ills." The idea that society can be "sick" and need "treatment" for "chronic disease" is relatively recent, probably dating from the early twentieth century. The Chicago school of sociology (Park, Burgess, etc.) was partially responsible for this linguistic change that altered people's way of seeing the world, for they were convinced that urban industrial life led to "social disorganization" and "social pathology." Thus, as they studied crime, deviance, juvenile delinquency, and other "pathologies," they helped to transfer medical and clinical language to the realm of urban life. At about the same time, the new field of psychoanalysis, in an attempt to gain legitimacy, began to apply the medical model to individual behavior. Where people were formerly labeled "sinful," "strange," or "eccentric," they now became mentally "ill."

Today, we routinely use medical language to describe people and societies. We often forget that the medical model of illness and problems is a mere metaphor that masks other ways of understanding. In particular, seeing disagreeable social conditions as "problems" conceals the political conflicts of interest that belie social problems, for a "conflict" requires observers to take a stand. But a "problem" is something anyone can safely oppose. Avoiding "conflict" and focusing on "problems" allows us to *not* see that social problem solving is far from neutral.

When problems were considered merely disagreeable social conditions, they were thought to be approachable through either the market mechanism or the political process. But once something is defined as a social problem, it logically calls for a technical solution. Here is the logic: Just as medical experts are needed to cure physical illness, social experts (social scientists) are needed to cure society's chronic ailments. Using technical experts—urbanists, for example—to solve social problems means transferring issues out of the political arena. This sidesteps public debate. It also turns social scientists into technocrats—as if they were value-free, with no ideological axes to grind. We have already seen how faulty that assumption is.

A classic case study by sociologist Scott Greer (1961) illustrates the problematic nature of problem solving. Looking at urban traffic and transportation, Greer asked, Whose problem is it? What kind of people, playing what social roles, define the nature of the metropolitan transportation problem? Who is concerned about it? After all, Greer said, traffic may not be a problem to drivers sitting and listening to car radios. Nor is traffic a major concern to suburbanites, who may pay the price of driving slowly through fumes rather than paying for antipollutants. But congestion may indeed be a major concern for downtown business merchants or suburban shopping mall

developers. In other words, it is wrong to assume that a social problem is everyone's problem. Greer advised researchers to analyze what groups in society have power to define a problem, as well as what interest groups benefit most from its solution.

Having looked at the transformation of social *conflicts* into more neutral social *problems*, let us touch briefly on a related matter: the proper role of social scientists in solving problems. This issue is rooted in much larger questions: Who should govern? Will government by experts turn out to be government in the interest of experts?

Since World War II, social scientists have become part of a giant knowledge industry. Armed with sophisticated research tools, many researchers think they can—and should—use their knowledge to build better cities—even a better world. Indeed, some see themselves as a priestly caste, possessing reason and analytical skills that can lead people into the good society. But others aren't so sure that social scientists *should* play the role of physician or social engineer. This view is epitomized by the late neoconservative urbanist Senator Daniel Patrick Moynihan in his book *Maximum Feasible Misunderstanding* (1969), a stinging appraisal of social scientists as problem solvers in the War on Poverty. Moynihan concluded that social scientists should evaluate the outcomes of public policy, not formulate it. Still others argue that the debate over the proper role of the scientific expert is academic, for professionals (afraid to risk the loss of community standing) are inherently conservative and thus end up serving the ends of those in power.

WHAT QUESTIONS TO ASK

"Research shows that…" sounds scientific, but consumers beware: So-called research can support almost any hypothesis, from the most outrageous to the most obvious. Poet Allen Ginsberg (1994) poked fun at what he considered the obvious: "Research shows that socialism is a failure if it's run by the secret police."

But it is not always easy to know what's obvious. And sometimes the obvious is wrong. So, how can we discriminate between good and questionable research? Here are some worthwhile questions to ask of any urban-oriented research study in order to assess more critically its "evidence" and the policy recommendations that may flow from it:

1. *Who says so?* What do we know about the author? Specifically, what is his or her (a) disciplinary background, (b) theoretical orientation, (c) practical experience that may be relevant, (d) set of assumptions and values, and (e) funding source(s)? What is the author's political ideology? Is it explicit, or does it hide under the neutral guise of "objective" social science? Can you tell by reading between the lines or by looking at the acknowledgments and footnotes? Is the study or tract published by an organization (or magazine) with a known point of view, such as the American Enterprise Institute (conservative), the Brookings Institution (centrist), the Institute for Policy Studies (radical), the Cato Institute (libertarian), or so-called Patriot groups (far right).

   How do your own values and biases affect your evaluation of information? Specifically, do you automatically accept as objective what some sources say, such as the *New York Times* or a favorite blog, but reject as slanted information (perhaps the same information) appearing in a European newspaper or on CNN?

2. *What's been neglected?* Is there evidence that might contradict the basic point of the study? Does the author use micro-level analysis alone when macro-level analysis would have added an important dimension, or vice versa? Could the study have been improved by combining several methods of investigation? What points of view seem to be overlooked? These are important questions because in research, as in life, sins of omission can be as deadly as sins of commission.

3. *So what?* Some urban studies may be sophisticated methodologically, but their findings may be trivial, their conclusions relatively meaningless. Hence the "so what?" question: Does the study enrich our understanding of the topic under investigation?

To conclude: By routinely asking and trying to answer these questions—Who says so? What's been

overlooked? So what?—we can begin to separate sense from nonsense. And we can strengthen our ability to understand and act on the urban world in which we live.

KEY TERMS

Deductive reasoning The process of reasoning from general principles to particular examples. Contrast: *inductive reasoning.*

Empirical evidence Evidence derived from direct observation and sense experience. Contrasts: *intuitive insight, metaphysical speculation,* and *pure logic.*

Hypothesis A tentative statement suggesting a relationship between two or more variables. A hypothesis is intended to be tested empirically or at least to be testable.

Ideology A set of beliefs and ideas that justify certain interests. An ideological position reflects and rationalizes particular political, economic, institutional, and/or social interests.

Inductive reasoning The process of reasoning from particular examples to general principles. Contrast: *deductive reasoning.*

Liberaltarianism Term coined by a libertarian to mean a fusion of two contemporary U.S. ideologies, liberalism and libertarianism. It stresses commonalities between the two ideologies, such as the dislike of government intrusion into private matters. The sticking point to such an alliance: vastly differing ideas on capitalism and the market.

Model A tentative and limited tool that represents some aspect of the world in words, mathematical symbols, graphs, or other symbols. Models attempt to duplicate or illustrate by analogy a pattern of relationships found in the empirical world. They are used to guide research and build theory in the sciences.

Participant-observation A research method commonly used by sociologists, anthropologists, and journalistic feature writers. The investigator becomes or poses as a member of a group under study in an attempt to gain an intimate, firsthand acquaintance with the group and understand how group members interpret the world.

Positivistic science or positivism The philosophical stance claiming that all true knowledge can be derived from sense experience (empirically-based knowledge). It rejects intuitive insight, subjective understanding, and metaphysical speculation as bases of knowledge.

Scientific method A method for doing science based on the assumption that all true knowledge is verifiable using empirical evidence. Well-ordered, successive stages—defining a research problem, constructing hypotheses, data gathering and analysis, and prediction of facts—are outlined.

Theory A comprehensive explanation of something. Its functions are to summarize and order information meaningfully, to permit prediction, and to suggest new lines of scientific inquiry. A theory is a generalization that is intermediate in degree of verification between a scientific law and a hypothesis.

Unobtrusive measure A research method that seeks to remove the observer from the event under study and thereby to eliminate possible reactive effects. Examples are content analysis of television programs and archival research.

Variable A trait or factor that can vary among a population or from case to case (e.g., sex, size of firm, cost per square foot, social class). Opposite: *constant*.

PROJECTS

1. **Constructing hypotheses.** Using poverty status as the dependent variable, construct three different hypotheses (with different independent variables) to explain why some people are poor. These three hypotheses should reflect the liberal, conservative, and neo-Marxist points of view.

2. **Reading between the lines.** Examine two works of urban scholarship on the same topic—for instance, slums or metropolitan unemployment. Do the authors agree? If not, why not? Try to analyze their assumptions, research methods, political biases, disciplinary perspectives, and levels of analysis used.

SUGGESTIONS FOR FURTHER LEARNING

Doing science can be messy and not altogether high-minded. A highly readable novel about a research lab that captures the petty jealousies, vengefulness, and fears of not being first with a scientific breakthrough is Allegra Goodman's *Intuition* (New York: Dial Press, 2006).

What it means to "do science" remains much debated. For one postmodernist viewpoint, see French theorist Bruno Latour, *We Have Never Been Modern* (Cambridge, Mass.: Harvard University Press, 2007; Catherine Porter, trans.). Latour wonders about a science that can connect nature and culture, past and present.

The women's movement in America has encouraged a reexamination of many assumptions underlying social science methods. For timely articles and policy suggestions, see *Feminist Economics: Journal of the International Association for Feminist Economics*, published quarterly. The journal says that its goal is "not just to develop more illuminating theories, but to improve the conditions of living for all children, women, and men." Drucilla Barker and Susan F. Feiner discuss the changing roles of families, the private costs and social benefits of caring labor, and the impact of globalization on social reproduction in *Liberating Economics: Feminist Perspectives on Families, Work, and Globalization* (Ann Arbor: University of Michigan Press, 2004).

For a spirited defense of the free market, see Milton Friedman's classic *Capitalism and Freedom: Fortieth Anniversary Edition* (Chicago: University of Chicago, 2002) and Andrew Bernstein's *The Capitalist Manifesto: The Historic, Economic and Philosophic Case for Laissez-Faire* (Lanham, Md.: University Press of America, 2005). In *Cowboy Capitalism: European Myths, American Reality*, also published in 2005 (by a leading U.S. libertarian think tank, The Cato Institute, Washington, D.C.), German reporter Olaf Gersemann compares economic conditions and policies in the United States favorably with those in Germany, France, and Italy, countries where free-market capitalism is moderated by heavy state intervention.

For a much less sanguine view of U.S. capitalism, read a Marxist or neo-Marxist critique. These include Michael Parenti's political science text *Democracy for the Few* (Belmont, Calif.: Wadsworth, 2007). For a devastating critique of the recent role of the United States in international affairs from a socialist point of view, see Jean Bricmont, *Humanitarian Imperialism: Using Human Rights to Sell War* (New York: Monthly Review Press, 2006). Bricmont, a Belgian theoretical physicist, argues that U.S. intervention in such places as Yugoslavia and Afghanistan is more arbitrary and self-serving than humanitarian-based. He suggests that, since the end of the cold war, "human rights" has become a justification for intervention by imperialist powers, particularly the United States.

There is no shortage of literature on ideology. Here are just a few examples from various decades: In *A Conflict of Visions: Ideological Origins of Political Struggles* (New York: Basic Books, 2002), conservative economist Thomas Sowell suggests that two competing visions—of "constrained" and "unconstrained" human beings—underpin political ideologies. For visions of the nature of human beings and their effect on political ideology, see Sheldon Wolin, *Politics and Vision* (Boston: Little, Brown, 1960), and C. B. Macpherson, *Political Theory of Possessive Individualism: Hobbes to Locke* (New York: Oxford University Press, 1962).

Two scholars at the Université de Montreal, Alain Noël and Jean-Philippe Thérien, contend that the left–right opposition is here to stay. In *Left and Right in Global Politics* (New York: Cambridge University Press, 2008), they argue that the conflict between progressives and conservatives has structured both domestic and international politics, and it will continue.

A novel by Ayn Rand, *Atlas Shrugged* (New York: Dutton, [1957] 2005), has been called one of the most influential business books ever written. Viewed as a moral defense of capitalism, it glorifies the right of anyone to live only for his or her interest. Over the years, some have dismissed the book as merely an homage to greed and immorality. Others, including former chair of the Federal Reserve Alan Greenspan, became devotees of Ayn Rand and her philosophy, objectivism.

Writing from a different angle, Martin W. Lewis announces his viewpoint in his title: *Green Delusions: An Environmentalist Critique of Radical Environmentalism* (Durham, N.C.: Duke University Press, 1992). Geographer Lewis claims that there are at least five main types of "eco-extremism": antihuman-ist anarchism, primitivism, humanist eco-anarchism, green Marxism, and radical eco-feminism.

For a discussion of historical and contemporary theoretical perspectives, particularly the various strands of radical theory (including critical theory, structural Marxism, Hegelian Marxism, Harry Braverman's economic sociology, and Immanuel Wallerstein's historically oriented world systems theory), see George Ritzer and Douglas J. Goodman, *Sociological Theory*, 6th ed. (New York: McGraw-Hill, 2004).

Mass-market movies often shy away from visions that could be interpreted as left-wing. Exceptions here include Oliver Stone's *Wall Street* (1987), which focuses on the stock market, and Michael Moore's documentary *Sicko* (2007), which focuses on the U.S. health-care industry.

The subdiscipline of economic sociology is based on the proposition that economic institutions are social, not natural, constructions. For a range of views on how market capitalism works from this perspective, see Mark Granovetter and Richard Swedberg, eds., *The Sociology of Economic Life*, 2nd ed. (Boulder, Colo.: Westview Press, 2001). In *The New Economic Sociology: A Reader*, edited by Frank Dobbin (Princeton, N.J.: Princeton University Press, 2004), four themes of the subdiscipline are explored in 20 articles: institutions, networks, power, and cognition.

An anthropological study, *Learning Capitalist Culture: Deep in the Heart of Tejas* (Philadelphia: University of Pennsylvania Press, 1990), examines how youth in a southwestern town learn American values through football, dating, classroom interactions, and so on. Author Douglas E. Foley, a professor of anthropology and education, uses data gathered over 14 years of fieldwork.

Social science texts on methodology discuss micro and macro levels of analysis but not the cosmic perspective. Why? Because it is not used in the *social* sciences—at least not yet. For a highly readable introduction to the cosmic perspective, see *The View from the Center of the Universe* by Joel R. Primack and Nancy Ellen Abrams (New York: Riverhead Books, 2006).

For discussions of technologists' "proper" role in politics, see Thorstein Veblen's classic *The Engineers and the Price System* (New York: Kelley, [1921] 1965), a defense of a form of technocracy in advanced technological society, and Robert Boguslaw's *The New Utopians* (Englewood Cliffs, N.J.: Prentice Hall, 1965), a description of the computer manufacturers, operations researchers, systems engineers, and other technological experts who aspire to transcend present reality.

Homelessness has been studied in the United States since at least the 1920s. A pioneer in the study of the homeless, Nels Anderson (1889–1986) was a hobo himself when he started gathering ethnographic data about his fellow hobos for his University of Chicago master's thesis in sociology. Due to academic snobbery in the 1920s, Anderson hid his hobo identity until long after his thesis was published in 1923 as *The Hobo*. The study was republished in 1999 as *On Hobos and Homelessness* by Nels Anderson and Raffaele Rauty (ed.) (Chicago: University of Chicago Press). Christopher Jencks calculated that there was a fourfold increase in U.S. homelessness between 1980 and 1988. In *The Homeless* (Cambridge, Mass.: Harvard University Press, [1994] 2005), a model for clear, well-balanced argument, sociologist Jencks discusses both liberal and conservative rationales for homelessness.

Political satire is alive and well in the United States. For a send-up of various ideologues, listen to Harry Shearer's weekly program *Le Show* on National Public Radio and watch Jon Stewart's *The Daily Show* and Stephen Colbert's *The Colbert Report* on Comedy Central.

For evidence that intelligent people who disagree can talk to one another in a civil and interesting way, see Bill Moyers' interview with philosopher Daniel Dennett, author of *Breaking the Spell* (New York: Viking, 2006), aired on *The Charlie Rose Show* on PBS, April 4, 2006. Dennett, an atheist (or "bright" as he calls himself), and Moyers, a Protestant minister, conduct an edifying, hour-long discussion on the nature of faith and reason.

REFERENCES

Baker, Dean. 2008. "The welfare king of the 21st century." *Truthout/Perspective* (March 31): http://www.truthout.org/docs_2006/033108A.shtml#

———. 2006. *The Conservative Nanny State* (lulu.com).

Banfield, Edward. [1968] 1970. *The Unheavenly City.* Boston: Little, Brown.

———. 1974. *The Unheavenly City Revisited.* Boston: Little, Brown.

Bell, Daniel. 1960. *The End of Ideology.* New York: Free Press.

———. 1992. "Into the 21st century, bleakly." *New York Times*, national edition (July 26):E17.

Bobbitt, Philip. 2008. *Terror and Consent: The Wars for the Twenty-First Century.* New York: Alfred A. Knopf.

Buchanan, Patrick. 1992. Speech at the Republican National Convention, Houston, August 17.

Burgess, Ernest W., and Donald J. Bogue. 1964. "Research in urban society: A long view." Pp. 1–14 in Ernest W. Burgess and Donald J. Bogue, eds., *Contributions to Urban Sociology.* Chicago: University of Chicago Press.

Burke, Edmund. [1790] 1959. *Reflections on the Revolution in France.* New York: Holt, Rinehart and Winston.

Cohen, Patricia. 2007. "Proclaiming liberalism, and what it now means." *New York Times* (June 2) http://www.nytimes.com/2007/06/02/arts/02left.html?th&emc=th

Dahl, Robert. 1961. *Who Governs: Democracy and Power in an American City.* New Haven, Conn.: Yale University Press.

DeParle, Jason. [2004] 2005. *American Dream: Three Women, Ten Kids, and a Nation's Drive to End Welfare.* New York: Penguin.

Democraticunderground.com.n.d. "Helen Keller was a socialist, peace activist and member of the ACLU." http://www.democraticunderground.com/discuss/duboard.php?az=view_all&address=104x1610466

Edin, Kathryn, and Maria Kefalas. 2005. *Promises I Can Keep: Why Poor Women Put Motherhood Before Marriage.* Berkeley: University of California Press.

Galbraith, James. 2008. *The Predator State: How Conservatives Abandoned the Free Market and Why Liberals Should Too.* New York: Free Press.

Gans, Herbert J. 1962. *The Urban Villagers.* New York: Free Press.

Ginsberg, Allen. 1994. Poem read at the Tikkun Conference, New York City. Broadcast on *As It Happens*, CBC (January 21), 5:30 p.m. PST.

Gordon, David, ed. 1977. *Problems in Political Economy: An Urban Perspective.* Lexington, Mass.: Heath.

Greer, Scott. 1961. "Traffic, transportation, and problems of the metropolis." Pp. 605–650 in Robert K. Merton and Robert A. Nisbet, eds., *Contemporary Social Problems*. New York: Harcourt, Brace & World.

Hacker, Andrew. 1973. "On original sin and conservatives." *New York Times Magazine* (February 25):13+.

Harvey, David. 1973. *Social Justice and the City*. Baltimore: Johns Hopkins University Press.

———. 1989. *The Condition of Postmodernity: An Enquiry into the Origins of Cultural Change*. Oxford: Blackwell.

———. 2005. *The New Imperialism*. New York: Oxford University Press.

Hayek, F. A. [2004] 2007. Bruce Caldwell, ed. *The Road to Serfdom: Text and Documents—The Definitive Edition*. Chicago: University of Chicago Press.

Hobbes, Thomas. [1651] 1968. *Leviathan: or the Matter, Forme and Power of a Commonwealth Ecclesiasticall and Civil*. New York: Collier.

Howe, Irving. 1993. "Clinton, seen from the left." *New York Times* (January 20):A19.

Hunter, Floyd. [1953] 1963. *Community Power Structure: A Study of Decision Makers*. Garden City, N.Y.: Doubleday, Anchor.

Hyde, Kevin. 2008. "GM's 'Engine Charlie' Wilson learned to live with a misquote." (September 14): http://www.freep.com/article/20080914/BUSINESS01/809140308/

Kennedy, Edward M. 2006. *America Back on Track*. New York: Viking Adult.

Kingsolver, Barbara, et al. [2007] 2008. *Animal, Vegetable, Miracle: A Year of Food Life*. New York: Harper.

Klein, Daniel B. and Charlotta Stern. 2006. "Sociology and classical liberalism." (Summer) Independent Institute 6/22: http://findarticles.com/p/search/?qa=Daniel%20B.%hh20Klein%20Charlotta%20Stern

Kuhn, Thomas S. [1962] 1970. *The Structure of Scientific Revolutions*. Chicago: University of Chicago Press.

LaHaye, Tim, and Jerry B. Jenkins. 2006. *The Regime: Evil Advances Before They Were Left Behind*. Waterville, Maine: Thorndike Press.

Lewis, Oscar. 1961. *The Children of Sanchez*. New York: Random House.

Liebow, Elliot. *Tally's Corner: A Study of Negro Streetcorner Men*. 2nd ed. Lanham, Md.: Rowman & Littlefield.

Lindsey, Brink. 2006. "Liberaltarians." *New Republic* (December 4) on Cato Institute's website now at: http://www.cato.org/pub_display.php?pub_id=6800

Moynihan, Daniel Patrick. 1969. *Maximum Feasible Misunderstanding*. New York: Free Press.

Nuland, Sherwin B. 2008. *The Uncertain Art: Thoughts on a Life in Medicine*. New York: Random House.

Packer, George. 2008. "The fall of conservatism." *New Yorker* (May 26): http://www.newyorker.com/reporting/2008/05/26/080526fa_fact_packer/

Parenti, Michael. 2009. "Capitalism's self-inflicted apocalypse." (February 10):http://www.informationclearinghouse.info/

Phillips, Kevin. 1992. "The politics of frustration." *New York Times Magazine* (April 12):38+.

———. 2006. *American Theocracy. The Peril and Politics of Radical Religion, Oil, and Borrowed Money in the 21st Century*. New York: Viking Adult.

Pollan, Michael. [2006] 2007. *The Omnivore's Dilemma: A Natural History of Four Meals*. New York: Penguin.

Rand, Ayn. 1964. *The Virtue of Selfishness*. New York: Signet.

Reich, Robert B. 2007. *Supercapitalism: The Transformation of Business, Democracy, and Everyday Life*. New York: Alfred A. Knopf.

Roth, Gabriel, ed. 2006. *Street Smart: Competition, Entrepreneurship, and the Future of Roads*. Oakland, Calif.: Independent Institute.

Sagan, Carl. 1978. *Broca's Brain: Reflections on the Romance of Science*. New York: Random House.

Samuelson, Paul A. 1964. *Economics*, 6th ed. New York: McGraw-Hill.

Samuelson, Paul A., and William D. Nordhaus, with Michael J. Mandel. 1995. *Economics*, 15th ed. New York: McGraw-Hill.

Schumacher, E. F. 1973. *Small Is Beautiful: Economics as if People Mattered*. New York: Harper & Row.

Smith, Adam. [1776] 1970. *Wealth of Nations*. Baltimore: Penguin.

Sorkin, Andrew Ross. 2008. "On Wall Street, a year of living dangerously." *International Herald Tribune* (June 25):13.

Toffler, Alvin. 1970. *Future Shock*. New York: Random House.

Vargas Llosa, Alvaro. 2008. "Lessons from the poor." Independent Institute, *The Lighthouse* (September 22). www.independent.org/store/book_detail.asp?bookID

Wallerstein, Immanuel. 2008. "The depression: A long-term view." *Commentary 243* (October 15).

Warren, Rick [2002] 2007 *The Purpose Driven® Life: What on Earth Am I Here For?* Grand Rapids, MI: Zondervan.

Weisman, Steven R., and Jenny Anderson. 2008. "Can Hank Paulson defuse this crisis?" *New York Times* (July 27): http://www.nytimes.com/2008/07/27/business/economy/27hank.html?_r=1&th&emc=th&oref=slogin

Weissinger, George. 2005. *Law Enforcement and the INS*, 2nd ed., Lanham, Md.: University Press of America.

Wertheimer, Richard, et al. 2001. "Welfare recipients' attitudes toward welfare, nonmarital childbearing, and work." Urban Institute B-37 series (June 1) *New Federalism: National Survey of America's Families.*

Wolfe, Tom. [1987] 2008. *The Bonfire of the Vanities.* New York: Picador.

POLIS, METROPOLIS, MEGALOPOLIS

Bank of California

CHAPTER 4

FROM URBAN SPECKS TO GLOBAL CITIES

THE FIRST CITIES

DIGGING INTO URBAN HISTORY

Rising like a giant spaceport out of Turkey's Anatolian plain is a 58-foot mound of earth. Until 1961, it was just a big mound lying in the hot sun. Then an international team moved in to excavate and analyze this ancient site, named **Çatal Hüyük** (pronounced Chatal Hooyook, meaning "mound at the end of the road" in modern Turkish). Under the direction of archeologist James Mellaart, the team dug wide trenches into the urban past. As they cut through the mound, they uncovered a prehistoric community—perhaps even a city—constructed about 9,500 years ago or even earlier.

Archeological digs such as Çatal Hüyük and new scientific techniques for radiocarbon dating of ancient artifacts have been overturning long-held theories about why and where cities first came into existence. New evidence has also called into question the dates for the birth of cities, often referred to as the "dawn of civilization." Until recently, it was generally assumed that urban life started in the fertile river valleys of present-day Iraq around 3500 BCE. Newer theories have pushed back the date to 8000 BCE or earlier. Newer theories also suggest that the earliest city dwellers settled in the hills above the valleys or in places far from the great rivers of antiquity.

But these matters are far from settled. The origins of cities remain controversial. And as archeological teams uncover new mounds in their digs, we can expect even more controversy and theorizing about what prerequisites were necessary for the emergence of urban life.

Controversy and tentative knowledge thus typify scholarly discussions of the earliest cities. In fact, controversy and tentative knowledge seem to be our fate in studying many urban phenomena, whether in ancient earth mounds or modern cities. (In 2008, for example, Paris "became" 3,000 years older: Archeological digs on the southwestern edge of the city moved back Paris's first-known human occupation to about 7600 BCE, in the Mesolithic period between the New and Old Stone Ages.)

For some, this state of seemingly constant tentative knowledge may produce anxiety and a desire to enter another field or discipline, perhaps physics with its laws and certainties. Yet physicists on the cutting edge of research say that they too deal only with tentative knowledge and approximations of truths. Facing the limits of our collective understanding in so many important areas—from the origins of the universe and the birth of cities to the causes of and cures for human misery—could throw us into despair. Or it could (and, I argue, should) encourage us to join the long search for knowledge and meaning by seeking better answers to more informed questions.

Let us now begin the search by tracing the roots of urban life and culture through the millennia. En route, let us think about questions that have few definitive answers: Why did people originally form cities? What features do the varied cities invented and sustained by human beings have in common? Why did cities grow and prosper in certain historical periods? What roles do **technology**, social organization, physical environment, and population play in city growth?

WHAT IS A CITY?

Before attempting to date the origin of cities, we run into a problem of definition: What exactly is a **city**? The ancient Romans made a sharp distinction between the community of people who banded together to form a settlement, which they called *civitas* (from which our words "city" and "civilization" are derived), and the physical place they formed—an *urb* (from which our word "urban" is derived). The earliest Roman cities were created by a solemn religious ceremony—the banding together of a group of people to form a community at a definite site.

Today, there is no precise or agreed-on definition of the word "city." It has been applied to so many different settlement types that the original Roman use of the word is obsolete. This is one reason it is so difficult to discuss when the first cities were invented or whether some communities were indeed cities.

In most definitions of "city," however, there are common elements. These include notions of *permanent residence, large population, high density,* and *heterogeneity.* But how large is large? How densely settled must a community be to be classified as a city rather than a village—200 people per square mile, 400, more? And how differentiated by occupation and kin group must a population be in order to be categorized as heterogeneous? Again, there are no precise criteria.

Another approach is to define a city in terms of its economic character. Using this approach, we can describe a city as a *market settlement*, a place "where the local inhabitants satisfy an economically substantial part of their daily wants in the local market" (Weber, [1921] 1963:66–67).

Yet another approach assumes that a city exists only when there are *cultural ingredients* considered essential to urban life—fine arts, exact sciences, and, in particular, writing. In this view, a collection of people—no matter how large—does not constitute a city unless these characteristics are present.

THE FIRST URBAN SETTLEMENTS: AN OVERVIEW

Using any of these definitions, should the most ancient sites yet excavated be called cities? It is unclear. Early settlements that might qualify as cities overlap two other settlement forms: agricultural villages and trading posts. Some add another permanent settlement form: the *pre*agricultural village. Indeed, an excavated site in present-day Israel is changing archeologists' views of why and when permanent settlements first arose. This site, **Wadi-al-Natuf**, was home to the Natufians (named for the site) about 13,000–14,000 years ago. The Natufians were foragers—not farmers—when they built what many archeologists now believe to be the world's first large, permanent habitat with storage facilities, elaborate buildings, and semiunderground houses. These settlements were so complete that, according to archeologist T. Douglas Price, the Natufians had practically "everything but mailboxes" (in Stevens, 1988:B11). Yet archeologists think these settlements were preagricultural villages, not true cities.

Jarmo, in present-day Iraq, is the most widely studied example of a large Neolithic agricultural village. Around 7000–6500 BCE, an estimated 150 people lived there at a low density, about 27 people per square mile. Perhaps it had the stirrings of a barter economy, a simple division of labor, and some cultural life. But it was not a city by anyone's definition.

Ancient **Jericho** is harder to classify. Some archeologists believe that Jericho is indeed the earliest city. When Dame Kathleen Kenyon and her team of archeologists started digging up Jericho in the 1950s,

they found ruined walls that apparently came tumbling down around 1400 BCE, when Joshua "fit the battle of Jericho" in the biblical story. Beneath these ruined city walls, they kept finding remains of earlier Jerichos. Finally, some 70 feet down, they unearthed a substantial settlement, the first Jericho—a Neolithic community, inhabited perhaps as early as 10,000 years ago. Kenyon (1957:65) estimates that it contained about 3,000 residents, called the "hog-backed brick people" after the round houses with humps at the top that they built.

Although Kenyon calls ancient Jericho the first "town" (a settlement bigger than a village but smaller than a city), its status remains controversial. To many, it is a mere trading post.

If Jericho's status is disputed, if Wadi-al-Natuf is viewed as a preagricultural settlement, and if Jarmo is certainly not a city, what is the earliest true city? Perhaps archeologists will find an early site near the great Sphinx of Egypt. (About a generation ago, its age was reevaluated by a team of geologists and geophysicists, who say that it was carved between 5000 and 7000 BCE—that is, millennia before Mesopotamian cities and some 2,500–5,000 years earlier than is generally thought. To date, no early site there has been uncovered.) Or was it Çatal Hüyük on Turkey's Anatolian plain?

Çatal Hüyük was probably established shortly after Jericho. Apparently, its population was twice that of Jericho. Residents produced some spectacular artwork and engaged in extensive trade. By some people's definitions, it qualifies as one of the earliest cities.

Bigger and much more sophisticated were a number of cities in ancient Mesopotamia that arose about 3500 BCE. Until the discoveries at Jericho, Çatal Hüyük, and Wadi-al-Natuf, conventional wisdom held that these **Mesopotamian** cities in the Sumer region were the earliest cities.

Four other centers of early urban civilization have been identified, the first in the Indus Basin in present-day India and Pakistan. Here, twin capital cities, Mohenjo-daro (about 240 miles north of present-day Karachi, Pakistan) and Harappa (about 350 miles farther north) flourished around 2300–1750 BCE. Physically, these were large cities, about 1 square mile in size. Carefully built according to identical city plans, they housed perhaps as many as 250,000 persons each. And, the archeological record shows, Mohenjo-daro and Harappa were technologically sophisticated centers as well as trade centers.

The second early center of urban life was in the valley of the Huang Ho River in China. The first Chinese dynasty, the Shang, built large cities at Cheng Chou and An Yang in approximately 1300–1500 BCE. One archeologist estimates that it would take 19,000 workers, working full time for at least 18 years, to build the massive packed-earth walls that surround An Yang, the largest of the Shang cities.

The third early urban center was in **Mesoamerica**: present-day Mexico, Guatemala, and other parts of

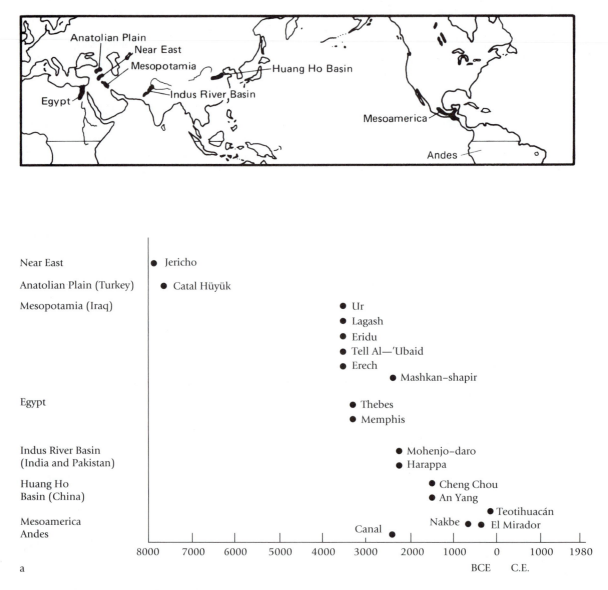

Fig. 4.2   (a) WHERE AND WHEN EARLY CITIES AROSE.

b

Fig. 4.2 (*b*) CARAL, PERU. Recently unearthed ruins in Caral, Peru, include a pyramidal structure. (Alessandro Catenazzi)

Central America. Various Amerindian cultures, including the Olmec, Maya, and Aztecs, developed large cities with elaborate buildings and political structures. For example, a recently excavated Mayan city of apparent grandeur, Nakbe, existed in what is now a remote tropical forest in Guatemala. Archeologists think that Nakbe reached its population peak between 600 and 400 BCE. On the basis of finds like Nakbe, archeologists are revising conventional wisdom about when Mesoamerican city cultures began.

Recently, archeologists added a fourth center of early urban civilization: the Peruvian Andes. That anyone at all lived there is surprising. The area's high altitude and dry cold make it hostile to human beings.

Yet well-preserved ruins (thanks to the height and dry cold) reveal numerous planned ancient communities, excavated since the late 1970s. Other Andean cities are well preserved due to desertlike conditions.

Conventional wisdom changed again in 2001 when a Peruvian–American team of archeologists announced the discovery of Caral, Peru, as the oldest known city in the Americas (see Shady Solis et al., 2001). According to team member Winifred Creamer, Caral "may actually be the birthplace of civilization in the Americas" (http://www.niu.edu/pubaffairs/nnow/fall01/universe6.html). Caral today is a sparsely populated shadow of its former self. "The real irony," Professor Creamer says, "is that the peak of civilization in this area happened before 2000 BCE....Nothing much has happened in this valley since." Radiocarbon dating suggests that the ruins of a once bustling city at Caral date to as early as 2627 BCE, about the same time as the great Egyptian pyramids.

Nestled in the Andes' Supe Valley about 120 miles north of Lima, the ancient civilization of Caral was established at 350 meters above sea level. It—or, rather, its ruins—lie 12 miles inland from the Peruvian coast. Caral's ruins, buried under sand and rock, include six flattop pyramids; two sunken plazas; evidence of an irrigated agricultural system, domesticated plants, and large-scale cultivation of cotton; and the remnants of upper-, middle-, and lower-status housing. The pyramids and irrigation system at Caral suggest an organized society in which large numbers of people were paid, or forced, to work on centralized projects (BBC, 2001). From this observation, archeologists deduce that power and wealth were held by an elite group at a time when, in most of the Americas, people were still hunting and gathering in much smaller communities.

Why did the ancient Andean civilizations disappear? That remains a mystery. So does the disappearance of the largest of the Mesoamerican early cities, **Teotihuacán**, "place of the Gods," so named by the Aztecs when they uncovered it about 700 years ago. It is located just outside Mexico City and now faces encroaching slums. (An archeological dig in 2008, beneath the Pyramid of the Sun, may begin to answer some enduring questions.) Teotihuacán was established much later than the Andean settlement, about 150 BCE. Flourishing for more than 1,000 years, its ruins today show an impressive city of pyramid-type structures and religious buildings. At its height, the multiethnic city became a major market and pilgrimage center; it may have had as many as 200,000 residents, or as many as ancient Rome (Gutierrez, 2008).

Teotihuacán, however, lacked what some consider a prerequisite for the birth of cities: a fertile environment. Teotihuacán emerged on a high, arid plain. Furthermore, some view the wheel and writing as prerequisites of early urban growth. Yet, even at their height, neither the ancient Peruvian civilization nor Teotihuacán had these inventions.

A final puzzle concerns cultural diffusion. Some archeologists think that the Peruvian and Mesoamerican civilizations had common roots: Stone Age chiefdoms in the central Amazon basin about 7,000–8,000 years ago. A few think that Teotihuacán borrowed elements from already-established urban cultures in Sumer or Egypt. (There are striking parallels, including religious pyramids similar to Mesopotamian ziggurats.) In one ingenious test of the cultural diffusion thesis, explorer Thor Heyerdahl built a reed boat, the *Ra II*, to demonstrate that Egyptian sailors might have reached Mesoamerica centuries ago. It sank.

Caral and other cities, not yet uncovered, may be as old as Mesopotamian cities. But let us now return to Mesopotamian cities, cities which captured the imagination of so many archeologists for so long, exploring questions about why early cities came into existence.

THE CHILDE THESIS: THE URBAN REVOLUTION IN MESOPOTAMIA

Australian–British archeologist V. Gordon Childe (1892–1957) spent a scholarly lifetime studying the rise of civilization in Mesopotamia: the Fertile Crescent located between the Tigris and Euphrates rivers (which flow into the Persian Gulf) in what is now Iraq. In his very readable books *Man Makes Himself* ([1936] 1952) and *What Happened in History?* ([1942] 1964), Childe detailed his thesis about what he considered to be the evolutionary development and progress of humankind from prehistoric food gatherer to food producer in the Neolithic revolution to city builder in the second revolution, the **urban revolution**.

According to the **Childe thesis**, the long march of human development started in the fertile river valleys of the Tigris–Euphrates. At the end of this developmental sequence was the emergence of cities around 3500 BCE. In brief, Childe's logic goes like this: The transition from hunting and gathering to food cultivation and the domestication of animals—the agricultural revolution—was a necessary precondition for the emergence of village and city life. Agriculture and the consequent production of a food surplus permitted people to stop their nomadic wandering and form settled communities. Thus, in Childe's view, agriculture is the key factor in the revolutionary change from nomadic wandering to settled, village/urban life.

In a fertile environment such as the Tigris–Euphrates river valley, the Childe thesis continues, farmers could and did produce and store a food surplus. Population in the agricultural villages then increased, for a constant food supply allowed more people to survive. Over the millennia, larger and larger villages developed. In turn, larger villages led to the need for more complex social organization and social control. To feed the ever-increasing population, intensive agriculture was invented. Eventually, a whole series of technological innovations and political changes followed as a result of larger populations and the need to handle and ensure the food surplus. For instance, the Childe thesis holds that ruling elites or classes developed to oversee the organization of the surplus. These elites invented systems of recording to ensure the surplus, as well as peace and security. This long historical chain of events set the stage for the emergence of cities in Mesopotamia: the urban revolution.

Childe's thesis assumes that the urban revolution in Mesopotamia was the product of four inextricably linked factors:

1. *Population.* Increased numbers encouraged by the agricultural surplus.
2. *Organization.* An increasingly complex division of labor, particularly the evolution of ruling religious and secular elites to organize the surplus and a variety of specialists such as craftspeople, metallurgists, and scribes.
3. *Environment.* A hospitable physical setting, such as a fertile river valley, capable of producing an agricultural surplus.
4. *Technology.* Innovations that first brought food cultivation and food surplus and gradually led to such inventions as the wheel and writing.

Thus, according to the Childe thesis, the earliest cities resulted from the interaction between these demographic, environmental, social, and technological factors, easily remembered by their acronym, POET.

Childe uses the term "revolution" on purpose to emphasize a total transformation in a very short period of time. It is as if a chemist slowly added ingredients to a test tube until suddenly the mixture was just right to produce a sudden transformation into a new compound.

What were the Mesopotamian cities like? And how well do they fit the several definitions of a city discussed earlier? The case of ancient **Ur**, the largest of the Mesopotamian cities, is instructive.

The population of Ur was large compared with that of any settlement that preceded it. At its height, Ur's population may have numbered as many as 34,000 within the walled city itself and perhaps as many as 360,000 in "Greater Ur" (Sjoberg, [1960] 1965:36–37). Ur was densely settled. The total area within the wall and moat in 3000 BCE was 220 acres, and the entire population was compressed into this space.

The population of Ur was socially heterogeneous, reflecting a well-developed system of classes and specialization of function. Wide differences in wealth and power existed between elites and the rest of the population. There were also finely-graded occupational divisions, including full-time soldiers, herders, artisans, and musicians. Cuneiform clay tablets from Ur record the specialization of labor at the royal palace: gatekeepers, cooks, stewards, servants, messengers, a harem official (hence, a harem), and a royal cupbearer (Adams, 1966:143).

Using conventional criteria, then, Ur may be defined as a city. It was a relatively large, dense, and heterogeneous community. Ur also qualifies as a city in terms of market functions and urban culture. It served as the marketplace for an extended region. Artifacts unearthed at the site show trade with countries as far away as Egypt, Armenia, and Oman in the Persian Gulf. Culture in Ur also advanced to high levels. The city itself was a handsome, planned area with wide streets and large civic buildings. The dominant architectural feature was a **ziggurat**—a pyramid with stepped sides central to the religious functions of the community. Further, residents developed writing, an accurate solar calendar, musical instruments, fine art, and handicrafts.

Reflecting on how radically different Ur and other cities in the Sumer region were from the scattered, humble farming villages that preceded them, Childe generalized about what distinguishes any early city from such villages: 10 criteria, deducible from archeological data (Box 4.1). These criteria remain influential—and controversial.

BOX 4.1 CHILDE'S CRITERIA

How to Distinguish an Early City from Other Forms of Human Settlement

1. Larger size and denser population (Ur and other Sumerian cities contained 7,000–20,000 persons by 3000 BCE).
2. Classes of nonfarming specialists, including artisans, merchants, administrators, and priests, all supported by the agricultural surplus.
3. Taxation and capital accumulation (taxes or tithes paid to gods or kings, who concentrated the surplus).
4. Monumental public buildings, such as the stately temples of Sumer with their ziggurats.
5. Ruling elites or classes who absorbed, accumulated, and organized the surplus.
6. Exact sciences, needed to predict, measure, and standardize (e.g., arithmetic, geometry, astronomy).
7. The invention of writing or scripts, enabling the "leisured clerks" to elaborate the exact and predictive sciences.
8. Specialists in the arts, supported by the surplus.
9. Long-distance trade in vital materials.
10. Community membership based on residence alone, rather than kinship.

Source: Adapted from V. Gordon Childe. 1950. "The Urban Revolution." *Town Planning Review* 21:9–16. Published in Liverpool at the University Press. Reprinted by permission.

In other words, Childe set out his own list of prerequisites for urban life. All existed in the Mesopotamian cities by definition, for he deduced them from archeological evidence.

COUNTERVIEWS ON THE ORIGIN OF CITIES: TRADE, THE SACRED, AND THE SPIRIT OF THE PEOPLE

Childe's evolutionary thesis dominated scholarship throughout his lifetime. His views became conventional wisdom. It was generally assumed, for instance, that agriculture was invented as populations started to increase—that is, as a response to social stress or, alternatively, as a response to shrinking natural resources or environmental pressure. In addition, it was assumed that cities emerged after a long linear sequence: from nomadic wanderings to agricultural villages to cities.

Recent discoveries, however, pose new questions about when cities arose. These findings are causing archeologists to radically revise their theories. Here we'll consider a few of the leading competitors to Childe's thesis, including a still-emerging theory.

Shortly after Childe's death in 1957, Kenyon's findings at Jericho upset conventional wisdom about the slow progression of agricultural settlements. Later, in 1961, at Çatal Hüyük, archeologist James Mellaart dug deep into something Childe said could not exist: a Neolithic city.

The settlement lies in south central Turkey about 250 miles from Ankara. It is situated on a high mountain plain, not in a fertile river valley. Environmentally, Çatal Hüyük was not particularly favored. In Neolithic times a freshwater lake nearby may have made its environment somewhat more fertile but certainly far less so than the swampland of Mesopotamia.

Çatal Hüyük's population was probably 5,000–6,000 (Mellaart in Todd, 1976:122). Since the mound from which the settlement is being excavated covers only 32 acres, it was densely settled.

While Çatal Hüyük had a somewhat heterogeneous population, there is no evidence of anything like the elaborate class structure in the Sumerian cities. Distinct skeletal types unearthed show that at least two different racial groups inhabited the settlement. Religious buildings suggest the existence of a priestly class, and art and trade artifacts suggest some social differentiation and specialization of functions. But this is far removed from the elaborate Mesopotamian social structure with a royal cupbearer.

Does Çatal Hüyük qualify as a city in terms of its cultural level? In the judgment of Mellaart, it "shines like a supernova among the rather dim galaxy of contemporary peasant cultures" (Mellaart, 1967:77). Representational and abstract wall paintings include striking scenes of bulls, people, and cattle; and one macabre room is decorated with vultures and decapitated human beings. Other artifacts reveal rather subtle clay-baked seals and fine obsidian daggers. But there was no writing. Thus, by Childe's standards—which placed great weight on the invention of writing—Çatal Hüyük falls short of city culture. But in Mellaart's view, it was a stellar cultural achievement even when compared with some cultures today.

Çatal Hüyük would qualify as a city under Weber's definition, for it was a market center. Çatal Hüyük apparently carried on brisk trade with its neighboring region.

In *The Economy of Cities* (1970), the late, much lamented amateur urbanist and professional iconoclast Jane Jacobs described New Obsidian, the "first city." Jacobs's first city is an imaginary creation, but she drew heavily on the discoveries and theories of Mellaart. In fact, New Obsidian closely parallels Çatal Hüyük. Mellaart, the patient archeologist taking years to sort through the dust and rubble, is more cautious about constructing theories than Jacobs. Yet their ideas on the possible role of trade in Çatal Hüyük are similar.

Jacobs's **trade thesis** turns Childe's thesis on its head. In her imaginary scenario, the city becomes the independent variable, explaining the development of agriculture—not the reverse. Moreover, factors that Childe stressed as vital in setting the stage for the urban revolution (a favorable environment, technology, a large population base, and elaborate social organization) are relatively unimportant in her vision. *To Jacobs, the first cities arose because of trade.* Location was a key factor; early cities had to be located near the source of prized goods such as salt and obsidian. And they had to be situated along trade routes that bypassed geographical barriers.

In Jacobs's scenario, the survival of the first city dwellers, the New Obsidianites, was based on exchanges of vital commodities for food from their trading partners, not on agriculture. Furthermore, Jacobs believed that agriculture was invented by ancient city dwellers and diffused by trade. In her view, then, intensive farming didn't lead to the development of cities. To the contrary, *agriculture developed because of cities.*

If correct, the trade thesis does overturn Childe's thesis. It implies that agriculture was not an absolute prerequisite for the rise of cities. It also implies that Childe's notion of slow evolutionary development—a Darwinian concept whereby each stage of life represents an advance over the previous stage—is wrong. In other words, some cities could have been established as cities from the start, without a gestation period of several millennia and without the

linear progression from nomadic wandering to food production to settled village to city. Finally, the trade thesis calls into question Childe's list of 10 criteria as universal.

Both Childe's evolutionary thesis and Jacobs's trade thesis are called into question by a third and competing view of city origins and growth: the sacred meanings-symbolic thesis. In this view, both Childe's thesis and Jacobs's thesis are incomplete because they neglect *nonmaterial* factors in city development.

Urbanist Lewis Mumford, representing this third viewpoint, wrote that

> early [people's] respect for the dead, itself an expression of fascination with [their] powerful images of daylight fantasy and nightly dream, perhaps had an even greater role than more practical needs in causing [them] to seek a fixed meeting place and eventually a continuous settlement.
>
> *(1961:6–7)*

Mumford states that practical needs did draw families and tribes together in campsites, but "the very reason for the city's existence" was sacred in nature: "The first germ of the city, then, is the ceremonial meeting place which has 'spiritual' or supernatural powers" that are endowed with a "cosmic image" (10).

Other scholars in this tradition (e.g., Fustel de Coulanges, [1864] 1955; Adams, 1966) emphasize the idea that a strong ideological core, holding together early urbanites in a sense of community, is a key variable in the origin or growth of cities. In this third view, then, what brought people together in settlements in ancient times had to do with much more than physical survival and economic subsistence. As Mumford put it, "fixed landmarks and holy meeting places called together, periodically or permanently, those who shared the same magical practices or religious beliefs" (1961:8).

Using the religious-symbolic thesis, it could be argued that Çatal Hüyük was a shrine city, attracting the faithful. Its central purpose was to serve as a holy meeting place. If so, many materialist social science theories are called into question, for materialist theories assume that culture (including religion) is a *dependent* variable, reflecting the material base of culture, not an independent variable.

A variant of the religious-symbolic thesis centers on an early Neolithic site near Urfa in southeastern Turkey. Named Göbekli Tepe, this site contains the world's oldest-known stone temples, dating to before 9000 BCE. (The site was discovered in 1963 and has been excavated since the mid-1990s.) Göbekli Tepe's mere existence calls into question the long-held theory that agriculture preceded the construction of big buildings. That is, it contradicts the Childe thesis.

Archeologists say that Göbekli Tepe was created by hunter–gatherers, not settled farmers. One school of thought proposes that agriculture may have started there by chance: as a result of wild einkorn wheat, gathered to feed the temple and homebuilders, which took hold and then became the first domesticated cereal. (Göbekli Tepe is situated in a part of the Fertile Crescent that has been identified as a likely place of origin of flat, black-headed einkorn wheat, a type of grain which resembles the heads of crested wheatgrass.)

Many scholars agree with Childe: The domestication of cereal grasses (wheat) *preceded* permanent settlements, not the other way around. That is, wheat varieties were domesticated, allowing for permanent settlement. As a result, trade increased and wheat was introduced far and wide.

Yet, *if* Göbekli Tepe developed as a city of temples and houses before wheat was domesticated and before widespread trade occurred, then both Childe's evolutionary theory and Jacobs's trade theory appear limited in value—or wrong.

And there is yet another point of view, one that calls into question all the foregoing theories. Very briefly, this fourth view, associated with the late architectural historian Spiro Kostof, holds that neither religion, trade, environment, nor the evolution from agricultural village to city was a key to the origin of cities. Economics and environment, in this view, are not nearly as important as the *spirit of people*. According to Kostof (1991), city creating always entails an act of will by a leader or a collectivity.

AN EMERGING THEORY OF EARLY CITY MAKING

In recent decades, excavations in many parts of the world—present-day Russia, Israel, Peru, Guatemala, Iraq, and western Europe—have led archeologists to question, even reject, Childe's evolutionary thesis in favor of a still-emerging theory of the origin of cities. According to this emerging thesis, hunter–gatherers had permanent communities thousands of years *before* the development of agriculture.

Here's the thinking: Stone Age hunter–gatherers were not simple nomadic folk. To the contrary, preagricultural foragers such as the ancient Natufians tended to stay put, establish decision-making hierarchies, develop a system to store the food surplus, trade goods over long distances, and make a variety of tools. Preagricultural, settled foragers were often culturally complex, designing social and political hierarchies. In central Russia, for instance, burial grounds of these foragers reflect sumptuous graves for the rich, while the poor had almost nothing.

Why did these complex foraging societies appear? It's not yet clear. Some archeologists point to changes in climate—warmer and wetter weather as the glaciers retreated—that led to the explosive growth of wild grains, which in turn allowed people to store wild resources. Others think that hunter–gatherers settled down because their main food source (mammoths and other large animals) became extinct at the end of the Ice Age, forcing the preagriculturalists to develop more complex forms of social organization in order to store surplus food. Still others say that population increase is the key to understanding why settled communities began. In this view, more complex institutions developed to manage the food surplus and handle the increased social conflict that apparently accompanied non-nomadic life.

There is no consensus on how these early complex societies came about. But a consensus is developing around this new, still-emerging thesis: Long before agriculture, human beings developed complex cultures.

To conclude: If correct, the emerging thesis overturns Childe's conventional wisdom. Like Jacobs's trade thesis, it suggests that agriculture was not a prerequisite for the rise of cities, and that there was no slow evolution from nomadic hunting–gathering to farming to settled villages to an urban revolution and early cities. Recent evidence, particularly discoveries about the Natufian culture and ancient Andean civilization, does pose a serious challenge—perhaps a death knell—to Childe's evolutionary thesis. Yet, at this time, there is no definitive conclusion about the puzzles of early agriculture or cities. Indeed, when thinking about the origin of cities, it is wise to recall what Childe himself said on his opening page: "Almost every statement in prehistory should be qualified by the phrase 'On the evidence available today the balance of probability favors the view that'" ([1936] 1952:v).

One more thing: The debate about when and where cities really began is essentially a debate over two issues: (1) the definition of a city and (2) when and where *civilization* began. (The words "city" and "civilization" are connected not only through a common Latin root—*civitas*—but also by a belief that cities are produced by civilizations—and that great cities are produced by great civilizations). Indeed, the links between being "civilized" and "citified" go back at least to Mesopotamia. In the ancient city of Babylon, urbanites stood at the "gates of God," for their city was "a visible heaven on earth, a seat of the life abundant—in other words, utopia" (Mumford, 1966:13). Later, during the Roman Empire, to live meant to live in Rome.

TRYING TO CLASSIFY CITIES

The controversy about the emergence of cities is just one of many current debates about urban life. We now turn to another. This debate focuses not on the desirability but rather on the success of attempts to generalize about the nature of cities.

PREINDUSTRIAL VERSUS INDUSTRIAL CITIES (SJOBERG)

Sociologist Gideon Sjoberg thinks that cities share certain general features and can be classified accordingly. Sjoberg's central hypothesis is that "in their structure or form, preindustrial cities—whether in medieval Europe, traditional China, India or elsewhere—resemble one another closely and in turn differ markedly from modern industrial-urban centers" ([1960] 1965:4–5). In other words, Sjoberg looks for what he calls "structural universals" that typify preindustrial cities and distinguish them from modern industrial cities.

According to Sjoberg, all cities that utilize animate energy sources (human beings and other animals) rather than inanimate energy sources (steam, electricity, nuclear fission, etc.) are classified as "preindustrial." This means, in Sjoberg's view, that cities as diverse in culture and context as ancient Ur, the lost cities of Africa, Periclean Athens, seventeenth-century London, and modern Kathmandu "share numerous patterns in the realms of ecology, class, and the family, as well as in their economic, political, religious, and educational structures, arrangements that diverge sharply from their counterparts in mature industrial cities" ([1960] 1965:6).

Sjoberg argues that the demographic and ecological structures of all preindustrial cities are remarkably similar and transcend cultural boundaries. For instance, he notes the common features of small size (under 100,000 inhabitants), cramped conditions (because transportation and building technology are limited, people live close together in low-rise structures within walking distance of central facilities), widespread residential segregation by ethnic and occupational groups (the poorest castes or classes live farthest away from the city center, where the elites are concentrated; special quarters are set aside for particular economic pursuits, such as goldsmithing or pottery making), and little specialization in land use (due to the lack of industrial technology, such as rapid transit, which permits high specialization of land use in industrial cities).

Similarly, Sjoberg hypothesizes that class and status structures in all preindustrial cities have common features. These include a small elite, generally composed of political and religious leaders and sometimes military leaders, educators, and wealthy merchants; a large lower-class group of laborers, artisans, and small merchants; and, commonly, an outcaste group, such as India's untouchables or a slave population. These class and caste barriers were and are nearly impossible to cross, for social position is determined by one's family background rather than one's personal achievements, including education. Thus, he says, there is little mobility within the rigid social structure of preindustrial cities.

In many other areas—family, the economy, politics, communication, and the nature of education—Sjoberg

a   b

Fig. 4.3 SJOBERG'S PREINDUSTRIAL CITY. Essaouira, Morocco, displays many characteristics that Gideon Sjoberg associates with the preindustrial city, including (*a*) the hiding of female attractiveness and (*b*) governmental and religious structures that dominate the urban horizon. (© Andrée Abecassis, 1980)

notes recurring patterns among preindustrial cities. These range from the "purposive adulteration of goods" ([1960] 1965:211) and periodic public festivals that provide entertainment and promote social cohesion (though outcaste groups may be excluded) to the treatment of books as sacred and holy.

While tidy, how useful is Sjoberg's way of approaching the nature of preindustrial cities? Here, urbanists disagree. A few consider the concept of the preindustrial city a notable contribution to urban studies. The majority, however, attack Sjoberg for bringing more confusion than clarity to the study of preindustrial cities. Critics charge him with imprecision on concrete historical matters, technological

determinism, and neglect of the role that culture plays in city form and structure. In addition, urbanists point to a basic fallacy in Sjoberg's approach: He incorrectly treats all cities before the Industrial Revolution as dependent subsystems within larger feudal societies. This is historically wrong, critics hold, pointing to such ancient cities as Athens, Rome, and Constantinople, which did not exist under feudalism, and such medieval cities as Venice, which were autonomous—not dependent subsystems within feudalism—to support their challenge. As one critic puts it, "The preindustrial city type lumps so many disparate societal systems [feudalism, capitalism, etc.] that its value as an operational instrument seems nullified" (Cox, [1964] 1969:26). Or, in plainspeak, it is useless.

In 1996, decades after the publication of *The Preindustrial City* (1960), Sjoberg and his wife responded to some criticisms lobbed at his typology (see Sjoberg and Sjoberg, 1996). They stood by his typology as useful (see Chapter 6).

A SAMPLER OF CITIES

Despite Sjoberg's later defense of his typology, his critics are convincing. Thus, we will not use his dichotomy to examine the wide variety of cities and urban cultures created over the millennia, including *Lost Cities of Africa* (Davidson, [1959] 1970) and *Victorian Cities* (Briggs, 1963). Instead, here's a sampler of various sorts of cities through time and space.

THE GLORY THAT WAS GREECE

"Frankly, Scarlett, I don't give a damn" may be the best-remembered exit line of the U.S. cinema. Delivered by Rhett Butler (Clark Gable) in *Gone with the Wind* (1939), it signals more than the hero's rejection of a woman. It brings down the curtain on a way of life embodied by Tara, the stately southern plantation house built during the Greek Revival period of architecture in the United States (1830–1860). In a nation moving toward industrialization after the Civil War, Rhett Butler turns his back on a way of life: an agrarian way of life symbolized by Tara's perfect proportions and pure form in harmony with its natural setting.

Ironically, Greek templelike plantation homes such as Tara (and county courthouses and other public buildings constructed in the Greek Revival period) may be considered some of the many expressions of antiurban tendencies and thoughts in the United States. "The Greek temple," one architectural historian notes, "does not really want to get along with other buildings in a street, but to stand free outside....As revived, it demonstrates the puristic instinct to the utmost" (Scully, 1969:64–65). What's ironic is that the original ancient Greek temples and public monuments crowned the glory that was Greece—an urban glory—and celebrated city life.

In ancient Greece, monumental public buildings—theaters, stadia, gymnasia, and temples—were erected to enrich the beauty of the city. Consistent with the Greek emphasis on collective civic endeavor (detailed in Chapter 6), private houses were small and unpretentious. The Greeks devoted their energy to public institutions such as the *agora* (literally, "the place where people get together"), which dominated the city center. The everyday life of ordinary Greek citizens focused on the *agora*: a mixture of markets, courts, temple shrines, and government buildings. Here, Greeks of the fifth century BCE could get fish, discuss their leader Pericles's policies toward Persia, pay tribute to their gods and goddesses, and gossip.

In Greek cities before the fifth century BCE, an **acropolis**, such as Athens's famous Parthenon, dominated the city (Figure 4.4). Built on hills with commanding views, the acropolis consisted of a fortified palace, temple, and fort complex. Later, as the Greeks evolved democratic institutions, the acropolis declined in importance.

Cities built during the height of Greece's glory—the democratic period, particularly Periclean Athens—were constructed mainly on the principles of one architect–town planner: Hippodamus of Miletus (in Asia Minor), born in the fifth century BCE. Integrating architectural and planning principles, Hippodamus urged the use of simple, functional, and pure forms blended harmoniously with the natural environment. The outcome was not only a magnificent beauty but, according to Thucydides ([411 BCE] 1956:19), a sense of overwhelming power. In its own day, then, Athens's mix of a commanding acropolis and Hippodamus-inspired buildings was recognized as architecture that magnified the city's strength.

Ancient Greeks viewed their cities' monuments from streets laid out in a grid system. The grid, introduced earlier, was continued by Hippodamus in his city plans. (His grid plan may have influenced cities in Asia.) Centuries later, it became the dominant scheme in U.S. cities, appearing as early as 1641 in the plan of New Haven, Connecticut.

KYOTO: "THE MOST JAPANESE OF JAPANESE CITIES"

Most people associate Kyoto, Japan's capital from 794 to about 1867 (still considered the capital of traditional Japanese arts and spirituality), with

Fig. 4.4   THE PARTHENON IN ATHENS. (Alison Frantz)

Buddhist temples, museums, and the famous rock garden at Ryo-anji. So, when most travelers arrive at the railway station (there's no airport nearby), they are greeted by an unexpected, if not shocking, structure: a huge, postmodern rail station designed by Hiroshi Hara. Completed in 1999, the $1 billion station contains businesses (e.g., a theater, a hotel, a department store) and enormous public spaces set off by soaring expanses of glass and metal.

Not everyone appreciates Kyoto's postmodern railway station. Indeed, vocal protesters see it as an attack on the city's heritage. But, according to a Harvard art historian, a tension between modernity and tradition has been a recurrent theme in Kyoto's long history. From its beginnings in the eighth century until the present, Kyoto has struggled over its spatial pattern and its identity (Rosenfield in Gewertz, 2002).

Ironically, long known for its Buddhist temples and Shinto holy places, Kyoto's beginning as Japan's capital started with an effort to break away from religion. Government officials, fearing that Emperor Kammu's daughter wanted to turn over the throne to a Buddhist monk, moved the capital to Kyoto and limited the number of temples within the city limits.

Once known as Heian-kyo, "capital of peace and tranquility," Kyoto was the emperor's home for almost 1,100 years. Despite its status as capital (which, in Japanese, is equivalent to "the place where the emperor lives"), Kyoto was not always Japan's *political* powerhouse or capital.

Often called the "heart of Japan" and "the most Japanese of Japanese cities," Kyoto borrowed its original spatial pattern from China (and perhaps from Greece. A few Chinese archeologists [e.g., Fanren Meng, 1994, in Wang, n.d.:8] contend that the Greek grid pattern arrived in Asia via Alexander the Great's conquests and then was carried east by people of nomadic origin. But most scholars doubt it. See Ohji, 2003; Pstrągowski, 2003.) Most scholars think that Kyoto's form is based on a Chinese grid pattern in Chang'an (present-day Xian), the former imperial capital of the T'ang dynasty, 618–907 CE. (At its height

a

Fig. 4.5 THEN AND NOW IN KYOTO. Monuments to Kyoto's past, still standing, include (*a*) a traditional water temple. (*b*) The postmodern railway station represents the city's present, perhaps future. (*a, b* Arlene DeLeon)

during the T'ang dynasty, Chang'an probably numbered over 1 million inhabitants.)

Whatever its provenance—China and/or Greece— the *meaning* of the grid in Kyoto and Chang'an is very different from that in ancient Greek (and U.S. colonial) cities. Grids in imperial China and, by extension, Kyoto may "look to be in the spirit of Hippodamus," but they served a different purpose: social control, the central task of imperial government (Kostof, 1991:233). Maintaining both symbolic power and social control, the blocks in Asian grid cities were individually walled. They were constructed to help prevent the exit of settled populations.

In Asia, Chinese cosmology played an all-important role in laying out the grid: "The layout suggests that the City is the seat of a benevolent ruler whose reign is in harmony with the forces of nature" (Rosenfield in Gewertz, 2002). Other factors, particularly Chinese notions about the ideal city, geomancy (an ancient form of divination), and feng shui (see Chapter 17), influenced Chinese spatial patterns too.

As the home of royalty, Kyoto had a special and exalted position. Its orthogonal grid symbolized imperial power. Kyoto's Imperial Palace lay at a grand avenue's northern terminus.

Like Chang'an, Kyoto is a *to-jo*, that is, a capital city protected by a castle wall and moat. A grid system of streets divided Kyoto into more than 1,200 blocks, all the same size. The entire area of roughly 6,000 acres was enclosed by a light earthen embankment and moat construction that served as protection for the city.

b

Fig. 4.5 (continued)

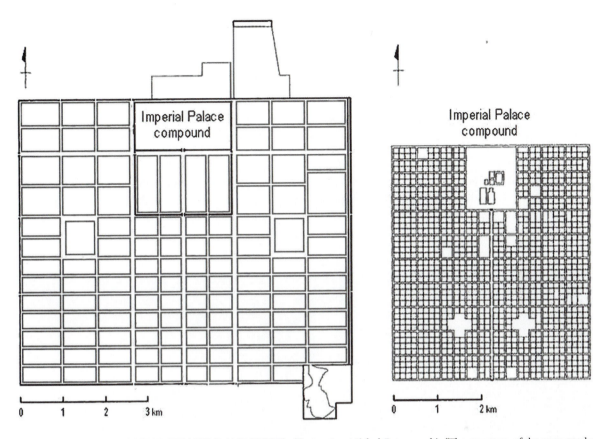

Fig. 4.6   PLANS OF ANCIENT CHANG'AN AND KYOTO. (*Source*: Jan Michał Pstrągowski, "The structure of the man-made environment—image and meaning," Fig. 7, p. 3: http://ws3-er.eng.hokudai.ac.jp/egpsee/alumni/abstracts/John.doc)

In brief, Kyoto's spatial grid carries spiritual as well as administrative/political meanings. One meaning can be summarized like this: *Tian-Yuan-Di-Fang*, translated as "the sky is round and the ground is quadrilateral (Ohji, 2003:193). Indeed, Kyoto is divided into four quarters, with east–west and north–south thoroughfares. This spiritual (and political) grid form in Kyoto imitates Chinese spatial forms, particularly that of Chang'an.

Little remains from early Kyoto, particularly the city's glorious Heian period (794–1185 CE). Fires, wars, and the passage of time have taken their toll. Yet, most think that Kyoto's early attempt at urban planning remains modeled on imperial Chang'an and is reflected in the city's street patterns.

Because Kyoto was not bombed in World War II, visitors today can sense the city's medieval past if they walk down streets lined by wooden structures where Kyoto's artisans, courtiers, merchants, and samurai once lived. And they can also sense the present, if not the future, at the railway station (Fig. 4.5b).

FROM ROME TO MEDIEVAL EUROPEAN CITIES

For complex reasons, the glory that was Greece faded (see Chapter 6). It was later replaced by the grandeur that was Rome. The vast Roman Empire stretched from the Sahara and the Euphrates to Gaul, creating such grandiose structures as the Roman Forum; the Temple of Bacchus at Baalbek, Lebanon; and the Pont du Gard near Nîmes, France.

What produced and sustained this vast empire and its sparkling cities, particularly its jewel, Rome? According to the eminent Belgian historian Henri Pirenne ([1925] 1956), commerce was the key. Roman civilization was built on trade, and the Mediterranean Sea was the crucial element in Rome's maritime empire. Even after the fall of Rome in 476 CE to the Goths, Vandals, and other invaders, trade continued on the Mediterranean and the economy of the Mediterranean commonwealth, created by the Roman Empire, remained unified.

But in the seventh century CE, this long-lived unity and world order that had survived the fall of Rome collapsed. Islamic expansion changed the face of the world, spreading from the China Sea to the Atlantic Ocean. And in its wake, the Mediterranean Sea, which had for so long united the cultures of eastern and western Europe, became a barrier between them.

According to Pirenne, the closing off of the Mediterranean Sea by the Islamic invasion led to the stagnation of the old Roman cities. But by the twelfth century, conditions stabilized and western Europe was back on the road to economic progress: "[T]he new Europe resembled...more the ancient Europe than the Europe of Carolingian times....She regained that

Fig. 4.7 BUILDING THE IDEAL CITY, WITH A LITTLE HELP FROM SOME FRIENDS. Christine de Pizan wrote *The Book of the City of Ladies* in 1405. It was the first book by a woman in praise of women. (She is considered to be an early feminist.) In one illustration published in the book, three celestial ladies—Reason, Rectitude, and Justice—help Christine construct the ideal city, a City of Ladies. (Photo: Ruth Wardrop of copy of the illustration [from the original Harley manuscript 4431, folio 290] in the British Library, London)

essential characteristic of being a region of cities" (Pirenne, [1925] 1956:73).

Pirenne painted a picture of many medieval towns built around the physical shell of an ancient Roman city. These towns contained an old *burg* (walled fortress or town) occupied by a Catholic bishop or other religious officials but were surrounded by a new burg, a fortified area for storing goods plus living quarters for traders.

It was in twelfth-century towns operating as autonomous trading centers—Venice and Bruges, for instance—that a new merchant class acted as a catalyst, pushing forward economic and social change. Unlike the vast feudal masses of western Europe, people in these autonomous cities were not tied to tradition. The secular, commercial towns encouraged innovation and entrepreneurial activity.

Residents of commercial suburbs were referred to as "burghers" or members of the "bourgeoisie" (from the root *burg* or *bourg*). From their origins in the twelfth century as a fledgling merchant class, they came to dominate England and other nations in the throes of the Industrial Revolution in the eighteenth century. By the nineteenth century, the word "bourgeoisie" had turned into a contemptuous epithet and the overthrow of this class had become an objective of revolutionary intellectuals like Karl Marx and Friedrich Engels.

MUSLIM CÓRDOBA, SPAIN: "THE ORNAMENT OF THE WORLD"

Following Pirenne, the keys to Rome's success were trade and commerce. Later, the merchants of Venice and other secular, commercial towns encouraged innovation and entrepreneurial activity, which helped to ensure their success.

But tenth-century Córdoba (Arabic, قبطرق Qurtuba), Spain, suggests another model of cultural vitality and economic prosperity. What follows is a brief history of this sophisticated city from its beginnings to its glorious period centuries ago. Today, Córdoba is but a shadow of its former self. Yet, with a population of over 320,000 in 2005, it remains very much alive.

By the eighth century, the borders of the Islamic empire had spread, filling almost exactly the area of the former Roman Empire in the second century. By the tenth century, Muslim-ruled Córdoba was arguably the richest and most sophisticated city in western Europe. (At the time, Constantinople and Baghdad were leading cultural centers of the eastern medieval world.) By 936, Córdoba was considered by many to be the most civilized place on earth. As Pirenne suggested, not until the twelfth century did cities in western Christendom begin to reach comparable levels.

Córdoba's ascent began in May 756 when half-Berber/half-Syrian Abd al-Rahman won a battle outside the city walls, founded the Umayyad dynasty in Spain, and became the new governor of al-Andalus (Andalusia), Spain, the westernmost province of the Islamic world. This battle, according to Iberian scholar Maria Rosa Menocal (2002:8), "decisively changed the face of European history and culture."

It was here in Córdoba, called "the ornament of the world" by a tenth-century Saxon nun, where Umayyad Muslims crafted a new culture: a culture of tolerance among Muslims, Jews, and Christians. In the process, a distinctive Andalusian identity was forged out of intermixed cultural origins, intermarriage, and the adoption of the Arabic language by the *dhimmi* (Arabic for the protected "peoples of the book"—Jews and Christians, both Abrahamic monotheists like Muslims), who were culturally assimilated into Arabic-Muslim Spain but not forced to convert to Islam.

Córdoba under the Umayyads was famed not only for its running water and noble gardens but also for its 70 libraries (the biggest containing about 400,000 volumes), 900 public baths, and 80,000+ shops. Moreover, it was home to Arabic poetry, scientific learning, and intellectual opulence. At its height, the city was home to perhaps 500,000 inhabitants. (Only 40,000 lived in Paris at the time). There were as many as 1,600 mosques, including Córdoba's great (and surviving) monument, *La Mezquita* (the Mosque), begun by Abd al-Rahman I in 786 on the sight of a Roman temple and a Visigothic church.

This vibrant city-based culture, according to Menocal (2002), was largely the result of Córdoba's Muslim rulers' tolerance toward Jewish and Christian cultures plus their patronage of art and culture. Others (e.g., Lapidus, 2002:310–314) focus on more economic and technological reasons, noting that

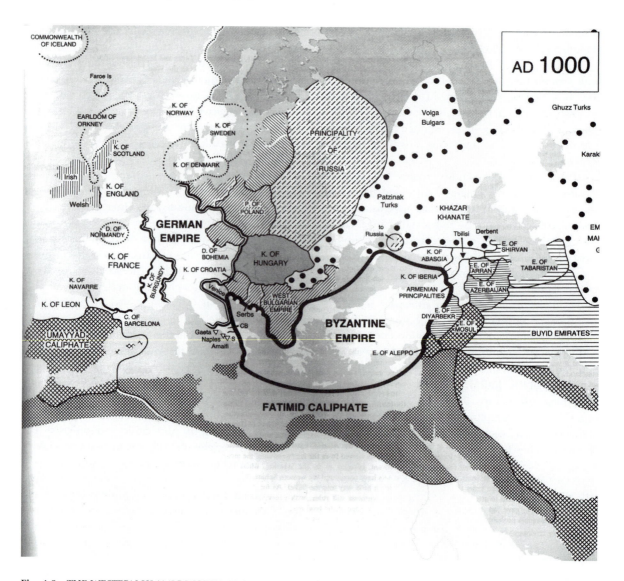

Fig. 4.8 THE WESTERN ISLAMIC WORLD ABOUT 1000 CE. This map shows towns and trade routes about the time when Córdoba—the jewel in the crown of European Muslim cities—had tarnished. (*Source*: adapted from Colin McEvedy and David Woodroffe, illustrator, *The New Penguin Atlas of Medieval History*, rev. ed. New York: Penguin, 1992, pp. 51 and 57)

during this era Arabic-Muslim Spain had entered a phase of commercial prosperity (based in part on the Byzantine navy's loss of control over the western Mediterranean), significant growth of international trade, and irrigation agriculture that led to the cultivation of pomegranates, cherries, and other valuable crops (Lapidus, 2002:316).

Whichever, the "ornament" soon rusted. Internal conflicts (e.g., hostilities between urban and provincial merchant elites, internecine Muslim warfare) led to the collapse of Umayyad rule by 1030. The descent of Córdoba accompanied the Umayyad's fall. Córdoba soon became only one of about 20 petty warring governments throughout Arabic-Muslim Spain.

Yet the spirit of Córdoba lives on. As described by Madeleine Albright (2006), former U.S. secretary of state, "the Córdoba process" seeks to find common threads among the three Abrahamic religions in order to better understand issues—for example, Jerusalem—not merely as issues of real estate but as spiritual concerns also.

MEXICO CITY: IMPERIAL CITY, COLONIAL CITY, MEGALOPOLIS

On June 8, 1325, the Aztecs started to build their capital city, Tenochtitlán, in the center of an enormous lake in present-day Mexico City. Why there? Because, according to legend, Huitzilopochtli (left-handed hummingbird and war god) appeared in a vision to the Aztec chieftain, telling him that the Aztecs' new homeland would be on the island in Lake Toxcoco. When the Aztecs reached the island, the god said they were to look for an eagle devouring a snake while perched on a cactus from a rock or cave, surrounded by water. There, they should build their city. (An eagle perched on a cactus with a snake in its beak remains Mexico's national symbol.)

In about 200 years, the Aztecs—led by some extraordinary leaders and their disciplined warriors, combined with well-heeled craftsmen and traders—conquered surrounding tribes and expanded their empire geographically to distant lands. During this time, their capital, Tenochtitlán, grew to an estimated population of 200,000, outgrowing their city-island (*Aztlan*) home. To deal with the need for more space, the Aztecs connected the city-island to the mainland via causeways that ran next to dikes; these dikes protected agricultural floating gardens (*chinampas*). Canals, which ran between the floating gardens, conveyed traffic through the city.

In 1518, the Aztecs' imperial capital, Tenochtitlán, was a city of great magnificence. It was comparable to great cities anywhere in the world. The most visible landmark of the city's vast urban infrastructure was the *Templo Mayor* (Main Temple), a double pyramid dedicated to Tlaloc (god of water and rain, key to the crop cycle) and Huitzilopochtli. The Main Temple, Tenochtitlán's central religious center, also represented the cosmic center of the universe to the Aztecs. Other important Aztec temples were dedicated to Quetzalcoatl (hero-god, father of civilization) and Tezcatlipoca (god of destiny).

Conquistador Hernán Cortés (1485–1547) and his Spanish invaders captured the city in 1519. They took Aztec Emperor Montezuma II hostage. Aside from technological and military advantages, including armor-clad horses and crossbows, the Spanish warriors brought smallpox, which devastated the Aztec population.

When the invaders came, what did they find? According to Cortés himself (1972:104), in letters back to the king of Spain, Tenochtitlán was as large as Córdoba with wide streets and plazas where "every sort of vegetable" and "many sorts of fruit" and a wide variety of silks were readily available. There were an estimated 200,000 inhabitants in Tenochtitlán when Cortés and his conquistadors arrived. Then, a smallpox epidemic wiped out an estimated 170,000 (Reader, 2004:182–185). Indeed, the population of the entire basin fell from about 1.5 million to fewer than 100,000 in the century after the Spanish Conquest.

After completely defeating the Aztec Empire in 1521, Cortés destroyed most Aztec buildings and constructed a new, colonial Spanish city atop the ruins. Perhaps symbolically, Cortés built his home atop Montezuma's palace and a cathedral atop the Aztec temple. Later, after a battle in 1692, Spanish settlers destroyed most Aztec art in the name of Christianity.

Like other Spanish colonial cities, the new European-style city, now called "Mexico City," followed a grid pattern. The cathedral and the principal administrative buildings were built around a central plaza, known today as the "Zócalo." (From Aztec times until the present, the Zócalo has been the hub of the city.) Elites, most of whom were appointees from Spain, lived in large homes and palaces on streets running off the Zócalo. Poor people lived farther away or slept in the streets. Native Americans tended to live in hut villages at the city's edge.

Mexico City soon became the most important settlement in Spain's American colonies, "New Spain." It became a key military outpost, an administrative center, and an economic powerhouse: the base for exporting mineral and agricultural wealth from the Americas to Spain.

Spanish colonial rule of Mexico lasted 300 years, from 1521 until independence in 1821. During most of that time—and long after—Tenochtitlán remained buried under colonial Mexico City. In 1790, digging for water pipes uncovered two Aztec sculptures near the Main Temple, but excavation was minimal. However, in 1978, electrical workers made a major archeological find near the Zócalo, spurring excavation of Tenochtitlán's ruins below Mexico City's streets. As a result, some Spanish colonial buildings were razed, revealing the Templo Mayor. Ever since, people have been visiting the dig as well as the Templo Mayor Museum that opened in 1987.

In population terms, Mexico City in 1900 was only a little larger than it was in 1519. But explosive growth, both in land expansion and in population, changed that quickly: Surrounding communities and rural areas were absorbed into the metropolitan area, and the population increased from 250,000 around the turn of the twentieth century (in a 29-square-mile area) to 3.2 million by the early 1950s (in a 150-square-mile area).

The metropolitan area's rapid growth and unchecked sprawl resulted in or exacerbated a variety of conditions, including poor housing, lack of public services, massive joblessness, high infant mortality rates, malnutrition, inadequate sanitation, violent crime (e.g., 3,000 kidnappings in one recent year), traffic congestion, police corruption, and uncertain water supplies. Nonetheless, in 2000, a leading political party introduced a new nickname for Mexico City: *la Ciudad de la Esperanza* ("The City of Hope").

Metropolitan Mexico City is now a giant megalopolis, perhaps (estimates differ) the second largest in the world, population-wise. By 2003, the metro area's population topped 18.7 million. Based on a number of sources, including the United Nations, Mike Davis (2006:31) estimates that 27 percent in the inner city and 73 percent in the rest of Mexico City's metro area are slum dwellers.

And what of the future? According to Juan Ramón de la Fuente, a former Mexican minister of health and later head of Mexico's largest university, the challenges facing the country (and thus Mexico City, where more than an estimated 50 percent of the nation's population live) can best be met by becoming "more competitive in the global economy." This goal, he said, depends on more education:

> Over the next 30 years, Mexico's working age population will increase by nearly 50 percent. The country must capitalize on this population shift in order to become more competitive in the global economy. The key to meeting this challenge is to educate more of the young people who will soon be part of the working age population.
>
> *(Fuente,* **2005)**

Others disagree. For one, Nobel Prize–winning economist Joseph E. Stiglitz believes that increased education is important but "not enough." According to Stiglitz (2006), globalization should be reshaped to make it more democratic and to help countries such as Mexico, one of the three members (along with the United States and Canada) of the North American Free Trade Agreement (NAFTA):

> Countries trying to compete are repeatedly told to increase labor-market flexibility, code words for lowering the minimum wage and weakening worker protections.
>
> Competition for business puts pressure to reduce taxes on corporate income and on capital more generally, decreasing funds available for supporting basic investments in people and the safety net. And international agreements, such as Chapter 11 of NAFTA [a controversial provision concerning investment that, critics say, gives multinationals the right to undermine local, state, and national governments' health and environmental regulations]...have been used to short-circuit national democratic processes....Coping with globalization entails recognizing both the consequences of globalization and the limitations in the standard responses. Increased education is important, but it is not enough.
>
> *(Stiglitz, 2006)*

Stiglitz is not alone. Indeed, there are some unexpected critics of globalization. These include the never-known-as-a-radical-rag the *Wall Street Journal.* On May 24, 2007, the *Wall Street Journal* headlined its two-page report "Unexpected Results: Globalization Has Widened Income Disparity." According to *International Herald Tribune* columnist William Pfaff (2007:9), this widening of the income gap was unexpected—and probably unwelcome—news to the editorial writers of the *Wall Street Journal*, "whose unswerving position has always been that it is anti-capitalist and anti-American to suggest that globalization might have ruinous consequences for the lives of millions of poor workers in countries like Mexico and even China, as well as in the United States." Pfaff (2007:9) also notes that many European thinkers believe globalization is the most "profoundly destabilizing force the world has experienced since World War II," tied to radicalization in the world's poorest countries.

MANCHESTER, ENGLAND: SYMBOL OF THE NEW INDUSTRIAL CITY

Beginning in the late eighteenth century, a series of technological changes in textile machinery in England made possible large-scale, mechanized, capital-intensive industry unlike anything the world had previously seen. In two generations, textile workers who labored on hand looms in their cottages were replaced by an urban-industrial proletariat toiling in giant spinning factories. Many other sectors of the British economy also experienced the Industrial Revolution. Water and steam power replaced hand labor, machinery grew in complexity, and the small-scale familial workplace was replaced by massive industrial establishments.

Engels noted that in 1760,

> England was a country like every other, with small towns, few and simple industries, and a thin but *proportionally* large agricultural population. Today [1844] it is a country like *no* other, with a capital of two and a half million inhabitants; with vast manufacturing cities; with an industry that supplies the world, and produces almost everything by means of the most complex machinery; with an industrious, intelligent, dense population, of which two-thirds are employed in trade and commerce, and composed of classes wholly different.
>
> *([1845] 1950:15)*

"Composed of classes *wholly different*." In Engels's view, that was the key. The bourgeoisie, or capitalist class, formed a relatively small, privileged group. In contrast, a large, oppressed mass—the industrial proletariat—was developing. "What is to become of these destitute millions," Engels asked, "who consume today what they earned yesterday; who have

created the greatness of England by their inventions and their toil; who become with every passing day more conscious of their might and demand with daily increasing urgency their share of the advantages of society?" (17). Engels's prescription was socialist revolution.

Manchester is often taken as the symbol of the new industrial city, and few were neutral about it. Like the Chicago painted by Nelson Algren (Chapter 1), "Manchester forced to the surface the problems of 'class' and the relations between rich and poor" (Briggs, 1963:93).

Like Chicago in the 1890s and early 1900s, some saw Manchester as a grand city, a symbol of progress and civilization. Engels did not deny the grandeur of parts of Manchester, but he loathed the brutality of the city toward its working-class residents. And he connected "the marvels of civilization" for the few to the "nameless misery" for the many. The price paid for progress under capitalism, in Engels's view, was "brutal indifference," "unfeeling isolation," and "reciprocal plundering" (24).

Manchester was not what a city planner would call a planned community. But Engels thought that private forces—the workings of the capitalist economic system—had patterned the city and its environs in a certain fashion: to serve the interests of the bourgeoisie. Members of the capitalist class, living in villas and breathing the clean air of the suburbs, could catch a horse-drawn omnibus to work and ride along broad boulevards, walled off from human misery by the shops of the petty bourgeoisie. They did not even see the working-class slums.

In many ways, Engels's writing on Manchester prefigures the work of later urban sociologists, as we shall see in Chapter 5. According to Engels, the new urbanites

> crowd by one another as though they had nothing in common....The brutal indifference, the unfeeling isolation of each in his private interest becomes the more repellant and offensive, the more these individuals are crowded together....This isolation of the individual, this narrow self-seeking is the fundamental principle of our society everywhere, [but] it is nowhere so shamelessly barefaced, so self-conscious as just here in the crowding of the great city. The dissolution of mankind into monads, of which each one

has a separate principle, the world of atoms, is here carried out to its utmost extreme.

([1845] 1950:24)

Thus atomism for all, crushing poverty for wage earners, and the marvels of civilization for those who owned and controlled the industry that made Manchester and other English towns great—such was, in Engels's view, the new industrial city in the capitalistic society.

A dissenting view: Recall from Chapter 2 what Lewis Mumford said about "slum, semi-slum, and super-slum" in Manchester. According to Mumford, even Engels didn't realize "the fact that the upper-class quarters were, more often than not, intolerable super-slums" (1961:465). In this view, there were few marvels of civilization for any class to enjoy in Manchester or other industrial powerhouses: The new industrial cities were just as intolerably ugly, overcrowded, and unsanitary for the rich as for the poor.

HUIS TEN BOSCH, JAPAN: THEME-PARK CITY

Huis Ten Bosch, Japan, is neither industrial, ugly, unsanitary, nor overcrowded. Quite the opposite. This postindustrial theme-park town, opened in 1992, is named for a palace of the Dutch royal family in the Hague. A faithful replica of the Dutch royal residence, Huis Ten Bosch (Dutch for "house in the woods") forms the centerpiece of the town. (Started in 1645, the "real" palace became home to many rulers, including the king of Prussia, Napoleon Bonaparte's brother, and Queen Beatrix of the Netherlands.) Indeed, the whole town is a faithful replica (or imitation, depending on your viewpoint) of a seventeenth-century Dutch town. And, like nearly 40 percent of the Netherlands, the town is built on reclaimed land.

Mr. Yoshikuni Kamichika, the founder of Huis Ten Bosch, constructed the town using Dutch city planning, Japanese technology, and Japanese–Dutch history. The small island of Hario-jima in Omura Bay, the home of Huis Ten Bosch, was formerly a Dutch trading post when only the Dutch were allowed to conduct trade during Japan's period of national isolation (1600–1868).

An online ad for the theme-park town touts Huis Ten Bosch as a throwback to a romanticized, preindustrial enchantment:

Just outside Nagasaki, travelers can enter a time machine that takes them to another world—the enchanted countryside of 17th-century Holland. Here canals wind between replicas of gracious historic buildings, and visitors can wander through parks....

Visitors say they're impressed by the ambiance of this provincial Dutch town of yesteryear. Attention to detail (even the bricks were imported from the Netherlands) is a hallmark of this ersatz Dutch community: From nostalgic sounds of carillons and music boxes to sweeping views of windmills and 300,000 tulips, it recreates the sounds and smells of a Dutch village in the 1600s. A self-described English "road junkie" put it like this:

I found myself transported into beautiful rural Holland....I felt as if I had stepped out of Japan and into an Old Master canvas, depicting an age more noble.

(Blazdell, 1999)

Being transported to "an age more noble" indeed! The seventeenth century was the golden age of Dutch art, including Rembrandt, Franz Hals, and Vermeer. It was also a prosperous time for the Netherlands. During the seventeenth century, the Dutch extended their trade worldwide, including Japan.

Yet, like many theme-park towns, Huis Ten Bosch is faithful only to parts of the historical record—the uncomplicated, conflict-free parts. Decades of Dutch warfare and struggle against Spain and France are not depicted, for example. Neither are any negative impacts of the expansion of Dutch commerce and imperialism in south Asia during the 1600s.

Undoubtedly, its selective, sunny memory is one of Huis Ten Bosch's charms. After all, visitors do not travel to theme-park towns (e.g., Wauchope, Australia, a recreated timber town of the mid-1880s) primarily to learn history. No, they want to be entertained, to be happy, and to experience a romanticized past. They come to flee ugliness, overcrowding, street crime, slums, and slum dwellers. In a word, to *escape* the seamier side of life.

BOM BAHIA/BOMBAY/MUMBAI/"SLUMBAY"

A seaside megalopolis in western India, Mumbai (formerly known as Bombay) has a multireligious past and probably a similar future. Although Mumbai is majority Hindu (about 68 percent of the population), many other groups are represented, including Muslims, Buddhists, Parsis, Jains, Sikhs, Jews, and atheists. Over the centuries, Mumbai has been ruled by Buddhists, Hindus, Muslims, and Christians.

Part of the Buddhist empire in India under Emperor Ashoka (304—232 BCE), the city was later ruled by Hindus. Muslims took it by arms and ruled the city for more than 200 years: 1343–1543. Then, Roman Catholic Portuguese, who had already established trading centers in India, took the city by force, naming it "Bom Bahia" ("Good Bay" in Portuguese).

In 1662 Bom Bahia passed into the possession of the English king as a result of a marriage dowry. Shortly after, Bom Bahia (later corrupted to "Bombay") was leased by the English Crown to the English East India Company. The population quickly rose from 10,000 in 1661 to 60,000 in 1675.

By the mid-1600s, Bom Bahia was a multireligious stewpot. Aside from English Protestants, Catholic Portuguese, and local Hindus and Muslims, there were Parsis (followers of Zoroastrianism from present-day Iran, who came in the seventeenth century. Zoroastrian Towers of Silence and fire temples, built in 1672, are still visible today.)

First under the East India Company and then under direct British rule, Mumbai (then called Bombay) became an important trading center. (India had become the "jewel in the Crown" of the British Empire. Here, we focus on Mumbai, not colonial India or the East India Company's Raj. But a little history is worth mentioning: The British Crown took control of the East India Company in 1773. However, not until 1857, the time of the Sepoy Rebellion—or the First War of Independence, depending on whose side wrote history—did the Crown directly rule India.)

By the 1860s, Bombay thrived economically. Why? Key were new, industrial-era communications and transport, including a regular steamer service and rail service. Faraway events also played important roles, particularly the opening of the Suez Canal and the 1861–1865 war in the United States (the "Civil War," the "War of Northern Aggression," or the "War Between the States," depending on who writes history); the war increased western European and American demands for cotton. Indeed, during the U.S. war, Mumbai became the world's premiere cotton trading market.

After the Suez Canal opened in 1869, Mumbai became a busy seaport. (Textile mills and the seaport remained prime job centers for over a century.) Over the next 30 years, Mumbai grew into a major urban center, with a population reaching 1 million by 1906.

A century later, the city's population reached an estimated 13 million, living in an area of 169 square miles. With its surrounding suburbs, Mumbai (its name changed from Bombay to Mumbai in the 1990s) reached an estimated 20 million by 2006, making it the world's fifth most populous metro area by most accounts.

Now home of a diversified economy, including important commercial and financial institutions (Figure 4.9), state government, and "Bollywood" (the Hindi film and TV industry), the city and metro area continue to attract migrants from all over India. Like elsewhere, the bright lights of the big city nurture dreams of mere survival or a higher standard of living.

Mumbai also attracts international tourists. According to 1998 Nobel Prize–winning economist Amartya Sen, Mumbai attracts a particular kind of international visitor—sex tourists. Professor Sen writes that the government of his native India encourages sex tourism because it brings in so much foreign exchange:

> …mass recreational tourism fuels prostitution, [and the Indian] government has firmly set its sights on precisely this kind of tourism.…[T]he lure of the short-term foreign exchange gain seems far more promising than attempts to remedy the causative factors of poverty, inequality, and justice.…
>
> *(in Goldstone, 2001:66)*

(*Sidenote*: Mumbai is hardly alone here. Even better known for sex tourism are Phnom Penh, Cambodia; Bangkok, Thailand; and cities in the Philippines. In *Making the World Safe for Tourism*, Patricia Goldstone [2001:67] writes that in the 1990s prostitution emerged as a multinational growth industry, paralleling the growth of tourism. She notes that "Sex, after all, is the original cheap vacation.")

Fig. 4.9 A SUBURBAN BUSINESS CENTER, MUMBAI. This modern business–financial center is located in Bandra Kurla, outside Mumbai. Many multinational companies and banks have offices there. (Kiran Shroff)

Recently, Mumbai has attracted other controversial tourists: so-called reality tourists. Critics accuse them of practicing "poorism," not tourism. Just as visitors (and their money) have been attracted to Rio de Janeiro's *favelas* and Johannesburg's townships, so too have they come to Mumbai's sprawling slum, Dharavi. One British tour has been criticized for treating human beings like animals in a zoo. But one who took the reality tour wondered whether critics were embarrassed by the poverty exposed on the tour, not the tour itself.

India's financial hub, Mumbai contains India's most expensive real estate at its core (some of it more expensive, per square foot, than equivalent real estate in New York City). And Mumbai is a stewpot of cultures and subcommunities.

Perhaps because it is such a financial and sociopolitical powerhouse, Mumbai also attracts terrorists. These include bombers who killed more than 200 and wounded more than 700 on crowded commuter trains in 2006 and others, including suicide bombers, who killed hundreds more in late 2008.

Mumbai has long attracted visitors that many cities would rather not talk about: rats. Mumbai employs full-time rat catchers, including Behram Harda, a former Bollywood film dancer before his tenure (33 years in 2007) as a rat catcher. Reporter Anand Giridharadas (2007:2) suggests that "Behind

Fig. 4.10 DHARAVI SLUM, MUMBAI. (Kiran Shroff)

every great city there is, or perhaps ought to be, an obsessive, fearsome rat catcher [like Harda], toiling silent so that bankers can bank, film stars film and vendors vend."

Despite its rats and fearsome rat catchers, Mumbai enjoys a relatively higher standard of living compared to many Indian cities. But it has earned a lowbrow nickname: "Slumbay." Why? Because in 2006 over 50 percent—and perhaps nearer to 60 percent—of Mumbai's residents lived in "a multiplying labyrinth of slums, covering a third of the city and sheltering more than five million people in squalid conditions, with a shortage of water and toilets, a surfeit of disease and the constant odor of feces mixed with garbage" (Giridharadas, 2006).

One such slum, Dharavi, is located in the middle of Mumbai. Dharavi is arguably Asia's largest shantytown: a neighborhood with over 600,000 inhabitants, open sewers, and ramshackle residences, as well as many cottage industries. In the stinging words of Mike Davis (2006:92), mega-slums like Dharavi have achieved "densities comparable to cattle feedlots."

(For a vivid look at Dharavi, as well as changes there over time, particularly recent high rises, see the Oscar-winning film, *Slumdog Millionaire* [2009] based on the novel *Q & A* by Vikas Swarup [2005, 2008]. The film's title word "slumdog," a play on the word "underdog," lies at the heart of protests by some critics. Others criticize the film because it does not show the high level of organization in Dharavi. They say, for example, that small businesses and entrepreneurs thrive there, producing about half a billion dollars annually in receipts.)

Private developers want to change this. Some give slum dwellers free apartments in order to make room for more high-rise buildings for the wealthy: Under an inventive government scheme in Mumbai, worked out over many years in conjunction with activist slum dwellers, builders raze entire slum neighborhoods and use part of the land for new apartments (tenements) to house the original residents. However, many former slum dwellers don't like their new digs. The 225-square-foot apartments don't let much daylight in, and they are located far from open space and needed facilities but close to the garbage dump and its smells. Some planners fear they'll deteriorate into new, vertical slums (Fink, 2006).

Still, Mumbai's housing boom ties the housing of desperately poor shantytown dwellers to the housing of wealthy people who live in the highly profitable towers (built by developers on the rest of the slum dwellers' land). According to one reporter, the rich in the new towers and the poor (about 600,000 in 2006) in their free apartments are "separated by the Dickensian disparities of the new India" (Giridharadas, 2006).

Private developers plan to transform Mumbai's (and perhaps Asia's) largest slum, Dharavi, into a middle-class area. The new Dharavi will have modern apartments, industrial parks, and a cricket museum. However, some are skeptical. For one, the head of the National Slum Dwellers Federation fears the lack of involvement of Dharavi residents in the project (Jockin in Thanawala, 2006:A19). Others suspect the developers' motives; they fear that the vast urban renewal project is really an urban removal project aimed at transferring newly valuable land (thanks to Dharavi's proximity to airports and emerging commercial areas) to private hands.

Note: Making judgments about slums is risky. Slum life anywhere may *look* chaotic to outsiders. However, it may be highly structured. In Mumbai's slums, for example, various interests—economic, religious, caste, and political—are routinely taken into account. While conditions in Dharavi and other slums may be very difficult, even horrific, in the eyes of a non–slum dweller, life there may also be lively, animated by a *joie de vivre*.

Whether or not slums like Dharavi are rebuilt, Mumbai's future will probably include explosive urban growth—and slums (*zopadpattis*). As one geographer blogged,

> Despite all the attempts to remedy the slum problem of Mumbai, slums are still growing. The slum growth rate is actually greater than the general urban growth rate. (http://www.macalester.edu/courses/geog61/espencer/slums.html)

SILICON VALLEY

Like Mumbai, cities in California's Silicon Valley experienced dizzying growth in recent decades. But comparisons end there.

The prosperity and population growth of the San Francisco Bay Area's Silicon Valley—a 40-mile by 10-mile strip in Santa Clara County, part of the San Jose–Sunnyvale–Santa Clara metropolitan area—was fostered by the interaction of external and internal forces (Hall, [1998] 1999:450). These include (1) a build-up of national defense industries during World War II in the nearby San Francisco Bay Area; (2) pressure by the military to develop solid-state electronics for cold war weaponry; (3) a long-standing tradition of close industry–university relations (particularly at nearby Stanford University, long a leader in radio/electrical engineering and research); (4) at least hundreds of small, highly competitive firms, many of which were spin-offs from the "Silicon Valley maternity ward" (Miller and Côté, 1987:5); (5) a few special individuals, particularly Frederick Terman and two of his Stanford students, William R. Hewlett and David Packard; and (6) the macro-level shift from an industrial to a postindustrial information society.

Best known as the prune capital of the United States, the Santa Clara Valley—the future Silicon Valley—was mainly agricultural in 1950. Twenty years later, the valley had become a major industrial center, rooted in high-tech electronics. By 1970 most large U.S. semiconductor firms called the valley their headquarters.

According to city historian Peter Hall ([1998] 1999:423), the valley's growth from the 1950s

Fig. 4.11 GOOGLEPLEX. The corporate headquarters of Internet giant Google in Silicon Valley's Mountain View. *Note*: The name "Googleplex" is a play on words that computer geeks may recognize. (Leesa Curnan)

onward is based on the "industrialization of information." Birthplace of home computers, laser technology, cordless phones, and video, to name just a few innovations, Silicon Valley has attracted over 6,000 Ph.D.s, as well as countless venture capitalists, entrepreneurs who shepherded inventions to market, marketeers and support people, and thousands of electronics manufacturing firms. For decades, "Silicon Valley," a name coined in 1971 by a microelectronics newsletter editor, has been synonymous worldwide with innovation and a noncorporate subculture of long-working, free-wheeling geeks, particularly 20-something males in blue jeans, T-shirts, and running shoes, whose dogs sleep at their feet.

A data snapshot of Santa Clara County shows explosive growth. In 1940, the county numbered under 175,000 residents. Ten years later, there were just over 290,000. By 1960, the county had over 642,000 people; by 1970, over 1 million; by 1980, nearly 1.3 million; by 1990, nearly 1.5 million; and by 2000, nearly 1.7 million people. The U.S. Census Bureau predicts that growth will continue but more slowly: By 2020, Santa Clara County's population is predicted to increase to 2,007,500.

(*Sidenote*: AnnaLee Saxenian [in Whiting, 2006], a leading observer of the valley and dean of the University of Berkeley School of Information, predicted, wrongly, in 1980 that Silicon Valley would stop growing for various reasons, including the high cost of housing, traffic congestion, and the consolidation of the semiconductor industry. By 1989, when she completed her Ph.D. about the valley, she had changed her mind.)

Unlike Mumbai, neither high population densities nor enormous slum growth accompanied Silicon Valley's population explosion. Quite the contrary. Silicon Valley has a population density of 503 per square kilometer, compared to Mumbai's population density estimated at 29,000 per square kilometer. In 2000, fewer than 5 percent of families in Santa Clara County lived below the poverty line and the county enjoyed the highest median household income—$74,335—of any county in California.

In recent years, new Silicon Valley-type centers have been developing globally. Bengaluru, India, is exemplary. (In her 2006 book *The New Argonauts* [her

term for global commuters employed in the high-tech sector], AnnaLee Saxenian discusses Silicon Valley's seeding of new centers of entrepreneurship such as Bengaluru, Shanghai, Taiwan, and towns in Israel.)

Yet, the luster of Silicon Valley remains. Even after a serious economic downturn in the late 1990s and early 2000s, Silicon Valley expanded. Perhaps it is a combination of good weather, beautiful landscape, easy access to the ocean and mountains, a reputation for innovation and quirkiness, proximity to great universities and San Francisco, and a diverse population (in 2000, the county where Silicon Valley is located numbered 47 percent nonwhite—of these, 26% were Asian and Pacific Islander and about 24% considered themselves either Latino or Hispanic, of any race) that continue to attract U.S. and global migrants (*if* they can secure a U.S. visa, a post-9/11 concern).

A final note: One holiday is celebrated in Silicon Valley as well as Mumbai: India's Independence Day. January 26 (1947) was proclaimed a holiday by Santa Clara County's Board of Supervisors in 2005, reflecting the numbers and contributions of its Indian-born and/or Indian American residents.

SHANGHAI, CHINA

Unlike many Chinese cities, Shanghai's history is relatively short. Although its beginnings date to about 1,000 years ago, for centuries it was little more than a sleepy fishing, farming, crafts, and market community. By the early 1400s, there were an estimated 64,000 households. By the 1700s, the city prospered as a cotton-growing and garment-producing center during the Qing dynasty (1644–1911).

But it was not until 1842 that Shanghai entered world history. Before that, Great Britain smuggled opium into China, which led to great financial profits for the British—and exploitation, degradation, and addiction for many Chinese. China's Qing dynasty rulers responded by dumping opium into Hong Kong. This subsequently led to the Opium Wars between Great Britain and China, ending in China's humiliating defeat at the hands of better-equipped British armies. The spoils of victory included Britain's declaring Shanghai (and Hong Kong, among others) a "treaty port" under the Treaty of Nanking in 1842. By this treaty (and a supplemental treaty the following year), China was forced to open Shanghai to British trade and settlement.

Other countries soon demanded and got similar privileges. British, then French and American citizens were awarded small, autonomous zones (called "concessions") north of the original walled Chinese city. (During the 1860s, the American and British concessions were combined into the International Settlement.) These concessions were extraterritorial in nature that is, they were immune to Chinese law. (Officially, extraterritoriality endured until 1943, but it was essentially dead by the late 1930s.)

The architecture of the concessions reflected their settlers. Most chic was the French concession. It boasted beautiful, European-style, three- and four-storey residences. (Many stood until the 1990s, when more than 1,000 high-rises were built in the former concessions, dramatically changing the appearance and feel of Shanghai.) No concession was overcrowded, for there were only a few hundred foreigners by the late 1800s.

Soon after, however, Shanghai's International Settlement grew quickly, mainly as a result of another war and its aftermath: In 1895 Japan defeated China in the first Sino–Japanese War. Japan emerged from the war (fought over control of Korea) as another foreign power in Shanghai. Indeed, Japan built the first factories in Shanghai. Other foreign powers followed. Before long, Shanghai was not only the

Fig. 4.12 COFFEE OR TEA? Shanghai, a former tea-drinking city, now is swimming in Starbucks coffeehouses. (John Randall)

biggest financial city in the Far East but also a leading manufacturing center.

The spoils of the first Sino–Japanese War included China's being forced to allow both Westerners and the Japanese to invest directly in China. This led to increased foreign commercialization, industrialization, and foreign trade, as well as a substantial increase in Japanese residents. Shanghai quickly prospered. Or at least some residents did.

As the rich got richer, many Chinese got poorer—and even more exploited at the hands of foreigners and their own corrupt rulers. Resentment festered. Rebellion followed. First, in 1911, the weak Qing dynasty was overthrown. Then, a new Republic of China with Sun Yat-sen as president was born in 1912. Less than a decade later, in Shanghai, Chinese intellectuals formed the Communist Party.

Often, Shanghai is viewed as the birthplace of everything modern in China. It was in Shanghai where the first car was driven and where the first modern sewers were laid. It was also an intellectual battleground: Socialist writers and those considered "bourgeois" (for their romantic style and ideas) by socialist writers were fierce rivals.

Unsurprisingly, twentieth-century Shanghai was important intellectually and politically. One of China's premier universities, Fudan, was founded there in 1905. The Chinese Communist Party was founded there in 1921, and Communist revolutionaries staged an uprising in Shanghai in 1925. (Young Mao Ze Dong was a Party member.) At first, the revolutionaries supported Chiang Kai-shek's powerful Nationalist Party. But Chiang violently suppressed a Communist uprising in Shanghai in 1927. Thus, the uneasy Communist–Nationalist alliance (formed to reunify China and reassert Chinese sovereignty) fell apart.

Between the first Sino–Japanese War and World War II, Shanghai developed a distinctly Western character. It also experienced substantial commercial, cultural, and industrial development. And it continued to be an important seaport. Foreigners flocked to the prosperous and increasingly sophisticated city. While many, if not most, local Chinese lived in horrific poverty, foreign *tai-pans* (great merchants or tycoons operating in China) led a life of luxury and, in the eyes of many, self-indulgence.

By the 1920s and 1930s, global financial and commercial firms were operating in Shanghai. Foreigners listened to jazz at Shanghai's Peace Hotel, gambled, and visited opium dens, casinos, and other places of ill repute. (Rumor had it that gangsters controlled much of the illegal activities.) They looked up at the tallest buildings in Asia. More cars drove around its streets than the rest of China combined. Marines and soldiers from the United States, France, Italy, Great Britain, and Japan guarded the foreigners' peace and prosperity.

Before (and after) the Chinese Revolution in 1949, Shanghai's most famous landmark was known as "the Bund," a name derived from an Anglo–Indian word meaning a muddy embankment on the waterfront. The 4-kilometer-long Bund was home in the 1930s to Shanghai's centers of finance and commerce. European-style buildings lined the boulevard in the late nineteenth and early twentieth centuries, and it was here that ocean liner passengers first set foot in Shanghai. Today, its official name is "Zhongshan Lu Boulevard," but many still refer to it as "the Bund."

Whatever it's called—the Bund or Zhongshan Lu Boulevard—it retains much of its colonial atmosphere (Figure 4.13). Western banks and office blocks still dominate the boulevard. It remains home to many of Shanghai's tourist hotels and bars. Also, there is a feeling of spaciousness there, unlike most of contemporary Shanghai.

Although Shanghai developed a distinctly Western character, Japan's influence after the first Sino–Japanese War was considerable. Notably, it brought factories and settlers there. Further, Shanghai became a battleground between China and Japan. Japan won. The Japanese Navy bombed Shanghai in 1932, ostensibly to crush Chinese student protests. By 1937, after various "incidents," the Japanese invaded and occupied all Shanghai except the international and French concessions. (On December 8, 1941, Japanese troops occupied the International Settlement but not the French concession, which was never invaded. However, it was dissolved by Japan in 1942.)

To conclude: By the 1920s and 1930s, the once-sleepy fishing village of Shanghai had become the most glamorous and cultured (some said "decadent"

Fig. 4.13　THE BUND, SHANGHAI. (John Randall)

and "vice-ridden") city in all Asia, earning the nicknames "Paris of the East" and "Pearl of the Orient." (Popularly, Shanghai may be better known by some English speakers by a verb: "shanghaied." To be "shanghaied" referred originally to the long-gone custom of kidnapping sailors to serve on China-bound ships; now, more generically, it carries the sense of fraudulently or forcibly inducing someone to do something.)

What lay behind Shanghai's swift transformation between 1842 and the 1930s? In brief, geography, war, trade, colonial arrangements, and commercial/industrial development. (After the 1930s, the national economic policies of China and migration played key roles in the city's fortunes.)

First, geography. Shanghai, often translated as "on the sea," is strategically located in eastern China: It lies on a tributary of the Yang Tze near that river's mouth at the East China Sea, an ideal location for trade with Europe and America. (Contemporary Shanghai still benefits greatly from its location; it commands the entrance to the Yang Tze Basin, a heavily populated and economically important region in central China. Indeed, contemporary Shanghai is not only an important port and home of China's very modern stock market but also China's industrial, financial, cultural, and commercial center, poised to regain its 1920s–1930s status as East Asia's most cosmopolitan city.)

Next, war, colonial arrangements, and consequent commercial/industrial development. China's losses to Great Britain and Japan resulted in colonial arrangements that fueled investment and commerce in Shanghai. Aided greatly by its strategic geographic location, Shanghai became China's largest and most industrialized city as well as an important trade and cargo port.

In former times, as now, most residents of Shanghai were ethnic Han Chinese. Some Chinese minorities, as well as foreigners, settled there too. In recent years, substantial numbers of Chinese migrants from the countryside have come there.

(*Sidenote*: Historically, two major groups of refugees have also called Shanghai home. First, substantial numbers of Russians. They were fleeing revolution, civil war, or pogroms and settled there before 1920. So many fled to Shanghai that the Russian community was the second largest foreign group, after the Japanese, by the 1920s. Second, during World War II, European Jews found refuge from Hitler there. Shanghai was the only city worldwide that opened its doors—without conditions—to Jews, and an estimated 32,000 Jews settled in Shanghai in the late 1930s. Indeed, some say that Shanghai saved more Jews from the Nazi Holocaust than Otto Schindler and all the Commonwealth countries combined. Among the Shanghai Jews who later made their way to the United States were Hollywood movie mogul Michael Medavoy, pop artist Peter Max, and Jimmy Carter's treasury secretary, Mike Blumenthal. In 1941, the Japanese who ruled Shanghai, under pressure from their ally Nazi Germany, ghetto-ized Jews but refused Nazi requests to deport the Shanghai Jews.)

After World War II, Shanghai reemerged as China's most important domestic and international trading, banking, and port center. But in 1949 armed forces of Mao Ze Dong's new Communist government occupied the city and moved rapidly to downplay Shanghai's economic importance in the new nation. Foreigners left. Businesses left behind were taken over by the government. Government funds were redirected from Shanghai to use in other areas of the country. Why? Because the new Communist rulers disapproved of Shanghai, considered "sin-ridden" and corrupted by Western influence. They viewed it as a consumer haven tied to a worldwide capitalist economy.

From about 1949 to 1979, Shanghai's reign as the most cosmopolitan city in China, and arguably all of Asia, fizzled. Those years were difficult for Shanghai; it suffered from famine, the Cultural Revolution, and power struggles. But in 1979 Mao Ze Dong's successor, Deng Xiao Peng, initiated reforms that particularly benefited Shanghai. For example, Shanghai was designated as an economic development zone with an emphasis on foreign investment in 1984.

Beginning with economic reforms in the 1970s, Shanghai blossomed once again. Since 1990, the central Chinese government has relaxed regulations and lessened bureaucratic procedures, thereby encouraging foreign investment, commerce, and trade. Investment in Shanghai increased substantially, giving rise to a huge construction boom.

Retailing and industry also grew substantially. China's largest integrated iron and steel plant, for example, is located in suburban Shanghai. "Shanghai, Inc.," as the business model is widely known, is back in business with explosive growth, in terms of both population and commerce, inspiring dreams of a Chinese century.

Estimates of Shanghai's population vary widely. (Partially, this is due to problems in counting migrants and temporary workers, who often do not register with city authorities.) In 2003, Shanghai's mayor claimed the city's population had topped 20 million. However, other Chinese sources (e.g., Xinhua, 2006) say that the city's population in 2005 was millions fewer—about 18 million, including 4.38 million migrants from other parts of China. (Echoing the debate over immigrants in the United States and Europe, Chinese observers disagree on the role of city newcomers. One Chinese researcher at the Shanghai Academy of Social Sciences says that immigrants to the city have become "indispensable" to Shanghai's economy because they do things "local residents are not willing to do" [in Xinhua, 2006], but others blame migrants for increased crime and loud behavior. And some complain that they add to the city's congestion and crowding.)

As in Mumbai, local government is relocating some migrants to high-rises in suburban Shanghai areas. Some relocatees complain that while they have gained good plumbing, they have lost a sense of community.

Fig. 4.14 THE CRANES OF SHANGHAI. Cranes symbolize the city's go-go growth in the early twenty-first century. (John Randall)

A word about Shanghai's population and suburban growth: The suburbs of Shanghai have mushroomed since the 1970s. Former farmland has been converted to industrial, transportation, and residential uses. One massive development project is Pudong, a large area on the east bank of the Huangpu River, transformed from an older, industrial area into a modern city. Its aim is to relieve some of Shanghai's congestion and crowding.

While the exact number of residents in Shanghai (and its suburbs) remains disputed, this much is crystal clear: Shanghai is already one of the world's most populous cities. (Some expect it to be the world's largest city population-wise sometime soon.) And Shanghai continues to grow up, down, and across as well as population-wise: Construction cranes dot the landscape, while new underground stations and highways crisscross the city. (This renaissance began after the Chinese government chose Shanghai in 1990 to be the nation's economic powerhouse. Shanghai started its cultural rebirth and economic comeback. Construction boomed. Private business and foreign investment increased. So did personal incomes—for some.)

The city may soon reclaim its former crown as Asia's most cosmopolitan city. Yet, amidst the hustle and bustle, the prosperity and prestigious universities, the modern cultural institutions and the sophistication, Shanghai remains a city of contradictions. Poverty is as prevalent as new, glitzy tower residences.

Again, reliable poverty numbers are very hard to come by. The United Nations Development Programme (UNDP, 2005) noted that if Shanghai were a country, it would not score high on its Human Development Index, a composite index measuring a country's average achievements in three areas: longevity, knowledge, and a "decent" standard of living. (This index, developed by a former finance minister in Pakistan, takes for granted that it reflects "real" goals of development: not factories, highways, or more stuff but, instead, fuller lives and more options. See Lewis [1993].)

Globally, the bright lights of the city may exist primarily for those wealthy enough to enjoy urban amenities. That is the verdict of UN-HABITAT, a United Nations agency dedicated to working for "decent" housing for people globally. It notes that, although many people assume that urban populations are healthier, more literate, and more prosperous than rural populations, it is probably a false assumption. In general (not specifically Shanghai), UN-HABITAT (2004–2005) reports that slum dwellers in poor countries are often far worse off than their rural cousins. Still, that finding has not ebbed the flow of migrants from China's countryside to the city and suburbs of Shanghai (or in much of Africa), hoping for a better life.

U.S. URBAN ROOTS

SPECKS IN THE WILDERNESS

Now we turn back the clock. Let us consider preautomobile cities in the United States. We'll focus on just one colonial city: Philadelphia.

America's first European settlers founded tiny, compact colonial cities, "specks in the wilderness" (Bridenbaugh, 1938:467). Between their founding in the seventeenth century and the American Revolution, these first settlements matured into larger cities. Let's look at late eighteenth-century Philadelphia to get a feeling for the colonial city.

Historian Samuel Bass Warner, Jr. (1968), characterized Philadelphia on the eve of the revolution as a "private city." The vast majority of its 23,700 residents were artisans or independent shopkeepers, contracting out on a daily basis. A small merchant elite engaged in production and trade, and a small underclass of indentured servants, slaves, and hired servants toiled at the bottom of the heap. Most Philadelphians, however, were modest, independent businessmen (and their families) with a privatistic ethic.

Colonial Philadelphia, according to Warner, was a town of abundant opportunity. Workers were in great demand. People could find work, save money, and move into most trades, for the guilds had failed in their attempts to restrict access to their crafts. If there was great social mobility in Philadelphia at the time, what was its cause? Property ownership, in Warner's analysis.

The physical form of colonial Philadelphia was consistent with its social structure. The city was compact—a classic **walking city**. All points were easily accessible on foot. Blocks tended to be economically and socially mixed. The clustering effects of ethnic or occupational groups were not consequential.

The city's political structure also reflected the privatistic ethic. Citizens wanted little government. The formal city government consisted of a "club of wealthy merchants without much purse, power, or popularity" (Warner, 1968:9). Its only significant functions were to manage the market and run the local records court; there were no public schools, and there was no public water supply; most streets were unpaved. Philadelphia had independent commissions of assessors, street commissioners, city wardens (in charge of the night watch and street lighting), and a board of overseers for the poor. But these groups accomplished little. Warner concluded that things got done in Philadelphia less through formal government structures than through the clubbiness of a small community that functioned by a set of informal rules and power relationships (a common theme in urban government, as we shall see in Chapter 14).

Warner depicted a city of small-scale entrepreneurs, abundant opportunity, and social fluidity, without the geographic segregation that characterized Philadelphia (and other American cities) in later years. But he pointed out that Philadelphians were not socially or economically equal by any means. Indeed, the tax list for 1774 shows that the upper 10 percent of the taxpaying households owned 89 percent of the city's taxable property.

The little private city of Philadelphia described by Warner did not have the great extremes of wealth and poverty, the teeming slums, the unhealthy conditions, or the social discord of European industrial cities that emerged shortly thereafter. Nor did it have the urban problems of contemporary Newark, East St. Louis, or Detroit.

Indeed, most of the U.S. population at the time was rural. Only 5.1 percent of the population was classified as urban by the first U.S. census in 1790. Nonetheless, the predominantly rural intellectuals of the day generally disliked and distrusted the city. As cities grew larger, more heterogeneous, and less tied to rural ways during the nineteenth century, this animosity increased.

ANTIURBANISM OF THE INTELLECTUALS

"The mobs of great cities," wrote Thomas Jefferson in 1784, "add just so much to the support of pure government, as sores do to the strength of the human body." In this negative judgment, he was in good company; few American intellectuals liked cities. Jefferson's blast at city mobs in 1784 was indicative of his early antiurbanism. He disliked cities on medical, moral, and political grounds (White and White, [1962] 1964). Later in life, Jefferson's attitude toward cities changed.

One reason why the concentration of people in cities in eighteenth-century America was undesirable to Jefferson (and others) was purely medical. Periodically, yellow fever ravaged colonial cities, and Jefferson based part of his urban opposition on medical grounds.

But Jefferson's critique went much deeper. Jefferson was somewhat torn between the values of the country squire and those of the city gentleman. As a child of the Enlightenment, he enjoyed the good things of civilized urban life: art, literature, witty conversation, painting, science, and other "elegant arts." Yet he more dearly loved the simple pleasures of the country farmer. Further, he viewed great cities as "pestilential to the morals, the health and liberties of man" (in White and White, [1962] 1964:28).

Another basis for his concern was political stability. Jefferson's writings reflect a fear of the political consequences of city mobs. The words of Alexis de Tocqueville, a generation later, echo this fear. Tocqueville viewed the largest American cities in the 1830s with alarm, even predicting that the United States and other republics would perish from the

unruly, self-interested mobs of cities "unless the government succeeds in creating an armed force which, while it remains under the control of the majority of the nation, will be independent of the town population and able to repress its excesses" (in White and White, [1962] 1964:35). Similarly, Jefferson believed that a dispersed agricultural population, tied to the land and concerned with private property, was most conducive to political stability and personal freedom.

Jefferson's antiurban views survived decades of politics and travel to Paris. But late in life, they changed. During the War of 1812, Britain cut off imports from Europe and the United States, lacking industries of its own, suffered. Jefferson concluded that the United States must develop its own manufacturing (and, by implication, cities) rather than face dependence or want in time of war or national crisis.

During and after Jefferson's time, antiurbanism was a dominant attitude among U.S. philosophers, novelists, poets, and social critics. Transcendental poet and essayist Ralph Waldo Emerson reportedly shuddered when approaching New York City (population 200,000 by the 1830s). He wrote, "Cities force growth and make men talkative and entertaining, but they make them artificial" (in White and White, [1962] 1964:40). Accordingly, transcendentalists "prefer to ramble in the country and perish of ennui, to the degradation of such charities and such ambition as the city can propose to them." Henry David Thoreau carried the logic of the "cities corrupt—nature restores" philosophy to its logical extreme, repudiating cities, towns, and eventually the society of other human beings. Thus, while Jefferson disliked cities on political grounds, the transcendentalists attacked them on metaphysical grounds.

Meanwhile, major U.S. novelists and poets described the city as a bad dream. Edgar Allen Poe (1886:170) painted a surreal setting in which a nightmarish city, disembodied from space and time, is destroyed:

Down, down that town shall settle hence,
And when amid no earthly moans,
Down, down that town shall settle hence,
Hell, rising from a thousand thrones,
Shall do it reverence.

Similarly, Hawthorne, in *The Marble Faun* ([1860] 1950), described the streets of Rome as "uneasy," "evil," and "stony-hearted" and the city itself as "chilly," "gloomy," "melancholy," "sickly," "dreary," "filthy," and "foul."

U.S. writers, using nightmarish imagery, tended to set their fantasies in Europe, not the United States. But as the United States began to experience the first strains of industrialization and urbanization in the 1830s and 1840s, these authors looked with fear at the potential consequences.

How much do the views of novelists and philosophers count? What impact did they have on policymakers and the masses? Some argue that they had a great impact. For example, White and White ([1962] 1964) say that the antiurban bias of U.S. intellectuals and writers helped not only to shape the values and attitudes of people in the United States for generations but also to shift public-policy concerns away from cities.

FROM WALKING CITY TO STREETCAR SUBURB

The cities described in nightmarish terms by the antiurban intellectuals were small and compact by today's standards. Indeed, until the 1850s, even the largest U.S. cities could be crossed on foot in about 30 minutes, hence the name "walking city."

As we confront the effects of increased costs and decreased availability of energy on city life, historical studies of the relationship between transport technology and city form take on renewed interest. Here is one: Speaking in 1895, an observer, a Mr. Kingsley, noted the role of three new technologies: the trolley, bicycle, and telephone. Mr. Kingsley said that already they had added 5 to 15 miles to the radius of every large town (in Banfield, [1968] 1970:25). In other words, a change in transport or communications technology leads to changes in city structure, and no one can predict with certainty where they will lead.

The demise of the compact walking city can be traced to a series of innovations in transport technology. Trolleys, bicycles, and, later, cars expanded the limits of the walking city.

The centrifugal forces that ultimately destroyed the walking city were put into motion as early as 1829 when a New York City entrepreneur initiated the first omnibus route in the United States. A decade later, similar operations had spread to all major U.S. cities. Although some riders found buses uncomfortable and inconvenient, bus companies proliferated and ridership testified to the popular desire for improved transportation. Soon the omnibus was followed by horsedrawn buses on rails and commuter railroads, further accelerating the sprawl of the city.

But it was the invention of the electric trolley in 1886, coupled with that of the telephone in 1876, that wrought a major change in the structure of cities. These two inventions greatly increased people's ability to work in cities and travel to suburban homes, to live on the outskirts of town and communicate to central locations.

In his study of three Boston **streetcar suburbs** (1962), historian Samuel Bass Warner, Jr., noted that the electric trolley pushed Boston's urban fringe out to 6 miles in the 1880s and 1890s. By 1900, the old walking city had become primarily a region of cheap housing. Warner concluded that early streetcar suburbanization around Boston produced an urban area characterized by housing segregation, by both ethnicity and class. In addition, the new trolley technology made possible what many builders, large institutions, and upper-class homeowners wanted: the physical separation of work from residence.

To conclude: Despite Jefferson's lament, U.S. cities continued to grow apace in the nineteenth century, changing from colonial walking cities to more sprawling places with suburbs reached by streetcars and trolleys. Such technological innovations in the 1880s influenced the shape of housing patterns, as well as other social and political patterns.

ANOTHER LOOK

Looking back on this turbo-tour of several millennia of urban history, several themes emerge. First, scholars disagree on why and where cities arose. These disagreements have little to do with their disciplinary backgrounds. Clearly, archeologists differ among themselves, as do sociologists and historians. Their dissent turns primarily on (1) how they define cities and (2) the relative weights they assign to various factors associated with the birth and development of cities. Some scholars, notably Childe and Sjoberg, placed great emphasis on the role of technology. Others, such as Mumford and Kostof, stressed the role of nonmaterial factors such as spirituality in the development of human institutions. This split—between those who think that ideas and culture can act as independent variables in determining social and political institutions and those who see ideas and culture as dependent upon people's material existence—is deep and irreparable. And it extends to many aspects of urban scholarship.

A second theme concerns conventional wisdom: Today's truth can quickly become tomorrow's folly. New evidence often challenges or changes long-accepted explanations of urban-related phenomena. Such is the case with Childe's thesis. Thus, it is wise to consider all urban "truths" as tentative, not timeless.

A third theme concerns language and definitions. Often, scholars do not share a definition of a very basic concept, including that of a city. Perhaps the best strategy is to accept dissensus as a given and then try to understand how a particular theorist uses a concept.

KEY TERMS

Acropolis In early classical Greek cities, a combined palace–fortress–temple complex built on a defensible hill within the city.

Çatal Hüyük An early (perhaps the earliest) trade city, dating from about 9,500 years ago. It was located on high, arid land in present-day Turkey. Its economy was apparently based on trade in salt, obsidian, and other goods, not agriculture.

Childe thesis Evolutionary thesis about the origin of cities formulated by V. Gordon Childe. Childe argued that after a necessary agricultural revolution, cities emerged about 3,500 BCE in Mesopotamia. He linked the development of ancient Sumerian cities to a fertile environment, increasing population, the growth of social organization, and introduction of technology. Although it was once conventional wisdom, many now reject the notion that the urban revolution was a prerequisite for the development of ancient cities.

City No single definition exists. Definitions often assume a relatively large population, high population density, and heterogeneity in terms of job specialization. Alternatively, a settlement may be defined as a city if it performs certain market functions or cultural roles.

Jericho Ancient urban center in the Near East, located in mid-desert. Scholars dispute the claim that it was the first city.

Mesoamerica The area in which pre-Columbian (pre-1492) Indian civilizations flourished, now thought to begin about 600 BCE. It encompasses the southern two-thirds of mainland Mexico, Guatemala, Belize, a western strip of Honduras, El Salvador, the Pacific coast of Nicaragua, and northwestern Costa Rica.

Mesopotamia The Fertile Crescent region (in present-day Iraq), where some, notably V. Gordon Childe, believe the first true cities arose about 3500 BCE.

Streetcar suburbs First wave of U.S. suburbs resulting from improved transport technology during the last quarter of the nineteenth century.

Technology Tools and cultural knowledge used to control the physical environment to achieve practical ends. In Sjoberg's typology, it is the key variable in distinguishing city types. In Childe's thesis, it is one of four important variables (the T in POET) used to explain early city creation.

Teotihuacán Largest of the Mesoamerican cities, located on a high, relatively infertile plain near present-day Mexico City. At its height, its population may have reached 200,000.

Trade thesis One thesis on the origin of cities. Unlike V. Gordon Childe, Jane Jacobs and some others claim that trade, not agriculture, was the basis for the emergence of the earliest cities, notably Çatal Hüyük.

Ur Largest of the ancient Mesopotamian cities in the Fertile Crescent. It emerged in a fertile, swampy area of Sumer in lower Mesopotamia between the Tigris and Euphrates rivers. A well-planned, compact city of perhaps 34,000 persons, it served as a religious and organizational center and a distribution point for the agricultural surplus of a larger agricultural area.

Urban revolution Term used by the late archeologist V. Gordon Childe to refer to what he deemed profound changes in civilization that concurred with the rise of cities in ancient Mesopotamia.

Wadi-al-Natuf What some archeologists think was the world's first large, permanent habitat about 13,000–14,000 years ago in present-day Israel.

Walking city A city prior to the introduction of transport technology that expanded its outer limits beyond comfortable walking range. Prior to 1850, all American cities were walking cities: The edge of the urbanized area could be reached in a half-hour's walk.

Ziggurat Religious temple in ancient Mesopotamian cities shaped like a pyramid, with steps rather than smooth sides and a temple on top.

PROJECTS

1. **Urban history**. For the city in which you live (or a nearby one) and a city on another continent, identify and determine the location of key transportation routes and their history. For instance, when were major roads, trolley lines, and highways built? Have these cities been affected by water transport or air hubs? What effects on the present form of the cities are evident from these early developments?

2. **Urban history**. Select an older inner-city neighborhood. Walk through the area. First, differentiate the architectural styles of the houses: When were they built? For whom? Then, examine other buildings, such as churches and ethnic clubhouses, if any: What do their architecture and size say about the ethnic roots of the neighborhood? Do they indicate when ethnic groups arrived or were present in large-enough numbers with enough wealth to build a church or ethnic meeting place? Are these buildings still used for their original purposes? If not, what functions do they now serve?

3. **Urban history: Katrina and New Orleans**. Explore how a variety of voices—religious, ideological, scholarly, disciplinary, and/or artistic—describe the impacts of Hurricane Katrina on New Orleans in 2005. Who or what comes in for blame? What was the "official" explanation of post-Katrina events? What were the "unofficial" explanations? Compare and contrast at least three points of view, analyzing the bases of their possible disagreements.

SUGGESTIONS FOR FURTHER LEARNING

There has been an explosion of new evidence and theorizing about early human settlements in recent years. This outpouring continues as new sites are found, particularly in South America.

Many scholars, including V. Gordon Childe, note that environment is a key variable in the development of early cities and/or dominant civilizations. In *Guns, Germs, and Steel: The Fates of Human Societies*, Jared Diamond (New York: W.W. Norton, [1999] 2005) argues that environment played a key role in Western civilization's near-global hegemony. According to Diamond, history followed different paths for various peoples—not because of any biological differences among the groups themselves but rather because of differences among their environments. Further, Diamond claims, those who domesticated plants and animals early got a head start on developing writing, government, technology, weapons of war, and immunity to deadly germs.

Environment is one of four elements—population, organization, environment, and technology (POET)—named by V. Gordon Childe in his analysis of an urban revolution in Mesopotamia. Childe's now much-disputed notions are available in two of his highly-readable books: *What Happened in History* (Harmondsworth: Penguin, [1942] 1950) and *Man Makes Himself* (New York: Mentor, [1936] 1952).

Childe's thesis about the origin of early cities is far from the only historical debate about cities. In his now classic study, *The Urban Frontier: The Rise of Western Cities, 1790–1830* (Urbana: University of Illinois Press, [1959] 1996), urban historian Richard C. Wade put forth a thesis that turned then-conventional wisdom, Frederick Jackson Turner's so-called frontier thesis, on its head. In a nutshell, Wade argued that Turner got it backward: Urbanization in the U.S. West did not follow the farmer; it made the development of farming possible. Shades of similar debates about the earliest cities!

Anthropologist, professor, and winner of the MacArthur "genius award," Guillermo Algaze, representing accepted theory, thinks that ancient colonialism sprang—inevitably—from the early urban states. He thinks that Mesopotamia (as well as Teotihuacán, Harrappa, and Sumer) expanded in order to get resources and territory. His ideas are detailed in his influential study, *The Uruk World System: The Dynamics of Expansion of Early Mesopotamian Civilization* (Chicago: University of Chicago Press, 2005).

A CD-ROM for Macintosh or Windows, *Exploring Ancient Cities* (San Francisco: Sumeria, with *Scientific American, 1995*) offers an interactive tour of Petra, Teotihuacán, Pompeii, and Minoan Crete. It features textured maps, a 20- to 35-minute slide show of each society, and discussions of cultural features, such as architecture, in the ancient cities.

Former U.S. Secretary of State Madeleine Albright (on *The Newshour*, PBS-TV, May 10, 2006) discussed the "Córdoba process" as a tool in international diplomacy. It is named for the medieval Muslim city's culture of tolerance.

For a broad, interdisciplinary look at recent Mumbai, see *Bombay: Mosaic of Modern Culture*, edited by Sujata Patel and Alice Thorner (New York: Oxford University Press, 1997). It deals, inter alia, with Mumbai's architecture. Jim Masselos's *The City in Action: Bombay Struggles for Power in the 19th and 20th Century* (New York: Oxford University Press, 2007) presents 14 essays about the politics and socioculture of the city during the last 100 years. A provocative film, *Barah Aana* (2008), directed by Raja Menon, takes place in Mumbai. It recounts the stories of three migrants to the city, working as a chauffeur, a waiter, and a security guard, showing the separate realities of an affluent employer and poor servants who live nearly as two different species.

For U.S. urban history, see Howard P. Chudacoff and Judith E. Smith, *Evolution Of American Urban Society.* (Upper Saddle River N.J.: Prentice Hall, 2004). This text is particularly strong on the connection between technological change and the evolution of city form, social and cultural history, and urban politics.

Long before he became famous for his documentaries on 9/11 and the U.S. health-care industry, Michael Moore had a program on NBC-TV, *TV Nation*. In the first program, broadcast in July 1994, Moore toured Reynosa, Mexico, a town with over 200 *maquiladoras*, near the Texas border. Moore's bilingual guide explained that Mexican workers lived in slums, earned little, and could not pay for home mortgages or cars, all in stark contrast to the people from the United States who manage the plants.

REFERENCES

Adams, Robert M. 1966. *The Evolution of Urban Society: Early Mesopotamia and Prehispanic Mexico.* Chicago: Aldine.

Albright, Madeleine. 2006. Interview with Ray Suarez. *The Newshour*, PBS-TV (May 10).

Banfield, Edward. [1968] 1970. *The Unheavenly City.* Boston: Little, Brown.

BBC. 2001. "Oldest city in the Americas." (April 26): http://news.bbc.co.uk/2/hi/science/nature/1298460.stm

Blazdell, Philip. 1999. "Huis ten Bosch, Japan—September 1999." *Bootsnall Travel* http://www.bootsnall.com/articles/99-09/huis-ten-bosch-japan-september-1999.html

Bridenbaugh, Carl. 1938. *Cities in the Wilderness.* New York: Knopf.

Briggs, Asa. 1963. *Victorian Cities.* New York: Harper & Row.

Childe, V. Gordon. [1936] 1952. *Man Makes Himself.* New York: New American Library.

———. [1942] 1964. *What Happened in History?* Harmondsworth: Penguin.

———. 1950. "The urban revolution." *Town Planning Review* 21:3–17.

Cortés, Hernán, trans. A. R. Pagden. 1972. *Letters from Mexico.* London: Oxford University Press.

Cox, Oliver C. [1964] 1969. "The preindustrial city reconsidered." Pp. 19–29 in Paul Meadows and Ephraim H. Mizruchi, eds., *Urbanism, Urbanization, and Change: Comparative Perspectives.* Reading, Mass.: Addison-Wesley.

Davidson, Basil. [1959] 1970. *Lost Cities of Africa.* Boston: Little, Brown.

Davis, Mike. 2006. *Planet of Slums.* London: Verso.

Engels, Friedrich. [1845] 1950. *The Condition of the Working Class in England in 1844.* London: George Allen and Unwin.

Fink, Sheri. 2006. "Cities of the Poor: Mumbai." *The World*, WGBH-radio.

Fuente, Juan Ramón de la. 2005. "Education, competitiveness and reforms in Mexico." (April 7) (001/Events/spring2005/04-07-05-delafuente/index.html).

Fustel de Coulanges, Numa Denis. [1864] 1955. *The Ancient City*. Garden City, N.Y.: Doubleday, Anchor.

Gewertz, Ken. 2002. "Kyoto first city in series on art and architecture." *Harvard Gazette Archives*. www.hno.harvard.edu/gazette/2002/11.07/15-kyoto.

Giridharadas, Anand. 2006. "Free apartments in Mumbai, but not everyone is happy." *International Herald Tribune* (December 12).

———. 2007. "From Bollywood to the rat pack." *International Herald Tribune* (July 19):2.

Goldstone, Patricia. 2001. *Making the World Safe for Tourism*. New Haven, Conn.: Yale University Press.

Gutierrez, Miguel Angel. 2008. "Pyramid cave may solve ancient mystery." (July 3): http://news.aol.com/story/_a/pyramid-cave-may-solve-ancient-mystery/20080703150109990001?icid=100214839x1205165845x1200231716

Hall, Peter. [1998] 1999. *Cities in Civilization: Culture, Innovation, and Urban Order*. London: Orion Books, Phoenix.

Hawthorne, Nathaniel. [1860] 1950. *The Marble Faun*. New York: Arcadia House.

Jacobs, Jane. 1970. *The Economy of Cities*. New York: Vintage.

Kenyon, Kathleen M. 1957. *Digging Up Jericho*. New York: Praeger.

Kostof, Spiro. 1991. *The City Shaped: Urban Patterns and Meanings Through History*. Boston: Little, Brown.

Kostof, Spiro, Gregory Castillo, and Richard Tobias. 1995. *A History of Architecture: Settings and Rituals*, 2nd ed. New York: Oxford University Press.

Lapidus, Ira M. 2002. *A History of Islamic Societies*, 2nd ed. Cambridge: Cambridge University Press.

Lewis, Paul. 1993. "New U.N. index measures new nations' quality of life." *New York Times* (May 23): http://query.nytimes.com/gst/fullpage.html?res=9F0CE7DC1531F930A15756C0A965958260&sec=&spon=&pagewanted=1

Mellaart, James. 1967. *Çatal Hüyük: A Neolithic Town in Anatolia*. London: Thames and Hudson.

Menocal, Maria Rosa. 2002. *Ornament of the World: How Muslims, Jews, and Christians Created a Culture of Tolerance in Medieval Spain*. Boston: BackBay Books, Little, Brown and Company.

Miller, Roger, and Marcel Côté. 1987. *Growing the Next Silicon Valley*. Lexington, Mass.: Lexington Books.

Mumford, Lewis. 1961. *The City in History*. New York: Harcourt, Brace & World.

———. 1966. "Utopia, the city and the machine." Pp. 3–24 in Frank E. Manuel, ed., *Utopias and Utopian Thought*. Boston: Beacon Press.

Ohji, Toshiaki 2003. "Tojo in Asia and cosmology." Pp. 191–253 in Funo Shuji, ed., *Architecture History of Asian Cities*. Kyoto: Showado: http://www.spacesyntax.tudelft.nl/media/longpapers2/tsuyoshikigawa.pdf

Pfaff, William. 2007. "Debunking globalization." *International Herald Tribune* (June 5):9.

Pirenne, Henri. [1925] 1956. *Medieval Cities*. Princeton, N.J.: Princeton University Press.

Poe, Edgar Allan. 1886. *The Complete Poetical Works of Edgar Allan Poe*. Chicago: Belford, Clarke.

Pstrągowski, Jan Michał . 2003. "The structure of the man-made environment—image and meaning." Doctoral diss., Hokkaido University, Urban Engineering and Planning: http://ws3-r.eng.hokudai.ac.jp/egpsee/alumni/abstracts/John.doc

Reader, John. 2004. *Cities: A Magisterial Exploration of the Nature and Impact of the City from Its Beginnings to the Mega-conurbations of Today*. New York: Atlantic Monthly Press.

Saxenian, AnnaLee. 2006. *The New Argonauts: Regional Advantage in a Global Economy*. Cambridge, Mass.: Harvard University Press.

Scully, Vincent. 1969. *American Architecture and Urbanism*. New York: Praeger.

Shady Solis, Ruth, Jonathan Haas, and Winifred Creamer. 2001. "Dating Caral, a preceramic site in the Supe Valley on the central coast of Peru." *Science* 292:723–726.

Sjoberg, Gideon. [1960] 1965. *The Preindustrial City*. New York: Free Press.

Sjoberg, Gideon, and Andrée F. Sjoberg. 1996. "The preindustrial city: Reflections four decades later." Pp. 94–103 in George Gmelch and Walter P. Zenner, eds., *Urban Life*, 3rd ed. Prospect Heights, Ill.: Waveland Press.

Spencer, E. N. D. "Zopadpatlis." http://www.macalester.edu/courses/geog61/espencer/slums.html

Stevens, William K. 1988. "Life in the Stone Age: New findings point to complex societies." *New York Times* (national edition) (December 20):B5+.

Stiglitz, Joseph E. 2006. "Taming global capitalism anew:" http://www.thenation.com/doc/20060417/forum

Swarup, Vikas. [2005] 2008. *Q & A*. New York: Scribner's.

Thanawala, Sudhin. 2006. "Slums separate Bombay from its future." *San Francisco Chronicle* (October 12):A19.

Thucydides. [411 BCE] 1956. *History of the Peloponnesian War*, Books 1, 2, Vol. 1. Trans. Charles Forster Smith. Cambridge, Mass.: Harvard University Press.

Todd, Ian A. 1976. *Çatal Hüyük in Perspective*. Menlo Park, Calif.: Cummings.

UN-HABITAT. 2004–2005. "State of the world's cities." www.unhabitat.org

Wang, Tao. n.d. "A city with many faces: urban development in pre-modern China, c.3000 BC–AD 900." http://www.arkeologi.uu.se/afr/projects/BOOK/wangtao.pdf

Warner, Samuel Bass, Jr. 1962. *Streetcar Suburbs: The Process of Growth in Boston, 1870–1900*. Cambridge, Mass.: MIT Press.

———. 1968. *The Private City: Philadelphia in Three Periods of Its Growth*. Philadelphia: University of Pennsylvania Press.

Weber, Max. [1921] 1963. *The City*. Trans. and ed. Don Martindale and Gertrude Neuwirth. New York: Free Press.

White, Morton, and Lucia White. [1962] 1964. *The Intellectual Versus the City*. New York: Mentor.

Whiting, Sam. 2006. "Facetime: AnnaLee Saxenian on the future of informationists and admitting error." *San Francisco Chronicle* (October 29): CM3.

Xinhua, 2006. "Migrant wave drives Shanghai's population growth." (April 26): http//english.sina.com/China/1/2006/0406/72038.html

CHAPTER 5

URBANIZATION AND THE URBAN SYSTEM

URBANIZATION OF THE WORLD'S POPULATION

It was not until about the turn of the twentieth century that the first urbanized society came into existence: Great Britain. It became the first society in history whose urban population exceeded its rural population. (As noted earlier, at the time of the first U.S. census in 1790, only 5.1 percent of the population lived in cities.)

In 1850 no society in the world could be called urban. Only since around 1900 has there been a profound change in the number of cities worldwide, their size, and the *proportion* of the world's population that lives in (or around) them. Demographer Kingsley Davis (1965) called this profound change "the urbanization of the human population."

THE PROCESS OF URBANIZATION

Early cities were nothing more than urban specks in a rural world—and small ones at that. Ancient Sumerian cities and Periclean Athens had populations no larger than those of many contemporary suburbs. Moreover, Ur, ancient Athens, Teotihuacán, medieval Venice, and all cities before the Industrial Revolution accounted for only a tiny proportion of the population of their societies. In other words, being a city dweller and being urbanized aren't the same thing.

Urbanization refers to population concentration. The term typically refers to the proportion of the total population in a society or nation living in urban settlements. It can also refer to a rise in the proportion of urban residents within the society or nation. Finally, urbanization may also refer to the process of becoming urban in terms of social, technological, political, and spatial organization.

Urbanization should not be confused with city growth. Urbanization refers to the *proportion* of an entire society's or nation's population living in urban or metropolitan places. So, it is quite possible for cities to increase in population enormously without urbanization taking place. This can occur if the rural population grows as rapidly as, or more rapidly than, the urban population. For instance, both China and India have several of the world's largest cities, yet neither is an urbanized *society*, at least as of 2008.

Two factors are crucial in the urbanization process: (1) *out-migration* from rural areas to cities and (2) *natural increase* (population increase due to an excess of births over deaths). The movement of people from rural to urban areas can change the total proportion of people living in cities. Natural increase can also alter the demographic structure of a society. If birth rates are lower or mortality rates higher in cities than in the countryside, they may retard urbanization. In many eighteenth- and nineteenth-century cities, poor sanitation and health conditions led to just such a differential in mortality rates.

INDUSTRIALIZATION AND URBANIZATION IN WESTERN EUROPE AND NORTH AMERICA

Kingsley Davis (1965) concluded that between the sixteenth and eighteenth centuries, the average rate of urbanization was barely perceptible—about six-tenths of 1 percent a year for the European cities he examined. Since that time, industrialized nations in Europe and North America passed through a recognizable pattern of urbanization: an S-shaped curve, beginning slowly, moving sharply upward, then leveling off. In rural, preindustrial societies, urbanization proceeds slowly. Then, if the society experiences an industrial revolution, it shoots up. At the most advanced stages, it tends to level off.

Generally speaking, urbanization accompanied industrialization in western Europe and North America. Thus, when Britain became the first urban society in human history around 1900, rural migrants to the city were working in the factories and shops of an industrialized nation. This is not the case in many poor countries today.

URBANIZATION IN POOR COUNTRIES

Before examining the dramatic urban population growth in many countries of Africa, Latin America, and Asia, we should note that there is no agreed-on name for these countries. They are variously called "emerging markets," "underdeveloped," "less developed," "backward markets," "advanced developing" (e.g., Brazil, China), "modernizing," "economically dependent," "South," and "Third World." But **Third World** is outdated: Politicians once described anti-Soviet, industrialized nations as the "First World," the Soviet bloc as the "Second World," and nations neutral in the struggle between the Soviet bloc and the so-called free world as the "Third World," a term coined by Charles de Gaulle and used at the Bandung Conference in 1955. With the disappearance of the Second World, the term "Third World" became obsolete. Now it is often used to mean poor, underdeveloped nations. It is also used as a synonym for people of color.

Here, I use the term **poor countries** because so-called Third-World nations display enormous cultural richness and diversity, but they share an economic situation: mass poverty. (Of course, not everyone in a poor country is poor; some billionaires live and/or made their billions in poor countries. China is a prime example. Its numbers of billionaires will soon rival the U.S. number.) Similarly, the term "rich countries" is used instead of "First World."

Especially in poor Asian and African countries, cities are growing rapidly. Indeed, in Africa, the least urbanized continent, some cities double in population every 12 years. Urbanization in Africa is happening more rapidly than it did in western Europe's and North America's periods of rapid industrialization .

Chinese rural-to-urban migration is in a class by itself. More than 100 million people moved from the countryside to cities in just a decade, from the mid-1990s to the mid-2000s (TVE Madrid, 2005).

Many predict that the world's urban population will grow from 2.86 billion in 2000 to 4.98 billion by 2030. Most of this growth will occur in poor countries; high-income countries will account for only 28 million out of the expected increase of 2.12 billion.

Every year, 20–30 million of the world's poorest people migrate from rural to urban areas. Where do they go? Very often to mega-cities in poor countries such as Mexico.

According to Davis, a population boom, not rapid urbanization, is the primary cause of urban growth in poor countries. Others are not so sure. Dissenters argue that *overconsumption* in the rich countries, such as the United States—not overpopulation in the poor countries—underlies urban problems in the poor countries. They note, for example, that in 1990, one American used as much electricity as 200 people in China. But this ratio is quickly changing as China industrializes. Indeed, in terms of carbon emissions, China topped the United States for the first time in 2007.

There is wide disagreement about both the causes and the effects of urbanization in poor countries. There are three general perspectives: (1) modernization, (2) urban bias, and (3) economic dependence. Briefly, (1) modernization theorists believe that as traditional, agrarian societies modernize, they will experience rapid urbanization, a positive trend that should be encouraged. (2) Urban bias scholars and policymakers claim that government policies are biased in favor of metropolitan areas; these policies promote migration from rural area to city, a long-term negative effect in poor countries. Some claim that policymakers worldwide are promoting—not controlling—growth by wrongheaded policies such as subsidizing urban transport, energy, and water. (3) Economic dependence theorists argue that the capitalist world economy, dominated by the advantaged **core** powers (western Europe, the United States, Canada, and Japan) use areas on the **periphery** (poor, dependent countries such as Uganda, Ethiopia, and Bangladesh) and **semiperiphery** (middle countries, such as Argentina) as sources of cheap labor, raw materials, and environmental dumping grounds. In this view, development and underdevelopment are flip sides of the same coin: Industrialized countries became rich by exploiting poor countries. Foreign investment is an obstacle, not an aid, to balanced urban development. It forces farmers into cities by reducing the land available to them,

distorts urban labor markets, and increases the poor countries' dependence on the rich countries.

WORLDWIDE, THE PRESENT (AND FUTURE) IS URBAN

As of 2008, more than half the world's human population—about 3.3 billion people—lived in urban areas (UNFPA, 2007). Worldwide, urbanization is expected to continue on a massive scale, particularly in poor countries: By 2030, about 60 percent of the world's population will live in cities (UN-HABITAT, 2004–2005).

No doubt, the pace will only quicken. The United Nations (UN) Population Fund reports that the next few decades will see "an unprecedented scale" of urban growth in poor countries, notably Africa and Asia, where the urban population is predicted to *double* between 2000 and 2030. This growth is historic: "the accumulated urban growth of these two regions during the whole span of history will be duplicated in a single generation. By 2030, the towns and cities of the developing world [read "poor countries"] will make up 81 per cent of urban humanity" (UNFPA, 2007).

In 2003, worldwide, there were 39 cities with over 5 million people and 16 cities with over 10 million. If UN forecasts prove accurate, in coming decades there will be a *weekly* increase in the world's urban population of about 1 million persons. (Otherwise said, enough people will make the rural-to-urban move to build a new city the size of Ha Noi or Pittsburgh every 7 days.)

By 2020, it is estimated that the world's population will grow to at least 8.1 billion. Only 37 percent of the population will inhabit rural areas.

Globally, large cities (over 1 million persons) will absorb much of the population increase. (This is especially so in poor countries.) A few statistics show the dramatic growth: In 1900, 12 percent of the world's population lived in cities of more than 1 million; in 2020, 35.4 percent will live in cities of at least 1 million.

It is noteworthy that most **mega-cities**—giant metropolises of over 10 million inhabitants (originally defined as 7 million by the year 2000)—are located in countries facing seemingly unmanageable conditions. These include high rates of unemployment and underemployment; inadequate sanitation and water; unstoppable migration from rural areas based on the hope for opportunity; overloaded transportation systems; air, water, and noise pollution; and lack of housing.

Nairobi, the capital of Kenya, is exemplary. From 1950 to 1979, Nairobi grew 600 percent. By 1988, the city held about 2 million people, with over 250,000 living in rock-bottom poverty. Bread and sugar became unaffordable luxuries for countless slum dwellers. By 1999, Nairobi was home to an estimated 2.5 million people (http://www.citypopulation.de/index.html) with an estimated 78 percent of the population in some neighborhoods considered poor.

(*Cautionary notes*: Population statistics are often based on estimates. These can vary widely, primarily due to issues of data collection and definitions. Some

use "city" and others use "agglomeration." Typically, agglomerations include a central city and neighboring communities linked to it by continuous built-up areas or commuters. In addition, all city population data, particularly in poor countries, should be treated with extreme skepticism, including the data in Figure 5.2. Further, it is very hard to determine the population of metro areas. Some consider Seoul, South Korea (with a population that topped 10.2 million in the early 2000s), as the world's largest city in terms of population, followed by São Paulo, Brazil, with a population of just over 10 million. But other sources say that Greater Tokyo stands unrivalled at number one in terms of population. In 2006, the National League of Cities (2007) said that "the Japanese capital and its surrounding towns are home to an estimated

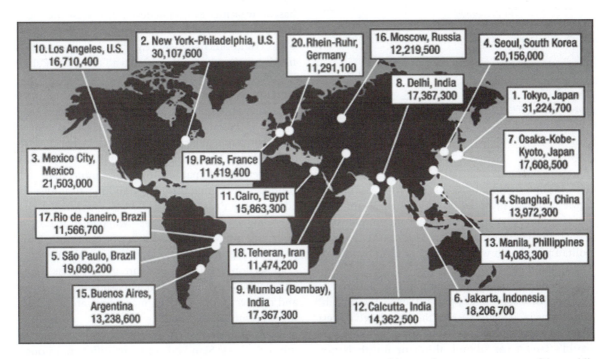

Fig. 5.2 (*a*) TOP 20 METRO AREAS WORLDWIDE, 2004: ASSESSMENT ONE. This map shows one assessment of the world's 20 most populous urban agglomerations in 2004. Mexico City ranks third here, but some sources rank Mexico City first or lower (see *b*). Today, more people live in cities and metro areas than outside them. This urban growth will continue: Before 2020, it is estimated that about 60 percent of the world's population will live in urban agglomerations. In recent years, the most explosive growth has occurred in poor countries. (Data courtesy the *World Gazetteer*; illustration Mike Shibao.) *Sources*: National Center for Atmospheric Research and the University Corporation for Atmospheric Research, June 2005, both part of the U.S. National Science Foundation (http://www.ucar.edu/communications/staffnotes/0506/mirage.html).

5.2b TOP 20 METRO AREAS (CITIES AND SUBURBS) WORLDWIDE: ASSESSMENT TWO

1. Tokyo, Japan	2003	34,997,000
2. Seoul, South Korea	2003	23,239,900
3. New York, United States	2003	21,578,900
4. Mexico City, Mexico	2003	18,660,000
5. São Paulo, Brazil	2003	18,628,400
6. Mumbai, India	2003	17,400,000
7. Los Angeles, United States	2003	17,262,700
8. Delhi, India	2003	14,146,000
9. Calcutta, India	2003	13,800,000
10. Shanghai, China	2003	13,417,700
11. Jakarta, Indonesia	2003	12,296,000
12. Buenos Aires, Argentina	2001	12,046,800
13. Teheran, Iran	2003	11,931,700
14. Dhaka, Bangladesh	2003	11,560,000
15. Beijing, China	2003	11,488,200
16. Rio de Janeiro, Brazil	2003	11,226,700
17. Osaka, Japan	2003	11,200,000
18. Karachi, Pakistan	2003	11,100,000
19. Cairo, Egypt	2003	10,834,000
20. Istanbul, Turkey	2003	10,834,000

Source: Statistics Finland, in Statistics Norway, *Statistical Yearbook,* 2006 (http://www.ssb.no/en/yearbook/tab/tab-054.html).

35.5 million people. By 2020, it is forecast that this figure will have increased to more than 37 million." But guesstimates can prove wrong. For example, in the 1990s, the UN estimated that Mexico City's metropolitan population would top 25 million by the year 2000. (It did not.)

Whether accurate or not, population statistics are limited. For instance, they give no sense of the health conditions in any city, such as those endured by residents of Mexico City and its metropolitan area—the world's largest (or second, third, or fourth largest, depending on definitions). These unhealthful conditions include some of the world's most polluted air. Mexico City's air has gotten worse, not better, over the years. Teachers there report that schoolchildren use shades of brown and gray, not blue, to paint the sky.

Is there any hope of improving living conditions in mega-cities? Some religious movements and activists think so. Let's briefly look at some urban religious movements, worth noting because they run counter to urban theory, before noting some activists' efforts.

In many places, the move from countryside to city has been accompanied by a growth of urban religious movements (UNFPA in Toler, 2007). These include Pentecostal Christianity in Latin America, radical Islam in the Mideast, and the Shivaji cult in India. Such movements are unexpected; they run contrary to urban theory, for secular values are most often associated with urban life. Perhaps these religious movements signal hope in the future. Or they could just as well signal the opposite: hopelessness on earth.

Whatever religious leaders preach, secular activists try to make a difference on earth. Activists at the U.S.-based Megacities Project believe that diverse metropolises such as Bangkok, Buenos Aires, and Beijing face many common challenges (e.g., housing poor people, moving garbage around) and that all can gain by sharing information.

Others, trying to foster global dialogue between urbanites and policymakers, are using "wikis" and other Web-based devices. Exemplary is Habitat Jam, an open conversation used to prepare for UN-HABITAT's 2006 World Urban Forum. The World Urban Forum had over 10,000 participants from more than 100 countries discussing innovative and practical ideas to address urban issues.

Many say that mega-cities—whether in rich or in poor countries—have something in common: Every poor city has a rich section, and every rich city has a poor section. Poor metropolitan areas such as Lagos, Nigeria, have rich areas such as posh suburban Ikoyi; and rich New York City has many poor areas, including the South Bronx.

Economic dependence theorists might explain the mix as follows: Standards of living differ enormously *within* a city. In part, these differences occur because a few high-paid managers in poor countries, working in global offices of multinational corporations and their subsidiaries, create a core inside the periphery or semiperiphery. Meanwhile, low-paid immigrants from poor countries, working in sweatshops of U.S. cities or cities in other rich countries, create peripheral areas inside the core. This brings us to a broader discussion of linkages between cities everywhere.

THE WORLD URBAN SYSTEM

GLOBALIZATION OF CITIES

Generally, theorists agree that San Francisco, Paris, Lagos, Lima, New Delhi, and Beijing have quite distinct histories and personalities yet confront many common practical challenges. Theorists also point to two forces that are *decreasing* cultural diversity among cities while *increasing* their economic interdependence: (1) the *globalization of cultural life*, including the production and diffusion of films, TV series, and news from multinational corporations (e.g., IBM, Sony, CNN, Time Warner), and (2) the *globalization of economic life*.

Cultural and economic life is becoming ever more globalized. At the same time, the feeling of cultural uniqueness can inspire people to fight legally or extralegally for a separate identity, as in the case of the Scots, Kurds, Tamils, and Basques, to name just a few examples.

The threat of economic or cultural loss can also lead to cultural protectionism. For example, the French curbed the import of U.S. movies in the early

a

Fig. 5.3 GLOBALIZATION VS.LOCAL TRADITION. Two store windows (a) in Cairo, Egypt, and (b) Amman, Jordan, are miles—and worlds—apart. (a, b Susan Hoehn)

b

Fig. 5.3 (*continued*)

1990s, and they tried (unsuccessfully) to ban English-language words from their commercial signs.

THE INTERNATIONAL DIVISION OF LABOR, OLD AND NEW

Citizens and scholars alike have been realizing that a very abstract concept—the internationalization of the economy and culture—is having a significant impact on Main Street. This consciousness of connection may be recent, but in the view of economic dependence theorists, the phenomena themselves are not: "For the past three centuries at least, world-economic, political, and cultural forces have been major factors shaping cities" (King, [1990]

1991:1–2). In this view, it was colonialism that shaped cities worldwide.

And, in this view, it was colonialism that created the **old international division of labor (OIDL)**. Using the example of British colonialism, here's how the OIDL worked: Peripheral colonies in Africa, India, and elsewhere in the British Empire produced primary products and raw materials (e.g., cotton, tea, rubber) for the core industries in Liverpool and Manchester and the dinner tables of London. In exchange, people in the empire got machine tools, cotton cloth, railway cars, and other manufactured goods from Britain (Taylor, 1985). Under this arrangement, Britain's largest cities grew rapidly in the eighteenth and nineteenth

a

Fig. 5.4 GLOBALIZATION OF CULTURAL AND ECONOMIC LIFE. (*a*) U.S. movies, often produced by multinationals such as SONY, are popular in many cities globally, including Riga, Latvia, and Shanghai, China. *Memoirs of a Geisha* (2005), advertised in Riga, is based on a novel written by an American; it tells a story about Japan. It was filmed in California and Japan with an international cast. (By the early 1990s, Hollywood had captured about 80 percent of the European film market. Some nations, including France, tried to protect their own movie industries from extinction—or, some say, their culture from corruption—by a system of quotas and subsidies.) (*b*) Even though slightly misspelled on the poster that adorns Shanghai's Grand Theatre, Bruce Willis's name and face are recognizable worldwide. (*c*) U.S.-style "french" fries (briefly dubbed "freedom" fries by some in the United States during the early years of the Iraq War) are popular in France. An ad for McDonald's, complete with golden arches, adorns nineteenth–century Parisian rooftops. (*d*) The Poitevin family of Montmartre in Paris celebrates the victory of its preferred U.S. presidential candidate in November 2008. ([*a*] Gesche Würfel, [*b*] John Randall, [*c*] Tim Teninty, [*d*] Jeff Berner)

b

Fig. 5.4 (*continued*)

centuries; their growth and prosperity depended on Britain's key role in the international economy. Conversely, by the 1930s, Britain's global role had declined greatly and, consequently, so did the economic fortune of its largest industrial and port cities.

By the late 1960s, the OIDL was replaced by the **new international division of labor "Needle"** an acronym coined by former San Francisco State student Erica Perkins, suggesting that people are knit together by the thread of global specialization. Here is a key difference between the old and the new: The OIDL depended on nation-states such as Great Britain; Needle depends just as much, or perhaps more, on transnational corporations. Already by the 1980s, the majority of the largest economic units globally were multinational companies, not nation-states.

In a nutshell, the thinking behind Needle is as follows: Global and local issues can no longer be separated because there is a new international division of labor. That is, cities everywhere are economically interdependent, linked by a network of giant transnational corporations that engage in production, exchange, finance, and service functions. Theorists of Needle (e.g., Henderson and Castells, 1987) say that Needle started happening in the 1960s as multinational corporations relocated manufacturing production from high-wage cities in rich nations to low-wage cities in poorer countries.

c

d

Fig. 5.4 (*continued*)

Let's take one industry—automobiles—to get an idea of how Needle works. The car industry dominated the industrial organization of rich countries after World War II. But the industry has been undergoing a crisis since the early 1970s, and automakers responded by restructuring their global operations. One result was that in the United States hundreds of thousands of jobs were lost, not only in car manufacturing but also in allied industries—steel, machine tools, electronics, and automotive components—that depend heavily on auto production. Detroit, Flint, Gary, and Pittsburgh are a few of the many cities that have experienced structural unemployment, underutilized plant capacity, and disinvestment.

After global restructuring, cars were partially manufactured at various lower-cost industrial sites all over the world, creating the "global factory." This restructuring was accomplished by a small number of large transnational or multinational corporations ("planetary enterprises," in the language of Barnet and Müller [1974]) that control the auto industry globally; by the early 1980s, 22 firms produced about 90 percent of all cars in the world (Tolliday and Zeitlin, 1987).

As a result of restructuring, it is now difficult to buy an "American car" or a "foreign" (a word long ago banished from CNN in favor of "international") car because so many vehicles are "world cars":

international hybrids or products of joint ventures. For example, Ford's Fiesta was designed as a world car to appeal to consumers everywhere and is manufactured on several continents. (Marketed worldwide, the Fiesta remains one of Ford's most successful cars: Over 10 million have been sold since 1976. An eighth generation of the car was projected for 2008. Other Ford cars have not done that well.) Before consumers' environmental concerns and global competition bedeviled Ford (and other U.S.-based auto manufacturers), Barnet and Cavanagh (1994:17) wrote that Ford "most successfully adapted to the post-mass-production era" in the 1990s by becoming the "most avid in trying to develop a car that can be sold anywhere in the world."

These data suggest that in an age of globalization, *multilocational, transnational firms are hard to identify as "American" or "not American," "Japanese" or "German" or whatever!* One observer notes that IBM is Japan's largest computer exporter, and Sony is the largest exporter of television sets from the United States. It is the world in which Brother Industries, a Japanese concern assembling typewriters in Bartlett, Tennessee, brings an anti-dumping case before the U.S. International Trade Commission against Smith Corona, an American firm that imports typewriters into the United States from its offshore facilities in Singapore and Indonesia (Rugie, 1998:196).

Fig. 5.5 WHAT NATIONALITY IS THIS CAR? (Lisa Siegel Sullivan)

Here's a difficult question: What nationality is an automaker that borrows money from banks in Dubai and Tokyo, airmails word processing to a back office in Bucharest, buys tires from a subsidiary in Brussels, assembles parts outside Mexico City, uses a London-based ad agency, and coordinates all of these activities in its suburban New York City corporate headquarters? In today's global economy, that question seems pointless (Figure 5.5). Economist William K. Tabb (2001:175–176) puts it succinctly: "To think in terms of U.S. corporations versus foreign corporations…is anachronistic."

To conclude: By 2006, global competition spelled near-disaster for Detroit carmakers and thousands of laid-off U.S. workers in auto and auto-related industries, such as tires. As they closed plants in the United States, Ford and other former automotive giants (and former giants in automotive-related industries) tried to figure out their future. They realized that consumers are fickle and may care more about environmental

technology than where cars come from. As a *New York Times* reporter noted, "While some national loyalty lingers in Europe, as it does in the United States, no company can rely on such loyalty to sell cars" (Maynard, 2006). True enough. By 2007, Toyota outranked GM as the biggest carmaker in the world.

Global consumers care less and less where their cars are made. A good thing too for the industry: For at least a generation, many cars have been multinational products. For example, "Japanese" cars, including Honda and Toyota, may be made in the United States, not Japan.

Here is a short history of a car branded "American": Chrysler. Ironically, in the late 1980s, while it advertised its cars as "Born in America," Chrysler imported machine tools from Japan. Less than a decade later, in 1998, Chrysler was taken over by Germany's Daimler. Then, less than another decade later, in 2007, DaimlerChrysler dumped its controlling share in its very unprofitable Chrysler division. The buyer? Cerberus Capital Management, an investment group—not a car maker—which experienced a drop in U.S. sales of 23 percent in 2008, more than twice the industry average (Vlasic, 2008:11). Similarly, in 2007, when Ford asked for potential buyers to bid on their two British-identified brands, Land Rover and Jaguar, Thomas Stallkamp, a former president of Chrysler, was an initial bidder on behalf of the private investment group he then headed, Ripplewood Holdings. By spring 2008, former Chrysler head (and still at Ripplewood) Stallkamp predicted that Chrysler couldn't survive if Cerberus didn't take a partner (Gupta, 2008:15); later in 2008, Chrysler/Cerberus entered merger talks with GM (which had its own survival issues). Later, Chrysler entered bankruptcy.

Yet, not everyone understands that "Buy American" is not always what it seems. For example, in August 2008, the mayor of Warren, Michigan, a suburban Detroit city where GM and Chrysler have plants (and are the city's biggest taxpayers), told his department heads that he expected them to buy either GM or Chrysler cars the next time they buy a car. (in Ransom, 2008).

U.S. CITIES IN THE WORLD URBAN SYSTEM

It may be pointless to ask which flag an automaker or computer maker salutes. In contrast, the following question seems all-important: What impacts will the transnationalization of production, distribution, and corporate organization have on cities everywhere?

Sociologists John R. Logan and Harvey L. Molotch (1987:chapter 7) address this question, focusing on U.S. cities. Taking for granted that "U.S. cities are tied to a transnational system" (257), Logan and Molotch suggest that there are at least five types of U.S. cities, each playing a different economic role within the new international division of labor: (1) headquarters, (2) innovation centers, (3) module production centers, (4) Third-World entrepots (warehouses), and (5) retirement centers.

To Logan and Molotch's list, I have added one more type: (6) leisure-tourist playgrounds (Table 5.1). Why? Because tourism is arguably the biggest *legal* business in the world: By some estimates, it is "a major factor in international trade and the balance of payments"

(Goldstone, 2001:45), contributing over $65 billion in taxes to governments. In 2006, the UN World Tourism Organization estimated that tourism—including everything from hotels to airlines—brought in $730 billion (in Nortey, 2007:12). In Turkey, for example, tourism by international visitors brought in $16.9 billion in 2006, and this was a drop of about 7.2 percent from 2005 (Bloomberg, 2007), perhaps due to tourists' fear of bird flu, terrorist attacks, and conflict in neighboring Iraq.

By 2010, tourism is expected to beat oil as the planet's largest legal industry (van Rijk in Nortey, 2007:12). (Note, however, that this prediction could fizzle swiftly: Soaring oil prices, fear, and widespread feelings of economic insecurity may persuade prospective travelers to stay home instead.) By 2016, some predict that money spent on travel and tourism will more than double). (Note, however, that such predictions predate the global financial crises that began in 2007.)

Interestingly, one fast-growing sector among affluent people in the United States is cruises. According to one newsletter, high-end cruise lines reported record occupancy levels in the early 2000s, even at rates ranging from $400 to $1,000 per person per day (Fox, 2007).

Natural wonders, cherished climate, amusement and entertainment, gambling, and/or accessibility to sports are key tourist attractions. In the United States, Las Vegas, Lake Tahoe, and Honolulu are among the centers that draw many tourists.

Theme parks are another draw. Indeed, over 42 million visited Disney's Magic Kingdom and EPCOT center in Florida and Disneyland, California in 2008 (Beach California.com), more than all overseas visitors to the United Kingdom (31.9 million) in 2008 "*International Travel*," 2009.

According to Logan and Molotch (1987), each city type contributes to the permanent advantage or disadvantage of individuals and social groups. Specifically, each city type has distinct and unequal consequences for residents in terms of local rents, wages and wealth, taxes and services, and daily life. They cite the following examples: Affluent residents of innovation centers (e.g., Silicon Valley cities) have "much of the best of all worlds" because their places are in high demand. Hispanic migrant populations

TABLE 5.1 LOGAN AND MOLOTCH'S U.S. CITY TYPES PLUS ONE ADDITION

Type	Examples	Key Functions
Headquarters	New York City, Los Angeles	Corporate centers: dominance in cultural production, transportation, and communication networks; corporate control and coordinating functions of many large transnational corporations and international banks
Innovation centers	Silicon Valley towns, including Santa Clara, Calif.; Austin, Tex; and Research Triangle, N.C.	Research and development of aerospace, electronics, and instruments; some are (or were) so involved in military contracting that they are "war-preparation centers"
Module production places	Alameda, Calif, (military base);* Hanford, Wash, (nuclear waste); Omaha, Neb. (the "800" phone exchange center); Detroit and Flint, Mich, (cars)	Sites for routine economic tasks (e.g., assembly of autos, processing of magazine subscriptions or credit-card bills), some located near a natural resource (e.g., mining center) or government function (e.g.. Social Security main office in Baltimore)
Third World entrepots (warehouses)	Border cities such as San Diego, Calif.-Tijuana, Mexico; Miami, Fla.	Trade and financial centers for importing, marketing, and distributing imported goods, including illegal goods such as drugs and pirated music; major labor centers because of their large numbers of low-paid workers in sweatshop manufacturing and tourist-oriented jobs such as hotel maids
Retirement centers	Tampa, Fla.; Sun City, Ariz.	Home to growing numbers of aging Americans. *Range*: affluent towns that maximize services to less affluent cities dependent on pensions, Social Security, and other public programs to support the local economy
**Leisure-tourist playgrounds	Tahoe City, Calif.; Las Vegas, Nev.; Atlantic City, N.J.; Disney World, Fla.; Williamsburg, Va.	*Range:* theme parks, sport resorts, spas to gambling meccas, historical places, and cultural capitals

* Closed,, in large port, since the publication of Log.m and Molotch's book.

** This category is my addition.

Source: John R. Logan and Harvey L. Molotch, *Urban Fortunes* (Berkeley: University of California Press, 1987), chap. 7.

will continue to increase in the entrepot cities, invigorating barrio culture and discouraging assimilation (288). Module production centers (e.g., Flint, Michigan) and most retirement cities (e.g., Sun City, Arizona) are unlikely to provide income redistribution through taxes. Growing headquarters cities (e.g., New York City) and innovation centers have the highest rates of housing-price inflation. Tourist playgrounds, I would add, tend to have a two-tier local economy: many low-wage service personnel (e.g., hotel maids, swimming-pool attendants, cleaning crews, amusement-ride ticket takers) and relatively few highly paid top managers.

Update: Perhaps another city type—recovery communities— should be added to Logan and Molotch's list. These communities are springing up near rehab centers such as the Hazelden Clinic in Minnesota and a treatment center in Delray, Florida. In Delray, for example, over 5,000 people attend 12-step meetings, and special institutions—from halfway houses, radio shows, and coffeehouses—that cater to alumni of rehab centers.

To conclude: There is a global system of cities (see also Chapter 16). This is often called a **world urban system**: an interdependent system of "people, knowledge, images, and ideas" and, to varying degrees, "capital, labour, and goods" (King, [1990] 1991:2).

Cities perform differing economic roles in the new international division of labor, and their roles lead to disadvantages or advantages for residents. Places at the bottom of the urban heap may compete for garbage, nuclear waste, or potential toxic spills, often becoming "contaminated communities" (Edelstein, 2003), such as Love Canal in New York State.

Meanwhile, the top four cities at the top of the heap, so-called command or headquarters cities—such as New York, London, Paris, and Tokyo—attract heavy concentrations of top corporate decision makers from finance, industry, commerce, law, and the media.

According to one ranking system (Beaverstock et al., 1999) (see Table 16.2), just below the top four on measures of "world city-ness" are these cities: Chicago, Frankfurt, Hong Kong, Los Angeles, Milan, and Singapore. Ranked below these 10 so-called alpha cities are second-tier, or "beta," cities (world cities with high levels of advanced producer services, including advertising, banking and finance, law, and accountancy): San Francisco, Sydney, Toronto, Zurich, Brussels, Madrid, Mexico City, São Paulo, Moscow, and Seoul.

(Note that not all mega-cities, such as Mumbai, are considered global cities. Conversely, not all global cities are considered mega-cities. Zurich, for example, is a second-tier global city but not a mega-city. Also

Fig. 5.6   THE FINANCIAL CENTER OF LONDON, AN ALPHA CITY. (Gesche Würfel)

note that any rankings are time-sensitive. In future decades, we should expect some big changes.)

Economic functions are coordinated in global command cities such as New York and London. Some observers say that it is in such cities that multinational corporations create a truly transnational economy.

CITIES IN THE GLOBAL ENVIRONMENT

China's ever-increasing emissions of carbon dioxide (by 2007 China had surpassed the United States as the biggest emitter of carbon dioxide, the primary heat-trapping gas) made all aware that what happens in one place can have serious consequences for far-away people.

Many (but not all) scientists think that carbon from fossil fuels emitted in industrial or postindustrial nations (notably China, the United States, and Canada, nations with the highest per capita emission of fossil fuel) contributes to global warming; gases from fossil fuels act like panes of glass in a greenhouse, trapping heat from the sun and raising temperatures, particularly in the middle latitudes of the Northern Hemisphere. Carbon is also released when trees are burned in tropical rain forests, contributing to climatic change in far-flung metropolises.

Alternative, nonpolluting energies, including the sun, are now being explored. Yet, it is estimated that by 2020 rich and poor countries will each contribute 50 percent shares of carbon dioxide, a gas said to be responsible for about half of the global-warming effect.

Awareness of a shared ecosphere has expanded greatly since the disaster at Chernobyl in 1986. But this awareness is not matched by political mechanisms to control (or prevent) transnational environmental assaults.

What can be done to protect the ecosphere? Once again, there is no agreement. Ecologist Paul Ehrlich (once known as a leading advocate for population control, warning that population growth was outstripping the earth's food supply) and coworkers (see Liu et al., 2003) argued recently that it is not the size of a population but rather the number of households (increasing faster than the number of humans, an increasing divorce rate being one reason) that creates serious environmental problems in many places. Indeed,

"solutions" range from population control and reducing pollutants to the abandonment of industrialism with a return to a hunting–gathering way of life compatible with a healthy land.

To conclude: In a remarkably short time, a world of urban specks was replaced by a predominantly urban world. Estimates vary, but most agree that more than 50 percent of the world's population are now city dwellers.

ANOTHER LOOK

This chapter points up the difficulty of trying to draw boundaries around "urban" studies. Increasingly, we are learning that to understand what's happening in Detroit or Singapore, we must understand how the global economy and culture work.

KEY TERMS

Core, periphery, semiperiphery Terms used by economic dependence theorists and world-systems theorists, notably Immanuel Wallerstein. In this view, a world system is an interrelated economic—not political—unit divided into three zones, distinguished by different economic functions in the international division of labor, forms of labor control, political organization, and class structures. Today, richer industrial core areas, such as North America and Japan, perform control functions for the world economy. Poorer areas on the semiperiphery (e.g., Brazil) and the poorest areas on the periphery (e.g., Ethiopia, Bangladesh) are sources of cheaper labor and raw materials.

Mega-cities Giant metropolises with populations of at least 10 million. (Before 2000, the number was set at 7 million.)

New international division of labor (Needle) Economic interdependence between nations rooted in the specialization of economic tasks carried out through a global network of transnational corporations and cities. It connotes a restructuring of the world economy, starting in about the late 1960s, with these features: (1) a shifting global market for workers that results in plant closures in rich countries and plant start-ups in poor countries; (2) the worldwide integration by large multinational corporations of basic economic functions—production, exchange, finance, and corporate services—arranged in a hierarchical system of cities; and (3) the production of goods for the world market subdivided into smaller fragments, manufactured wherever it is most profitable. Contrast: *classical* or *old international division of labor* (where an integrated world market consisted of a few industrial nations producing capital goods and consumer goods and the vast majority of underdeveloped countries producing raw materials).

Old international division of labor (OIDL) Peripheral zones (colonies) produced primary products and raw materials (e.g., cotton, cocoa, copper) for industries of the core countries (imperial powers) and received finished goods in return.

Poor countries One term for nations with diverse cultures that face a common situation: economic poverty. This name avoids the ideologically loaded, negative term "underdeveloped nations" and the now obsolete "Third World."

Third World Term coined by de Gaulle to refer to nations neutral in the cold war struggle. Later, it referred to poor nations.

Urbanization Process by which the proportion of a society's or nation's total population living in urban settlements becomes greater and the proportion living in rural areas decreases. Some scholars use the term to refer to the process of becoming urban in terms of social, technological, political, and spatial organization. Urbanization is not the same as the growth of cities.

World urban system Systematic interconnection of interdependent cities in terms of people, knowledge, images, ideas, capital, labor, and commodities.

PROJECTS

1. **Cities and the environment**. Find out what policymakers and scholars believe to be the chief environmental culprits in your area—such as air pollution, toxic waste, or rotting garbage. What proposals exist to deal with these conditions? Do they represent a wide spectrum of ideas or not?

2. **World cities**. Choose three large cities or megalopolises located on each of three continents—say, Tokyo, London, and São Paulo. First, find out some basic information, including population numbers, percentage of people below the poverty line, economic activities of the population, physical setting (e.g., built on a river or ocean, constructed in a valley) and layout (a grid?). Next, investigate what ongoing issues these cities may share. For example, do they face common issues of garbage collection and high crime rates? If an extreme gap between rich and poor exists, is this defined as a problem or nonproblem? Then, explore what policies, if any, the three cities have used to approach these issues. Finally, discounting weather, answer this question: Which of the three cities would you prefer to live in—and why?

3. **The T in POET: The role of one technology today**. Wireless networks are the fastest-growing communications in history. Determine the approximate number of people using this communications technology in various world areas and then discuss its potential impacts, if any, on European and North American cities plus particular groups (e.g., teens, the poor) in cities.

SUGGESTIONS FOR FURTHER LEARNING

There is an ever-growing literature on cities in a global society. Early studies of global cities and the international division of labor include Saskia Koob (later Sassen-Koob and, still later, Saskia Sassen), "The New Labor Demand in Global Cities" in *Cities in Transformation: Class, Capital, and the State*, edited by Michael Peter Smith (Beverly Hills, Calif.: Sage, 1984), pp. 139–171.

In *Camden After the Fall: Decline and Renewal in a Post-Industrial City* (Philadelphia: University of Pennsylvania Press, [2005] 2006), historian Howard Gillette, Jr., looks at urban-renewal efforts in one New Jersey city, which was first transformed from an industrial powerhouse into the nation's third poorest city. In his biography of a city, Gillette weaves a narrative of postwar urban decline and renewal.

For a look at what Sir Peter Hall has called "the superheated hyperurbanization" of China, see *The Concrete Dragon: China's Urban Revolution and What It Means for the World* (Princeton, N.J.: Princeton Architectural Press, 2008) by Thomas J. Campanella. Urbanist Hall says that China's urbanization is "the most amazing phenomenon" of the early twenty-first century.

For the key work on core–periphery relations in a global economic system, see Immanuel Wallerstein's *The Modern World System* (New York: Academic Press, 1976). This classic traces the world system and world economy to the late fifteenth and early sixteenth centuries in Europe.

In the sixth edition of *The State of the World Atlas* (London: Penguin, [1999] 2001), Dan Smith uses statistics to discuss the quality of life and the global economy, including international tourism. For a particular kind of tourism—sex tourism—see Denise Brennan's 2004 ethnographic study *What's Love Got to Do with It?: Transnational Desires and Sex Tourism in the Dominican Republic* (Durham, N.C.: Duke University Press). She shows how women in one town, Sosúa, are caught in a web of global economic relations and how they try to take advantage of the foreign men who come there to take advantage of them.

In *Global Metropolitan* (Oxford: Taylor and Francis, 2007), John Rennie Short joins an ever-increasing group of scholars seeking to explain the deep economic and social changes that affect contemporary cities as they compete in a globalizing world. He suggests a new paradigm for urban studies.

Some people are more observant tourists than others. Paul Theroux (born Medford, Massachusetts) is one of the best travelers in terms of "seeing" things that others miss. In 1975 he took a 28,000-mile intercontinental rail journey from London to Tokyo and back; he reported what he saw in a classic of travel literature, *The Great Railway Bazaar* (New York: Mariner Books, [1975] 2006). More than 30 years later, Theroux repeated the train trip to places many of us only dream about. The results, revealing how he as well as the places he visited had changed, are chronicled in *Ghost Train to the Eastern Star: On the Tracks of the Great Railway Bazaar* (New York: Houghton Mifflin, 2008).

REFERENCES

Barnet, Richard J., and John Cavanagh. 1994. *Global Dreams: Imperial Corporations and the New World Order*. New York: Simon and Schuster.

Barnet, Richard J., and Ronald E. Müller. 1974. *Global Reach: The Power of the Multinational Corporation*. New York: Simon and Schuster.

BEACH california.com. n.d: http://www.california.com/california_theme_parks.html

Beaverstock, J. V., R. G. Smith, and P. J. Taylor. 1999. "A roster of world cities." *Cities* 16(6):445–458.

Bloomberg (news service). 2007. "Tourism in Turkey jumps 17 percent over last year." *International Herald Tribune* (July 25):18.

Davis, Kingsley. 1965. "The urbanization of the human population." *Scientific American* 213:40–53.

Edelstein, Michael R. 2003. *Contaminated Communities: Coping with Residential Toxic Exposure*, 2nd ed. Boulder, Colo.: Westview Press.

Fox, Alan. 2007. VacationsToGo.com (October 29).

Goldstone, Patricia. 2001. *Making the World Safe for Tourism*. New Haven, Conn.: Yale University Press.

Gupta, Poornima. 2008. "Cerberus feels weight of its Chrysler burden." *International Herald Tribune* (June 19):15.

Henderson, Jeffrey, and Manuel Castells, eds. 1987. *Global Restructuring and Territorial Development*. Newbury Park, Calif.: Sage.

"International travel," 2009. (July 6): http://www.statistics.gov.UK/CCT/hugget.asp?ID=178

King, Anthony D. [1990] 1991. *Urbanism, Colonialism, and the World-Economy: Cultural and Spatial Foundations of the World Urban System*. London: Routledge.

Logan, John R., and Harvey L. Molotch. 1987. *Urban Fortunes: The Political Economy of Place*. Berkeley: University of California Press.

Liu, Jianguo, Gretchen C. Daily, Paul R. Ehrlich, and Gary W. Luck. 2003. "Effects of household dynamics on resource consumption and biodiversity." *Nature* 421:530–533.

Maynard, Michelline. 2006. "Now playing in Europe: The future of Detroit." *New York Times* (October 29): www.nytimes.com/2006/10/29/business/yourmoney/29plants.htm

National League of Cities. 2007. City Mayors Urban Statistics: http://www.citymayors.com/sections/rankings_content.html

Nortey, Sam, Jr. 2007. "Next destination: Sustainable tourism." *International Herald Tribune* (June 5):12.

Ransom, Kevin. 2008. "Buy American or get out? A Detroit mayor tells his employees what car to drive." AOL Autos.(September 12): http://autos.

aol.com/article/car-news/buy-american-cars-or-not/20080906161909990001

Rugie, John Gerard. 1998. *Constructing the World Polity: Essays on International Institutionalization*. London: Routledge.

Tabb, William K. 2001. *The Amoral Elephant: Globalization and the Struggle for Social Justice in the Twenty-First Century*. New York: Monthly Review Press.

Taylor, Peter J. 1985. *Political Geography: World-Economy, Nation-State and Locality*. London: Longman.

Toler, Lindsay. 2007. "UN: Half the world soon to be in cities." *Associated Press* (June 27): 12:21 p.m. EDT.

Tolliday, Steven, and Jonathan Zeitlin, eds. 1987. *The Automobile Industry and Its Workers: Between Fordism and Flexibility*. Cambridge, Mass.: Harvard University Press.

TVE Madrid. 2005. "China: A million steps ahead."

UNFPA (United Nations Population Fund). 2007. "State of world population 2007." http://www.unfpa.org/swp/2007/english/introduction.html

UN-HABITAT. 2004–2005. "State of the world's cities." www.unhabitat.org

Vlasic, Bill. 2008. "Chrysler, yet again, is seeking salvation." *International Herald Tribune* (August 20):11.

CHAPTER 6

THE TIES THAT BIND

World
Pho

Poet John Donne (1572–1631) expressed his view of the human condition in a memorable phrase: "No man is an island" (the first line in *Meditation 17*, from *Devotions Upon Emergent Occasions*, 1624). Were he alive today, he might have put it this way: No person is an island.

If, as Donne implies, people are social animals whose fates are intertwined, then why do so many people feel disconnected and alone in the world? What ties people together? How do we prevent insecurity and loneliness? The idea of community is central to such questions of personal security and social connectedness. Although the abstract concept has many meanings, "community" hinges on the notions of togetherness and sharing.

Chapters 6–9 focus on the ties that bind people together—and tear them apart. This chapter begins with a discussion of the concept of community and then examines a form of community that Aristotle (and many since) held up as an ideal: the polis of ancient Athens. Next, the chapter looks at various explanations of the shift from rural to urban life in western Europe and North America. The effects of this rural–urban shift on human personality are evaluated in terms of their basic assumptions and contemporary relevance. For example, nineteenth-century urban theories predict an *inevitable* breakdown in community within urban-industrial society. Did this happen? That leads us back to the issue of metropolitan community today, a major topic of Chapter 7. Then in Chapter 8, we continue the search for modern community, asking what, if anything, binds people together in large, sprawling urban–suburban areas. Do computer chat groups on the Internet promote a new type of community, one that is both placeless and faceless? And what about community life in the future—in proposed space-age cities above the earth and beneath the water? Chapters 9 and 10 continue with related questions, particularly this one: Is it possible to have multicultural, multiethnic societies with unity in diversity?

Chapters 6–10 pose many questions—and not merely abstract ones. What makes us feel like insiders or outsiders in a neighborhood or a nation? Why do we tend to trust people like ourselves but mistrust people unlike ourselves? What are the pluses and minuses of hanging out solely with people like ourselves? When do we feel cut off and alone, disconnected from the fates of others?

Finally, can any events bring us—a diverse bunch with varied concerns and interests—together in community? These questions confront us all, often in deeply emotional ways. How beautiful it would be, we may fantasize, to live in peace and harmony like the 1,000 members of the isolated Aché tribe who hunt and gather in the Paraguayan subtropical forest. Can any group in postindustrial society succeed in building a community based on trust and self-sufficiency?

So many questions, so few answers....Of course, there are many *proposed* answers to questions of community. The essence of many solutions is this: *If only* we could do X or Y, *then* we could create an atmosphere in which human beings live in harmony. Solutions have taken various forms—altering basic institutions through civil war or revolution; organizing separatist political or religious movements such as those in Baghdad, Iraq, and the Basque areas of Spain; and segregating, exiling, or killing people defined as outsiders (e.g., Hitler's Final Solution—a national policy of killing Jews, people with disabilities, gays, and Gypsies [Roma]—"ethnic cleansing" in many places).

These often deadly solutions suggest the power of community.

Meanwhile, philosophers and writers wonder aloud whether there are any answers. Are we doomed to be eternally *Waiting for Godot*, in the phrase of playwright Samuel Beckett? Is there *No Exit*, as Jean-Paul Sartre implies?

My purpose here is not to provide definitive answers to the problems of human community because, in my view, there are none. Rather, I hope that by openly discussing issues of community, all of us may make more conscious choices, both in our personal lives and in our collective life.

WHAT IS A COMMUNITY?

Like love, truth, and other abstract concepts, **community** has no agreed-on meaning. In the discipline of sociology alone, there are at least 90 definitions of the word.

However, in general terms, a human "community" usually refers to either (1) a group sharing a physical space (e.g., residents of Chicago's Austin neighborhood), (2) a group sharing a trait (e.g., a student or lesbian community, the Falun Gong in China), or (3) a group sharing an identity and a culture typified by a high degree of **social cohesion** (e.g., the Amish, the Nation of Islam, medieval Cathar heretics in southwest France, and the seventeenth-century Massachusetts Bay Colony settlers). Sometimes, but not always, this last group is called a "traditional community."

COMMUNITIES BASED ON TERRITORY

As just noted, a physical concentration of people—in a neighborhood, city, or nation—may be called a "community." If asked "What community are you from?" most of us would probably respond by naming a place—say, Chicago, the West Side, or Austin, depending on the context and geographical knowledge of the questioner. Few would answer with a number—a ZIP code. Yet, as discussed in Chapter 8, some researchers think that a ZIP code is the single most important bit of information about people in the United States (and in many other places). It identifies us as birds of a feather: members of residential communities where neighbors share preferences for food, cars, and presidential candidates.

Here, we are not concerned with communities based solely on the sharing of space. Rather, we focus on communities rooted in social relationships. In this context, community is based on a feeling of **"we-ness"**—that is, a sense of shared identity and interdependence. Such a community may or may not share a physical territory.

COMMUNITIES BASED ON COMMON CULTURE

Some groups share both a physical territory and a cohesive social existence—the traditional community mentioned earlier. For instance, the Hopi inhabit a common physical space and accept the group's rules and goals.

However, many groups called communities today are not bound to a plot of land. For instance, a close-knit ethnic or religious community (e.g., Armenians, Sikhs, Wahhabi Muslims, Hasidic Jews) can be widely dispersed. Yet its members share a culture and origins that bind them and set them apart from others in the society.

Similarly, members of an occupational community do not inhabit a common territory. They can be spread throughout the world, and rarely do they share origins. Yet, certain occupational groups—lawyers, nurses, soldiers, and priests, to name a few—engage in activities that give rise to a shared culture, attitudes, and values in urban society. Police and public safety officials, at least as portrayed in U.S. TV series, notably *Law and Order* (NBC, 1990–), *CSI* (CBS, called *Les Experts* in Canada, 2000–), and *Without a Trace* (CBS, 2002–), exemplify such an occupational community. So do navy personnel aboard a carrier ship or an army platoon.

Many consider a professional group (such as doctors or cancer researchers) to be a community because it has the following characteristics:

1. Members are bound by a sense of shared identity.
2. Once in the profession, few leave.
3. Members share a language (or jargon) that can be understood only partially by outsiders.
4. Members share values.
5. In a social sense, members collectively reproduce the next generation.
6. Insiders are easily distinguished from outsiders in the professional community.
7. Requirements for membership are the same for all members.

8. The professional group has power over its members (Goode, 1957).

This list stresses that a professional group is a community without a physical location. Still, it is often called a community because its members have a common identity, culture, and occupational goals.

Many universities call themselves communities. But, as a former president of the University of California, the late Clark Kerr, once joked (in earnest), a university is "a series of individual faculty entrepreneurs held together by a common grievance over parking ([1963]2001:15)." Faculty in a university program or department, however, sometimes consider themselves to be a community of scholars.

Nonoccupational groups can also be considered communities if they meet the eight criteria. Examples here include some—but not all—religious, ethnic, political, spiritual, age-based, economic, and gender-specific groups: Alcoholics Anonymous; college sororities; l'Union des Jeunes Musulmans in France; the Vietnamese American community in San Jose, California. Such groups may constitute **subcultures**—subcommunities that share some cultural elements of the dominant culture but also have their own symbols, beliefs, and values. Alternatively, they may constitute **countercultures**—subcommunities whose beliefs, symbols, attitudes, and values *oppose* those of the dominant culture (e.g., 1960s hippies, today's "freegans").

Some social scientists distinguish between communities and **collectivities**. Communities, they say, derive from common *origins*, while collectivities are established on the basis of common *ends*. Using this distinction, occupational groups such as doctors, as well as other nonkin groups, would be considered collectivities, not communities.

A SENSE OF COMMUNITY

A sense of belonging—a we-ness—typifies many traditional communities. But is this we-ness possible today? Many theorists think not. They argue that contemporary urban-industrial or postindustrial society is too large, too diverse, and too individualistic to promote a sense of community except in subcommunities (e.g., ethnic groups) or collectivities (e.g., occupational groups).

Perhaps that is one reason some in the United States, including Muslims, Orthodox Jews, Hindus, and evangelical Christians, are turning more and more to arranged (or "assisted") marriages to preserve their culture. (*Note*: Critics point to what they view as downsides, including the yen to preserve "ethnic purity" and the furthering of rigid male–female roles that can lead to gender inequities. In other words, critics note the two-headed face of community. On one hand, there is closeness within the group. On the other, there is distance from outsiders. Similarly, communities offer clear expectations of a person's social roles. However, those roles are often frozen.)

In recent years, some groups in the United States, notably the well-educated and religious modernists, have been feeling less a sense of community than others. Why? Key institutions themselves, notably education and certain religious denominations, are biased toward individualism. That is the conclusion of sociologists Ryle and Robinson (2006:53). Based on their analysis of national survey data, they argue that the U.S. educational system "inculcates an individualistic ideology that disposes highly educated people to a weaker sense of community" and that a "theologically modernist moral cosmology" is inherently individualistic, relative to more orthodox religious traditions.

Some lament a loss of shared values. This is reflected in the words of Swedish lawyer Henrik Ponten, who noted the prevalence in Sweden of illegal downloading: "A hundred years ago we were Christians. Today we are file sharers" ("On the record," 2006:18).

Is it possible to reweave the modern social fabric? Some social scientists (e.g., Putnam, 2000) believe—or hope—so. Web "communities" or "social networks" such as Craigslist.org, Facebook.com, and MySpace.com, are exemplary. Consider these observations: (1) Craig Newmark, founder of the Internet's mainly free, open, easy-to-use, innovative Craigslist.org, insists that the localness of the Craigslist sites leads to a Web community connection (in Putnam and Feldstein, 2003:231). (2) An estimated 161 million plus (and growing) people are members of Myspace.com. A free social networking site, it advertises itself as a place where you can "meet people from your area in the country and keep in touch." (Note that many warn of dangers inherent in such sites, which display private information.) Indeed, Buckley's *The Rough Guide to MySpace & Online Communities* (2006:viii) starts like this: "The Internet has always been about communities, and in the last few years the most cohesive type of online community yet has evolved." Here, Buckley names MySpace, Bebo, and Friendster as cohesive online communities. (New online communities are proliferating, with cutesy-poo names to make it easier to remember which is which.)

Still, we should ask, are these Internet groups truly "communities"? Before considering either possibility—that community is or isn't possible in postindustrial society—let us examine forms of community in times past. We begin with what some scholars believe to be the most highly developed community in the Western world: the polis in ancient Athens.

THE ATHENIAN POLIS OF ANCIENT GREECE

In the fifth century BCE, Greece was composed of a number of independent, economically self-sufficient, and self-governing political units called *poleis* (singular, *polis*). The word **polis** is usually translated as "city-state," but this is a bad translation. The polis was not much like a modern nation-state, and it was much more than a city. For this reason, following a historian of the Greeks, H. D. F. Kitto, we use the Greek word *polis*.

By current population standards, a polis was small. Only three poleis—Athens, Syracuse, and Acragas—numbered more than 20,000 citizens. (*Note*: Not all inhabitants were granted citizenship. Slaves, who were foreigners, and other foreigners were not citizens. Further, women had no political rights. Thus, a citizenry of about 10,000 persons implies a total population of about 100,000.)

The small population of the polis is important in understanding its ethos. Greek philosophers insisted on this point. Plato wrote that the ideal polis should contain no more than 5,000 citizens (about 50,000 people). Aristotle maintained that the polis should not be too small or too large. He reasoned that it should be small enough so that all citizens could recognize one another on sight and be properly governed. But it should not be too small because it would not be economically self-sufficient. The idea of a metropolitan community numbering several million or a nation-state with over 300 million people, such as the United States today, would have seemed absurd to the ancient Greeks.

By contemporary standards, the physical scale of the polis was also small. Corinth, a commercial center, encompassed only 330 square miles. Sparta, covering 3,200 square miles, was considered enormous. To think in such small terms is difficult today. After all, the Los Angeles metropolitan area, covering over 4,000 square miles, is larger than any ancient Greek polis. Ancient Greeks would not have liked living in a huge modern state like the United States. The Greeks were in contact with one such vast state, the Persian Empire; and they thought it suitable only for barbarians, not civilized people like themselves.

Why did the Greeks live under the small-scale polis system rather than consolidating into larger political units? Surely, economic factors and geographical barriers (particularly mountains) contributed to maintaining the polis system; but the "real explanation," according to Kitto (1951:69), was the character of the Greeks: Fearing that differences in scale would become differences in kind, they chose to live in poleis.

A COMMUNAL WAY OF LIFE

Most citizens of a polis were farmers. Although agriculturalists, they preferred to live in a town or village, walk to their fields, and spend any leisure time talking to fellow citizens in the public square.

To these ordinary citizens, the polis was a community where all issues of common concern were public, not private. Citizen participation was widespread; about 15–20 percent of the citizens in the Athenian polis served the community in some capacity each year, filling offices by lot and rotating administrative responsibilities. Legislation took place in large popular assemblies. (Again, note that slaves and other foreigners were barred from public affairs. Further, women took no public role; they remained secluded in their homes, for Athens was a male-dominated community where men and women had separate spheres.)

From our vantage point, it is hard to comprehend what the Athenian polis meant to ordinary Greek citizens, particularly in the so-called golden age of Pericles (roughly 448 BCE to either the death of Pericles in 429 BCE or the end of the Peloponnesian War in 404 BCE).

Depending on our political ideology, we see modern government as a mechanism to prevent "the war of all against all" (the classical liberal approach based on Thomas Hobbes's philosophy); as a means of regulating who gets what when the market mechanism of supply and demand needs adjustment (the liberal approach); or as a weapon serving the interests of the powerful against the powerless (the radical approach). But to the Greeks, the polis represented a positive force. It was the only framework in which people could realize their human potential: intellectual, spiritual, and moral.

The democratic leader of the Athenian polis, Pericles, gives a clue to communal life in the polis in his famous funeral oration (cited in Book 2 of Thucydides's *The History of the Peloponnesian War*:

"Each individual is interested not only in his own affairs but in the affairs of the polis as well. . . . We do not say that a man who takes no interest in politics is a man who minds his own business; we say that he has no business here at all."

Pericles's funeral oration and the Athenian Oath of Citizenship (Figure 6.2) indicate the public-spirited attitude of the Greeks. They were social animals, living in and through the polis. For the Greeks, the polis was a community and a way of life. It was an active agent, training the minds and characters of its citizenry. It was a living entity, and citizens were like members of a large extended family.

Kitto concludes that the Greek citizen was essentially an individualist *only* in economic affairs. In the rest of life, he was essentially communal: "Religion, art, games, and the discussion of things—all these were needs of life that could be fully satisfied only through the polis" (1951:78). This situation stands in stark contrast to current conceptions of self-fulfillment.

To conclude: The polis was built on a common cultural life. Its geographic area was compact, so people identified with their locality; and its population was small enough so that citizens were personally known to one another. Unlike a city or nation-state in urban-industrial society, the polis was a self-sufficient entity with an ethos of public, not private, interest.

The Athenian polis was ancient Greece's crowning glory. Why, then, did it disappear as a way of life? Some accounts of the decline and fall of the polis system

FROM THE OATH OF THE ATHENIAN CITY-STATE

WE WILL EVER STRIVE FOR THE IDEALS AND SACRED THINGS OF THE CITY, BOTH ALONE AND WITH MANY; WE WILL UNCEASINGLY SEEK TO QUICKEN THE SENSE OF PUBLIC DUTY; WE WILL REVERE AND OBEY THE CITY'S LAWS; WE WILL TRANSMIT THIS CITY NOT ONLY NOT LESS, BUT GREATER, BETTER AND MORE BEAUTIFUL THAN IT WAS TRANSMITTED TO US.

Fig. 6.2 EXCERPT, ATHENIAN OATH OF CITIZENSIP. Citizens pledged to transmit the polis's cultural heritage and to improve Athens as part of their civic duty. (Athenian oath as it appears at the Maxwell School of Citizenship and Public Affairs, Syracuse University. Reproduced by permission.)

focus on the effect of trade and markets. According to economic anthropologist Karl Polanyi and coauthors (1957), the Athenian polis under Pericles was governed by laws of economic reciprocity. The concept of profit hardly existed. Instead, economic exchanges were seen more as gift giving than as trade; their chief function was to ensure social solidarity, not to redistribute wealth. This system of economic reciprocity faded with the emergence of a market economy (where prices are set by supply and demand) in the fifth century BCE. With the market economy came new ideas—profit and individualism.

In Kitto's view, what destroyed the polis system was progress. The polis was suited for amateurs, not professionals or specialized experts. Indeed, the polis discouraged specialization and efficiency, for its ideal was

participation: Every citizen could and should play a role in public affairs. To accomplish this, no role could be very difficult for an ordinary person to play. When life became more complex in the fourth century BCE, new experts were needed. Commerce had expanded on the Mediterranean, and Philip of Macedonia had introduced new military tactics in a war against the poleis. In short, the world was shrinking, and specialized skills—military tactics and commercial skills in particular—were needed to meet the challenges. Athens responded by employing professional soldiers (mercenaries) instead of citizen-soldiers. This act denied the very ideal of citizen participation.

In addition, Athenian education changed. Under Pericles, education was free and available to all citizens; it was part of living in the polis. But to meet the new challenges in the fourth century BCE, education became specialized and available only to those who could pay.

Soon, divisions between the educated and uneducated appeared, and specialist experts separated from laypersons. At his educational academy, Socrates taught students that government should be left to experts instead of being decided by democratic vote and popular debate; these teachings—not the expression of unpopular opinions—may have led to his condemnation to death (Stone, 1979).

These educational changes had wide-ranging effects. The educated of all poleis now had more in common with one another than with uneducated members of their own polis; this weakened the bonds of community. Further, the division between experts and laypersons destroyed the common knowledge base and culture upon which the polis was built.

It was at this time, the fourth century BCE, that the word **cosmopolis** was coined. It meant that people owed allegiance not to their own local community but to a larger group, the community of humankind. This new notion of cosmopolitanism, signaling the individual's connection to a wider community, helped to break down the traditional sense of community.

To conclude: As the educated became cosmopolitan in outlook, the ideal of the polis as a community waned. And as specialized experts in military and commercial affairs arose, the ideal of community gave way to the ideal of cosmopolitan life.

This brief account of the rise and fall of the polis, especially in Athens, suggests that a sense of traditional community could not be sustained in the face of growing complexity and specialization. The preconditions for its existence—a simple, small-scale, self-sufficient, relatively unspecialized local way of life—gave way to a wider world and a more cosmopolitan outlook.

Now let us begin a more systematic examination of some issues touched on in the history of the polis. For instance, does functional specialization necessarily lead to the breakdown of community? Can a sense of traditional community exist in a world shrunk to the point where a moon landing can be telecast to a global audience? Are individualism and loss of community inevitable companions of large-scale, complex

society? We turn to urban scholars whose theoretical constructs deal with these very issues.

CLASSICAL URBAN THEORY

By the 1870s, western Europe had experienced the effects of twin revolutions: the French Revolution and the Industrial Revolution. The giant broom of the twin revolutions was sweeping traditional community into the dustbin of history. The foundations of small-scale rural community—family, social hierarchy, church, relatively simple technology, property in land—were crumbling in the wake of industrialism, urbanism, and industrial capitalism. Great population shifts from countryside to city were in process, and England was on its way to becoming the first urban society in human history. It is not surprising that at this time the idea of community became a dominant theme in European social thought (and art).

Theorists living through the demise of traditional community formed differing judgments about the new urban–industrial–capitalist order. Ferdinand Tönnies, for one, romanticized the medieval small town as the home of the humane life and mourned the passing of traditional community. Karl Marx, however, viewed the slow transformation from feudalism to industrial capitalism as a positive step, ending what he called "the idiocy of rural life." For Marx, the twin revolutions were liberating forces, freeing the political spirit and setting in motion the forces that would someday lead to a new basis for community—the solidarity of the working classes of the world.

Nineteenth-century theorists viewed the transformation of Europe in different ways, but they interpreted these changes in a similar fashion: *as inevitable evolutionary developments from one form of social organization to another*—from rural to urban, from simple to complex, from feudalism to capitalism, from small-scale to large-scale, from religious to secular. Hence, classical urban theory is based on polar contrasts between two forms of social organization and human personality.

TYPOLOGIES OF THE RURAL-URBAN SHIFT

Theorists express these polar contrasts in the form of typologies (classification schemes). As noted in

Chapter 2, *typologies* are designed to be tentative models of the real world, not to correspond exactly to every observable case. A typology is composed of two or more **ideal types** that can be used to describe, compare, and test hypotheses, such as the rural and urban types of society.

Despite their unique features, the various typologies of the rural–urban shift share some important assumptions. Most important is their evolutionary bias. The shift from rural life to city life is viewed as a one-way street: a unilinear, inevitable, and irreversible development. At one end of the evolutionary process lies simple rural life, and at the other end lies complex modern society. However, a continuum between the two poles is implied.

Let us take a closer look at some of the many rural–urban typologies, examining several classical nineteenth-century formulations and other more recent ones. We begin with arguably the best-known: Tönnies's *Gemeinschaft–Gesellschaft* dichotomy.

GEMEINSCHAFT AND GESELLSCHAFT (TÖNNIES)

Like other nineteenth-century theorists, Ferdinand Tönnies (1855–1936) based his typology on changes in peasant communities in western Europe. From that vantage point, he constructed a typology contrasting two forms of social organization: community and society. *Gemeinschaft* (community) lies at one end of the continuum, and *Gesellschaft* (society) lies at the other.

According to Tönnies, social life evolves in the following way: from family units to rural villages, towns, cities, nations, and finally cosmopolitan life. At the beginning stages of this evolutionary development lies *Gemeinschaft*, the traditional community that existed prior to the twin revolutions in Europe.

In *Gemeinschaft* social organization, people are bound together by common values, sacred traditions, and blood ties. They share a physical territory, experience, and thoughts. They are linked by a "reciprocal, binding sentiment." Kinship, land, neighborhood, and friendship are the cornerstones. These key elements are embodied in the family, the primary social unit.

By contrast, kinship, land, and friendship count little in *Gesellschaft*. In *Gesellschaft* (a form of social organization that accompanied the rise of industrialism, capitalism, and cities), there is a lack of close-knit family and friendship ties. Tönnies argued that in urban-industrial capitalist society, human relations are based on contracts and laws, not binding sentiment. Attachments to land and neighborhood lose their meaning; money and credit become paramount concerns.

Tönnies, like his contemporary, Karl Marx, insisted on the importance of the money economy in determining human interaction. For Tönnies, people in *Gesellschaft* measure all values, including self-worth, in terms of money. This cash nexus replaces community values based on traditional authority, binding sentiment, religious traditions, and kinship.

As described by Tönnies, *Gemeinschaft* is typified by small rural communities where people know one another and their place in the social system. In contrast, *Gesellschaft* is marked by large urban centers where people are strangers whose place in the social system can shift.

Individualism, not community interest, is the hallmark of *Gesellschaft*. Since no common morality exists in the heterogeneous city, people are free to calculate rationally what is in their own self-interest. The U.S. TV series *24* (Fox, 2006–) illustrates Tönnies's point. In *24*, the main character, agent Jack Bauer (Kiefer Sutherland), flaunts norms of behavior to do what he—and sometimes he alone—thinks is right. In *Gemeinschaft*, Tönnies maintained, the opposite is true: People conform to accepted standards of behavior and share a definition of right and wrong.

Why did *Gemeinschaft* evolve into *Gesellschaft*? For Tönnies, *Gesellschaft* arose with the growth of commerce and capitalism. It serves the interests of merchant-capitalists, who trade commodities on the basis of contracts, not friendship or blood ties.

How did Tönnies evaluate this movement from the simple rural community to the complex industrial city? Mainly negatively. He romanticized European medieval towns and their feudal institutions—symbolized by church spires, fortifications, and castles—as the source of the humane life.

Tönnies believed that the shift from *Gemeinschaft* to *Gesellschaft* meant an inevitable loss of community, a loss he tended to mourn with a sense of nostalgia.

Fig. 6.3 A *GEMEINSCHAFT*-LIKE COMMUNITY. The church steeple is the tallest structure in many European towns built before the twin revolutions. Pictured here is St. Cirq Lapopie, a preserved medieval village in southwest France today. (Tim Teninty)

Fig. 6.4 *GEMEINSCHAFT, GESELLSCHAFT, TECHNO$CHAFT.* (Lisa Siegel Sullivan)

At the same time, he noted what he considered *Gesellschaft*'s positive aspects, particularly the rise of cities as cultural and scientific centers. (See "Adding a Third Type: Techno$chaft" later in this chapter for an update to Tönnies's typology.)

MECHANICAL AND ORGANIC SOCIAL SOLIDARITY (DURKHEIM)

French sociologist Emile Durkheim (1858–1917) described the rural–urban shift in terms of changes in social bonds among people, or social solidarity. At the rural end of the continuum, people are mentally and morally homogeneous. In this form of social solidarity—**mechanical solidarity**—communities are not atomized.

At the other end of the continuum, the urban-industrial end, lies a society characterized by **organic solidarity**. Here, the mental and moral similarities among people disappear, the collective conscience (shared beliefs, values, sentiments, and morality) weakens, and the **division of labor** stimulates individualism. People become highly differentiated according to their jobs.

To Durkheim ([1893] 1964), Western civilization was inevitably moving from mechanical to organic solidarity. That is, it was changing from a form of social organization based on unity of thought, beliefs, sentiments, and manners to one based on unity of heterogeneous individuals bound together by functionally interrelated tasks.

For Durkheim, the prime force behind this evolution is the increasingly complex division of labor. In organically solid societies such as the United States, tasks are highly specialized. This specialization is reflected in the U.S. Labor Department's O*NET system, which consists of more than 950 job titles known to the U.S. federal government.

Both mechanically solid and organically solid societies, in Durkheim's view, are natural forms of social organization. Both are rooted in social unity; only the type of unity differs. The unity and homogeneity of rural society are replaced by unity consisting of functional interdependence in industrial society. (Tönnies, in contrast, defined *Gemeinschaft* as a natural social form and *Gesellschaft* as artificial.)

What are the consequences of the evolution from rural, mechanically solid society to urban-industrial, organically solid society? Durkheim thought that the collective conscience weakens as a society becomes more specialized and differentiated by function. Contracts and a belief in the individual replace the collective conscience. In urban-industrial society, moral order is upheld by contracts and restitutive law, not by a common morality and repressive law.

To Durkheim, then, the two forms of social organization can be distinguished by their legal base: "Law reproduces the principal forms of social solidarity" ([1893] 1964:68). In mechanically solid society, the legal system represses offenses against the common morality or collective conscience; such offenses are symbolically repressed because they threaten the moral order. Retaliation and punishment are typical sanctions applied in mechanically solid society. But in organically solid society, few offenses are seen as threats to the entire moral order. In many cases, an offense is handled by making amends (restitution) to the injured party in the form of money.

Here is an example of the difference between repressive and restitutive legal systems. Suppose your gun accidentally goes off, killing another person. Everyone agrees that this was a freak accident. Would a court imprison or exile you? Not in organically solid society, for this action would not be considered a threat to morality. At worst, you could be judged negligent and ordered to pay restitution to the victim's survivors. This same freak accident in mechanically solid society, however, could be punished in a repressive way. In *Things Fall Apart* ([1959] 1996, 2003), Nigerian novelist Chinua Achebe describes just such an incident. In the novel, the gun of an Ibo tribesman accidentally goes off, killing a 16-year-old boy. The punishment is 7 years in exile. Why? Because it was a crime against the earth goddess to kill a clansman; a man who committed such a crime had to flee from the land.

To conclude: Durkheim draws a polar distinction between two forms of social solidarity: mechanical and organic. The law, either repressive or restitutive, provides an index to a society's form of social solidarity. In both forms, the division of labor functions to cement social bonds. In rural, mechanically solid society, the simple division of labor promotes a common morality (collective conscience); in urban, organically solid society, the complex division of labor promotes functional interdependence. As simple, homogeneous, rural society is transformed (by population growth, increased communication, and larger territory), the division of labor evolves toward higher and higher specialization of function. This specialized division of labor can—*but does not necessarily*—lead to social dislocations: If the complex division of labor malfunctions in urban-industrial society, Durkheim warned, it could not play its role of cementing social solidarity. For example, the division of labor can become so complex that people work at very specialized tasks, not knowing how their task fits into any larger whole. Under such conditions, people can experience feelings of anxiety and meaninglessness, not a sense of social solidarity. This point of view, as we shall see in Chapter 19, is especially relevant to contemporary job dissatisfaction.

CULTURE AND CIVILIZATION (SPENGLER)

Oswald Spengler (1880–1936) was so unlike his predecessors in the typological tradition that the differences deserve comment. Spengler was an obscure high school teacher, not a respected scholar. But the book he wrote—translated as *The Decline of the West* ([1918] 1962)—had much more popular impact than the writings of Tönnies and Durkheim combined.

Spengler was not a social scientist. The label "agrarian mystic" comes closest to describing him. In *The Decline of the West*, Spengler celebrates the triumph of the will and intuition over reason and intellect, glorifying the notion of destiny and denigrating social science. This brand of mystic romanticism is echoed in Hitler's propaganda of the 1930s, particularly the Nazi film *The Triumph of the Will* (1936), which stresses the superiority of so-called Aryan community over heterogeneous society.

Spengler draws a fundamental contrast between country and city. To him, the country is the home of all things bright and beautiful. He refers to rural, preindustrial life as the home of a living, organic entity (culture). In contrast, the city is a dead, mechanical shell, the home of civilization.

To express his evolutionary view of the shift from country to city, Spengler uses the metaphor of the seasons. In the spring of history, there are rural communities typified by intuition and unity. Then comes summer, the time of early urban stirrings. Religion becomes impoverished, mathematical and scientific thought expands, and rationality starts to replace mystical views of the universe. The autumn of a culture's history soon follows. Here is the "intelligence of the city," the height of intellectual creativity. And a cult of science, utility, and prosperity is not far behind; it follows in the winter season, that time of megalopolitan civilization and irreligious cosmopolitanism. It is in winter that civilization finally withers and dies. Birth, growth, death, and rebirth. That, in Spengler's cyclical view of history, is the evolutionary sequence from culture to civilization and back again to culture.

The central focus of Spengler's analysis is sociopsychological: the urban and rural personalities. In the preindustrial-rural community, Spengler writes, people interact on the basis of feelings. But in urban-industrial life, money becomes paramount, intellect takes over from intuition, and human interaction becomes shallow.

URBAN PERSONALITY (WIRTH)

Louis Wirth (1897–1952), a member of the Chicago school of sociology, was not at all attracted by Spengler's antiscientific mysticism. But he was vitally concerned with the social psychology of modern city dwellers. He asked, and answered, this question: Is there an urban personality?

In his still influential essay," Urbanism as a Way of Life" (1938), Wirth argued that **urbanism**—patterns of social interaction and culture that result from the concentration of large numbers of people in small areas—affects the human personality. In his essay, Wirth implies a polar contrast between urban and rural personalities, and he theorizes that the way urbanites think and act is linked to the characteristics of modern cities (Box 6.1).

More specifically, Wirth says that cities are large, dense settlements with heterogeneous populations. These three variables—large size, high density, and heterogeneity—promote a certain kind of emotional and mental response. Urbanites typically react by becoming sophisticated, rational, and relativistic. They become indifferent and seemingly uncaring toward one another because that is the only way they can protect themselves against "the personal claims and expectations of others." Human interaction becomes "impersonal, superficial, transitory, and segmental" (Figure 6.5).

The lone individual counts for little in the modern city. Thus, to accomplish their goals, individuals with similar interests join together to form organizations. Unlike rural folk, city dwellers do not owe their total allegiance to any one group or community. A woman might simultaneously be a member of Save the Whales, a political party, a cousins' club, a baseball team, a church-sponsored social group, and a labor union. Each group represents merely one part of the woman's total interests; none commands her undivided loyalty. Similarly, urbanites relate to one another on the basis of segmented roles—as teachers and students in a classroom, for example, rather than as total human beings who know one another's families, interests, concerns, and so forth.

Like Tönnies, Spengler, and Marx, Wirth insisted on the importance of the money economy as a determinant of the urban personality. According to Wirth, the "pecuniary nexus" replaces personal relations as the basis for association in the city. Utility and efficiency replace emotion and intimacy. The result is depersonalization.

For Wirth, then, urbanism leads inevitably to specific forms of social action and personal behavior. For example, urbanites come into contact with too many people to interact in any but a superficial way. Wirth implies that the large, dense, heterogeneous city is such a powerful force in people's lives that they react to this entity in similar ways. That is, urbanites—regardless of race, color, creed, or social rank—react to their physical and social surroundings in a typically urban fashion.

PREINDUSTRIAL AND INDUSTRIAL CITIES (SJOBERG)

U.S. sociologist Gideon Sjoberg ([1960] 1999) is not, strictly speaking, in the rural–urban tradition. His typology contrasts two city types: preindustrial and industrial. But Sjoberg's categories essentially deal with two types of societies, not cities: those his predecessors call rural and urban, mechanically solid and organically solid.

In Sjoberg's view, technology dictates social, political, and ecological organization. Taking energy sources (animate, such as people or animals, versus

Fig. 6.5 URBANISM AS A WAY OF LIFE. Wirth (1938) says that a modern urbanite does not owe allegiance to a single group but instead acquires membership in many different groups; each group represents only a particular segment of his or her personality. One group that functions like this is the Pagan Alliance. (T. S. Whitmore)

inanimate, such as steam or electricity) as his key variable, Sjoberg argued (and still does) that extensive industrialization requires particular economic, social, and political institutions. An industrial city (dependent on inanimate energy sources) requires a centralized economic organization, a flexible kinship system, mass education, mass communication, and an achievement-oriented social-class system. By contrast, he says, a preindustrial city (dependent on animate energy sources) requires face-to-face communication, rigid social differentiation by age and gender, and informal social controls based on kinship, religion, and social rank.

Interestingly, 40 years after his article about the preindustrial city, Gideon Sjoberg and his wife Andrée Sjoberg (1996) took another look at his typology. Rethinking the original formulation (and responding to critics) of their city type, the Sjobergs say that they would make some updates. For example, they would now pay more attention to the literature of preindustrial civilizations (e.g., India's *Ramayana*), and they would "analyze the differences between earlier and later forms of the preindustrial city" (99). Yet, they insist on the importance of traditional norms that continue to affect "family, religious, and stratification even in the face of the great transformation [in Eurasia] that has resulted from industrialization" (101).

BOX 6.1 SIZE, DENSITY, AND HETEROGENEITY

"Urbanism as a Way of Life" by Louis Wirth

A Sociological Definition of the City

For sociological purposes a city may be defined as a relatively large, dense, and permanent settlement of socially heterogeneous individuals.

Population Aggregate Size

Ever since Aristotle's *Politics*, it has been recognized that increasing the number of inhabitants in a settlement beyond a certain limit will affect the relationships between them and the character of the city. Large numbers involve...a greater range of individual variation. Furthermore, the greater the number of individuals participating in a process of interaction, the greater is the *potential* differentiation between them. The personal traits, the occupations, the cultural life, and the ideas of the members of an urban community may, therefore, be expected to range between more widely separated poles than those of rural inhabitants.

That such variations should give rise to the spatial segregation of individuals according to color, ethnic heritage, economic and social status, tastes, and preferences may readily be inferred. The bonds of kinship, of neighborliness, and the sentiments arising out of living together for generations under a common folk tradition are likely to be absent or, at best, relatively weak in an aggregate the members of which have such diverse origins and backgrounds. Under such circumstances competition and formal control mechanisms furnish the substitutes for the bonds of solidarity that are relied upon to hold a folk society together.

Increasing the number of inhabitants of a community beyond a few hundred is bound to limit the possibility of each member of the community knowing all the others personally....The increase in numbers...involves a changed character of the social relationship....

Characteristically, urbanites meet one another in highly segmental roles. They are, to be sure, dependent upon more people for the satisfactions of their life-needs than are rural people and thus are associated with a great number of organized groups, but they are less dependent upon particular persons, and their dependence upon others is confined to a highly fractionalized aspect of the other's round of activity. This is essentially what is meant by saying that the city is characterized by secondary rather than primary contacts. The contacts of the city may indeed be face to face, but they are nevertheless impersonal, superficial, transitory, and segmental. The reserve, the indifference, and the blasé outlook which urbanites manifest in their relationships may thus be regarded as devices for immunizing themselves against the personal claims and expectations of others.

The superficiality, the anonymity, and the transitory character of urban social relations make intelligible, also, the sophistication and the rationality generally ascribed to city-dwellers [italics mine]. Our acquaintances tend to stand in a relationship of utility to us in the sense that the role which each one plays in our life is overwhelmingly regarded as a means for the achievement of our own ends. Whereas the individual gains, on the one hand, a certain degree of emancipation or freedom from the personal and emotional controls of intimate groups, he loses, on the other hand, the spontaneous self-expression, the morale, and the sense of participation that comes with living in an integrated society. This constitutes essentially the state of *anomie*, or the social void....

The segmental character and utilitarian accent of interpersonal relations in the city find their institutional expression in the proliferation of specialized tasks which we see in their most developed form in the professions. The operations of the pecuniary nexus lead to predatory relationships which tend to obstruct the efficient functioning of the social order unless checked by professional codes and occupational etiquette. The premium put upon utility and efficiency suggests the adaptability of the corporate device for the organization of enterprises in which individuals can engage only in groups. The advantage that the corporation has over the individual entrepreneur and the partnership in the urban-industrial world derives not only from the possibility it affords of centralizing the resources of thousands of individuals or from the legal privilege of limited liability and perpetual succession, but from the fact that the corporation has no soul....

The dominance of the city over the surrounding hinterland becomes explicable in terms of the division of labor which urban life occasions and promotes. The extreme degree of interdependence and the unstable equilibrium of urban life are closely associated with the division of labor and the specialization of occupations....

...Typically in the city, interests are made effective through representation. The individual counts for little, but the voice of the representative is heard with a deference roughly proportional to the numbers for whom he speaks....

Density

An increase in numbers when area is held constant (i.e., an increase in density) tends to produce differentiation and specialization, since only in this way can the area support increased numbers. Density thus reinforced the effect of numbers in diversifying men and their activities and in increasing the complexity of the social structure....

The different parts of the city acquire specialized functions, and the city consequently comes to resemble a mosaic

Continued

BOX 6.1 *Continued*

of social worlds in which the transition from one to the other is abrupt. The juxtaposition of divergent personalities and modes of life tends to produce a relativistic perspective and a sense of toleration of differences which may be regarded as prerequisites for rationality and which lead toward the secularization of life.

The close living together and working together of individuals who have no sentimental and emotional ties foster a spirit of competition, aggrandizement, and mutual exploitation [italics mine]. Formal controls are instituted to counteract irresponsibility and potential disorder.... The clock and the traffic signal are symbolic of the basis of our social order in the urban world. Frequent close physical contact, coupled with great social distance, accentuates the reserve of unattached individuals toward one another and, unless compensated by other opportunities for response, gives rise to loneliness. The necessary frequent movement of great numbers of individuals in a congested habitat causes friction and irritation. Nervous tensions which derive from such personal frustrations are increased by the rapid tempo and the complicated technology under which life in dense areas must be lived.

Heterogeneity

The social interaction among such a variety of personality types in the urban milieu tends to break down the rigidity of caste lines and to complicate the class structure.... The heightened mobility of the individual... brings him toward the acceptance of instability and insecurity in the world at large as a norm. This fact helps to account, too, for the sophistication and cosmopolitanism of the urbanite. No single group has the undivided allegiance of the individual.... The individual acquires membership in widely divergent groups, each of which functions only with reference to a certain segment of his personality....

There is little opportunity for the individual to obtain a conception of the city as a whole or to survey his place in the total scheme. Consequently *he [or she] finds it difficult to determine what is in his [or her] own "best interests"* [italics mine] and to decide between the issues and leaders presented to him [or her] by the agencies of mass suggestion. Individuals who are thus detached from the organized bodies which integrate society comprise the fluid masses that make collective behavior in the urban community so unpredictable and hence so problematical.

Although the city... produces a highly differentiated population, it also exercises a leveling influence.... This leveling tendency inheres in part in the economic basis of the city.... Progressively as cities have developed upon a background of [mass production of standardized products for an impersonal market], the pecuniary nexus which implies the purchasability of services and things has displaced personal relations as the basis of association. Individuality under these circumstances must be replaced by categories. When large numbers have to make common use of facilities and institutions, those facilities and institutions must serve the needs of the average person rather than those of particular individuals... the cultural institutions, such as the schools, the movies, the radio, and the newspapers, by virtue of their mass clientele, must necessarily operate as leveling influences. The political process as it appears in urban life could not be understood unless one examined the mass appeals made through modern propaganda techniques. If the individual would participate at all in the social, political, and economic life of the city, he must subordinate some of his individuality to the demands of the larger community and in that measure immerse himself in mass movements.

Source: Louis Wirth, "Urbanism as a Way of Life," *American Journal of Sociology* 44 (1938):1–24. Copyright 1938 by the University of Chicago Press. Reprinted by permission.

ADDING A THIRD TYPE: *TECHNO$CHAFT*

Call it postindustrial, postsuburban, or postmodern society. Call it the world information economy, the global village, the third wave, or *Techno$chaft* (so named by my San Francisco State students some years ago). Whatever it's called, many theorists think it is a new form of social, spatial, and economic organization.

In general terms, *Techno$chaft* (postindustrial society) is viewed as a type of society where wealth is based on the capacity to get, understand, and use information. One key difference between

urban-industrial and postindustrial society is this: In *Gesellschaft*, manufacturing (particularly textiles, steel, and cars) dominates the economy; in *Techno$chaft*, global finance and electronic entertainment dominate the economy.

This shift from *Gesellschaft* to *Techno$chaft* is facilitated by information technologies. One result: Neither the shape of cities nor the range of a firm's business is inextricably tied to the physical location of factories, finance centers, and so on. Instead, there is a global urban system run, to a great extent, on information.

The case of the Italian-based chain Benetton is instructive. It suggests that the global fashion business resembles electronic entertainment more than *Gesellschaft* manufacturing. It also suggests how important globalization has become to merchandisers.

Benetton was staggeringly successful in the mid-1980s and early 1990s because it operated thousands of shops with up-to-date information regarding color and consumer habits. But, for years after that, it lost out to new competitors. Despite hard times, Benetton never abandoned its politically controversial ads, which celebrated racial diversity and integration. Then, in 2006, it rebounded. How? In large part by streamlining its deliveries, not changing its styles (Meichtry, 2007:B1).

Given Benetton's celebration of racial diversity and integration as key to their corporate image, increased immigration to Europe could have impacted their sales. In Italy, for example, there has been a "substantial hardening of attitudes" against immigrants of many colors—whether African, Muslim, Chinese, Romanian, or other (Wilkinson, 2007). Indeed, the hardening of attitudes against immigrants of various colors meant that Benetton's message became more provocative. Even in Treviso, Italy, Benetton's hometown, an unknown person or persons defaced a Benetton billboard showcasing people of different races, scribbling "these colors do not mix" (Martin, 2007). Moreover, Treviso's longtime mayor (and later deputy mayor, due to term limits), an ultra-rightist, told a *New York Times* reporter that "Italians have a 2,000-year-old civilization" behind them but African immigrants in Treviso "know only the civilization of the savanna and the jungle," where they used to chase gazelles and lions (in Bruni, 2002).

Now that its ads run contrary to the sentiments of so many Europeans (and potential customers), how does Benetton proceed? So far, its ads celebrating racial diversity continue. The company's image as socially conscious, together with its founders' deep-seated values, may be important. But globalization may be pivotal: Benetton operates in 120 countries, and most of its sales lie outside Italy. (In 2001, all of Europe generated 68.7 percent of total sales volume [Chun et al., 2003]. In 2006, Europe accounted for an even higher percentage of its sales—over 82 percent—but Asia, the Americas, and the rest of the world were good customers too; they bought a growing share of 150 million garments in 5,000 stores whose total turnover amounted to over 1.9 billion euros [Benetton Press Area, 2007]).

Benetton, like many companies today, depends on borderless communication. In this *Techno$chaft* world of communication without borders, nations mean less and less. Anthony Smith suggests why:

> The whole history of the nation as a political unit of [hu]mankind has been predicated upon territoriality; the technology of printing came into being in the same era as the nation-state and both seem to be reaching the end of their usefulness in the era of the computer; it is physically impossible to impose upon data the same kinds of controls that are imposed upon goods and paper-borne information....
>
> *(Smith in Brand, 1987:239)*

In this tantalizing (and disguised) hypothesis, Smith posits that technology is a key influence on political change: The rise of the nation-state and the rise of print occur at the same time, as do the fall of the nation-state and the rise of the computer, because computer data, unlike printed books, are essentially borderless and thus uncontrollable by sovereign states.

HOW USEFUL ARE THE RURAL–URBAN TYPOLOGIES?

The late anthropologist Margaret Mead, noted for her outspoken wit as well as her scholarship, once gave this explanation for migration from the countryside to cities: "At least 50 percent of the human race doesn't want their mother-in-law within walking distance." Mead's remark may tell us as much about rural-preindustrial life as the typologies do.

The typologies were constructed as tools for understanding the changes from rural-preindustrial to urban-industrial life in western Europe. But they remain very limited tools. Essentially, four kinds of criticism can be leveled at the typologies. These deal with their major hypotheses, empirical evidence, analytical rigor, and contemporary relevance.

TABLE 6.1 TYPOLOGIES OF THE RURAL-URBAN-GLOBAL SHIFT IN WESTERN EUROPE AND NORTH AMERICA

Characteristics	Rural-Preindustrial Community (*Gemeinschaft*)	Urban-Industrial Society (*Gesellschaft*)	Global-Postindustrial Association (*Techno$chaft*)
SPATIAL-GEOGRAPHIC	Cities organized around religious/public buildings, market centers. Symbols: church spires, forts, palaces. Urban places but no urban society. Close links to surrounding, immediate environment. Well-defined neighborhoods by ethnic/tribal group.	Cities organized around economic institutions, business/industry. Symbol: factory smokestacks. Urban society, dense settlements. Urban sprawl. Links to faraway places via communications and transport technology.	Cities organized around electronic communication. Symbol: skyscraper, temple of corporate finance and communications. Fragmented, collage cities. Continuous spatial restructuring. Shape of cities results from interplay of market forces, government policies, and community resistance. No single spatial pattern. Global urban system. "World cities" (e.g., Tokyo, New York City) play key roles. Sense of place fades. Time–space compression due to advanced information technology and firms' ability to use various spaces for various purposes.
ECONOMIC	Nonmarket economy: barter, exchange, or money exchange at a simple level. Wealth measured in land (or cattle, etc.), not money. Agricultural base. Relatively self-sufficient communities. Cottage, handicraft industries. Simple division of labor. Relative self-sufficiency.	Market economy. Cash nexus. Wealth measured in money, capital. Heavy manufacturing base. Interdependence at regional, national, international levels. Complex division of labor. Functional interdependence.	Late capitalism. Global interdependence. Agribusiness, transnationals, trading networks. Wealth based on ability to get and use information. Decentralization of production, centralization of control. Demyasstified, customized products. Flexible work practices. Heightened intercity competition for development. Information, communications, and service base. Power of market over cultural production. Growing gap between rich and poor.

The rural–urban typologies have unique aspects, but they share a basic assumption: that people think, feel, behave, and organize their activities differently in rural and urban cultures. (These differences, in general terms, are outlined in Table 6.1, with one addition: alleged differences in *Techno$chaft*.) Further, the theoretical constructs assume that modern urban-industrial life requires or inevitably leads to particular forms of urban personality structure, social organization, and economic–political institutions.

UNTESTED HYPOTHESES

In 1951, Louis Wirth said that the hypotheses embedded in the typologies had not been thoroughly tested empirically (in Hauser, 1967:506–507). Unfortunately, Wirth's criticism stands to the present day.

TABLE 6.1 *CONTINUED*

Characteristics	Rural-Preindustrial Community (*Gemeinschaft*)	Urban-Industrial Society (*Gesellschaft*)	Global-Postindustrial Association (*Techno$chaft*)
SOCIOCULTURAL	Blood ties, extended family and kinship networks, neighborhood, friendship. Sense of community, belongingness. Face-to-face communication. Primary groups important. Tribal or ethnic cohesion. Homogeneity of culture, beliefs within tribal/ethnic group. Ascribed status. Religions, sacred explanations.	Blood ties relatively unimportant, individual as primary unit. Segmented roles. Social mobility. Heterogeneity. Urban, urbane culture. Mass communication. Secondary groups important. Alienation, anomie. Achieved status. Scientific, secular explanations.	Extended social networks. City as giant electronic screen or collage. Denationalized, world entertainment culture. Distinctions based on social status and taste all important. Multiple viewpoints. "Reality" negotiated between social groups. Fragmentation and eclecticism. Acceptance of deep chaos in urban process. *Gemeinschaft*-like groups remain. Plural systems of knowledge. An aesthetic that celebrates cultural differences and quick changes.
POLITICAL	Traditional authority. Sacred traditions. Some experts (e.g., priests) with monopoly over knowledge, but generally widely shared knowledge base. Informal sanctions. Repressive law. Lack of contracts. Dominance by traditional religious/political elites. Family background, connections important.	Legal/rational authority. Secular traditions. Knowledge gap between experts and laypersons. Dominance by merchants, capitalists. Power elites. Occupations and professions among important interest groups. Bureaucracy. Restitutive law, contracts. Merit as principle of advancement rather than family background.	Corporate power dominates. Nation-state fades. Pre-eminence of professional-scientific technical personnel. Meritocracy. Bureaucratic state. Democracy of consumers rather than citizens. Possibilities for both centralization and decentralization of political knowledge.

CONTRARY EVIDENCE

Existing empirical evidence, however, does call into question the major hypotheses. Wirth himself drew attention to the U.S. city as a mosaic of local cultures, maintained by social isolation. In his study of Chicago's Jewish ghetto ([1928] 1956:284–287), he noted that many *Gemeinschaft*-like groups (e.g., French Canadians, artistic rebels, hobos) had their own distinct type of dominant personality and moral code.

The work of George M. Foster goes to the heart of the matter. It questions the assumption that urban and rural modes of life are fundamentally different. Long ago, anthropologist Foster (1965) found many so-called urban personality traits in rural society.

According to Foster, peasant societies have an "image of limited good." That is, the good life is seen as finite and nonexpandable, and an individual can progress only at the expense of others. Cooperative behavior among peasants is perceived as dysfunctional to community stability. The result is that "extreme individualism is chosen over cooperation in preserving peasants' security," discouraging any changes in the status quo (Foster, 1965:310).

Indeed, Foster finds that peasants typically express distrust of others, friendlessness, and suspicion of people outside the family. Such an orientation does not lead to the mechanical solidarity or the caring–sharing community that Durkheim and Tönnies envisioned. To the contrary, it leads to structural and psychological atomism.

Through the decades, writers of varying ideological stripes (e.g., Banfield and Banfield, 1958; Talese, 1992) have supported Foster's vision of preindustrial communities as fiercely competitive, uncooperative, and contentious. In addition, some (e.g., Springborg, 1986) claim that relationships in many ancient societies were contractual, not based on love or kinship. In light of such evidence, Tönnies's conception of *Gemeinschaft* seems a rather romantic vision of a past that never was.

If Foster and others find indifference and friendlessness in the rural countryside, other researchers find so-called rural personality traits in the city. The fieldwork of Oscar Lewis is illustrative. Anthropologist Lewis studied the "citification" of peasants in Mexico over a number of years. One such rural emigrant, Jesús Sanchez, had lived for over 20 years in a Mexico City slum tenement when Lewis interviewed him again, along with his four children. Their autobiographical statements, recorded by Lewis in *The Children of Sanchez* (1961), show them to be living refutations of Wirth's urban personality type; they are not uncaring, utilitarian, or blasé.

The thrust of Lewis's research was that there is no such thing as a typically urban personality. He showed that various city dwellers have different responses to city life. Lewis (1967) argued that Wirth's key variables (large size, high density, and heterogeneity) are not the crucial determinants of urban personality or urban social life. Lewis advocated studying the varied social areas or neighborhoods in a city, not the city as a whole, in order to understand the various urban personalities.

Years ago, sociologist–planner Herbert Gans ([1962] 1982) did study one neighborhood: an Italian American working-class community in Boston. There, he found an "urban village" based on social intimacy, not alienation and loneliness.

DETERMINISTIC ASSUMPTIONS

This brings up a related criticism of the typological tradition: its determinism. The typologies leave no room for varied cultural adaptations to urban-industrial life. Instead, they assume that urbanization and industrialization are such powerful processes that they stamp out cultural and ideological differences.

Yet many examples show that differing cultural traditions do count in people's adaptations to urban life. In addition to Oscar Lewis's research in Mexico, there are other examples of differential responses to urban life from other continents. In Uganda, for instance, some middle-class Ganda tribespeople work in the capital city of Kampala, but they try to live in surrounding rural areas so that they can raise their own subsistence crops. This arrangement permits strong continuity between rural and urban environments. In Timbuktu, Mali, and Cairo, Egypt, researchers did find strong kinship relationships, not anonymity, superficiality, and transitory social associations, as Wirth predicted.

Bangkok, Thailand, exemplifies another non-Western response to urban life. In the sprawling city of Bangkok, traffic seems death-defying to foreigners. Since 1945, Bangkok's population has mushroomed, surpassing 10 million in the year 2000. Its rapid growth has led to a severe strain on facilities and heavy traffic congestion. Streets are packed with people and noisy vehicles. Parts of the city are sinking due to the pumping of water from wells to supply suburban areas. But despite this apparent chaos, Bangkok works rather harmoniously. A Thai architect–city planner thinks he knows why: Bangkokites were once water people. For centuries they lived on canals, now mainly filled in. But the people still live like water people. They drive their cars and trucks as they used to drive riverboats, accommodating other drivers and pedestrians as they once did on the canals. According to Mr. Jumsai, "Water people adapt to the flow of the current. They go with the forces of nature, not against" (in Kamm, 1978). This sense of accommodation—literally and figuratively going with the flow—seems to pervade the social fabric of Bangkok, where overseas Chinese and other ethnic minorities live without apparent friction, unlike the inhabitants of so many cities in South Asia.

These examples suggest that we cannot make gross generalizations about *the* nature of city life or *the* personality of urbanites. In short, beating the traffic and living in crowded spaces are common features of urban-industrial life. But the responses to these constants may be different.

Of course, we should not forget the eastern European proverb: "'For example' is no proof." That is, for every example of how culture mediates a group's adaptation to urban-industrial life, a determinist could respond, "Hey, just wait. It's only a matter of time. Eventually, societies with similar economic systems will resemble each other (converge) in their basic institutional structures and world views—despite their cultural differences." This is the core of **convergence theory**. And it is not new. Many eighteenth- and nineteenth-century social thinkers, including the French *philosophes*, the Scottish moral philosophers, Tönnies, Marx, Spencer, Weber, and Durkheim, thought that societies with similar economic structures would converge. In recent years, changes in the family-like Japanese factory (where labor–management relations were once—but are no longer—typified by lifetime employment and loyalty, not worker alienation) and studies of Eastern European nations after the breakup of the former Soviet Union in 1989 as well as studies of the postindustrial society tend to reflect convergence theory. (*Note*: Social scientists do not always share a definition of a term, making it difficult to do interdisciplinary research. Such is the case here. In economics, for instance, the theory of convergence refers to one particular measure of similarity, per capita income: Poorer economies tend to grow faster than wealthier economies, resulting in a convergence of all economies in terms of per capita income.)

To be evenhanded, there is a great deal of evidence pointing to convergence. Here are a few examples:

1. Years ago, a Spanish sociologist lamented that young urbanites in Spain were catching up with other western Europeans, becoming "a nation of narcissists, concerned mainly with the cult to the body, to comfort, to consumption, to money" (de Miguel in Riding, 1991:4). This narcissism does not seem to have been reversed in recent years.

2. Increasing global economic interdependence, decreasing importance of national borders, and widespread use of communications technologies are leading to similar urban challenges, including unemployment, residential segregation by social class, and decaying housing. Thus, industrial cities as different as Detroit, Brussels, and Kiev face the same economic forces, with similar results.

3. Cross-cultural data show that the same occupations rank high or low in social esteem in all urban-industrialized societies. (Chapter 11 details this point.)

4. Cross-cultural data also suggest that the definition and expectations of the family are changing throughout the urban-industrial and postindustrial worlds. For one thing, government, professional experts, and business are taking over traditional family functions, including financial support and emotional warmth. Here is a stark case from Japan, a society once known for its extended family ties: A Tokyo company, Japan Efficiency Corporation, is in the rent-a-family business. Mainly older couples pay top yen for "family visits," where professional stand-ins play the roles of children and grandchildren.

5. Cultural tastes around the world seem to be similar. For example, as of 2008, Hollywood's *Titanic* (1997) was not only the all-time top-grossing movie in the United States but also the biggest box office hit internationally. *Lord of the Rings* (2003), directed by New Zealand's Peter Jackson, placed second on the all-time top–grossing movies list, both in the United States and worldwide.

6. Among industrialized, labor-importing nations, there is a growing similarity in policies aimed at controlling immigration (Cornelius et al., 1995:3).

7. Many Japanese factories are no longer family-like, keeping employees on the payroll even if they no longer need them. Instead, some "downsize" and fire long-time workers.

Such examples lead followers of Durkheim to reaffirm his sense of evolutionary development. In Durkheim's view, increases in the specialization of function *inevitably* lead to particular forms of social solidarity.

No matter which side of the convergence–cultural adaptation debate one finds more convincing at the present time, there are other serious criticisms of the typologies. These concern their contemporary relevance and their analytical rigor.

CONTEMPORARY IRRELEVANCE

First, let's consider their relevance in the contemporary world. A rural speck today—whether in Nepal or Mexico—is hardly a self-sufficient island. Satellites, the Internet, transistor radios, and international trade agreements provide direct links between countryside and city. Even remote villages exist within a global political economy.

So, if rural communities are tied to far-flung nations as well as to nearby cities, what rural–urban contrasts make sense today? Should we expect to find meaningful differences in people's attitudes and behavior, depending on their rural or urban residence? Scholars disagree here too. One view, called the *massification thesis*, holds that rural people in advanced industrial societies become indistinguishable from their city cousins. In this view, mass media, mass education, and other influences break down rural isolation and diffuse urban culture into the countryside. Another view might be called the "global culture/ consumption thesis." It holds that the internationalization of culture and consumption patterns tends to homogenize cultures, tearing down national boundaries. If correct, the tendency toward sameness everywhere could result in the *intensification* of rural–urban distinctions. But why? And how? In an increasingly homogenized global society, tourists (an important economic resource) tend to seek out unique rural communities because they represent "the last vestiges of traditional ways-of-life" (Bartmann and Baum, 1998:692–693). Thus, it is in the interests of governments with rural hamlets in a scenic countryside to maintain the rural–urban distinction in order to attract tourists.

Appealing to a romanticized vision of the rural past can be a savvy advertising strategy, aimed at attracting visitors. As geographer David Lowenthal put it in *The Past is a Foreign Country* (1988), the future can be frightening because it is uncertain. The past, on the other hand, is safe and secure. (This may help explain the popularity of some theme parks and theme-park towns, discussed in Chapter 5, as well as attempts to combine urbanism and traditionalism, discussed in Chapter 17.)

Another view is that appreciable rural–urban differences persist even in advanced industrial societies. However, as the information superhighway replaces the Route 66s on many continents, my hunch is that more romantics than social scientists will find appreciable urban–rural differences.

The contemporary relevance of the typologies can be questioned on still other grounds. Importantly, the nineteenth-century typology builders assumed that European patterns of change would be universal. But this pattern—the nearly simultaneous rise of big cities, industrialism, and capitalism—is not being repeated in many poor countries. Hence, attitudes and behavior assumed to be associated with urbanization in western Europe (and North America) may not characterize poor societies now undergoing urbanization.

JUMBLED VARIABLES

This brings us to the problem of analytical rigor. The typologists did not separate the key variables in their hypotheses on urbanization and social change. Which variable—urbanization, industrialization, or capitalism?—supposedly leads inevitably, invariably, and necessarily to urbanism as a way of life? The typologies do not specify. Rather, they assume that these three processes go hand-in-hand. But individualism, to take just one supposed trait of the urban personality, may not be a necessary ingredient of urbanization per se. For example, in Japan, a postindustrial society, group loyalty and collective responsibility remain highly valued.

This is a serious criticism of the typologies: They make too much of the supposedly fundamental differences between rural and urban traits. The assumption that modern urbanites have greater faith in science than in religion for controlling events merits special attention in this regard. If correct, how can we understand some preachers who claimed in 2005 (not 1305) that Hurricane Katrina was God's retribution for human sins. In other words, differences between so-called urban (industrial and postindustrial) and rural (preindustrial) personalities do not seem all that clear.

To conclude: The rural–urban typologies are limited tools for understanding the shift from rural-preindustrial to urban-industrial life. First, they have never been systematically tested. They remain *articles of faith*, based more on historical imagination than on scientific research. Second, they are *deterministic*. The typological tradition comes out of a nineteenth-century Darwinian worldview of unilinear, one-way evolution. It cannot account for significant differences within preindustrial communities or industrial societies. Third, the typologies are *ethnocentric*. They assume that what happened in western Europe—particularly the hand-in-hand development of urbanization, industrialization, and capitalism—will happen universally. This has not been the case in much of the world. Fourth, they rest on a dubious assumption: that the transformation from agricultural to industrial life requires, or inevitably leads to, a radical change in the nature of human personality. To begin with, they make too much of the differences between city and country, between traditional community and modern society. The late, distinguished anthropologist Clifford Geertz put it this way: "Stark 'great divide' contrasts between 'modern' and 'premodern' societies, the one individualistic, rational, and free of tradition, the other collectivistic, intuitive, and mired in it, look increasingly mythical, summary, and simple-minded" (1994:3).

Instinctively, we may feel that the sense of community is not the same in the Athenian polis and the U.S. metropolis. We sense that life in a tribal village and medieval London is somehow different. Of course, there *are* differences between everyday life in a polis and a metropolis. But it is dangerous to attribute the differences to urbanization alone. The effects of industrialization, cultural values, and other variables have to be carefully unscrambled when assessing the ruran–urban shift in various societies. So far, this has not been done. Instead, theorists have accomplished only what poet William Carlos Williams (1953:11) advised against:

> up to the sum, by defective means.
> to make a start
> out of particulars
> and make them general, rolling
> up to the sum, by defective means.

ANOTHER LOOK

Looking back on the ties that bind, one basic theme emerges: Theorists fundamentally disagree on the nature of urbanization and urbanism. Their disagreements are not rooted in either their disciplinary backgrounds or their research methods. For example, two anthropologists (Robert Redfield and Oscar Lewis) studied the same Mexican village using the same method (fieldwork) but came to different conclusions about the nature of rural life.

Similarly, theorists do not agree on the nature of urban life. Their disagreements, however, do stem from differences in (1) levels of analysis, (2) theoretical orientations, or (3) attitudes toward "progress."

1. *Levels of analysis*. Tönnies, Durkheim, and Spengler were macro-level theorists interested in the broad sweep of change from rural to urban society. Hence, they focused on entire social systems in their analysis of urbanization and urbanism. Louis Wirth, investigating the urban personality, used the entire city as his unit of analysis. Other theorists, notably Lewis, argued that neither entire social systems nor the city as a whole are proper units for studying social life or human personality. Lewis claimed that large numbers, high density, and heterogeneity are *not* crucial determinants of either urban social life or the urban personality because both occur in smaller universes—families, neighborhoods, and so on. Thus, Lewis advised using smaller units of analysis to study the urbanization process and urbanism. Using micro-level analysis, as Lewis proposed (and Herbert Gans carried out in Boston), theorists often find many ways of life coexisting within the same city, not a single urban way of life.

2. *Theoretical orientations*. Structural–functionalists and many (but not all) Marxist-oriented scholars pay little attention to cross-cultural differences in their analysis of modern urban life. They think that, in the long run, technological and economic imperatives will render cultural differences insignificant. This determinism is

rejected by theorists who insist that values, cultural traditions, and particular historical conditions can influence social organization in important ways. Thus, structural–functionalists (e.g., followers of Durkheim) and many Marxist-oriented theorists tend to view urbanization in capitalist western Europe and North America as a single, unitary process with similar effects on human personality; others tend to stress the different forms and meanings that urbanization and urbanism have taken.

3. *Attitudes toward "progress."* Do urban-industrial society (*Gesellschaft*) and/or postindustrial society (*Techno$chaft*) represent human liberation and "progress"—or human enslavement and regression? Here, thinkers profoundly disagree. In one camp are thinkers and activists who agree with poet Robinson Jeffers's rejection of "progress"; he thought that industrial civilization distorted human nature and led to the loss of contact with the earth. Similarly, Mahatma Gandhi became convinced that people could flower only in small communities bound by ties of vision and service. More recently, American author Wendell Berry (2001) argued that modern industrialism, free trade, and economic growth triumphed in the modern West at a terrible price: an economy based on waste, violence, and war. Berry calls for a new era based on the decentralization of the economy, economic justice, and ecological responsibility.

The late French theologian–historian Jacques Ellul despaired of *The Technological Society* (1965) in which life is a disconnected set of activities. Post–World War II playwrights, notably Samuel Beckett and Eugène Ionesco, seem to share this vision, portraying discombobulated wanderers staggering around on a barren stage in a senseless universe.

From a very different perspective, some question the very notion of "progress." First, the late evolutionary biologist Stephen Jay Gould (2003) claimed that Darwinian thought does not imply progress. Second, some art historians say that although the meanings may be very different, the abstractions of Neolithic rock artists and those of modern painters share an

economy of line and perhaps a hallucinatory vision. They ask, Can we call this "progress"?

In a second camp are a range of thinkers who believe that the technology and modern attitudes associated with *Gesellschaft* helped to free people from the shackles of tradition, enslavement or serfdom, scarcity, superstition, and parochialism. These include Karl Marx, who disdained the "idiocy of rural life"; inventor Buckminster Fuller, who suggested that people can evolve and transform their environment by using new technologies; political scientist Barrington Moore, who wrote that technological progress brings changes in social structure that provide the "prerequisites of freedom" (in Lasch, 1991:43); and conservative sociologist Robert Nisbet, who thought that the idea of progress is the single most important idea in Western history. This view is held by most liberals who envision a world progressively redeemed by human reason from poverty and ignorance.

But another camp, one we might call the "third way," disagrees with both extreme pessimists and optimists. Proponents point to the failure of *Gesellschaft* science and reason to eliminate poverty or to provide both individual freedom and community; they think it is possible to build social systems that are at once high-tech, democratic, and ecologically sound. For example, in *Eco Civilization 2140: A 22nd Century History and Survivor's Journal* (2006), Roy Morrison argues that democracy and free-market incentives (e.g., taxing pollution, not income) can point the way to a prosperous and sustainable future. Social critic and historian Theodore Roszak argues that "deurbanizing" the world—scaling down the size and power of cities and placing cities in a balance with rural society—will serve the needs of both *Person/Planet* (1977–1978).

And then there are thinkers–activists who eschew all the above. For example, U.S. exile-in-India Jeff Knaebel (2006) gives seminars across India asking participants to "generate an evolutionary quantum leap into a higher consciousness of nonviolence" for species survival. Among other things, he calls for "a revolution from fear to love" and from "corporate enslavement to individual liberty."

Attempting to integrate insights from these opposing camps seems like a worthy cause. However, it may be an impossible dream. No synthesis can occur, for proponents clash on core issues such as the nature of rural life and the impacts of capitalism and urbanization.

KEY TERMS

Collectivity A group with common ends, but not common kinship origins. Examples: social science professors, computer networkers, and owner-workers of cooperative business.

Community A concept with many meanings, often used without precise definition. It can refer to a traditional community in the sense of *Gemeinschaft*, a group that shares only a territorial area, or a group that shares values and culture without a common territory (e.g., an occupational group).

Convergence theory Macro-level social theory that predicts that, over time, advanced industrial societies will develop similar traits despite their cultural or ideological differences in order to fulfill similar functions.

Cosmopolis From the Greek, meaning "world city." A cosmopolitan person is one whose identification and involvement are with a larger social universe than the local community.

Counterculture A group of people whose beliefs, symbols, attitudes, and values oppose those of the dominant culture. In the United States, 1960s hippies and 1990s streetwise slum youth are considered to be countercultural groups.

Division of labor Social differentiation by work specialization or occupational role. Term especially associated with Emile Durkheim.

Gemeinschaft-**like** A quality describing some close-knit religious, occupational, ethnic, and common interest groups (e.g., the Amish; Moonies; Hasidic Jews; God's Little Acre mobile home park in Apache Junction, Arizona; many Native American tribes; San Francisco's gay and lesbian community; a Marine battalion) existing within *Gesellschaft*. Members of a *Gemeinschaft*-like group share values, meanings, and goals, and they maintain kin-like, face-to-face relationships within their groups.

Ideal type A mental construct used as a heuristic device to describe, compare, and test hypotheses. An ideal type is not meant to correspond exactly to any particular case in the observable world; rather, it is designed as a tentative model. Two or more ideal types form a classification scheme or typology. Examples: *Gemeinschaft, Gesellschaft, Techno$chraft*.

Mechanical and organic solidarity Durkheim's contrasting types of social solidarity. Mechanically solid societies are based on similar values, traditions, kinship, and a simple division of labor; organically solid societies are based on a complex division of labor requiring cooperation among heterogeneous people. Organic solidarity is so named because, in Durkheim's view, it is similar to the human body, in which specialized organs have to function interdependently if the entire organism is to survive.

Polis From the Greek, usually translated (wrongly) as "city-state." A self-sufficient, small-scale political unit. It was not much like a modern nation-state, and it was much more than a city.

Social cohesion Integrated group behavior resulting from social bonds or social forces cementing members over time. To achieve it, group members accept the group's goals and standards of behavior.

Subculture A group of people who define themselves as different from the dominant culture in terms of some standards of behavior and values but who do not constitute an entirely different culture. Occupation, ethnicity, age, sexual orientation, religion, and social background can be bases for subcultures. In the United States, the Marines, circus performers, teenagers, and Mormons are considered subcultural groups. But the Amish and Hopi are considered separate cultures, not subcultures.

Techno$chaft A form of social, spatial, and economic organization based on information. Synonym: *postindustrial society*. Contrasts: *Gemeinschaft, Gesellschaft*.

Urbanism Presumed patterns of social interaction and culture that result from the concentration of large numbers of people in small physical areas. The concept is also used to convey the idea that in advanced industrial societies, urban values, culture, and modes of social organization have spread even to rural areas.

We-ness A sense of shared identity and interdependence found among members of a community. Members of communities may or may not share a physical territory.

PROJECTS

1. **The division of labor.** Using historical materials and current U.S. Department of Labor data and/or relevant non-U.S. governmental sources, compare and contrast the range of occupations in the Athenian polis, a medieval European town, and a modern American, European, or Asian city. Do your findings support Durkheim's dichotomy between a relatively simple division of labor in a mechanically solid society and a complex division of labor in an organically solid society?

2. **Urbanism as a way of life: the view from Hollywood.** Whether or not mass-media productions reflect or create social reality is much debated. Either way, we can assume that a mass medium is an important conveyor of social values and images. In terms of urban life, do commercial movies present images that reinforce or contradict Wirth's concept of urbanism as a single way of life? To investigate this question, view five or six films (e.g., *Taxi Driver, Manhattan, Salaam Bombay, The Godfather, Blue Collar, Atlantic City, Tin Men, My Beautiful Laundrette, Dim Sum, Do the Right Thing, Lost in Translation, Sin City, Crash, Hustle and Flow*) and analyze their content in terms of Wirth's notions of (a) the superficial, transitory character of urban social relations and (b) competition and formal control mechanisms as substitutes for bonds of kinship and common values.

3. **Sense of community.** In your physical area, which groups may feel a sense of community? Here are some possibilities: groups of cancer survivors, a church, sorority, war veterans, members of an ethnic group, and/or members of a professional group. Conduct oral interviews with several members of at least three groups. Asking each person the same questions, evaluate what group values they share, if any, and the level of their commitment to their group.

4. **Honor killings.** You have been asked by your local radio station to explain some recent honor killings, including one in Mosul, Iraq (of a young Kurdish, Muslim woman who fell in love with a Sunni Muslim, shown briefly on YouTube). Using the ideas of theorists mentioned in this chapter, how might you explain this event? What roles might modern technology (e.g., the Web, cameraphones, and YouTube) play in attitudes toward honor killings within communities which practice it?

SUGGESTIONS FOR FURTHER LEARNING

Few topics in social science and the humanities have drawn more ink than the concept of community. A good starting place is the discipline of sociology because the concept of community is a fundamental idea of sociological thought.

Classic works on community include Emile Durkheim, *The Division of Labor in Society* (New York: Free Press, [1893] 1964); Karl Marx, *Das Kapital* (New York: Modern Library, [1867] 1936); Claude-Henri de Saint-Simon, *On the Reorganization of European Society* (1814); Georg Simmel, *Philosophy of Money* (London: Routledge and Kegan Paul, [1900] 1978); Ferdinand Tönnies, *Community and Society* (New York: Harper & Row, [1887] 1963); and Auguste Comte, *The Positive Polity* (New York: Burt Franklin, [1851–1854] 1966). Essays of the German school (Weber, Simmel, Spengler) and the Chicago school (Park, Wirth, Redfield) appear in Richard Sennett's reader *Classic Essays on the Culture of Cities* (New York: Appleton-Century-Crofts, 1969). See also the chapter on community in Robert A. Nisbet, *The Sociological Tradition* (New York: Basic Books, 1966).

In *Cracks in the Pavement: Social Change and Resilience in Poor Neighborhoods* (Berkeley: University of California Press, 2008), Martin Sanchez-Jankowski explores five community mainstays—the housing project, small grocery store, barbershop and beauty salon, the gang, and local high school—in urban, poor areas. He discovered that these institutions provide a sense of community and social stability in an environment often thought to be chaotic.

Day-to-day life in a traditional community is perhaps best described by artists. Two favorites come from Italy. *The Leopard* (New York: Pantheon [1958] 2008) by Giuseppe Tomasi di Lampedusa (the Sicilian aristocrat's first and only novel) was published in 1958 and reissued on its fiftieth anniversary. It tells the story of the decline and fall of an aristocratic Sicilian family uneasily adjusting to the new society under the Italian republic; it identifies much about the shift from community to society. In a class by itself is a moving account of the shift in Italy from community to society: Ermanno Olmi's remarkable film *The Tree of Wooden Clogs* (1978). In telling the story of peasant life in Italy around the turn of the twentieth century, Olmi captures the ethos of *Gemeinschaft* and the ironies of its alleged social cohesion and bonds of friendship.

Other evocations of preindustrial, rural life can be found in histories, film, and memoir. Here are just a few: historian Emmanuel Le Roy Ladurie's dramatic history of a town in southern France during the Catholic Church's inquisition against the heretic Cathars, *Montaillou* (New York: Braziller, 1978); Camara Laye's *The African Child: Memories of a West African Childhood* (London: Fontana, 1962); and Robert Flaherty's pioneering documentary film *Nanook of the North* (1922).

Ngugi wa Thiong'o, exiled Kenyan playwright, novelist, and professor at the University of California at Irvine, sets his novel *Wizard of the Crow* (New York: Random House Harvill Secker, 2006) in the fictional Free Republic of Aburiria. A satiric political allegory, the novel's aim, Ngugi says, is "to sum up Africa of the twentieth century in the context of two thousand years of world history." The novel details a battle for the control of the souls of the Aburirians. Among the contenders: the nefarious Global Bank and the Wizard, an embodiment of folkloric wisdom.

Day-to-day life in a modern subculture—gay pre–World War II New York City—is chronicled by George Chauncey in *Gay New York: Gender, Urban Culture, and the Making of the Gay Male World, 1890–1940* (New York: Basic Books, 1994). Called a "pioneering work of scholarship," it shows that before World War II New York City had a large, communal gay world.

In *Casa Susanna* (New York: PowerHouse Books, 2005), Michel Hurst and Robert Swope tell the story of an oft-hidden subculture: heterosexual cross-dressers. Starting in the mid-1950s, professional men were free to play Scrabble in dresses, trade makeup tips, and walk around in high heels at Casa Susanna, a home in Hunter, New York. Many were married with children and wore gray flannel suits during the week. Meeting on weekends as Susanna, Felicity, Cynthia, etc., they escaped their strict gender roles and formed a tight subculture.

A documentary by Guillaume Dreyfus, *Lia* (2008), highlights the life of one woman in her nineties who lives in a small French village, Varaire, and whose life has been tied to the earth. The film is a paean to the peasant soul, portraying Lia's strength and independence. It also suggests, very obliquely, the strengths and weaknesses of community: the Janus-like nature of strong local ties and the lack of ties to anyone outside the small circle.

The shift from self-sufficient rural community to modern urban society is the theme of many artworks. A vivid account of the rural–urban shift in France is found in the novels of Honoré de Balzac, a conservative, aristocratic writer who mourned the passing of traditional community and despised bourgeois capitalism. Novelist Chinua Achebe's work *Things Fall Apart* (Portsmouth, N.H.: Heinemann, [1959] 1996) offers a sensitive inside look at the rural–urban shift in Nigeria.

Gaston Kaboré's award-winning film from Burkina Faso in West Africa, *Zan Boko* (1988), focuses on the impact of city expansion on rural communities (available in Mossi and French with English subtitles from California Newsreel, San Francisco). Orson Welles's film *The Magnificent Ambersons* (1942), based on a Booth Tarkington novel, depicts the impact of industrialization, particularly the automobile, on a small American town and the consequent changes in social structure.

In *All That Is Solid Melts into Air: The Experience of Modernity* (New York: Penguin, [1982] 1988), political scientist and urbanist Marshall Berman considers the writings of Marx, Goethe, and others who contributed to the modernist consciousness. Berman notes that one of Marx's images of modernity—"all that is solid melts into air" (from the *Communist Manifesto*)—is the inspiration for poet Yeats's famous line, "Things fall apart, the center does not hold." Note that Chinua Achebe's novel about the shift from *Gemeinschaft* to *Gesellschaft* in Nigeria is also entitled *Things Fall Apart*. (For a guide to Achebe's novel, see

Chinua Achebe's *Things Fall Apart: A Routledge Guide* [New York: Routledge, 2007] by David Whittaker.)

A group's struggle to retain community-like features within modern society is portrayed in many documentaries. For an offbeat look at the interaction between an Amish community and outsiders, see the documentary *The Amish and Us* (1998), directed by Dirk Eitzen and David Tetzlaff.

Joe Studwell describes what might be a *Gemeinschaft*-like group in *Asian Godfathers: Money and Power in Hong Kong and Southeast Asia* (Boston: Atlantic Monthly Press, 2007). According to Studwell, a 15-year veteran of economic journalism in Asia, South Asian billionaires (many of whom share a Chinese heritage, whatever their nationality), together with colonial interests, became an entrepreneurial elite. Now, Studwell claims, they form a coterie of crony capitalists, dominating the economies of Hong Kong, Singapore, Thailand, Malaysia, Indonesia, and the Philippines. He claims that these "godfathers," including politically connected Stanley Ho and Richard Li (son of Hong Kong billionaire Li Ka-shing) run their dealings like a family business.

Set in the California desert, *Bagdad Café* (called *Out of Rosenheim* outside the United States), a feature film (1987) and a musical comedy (2006) directed by Percy Adlon, is a poetic tale of two women: a Bavarian tourist and an African American café-restaurant owner. In some places, the film achieved cult status, perhaps because it is a fable offering the possibility of life in community and the acceptance of differences.

Great Britain's New Villages Project aims to create urban communities built around sustainable, mixed-use neighborhoods. See Peter Neal, ed., *Urban Villages and the Making of Communities* (London: Spon Press, 2003).

Some groups try to live in harmony with nature instead of conquering it. This is a theme of Pat Ferrero's compelling film *Hopi: Songs of the Fourth World* (58 minutes, New Day Films). The film depicts the Hopi's *Gemeinschaft*-like existence within *Gesellschaft*.

The late anthropologist Barbara Myerhoff's fieldwork among urban Hasidic Jews is highlighted in Lynne Litman's documentary film, *In Her Own Time* (1985). Made a generation ago, the film remains particularly moving because it suggests Myerhoff's personal dilemmas: faith or rationality, primacy of the group or the self. During the filming, Myerhoff discovered that she was terminally ill. While drawn to the community and spirituality of the Hasidim, she was uncomfortable with their restrictions and conformity.

Heroes in the novels of Ayn Rand are not tempted by a communal ethic. Instead, they laud individualism, the "virtue" of selfishness and capitalist values. See, for example, *The Fountainhead* (New York: Signet, [1943] 2005), made into a movie in 1949 (and DVD, 2006) featuring Gary Cooper as hero Howard Roark. Rand's ideas were codified into a philosophical movement called "objectivism." Alan Greenspan, chair of the Federal Reserve in the United States from 1987 to 2006, was once a member of Rand's inner circle.

Social scientists are not alone in constructing evolutionary typologies (e.g., the rural–urban shift). Various philosophers and spiritual leaders see a shift from one societal form of organization to another. Indian religious leader Sri Aurobindo described *The Human Cycle* (Pondicherry, India: Sri Aurobindo Ashram, [1916–1918] 1949) as a transition from the Age of Individualism and Reason to the Subjective Age and later the Spiritual Age. In *The Future of Man* (New York: Harper & Row [1959] 1964), Pierre Teilhard de Chardin describes five phases of development, culminating in the "noosphere," or thinking sphere, which results from social ties. In *At the Edge of History: Speculations on the Transformation of Culture* (New York: Harper & Row, 1971), William Irwin Thompson postulates four phases: tribal community, agricultural society, industrial civilization, and scientific–planetary civilization. Interestingly, the last phase is much like the first phase, only on a global scale.

The third type—variously named "informationalism," "post-*Gesellschaft*,: "Techno$chaft," or "postmodernism"—is the subject of geographer David Harvey's wide-ranging *The Condition of Postmodernity* (Oxford: Blackwell, 1989). An important contemporary urban theorist, Harvey links what happens in cities to macropatterns of political–economic change. In particular, see Chapter 4, "Postmodernism in the City: Architecture and Urban Design," which argues that postmodernism cultivates a concept of "the urban fabric as necessarily fragmented...and 'a collage' of current uses....[P]ostmodernists design rather than plan" (66).

For a discussion of the close relationship of economics to culture in post-*Gesellschaft* society, see the now classic article by F. Jameson, "Post-Modernism, or the Cultural Logic of Late Capitalism" (*New Left Review* 146[1984]:53–92). It is also the subject of *Global Dreams: Imperial Corporations and the New World Order* (New York: Simon and Schuster, 1994) by Richard J. Barnet and John Cavanagh. This excellent study continues Barnet's longtime interest in the global reach of corporations.

The late evolutionary biologist Stephen Jay Gould disputed the notion of linear "progress" so key to nineteenth- and twentieth-century typologists. See Gould's numerous essays collected in over 20 books.

Les Blank's ethnographic films (available from Flower Films, El Cerrito, Calif.) celebrate the persistence of community within society. Among the studies of *Gemeinschaft*-like groups are *Ziveli: Medicine for the Heart*, a documentary about Serbian American communities made in association with anthropologist Andrei Simic (1987). Blank's films often focus on shared food and music reflecting communal tradition.

Although he does not use the words, journalist Roger Cohen compares *Gesellschaft* to *Gemeinschaft*. In "In touch with time, like there's no tomorrow" (*International Herald Tribune*, September 2–3, 2006:2), Cohen says that change in the United States is disconcerting: "Your favorite restaurant is no more, gone in the night. The Pan Am sign disappears from Park Avenue. Pan Am itself disappears....Enron evaporates. Families disintegrate....Mom gets packed off to a home. Nothing is still...." Cohen contrasts that to Italy, where "everything and everybody seem to be where you left them....This familiarity reassures. It imbues time with a gentler quality and suggests that, if nothing else, we can all grow old together. What you have seems less important than who you have."

Individuals lost in the modern world without community or spirituality is a common theme in U.S. media. *Big Love* (2006–), on HBO-TV in the United States, features a polygamous Mormon family, advertising itself as just "another suburban family trying to live the American dream, struggling to balance the needs of seven kids, three wives, three separate houses, and one husband-in-chief." The series also features a controversial (and presently illegal) way of staving off loneliness: a polygamist commune in rural Utah.

Novelist Rosellen Brown says that U.S. movie audiences hunger for connectedness, "for a love beyond expediency, for a life in which an individual can still see her shadow." One movie that provides this connectedness, in her opinion, is *Fried Green Tomatoes* (1992), about women who "hang together in an unspoken conspiracy of affection and concern."

Jonathan Berman's 1993 movie *Shvitz* (Yiddish for "sweat") is a quick immersion into the lost culture and community of the male steam parlor. Before most homes had bathtubs, going to the *shvitz* was a weekly big-city ritual for male immigrant Jews. The steambaths were a democratic institution: factory pressers, doctors, lawyers, and gangsters sweated, schmoozed, and noshed together. Gerald Nachman, a former *San Francisco Chronicle* critic, once compared the schvitzers to those who use Nautilus for workouts: Their "idea of a good workout is bending over to tie their shoelaces."

Master French filmmaker Alain Resnais's *Private Fears in Public Places* (2006, known in French as *Coeurs*) is a movie about six lonely people in Paris struggling to make connections. It is not totally pessimistic.

Over the years, many U.S. television series have portrayed community-like work groups. *Grey's Anatomy* (ABC, 2005–) is a recent example. It often shows friendship and group solidarity winning out over romance and monetary gain.

Do significant rural–urban differences remain in postindustrial society? In "Between the County and the Concrete: Rediscovering the Rural–Urban Fringe," Jeff S. Sharp and Jill K. Clark (in *City & Community*, March 2008, 7(1):61–79) found in Ohio that rural-urban distinctions were less helpful than understanding rural–urban fringe differences.

REFERENCES

Achebe, Chinua. [1959] 1996. *Things Fall Apart*. Portsmouth, N.H.: Heinemann.

———. 2003. *Things Fall Apart*. Audio CD. Peter Francis James, narrator. White Plains, N.Y.: Recorded Books.

Banfield, Edward, and L. F. Banfield. 1958. *The Moral Basis of a Backward Society*. New York: Free Press.

Bartmann, Barry, and Tom Baum. 1998. "Promoting the particular as a niche cultural strategy in small jurisdictions." In Herbert William Faulkner, ed., *Proceedings, Progress in Tourism and Hospitality Research*. Gold Coast, Australia: Australian Tourism and Hospitality Research Conference.

Benetton Press Area. 2007. "About Benetton." (October 24): http://press.benettongroup.com/ben_en/about/

Berry, Wendell. 2001. *In the Presence of Fear: Three Essays for a Changed World*. Great Barrington, MA: Orion Society.

Brand, Stewart. 1987. *The Media Lab: Inventing the Future at MIT*. New York: Viking.

Bruni, Frank. 2002. "Treviso journal; In Benetton's hometown, colors are not united." *New York Times* (November 8): http://query.nytimes.com/gst/fullpage.html?res=9903E2DB1E39F934A1575AC0A9649C8B63

Buckley, Peter. 2006. *The Rough Guide to MySpace & Online Communities*. New York: Rough Guides.

Chun, Eunjung Jenny, Juliet Freedman, Nicole Parker, and Sonia Ketkar. 2003. "Benetton." Case study, the Fox School of Business and Management, Temple University: higheredbcs.wiley.com/legacy/college/kotabe/047123062

Cornelius, Wayne A., Philip L. Martin, and James F. Hollifield. 1995. "Introduction. The ambivalent quest for immigration control." Pp. 3–42 in Philip L. Martin, Wayne A. Cornelius, and James F. Hollifield, eds., *Controlling Immigration: A Global Perspective*. Stanford, Calif.: Stanford University Press.

Durkheim, Emile. [1893] 1964. *The Division of Labor in Society*. New York: Free Press.

Ellul, Jacques. 1965. *The Technological Society*. New York: Knopf.

Foster, George. 1965. "Peasant society and the image of limited good." *American Anthropologist* 67:293–315.

Gans, Herbert. [1962] 1982. *The Urban Villagers: Group and Class in the Life of Italian-Americans*. New York: Free Press.

Geertz, Clifford. 1994. "Life on the edge." *New York Review of Books* (April 7):3–4.

Goode, William. 1957. "Community within a community: The professions." *American Sociological Review* 22:194–200.

Gould, Stephen Jay. 2003. *I Have Landed: The End of a Beginning in Natural History*. New York: Three Rivers Press.

Hauser, Philip M. 1967. "Observations on the urban-folk and urban–rural dichotomies as forms of western ethnocentrism." Pp. 503–517 in Philip M. Hauser and Leo F. Schnore, eds., *The Study of Urbanization*. New York: Wiley.

Knaebel, Jeff. 2006. "Experiments in moral sovereignty: Notes of an American exile." (December 21): http://www.lewrockwell.com/orig6/knaebel7.html

Kerr, Clark. [1963] 2001. The Uses of the University: Fifth Edition. Cambridge, MA: Harvard University Press.

Kitto, H. D. F. 1951. *The Greeks*. Baltimore: Penguin.

Lasch, Christopher. 1991. *The True and Only Heaven: Progress and Its Critics*. New York: Norton.

Lewis, Oscar. 1961. *The Children of Sanchez*. New York: Random House.

———. 1967. "Further observations on the folk–urban continuum and urbanization with special reference to Mexico City." Pp. 491–503 in Philip M. Hauser and Leo F. Schnore, eds., *The Study of Urbanization*. New York: Wiley.

Lowenthal, David. 1988. *The Past Is a Foreign Country*. New York: Cambridge University Press.

Martin, Philip. 2007. "Race as a marketing tool." *The World*, KQED-radio, November 8.

Meichtry, Stacy. 2007. "Benetton picks up the fashion pace." *Wall Street Journal* (April 10):B1+.

Morrison, Roy. 2006. *Eco Civilization 2140: A 22nd Century History and Survivor's Journal*. Warner, N.H.: Writer's Publishing Cooperative.

"On the record." 2006. *International Herald Tribune* (June 10–11):18.

Polanyi, Karl, Harry W. Pearson, and Conrad M. Arensberg. 1957. *Trade and Market in the Early Empires: Economics in History and Theory*. Glencoe, Ill.: Free Press.

Putnam, Robert D. 2000. *Bowling Alone: The Collapse and Revival of American Community*. New York: Simon & Schuster.

Putnam, Robert D., and Lewis M. Feldstein. 2003. *Better Together: Restoring the American Community*. New York: Simon & Schuster.

Riding, Alan. 1991. "Politics? The generation gap yawns." *New York Times* [international edition] (June 17):A4.

Roszak, Theodore. 1977–1978. *Person/Planet*. Garden City, N.Y.: Doubleday.

Ryle, Robyn R., and Robert V. Robinson. 2006. "Ideology, moral cosmology, and community in the United States." *City & Community* 5(1):53–69.

Sjoberg, Gideon. [1960] 1999. *The Pre-Industrial City: Past and Present*. New York: Free Press.

Sjoberg, Gideon, and Andrée F. Sjoberg. 1996. "The preindustrial city: Reflections four decades later." Pp. 94–103 in George Gmelch and Walter P. Zenner, eds., *Urban Life*, 3rd ed. Prospect Heights, Ill.: Waveland Press.

Spengler, Oswald. [1918] 1962. *The Decline of the West.* New York: Knopf.

Springborg, Patricia. 1986. "Politics, primordialism, and orientalism: Marx, Aristotle, and the myth of the *Gemeinschaft.*" *American Political Science Review* 80: 185–211.

Stone, I. F. 1979. "I. F. Stone breaks the Socrates story." *New York Times Magazine* (April 8):22.

Weber, Max. [1906] 1960. "Capitalism and rural society in Germany." Pp. 363–385 in H. H. Gerth and C. Wright Mills, trans. and eds., *From Max Weber.* New York: Oxford University Press.

Williams, William Carlos. 1953. *Paterson.* London: Peter Owen.

Wilkinson, Tracy. 2007. "Immigrants find no welcome mat in Italy: Fears of terrorism, crime feed backlash." *Los Angeles Times* (October 28): http://www.commercialappeal.com/news/2007/oct/28/focus-italy-immigrants-find-no-welcome-mat-in/

Wirth, Louis. [1928] 1956. *The Ghetto.* Chicago: University of Chicago Press.

———. 1938. "Urbanism as a way of life." *American Journal of Sociology* 44 (July): 1–24.

Kathy Richland

CHAPTER 7

METROPOLITAN COMMUNITY

All those lonely people…strangers everywhere, going who knows where. Nowhere people. Lonely crowds, hearing only the sounds of silence. People who don't care about other people…

That is a popular image of life in the big city. As a friend from a small town in Texas asked when she moved to a major **metropolis**, "Don't people here know we're all in the same cotton field together?"

Many popular images have some grounding in everyday experience. Yet this view of urbanites as isolated and unfeeling needs to be qualified. City dwellers aren't as disconnected from one another as many images would lead us to believe.

Also, the image of the rural, small-town past—where like-minded people cared deeply for one another in a well-ordered, stable community—is rather idyllic, existing more in theory than in reality. Still, that cozy, imagined world is compelling, especially for those of us who have lived in lonely crowds. How humane the ideal of traditional community seems: a way of life built on close social bonds, friendship, mutual caring, and personal security.

But recall, too, the other face of traditional life. How many of us today would choose to submit to authority in the form of a mother-in-law or a hereditary ruler? How many of us would want to spend our whole lives interacting mainly with blood relatives? As Margaret Mead implies (*The House of Murphy*, n.d.), there is another and *less attractive face of community*: distrust of outsiders, lack of privacy, conformity to convention and authority, and adherence to tradition. In addition, both social and geographic mobility are very limited in a traditional community. This feature seems especially unattractive for most of us who would have been unfortunate enough to be born serfs, slaves, and underlings, not princesses or rulers.

Many contemporary voices bemoan the loss of community and seek to reestablish it. Some advocate a rejection of Western individualism and democratic tradition, substituting a religious way of life for modernism or postmodernism. The Taliban in Afghanistan and Osama bin Laden exemplify this approach. Others want to establish a sense of we-ness within advanced technological societies, looking to support groups, cohousing settlements, or worker cooperatives as vehicles for creating community.

Is it only in fictional towns, like Cicely, Alaska (the site of TV series *Northern Exposure*, CBS, 1990–1995), where people can have both personal freedom and close social ties? Does *Northern Exposure*'s Cicely reflect a new American dream—the enjoyment of a sense of community and individuality simultaneously?

Some think that the Internet can promote both personal freedom and social ties. For example, members of Internet support groups for cancer survivors or crime victims share personal information and stories without ever meeting in person.

There seem to be many avenues within modern or postmodern society that aim to find a sense of community. One of the rather unusual ways depends on trying to find others with your name. Typically, people Google others with their name and then try to connect. This kind of connection among name-sharers is called "Google twins" or *Googlegängers* (in Rosenbloom, 2008). (The world record as of April 2008 was held by over 1,220 people named Mohammed Hassan.)

Do some name-sharers seek a newfound sense of community? And what about lost communities—or at least neighborliness? Not long ago, as sociologist Douglas Harper (2001) points out, farmers in the United States routinely helped neighbors, but this practice died out mainly when new farm technologies entered the picture around the mid-twentieth century. Will the end of cheap fossil fuel in the United States signal a return of sharing trips and chores, neighborliness, and community, as some think or hope (see McKibben, 2008)? We will return to various types of community seekers after examining what is called, rightly or wrongly, "metropolitan community."

SOCIAL CEMENT IN THE METROPOLIS

V. S. Naipaul, whose novels deal with poor countries emerging from a tribal or caste tradition into an uncertain modernity, once said that he felt no nostalgia for the miserable security of old customs. For most people in modern society, the miserable security of old customs is not even an option. Urbanism may not be a single way of life, as Wirth theorized; but it certainly does entail constant change, not the continuity of traditional community. Institutions and traditions that once promoted a sense of personal security, however miserable, no longer fulfill that function for many urbanites or suburbanites.

What, then, helps to bind contemporary people in the modern metropolis? Not much, warned economist and one-time Clinton cabinet member Robert Reich (1991a, 1991b). In the early 1990s, Reich wrote that the top one-fifth of U.S. income earners were disengaging from (and losing interest in) the fate of the bottom four-fifths. The elite 20 percent may be charitable, Reich noted, but their generosity typically supports institutions that serve or educate people like themselves—symphonies, private hospitals, museums, elite universities, and so on—not social services for the poor.

By the early 2000s, the rich and even less-than-rich were privatizing their residential space, often living in guarded or gated economic enclaves. According to Ed Blakely, author of *Fortress America: Gated Communities in the United States* (1999), this is increasingly the case worldwide, from Great Britain and China as well as the United States. The Census Bureau's 2001 American Housing Survey, based on a sample representative of the nation's then 119 million households, showed that more than 7 million households in the United States lived in developments behind walls and fences. A decade earlier, as many as 300,000 Californians were "forting up"—one critic's term for living in walled, private neighborhoods (Blakely in Schreiner, 1992:A1).

There are differences among racial/ethnic groups regarding "forting up." For example, in the United States, Hispanics—whether they own or rent—are more likely to live in gated communities than non-Hispanic whites or African Americans. Affluent African American homeowners are less likely to live in gated communities than affluent non-Hispanic whites and Hispanics.

Whatever the ethnicity of those behind gates, the result is often an "us" versus "them" mentality. Physically and psychologically separate, the top 20 percent feels little sense of community with or responsibility for "them"—the bottom 80 percent.

As noted earlier, gated communities are becoming popular globally, from Shanghai and Great Britain to Los Angeles and beyond. One Dominican, Vinela Arias, a housekeeper in Boston and Cambridge, Massachusetts, prepared to return to her native country in style; she and her boyfriend put a bid on a large colonial home in an elite gated community in Santo Domingo (Sacchetti, 2008).

Some gated enclaves seem to have containment as their sole purpose. For example, a gated community built in 2007, constructed by the U.S. military in a lower middle-class Baghdad neighborhood, separates Shi'a and Sunni inhabitants: The U.S. military tried to contain Iraq's "civil war" by building huge, concrete barriers between the factions. One U.S. army colonel envisions small, homogeneous, gated communities, each built around a market, a mosque, and a generator (Jaffe, 2007:A1+).

In terms of the United States, Robert Reich (1991a) concluded in the early 1990s that successful people were gradually seceding from the union. This secession, he noted, was speeded by the federal government's shift of responsibility for many public services to state and local governments, which were already financially strapped and often unable to provide good services. Public services (e.g., public parks, playgrounds, police) deteriorated even more as the rich withdrew their funds, switching to private services such as health clubs, golf clubs, spas, and hired security guards. (No data since the early 1990s seem to upend Reich's earlier conclusions. For example, the number of private security guards in the United States now exceeds the number of public police officers by about 2 to 1.)

Reich thought that even more than a ZIP code and private tennis clubs separate the successful elite: They "inhabit a different economy from other Americans." Typically, this elite of "symbolic analysts" (who analyze or manipulate words, numbers, or visual images in their work as ad executives, research scientists, corporate executives, lawyers, software engineers, etc.) is linked by jet, modem, BlackBerry, and other electronic media to people in world headquarters' cities and resort centers but retains few ties to the activities of the other 80 percent. Following this logic, a corporate executive in New York City is more involved with and at home with the world marketplace and acquaintances in Tokyo and the European Union than with the local public school or homeless people in the next county. In other words, the notion of "hometown" is losing both its emotional and its economic clout.

To conclude: Reich echoes a familiar theme: the breakdown of communal feeling in cosmopolitan, highly-specialized society. As we saw earlier (Chapter 6), cosmopolitanism, the privatization of formerly public services (e.g., education), and increasing specialization were associated with the fall of the Greek polis centuries ago. And, as Chapter 6 details, a host of thinkers theorize that both urbanites and suburbanites in *Gesellschaft* tend to relate to one another on the basis of the cash nexus, not community ties.

Reich added more factors—income level and global work role—that separate people in the contemporary metropolis. The result, he posited, was the short-circuiting of local emotional and economic interdependence.

So, once again, we ask, "What, if anything, helps to bind contemporary urbanites together?" We get a few clues from popular culture. Many films set in global cities—Martin Scorsese's *Goodfellas* (1990) and *Taxi Driver* (1976), Oliver Stone's *Wall Street* (1987), Spike Lee's *Do the Right Thing* (1989), Curtis Hanson's *L.A. Confidential* (1997), Sofia Coppola's *Lost in Translation*

Fig.7.2 GATED COMMUNITIES GO GLOBAL. In recent years—from London to Shanghai and beyond—urbanites and suburbanites are flocking to gated communities. This one, located in London's Bow Quarter, houses educated cosmopolitans, many of whom work in London's financial district. (Critics accuse those in gated communities of "forting up" against "them.") Note that in some cities, including Quito, Ecuador, middle-income people often erect their own, private version of a gated community: They ring their homes with barbed wire. (Gesche Würfel)

(2003), Justin Lin's *Fast and Furious: Tokyo Drift* (2006), and Paul Thomas Anderson's *Punch-Drunk Love* (2002), for example—depict New York City, suburban Los Angeles, and Tokyo as alienating and/or corrupting. Violence, dog-eat-dog exploitation, lovelessness, interethnic mistrust, and intraethnic betrayal are presented as normal. Even in Woody Allen's classic love letter to the city, *Manhattan* (1979), the main characters seem like aliens struggling to find affection in a lonely world. These movies show few forces or institutions—family, neighbors, religious groups, friends, ethnic subcommunities, and so on—that effectively provide emotional or financial support.

What movies like *Lost in Translation* do not—perhaps cannot—portray is an unseeable, abstract force that ties people together economically (not emotionally): functional interdependence. *How* and *at what level* this works are matters of current debate.

METROPOLITAN COMMUNITY: ALIVE OR EXTINCT?

ONE VIEW: METROPOLITAN DIVISION OF LABOR

Some theorists stress the functional interdependence that stems from the complex division of labor. This perspective, rooted in Emile Durkheim's ideas about organically solid society (Chapter 6), focuses on population density, interpersonal communication, and functional differentiation as factors cementing members of a metropolitan community. Among others, Robert Park (1916) and Ernest Burgess ([1923] 1925), creator of the concentric zone model of urban growth; Roderick D. McKenzie (1933); Amos Hawley (1950); and geographer Brian Berry and sociologist John Kasarda (1977) are associated with this perspective. All are urban ecologists who, like biological ecologists, focus on a population's adaptation to its environment. (Chapter 16 contains a more detailed discussion of urban ecology.)

We who live in the urban world may not realize it, but we depend on absolute strangers for a wide range of goods and services. For example, unless you grow your own food, limit travel to places where your feet can take you, entertain yourself without mass media, fix your own broken toilet (without calling a plumber from the Yellow Pages), receive no government benefits, and buy nothing that must be paid for in money, you depend on countless anonymous people to sustain your daily existence.

Indeed, we are so interdependent and specialized that we need one expert to find another expert! This is clear to anyone suffering from a rare illness. Finding a specialist to diagnose and treat the ailment requires the advice of other specialists. With the continuing expansion of knowledge and the "expertization" of almost everyone, we are becoming increasingly dependent on the skill and good will of strangers just to survive.

Let's pause here for a few notes on terminology. *Population core* is synonymous with **central city**. However, *central city* is not synonymous with *inner city* or *center city*. The central city is—or was, due to recent changes, as we shall soon see—seen as central because (1) all goods coming into and going out of the region come through this city and (2) it organizes the economic activities of its surrounding hinterland. The term *suburb* is synonymous with *hinterland* and **outside central city**.

The central city and its suburbs are the two basic components of a metropolitan area or metropolitan community. At the local level, a complex network of mutually sustaining activities links (or once linked) people in the population core and its suburbs.

In the urban ecologists' view, the commuting pattern is the key indicator of metropolitan interdependence. The U.S. Census Bureau agrees; it makes the journey-to-work pattern between a city and its surrounding suburbs the primary measure of metropolitan community. Thus, from this viewpoint, a metropolitan area is essentially an *integrated labor market*, measured by the number of people who live in the suburbs and commute to the central city for work.

How, then, do urban ecologists explain the massive exodus from U.S. central cities to suburbs, starting after World War II, that has transformed many metropolitan areas? They begin by looking at the interplay of ecological factors, known by their acronym POET: *p*opulation, social *o*rganization, *e*nvironment, and *t*echnology (see Chapter 4). Their explanation for individuals and corporations relocating to U.S. suburbs centers on changes in transportation and communication technology. In particular, they point to the mass production and affordability of the private automobile as the key factor in suburban growth (e.g., Berry and Kasarda, 1977). As we shall discuss shortly, their explanation does not go unchallenged by the "new" urban theorists.

To conclude: Following Durkheim, urban ecologists stress functional interdependence in modern society based on the complex division of labor. They see society *naturally* tending toward equilibrium or balance. Parts of a social system, like the organs of a human body, fit together and run smoothly until some external disruption occurs; then societies, like bodies, adapt to the change. In their analysis of metropolitan life, urban ecologists focus on ecological factors and ignore or underplay social psychological factors (e.g., attitudes) and political factors, including the role of the state.

ALTERNATIVE VIEW: NEW INTERNATIONAL DIVISION OF LABOR ("NEEDLE")

Dissenters don't deny that functional interdependence is important, but they put it in a very different context: the new international division of labor (Chapter 5). This view is associated with the so-called new urban theorists, a group of interdisciplinary social scientists including David Harvey (1985), Manuel Castells (1983), and Joe R. Feagin (1988). New urban theorists draw insights from diverse disciplines (geography, sociology, economics, planning, political science, cultural studies) and theoretical traditions (e.g., world systems theory and neo-Marxism to postmodernism).

"New" urban theorists (no longer so new but still referred to as such) think that the global capitalist economy is the abstract glue that cements people worldwide, albeit very unequally. Indeed, they theorize that "every major dimension of city life today is related to the shifts produced by changes in investment deriving from a hegemonic, global system of capital" (Gottdiener, 1987:77). One event serves to illustrate their view of borderless interdependence: In 2007 and beyond, the so-called subprime mortgage market meltdown in the United States brought some Wall Street securities firms and banks to their knees. It reverberated throughout Europe and elsewhere; banks, notably Switzerland's UBS, suffered huge losses as a result of the "mortgage meltdown" in the United States.

Unlike urban ecologists, new urban theorists tend to incorporate political and cultural factors into their analyses, paying special attention to the influence of political individuals and organizations—citizens' groups, multinational managers, real estate developers, and so on—on metropolitan outcomes. In this view, the impact of the *global* capitalist economy on *local* development, federal and local government policies, and local political coalitions—not population increase, new technologies, and other ecological variables (as the urban ecologists think)—best explains spatial and social change in metropolitan areas (Gottdiener and Feagin, 1988).

URBAN ECOLOGISTS VERSUS "NEW" URBAN THEORISTS: A CASE STUDY

The case of U.S. suburbanization illustrates some major differences between urban ecologists and new urban theorists. Very briefly, urban ecologists claim that the automobile was the key factor in suburban development. New urban theorists disagree. They argue that technology played only one part, for decentralization to the hinterland started before the introduction of the automobile. Instead of technology, they focus on the *political decision-making context* that resulted in the dominance of the auto over alternative transit forms (e.g., rail mass transit) as well as the particular actors that shaped the auto-centered transport system in the United States.

Finally, urban ecologists think that the *highly specialized division of labor*, *new technologies*, and *increased population density* spurred suburban growth. New urban theorists point to a different set of incentives and forces, including the following: *labor force considerations* (e.g., corporate owners and managers chose to relocate in the suburbs to control labor militancy in central cities); *national and local government intervention* (e.g., post–World War II programs to build suburban freeways, provide low-interest loans to suburban home builders, and subsidize defense-related industries that located in the suburbs); and the *role of political–economic players* (e.g., real estate speculators and developers) in the promotion of growth. In this view, the automobile and other technological innovations are important but only as a means, not a cause, of suburbanization (Gottdiener, 1985, 1994).

To conclude: So-called new urban theorists see metropolitan shifts as part of larger processes with local repercussions—global capitalism and government intervention. In their view, these are the major forces shaping metropolitan areas, and they are neither natural nor neutral (i.e., they do not serve everyone's interests equally). However, local outcomes are not entirely determined by these macro-level processes; individuals and organizations (grassroots citizens' groups, real estate developers, etc.) can have important local impacts. Urban ecologists, by contrast, see metropolitan shifts as results of technological change (e.g., new communications technologies) and shifts in social organization (e.g., mass production, consumers' ability to pay for cars).

Now we turn from this theoretical debate to a related practical issue: how to measure a metropolitan area. This sounds rather unimportant and exceedingly boring. It is not unimportant.

MEASURING FUNCTIONAL INTERDEPENDENCE

At present, measurement is based on the urban ecologists' concept of functional interdependence. The journey-to-work pattern between a central city and its surrounding suburbs is probably the most common measure of metropolitan interdependence. Yet, using this measure, we conclude that many areas now called "metropolitan" are far from functionally interdependent: *By 1990, twice as many people in the U.S. commuted from suburban residence to suburban job as commuted from suburb to central city.* This decentralization has reached the point where most urbanists now believe that "the central city is no longer essential to the economic functioning of a metropolitan area" (Frey and Speare, 1988:19).

(*A note about U.S. census data*: In development since 1996, the annual American Community Survey was first used by the U.S. Census in 2003. It is sent to a sample of U.S. households. As of 2010, it replaces the long-form census. Questions and categories for decennial censuses are decided 2 years prior to a census. Thus, questions for the 2010 Census were decided by 2008.)

During the past several decades, people all over the world have become more aware of some effects of car travel, including congestion, air pollution, and greenhouse gases that many scientists say contribute to global warming. In 2001, a small but growing number in the

United States (about 6 percent, just over 5 percent a decade earlier) avoided a commute by working at home (Gordon et al., 2004). Nonetheless, commuting behavior in the United States can best be described like this: more people in more cars traveling to more places.

By 1996, the suburb-to-suburb commute had become the dominant commuting pattern in the United States (University of South Florida, 2008). Yet, people in the United States still commute from suburb to city. In the nation's largest city, New York, city for example, the number of people commuting into all five boroughs increased from 655,000 to 775,000 between 1980 and 2000. The number of people who "reverse commuted" out of the city into suburbs also increased— from 171,000 to 242,000. Thus, at least in one global city and its environs, "reverse commuters showed a much larger percentage increase—42 percent compared with 18 percent" but "the inbound commuters outnumbered them three to one" (Bram and McKay, 2005).

THE NEED FOR NEW CONCEPTS

What is an important implication of reverse commuting and suburb-to-suburb commuting? That *the very concept of a metropolitan area as an urban core with dependent suburbs is outdated in many cases.* In other words, many U.S. suburbs have become independent of their mother cities.

Official record keepers have not yet fully come to grips with this spatial shift. The U.S. Office of Management and Budget (OMB), originator of the metropolitan area concept, did review present concepts for the 2000 census (Forstall, 1991); and the Council of Professional Associations on Federal Statistics did sponsor a seminar that asked "Should the metropolitan concept be eliminated?" (Fitzsimmons, 1995). Meanwhile, the OMB and the U.S. Census Bureau retain the metropolitan area as a core concept. In part, this may reflect data-collection problems; the metro area concept offers a standardized measure and the promise of comparable data to scholars, planners, and so on.

Predictably, both theoretical and political disputes will accompany any process to reconceptualize the nature of metropolitan community. So will policy disputes. We can expect groups representing the interests of cities to resist the notion of *in*dependence between cities and "their" suburbs. For example, the

National League of Cities (NLC), an advocate for more than 18,000 cities, villages, and towns, argues that cities and suburbs are *inter*dependent. The NLC has long held that "metropolitan areas are a single regional economy" (Ledebur and Barnes, 1992:12). Further, the NLC claims that "cities and suburbs have a common and essential stake in their shared economies. Growing disparities between these jurisdictions erode and eventually undermine the vitality of the regional economy and, hence, the welfare of both cities and suburbs."

Is there any evidence that, as the NLC puts it, "the economic fate and fortunes of cities and suburbs are inextricably intertwined" (Ledebur and Barnes, 1993:4)? That depends on how interdependence is measured: The NLC abandons the more common measure of city–suburban interdependence—commuting patterns—in favor of changes in per capita incomes of cities and suburbs, reasoning that city–suburban incomes "tend to rise and fall together" (Ledebur and Barnes, 1992:15).

METROPOLITAN STATISTICAL AREA (MSA) AND MICROPOLITAN AREA IN THE UNITED STATES

To standardize the measurement of a metropolitan area, the OMB developed the concept of a **Metropolitan Statistical Area (MSA)**. As its name implies, the MSA is not a political unit; like many entities, it is only a geostatistical creation. It is used as a uniform area for data gathering and analysis.

Introduced in the 1950 census (in a slightly different form) and modified several times (e.g., in 1983 from Standard Metropolitan Statistical Area [SMSA] to MSA), the general concept of a metropolitan area has remained constant: a large population center or "nucleus" (central city) together with its adjacent, socially and economically integrated communities (outside central city or suburban area). In other words, the concept is based on a parent–child relationship: The "mother" (the Greek root of *metro*polis) dominates her dependents (hinterland, sphere of economic influence, or suburbs), which could not exist on their own.

Micropolitan Statistical Area is a rather recent U.S. Census designation. Created in 2003, a U.S. micro area is defined as an urban area containing an urban core city or town of at least 10,000 but less than

50,000 population. Like the MSA, it is a geostatistical measure. The Census Bureau identified 577 U.S. micro areas in 2005. (Most credit G. Scott Thomas and his 1990 book, *The Rating Guide to Life in America's Small Cities*, with the term "micropolitan.")

Now, back to big. An MSA more accurately reflects the number of people in an area than looking just at a city's population. For instance, Boston ranks only twentieth in terms of size but, counting its metropolitan area residents, it is ranked as the nation's seventh largest metropolitan area, according to the 2000 Census. On the contrary, the population of the city of San Diego—more than 1.2 million in 2000—meant that it ranked seventh largest in the nation in terms of population. But it ranked as the seventeenth largest metro area.

Figure 7.3 displays the component parts of an MSA for which census data are readily available: MSA, county, central city, urbanized area, place, minor civil division, **census tract**, block group, and block. (Not illustrated but available are data for user-defined units, such as neighborhoods, school attendance areas, business zones from the U.S. Census Bureau's User-Defined Areas Program.) The Census Bureau's Topologically Integrated Geographic Encoding and Referencing database (TIGER) is also a handy resource for researchers; the database contains information about such features as railroads, streets, and the geographic relationship to other features.

Before describing the criteria used to define an MSA, we should note how the U.S. Census Bureau defines and operationalizes some rather ambiguous terms, such as *urban* and *rural*. (Note that U.S. Census definitions are often long and complex.) Here are just a few definitions used in the 2000 Census:

Urban All territory, population, and housing units located within an urbanized area (UA) or an urban cluster (UC). It delineates UA and UC boundaries to encompass densely settled territory, which consists of

- core census block groups or blocks that have a population density of at least 1,000 people per square mile and
- surrounding block groups and census blocks, each with an overall population density of at least 500 people per square mile

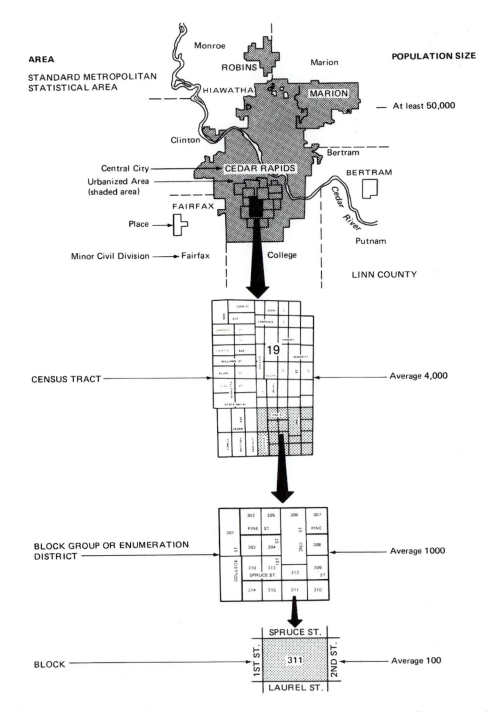

Fig.7.3 COMPONENTS OF A U.S. METROPOLITAN STATISTICAL AREA. An MSA is an integrated economic and social unit with a large population center, the central city. This chart illustrates the hierarchical relationship among units within the MSA. Since 1992, U.S. Census data have been available for each of these components, plus many user-defined components such as ZIP codes and neighborhoods. (*Source*: Adapted from U.S. Bureau of the Census, *Census Geography* [October 1978])

(In addition, under certain conditions, less densely settled territory may be part of each UA or UC.)

Urban cluster (UC) Consists of densely-settled territory with at least 2,500 people but fewer than 50,000 people. Introduced in Census 2000 to provide a more consistent and accurate measure of population concentration in and around places. (UCs replace earlier census categories that defined as urban only those places with 2,500 or more people located outside of urbanized areas.)

Urbanized area (UA) Consists of densely-settled territory with 50,000 or more people. This designation aims to provide a better separation of urban and rural territory, population, and housing around large places. Because of different density requirements in the 1990 Census, some territory then classified as urbanized has been reclassified as rural.

Rural All territory, population, and housing units located outside of UAs and UCs. The rural component contains both place and nonplace territory.

Extended place Any place that is split by a UA or UC boundary; that is, it is partly urban and partly rural. Used first in Census 2000.

Census tract Small, relatively permanent statistical subdivisions of a county or statistically equivalent entity. As of Census 2000, the entire United States is covered by census tracts. Generally, census tracts have 1,500–8,000 people. Optimum size is 4,000 people. (Census tracts in U.S. Samoa, Guam, and the Northern Marianas are smaller, population-wise.) They are designed to be homogeneous with respect to population characteristics such as living conditions and economic standing.

Block group (BG) A cluster of census blocks having the same first digit of their four-digit identifying numbers within a census tract. For instance, block group 3 (BG 3) within a census tract includes all blocks numbered from 3000 to 3999. Optimum size is 1,500 people.

Central city The MSA's core—the city (or cities) around which an MSA is formed. It must meet minimum population standards.

Outside central city Every place in the MSA minus the central city.

Counties (or equivalent entities) Counties form the geographic "building blocks" for metropolitan and micropolitan statistical areas throughout the United States and Puerto Rico.

Core-Based Statistical Area (CBSA) Created by the U.S. Census Bureau in 2000, the term refers collectively to metro and micro statistical areas.

New England City and Town Area (NECTA) Defined using the same criteria as Metropolitan and Micropolitan Statistical Areas. Identified as either metropolitan or micropolitan, based, respectively, on the presence of either a UA of 50,000 or more population or a UC of at least 10,000 but less than 50,000 population. If the specified criteria are met, a NECTA containing a single core with a population of at least 2.5 million may be subdivided to form smaller groupings of cities and towns referred to as New England City and Town Area divisions.

These census designations do not solve all the problems of classification. But at least the categories are standard so that uniform data can be collected.

As noted, census definitions can change over time. For example, in 2000, a new term—"core-based statistical area" (CBSA)—was added, referring collectively to Metropolitan and Micropolitan Statistical Areas. Each CBSA must contain at least one urban area of 10,000 or more population. However, the general concept of an MSA remains the same: a core area containing a substantial population nucleus, together with adjacent communities having a high degree of economic and social integration with that core.

Now, back to the MSA. Except in the six New England states (where cities and towns are used rather than counties), Alaska (which uses county equivalents), and a few other areas (which use county equivalents), an MSA consists of an entire county or a group of contiguous counties that contain (1) at least one central city with at least 50,000 inhabitants (or "twin cities" with a combined population of at least 50,000) or (2) an urbanized area surrounding the central city with a population of at least 50,000 and a total metropolitan population of at least 100,000 (or 75,000 in New England). *Counties surrounding the central city are*

CALIFORNIA - Core - Based Statistical Areas and Counties

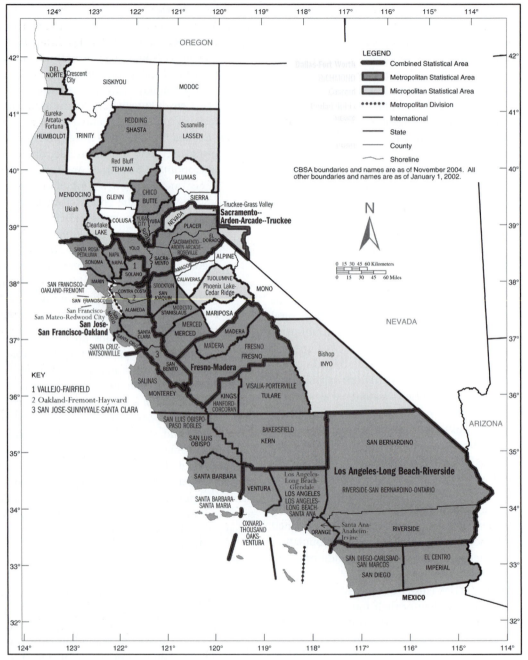

Fig. 7.4 ONE STATE'S CORE-BASED STATISTICAL AREAS AND COUNTIES: CALIFORNIA, 2004. (*Source*: U.S. Census, http://ftp2.census.gov/geo/maps/metroarea/stcbsa_pg/Nov2004/cbsa2004_CA.pdf)

included in an MSA if they meet certain criteria of "metropolitan character" and socioeconomic integration with the central city. These criteria are based on high population density or high level of commuting to the core. These criteria also show that the U.S. Census Bureau defines the metropolitan area as an integrated labor market, the smallest area containing most of the workplaces and residences of those who work there.

A county contiguous to the central city's county must meet criteria of metropolitan character and integration to be included in the MSA. The criteria have changed over the years, but commute patterns and population density remain key indicators of a metropolitan system. Using Figure 7.3, for example, here is how to determine the extent of the metropolitan area: If a county surrounding Linn County, home county of the central city of Cedar Rapids, has either (1) 50 percent of its workers commuting to the urban core and a density as low as 25 persons per square mile or (2) 15 percent commuters with a density of 50 persons per square mile and other evidence of "metropolitan character," it would be included in the MSA.

Before proceeding, a few words about the U.S. county and its equivalents are in order. *The entire county is the basic political unit of an MSA, except in the six New England states, Louisiana, Alaska, four other states, D.C., and Puerto Rico.* Why the exceptions? A variety of reasons. First, New England. Historically, cities and towns have more political significance than counties in New England; thus, New England's MSAs are composed of cities and towns. In addition, based on its French heritage, Louisiana has a history of "parishes," which are like counties. Alaska does not have counties but, since 1980, uses county equivalents: boroughs or "census areas." The District of Columbia is considered to be the equivalent of a county. Four states (Maryland, Missouri, Nevada, and Virginia) have independent cities, which constitute primary divisions in their state. But most states use the county as the basic political unit. Finally, in Puerto Rico the primary divisions are *municipios*; they are treated as county equivalents.

Two more notes on New England's MSAs: (1) In the 1990 Census, metro areas in New England used minor civil divisions, not counties, as the basic unit. This changed in the 2000 Census. As of 2000, metro and micro statistical areas are defined using counties or county equivalents nationwide. (2) The minimum population standard for New England's central cities is 75,000, not 50,000. There are also alternative county-based metropolitan areas defined since the 1970s called "New England County Metropolitan Areas" (NECMAs), which are more similar to MSAs in the rest of the United States.

Because metropolitan areas are defined on the basis of (presumed) economic and social interdependence—not political ties—MSAs can and do cross state lines. Interstate MSAs are common in the Northeast and Midwest but rare in the far West. A couple of examples from the 2000 Census: Huntington–Ashland, West Virginia–Kentucky–Ohio and Minneapolis–St. Paul–Bloomington, Minnesota–Wisconsin.

Also, metropolitan systems change over time. MSA boundaries shift with economic growth or restructuring. For example, before 1963, Solano County, California, was included in the San Francisco–Oakland metropolitan area; in 1963 it became part of a new two-county metropolitan area as movers, working at newly-created jobs or retiring there, stopped commuting to the Bay Area in large numbers.

Over time, the number of MSAs has changed. In the 1970 Census, there were 243 metropolitan areas (then called SMSAs) in the United States and four in Puerto Rico, for a total of 247. By 2005, there were 361 MSAs in the United States plus eight in Puerto Rico.

CONSOLIDATED METROPOLITAN STATISTICAL AREA (CMSA) OR MEGALOPOLIS

Popularly, a supermetropolitan area—a large metropolitan complex with at least 1 million in population—is often called a **megalopolis**. The U.S. Census Bureau calls it a **Consolidated Metropolitan Statistical Area (CMSA)**. A CMSA is defined as an MSA with a population of 1 million or more that also contains separate, component areas. A CMSA's component areas are called **Primary Metropolitan Statistical Areas (PMSAs)**. Solano County, California (mentioned in the previous section), was part of the Vallejo–Fairfield–Napa PMSA, one of six PMSAs that made up the nation's fifth largest CMSA in 2000, San Francisco–Oakland–San Jose. (Planners predict that formerly-rural Solano County will soon be the link connecting the Sacramento Valley to the Bay Area, resulting in a new megalopolis of over

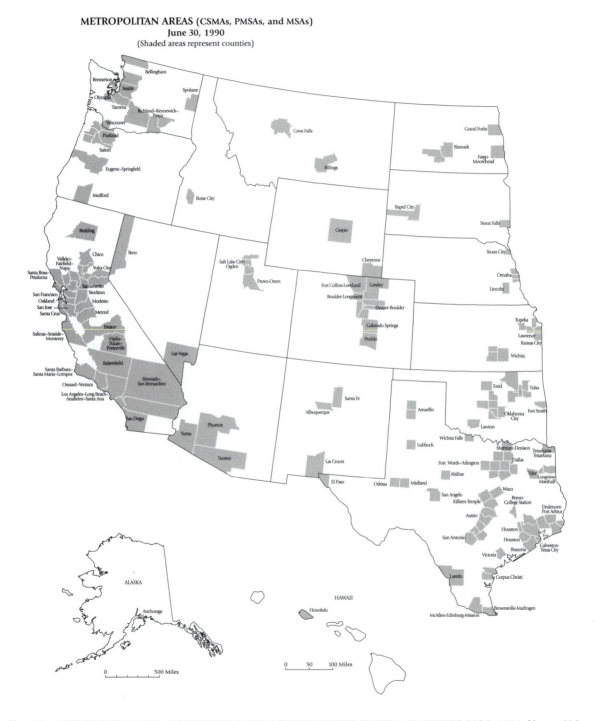

METROPOLITAN AREAS (CSMAs, PMSAs, and MSAs)
June 30, 1990
(Shaded areas represent counties)

Fig. 7.5 METROPOLITAN AND MICROPOLITAN AREAS OF THE UNITED STATES AND PUERTO RICO, 2005. (*Source*: U.S. Census Bureau, *Statistical Abstract of the United States, 2007*, p. 897 http://www.census.gov/geo/www/maps/msa_maps2005/ msa2005_previews_html/cbsa_csa_us_wall_1205.html)

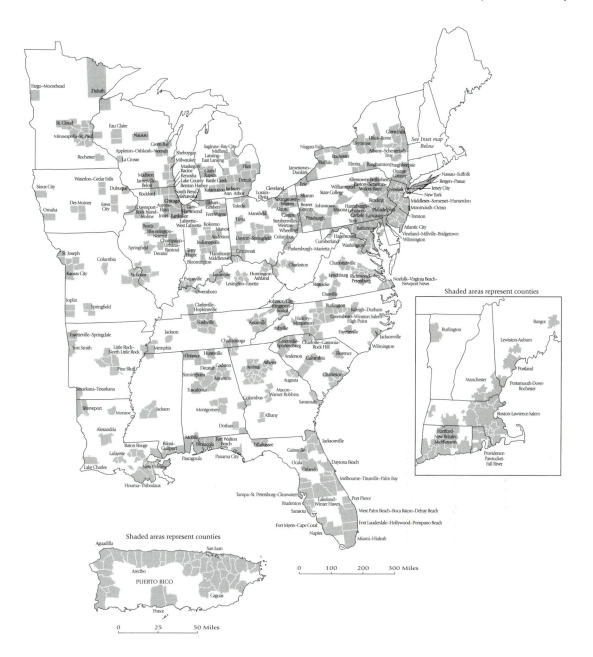

Shaded areas represent counties

Shaded areas represent counties

PUERTO RICO

9 million people.) Another example of a CMSA's component parts from the U.S. Census 2000: The New York CMSA included the PMSAs of Nassau and Suffolk Counties on Long Island, Bergen and Passaic Counties in New Jersey, and Brideport and Milford Counties in Connecticut. (PMSAs, like the CMSAs that contain them, are composed of entire counties except in the six New England states, where they are composed of cities and towns.)

Population continues to concentrate in U.S. megalopolises. By 2000, 50 MSAs had more than 1 million inhabitants. Here's another measure of population concentration: As of 2000, MSAs comprised only about 16 percent of U.S. land, but more than 80 percent of people in the United States lived in them.

RURAL AND MICROPOLITAN AREAS

In 2000, most people in the United States—about 80.3 percent or 226 million people—lived in metropolitan areas. This percentage grew enormously over the decades of the twentieth century. It continues to grow, albeit at a much slower pace.

There are, however, other Americas: (1) nonmetropolitan, very sparsely settled rural areas and (2) micropolitan areas. In recent years, nonmetropolitan America has captured the imagination of radio and TV writers, giving us such creations as Garrison Keillor's Lake Wobegon, Minnesota.

But in real life, nonmetropolitan America is dying out. For a period in the early 1970s, rural areas grew faster than metropolitan areas, but this **counterurbanization** (decreasing size, density, and heterogeneity) was short-lived. By 1990, "The American small town, which has long occupied a revered place in the nation's history and mythology, [was] becoming something of a museum piece" (Johnson, 1990:A10). From 1990 to 2000, one in four nonmetro counties in the United States lost population.

Why have rural places and small towns in the United States been losing population? The reason is not cultural: Norman Rockwell's sentimental picture of small-town America still seems to dominate the popular imagination, crowding out darker counterimages, such as Sherwood Anderson's grotesques of *Winesburg, Ohio* (1919); Sinclair Lewis's provincial, drab, small Midwestern *Main Street* (1920); and

David Lynch's hidden world of depravity beneath the blissful small-town exterior in the movie *Blue Velvet* (1986). Rather, the demise is primarily economic: "In an economic sense, a lot of these little places just aren't needed anymore" (Beale in Johnson, 1990:A10).

However, times change. In the twenty-first century, some small towns, as depicted by Hollywood, were either places to escape from, as in *Swing Vote* (2008), or the locus of extreme violence, as in the Oscar-winning film *No Country for Old Men* (2007).

Some U.S. rural communities, unlike the one depicted near the Rio Grande in *No Country for Old Men*, have been beset in recent decades by job losses from farming, mining, and manufacturing. They are trying to retain residents and attract new ones by developing their recreational appeal.

Typically, tourism works best in scenic areas. For one, Salmon, Idaho, is located on a fork of the Salmon River, "The River of No Return." The larger area features outdoor recreation including white-water rafting, hunting, and pack expeditions into the Bitterroot Mountains.

But tourism has not offset population loss throughout the United States. A few numbers show the population decline in rural America. At the mid-twentieth century, about 44 percent of the U.S. population lived in small towns and on farms. By 1990, this proportion had declined to less than 23 percent. By 2000, this proportion had declined to less than 21 percent. (This statistic hides one group's preference for rural places in the United States: Hispanics/Latinos [Kandel and Cromartie, 2004]. Since 1980, the *nonmetro* Hispanic/Latino population in the United States doubled. By 2000, Hispanics/Latinos were the most rapidly growing demographic group in U.S. rural areas and small towns.)

Still, the sentimental attachment remains. More Americans prefer to live in small towns than in any other place. The vast majority of people—over 80 percent by 2000—in the United States live in metro areas, but polls confirm the long-standing American antimetropolitan bias. For example, one poll asked respondents if they would rather live in a city, suburb, small town, or farm: Small towns were the top choice (See Appalachian Resource Center, n.d.).

As noted, the U.S. Census Bureau adopted Micropolitan Statistical Area as a category, designating 577 micro areas (as of December 2005); these included Brownsville, Texas; Bishop, California; and North Platte, Nebraska. Just as there is no "typical" metro area, there is no "typical" micro area. But residents of micropolitan and metropolitan areas do differ in significant ways. In general, metropolitan dwellers go to school longer and earn more money. Micro areas tend to be less racially and ethnically diverse.

WHERE ARE WE HEADED IN THE UNITED STATES?

Will new communications and transport technologies reverse the population decline in rural America, allowing people to telecommute or to commute via high-speed trains? Or, with seemingly ever-increasing energy prices, will most people in the United States soon be living in a handful of giant CMSAs with 10–50 million inhabitants? Which future is it—or are we headed in both directions?

We can't forecast the future with certainty. Even so, we have no rational choice but to try to anticipate it. Before looking ahead to alternative futures—ranging from a high-tech rural society and supercities to skybound cities—let us reexamine where we have been. This time we'll focus on major population shifts and the transformation of community life in the United States.

U.S. POPULATION SHIFTS

Looking backward, we see how rapidly the United States was transformed from a collection of farms and small towns into a metropolitan nation. A few numbers illustrate this shift.

FROM RURAL TO URBAN

In 1790, only 5.1 percent of the U.S. population lived in urban places. By 1850, this number had increased to only 15 percent. The year 1920 was a landmark. For the first time in U.S. history, more people lived in urban centers than in rural areas.

But urban growth in the United States was uneven—and remains so. Very large cities grew faster than smaller ones due to the centralization of industry and postindustrial services there. This pattern of centralization of people and industry meant that in 1970 45 percent of the nation's population lived on 15 percent of the land area in the continental 48 states. (This small core produced much more than its share of economic wealth and power: They generated 55 percent of the national income.) By 2000, over 80 percent of the population lived on 16 percent of the land.

FROM URBAN TO SUBURBAN AND POSTSUBURBAN

The year 1920 also marked the start of another long-standing trend: the movement away from central cities. Just as the United States became an urban nation in 1920, suburbs started growing at a faster rate than central cities. By 1970, more people lived around U.S. cities than within them.

This major population shift—from central city to outside central city—has various names: "suburbanization," "metropolitanization," and "urban sprawl." Whatever it is called, it happened quickly. In fact, the transformation of America from an urban to a suburban nation took place in only 50 years (1920–1970), much faster than the rural–urban shift.

By 1970, the United States was a metropolitan nation. The majority of people—140 million, or 70 percent—lived in metropolitan areas. More importantly, of this 140 million, the majority (76 million) lived outside central cities.

Out-migration from central city to outside central city began in the nineteenth century. Streetcars and railroads made suburban areas more accessible to the well-to-do and socially-prestigious groups.

Suburban development in the United States did not boom, however, until after World War II. Between 1950 and 1970, suburbs grew from 30 million to 76 million residents. As the "new" urban theorists remind us, this massive population shift was encouraged by a host of federal government programs, ranging from a $2 billion-a-year highway construction program to Federal Housing Administration and Veterans Administration mortgage guarantees. Such federal support led to a suburban housing boom, permitting a mass exodus from central cities by white, middle-class, and some working-class, Americans.

Starting in the late 1960s, people in the United States moved to a new kind of outside central city location: "technoburb," "edge city," or "postsuburbia." Whatever it's called, it is neither a traditional city nor a suburb. As detailed in Chapter 8, this form is a culturally diverse, economically viable, multi-centered region (such as Orange County, California) that reflects various societal trends in production and consumption.

BACK TO THE LAND?

For a brief moment over a generation ago, many rural places in the United States once regarded as "nowhere" became "somewhere." Entirely rural counties (not adjacent to metropolitan areas and having no urban places) were the fastest-growing areas. But this reversal of the long-term trend toward metropolitanization was short-lived.

Why did this U.S. "rural renaissance" happen? Theorists disagree, but among the factors often mentioned are deconcentration (due particularly to improvements in communications technologies) and the spread of retirement communities.

In the near future, another rural renaissance—based primarily on high-speed communications—might take hold, bringing numerous people, particularly professionals in hi-tech fields and people who wish to grow their own food. Some urban refugees—called "location-neutrals"—have already made the transition, including a former Chicago lawyer who runs his business from a small, bucolic town in the Rockies. Indeed, small, recreational towns (e.g., Jackson, Wyoming; Steamboat Springs, Colorado) may experience "virtual suburbanization" (Schechter, in Leland, 2007).

In many places, technology is enabling people to live and work wherever they want. Some in the U.S. are clustering in "resort playgrounds" like Steamboat Springs, Colorado (pop. 9,315) that have natural amenities, good weather—and, now, lots of people like themselves (Leland, 2007). Indeed, from 2000 to 2006, those 297 counties that ranked highest in natural amenities (e.g., beautiful scenery) by the U.S. Department of Agriculture grew at 10 times the rate for the 1,090 rural counties with below-average amenities (in Leland, 2007).

FROM FROSTBELT TO SUNBELT

Another important population shift in the United States, starting about 1950, concerns interregional migration. Popularly, this is called the move from Frostbelt to Sunbelt. Some call it the shift from *Rustbelt* (symbolizing the **deindustrialization** that transformed many northern factories into rusted-out plants) to *Gunbelt* (symbolizing the postwar growth of defense-related centers in the South and West).

Before 1950, people moved from economically-depressed southern states to northern industrial cities. In the 1950s, this pattern was reversed; population began flowing to the South and the West. By 1990, the majority of people in the United States lived in the South and West.

The Sunbelt (the broad band of southern states from Florida to southern California) led U.S. population growth between 1950 and 1970. A sunnier climate had some impact, but more important were jobs and economic expansion. Gigantic post–World War II industries spread throughout the Sunbelt. Leading the list of new or expanded Sunbelt industries were oil and gas extraction, electronics, agribusiness, aerospace, and defense-related production. (After World War II, the federal government spent billions of dollars to provide infrastructure to the Sunbelt and to support the newly established defense-related industries there.)

Note, however, that the Snowbelt–Frostbelt distinction may not be as useful as once thought. Indeed, over a generation ago, Noyelle and Stanback (1984:222) indicated that the economic transformation of most U.S. cities is a complicated process in which many Snowbelt cities held their own. Further, they noted, many key economic resources (e.g., finance) didn't flow to the Sunbelt. They were right: A generation later, New York City—a Snowbelt city—remains a headquarters city, and Los Angeles is the only Sunbelt city with that distinction in the United States.

Still, it is noteworthy that people in the United States keep moving to the Sunbelt. From summer 2006 to summer 2007, the Sunbelt was home to the fastest-growing areas in the United States. However, a year later, some Sunbelt states led the nation in terms of percentage of homes foreclosed. Will those foreclosed-upon stay put or move to less sunny climes where housing may be more affordable? Again, stay tuned!

INTERPRETING THE POPULATION TRENDS

What do all these U.S. internal migrations—from Frostbelt to Sunbelt, urban to suburban to postsuburban, metropolitan, and supermetropolitan—add up to? The picture is muddy. In the decade 1990–2000, nine of the 10 fastest-growing metro areas were located in the Sunbelt. But, as a former director of the U.S. Bureau of the Census said decades ago, "Population shifts can be shifty....Not all the sunshine is in the sunbelt" (Keane, 1985:6).

Indeed, one state whose population grew enormously in the 1990–2000 decade was not in the Sunbelt: Alaska (up 14 percent). However, Nevada, often considered part of the Sunbelt, topped the nation's growth with a 66 percent population increase. (What a difference a near-decade can make: With job losses and unemployment, by 2008, the state of Nevada—for the twenty-third straight month—had the highest rate in the United States of home foreclosures: one in 76 households, more than six times the national average. How this will translate to population loss remains murky.)

Several other population trends are noteworthy:

1. *More footloose Americans.* Mainly elderly and extremely elderly retirees (age 85 and up, whose numbers have nearly tripled in recent decades), the footloose can take their pensions, Social Security, and other nonwage income to the Florida sun, the Oregon seaside, a Mexican village, or the daughter's spare room; they don't need to consider job opportunities when moving.
2. *More immigrants.* In past decades, millions of immigrants from Mexico, the Caribbean, and Asia settled in southwestern MSAs and in non-metro areas. This trend signals a shift with vast political, social, and economic implications. For one, the U.S. Census Bureau predicts that by 2020 people of Latino/Hispanic descent will remain the largest U.S. "minority" (guesstimated at 15.7 percent in 2020).
3. *More supermetropolitanization.* By 1990, for the first time in U.S. history, a majority of people (50.2 percent) lived in CMSAs. In 2000, the New York metropolitan area remained the

nation's biggest (over 21 million people) and the Los Angeles CMSA, with a population over 16.3 million, held the "second city" title.
4. *Coastalism.* During the 1990–2000 decade, California grew 13.8 percent to nearly 34 million. By 2020, the U.S. Census Bureau expects California to be the biggest population gainer, increasing to 47.9 million people.
5. *Continued suburbanization (perhaps).* Although the trend toward suburbanization has remained constant since 1920, it may be slowed or even reversed. The near future may depend on the price of gas (and thus commuting-by-car costs) and other economic factors. There has been another recent twist: increased poverty in the suburbs. Indeed, in 2005, for the first time in U.S. history, the number of poor was higher in many suburbs than in the large central cities which they ringed.

One prediction that outdid itself: By 2005, the number of telecommuters in the United States had been expected to triple, to about 15 million people. It did that—and more: By 2006, the number reached 28.7 million (Management-Issues Ltd., 2007).

In the future, more are expected to work at home or in small neighborhood satellite offices. Since the first telecommute center was set up near Honolulu in 1989, the concept has spread to many metro areas, including Vienna, Austria. Globally, this trend will probably spur further deconcentration of population, particularly around edge cities in rich nations. Yet, this may depend in large measure on the availability of public transport and the price of gas.

ANOTHER LOOK

Industrialization, urbanization, and capitalism transformed western European and U.S. cities, changing the nature of urban space, work, and human relationships. Decades later, new communications technologies and the restructuring of the world economy once again are transforming metropolitan life. Bigness (supermetropolitanization) and sprawl (continuing population deconcentration out from the urban core) reflect these technological and organizational innovations.

Growth patterns such as bigness and deconcentration may be neither inevitable nor desirable. Land-use patterns reflect human decisions and cultural values. For instance, whether or not they can afford it, people in the United States tend to see the single-family home in a low-density suburb as ideal for children's growth. (To the contrary, the French tend to idealize big-city apartment life as healthy for their children's development.) Further, suburbanites tend to see an expansive green lawn as a symbol of healthy living, while urban critics see it as an ecological outrage as well as a waste of time and energy.

Most people in the United States now live in metropolitan areas but outside central cities. Did they move to the suburbs in a vain quest for community? Do particular neighborhoods (or ZIP-code clusters) in cities and suburbs represent *Gemeinschaft*-like communities? Are so-called edge cities, technoburbs, or postsuburbs new types of communities, typical of *Techno$chaft*? We turn to such questions in Chapter 8.

KEY TERMS

Census tract A small subdivision of a U.S. city within an MSA, devised by the U.S. Census Bureau to help tabulate and analyze census data. Generally, census tracts have 1,500–8,000 people. Optimum size is 4,000 people.

Central city In the United States, the population center of an MSA, containing at least 50,000 people (or twin cities with a combined population of at least 50,000). This is not to be confused with the popular terms *center city* or *inner city*.

Consolidated Metropolitan Statistical Area (CMSA) U.S. Census Bureau term used to refer to regions comprising more than one MSA that are closely related socially and economically. A CMSA always includes two or more contiguous MSAs that meet specific criteria of size, urban character, integration, and contiguity of urbanized areas. One of the constituent MSAs must have a population of at least 1 million people, and at least 75 percent of the population of each MSA must be classified as urban.

Core-Based Statistical Area (CBSA) A U.S. Census Bureau term, as of 2000, referring collectively to metropolitan and micropolitan statistical areas.

Each CBSA must contain at least one urban area of 10,000 or more population.

Counterurbanization In an urbanized society, the process whereby the proportion of nonmetropolitan residents increases relative to the proportion of metropolitan residents and cities become less dense, less heterogeneous, and smaller.

Deindustrialization The process of job shifting in the economy from manufacturing to services/information and the accompanying "outsourcing" of manufacturing jobs to other, lower-wage countries. In the United States, the general process has resulted in the demise of high-wage manufacturing jobs in older industrial cities like Detroit, Michigan, and Youngstown, Ohio, and the creation of lower-wage service jobs.

Megalopolis Term for a supermetropolitan area (Greek: *mega* = big) or CMSA, an urban complex with at least 1 million in population.

Metropolis A big city that dominates the surrounding area economically, socially, and culturally. From the Greek, meaning "mother city."

Metropolitan Statistical Area (MSA) As defined by the U.S. Census Bureau, a contiguous territorial unit economically and socially integrated around a U.S. central city or twin cities containing at least 50,000 people. The entire county in which the central city is located is always included in the MSA. (In New England, cities and towns are used instead of counties.)

Micropolitan Statistical Area Since 2003, a U.S. census term. A U.S. micro area is defined as an urban area containing an urban core city or town of at least 10,000 (but less than 50,000) population. Like the MSA, it is a geostatistical measure. (As originally defined by G. Scott Thomas in the late 1980s, it was a single county with at least 40,000 residents, including the population of the core city, which has at least 15,000 residents, or any independent city with at least 15,000 residents.) As of 2005, using the new definition, the U.S. Census Bureau identified 577 Micropolitan Statistical Areas in the United States and five in Puerto Rico.

Outside central city Every place in the MSA minus the central city.

Primary Metropolitan Statistical Area (PMSA) A major component of a Consolidated Metropolitan Statistical Area (CMSA). A county or group of counties recognized as a separate MSA or any additional county or counties recognized by local opinion if it meets certain population and commuting criteria. There are four levels of PMSA, according to total population: level A, MSAs of 1 million or more; level B, MSAs of 250,000 to 1 million; level C, MSAs of 100,000–250,000; level D, MSAs of less than 100,000.

PROJECTS

1. **Metropolitan areas** Using U.S. census data, look at the changes over time in your own or a nearby MSA. Did the population grow or decline since 1950? Did the number of counties in the MSA remain the same? In 1960 and 2000, what percentages lived in the central city and outside central city? What factors account for the demographic changes (or lack of change)?

2. **CMSAs** In the 1980s, 90 percent of U.S. population growth happened in metropolitan areas of more than 1 million people. Why? Show via a chart if this trend is continuing or not.

SUGGESTIONS FOR FURTHER LEARNING

U.S. community life is a continuing, lively subject in both the arts and social sciences. Over the years, the popular arts have presented contrasting visions of neighborhood and small community. On one end of the spectrum lies the 2007 Oscar-winning film *No Country for Old Men* (based on a novel by Cormac McCarthy), which shows a rural West Texas town as the setting for individual greed and morally bankrupt or compromised individuals. Wisteria Lane, the site of TV's globally popular *Desperate Housewives* (ABC, 2004–), is fraught with suspicion and juicy gossip—with caring and neighborliness thrown in. Emmy-winning TV show *Everybody Loves Raymond* (CBS, 1996–2005 and in syndication), set in a village on Long Island, is a sitcom built on the theme of family. Featured are an Italian American sportswriter and his family, with its share of obnoxious members who care about one another just the same. The show is nostalgic but adds the twist of unappreciated family members living nearby, which recalls Margaret Mead's putdown of "community." Popular culture works that emphasized positive attributes of neighborhood and community within modern society were more the norm a generation ago in the United States than now.

For a strong argument that the small town in America is not the polar opposite of urban society but instead is permeated by the culture and politics of mass society, see Arthur J. Vidich and Joseph Bensman, *Small Town in Mass Society* (Princeton, N.J.: Princeton University Press, [1958] 1968).

Studies of *Gemeinschaft*-like communities within urban-industrial or industrializing societies include Charles Nordhoff's observations of utopian communities in nineteenth-century America, *The Communistic Societies of the United States* (New York: Dover, [1875] 1966). Of special note is Jacquelyn Dowd Hall et al., *Like a Family: The Making of a Southern Cotton Mill World* (New York: Norton, 1987); interviewees use the imagery of family to describe their own social relationships in a mill village.

William H. Whyte depicts what he views as the loss of individualism to corporate values, both in managerial work and in home life, in Park Forest, Illinois (and by extension other suburbs), after World War II. See *The Organization Man* (New York: Simon and Schuster, 1956).

Can new communities be constructed with democratic decision-making structures, ecological awareness, and communitarian social relations? Some think so. In *We Build the Road as We Travel* (Santa Cruz, Calif.: New Society, 1991), Roy Morrison tells the story of the Mondragon cooperatives in the Basque region of Spain. Started by a parish priest and a few students in the early 1950s, the network has grown to employ some 21,000 people. They have developed their own nongovernmental social welfare and educational systems, as well as businesses.

In the United States, Rancho Linda Vista, 35 miles north of Tucson, Arizona, is a communally-owned, close-knit community. Founded in 1968, it remains dedicated to providing its members with an environment organized around promoting artistic purposes. What has held it together for all these years?

"Art," says one resident painter. (For information about the community, see: http://interstice.us/rlvweb/index.htm)

Connecting via the Internet with others who have the same name may or may not promote community. But it is the subject of at least one book, *Finding Angela Shelton* (Toronto: Meredith Books, 2008), by filmmaker/actress Angela Shelton. She describes her getting together with 40 other Angela Sheltons, the majority of whom (like herself) suffered abusive family relationships.

REFERENCES

Anderson, Sherwood. 1919. *Winesburg, Ohio.* New York: Huebsch.

Appalachian Resource Center. n.d. "Historical patterns of growth and decline in the 20th century." Online Resource Center: http://www.arc.gov/index.do?nodeId=2764

Berry, Brian, and John Kasarda. 1977. *Contemporary Urban Ecology.* New York: Macmillan.

Blakely, Edward J. 1999. *Fortress America: Gated Communities in the U.S.* Washington, D.C.: Brookings Institution Press.

Bram, Jason, and Alistair McKay. 2005. "The evolution of commuting patterns in the New York City metro area." Federal Reserve Bank of New York. (October): http://www.newyorkfed.org/research/current_issues/ci11-10/ci11-10.html

Burgess, Ernest. [1923]. 1925. "Growth of the city." Pp. 47–62 in Robert E. Park, Ernest W. Burgess, and Roderick McKenzie, eds., *The City.* Chicago: University of Chicago Press.

Castells, Manuel. 1983. *The City and the Grassroots.* Berkeley: University of California Press.

Feagin, Joe R. 1988. *Houston—The Free Enterprise City.* New Brunswick, N.J.: Rutgers University Press.

Fitzsimmons, James D. (U.S. Census Bureau). 1995. Personal phone communication. May 2.

Forstall, Richard L. (U.S. Census Bureau). 1991. Personal phone communication. August 1.

Frey, William H., and Alden Speare, Jr. 1988. *Regional and Metropolitan Growth and Decline in the United States.* New York: Russell Sage Foundation.

Gordon, Peter, et al. 2004. "Travel trends in U.S. cities: Explaining the 2000 Census commuting results." (April): http://www.rcf.usc.edu/~pgordon/pdf/commuting.pdf

Gottdiener, M. 1985. *The Social Production of Urban Space.* Austin: University of Texas Press.

———. 1987. *The Decline of Urban Politics.* Newbury Park, Calif.: Sage.

———. 1994. *The New Urban Sociology.* New York: McGraw-Hill.

Gottdiener, M., and Joe R. Feagin. 1988. "The paradigm shift in urban sociology." *Urban Affairs Quarterly* 24:163–187.

Harper, Douglas. 2001. *Changing Works.* Chicago: University of Chicago Press.

Harvey, David. 1985. *The Urbanization of Capital.* Baltimore: Johns Hopkins University Press.

Hawley, Amos. 1950. *Human Ecology.* New York: Ronald Press.

(The) House of Murphy. n.d. http://members/lycos.fr/The Walrus/m.html

Jaffe, Greg. 2007. "In Iraq, an officer's answer to violence: build a wall." *Wall Street Journal* (April 5):A1+.

Johnson, Dirk. 1990. "Population decline in rural America: A product of advances in technology." *New York Times* [national edition] (September 11):A10+.

Kandel, Jonathan, and John Cromartie. 2004. "New patterns of Hispanic settlement in rural America." Rural Development Research Report RDRR99, 49 pp., (May): http://www.ers.usda.gov/publications/rdrr99/

Keane, John G. 1985. "Our cities: Trends and times." Address to U.S. Conference of Mayors, Anchorage, Alaska (June 18): https://catalog.lib.ecu.edu/ipac20/ipac.jsp?session=12244052297DC.68092&profile=joyner&uri=link=3100020~!2817785~!3100001~!3100002&aspect=subtab13&menu=search&ri=1&source=~!alsdb&term=Our+cities+%3A+trends+and+times+%2F&index=UTL

Ledebur, Larry C., and William R. Barnes. 1992. *City Distress, Metropolitan Disparities and Economic Growth.* Washington, D.C.: National League of Cities.

———. 1993. *"All in It together": Cities, Suburbs, and Local Economic Regions.* Washington, D.C.: National League of Cities.

Leland, John. 2007. "Off to resorts, and carrying their careers." *New York Times* (August 13): http://www.nytimes.com/2007/08/13/us/13steamboat.html?th&emc=ths

Lewis, Sinclair. 1920. *Main Street.* New York: Harcourt.

Management-Issues Ltd. 2007. "US sees big rise in teleworking." (February 13): http://www.management-issues.com/2007/2/13/research/us-sees-big-rise-in-teleworking.asp

McKenzie, Roderick D. 1933. *The Metropolitan Community.* New York: McGraw-Hill.

McKibben, Bill. 2008. "Where have all the joiners gone? A declaration of dependence." *Orion Magazine* (March/April): http://www.orionmagazine.org/index.php/articles/article/2874

Noyelle, Thierry J., and Thomas M. Stanback, Jr. 1984. *The Economic Transformation of American Cities.* Totowa, N.J.: Rowman & Allanheld.

Park, Robert. 1916. "The city: Suggestions for the investigation of human behavior in the urban environment." *American Journal of Sociology* 20:577–612.

Reich, Robert B. 1991a. "The secession of the successful." *New York Times Magazine* (January 20):16+.

———. 1991b. *The Work of Nations: Preparing Ourselves for 21st Century Capitalism.* New York: Knopf.

Rosenbloom, Stephanie. 2008. "Names that match forge a bond on the Internet." *New York Times* (April 10): http://www.nytimes.com/2008/04/10/us/10names.html?_r=1&th=&adxnnl=1&oref=slogin&emc=th&adxnnlx=1207854006-/nKfevhbRKAlHkxcVf18/g

Sacchetti, Maria. 2008. "More immigrants buying land in native countries." Boston Globe (July 7): http://www.boston.com/news/local/articles/2008/07/07/american_dream_goes_global/

Schreiner, Tim. 1992. "Suburban communities 'forting up.'" *San Francisco Chronicle* (September 21):A1+.

Thomas, G. Scott. 1990. *The Rating Guide to Life in America's Small Cities.* Buffalo, N.Y.: Prometheus.

University of South Florida.2008. Clearinghouse: http://www.nctr.usf.edu/clearinghouse/about.htm

MAKING CONNECTIONS

Gesche Würfel

SEARCHING FOR COMMUNITY, OR NEW HOUSES?

Millions of people in the United States voted with their cars between 1950 and 1970. They moved from the urban core to the suburbs. By 1970 more Americans lived around cities than within them.

SUBURBANIZATION: AN ALMOST WORLDWIDE PHENOMENON

From Marin County, California, to the rings around Vienna, Austria, many are now rethinking their suburban lifestyles. This is particularly so if their work is far

from home, they use high-priced gas to get there, and worry over carbon emissions as an element in climate change.

However, in the 1950s, gas in the United States was relatively cheap, climate change was not a concern, and millions moved to U.S. suburbs. And they were far from alone: Suburbanization occurred in metro areas worldwide (Mills and Tan, 1980).

Note: Typically, "suburbs" around cities that grew up before industrialization (e.g., Paris, Lima) do not fit the U.S. stereotype. Indeed, *globally, many areas outside the central city are the opposite of what are called suburbs in the United States*: squatter settlements, slums, or poverty-stricken zones with substandard housing and extremely crowded conditions. (The stereotype of "suburbia" may be changing in the United States too. As noted in this chapter and elsewhere, the poverty rate is often higher in the inner suburbs than in their nearby central cities.)

The population shift from city to suburb proceeded more quickly in the United States than in most other nations. One major exception is Canada. Canada became a suburban nation by 1960 (Harris, 2004). Vancouver, British Columbia, for instance, experienced rapid suburban growth from 1900 to 1930.

Since the 1980s, suburbanization has proceeded apace in many nations, fueled by personal preferences. In Estonia, as in many countries of the former Soviet Union (but not those of East Central Europe),

the major population movement has been to suburbs; the more highly educated and those with families have been the most likely to move there (Kontuly and Tammaru, 2006).

Turkey's suburbanization is following another path. It began in the 1980s as upper-class professionals voted with their cars and began acquiring "villas" in gated communities outside of cities, such as Kemer Country, a resort village outside Istanbul.

Suburbanization can also result from government policy, as in Shanghai, China. City officials in Shanghai, a city with one of the densest urban cores in the world, plan to move 5.4 million residents out of older, low-rise buildings in the core and relocate them to nine new satellite suburbs and 60 new small towns with populations of about 50,000 each (Peralta, 2006).

Fig. 8.2   GATED COMMUNITY IN SUBURBAN SHANGHAI. (John Randall)

Why did suburbanization occur very quickly in Canada but more slowly in Europe and Japan? Some (e.g., Montgomery, 2003:81) say that auto-love and suburbanization go together with national prosperity. Others say culture plays a role: personal preferences to live in single-family homes with space rather than high-density, city settlements. And some point to government strategies as a key factor: prosuburban policies, such as the building of highways to make commuting easier, or antisuburban public policies, such as higher taxes past city limits.

Why did suburbanization *not* happen in much of Latin America? Some say that land limits and transport deficiencies inhibited the suburbanization of high-income people.

Suburbanites were not—and are not—all the same. As noted, historically (and even now), the poor often live on the fringes of big cities which predate the Industrial Revolution. Furthermore, in the United States, poverty reached the suburbs in record numbers by 2005, particularly in inner suburbs.

Here, we'll focus on suburbs in the United States, starting after World War II and moving forward. First, what kinds of people were the post–World War II migrants? What kind of life did they lead once they got to the suburbs? A host of social critics thought they knew.

DIATRIBES AGAINST "SUBURBIA"

Shortly after the mass exodus from central city to suburb began after World War II, U.S. social critics looked at "**suburbia**," and here is what they saw:

> Boring couples with small children, spending Saturday picking crabgrass out of their lawns.
> Ugly, poorly planned tract developments called "Merry Meadows" or "Happy Acres," high-sounding names that masked cheap construction and dull lives.
> A land of joiners and conformists.

That was the stereotype of the U.S. suburb: a vast wasteland. This negative image dominated novels and even so-called empirical studies in the 1950s.

With little evidence but much venom, most of the supposed social science studies in the 1950s crucified the suburbs. John Keats's antisuburban study

The Crack in the Picture Window (1956) is exemplary. According to Keats, John and Mary Drone decorate their shoddily-built, look-alike tract home in Rolling Knolls with plastic reproductions of high art. Further, the Drones live in a "jerry-built, homogeneous, post-war hell that destroys individualism" (61).

To Keats and numerous other critics, suburbia was the American nightmare, not the American dream. It symbolized middle-class mediocrity, spiritual malaise, and materialism.

Who were these critics who painted such a devastating picture of suburban life? Why did they attack with such venom? It is significant that the negative suburban image was the work of a small segment of people in the United States: urbane, upper-class, white intellectuals. Overwhelmingly, the critics were well-educated white, Anglo-Saxon, Protestant (WASP) males who lived in either the rural countryside or the major metropolitan centers, not in the suburbs.

These elite critics fell into two major categories, both tinged with romanticism. Some critics of suburbia looked backward, glorifying a rural past. Either they dreamed of recapturing Tönnies's vision of *Gemeinschaft* (people living in harmony with nature and one another in a tight-knit community) or they idealized Thomas Jefferson's American dream (a rural nation populated by self-sufficient, individualistic gentlemen farmers). Jefferson thought that democratic traditions needed to be nourished in the soil of yeoman farmers' fields.

Jefferson's ideal underlies the most influential attack on suburbia of the era, William H. Whyte's best-seller *The Organization Man* (1956). Whyte's analysis "The New Suburbia: Organization Man at Home" is one of the few empirically grounded studies of the 1950s, and his treatment of suburban Park Forest, Illinois, is more even-handed than other critics' antisuburban tracts. Yet, on balance, Whyte concludes that the group tyrannizes the individual: "group immersion" equals "imprison[ment] in brotherhood" (404). Whyte's verdict: The price of a tight-knit community is tyranny of the individual, a price too high to pay.

Whyte looked back to self-sufficient communities. Other critics of suburbia looked forward to an imagined urban future. In this romantic vision, cities would be centers of high culture, social order, and true sophistication. (Contemporary cities, these critics bemoaned, were disorderly and barbaric.)

To both kinds of romantics—the traditionalists and the futurists—suburbia was a dismal failure. Neither countryside nor city, the suburbs seemed to combine the worst features of both.

This antisuburban literature has a familiar ring, for the same themes run throughout U.S. intellectual history. Indeed, the antisuburban diatribes of the 1950s echo the antiurban harangues of earlier times. In both cases, members of the traditional WASP elite led the attack. They seem to have been reacting to an alien presence in their midst that threatened their most cherished dreams for their nation.

Comparing the antisuburban diatribes to the antiurban attacks of the 1880s, we can see what fears these social critics shared. In the late nineteenth century, upper-crust, educated WASPs worried that the immigrant "mobs" would destroy "their" cities and U.S. high culture. Such literary figures as novelist Henry James did not hide their disdain for the lower-class ethnics streaming into New York City. To James, they represented the first stage of "alienism."

Patrician James also criticized the newly rich business tycoons, whom he called the "vulgar rich," for their bourgeois values. (Today, some refer with disdain to such folks as "nouveaux riches," a category that typically includes newly rich people of all sorts, not just business tycoons.) James especially disliked tycoons who made their fortunes in U.S. cities and then deserted them for the "non-descript excrescences" of fashionable suburbs.

Henry James was a patrician or "blue blood." The United States did not have an aristocracy, but James no doubt considered himself aristocratic and feared the spread of two alien traditions: (1) mass culture and (2) bourgeois values.

Similarly, Whyte and other antisuburban critics in the 1950s found fault with mass culture and bourgeois values, this time symbolized by a new mass migration: the move to the suburbs. But this time the "aliens" weren't lower-class ethnics; they were members of the white, new middle class of corporate America.

To conclude: Lurking behind the 1950s critique of suburbia is the specter of George Orwell's nightmare world of *1984* (see Orwell, 1949). There, mass-produced people live in authoritarian **mass society**. Critics like Keats and Whyte feared that mass society, symbolized by suburbia, would destroy individualism. (There is a certain irony here, for according to Durkheim, Tönnies, and others in the typological tradition, individualism can flourish *only* in urban-industrial society.) These fears were fueled by the cold war vision of the then Soviet Union, depicted—like suburbia in the United States—as the quintessence of conformity.

THE MYTH OF SUBURBIA

When the dust started settling on the newly paved roads of tract homes, social scientists began to paint a more complex portrait of suburban life. Post-1950s studies show that life beyond the city limits is hardly a wasteland of drab conformity and dreary, look-alike lives.

By the 1960s, researchers dropped the label "suburbia." It was, they inferred, a myth. Suburbs do not look alike, nor do their inhabitants share a lifestyle. Instead of homogeneity, the 1960s studies revealed a variety of suburban types: from enormously wealthy to middle income and dirt poor, Democratic and Republican, and from high- to low-density communities. Some urbanists (e.g., Schnore, 1963) distinguished suburbs on the basis of function: (1) residential bedroom suburbs, (2) industrial-manufacturing suburbs, and (3) mixed residential–industrial suburbs. Whatever their function, few fit the 1950s stereotype of suburbia. Take, for example, Levittown.

LEVITTOWN

Constructed by a single developer in the late 1950s, Levittown, New Jersey, is a bedroom suburb outside Philadelphia. (Residents later changed its name back to "Willingboro.") From the outside, it could have served as a model for Keats's dread "Rolling Knolls," home of the Drones. But from the inside, as Herbert Gans's monumental study *The Levittowners* (1967) documents, this then mainly working-class and lower middle-class suburb did not fit the stereotype of suburbia.

Sociologist Gans lived in Levittown during its first years, gathering data as a participant-observer on the new suburb's way of life and politics. He found that the generally young residents were not marked by crushing conformity and homogeneity. He also found, among other things, that "by any yardstick one chooses, Levittowners treated their fellow residents more ethically and democratically than did their parents and grandparents. They also lived a 'fuller' and 'richer' life" (1967:419).

Gans noted that most Levittowners were neither rich nor poor. The middle-income population was a result of the developers' key decision: to build houses in the $12,000–$15,000 price range (in 1950s dollars). In essence, this one decision by the builders (William J. Levitt, his father, and his brother) determined who lived there and what kinds of groups developed in the new community.

Note: When various Levittowns were built in the late 1940s and early 1950s, racial discrimination was legal in the United States. At that time, Levitt refused to sell to African Americans because he feared losing potential white home buyers. He told the *Saturday Evening Post* in the mid-1950s that "as a company, our position is simply this: we can solve a housing problem or we can try to solve a racial problem. But we cannot combine the two." In 1954, he said that "As a Jew, I have no room in my mind or heart for racial prejudice." But, he added, "if we sell one house to a Negro family, then 90 to 95 percent of our white customers will not buy into the community. That is their attitude, not ours" (in Blackwell, n.d.).

Among white residents, there was a limited range of occupations, mainly in the technical and service areas. But people did come from various white ethnic backgrounds. And, after a court order and some original homeowners reselling houses to them, some African Americans.

Most Levittowners saw their homes as the center of their lives. But, Gans noted, they were much more "in the world" and less parochial than their ethnic or WASP grandparents or parents.

According to Gans, there was little evidence in Levittown of what Whyte and others so feared: tyranny of the majority over the individual. Levittown neighbors did apply peer pressure to conform in minor ways (say, to keep the front lawn trimmed), but this did not lead to sameness of thought and action.

In general, Gans (1967:417–420) found that the young Levittowners did *not* resemble Whyte's and Keats's suburbanites. They were neither fearsome "apathetic conformists" nor frightful "organization men." Nor did they resemble the residents of upper-class, prestigious suburbs.

To conclude: Was Levittown a community? No. According to Gans, it was neither an economic unit (where members depend upon one another for their livelihood) nor a social unit nor a symbolic unit (for the sense of community was weak (1967: Chapter 7).

Then what was it? In Gans's view, Levittown was only a loose network of groups and institutions. Mainly, it was an administrative–political unit (with many community-wide associations). Levittowners, Gans concluded, did not come to find a sense of community; they came to carry on old ways of life in new houses (149). They were trying to re-create old life styles and institutions—but on new soil. Sociologist and planner Gans decided that social planners shouldn't waste their time trying to recreate something that never existed in the first place: the cohesive community.

Updates to Gans's classic study: (1) After the "whites-only" policy was declared illegal, Willingboro (Levittown) became split almost evenly between black and white. Ironically, real estate agents, who had earlier told prospective white home buyers that the suburb was "homogeneous" (read "all white"), then touted Willingboro's peaceful diversity as a selling point. (2) By 2007, the company that built Levittown was in bankruptcy.

Gans's study of Levittown—plus other early social science studies of more affluent suburbs such as Princeton, New Jersey (Sternlieb et al., 1971), and poor suburbs like East St. Louis (Bollens, 1961)—suggest that *suburbanism is no more a single way of life than is urbanism*. Years ago, these scholars found that communities on the city's rim shared a label—"suburb"—but not one way of life.

In the United States, this conclusion still holds today, perhaps even more so. By 2005, many inner suburbs of large cities had poverty rates higher than areas inside those cities. Further, some suburbs featured cultural palaces, media outlets, and an array of ethnic restaurants as well as locally-based jobs (see Figure. 8.3).

In other words, unlike Gertrude Stein's proverbial rose, a suburb is not a suburb is not a suburb. And, moving beyond Stein's rose, a suburb may no longer be sub-anything.

But the negative reputation of the U.S. suburb dies hard. James Howard Kunstler (1994) wrote that suburbs were *The Geography of Nowhere*, and Bonnie Menes Kahn compared suburbs, unfavorably, to the cosmopolitan culture of cities (1987:107).

In other nations, critics continue to lambast contemporary suburbs. Australian architect–trained journalist Elizabeth Farrelly, for one, writes about what she calls *Blubberland* (2008). There, in her view, bloated, bored, and miserable residents suffer from "affluenza." To Farrelly, Blubberland is not only a place but a state of mind where people live in McMansions or gated communities and leave a destructive eco-footprint.

TAKING THE *SUB* OUT OF SUBURBAN

Suburbs, as historian Lewis Mumford stated long ago, originally were "a collective effort to live a private life" ([1938] 1970:215). Modern suburbs—first on the outskirts of eighteenth-century London, then on the fringes of U.S. industrial cities in the late nineteenth century—housed the rich and powerful. Indeed, these strictly segregated (by class and function) bedroom suburbs of substantial houses on tree-lined lots have been called "bourgeois utopias," blending ideas of "property, union with nature, and family life" (Fishman, 1989:15).

However, by the twentieth century, the dream of a suburban life reached beyond the elites. Los Angeles—"Autopia," as architectural historian Reyner Banham ([1971] 1976:chapter 11) called it—best represents

a

Fig. 8.3 FROM SUBURBIA TO CYBERBIA, A PHOTO ESSAY.
(*a*) In the 1950s, Dublin, California, had a population of 1,000 ("most of them cows") plus "15 gas stations, six supermarkets, two department stores and a K-Mart." By 1973, when Bill Owens profiled Dublin in *Suburbia* (1973, reissued and revised in 1999, New York: Fotofolio), the San Francisco suburb was a fast-growing, lower middle– and middle-income community. By 1990, it had grown to over 23,000 people. (And had passed an "anti-ugly" ordinance, prohibiting peeling paint and drying clothes outside, among other things. Why such an ordinance? Some said it aimed to keep property values high; others said it aimed to beautify the community.) By 2000, its population, numbering almost 30,000, had become more diverse; it included 13.5 percent Latinos, 10.1 percent African Americans, and 10.4 percent Asian Americans. (Dublin is still famous locally for its annual St. Patrick's Day Parade.) By 2000, residents' median household incomes soared to $77,283, much above the U.S. household median income ($49,995). Nielsen Claritas described it in 2006 as a SER 12 "Brite Lites, L'il City" community (see Box 8.1 in this chapter). According to Joel Garreau (1991:436), Dublin, together with three East Bay cities on the Interstate-680 corridor, constitute an edge city. Others call it "postsuburbia" or "cyberbia." (Bill Owens)

b

Fig. 8.3 (*b*) Few walnuts remain in Walnut Creek, California (2000 population 64,296), now a postsuburban development or edge city. It is located only a few miles from Dublin on the I-680 corridor and about 1 hour from San Francisco by Bay Area Rapid Transit. Its downtown, seen here in the distance, features both big department stores and upscale boutiques. (Deborah Mosca)

c

Fig. 8.3 (*c*) The Walnut Creek Arts Center, festooned with flags. According to Joel Garreau (1991: 443), flags are often added to overcome sterility and to suggest "animated space" in edge cities. (Victoria Sheridan)

d

Fig. 8.3 (*d*) Residents of edge cities often feel quite separate socially and politically from nearby central cities. This is what Larry, an edge city resident, says: "About twice a year we get to San Francisco. We live here [in Walnut Creek], go out to the movies and restaurants here. We shop here, and we go to the doctor and vet here." (Deborah Mosca)

the fulfillment of the U.S. dream: money, speed, freedom, mobility, and a single-family suburban home. (*Note*: Most often, this is called the "American dream" as if the United States constituted North, Central, and South America.)

Los Angeles, the quintessential suburban metropolis of the twentieth century, is a 70-square-mile area of "limitless horizontality" (Baudrillard, [1986] 1989:52). It is bound by a network of freeways and "shaped by the promise of a suburban home for all" (Fishman, 1987:15).

This metropolitan form, developed in the 1920s and 1930s, features a complex mix of urban, suburban, and rural spaces. Its basic unit is the decentralized suburb, or what we could call the "California Dreaming" utopia (my term)—in contrast to the "bourgeois" utopia (Fishman's term). In the California Dreaming utopia, offices, shopping, services, and industries, formerly concentrated in the industrial city's core, are dispersed throughout the suburban area.

By 1945, its suburbs were no longer satellites of Los Angeles. Instead, the suburb had become the heartland of the fastest-growing elements of the late twentieth-century economy.

The image of the suburb as a borderland—a privileged zone between city and country—became superseded by what some call a "posturban era," where hi-tech research centers sit in former farm fields and abandoned factory sites in the core are surrounded by growing grass.

Sociologist Fishman wondered, "As both core and periphery are swallowed up in seemingly endless multicentered regions, where can one find suburbia?" He answered his own rhetorical question as follows: The movement of houses, industry, and commerce to the outskirts has created

perimeter cities that are functionally independent of the urban core. In complete contrast to the residential or industrial suburbs of the past, these new cities contain along their superhighways all the specialized functions of a great metropolis—industry, shopping malls, hospitals, universities, cultural centers, and parks. With its highways and advanced communications technology, the new perimeter city can generate urban diversity without urban concentration.

(1987:17)

The basis of this new city, Fishman wrote, is "the invisible web of advanced technology and telecommunications that has been substituted for the face-to-face contact and physical movement of older cities" (17).

To distinguish this new peripheral city from dependent, suburban bedroom communities, Fishman dubbed it a **technoburb**. Others call this new city or zone **postsuburbia**, a form organized spatially around many distinct, specialized centers (Kling et al., 1991) or an **edge city** (Garreau, 1991), which has 5 million square feet or more of leasable office space (the workplace of *Techno$chaft*) and 600,000 square feet or more of leasable retail space, has more jobs than bedrooms, is seen by locals as one place, and was a bedroom community or cow pasture as recently as the early 1960s. Lastly, this relatively new type of settlement is also called **cyberbia**, a science fiction–sounding term that evokes an image of people connected by high-tech electronic communications.

Whatever it's called—perimeter city, technoburb, postsuburbia, edge city, or cyberbia—it has become the center of most people's lives in the United States, replacing traditional categories of urban, rural, and suburban areas. Driving time, not space, determines its fluid boundaries: how long it takes to reach work, shopping, college, and so on by car conveniently.

ENERGY COSTS AND SUBURBS

Although much maligned—notably as unsuited to family patterns and needs (e.g., single moms who commute to faraway workplaces), as eco-unfriendly and energy-inefficient, and/or as designed mainly by traffic engineers—car-based suburbs are not disappearing in the United States or elsewhere.

At least not yet. High energy prices, some think, may fuel a suburban demise. For one, planning professor and real estate developer Christopher B. Leinberger predicted in 2008 that "today the pendulum is swinging back toward urban living, and there

are many reasons to believe this swing will continue." If it does, the consequences will be considerable: "many low-density suburbs and McMansion subdivisions, including some that are lovely and affluent today, may become what inner cities became in the 1960s and '70s—slums characterized by poverty, crime, and decay" (2008).

Others are not so sure. Some say that if high energy costs continue, what the United States will more likely see is a gradual reordering of the city–suburban landscape.

Still, many tend to support the demise-of-the-suburbs scenario, at least in the United States. A *New York Times* reporter put it like this: "Basic household arithmetic appears to be furthering the trend [back to the city]: In 2003, the average suburban household spent $1,422 a year on gasoline…by April, [2008]…the same household was spending $3,196 a year, more than doubling consumption in dollar terms in less than five years" (Goodman, 2008). However, a global recession could change much and quickly, so this trend bears close watch.

THE TRANSFORMATION OF MILPITAS, CALIFORNIA, 1954–2000

Post–World War II Los Angeles pioneered the technoburb. This postsuburban form now exists in many hi-tech areas, typically near research universities—from Boston's Route 128 (MIT) and North Carolina's Research Triangle (Duke, University of North Carolina, North Carolina State University) to Silicon Valley, California (Stanford).

A brief history of Milpitas, California, located in northern California's Silicon Valley (see Chapter 4), the hi-tech complex near Stanford University, illustrates one place's swift transformation. In little more than one generation, Milpitas ("little cornfield" in Spanish) evolved from a semirural community to a working-class suburb to a multicultural technoburb.

During World War II, only 600 people lived in semirural Milpitas. It didn't become a city until 1954. One year later, it was transformed into a residential-industrial suburb when the Ford Motor Company opened a new plant there. Virtually all Ford autoworkers moved from industrial Richmond, the former Ford plant site, to Milpitas in 1955. Two years later, sociologist Bennett M. Berger interviewed 100 Ford workers and their spouses. As he documented in *Working-Class Suburb* ([1960] 1971), these autoworkers and their wives were apparently unaffected by their move from industrial city to suburb; they didn't take on the habits, attitudes, and aspirations of the middle class when they became suburban homeowners.

During its early years, Milpitas was the butt of wisecracks by TV comedians, perhaps because "the local fragrance was a gagging mix of sewage and drainage ditch water" or perhaps because "the city's night life was an adult drive-in theatre across the road from the Ooh La Lodge Motel" (Tessler, 1989:A2). Then, the jokes turned sour. Over 2,400 workers lost their jobs in 1983 when the Ford plant closed.

Then, Milpitas was reborn. Again. The once blue-collar city joined upscale Silicon Valley. It developed 24 industrial parks, 23 retail-professional centers, and 120 manufacturing plants (largely electronics). Its households had the highest income growth in the Bay Area—over 60 percent—from 1980 to 1987. And a $100 million giant shopping mall opened in 1994 on the very site of the former Ford assembly plant in Milpitas.

By 2000, Milpitas was an affluent, ethnically diverse, well-educated community. Its median family household income was $93,531. The majority of its residents were Asian (52%), with white non-Hispanic (27%) and Hispanic (17%) minorities plus a small African American presence (3%). (The percentage of Asian American residents in Milpitas skyrocketed from 12% in 1980 to 51% in 2000.) More than one-third of its residents held a college or graduate degree.

To conclude: As the head of the Milpitas Chamber of Commerce noted years ago, "You can live here, work here, play here. It's a complete community. You can even die here. We have senior citizen centers" (in Tessler, 1989:A2). This statement sums up the new technoburban reality. Milpitas originated on the suburban periphery of another urban core (in this case, San Jose). Then it broke away economically and socially. Now, like other postsuburban developments, Milpitas is much more than a *sub*-urb. It is something relatively new: a conglomerate of residences, technologically-advanced industries, services, cultural activities, and information processing.

ZIP CODES AS NEIGHBORHOODS

Conscious, perhaps touchy, about its former reputation, Milpitas launched a public-relations campaign to change its image. Starting in 1989, the mayor worked hard "to let people know this is not a one-gas-station town anymore. It's upscale. My address is as good as the next guy's" (in Tessler, 1989:A2).

Address, as Milpitas's mayor implies, has important symbolic value. For example, *Beverly Hills, 90210*, a TV series (FOX, 1990–2000; available on DVD), and its update *90210* (CW, 2008–) cram a great deal of information about its characters into an address: a five-digit ZIP code. Why? Because, like it or not, in the United States, your ZIP code symbolizes much more than a postal zone.

The United States is not alone. ZIP codes (often called "postal codes" outside the United States) reveal a great deal about their residents. This is true in Canada, South Africa, Japan, or Australia, to name just a few places.

Market researchers were quick to see that a ZIP (or postal) code represents the social status, values, even political beliefs of a neighborhood. Journalist Michael J. Weiss put it this way: "You are where you live." Maybe not to your mother, but to people who want to sell you things and ideas your ZIP code has become "a yardstick by which your lifestyle is measured" (Weiss, 1988:xi).

A related notion, one long recognized by social scientists, may be a better motto: "In the eyes of others, you are what you buy." (The eminent sociologist Max Weber, among others, based his ideas of social status on shared consumption patterns or lifestyles; see Chapter 11.)

Blending census data, market research, and consumer surveys, analysts can predict a great deal about the consumption patterns, political preferences, and social backgrounds of residents in a ZIP code. The creator of one market research system, PRIZM (an acronym for Potential Rating Index for Zip Markets), goes as far to say this: "Tell me someone's zip code, and I can predict what they [sic] eat, drink, drive—even think" (Robbin in Weiss, 1988:1).

Many resist the notion that they can be pigeon-holed by any social marker, particularly a ZIP code. They see themselves as totally self-willed. Marketeers and sociologists do not agree.

a

Fig. 8.4 WHAT SER IS THIS? In Nielsen Claritas's PRIZM system, neighborhood types are assigned a SER (socioeconomic rank, formerly called a ZQ, or zip quotient) based on residents' household income, home value, education, and occupation. (All examples except [g] are based on Nielsen Claritas's 2006 data; [g] is based on Global Mosaic's 2000 data. [Note that Claritas became Nielsen Claritas in 2008 and is referred to here as "Nielsen Claritas"].) (a) SER 01 Upper Crust was the highest-ranked neighborhood in the United States in 2006. This SER 01 home, located in the San Francisco Bay Area, is superexpensive. SER 01 homes are filled with artisan touches and original art, not unframed posters and brick-and-board bookcases. Typically, there is no TV set in the living room and no rap music playing. (b) SER 04 Young Digerati is an area of sophisticated, affluent, and educated professionals such as Chicago's Lincoln Park neighborhood. (SER 04 appeared in 2006. Formerly, Lincoln Park was part of SER 03 Urban Gold Coast, a PRIZM cluster that disappeared by 2006.) (c) Bohemian Mix, a SER 16 neighborhood (formerly ranked ZQ 11), is an urban area with liberal, ethnically diverse, culturally bohemian lifestyles and a high percentage of college graduates like this neighborhood, the Haight-Ashbury section of San Francisco. (d) White Picket Fences (SER 34) is an ethnically mixed, middle-class, blue-collar area like this one in northern Indiana. (e) American Dreams (SER 29) is a multilingual area (one person in 10 speaks a language other than English) and home to middle-income, immigrant, ethnic families. (f) Shotguns and Pickups (SER 51) is a rural crossroads village or small town, characterized by U.S.-branded pickups and mobile homes. (g) Clever Capitalists, Great Britain's top cluster in 2000, live in once-aristocratic "digs" such as this former baronial mansion in London. Inhabitants of Upland and Small Farms, Great Britain's poorest cluster, live outside London in places described by the cluster title. ([a, c, d, e]) Deborah Mosca; [b] iStock Photo, [f] Tim Teninty, [g] Gesche Würfel)

b

Fig. 8.4 (*continued*)

c   **Fig. 8.4**   (*continued*)

d

Fig. 8.4 (*continued*) e

f

g

Fig. 8.4 (*continued*)

Examples of social markers by ZIP code follow. They come from Michael Weiss's 2000 book *The Clustered World*. (*Note*: PRIZM updated these data online in 2006. See Box. 8.1.) In the United States, Weiss wrote in 2000, a small percentage of households (1.2%) lived in suburbs that served as "executive suites," which mainly consisted of upper middle-class subdivisions. Mainly, residents in executive suites were 25–44 years of age. They voted moderately independent, bought gourmet coffee and Brie cheese, read business and cooking magazines, and stayed away from auto races and lottery tickets. In such communities, such as Piermont, New York (10968), and Huntington Beach, California (92649), residents drove Lexuses, Volvos, and Alfa Romeos. Residents tended to be comfortable but not rich.

In contrast, those in "upward-bound" neighborhoods (2% of U.S. households) shared the same age range (25–44) but not consumption habits. Upward-bounders tended to be upper middle-class families living in suburban satellite cities, such as Marietta, Georgia (98023), and Columbia, Maryland (21045). Typically, these folks were soccer moms and dads, drove GMC Suburbans, voted conservative Republican, listened to golden-oldies radio, and shopped at Costco.

Another group, mainly in the same age range (24–44, but some also under 24) lived in a cluster called "mid-city mix." This neighborhood was urban, middle-class, and mainly African American. (About 1.3% of U.S. households fell into this category.) In mid-city mix, the median household income was much lower than in upward bound and executive suite communities. Further, it was characterized by a different set of social markers: Residents voted for liberal Democrats, drove Hyundais and Pontiac LeManses, bought *Essence* and *Ebony*, and drank malt liquor. They lived in such ZIP codes as 07017 (East Orange, New Jersey), 90221 (Compton, California), and 60620 (Auburn Gresham, a community on Chicago's far southside).

In the PRIZM system, clusters come and go. By 2000, PRIZM's original 40 clusters had morphed into 62. ("Mid-city mix" had disappeared by 2006.) No doubt, housing foreclosures and the global economic crisis will impact future cluster rankings in the United States and elsewhere (see Box 8.1).

To conclude: Groups with similar demographic characteristics, such as age and income, can lead very different lifestyles. The three groups mentioned share one key characteristic—age—but *not* lifestyles.

Based on Weiss's data, we can assume that Milpitas residents (ZIP codes 95035 and 95036) bought Ford Escorts when it was a working-class suburb. Now, its white-collar and "no-collar" (Chapter 19) technoburbanites probably buy higher-end Toyotas instead.

Weiss's data come from a computer-driven market research tool, PRIZM (an acronym for Potential Rating Index for Zip Markets). PRIZM was developed by social scientist-turned-entrepreneur Jonathan Robbin. Its original use was to target audiences for Robbin's marketing company, Claritas (since sold and known as Nielsen Claritas). There is no use, for example, in advertising Ford pickup trucks in a Volvo neighborhood.

PRIZM is a for-profit, entrepreneurial tool geared to delivering potential buyers to sellers. But it has much wider applications, both practical and scholarly. It can be useful for planning a global vacation, finding potential voters for your cause, or operating across-border, nonprofit organizations. For example, residents of the same cluster—whether in Italy or Australia—will tend to drive the same cars, enjoy similar entertainment, and worry about similar political issues. Thus, if trolling for donors to support a nonprofit concerned with the environment or gun rights or health-care insurance, staffers would be wise to look in certain neighborhoods and not in others, whether in the United States or Australia.

Advisers to political candidates may want to know what's for dinner in a household. Why? Because it can be a clue to their voting choice! White wine and butter in the fridge can signal one preference, while crusty pizza would signal another (Severson, 2008). This practice, called "microtargeting," mirrors Weiss's cluster analysis.

Practically speaking, if you're moving to an unfamiliar place, the PRIZM cluster system can help you select new neighbors and preferred nearby activities: singles bars, bowling alleys, ranch houses with teenagers, gas chainsaws, novellas (Spanish soap operas), CB radios, college basketball games, health-food stores, conservative politics, union meetings, cafés, funky brownstones, and/or fast-food restaurants. If you work as a fund-raiser or door-to-door magazine salesperson, it can assist you to pinpoint potential donors to the local symphony or subscribers to *Ebony*.

Indeed, PRIZM contains much more cultural and economic information about individuals than countries' censuses. But, unlike data collected by national census bureaux, data collected by Nielsen Claritas and other marketeers are privately held (proprietary). In cost terms, they are not free.

What's interesting to social scientists about PRIZM is its approach to the study of community and metropolitan differentiation. Essentially, it divides the United States's 36,000 ZIP codes into neighborhood types or **lifestyle clusters**.

Cluster analysis doesn't stop at U.S. borders. As journalist Weiss notes in *The Clustered World* (2000), market research companies expanded cluster analysis to Canada (60 dominant lifestyles) and the global village (based on Global MOSAIC, a system classifying 800 million people who produce about 80 percent of the world's gross national product). According to MOSAIC (Weiss, 2000:144), groups with the same demographics can lead very different lifestyles. Take, for example, young middle-class British singles. One group, named "Studio Singles," tend to drink about four times the amount of red wine, play less bingo, and own more computers than another British group of similar age, marital status, and income level: Military Bases. Residents of military base neighborhoods are disproportionately male; they tend to spend money on home entertainment, music, and sporting goods. They play more bingo than Studio Singles but chow down less often in eat-in restaurants.

As of 2000, 19 countries had been "clustered." These include Great Britain, Australia, Belgium, South Africa, and the United States. Clusters reflect a nation's culture, not size. For example, Norway had about 2 million households, divided into 30 clusters or lifestyles (e.g., "Maritimers," "Mountain Farmers"). Belgium, with twice the number of households, had only 27 clusters (e.g., "Active Retired People," "Mining Villages").

Clusters reflect a culture's history too. For example, many of the poorest European clusters are rural. These include France ("Agrarian Decline"), Belgium ("Farmers & Agricultural Areas"), and Great Britain ("Upland and Small Farms"). By contrast, Japan's poorest cluster—"Old People's Home"—is not necessarily rural. Meanwhile, South Africa's largest cluster, predominantly black, is called "Matchbox Houses": more than 11 percent of the population live in small, modest houses built during apartheid times.

How can it be that people of similar status— whatever their nationality—share similar tastes? In Weiss's view, one key reason is *globalization*: Globalization of brands helps to create common tastes for a variety of products, from food to media. Indeed, Weiss says, "The net effect of these globalizing forces e.g., Internet sites; Starbucks, CNN, U.S. multinational retailers like Levi Strauss, McDonald's is the creation of similar desires and cookie-cutter stores everywhere on the planet" (2000:164).

Concerning the United States, Weiss thinks that clustering represents a newer way of looking at the nation: *not as 50 states but as neighborhood types*—40 in the late 1980s, 62 in 2000, and 66 by 2006, "each with distinct boundaries, values, consuming habits and political beliefs." Each neighborhood type, Weiss says, has a particular personality, described in 2006 by such colorful names as "Multi-Culti Mosaic," "Mayberry-ville," "Gray Power," "Big Fish, Small Pond," "Park Bench Seniors," and "Shotguns and Pickups" (Box 8.1).

By 2006, Nielsen Claritas, working with data from the 2000 U.S. Census and other sources, defined 66 U.S. clusters. These included some new high-income and low-income additions. Also, some clusters disappeared altogether. For example, SER 3 Urban Gold Coast disappeared. At the highest end was a new cluster, SER 01 Upper Crust, the United States's "most exclusive address." Other new, high-end clusters were added, including SER 03 Movers and Shakers (home to the U.S. up-and-coming business class) and SER 04 Young Digerati (tech-savvy, highly educated, ethnically mixed singles and couples in trendy neighborhoods). In 2006, two new low-end clusters were also added, including the lowest: SER 66 Low-rise Living (a transient world for young, ethnically diverse singles and single parents in a struggling area of mom-and-pop commercial stores) (Nielsen Claritas, 2006b).

Notes: Here I use both the 62 neighborhood types outlined in Weiss's 2000 book, *The Clustered World*, and the 66 clusters posted online in 2007 for 2006. Box 8.1 is based on the 2006 data. Why both? Because Nielsen Claritas's online update, based on the 2000 U.S. Census and other data, are incomplete—purposefully—for nonpaying visitors. Most kindly, a Nielsen Claritas representative made these data available to me, gratis. But, as of this writing, the 2006 data were not widely accessible to citizens or scholars. Thus, I use both published, pre-2000 data and 2006 data, published in 2007 but only online. Estimates for 2008 and 2013 projections are available from Nielsen Claritas too. With the U.S. subprime mortgage "meltdown" or "crisis" of 2007 onward, many clusters have recently experienced big changes; but as of this writing, no data confirm the particulars. Still, it is noteworthy that some ZIP codes, such as 94806 in suburban San Francisco, lost almost 41 percent of their square-foot price between 2007 and 2008.

PRIZM neighborhood types are ranked in terms of status, from highest to lowest. Ranks, now called SERs (socioeconomic ranks, formerly ZQs or zip quotients), are based on *residents' household income, home value, education, and occupation.*

At the top of the pre-2000 U.S. Census status ladder was SER 1 Blue Blood Estates (followed by SER 2 Winner's Circle and SER 3 Urban Gold Coast). By 2006, a new, wealthier neighborhood type replaced Blue Blood Estates as the top-ranked cluster: SER 01 Upper Crust, the nation's "wealthiest lifestyle." Who lives in SER 01? Many empty-nester couples over 55 years old. SER 01 has the highest concentration of residents earning over $200,000 a year and possessing a postgraduate degree. No cluster "has a more opulent standard of living" (Nielsen Claritas, 2006b).

The lowest-status neighborhood in 2006 was SER 66, Low-rise Living. It is mainly characterized by renters earning less than $23,000 per year.

According to Weiss, neighborhoods separated geographically can be virtually identical in lifestyle. Take, for example, U.S. ZIP codes 08003 (East Cherry Hill, New Jersey) and 91367 (Woodland Hills, California) just before 2000. Geodemographically, both were classified SER 02 neighborhoods. They had similar consumption habits as well as personal backgrounds. (*Note*: By 2006, Woodland Hills dropped in rank from 2 to 15, while East Cherry Hill climbed the status ladder to the highest rank: SER 01 Upper Crust.)

In any SER 02 neighborhood, you can expect to find sophisticated, well-heeled, college-educated suburbanites who live in million-dollar homes, go to exclusive clubs, play tennis or racquetball, ski, own or lease a new Mercedes or BMW, take three or more cruises a year, and do not smoke or listen to rap music. You can expect to find cappuccino bars but not fast-food eateries nearby. Clearly, if you like to hunt, fish, listen to CB radio, and watch the roller derby, this is not the neighborhood for you. Even if you could afford it.

One implication here is that *people in the United States, known for their propensity to move, do not really move; instead, they merely go to and from the same neighborhood*, say, from New York's Greenwich Village (10014) to San Francisco's Haight-Ashbury (94117) to Washington, D.C.'s Dupont Circle (20036), all primarily Bohemian Mix neighborhoods.

Whether in the United States or elsewhere, clusters are not randomly distributed over space. Some are rural or small-town and others urban or suburban. Some are found nationwide, or nearly, while others are regional or concentrated in a particular area. And some cross boundaries.

Over time, some clusters change their identity. Take, for instance, 80110 (Englewood, Colorado). In PRIZM's late 1980s analysis, this ZIP code was ranked 15 (New Beginnings). By 2000, it had become a SER 28 Upstarts & Seniors cluster. By 2006, the neighborhood

again changed: The top two groups living there were SER 30 Suburban Sprawl and 52 Suburban Pioneers. In other words, over time, neighborhood types can change status.

To conclude: Residents of the highest-status SER neighborhoods in the United States and elsewhere are the very people that Robert Reich described sometime ago in "The Secession of the Successful" (1991)—part of the top 20 percent working mainly as symbolic analysts and living in aesthetically-pleasing neighborhoods, often protected by gates or private guards. It is the same group that a *New York Times* reporter calls "the checked-out classes," referring to middle-class people in India who dream of living "in a foreign-style villa in a gated township outside the city, with its own privately built roads, hospitals, corporate offices and schools" (Giridharadas, 2008:2). Typically, in the United States, residents are white or Asian American, conservative or moderate in their politics, well-paid, and college-educated.

Does—or can—this financially successful elite feel a sense of community with the bottom 80 percent? Weiss thinks not. He offered this explanation: Most Americans have a narrow "bubble of consciousness" that allows only a close circle of acquaintances inside; these acquaintances tend to live in SERs near their own socioeconomic level (1988:268). (We might add that this is probably true in many places, including London.) Moreover, Weiss claims that "people who live 3,000 miles apart yet share the same neighborhood type have more in common with each other than with those people who live only three miles away" (6).

In other words, *birds of a feather not only flock together, they exclude all others from their consciousness*. This implies that reaching across barriers—of status and neighborhood, income, education, ethnicity, political and social preferences—is rare. As a historian so nicely phrased it, "Walls and gates assume a world of strangers" (Leed, 1991:18). In contemporary society, the barriers may be literal (gated communities) or figurative (communities that erect an invisible wall against the lower middle class via zoning ordinances).

Whether or not some observers (e.g., Bishop, 2008) decry the clustering of "like-minded" people in

BOX 8.1

Rank/Name	For Selected Clusters: Date Defined as Cluster/Previous Rank	Thumbnail Demographics	Some High-Usage Products & High Media Uses	Sample Neighborhoods	% of the U.S. Population	MHI (Median Household Income)
Elite, Suburban/Exurban Households						
SER 01 UPPER CRUST	New in 2006	The U.S.'s most exclusive address. Graduate plus. White, Asian mix. Mainly empty-nesters, 45–64.	Shop at Costco, Bloomingdale's. Drive Jaguar XK. Luxury international travel. Give to NPR, PBS. Drink domestic & imported wine. Read *Atlantic Monthly, Wall St Journal (WSJ), New York Times (NYT), Architectural Digest.*	Potomac, MD (20854), McLean, VA (22101), Mill Valley, CA (94941); Benecia, CA (94510)	1.51%	$110,142
SER 02 BLUE BLOOD ESTATES	SER 01 in 1988	Very rich. Graduate plus. White, Asian. Management (mgt). 45–64 with kids.	*The New Yorker, WSJ, NYT, Scientific American,* NPR. German luxury car. Luxury international travel, country clubs, skiing, racquetball. Shop at Costco, Nordstrom's. Buy Apple iPod.	Derwood, MD (20855)	0.98%	$115,814
SER 03 MOVERS & SHAKERS	new in 2006	White, Asian. Wealthy, suburban world of dual-income couples. Home of up-and-coming business class; folks here are more likely to own a small business and have a home office than in any other cluster. Executives, white collars. Graduate plus. Mainly no kids, 35–64.	Luxury European car. Shop at Banana Republic, Bloomingdale's. First-class air travel.	Clayton, CA (94517), Avon Lake, Ohio (30311)	1.61%	$99,130

High Income, Sophisticated Tastes, Urban

Affluent, Town/Rural, exurban or smaller cities

SER 05 COUNTRY SQUIRES		Mostly White, exurban families. Graduate plus. 35–64 with kids.	Country club. Skiing, biking, tennis. Order from on-line retailers. *WSJ, Fortune, PC World, O* (the Oprah magazine). Lexus SUV.	Avon, Ohio (44011).	1.90%	$102,263
SER 06 WINNER'S CIRCLE	SER 02 in 2000	The youngest of the wealthy, suburban lifestyles. White, Asian. Graduate plus. 25–44 with kids.	Big spenders who ski, eat out. *Fortune, Architectural Digest, WSJ, Travel & Leisure.* Disney Channel. Infiniti SUV.	Brentwood, CA (94513), Antioch, CA (904531)"	1.10%	$102,213
SER 04 YOUNG DIGERATI	new in 2006	White, Asian. Tech-savvy singles plus family mix. 25–44.	Visit Disneyland, Buy Apple iPods. Travel internationally. *NYT, Esquire.* NPR, alternativer rock radio. Shop at Banana Republic, Bloomingdale's, Nordstrom's. Mercedes, Range Rover.	Lincoln Park, Chicago (60614), various ZIP codes in Silicon Valley, CA, Cambridge, MA (02140)	1.23%	$80,782
SER 07 MONEY & BRAINS	SER 03 in 2000	Multi-ethnic: White, Asian, Hispanic. Graduate plus. 45–64. te plus. 45–64. Family mix.	Shop at Nordstrom's. *The New Yorker, Fortune, WSJ, NYT,* NPR, all-news radio. Mercedes Benz E class, European luxury car. Travel outside the U.S. 3+ times per year.	Berkeley, CA (94707), Boston, MA (02110), New York City (10021)	2.02	$84,506
SER 08 EXECUTIVE SUITES	SER 08 in 2000	White, Asian. College grad. Upper-middle class singles, couples. 35–54.	Golf, snowboarding, in-line skating. Shop Saks Fifth Avenue, Victoria's Secret. NPR. *Esquire, Fortune, WSJ.* New VW, Acura TSX.	Redmond, WA (98052), Piermont, NY (10968)	0.91%	$71,804

Continued

BOX 8.1 *Continued*

Rank/Name	For Selected Clusters: Date Defined as Cluster/ Previous Rank	Thumbnail Demographics	Some High-Usage Products & High Media Uses	Sample Neighborhoods	% of the U.S. Population	MHI (Median Household Income)
SER 09 BIG FISH, SMALL POND	SER 18 in 2000	Older, upscale, empty-nesting couples. Mainly White. Graduate plus. Mgt. 45–64 w/o kids.	Large investment portfolios. Country club. Own motor home. Give to NPR. Read *Atlantic Monthly*. Lexus LS430.	Cedar Crest, NY (87008), Orinda, CA (94563), Concord, MA (01742)	2.26%	$82,416
SER 10 SECOND CITY ELITE		Mainly White, prosperous executives. Graduate plus. 45–64 w/o kids.	Enjoy attending theater, dance productions, reading. CNBC. *WSJ, Travel & Leisure, Inc.* Order from *Readers' Digest*. Multiple computers. Largescreen TVs, nice wine collections. Toyota.	Kailua, HI (96734), Pleasanton, CA (94566)	1.18%	$74,375
SER 11 GOD'S COUNTRY		Mainly White, affluent, exurban. High-power jobs and laid-back leisure time. Spacious homes. College grad. 35–54 w/o kids.	Golf vacation. Skiing. Outdoor Life network. Toyota Land Cruiser SUV.	Chantilly, VA (20152), Ben Lomond, CA (95005)	1.55%	$83,827
SER 12 BRITE LITES, LI'L CITY	new in 2006	White, Asian. College grad. Mainly middle-aged couples in satellite cities.	Racquetball, water skiing. New BMW. Order from priceline.com. MTV, "Comedy Central," sports TV. Macworld. Toyota Land Cruiser SUV.	Dublin, CA (94565), Pleasant Hill, CA (94523)	1.50%	$69,380
SER 13 UPWARD BOUND	SER 13 in 2000	Multiethnic: White, Asian, Hispanic. College grad. 34–54 with kids.	Visit Disneyland, go to the zoo. Skiing Vacation. Men's Health. All-talk radio, sports radio. Toyota Sequoia SUV.	Edmond, OKLA (73003), Pittsburg, CA (94565)	1.60%	$80,345
SER 20 FAST-TRACK FAMILIES		Mostly White, upper-middle-class, child-filled families in their prime acquiring years. College grad. Rustic locales. 35–54 with kids.	New computers. Home theatre systems. Boating, fishing, ice hockey games. Order from walmart.com. Contemporary Christian music. Country music. *Parenting Magazine, Field & Stream, Redbook.* Dodge Ram minivan.	Waddell, AZ (85355)	1.74%	$74,562

Affluent, Suburban

SER 14 NEW EMPTY NESTS		Mainly White, retired (age 65+). College grad, w/o kids.	Take cruises. Shop Nordstrom's. Give to PBS. Order from L.L. Bean. Buy classical music. *AARP, the Magazine. The New Yorker.* Watch "Antiques Roadshow." *WSJ.* Cadillac Seville.	St.Louis, MO (63126)	1.05%	$69,595
SER 15 POOLS & PATIOS	SER 09 in 2000	White, Asian. College grad. Stable neighborhoods, evolved from young-to-mature empty-nesters. 45-64 w/o kids.	Homes built in the 1960s. Read *Sunset.* Own motor home, new European luxury car. Listen to all-news radio, religious radio. Shop high-end department stores. Mercury Mariner SUV. Mercedes.	Escondido, CA (92029), Catonsville, MD (21228)	1.31%	$69,382
SER 17 BELTWAY BOOMERS		Multiethnic: White, Asian, Hispanic. Upper-middle class Baby Boomers. College grad. Kid-centered lifestyles. Comfortable suburban subdivisions. 45-64 w/kids.	Buy Apple iPods. Shop Ethan Allen. Minivan. *PCWorld, Vibe, Essence, Seventeen, Parenting, Star.* Sports radio,religious radio. Izusu Ascender.	American Canyon, CA (94503).	0.96%	$72,262
SER 18 KIDS & CUL-DE-SACS		Multiethnic: White, Asian, Hispanic. Upper-middle class, married couples with kids. College grad. 25-44. Recently-built subdivisions.	Buy toys on Internet, go to zoo. Disney Store. Roller-blading, soccer. Minivan. *Parenting* magazine. Cartoon network. Rock music. Nissan Armada SUV.	Laguna Hills, CA (92653)	1.63%	$70,034
SER 19 HOME SWEET HOME		Multiethnic: White, African-American, Asian. Under 55, w/o kids. Upper-middle-class married couples. College grad. Professionals.	Mountain biking. Inc., *NYT, NPR, Rolling Stone, Vibe, Essence, Parenting.* MTV. Saturn Vue SUV.	Parkville, MD (21234), Fox Lake, IL (60020), Crockett, CA (94525), Orangedale, CA (95662)	1.74%	$74,562

Continued

239

BOX 8.1 *Continued*

Rank/Name	For Selected Clusters: Date Defined as Cluster/ Previous Rank	Thumbnail Demographics	Some High-Usage Products & High Media Uses	Sample Neighborhoods	% of the U.S. Population	MHI (Median Household Income)
Affluent to Comfortable, Urban						
SER 16 BOHEMIAN MIX	SER 17 in 2000	Multiethnic: African-American, White, Asian, Hispanic. College grad. Renters. Under 55, mobile. Most liberal cluster.	Go dancing once monthly +. Buy Apple iPods, use laundromat, drink imported beer. Mini Cooper car. *New York* magazine.	Burlingame, CA (94010)	1.79%	$51,588
SER 21 GRAY POWER		Mostly White, retirees. College grads. 65 +.	Take cruises.Give to PBS. Shop Costco, Lord & Taylor. Belong to veterans' clubs. *AARP, the Magazine, WSJ Report.* "Jeopardy." Buick LaCrosse.	Indianapolis, IN (46228), Healdsburg, CA (95448)	0.92%	$51,053
SER 26 THE COSMOPOLITANS		Multiethnic: Asian, White, African-American, Hispanic. Some college. White-collar mix. 55+ mostly w/o kids. Concentrated in just a few metro areas, including Miami, Albuquerque.	Shop at Bloomingdale's, Saks Fifth Avenue, Macy's. Drink imported wine. Take cruises. *WSJ report. Black Enterprise.* Jazz radio. *AARP the Magazine.* New Mercedes, Infini 136.	Monterey Park, CA (91754), El Cerrito, CA (94530)	0.17%	$54,229
SER 29 AMERICAN DREAMS	SER 13 in 2000	Multiethnic: Asian, White, Hispanic, African-American. Multilingual (1 in 10 speaks a language other than English) and middle-class comfort. Some college. 35–54.	Shop at Bloomingdale's, Saks Fifth Avenue, Macy's. Drink imported wine. Take cruises. *WSJ report. Black Enterprise.* Jazz radio. New Mercedes, Infini 136.	Forest Park, IL (60130), Calumet City, IL (60409), San Pablo, CA (94806)	2.18%	$52,863

Affluent to Comfortable Suburban town/Smaller cities/Rural

Segment		Description	Interests/Products	Location		
SER 22 YOUNG INFLUENTIALS		Multiethnic: White, African-American, Asian. College grad. Suburban renters, under 45, middle-class singles/couples (once called "yuppies") who try to balance work & leisure.	Play soccer, go to auto races. Buy rap music, Spanish/Latin music. MTV, *Rolling Stone*, *Essence*. Mazda 3.	Manchester, NH (03102)	1.46%	$47,717
SER 23 GREENBELT SPORTS	new in 2006	Mostly White, ex-urban couples. College grad. 35–44.	Active lifestyles. Mountain biking, power boating. Own motorcycle, RV. Motor Trend, rock radio, country music radio & TV. Suburu Impreza	Forestville, CA (95436)	1.44%	$57,042
SER 25 COUNTRY CASUALS		Mainly White in small towns or rural areas with a laid-back feel. 35-54 with kids. Upper-middle class. College grad. Many two-income, Baby Boomer households.	*Guns and Ammo*, *Field & Stream*. BBC America. NASCAR, Country radio. GMC Sierra.	Red Wing, MN (55066), Santa Claus, IN (47579)	1.61%	$71,266
SER 27 MIDDLEBURG MANAGERS	SER 20 in 2000	Mainly White in satellite communities. Solid managerial jobs or comfortable retirement in older homes. 45–64.	Do needlepoint, play musical instruments, refinish furniture. Belong to country club. Give to NPR. Own motor home. *AARP, The Magazine*. TV figure skating. "Jeopardy." All-talk radio. Mercury Sable.	Fort Mitchell, KY (41047)	1.85%	$49,468
SER 28 TRADITIONAL TIMES		Mostly white. Some college. Small-town couples beginning to enjoy empty nests. 55+	Own motor home, camper. Belong to country club. Order from Land's End. Drive RV. Satellite dish or disc. Bird watching. Member of fraternal order. *AARP, The Magazine*. "Antiques Roadshow." Buick LaCrosse.	Pollack Pines, CA (95726), Myrtle Beach, SC (29572)	2.84%	$54,801

Continued

BOX 8.1 *Continued*

Rank/Name	For Selected Clusters: Date Defined as Cluster/ Previous Rank	Thumbnail Demographics	Some High-Usage Products & High Media Uses	Sample Neighborhoods	% of the U.S. Population	MHI (Median Household Income)
SER 30 SUBURBAN SPRAWL		Multiethnic: White, African-American, Asian. College grad. Suburban Professionals.	Play billiards, tennis. Laptop/ Notebook PC. *Rolling Stone, Car & Driver, Black Enterprise.* Rock & alternative rock radio. MTV. Ford Escort.	Baton Rouge, LA (70181)	1.31%	$49,233
SER 33 BIG SKY FAMILIES		Mostly White & youngish (25–44) with kids,	Own a camper, horse, all-terrain vehicle, motorcycle. Hunts with gun. Dodge Ram. "Noticiero Telemundo." *Vibe, Essence,* TV soccer. "The Simpsons."	Limington, ME (04099), Forest Hill, LA (71430)	1.79%	$55,473

Midscale City Districts, Mid-to-small Towns & Suburbs & Rural Settings

Rank/Name	For Selected Clusters: Date Defined as Cluster/ Previous Rank	Thumbnail Demographics	Some High-Usage Products & High Media Uses	Sample Neighborhoods	% of the U.S. Population	MHI (Median Household Income)
SER 32 NEW HOMESTEADERS		Mostly White, young, middle-class families in small, rustic towns. White-collar & service jobs. College grad.Dual-income couples. Child-centered lifestyles.	Play softball, golf. Contemporary Christian music. Own tent. Read off-road magazines, *Parenting, Field & Stream.* County music, religious radio. Kia Sedona.	Indianapolis, IN (46231), Hyde Park, NY (12538)	2.01%	$56,184
SER 34 WHITE PICKET FENCES		Multiethnic: Asian, White, African-American, Hispanic. Young (25–44),married with kids, middle-class. Some college. Modest homes.	Own a treadmill, tent, fishing equipment. Visit Six Flags Park. Buy kids' bikes. Attend pro football games. Hispanic radio, BET, MTV. *Seventeen.* "Noticiero Telemundo." Mitsubishi Montero sport.	Fairlield, CA (94533), Oxnard, CA (93030)	1.25%	$49,545

Segment	2000 Rank	Description	Lifestyle / Media	Location	%	Income
SER 35 BOOMTOWN SINGLES	SER 27 in 2000	Thriving singles' scene in fast-growing, satellite cities. Working-class, young singles with some college, renting in apt. complexes. Bars, laundromats nearby. Under 45 w/o kids.	Snowboarding, in-line skating, volleyball, bowling. "Noticiero Telemundo," BET, MTV, classic rock radio. Nissan Sentra.	Boise, ID (83705), Columbia, SC (29201)	1.30%	$38,616

Urban Gateway Communities

Segment	2000 Rank	Description	Lifestyle / Media	Location	%	Income
SER 24 UP-AND-COMERS	SER 22 in 2000	Multiethnic: Asian, White, Hispanic. Colleger grad. Professional. A Stopover for some young singles before marriage. Mobile 20somethings, 25-44.	Snowboarding. Attend ice hockey games. First-class international travel, Golf vacations. MTV, Sundance Channel. *Car and Driver*, *Men's Health*. Mitsubishi Eclipse Spyder.	Walnut Creek, CA (i94596).	1.21%	$48,620
SER 31 URBAN ACHIEVERS	SER 22 in 2000	Multiethnic: White, African-American, Asian, Hispanic. Mainly in U.S. port cities. Often, the first stop for up-and-coming immigrants. Young (under 45) singles. Some college.	Buy rap music. Go snowboarding.Use laundromat. Buy Spanish/Latin music. Watch "Jerry Springer Show," "Maury," "Noticiero Telemundo," cartoon network, BET. *Essence*, *Vibe*. Nissan Sentra	West Vern, LA (90062), Pawtucket, RI (02860)	1.71%	$34,070

Midscale City Districts or Mid-to-small Towns & Suburbs

Segment	2000 Rank	Description	Lifestyle / Media	Location	%	Income
SER 36 BLUE-CHIP BLUES	SER 30 in 2000	The nation's largest lifestyle cluster in the 1980s, shrunk by one-half following the decline in blue-collar jobs. Multiethnic: White, African-American,	Go roller skating,buy rap music. Visit Six Flags Park. *Parenting, Essence, Vibe, Soap Opera Digest*. BET, MTV. Izuzu Ascender.	Baton Rouge, LA (70814)	1.25%	$49,138

Continued

BOX 8.1 *Continued*

Rank/Name	For Selected Clusters: Date Defined as Cluster/ Previous Rank	Thumbnail Demographics	Some High-Usage Products & High Media Uses	Sample Neighborhoods	% of the U.S. Population	MHI (Median Household Income)
SER 36 *(cont.)*		Asian, Hispanic. Comfortable, suburban lifestyle for young families with good, blue-collar jobs. Some college. Modestly-priced homes near commercial centers catering to child-filled homes. 25–44 with kids.				
SER 37 MAYBERRY-VILLE		Mostly White in small towns. Middle-class couples & families who like to fish, hunt, stay home, watch TV at night. Good paying blue-collar jobs. 35–54 w/o kids.	Hunt with gun. Own pickup truck, camper, horse, motorcycle. Go to auto races. Country music TV, radio. Rock radio. Fishing/hunting magazines. *Field & Stream.* Chevy Silverado.	Interlochen, MI (49643)	2.49%	$53,563

Midscale Blue-Collar (or former Blue-Collar) & White-Collar in Towns/rural places/suburbs

SER 38 SIMPLE PLEASURES		Mainly White, high school grads. Mostly a retirement lifestyle with lower-middle-class singles & couples in modest homes. 65+. Very large % served in the military.	Member, veterans' club. "Jeopardy," "Wheel of Fortune," "Antiques Roadshow." Order from *Readers Digest.* Travel by motor home. Bird watching. *AARP, The Magazine.* Ford Crown Victoria.	Alden, KS (56712), Cumberland, WS (54829)	2.30%	$42,732

244

Continued

Segment	Description	Location	%	Income
SER 39 DOMESTIC DUOS	White, African-American. Mix of over-55 singles & married couples in older, suburban homes, w/o kids. High school. Fixed incomes. White-collar mix.	Bowling. Member, veterans' club. Attends pro baseball games. Own motor home. Give to PBS. Order from Home Shopping Network. Chevy Cobalt. TV bowling. *AARP, The Magazine.* "Antiques Roadshow."	Atlanta, GA (30310), Chicopee, MA (01020) Schnectady, NY	1.19%	$48,115

Lower-middle Class, Mainly Older & Urban

Segment	Description	Location	%	Income
SER 40 CLOSE-IN COUPLES	Multiethnic: African-American, White, Asian, Hispanic. Mostly retired in older homes in mid-sized metro areas. Some college. 55+.	Order from *Readers Digest.* Watch TV bowling, "People's Court." Eat at Denny's. Member, veterans' club. Shop Bloomingdale's, Macy's. *Black Enterprise.* All-news radio. Suzuki Grand Vitara SUV.	Baltimore, MD (21229)	1.18%	$39,220
SER 41 SUNSET CITY BLUES	White, African-American. High school grad, living in older areas of small cities. Many retired or near retirement. Under 55 w/kids.	Low-key lifestyle. Family-style restaurants. Member, veterans' club. Travel by motor home. Do needlepoint. College basketball games. "Maury," TV pro wrestling. *Wrestling* magazine, *Esquire, Black Enterprise.* Hispanic radio. Kia Rio.	Bangor, ME (04401)	1.17%	$28,460

Rural/Town/Satellite Cities—Middle Class & Poverty Areas

Segment	Description	Location	%	Income
SER 45 BLUE HIGHWAYS	Mainly White. Remote stretches of the U.S. landscape. Lower-middle-class couples, families in isolated downs, farmsteads. High school grad. 35-54.	Hunting, fishing. Sewing, crafts. Country music. Own horse, all-terrain vehicle, tent. Hunt with gun. *Guns & Ammo, Field & Stream.* Dodge Ram.	Homer, GA (30547), Louisa, VA (23093)	1.46%	$42.88

BOX 8.1 *Continued*

Rank/Name	For Selected Clusters: Date Defined as Cluster/Previous Rank	Thumbnail Demographics	Some High-Usage Products & High Media Uses	Sample Neighborhoods	% of the U.S. Population	MHI (Median Household Income)
SER 48 YOUNG & RUSTIC		White, African-American. Young, restless singles with lower incomes. High school grad. Tiny apts in exurban towns. Under 55.	Car, dating, and sports-centered lifestyles. Go to auto races. Hunt with gun. Order from priceline.com, QVC. Own motorcycle. Roller skating. TV wrestling. Dodge Neon.	Spartanburg, SC (29301), Tonopah, AZ (84354) Cynthiana, KY (41031)	2%	$32,338
SER 51 SHOTGUNS & PICKUPS		Mostly White, working-class couples with large families, many (nearly 33 %)in mobile homes. High school grad. 25–44 w/kids.	Own tent, horse, all-terrain vehicle, motorcycle. Go fresh wter fishing. Attends auto races. Hunt with gun. Watch country music TV. *Field & Stream. Parenting.* Satellite dish. Dodge Ram.	King Hill, ID (83633), Moundville, ALA (35474).	1.61%	$41,673
SER 55 GOLDEN PONDS		Mainly White, retirement lifestyle in bucolic, small towns or rural area. Some high school. 65+ w/o kids.	Member, veterans' club. Do needlepoint. Buy gospel music. Use magazine coupons. TV bowling. "Jeopardy," Oprah Winfrey, "Antiques Roadshow." *AARP, The Magazine.* Mercury Grand Marquis.	Wellton, AZ (85356)	1.58%	$31,029
SER 56 CROSSROADS VILLAGERS		White, African-American mix. Middle-aged, blue-collar couples & families. Classic rural lifestyle: modest homes with 1/4th in mobile homes. Fishing, gardening, hunting. High school grad. 35–44 w/o kids.	Own motor home. Play soccer, go whitewater rafting.Shop at Saks Fifth Avenue, 7/11. NASCAR radio. *Soap Opera Digest, Guns & Ammo.* Dodge Neon.	Raceland, LA (70794)	2.10%	$32,275

246

Cluster	Demographics	Activities/Media	Example Locations	%	Income
SER 57 IKD NUKKTIWBS	White, African-American. Once-thriving manufacturing, mining towns—aged as have most of their residents. Retired singles, couples. Some high school. 65+, mostly w/o kids.	Gardening, sewing, socializing at veternas' clubs. Watch soap operas, play bingo. Oprah Winfrey, TV figure skating. Cable TV. Chevy Cobalt.	Dowagiac, MI (49047), Wabash, IN (46992)	1.59%	$30,235
SER 58 BACK COUNTRY FOLKS	White, African-American. Tend to be poor, over 55, living in older, modest homes or manufactured housing. Some high school. Mostly retired, w/o kids.	Own motor home, horse. Daytime TV, "Antiques Roadshow," "the Jerry Springer show," TV horse racing. *WSJ Report.* GMC Sierra 3500 pickup.	Richwood, WV (26261), Waynesboro, TN (38485)	2.18%	$31,811
SER 60 PARK BENCH SENIORS	White, African-American. Typically, retired single renters in racially-mixed neighborhoods in "second cities." Some high school.	Daytime TV, TV bowling. Play bingo. Watch Game Show network, "Noticiero Telemundo." Eat at Sizzler. *AARP, The Magazine.* Kia Rio.	Manchester, NH (03101)	1.07%	$23,073
SER 62 HOMETOWN RETIRED	Multiethnic: African-American, White, Hispanic. Majority are retired homeowners in second cities. Over 65 w/o kids at home. Some high school.	Watch soap operas, bowling, "Noticiero Telemundo." *AARP, The Magazine.* Travel the U.S. by bus. Chrysler Sebring.	West Palm Beach, FL (33404)	1.11%	$26,269
SER 63 FAMILY THRIFTS	Multiethnic: White, African-American, Hispanic. Young parents in second cities working in entry-level service jobs. High school grad. Under 45 w/ kids.	Buy rap music, Spanish/Latin music. Go roller slating, visit Six Flags Park. Eat fast food. *Vibe.* Daewoo, Hyundai, Kia Spectra.	Petersburg, VA (23803), Montgomery, ALA (36104), Cumberland, MD (21502)	1.69%	$29,346

Continued

BOX 8.1 *Continued*

Rank/Name	For Selected Clusters: Date Defined as Cluster/ Previous Rank	Thumbnail Demographics	Some High-Usage Products & High Media Uses	Sample Neighborhoods	% of the U.S. Population	MHI (Median Household Income)
SER 64 BEDROCK AMERICA		Multiethnic: African-American, White, Hispanic. Blue-collar jobs. Living in towns or rural places. One-quarter in mobile homes. High school grad or some high school. Under 45 w/ kids.	Haven for fishing, hunting, hiking, camping. Own tent, horse. Buy rap music. Go rollerskating. *Vibe, Parenting, Soap Opera Digest.* "Maury," "The Jerry Springer show." Pro wrestling fans. Chevy Silverado.	Greenville, MS (38701)	1.81%	$27,581
Urban Poor or Nearly Poor						
SER 59 URBAN ELDERS		Multiethnic: White, Asian, African-American, Hispanic. Living in downscale apts in down-town areas of bigger metro areas. Mostly retired renters. Some high school. 55+ w/o kids.	Daytime TV, "Noticiero Telemundo," "Maury," Hispanic radio. *Black Enterprise.* Eat fast food hamburgers. Toyota Corolla.	Roxbury, MA (02019), Chicago, IL (60612)	1.32%	$23,301
SER 61 CITY ROOTS		Multiethnic: White, African-American, Hispanic. Lower-income, urban retirees. Many widows, widowers on fixed incomes with low-key lifestyles. Some high school. 65+.	Daytime TV, "Noticiero Telemundo." Member, veterans' club. Stamp collecting. *WSJ Report. AARP The Magazine.* Hyundai Accent.	Detroit, MI (48214)	1.15%	$36,943

SER 65 BIG CITY BLUES	Multiethnic: African-American, White, Asian, Hispanic. More than 50 % Latino. Concentrated in major metro areas. Young singles, single parent families. Some high school. Under 45. Renters.	Play soccer. Eat at Sizzler. Do needlepoint. Buy rap music. Use laundromat. "Noticiero Telemundo," "Maury," Hispanic radio. *Vibe*. Nissan Sentra.	Sections of the Bronx, New York City (e.g., 10460)	1.12%	$29,946
SER 66 LOW-RISE LIVING	Multiethnic: African-American, White, Hispanic. Transient, poorest urban cluster. Young singles & young parents (under 45). Some high school. Low home values, mostly renters.	Watch syndicated TV. East fast food burgers. Buy Spanish/Latin music, rap music. Eat at White Castle, Sizzler, Jack in the Box. Use laundromat. "Noticiero Telemundo," "Maury." *Vibe, Essence, Black Enterprise.* Hispanic radio. Hyundai Accent.	Sections of the Bronx, New York City (in ZIP Code 10460)	1.43%	$22.88

* A ZIP code can, and often does, contain multiple lifestyle clusters. Claritas Nielsen uses the cluster most-often occuring in each ZIP code to define the cluster rank. For clusters SER 65 and SER 66, I could not find any Zip codes (there is no information given for many ZIP codes) that were primarily defined as above, but there were sections in the ZIP codes so defined.

** Change can happen fast. Fallouts from U.S. subprime mortgage lendind situation and the financial crisis will undoubtedly impact PRIZM's next rankings. Take, for example, a Winner's Circle cluster of 2006: 94531: From January to August, 2007, ZIP Code 94531 in Antioch, California, experienced 525 foreclosures, the highest rate—23.1 per 1,000 homes—in the San Francisco Bay Area (home to 236 ZIP Codes). Antioch, CA also experienced the region's biggest drop in housing prices: a 15 percent from May 2006 to August 2007. (See Kelly Zito et al, "Neighborhoods Crumble in Wave of Foreclosures," *San Francisco Chronicle,* October 14, 2007: 1+.) If these conditions continue, we can expect Antioch's rank—as well as many other ZIP Code areas—to change radically in future PRIZM rankings.

the United States as separating individuals into thousands of insular tribes, it is happening. People in the United States cluster in increasingly homogeneous communities. And they are far from alone globally.

This brings us back to the two-sided face of community. To live near people one has "more in common with" or feels "comfortable with" usually means to live near people like oneself. To some, this is an ideal. For example, the St. Johnsbury, Vermont's, Preface to the Town Plan suggests that people *need* "spiritual unity" and to pass on "*the* basic cultural inheritance." But whose inheritance? Only in a homogeneous community is there one agreed-on culture.

This brings us to the other face of community: parochialism and insularity. In other words, the price of feeling a sense of we-ness and community with members of a small group is estrangement from people unlike those in the group.

Questions of democracy also arise. In a small community, the possibility of the majority's tyranny over the minority looms large. There is also the problem of scale: "Democratic" decisions at the micro-level can be restrictive, even oppressive, to outsiders and harmful to the society as a whole. For instance, is it democratic if a group of 2,000 or 20,000 keeps people unlike themselves out of the neighborhood (e.g., by passing restrictive zoning regulations or by prohibiting children), thus ensuring homogeneity?

Are we doomed to live either without individual freedom in local community or without close bonds in cosmopolitan society? Can any real-life community meet the dual challenge of (1) encouraging personal freedom and openness to new ideas and (2) providing intimacy and cohesive social bonds? There seem to be no easy answers to these questions.

PLACELESS, FACELESS COMMUNITIES: INTERCONNECTIVITIES

There are a few "places" that don't identify "residents" as members of either high-, middle-, or low-status ZIP codes. These places (or "nonplaces") may be instrumental in forging a new sense of we-ness among people of different ages, backgrounds, status positions, and tastes. To some, these "communities" meet the challenge: They guarantee freedom and provide intimacy.

"Residents" may be shut-ins, geographically distant folks, family members, students, or people sharing a particular interest (chess, games, conspiracy politics, etc.). Whichever, growing numbers of such "residents" spend hours daily communicating electronically with people they've never seen or met in any traditional manner. Students and faculty have a particular interest in the Internet, mobile phones, and allied telecommunications because they can be academic goldmines. First, courses offered online increase annually. Second, teleconferences can cross costly travel barriers, bringing together distant students and teachers. Third, scholars and students can share their findings and get feedback quickly, thus bypassing the much longer process of publishing an article or book.

In addition, Internet use is changing how many people, especially young people, communicate. A 2008 study by the Pew Internet and American Life Project (in Jesdanum, 2008:A5) showed that teens who blog or use sites like Facebook or MySpace often use "nonstandard" elements of speech–such as "LOL"—in written school assignments. This means, perhaps, that the digitally connected may increasingly share a language of informal writing that their elders neither comprehend nor respect.

Mobile phones may be changing communication patterns too. In European Union (EU) member countries (which had over 85 percent "teledensity" by 2004, the highest rate in the world [see Castells et al., 2007:12]; the EU has since expanded) and other places, notably the United States, the widespread diffusion of mobile phones may be leading to a separate youth subculture with peer-to-peer networks.

Do such mobile phone users and computer networkers constitute a community? On the one hand, social relationships carried on by impersonal technologies seem to be an oxymoron like "jumbo shrimp." [deleted standard deviation à la Andrew's note, now disappeared; comma may remain-I cant tell...] On the other hand, computers and mobile phones promote a new sort of interconnectivity that is both placeless and faceless. People meet in no place or cyberspace—a keyboard-connected computerland of shared information and inner secrets.

Most computer users think that some cyberspace meet-up groups are virtual communities—"places that are no place." Some say that they feel "in" something. Many who share an issue, say, surviving breast cancer, use online "communities" to share emotions as well as information. Many such users see themselves as members of a real community. Members of some online networks, such as abuse support groups, agree.

But critics are not so sure. Some claim that there is a significant difference between virtual and real communities: Only in real communities is there a sense of responsibility to fellow members.

To conclude: "Human identity," philosophizes architect Christian Norberg-Schulz, "is to a high extent a function of places and things" ([1979] 1984:21). He argues that individual identity and physical environment have been linked for centuries. But if the human identity–physical place relationship existed historically, it is being changed, perhaps destroyed, by computers and telecommunications. Indeed, "the digitization of the entire world," as reporter John Markoff (1994) once called the global spread of electronic media, may change the very definitions of "human identity" and "place." Manuel Castells and his coauthors (2007) imply that social life and individual identity are being transformed by mobile communications.

Observers from many disciplines and fields insist that electronic media affect social relationships and human identity in deeply significant ways. Some stress the impact of television or newer technologies, such as texting, in changing our feeling of connectedness and offering users a wider but shallower sense of community.

Ever-increasing numbers of people spend hours "together" on the Internet. These exchanges of ideas depend on having unique e-mail addresses, not similar SERs or lifestyles. Indeed, in this setting, the concepts of local—and national and international—addresses become meaningless.

The impacts of newer, citizen-based media such as YouTube and Godtube are being studied now. Already, we have seen a few impacts. For one, reputations can be affected in a nanosecond. Take the 2006 political campaign for the U.S. Senate. A cameraphone captured one candidate's unscripted racist remark, which was played almost instantaneously on YouTube. The upshot: The candidate dropped out of the race.

SOCIAL NETWORKS

A STRUCTURAL APPROACH TO COMMUNITY

Excluding hermits, people are not isolated. Instead, they belong to "communities" and/or social networks. Analyzing these networks is another approach to studying how contemporary people maintain a sense of connection.

Network theory was pioneered by Elizabeth Bott (1957). It is associated with the work of sociologists Barry Wellman (1979), Mark Granovetter (1973), and Claude Fischer (1982). (John P. Scott's 2000 text tries to simplify some of the more complicated mathematical procedures used in applying this approach.) It is based on four interrelated premises:

1. *Gesellschaft* and *Techno\$chaft* are not socially "disorganized" (as Tönnies and early urban theorists thought); modern institutions and processes, particularly the highly specialized division of labor and physical and social mobility, are tools for individual freedom.
2. People are involved in a "web of group affiliation" (Simmel, [1922] 1955), with varying intensities and degrees of stability.
3. Social structure is not spatially bounded in contemporary life.
4. Social networks play a variety of roles, from helping people to find jobs, spreading gossip, and offering social support and friendship to bridging the gap between different social worlds.

To illustrate this perspective's basic concepts, consider one of your networks—say, your friendship or work network. First, put yourself at the center of the network (called an "egocentric network" because you are at the center). Then try to determine your network's *range* (from narrow to wide, depending on the number of direct contacts you have within the network), its *stability* over time, and its *density* (from close-knit to loose-knit; density is the proportion of actual connections among network members compared with the possible number of connections if all members were connected to the entire network). Next, look at the nature of the social ties. Are they *single-stranded* (one-dimensional, as in the case of you and a bank teller, who interact only about a banking transaction) or *multistranded* (multidimensional: say, you and the bank teller interact in many roles—you raise children together as mates, play soccer, and care for your aged aunt together)? Are the ties strong, as in warm friendships with reciprocity, emotional intensity, and frequent contact, or weak, as in acquaintanceships that are peripheral and less intense?

Network analysts offer the following kinds of insights based on their empirical studies:

1. *Ubiquity.* Most people, whether urban, suburban, or rural, maintain close social ties with people outside their own households.

2. *Number and kinds of ties.* Rural dwellers have no more close social ties than urbanites or suburbanites; all have about the same number of close bonds. However, the kind of involvement differs: People in small towns and nonmetropolitan areas are more involved with kinfolk; urbanites and suburbanites are more involved with nonkin friends.

3. *Homogeneity.* Close associates tend to be similar in age, income level, religious preference, education, marital status, and occupational level. However, some groups tend to have more heterogeneous networks than others in terms of ethnicity and religion (ethnoreligion). For example, Laumann (1973) found that urban Protestants were more likely to be in networks that were occupationally alike but ethnoreligiously much more mixed than either Catholics or Jews.

4. *Strength of weak ties.* Weak ties are very useful; they can bridge diverse networks. Typically, strong ties are forged with people of similar backgrounds. While strong ties may provide emotional security, they can limit opportunities. For example, Boston's Italian American "urban villagers" studied by Gans ([1962] 1982) had such strong ties in the West End and so few weak ties outside the close-knit circle that they missed out on valuable information carried by weak ties, including political gossip about the city's plans to tear down their neighborhood.

Note: People located anywhere in cyberspace can share interests and information, from job openings and recipes to wellness hints, without meeting face-to-face. Developing "friends" or social contacts online at social networking sites may represent a new kind of weak tie. (Already, employment counselors suggest buoying up networks in flush times as well as lean times.) No doubt this will be the subject of future social science research.

5. *Strength of strong ties.* In general, urban villages—low-income, ethnic city neighborhoods such as Boston's former West End—are characterized by strong ties; they tend to function more as subcommunities than do upper-income, more ethnically heterogeneous neighborhoods. In such parochial (rather than cosmopolitan) urban enclaves, strong ties provide an important support system where residents routinely exchange tools, resources, and favors. However, Gans is careful not to romanticize the West End's distinct working-class subculture. He says that the area was "not a charming neighborhood of 'noble peasants' living in an exotic fashion...and overflowing with a cohesive sense of community"; rather, it was a "run-down area of people struggling with the problems of low income, poor education, and related difficulties" ([1962] 1982:16).

6. *Mobility.* Both geographic mobility and social mobility are heavily influenced by social ties. Most often, job seekers find employment information and get chosen over others with the same qualifications for a job because they have connections (the "who you know" factor) through weakly tied persons. In terms of geographic mobility, close ties play a key role in the creation of ethnic neighborhoods via "chain migration." *Chain migration* happens when prospective movers get survival information and jobs in a new place arranged for them by closely tied previous migrants, normally kinfolk or coethnics. In recent times, chain migration has become an issue for those wanting to limit immigration to the United States. For example, a blog in 2008 posted this excerpt from Americans for Better Immigration, a nonprofit, nonpartisan organization which

Fig. 8.5 A COMMUNITY OF EXTREMELY LIMITED LIABILITY. Dogs cavort at an off-leash dog park in Berkeley, California, while their human companions schmooze. The dog park is somewhat like a neighborhood bar; most human visitors (predominantly women in this case) are regulars, arriving at about the same time of day and talking to the same people. Rarely do the humans know one another's names, but many know the names of each dog regular. (Barbara Cohen)

"lobbies Congress for reductions in immigration numbers."

Chain Migration refers to the endless and often-snowballing chains of foreign nationals who are allowed to immigrate because previous immigrants can send for ADULT relatives.... Because each of those can then bring in their own adult relatives and nuclear family, a single immigrant can eventually be responsible for the arrival in the United States of his/her aunts, uncles, nephews, nieces, first cousins, second cousins once-removed, in a spiraling chain that eventually could reach most of the world's 6 billion-plus residents. (http://michiganredneck.wordpress.com/2008/03/08/no-milk-and-cookies/).

7. *Single-stranded ties*. A person's neighborhood is not the only warm nest for birds of a feather. As Louis Wirth and many others have suggested, shared interests bring the flock together too. A shared interest is often the basis for a single-stranded tie, resulting in only minimal mutual responsibility. In some cases, it is the foundation for what might be called "communities of extremely limited liability." (Sociologist Morris Janowitz coined the term "community of limited liability" back in 1952. He meant that a local community today resembles a corporation: Neither has total liability for its members.) Members—if we can even call them by such a

name—of a community of extremely limited liability have very limited expectations of one another, but they maintain regular social interaction (Figure 8.5). Here are some examples:

a. The Chicago "Court Buffs" are a group of men and women—mostly not lawyers—who watch federal trials every day. They debate and analyze the lawyers' performances. They have a kind of bond, but they rarely see one another outside a Federal court.

b. Members of 12-step groups offer support focused on a particular need—say, avoiding alcohol, gambling, overeating, or cocaine.

c. People who pray or study Scripture together—the most common type of limited-liability community in the United States.

Interestingly, these groups complement (rather than clash with) U.S. values of individualism and personal growth. Such groups demand little but give participants a sense of feeling good about themselves (Wuthnow, 1994).

To conclude: Even without formal study, many people understand the importance of social networks. Indeed, understanding how social networks operate is relevant to a range of practical and theoretical pursuits, including getting a job and choosing a college or university. (Some families understand this and are willing, if able, to pay for family members to profit from, say, graduating from prestigious Harvard University rather than a community college. Why? Better educational opportunities may be only part of the reason; the hope for better social connections may play a significant role.)

WHAT NOW, WHAT NEXT?

GATED COMMUNITIES

Privacy, prestige, and protection—those are the promises of a relatively recent international phenomenon: gated communities (GCs) (Blakely and Snyder, [1997] 1999). Few residents of GCs see themselves as living in architecturally or environmentally cutting-edge communities. That is not their draw. But GCs, in both cities and suburbs, are proliferating across the globe today (see Chapter 7).

GCs are residential neighborhoods enclosed by fences, walls, landscaping, or other physical barriers designed to protect the people, homes, and all facilities (e.g., pool) from "them" or "outsiders"—those who don't live there. Typically, GCs are run by self-governing homeowner associations, which can establish restrictions, including who can live there.

Although such privatized areas in the United States began in the nineteenth century for the wealthy and white (e.g., Tuxedo Park in New York), one researcher and her colleagues (Vesselinov et al., 2007) believe that this is no longer the case. They say that gated living is no longer only for the top tier of U.S. society. Rather, gated enclaves are spreading across the middle class, as well as across minority groups.

Why do so many people choose GCs? Some move into GCs because their options are limited: Developers build most new homes there, as in Las Vegas. Some movers seek security from fear and crime. Others wish to avoid rubbing shoulders with people unlike themselves. Some are concerned with maintaining their property values. Others seek a sense of community. Sociological researchers Vesselinov et al. (2007) conclude that the increase of GCs in the United States results from both (1) consumers' wants and (2) the marketing strategies of planners and developers. We can intuit from Mike Davis's book *City of Quartz: Excavating the Future in L.A.* ([1990] 1992:chapter 15) that he would add a particular consumer desire: escape from fear.

What about the social impacts of GCs? Many scholars (e.g., Blakely and Snyder [1997] 1999) are alarmed by the recent and rapid increase in the number of U.S. GCs because they fear that "gating up," or "forting up," extends residential segregation, increases social separation and fragmentation, and leads to more urban inequality.

GCs are increasing worldwide. From Shanghai (Fig. 8.2) to the Côte d'Azur, residents are gating up. In India, for example, many exclusive enclaves have emerged outside prospering cities. A resident of Hamilton Court, a suburban GC outside high-tech Bengaluru, India calls it "a kind of self-contained island" (in Sengupta, 2008); Hamilton Court boasts a private school, manicured lawns, and security guards;

and it's located just across the street from a shanty-town, which houses its servants.

GRAND DREAMS AND GRANDIOSE SCHEMES

Living in GCs, technoburbs, and megalopolises. Romanticizing rural retreats. These are some responses to urban growth in the past 30+ years.

What about the next 30 years? Here, we enter a mind-boggling realm where proposals range from cities floating in space to cities below the earth and sea. Imagine, for example, "commuting" daily from Los Angeles to Boston. It might take only 21 minutes by a passenger train powered by pollution-free magnetic levitation.

Gerard K. O'Neill, professor of physics at Princeton University, envisioned even grander technological projects before his death in 1992. It may sound like science fiction, but he wrote in 1977 that it is "almost inevitable" that humans will "break out" from earth, creating permanent colonies in space that could house up to 10,000 people. And what would life be like in these orbiting cities? (*Note*: O'Neill died before an earth-like planet was detected in 2007, ingloriously named Gliese 581c. Located over 120.5 trillion miles from earth, Gliese 581c may be habitable, astronomers say; this led London bookies to lower the odds on extraterrestrial life from 1,000 to 1 to 100 to 1.)

While O'Neill touted human colonies in space, others look to a Jules Verne-like vision: cities beneath the sea. Some envision a marine civilization with underwater urban structures.

At present, cities below and above the earth are only a twinkle in the visionaries' eye. But even if they remain just a twinkle, the potential of such space-age cities may spur our collective imagination to redesign earthbound settlements. Likewise, imaginings of the future—from cultural historian William Irwin Thompson's (1978) generation-old vision of new "metaindustrial" villages and smaller, decentralized, symbiotic cities and Richard Register's (1987) carless "eco-city" to Robert Reich's (1991) two-tier society, composed of the successful 20 percent and the unsuccessful 80 percent, to some socialist-feminist visions of a classless, gender-equal society shake our most basic assumptions about what is and what ought to

be (see Chapter 17). Essentially, visionaries, whether scholars, mystics, science fiction writers, or artists, are moralists; they comment on good and evil in the present while presenting alternatives for the future. Long may the imaginers live to enliven our sense of possibility! As a congressperson put it some years back, "Unless we try to visualize what is beyond the horizon, we will always occupy the same shore" (Brown, 1993:B2).

ANOTHER LOOK

For a change, theorists seem to agree on a basic point: Urban–industrial–capitalist society is too big, too specialized, and too heterogeneous to promote a sense of community except within smaller subcommunities. But on the question of what to do about this situation, if anything, consensus breaks down.

Differences in ideology and historical perspective are the basis of dissent over questions of modern community. Decentralists like William Irwin Thompson (1978) think that communications technology permits a return to a smaller-scale, more humane village life without the parochialism of preindustrial communities. In this view, the global village is possible without reinventing what Marx called the "idiocy of rural life." Centralists, on the other hand, tend to be prourban. Those in the Marxist tradition look to the radical restructuring of economic and political institutions as the precondition for reconstituting a sense of community by abolishing inequality and oppression. Ultraconservatives argue that secular modern urbanites cannot handle freedom, democracy, and advanced technology; a return to benevolent, authoritarian, religious rule is one answer for them. Other conservatives wish for a Jeffersonian past. Meanwhile, numerous philosophers are skeptical about whether *any* form of human social organization—urban, suburban, or rural—can encourage both personal freedom and intimate social bonds.

Theory aside, there seems to be a growing recognition that members of the global community share common concerns, perhaps a common fate. Since Hiroshima, Chernobyl, and melting ice caps, an understanding of the destructive power of technology—destruction that cannot be contained by political borders—combined with the spread of a global economy and culture have alerted us to our interdependence.

This situation is reflected in language. "Afghanistanism" was once a term newspaper editors used to refer to the preference for stories about far-away, exotic places over hard-hitting, close-to-home news. That term disappeared almost overnight in 1980 when Soviet troops marched into Afghanistan, and no term has replaced it. Perhaps this signals the idea that no place on earth is now so remote as to deserve our ignorance or lack of concern.

KEY TERMS

Cyberbia A postsuburban human settlement in an information-based, electronic (cybernetic) society.

Edge city Joel Garreau's book title (1991) and term for any place outside the central city that contains the following: (1) at least 5 million square feet of leasable office space, which is more than down-town Memphis; (2) at least 600,000 square feet of leasable retail space—the equivalent of a fair-sized mall; and (3) more jobs than bedrooms. In addition, these places (4) were merely bedroom communities or semirural places as recently as the early 1960s but now (5) are seen by the local population as one place that "has it all"—jobs, shopping, and entertainment.

Lifestyle cluster A term used by Nielsen Claritas, a marketing firm, to distinguish neighborhoods in the United States and elsewhere. Clusters, given colorful names such as "Blue Blood Estates" and "Shotguns and Pickups," are ranked from top to bottom. Status rankings are based on residents' household income, home value, education, and occupation. A key assumption of cluster analysis (and other geodemographic systems) is that birds of a feather flock together.

Mass society An imprecise term, used in the sense of *Gesellschaft*. Usually viewed as large-scale, urban-industrial society characterized by loss of traditional community ties, dependence on mass (instead of face-to-face) communications, and impersonal social relations.

Postsuburbia A spatial form pioneered in Los Angeles in the 1920s and 1930s and developed elsewhere after World War II, characterized by a complex, decentralized mix of urban, suburban, and rural space and a mix of residents in terms of class and ethnicity.

Suburbia Negative term, a stereotype of the suburbs created by social critics in the 1950s, connoting ugliness, tacky construction, middle-class mediocrity, and conformism.

Technoburb A perimeter city or zone, perhaps as large as a county, that is functionally independent of the central city and can generate urban diversity without urban concentration; it is made possible by technologically advanced industries. Its residents meet their work, housing, and other needs in their immediate surroundings. The term was coined by Robert Fishman, author of *Bourgeois Utopias* (1987).

PROJECTS

1. **ZIP codes and postal codes as communities.** First, walk through two residential neighborhoods that appear, on the surface, to represent different neighborhood types or SERs. Record—but do not judge—what you see: Alfa Romeos? motorcycles? pickup trucks? private security? tricycles? single-family, large houses on tree-lined streets? condos? multiunit apartments? the *New York Times* on the doorstep? ale bottles? toy-sized dogs? remnants of TV dinners? imported French wine bottles and/or freeze-dried coffee jars in the curbside recycle container? Then, using U.S. Census of Population and Housing data (plus any proprietary data you can find, perhaps in a business library, organized by ZIP codes), check out the residents' median income, ethnic background, presidential voting records, home value, and occupations. Based on the information you've collected, in what SERs would you place the two neighborhoods?

2. **Neighborhoods as communities.** Do people in your city's neighborhoods feel a sense of community? Choose two neighborhoods and try to find out how residents perceive and feel about social relationships there. Construct a short questionnaire, including background questions on age and ethnicity and questions on the use of neighborhood facilities. Personally administer the question-

naire to residents, perhaps a nonrandom sample of 20 persons. Are there differences between respondents in the two neighborhoods concerning their social relationships? If so, why might this be? (*Note:* Don't generalize on the basis of your nonrandom sample. That is, avoid all claims about what "people" say or do; report only what your *respondents* say or say they do.)

3. **Social networks.** Choose two novels and trace the social networks of the main characters in each. Are their relationships close- or loose-knit, multi- or single-stranded? Do their webs of affiliation differ? If so, what difference does it make to the story and to the characters' feelings?

4. **Social networks.** How might the Internet be affecting social networks, particularly those of young adults and elders? First, see what others have written about the possible impacts and do a review of the key notions. Then, weigh in with your own observations.

SUGGESTIONS FOR FURTHER LEARNING

The social science literature on suburbs is extensive. Unsurprisingly, scholars hold a variety of opinions on the topic. Marxist David Harvey contends that suburban growth served an extremely political purpose. In his major study *The Urbanization of Capital* (Baltimore: Johns Hopkins University Press, 1985), geographer Harvey argued that suburbanization was but one "bourgeois response" to the ghetto riots of the 1960s; the aim was to disperse potential revolutionaries who were highly concentrated in cities.

For a historical study of one suburb, see *Westchester: The American Suburb, 1875–2000*, Roger Panetta, editor (New York: Fordham University Press, 2006). The forward was written by one of the United States's keenest observers of suburbs, Kenneth T. Jackson.

In "Between the County and the Concrete: Rediscovering the Rural–Urban Fringe," Jeff S. Sharp and Jill K. Clark (in *City & Community* 2008;7(1):61–79) find in their research in Ohio that rural–urban distinctions are not as helpful as rural–urban fringe differences. For example, they found that people living in the urban fringe differ from both urbanities and suburbanites (74).

Rants against suburbia did not end in the 1960s. See, for example, James Howard Kunstler, *The Long Emergency: Surviving the End of Oil, Climate Change, and Other Converging Catastrophes of the Twenty-First Century* (New York: Grove Press, [2005], 2006), and Elizabeth Farrelly, *Blubberland: The Dangers of Happiness* (Cambridge, Mass.: MIT Press, 2008).

One strain of anti-suburbanism concerns the supposed lack of spirituality and/or religiosity there. Two books in this tradition are *Death by Suburb: How to Keep the Suburbs from Killing Your Soul* (New York: Harper One, 2007) by Dave L. Goetz and Albert Y. Hsu, *The Suburban Christian: Finding Spiritual Vitality in the Land of Plenty* (Westmont. IL: InterVarsity Press, 2006). (Note that the publisher of Hsu's book is a division of the InterVarsity Christian Fellowship/USA.)

First published in 1961 and made into a motion picture in 2008 (starring Leonard DiCaprio and Kate Winslet), Richard Yates's *Revolutionary Road* (New York: Vintage, 2008) is a searing critique of U.S. suburban life. The novel and movie suggest that the United States may have been founded on revolutionary principles, but it now (and in the 1950s) celebrates spirit-crushing conformity, symbolized by the suburbs.

TV satires of the suburbs are alive and well. One, critically acclaimed cable TV's *Weeds* (Showtime, 2005–), stars Mary Louise Parker as a suburban U.S. housewife whose husband dies of a heart attack and who then turns to drug dealing to support her family.

Thirty-five years after William Whyte's *The Organization Man* (New York: Simon and Schuster, 1956), Paul Leinberger, a son of one of the original "organization men," and Bruce Tucker published their study, *The New Individualists: The Generation After the Organization Man* (New York: HarperCollins, 1991). They claim that while their parents valued consumption, sociability, and a sales mentality, their generation values creativity, subjectivity, and the artistic.

More than a half-century after three Levittowns were built in New Jersey, New York, and Pennsylvania, two of the three still fit the former stereotype. But Levittown, New Jersey (renamed Willingboro), does not. Ironically, this suburb—where builder Levitt once refused to sell to African Americans—is now majority

African American. In "Race and Place in Willingboro, NJ," Karen Beck Pooley comments that

> In today's Willingboro, the homes look the same but the faces have changed. And because the faces are different, the perception of the town's condition and the level of its property values stand in stark contrast to the New York and Pennsylvania Levittowns—confirming that the link between race and real estate is alive and well decades after the judicial and legislative repudiation of exclusionary zoning and other discriminatory practices. (June 2003): http://www.dreampioneers.org/id20.html.

In just one generation, very rich people in the United States seem to have changed their wants. According to Les Cristie's article, "Living Rich: What the Wealthy Want in a Home" (CNNMoney.com/Netscape May 9, 2006), the wealthiest people in the United States—the top 0.05% of the population in terms of assets–want very large homes, what others call "McMansions."

Those interested in telecommuting or working near home will be buoyed in spirit by some current practices. In some cities, people can drive a few miles to a telecommuting center. Or they can use groupware to work together. And some businesses and government agencies encourage employees with computer-related jobs to work at home a few days each week.

In his often amusing and pointed study *Richistan: A Journey Through the American Wealth Boom and the Lives of the New Rich* (New York: Crown, 2007), *Wall Street Journal* columnist Robert Frank looks at what Nielsen Claritas considers the top SERs in the United States.

For a discussion of network analysis that requires some sophisticated understanding of math, see Ulrik Brandes and Thomas Erlebach, *Network Analysis: Methodological Foundations* (New York: Springer, 2005). Several chapters involve connectivity.

REFERENCES

Banham, Reyner. [1971] 1976. *The Architecture of Four Ecologies*. New York: Penguin.

Baudrillard, Jean. [1986] 1989. *America*. London: Verso.

Berger, Bennett. [1960] 1971. *Working-Class Suburb*. Berkeley: University of California Press.

Bishop, Bill. 2008. *The Big Sort: Why the Clustering of Like-minded America Is Tearing Us Apart*. New York: Houghton Mifflin.

Blackwell, Jon. n.d. "1951: American dream houses, all in a row." http://www.capitalcentury.com/1951.html

Blakely, Edward J., and Mary Gail Snyder. [1997] 1999. *Fortress America: Gated Communities in the United States*. Washington, D.C.: Brookings Institution Press.

Bollens, John, ed. 1961. *Exploring the Metropolitan Community*. Berkeley: University of California Press.

Bott, Elizabeth. 1957. *Family and Social Network*. London: Tavistock.

Brown, George E., Jr. 1993. "Technology's dark side." *Chronicle of Higher Education* (June 30):B1–B2.

Castells, Manuel, Mireia Fernandez-Ardevol, Jack Linchuan Qui, and Araba Sey. 2007. *Mobile Communication and Society: A Global Perspective*. Cambridge, Mass.: MIT Press.

Davis, Mike. [1990] 1992. *City of Quartz: Excavating the Future in L.A.* New York: Vintage.

Farrelly, Elizabeth. 2008. *Blubberland: The Dangers of Happiness*. Cambridge, MA: MIT Press.

Fischer, Claude S. 1982. *To Dwell Among Friends: Personal Networks in Town and City*. Chicago: University of Chicago Press.

Fishman Robert. 1987. *Bourgeois Utopias: The Rise and Fall of Suburbia*. New York: Basic Books.

Gans, Herbert. [1962] 1982. *The Urban Villagers: Group and Class in the Life of Italian-Americans*. New York: Free Press.

———. 1967. *The Levittowners*. New York: Random House.

Garreau, Joel. 1991. *Edge City: Life on the New Frontier*. New York: Doubleday.

Giridharadas, Anand. 2008. "With influence rising, where are the ideas?" *International Herald Tribune* (August 15):2.

Goodman, Peter S. 2008. "Fuel pices shift math for life in far suburbs." *New York Times* (June 25): http://www.nytimes.com/2008/06/25/business/25exurbs.html?_r=1

Granovetter, Mark. 1973. "The strength of weak ties." *American Journal of Sociology* 78:1360–1380.

Harris, Richard. 2004. *Creeping Conformity: How Canada Became Suburban, 1900–1960*. Toronto: Toronto University Press.

Janowitz, Morris. 1952. *The Community Press in an Urban Setting*. Chicago: University of Chicago Press.

Jesdanum, Anick. 2008. "Instant-message lingo slips into teens' formal writing." *San Francisco Chronicle* (April 25):A5.

Kahn, Bonnie Menes. 1987. *Cosmopolitan Culture: The Gilt-Edged Dream of a Tolerant City*. New York: Atheneum (reprinted in paperback by New York: Scribner, 2002).

Keats, John. 1956. *The Crack in the Picture Window*. Boston: Houghton Mifflin.

Kling, Rob, Spencer Olin, and Mark Poster, eds. 1991. *Postsurburban California: The Transformation of Orange County Since World War II*. Berkeley: University of California Press.

Kontuly, Thomas, and Tiit Tammaru. 2006. "Population subgroups responsible for new urbanization and suburbanization in Estonia." *European Urban and Regional Studies* 13(4):319–336.

Kunstler, James Howard. 1994. *The Geography of Nowhere: The Rise and Decline of America's Man-Made Landscape*. New York: Free Press.

Laumann, Edward O. 1973. *Bonds of Pluralism*. New York: Wiley.

Leed, Eric J. 1991. *The Mind of the Traveler: From Gilgamesh to Global Tourism*. New York: Basic Books.

Leinberger, Christopher B. 2008. "The next slum?" *Atlantic Monthly*: http://www.theatlantic.com/doc/200803/subprime

Markoff, John. 1994. "The frontiers of new media." Speech delivered at "Media after convergence: Pacific perspectives." Conference sponsored by The Freedom Forum Pacific Coast Center and The Freedom Forum Media Studies Center at Columbia University, New York City. November 4, Oakland, Calif.

Mills, Edwin S., and Jee Peng Tan. 1980. "A comparison of urban population density functions in developed and developing countries." *Urban Studies* 17(3):313–321.

Montgomery, Michael R. 2003. "Book Review, *Smarter Growth: Market-Based Strategies for Land-Use Planning in the 21st Century*, Randall G. Holcombe and Samuel R. Staley, eds. Westport, CT: Greenwood Press, 2001." *Quarterly Journal of Austrian Economics* 6(1):81–88.

Mumford, Lewis. [1938] 1970. *The Culture of Cities*. New York: Harcourt Brace Jovanovich.

Nielsen Claritas. 2006a. "Welcome to MyBestSegments. com: Consumer Segments, defined and described detailed customer segmentation profiling." http://www.claritas.com/MyBestSegments/Default.jsp

———. 2006b. "My Best Segments: 2006 PRIZM NE Segmentation System." http://www.claritas.com/MyBestSegments/Content/tabs/filter-MenuFrameWork.jsp?page=../Segments/snapshot.jsp&menuid=91&submenuid=911

Norberg-Schulz, Christian. [1979] 1984. *Genius Loci: Towards a Phenomenology of Architecture*. New York: Rizzoli.

O'Neill, Gerard K. *The High Frontier: Human Colonies in Space*. New York: Morrow.

Orwell, George. 1949. *1984*. New York: Harcourt, Brace.

Peralta, Christian. 2006. "Shanghai's suburbanization plan," from *China Daily* (July 3), in Planetizen/Archnet (July 5): http://www.planetizen.com/node/20424

Register, Richard. 1987. *Ecocity Berkeley: Building Cities for a Healthy Future*. Berkeley, Calif.: North Atlantic.

Reich, Robert. 1991. "The secession of the successful." *New York Times Magazine* (January 20):16+.

Schnore, Leo F. 1963. "The socio-economic status of cities and suburbs." *American Sociological Review* 28:76–85.

Scott, John P. [1991] 2000. *Social Network Analysis: A Handbook*. Thousand Oaks, Calif.: Sage Publications.

Sengupta, Somini. 2008. "Inside gate, India's good life; outside, the slums." *New York Times* (June 9): http://www.nytimes.com/2008/06/09/world/asia/09gated.html?_r=1&th&emc=th&oref=slogin

Severson, Kim. 2008. "What's for dinner? The pollster wants to know." *New York Times* (April 16): http://www.nytimes.com/2008/04/16/dining/16voters.html?th&emc=th

Simmel, Georg. [1922] 1955. *Conflict and the Web of Group Affiliations*. Trans. Kurt Wolff and Reinhard Bendix. New York: Free Press.

Sternlieb, George, Robert W. Burchell, and Lynne Sagalyn, with Richard M. Gordon. 1971. *The Affluent Suburb*. New York: Dutton.

Tessler, Ray. 1989. "Milpitas outgrows the jokes." *San Francisco Chronicle* (February 14):A2.

Thompson, William Irwin. 1978. *Darkness and Scattered Light*. Garden City, N.Y.: Doubleday, Anchor.

Vesselinov, Elena, et al. 2007. "Gated communities and spatial inequality." *Journal of Urban Affairs* 29(2):109–127.

Weiss, Michael J. 2000. *The Clustered World*. Boston: Little, Brown.

Weiss, Michael J. 1988. *The Clustering of America.* New York: Harper & Row.

Wellman, Barry. 1979. "The community question: The intimate networks of East Yorkers." *American Journal of Sociology* 84:1201–1231.

Whyte, William H. 1956. *The Organization Man.* New York: Simon and Schuster.

Wuthnow, Robert. 1994. *Sharing the Journey: Support Groups and America's New Quest for Community.* New York: Free Press.

PLURIBUS VERSUS UNUM

PART

III

Richard Steven Street

Dorothea Lange

CHAPTER 9

MOVIN' ON

We don't know where we're going, but we're on our way!

        Stephen Vincent Benet's "Prelude" to
                Western Star, 1943

Movin' on is what people in the United States do all the time. Outsider Alexis de Tocqueville spotted this restlessness as far back as the 1830s: "An American will take up a profession and leave it, settle in one place and soon go off elsewhere."

Although residential mobility rates slowed in recent decades, people in the United States remain big movers. About 20 percent moved in 1980. By 2002–2003, the rate declined to 14 percent: yet, in that one year, 40 million people moved their residence (Schachter,2004)). Some (e.g., Stuart, 2002:17) say that people in the United States move, on average, once every 6 years.

Why do people in the United States move so much? Changes in life cycle (growing families, divorce, retirement), changes in income (more or less money available to spend on housing), and changes in job location are some key reasons. Government policies, such as housing subsidies (or lack thereof), and homeownership (or lack thereof) also play a role in decisions to move or stay put. In addition, when energy prices soar, we can expect more moves—suburbanites are rethinking the costs of filling up their gas tanks and their propane gas tanks (Goodman, 2008).

Comparatively speaking, people in the United States are big movers. About 12 percent of the English population moves each year (Weiss, 2000:145), and only 5.1 percent of Japan's population changes residence in any year (Seko, 2006).

Today, moving to the big city—or far from it—is no big deal. A rural Texan can go to Houston and a Londoner can "move house" to Normandy or Tokyo without feeling totally cut off from family and familiar things. In mass societies (e.g., the United States, Japan, Germany), McDonald's, CNN, the Internet, picturephones, and text messaging reach into the backwoods.

Even if they live in Podunk, only a few rural people in the United States are unfamiliar with urban life. Indeed, for most, *urbanism is a way of life*. Why? Because, as a sociologist remarked a generation ago (and it is more the case now and not only in the United States): "The attitudes, behaviors, and cultural patterns of rural areas of the United States are dominated by urban values, urban attitudes, and urban lifestyles" (Palen, 1987:12).

Urban culture has spread worldwide, or almost. With the near-global diffusion of Coca-Cola, cell phones, and the Internet, farmers from outside Ha Noi or Kiev would not feel totally out of place in cities anywhere. How different were the experiences of earlier generations of migrants! Imagine what Tevye the milkman in *Fiddler on the Roof* might have felt, uprooted from his east European *shtetl* and rerooted to New York City, trying to adjust to the rhythms of urban-industrial life.

MIGRANT EXPERIENCES IN THE UNITED STATES

THE OLD MIGRATION

According to iconoclast Gore Vidal, "history is nothing more than the bloody record of the migration of tribes. When the white race broke out of Europe 500 years ago, it did many astounding things all over the globe" (1992:56). One astounding thing it did was to establish settlements in the Americas.

English, Dutch, and other western European settlers came to North America to live on farms and build colonial cities in the seventeenth and eighteenth centuries. Blacks from Africa arrived shortly after the English settlement at Jamestown, Virginia, in 1619.

But it was not until the era of rapid industrialization that mass immigration to the United States took place: From the 1840s to the 1910s, about 35 million Europeans fled their plots of land, villages, and *Gemeinschaft*-like communities to resettle in U.S. cities. They came from all over Europe—Sweden, Germany, Ireland, southern and eastern Europe. They came from Japan and China too, first to work on the railroads and perform hard labor.

Many, perhaps one-third, of all western European immigrants had no intention of staying in the United States. About one-third of Italian immigrants, for instance, worked hard for years, scrimped and saved up to buy land in Italy, and then returned "home" (Wyman, 1993).

Mainly peasants and rural folk, most immigrants were ill-prepared for urban life in the United States. They were the uprooted—from rural rhythms, traditional ways of life, and often family. Some believed they would find streets paved with gold in the New World. Instead, many met hostility and discrimination—or racism, in the case of the Japanese and Chinese.

Ethnic stereotypes were nearly universal. "No Irish Need Apply" signs greeted Boston's Irish in the 1850s when they searched for work. Old-stock Americans accused the "foreign element" of having "animal pleasures" and a "pigsty mode of life."

Fear was pervasive in the United States during much of the nineteenth century. There was fear of cheap immigrant labor and unemployment, fear of "inferior races" overwhelming white Anglo-Saxon Protestant (**WASP**) culture, fear of papism and international economic conspiracy, and fear of "them" or the unknown. In other words, xenophobia, racism, anti-Semitism, and anti-Catholicism.

In 1882, the Chinese Exclusion Act effectively ended Chinese immigration to the United States. By the

Fig. 9.2 ELLIS ISLAND, GATEWAY TO THE "PROMISED LAND:" European immigrant women and children arrive at Ellis Island, off New York City, around 1907. (Museum of the City of New York)

1920s, all immigration to the United States. was drastically curtailed by new restrictive legislation; the "immigrant hordes," as critics called them, were shut out.

INTERNAL MIGRATION

In the 1920s, immigration from abroad to the United States came to a halt, but another large-scale migration began: an internal U.S. population shift. Once again the cities served as entry points for rural people—this time, black and white Americans.

In terms of numbers, the most significant internal movement was the migration of African Americans out of the South and into northern and western cities. Between 1910 and 1970, over 6.5 million African Americans left the South. Of those who remained, many also moved—from rural areas to cities. Today, the majority of African Americans live in U.S. cities.

Since World War I, two kinds of forces have worked to move people in the United States from the countryside to the city: *push* and *pull*. Economic and natural forces (e.g., poverty, landlessness, dust storms) pushed some off the land and pulled others into urban areas, more precisely, into what Burgess (1964) called the "zone of transition" (zone II). Southern dirt farmers, displaced by mechanized agriculture or beset by constant poverty, sought economic survival in cities. During the 1930s, Oklahoma whites (disparagingly called "Okies") moved west when the Dust Bowl engulfed their land.

By World War II, large numbers of people in the United States were moving geographically, hoping to move up socially too. Southern blacks and rural whites were drawn to war-related industries in the North and West. Puerto Ricans moved to New York City seeking jobs. Chicanos (Mexicans and Mexican Americans) and other Latinos in the Southwest came to western cities. Today, most Latinos in the United States, like most African Americans, live in cities.

a

Fig.9.3 THE PEOPLE LEFT BEHIND. Badlands, dust storms, and rural poverty *pushed* people off the land in the United States in the 1930s. And the hope of economic survival *pulled* many to cities. (*a*) Dust storm, Cimarron County, Oklahoma, 1936. (*b*) Rural poverty near Wadesboro, North Carolina, 1938. (*c*) Southern sharecropper family. (Library of Congress: [*a*] Arthur Rothstein; [*b*] Post Wolcott; [*c*] Walker Evans)

However, one recent development looks like it may be a trend: the move of African Americans to the South. According to the U.S. Census Bureau (in Associated Press, 2003), more than 680,000 African Americans over the age of 5 years moved to the South from other regions in the 1995–2000 period. In the largest U.S. city, New York, preliminary census figures showed an exodus of U.S.-born African Americans in the 2000–2004 period, a population loss that reversed a long-standing pattern for the first time since the Civil War. Where did they go? Seven in 10 African American movers from New York City went south, especially to Florida, the Carolinas, and Georgia.

Since 2000, why did African Americans and others in northern U.S. cities move south? Historian Charles Ross at the University of Mississippi (in Associated Press, 2003) argues that "Many blacks left

[the South] not only because of [the lack of] economic opportunities but because of the political and social constraints of segregation," implying that a stronger economy and better relations between the races seem to be the chief lures back to the South for their children and grandchildren.

In recent times there seems to be another trend, or minitrend, in the United States, one that crosses ethnic, racial, and economic lines: multigenerational households. As of 2000, multigenerational households (typically, a grandparent living with a child and a grandchild) represented only a small percentage of U.S. living arrangements—fewer than 4 percent of all U.S. households. But U.S. households with *three or more generations* living under the same roof rose 38 percent from 1990 to 2000. This suggests that many people in the United States are starting to reverse the long-term pattern of living independently. The

b

Fig. 9.3 (*continued*)

key reason? The high cost of housing. According to a sociologist specializing in family matters (Frances Goldscheider, in Miller, 2005), when U.S. home prices increase, "it is harder and harder for people to live independently."

THE NEW MIGRATION

"New" immigrants to the United States overwhelmingly trace their heritage to Asia or Latin America. As Figure 9.4 shows, in one year, 2006, the majority of legal newcomers to the United States (a category which includes those whose status was "regularized" in 2006 but who may have migrated earlier) were born in Mexico (about 14.4 percent), India (about 7.5 percent), or China (about 6.2 percent).

The "new" migration started in the 1960s after U.S. immigration laws changed. From 1968 to 1990, about 14 million people immigrated to the United States (10 million legally and approximately 4 million illegally). During the 1990s, an average of more than 1.3 million immigrants—legal plus "nondocumented" or "illegal"—settled in the United States each year. Between January 2000 and March 2002, 3.3 million additional immigrants arrived.

As of 2006, the foreign-born population of the United States was about 33.1 million. The U.S. Census Bureau estimates that about 8–9 million of these newcomers are nondocumented or illegal immigrants (in Center for Immigration Studies, 2006).

While old immigrants were mainly penniless European peasants, new non-European immigrants come from a variety of backgrounds, from millionaires and top engineers and scientists to destitute refugees. Some newcomer groups, particularly from India and Taiwan, tend to be predominantly college-educated, high-status, urban professionals.

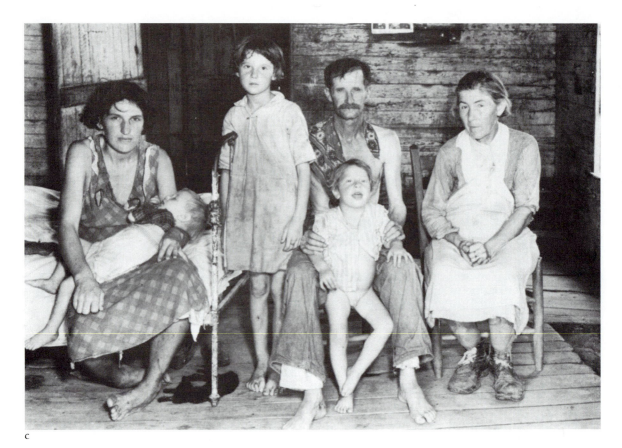

c

Fig. 9.3 (*continued*)

Note, however, that since 9/11 and new visa requirements, many have been turned away. Still, in 2005, more people from Muslim countries became legal permanent U.S. residents—nearly 96,000—than in any year in the previous two decades (Elliott, 2006). According to John Tirman of the MIT Center for International Studies (2006), this rise in the legal status of Muslim residents may reflect changes in security concerns in the United States: a shift from rounding up suspect Arabs and Muslims to shoring up the Mexican border.

More immigrants arrived in the United States in the 1990s than in any other decade. (Previously, the peak years were during the 1900–1910 decade when a record 8.2 million European immigrants arrived at Ellis Island.) However, numbers alone do not tell the whole story. Immigration in 1990–2000—*as a percentage of the total U.S. population*—was much lower than in the 1900–1910 decade: In 1910, almost 33 percent of U.S. residents were foreign-born; in 2000, the percentage was much lower—about 11 percent (Singer, 2006:6).

Each year, an estimated 200,000–300,000 nondocumented or illegal immigrants risk suffocation, drowning, disease, and virtual enslavement to come through the so-called Golden Door. What brings these newcomers in record numbers? Not destitution. Generally, people at the bottom of the income distribution in the sending country do not migrate; they lack the resources. (There are important exceptions, notably those who pay off their illegal passage by enslaving themselves for years to smuggling gangs.) Both push and pull

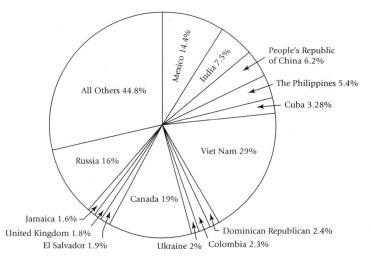

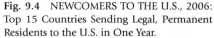

Fig. 9.4 NEWCOMERS TO THE U.S., 2006: Top 15 Countries Sending Legal, Permanent Residents to the U.S. in One Year.

Source: Kelly Jefferys, Table 3, p. 3 *Annual Flow Report,* U.S. Department of Homeland Security, 2007. (http://www.dhs.gov/xlibnargassets/statistics/publications/IS-4496_LPR#LowReport.04vaccessible.pdf)

factors—religious persecution and political upheaval in the homeland, changed U.S. immigration laws, the promise of (low-wage) industrial and service jobs in the United States associated with global economic restructuring, and family reunification—contribute to the new immigration. In addition, a few come to commit acts of terrorism in the receiving country.

But a basic reason for the new migration seems to be hope. More specifically, it is a gap between what people have as life aspirations and the means to fulfill them in the sending countries.

Where in the United States do migrants settle? In 2000, nearly 29 million immigrants were living in metropolitan regions throughout the United States. Most new immigrants, including nondocumented or illegal workers, come from cities and settle in cities, particularly the largest ones. However, increasing numbers (particularly Hispanics/Latinos) are also settling in small towns and rural areas.

Since the 1960s, from one-quarter to one-third of all immigrants settled in just a handful of cities: New York (which remains the preferred site of arrival), Los Angeles, Chicago, or Miami. This spatial concentration of immigrants is linked to economic and political factors, particularly the global restructuring of work that dislocates people in their home countries and creates a demand for them across national borders in large headquarters or global cities such as New York and Los Angeles.

Yet, some new immigrants do settle in small towns. Take, for example, Garden City, Kansas. Literally in mid-America (it lies halfway between the Atlantic and the Pacific), Garden City's Main Street and downtown buildings reflect the recent influx of immigrants from Mexico and Southeast Asia, many of whom work at a local meatpacking plant, a tortilla factory, a Laotian market renting Thai videos, and a Vietnamese-run karaoke bar. By 2000, about 44 percent of Garden City's residents identified as Hispanic (ERsys.com, n.d.). Remarking on the multiculturalism of this "cow town," a Garden City schoolteacher said, "We've become a little New York City in the land of Dorothy, Toto and Auntie Em" (in Sontag, 1993:1).

Finally, it bears noting that since 9/11 many immigrants—and not only Muslims—fear coming to the United States. What exactly do they fear? Not enough money and finding a "different" country, among other things. Here is reporter A. Craig Copetas's own family story: His impoverished Sicilian grandfather, Salvadore Di Bennedetto, emigrated from Sambuca di Sicilia a century ago with nothing "but raw optimism in his wallet." But, Copetas (2007) says, the triumphant tales of his and other Sicilian emigrant ancestors no longer resonate with younger generations. Instead, Copetas says, young Sicilians talk of a "different America, where money rules and not everyone is welcome," where—after the "fear-mongering" in post-9/11 times—all people are no longer created equal. In

Fig. 9.5. GIVE ME YOUR TIRED, YOUR POOR.... Historically, European immigrants came to the United States to escape famine, political oppression, economic hardship, and religious persecution. This tradition brought many eminent scholars to the United States during Hitler's time, including Albert Einstein, shown here taking the oath of citizenship with his stepdaughter in a Trenton, New Jersey, courtroom, October 1, 1940. (Peter C. Marzio, National Archives)

the minds of many young Sicilians, the United States "is broken," and they are choosing to stay put rather than emigrate. Journalist Copetas explains the difference like this: Generations ago, when his grandfather emigrated, Sicilian peasants were

> [l]abeled dirty, diseased and mostly anarchist... [they] debarked at Ellis Island speaking Parrati, a patois of Italian, Arabic, Greek and a half-dozen other languages that evolved into a regional tongue with no future tense.
>
> *For them, tomorrow was America.* Despite internment camps during World War II, decades of stereotyping and even lynchings, my grandfather's generation never lost its belief that America was the greatest place on Earth. [italics mine]

But today, Copetas says, Sicilian would-be emigrants are staying home; in their minds, tomorrow is no longer the United States. The country is "more dangerous" and "all about money," according to one Sicilian who emigrated to Boston in 1968 but returned to Sicily in 2002 (Friscia in Copetas, 2007:2).

SOME IMPACTS OF THE NEWCOMERS

If current population trends continue, so-called minorities will be the numerical majority in the 10 largest cities in the United States in less than one generation. Guesstimates vary, but some say that by 2089 the majority of people in the United States will trace their heritage to groups other than white Europeans.

In 2004, the largest minority group in the United States (about 14 percent or nearly 40.5 million persons) identified as Latino or Hispanic (Pew Hispanic Center, 2005:4). By 2050, the U.S. Census Bureau projects that the nation will include over 24 percent Hispanic (of any race), over 14 percent African Americans, 8 percent Asians, about 5 percent "others" (including Pacific Islanders and Inuits), and about 50 percent non-Hispanic whites (U.S. Census Bureau, 2004). Others think Census projections underestimate Hispanics/Latinos. For one, Sonia M. Pérez thinks that "Owing to both high fertility and immigration, by 2030 one in four Americans will be of Hispanic origin" (Pérez, 2000).

This demographic shift is happening sooner in some U.S. places than in others. For example, in California ethnic and racial minorities constituted a *majority* of the state's population by 2003. As of 2000, California was the primary destination of most immigrants to the United States: about 9 million (or 28 percent of the nation's immigrant population).

Prize-winning author and Vietnamese American Andrew Lam lives in San Francisco, California. In his adopted city, no one race constitutes over 50 percent of the population. According to Lam, "to live in California is to live at the crossroads of a global society" (2005). But, Lam continues, diversity is far from *just* being a California experience: "San Francisco is not an anomaly. It is the trend, the future. By the year 2050, there will be no majority left in America." Lam (2006) concludes that the very notion of "majority" race is becoming obsolete.

BOX 9.1 A POTPOURRI OF U.S. MIGRANT MEMORIES

The Uprooted

Over 56 million immigrants walked through the "Golden Door" from 1820 to 1991. Once inside the United States, millions more migrated from south to north and from east to west.

During the 1990s and beyond, millions came any way they could, escaping poverty, repression, sexual slavery, war, and other conditions. Post-9/11, much changed.

Here is a sampler of migrant memories. These remembrances, dealing with their old lives and new starts, span a period from the late nineteenth century to the early twenty-first century.

Dreams of America

Sitting in nineteenth-century Plotzk or Kiev, what did future emigrants think life in America would mean? Mary Antin, an east European Jewish immigrant who arrived in 1889, gives us an inkling:

America was in everybody's mouth. Businessmen talked of it over their accounts; the market women made up their quarrels that they might discuss it from stall to stall...children played at emigrating; old folks shook their sage heads over the evening fire, and prophesied no good for those who braved the terrors of the sea...all talked of it, but scarcely anyone knew one true fact about this magic land.

(Antin, 1899:11)

Stark Realities

Once here, "this magic land" turned into something else: sweatshops, tenements, and discouragement. Social reformer Jacob Riis describes a typical situation in New York City's seventh ward around 1890:

There were nine in the family: husband, wife, an aged grandmother, and six children; honest, hard-working Germans, scrupulously neat, but poor. All nine lived in two rooms, one about ten feet square that served as parlor, bedroom, and eating-room, the other a small hall-room made into a kitchen....That day, the mother had thrown herself out of the window, and was carried up from the street dead. She was "discouraged," said some of the other women from the tenement.

([1890] 1970:41)

From Dust Bowl to Peach Bowl

When the Dust Bowl hit during the Depression, some farmers in the Southwest traded their land for a Ford and headed west. They arrived in California hungry and broke, eating a potato stew so thin that they could read a magazine through it. Soon, the Dust Bowl refugees were part of the Peach Bowl, wandering the open highways as migrant field labor.

The refugees' plight has been celebrated in song and story. John Steinbeck's saga *The Grapes of Wrath* ([1939] 1972) follows the Joad family to California, which did not turn out to be the promised land after all.

Harlem: Seventh Heaven

At age 16, Malcolm X took a railroad job, mainly to visit Harlem. Here is how he remembers his first look at "This world...where I belonged":

Up and down along and between Lenox and Seventh and Eighth Avenues, Harlem was like some technicolor bazaar...combed not only the bright-light areas, but Harlem's residential areas from best to worst, from Sugar Hill up near the Polo Grounds, down to the slum blocks of old rat-trap apartment houses, just crawling with everything you could mention that was illegal and immoral. Dirt, garbage cans...drunks, dope addicts, beggars. Sleazy bars, store-front churches with gospels being shouted inside, "bargain" stores, hockshops, undertaking parlors. Greasy "home-cooking" restaurants...barbershops advertising conk experts. Cadillacs, secondhand and new...Harlem was Seventh Heaven!

(Haley and Malcolm X, [1964] 1966:74–76)

Forced Migration

This haiku by Sankuro Nagano reflects the irony of the Japanese American internment camp experience in the land of "freedom":

Against the New Year sky,
Beyond the fence flutters
The Stars and Stripes

(in Hosokawa, 1969:359)

Aztec Heritage of Migration

As the capital of *La Raza* in the United States, Los Angeles "is to the Mexicans what Boston has been to the Irish and New York City has been to the Jews" (Steiner, 1970:141). The heart of Los Angeles's Chicano population is the barrio (Spanish, originally meaning "neighborhood," later "native quarter" under colonial rulers). The barrio is a city within a city—a collection of urban villages, each with its own character, shrines, village patriarchs, gangs, and history.

Considered to be the founder of modern Chicano theater and film in the United States, actor–movie director Luis Valdez (*La Bamba*, 1989) says that Mexicans have a long tradition of migration, one rooted in the legend of the founding of Mexico: The sun and war god of the Aztec's ancestors forecast that if his people migrated south, they would establish a powerful kingdom. According to Valdez,

Continued

BOX 9.1   *Continued*

In that march [the sun and war god] prophesied that the children would age and the old would die, but their grandchildren would come to a great lake. In that lake they would find an eagle devouring a serpent, and on that spot they would begin to build a great nation. The nation was Aztec Mexico.

(in Steiner, 1970:130)

Of more recent migrations, Valdez says that "we put our old history on wheels of jalopies. Culture of the migrants! It is nothing but our Aztec heritage of migrations, mechanized" (132).

Freedom, Work, Family, and Hope

America's cities remain a popular destination of the world's recent immigrants. What are the chief pulls? Here is what a few new immigrants say.

Le Xua, a political refugee from Vietnam:

I loved my country and didn't want to leave my motherland, because my ancestors are buried there and also because I had to leave my brothers and sisters behind. But living conditions…became impossible.…So we came here for freedom, but we also found that life is easier here than it was in Vietnam.

Mariya Kovaleva, a Pentecostal Christian from Ukraine:

We felt like we couldn't practice our faith because people discriminated against us.…[I]n the United States…we can go to church and practice our religion without discrimination.

(in Holmstrom, 1992:10–11)

Safe Haven

Colombian refugee lawyer Camilo Perdomo (formerly the second in charge at the Columbian equivalent of the Federal Aviation Authority) and his lover Juan Carolos Veloza (a Colombian marketing manager) came to Queens, New York, seeking asylum. In Colombia, Perdomo had received harassing and threatening phone calls in Bogotá because he is gay. His office had been defaced with hate words, and later he was fired. Perdomo interpreted a visit from motorcyclists in trench coats and dark helmets in late 1998 as a "social cleansing squad." Perdomo and Veloza decided to leave the country to avoid being killed. Packing some clothes, a baby Jesus, a few saints, rosaries in one pocket, and $80 in the other, they prepared to come to New York City. First, they rented a room from a Colombian woman in Flushing, Queens. Perdomo says,

We miss our families. We miss our country. We did not come here to have money to buy our first osterizer, because we had an osterizer and a car and a house and a garden in our country. We just can't live there anymore without being dead.

(in Lehrer and Sloan, 2003:146)

In 1997 Bovic (not his real name) went from the Democratic Republic of the Congo, formerly Zaire, to JFK International Airport in order to escape serving in anyone's military. First, he went to a neighboring country. Later, he returned home. Then, his home was ransacked by the army, he was called "dangerous," and locked up. He escaped and, through a helpful Russian friend, sought asylum at JFK. He spent years in a detention center in New York City with no windows or fresh air or sun, which was "the darkest period in my life." After years of waiting, Bovic was released from the detention center and found work at a youth hostel, welcoming people from all over the world. He says,

If I meet someone new to this country, I'm going to give them hospitality that I did not receive.…I'm going to enjoy the life because I have the human right now to enjoy.

(in Lehrer and Sloan, 2003:85)

Post-9/11: A Paler Shade of Green

Writing after St. Patrick's Day, 2007, reporter Kevin Cullen noted that "Ireland's booming economy and the crackdown on illegal immigration that followed the September 11, 2001, terrorist attacks have combined to produce a reversal of migration patterns for those who have long made up the biggest, and most influential, ethnic group in Boston" (2007a).

This migration pattern started in the 1840s when a potato blight in Ireland killed about 1 million people and sent double that number to find food and fortune elsewhere, particularly Boston. Indeed, in one generation, Boston was transformed from an overwhelmingly English American, Protestant city to a largely Roman Catholic city where thousands had Irish roots. Over the decades, the Irish came to dominate Boston and the metropolitan area's politics, then its businesses.

Even now, Boston is viewed as the most Irish city in North America. (Other U.S. cities, including New York, Chicago, and San Francisco, have significant numbers of Irish-identified residents; but Irish influence waned when other ethnic groups arrived.) Still, between 1990 and 2000, Boston's Irish-identified population shrank 27 percent, and if current trends hold, it will continue to decrease. (In 1990, 23,000 Irish headed for the United States, many for Boston. By 2006, only 1,700 emigrated from Ireland to the United States.)

According to Cullen (2007a), "The cachet and freedom, both economic and social, that drew young Irish immigrants even as Ireland's economy boomed has been diminished. In its place are the unsettling realities of life for immigrants of any nationality who outstay their visas." As one immigration

Continued

lawyer put it, "It's a new world since 9/11." One sign of the times is the changing role of some Irish pubs in Boston: They now host legal clinics, advising immigrants "how to navigate living in a place that is less hospitable to them than it was to members of their parents' and grandparents' generations" (Cullen, 2007a).

Jenny and Paul Ladd are one of many Irish couples living in Boston without proper documents. He worked as a roofer until he was arrested for driving with an expired license. They do not want to leave the country but face deportation. Jenny

says, "Our American dream became our American nightmare" (in Cullen, 2007a). Baffled, an Irish-born American, Connie Kelly, says that "America has always been good to the Irish, and the Irish have been good to America. I don't understand why it has to come to this" (Cullen, 2007a).

Coming full circle: Once upon a time there was a neighborhood near Boston called "Little Kerry" because so many residents came from County Kerry in Ireland. Now, in County Kerry, there is a neighborhood called "Little Boston" because so many residents used to live there (Cullen, 2007b).

What these newcomers mean for politics, culture, and everyday metropolitan life is not altogether clear. The response of urban/suburban institutions and groups is one important factor, particularly in hard economic times. Much also depends on the political leadership developed within ethnic communities and possible coalitions or conflicts.

Yet, nationwide, some things are already clear. First, more voters and politicians in the United States are listening to groups lobbying to restrict immigration. Anti-immigration voices, which often cross liberal–conservative lines, may have increased in recent years; but none of the major presidential candidates in 2008 made immigration policy a key plank in the campaign. (Indeed, the subject was barely mentioned by any major candidate!) Second, at the same time, U.S. employers across the country are fighting at various levels—in state legislatures, the federal courts, and city halls—to reverse a recent crackdown on illegal or undocumented immigration. Business-driven appeals to end such crackdowns are bound to cause rifts in traditional U.S. party politics, particularly within the Republican Party. Third, the recent influx of Asian and Latino immigrants has changed the long-standing bipolar model of race relations in the United States, away from black and white to much more complex, multiethnic models. Fourth, the newcomers, particularly Hispanics/Latinos, were often ignored or neglected in past decades, but recently they have been actively courted by political parties.

Here are just a few questions scholars and politicians are sure to ask: What will the impacts be, if any, of having a Hispanic "majority-minority" in the United States rather than an African American majority-minority? What does it mean that there are

a million *black Hispanics* in the United States who are more similar to non-Hispanic blacks than to other Hispanics? (Both the level of income and the integration of Hispanics, sociologist John R. Logan found [in Fears, 2003], depend in large measure on the shade of their skin.) Will major political parties neglect the needs of African Americans as their numbers decrease relative to Hispanics?

Both groups, newcomers and long-established citizens, include a number of Muslims. But how many? No one knows. The U.S. Census does not collect information on religious affiliation. Totals are a political football; there are consequences for groups with either high or low numbers. (Truth is often the first casualty not only in war but also in religion.) Guesstimates range from a low of about 1 million adult Muslims residing in the United States to just over 4 million. Whichever, it is a tiny percentage of the U.S. population. But since 9/11, the U.S. Department of Justice reports that one in five so-called hate crimes in the United States involves an attack on a Muslim, an Arab, or someone assumed to be a Muslim or Arab (in Spiegel, 2006).

FROM ELLIS ISLAND TO LAX

ADJUSTMENTS TO URBAN LIFE

Few generalizations can be made concerning migrants' responses to urban life in the United States. Some felt lost in the U.S. city, overwhelmed with longing for the structure and order of rural life, whether in the old country or the U.S. countryside. Others relished the fast tempo, the opportunities to get ahead, and the chance to break away from domineering in-laws. Some recent refugees, like the Hmong from Laos, remain collectivist in their outlook, while Cambodians are much more individualistic; their adaptations to U.S. life reflect their cultures and histories (Hein, 2006).

In brief, then, culture, ethnic background, religion, social class, the health of the local and global economy, and time of arrival in the city influence how migrants adapt to U.S. metropolitan life. For instance, eastern and southern Europeans arriving before 1920 came at the "right" time. At least some of these uprooted rural folk, or their children, could begin at the bottom of the socioeconomic ladder and move up as the country grew economically and prospered. In other words, the "American dream" did in fact work for many of these early immigrant families. Starting in the slums and sweatshops pictured in Jacob Riis's 1890 photos, many children or grandchildren of the European immigrants moved up and out.

But those who arrived in the city at a later date, especially Appalachian whites and African Americans from the South, came at the "wrong" time. Social mobility has been more difficult in recent decades due to structural changes in the economy, technological innovation, and—in the case of blacks—institutionalized racism. Unskilled jobs, once the point of entry for moving up, now tend to be dead ends. Few, if any, janitors become corporate board members.

African Americans faced overwhelming obstacles. Their chances for economic advancement and social equality after 1920 were limited by segregation and discrimination, exclusion from many labor unions, and chronic injustice—all legal until the 1950s and 1960s. Desegregation laws, civil rights acts, affirmative action, and other public policies aimed at creating equal opportunities have not yet significantly improved the life chances of most African Americans. Like Native Americans and Latinos, they remain disproportionately poor and outside the mainstream of the U.S. economy.

Some scholars, notably William Julius Wilson (1978, 1987), argue that class—not race or racism—is now the key variable explaining African American and Latino impoverishment. Wilson says that the mass of African American workers constitute a permanent "underclass" due to changes in the macroeconomic structure, particularly deindustrialization (see Chapters 10, 11). (In a more recent book [2009], Wilson argues that structural and cultural forces are

inextricably linked, and that public policy can change the racial status quo—by reforming institutions that reinforce it.)

Many others name race or racism, not class, as the major contributor to black poverty. In this view, typified by the 2008 Nobel Prize winner in economics, liberal Paul Krugman ([2007]2009), race remains the major reason America treats its poor so harshly. Sociologist Robert D. Bullard, often called "the father of environmental justice," agrees. He thinks that race continues to be a "potent variable" in explaining much about the United States, including the spatial pattern of urban housing. Years before Hurricane Katrina, Bullard wrote about toxic, industrial poisons spewed forth in poor, black, and minority neighborhoods. One place he discussed was (and remains) "Cancer Alley," the 100-mile stretch between New Orleans and Baton Rouge, Louisiana; it earned its name from vinyl chloride and other cancer-causing by-products from hundreds of heavy industries, including oil and gas refineries, which enter the local environment. Pre-Katrina, Bullard ([1990] 2000:6) argued that race—not class—is a key variable in city life. Why? He cites various reasons, including this one: racial barriers in education, employment, and housing that affect members of the black middle class as well as the black underclass.

Others, however, think that both race and class are keys to understanding poverty (and more) in the United States. The aftermath of Hurricane Katrina in 2005 reinforced this view for some scholars and citizens. For one, radical Henry A. Giroux, a professor of education and communication studies, writes that Katrina "shamed [people in the United States] into seeing the plight of poor blacks and other minorities," thus rupturing "the pristine image [of the United States] as a largely, white middle-class country modeled after a Disney theme park." For Giroux, "The bodies of the Katrina victims laid bare the racial and class fault lines" in the United States (2006:187, 188).

Some scholars vacillate on which is more important, class or race/ethnicity. For example, sociologist Stephen Steinberg wrote a book whose title announced his viewpoint: *The Ethnic Myth* (1981). Steinberg said that "class difference is far more important than the fact of ethnic difference" (170). That was in 1981. A decade later, he had second thoughts. In 1992 Steinberg named "racism, which still pervades the occupational world, especially in the service sector" (744) as a key factor in the making of the African American underclass. Many respected social scientists agree, including political scientist Andrew Hacker (1992). Cornel West stated this viewpoint most succinctly in his book title: *Race Matters* (1993).

This debate over the relative importance of race and class to understanding the plight of the poor, particularly African Americans, continues to engage scholars and citizens. (And it is discussed in various chapters in this book.)

Now, back to the role that ethnicity can play in immigrants' adjustment to cities in the United States. Let's look at two sets of newcomers: (1) old migrants to New York City, who entered through Ellis Island, and (2) newer migrants to Los Angeles, many of whom landed at Los Angeles Airport (LAX).

IRISH CATHOLICS AND EAST EUROPEAN JEWS IN NEW YORK CITY

The Irish started arriving after a potato famine in the old country during the 1840s. Waves of Russian, Romanian, and other east European Jews flocked to the New World after 1881; many were refugees, victims of pogroms like the one that struck Tevye's village in *Fiddler on the Roof*.

According to a descendant of Irish Catholic immigrants, the late urbanist and senator Daniel Patrick Moynihan (in Glazer and Moynihan, 1963), the Irish brought from rural Ireland certain habits of mind that influenced their reaction to U.S. city life: experience with mass politics, suspicion of legal niceties, indifference to proprieties such as not stuffing ballot boxes, a capacity for political bureaucracy, a preference for informal over formal political institutions, and pride in taking orders from a chain of command (starting with an oligarchy of stern elders). These qualities, Moynihan wrote, were easily transferred from the Irish countryside to U.S. city politics. Eventually, they led to Irish control over machine politics from the early 1870s to the 1930s in New York City and elsewhere.

However, Irish American political power didn't lead to control in the private business sector or to a push for social change. According to Moynihan, "the Irish did not know what to do with power once they got it" (Glazer and Moynihan, 1963:229). While they were "immensely successful" in politics, "the very parochialism and bureaucracy that enabled them to succeed [there] prevented them from doing much with government" or using their political base to gain economic power.

The experience of the east European Jews was very different. Unlike the Irish in Ireland, east European Jews had long been a minority group within a larger hostile culture. While the Irish and many other immigrant groups came to America with one culture, Jews came with two—or more than two—cultures. Thus, the Jews didn't need to get used to minority group status, which sapped so much of the energy of other immigrant groups.

Further, east European Jews had a loose pattern for their collective existence; the Irish community tended to be more clannish. Most immigrant Jews wanted to keep their separate cultural life. At the same time, they did not depend on their ethnic ties to enter U.S. social and economic institutions; this they did on an individual basis.

While the Irish Catholics used their communal experience in the sphere of city politics, the east European Jews channeled their energies into the professions and business (although most first-generation immigrants were manual laborers and factory workers). The Jews had long been dependent on the sufferance of potential pogrom-makers and Jew-haters. Working for themselves—not joining the corporate bureaucracy—meant that they didn't have to depend on the good will or reaction of a person who may hold anti-Semitic views. In other words, Jews in the United States tried to avoid getting into situations where discrimination could seriously affect them. (This may have been the case decades ago, when signs in some hotels warned "No Jews allowed," and many country clubs barred them from membership. But it may no longer apply widely. More people from all ethnic/religious backgrounds seem to work for corporate bureaucracies. Trustworthy data on Jews and others in corporate bureaucratic jobs are hard to come by.)

Other important ethnic differences also affected the response of the two groups to U.S. urban life. For one thing, by the turn of the twentieth century, political dissent—especially socialism—had become a vigorous strand within Jewish immigrant life. For various reasons, this didn't happen in the Irish American community. Also, the two groups developed into distinct subcultures based on worldviews, values, and religious doctrines. The east European Jewish culture, as Glazer and Moynihan put it, is or was "secular in its attitudes, liberal in its outlook on sexual life and divorce, positive about science and social science," and passionate about education. Irish Catholics, by contrast, at least in the early 1960s, remained religious in their outlook, resisted liberalized sexual mores, and strongly felt the "tension between moral values and modern science and technology" (1963:298).

These differences showed up (and still do) in many areas, from choice of occupation to participation in civic activities. For instance, the Jews' positive attitude toward modern science is reflected in the fact that some "disciplines such as psychoanalysis, particularly in New York, are...largely staffed by Jews" (Glazer and Moynihan, 1963:298).

One might think that over the generations these differences would become less important and that the values of the two groups would grow more alike. Not so, say Glazer and Moynihan. They argue that over the passing decades, the values and attitudes of Irish Catholics and east European Jews have grown farther apart.

Looking at five ethnic groups in New York City—the Irish, east European Jews, Puerto Ricans, Italians, and African Americans—Glazer and Moynihan conclude that race and ethnicity are significant, often independent, variables affecting city life. In their estimation, "Ethnicity is more than an influence on events; it is commonly the source of events. Social and political institutions do not merely respond to ethnic interests; a great number of institutions exist for the specific purpose of serving ethnic interests" (1963:310).

Glazer and Moynihan wrote that decades ago. At that time, the early 1960s, and since, a number of distinguished social scientists disagreed with them, at least in the case of white ethnics. Herbert J. Gans, for one, thinks that race and ethnicity are no longer important determinants of social life and politics for most whites. (Gans's views will be detailed in Chapter 10.) And Glazer has come to terms with some

changes in the United States since *Beyond the Melting Pot* was published. His [1998] 2003 book's title, *We Are All Multiculturalists Now*, offers his assessment but not his opinion about that process.

Now, let's consider two groups of newer immigrants in Los Angeles, Chicanos and Koreans, and another group of immigrants who transformed Miami, the Cubans.

CHICANOS AND KOREANS IN LOS ANGELES

After New York City, Los Angeles is the second largest city in the United States. It is located in a sprawling county that encompasses 4,070 square miles. It is also a global, headquarters or world city.

Years ago, two political scientists wrote that Los Angeles presented an "unsettling vision" of the future (Riposa and Dersch, 1992:vii). Since then, the "future" arrived. And immigrants played a significant role in that "future."

Los Angeles is the new Ellis Island or, as UCLA urban geographer Edward W. Soja once put it, "the only place on earth where all places are." A generation ago, Soja (1989:223) noted an irony: Los Angeles was long ignored as bizarre or exceptional, but paradoxically, the metro area became the paradigm for the nation for a half-century: from 1950 until 2000. That is, Los Angeles had already become a warehouse to the world, a global or headquarters city inhabited by a "pool of cultures" representing a hundred different homelands.

Los Angeles's diverse and colorful pool of cultures representing the world is fairly recent. Indeed, in just one decade, 1980–1990, Los Angeles experienced a population transformation: In 1980, the L.A. metropolitan area was mainly white ("Anglo") and by 1990 the U.S. Census showed that the city was about 40 percent Hispanic, 37 percent non-Hispanic white, 13 percent African American, and 10 percent Asian. Spanish was (and is) the primary foreign language spoken there, but within the school district some 160,000 students speak more than 90 languages, from Afrikaans and Amharic to Urdu, Yoruba, and Yiddish.

Central to understanding Los Angeles's new status and rapid transformation are two connected factors: (1) its role in the world economy and (2) massive immigration. Following in New York City's footsteps,

Los Angeles emerged as a *headquarters city* (Logan and Molotch's term, see Chapter 5): a command post of the international economic system. New immigrants—semi-skilled and unskilled labor plus professionals and managers—are attracted to jobs in Los Angeles's headquarters economy of manufactured products, services, and financial goods. This mix of high- and low-income jobs has social and spatial impacts: a bipolar income distribution and residences segregated into rich and poor areas.

Los Angeles's role as a headquarters or **global city** (Sassen's term, 1991) has been evolving for decades. Edward Soja noted that for most of the twentieth century Los Angeles was one of the most "superprofitable industrial growth poles in the world economy." By 1987, southern California, a five-county urban region centered on the city of Los Angeles, had a regional economic product larger than the gross national product of all but 10 countries (Soja, 1989:191).

The Los Angeles region was the world's largest "job machine" up to the late 1980s. That was before the end of the cold war and massive unemployment in defense industries, economic recession, earthquakes, wildfires, riots, an upsurge in the rate of serious crime, and the loss of tourist dollars that hit the area particularly hard. Still, Los Angeles has been the most common U.S. destination for both Mexicans and Koreans.

Perhaps it is for all these reasons—economic, cultural, political, and social—that Los Angeles is arguably the most studied city in the world. (A cynic might add that scholars prefer its weather to London's fog, Moscow's snow, or New Delhi's heat.) Plus by the early 1990s Los Angeles and New York, taken together, were home to two-fifths of all immigrants in the United States (Logan and Mollenkopf, 2003).

Los Angeles—like Chicago decades earlier—became the center of a "school" or perspective on urban theory. Thinkers associated with this perspective, sometimes called "postmodern," include Michael Dear (2001) and Mike Davis (1992, 2007).

Chicanos

First let's consider Mexican immigrants in Los Angeles, starting with the name game: There is no agreement on which name to use—"Hispanic," "Latino," or "Chicano"—and the distinction is not always clear.

Here, I use "Chicanos" to mean only Mexicans and Mexican Americans. The broader term "Latinos" refers to Latin Americans in the United States of any national or racial background. "Hispanic" is the federal government's term, referring to the language community of Spanish-speaking people from all racial/ethnic backgrounds. Hence, Cuban-born singer Gloria Estefan is Latina and/or Hispanic. The late Arizona-raised farm workers' organizer Cesar Chavez was Chicano, Latino, and/or Hispanic. Spanish heritage, Filipino-born, Stanford University sociologist Francisco Ramirez is Hispanic but not Chicano or Latino.

In Los Angeles, the community of Chicanos is composed of old-timers and newcomers. At the time of the U.S. war with Mexico (1846–1847), there were at least 80,000 Mexicans in territory that the United States later annexed, probably 20,000 of these in California. By 2007, persons of Hispanic or Latino origin represented at least over 44 percent of the population of Los Angeles County, a county so large that it would rank eighth in population if it were a U.S. state. (Sources disagree on the exact percentage: The U.S. Census Bureau [2008] reported a population of 47.3 percent in 2006, but the Los Angeles Economic Development Corporation reported 44.6 percent in mid-2007.)

Los Angeles is a manufacturing powerhouse. In 2007 it remained the nation's leading county for manufacturing goods. International exports and tourism are also very important to its post-2000 economy, which is why it remains so attractive to migrants. In part, the choice of settling in Los Angeles County is a matter of higher wages attracting poor workers.

Traditionally, emigration from Mexico has appealed particularly to young, propertyless males with a growing family. In recent years, there has been an increase in female immigrants from Mexico to Los Angeles, who typically come as cheap labor.

Also important to Mexican (and other groups') emigration are preexisting social networks or "migration chains": Older migrants from the same community link newcomers to jobs with U.S. employers and labor contractors (see Chapter 8). For low-wage workers without money, college education, or technical skills, migration chains can be the most important factor in determining where to locate. (*Note*: In contrast, professionals depend much less on the help of eth-nicity-based migration chains. No national group is composed only of professionals and their kin, but a few, such as East Indian and Iranian immigrants, have high percentages of professionals; they tend to rely more on their own skills than on migration chains, and they tend to disperse spatially. For one, the high-income, highly-educated Iranian population in Los Angeles is widely dispersed. The biggest "Persian" bookstore outside Iran is located in Los Angeles, and about 10 newspapers in Farsi, the language of Iran, are published in Los Angeles.)

Now, back to Mexican Americans in Los Angeles. Once there, how have they been treated? Historically, Mexican Americans met pervasive and blatant hostility from police, discrimination by employers and public officials, and paternalism by Anglo church leaders. During World War II, ethnic hatred erupted in the so-called Zoot Suit riots in 1942 and reerupted in 1943 when aggression against young Chicano males by sailors and military police resulted in a reign of terror. The Los Angeles sheriff justified Chicanos' mass arrests by saying that their "desire to kill, or at least let blood" was an "inborn characteristic" (in Steiner, 1970:233). Further, Chicanos were barred from learning trades in defense plants and faced discrimination in public schools. Symbolizing the dominant white attitude toward them, Chicanos were allowed to swim in public pools only on days just prior to pool cleaning (Daniels, [1990] 1991:chapter 12).

In the last half-century or so, some blatant forms of economic oppression and cultural discrimination have been mitigated. But the Chicano/Latino community in Los Angeles still suffers from negative stereotypes, particularly in the mass media.

Media neglect adds to Chicano and Latino frustration and anger. This can lead to feeling forgotten. Here's one example: In 2007, prize-winning documentary filmmaker Ken Burns (*The Civil War, Jazz*) produced a seven-part series for the Public Broadcasting System (PBS) about World War II, called simply *The War*. Spokespersons for Latinos protested to corporate sponsors, Hispanic congresspersons, and PBS that the series neglected the role of over 500,000 Latinos in the war effort. (The upshot: Burns agreed to make changes, adding voices of Hispanic vets to the film.)

Beginning with modest resources and social origins and facing discrimination, most Chicanos have had few chances to "make it" by two common routes: working at a high-paid, professional-managerial job or owning a business. The proportion of Chicanos in professional-managerial jobs is low, and Mexico is the primary source of immigrant cheap labor in the United States. In 2000, the poverty rate among Mexican Americans nationwide was 23.5 percent.

A few more statistics give a bleaker picture for Mexican Americans nationwide. Between 1970 and 2000, the number of all people in the United States in poverty increased by 24.6 percent but the number of Hispanic Americans in poverty leaped by 262 percent (*Sacramento State News*, 2005).

The lack of economic empowerment is only one aspect of a group's status. Here's another: political empowerment. In this regard, in Los Angeles, there may be a less bleak picture. And it begins with a possible irony: The election of a conservative Republican businessman (Richard Riordan) as Los Angeles's mayor in 1993 may have fueled an era of Latino political empowerment. In a plot twist worthy of mystery writer Scott Turow, it turns out that the Catholic Church's cardinal in Los Angeles, Roger Mahony (once known as "Red Roger" for his advocacy on behalf of illegal immigrants and farm workers), forged a close working relationship with Riordan, an Irish American millionaire.

Aside from demographic shifts and other changes, the Riordan–Mahony alliance in government may have been one factor that led to a deeper Chicano/Latino voice—and vote: In 2005 voters elected former labor organizer and long-time Democratic politician Antonio Villaraigosa, a Chicano, as mayor. His win as the forty-first mayor of Los Angeles (and the city's first Chicano mayor since 1872) can also be attributed to alliance building; significant numbers of African Americans were added to his earlier coalition of Latinos, labor, and white liberals.

Electing one highly visible Chicano such as Mayor Villaraigosa or even a few (including Los Angeles's City Council president) may increase Chicano/Latino pride. But it does not pay the rent or quickly change daily lives. Issues of employment, education, and economic well-being remain of particular concern to the Latino plurality in Los Angeles.

We might add that questions of community remain important too. Perhaps the desire for a feeling of community is key to understanding young people's attractions to Chicano gangs in Los Angeles. According to Professor Martín Sánchez Jankowski, Chicano gangs in Los Angeles provide a *Gemeinschaft*-like brotherhood; many members are kinfolk or treat one another like family. Gangs open up an avenue of upward mobility to low-income young males and provide rites of passage to adulthood, much as the Little League does for boys in more affluent neighborhoods. For Chicanos in ethnic enclaves such as East Los Angeles, gangs are a source of solidarity (1991:199–200).

In recent years, there has been an increase in the city's interracial violence, typically springing from rivalries between African American and Chicano gangs, particularly in "changing" neighborhoods where the African American population has been declining and the Chicano population surging. In one year, 2006, a 14 percent increase in gang violence and gang crime was reported—at a time when overall violent crime was down (Archibold, 2007). What to do? A city-funded report advises nothing less than a "Marshall Plan" to deal with Los Angeles's gang violence.

To conclude: As of 2000, the majority of Latinos in Los Angeles were poor: More than one out of two lived below the poverty line. In 2000, according to some sources, Latinos constituted 37 percent of the population—and 54 percent of the poor in the Los Angeles region (McConville and Ong, 2006:8). (available data lump Chicanos, Central Americans, and "other" Hispanics together.)

Further, Chicanos are not being acculturated or assimilated. More than any other immigrant group, Chicanos can hold on to their ancestral culture because modern communications and geographical proximity enable them to maintain close ties with their country of origin, Mexico.

Some observers predict that Chicanos may evolve into a bicultural, bilingual culture. David Hayes-Bautista (2004), a third-generation Chicano and former head of the Chicano Studies Research Center at the University of California at Los Angeles, predicts that in less than 100 years Chicanos will not have assimilated in the classic sense; they will still "feel" Chicano.

If Hayes-Bautista's prediction proves correct, Latinos in California will pioneer another model of immigration: neither complete assimilation nor complete separatism. Instead, Latinos will forge a distinctive regional identity, and it will be based on Chicano (Latino) definitions of what it means to be "American" (i.e., a U.S. resident).

In part, Chicanos' (and Latinos') lack of incorporation into the mainstream reflects their position in general: Most remain a "them" to mainstream people in the United States—separate and less than equal. Otherwise stated, they feel like a group without a ladder to move up (see Chapter 11). Chicano poet Rodolfo Gonzales, writing a generation ago, put it this way: Many Mexican Americans feel

Lost in a world of confusion
Caught up in the whirl of an Anglo society,
Confused by the rules, Scorned by attitudes
Suppressed by manipulations, And destroyed by
    modern society.

(in Steiner, 1970:240–241)

Some predict that Chicano ethnicity will not only survive but thrive, acting as a tool to protect or enhance status. Others predict a very different future for Hispanics: one of assimilation and acceptance.

On the surface, Chicanos and Koreans in Los Angeles share little, for they seemingly have a different past, present, and future. But they share more than what is readily apparent, including mass migrations related to the global economy.

Koreans

Los Angeles is home to the largest Chicano and Korean communities in the United States. Unlike Mexican migration, this happened quickly for Koreans. A handful of Koreans, mostly farm workers, lived in California by World War I; but massive emigration started only in the mid-1960s. These newcomers were mainly middle-class urbanites; about 70 percent of Korean immigrants in Los Angeles came with college degrees in the 1960s (Takaki, 1989:437). Many were doctors, teachers, and other professionals. In the early 2000s, post-1965 Korean immigrants and their children constituted about two-thirds of Koreans and Korean Americans in the United States.

Most often, Koreans and Korean Americans work in small business, from fashion and small groceries to gas stations, 1-hour photo shops, liquor stores, and flea market stores. Hard work, long hours, networking among fellow/sister ethnics, and rotating credit associations (*kye*) have helped build many successful enterprises.

Indeed, in Los Angeles, Koreans have the highest self-employment rate among all minority and immigrant groups (Min, 1996:46). Sociologist Pyong Gap Min (1996:46) thinks that self-employment in small business was the best option for most Korean immigrants; they suffered serious job disadvantages, particularly a language barrier. According to Min, Koreans in Los Angeles (and elsewhere) reluctantly turned to small business as an alternative to low-level, blue-collar work, which they considered undesirable. (Other possible reasons for Korean immigrants' self-employment are discussed later in this section.)

Emigrants left their homeland of South Korea for various push reasons, including military dictatorship, political and religious repression, few educational opportunities, very high population density, and economic dislocation. Sociologists Ivan Light and Edna Bonacich argue that the first big wave of Korean émigrés was pushed out for another reason: Korea's "involvement in world capitalism." Specifically, they wrote, it was in the late 1960s and 1970s, when the "economic and political consequences of Korea's role as a producer of cheap manufactured exports" led to the dislocation and discontent of certain classes. The émigrés came from those dislocated classes (1988:124).

In terms of pulls, Korean emigration is intimately tied to U.S. immigration policy. Before 1965, Korea and other Asian countries came under restrictions that started with the Chinese Exclusion Act of 1882. The 1965 immigration law overturned the anti-Asian regulations and dramatically increased Asian immigration to the United States.

Korean immigration nationwide peaked in 1987 (almost 36,000 that year). In 1990, before the Rodney King "riots" (or "civil unrest" or "civil rebellion" in Los Angeles, depending on who's talking), there were nearly 73,000 Koreans in the city of Los Angeles and over 145,000 in the city and county of Los Angeles (U.S. Census in Min, 1996:Table 3, 34). By 2000, the estimated population of Koreans in Los Angeles had more than doubled: an estimated 186,000+, despite the moving out—at least for a while, after the Rodney King troubles—to Los Angeles suburbs already laden with Koreans. (The actual number is likely much higher due to the large number of undocumented and/or illegal immigrants living in Los Angeles.)

By the millennium, the name "Koreatown" did not fit the area of Los Angeles made infamous in the so-called Rodney King riots. Latinos made up over 75 percent of its population (but Koreans remained the predominant business owners). In recent years, Koreatown (an area about 5 miles west of Los Angeles's City Hall; its boundaries—roughly—are Beverly Boulevard and Pico Boulevard to the north and south and Hoover and Crenshaw on the east and west) has morphed. It has become an area with construction cranes, toney apartment buildings, lively commerce, and a vibrant nightlife.

By 2005, there were an estimated 2 million+ ethnic Koreans living in the United States, mostly in metropolitan areas. The Los Angeles area was their number one choice to live, making it home to the largest population of Koreans outside of Asia.

Once in Los Angeles, how have Koreans and Korean Americans been treated? That depends mainly on their occupation. Liquor store owners, grocers, and other merchants in South Central Los Angeles and Koreatown were targets of hatred by other minorities during the so-called Rodney King riots a generation ago (1992).

For starters, Koreans and Korean Americans in the Los Angeles area can enjoy a rich, ethnically-based cultural life (e.g., multiple newspapers in the Korean language), enhanced by an active Korean Consulate which, inter alia, promotes a plethora of activities, including heritage events such as an international summer camp, in Korea, for children 13–17 years old. (In summer 2008 this camp—the Seventh International Camp for Being Korean—featured traditional Korean arts.)

But what about Koreans in the larger society? In *Blue Dreams: Korean Americans and the Los Angeles Riots* (1997), Nancy Abelmann and John Lie argue that Korean American merchants in Los Angeles suffered shattered dreams post-1992. Similarly, sociologist Min

(1996:1) claims that a disproportionately large number of Korean-owned stores in Koreatown suffered during the 1992 riots.

Many Korean immigrants who arrived with professional experience or credentials found limited job opportunities, in part due to cultural and economic discrimination by whites. A generation ago, a survey found that only 35 percent of Korean professionals in Los Angeles were able to enter professional occupations there (Takaki, 1989:440). Seung Sook Myng's story is common: A pharmacist in Korea for 10 years, she could not take the licensing exam in California and became a knitting-machine operator in a Los Angeles garment factory, locked into a low-wage job (in Takaki, 1989:439–440).

Most Korean immigrants were not shopkeepers in Korea. But, as noted, once in the United States, many opened small businesses. Why? Some draw a parallel here between self-employed Koreans and other ethnic minorities who cluster in self-employed small businesses rather than large corporations, such as Jews in New York City; in both cases, self-employment serves as a shield against job discrimination by non-coethnics. Other analysts believe that this occupational choice is related to Korean culture, particularly the Confucian ethic of hard work, close-knit families, and inner-directedness. Still others say that the Korean immigrants were pushed into self-employment for various reasons, including the language barrier and the lack of professional opportunities noted. Whatever the reasons, it is ironic that Koreans "had left white-collar jobs in a modernized economy in Korea and had become old-fashioned shopkeeping capitalists in America" (Takaki, 1989:442).

According to *Immigrant Entrepreneurs: Koreans in Los Angeles 1965–1982*, a study by sociologists Ivan Light and Edna Bonacich (1988:24), once in the United States, Korean immigrants had the motive, money, education, and ethnic resources to open and run small business enterprises. Indeed, when these sociologists conducted their analysis in 1982, the extent of Korean small business ownership in Los Angeles was remarkable: The *Yellow Pages* of the Korean phone directory listed 4,266 Korean-owned businesses in Los Angeles County. Further, Koreans tended to hire coethnics so that "about 62 percent of employed Koreans in Los Angeles County were either self-employed or employees of Korean-owned firms, mostly service and retail proprietorships" (1988:3–4).

Typically, entrepreneurial minorities settle in large urban areas that offer close proximity to markets and workers. Koreans were (and are) no exception. Many Koreans did open small businesses inside the city of Los Angeles, the region's core, at the moment of "white flight." (The city of Los Angeles was a slow-growth area compared to the four adjacent counties in the metropolitan area.)

From 1960 to 1980, the white population of Los Angeles decreased from 71.9 to 44.4 percent, reflecting increased residential segregation of whites from African Americans, Asians, and Latinos. (*Note*: Some say, by 2000, the white population of the city had decreased to 29.7 percent.) White proprietors were abandoning inner-city ghetto neighborhoods, leaving a retail niche for Koreans. It was this void that Korean businesses filled, and many Koreans located their small businesses in ethnic enclave economies such as "Koreatown," then a superblock of residences and highly visible and concentrated, immigrant-owned businesses. (Despite its name, Koreatown has been a cosmopolitan area for years. As noted, in 2000, the majority of residents of Koreatown traced their ancestry to Mexico and Central America, not Korea.)

Generally, immigrants who own their own businesses earn much more than immigrants who work for wages. Thus, in most people's minds, it follows that Korean entrepreneurs are more independent than Chicano wage laborers. But Light and Bonacich suggest a different reality. They argued a generation ago that although many Koreans owned their own businesses, they remained economic pawns: "Koreans came to the United States as cheap labor," and "Korean immigrant entrepreneurship was a disguised form of cheap labor utilization by U.S. capitalism" (1988:27).

How can it be that Korean business owners in Los Angeles were (and perhaps remain) mere pawns? First, Light and Bonacich say, Koreans arrive with different expectations and experiences than U.S. workers. For one thing, South Korea has the longest workweek of all industrial nations—44+ hours at last count (and about 55 hours per week in earlier decades). Koreans expect to work very long and very hard each day for relatively little money; they don't necessarily share the North American and Western European expectation that they will be protected by labor unions or government agencies.

Further, much more than the U.S. norm, Korean shopkeepers depend on the unpaid labor of spouses and children to earn their living. It is not unusual for Korean small businessmen and their wives to work 6 days a week without one day of vacation for 8 or 9 years in order for their children to get ahead. Korean wage laborers work just as long and hard. Second, big corporations subcontract work at lower labor costs to small Korean garment factories and firms. Third, Korean small businesses (e.g., service stations, liquor stores, groceries, real estate offices) are often franchise businesses located in low-income, ghetto neighborhoods—considered risky both financially and physically by corporate executives. Large U.S. corporations that sell the franchises take no risk but penetrate markets that would otherwise be closed to them. In addition, franchisers gain from Korean family members' unpaid labor. In all these ways, Light and Bonacich argue, Korean small businesses provide profits for U.S. corporations.

In their business relations, Koreans, like other ethnic entrepreneurial groups before them, often find themselves in the potentially volatile position of **clientelistic hostility**: Clients of one ethnic group show hostility toward neighborhood vendors of another ethnic background. When clients of one ethnic group feel slighted or demeaned by vendors of another ethnic group, contempt and hatred can lie dormant, waiting to explode. Some argue that this was at the heart of the "riots" in Koreatown in 1992. Relations between Korean shopkeepers and their African American, Chicano, and other Latino clients in Los Angeles exploded, ending in the destruction of more than 2,500 Korean-owned stores during the Rodney King troubles.

Light and Bonacich suggest another reason for clientelistic hostility: Ethnic entrepreneurial groups, including Koreans, "tend to draw a tight line around their realm of social responsibility. It ends at the boundary of their ethnic community. With the rest of the world they can act as ruthless competitors" (1988:435). In other words, *they divide the world into "us" and "them" on the basis of ethnicity.* The result,

Light and Bonacich claimed, is a society where ethnic division is encouraged but class division is ignored: "Because ethnic entrepreneurship, on the one hand, fosters cross-class ethnic solidarities instead of cross-ethnic class solidarities, it helps to create an ethnically divided society. On the other hand, it inhibits the development of class conflict by fragmenting the working class along ethnic lines" (434–435).

Sociologist Min has a different take. Min focuses on Koreans' role as middlemen. He says that Koreans, more than other immigrant groups in Los Angeles (and New York City), are *Caught in the Middle* (1996:6–7) between low-income minorities as customers and large, white-owned corporations as suppliers. This minority-as-middleman role, Min says, increases interethnic conflicts, particularly with African Americans, but it has the opposite effect inside the group: interethnic conflict enhances Korean ethnic solidarity. (Not all scholars agree here. For instance, based on her ethnographic observations, sociologist Jennifer Lee [2006] says that conflict between Koreans and other ethnic minorities is far from the norm. On the contrary, Korean–interethnic relations, she says, are marked by civility and routine.)

Min concludes that Korean Americans are "not well prepared to live in a multiethnic society like the United States" (226). His suggestion for improving the Koreans' situation: "By learning about other cultures, Koreans will make it possible to live in peace and harmony with other ethnic groups" (226).

This is not at all what Light and Bonacich (1988:435) concluded. Writing several years before the 1992 riots, they thought that Korean immigrant entrepreneurs were themselves both victims and victimizers: Driven from their homeland, suffering hardship, and working extremely long hours, they were "victims of world capitalism" who "help to perpetuate the system that created their own oppression" (435).

Linkages?

Earthquakes and mudslides in metropolitan Los Angeles became a metaphor for the region's shifting economic and cultural ground in the 1990s and beyond. National recession, the end of the cold war (which brought a big loss of military-contracting jobs in the Los Angeles region), the civil unrest following the Rodney King verdict, and the loss of tourist dollars had far-reaching and negative impacts on Los Angeles's work force. Jobs in the aerospace industry declined by nearly one-third from 1986 to 1992. Plant shutdowns in the 1980s meant unemployment for hundreds of thousands, including over 70,000 blue-collar workers in South Central Los Angeles, the area where the Rodney King uprisings began.

Even before the uprisings, Korean newcomers nationwide were squeezed by recession and started leaving the United States, but the percentage grew over the years: In 1980, only 2 percent returned to Korea; by 1990, 27 percent returned in a reverse migration. In a related development, the "brain drain" from Korea (and some other countries, including Taiwan) ended in large measure by the early 2000s. In the case of South Korea, more than 80 percent of the students who received PhDs in the United States returned to their homeland.

To conclude: At first glance, Korean Americans and Chicanos in metropolitan Los Angeles appear to share little aside from vulnerability to earthquakes and other natural upheavals. After all, they have nothing in common: language, culture, job skills, neighborhood, or educational background. In addition, their rates of business ownership differ widely, with Koreans owning many more businesses than Chicanos.

But perhaps the two seemingly disparate groups are linked. If Light and Bonacich are correct, a significant irony connects Chicanos and Koreans: They share a basic economic relationship—both provide cheap labor for large U.S. corporations.

INTERNATIONAL MIGRATION AND INTERNAL MIGRATION GLOBALLY

NUMBERS, DEFINITIONS, AND DATA ISSUES

As of 2000, the total world population of people living outside their country of birth, citizenship, or usual residence—that is, immigrants—was estimated to be about 160 million (Massey and Taylor, 2004:1). Most immigrants live in so-called developing or Southern countries, that is, *poor* countries. Just a few examples: (1) During long-standing ethnic and civil conflict, hundreds of thousands of political refugees and stu-

dent activists escaped Myanmar (Burma), typically migrating to Thailand. (2) Economic refugees left Thailand for the Middle East and other places before the 1980s; but afterward Thailand's economy grew, and it became a nation of destination for other Asians. (3) Contemporary civil wars in Ivory Coast, Somalia, Iraq, Kashmir, Georgia, and Ossetia, among other places, have sent millions of migrants to both near and far places. (Exact numbers of migrants are guesstimates.) For instance, during the war in Iraq, the exodus of middle-class Iraqis, typically to nearby countries such as Syria and Jordan, was estimated to be about 2 million refugees in early 2007 (Caryl, 2007:32). In Iraq, another estimated 280,000 families were swept up nationwide in a massive, internal migration (Glanz and Rubin, 2007).

In recent years, there have been some changes in the countries of destination, the numbers of one kind of migrant— refugees—and the composition of international migrants. First, there has been an increase of immigrants to "Northern" (richer) countries. Second, the number of people displaced by conflict and/or persecution and under the care of the United Nations (UN) Office of the High Commissioner for Refugees reached 11.4 million in 2007 (in Cumming-Bruce, 2008:3). Third, international migrants have become much more diverse in terms of origins, destinations, and skill levels.

Starting with the fall of the so-called Iron Curtain in Eastern Europe and the growing globalization of economic activity, policymakers and voters in many countries, including the United States, Spain, and France, have paid more attention to cross-border migration, legal and otherwise. Photos or reports of African children drowning off the Sicilian island of Lampedusa, smugglers forcing Somali migrants out of boats and into shark-infested waters near Yemen, or Mexicans foiling U.S. border patrols, for example, plus loud voices decrying the entrance of nondocumented newcomers have helped to transform immigration into a serious issue in the United States, European Union countries, and Australia, among others.

Yet, despite heightened concern, data on international migration remain suspect (Lemaitre, 2005). First, definitions of international immigrants differ. The UN's definition, for instance, is not the same as definitions used by some nations and private groups. This makes it difficult to collect comparable data. Second, the term "immigrant" lumps together many cross-border movers (e.g., asylum-seekers, long-term students, conflict-diamond runners, children joining their family). So beware: The reasons why people move across national borders—which could be important to policymakers and citizens alike—exist only in guesstimates. And without knowing why movers move (e.g., lack of jobs, persecution, drought), it is difficult to design workable policies to respond to cross-border migration.

Still, we do know that in recent years immigration to richer countries has increased. Indeed, in Europe immigration has started to change the faces of the continent. African and North African migrants may be the most talked about (or feared?) in some capitals, but Eastern Europeans and Chinese are moving westward in unprecedented numbers. For example, in 2004 when Latvia and nine other countries joined the European Union, nearly 450,000 migrants, mainly from the poorest edges of former Soviet-controlled Eastern Europe, legally migrated to the then job-rich economies of Western Europe, especially Ireland, Britain, and Sweden.

Also, Chinese migration to Europe mushroomed, particularly to Italy and Spain. In less than one decade—1991–2000—Chinese residents rose in Italy from 18,700 to 48,650, an increase of 260 percent. Spain saw a sixfold increase during the same decade. By 2000, the number of Chinese legally resident in Europe was estimated to be 200,000 (Laczko, 2003).

With such increases, debates over "proper" public policies toward immigration—long volatile concerns—have become even more explosive. In Europe, voices in the migration debate range from "Euroskeptic" restrictionists to open-border advocates; multiculturalists to assimilationists; those seeking national solutions to those looking for global solutions to those who disagree about asylum (arguing it is or isn't in crisis). Politically, Far Right parties (e.g., the National Front in France) define immigration as a key issue, but they are not alone. Swiss elections in 2007 focused on immigration issues, and no doubt, being "tough" on immigrants did not harm Nicolas Sarkozy's successful bid for the presidency of France in 2007.

For complex reasons of identity and history, resistance to migration may be stronger in Europe than in the United States, Canada, Australia, New Zealand, and other countries built on immigration. At least one might expect that. Nonetheless, anti-immigration parties and calls for harsher treatment of asylum-seekers have emerged in Australia and other countries built on immigration, including New Zealand. A post-2000 survey in New Zealand shows that a large group there believes that there are "too many Asians" in the country (Lintner, 2003).

In the United States, how (and how much) to control immigration (of mainly illegal or nondocumented migrants) is an issue of highly-contested national concern. Controversy and emotion envelop discussions of the presumed effects of the newcomers on the economy, the polity, and the society. Among the hot-button issues: language. For example, in anticipation of the Bears–Colts Super Bowl game in 2007, the *Chicago Tribune* ran a headline in Spanish—"Vivan los Osos" (and underneath, in smaller type, "Spanish for 'Long live the Bears'"). Some readers responded angrily. One said, "Do you people understand that the national language in this country is English, not Spanish, and to have to look at this is incredibly offensive. It is offensive! These people, these Hispanics, come to this country…[and] give nothing to this society…" (in Poynter Institute, 2007). Furthermore, proponents and opponents of less open borders cite different statistics to buoy their deeply-held opinions.

Research studies do not agree on the impact of immigrants on U.S.-born workers. On the one hand, University of California at Davis economist Giovanni Peri concludes that "Most of the immigrants [who come to California]—because of skills that are different from U.S.-born workers—take different jobs than American workers take" (in Henricks, 2007:B10). But a study by Harvard economist George J. Borjas (2004) shows the opposite: There are negative effects on U.S.-born workers by immigrants. According to Borjas, "By increasing the supply of labor between 1980 and 2000, immigration reduced the average annual earnings of native-born men by an estimated $1,700 or roughly 4 percent."

Whichever, attitudes seem to be hardening against immigrants, legal or not. In richer, receiving nations, such as England, the United States, and France, fear and loathing of the "other" are common. For example, a 2005 survey (Rohan, 2006) found that more than one-third of French respondents said they were "racist." Asked about their main fears for French society, the respondents' list was topped by unemployment (27 percent) and insecurity (16 percent); "different cooking smells" and lifestyles were others. (These are often code words for fear of "them": in this case, non-Christian non-Europeans, Christian black Africans, or Christian Eastern Europeans.) Similarly, in Great Britain, a major BBC survey (Cowley, 2002) revealed that 44 percent of Britons polled believed immigration had damaged Britain over the last 50 years. A Field Poll of California voters (released in November 2007) showed that immigration and border protection topped the list of voter concerns in the state, well ahead of public education and the economy (Chorneau, 2007:B1). (For various reasons, immigration was barely mentioned by any U.S. presidential candidate in 2008.)

The reasons for such opinions are much disputed. But contemporary anti-immigrant sentiments in the United States often seem like echoes of nineteenth-century fears, discussed earlier in this chapter, by white Protestants toward Catholic, European immigrants.

INTERNAL MIGRANTS

There is yet another group of migrants—some 25 million persons in about 50 countries—who receive far less publicity or are overlooked altogether (Deng, 2007): people who are *internally displaced* and remain unprotected by any government. (The UN's Guiding Principles on Internal Displacement define internally displaced populations, or IDPs, like this: "persons or groups of persons who have been forced or obliged to flee or to leave their homes or places of habitual residence, in particular as a result of or in order to avoid the effects of armed conflict, situations of generalized violence, violations of human rights or natural or manmade disasters, and who have not crossed an internationally recognized state border.") [The Office of the High Commissioner for Human Rights, 1998] MIT's Francis Deng (2007) claims that the crisis is global, but "the worst hit is Africa, with more than half the world's internally displaced."

To conclude: Fear of being overwhelmed by "them" is far from new. In western Europe, it may date (at least) to 25,000 years ago: to confrontations in southwest France between the intellectually- and technologically-superior Cro-Magnons and the smaller, sloped-headed Neanderthals. Cro-Magnons probably engaged in ethnic cleansing, wiping out Neanderthals. (*Sidenote:* One notion holds that the Cro-Magnons were victorious because they domesticated dogs, which barked and thus warned when attackers neared. But we can only guess about that because no written records exist. What the Cro-Magnons did leave for posterity are still-exquisite cave paintings in southwest France.)

In recent times, more people from poor countries have been migrating to richer countries. Their reasons vary, from hope for a better life to survival from persecution or worse. Likewise, attitudes toward newcomers vary widely. In richer countries, a person's stand on immigration often depends upon where he or she sits: Employers seeking cheap labor and landlords seeking renters for low-end dwellings, to take just two examples, may welcome unskilled immigrants. But middle-class taxpayers, nationalists, and people living on borders may feel overwhelmed and overrun. Further, some worry about environmental damage caused by people fleeing their homelands. In the meantime, immigration remains an extremely divisive and hotly-debated issue in many countries.

THE NEED FOR NEW U.S. MODELS

Decades ago, Chicago became a lab for social theorists as European immigrants poured into the City of the Big Shoulders. Researchers at the University of Chicago constructed models charting the immigrants' adaptations to urban-industrial life. Louis Wirth wrote about *The Ghetto* ([1928] 1956) and how its eastern European Jewish residents dispersed over time. E. W. Burgess constructed his zonal model of urban space, hypothesizing a link between immigrants' economic success and their assimilation over time. Burgess's notion of assimilation has been summed up as follows: "[European immigrants] came in, struggled hard, were discriminated against, lived in the ghetto. Eventually they climbed up, their children of the third generation went to a university, they joined the mainstream, and they are now Americans" (Portes in Coughlin, 1993:A11).

Does Burgess's model work for post-1965 immigrants from Latin America and Asia? Are new immigrants following the pattern of earlier immigrants, assimilating as they climb the ladder of economic success? Some think so. Sociologists Richard Alba and Victor Nee ([2003] 2005) write that assimilation continues to mold the immigrant experience even if the geography of immigration has changed, from Europe to Latin America and Asia. This assimilation, they say, is fueled by the decisions of immigrants and their children to better their social and material circumstances in the United States. Exploring several domains, including intermarriage, language, and housing patterns, they hold that assimilation continues to be important.

Others disagree. A leading contemporary immigration researcher, Alejandro Portes, thinks that older models of immigration don't explain what's happening now. Indeed, Portes and his colleagues say that at least one group of new immigrants, Cubans in Miami, are turning the old model on its head. Plus, according to Portes (2002), there are new "global villagers" who defy previous models.

CUBANS IN MIAMI

Just as Chicago once served as a laboratory for the study of eastern and southern European immigration, Miami has become a social lab for Latin American immigration. Why? Partly because Miami is a polarizing concept as well as a city: Anti-immigration voices view Miami as a nightmare, where immigrants dominate and Denny's is an ethnic eatery. But for others, Miami stands as a rather new model of accommodation, where immigrants are neither totally assimilated nor totally marginalized.

In less than one generation, Miami and its county, Miami-Dade, were transformed from a somewhat down-at-the-mouth retirement and tourism center into the transcultural, northern capital of Latin America. This began in 1959, during the so-called cold war and an anti-Castro exodus from Cuba. During the first wave of immigration, mainly well-off, educated Cuban immigrants flocked to south Florida, particularly to Miami-Dade County. It is noteworthy that

these Cubans were welcomed into the United States, seen generally as refugees from Communism.

By the year 2000, "Little Havana," a predominantly Cuban neighborhood just west of Miami's downtown, had a population of more than 91,000. Hialeah, another city in Miami-Dade County (best known for its once-gracious racetrack) had a population of 226,419 residents with a Cuban majority (62 percent).

By 2000, Cubans and other Latinos made up about 66 percent of Miami's total population. These relative newcomers changed—and strained—relationships with several non-Latino groups in Miami. For example, working-class whites left Miami as Spanish-speaking enclaves grew. White business leaders didn't understand how Cubans could be so economically successful without joining mainstream business and civic organizations. Later, Haitians, who faced widespread prejudice, were frustrated by the special treatment that Cubans received in immigration matters.

As Cubans were making a new life for themselves in Miami, scholars explored the possibility that they exemplified a new model of immigration. At the forefront of this scholarly interest were two social scientists: Cuban-born sociologist Alejandro Portes and California-born anthropologist Alex Stepick. They said in 1993 that the city was being transformed by Cuban newcomers, not the reverse: Instead of Cuban immigrants adapting to Miami, Miami adapted to the waves of Cuban immigrants. For example, instead of learning English and picking up American customs and *then* reaping political power and/or economic success—as many European immigrants did before them—Miami's Cubans *first* gained political and economic success and then began to adapt culturally.

As Portes and Stepick tell the city's story, Miami was a southern city founded in 1896. Unlike other U.S. cities of its day (which grew as centers of commerce or transportation or as central places), Miami had natural beauty on its side; it was developed as a tourist and retirement spot simply because it was a lovely site.

Then, in 1959, things started to change quickly. After the Cuban Revolution, groups of privileged Cubans fled to Miami. From 1959 to 1973, 500,000

Cuban refugees came to the city. Typically, these first Cuban immigrants were skilled, educated landowners or businesspeople. Some later moved out of Miami, but a large, occupationally diverse group remained—and prospered.

In large part, the first wave's prosperity was linked to a high degree of social cohesion (what Portes and Stepick call a "bounded solidarity") fueled by anti-Castro politics and a collective image of themselves as exiles waiting to return home. Many became successful in business and helped their compatriots. Some became bankers, granting "character loans" to fellow immigrants on the basis of their reputations alone (instead of the usual economic collateral).

In 1980, the second wave of over 100,000 Cuban immigrants came to Miami by boatlift. These immigrants, the so-called *marielitos* (named after the port of Mariel, Cuba), were less educated, less well-off financially, and less welcome (by both U.S. government officials and numerous first-wave Cubans). Many *marielitos* were black, and they faced prejudice and ostracism from some white Cuban exiles, African Americans, and black Haitians.

According to Portes and Stepick, 1980 was a turning point for Miami: The *marielitos* arrived, Haitian immigration reached its high point, and African Americans (many of whom considered themselves twice oppressed, by Cubans as well as by whites) rioted in Liberty City. In addition, the white power structure in 1980 was no longer sure that "they" (Cubans) would turn into "us" (Anglos). By this time, it was becoming clear that the immigrants would not fade into Miami's background and assimilate.

To date, Miami's Cubans have neither faded away nor melted in. Instead, they have maintained an ethnic enclave. And they have played key roles in mainstream politics and economics. Further, in a relatively short time, they have helped to transform Miami into a bicultural metropolis.

Various observers point to the Cubans' networks and cultural practices as key to their rather spectacular economic success in Miami (e.g., Portes and Zhou, 1992). But Ramón Grosfoguel (2003), to take just one dissenting voice, thinks that such thinking is merely a new version of the "culture of poverty" concept—and wrong. Sociologist Grosfoguel says that the "neoculture of poverty" approach blames the victims who did not climb the success ladder, dismissing or underplaying massive U.S. government aid to Cubans in south Florida, including English-language training and health assistance.

Some observers, including Stepick, claim that Miami is the most internationalized U.S. city because in Miami, they say, the rules of the game for newcomers were not dictated by white Protestants. Instead, Miami-Dade County has undergone a dramatic upsurge of biculturalism, notably the effort (opposed by organizations such as U.S. English) to include Spanish as well as English as a language of record for some city and county proceedings.

To conclude: Miami, Florida, is unlike most U.S. cities. First, it is dominated by immigrants (Latinos, mainly Cubans) and their language (Spanish), not English. Second, it is widely viewed as the *de facto* capital of another geographical region: Latin America.

In the United States, feelings about Miami tend to mirror ideological positions. Some (typically not liberals or libertarians) fear that Miami's immigrants and their language represent a trend that is undermining American culture and identity. For social conservatives in particular, and those opposed to immigration in general, Miami is a bad dream come true. For some radicals, Miami's immigrant population is not just any old success story. Rather, it shows how government policy can help some groups (i.e., the first wave of Cubans) to "make it." For some scholars, the case of Cubans in Miami suggests the notion that bicultural living can be an alternative to assimilation in U.S. cities. But, Miami's bicultural model may have very limited application in the United States. First, there was a critical mass of Cubans and other Spanish speakers; by 1990 metropolitan Miami was 49 percent Hispanic. Second, the first wave of Cubans included many who were already economically successful and who brought "cultural capital," including education, particular attitudes, and social know-how. (See Chapter 11 for a discussion of this concept.) First-wave Cubans were also united by political ideology and self-image, enabling them to surmount many obstacles typically faced by immigrant groups. In other words, Miami may represent a unique case.

Finally, a word on Miami's biculturalism. It is important to note that racial and ethnic tension have not disappeared in Miami. Quite the contrary. Biculturalism for Latinos has not brought acceptance for all other ethnic groups—least of all for black people. Haitian immigrants, for one group, face enormous prejudice and have not been welcomed to south Florida (Stepick and Foner, 1997). According to a study by Dario Moreno of Florida International University [in Williams, 2008:2], Miami-Dade County (with about an 18 percent African American population as of 2008) was the scene of occasional riots directed at Hispanics, complaints by non-Spanish-speaking citizens that jobs are hard to get, and the consequent flight and "brain drain" of middle-class African Americans. These events, plus racial slurs by Hispanics against African Americans, portend an uneasy future for racial and ethnic harmony in Miami.

Chicanos–Latinos in Miami or Los Angeles are not united by political ideology or self-image, but they may represent another bicultural alternative. And there is yet another possible model: "global villagers."

"GLOBAL VILLAGERS"

According to Alejandro Portes (2002), there is a fairly recent phenomenon that bears notice: communities that span national borders. A cross-border Mexico–Brooklyn network is exemplary: When farmers in Ticuani, Mexico, wanted cleaner water, they asked a private civic group, the Ticuani Potable Water Committee, to assist. And it did, quickly raising money for and installing new tubing to bring clean water to Ticuani. Unremarkable? On the contrary. Why? Because the water committee was located in faraway Brooklyn, New York, not Mexico; and it was not composed of immigrants sending money home or flying back to assist with the laying of water tubing. Instead, thanks to modern communications, the water committee was able to complete this transnational project, far from its first in 20+ years of existence. The transnational group's motto succinctly states its attitude: "Por el Progreso de Ticuani: Los Ausentes Siempre Presentes. Ticuani y New York"("For the Progress of Ticuani: The Absent Ones, Always Present").

According to Portes (2002), these transnational communities are a by-product of improved communications, better transportation, and free-trade laws. In a sense, Portes claims, these transnational communities are labor's analogue to the multinational corporation. Unlike their corporate siblings, however, their assets consist chiefly of shared information, trust, and contacts. As the members of these communities travel back and forth, they carry cultural and political currents in both directions.

Portes says that most people in the United States expect immigrants to come to the United States, earn a living, and send money home to relatives. But "in transnational communities the money often flows in the other direction." He cites, for example, a study of Chinese immigrants in the New York area, which shows that Chinese immigrants troll for capital abroad in Hong Kong and Taiwan, among other places, to finance new banks in the Flushing area of Queens in New York City.

Portes (2002) concludes that the emergence of such transnational communities complicates our understanding of global trade, immigration, and national identity. (*Note*: Portes is far from alone in studying transnational communities. For example, members of the multidisciplinary Urban China Research Network examine both internal Chinese migration and Chinese–U.S. migration.)

Clearly, such transnational communities do not fit neatly into any classic models of city form and space (Chapter 16) or immigration to the United States. Thus, implicitly, Portes calls for new models.

ANOTHER LOOK

People have been on the move since time immemorial. Fossil evidence and genetic studies suggest that the ancestors of modern humans began leaving Africa 100,000–50,000 years ago; geneticists and paleoanthropologists disagree on the exact timing (Gibbons, 2007).

Historically, how important are these migrations? Very, according to many. A UN document claims that exoduses and migratory flows have been "a major determinant" of human history (United Nations, 2006), and an anthropologist says that human migration is "one of the greatest untold stories in the history of mankind" (Goebel in Perlman, 2007:A9).

Early human migration is dimly understood. But discovered tools, genetic studies of human fossil remains, and a skull from South Africa offer hints about early migration. In particular, a treasure trove site on the Don River in Russia, called Kostenki, shows that humans reached as far north as Russia about 42,000–45,000 years ago.

Large, intercontinental movements began in the sixteenth century, when Europe settled colonies. Since about 1800, migration rose to an unprecedented level, owing mainly to the impact on labor of economic globalization.

Today, the number of people living outside their country of birth is larger than at any other time in history. The number nearly doubled during the last 50 years, reaching 191 million in 2005.

Women now constitute almost half of all migrants. The number of those *forced* into migration—for virtual sexual or economy slavery—is highly disputed.

Worldwide, over 36 million people migrated to another country between 1990 and 2005, and the vast majority (33 million) settled in richer, industrialized countries: Today, one of every four migrants lives in North America and one of every three in Europe. Why? Hope, in large measure: People from poorer countries hope for better lives in richer nations, particularly as the global economy has emphasized, not reduced, inequality between nations.

In coming years, demographers predict even greater mass migrations globally. Given economic hard times, we can predict that some newcomers to rich, receiving countries will be greeted with distrust or a racist backlash. European nations and the United States already face either deadly anti-immigrant sentiment and/or efforts to limit immigration.

Issues surrounding migration are complex and sensitive. When people from one culture are introduced into another culture, suspicion, fear, and/or xenophobia can—and often do—follow.

In scholarly work about U.S. cities, there is an ongoing debate about immigrants' adjustment. On the one hand, some theorists see *cultural characteristics* as the primary reason that one group "makes it" or lags behind. In this view, factors such as family structure, moral values, and attitudes toward time and education lie behind a group's success or failure. Research in the "culture of poverty" tradition exemplifies this view. On the other hand, some theorists focus on *structural factors* such as the immigrants' social class backgrounds and role in the global economy. Light and Bonacich's (1988) study of Korean immigrant entrepreneurs is exemplary.

Shall never the twain meet? Are structuralists and culturalists doomed to talk past each another? As we shall see in Chapter 10, there are fledgling attempts to merge the two traditions of culture and structure.

KEY TERMS

Clientelistic hostility Hostility triggered by a situation in which neighborhood small businesses are owned by members of one ethnic group and shoppers come from other ethnic groups.

Ethnic Refers to people with a sense of group identity different from that of other subgroups within a society. Ethnicity can be based on secular or sacred identity, national ancestry, race, or religious background (and, in some observers' view, sexual orientation).

Global city Sociologist Saskia Sassen's term for cities such as New York, London, and Tokyo that act as command posts in the international economy. Typically, international finance and advanced business services undergird a global city's worldwide role. Synonym: *headquarters city* (Chapter 5).

WASP Acronym for white Anglo-Saxon Protestant.

PROJECTS

1. **Ethnicity**. Determine the two largest ethnic groups in your community. Find out when each group first settled there, where they lived, what work they did, and what institutions they built (e.g., churches, newspapers, private schools, clubs). Trace the changes over time from their arrival until today. Do members of each group cluster together in residential sections? What areas do they live in? What kinds of jobs do they hold now? Are their institutions still viable?

2. **Family history**. Use available research tools—including oral histories of relatives, genealogy charts, library documents, archival materials, family diaries, and Internet sites—to establish your family's ethnic

history and consciousness. If Native American, where is your family rooted? If not Native American, when did they arrive here? What type of work did they do upon arrival in this country? What is their occupational profile today? Have family members spread out geographically? If they spoke another language, can your generation speak this language? Are there any regular gatherings (e.g., annual family reunions, cousins' club get-togethers)? What distinctive ethnic traditions do you retain, if any? Do most of your friends come from your ethnic background? In what ways, if any, do you feel set apart from members of other ethnic groups?

3. **Immigration, past and present**. Compare and contrast attitudes toward "old" immigrants from earlier decades and "new" immigrants who arrived in the past decade or so. Using the method of content analysis, examine the positions and logics of a range of social and political groups toward immigrants. Next, analyze the rhetoric describing newcomers from various commentators and citizens.

SUGGESTIONS FOR FURTHER LEARNING

A growing number of museums celebrate immigrant and emigrant experiences. Edward Rothstein notes in "Mining the Past, Identity Museums Forge a Future" (*International Herald Tribune*, July 2, 2008: 20) that a museum in the Seattle, Washington, neighborhood of Ballard—in a state where 17 percent of the residents claim Nordic ancestry—celebrates Nordic peoples.

Among the most exciting heritage museums are New York City's Ellis Island Immigrant Museum, the building (now restored) where 12 million immigrants landed, and the Deutsches Auswanderer Haus (Emigrant Center) in Bremerhaven, Germany. The Emigration Center, opened in 2005. Winner of the European Museum of the Year Award in 2007, it features exhibits about the ocean voyages of some of the 7+ million Germans to Ellis Island and beyond between 1830 and 1974.

The darker side of arriving at Ellis Island is captured in Stephen Wilkes's images of *Ellis Island: Ghosts of Freedom* (New York: W.W. Norton, 2006). Wilkes's photos depict the south side of Ellis Island, where would-be immigrants who did not pass health inspection were held. Some perished in confinement there, a mere mile away from new beginnings in New York City.

On New York City's Lower East Side (Figure 9.6a), one tenement where many immigrants first lived is preserved as part of the Lower East Side Tenement Museum (Figure 9.6b). The museum offers tours of the restored 1863 tenement and the Lower East Side. On the West Coast, the Japanese American National Museum in Los Angeles documents various aspects of *Issei* pioneers (first-generation immigrants from Japan) from 1885 to 1924 as well as later emigrants. In the Midwest, the Immigration History Research Center at the University of Minnesota in Minneapolis has storerooms of materials on European immigration.

Perhaps the most widely-read book on the history of the mass migrations from Europe to the United States in the nineteenth century remains Oscar Handlin's *The Uprooted* (Boston: Little, Brown, 1952). Winner of the Pulitzer Prize when first published, it is an impressionistic account with relatively little empirical evidence. Handlin focuses on the loss of the Old World peasant community and the sense of alienation resulting in a new individualism. He makes few distinctions between differential adjustments to urban life among various European immigrant groups. Today, this classic work is widely viewed as Eurocentric.

Scholarly study of the immigrant experience is enhanced by a series published by Arno Press (New York). A multivolume series on the experience of Italian Americans, the American Catholic tradition, the Puerto Rican experience, the Chicano heritage, and the Chinese and Japanese in North America includes literary chronicles as well as social science and personal accounts. Arno Press also publishes two series, called The American Immigration Collection (74 books) and The Reports of the Immigration Commission, popularly known as the Dillingham Reports. This 41-volume series, originally published between 1907 and 1910, provides fascinating clues to the legislation enacted between 1917 and 1924 that closed America's gates to immigrants. The Dillingham Reports presented what they felt to be scientific proof of the inferiority of eastern and southern Europeans.

Personal memoirs of immigrants include Mary Antin, *From Plotzk to Boston* (Boston: Clarke, 1899), and Thomas C. Wheeler, ed., *The Immigrant Experience: The*

a

Fig. 9.6. (*a*) HESTER STREET. In the 1890s, east European Jews lived on the Lower East Side, New York City's most densely populated area. One of the neighborhood's most crowded spots was Hester Street. Almost anything could be purchased there, and new arrivals would line up, waiting for employers seeking cheap labor. Over a generation ago, a feature film about the assimilation process of two young Russian Jewish immigrants, titled *Hester Street* (1975), focused on two young Russian Jewish immigrants' different adjustments to New York City in 1896. (*b*) 97 ORCHARD STREET. Once a six-storey tenement that housed immigrants straight off the boat, this building is now part of the Lower East Side Tenement Museum. Scholars are trying to identify each of its approximately 7,000 residents from 1863 to 1939, including waves of Germans, east European Jews, Sephardic Jews, Irish, and Italians in the 1920s. The project is one of relatively few urban historic preservations amid preserved log cabins, antebellum mansions, and other rural U.S. sites. ([*a*] Library of Congress, [*b*] Martin Gorosh)

b

Fig. 9.6 (*continued*)

Anguish of Becoming American (New York: Pelican, [1971] 1977). Selections include "A Chinese Evolution" by Jade Snow Wong, "Italians in Hell's Kitchen" by Mario Puzo, and "Norwegians on the Prairie" by Eugene Boe.

In *Immigration and American Popular Culture: An Introduction*, Rachel Rubin and Jeffrey Melnick (New York: New York University Press, 2006) showcase contributions of immigrants to U.S. popular culture as performers and entrepreneurs.

The internal migration of African Americans and whites from the South to the North from 1900 to 1950 is detailed in Neil Fligstein's *Going North* (New York: Academic Press, 1981). After 1930, Fligstein concluded, the chief reason for both black and white migration north was the transformation of cotton agriculture from a labor-intensive, tenant economy to a capitalist, machine-oriented economy.

In *The Promised Land: The Great Black Migration and How It Changed America* (New York: Knopf, 1991), Nicholas Lemann focuses on African American migration from the South to Chicago since the 1950s. It describes the impact of the War on Poverty by following specific families north from the sharecropper culture of the Mississippi Delta, creating a tale of three cities: Clarksdale, Mississippi; Washington, D.C.; and Chicago. Among other things it shows that scholars can influence government policy: Sociologists Richard Cloward and Lloyd Ohlin actively contributed in the effort to alleviate ethnic tensions in Chicago and the nation. Author and scholar Gary Wills deems this book "indispensable" for understanding African American history. He puts Taylor Branch's *Parting the Waters* (New York: Simon and Schuster, 1988) in the same category.

Painter Jacob Lawrence chronicled the African American exodus from the South to northern cities after World War I. His Migration Series, a cycle of 60 paintings finished in 1941 when he was 23, traveled to nine U.S. cities in the mid-1990s.

The plight of rural migrants is told in the works of John Steinbeck, particularly *The Grapes of Wrath* (New York: Viking, [1939] 1972). The movie version of Steinbeck's novel of the Joad family, starring Henry Fonda, appeared in 1940.

The Worst Hard Time: The Untold Story of Those Who Survived the Great American Dust Bowl by Timothy Egan (Boston: Houghton Mifflin, 2005) details how drought, the Depression, and reckless farming produced an ecological and human disaster in spring 1935. The plains—from the Dakotas to parts of Texas—weren't suited to farming, but grassland was plowed up to plant wheat. (Buffalo there had long since been decimated.) The result in the view of many: an un-natural disaster—millions of acres of topsoil were lifted by winds in black blizzards and resultant human tragedy.

In his autobiography *Black Boy* (New York: Signet, [1937] 1963), Richard Wright related his hopes when heading north on a train for Chicago: "With ever watchful eyes and bearing scars, visible and invisible, I headed North, full of a hazy notion that life could be lived with dignity" (285). The escape from the home of an uncle who had just been lynched by a white mob was just one memory of his early life in Mississippi.

Starting in the early 1990s, global migration and transnational identities became popular topics in many disciplines and interdisciplines. See, for example, Karen McCarthy Brown's *Mama Lola: A Vodou Priestess in Brooklyn* (Berkeley: University of California Press, 1992). Brown, a professor of sociology and anthropology of religion, traces five generations of voodoo priesthood in Mama Lola's family, from Haiti to Brooklyn, and the mix of Catholic, French, and West African influences in the practical religion of voodoo. See also Ron Kelley, Jonathan Friedlander, and Anita Colby, eds., *Irangeles: Iranians in Los Angeles* (Berkeley: University of California Press, 1993).

The film *Menace II Society* (1993) opens with a shocking murder of Korean grocery store owners in Los Angeles and ends with the death of a teenager in the ghetto. In between, it shows what Allen and Albert Hughes, the then 21-year-old twins who directed the movie, called the ghetto: "a concrete Vietnam" where people kill over dollars, women, and turf.

Los Angeles's Olvera Street (San Francisco, Calif.: Arcadia Publishing, 2006) by William D. Estrada features the "home of Latino culture" in the Los Angeles region. Historian Estrada, curator of El Pueblo Historical Monument, highlights the marketplace and 1820s-built plaza on this downtown street where over 1 million people visit each year.

People on the borders of two nations live in a special human environment. For a historical account of the French and Spanish on the Pyrenees Mountains' frontier, in French, see *Frontières et identités nationals: La France et l'Espagne dans les Pyrénées depuis le XVIIe siècle* by Peter Sahlins, Bernard Lepetit, and Geoffroy de Laforcade (Paris: Belin, 2000).

The Namesake (2007), a movie directed by Indian-born, Harvard-educated Mira Nair, tells the tale of one upwardly mobile family of immigrants who move from Calcutta to New York City. They are torn between tradition and modernity.

In *This Land Is Our Land: Immigrants and Power in Miami* (Berkeley: University of California Press, 2003), Alex Stepick and his social scientist coauthors focus on interethnic relations, arguing that immigration is not a simple "us" vs. "them" phenomenon. They start with the notion that "becoming American" is not a one-way street.

Cuban Miami by Robert M. Levine and Moises Asis (New Brunswick, N.J.: Rutgers University Press, 2000) presents a photographic record of Cuban migration to Miami. The book is a feast for the eyes, including over 180 photographs plus original cartoons drawn for the book.

Dominican American Junot Diaz's Pulitzer Prize–winning novel *The Brief Wondrous Life of Oscar Wao* (New York: Riverhead Books, 2007) tells the story of Oscar, a first-generation Dominican American. The novel deals with issues of immigration, nationhood, and nationality. It carries a motif of *fukú*, the curse and doom of the New World.

For a social anthropological discussion of various groups living outside their original homeland, plus a theoretical perspective, see the work of Michel S. Laguerre. For a scholarly discussion of one group's diaspora, particularly in New York City, see *Diasporic Citizenship: Haitian Americans in Transnational America* (New York: Palgrave Macmillan [1998] 2006) by Michel S. Laguerre. Professor Laguerre, a Haitian American, argues that the role of the nation-state has changed, becoming more and more impotent in the presence of transnational practices used by residents. In *Urban Multiculturalism and Globalization in New York City: An Analysis of Diasporic Temporalities* (New York: Palgrave Macmillan, 2004), Laguerre discusses various cultural rhythms in the United States, a transglobal nation, including those of Muslim and Jewish life. In *Diaspora, Politics, and Globalization* (New York: Palgrave Macmillan, 2006), Laguerre looks at the Haitian diaspora from a global perspective, offering a new theory of interconnectedness in migration.

English novelist Zadie Smith creates a multiracial cast of characters who inhabit a world of class, race, and political conflicts in *On Beauty* (London: Penguin, 2006). Writing in an often hilarious tone, Smith presents a cast of characters who surround two opposing scholars in a U.S. college town (1) a self-absorbed, working-class British white man married to an African American woman, parents of three light-skinned children, and (2) a West Indian stuffed-shirt.

Race and ethnicity in U.S. cities is a continuing theme in both social science and literature. For essays on a variety of contemporary ethnic groups in New York City, including Greek Americans, Italians, Muslims, and Puerto Ricans, see *Race and Ethnicity in New York City*, volume 7 (Greenwich, Conn.: JAI Press, 2005) edited by J. Krase and Ray Hutchison.

In *Ethnic Origins: The Adaptation of Cambodian and Hmong Refugees in Four American Cities* (New York: Russell Sage Foundation, 2006), Jeremy Hein notes that culture and history count in the adaptation of immigrants. His comparison of the experience of two Southeast Asian refugee groups, marked by similar regional origins and levels of competence in English, reveals differing patterns of adjustment, which, he claims, are related to their culture. For example, Hein says the Hmong are highly collective in their outlook, while the Cambodians are individualistic. Thus, Hein says, Hmong tend to preserve their group solidarity and discourage intermarriage, but Cambodians have a weak collective identity in the United States and are more open to pan-Asian identities. Hein also says that refugees in small towns face much more racism than those in large cities.

Among novels with themes of immigration and ethnicity, one stands out for the controversy it inspired: *The Camp of the Saints*. First published in 1973 in French and translated into English by Jeremy Leggatt in 1994, it was republished in 2000 (New York: Ace Books). In this parable, perhaps meant to scare Europeans, author Jean Raspail argues that immigration (legal or not) negatively impacts a nation's national security as well as its environment, crime, and economy. Raspail claims that immigration from poor, non-European countries to the West threatens the relatively democratic and "civilized," Western cultures. Many immigration restrictionists praise this novel as a clear view of the future; critics call it racist and wrong.

In the United States, interest in Raspail's novel grew after *The Atlantic Monthly* magazine featured a cover story by historians Matthew Connelly and Paul Kennedy, "Must It Be the Rest Against the West?" in December 1994; the cover featured a reference to Raspail's novel. However, the article suggested ways to *avoid* Raspail's implied scenario: global apartheid of rich vs. poor. For a scathing rebuttal to Raspail and to Connelly and Kennedy, see "The White Man's Barbecue" by the Committee on Women, Population and the Environment (http://www.cwpe.org/issues/dangerous_html/dangerous2.html).

One-time U.S. presidential nominee and longtime conservative TV commentator Patrick J. Buchanan shares Raspail's vision. In *State of Emergency: The Third World Invasion and Conquest of America* (New York: Thomas Dunne, 2006), Buchanan warns that Western countries risk death by drowning under waves of non-Western immigrants.

Why do migrants come from Mexico to the United States? Do migrants go home again? Such questions are explored by Sam Quinones in *Antonio's Gun and Delfino's Dream: True Tales of Mexican Migration* (Albuquerque: University of New Mexico Press, 2007). U.S. reporter Quinones spent 10 years in Mexico, traveling to Mexican villages and interviewing migrants.

Spike Lee's 1989 movie *Do the Right Thing* (available on DVD) is widely considered to be a "classic." It dramatizes two instances of clientelistic hostility in the Bedford-Stuyvesant neighborhood of Brooklyn: (1) Sal, an Italian American pizza parlor owner, versus his African American customers and (2) a Korean small businessman versus his African American customers.

Films and video that depict immigrants' adjustment to urban America include *Becoming American* (New Day Films), a documentary which follows a preliterate tribal farm family from Laos to refugee camps in Thailand and their new home in Seattle. It records their culture shock, community reactions, and their gradual adaptation to urban life.

A Chicano arts movement, born about a half-century ago in Los Angeles, was the subject of a show at the Los Angeles County Museum of Art in 2008. Art in the collection of actor Cheech Marin, including works by arts pioneer Diane Gamboa (b. 1957), were featured.

In *Deflecting Immigration: Networks, Markets, and Regulation in Los Angeles* (New York: Russell Sage, [2006] 2008), Ivan Light, whose joint study of Koreans in Los Angeles was discussed in this chapter, argues that chain migration can be effected by local policy. In Los Angeles, between 1980 and 2000, Light says, about 1 million Latinos were "deflected" to other U.S. cities, serving to help "nationalize" a regional immigration issue. Los Angeles accomplished this by various measures, including the enforcement of housing ordinances that made homeownership in the city's suburbs unaffordable.

Journalist Robert Scheer's essay "The Jews of Los Angeles" in *Thinking Tuna Fish, Talking Death* (New York: Hill and Wang, 1988) remains a fascinating study of some descendants of east European Jews. Irving Howe wrote about their ancestors in *World of Our Fathers: The Journey of the East European Jews to America and the Life They Found and Made* (New York: Simon and Schuster, 1976).

In *Whitewashed Adobe: The Rise of Los Angeles and the Remaking of Its Mexican Past* (Los Angeles: University of California Press, 2005), history professor William Deverell chronicles six events in Los Angeles, including the outbreak of bubonic plague in 1924. He argues that Los Angeles, once part of Mexico, obliterated the area's Mexican connections.

Most literature on international migration focuses on freer trade and the mobility of capital—but not the mobility of workers. One exception is *International Migration: Globalization's Last Frontier* by Jonathon W. Moses (London: Zed Books, 2006). Moses argues for the free mobility of people across borders, just as there is free movement of goods and capital.

Since the mid-1990s, there has been an outpouring of novels chronicling the lives of new U.S. immigrants. These include Ethiopian-born Dinaw Mengustu's *The Beautiful Things that Heaven Bears* (New York: Riverhead Press, 2007); Korean-born Chang-rae Lee's *Native Speaker* (New York: Riverhead Press, 1996), and Chinese-born Ha Jin's *A Free Life* (New York: Pantheon, 2007).

Numerous feature films capture aspects of migration and ethnic life. The rhythms of preindustrial life for late nineteenth-century peasants in northern Italy, eventually kicked off the land, are portrayed in Italian director Ermanno Olmi's masterpiece *The Tree of Wooden Clogs* (1978). Charlie Chaplin's silent film classic *The Immigrant* (1917) contrasts the promise and pain of immigration through the character of the baggy-trousered Little Tramp. Franco Brusati's *Bread and Chocolate* (1974) is a poignant satire about an Italian immigrant in Switzerland who wants to assimilate so badly that he dyes his hair blond. Khaled Hosseini's 2005 novel (New York: Riverhead Press) about an Afghani-American who returns to Afghanistan, *The Kite Runner*, was made into a movie in 2007. Wayne Wang's *Eat a Bowl of Tea* (1989) and Peter Wang's *A Great Wall* (1986) deal with Chinese American adjustments and readjustments to urban America.

Sociologists Min Zhou and Carl L. Bankston ask hard questions about why some immigrant groups do better than others in *Growing Up American: How Vietnamese Children Adapt to Life in the United States* (New York: Russell Sage Foundation, 1999).

Among the numerous studies about groups living outside their original homeland in the diaspora is Minoo Moallem, "Ethnicity for Sale: The Gendering of Persian Carpets in the National and Transnational Markets." She argues that for over 100 years the Persian (note: not "Iranian") carpet "has become an important part of the Iranian national identity." Her paper was presented at the Diaspora and Homeland Development Conference held at the University of California at Berkeley on April 13, 2004, sponsored by the Berkeley Center for Globalization and Information Technology.

The telephone, the Internet, and an older technology—radio—help keep some in the diaspora connected to their original homeland. For one, Radio Bilingüe, a multilingual public radio network (with over 60 affiliates in the United States and Canada) in Fresno, California, links families and friends. News and information is read in Spanish, Mixteco (the language of Oaxaca, Mexico), English, and Hmong (a Laotian language).

Rap music often reflects the rage of people who feel disenfranchised. Looking backward, rapper Ice Cube's "Black Korea" (1991) has a prophetic ring. Recorded before the burning of Los Angeles's Koreatown in 1992, it warns Korean merchants to show more respect to African Americans or face the possibility that their stores will be burned down.

REFERENCES

Ablemann, Nancy, and John Lie. *1997. Blue Dreams: Korean Americans and the Los Angeles Riots* . Cambridge, MA: Harvard University Press.

Alba, Richard D., and Victor Nee. [2003] 2005. *Remaking the American Mainstream: Assimilation and Contemporary Immigration*. Cambridge, Mass.: Harvard University Press.

Antin, Mary. 1899. *From Plotzk to Boston*. Boston: Clarke.

Archibold, Randal C. 2007. "Racial hate feeds a gang war's senseless killing." *New York Times* (January 17): http://www.nytimes.com/2007/01/17/us/17race.html?th&emc=Th

Associated Press. 2003. "Census: Blacks moving back to the South at record pace." *St. Petersburg Times* (Oct. 31): http://www.sptimes.com/2003/10/31/Worldandnation/Census_Blacks_moving.shtml

Benet, Stephen Vincent. 1943. *Western Star*. New York: Farrar & Rinehart.

Borjas, George J. 2004. "Increasing the supply of labor through immigration: Measuring the impact on native-born workers." *Center for Immigration Studies* (May): http://www.cis.org/articles/2004/back504.html

Bullard, Robert D. [1990] 2000. *Dumping in Dixie: Race, Class, and Environmental Quality*. Boulder, Colo.: Westview.

Burgess, Ernest W., and Donald J. Bogue. 1964. "Research in urban society: A long view." Pp. 1–14 in Ernest W. Burgess and Donald J. Bogue,eds., *Contributions to Urban Sociology*. Chicago: University of Chicago Press.

Caryl, Christian. 2007. "Iraq's young blood." *Newsweek* (January 22):24–34.

Center for Immigration Studies. 2006. (http://www.cis.org/topics/currentnumbers.html)

Chorneau, Tom. 2007. "California voters grow pessimistic about future." *San Francisco Chronicle* (November 2):B1 http://www.uic.edu/cuppa/gci/programs/The%20New%20Chicago%20School%2024%5B1%5D.TextandFigures.pdf

Copetas, A. Craig. 2007. "Letter from Europe: The view from Sicily: 'America is broken'." *International Herald Tribune* (September 4):2.

Cowling, David. 2002 "BBC race survey: What it reveals." *BBC News*. (May 19): http://news.bbc.co.uk/2/hi/uk_news/ht.

Cullen, Kevin. 2007a. "Boom times, crackdown slow emerald wave." *Boston Globe* (March 18): http://www.boston.com/news/local/articles/2007/03/18/boom_times_crackdown_slow_emerald_wave/

———. 2007b. "Going full circle: Native land's new prosperity has many reversing their exodus." *Boston Globe* (March 19): http://www.boston.com/news/local/articles/2007/03/19/going_full_circle/

Cumming-Bruce, Nick. 2008. "UN warns of swelling global tide of refugees." *International Herald Tribune* (June 18):3.

Daniels, Roger. [1990] 1991. *Coming to America: A History of Immigration and Ethnicity in American Life*. New York: Harper Perennial.

Davis, Mike. 1992. *City of Quartz: Excavating the Future in Los Angeles*. New York: Vintage.

———. 2007. "The urbanization of empire." Pp. 122–131 in Mike Davis, ed., *In Praise of Barbarians: Essays Against Empire*. Chicago: Haymarket Books.

Dear, Michael. 2001. *From Chicago to LA: Making Sense of Urban Theory*. Thousand Oaks, Calif.: Sage.

Deng, Francis. 2007. "As conflict rages across the globe, people are not protected in their own country." (June 4): http://www.alternet.org/audits/52544/

Elliott, Andrea. 2006. "More Muslims arrive in U.S., after 9/11 dip." *New York Times* (September 10): http://www.nytimes.com/2006/09/10/nyregion/10muslims.html?_r=1&pagewanted=print&oref=slogin

ERsys.com. n.d. www.ersys.com/usa/20/2025325/index.htm

Fears, Darryl. 2003. "Race divides Hispanics, report says." *Washington Post* (July 14):A3.

Gans, Herbert. 1999. "The possibility of a new racial hierarchy in the twenty-first century United States," pp. 371–390 in Michelle Lamont (ed.), *The Cultural Territories of Race*. Chicago and New York: University of Chicago Press.

Gibbons, Ann. 2007. "New clues from an old skull." ScienceNOW Daily News (January 11): http://science-now.sciencemag.org/cgi/content/full/2007/111/2

Giroux, Henry A. 2006. "Reading Hurricane Katrina: Race, class, and the biopolitics of disposability." *College Literature* 33(3):171–196.

Glanz, James, and Alissa J. Rubin. 2007. "Internal migration soars in Iraq, altering sectarian landscape." *International Herald Tribune* (September 19):1.

Glazer, Nathan. [1998] 2003. *We Are All Multiculturalists Now*. Cambridge, Mass.: Harvard University Press.

Glazer, Nathan, and Daniel Patrick Moynihan. 1963. *Beyond the Melting Pot*. Cambridge, Mass.: MIT Press.

Goodman, Peter. 2008. "Rethinking the country life as energy costs rise." *New York Times* (June 25): http://www.nytimes.com/2008/06/25/business/25exurbs.html?_r=1&th=&adxnnl=1&oref=slogin&emc=th&adxnnlx=1214381650-T4FsP/603SyVcuKxFLF+aA

Grosfoguel, Ramón. 2003. *Colonial Subjects: Puerto Ricans in a Global Perspective*. Berkeley: University of California Press.

Hacker, Andrew. 1992. *Two Nations: Black and White, Separate, Hostile, Unequal*. New York: Scribner.

Haley, Alex, and Malcolm X. [1964] 1966. *The Autobiography of Malcolm X*. New York: Grove Press.

Hayes-Bautista, David. 2004. *La Nueva California: Latinos in the Golden State*. Berkeley: University of California Press.

Hein, Jeremy. 2006. *Ethnic Origins: The Adaptation of Cambodian and Hmong Refugees in Four American Cities*. New York: Russell Sage Foundation.

Henricks, Tyche. 2007. "Study says immigrants vie with earlier arrivals." *San Francisco Chronicle* (February 28):B10.

Holmstrom, David. 1992. "The new Americans." *Christian Science Monitor* (June 17):9–12.

Hosokawa, Bill. 1969. *Nisei: The Quiet Americans*. New York: Morrow.

Jankowski, Martín Sánchez. 1991. *Islands in the Street: Gangs and American Urban Society*. Berkeley: University of California Press.

Krugman, Paul. [2007[2009. *The Conscience of a Liberal*. New York. W.W.Norton.

Laczko, Frank. 2003. "Europe attracts more migrants from China." International Organization for Migration (July 1): http://www.migrationinformation.org/Feature/display.cfm?ID=144

Lam, Andrew. 2006. "Commentary: Diversity—not just a California experience." *New America Media* (December 16): http://news.newamericamedia.org/news/view_article.html?article_id=90ae4dd0398f8eee8b47389d20b7aaa3

———. 2005. *Perfume Dreams: Reflections on the Vietnamese Diaspora*. Berkeley, Calif.: Heyday Books.

Lee, Jennifer. 2006. *Civility in the City: Blacks, Jews, and Koreans in Urban America*. Cambridge, Mass.: Harvard University Press.

Lehrer, Warren, and Judith Sloan. 2003. *Crossing the Blvd: Strangers, Neighbors, Aliens in a New America*. New York: W.W. Norton.

Lemaitre, Georges. 2005. "Problems and prospects: Statistics brief n°9: The comparability of international migration statistics." OECD (Organization for Economic Cooperation and Development) (November): http://www.oecd.org/dataoecd/4/41/35082073.pdf

Light, Ivan, and Edna Bonacich. 1988. *Immigrant Entrepreneurs: Koreans in Los Angeles, 1965–1982*. Berkeley: University of California Press.

Lintner, Bertil. 2003. "Illegal migration in the 21st century." *YaleGlobal* (January 10): http://yaleglobal.yale.edu/display.article?id=704

Logan, John A., and John Mollenkopf. 2003. "People and politics in America's big cities." (May 15): http://mumford.albany.edu/census/report.html; http://mumford.albany.edu/census/2003newspdf/People%20&%20Politics%20report.pdf

Massey, Douglas S., and J. Edward Taylor. 2004. *International Migration: Prospects and Policies in a Global Market*. New York: Oxford University Press.

McConville, Shannon, and Paul Ong. 2006. "The trajectory of poor neighborhoods in Southern California, 1970–2000." *Brookings Institution:* ttp://www.brookings.edu/es/urban/publications/20031124_Ong.pdf

Miller, Sara B. 2005. "3-Generation households increase due to necessity." *Christian Science Monitor* (September 10): www.csmonitor.com/2005/0822/p02s01-ussc.html.

Min, Pyong Gap. 1996. *Caught in the Middle: Korean Merchants in America's Multiethnic Cities.* Berkeley: University of California Press.

Palen, John. 1987. *The Urban World,* 3rd ed. New York: McGraw-Hill.

Pérez, Sonia M. 2000. Visiting Scholars Program, 1999–2000. "Reports on current research." *Institute for Research on Poverty:* http://www.irp.wisc.edu/initiatives/funding/vscholars/vs1999-00.htm

Perlman, David. 2007. "New evidence on migration of earliest humans." *San Francisco Chronicle* (January 12):A1+.

Pew Hispanic Center. 2005. "Hispanics: A people in motion." (January): http://pewhispanic.org/files/reports/40.pdf

Portes, Alejandro. 2002. "Global villagers: The rise of transnational communities." *American Prospect* (November 30): http://www.prospect.org/cs/articles?article=global_villagers

Portes, Alejandro, and Min Zhou. 1992. "Gaining the upperhand: Economic mobility among immigrant and domestic minorities." *Ethnic and Racial Studies* 15(4):491–522.

Portes, Alejandro, and Alex Stepick. 1993. *City on the Edge: The Transformation of Miami.* Berkeley: University of California Press.

Poynter Institute. 2007. "*Chicago Tribune* gets complaints about 'Vivan los osos' hed." (February 9): newsletters@poynter.org

Riis, Jacob. [1890] 1970. *How the Other Half Lives: Studies Among the Tenements of New York.* New York: Dover.

Riposa, Gerry, and Carolyn Dersch, eds. 1992. *City of Angels.* Dubuque, Iowa: Kendall/Hunt.

Robinson, Eugene. 1993. "U.N. calls mass migrations global problems." *San Francisco Chronicle* (July 7):A1+.

Rohan, Brian. 2006. "One third of French say they are racist: Survey." (March 21), *Reuters:* http://www.redorbit.com/news/oddities/437927/one_third_of_french_say_they_are_racist_survey/

Sacramento State News. 2005. "Study by Sacramento State professor shows differences in poverty rates for Hispanics" (November 17): http://www.csus.edu/news/111705hispanic.stm

Sassen, Saskia. 1991. *The Global City: New York, London, Tokyo.* Princeton, N.J.: Princeton University Press.

Schachter, Jason P. 2004. "Geographical mobility: 2002 to 2003." Current Population Reports series. *U.S. Census Bureau.* (March): http://www.census.gov/prod/2004pubs/p20-549.pdf

Seko, Miki. 2006. "Barriers to residential mobility in Japan: Housing equity and the rental act." (July 8): http://faculty.ccer.edu.cn/zxzeng/icrem/papers/seko-paper.pdf

Singer, Audrey. 2006. "The new metropolitan geography of U.S. immigration." *Brookings Institution, Metropolitan Policy Program* (February 21–23): http://www.brookings.edu/metro/speeches/20060221_immigeography.pdf

Soja, Edward W. 1989. *Postmodern Geographies: The Reassertion of Space in Critical Social Theory.* London: Verso.

Sontag, Deborah. 1993. "New immigrants test nation's heartland." *New York Times* [national edition] (October 18):1.

Spiegel, Lisa. 2006. "Shouting across the divide." *This American Life* (December 16) PRI International, KALW 1 p.m., PST.

Steinbeck, John. [1939] 1972. *The Grapes of Wrath.* New York: Viking.

Steinberg, Stephen. 1981. *The Ethnic Myth: Race, Ethnicity, and Class in America.* Boston: Beacon Press.

———. 1992. "Occupational apartheid." *The Nation* (December 9):744+.

Steiner, Stan. 1970. *La Raza: The Mexican Americans.* New York: Harper.

Stepick, Alex, and Nancy Foner. 1997. *Pride Against Prejudice: Haitians in the United States.* Boston: Allyn & Bacon.

Stuart, Guy. 2002. "Integration or resegregation: Metropolitan Chicago at the turn of the century." (May): http://www.civilrightsproject.harvard.edu/research/metro/Chicago%20Study4.pdf

Takaki, Ronald. 1989. *Strangers from a Different Shore: A History of Asian Americans.* New York: Viking Penguin.

Tirman, John. 2006. "Immigration and insecurity: Post 9/11 fear in the United States." (June): http://web.mit.edu/cis/pdf/Audit_Tirman_Immigration_6.06.pdf

United Nations. 2006. "The good, the bad, the promising: Migration in the 21st century." In *State of World Population 2006:* http://www.unfpa.org/swp/2006/english/chapter_1/index.html

U.S. Census Bureau. 2004. "U.S. interim projects by age, sex, race, and Hispanic origin." (March 18): http:www.census.gov/ipc/www/usinterimproj/

———. 2008. "State and county quickFacts." http://quickfacts.census.gov/qfd/states/06/0644000.html

Vidal, Gore. 1992. "Monotheism and its discontents." *The Nation* (July 13):1+.

Weiss, Michael J. 2000. *The Clustered World: How We Live, What We Buy, and What It All Means About Who We Are.* Boston: Little, Brown.

West, Cornel. 1993. *Race Matters.* Boston: Beacon Press.

Williams, Daniel. 2008. "Letter from America: A post-racial nation: No, a shift of enmities." *International Herald Tribune* (August 20):2.

Wilson, William Julius. 1978. *The Declining Significance of Race: Blacks and Changing American Institutions.* Chicago: University of Chicago Press.

———. 1987. *The Truly Disadvantaged: The Inner City, the Underclass, and Public Policy.* Chicago: University of Chicago Press.

———. 2009. *More than Just Race: Being Black and Poor in the Inner City.* New York: W.W. Norton.

Wirth, Louis. [1928] 1956. *The Ghetto.* Chicago: University of Chicago Press.

Wyman, Mark. 1993. *Round Trip to America.* Ithaca, N.Y.: Cornell University Press.

Bill Owens

CHAPTER 10

IDENTITY CRISIS

WORLDWIDE ETHNOSCAPES

GLOBAL IDENTITY . . .

Ever dream of writing the great American novel or directing the great U.S. movie? Too bad, bad timing. Sensitivity to differences in ethnicity, race, gender, and class makes it difficult to even define a North American novel or movie.

Besides, an emerging genre is taking its place: the global artwork. Global novels and movies leap across national boundaries. They include sophisticated characters from various cultures who happen to collide, often in world cities such as New York, Mumbai, and London. They often mirror globalization and demographic shifts (e.g., the emergence of Latinos as the United States's largest so-called minority). These artworks also mirror supranational *Techno$chaft*, where cosmopolitans commune in a global village. One such movie, *Babel* (2006), directed by Mexico's Alejandro González Iñárritu, earned an Oscar nomination plus the disapproval of *The New Yorker's* film critic, David Denby (2007:84) as "the first example of a new genre—the highbrow globalist tearjerker."

Not surprisingly, many global writers and filmmakers are themselves exiles or "shufflers." They shuffle between cultures, like Mumbai–Berkeley writer Vikram Chandra (author of *Sacred Games*, 2007) and the late French director Louis Malle, who seemed at home in various settings, including *Atlantic City* (1981) as well as his houses in Beverly Hills and the hamlet of Lugagnac in southwest France. Similarly, a U.S. writer, Jonathan Littell, writes in French and won France's top literary prizes in 2006.

Many shufflers often see with prescient eyes. Such is the case with Louis Malle's film *Alamo Bay* (1985). It was an early example of an artwork in what some call "the racism genre." The movie tells the story of a Vietnam vet whose livelihood is endangered and pushed to the edge when Vietnamese immigrants move into the fishing industry in Alamo Bay, Texas.

These writers and artists embody a citizen-of-the-world identity: Boundaries of ethnicity, nationality, race, and religion are of secondary importance at best. Implicitly, citizens of the world reject the **insider-as-insighter doctrine**, where members of a group claim a monopoly of knowledge unavailable to "outsiders."

Another recent development challenges many boundaries: Bollywood meets Hollywood. Film moguls from Mumbai (formerly Bombay, hence the nickname "Bollywood," for the city's huge movie industry) have invested in U.S. movies and may be introducing their techniques (and plots) to U.S. cinema.

. . . VERSUS THE PULL OF "LESSER LOYALTIES"

Simultaneously, there are powerful, some say primordial, forces antagonistic to global identity. Novelist and essayist V. S. Naipaul once said that patriotic feelings for region, caste, and clan were disruptive, lesser loyalties. Winner of the 2006 Nobel Prize for Literature, Orhan Pamuk, a native of Istanbul, Turkey, put it this way in *Snow* (2005:393): "any citizen of an oppressive and aggressively nationalistic country" will understand "the magical unity conjured by the word *we*."

The flames of "lesser loyalties" have burned bright in recent years. After the breakup of the Soviet Union, ethnic secessionist movements in former republics, including Georgia, have led to marauding and sometimes murder and "ethnic cleansing." In Somalia, contemporary warfare or discord is typically clan-based.

(The word "clan" is loosely used for large family networks such as the large Hawiye clan and a smaller network like the Ayr. You cannot join a clan—you are born into one or not.)

One group, the Roma, divide the world into *gadjikano* ("them," the non-Roma or non-"Gypsy", considered dangerous and untrustworthy) and "us." Indeed, the Roma's fundamental value is "us" against the world (Fonseca, [1995] 1996:13). This flame of lesser loyalty has served the Roma both well and ill. On the one hand, it has allowed the Roma, numbering about 12 million worldwide, to resist assimilation for over 1,000 years, a key to their survival (assimilation equals surrender to them) (Fonseca, [1995] 1996:15). But the Roma have paid high prices for their group survival, including persecution and death. Often, they are targeted as outsiders: In 2007, four Roma children near Livorno, Italy, were burned to death. Ironically, about the same time, people all over the world seemed to embrace Roma culture via films, festivals, plays, and music.

Ethnic hate and conflict know no national boundaries. In the past two decades, U.S. cities from Miami and New Orleans to Los Angeles have experienced ethnic (and economic) hatred that exploded in uprisings. Globally, from the former Yugoslavia and Soviet Union to Iraq, Thailand, and the Sudan, neighbors became enemies, fighting to preserve tribal, religious, cultural, and/or ethnic communities.

In one 5-year period during the late 1980s–early 1990s, ethnic conflict sparked record-high migrations of refugees: Over 23 million people—one in every 114 people in the world—were uprooted and forced to move elsewhere (Darnton, 1994). Twenty-six million more people became refugees within their own countries (United Nations High Commissioner for Refugees, 1993).

In one recent year, 2007–2008, ethnic distrust and hatred did not abate. To the contrary. In Tibet, Chinese soldiers killed unknown numbers of protesters. In Indonesia, a village of the Ahmadiya, a Muslim sect, was attacked by fundamentalist Muslims. In Italian cities, violence against "outsiders" ("them") led to the deaths of Roma. In South Africa's poorest slums, immigrants from other African countries were murdered. In the Caucasus, ethnic Ossetians slaughtered ethnic Georgians—and perhaps vice versa. And so on.

In recent years, Europe's right–wing parties have openly espoused xenophobia and extremism. Further, they have secured money, talking time, and political influence in the European Union (EU)'s Parliament. As one headline succinctly put it, "Gypsy-Haters, Holocaust-Deniers, Xenophobes, Homophobes, Anti-Semites: The EU's New Political Force" (Castle, 2007). This ultranationalist force claimed the backing of 23 million Europeans in 2007. One outcome: a formal political group called Identity, Tradition, Sovereignty (ITS). A reporter noted that for the first time since World War II European elections swept Far-Right parties into office in municipal, regional, national, and European parliamentary elections. The admission into the EU of Romania and Bulgaria in January 2007 brought in enough Far-Right members of the European Parliament to form a bloc (Castle, 2007).

The case of Germany's neo-Nazis illustrates how a search for community can be the flip side of hatred for outsiders. German neo-Nazis hope to create a Fourth Reich, a "pure race" German state without "outsiders" (i.e., devoid of Jews, foreigners, and capitalists), ruled by a Nazi dictatorship. In other words, they seek an oxymoron: a modern *Gemeinschaft*. (Hitler used the same myth of racial purity as an ideal; the 1936 film *The Triumph of the Will* exhorts Germans to respect the cornerstones of *Gemeinschaft*: blood, land, and friendship.)

In Germany and other nations of Europe, hatred and/or fear of the outsider may reflect an identity crisis. Some observers think that this crisis of identity is encouraged by a deadly mix of unemployment, humiliation, and resentment—a mix similar to the one that gave rise to the Nazis in the 1930s.

What sparks this European identity crisis? In a phrase, changes in culture and ethnicity: A white, Christian continent is becoming multicultural and multiethnic.

At the same time, migrants from Africa, Southeast Asia, and China are literally dying to get into Europe. And, in some places, young people, judged "outsiders" are being recruited by terrorists to inflict harm or death on their adopted homelands. In addition, some extremists and nationalists blame easy targets, such as foreigners and Jews, for all that is wrong because they seek easy answers to complex problems.

Alas, in a complex world, some people are drawn to simple answers, such as neo-Nazism. The result: In many cities—from Rome to Moscow and beyond, members of poor immigrant communities have been the targets of simmering xenophobia and racist violence.

Ethnic and religious loyalties will probably prevail in many parts of the world. Take Central Asia, for one. Shortly after the end of the cold war, the chief cleric in the Central Asian Republic of Tajikistan, formerly part of the Soviet Union, predicted a key role for religion in shaping the region's future. He noted that Islam constitutes 90 percent of his people's culture and tradition, which are inseparable from national feeling (in Wright, Robin, 1992:75). Recent history has not proved him wrong.

Some keen observers predict even more conflict based on identity politics. For one, Iranian-born, MIT-trained professor Vali Nasr describes the conflict between two branches of Islam (the Shi'a and the Sunni) in part as a "contemporary clash of identities" ([2006] 2007:20): "a manifestation of the kind of tribal wars of ethnicities and identities" that is much more than a religious dispute. He concludes that while we live in an age of globalization, we also live in a world of identity politics: "It is as if our world is expanding and contracting at the same time" (23).

Many places—from Baghdad to Basque country—are synonymous with sectarian and ethnic differences. Trying to make theoretical sense of this, a geographer in Belfast devised a typology laying out five ways that racial and ethnic groups live together (or not) in "divided cities": assimilation, pluralism, segmentation, polarization, and ethnic cleansing (Boal, 1999).

Ethnic loyalties may prevent subordinate groups from coming together around common economic interests. So argues sociologist Orlando Patterson. In his book of a generation ago, Harvard sociologist Patterson chided both black power and white ethnic movements for celebrating a "tyranny of the lesser loyalties" (1977). Some years later, Patterson thought that ethnic particularism was helping to tear nations apart (Patterson in Raymond, 1992:A12). Since he wrote that, ethnic chauvinism has been tearing neighborhoods apart too, as in the case of ethnic or "sectarian" cleansing in many places, including Bosnia, Burundi, and Baghdad.

Patterson's critique of ethnic particularism has had little impact. A few names remind us of particularism's lethal consequences: Shi'a vs. Sunni vs. Kurd in Iraq, black Africans vs. Arabs in Darfur, and Tamils vs. Sinhalese in Sri Lanka.

As an antidote to ethnic chauvinism, George Soros, a major funder of university education in eastern and central Europe, advocates an "open society." (To Soros, an open society is one where the individual is not at the mercy of the state and minorities are tolerated, if not respected.) Soros, a U.S. citizen and Hungarian-born Jew, recounted that he learned the urgency of establishing an open society at an early age because he nearly ended up in a gas chamber on account of his ethnic origin (1993).

Let us also remember that other accidents of birth divide human beings into "us" and "them." For one, caste. In India, Dalits (formerly called "Untouchables") were the worst hit by floods in Bihar Province in 2007. The flooding killed thousands and affected millions, but it hit low-caste villagers harder than others because, as one human-rights worker put it, "The culture of discrimination which runs through Indian society intensifies in times of crisis" (Divakar in Gentleman, 2007).

CIVICS VERSUS ETHNICS

Hoover Institution political scientist Ken Jowitt (in Kriesler, 1999), widely considered as a neoconservative spokesperson, draws a distinction between two types of identity in the world today: civics versus ethnics. (This distinction is similar to Soros's open society versus closed society and Tönnies's *Gesellschaft* cosmopolitanism versus *Gemeinschaft* localism.) Those who identify as civics, Jowitt says, stress the individual; those who identity as ethnics stress the group. In addition, civics stress the ability to view the world critically; ethnics see the world divided into us (insiders) and them (outsiders). That is, *civics are inclusive, ethnics are exclusive.*

Dozens of twentieth and twenty-first century political figures symbolize the primacy of ethnic over civic identity. These include Hitler, Osama Bin Laden, the late U.S.–Israeli citizen Rabbi Meir Kahane, and Elijah Mohammed (one-time leader of the Nation of Islam in the United States).

According to Jowitt, a conflict between civics and ethnics is now a major feature of politics almost everywhere, including the United States. He fears a "Tower of Ethnic Babel" where ethnicity becomes *primary*: An individual's identity is first and foremost white or Shi'a Muslim or Pacific Islander and so on. Jowitt fears that the United States, "the one nation indivisible, is being multiplied and divided."

It is in U.S. cities, Jowitt notes, that movements of ethnic rage combine with economic frustration to produce a boiling cauldron. If so, did this replace the proverbial "melting pot"?

WHAT HAPPENED TO THE U.S. MELTING POT?

"These States," wrote poet Walt Whitman "are the amplest poem. Here is not merely a nation, but a teeming nation of nations." A nation of nations—that was the vision: a great **melting pot**, a fusion of all immigrants into a new American. "Here," proclaimed naturalized American Jean de Crèvecoeur in 1782, "individuals of all nations are melted into a new race of man." Thus, from the very beginning, America was viewed as a new nation, a nation unlike all others that would fuse people of different origins into one people.

But this ideal waned over the generations. When European Catholic and Jewish immigrants came in massive waves, many old-stock white Anglo-Saxon Protestants (WASPs) wondered whether the melting pot was possible—or desirable. By the 1880s and 1890s, several reactions to the immigrant tide had surfaced.

One reaction came from upper-crust WASPs: the founding of ancestral associations such as the Daughters of the American Revolution (DAR) in 1890. During the 1890s, some 35 hereditary, historical, and patriotic associations were formed as these old-stock WASPs searched for their roots.

Old-stock Americans also took direct action, trying to shut the floodgates. The American Protective Association (1886) and other groups aimed at restricting immigration were formed by those calling themselves "native Americans"—and they did *not* mean

Fig. 10.2 TURNING "THEM" INTO "US." Through Americanization classes, like this one at the Barrett Plant, Chicago, in 1919, reformers taught immigrants the "American way of life" and the English language. (Chicago History Museum, formerly Chicago Historical Society)

Indian or what today is oft-referred to as Native American.

Liberal reformers had another approach: turning "them" into "us." Schools, military academies, sports clubs, and settlement houses became vehicles for **assimilation**, not **acculturation**. Their goals: to inculcate the "American way of life" and to "Americanize" the immigrants.

Another reaction was to deny that some immigrant groups were capable of being assimilated. The San Francisco School Board, for instance, declared in 1905 that it would segregate Japanese children to prevent white children from being adversely affected by "association with pupils of the Mongolian race" (in Hosokawa, 1969:86).

By 1908, when Israel Zangwill's play *The Melting Pot* appeared on Broadway, the Chinese had been barred from further immigration; the Japanese in California were officially classified as "aliens ineligible to citizenship"; blacks were segregated and denied civil rights; upper-class WASPs were busy finding their roots; and millions of Catholic and Jewish immigrants lived and died in unsanitary, overcrowded, oppressive urban slums. Still, Zangwill's play was a great success. It celebrated "the great Melting Pot where all the races of Europe are melting and reforming!...The real American has not yet arrived. His is only in the Crucible. I tell you—he will be the fusion of all races, the coming superman" (Zangwill, 1909:37–38).

RACE, ETHNICITY, AND MINORITY GROUPS

Today, many believe that the U.S. ideal of the melting pot has disappeared. In its place is the stewpot or salad bowl of **multiculturalism**.

Some keen observers disagree. For one, Mabry (2008:6) believes that people who came of age in a post–civil rights era, including Barack Obama, share a popular culture, such as hip-hop, that has forged a new U.S identity. They argue that this new "ecumenical" identity replaces the multicultural ideal.

Others are not so sure. As a vice president of the National Association for the Advancement of Colored People (NAACP) in Miami put it when discussing a racial slur by a Cuban American politician against an African American school superintendent: "If Obama is post-racial, Miami isn't there yet" (in Williams, 2008:2).

What exactly are race and **ethnicity**? Slippery terms—social labels that humans pin on themselves and others.

Racial and ethnic labels are far from universal. For instance, the U.S. State Department sent a light-skinned African American scholar to West Africa as an ambassador in the 1960s; Africans viewed him as white, not black.

Neither are labels timeless. Here are a few examples: Local whites first classified Mississippi Delta Chinese as blacks, then reclassified them as whites. The 1930 U.S. Census classified white persons of Mexican birth or ancestry in the group "other races"; in 1940, they were reclassified as "white."

Human beings also create new racial–ethnic categories. For instance, the Nazis deemed the Japanese "honorary Aryans" during World War II, and *mestizo* is a term rooted in Cortés's conquest of Mexico (Carrasco, 1992).

Neither geneticists nor social scientists agree on what constitutes a race or an ethnic group. Here are just a few ways that race has been defined or viewed: (1) a concentration of gene frequencies; (2) not a scientific concept—at the level of the human genome, all human beings are essentially identical twins; (3) a group that is defined socially, on the basis of physical criteria; (4) a group that is defined by class, not skin color or other biological traits (e.g., at one time, the English defined the Irish as a "lower race");

(5) a socially-constructed (not biological) category used by its creators, white Europeans, to assign non-whites such as Amerindians and Africans to the lower orders and thus maintain power and privilege over them—that is, social hooey with enormous, negative ramifications for those not defined as white.

Until recently, in much of Europe, race had little to do with physical traits. In France, for instance, people with a common ancestry, history, and political heritage—not biological heritage—were considered a race (Chapman and Frader, 2004). Leaders typically embraced "color-blindness" as the preferred approach to conflicts that can arise in a multiracial or multi-ethnic society. (French intellectuals tend to avoid the word "race"; they view the very word as racist. They prefer the term "ethnicity.")

France's history with race is instructive. At the time of the French Revolution, revolutionaries emphasized the universalist nature of the Republic, based on *individual*, not *group*, rights. There was little or no recognition of group differences. (In Jowitt's terms, the revolutionaries emphasized civic over ethnic identity). French revolutionaries insisted that religion, ethnic background, and race were not important to exercise the rights of citizenship. France's Declaration of the Rights of Man repudiated any form of segregation or distinction based on race, religion, or ethnic origin. The Napoleonic Code of 1804, which remains the basis of French law, also embodies these principles.

The ideal of individual (rather than group) rights exists to this day in France. For example, data in France are not gathered by race or ethnicity (unlike in the United States and Great Britain).

However, France's republican model of color-blindness and religion-neutrality has not prevented prejudice and discrimination. Over time, many groups have suffered segregation, ostracism, discrimination, and worse. These groups include Africans, Jews (who, in the late Middle Ages, were defined as a people different from Christians), and people of color (who were colonized and/or enslaved). Religious doctrine, later joined by pseudoscience, justified bigotry and the notion that people of color were inherently inferior. By the mid-1850s, several French pseudoscientists advocated "polygenetic" theories claiming separate origins of the world's "races," some of which were inferior. It was about this time, the mid-nineteenth century, that race lost its earlier meaning: a group sharing a common history and political heritage (what many define as an "ethnic group" today). Thus, the notion of race in France became biologized by the 1850s.

Currently, in France, as in much of Europe, the concept of race remains contentious. For instance, the notion that white Europeans are inherently superior, say, to North Africans, remains alive and well today among segments of the population, notably, the extreme Right.

Globally, how is race understood by most people today? There is no simple answer. Ideology and place, as the French and U.S. examples show, play key roles.

Popularly, in the United States, race is a biologically-based concept, referring to members of a group who see themselves—and whom others see—as having specific physical traits that set them off as different. (Racist ideology links race to *non*physical traits such as morality and intellect. Many examples exist, including writings by some former French settlers, including educated professionals, in Algeria.)

It is worth noting that in the United States attitudes toward race may be changing—rather rapidly. Indeed, sociologist Orlando Patterson (in Mabry, 2008:6) notes that younger people hold less racist attitudes than older people. While race remains relevant, Patterson says, younger people are part of a more "ecumenical," unself-consciously multiracial U.S. culture. Various polls in the United States show that about one in five whites continues to hold racist views but that those under 44 years of age are much less likely to hold such views (see Mabry, 2008:6).

Census Definitions

Changes in U.S. Census definitions often reflect changes in perception—and political clout. Data on race, for example, have been collected since the first decennial U.S. census in 1790. But definitions concerning race have greatly changed over the years.

In 1990, the U.S. Census recognized the following major racial groups: whites; blacks (African Americans); American Indians, Eskimos, and Aleuts; Asians and Pacific Islanders. Respondents could define themselves as belonging only to one race. Traditionally, the Census Bureau classified anyone with mixed-race

parentage by the race of the nonwhite parent (U.S. Bureau of the Census, 1972:appendix B-6).

This pre-2000 definition of racial identity reaffirmed what Andrew Hacker reported years ago (1992a): There is a hierarchy of color in the United States, and for whites, whiteness is highly prized over color.

But in the 2000 Census, there was a profound change in racial categorization. For the first time, respondents were allowed to identify one *or more* races to indicate their racial identity. About 2.4 percent of the population (6.8 million people) did identify themselves as multiracial. Guesstimates are that this number will grow in the future. According to a recent National Academy of Science study, self-identified multiracial people in the United States could soar to 21 percent by 2050.

There were other changes concerning racial categories in the 2000 Census. These included a new write-in category, Some Other Race (intended to capture responses such as Mulatto, Creole, and Mestizo). In addition, American Indians, Eskimos, and Aleuts were combined into one category (American Indian or Alaska Native), and the Asian and Pacific Islander category was split into two categories (Asian, Native Hawaiian and Other Pacific Islander).

Starting with the 2010 Census, U.S. respondents can identify themselves even more precisely in terms of race, including "some other race." In census tests, some defined themselves as Creole, rainbow, and cosmopolitan (Kronholz, 2007:B2); this may prove to be highly problematic because other federal agencies, such as the Social Security Administration, do not recognize those as races. So census officials will impute a race to those answers. As one official said, "Maybe I get it right and may I get it wrong" (Waite in Kronholz, 2007:B1).

Further, some Mexican Americans are not happy with the concept of "Latino" as a nationality group. Some say that the very concept—Latino—is not recognized by most Hispanic immigrants.

To conclude: Racial categories in the United States have changed dramatically since 1950, reflecting the recognition of new social identities. In 1950 and 1960, the U.S. Census Bureau recognized only two groups: white and nonwhite. By 1990, there were 25 categories,

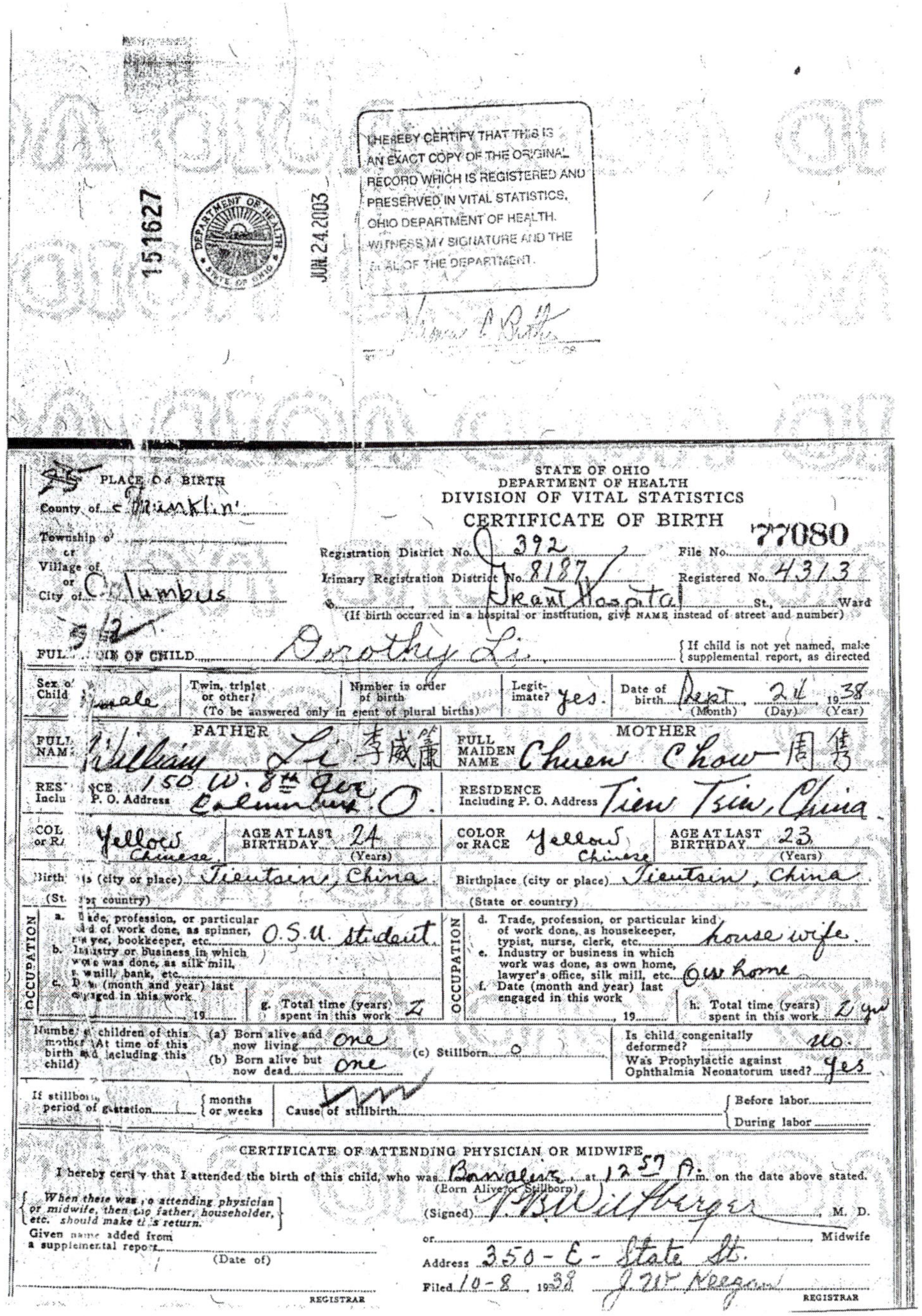
151627

JUN 24 2003

DEPARTMENT OF HEALTH STATE OF OHIO

I HEREBY CERTIFY THAT THIS IS AN EXACT COPY OF THE ORIGINAL RECORD WHICH IS REGISTERED AND PRESERVED IN VITAL STATISTICS, OHIO DEPARTMENT OF HEALTH. WITNESS MY SIGNATURE AND THE SEAL OF THE DEPARTMENT.

STATE OF OHIO
DEPARTMENT OF HEALTH
DIVISION OF VITAL STATISTICS
CERTIFICATE OF BIRTH

77080

PLACE OF BIRTH
County of Franklin
Township of
or
Village of
or
City of Columbus

Registration District No. 392 File No.
Primary Registration District No. 8187 Registered No. 4313
Grant Hospital St., Ward
(If birth occurred in a hospital or institution, give NAME instead of street and number)

FULL NAME OF CHILD Dorothy Li

{If child is not yet named, make supplemental report, as directed

Sex of Child	Twin, triplet or other? (To be answered only in event of plural births)	Number in order of birth	Legitimate?	Date of birth
female			yes.	Sept. (Month) 21 (Day) 1938 (Year)

	FATHER		MOTHER
FULL NAME	William Li 李威廉	FULL MAIDEN NAME	Chuen Chow 周隽
RESIDENCE Including P. O. Address	150 W. 8th Ave Columbus O.	RESIDENCE Including P. O. Address	Tien Tsin, China
COLOR or RACE	Yellow Chinese	COLOR or RACE	Yellow Chinese
AGE AT LAST BIRTHDAY	24 (Years)	AGE AT LAST BIRTHDAY	23 (Years)
Birthplace (city or place) (State or country)	Tientsin, China	Birthplace (city or place) (State or country)	Tientsin, China
OCCUPATION a. Trade, profession, or particular kind of work done, as spinner, sawyer, bookkeeper, etc.	O.S.U. student	OCCUPATION d. Trade, profession, or particular kind of work done, as housekeeper, typist, nurse, clerk, etc.	house wife.
b. Industry or business in which work was done, as silk mill, saw mill, bank, etc.		e. Industry or business in which work was done, as own home, lawyer's office, silk mill, etc.	Own home
c. Date (month and year) last engaged in this work 19	g. Total time (years) spent in this work 2	f. Date (month and year) last engaged in this work 19	h. Total time (years) spent in this work 2 yrs

Number of children of this mother (At time of this birth and including this child) (a) Born alive and now living one (b) Born alive but now dead one (c) Stillborn 0

Is child congenitally deformed? no.
Was Prophylactic against Ophthalmia Neonatorum used? yes

If stillborn, period of gestation { months or weeks Cause of stillbirth { Before labor During labor

CERTIFICATE OF ATTENDING PHYSICIAN OR MIDWIFE

I hereby certify that I attended the birth of this child, who was Born alive at 12 57 A.m. on the date above stated.
(Born Alive or Stillborn)

{When there was no attending physician or midwife, then the father, householder, etc. should make this return.}

(Signed) P. B. Wilberger M. D.
or Midwife

Given name added from a supplemental report (Date of)

Address 350 - E - State St.

Filed 10 - 8 1938 J. W. Keegan

REGISTRAR

REGISTRAR

Fig. 10.3 COLOR-CODED IDENTITY. When she was born in 1938, Dorothy Li's birth certificate from Ohio was marked "yellow" as well as Chinese for race. (MeiSun Li)

including "Other." By 2000, respondents could mark themselves biracial, and in 2010 there will be even more categories.

It is worth noting that the U.S. Census officially recognizes biracial people, but many people in the United States do not. Countless numbers of biracial or multiracial persons—however they define themselves—are generally viewed as nonwhite in the United States if one parent is not white. This is particularly the case if one parent is black. That is, whether the offspring of a white mother and African or African American father (e.g., President Barack Obama) or vice versa (e.g., Rachel Walker, writer Alice Walker's daughter), a person is considered African American, not white or biracial. Indeed, the social definition of biracial is not widely available. At least not yet.

The federal government's Office of Management and Budget (OMB, the agency that sets policy on gathering federal statistics) began a review of its racial and ethnic classifications in 1994. It was responding to demographic change and political pressure: (1) increased numbers of interracial marriages and unions plus (2) complaints by groups displeased by their current classification, particularly Arab Americans, Hawaiian Islanders, and multiracial people. The 2000 U.S. Census was the first to incorporate the OMB's newer categories.

Politically speaking, ethnic and racial reclassification is a can of worms. The multiracial category is distrusted by some established ethnic organizations, which fear that it reduces their group's counts in the U.S. census and thus reduces their influence. Other groups want to drop all classification by race or ethnicity. Their chief argument: A democratic society should be color-blind. (Typically, a color-blind society is championed by conservatives, who thus fight affirmative action programs. Many liberals and radicals see this as an ideal, not a reality.)

Furthermore, racial and ethnic classification is being changed radically with recent scientific developments, especially "genetic genealogy," which maps a person's haplotype. Human genomes are 99.9 percent identical. Yet, that minute 0.1 percent difference holds clues to our ancestors. According to some sources, many Europeans and Native Americans share a mutation in their genes, suggesting that they arose from the same Central Asian population some 20,000 years ago.

For a few hundred dollars or euros and a swab from a cheek, a human being can now discover his or her ancestral heritage (as well as susceptibilities to certain illnesses) via DNA testing. And it can be mind-blowing. Take the case of Harvard's Henry Louis Gates. For a long time Gates thought that he was not 100 percent African American; he believed he was descended in part from a slave owner named Brady. But DNA analysis turned his world upside down. He learned that one of his white ancestors was probably an Irish servant who met a sixth or seventh great-grandfather before 1700. Gates (in Kalb, 2006:48) says, "I'm thinking I'm a Brady and maybe I'm from Nigeria, and here I am descended from some white woman....It's incredible!" Or take the case of Father Bill Sanchez in Albuquerque, New Mexico. Through DNA testing, the Catholic priest discovered that his DNA contains some characteristics of an ancient Jewish priesthood, the Cohanim (in Kalb, 2006:50–51).

(*Sidenote*: In the 2010 U.S. Census, the long form—with questions about house size, commuting to work, and others aspects of daily life—is being retired. A new, annual American Community Survey, which asks questions of a sample of about 3 million households, is already in place; and it replaces the long form.)

Peoplehood

Most generally, the term "ethnicity" connotes a "consciousness of kind," a sense of peoplehood (*eth* is the Greek root for "people"). This is a subjective belief; an objective blood relationship may or may not exist. According to the eminent German sociologist Max Weber, an ethnic group holds a subjective belief in its "common descent because of similarities of physical type or of customs or both, or because of memories of colonization and migration" ([1921] 1968:389). In Weber's definition, the defining element of an ethnic group is the sharing of an identity based on a shared history. Hence, African Americans, Amish, Hopis, and Italian Americans are considered ethnic groups. But what about many others—for instance, persons with a multiracial or multiethnic background—Vietnamese African Americans or Jewish Cuban Americans? It all depends on how individuals define themselves and how the larger society defines them.

Who's a "Minority"?

Changes in racial and ethnic consciousness are reflected in language. Take, for instance, the term **minority**. After World War I, it referred to European national groups—Serbs, Latvians, Czechs, and other groups involved in the Treaty of Versailles. By the 1930s and 1940s, the term designated ethnic and racial groups in the United States.

Nations define "minorities" differently. Indeed, some deny the existence of minority groups altogether. In France, for example, the notion of an ethnic or religious "minority" is not recognized. (Jowitt might say that this exemplifies a nation that promotes "civic" rather than "ethnic" identity.)

In the United States, it was Louis Wirth (Chapter 6) who first tried to define and comprehensively type the nation's minorities. In 1945, Wirth said that a minority is a group of people that is "singled out from the others in the society in which they live for differential and unequal treatment and who therefore regard themselves as objects of collective discrimination" (1945:347). Note that Wirth makes no specific mention of race, ethnic background, religion—or numbers. Instead, he emphasizes social oppression: minorities-as-victims. Using Wirth's definition, gays and lesbians, people in wheelchairs, and people weighing over 350 pounds, among other groups, qualify as minorities.

How minorities are defined is no small issue. For one thing, "perks" and big money are at stake. Government agencies in many countries, from Brazil, India, Malaysia, Sri Lanka, and Nigeria to the United States, set aside money and/or perks specifically for racial/ethnic minority groups. For example, in Brazil, the Federal University of Brasilia reserves 20 percent of its places for black students (Davies, 2003). In one pre-Katrina year, the city of New Orleans earmarked about 20 percent of its $300 million budget for minority-owned businesses. (In a controversial ruling, Louisiana lawmakers defined the state's 200,000–300,000 Cajuns as a minority, thus qualifying them for these "minority set-asides." A Cajun spokesperson argued that his people had suffered cultural discrimination historically, particularly repression in the exercise of their French language, and that some had been enslaved or indentured. Thus, according to Wirth's definition, the Cajuns qualify as a minority. But many

in Louisiana felt that calling Cajuns a minority was a bad joke, mocking affirmative action programs in general and the discrimination and economic hardship faced by the state's 1 million African Americans in particular.)

Clearly, there is no agreed-on definition of "minority." Some Americans use the word as Wirth intended: as a social–psychological badge of discrimination. Some use the word interchangeably with "people of color," a term that returned to favor a generation ago. Others use it to mean an economically-disadvantaged ethnic group. Now, many social scientists refer to groups once called minorities as "subcultures" or "subcommunities"—that is, groups defining themselves as different from other groups and from the dominant culture in terms of worldview and/or lifestyle. In this usage, there is a sense of difference—but not of discrimination or oppression.

FROM MINORITY TO MAJORITY

However defined, *the term "minority" has nothing to do with numbers*. In many U.S. cities—including New York, Miami, Gary, Washington, Honolulu, El Paso, New Orleans, Chicago, Atlanta, and Baltimore—so-called minorities have become numerical majorities.

Such is also the case in many California cities, including Los Angeles, Oakland, Milpitas (Chapter 8), and "Everyone's Favorite City"—San Francisco. At the very least, this demographic development affects political coalitions and public school curricula. For whites, it may also affect deep-seated psychological assumptions: For 200 years whites assumed that the United States was basically an European country with pockets of minorities, but the present generation of Euro-Americans (whites) in California and in many U.S. cities faces a new reality: They represent a minority, not a majority, in terms of numbers.

Indeed, in the United States, according to analyses of census data released in August 2008, one in four counties is already—or is approaching—the point where Hispanic, African American, and Asian children and young adults constitute a majority of the population under 20 years of age. Among people of all ages, "minorities" make up at least 40 percent of the population in more than one-sixth of the nation's counties, which include many U.S. cities (Roberts, 2008b).

Does this shift in many U.S. cities—from numerical majority to minority—mean that whites will consider themselves just one among many groups? Perhaps. Perhaps not. This shift may test whether the United States can peacefully change from an European-dominated society with minorities to a "world society" where everyone is considered a minority.

Indeed, from 2006 to 2007, according to the U.S. Census Bureau, the Hispanic population in the United States grew by 3.3 percent compared with 2.9 percent for Asians, 1.3 percent for blacks, and 0.3 percent for non-Hispanic whites (in Roberts, 2008a). During the same period, the number of Asians increased even faster than the number of Hispanics in 14 states. The upshot, as of 2007: "Members of racial and ethnic minorities now account for more than one in three Americans," (Roberts, 2008a). (Since 2007, however, the population growth of Asians and Hiapanics in the United States slowed, probably due to a lackluster economy and immigration laws. As a result, the U.S. Census Bureau pushed back estimates on when "minorities" will become the majority by as much as a decade [Yen, 2009].)

In some cases, violence in U.S. metro areas (as well as elsewhere globally) has accompanied the arrival of "outsider" ethnic groups. But more often when people of color move in, whites pull up stakes, not an AK-47. Why? Because some whites are discomfited by immigrants and people from different cultures. Preferring to avoid such people, many move to segregated enclaves—if they can.

In the United States, gated communities (GCs) are fueling "segregated cities" and suburbs. That's the conclusion reached by many researchers (e.g., Vesselinov, 2008) who claim that increased economic and social residential segregation results from the expansion of GCs in the past two decades or so. (Ironically, immigrants have higher rates of moving to GCs than native-born people in the United States.)

One key reason that movers give for decamping to GCs is *fear of outsiders*. For example, in two GCs, one in San Antonio, Texas, and the other in Queens, New York, many residents feared "others" from "outside the gates" (Low, 2003). GC residents were particularly bothered by "ethnic change" in their former neighborhoods; this concern could well mask ethnocentrism and racism.

Note that in the United States there is a wide variety of homogeneous GCs. These range from Carefree Cove, a GC for gays and lesbians in Zionville, North Carolina, to Aegis Gardens, an assisted-living center in Fremont, California, where the food and the building design are Chinese. Homogeneity is built into such GCs by admission policies. Perhaps this reflects a desire for living "with one's own kind"—however defined.

Finally, and importantly, it is no longer only "white flight" in the United States that fuels residential segregation. In recent years, Latinos have proportionally been bigger movers to GCs than many racial or ethnic groups, particularly African Americans (see Vesselinov, 2008). Asian Americans too have chosen to live in walled communities much more often than African Americans and some other groups.

A CLASH OF VALUES: WHITE ETHNICS VERSUS WASP SUPERCULTURE

Of course, whites in the United States are far from homogeneous. One division that remains important is WASP versus white ethnic.

A generation ago, Michael Novak, a conservative, Catholic philosopher, and descendant of Slovak immigrants, wrote that white ethnics had been made to feel stupid, backward, and immoral by what he called the WASP *superculture* in America. In *The Rise of the Unmeltable Ethnics* (1971), Novak described and contrasted white ethnic working-class culture and WASP "superculture," so-called because he felt it only tried to overwhelm and stamp out competing ways of life:

> The WASP home cherishes good order, poise, soft voices, cleanliness...[such a home] offers culture shock to non-WASPs. Decorum and self-control. Tight emotions....To the WASP, the direct flow of emotion is childish; his acculturation requires cognitive control....The WASP way—the almost universal industrial way of the modern age—is to put a harsh rein upon the impulses of man's animal nature...and to order him docilely to produce. It is a life geared to action, to "changing history," to progress.
>
> *(1971:179, 180, 185)*

Working-class, white ethnic homes, Novak (1971:26) said, are just the opposite, and the people in them don't share WASP values or goals. Noise, family get-togethers, and emotionality typify white ethnic home life. And instead of seeking to change history, white ethnic males see the world as a tough, violent place where hard work, family discipline, and gradual self-development are the routes to moderate success. To the women, the world outside remains "mainly unchangeable."

Other observers agree that family and neighborhood are centers of working-class ethnic life. And some, like the late Jane Jacobs (1916–2006), celebrated the vitality of such neighborhoods. She found ethnic neighborhoods to be alive with activity, especially the sidewalks. Before moving to Toronto, Canada, here is how she described the "intricate sidewalk ballet" on her stretch of Hudson Street in New York City, a scene that not only animates the city but, she says, helps keep its residents safe:

> When I get home after work, the ballet is reaching its crescendo. This is the time of roller skates and stilts and tricycles, and games in the lee of the stoop with bottletops and plastic cowboys; this is the time of bundles and packages, zig-zagging from the drug store back over to the butcher's; this is the time when teenagers, all dressed up, are pausing to ask if their slips show or their collars look right; this is the time when beautiful girls get out of MG's; this is the time when the fire engines go through; this is the time when anybody you know around Hudson Street will go by.
>
> *(1961:52)*

Urbanist Jacobs idealized the New York City street as a place made safe by having everyone's "eyes on the street"—people watching and watching over one another while they talk, flirt, play, and so on. No one could mistake Jacobs's description of her ethnic neighborhood for a portrait of a middle-class WASP street scene.

Some WASPs might feel uncomfortable on Hudson Street. For one, Richard Brookhiser, a senior editor at the conservative *National Review*, thinks that what made America great are not eyes on the street and an intricate sidewalk ballet but rather basic WASP values, which he defines as self-control, reserve, conscience, antisensuality, hard work, determination not to waste time, success, and civic-mindedness (1991). Perhaps that is what "traditional values" mean to WASPs—

but not necessarily to working-class white ethnics or people of color.

ONCE AGAIN, THE ENTANGLEMENT OF RACE/ ETHNICITY AND CLASS

For many white working-class ethnics, a life centered on family and neighborhood remains a deeply held value. Amid turbulence, even chaos, home and family can represent the comfort of a homogeneous island in a heterogeneous ocean. Take, for example, the life in Canarsie, a Brooklyn, New York, neighborhood of formerly mainly second- and third-generation Italians and Jews. There, neighborhood stability, particularly home and children, was once highly valued; "alternative lifestyles" found little support. Sociologist Jonathan Rieder, writing a generation ago, found that working-class whites of Canarsie experienced the period between 1960 and 1980 as a time of "danger and dispossession—culturally and internationally, but especially racially" (1985:1, 4).

But, a generation later, Canarsie's ethnic and racial makeup had changed enormously. Between 1960 and 1990, Canarsie lost population as the Italian American and Jewish residents aged, died, or left. Then, population spurted; from 1990 to 2000, it grew nearly 20 percent. Thousands of Caribbean immigrants moved to the neighborhood together with relatively affluent non-Hispanic African Americans. By 2000, Canarsie and the neighboring Flatlands District were majority African American.

Like those in pre-change Canarsie, white working-class families in U.S. multiethnic cities often see themselves as victims—"the objects of others' will"—of reverse discrimination, of bureaucrats, of liberal social policies, and of the values of so-called cultural elites. In pre-1990 Canarsie and similar white ethnic neighborhoods, residents often find themselves in the immediate line of fire; typically, racial tension shows up first and more intensely in such neighborhoods, for residents have fewer resources and escape valves than upper-middle-class whites. Here is a classic example: When the Irish took over the public schools in Boston and Cambridge in the first part of this century, Harvard University families moved their children out of public schools and started private ones. By 1962, only one out of over 50 members of the Harvard Graduate

School of Education had children in Cambridge public schools (Binzen, 1970:49–50).

An observer from Mars might wonder why working-class whites and African Americans don't recognize their common interests. After all, they often reside in side-by-side communities and share similar hopes. Yet, often they are separated by a gulf of fear and suspicion. Their worlds rarely intersect, and they live as if on different planets.

Sociologist William Julius Wilson once said that "if you could get these [white and African American working-class people] to recognize their common interests, it would go a long way toward alleviating racial hostility" (in Wilkerson, 1992:A12)—which brings us to the Grand Canyon.

THE GRAND CANYON

Countless observers have tried to understand the social–psychological gulf between African Americans and whites, what has been called the "American dilemma." Let's consider a few of their ideas.

One view is that *permanent racism* is the root of the grand canyon between blacks and whites. If so, what is at the root of racism? Here, there is wide disagreement. Author Gore Vidal traces white racism to the Bible: "As descendants of Ham, blacks are forever accursed.... Racism is in the marrow of the bone of the true believer. For him [or her], black is forever inferior to white" (1992:55).

Novelist James Baldwin had another explanation. He claimed that whites created the image of a lustful, lazy, stupid "nigger" to embody the very traits that they could not tolerate within themselves. Sociologist Douglas Massey (2007) believes that there is a universal human tendency to place others on social ladders—higher or lower—and that in the United States people of color as well as others (e.g., the poor, women) have been targets of stereotyping, resulting in discrimination and exploitation throughout U.S. history.

Other analysts think that racism is essentially about power: White elites promote a racist ideology in order to help maintain poor whites' perception of their own superiority over subordinate groups such as African Americans and Latinos; this ideology prevents poor people of color and poor whites with common class interests from making common cause. In this view, white elites thus maintain their power, even if few in number. Others think that racism is chiefly motivated by psychological sentiments internalized in childhood, not by rational self-interest.

Whatever the underlying causes of racism, sociologists Robert D. Bullard and Joe R. Feagin (1991) say that there are two types: individual racism and institutionalized racism. (*Individual racism* takes many forms, including a person's attempt to drive a black family out of a white neighborhood by burning a cross in the yard. *Institutionalized racism* refers to organizational actions that carry out discriminatory practices, such as real estate agents' steering black families away from white areas.)

They argue that in both the North and the South, "the modern American city has its roots in well-institutionalized racism" by whites against blacks, which is reflected in racially segregated housing, schools, and jobs (1991:72).

Political scientist Ira Katznelson (1981) offers a contrasting view, one based on capitalism and class. He argues that U.S. workers in major industrial cities act on the basis of class solidarity at work but on the basis of ethnic and territorial affinities at home. In Katznelson's view, this sharply divided consciousness—between the politics of work and the politics of community—is a divide-and-conquer tactic that has served to protect the core arrangements of capitalism. This pattern, he says, started in the post–Civil War era when workers were mobilized politically into labor unions at work and into city machines at home. Big-city machines (Chapter 14) used divide-and-rule tactics to pit ethnic group against ethnic group, thereby diffusing or coopting the energies of the working class. Additionally, new government services were delivered to citizens in their communities, not their workplaces. The result, according to Katznelson, is that the U.S. urban political system produced "a working class unique in the West: militant as labor, and virtually nonexistent as a collectivity outside the workplace" (1981:71).

From another angle, sociologist Erving Goffman's classic study *Stigma* (1963) offered an approach to social identity that can be adapted to better understand black–white relations in the United States. Goffman said that a stigmatized individual is one who is disqualified from full social acceptance by so-called normals (people whose identity is accepted). Disqualification may be based on perceived character blemishes, physical deformities, or "the tribal stigma of race, nation, and religion." Normals "believe the person with a stigma is not quite human." Based on this assumption, normals "exercise varieties of discrimination, through which [they] effectively, if often unthinkingly, reduce the life chances" of the stigmatized individual. Then "normals construct an ideology which rationalizes their animosity and also explains the stigmatized person's supposed inferiority" (1963:4, 5). Although Goffman doesn't mention them, we can interpret various historic public policies, including the Chinese Exclusion Act of 1882 and racial segregation in U.S. public schools, as outgrowths of such stigmatizing ideologies.

Political scientist Andrew Hacker has written about how the stigma of blackness operates in the United States. In his book *Two Nations: Black and White, Separate, Hostile, Unequal* (1992a) and in a radio interview about the book (1992b), Hacker said that an African American "bears the mark of slavery. Even after emancipation…blacks continued to be seen as an inferior species." According to Hacker, African Americans are still treated as a "subordinate caste." His examples included this one about dental hygiene, an occupation that (still) has one of the smallest percentages of blacks: "White people just don't want black fingers in their mouths. If that isn't racism, tell me what is" (1992b).

Hacker claimed that few whites ever think about how membership in the dominant race gives them power and privileges. Yet the greatest privilege any American can have is being white because "no matter how degraded their lives…. [whites] can never become black." (*Caution*: "Never" is one of those words to watch out for. Perhaps you know, as I do, a white person passing as black. Rare in the United States but possible. The opposite is more often the case, as with Anatole Broyard, a one-time *New York Times* book critic. Perhaps more widely known is novelist Philip Roth's creation, Coleman Silk, a classics professor who long passed as white, with various surreal consequences (see Roth's *The Human Stain*, [2000] 2001).

Just how important is it to be white in the United States? Hacker's experiment suggests that it's very important—to whites. He asked his white college students in New York City to put a price tag on having their white skin taken away and becoming black. On average, the white students thought that they should be indemnified $1 million—*annually*—for the loss of their whiteness.

Have attitudes changed in the past generation? Perhaps. Another study—asking similar questions of whites—was published in 2007 by Ohio State University professor of psychology Philip Mazzocco and Harvard professor of social ethics Mahajin Banaji (see Grabmeier, n.d.). They found that when white respondents in the United States were asked to imagine how much they would have to be paid to live the rest of their lives as a black person, most requested relatively low amounts, generally less than $10,000. (In contrast, they said they would have to be paid about $1 million to give up watching television for the rest of their lives.)

What has changed since Hacker's earlier study, if anything? How should these findings be interpreted? According to coauthor Mazzocco, the 2007 study suggests that most white people in the United States just don't get it—they don't understand the persistent racial disparities in the United States. Coauthor Banaji thinks that white people in the United States are not mean or uncaring or ethically flawed. Rather, he says, whites "suffer from a glaring ignorance about what it means to live as a black American" (in Grabmeier, n.d.).

Yet, there are signs that, as the classic Bob Dylan song put it, "the times they are a-changing." As many have noted, that an African American (of biracial heritage) was elected to the highest office in the land in 2008 means that prior attitude shifts, among numerous whites, had already occurred. At the same time, however, three in 10 white respondents in a June 2008 random sample poll conducted by the *Washington Post* and ABC News admitted to racist views (in Cohen and Agiesta, 2008:A1). At the same time, 51 percent of the respondents call the current state of race relations "excellent" or "good." The gap between whites and blacks on the issue of racism is now the widest it has been in polls dating to early 1992: "More than six in 10 African Americans now rate race relations as 'not so good' or 'poor,' while 53 percent of whites hold more positive views" (Cohen and Agiesta, 2008:A1).

Whatever racial (or ethnic) bias that respondents state or refuse to state, successful, educated, affluent African Americans and Latinos are not immune to discrimination. On the contrary. If hailing a late-night taxi, for example, educated/affluent people of color often assume a posture which says to the driver, "Please do not pass me by. Trust me."

Furthermore, economic discrimination hurts nonwhites much more often than whites. For example, in one recent year, high-income African Americans were rejected for bank home loans 2.83 times more often than high-income whites. (ACORN, 2003). In public places, African Americans often suffer hate crimes, avoidance, police harassment, or verbal epithets—solely because of their skin color. A poignant story told by the distinguished Harvard scholar Henry Louis ("Skip") Gates, Jr., may be years old but is not dated:

> I often find myself moving into upper-middle-class white neighborhoods, and the first thing I do when I move into a neighborhood is to check in with the police and introduce myself. "Hi. I am Doctor Gates. I go away often and I was wondering if there are any security precautions I should take during vacations." But of course that's not it. It's that sooner or later someone is going to see this Negro in a car and ask what he is doing there. I do it so often and they see this face. I've lived in all-white neighborhoods in Durham, N.C. and in Ithaca, N.Y., and now in predominantly white Lexington, Mass. I think it's disgusting to feel that you have to do that.
>
> *(1992:48)*

Update: As noted earlier, in a much-publicized—and much-disputed—case in July, 2009, Gates was arrested outside his Cambridge, MA home, he said, due to the color of his skin. (The arresting officer denied this.)

Gates's experiences and many studies suggest that in the United States a person's skin color—specifically blackness—remains an important, perhaps the most important, characteristic of the person, whatever the content of his or her character or station in life. Sadly, the United States has no monopoly on this color fixation.

SYMBOLIC ETHNICITY

Arguably, race and ethnicity are the most widely written-about topics in the United States. That is a

testament to their continuing centrality to the nation's conscience. Yet some scholars argue that many grand- and great-grandchildren of European immigrants (i.e., third- and fourth-generation white ethnics) may be characterized by **symbolic ethnicity**; that is, their ethnic identity may be more symbolic than real. Some claim that European ethnicity today—being Polish American or Italian American, for example—bears little relation to the ancestral European heritage. Instead, they say, white ethnic identity is more of a political and psychological defense mechanism against a lack of opportunities.

A generation ago, sociologist–urban planner Herbert J. Gans (1979:3) argued that, essentially, ethnicity was a white working-class style. By the third generation, however, most white ethnics had friends outside the ethnic group, depended little on fellow ethnics, and worked for companies where ethnic ties are either irrelevant or not very relevant. (Note that third-generation white ethnics are aided by the "strength of weak ties," detailed in Chapter 8.) In other words, ethnicity is not central to the lives of white ethnics in the United States by the third generation.

FEELINGS AND FOOD

By the third generation, ethnicity may not remain central to white ethnics, but, Gans argued, third-generation white ethnics do continue to see themselves as ethnics—whether they define ethnicity in terms of religion or national ancestry. This ethnicity expresses itself as a *feeling*—a feeling of being Italian or Polish or Jewish—that is primarily shown in nostalgia for the Old Country, pride in tradition, a desire to return to an imagined past, the practice of ceremonial holidays, and/or consumption of special foods.

Symbolic ethnicity, in my view, is often reinforced by a perceived need to fight negative stereotypes. For example, *fra noi*, a newspaper serving Chicagoland's Italian American community, often carries articles about food, wine, and celebrations—and, tellingly, an article about anti-Italian bigotry based on popular myths about the alleged links between organized crime and Italians, thus reminding coethnics of their collective image (http://www.franoi.com/).

Gans concluded that among European immigrants "symbolic ethnicity should become the dominant way of being ethnic by the time the fourth generation...matures into adulthood" (1979:16). It is noteworthy that Gans did not extend his concept of symbolic ethnicity to non-European immigrants. In recent years, he has written that some U.S. immigrants, who are people of color, are being "socially whitened" (Chapter 11). However, Gans and others say that this is not happening to African Americans.

We might add that even symbolic ethnicity seems problematic for some once-European groups. Take, for example, U.S. Jews. Since the mid-1960s the small U.S. Jewish population—5.5 million or 1.8 percent of the nation's population in 2005 (Jewish Virtual Library, 2005)—has been eroding, due largely to interfaith marriage. In just one generation, the rate of Jewish intermarriage increased more than five times—from 9 percent before 1965 to over 52 percent after 1985. This

trend has continued: In 2006, an estimated 50 percent of both Jewish men and women "married out" (Allen Schwartz, 2006). And, once Jews intermarry, their children seldom identify as Jewish (Steinfels, 1992:156).

My hunch is that Gans's prediction of symbolic ethnicity as a dominant mode for European ethnics will hold true for some non-European immigrant groups too. Here is my hypothesis: Symbolic ethnicity will become the dominant way of being ethnic for any fourth-generation immigrant group with either of two key characteristics: (1) very high out-marriage rates, such as Korean American and Filipino American women (see Lee, 2007) or (2) heavy representation in professional–technical occupations, such as Filipinos and East Indians (Portes and Rumbaut, 1990:19–20). My hypothesis is based on this truism: Both out-marriage and professionalization tend to blunt ethnic identification. People in professional–technical

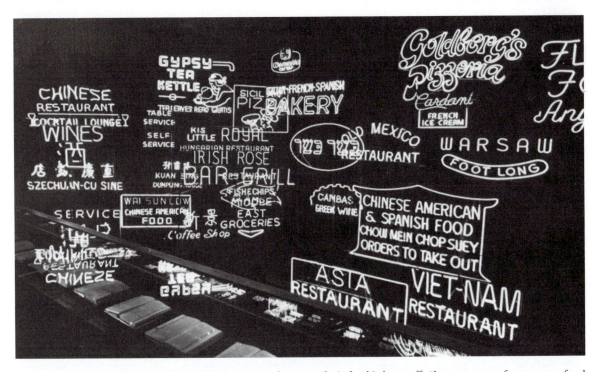

Fig. 10.4 U.S. DIET: ETHNIC POTPOURRI. In U.S. retail stores, ethnic food is hot stuff: About one out of every seven food dollars was spent on ethnic food in 2006, and salsa outsold ketchup. In both fine-dining and fast-food ("quick-service") restaurants, including McDonald's, Latin cuisine is now mainstream in the United States. According to a National Restaurant Association study, Italian food is the most popular ethnic cuisine in the United States, followed by Mexican food (in Wolfe and Ferland, n.d.). Decades earlier, the hot dog, a U.S. staple, was considered an ethnic (German) food. (Peter Garfield)

occupations rarely come from urban villages or tight ethnic communities. Further, out-marriage tends to create new cultural patterns. And, demographers predict, by 2020 nearly 20 percent of all Asian Americans will be multiracial; that figure will climb higher, to 36 percent, by the year 2050 (Le and Huang, 2008). If so, it means that out-marriage alone will have a significant impact on the identity and probable feeling of symbolic ethnicity among many Asian Americans.

THE STEWPOT

For some in the United States, ethnicity is mostly symbolic. But the persistence of racial and ethnic communities suggests that the United States is a **stewpot**—sometimes boiling over with anger, frustration, and hate—not a melting pot. After the turmoil (or "riots" or "civil disobedience") in Los Angeles following the Rodney King jury verdict in 1992, some called it a "boiling pot."

The Pennsylvania Amish and some groups have remained aloof and unassimilated by choice. But many groups, particularly African Americans, had no choice. Speaking specifically about African Americans, the late Supreme Court justice Thurgood Marshall put it this way in 1987: "If the United States is indeed the great melting pot, the Negro either didn't get in the pot or he didn't get melted down" (in Taylor, 1987).

At various historical periods, many non-WASP groups have been victims of discrimination, racism, or violence. Today, some argue that discrimination extends to some groups with WASP members too. Now let's take a closer look at some groups in the U.S. stewpot.

NATIVE AMERICANS: THE UNASSIMILATED

In Rapid City, South Dakota, the office of the weekly *Lakota Times* used to be festooned with baseball pennants. There was one for the "Cleveland Indians" and others for the "Pittsburgh Negroes," the "Kansas City Jews," and the "San Diego Caucasians." Beneath the pennants was this sign: "Now you know how Native Americans feel" (Johnson, 1991:A10). Responding to such feelings, several media organizations dropped nicknames that Native Americans consider offensive, using instead such terms as "Atlanta baseball team." Recently, the American Sociological Association (2007),

the professional association of U.S. sociologists, called for the elimination of the use of Native American nicknames, logos, and mascots in sports because social science research shows that they "reflect and reinforce misleading stereotypes of Native Americans" and their continued use "communicates implicit disrespect for [their] spiritual and cultural practices."

But new names don't change the Native Americans' bleak economic situation. As a group, Native Americans (called First Nations in Canada, a name that excludes Inuits and Métis people) and Alaskan Natives are poor. Some are desperately poor. For example, the Pine Ridge Reservation, home of the Lakota-Oyate (called the Sioux by white settlers) in South Dakota's well-named Badlands, had the sad distinction of being the nation's poorest community in 1990 and 2000. On the Pine Ridge Reservation, roughly the size of the state of Connecticut, residents suffered an unemployment rate in 1998 of 73 percent (according to an annual survey by the Oglala Sioux Tribe and the Bureau of Indian Affairs) or higher; some (e.g., Stephanie M. Schwartz, 2006) report the rate to be over 83 percent. In 2006, one reporter claimed that over 97 percent of the residents on the reservation lived in poverty and that the median income on the Pine Ridge Reservation was less than $3,500 per year (Stephanie M. Schwartz, 2006). Pine Ridge is located in two counties, one of which—Shannon County—was the second poorest county in the United States (based on per capita income) in the 2000 Census.

A dubious honor goes to Buffalo County, South Dakota, too. It was the poorest county in the nation as of the 2000 Census. The majority of its 2,000+ inhabitants are Crow Creek Sioux, living on a reservation. Living conditions on the reservation resemble those in very poor countries: about 7 out of 10 people are jobless, and neither plumbing nor electricity exists there.

Some small tribes, with "vibrant" casinos located near urban areas, have done well in recent years (Grover, n.d.). And about 221 tribal governments operate either class II (bingo) or class III (full-scale) casinos on their lands. Yet, many Native people in the United States do not have what others consider basic services such as plumbing, running water, telephone service, and electricity. Again, reports vary, but one source (Kraus, 2001) reports that 52 percent of Navajos lacked complete plumbing facilities and over 81 percent did not have telephone service in 2001.

In the 2000 U.S. Census, about 4.3 million persons (about 1.5 percent of the total U.S. population) identified themselves as Native American or Alaskan Native (Ogunwale, 2006:3). Many of them are not doing well economically. For example, in 2000, over 37 percent of the Navajos, the second largest Native American group, lived in poverty as defined by the federal government, and 37 percent had less than a high school education. (The Cherokee Nation is the largest in terms of numbers, but the Navajo Nation has the most populous reservation: 175,200 reside on the Navajo reservation and trust lands, which span portions of Arizona, New Mexico, and Utah.)

As of the 2000 U.S. Census, the majority— 66 percent—of Native Americans and Alaskan Natives lived in metropolitan areas, but this represented the lowest percentage of any racial/ethnic group in the nation. (Until about 1990, a majority of Native Americans and Alaskan Natives lived outside of metro areas, mainly on reservations or other trust lands.)

Whether in cities or on reservations or trust lands, Native Americans suffer from high rates of unemployment, suicide, alcoholism, car accidents, obesity, and diabetes. In addition, the economic future for many is limited. Statistics vary widely from reservation to reservation, but low educational attainment is the norm on many reservations.

Official U.S. government policy toward the first Americans has been assimilationist. But the policy has not worked. Forcibly removed from their ancestral homes, robbed of schooling in their tribal languages, and sent off to Bureau of Indian Affairs schools—and generally overwhelmed by white migrants—many Native Americans still retain their distinctive cultures.

Officially, the federal government vowed to assimilate Native Americans into the mainstream of U.S. culture. Yet they weren't granted citizenship until 1924. And by 2001 more, not fewer, nations were recognized by the U.S. government: There were 556 federally recognized tribes.

The unique plight of the first Americans can be summed up as follows: Most immigrants to the United States left their native lands due to dissatisfaction and,

thus, had to adjust to a new environment or enslavement. But this was not the case for Native Americans: They were conquered and overwhelmed by foreigners in their own land.

In contemporary life, as Figure 10.5 suggests, Native American cultures may be undermined or overwhelmed by more subtle means: television and other technologies. However, there are some signs that Native American culture has not been totally overwhelmed. One is a flourishing, tribally-controlled college in those same South Dakota Badlands: Oglala Lakota College. Chartered in 1971, the college follows a philosophy expressed in its motto: *Wa Wo Ici Ya*, a Lakota expression translated as "We can do it ourselves."

AFRICAN AMERICANS: PERMANENT UNDERCLASS?

Blacks from Africa first arrived in the English colonies in 1619. They were considered indentured servants who could work off their bonds after a period of time. This situation quickly changed, and by the mid-seventeenth century the enslaved black population in the South had increased. Northerners in colonial America also held slaves, mainly as house servants and farm workers.

The forced migration of black Africans to the fields and cities of the colonies and the early migration of British and European settlers to North America were inextricably linked: "They were both undertaken primarily in the hope of securing a better life—for whites" (Greene, 1976:89).

Yale historian David Brion Davis goes further, arguing that the very notion of "the American dream" was originally made possible by the availability of enslaved labor: "From the early West India trade of the northeastern colonies to the cotton exports that helped pay for northern railroads and industrialization, America's economy depended largely on slave labor" (1992:14).

Journalist–writer Ryszard Kapuściński puts it even more starkly: "Africa's contribution to world history has been immense—nothing less than a transformation of a centuries-old global hierarchy. By furnishing the New World its labor force, it enabled it to amass enough wealth and power to surpass the Old World" (2007:100).

From colonial days and the plantation South to the present, much has changed. African Americans now

Fig. 10.5 GENERATION GAP. In an Alaskan village, a Yupik renders a seal while her granddaughter watches TV. (Paul Souder)

have citizenship and civil rights. Most (86.5 percent as of 2000) live in metropolitan areas, not rural places. And yet, as victims of long-standing racism and economic discrimination, they are consigned as a group to lower socioeconomic status and marginalized.

Housing segregation is one measure of African American marginalization. In terms of the most commonly-used residential segregation, the dissimilarity index, the five most-segregated metropolitan areas in the United States in 2000 for African Americans were, in descending order, Detroit, Milwaukee–Waukesha, New York, Newark, and Chicago. (The five least-segregated metro areas were, in descending order: Orange County, California; Hickory–Morganton–Lenoir, North Carolina; Fort Walton Beach, Florida; Charlottesville, Virginia; and Auburn–Opelika, Alabama.)

There has been a "slow but steady" reduction in residential segregation of African Americans in most U.S. metro areas during the 1980–2000 period (U.S. Census Bureau, n.d.:15). Yet, many African Americans still live in virtual racial isolation: They live in neighborhoods that are at least 90 percent black. Some analysts (e.g., Patterson and Winship, 1992:A17) say that most blacks *choose* to live separately from whites and that housing segregation in itself is no problem. Others, including sociologist Douglas Massey, a leading analyst on migration and housing segregation, disagree. Massey says that extreme housing segregation leads to residential immobility based on race, and that this harms African Americans because "residential mobility [which they lack] is a major avenue of social mobility" (in Kilson and Bond, 1992:A16).

Massey and coauthor Nancy Denton charge that millions of African Americans live in hypersegregated neighborhoods. In their view, this is tantamount to *American Apartheid* (1998). Massey and Denton claim that housing segregation (and the consequent disassociation from other lifestyles) is the root of many problems facing African Americans today.

And how did this extreme segregation happen? Massey and Denton (1998) blame whites for creating or encouraging the making of African American ghettoes in order to isolate growing urban African American populations. They argue that housing segregation is being perpetuated by a combination of institutional practices, individual behavior, and public policies.

The conclusions of Massey and Denton challenge the views of William Julius Wilson and others, who think that race is declining in significance. We now turn to Wilson's influential ideas.

Sociologist William Julius Wilson's most influential and controversial study remains *The Declining Significance of Race* (1978). His later studies have also been influential and controversial: *The Truly Disadvantaged* (1987) and *When Work Disappears* (1996). In *When Work Disappears*, Wilson argues that it is joblessness and the disappearance of decently paid, blue-collar work, due mainly to changes in the global economy—not racism—that underlie the destruction of inner-city businesses and the consequent deterioration of inner-city ghettoes and flight of younger, more mobile African Americans to the suburbs.

In his 1978 book (which caused the most significant stir), Wilson argued that, primarily, it is structural changes in the metropolitan economy (e.g., deindustrialization, suburbanization of blue-collar work, and the consequent reduction in the pool of African American marriageable men)—not a culture of poverty, not immigration policy, and not racism—that created a huge black "underclass." (The term "underclass" generally refers to the urban impoverished [particularly African Americans and Latinos] who are chronically jobless and welfare-dependent. Radicals prefer the word "lumpenproletariat," a harsher term used by Marx to describe "the reserve army of the unemployed.")

In general, then, Wilson, a sociology professor at Harvard University since 1996, maintains that class is more important than race in determining blacks' life chances due to these structural changes. He is not alone. Historian Jacqueline Jones (1992) says that by the late 1980s, historical and economic processes had created a multitude of "underclasses" and that these people were not necessarily black or residents of northern cities. New immigrants from Latin America, China, and Southeast Asia, as well as Appalachian white migrants, she notes, often faced the same prejudice as African Americans from would-be employers, landlords, and public officials. She concludes that "black traits" which whites disliked most—presumed laziness, violent proclivities, welfare-seeking, unreliability, shiftlessness, lack of ambition—were associated more with lower-class position than with race.

The urban underclass has long interested Wilson as well as many other scholars. As a result of research he directed at the Urban Poverty and Family Life Project in Chicago from 1985 to 1989, Wilson thought that *no one factor explains why some disadvantaged groups are more likely to join the underclass than others* (in Raymond, 1991:A12). The Chicago researchers focused on 2,490 inner-city residents—1,177 African Americans, 458 Puerto Ricans, 474 Mexicans, and 381 whites—and investigated their work and family experiences, friendship networks, marriage and children, and use of welfare; they also looked at structural reasons for joblessness such as automation. Researchers found a combination of structural and cultural factors that account for the rise of chronic poverty among African Americans, including the following: living in the poorest neighborhoods among unemployed people (thereby cutting off "weak ties," discussed in Chapter 8, to job leads), racial discrimination, generally positive attitudes toward welfare, lack of access to cars, the presence of a sole adult in the house (preventing the sharing of child-care duties), and plant shutdowns.

The upshot, Wilson said, is that the mass of poor and poorly-trained African Americans have little hope or chance of escaping poverty and low status. Years earlier, Glazer and Moynihan came to the same conclusion. In 1963, they wrote that blacks and Puerto Ricans in New York City were a "submerged, exploited, and very possibly permanent proletariat" (299).

Although best known for his earlier stance on the significance of race, Wilson seems to be broadening his approach. In a more recent work, *More than Just Race* (2009), he emphasizes the interaction of cultural and structural factors involved in African American poverty. Discussing the persistence of the inner-city ghetto, the plight of low-skilled black males, and the fragmentation of the African American family, Wilson argues that structural and cultural forces are inextricably linked. Further, he argues, public policy can change the racial status quo by reforming the institutions that reinforce it.

To conclude: The notion that large groups of citizens may be permanently poor goes against the grain in the United States. As French historian-aristocrat Alexis de Tocqueville ([1840] 2006) long ago observed, Americans will endure poverty and even servitude but not fixed class differences. In the past, different standards of life were made tolerable either by the idea of equal opportunity for advancement or by the "American dream" of upward mobility through a sweaty brow and a pinch of luck. All were reassured that they too could move up socially and economically. This assumption provided hope for generations of people in the United States. But now this assumption is widely questioned as (1) both blue-, white-, and "no-collar" jobs disappear from the United States and (2) the gap between rich and poor grows wider. Still, countless people in the United States continue to "dream up and blame down" (Tim Teninty, personal conversation, 1992).

Finally, as detailed in Chapter 11, Herbert Gans (1999) and others predict that some U.S. ethnic groups—but not African Americans—will be "socially whitened," that is, blend into the larger culture and be accepted by whites as "us" rather than "them." If this prediction proves correct and even if a few African Americans ascend to the top ranks of national politics, the future of most African Americans probably will be one of being separate—and less than equal.

LATINOS/HISPANICS: CLIMBING UP?

Persons of Latin and Central American heritage in the United States, as we've discussed, disagree among themselves on one name that fits all. Additionally, they often fall into the category of "Spanish surnames," making identity issues even murkier.

As of Census 2000, people in the United States of Spanish/Hispanic/Latino origin could identify as Mexican, Puerto Rican, Cuban, or other Spanish/Hispanic/Latino. (The term "Latino" appeared on the census form for the first time in 2000.)

Whatever their name, the United States's largest "minority" is growing. The Hispanic population increased by 58 percent in one decade: from 22.4 million in 1990 to 35.3 million in 2000. As of Census 2000, half of all Hispanics/Latinos in the United States lived in just two states: California and Texas. (New Mexico had the largest proportion of Hispanics/Latinos of any state in 2000: 42 percent of the state's population.)

The nation's Hispanic/Latino community (or communities) is gaining political strength. That was made clear in the run-up to the 2008 presidential campaign by such news headlines as this one in the *New York Times*: "Hispanic Voters Gain New Clout with Democrats." As a reporter noted in the *New York Times*, the "battle for Hispanic voters" is a result of the decision by several states with large Hispanic populations to move up their presidential primaries to early 2008; these included California, Florida, and New York (Hernandez, 2007). (About two-thirds of the United States's Latino/Hispanic residents live in nine of the states which held Democratic primaries or caucuses on or before February 5, 2008.) Among other actions, candidates courted Hispanic voters by starting Spanish-language Web sites and talking to unions with mainly Hispanic/Latino members. Further, both Senators John McCain and Barack Obama focused on the same groups—particularly Latinos—in preparing their 2008 presidential campaign strategies.

Analysts think that proposed U.S. immigration legislation, which will disproportionately affect Hispanic/Latino communities, has energized Hispanic/Latino voters. Can political candidates be far behind?

In economic and social terms, Hispanics/Latinos have lower education and skill levels than non-Hispanics. This translates to lower wages and higher unemployment than many other groups. In addition, Hispanics/Latinos are disproportionately—and negatively—affected by a cooling off of the housing sector in the United States as that sector has been a key employer.

a

Fig. 10.6 THE CRIME WAS ANCESTRY. (*a*) A Japanese American child in Los Angeles awaits transport to a World War II "relocation center" like Manzanar. (*b*) Manzanar. Today, almost nothing remains of the 500-acre living area except a cemetery, stone guard houses with graffiti, and a plaque at the camp near Death Valley, California, where about 10,000 Japanese Americans were incarcerated for the duration of World War II. The plaque, placed by the California Department of Parks and Recreation in cooperation with the Manzanar Committee and the Japanese American Citizens League, is difficult to read because it has been defaced. It says:

> In the early part of World War II, 110,000 persons of Japanese ancestry were interned in relocation centers by executive order no. 9006 issued on February 19, 1942. Manzanar, the first of 10 such concentration camps, was surrounded by barbed wire and guard towers, containing 10,000 persons, the majority being American citizens. May the injustice and humiliation suffered here as a result of hysteria, racism and economic exploitation never emerge again.

(c) When Japanese Americans on the West Coast were evacuated to relocation camps, their businesses were taken over by whites. ([a] Library of Congress, [b] Tim Teninty, [c] National Archives)

b

Fig. 10.6 *(continued)*

What of the future? One observer (among many) reports that "almost 1 out of every 2 new jobs is filled by Hispanics" in the United States and predicts that "in the long-run, Hispanics will achieve higher educational levels and with it, higher incomes and better opportunities" (Amador, 2006).

MAKING IT: JAPANESE AMERICANS

Some ethnic groups prospered against all odds. Japanese Americans are a case in point. The Japanese in the United States have met prejudice, discrimination, and racism. On racist grounds they were denied the rights to naturalization, land ownership, and entrance into certain professions. Eventually, they were completely excluded.

In wartime, Japanese Americans faced worse. At the outbreak of World War II, about 110,000 Japanese Americans living on the West Coast were evacuated from their homes and put behind barbed wire in "war relocation camps," a euphemism for concentration camps. Many of their urban businesses were taken over by whites, and their rural land was confiscated. (The U.S. government also financed the transportation over international borders of 2,264 men, women, and children of Japanese ancestry living in Latin America, 80 percent of whom were Japanese Peruvians, and the incarceration of these Japanese Latin Americans in U.S. internment camps. Many were interned at a former migrant labor camp in Crystal City, Texas. The ostensible reason for taking Japanese Latin Americans forcibly from their homes and deporting them to U.S. internment camps: hostage exchange. Many Japanese Peruvians interned in the United States were deported to war-devastated Japan after the war, some stayed in the United States, and eventually about 100 returned to Peru.)

New Management White Americans

Free Room Rent The 3rd Week

Room · Close · In Clean · Modern

c

Fig. 10.6 (*continued*)

Yet, since World War II and their internment, the Japanese American community, a tiny minority group (2000 population: roughly just 0.4 percent of the nation's population or about 1.1 million, including those who consider themselves mixed race) has prospered economically and escaped ghettoization. Japanese Americans tend not to live in racial isolation from whites. Further, their educational attainment ranks very high.

Some scholars think that traditional Japanese culture and values have much to do with the high levels of Japanese American achievement. First-generation Japanese Americans (*Issei*) came from a culture in which "diligence in work, combined with simple frugality, had an almost religious imperative, similar to what has been called 'the Protestant ethic' in Western culture," and psychologically the *Issei* carried with them an "achievement orientation" (Petersen in Hosokawa, 1969:495). Such values were transmitted from *Issei* to *Nisei* (the second generation in America) and to succeeding generations by strong family ties and culture.

Some scholars dispute this cultural explanation. They suggest that Japanese emigrants started off with economic advantages: They tended to be skilled, literate nonpeasants whose technological know-how gave them a chance to grab onto the ladder of success (e.g., Ideda, 1973).

Will Japanese Americans retain their distinctive culture? Probably not. The out-marriage rate is high. Although some say that the rate has declined in recent years, others state that it is the highest of any ethnic group in the United States: 60 percent and increasing. Dr. Satsuki Ina, a Japanese American trauma psychologist who was born into and spent her childhood in an internment camp during World War II, thinks she knows why: "I wouldn't say it is a result of the fear of being Japanese, but more the fear of being ostracized, excluded and disempowered" (*Kyoto Journal*, 2007). Whatever the reasons, and whatever the exact figure, assimilation via intermarriage has had serious consequences for U.S. Japantowns (*Nihonmachis*). It is not only in the largest Japantown in California, San Francisco, that both Japanese American residents and merchants in Nihonmachis are dwindling.

For over a generation, Japanese Americans have been called part of an Asian "model minority." This stereotype is based partially on facts—for example, Japanese Americans are more likely than whites to go to college in the United States and, in 2000, their median family incomes were $70,000, or about $20,000 more than all U.S. residents' median income.

But the Asian "model minority" model obscures a great deal, including the following: numerous Chinese women work for illegally low wages in garment sweatshops; some Asian groups suffer from high poverty rates; in 2000, U.S. Cambodians had more than 29 percent living below the poverty line and the Hmong had nearly 38 percent below the poverty line. For Japanese Americans in particular, the "model minority" label hides discomfort, fear of hate crimes, discrimination, and violence fueled by Japan-bashing (or China-bashing, as some people in the United States do not seem to differentiate between the two).

GAYS AND LESBIANS: LIKE AN ETHNIC GROUP?

The idea that there is such a thing as a "gay identity" is fairly recent, probably dating to the mid-1970s (Epstein, 1987:10). At that time, gays and lesbians came to see themselves as a legitimate and stigmatized minority, like an ethnic group and deserving the same legal protections against discrimination, defamation, and hate crimes as ethnic groups.

Whether or not gays and lesbians constitute an ethnic group is much debated. Some conservative religious groups and politicians see homosexuals as "deviants" who "violate human nature," reject "family values," and have an unacceptable "alternative lifestyle," not as members of an ethnic group.

Nonetheless, many gay communities act like ethnic groups. And before AIDS started to decimate them, gay male communities often resembled ethnic urban villages. (Typically, lesbians spread out more geographically but maintain strong support networks.) For example, San Francisco's Castro District in the late 1970s was a gay urban village—a spatially segregated and culturally distant ghetto—of some 25,000–30,000 gay men. It contained about 150 gay institutions ranging from bars, political clubs, newspapers, churches, and singing groups to a business association (FitzGerald, [1981] 1987:27).

Politically speaking, gays act like highly-organized ethnic groups in many big cities. In San Francisco, to continue the example, "gays and lesbians can claim the highest level of electoral mobilization, representation, and political assimilation in the city's political system" (DeLeon, 1992:30).

Indeed, a generation ago, gay and lesbian clout changed San Francisco politics. According to Manuel

Fig. 10.7 GAY PRIDE. Activists at a Gay Pride Day in San Francisco. (Deborah Mosca)

Castells, "the gay community transformed the local political system, making it very difficult for conservatives [particularly business interests] to control the city, and creating an alternative power base relying on neighborhood associations, public workers' unions, and oppressed ethnic communities" (1983:168–169).

In the last generation, AIDS took a devastating toll on gay male communities throughout the United States. For thousands, living with AIDS replaced gay institution building. Still, in San Francisco, there has been great local commitment (and funds) to gay communities by public agencies, community groups, nonprofit organizations, and businesses (DeLeon, 1992:190). In 2008, gay and lesbian marriage, declared legal in Massachusetts, all of Canada, and some European countries, may lead to new institution-building efforts. (Or not.)

Paralleling many nationality-based ethnic groups, "first-wave" and "second-wave" gay immigrants distinguish between themselves on the basis of generation, manners, and style. But they show an opposite pattern: Second-generation gay organizations, such as Queer Nation, tend to be less establishment-oriented and more confrontational than first-generation groups; in contrast, second-generation, nationality-based ethnic organizations, such as the Japanese American Citizens League, tend to be hyperpatriotic and to distance themselves from the previous generation (Kitano and Daniels, 1988).

Some "third-wave" gays are joining organizations which assume gayness and then distinguish members by other factors. These include the Gay Asian Pacific Network, Black Lesbians in the United Kingdom (BLUK), gayyouth, GayDads, and the Lesbian & Gay Christian Movement. Such gay-assumed organizations, whether based on common roles, religion, age, interests, or ethnicity, mirror nongay ("breeder" or "straight") associations in their breadth.

At the same time as third-wave gays are joining organizations and unknown numbers of each wave are marrying in U.S. states where it is legal, one keen participant-observer proclaims the ending of gay culture. According to conservative author and gay journalist Andrew Sullivan (2005), in the United States there is no longer a single gay identity or "a single look or style or culture." "Slowly but unmistakably," he says,

"gay culture is ending." He notes, among other things, that "outsider rebellion" of decades past has turned, in many places, to "bourgeois organization." (Partially responsible for many changes in gay cultures, Sullivan claims, is the Internet, which dealt bars—"a fundamental social institution for gay men"—a "body-blow" because the first stop for most gay men when looking to find someone is now online, not a bar.

If Sullivan is correct and if gays can (or could) be seen as an ethnic group, does Gans's notion of symbolic ethnicity apply to them? It would seem so.

MULTICULTURALISM

"Who controls the present controls the past." This truism—that history is written by dominant groups—is not always true in the multicultural United States.

Since the 1960s, more U.S. textbooks and artworks have come to reflect the views of the once-vanquished or still-subordinated. Two key processes influenced this new outlook: (1) the arrival of millions of non-European immigrants who brought with them a great variety of cultures and languages and (2) social movements, particularly for civil rights and women's rights, which alerted the nation to the separate and often unequal condition of many people in the United States.

While some scholars applaud so-called multiculturalists for expanding the historical vision, others blame them for helping to "disunite" America. The late Allan Bloom led the conservative attack on "the new [multicultural] curriculum" in his best-seller *The Closing of the American Mind* ([1987] 1988:380). Bloom argued that multiculturalism is based on cultural relativism, a wrongheaded philosophy because human nature remains the same. Bloom's antidote? The "great books" approach, "in which a liberal education means reading certain generally recognized classic texts" (344), such as those of Plato and Shakespeare.

Some liberals, notably the late historian Arthur M. Schlesinger, Jr., joined the conservative outcry against multiculturalism. In *The Disuniting of America* (1991), Schlesinger revealed his fear that ethnocentric chauvinists and academic hustlers would manipulate students' emotions and preach romantic notions of separatism. Meanwhile, radical critics charge that Bloom was sexist, antidemocratic, and elitist. Further, radicals suggest that both liberals and conservatives tend to confuse cause and effect. They say that multiculturalists did not *cause* the disunity of the United States; rather, fragmentation happened because so many people were denied protection and resisted oppression.

Finally, a variety of observers want to broaden the definition of multiculturalism. They argue that differences in regional background, class, religion, age, and gender identity are more important than cultural differences. Further, they say, such variables (e.g., class, gender) are neglected in the contemporary discussion of multicultures, which spotlights ethnic–racial identity.

Today, whether broadly or narrowly defined, multiculturalism is an issue debated on most continents. Australia, to take just one example, has been struggling with multiculturalism and its sense of national identity. In 2007, Australia changed the name of its Department of Immigration and Multicultural Affairs to the Department of Immigration and Citizenship. This seems like a small change, but it reflects a big shift: from the celebration of the cultural diversity of its immigrant population to the promotion of an Australian cultural unity (Johnston, 2007).

A final word on U.S. multiculturalism: People in the United States often think that languages other than English are a threat to their cultural identity. But presidents and their spouses, at least, have a long tradition of multilingualism, starting with John Adams, second president, who spoke several languages. (Jefferson spoke between five and seven languages. Hoover not only was fluent in Mandarin; he and his wife translated a book from Latin into English. And Jackie Kennedy campaigned for husband JFK in three languages.)

The United States, where about 20 percent of residents speak a language other than English at home, remains one of the richest nations in the world when it comes to languages. Some tout this reality as a strength. Others do not.

Columbus: Hero or Villain?

To write history is to construct, not merely record, reality. To rewrite history from the viewpoint of the vanquished—not the victors—can change the meaning of events and lead to heated controversy. Take one example: the transformation of Christopher Columbus. The year 1992 marked the 500th anniversary of Columbus's arrival in the Americas. In many U.S. cities, this event was marked by celebrations, for conventional histories revere Columbus as the symbol of a triumphant European civilization, the hero who "discovered" America. But revised histories tell a different story. For example, *1492–1992: The Legacy of Columbus* (Zinn, 1991); *The Conquest of Paradise: Christopher Columbus and the Columbian Legacy* (Sale, 1990); *Dangerous Memories: Invasion and Resistance Since 1492* (Golden, 1992); and *Stolen Continents: The Americas through Indian Eyes Since 1492* (Ronald Wright, 1992) depict Columbus as an antihero who destroyed native cultures.

Many observers implicitly dispute the portrait of Columbus as hero. They point to sophisticated Native American cultures that thrived before Columbus set foot in the Americas. For one, Charles C. Mann (2005) claims that there were probably more people in the Americas than in Europe in 1491 and that some cities, including the Aztec capital, Tenochtitlán (Chapter 4), were more advanced in some ways than most of their European counterparts. For example, Mann asserts that Tenochtitlán had clean streets, running water, and beautiful botanical gardens (unlike, according to Mann, most European cities of its era). Further, according to Mann, pre-Columbian Indians had developed a very advanced form of breeding corn and a way to farm the Amazonian rain forest without destroying it. Similarly, University of Chicago anthropologist Alan L. Kolata (1993) excavated Tiwanaku (Tihuanacu), a Bolivian city which, a half-millennium before Columbus, had a population of as many as 115,000 residents, with another 250,000 living in the surrounding area. (Interestingly, Kolata [173] notes that Tiwanaku does not fit the Western conception of a "real city" at all; it lacked markets, a flourishing merchant class, and independent artisans. Instead, it was an "autocratic city," built for and dominated by local aristocrats.)

Influenced by such revised thinking, some U.S. cities no longer celebrate Columbus Day. Berkeley, California, for one, now celebrates October 12 as Indigenous Peoples Day.

No doubt as the United States becomes more colorful and multicultural, there will be more debates,

Fig. 10.8 POLITICAL PLURALISM, 1950. Billboard in front of the Lower Manhattan Republican Club shows that a "balanced ticket" in New York City at that time meant white ethnic pluralism—from WASP and Irish to Jewish and Italian. Since that era, the names of African Americans and Hispanics/Latinos have been added to the tickets of most political parties seeking election in the city.

even battles, over whose version of history to teach. Public schools are already a battleground.

To understate the case, college professors are divided on multiculturalism. Some fear politicization of the traditional European American–based curriculum ("the canon") and the breakdown of common discourse centered on "generic humanity." Others applaud the addition of new voices with new interpretations, arguing that U.S. colleges have long been politicized—promoting a narrow white European male view at the expense of subordinate groups such as people of color and women. Typically, conservatives fear what they call "political correctness" and the fragmentation of knowledge more than too narrow a vision; radicals fear what they call "Eurocentric monoculturalism" and "educational oppression" more than balkanization. Often, liberals, wishing to make some curriculum changes without changing academe's deep structure, suffer the deepest personal pangs as epithets such as "racist" and "elitist" are thrown around on campuses.

Is it possible to celebrate heterogeneity and to retain the notion of "one nation, indivisible"? Opinions differ. Apparently, the Tennessee State Senate thinks so. Aware that they represent people of many faiths, not only Christians, the senators opened a session with an Islamic prayer. But many French, echoing Ken Jowitt's distinction between civics and ethnics, think not: It is impossible, they reason, to protect both the rights of individuals and those of communities. (Historically, the French government has sponsored cultural homogeneity, not multiculturalism. Practically, this means that schools become the main vehicle for turning "them"—Algerian, Vietnamese, Senegalese, and other immigrants—into "us"—Frenchmen and Frenchwomen. As noted earlier, they do this by treating immigrants as individuals, not members of communities. In recent years, this policy underpinned the ban on head scarves by Muslim schoolgirls.)

Separatists of all colors, creeds, and pocketbooks—from white supremacists, black nationalists, and religious groups like the Amish and the Brooklyn Lubovicher communities to wealthy and not-so-wealthy folks living in gated communities protected by security guards—have chosen isolation or abandoned hope for multicultural togetherness. Some behind gates and walls (real or imagined) hope to protect themselves from harm, to maintain their community within society, to maintain property values, and/or to barricade themselves against all things unpleasant. Others wish to keep "them" out of sight.

Yet others hope to build multicultural understanding. How? Not through laws: Laws can break down barriers, but they cannot build bridges.

It may take powerful artworks to help us to cross the bridge. Anna Deavere Smith's theater pieces are just such works. In *Fires in the Mirror* (1992–1993), sometime drama professor and actress Smith acquaints audiences with 26 people—including radical thinker and activist Angela Davis, a Hasidic Jewish housewife, and the Reverend Al Sharpton—by drawing on their verbatim comments about emotionally-charged events in Crown Heights, Brooklyn, New York: an African American child's death in a car accident, a riot, and a retaliatory killing of a Hasidic Jewish student. As a whole, her work suggests that we need to discover our social glue.

Also, scholarship can cross, even redefine, boundaries. One groundbreaking book is the first volume of Martin Bernal's *Black Athena: The Afroasiatic Roots of Classical Civilization* (1987). Bernal argues that Afroasiatic influences on classical Greece were systematically suppressed since the 1900s—mainly for racist reasons. Another is a provocative literary study, *Was Huck Black? Mark Twain and African American Voices* (1993). Author Shelley Fisher Fishkin, a professor of American studies, suggests that Mark Twain based much of Huck's character and language on a black child he met in the 1870s. Her finding is important for many reasons, not least because Twain's *Huckleberry Finn*, published in 1884, is at the center of the American literary canon. Tracing Huck Finn's voice to a black source suggests that "African-american [*sic*] voices have helped shape what we have thought of a mainstream American literature" (Fishkin in Winkler, 1992:A6). Many literary scholars think that Fishkin's study is a major step in the emerging recognition of the overlap and interplay between ethnic cultures in the United States.

To conclude: Recognizing, even celebrating, ethnic differences brings back the enduring issue of community: insiders vs. outsiders. But can we retain enriching differences without retaining old prejudices?

In other words, cultural identity wears two faces. One is proud and strong, giving a sense of special belonging to individuals and a rich variety to urban life. It gives the Dutch Americans of small-town Pella, Iowa (with its annual Tulip Festival, its Vermeer windmill, and its nearly all-white population) and the former residents of Boston's Italian American West End a sense of community. But the other side is ugly, glowering with misunderstanding and hate. And it is in cities (which bring together heterogeneous individuals) where both faces of cultural pluralism are so prominently displayed.

ANOTHER LOOK

In any nation considered democratic and modern, such as the United States, positions assigned at birth—such as racial and ethnic status—are supposed to count for little. But this is just not the case. Persistent inequalities still exist among racial and ethnic groups, and our life chances are significantly influenced by the group into which we are born. This runs counter to democratic theory.

True, ethnicity is largely symbolic for some people today. Cosmopolitan citizens of the world (who tend to be affluent, college-degreed, idea workers) typically have more in common with each other than with fellow ethnics or coreligionists, whether they live in New York City, London, Mexico City, or Tokyo.

Yet for many others, ethnicity remains significant, even primary. This, too, runs counter to classical social theory. Tönnies, Durkheim, and Marx, among others, suggested that kinship and blood relations are not key factors in the social organization of capitalist, mass society. Marx, for one, believed that ethnic ties would be replaced by bonds of social class in capitalist society. But so far, at least, ethnicity remains one of the strongest ties that bind throughout the globe, often coexisting and competing with cosmopolitanism. Some whole nations are coming apart, apparently along ethnic lines.

So, we see two opposing trends: (1) religious community, ethnic brotherhood and sisterhood, and ganglike organizations growing in strength, anchoring those adrift in a worldwide search for identity and meaning, and (2) many citizens coming together on the basis of supranational and cross-ethnic concerns—toxic waste in the global environment, space exploration, and workplace safety, to name just a few. Thus, from Quebec, Canada; Flemish Belgium; northern Italy; and Basque Spain to the former Yugoslavia and the former Soviet Union, India, Iraq, Sudan, China's Xinjiang Uighur Autonomous Region, and Sri Lanka, *Gemeinschaft*-like, communal loyalties compete with a *Techno$chaft* identification in a global village.

Among some groups, ethnicity and identity remain inseparable. Typically, this occurs in tribes such as the Kawesqar in Chile, a very small (and nearly extinct), once-nomadic tribe (Navarro, 2006:A25). But for "moderns," including people reading this book, ethnicity and identity almost never overlap totally.

These are unsettling or exciting times, depending on your pessimism–optimism score. Or maybe both. In general, social conservatives are pessimistic about race relations, believing that "tribal" or ethnic feelings run so deep that they may be primordial, a part of "human nature." In this view, individual responsibility (not government programs such as affirmative action) and personal values are key components of good race–ethnic relations.

Historically, U.S. liberals have been more optimistic, counting on public programs to level the playing field for the disenfranchised. But their mood took a dark turn in the Reagan–Bush era and subsequent economic recessions. Later, many liberals regretted the voters' rejection of affirmative action programs in several states, including Michigan (which had fought and won the battle for affirmative action in admissions policies to the University of Michigan in 2003 before the U.S. Supreme Court voted against it in 2006). Despite electing or appointing people of color to high political office, many agree with Blanche Wiesen Cook's assessment of a generation ago (1992): "race is where Americans have put their hate marbles."

Many liberals support political scientist Andrew Hacker's grim assessment: There is endemic racism in the United States. Yet, other liberals, particularly William Julius Wilson, stress the role that joblessness (caused by structural changes in the global economy), not racism, plays in keeping the disenfranchised down.

In contrast, radicals tend to think that liberals are obsessed with race—using race rather than social class to explain many events, including "civil unrest" or "riots." They tend to criticize liberals such as Hacker for minimizing government and corporate policies that perpetuate poverty and racism.

Wherever you score on the optimism–pessimism scale, remember: We may be approaching the end of an era. If so, we can expect to see breakthroughs in social theory.

Meanwhile, it pays to be humble. In the recent past, most social scientists failed to foresee momentous changes affecting migration, race, and ethnicity, ranging from the disintegration of the former Soviet bloc and "ethnic cleansing" in Darfur and elsewhere to the global economic "downturn" that started after 2007.

KEY TERMS

Acculturation A process by which one culture is modified through contact with another. Many subcultural differences are retained in the process.

Assimilation (1) The merging of dissimilar subcultures into one common culture or (2) the absorption of one group by another, whereby the absorbed group loses its prior distinctiveness.

Ethnicity A "consciousness of kind" or sense of peoplehood based on a subjective sense of community. Ethnicity can be based on national, racial, or religious background or, according to Max Weber, a common identity based on a shared history.

Insider-as-insighter doctrine The principle that only members of a group can truly understand that group's experiences due to their privileged access to knowledge. Otherwise stated: "You have to be one to know one" (whatever "one" is—female, Polish, dancer, soldier, etc.). Generally rejected by social scientists and journalists.

Melting pot Process by which a unique American (i.e., a person in the United States) supposedly emerges from the blending together of immigrants with dissimilar backgrounds. Contrasts: *stewpot*, *salad bowl*.

Minority In the 1920s, this term referred to European national groups seeking self-determination after World War I (e.g., Latvians). In the 1930s, it referred to ethnic and racial groups in the United States. Sociologist Louis Wirth emphasized social oppression (minorities as victims) in his 1945 definition of minority groups.

Multiculturalism Two very different connotations, depending on the user's ideology: (1) the celebration of pluralism or heterogeneity in a society where ethnic and other minority groups retain their cultural identity in a stewpot or (2) the fragmentation and breakdown of shared culture into groups based on race, ethnicity, age, gender, and so on.

Stewpot My term, rejecting the idea that the United States is a true melting pot. It implies that ethnic groups retain important social, economic, and/or cultural distinctions. Synonym: *salad bowl*.

Symbolic ethnicity Sociologist Herbert J. Gans's term for a voluntary ethnic involvement emphasizing identity—the *feeling* of being Italian, Japanese, or Jewish, for example—which expresses itself in various symbolic ways, particularly a nostalgic allegiance to the immigrant culture, ceremonial holiday celebrations, and special foods. Contrast: *ethnicity as an important, taken-for-granted part of everyday life that is involuntary, public, and communal.*

PROJECTS

1. **Separatist movements.** Growing numbers of people worldwide—from Spanish Basques, Flemish speakers in Belgium, Scots in Scotland, and Tamil Tigers in Sri Lanka to religious fundamentalists in many countries—are eschewing the goal of ethnic–racial and/or religious harmony or national unity. Using archival materials and electronic resources (e.g., Internet blogs), analyze the appeal and rationales of separatists. First, try to determine the number and kinds of separatist movements worldwide today. Second, choose three groups and determine their ideologies, paying special attention to their definitions of "outsiders." Third, analyze the members of the three groups in terms of relevant factors (e.g., occupation, gender, educational background, age, ethnicity). Do patterns emerge? If so, construct a typology of separatist groups.

2. **Ethnicity-based institutions.** Historically, what ethnicity-based institutions—media, social clubs, marriage brokers, soccer clubs, churches, and so on—used to exist in your city or a nearby large city? How many remain viable today? Try to establish whether these organizations are central or peripheral to people's lives by interviewing media users, club members, and so on.

3. **Assimilation versus separation**. What do people lose and gain from leaving behind their cultural heritage (e.g., language, values) and joining—or attempting to join—the mainstream? First, examine what novelists and essayists say. Here are a few who write about these issues: Richard Rodriguez, Richard Wright, V. S. Naipaul, Aaron Wildavsky (in his writings about biblical personages), Jessica Hagedorn, Amy Tan, Chaim Potok, and Chinua Achebe. Then, if possible, interview a variety of newcomers and old-timers about U.S. immigration. Why and when did some "Americanize" their surnames? By the third generation, have some taken back their former surnames or created new first or last names as symbols of ethnicity? What value clashes occur in a family between the first generation born and raised in the United States and their parents born outside the United States?

SUGGESTIONS FOR FURTHER LEARNING

The literature on race and ethnicity in the United States and worldwide is voluminous. Studies range from general works to studies of one group, such as *The Columbia History of Latinos in the United States Since 1960* edited by David G. Gutiérrez (New York: Columbia University Press, 2004), and studies focused on one issue, such as *Transforming Politics, Transforming America: The Political and Civic Incorporation of Immigrants in the United States* edited by Taeku Lee, S. Karthick Ramakrishnan, and Ricardo Ramirez (Charlottesville: University of Virginia Press, 2006).

It is interesting to compare studies of the same ethnic group over time. For example, see Illsoo Kim's *New Urban Immigrants: The Korean Community in New York* (Princeton, N.J.: Princeton University Press, 1981) and Pyong Gap Min's *Caught in the Middle: Korean Communities in New York and Los Angeles* (Berkeley: University of California Press, 1996). Why might the two scholars come to differing conclusions?

What is the relationship between culture and politics? This is much debated. Note that the thunderous applause in the United States for some cultural groups, such as the Bolshoi Ballet, did not spill over into U.S.–Soviet political relations during the so-called cold war. Whether Roma cultural attractions and Roma bands such as Taraf de Haidouks will lead to wider acceptance of this ethnic group worldwide remains to be seen.

For a look at the world from the point of view of those in "the South"—or poor—countries, see *The World Guide: Global Reference, Country by Country*, 11th ed., by editors Amir Hamed and Chris Brazier (Oxford: New Internationalist Publications, 2007). It is published by a communications cooperative, which describes itself as "renowned for its radical, campaigning stance on a range of world issues."

In *Unequal Chances: Ethnic Minorities in Western Labour* Markets (New York: Oxford University Press, 2007), editors Anthony F. Heath and Sin Yi Cheung present the results of the first major cross-national study of ethnic minority disadvantage in the labor market. They focus on the experiences of the children of immigrants in western Europe, North America, Australia, and Israel.

In *Diaspora, Politics and* Globalization (New York: Palgrave Macmillan Press, 2006), Michel S. Laguerre analyzes the politics of diaspora. (The word "diaspora" comes from two Greek roots: *dia* ["through"] and *speiro* ["to scatter"]. Thus, it literally means scattering or dispersion. Originally, it applied to the dispersion of Jews after the Babylonian exile in 586 BCE and to the aggregate of Jews or Jewish communities scattered in exile outside Palestine. Today, however, the term is used to describe any group of scattered people.) Professor Laguerre stresses the importance of the multinational context, not only the relations in the host land and the homeland of people in the diaspora.

In *Ethnic Landscapes in an Urban World*, editors Ray Hutchison and Jerry Krase (London: Elsevier, 2007) bring together essays and case studies on immigration, globalization, and diaspora. Among the countries and cities discussed: Bolivia, Bulgaria, Italy, Jakarta, Haifa, Toronto.

Historian Yuri Slezkine started out to write a book about a residential building in Moscow that housed Soviet leaders in the 1930s. When he looked closer, he found that before the 1930s this building had been occupied by Jewish immigrants from the "Pale of Settlement," a region where Jews were forced to settle under the Russian Empire. (The common expression "beyond the pale" originally referred to the Pale of Settlement.) From this humble beginning came a work that examines much more than a mere residence: three great migrations of Russian Jews in the twentieth century and, more broadly, the role of Jews in modern times. The resulting book, *The Jewish Century* (Princeton, N.J.: Princeton University Press, [2004] 2006), has been called brilliant, multilayered, fascinating, infuriating, and provocative. His provocative thesis is that the twentieth century is the Jewish century because "modernization is about everyone becoming urban, mobile, literate, articulate, intellectually intricate. . . . Modernization, in other words, is about everyone becoming Jewish."

For an example of changing definitions of race, see James W. Loewen, *The Mississippi Chinese: Between Black and White*, 2nd ed. (Prospect Heights, Ill.: Waveland Press, 1988). The 1,200 Delta Chinese came to the state of Mississippi about 1869 as sharecroppers. Originally classed with blacks, they are now viewed as essentially "white."

Martin Scorsese's films often describe the importance of ethnicity. For instance, in *Goodfellas* (1990), the film's key character, Henry Hill, was denied privileged status ("made man") in the Sicilian gang organization because his father was not Sicilian.

According to Michael Ignatieff, ethnic conflict is often driven by what Freud called the "narcissism of minor differences." That is, basically similar populations make much out of small differences that set them apart in a search for identity. In *Blood and Belonging: Journeys into the New Nationalism* (New York: Farrar, Straus & Giroux, 1994), he argues that conflicts between Serbs and Croats in the former Yugoslavia and between working-class Catholics and Protestants in Northern Ireland—who are more alike in terms of customs, language, political culture, and shared memories than any other groups—exemplify such narcissism.

An important work of scholarship in the multiculturalism debate is the first volume of Martin Bernal's series *Black Athena: The Afroasiatic Roots of Classical Civilization* (New Brunswick, N.J.: Rutgers University Press, 1987). Bernal argued that ancient Egyptian civilization was essentially African but that racist tendencies in nineteenth-century classical studies led to the denial of the influences of ancient Egypt and Phoenicia on classical Greek civilization for 150 years.

Many artworks show the spread of U.S. culture to other cultures. See, for one, a novel by Haruki Murakami, *Dance Dance Dance* (New York: Kodansha International, 1993). The narrator of the book, a citizen of Tokyo, idolizes Clint Eastwood and snacks at McDonald's or Dunkin' Donuts.

Is racism in the United States against African Americans alive and well? Some think it has not much changed in past decades; they would agree with former New York City mayor David Dinkins who quotes an unknown observer: "A white man with a million dollars is a millionaire, and a black man with a million dollars is a nigger with a million dollars" (in Ellis Cose, *The Rage of a Privileged Class*, New York: HarperCollins, 1993).

Have gambling casinos helped the economic plight of Native Americans? This is a question posed by Jonathan P. Taylor and Joseph P. Kalt in their 10 year review (1990–2000), written in 2005: "*Cabazon*, the Indian Gaming Regulatory Act and the socioeconomic consequences of American Indian governmental gaming at *The Harvard Project on American Indian Economic Development* (January): http://www. ksg. harvard.edu/hpaied/pubs/documents/American IndiansonReservationsADatabookofSocioeconomic Change.pdf

James Ridgeway examines one part of the seething U.S. cauldron—the racialist Far Right—in *Blood in the Face* (New York: Thunder's Mouth Press [1990] 1996). He argues that the Far Right addresses the fear and anger of many people, particularly in smaller towns in the United States.

Donald Young's landmark book *American Minority Peoples: A Study in Racial and Cultural Conflicts in the United States* (New York: Harper, 1932) pioneered the concept of minority peoples in the United States.

Interestingly, Young did not link Europe's minorities (resulting from World War I) to the United States's minorities.

In *America Revised: History Schoolbooks in the Twentieth Century* (Boston: Little, Brown, 1979), Pulitzer Prize-winner Frances FitzGerald tells how Columbus has become a "minor character" in U.S. history as history gets remade in accord with the changing fashions and prejudices of the era.

That history is written by the victors—not the vanquished—is a central point of the Oscar-winning Argentine film, *The Official Story* or *La Historia Oficial* (1985). The DVD (2004) is in the original Spanish with English subtitles.

"Political correctness" has lost much of its bite in recent years, perhaps as people in the United States get accustomed to not making ethnic jokes or slurs, at least not in public. Dinesh D'Souza, Roger Kimball, and the late Allan Bloom are associated with a disapproving voice toward political correctness and (what they consider the excesses of) multiculturalism.

Among the many studies and first-person accounts that focus on enhancing multicultural awareness is *Paul Robeson Jr. Speaks to America* (New Brunswick, N.J.: Rutgers University Press, 1993). Robeson says that the controversy about multiculturalism is "at the heart of a profound ideological struggle over the values of American culture and the nature of U.S. civilization." Robeson, the son of the civil rights activist, actor, and singer, claims that "the inability of melting-pot liberalism to accommodate racial diversity along with ethnic diversity is the primary cause of racial conflict on predominately white campuses."

Betty Jean Craige argues that there are two types of multiculturalists: *globalists* (who promote public awareness of human diversity and "weaken the dominant culture by reducing national loyalty") and *ethnic preservationists* (who promote distinct cultural identities and "weaken the dominant culture by refusing to blend into it"). Both types, she says, have the potential for "ideologically disuniting the nation" and redefining the notion of "patriotism." (See her article, "Multiculturalism and the Vietnam Syndrome," *Chronicle of Higher Education*, January 12, 1994, p. B3.)

On June 12, 1967, the U.S. Supreme Court ruled unanimously that laws barring racial intermarriage in 16 states were unconstitutional. By the early 1990s, there were about 1 million interracial couples in the United States. The number increases with each decade. Some demographers suggest that 20 percent of Asian Americans will be in interracial couples by the year 2020.

Some individuals and groups maintain multiple identities. See, for example, "Cuban Jewish Women in Miami: A Triple Identity," a paper presented by Hannah R. Wartenberg at the 83rd annual meeting of the American Sociological Association, Atlanta, Georgia, August 1988.

Attempts to construct pan-ethnic identities have concerned scholars for decades. For an analysis of the emergence in the 1960s of an Asian American consciousness, mainly for a political reason—strength in numbers—see Yen Le Espiritu, *Asian American Panethnicity: Bridging Institutions and Identities* (Philadelphia: Temple University Press, 1992). For a discussion of the evolution of a "supratribal" identity among Native Americans, see Stephen Cornell, *American Indian Ethnic Renewal* (New York: Oxford University Press, 1993).

In contrast, *Raising Black Children* (New York: Plume, 1993) by two African American psychiatrists, Alvin F. Poussaint and James P. Comer, recognizes separate identity. The book is geared to child-rearing issues facing black children because, Poussaint says, "Parents ask, 'How do I raise a healthy black child in this racist society?'"

Taylor Branch begins his award-winning book *Parting the Waters: America in the King Years, 1954–1963* (New York: Simon and Schuster, 1988) with the maxim that "race shapes the cultural eye—what we do and do not notice." In his history of the civil rights movement, Branch also pays close attention to class divisions within the black community.

In *Against the Wall: Poor, Young, Black, and Male* (Philadelphia: University of Pennsylvania Press, 2008), editor Elijah Anderson brings together a series of articles, including one by William Julius Wilson and a forward by Cornel West, which discuss the legacy of racism on young black men in the United States. The collection includes discussions of structural bars to jobs and some life histories on harsh streets.

In *Gang Leader for a Day: A Rogue Sociologist Takes to the Streets* (New York: Penguin, 2008) Columbia sociology professor Sudhir Alladi Venkatesh (who grew up in southern California) tells about his 7 years befriending a crack-dealing gang in a Chicago housing project. Often crossing over from his observer role to participant, Venkatesh was a first-year doctoral student at the University of Chicago when he became involved with the ruthless and charismatic J. T. and his gang, the Black Kings (introduced to a wider public in Steven D. Levitt and Stephen J. Dubner's best-seller *Freakonomics*, [New York: William Morrow, 2005]).

In *The Collaborative City: Opportunities and Struggles for Blacks and Latinos in U.S. Cities* (New York: Garland, 2000), editors John J. Betancur and Douglas C. Gill bring together varying strategies for dealing with issues of concern to both urban groups, particularly housing concentration and socioeconomic disadvantage. Contributors do not avoid discussing bases of contentiousness between the two groups either.

A story of ethnic cleansing in the United States is told by Jean Pfaelzer in *Driven Out: The Forgotten War Against Chinese Americans* (Berkeley: University of California Press, 2008). Professor Pfaelzer says that Chinese Americans were rounded up in more than 300 U.S. communities in California and the Pacific Northwest from 1848 into the twentieth century.

No ordinary museum, the Museum of Tolerance in Los Angeles features hands-on exhibits dealing with racial discrimination in the United States and atrocities all over the world. Sponsored by the Simon Wiesenthal Center, the museum opened in 1993 with a "Whisper Gallery" where visitors see and hear a variety of ethnic slurs from a video screen. Another exhibit encourages visitors to exchange places with people of different races to promote empathy.

In *The Cinema of Globalization: A Guide to Films About the Economic Order* (New York: Cornell University Press, 2007), Tom Zaniello provides synopses of 213 films about various aspects of globalization. Among the topics covered: global labor, antiglobalization movements, and intellectual property rights.

History professor Marcia M. Gallo notes the importance of one group in securing lesbian rights in *Different Daughters: A History of the Daughters of Bilitis*

and the Rise of the Lesbian Rights Movement (Berkeley, Calif.: Seal Press, 2007).

REFERENCES

ACORN. 2003. "The great divide: Home purchase mortgage lending nationally and in 115 metropolitan areas." (October).

Amador, Jorge. 2006. "Hispanics economic status." (September 4): http://www.fxstreet.com/fundamental/analysis-reports/hispanics-economic-status/2006–09-04.html

American Sociological Association. 2007. "American "Sociological Association calls for the discontinuation of the use of Native American nicknames, logos, and mascots in sport." *Member news and notes.* (March 6): http://www.asanet.org/cs/native_american_sport

Bernal, Martin. 1987. *Black Athena: The Afroasiatic Roots of Classical Civilization.* Vol. 1, *The Fabrication of Ancient Greece, 1785–1985.* New Brunswick, N.J.: Rutgers University Press.

Binzen, Peter. 1970. *Whitetown USA.* New York: Vintage.

Bloom, Allan. [1987] 1988. *The Closing of the American Mind: How Higher Education Has Failed Democracy and Impoverished the Souls of Today's Students.* New York: Simon and Schuster, Touchstone.

Boal, Frederick W. 1999. "From undivided cities to undivided cities: Assimilation to ethnic cleansing." *Housing Studies* 14(5):585–600.

Brookhiser, Richard. 1991. *The Way of the WASP: How It Made America, and How It Can Save It, So to Speak.* New York: Free Press.

Bullard, Robert D., and Joe R. Feagin. 1991. "Racism and the city." Pp. 55–76 in M. Gottdiener and Chris G. Pickvance, eds., *Urban Life in Transition. Urban Affairs Annual Reviews*, vol. 39. Newbury Park, Calif.: Sage.

Carrasco, David. 1992. "The Spanish conquest." Audiotape. Boulder, Colo.: Alternative Radio.

Castells, Manuel. 1983. "Cultural identity, sexual liberation and urban structure: The gay community in San Francisco." Pp. 138–170 in *The City and the Grassroots.* Berkeley: University of California Press.

Castle, Stephen. 2007. "Gypsy-haters, Holocaust-deniers, xenophobes, homophobes, anti-Semites: the EU's new political force." *The Independent* (January 18): http://news.independent.co.uk/europe/article2157360.ece

Chandra, Vikram. 2007. *Sacred Games.* New York: HarperCollins.

Chapman, Herrick, and Laura Levine Frader, eds. 2004. "Introduction: Race in France." Pp. 1–33 in *Race in France: Interdisciplinary Perspectives on the Politics of Difference*. New York: Berghahn Books.

Cohen, Jon, and Jennifer Agiesta. 2008. "3 in 10 Americans admit to race bias." *Washington Post* (June 22):A1.

Cook, Blanche Wiesen. 1992. Convention coverage with Robert MacNeil. PBS (July 13).

Darnton, John. 1994. "Refugee crises growing trend worldwide." *San Francisco Chronicle* (August 8):A1+.

Davies, Rodrigo. 2003. "Brazil takes affirmative action in HE." *Guardian Unlimited* (August 4): http://education.guardian.co.uk/higher/worldwide/story/0,9959,1012157,00.html

Davis, David Brion. 1992. "The American dilemma." *New York Review of Books* (July 16):13–17.

de Crevecoeur, J. Hector, and Albert E. Stone.[1782] 1981. *Letters from an American Farmer and Sketches of Eighteenth-Century America* New York:Penguin.

DeLeon, Richard Edward. 1992. *Left Coast City: Progressive Politics in San Francisco, 1975–1991*. Lawrence: University Press of Kansas.

De Tocqueville, Alexis [1840] 2006. *Democracy in America, Volume II*: http://www.gutenberg.org/files/816/816-h/816-h.htm

Denby, David. 2007. "The new disorder: Adventures in film narrative." *New Yorker* (March 7):80–85.

Epstein, Steven. 1987. "Gay politics, ethnic identity: The limits of social constructionism." *Socialist Review* 93–94:9–54.

Fishkin, Shelley Fisher. 1993. *Was Huck Black? Mark Twain and African American Voices*. New York: Oxford University Press.

FitzGerald, Frances. [1981] 1987. *Cities on a Hill: A Journey through Contemporary American Cultures*. New York: Simon and Schuster, Touchstone.

Fonseca, Isabel. [1995] 1996. *Bury Me Standing*. New York: Vintage.

Gans, Herbert J. 1979. "Symbolic ethnicity: The future of ethnic groups and cultures in America." *Ethnic and Racial Studies* 2:1–20.

———. 1999. "The possibility of a new racial hierarchy in the twenty-first century United States," pp. 371–390 in Michelle Lamont, ed., *The Cultural Territories of Race*. Chicago and New York: University of Chicago Press.

Gates, Henry Louis, Jr. 1992. Comments in "Special report. Race: Our dilemma still." *Newsweek* (May 11):48.

Gentleman, Amelia. 2007. "Letter from India: In flood lands of India, caste prejudices thrive." *International Herald Tribune* (August 29):2.

Glazer, Nathan, and Daniel Patrick Moynihan. 1963. *Beyond the Melting Pot*. Cambridge, Mass.: MIT Press.

Goffman, Erving. 1963. *Stigma*. Englewood Cliffs, N.J.: Prentice Hall.

Golden, Renny. 1992. *Dangerous Memories: Invasion and Resistance Since 1492*. Chicago: Chicago Religious Task Force on Central America.

Grabmeier, Jeff. n.d. "Whites underestimate the costs of being black, study finds." Ohio State University Research News: http://researchnews.osu.edu/archive/blckcost.htm

Greene, Jack P. 1976. "'We the People'—the emergence of the American nation." Pp. 84–95 in Peter C. Marzio, ed., *A Nation of Nations: The People Who Came to America as Seen Through Objects, Prints, and Photographs at the Smithsonian Institution*. New York: Harper & Row.

Grover, Michael. n.d. "Demographic trends reveal mixed portrait of Ninth District reservations." http://www.indianlandtenure.org/resources/Reservation%20Demographic%20Trends.pdf

Hacker, Andrew. 1992a. *Two Nations: Black and White, Separate, Hostile, Unequal*. New York: Scribner.

———. 1992b. Interview with Terry Gross on *Fresh Air*, KQED-FM (March 30).

Hernandez, Raymond. 2007. "Hispanic voters gain new clout with Democrats." *New York Times* (June 10): http://www.nytimes.com/2007/06/10/us/politics/10hispanics.html?th&emc=th

Hosokawa, Bill. 1969. *Nisei: The Quiet Americans*. New York: Morrow.

Ideda, Kiyoshi. 1973. Review of *Japanese Americans: Oppression and Success*, by William Petersen. *Social Forces* 51:499.

Jacobs, Jane. 1961. *The Death and Life of Great American Cities*. New York: Vintage.

Jewish Virtual Library. 2005. http://www.jewishvirtuallibrary.org/jsource/Judaism/jewpop.html

Johnson, Dirk. 1991. "Paper gives a voice to Plains Indians." *New York Times* [national edition] (September 19):A10.

Johnston, Tim. 2007. "Australians debate immigration and national identity." *International Herald Tribune* (January 28): http://www.iht.com/articles/2007/01/28/news/oz.php

Jones, Jacqueline. 1992. *The Dispossessed: America's Underclasses from the Civil War to the Present*. New York: Basic Books.

Kalb, Claudia. 2006. "In our blood." *Newsweek* (February 6):46–55.

Kapuściński, Ryszard. 2007. *Travels with Herodotus*. Trans. Klara Glowczewska. New York: Alfred A. Knopf.

Katznelson, Ira. 1981. *City Trenches: Urban Politics and the Patterning of Class in the United States*. New York: Pantheon.

Kilson, Martin, and George C. Bond. 1992. "Marginalized blacks." *New York Times* (May 17):A16.

Kitano, Harry H. L., and Roger Daniels. 1988. *Asian Americans: Emerging Minorities*. Englewood Cliffs, N.J.: Prentice Hall.

Kolata, Alan L. 1993. *The Tiwanaku: Portrait of an Andean Civilization*. Oxford: Blackwell Publishers.

Kraus, Bambi. 2001. "Wealth, success and poverty in Indian country." (May/June): http://www.prrac.org/full_text. php?text_id=63&item_id=1778&newsletter_id=56& header=Poverty+%2F+Welfare

Kriesler, Harry. 1999 "The individual, charisma, and the Leninist extinction." (December 7): http://globetrot-ter.berkeley.edu/people/Jowitt/jowitt-con4.html

Kronholz, June. 2007. "Census 2010 plays six not-so-easy questions." *Wall Street Journal* (February 23):B1+.

Kyoto Journal. 2007. "Humanizing 'the other' through empathy—interview with trauma psychologist and filmmaker Dr. Satsuki Ina." *Kyoto Journal* 65: http:// www.kyotojournal.org/10,000things/058.html

Le, C. N., and J. J. Huang. 2008. "The landscape of Asian America." *Asian-Nation* (August 12): http://www. asian-nation.org/interracial.shtml

Lee, Alex. 2007. "Deconstructing color-blind love." *Korea Times* (August 28): http://www.koreatimes.co.kr/ www/news/special/2007/08/177_9141.html

Low, Setha. 2003. *Behind the Gates: Life, Security and the Pursuit of Happiness in Fortress America*. New York: Routledge.

Mabry, Marcus. 2008. "Race and politics: Obama tests politics in a changing land." *International Herald Tribune* (June 8):6.

Mann, Charles C. 2005. *1491 New Revelations of the Americas Before Columbus*. New York: Knopf.

Massey, Douglas S. 2007. *Categorically Unequal: The American Stratification System*. New York: Russell Sage Foundation.

Massey, Douglas S., and Nancy Denton. 1998. *American Apartheid: Segregation and the Making of the Underclass*. Cambridge, Mass.: Harvard University Press.

Nasr, Vali. [2006] 2007. *The Shia Revival: How Conflicts within Islam Will Shape the Future*. New York: W.W. Norton & Co.

Navarro, Lygia. 2006. "The voices of Chile's vanishing Kawesqar." *San Francisco Chronicle* (October 8):A25.

Novak, Michael. 1971. *The Rise of the Unmeltable Ethnics*. New York: Macmillan.

Ogunwale, Stella U. 2006. "We the people: American Indians and Alaskan Natives. *US Census Special Reports*." (February):1–23: http://www.census.gov/ prod/2006pubs/censr-28.pdf

Owens, Bill. 1975. *Our Kind of People: American Groups and Rituals*. San Francisco: Straight Arrow Books.

Pamuk, Orhan. 2005. *Snow*. Trans. from Turkish, Maureen Freely. New York: Vintage International.

Patterson, Orlando. 1977. *Ethnic Chauvinism: The Reactionary Impulse*. New York: Stein and Day.

Patterson, Orlando, and Chris Winship. 1992. "White poor, black poor." *New York Times* (May 3):A17.

Portes, Alejandro, and Rubén G. Rumbaut. 1990. *Immigrant America: A Portrait*. Berkeley: University of California Press (See also 3rd ed. published 2006).

Raymond, Chris. 1991. "Results from a Chicago project lead social scientists to a rethinking of the urban under-class." *Chronicle of Higher Education* (October 30):A+.

———. 1992. "Controversial Harvard U. sociologist relishes his role as a maverick." *Chronicle of Higher Education* (March 4):A8–A12.

Rieder, Jonathan. 1985. *Canarsie: The Jews and Italians of Brooklyn Against Liberalism*. Cambridge, Mass.: Harvard University Press.

Roberts, Sam. 2008a. "Rise in minorities is led by children, census finds." *New York Times* (May 1): http://www. nytimes.com/2008/05/01/washington/01census. html?_r=1&th&emc=th&oref=slogin

———. 2008b. "Minorities often a majority of the population under 20." *New York Times* (August 6): http://www.nytimes.com/2008/08/07/us/07census. html?_r=1&th&emc=th&oref=slogin

Roth, Philip [2000] 2001. *The Human Stain: A Novel*. New York: Vintage.

Sale, Kirkpatrick. 1990. *The Conquest of Paradise: Christopher Columbus and the Columbian Legacy*. New York: Knopf.

Schlesinger, Arthur M., Jr. 1991. *The Disuniting of America: Reflections on a Multicultural Society.* Knoxville, Tenn.: Whittle Direct Books.

Schwartz, Allen. 2006. "The emotional challenges of interfaith marriage." (December 12): http://psych-central.com/lib/2006/12/the-emotional-challenges-of-interfaith-marriage/

Schwartz, Stephanie M. 2006. "The arrogance of ignorance: Hidden away, out of sight and out of mind." (October 15): http://www.linkcenterfoundation.org/id24.html

Smith, Anna Deavere. 1992–1993. *Fires in the Mirror.* PBS-TV, *American Playhouse* (April 1993); audiotapes, Bantam Doubleday Dell Audio; book, New York: Anchor Doubleday.

Soros, George. 1993. "Bosnia and beyond." *New York Review of Books* (October 7):15–16.

Steinfels, Peter. 1992. "Debating intermarriage, and Jewish survival." *New York Times* [national edition] (October 18, 1992):A1+.

Sullivan, Andrew. 2005. "The end of gay culture: Assimilation and its meaning." *New Republic* (October 24)

Taylor, Stuart. 1987. "Marshall puts Reagan at 'bottom' among presidents on civil rights."(September 9): http://www.nytimes.com/1987/09/09/us/marshall-puts-reagan-at-bottom-among-presidents-on-civil-rights.html

United Nations High Commissioner for Refugees. 1993. *The State of the World's Refugees—The Challenge of Protection.* New York: Penguin Books.

U.S. Bureau of the Census. 1972. *1970 Census of Population: General Social and Economic Characteristics: United States Summary.* Appendix. Washington, D.C.: Government Printing Office.

———. n.d. "Residential segregation of blacks or African Americans, 1980–2000."http://www.census.gov/hhes/www/housing/housing_patterns/pdf/ch5.pdf

Vesselinov, Elena, 2008. "Members only: Gated communities and residential segregation in the metropolitan United States, "*Sociological Forum 23* (Sept.): 536–555.

Vidal, Gore. 1992. "Monotheism and its discontents." *The Nation* (July 13):1+.

Weber, Max. [1921] 1968. *Economy and Society*, vol. 1. Totowa, N.J.: Bedminister Press.

Whitman, Walt.[1855]2005. *Leaves of Grass: 150th Anniversary Edition.*New York: Oxford University Press.

Wilkerson, Isabel. 1992. "The tallest fence: Feelings on race in a white neighborhood." *New York Times* [national edition] (June 21):12.

Will, George. 1979. "Wagons in a circle." *Newsweek* (September 17):116.

Williams, Daniel. 2008. "Letter from America: A post-racial nation: no, a shift of enmities." *International Herald Tribune* (August 20):2.

Wilson, William Julius. 1978. *The Declining Significance of Race: Blacks and Changing American Institutions.* Chicago: University of Chicago Press.

———. 1987. *The Truly Disadvantaged: The Inner City, the Underclass, and Public Policy.* Chicago: University of Chicago Press.

———. 1996. *When Work Disappears: The World of the New Urban Poor.* New York: Alfred A. Knopf.

———. 2009. *More than Just Race: Being Black and Poor in the Inner City.* New York: W.W. Norton.

Winkler, Karen J. 1992. "A scholar's provocative query: Was Huckleberry Finn black?" *Chronicle of Higher Education* (July 8):A6–A8.

Wirth, Louis. 1945. "The problem of minority groups." Pp. 347–372 in Ralph Linton, ed., *The Science of Man in the World Crisis.* New York: Columbia University Press.

Wolfe, Kent, and Chris Ferland. n.d. "Estimated fresh salsa market for Georgia and bordering states." University of Georgia, College of Agricultural and Environmental Sciences: http://www.agecon.uga.edu/~caed/SalsaIndustry.pdf

Wolff, Michael, et al. 1992. *Where We Stand: Can Americans Make It in the Global Race for Wealth, Health, and Happiness?* New York: Bantam.

Wright, Robin. 1992. "Report from Turkestan." *New Yorker* (April 6):53–75.

Wright, Ronald. 1992. *Stolen Continents: The Americas Through Indian Eyes Since 1492.* Boston: Houghton Mifflin.

Zangwill, Israel. 1909. *The Melting Pot: A Drama in 4 Acts.* New York: Macmillan.

Zinn, Howard. 1991. *1492–1992: The Legacy of Columbus.* Audiotape. Boulder, Colo.: Alternative Radio.

PART

IV

RULES OF THE GAME

Susan Hoehn

Richard Hedman, revised by Lisa Siegel Sullivan

CHAPTER 11

SOCIAL LADDERS

"All people are created equal." That's what children learn in U.S. schools.

But growing up, we begin to realize that some people are more equal than others. Looking around town, we may notice that some people live in big houses on tree-lined streets, while others inhabit shacks by the railroad tracks. On prime-time television, we watch dramas in which people with badges of authority—police shields, white hospital coats, security clearance tags—wield **power** over those who don't. We may come across novelist F. Scott Fitzgerald's famous statement to Ernest Hemingway: "The very rich are different from you and me."

Before reaching voting age, most of us in the United States sense that—rhetoric and the Declaration of Independence aside—all people are not born equal and don't grow up equal. Most of us sense these inequalities in the United States— between rich and poor, powerful and powerless, socially esteemed and socially shunned. But rarely do we examine the *social* bases of these differences. Why? Because we haven't been taught to do so. Primary- and secondary-school textbooks rarely refer to inequalities that are linked to social factors. Hence, many people in the United States end up believing that existing disparities result from personal failure or bad luck.

Why is it that some people have more of the good things in life than others? How do occupation and other social structural variables affect a person's life chances? This chapter explores these questions. It looks at the influence of class, status, power, gender, age, religion, race, and ethnicity on a person's place in the social hierarchy. First, it outlines two general theoretical approaches to equality and inequality: the perspectives of Karl Marx and Max Weber. Next, it looks at some conceptual updates to Marx and Weber. Then, it examines social hierarchies in U.S. cities and metropolitan areas today.

This chapter, then, deals with the larger societal patterns that influence the games urbanites play. The next chapter focuses on the micro level of analysis— face-to-face social interaction; it concludes by demonstrating the virtue of combining macro and micro perspectives to gain a more complete understanding of urban social organization.

TWO WAYS OF LOOKING AT SOCIAL STRATIFICATION: MARX AND WEBER

The topic of **social stratification** (the process by which individuals and groups rank each other in a social hierarchy, from the Latin *strata*, meaning "layers") has occupied social thinkers for thousands of years. Over the millennia, many explanations have been offered to justify a society's inequalities and to explain why some possess more valuables (money, prestige, material goods, knowledge, power, etc.) than others. In the case of India, inequalities between **castes** (rigid social divisions based on status ascribed at birth) are justified by Hindu scriptures linking one's present position in the social hierarchy to one's past lives. In other religious belief systems, one's current position on the social ladder is tied to faith, good works, or divine providence.

With the birth of modern social science in nineteenth-century western Europe came new, nonreligious explanations for social inequality. Particularly important were the theories of Karl Marx and Max Weber.

Before discussing Marx's and Weber's theories in detail, we should note that pseudoscientists were not far behind scientists in explaining human inequality. Some claimed that intellectual superiority was related to skull size or body shape. Others proclaimed that criminals had particular physical characteristics.

The most famous of all pseudoscientific explanations for social inequality in the United States was—and, in some quarters, continues to be—social Darwinism. This ideology justified inequality on biological grounds as part of "natural selection." In 1911, the distinguished anthropologist Franz Boas assaulted social Darwinism and the idea of social evolution in general, arguing that there were no significant innate differences between racial or national groups.

In the past generation, Darwinism (social and biological) returned as an explanation for inequalities in the United States. Highly controversial—indeed, incendiary—studies claim that (1) different races have different brain sizes and, hence, different intelligence quotients (IQs) (Rushton, 1994); (2) IQs vary with race and ethnicity, leading to a polarization between smart, affluent elites and unintelligent poor people in the United States (Herrnstein and Murray, 1994); or (3) the United States is in economic and political decline because the least intelligent and most politically apathetic part of the population outbreed the intelligent and rich segment (Itzkoff, 1994). Critics call these studies "pornographic pseudoscience," not social science, charging that their authors use bad data, misuse statistics, depend on wrongheaded notions of both race and intelligence, make unwarranted conclusions, start from a conservative bias and agenda, and record little more than social prejudice.

Today, in many countries—including Brazil, Haiti, the UAR, and Pakistan—gross inequality exists, including modern slavery. Usually, the justification is economic: the chains of debt. (As the song about coal miners puts it, "I Owe My Soul to the Company Store.") According to some estimates, India and Pakistan keep up to 35 million people in bondage due to indebtedness. In Brazil, over 16,000 people remain enslaved. Mainly, landowners bind their cheap laborers by forcing them to run up unpayable debts at company stores. In the United States, laborers smuggled in from China are lured by stories of streets lined with gold; those who escape the immigration authorities typically end up as indentured servants to organized gangs, working 7 days a week for over 14 hours a day to pay off their passage. And these debt-ridden Chinese immigrants are far from alone.

Gross economic inequality exists in so-called advanced industrialized nations too. Indeed, the United States holds the dubious distinction of having the most unequal income distribution of any advanced industrialized (or postindustrial) nation in the world with the exception of one small country: Switzerland.

How one feels about this ever-increasing gap between rich and poor in the United States—and what one proposes doing about it, if anything—depends to a great degree on where one stands in the hierarchy and one's ideology. Princeton University sociologist Douglas Massey (2007) argues that among the culprits of this economic (and social) inequality are the U.S. federal government's "antipoor" policies (e.g., anti-union laws, drastic cuts in welfare spending, declines in the real value of the federal minimum wage) as well as the increasing residential segregation of neighborhoods by income, thereby insulating the affluent from the social consequences of poverty. (Nielsen Claritas and other marketeers predict that outcome.

See Chapter 8.) A conservative, libertarian, and radical would no doubt disagree on the roots of the inequalities as well as whether they are "good" or "bad."

Over the millennia, inequality has been justified on various grounds, notably biology, religion, special skills, and economics. Were he alive, this would not surprise philosopher Jean-Jacques Rousseau. In the eighteenth century, Rousseau wrote that "the strongest is never strong enough to always be master, unless he transforms his strength into right, and obedience into duty." In other words, those atop the social ladder need an ideology to legitimize their top spot. Ideologies of inequality, like alchemy, can help transmute might into right and special interests into the "common good."

We now turn to the theories of social inequality put forward by two nineteenth-century social scientists, Marx and Weber. Their ideas remain important—and controversial.

LIVING ON THE CUSP

The German philosopher Georg Hegel once wrote, "The owl of Minerva flies at dusk," meaning that wisdom appears at certain historical times: the approaching end of one era and the start of another. Some of us are living in such interesting times, in the shift from modern to postmodern, or from *Gesellschaft* to *Techno$chaft*.

In the nineteenth century, two German social thinkers, Karl Marx and Max Weber, lived at another such historical moment. Both witnessed the rapid rise of industrial cities, the rural–urban shift, and the changing social relationships that industrialization and urbanization brought. Profoundly influenced by these changing times, first Marx and then Weber formulated theories to describe and explain the bases of social stratification in different historical settings.

MARX AND WEBER: NO SPECIFICALLY URBAN THEORY

The models of Marx and Weber remain the leading theories of social stratification today. Often, they are viewed as competing models. But in important ways, the two intellectual giants agreed. Indeed, Weber's model can be seen as an extension of Marx's model, as well as an alternative to it.

Neither Marx nor Weber (nor Durkheim, for that matter) developed a specifically urban theory. They both viewed the modern city as a *dependent* variable, dependent on—not independent of—its larger context: a bureaucratic, industrial capitalist, state-centered society (Saunders, 1981:12). Marx analyzed western European history, capitalism, and capitalist societies, not cities per se (Katznelson, 1992:45). Weber, after visiting the United States in 1904, commented that its cities "served as a metaphor for capitalist modernity" (in Katznelson, 1992:10).

Marxist thinkers ignored the city for more than a century after Friedrich Engels published his 1845 portrait of Manchester, England (Chapter 4). But Marxists' inattention to cities took a U-turn by the 1970s. Indeed, Marxist-inspired theorists led to nothing less than an explosion of urban theory. Their theorizing was so different from conventional wisdom that some call it a paradigm shift.

Since the late 1980s, this so-called new urban theory reinvigorated urban studies. A variety of thinkers in a variety of cities—notably Henri Lefebvre in suburban Paris, David Harvey in Baltimore and Oxford, Manuel Castells in Berkeley and elsewhere, and an interdisciplinary group centered in Los Angeles—stirred up controversy and focused on a different set of issues: the interplay between local policies and state power, the role of class conflict in social change, the production of urban space, and the connections between the global system of production–consumption–exchange and the function of cities in poor and rich countries.

Many non-Marxists have been influenced by the new paradigm. This is ironic. For the first time in years, Marxist-inspired theories moved from the left margin to the mainstream in many U.S. universities at the very time that nations calling themselves "Marxist" or "socialist" began to repudiate Marxism. As one wag put it long after the fall of the Berlin Wall, "The only Marxists left teach at Berkeley or work in Havana!"

Now let's consider Marx's and Weber's general ideas about social inequality in capitalist–urban–industrial society. Then we'll look at a few conceptual updates that draw inspiration from Marx or Weber.

MARX AND THE CONCEPT OF CLASS

The late Pulitzer Prize–winning journalist J. Anthony Lukas once remarked, "America's dirty little secret is not sex. It is not power. Nor is it success. Rather, America's dirty little secret is class. It remains a secret even to some of its most cruelly treated victims." Noting a *New York Times* survey that found that one-quarter of all Americans don't consider themselves as belonging to any class at all, Lukas concluded, "To most of us, class is something only Germans with beards write about" (1978:9).

Most likely, Lukas was referring to one famous bearded German: Karl Marx. But he might have been noting another: Max Weber (see Fig. 11.3). Both Karl Marx (1818–1883) and Max Weber (1864–1920) insisted on the crucial importance of class in determining a society's system of individual rights and

Fig. 11.2 KARL MARX (Marx, Radio Times Hulton Picture Library)

privileges. Both thought that one's class position was a key to one's life chances. Yet the name of Weber, a political liberal in his own time, is not well known to most Americans. In contrast, Marx is widely recognized and, to put it mildly, his ideas on social class have been unpopular among most Americans.

At various times in U.S. history, even to be suspected of being a Marxist spelled disaster. This was true for a wide variety of people. Some lost their jobs, their friends, even their lives (by suicide) for real or suspected adherence to Marxism.

Why have Marx's ideas been considered alien and un-American? Why, even after the fall of Soviet-style Communism, are Marxist ideas still viewed as dangerous by so many Americans? Why is the concept of class "America's dirty little secret"? What did Marx think brought about social and political inequalities? And why do his ideas still fascinate scholars and activists today, generations after he sat in London's British Museum painstakingly working them out? Before we can begin to answer these questions, a little background on Marx's thought is called for.

As noted in Chapter 6, Marx was one of many European theorists trying to make sense out of what was going on in his own time. Most theorists—Marx, Durkheim, Tönnies, and so on—agreed on what they saw: rural folk streaming into the industrial cities to work in the expanding factory system. The nature and meaning of work were being transformed.

Marx had a unique slant on these events. To Marx, these changes signaled a historical event that became central to his analysis of history: the emergence of a new class of people, a mass of urban workers who controlled neither their work process nor their working conditions. He called this class of urban, propertyless workers the **proletariat**.

According to Marx, the proletariat was one of two major social divisions or classes to result from the development of capitalism. The other new class he called **capitalists** or the **bourgeoisie**: urban-based, propertied people who determined what the proletariat produced, how they produced it, and what wages they were paid. *Capitalists pay workers less than the value they produce—and pocket the difference. This is the root of capitalist exploitation.* Yet, workers don't realize they are being exploited, and often capitalists themselves are

unaware that they are exploiters. They attribute their profit to their own cunning, their investment in technology, their management skill, and so on. Further, Marx wrote, the structures of capitalism lead to human beings becoming alienated—from themselves, from the products of their labor, and in the end, from their nature as human beings.

To Marx, the development of medieval cities and mercantile capitalism in western Europe were inextricably linked. Marx's choice of the word "bourgeoisie" denotes this linkage, for a *bourg* is literally a town; thus, a bourgeois is an urbanite.

Very briefly, Marx reasoned as follows. Both the proletariat and the bourgeoisie developed out of the transformation from feudal to capitalist society between the sixteenth and nineteenth centuries in western Europe. As this historical shift proceeded, self-sufficient peasant economies died out. In their place arose city-based economies controlled by merchants and bankers, increasingly dependent on trade and commerce. The growth of mercantilist cities in medieval Europe, starting in the 1500s, marked the expropriation of rural people.

According to Marx, *the separation of the peasant from the soil was the basis of the whole capitalist process.* As rural people were uprooted from the land to work in urban manufacturing, they came under the domination of the bourgeoisie. Now, the urban workers had no land, no **wealth**—nothing except their labor, which they sold to factory owners. Living at a subsistence level with no public welfare system or unions to represent them, workers had few bargaining chips against their employers. In this situation, capitalist factory owners could set the wage scale and working conditions to suit their own class interests—specifically, the maximization of profit. Inevitably, the class interests of the proletariat would conflict with those of the bourgeoisie; the owners of capital wanted to maximize profit, not the welfare of their workers.

Up to this point, Marx's analysis of history doesn't seem very controversial. Marx's contemporaries of varying ideologies described the process of social change (e.g., from *Gemeinschaft* to *Gesellschaft*) in much the same way that Marx viewed the shift from feudal to capitalist society. (That these descriptions of the rural–urban shift transcended ideology is indicated by a footnote to history: Marx's favorite novelist was a French conservative, Honoré de Balzac, who mourned the passing of French aristocratic society but chronicled its demise in terms Marx thought brilliant.)

Marx did not invent the concept of class. It dates at least to ancient Rome, when people were ranked in six social divisions according to their wealth. Nor was Marx the first to recognize the existence of classes; many historians before him had used the concept. Then why are his ideas on social class considered un-American by so many?

First, Marx defined **class** in a way that *linked economic control to social domination.* Marx's logic was as follows. The nature and beliefs of human beings depend on what they produce and how they produce it. A person's social class is determined by his or her relationship to the **means of production** (inputs such as raw materials and tools, which produce or add to things of value in society, such as land in feudalism and factory machines in industrial capitalism). Class depends on how much the individual owns or controls of the means of production. By extension, Marx reasoned, those who own or control the means of production in a society also control the social organization of production. Thus, classes are not—repeat, *not*—income groups. Class is much more than an economic position; it also denotes the social relations that grow out of the way a society organizes its economy (e.g., private or collective ownership of the technology in use).

To a non-Marxist, "**capital** is just a thing (a machine, for example) or a sum of money. For a Marxist, that thing or that sum of money is only the facade for *a social relation of domination*: the machine has the mysterious power to compel people to obey 'its' rhythms, the money makes people dance to its tune" (Heilbroner, 1978:35). Under what Marx called the capitalist **mode of production** (the productive and social arrangements under capitalism, including the private ownership of the means of production), to be a capitalist or bourgeois ensures social as well as economic domination.

Second, Marx maintained that *human history could be understood best as a continuing struggle among classes for domination and control over scarce resources.* It is this idea—inherent class conflict—that has traditionally

gone against the grain in the United States. U.S. ideology stresses the opposite idea: harmony among social classes. The assumption of class harmony is captured in a favorite saying by laissez-faire economists: "A rising tide lifts all boats," meaning that economic prosperity and growth help rich and poor alike.

Conventional wisdom in the United States holds that workers' interests and the interests of business and industry are allied, not antithetical. The classic statement of this position came from "Engine Charlie" Wilson, head of General Motors in the 1950s: "What's good for GM is good for America." To a Marxist, this kind of thinking is, in itself, a form of capitalist domination. The concept of **hegemony**—cultural leadership or domination—helps to explain why. According to Italian Marxist Antonio Gramsci (see Lawner [1932] 1975:235), the masses do not have to be held in check by laws or police power because they accept a basic but false notion: that the dominant class represents the general interest of the nation, not its own class interest.

However, many people in the United States and Canada have been questioning the long-assumed harmony of interests between workers and owners. Most probably, their suspicion of conventional wisdom was jogged by the news of (or personal experience with) real-world events: Wall Street scandals, tax breaks for U.S. multinationals relocating jobs offshore, Enron's greed, corporate restructuring, union-busting, market panic, and so on.

Long before the U.S. market panic that spread globally in 2008, *New York Times* analyst Louis Uchitelle reported that a shared anxiety over the changing U.S. economy gave rise to class consciousness: "an awareness among millions of Americans that they occupy the same unsteady boat, even if they are doing well in high-paying jobs" (1994:A6). Mainstream publications, notably *Newsweek*, seemed to agree: It headlined that instead of a rising tide lifting all boats, "A Rising Tide Lifts the Yachts" (1995:62D).

By the late 1990s, the gap between rich and poor had widened so much that the United States led the industrialized world in the inequality of income. By 2001, wealth was even more concentrated: The top 1% of households held 39.7% of the wealth in the United States (Edward N. Wolff in Domhoff, 2006).

Still, the notion of a "class war" remains unpopular in the United States. So does Marx's idea that some are rich and powerful because others are poor and powerless. Instead of a class enemy, such as owners of capital and multinational corporations, people in the United States tend to direct their anger at the government, undocumented immigrants, and the poor in general.

Finally, what has seemed so alien about Marx's views is his predicted outcome of the class struggle between bourgeoisie and proletariat (the haves and have-nots). According to Marx, inherent contradictions within capitalism between the **forces of production** (e.g., the technology in use) and the **social relations of production** (e.g., private ownership of the technology in use) would work themselves out in a dialectical

---

BOX 11.1 SOCIAL THEORIST AS POLITICAL PAMPHLETEER: *THE COMMUNIST MANIFESTO*

Section 1: Bourgeois and Proletarians

The history of all hitherto existing society is the history of class struggle.

Freeman and slave, patrician and plebeian, lord and serf, guild-master and journeyman—in a word, oppressor and oppressed, stood in constant opposition to one another....

The modern bourgeois society that has sprouted from the ruins of feudal society has not done away with class antagonisms. It has but established new conditions of oppression, new forms of struggle in place of the old ones.

Our epoch, the epoch of the bourgeoisie, possesses however, this distinctive feature: it has simplified the class antagonisms. Society as a whole is more and more splitting up into two great hostile camps, into two great classes directly facing each other: Bourgeoisie and Proletariat.

From the serfs of the Middle Ages sprang the chartered burghers of the earliest towns. From these burgesses the first elements of the bourgeoisie were developed.

The discovery of America, the rounding of the Cape, opened up fresh ground for the rising bourgeoisie....

The feudal system of industry, under which industrial production was monopolized by closed guilds, now no longer sufficed for the growing wants of the new markets. The manufacturing system took its place. The guild-masters were pushed on one side by the manufacturing middle class; division of labour between the different corporate guilds vanished in the face of division of labour in each single workshop.

Meantime the markets kept ever growing, the demand ever rising....The place of manufacture was taken by the giant, Modern Industry, the place of the industrial middle class, by industrial millionaires, the leaders of whole industrial armies, the modern bourgeois. Modern industry has established the world-market, for which the discovery of America paved the way. This market has given an immense development to commerce, to navigation, to communication by land. This development has, in its turn, reacted on the extension of industry; and in proportion as industry, commerce, navigation, railways extended, in the same proportion the bourgeoisie developed, increased its capital, and pushed into the background every class handed down from the Middle Ages.

We see, therefore, how the modern bourgeoisie is itself the product of a long course of development, of a series of revolutions in the modes of production and of exchange.

Each step in the development of the bourgeoisie was accompanied by a corresponding political advance of that class. An oppressed class under the sway of the feudal nobility, an armed and self-governing association in the medieval commune; here independent urban republics (as in Italy and Germany); there taxable "third estates" of the monarchy (as in France)...the bourgeoisie has at last, since the establishment of Modern Industry and of the world-market, conquered for itself, in the modern representative State, exclusive political sway. The executive of the modern State is but a committee for managing the common affairs of the whole bourgeoisie....The bourgeoisie has subjected the country to the rule of the towns. It has created enormous cities, has greatly increased the urban population as compared with the rural, and has thus rescued a considerable part of the population from the idiocy of rural life....

Modern industry has converted the little workshop of the patriarchal master into the great factory of the industrial capitalist. Masses of labourers, crowded into the factory, are organized like soldiers. As privates of the industrial army they are placed under the command of a perfect hierarchy of officers and sergeants. Not only are they slaves of the bourgeois class, and of the bourgeois State; they are daily and hourly enslaved by the machine, by the overlooker, and, above all, by the individual bourgeois manufacturer himself.

Source: David McLellan, ed., *Karl Marx: Selected Writings* (New York: Oxford University Press, 1977), pp. 222–227. Copyright © 1977 by David McLellan. Reprinted by permission of Lawrence & Wishart, Ltd.

process and lead to a new form of society. He believed that the proletariat would develop a subjective **class consciousness**, realizing that they share an objective class situation (long hours, little pay, no control over their work process, domination by another class).

Ultimately, Marx thought, workers would act as a class to wrest control from the bourgeoisie. To Marx, this was inevitable. He wrote in *The Communist Manifesto* in 1848, a year marked by revolutions in Europe:

> The essential condition for the existence, and for the sway of the bourgeois class, is the formation and augmentation of capital; the condition for capital is wage-labour. Wage labour rests exclusively on competition between the labourers. The advance of industry, whose involuntary promoter is the bourgeoisie, replaces the isolation of the labourers, due to competition, by their revolutionary combination, due to association. The development of Modern Industry, therefore, cuts from under its feet the very foundation on which the bourgeoisie produces and appropriates products.
>
> *(in McLellan, 1977:231)*

To conclude: Marx used one measure of social stratification: class. For Marx, class denotes social as well as economic domination (or dependence). His model of social stratification is like a pyramid where people are ranked on the basis of their ownership or lack of ownership of the productive means in their society. At the top of the pyramid are the bourgeoisie, a small number of people who control most of the society's wealth and power. In the middle of the pyramid are strata that Marx felt would eventually be eliminated by capitalistic advances (e.g., small business owners, termed small or petite bourgeoisie). The bottom layer of the pyramid broadens out to include the vast majority of people who have neither wealth nor power.

For Marx, power and wealth are two sides of the same coin under capitalism: Those who control the means of production control the society's social relations. Thus, the bourgeoisie controls not only the mechanical process of production but also the dominant ideas of the time and the governmental processes.

Marx's vision of a new society—based on social equality, not inequality, and on a sense of community rooted in labor, not ethnicity, nationality, or religion—has provided inspiration for revolutionary movements throughout the world. It has also provoked feelings of fear, distrust, hatred, and cynicism in many places, including countries that once called themselves Communist or socialist. In the United States, most reject the notion of class struggle as the primary vehicle for social change.

"DREAM UP, BLAME DOWN"

Another reason that Marx's ideas have been unpopular in the United States is that to many people the United States represents the land of opportunity. In their minds, it is the place where a poor child can sell matchsticks on the corner and climb the ladder to success, as in the Horatio Alger stories of the nineteenth century. That is the **American dream**—self-made men and women, rugged individualists reaching the top by working hard and smart, playing by the rules, and having a pinch of good luck.

The Horatio Alger image of upward social mobility and an open class system has dominated U.S. thought. Historically, people in the United States have tended to "dream up and blame down" (Tim Teninty, personal conversation, 1992); that is, Americans tend to blame those below them on the social ladder for their lack of success while dreaming of reaching the top rung themselves.

In the United States, people seem to have had a love affair with (or at least an urge to identify with) the middle class. Whatever their job—ditchdiggers or doctors, cleaning women or CEOs—a big chunk of people in the United States think they are middle class. According to the General Social Survey (GSS), at no time between 1972 and 1994 did more than 10 percent of the American population classify themselves as either lower class or upper class.

Is class identification (or consciousness) in the United States changing? In the 2006 GSS, over 46 percent self-identified as middle class but 51 percent identified as lower or working class; less than 3 percent stated they were upper class (Tom Piazza, personal communication, July 7, 2008).

Still, to a Marxist or neo-Marxist, the fact that nearly one-half of the people in the United States see themselves as middle class indicates how powerful the wealthy few really are: They have succeeded in binding the weak by the chains of their own ideas. A neo-Marxist might accuse poor, powerless people who think they're middle class of living in self-deception (or, as Marx called it, **false consciousness).**

Typically, conservatives and libertarians scoff at the idea of false consciousness. Instead, they extol the rags-to-riches, Horatio Alger stories of just plain folks. They might interpret the annual Forbes 400 list of richest people in the United States as proof positive that the United States is an open economy where people like Oprah Winfrey, Sam Walton, and Steve Jobs can start off poor (or not rich) and end up very wealthy. They might point out that for years Bill Gates, Microsoft's founder—not a Rockefeller—was the richest person in the United States. Further, conservatives and libertarians might applaud a color-blind and gender-blind economy where "self-made" women and men of all hues make the *Forbes* list, including Bill Gates, Oprah Winfrey, Robert Johnson (founder, Black Entertainment Television), Margaret C. Whitman (eBay), French Iranian immigrant Pierre Omidyar (eBay), Stephen J. Biscotti (Aerotek), and Michael Dell (Dell Computer). Instead of bemoaning the growing income and wealth inequality in the United States, a conservative or libertarian might cheer a system that allows entrepreneurs to garner great wealth.

How might neo-Marxists and liberals respond? They might reexamine *Forbes* magazine's annual list (Miller and Serafin, 2006), pointing out that in 2006 there were many who inherited their wealth (including at least seven Waltons from Wal-Mart). They might also point out that the Horatio Alger stories work only for a tiny few; studies suggest that the United States is among the least economically mobile of the big industrial/postindustrial countries. Further, they might cite studies showing that the income gap in the United States widened since the millennium, with most economic benefits of the strong pre-2007 economy going to the wealthiest: By the early 2000s, the top 1 percent of income-earners garnered nearly 20 percent of the nation's income. That's more than double the share that the top 1 percent received 30 years ago (Ystie, 2007).

Neo-Marxists and liberals alike think this economic inequality bodes poorly for the nation. They point to what they see as "excessive" income inequality, unhealthy for a democracy and bad for economic growth. For instance, they say that not only has wealth in the United States become more concentrated since the 1970s (Wolff, [1995] 2002; Keister, 2004) but, when the top 5 percent of U.S. households in terms of income gained the most income of all income groups in 2005 (Center on Budget and Policy Priorities, 2006) such an income distribution is ill-suited to a democratic nation.

Unlike many (but not all) conservatives and libertarians, neo-Marxists and liberals tend not to put a positive spin on income inequality. They say, for example, that one negative impact of the U.S. wealth concentration is the slowing of upward social mobility (e.g., Beller and Hout, 2002; Hertz, 2005). They argue that wealth inequality restricts social mobility from father to son, that is, intergenerationally (typically not expressed as *mother*-to-*child* mobility).

A neo-Marxist or liberal might point out that people without nest eggs, including most African Americans in the United States, suffer a "wealth deficit." Specifically, the average African American family has only 18 percent of the wealth of the average white family (Wolff, 2003). Further, some claim that the subprime mortgage "meltdown," starting in 2007, hit low-income African Americans and Latinos the hardest. For example, in Fulton County, Georgia, which encompasses most of Atlanta's core and is heavily African American, one in 122 homes was in foreclosure in early April 2008 (Wright, 2008). Reporter Kai Wright (2008) concludes that the "mortgage meltdown" will "betray the promise of class mobility for tens of thousands of black families.... It's a loss black America can scarcely afford, because black wealth has long been enormously dependent on home equity. Without counting home equity, black net worth in 2004 was just 1 percent of that for whites.... "

Typically, then, the children of African Americans inherit less, have fewer chances to live in better neighborhoods and attend better schools, and thus have substantially less chance to be upwardly mobile. The cycle continues.

But, if one subscribes to either conservative or libertarian views, cycles can be broken. The fortunes of such people as Oprah Winfrey, who rose from a background of abuse and poverty to economic heights, suggests, in their view, that Horatio Alger lives.

MARX, THE INESCAPABLE CRITIC

However one evaluates Marx's ideas, they are inescapable. Marxists and non-Marxists alike are still engaged in sorting out what he "really" meant and what application Marx's ideas have to the contemporary world. Critics and followers debate his political message of revolutionary action (is it applicable to postindustrial societies?), his assumptions about human psychology (can they account for people's drives to power? even under socialism, won't individuals try to reassert domination in the name of virtue, sex, or bureaucratic efficiency, if not wealth?), his consistency (is there an "early" Marx concerned with issues of alienation and a "late" Marx concerned with "laws" of capitalism?), and his views on history (is it wholly determined by structural factors, as he implies in some passages of his work, or is it dependent on the revolutionary consciousness of the proletariat, as he implies in other passages?).

Contemporary Marxists, or *neo-Marxists*, don't agree among themselves on many points. Some even hold that the enemy is no longer capitalism but rather bureaucracy; they argue that bureaucracy—whether capitalist or socialist—is an instrument of domination and exploitation. As we shall soon see, this is not a new idea; Max Weber had the same notion.

If even those who consider themselves in the Marxist tradition question his ideas and view of human history, why do Marx's ideas continue to enthrall scholars, Marxist and non-Marxist alike? Economist Robert L. Heilbroner offers the following explanation:

> The reason for the magnetism that Marx [still] exerts...is that Marx had the luck, combined of course with the genius, to be the first to discover a whole mode of inquiry that would forever belong to him....I refer to Marx the inventor of critical social science, who "critiqued" economics....Marx invented a kind of social "criticizing"—that is, subjecting the social universe to a particular sort of questioning.
>
> *(1978:33)*

By the late 1980s, many conservatives were celebrating the death of Marxist thought in the Soviet bloc, the so-called socialist nations (nations that most neo-Marxists considered bureaucratic, state-capitalist

Fig. 11.3 MAX WEBER. (Alfred Weber Institut für Sozial and Staatwissenschaften der Universität, Heidelberg, Germany)

societies, not socialist or Communist). Yet, Marx's ideas remain central to social science, particularly to urban studies. Why? According to Heilbroner's argument, Marx continues to influence theorists "not because he is infallible" but rather because "he is unavoidable" for anyone who asks questions "about the nature of our thinking about society." "Sooner or later all such inquiries," Heilbroner says, "bring one to confront Marx's thought, and then one is compelled to adopt, confute, expand, escape from, or come to terms with the person who has defined the very task of critical social inquiry itself" (1978:33).

One scholar influenced by Marx (and the late French historian Fernand Braudel plus his own research in postcolonial Africa) is noteworthy here: Immanuel Wallerstein. Wallerstein ([1974] 1980,

2004) constructed a perspective called **"world-systems analysis,"** now widely used throughout the historical social sciences, particularly to discuss globalization.

Very briefly, sociologist Wallerstein's world-systems analysis does not focus on nation-states. Quite the contrary. It concentrates on a unit he calls the "world system." This world system, he argues, started evolving with the development of a capitalist world economy in the 1500s and continued developing through 200 years of liberal centrism, leading up to the French Revolution of 1789. Since then, Wallerstein notes, the world system continued expanding until it engulfed practically the entire globe by 1900. Global revolts of 1968, Wallerstein thinks, undermined that centrism.

In Wallerstein's view, we cannot understand the long evolution of the capitalist economy and social system by looking at individual countries. Why? Because, he claims, countries do not have separate economies; they are part of a world economy. Thus, the unit of analysis should be the world system of which they are a part. According to Wallerstein, the world system is comprised of interconnected nations, firms, households, classes, and identity groups of all kinds. It operates in core, semiperipheral, and peripheral zones, which are connected via the division of labor (where core zones dominate the most profitable economic activities).

WEBER'S VIEW OF SOCIAL STRATIFICATION: CLASS, STATUS, POWER

Max Weber was one of the most distinguished social inquirers who found Marx inescapable. He skillfully applied Marx's historical method, and his ideas on social stratification were influenced by Marx's previous work.

Weber did not refute Marx's notions on social stratification. Rather, he expanded on them. In fact, much of Weber's political sociology can be viewed as an attempt to "round out" Marx (Gerth and Mills, 1958:47).

Like Marx, Weber made capitalism a central theme in his scholarly work, calling it "the most fateful force in our modern life" (Weber, [1904–1905] 1958:17). Weber viewed Western capitalism as unique because of its rational, bureaucratic form. That is, it is organized on the basis of pursuit of profit by rational calculation;

it uses rational techniques, such as the legal separation of personal property from corporate property; and it depends on bureaucratic organization. According to Weber, this particular Western form of capitalism—"rational bourgeois capitalism"—linked profit making with the bureaucratic organization of the economy and high technology.

Weber and Marx agreed on the paramount importance of capitalism in modern life. They did not, however, share the same interpretation of capitalist institutions. Specifically, Marx saw capitalism as irrational in terms of meeting human needs. Weber viewed capitalist institutions, especially bureaucracy, as the epitome of rationality and efficiency. In fact, it was this ever-increasing movement toward bureaucratic efficiency and rationality that struck Weber as problematic; while efficient, it would inevitably lead to the depersonalization of the individual.

Weber agreed with Marx that under capitalism there is a class struggle between the haves and have-nots. But unlike Marx, he did not make class struggle the central dynamic of his work. Instead, the bureaucratization of everything, which went hand in hand with the development of capitalism in the West, was Weber's primary concern.

Weber felt that Marx did not go far enough. Agreeing with Marx that capitalism separates the peasant from the soil and the propertyless urban masses from the means of production, he extended the analysis. *Bureaucratic organization separates all people from their labor*—the scientist from the means of inquiry, the soldier from the means of violence, and the civil servant from the means of administration.

In brief, Marx and Weber had very different views of what was inevitable. To Marx, the "dictatorship of the proletariat" and socialism were inevitable. To Weber, only the "disenchanted garden" of rational calculation was inevitable, and it would lead to the depersonalization of the individual through efficient bureaucratic management.

Much more pessimistic than Marx, Weber commented that "for the time being, the dictatorship of the [corporate and government] official and not that of the worker is on the march" (in Gerth and Mills, 1958:50). Thus, while Marx looked forward to a socialist future in which people would control their

Fig. 11.4 WEBER'S VIEW OF BUREAUCRACY: EFFICIENT BUT DEADLY. (Richard Hedman)

work process and their lives, Weber felt that socialism (with its own bureaucracy) would be just another system for enslaving the individual.

Weber also felt that Marx's theory of history, with its emphasis on class struggle, was too one-dimensional. In his view, there were other important factors, especially the meanings that people brought to their situation.

Similarly, Weber felt that Marx's approach to social stratification was too simplified. For Weber, the economic order (class) was crucial to the social ranking process. But Weber contended that other institutional orders—the military, religion, politics, law, and so forth—were also important. All of these institutional orders were interrelated, but they were also separate and distinct. In his essay "Class, Status, Party" ([1922] 1958), Weber identified three interrelated but distinct social orders that influence a person's social rank:

1. The economic order (class)
2. The prestige order (status)
3. The political order (power)

Class

Weber thought that those sharing the same position in the economic order (class) also share similar "life chances" or market position. They can expect similar opportunities for income, material goods, living conditions, and personal life experiences.

Researchers in the Weberian tradition usually determine class position by some measure of income and wealth. They see class as a series of graded income groups. Some define these as upper class, upper middle class, middle class, working class, and the poor. Others pay attention to strata within one class, such as layers in the working class: self-employed, skilled workers, nonskilled in peripheral industries, marginally employed, and supervisors.

Applying Weber's notion of class as shared life chances, what do we find? The life chances of poor and rich people in the United States are not equal. Literally, the poor die younger—and have greater health problems—than the wealthy.

Countless studies show that life expectancy is linked to Weberian class. And race. For example, one study shows that among female twins in the United States, one who was working class fared worse healthwise than her professional twin (Krieger et al., 2005); the authors conclude that what they call "socioeconomic position" influences adult health.

In terms of race and gender, the same is true. For example, the U.S. Centers for Disease Control and Prevention (CDC) reported in 2007 that U.S. life expectancy had risen to almost 78 years but that U.S. whites will live longer than blacks and women longer than men (in Fox, 2008). Indeed, an African American man living in a high-crime U.S. city can expect to live 21 fewer years than a woman of Asian descent in the United States. Similarly, about 20 years ago researchers found that poor, white men had 6.7 times the death rate of rich white men and poor African American men had 5.4 times the death rate of rich African American men.

Also, being poor and Latino/Hispanic or African American makes the odds even worse. Nearly a generation ago, African American males in New York's

Harlem were less likely to live to the age of 65 than men in Bangladesh, one of the world's poorest nations (McCord and Freeman, 1990).

Applying Weber's notion of class as shared life chances, we find that in the United States the life chances of whites (not including Hispanics) and everyone else are not equal. Literally. Non-Hispanic whites in the United States live longer. As Table 11.1 shows, the longest-lived people in the United States, as of 2006, were Asian Americans who lived in counties where they did not compose the majority.

That life expectancy is linked to class is generally accepted. Why and how, however, is a matter of some discussion. Most researchers believe that, among other causal variables, the poor live and work in more toxic environments, eat less nutritional food, are exposed to more risks and dangers, suffer more stress, and have less health education. (However, some extreme

TABLE 11.1 EFFECTS OF RACE/ETHNICITY, CLASS, RURAL–URBAN RESIDENCE, AND REGION ON LIFE EXPECTANCY AMONG U.S. GROUPS, 2006

AMERICA	DESCRIPTION	DEFINITION	POPULATION, MILLIONS	Average Life Expectancy (years)
1	Asian	Asians living in counties where Pacific Islanders make up less than 40 percent of total Asian population	10.4	84.9
2	Northland, low-income, rural white	Whites in Northern Plains and Dakotas with 1990 county-level per capita income below $11,775 and population density less than 100 per square kilometer	3.6	79.0
3	Middle America	All other whites not included in U.S. 2 and 4, Asians not in U.S. 1, and Native U.S. not in U.S. 5	214.0	77.9
4	Low-income whites in Appalachia and the Mississippi Valley	Whites in Appalachia and the Mississippi Valley with 1990 county per capita income below $11,775	16.6	75.0
5	Western Native American	Native American populations in the mountain and plains areas, predominantly on reservations	1.0	72.7
6	Black Middle America	All other black populations living in counties not included in U.S. 7 and 8	23.4	72.9
7	Southern, low-income, rural black	Blacks living in counties in the Mississippi Valley and the Deep South with population density below 100 people per square kilometer and 1990 county-level per capita income below $7,500	5.8	71.2
8	High-risk urban black	Urban populations of more than 150,000 blacks living in counties with cumulative probability of homicide death greater than 1 percent	7.5	71.1

Source: PLoS Medicine, *Washington Post*, September 12, 2006: http://www.washingtonpost.com/wp-dyn/content/graphic/2006/09/12/GR2006091200162.html

conservatives turn this logic on its head, claiming that poor health might cause poverty, not vice versa. Or, they posit, a third factor—personal "shortcomings" such as laziness and substance abuse—might cause poverty.)

In London, it is the same story: The poor die younger. Indeed, throughout England and Wales, there appears to be a growing "health gap" between rich and poor. One document (in Kmietowicz, 2001) from the London Health Observatory based on data collected between 1997 and 1999 says that life expectancy in London depended largely on class. For example, a baby boy born in Westminster, one of London's richest boroughs, was likely to outlive a baby boy born in Newham, one of the poorest boroughs, by 6 years.

To conclude: A health gap between those higher on the income ladder and those below them exists in the United States and elsewhere. This gap has been widening, not narrowing, in recent years. Similarly, the poor in the United States have unequal chances of obtaining decent housing and education.

In brief, in the United States the poor—and especially poor African Americans—are more likely than affluent people of all races to live in substandard conditions. The poor are much less likely to be enrolled in institutions of higher learning; this is especially important because higher education is viewed as the stepping-stone to upward mobility. The poor are more likely to be victims of personal crimes of violence than the rich. For the same money, the poor often get shoddier merchandise and fewer groceries than the affluent. The poor often pay almost 10 percent more for an equivalent used car than middle-income shoppers ("Used cars," 1978:F17). The conclusion: A person's chances of obtaining a higher education, standard housing, and personal safety are directly tied to his or her economic position (class, in Weber's terms).

Race has a serious impact on health too. In West Oakland, California, to take just one example, an African American child is much more likely to be born prematurely and into poverty than a white child in upscale parts of Oakland. And he or she can expect to die nearly 15 years before his or her more upscale, white counterpart (Fernandez, 2008:A1). The deputy director of public health in Alameda County (where Oakland is located) put it like this: "People live longer in the hills...[because they] have higher incomes and education, better housing...[and] health insurance." In addition, those in the hills live farther from the freeway and have more access to healthy food. On the contrary, both African Americans and Latinos are highly concentrated in high-poverty areas (in Fernandez, 2008:A19).

Perhaps most chilling is the plight of the poor—and vulnerable—as human guinea pigs. The U.S. government revealed that from the 1940s to the mid-1970s, government agencies conducted or underwrote secret, potentially deadly experiments on many unknowing subjects. Most subjects "were drawn from the ranks of society's dispossessed, either by virtue of their race, age, income, or intelligence" (Healy, 1994:1). For example, cancer patients in Cincinnati (most of them poor and African African) got "treatments" laced with radiation between 1960 and 1972, Inupiat Eskimos in Alaska ate caribou that had absorbed radioactive debris, and children at a school for the mentally retarded in Massachusetts were given radioactive iron and calcium in their breakfast cereal that was served up by researchers at MIT (Healy, 1994:1). A physician and professor at Brown University, a critic of the so-called therapeutic radiation experiments conducted without informed consent, noted sarcastically, "For some reason, rich white people were deprived of all this wonderful research" (Egilman in Wheeler, 1994:A6).

That U.S. poor people of color suffer more from private as well as public policies is hardly an earthshaking discovery. For example, an Associated Press analysis of a little-known U.S. government research study showed that African Americans were 79 percent more likely than whites to live in neighborhoods where industrial pollution is suspected of posing the greatest health danger. A former head of the Environmental Protection Agency was not surprised. She commented, "Poor communities, frequently communities of color but not exclusively, suffer disproportionately" (Browner in Pace, 2005).

The links between social inequality and exposure to environmental pollutants and stress are not limited to the United States. In England, for example, case studies show a clear relationship between exposure to environmental pollution and low income due to housing (in Kempf, 2008).

Millionaire novelist Tom Clancy once called members of the U.S. Congress failures because "if [the then salary of] $120,000 a year is the best job you've ever had, you haven't really done much." Here the best-selling author reveals how much his value system is tied to the class system, as defined by Weber, and to what Wirth called the "pecuniary nexus." Clancy's comment suggests that in the United States people are judged by the numbers on their paycheck, not the number of good deeds completed or beautiful poems created.

Data based on Weberian measures of class affirm a related point: Class position makes a difference in determining what a person can expect to get out of life in the United States. As we shall see shortly, we come to the same conclusion if we use neo-Marxist measures of class.

Status

In Weber's view, the **status** order of prestige is related to the economic order (class) but separate from it. People who share the same position in the hierarchy of prestige share a similar lifestyle. They display similar symbols of consumption and respectability. PRIZM's SER clusters (Chapter 8) draw their inspiration largely from this insight.

Taking some contemporary American examples, a high-prestige group might share the following symbols: knowledge of languages long dead, like Latin or Greek; worn Persian carpets; subscriptions to the *New Yorker* or the *New York Review of Books*; refined tastes in modern art and French wine; classical record collections; tennis rackets; a television set outside the living room; homes or apartments at a "good address"; membership in exclusive social clubs; and old school ties to elite educational institutions. A lower-prestige group would share different symbols, perhaps a framed diploma, metal Venetian blinds, transparent plastic furniture covers, a "wall system" without books, an aquarium, homes in tract developments, bowling balls, a knowledge of home repair skills, copies of *Family Circle* or *Reader's Digest*, a television set in the living room, and ties to high-school buddies. (Nielsen Claritas's PRIZM clusters are largely based on Weber's insights on status.)

In many places, accent reflects status. In Great Britain, for one, an Oxford accent is much higher on the status hierarchy than a cockney accent. *My Fair Lady*, based on George Bernard Shaw's 1938 play *Pygmalion*, illustrates this "accent hierarchy." In the musical, London cockney Eliza Doolittle is made over to become an English lady by upper-class Henry Higgins. The make-over includes Eliza's dropping her cockney accent in order to speak "proper" (higher-status) English. In the United States, some people pay teachers such as Professor David Alan Stern, founder of Dialect Accent Specialists, to help them shed their accents, perceived as hindrances to their social or economic progress (Stern, 2007).

In brief, different status groups live in different worlds. Moreover, they suffer different fates. One longitudinal U.S. study, from 1968 to 1994, showed that occupation was an important risk factor: nonprofessionals were at higher risk of death than professionals in the United States across all sectors of the economy (Muntaner et al., 2004). Similarly, World Health Organization researchers conclude that in both poor and rich societies "cancer incidence and survival are related to socioeconomic factors" (Kogevinas et al., 1997).

U.S.-trained British epidemiologist Michael Marmot goes further. In *The Status Syndrome: How Social Standing Affects Our Health and Longevity* ([2004] 2005), Marmot found that in both Great Britain and the United States income, occupation, and education are directly related to health: *The lower a person (and his or her parents) ranks on the socioeconomic ladder, the worse is that person's health*. Similarly, Marmot found that those who stand higher on the ladder are healthier than those just a few rungs below.

Marmot's research suggests that inequality and a psychological sense of not being in control of one's fate—rather than poverty—lead to different health outcomes. Here is his basic chain of reasoning: The lower that people stand on the socioeconomic ladder, the less they feel in control of their own destiny. This psychological sense of lack of control often results in chronic stress, and chronic stress negatively affects health. On the contrary, those at the top of the income and occupation ladder tend to have greater control, more power, and better health. Thus, different status, income, and occupational groups live—and die—in much different circumstances and at different rates.

Fig. 11.5 WHO LIVES HERE? Not someone from a lower-status group. Lack of a visible television set, understated elegance, and original art from Asia indicate that this New York City apartment is inhabited by a professional (or professionals) who appreciates and is able to pay for quality and originality. (Susan Hoehn)

Different status groups also live in different "taste cultures" (Gans, 1974). A shared taste culture gives people a sense of belonging to the same kind of community. And, according to Weber, status groups are communities; people in similar status groups see themselves as having common interests and tastes. (On this point, Weber and Marx differed. Marx felt that class members would recognize their common class interests. Weber thought that a person's objective economic position would not necessarily lead him or her to feel a sense of community with others who share that same position.)

Following Weber's analysis, then, we can predict (correctly) the following: Members of similar status groups tend to marry each other. They tend to enjoy the same kinds of cultural events and display similar symbols of consumption. They listen to similar radio stations. A case in point is National Public Radio (NPR) in the United States. One audience survey found that "over one-half of all public radio listeners live in PRIZM's top four socio-economic neighborhoods in the United States" (Liebold, 1988). Another survey in the early 2000s found that NPR audiences were among the most affluent and educated in the nation; their average household income was $78,000 (Fonda, 2003). In other words, people with high incomes, professional jobs, and many years of education make up the majority of U.S. public radio listeners. And the majority of NPR listeners live in the highest-ranking SER neighborhoods.

Occupational groups, Weber noted, are also status groups. And in the United States the work one does is probably the single best indicator of a person's relative prestige. (This was not always so. In *Gemeinschaft*, the best indicator of prestige is the social esteem of one's family. "Who is your father?" was an all-important query to a marriage-minded person in eighteenth-century Boston. But individual leisure activities and residential neighborhood—not family or occupation—may be crucial status markers in *Techno\$chaft* or postindustrial society. If so, when adult strangers fall into conversation, the familiar "What do you do for a living?" will be replaced by "What are you into?" and "What's your ZIP code?")

Sociologists in the structural–functional tradition of Durkheim argue that the relative prestige of different occupations is essentially the same in all complex societies. Thus, in *Gesellschaft* societies, we should expect to find the same occupations at the top of the status ladder and the same occupations at the bottom. This is because all complex societies face similar "functional imperatives." To get these tasks accomplished, advanced technological societies organize themselves in similar ways (Table 11.2).

Briefly, the structural–functional argument is as follows. Social differentiation "inherently implies stratification. Specialization of functions carries with it inherent differences in the control over scarce resources, which is the primary basis of stratification." These resources—skill, knowledge,

TABLE 11.2A   PRESTIGE OF 23 PROFESSIONS AND OCCUPATIONS IN THE UNITED STATES 2007

	Very Great Prestige (%)	Considerable Prestige (%)	Some Prestige (%)	Hardly Any Prestige at All (%)	Not Sure/ Refused (%)
Firefighter	61	26	10	2	—
Scientist	54	28	13	4	*
Teacher	54	24	16	6	*
Military officer	52	29	15	4	*
Doctor	52	35	12	1	—
Nurse	50	29	17	4	—
Police officer	46	27	19	7	*
Priest/minister/ Clergy	42	23	26	9	*
Farmer	41	16	26	17	—
Engineer	30	37	25	6	1
Member of Congress	26	32	23	17	2
Architect	23	33	39	6	*
Lawyer	22	20	41	17	*
Athlete	16	20	45	19	*
Business executive	14	28	42	15	*
Journalist	13	24	47	16	*
Union leader	13	20	36	30	1
Stockbroker	12	17	46	25	1
Entertainer	12	16	42	31	—
Accountant	11	25	48	16	1
Banker	10	28	45	17	*
Actor	9	19	34	38	—
Real estate agent/broker	5	18	43	34	*

—, no response; *<0.5%.

These are some results of the annual Harris Poll measuring public perceptions of 23 professions and occupations, conducted by telephone between July 10 and 16, 2007, among a nationwide sample of 1,010 U.S. adults. The telephone interviewer said, "I am going to read off a number of different occupations. For each, would you tell me if you feel it is an occupation of very great prestige, considerable prestige, some prestige, or hardly any prestige at all?"

TABLE 11.2B OCCUPATIONAL PRESTIGE RANKINGS IN THE UNITED STATES, 1977–2007: HIGH-PRESTIGE OCCUPATIONS ONLY

	1977 (%)	1982 (%)	1992 (%)	1997 (%)	1998 (%)	2000 (%)	2001 (%)	2002 (%)	2003 (%)	2004 (%)	2005 (%)	2006 (%)	2007 (%)
Firefighter*	NA	NA	NA	NA	NA	NA	NA	NA	55	48	56	63	61
Scientist	66	59	57	51	55	56	53	51	57	52	56	54	54
Teacher	29	28	41	49	53	53	54	47	49	48	47	52	54
Military officer	NA	22	32	29	34	42	40	47	46	47	49	51	52
Doctor	61	55	50	52	61	61	61	50	52	52	54	58	52
Nurse	NA	NA	NA	NA	NA	NA	NA	NA	47	44	50	55	50
Police officer*	NA	NA	34	36	41	38	37	40	42	40	40	43	46
Priest/minister/ clergy*	41	42	38	45	46	45	43	36	38	32	36	40	42
Farmer	NA	NA	NA	NA	NA	NA	NA	NA	NA	NA	NA	36	41
Engineer	34	30	37	32	34	32	36	34	28	29	34	34	30
Member of Congress	NA	NA	24	23	25	33	24	27	30	31	26	28	26
Architect	NA	NA	NA	NA	26	26	28	27	24	20	27	27	23
Lawyer	36	30	25	19	23	21	18	15	17	17	18	21	22
Athlete	26	20	18	21	20	21	22	21	17	21	23	23	16
Business executive*	18	16	19	16	18	15	12	18	18	19	15	11	14
Journalist	17	16	15	15	15	16	18	19	15	14	14	16	13
Union leader	NA	NA	12	14	16	16	17	14	15	16	15	12	13
Stockbroker	NA	NA	NA	NA	NA	NA	NA	NA	8	10	8	11	12
Entertainer	18	16	17	18	19	21	20	19	17	16	18	18	12
Accountant	NA	13	14	18	17	14	15	13	15	10	13	17	11
Banker	17	17	17	15	18	15	16	15	14	15	15	17	10
Actor	NA	17	NA	NA	NA	NA	NA	NA	13	16	16	12	9
Real estate broker/agent	NA	NA	NA	NA	NA	NA	NA	NA	6	5	9	6	5

Source: (Tables 11.2A and 11.2B) Harris Poll® 77, August 1, 2007 (http://www.harrisinteractive.com/harris_poll/index.asp?PID=793).

*Before 2001, the words "policeman" (now "police officer") and "businessman" (now "business executive") were used. The word "fireman" was changed to "firefighter" in 2006. The word "clergyman" was changed to "clergy" in 2007. All name changes may have affected respondents' answers.

authority, property—function together to "create differential power.... Thus, the division of labor creates a characteristic hierarchy of occupations with respect to power exercised" and "this power leads to special privilege" (Treiman, 1977:5). So, in this view, power, privilege, and prestige become intertwined. A comprehensive study of 55 countries supports the view that there is indeed "a single, worldwide occupational prestige hierarchy" (Treiman, 1977:5–6).

In the United States, random sample polls show almost identical prestige rankings for occupations since the 1940s. In general, as Table 11.2 shows, professional, nonmanual jobs rank much higher than service jobs and manual labor. According to a poll by sociologists Bose and Rossi (in Kornblum, 1997:346–347), physicians, mayors, lawyers, and college professors are at the top of the U.S. status heap, while welfare recipients, parking lot attendants, and rag pickers are at the bottom.

The same pattern holds in high-tech societies worldwide. Heads of state and other high government officials such as ambassadors, doctors, university professors, physicists, and mayors of large cities occupy rungs at the top of the status ladder. At about the middle are the following occupations: professional athlete, advertising writer, television cameraperson, and police officer. At the bottom of the ladder are garbage collectors, contract laborers, shoe shiners, and recipients of public assistance. According to an international survey, agricultural gatherer is the least socially-esteemed occupation worldwide (Treiman, 1977:appendix A).

These occupational prestige rankings suggest a connection between the status order (prestige), the political order (power), and the economic order (class) in a complex society. That is, occupations that are prestigious are often highly paid and socially powerful. Yet, as Weber pointed out, this is not necessarily the case. His third dimension of social stratification—the power order—is related to, but separate from, class and status.

Power

For Weber, a person's position in the power order is determined by the amount of control he or she has over politics and administration. This includes the exercise of formal and informal power. Elected officials

and bureaucrats, for example, have formal power that goes with their office. Whoever becomes president of the United States or a member of the board of directors of AT&T has authority stemming from that position.

Soldiers, gang leaders, would-be revolutionaries, drug cartel chieftains, lobbyists, and bank presidents know that power also comes from either the barrel of a gun or the control over an organization's purse strings. A generation ago, Elaine Brown, the first woman to lead the Black Panthers, understood both formal power and informal power (**influence**). In *A Taste of Power* (1992), Brown reported that she began her initial address to several hundred Black Panther Party officials in 1974 like this: "I have control over all the guns and all the money of this party. There will be no external or internal opposition I will not resist and put down. I will deal resolutely with anyone or anything that stands in the way."

To summarize: Weber outlined three dimensions by which people rank and socially differentiate one another: class, status, and power. Each represents a distinct social order. The three are functionally interrelated, but in Weber's analysis they don't necessarily coincide. Hence, a person may enjoy high status but wield little political power. Or a low-status person without property could conceivably have great political clout. In other words, Weber felt that Marx's approach was too one-dimensional because noneconomic institutions are also important in determining where one fits in the social hierarchy.

CONCEPTUAL UPDATES

THE AMERICAN CLASS STRUCTURE

Long after their deaths, Marx and Weber remain the theorists whom others debate, refute, and update—but not discard. One leading contemporary theorist, sociologist Erik Olin Wright, draws mainly on Marx to reconceptualize the nature of class in advanced capitalist society.

According to Wright and Martin (1987:7), three forms of exploitation are crucial in advanced capitalist societies: exploitation based on (1) ownership of *capital* assets (which yield profits), (2) control of *organization* assets (which come from supervising others), and (3) ownership of *skill* assets such as valuable talents and credentials (e.g., a Ph.D. or law degree).

BOX 11.2 TWO APPROACHES TO SOCIAL STRATIFICATION

Dimensions of Stratification

Karl Marx

One Dimension: Class

A person's relationship to the means of production determines how much wealth he or she will have and thus the lifestyle he or she will be able to afford. The class that owns or controls the means of production also controls the ideas in that society.

Max Weber

Three dimensions

1. Class—shared life chances
2. Status—shared lifestyle, social esteem, prestige
3. Political power

Class, status, and power do not necessarily coincide. For example, members of political elites can be lower-class or low in social esteem.

Concept of Class

"Class" is a concept combining economic and social relations. A class is composed of individuals who share a situation in terms of their relation to the ownership of the means of production. *Classes are not income groups.* Nor are classes occupational groupings (e.g., two people may both be engineers, but one may be a propertyless employee and the other may be the owner of a large firm). In a capitalist system, there are owners of capital (bourgeoisie) who live off profits, landowners who live off rents, and wage laborers (proletariat) who live off wages. Under capitalism, society is split into two great classes: bourgeoisie and proletariat. Class conflict is the key to understanding history.

Basically, class is an economic concept. A class is composed of people who share a common situation in terms of the market (what goods and services they can afford to buy) and similar life chances. Class divisions are based on property relations: property owners and the propertyless. Class struggles begin in an urban economy, where a credit market operates and is developed by a small, powerful group (plutocracy).

Concept of Status

Marx didn't use this concept to differentiate people. He assumed that those with economic power also held social and political power in capitalist society. He also thought that under capitalism ideas and culture were produced by the ruling class (the capitalists or the bourgeoisie) in its own interests.

Status is not necessarily determined by or linked to class. Both propertied and propertyless people may belong to the same status group. Those who share a similar status tend to share a similar lifestyle (e.g., belong to the same kinds of clubs, display similar symbols of their station in life). In modern society, occupation is the single best indicator of status group.

Using Marx or Weber: What Difference Does It Make?

Using Marx's unidimensional approach, a social scientist tends to find a rather cohesive elite holding economic (and thus political) power in a city or nation.

Using Weber's three-dimensional approach, a social scientist tends to find a more pluralistic and open system in which wealth, power, and prestige are unequally distributed.

These types of exploitation correspond to the relationships between (1) capital and labor, (2) managers and workers, and (3) experts and nonexperts.

Wright's typology of classes in advanced capitalist societies has undergone several revisions (Wright, 1985, 2000 Wright et al., 1989; Wright and Martin, 1987). However, it retains Marx's basic assumption: Class depends on the ownership (or nonownership) of the means of production. Hence, Wright divides people into owners and nonowners. But Wright expands Marx's criterion for class membership by incorporating the other two types of exploitation mentioned above: control over organizational assets, operationalized as supervision of employees or control of labor power, and ownership of skill assets, operationalized as having a professional, technical, or managerial job. (The presumed percentage of each class in the United States is noted in parentheses.)

Owners

1. *Bourgeoisie.* Self-employed and employ (i.e., they purchase the labor power and control the labor of) more than 10 employees (1.8 percent).
2. *Small employers.* Self-employed and employ at least two persons in their business (6.0 percent).
3. *Petite bourgeoisie.* Self-employed or own a substantial part of the business in which they work; they have no employees, so they neither buy nor control the labor of others (6.9 percent).

Nonowners (Wage Laborers)

4. *Managers.* Not self-employed. They merely sell their own labor to the bourgeoisie; they do not employ others, but they do make policy decisions about their organization, whether or not they supervise others (12.4 percent).

5. *Supervisors.* Not self-employed but sell their own labor to the bourgeoisie. They do not employ others; they supervise others without making policy decisions about the workplace (13.7 percent).

6. *Nonmanagerial experts.* Not self-employed. They sell their labor to capitalists; they do not make policy decisions about their workplace and do not supervise others; they do have professional, technical, and managerial occupations (3.4 percent).

7. *Workers.* Not self-employed. They have only their own labor to sell to capitalists; they do not make policy decisions and do not have professional, technical, or managerial occupations (39.9 percent).

Under Wright's typology, then, the owner of a dress factory with 25 employees is a bourgeois (or bourgeoise, if female). A college professor is a nonmanagerial expert. A dry cleaner with three employees is a small employer. A vice president of a major bank is a manager. A self-employed jeweler or trucker with no employees is a petit bourgeois. A nursing administrator in a hospital is a supervisor. A file clerk, bridge toll taker, or auto assembler is a worker.

Note that there is *no middle-class category* in Wright's typology. To Wright (1985), the middle classes are truly in the middle—not in terms of income but in terms of relations of exploitation: They are part exploiter, part exploitee. They occupy "contradictory locations within class relations," sharing some traits with both the bourgeoisie and proletariat. For instance, middle managers in a big organization do not own capital, but as managers, they exploit others on the basis of their organizational assets and are themselves exploited by capitalists.

Using these criteria, Wright finds inequalities based on class position. For one thing, education helps managers and supervisors earn much more money than workers as a group. Managers and supervisors get about $1,169 for each increment to education; income returns to workers with the same increments to education are much less—$655 (Wright, 1978).

A note on class structure in the United States: "Of all the hokum with which [the United States] is riddled, the most odd is the common notion that it is free of class distinction." So quipped the late British novelist Somerset Maugham some years ago. But this "common notion" may be much less common today. "The anxious class," as Louis Uchitelle called them (mentioned earlier in this chapter), recognize growing inequalities—and the possibility of downward mobility in their own (and/or their children's) lives.

One does not have to be a follower of Marx or Wright to recognize growing inequalities in the United States. Generally speaking, radicals, conservatives, and liberals agree that the gap is widening between rich and poor and between high- and low-status people. The late conservative/libertarian economist Milton Friedman pointed out in 1991—and it remains the case almost a generation later—that there is a growing income gap among employed workers in the United States:

> In 1979, college-educated workers earned 47 percent more, on average, than those with just high-school education. By 1991, the gap was 67 percent. Similarly, in the mid-1980s, the chief executive officers of the nation's 300 largest companies made, on average, 20 times what the typical manufacturing worker made. By 1991, the multiple was 93 to 1.
>
> *(in Coffin, 1991:1)*

Further, white households continue to hold more than 10 times as much wealth as African Americans and eight times as much wealth as Latinos.

These inequalities in income and wealth have continued or grown through the years. For example, in 2004–2005, African American households had the lowest median income ($30,858) among U.S. racial groups. Median income for Hispanic/Latino households was $34,241, while that for non-Hispanic white households was $48,554. Asian households had the highest median income: $57,518 (U.S. Bureau of the Census, 2005). In 2001, the Census Bureau reported that 22.7 percent of blacks lived below the poverty line, while 7.8 percent of non-Hispanic whites lived below the poverty line.

What is the meaning of all these numbers? In a word, polarization. During the 1980s and 1990s and into the new century, the rich got richer, the poor got poorer, and the chasm between them increased. Kevin Phillips, one-time Republican strategist, called the 1980s a capitalist blowout where "the truly wealthy, more than anyone else...flourished under Reagan" (1990:26). This is perhaps more the case since that time. With a populist backlash flourishing too.

Perhaps for the first time in U.S. history, most young adults look ahead to having less—not more—than their parents in real and symbolic terms. Specifically, they look to a future where fewer will own their own homes, have as much money, or have as many skill credentials as their parents. All this adds up to fewer who will fulfill the "American dream."

Should this growing inequality be reduced? That depends on your ideology. While scholars debate, government officials talk, some citizens take to the streets or talk radio, and others experiment. The public schools of LaCrosse, Wisconsin, for one, have pioneered a novel approach: integrating primary-school students by social class. This approach suggests that class, not race, is the central inequality in education. Formerly, students attended neighborhood schools, which tended to be segregated on the basis of income. Starting in the 1990s, the children of affluent parents have been bussed across town to working-class areas and vice versa. Although the plan met resistance when first introduced, it has gained in popularity among students, teachers, and parents, who praise its mutual benefits (see Kahlenberg, 2001).

CURRENT DEBATE: DOES CLASS STILL MATTER?

Two social scientists sparked great debate by asking *Are Social Classes Dying?* (Clark and Lipset, 1991). After years of scholarly debate, primarily among sociologists and political scientists, the question changed a bit, but it remains much debated: In postindustrial societies does class matter—and if so, how much?

Unsurprisingly, honest scholars disagree. Their conclusions are tempered by their theoretical orientation and political ideology. On the one hand, sociologist Terry Nichols Clark and the late political sociologist Seymour Martin Lipset (2001) wrote that the links between class and politics are breaking down in some postindustrial societies. Others disagree. To their credit, Clark and Lipset offer some contrasting views, argued with subtle evidence, in their book *The Breakdown of Class Politics: A Debate on Post-Industrial Stratification* (2001).

One of the most vocal opponents of Clark and Lipset's position (not included in their book) is sociologist Erik Olin Wright. In *Approaches to Class Analysis* (2005), editor Wright includes various viewpoints on class: Some contributors assume that classes have largely dissolved; others hold that class remains a fundamental form of social inequality and social power.

CULTURAL CAPITAL

At one of the United States's leading technological universities, Caltech, there is a Cooking Basics class. Why? Because, notes a Caltech professor, "Many [of our students] haven't had exposure to some of the things that lead to success, like how to open a bottle of wine...or host a dinner" (Thomas Mannion in "Perspectives," 2006). In a similar vein, Alex (Swoosie Kurtz), one of four sisters in the Emmy Award–winning NBC-TV series *Sisters* (1991–1996, perhaps best remembered for introducing actor George Clooney and actress Ashley Judd to a wider audience) who lived in Winnetka (a SER 01 suburb on Chicago's North Shore), explained the difference between her plumber boyfriend and herself:

> When I hear "porcelain," I think Limoges, and he thinks American Standard.
>
> *(1992)*

Knowing how to open a bottle of wine or that Limoges is a type of French porcelain china or that American social scientists pronounce Weber as "Vay-bear" (not like the backyard barbeque grill) does not earn you a place in Paradise. Your ability or inability to discuss the virtues of a Manet versus a Monet painting is not a comment on the content of your character. But, like it or not, showing your familiarity (or lack of it) with these symbols is a badge of status, high or low.

High-status culture is the means that allows a high-status group to both maintain its solidarity and set itself apart from other societal groups. Having competence in and participating in a society's high-status culture (its behaviors, habits, and attitudes) give a person a great deal of **cultural capital**.

According to the late French social scientist Pierre Bourdieu ([1979] 2002), cultural capital includes the general cultural background, language competence, and behaviors that are passed from one generation to the next. He argued that upper-class children grow up with much different cultural capital from working-class children. Specifically, socially-advantaged parents typically transmit socially-advantaged cultural capital to their offspring, who then become socially-advantaged children. Schools play an important role too: Schools systematically devalue the attitudes and behaviors of working-class children and reward the cultural capital of upper-class students. In these ways, Bourdieu said, cultural capital becomes a vehicle through which class and status hierarchies are maintained and reproduced.

Cultural capital is more important in *Gesellschaft* and *Techno$chaft* than in *Gemeinschaft*. Why? Because high-tech societies depend more on democratic practices and merit promotion than family ties.

Theorist Bourdieu drew inspiration from Max Weber. Indeed, his concept of cultural capital draws primarily on Weber's ideas of status and lifestyle. Essentially, Bourdieu argued that taste—not class—is the key differentiator of people in modern times. True, Bourdieu said, different classes do tend to have different tastes, and class backgrounds tend to mold taste. But taste can be learned by mastering the symbols. In other words, people can recreate themselves by gaining cultural capital. (*Note*: Some cultures allow, even promote, recreated selves. And this has an impact on cultural capital's importance. For example, in the United States many believe that they can adopt—sometimes during a weekend seminar—new personalities or at least change the way others view them. People in the United States thus tend to accept that schooling the poor, for example, will provide them cultural capital, which will allow them to climb the status ladder. In contrast, the French put little faith in personality or school make-overs. This is reflected in the French saying *La caque sent toujours le hareng* ("The barrel will always smell of herring"), meaning that a

person always bears the stamp of his or her origins and past.

Bourdieu also expanded on Marx. Just as Marx thought that capital yielded income profit, Bourdieu thought that cultural capital yields *symbolic profit*: being seen by others as having good taste or distinction. In other words, a degree from Stanford or Brown, a living room with a Kazakh carpet on a hardwood floor, and a slim body all confer social esteem. Capital in the arena of culture gives symbolic profits: the conferring of prestige.

Symbols of good taste do not emerge from all strata in the population. Quite the contrary. Cultural capital most often reflects the culture of the dominant class.

However, a few symbols and goods start on the street and move up. This is particularly the case in fast-changing taste businesses aimed at young people. Indeed, some businesses, particularly fashion and music, pay people to tell them what's happening on the streets so that they can mass-produce it.

George Bernard Shaw instinctively understood that cultural capital mainly reflects the symbols of dominant groups. In his 1913 play *Major Barbara*, Undershaft, a millionaire munitions maker, proclaims that he will not give Greek teacher Adolphus Cusins part of his business. Why? Because Cusins brings no capital with him. Cusins counters, "What! no capital! Is my mastery of Greek no capital? Is my access to the subtlest thought, the loftiest poetry yet attained by humanity, no capital? My character! my intellect! . . . are these no capital?" Later in the play, Cusins suggests that cultural capital and machine guns are not very different in the war of rich against poor: "As a teacher of Greek I gave the rich man an intellectual weapon against the poor man."

A study of cultural capital done a generation ago found that familiarity with, and interest in, high culture does directly affect both educational and marital outcomes for men and women (DiMaggio and Mohr, 1985). The sociologist authors reported that "the most important finding of our separate analyses for men and women is the great similarity in the effects of cultural capital between genders" (1254). For example, in terms of mate selection, they found that both men and women "desire intimacy based on cultural similarity," not transactions in which "goods" (e.g., attractiveness and earnings) are exchanged.

Now, let us reconsider the battle over multiculturalism outlined in Chapter 10. Using Bourdieu's concept of cultural capital and Gramsci's concept of hegemony, we can construct the following hypothesis: *Because multiculturalism democratizes the content of cultural capital (by including symbols from subordinate groups), it dilutes the hegemony of the dominant class and thus will be fought with vehemence by the dominant class and its representatives.* This hypothesis predicts that some language variants (e.g., so-called black English) and class- or status-coded symbols (e.g., creating Spanish lyric music, knowing how to find a flea-market bargain) will be devalued by keepers of the "canon."

In the past few decades, fashion and pop music have often started on the street (i.e., in poor and working-class areas, often among people of color) and moved upward through social layers. Baggy blue jeans and hip-hop music exemplify the appropriation of street-originated symbols by higher social groups. If the above hypothesis is correct, we can predict that keepers of the canon will pooh-pooh such fashion and music statements.

A dissenting view on "somebodies" and "nobodies": One non-social scientist's take on status and status differences is worth noting for its audaciousness. Former Columbia University physics professor and president of Oberlin College Robert W. Fuller blames "rank-based discrimination" or "rankism" (status distinctions) for a host of events from Columbine-style school shootings to genocide. Here is his reasoning. First, Fuller asks a sky-blue question: "What makes it possible for one group to discriminate against another?" (5). His answer: power differences between *Somebodies and Nobodies* (2004). According to Fuller, "Color, religion, gender, and sexual orientation are simply pretexts for constructing and exploiting social stratifications; they are not the actual cause of ongoing injustice" (5). The actual cause, he believes, lies in power differences, bolstered by customs and laws (5–6). Then, Fuller claims, rankism leads to indignity and loss of pride, which in turn are sources of many happenings considered social pathologies: "The indignity suffered by those who've been 'nobodied' festers," building to indignation and often violence. The "nobodied," he argues, are vulnerable to leaders like Hitler and Milosevic, who promise to restore individual dignity and national pride. (Although he did not use the terms "somebodies" and "nobodies," Iranian-born U.S scholar Vali Nasr made a similar point when discussing how the United States might deal with Iran, a proud nation which, he noted, felt that it had been disrespected by key powers [2008]).

The key to turning nobodies into somebodies, Fuller thinks, lies in "redistributing recognition." (In his view, the individual, national, and international redistribution of recognition—not of income—would help address conflicts at all those levels.) How to bring this about? Fuller suggests developing supranational institutions "capable of taking a nonpartisan, comprehensive view of the legitimate interests of all parties and then mediating so that in the end everyone feels their [*sic*] concerns have received fair treatment" (169–170).

One person who seems to welcome all into his private world on an equal footing is art critic–writer John Berger, an Englishman by birth who has been living in France for over 30 years. (See Chapter 1 for some of his views on "reality.") A dinner guest at Berger's home in a tiny French mountain village recalls that his fellow diners included the local plumber and the renowned photographer Henri Cartier-Bresson. The guest later wrote that Berger "is a democratic person. The notion of a hierarchy, social or otherwise, is anathema to him..." (Dyer in O'Hagan, 2005).

STUDIES OF URBAN SOCIAL STRATIFICATION IN THE UNITED STATES

American social scientists generally adopt the Weberian approach when investigating how U.S. cities are socially stratified. But—and this is important—researchers in this tradition have not kept Weber's categories of class and status separate. Instead, they have joined class and status into a single concept: **socioeconomic status (SES)**. A person's SES is determined by a composite measure based on three variables: (1) income, (2) education, and (3) occupation. The rationale behind this composite measure is that the three variables tend to co-vary in complex societies, which means that high-skill occupations require a high level of education and are highly rewarded in terms of income.

What difference does it make if a researcher uses SES or separate measures of class and status? For one thing, SES ignores what Marx meant by class. It does not distinguish between owners and controllers of capital (including managers, large stockholders) and those who have little or no control over other people's work and social lives. For another, essentially SES is synonymous with prestige (the status order) exclusively. Consequently, studies that use SES as their indicator of social rank ignore what Weber originally meant: that class, status, and power (the three dimensions of stratification) are separate and distinct, although interrelated. And, of course, using SES as an indicator of social stratification ignores class and the consequences of class. This is an ironic twist, for many U.S. scholars who criticize Marx for being too one-dimensional turn out to be equally at fault. The difference is that most U.S. scholars use status, not class, as their one dimension of social rank.

There are other problems with making status the only measure of social stratification. Most important, it assumes that status concerns are of paramount importance to everyone in the United States. Yet as many studies, dating from the 1950s onward (e.g., Form and Stone, 1957) suggest, this is not always the case. Blue-collar workers, for example, seem to be less interested in social respectability and prestige than in working conditions and monetary rewards.

To conclude: The concept of SES is not neutral. Using SES (rather than measures of status and class) as a filter through which to see the social system of American cities helps to perpetuate the notion that classes don't exist in the United States.

Once again, what you see depends on how you look at it. Remembering that what is defined as empirical evidence depends on what researchers already believe, let's review some leading studies on urban social stratification in the United States.

We begin with a classic and influential series of studies that established the pattern of research for future generations: the Yankee City series by social anthropologist W. Lloyd Warner and his associates. Next, other "classic" studies are discussed. Then, a few snapshots of single cities are discussed.

YANKEE CITY: LIFESTYLES IN A NEW ENGLAND TOWN

Beginning in 1930, W. Lloyd Warner and his research group studied the system of social ranking in a small New England town they called "Yankee City." (The actual city was Newburyport, Massachusetts, which then had a population of about 17,000.) To do this, Warner developed two techniques that set the research pattern for future researchers of urban social stratification. Both techniques were designed to measure what Warner called "social class," which he defined as "two or more orders of people who are believed to be, and are accordingly ranked by the members of the community, in socially superior and inferior positions" (Warner et al., [1941] 1963:36). That's exactly what Weber meant by status. Thus, Warner's techniques to measure class actually measure status.

Warner determined that Yankee City had six separate social strata (actually status groups), each with its own particular lifestyle. He identified the following strata and the percentage of townspeople in each: upper upper (1.4 percent), lower upper (1.6 percent), upper middle (10 percent), lower middle (28 percent), upper lower (33 percent), and lower lower (25 percent). Thus, most people in Yankee City were in the two lowest status groups (58 percent).

JONESVILLE: A TYPICAL TOWN AND HOW ITS PEOPLE JUSTIFY INEQUALITY

Warner studied a small town near Chicago, dubbed "Jonesville" because it was considered to be a typical U.S. community. Since it seemed to be representative, Warner used this town (actually Morris, Illinois) as a laboratory in which to look at status hierarchies in the United States.

What did Warner find in this typical town? First, he found what he had found in Yankee City: *six distinct status groups, each with its own particular lifestyle.* Most people in Jonesville lived at the "level of the common man," or what others term the "middle class." Above that level was a layer divided into two parts and "crowned by an elite"; the one below was filled with a "mixed old American and ethnic proletariat." And there was the "highest crust," which was rewarded with deference, while the lowest often received "ridicule, pity, or scorn" ([1949] 1964:23).

Second, Warner et al. found that the status system of inequality in Jonesville (and, by extension, the United States) operated according to two competing systems of logic: "1) All men are equal and 2) Some men are superior in status, others inferior" ([1949] 1964:293).

These two contradictory propositions supported the following practices and beliefs in Jonesville:

1. People in Jonesville rank skilled jobs above less-skilled jobs.
2. Being a self-made person is good, but even better is to be born wealthy.
3. Recipients of public welfare are lowest on the social ladder.
4. People exposed to higher education were judged "superior."
5. People could move up or down the status ladder, principally by accumulating money and transforming it into socially-approved symbols: educational advancement; marrying up; learning the proper social skills, such as speech patterns; and joining the right churches and clubs ([1949] 1964:294–296). (*Note*: Today, we would say that such people possess cultural capital.)

How can the acceptance of inequality in Jonesville be reconciled with the U.S. ideal of equality? Warner and coauthors said that the shared belief in the "American dream" (the idea that anyone who works hard can make it to the top) is the key. The American dream provided "the moral code which enforces the rules of social mobility by insisting that all able [people] who obey the rules of the game have 'the right' to climb" ([1949] 1964:297).

Furthermore, Warner and associates saw the American dream as very functional. Without it, "there would be little or no movement between the classes [status groups]." They concluded that there is no fixed social rank order in Jonesville—or U.S. cities generally. Rather, there is a "system of open classes [again, status groups]" ([1949] 1964:297).

Clearly, this is a decades-old vision, filtered through particular ideological assumptions and research techniques. Not all researchers agreed with Warner et al.'s portrait. Other researchers painted a different community portrait of so-called typical U.S. towns (see Thernstrom [1965] for a different look at Yankee City). Writing about another typical town, called Middletown (in reality, Muncie, Indiana), Lynd and Lynd ([1929] 1956) found a fairly rigid class system.

To conclude: The composite measure of SES, based on income, education, and occupation, blurs Weber's distinctions. It also raises status to paramount importance and perpetuates the notion that classes don't exist in the United States. This distortion of Weber's original meaning began with W. Lloyd Warner's influential series of urban studies, which set the pattern of research for future scholars. In their studies of Yankee City and Jonesville, Warner and his associates stated that they were studying class. In actuality, they studied what Weber meant by status.

Warner and associates found inequality in Yankee City and later in Jonesville. They also found that the U.S. ideal of equality and the practice of inequality were rationalized by a deep-seated belief in the "American dream" of social mobility.

STUDIES OF PARTICULAR STRATA IN THE CITY

Warner and his associates looked at the entire social system in a U.S. city. Other researchers focus on a particular stratum. *Hard Living on Clay Street* ([1973] 1991) by Joseph T. Howell is one example. It looked at a white working-class neighborhood in Washington, D.C. Using participant-observation, Howell painted a portrait of two distinct types of blue-collar families: "hard-living" and "settled" families, all migrants from the South.

Howell noted that the hard-living families cope with everyday life in one way, the settled families in another. Generally, the lifestyle of the hard-living families was characterized by heavy drinking, marital instability, tough and profane manners, political alienation, strong individualism, rootlessness, and a present time orientation (Howell, [1973] 1991:263–264). Meanwhile, the settled families attended church regularly, had roots in the community, stayed away from liquor, held politically-conservative ideas, had refined manners, and were concerned with their reputations. In the settled families' eyes, the hard-living folk were "white trash." In popular terms, the difference between the two groups is often expressed by the following dichotomy: the "respectable" poor (settled) and the "disreputable" poor (hard living).

Howell's study raises several issues pertinent to our discussion of status and class. First, it suggests that two different status groups can live side by side. The settled and hard-living families, both in the same economic position, do not share a set of symbols, attitudes, or values. Thus, Howell may call his research a study of a working-class neighborhood, but he is really dealing with *two status groups residing as neighbors.*

Second, Howell's portrait of blue-collar families suggests that people in the same objective economic situation don't necessarily react in similar ways. To a Marxist, the reaction of the settled families might indicate false consciousness about their "real" class situation. To a follower of Warner, however, the settled families' more cautious and refined lifestyle shows the power of belief in the American dream. Many children from settled families went to college; no children from hard-living families did so, and most didn't even finish high school. The settled families, concerned with what others thought of them (status concerns of social respectability), were more upwardly mobile than the hard-living families. As noted in Chapter 12, the same objective situation (in this case, being part of the urban working class or proletariat) can be interpreted subjectively in different ways, and people's interpretation of their situation influences their behavior.

Finally, Howell doesn't suggest it, but his study indicates that class and status are more significant variables than race in explaining social behavior. In many important ways, the hard-living folks on Clay Street resemble the African American streetcorner men observed across town hanging out at *Tally's Corner* (Liebow, 1967).

Like Howell, many researchers have analyzed the lifestyles or life chances of poor Southerners rerooted in northern cities (e.g., Liebow, 1967). Some focus on white (when studied) working-class communities, such as Brooklyn's Canarsie (Rieder, 1985). Some describe inner-city communities of Chicano youth (e.g., Horowitz, 1983). And some focus on the poor who stay where they are—until disaster hits, such as post-Katrina New Orleans. Here, we focus on one scholarly study, edited by planner Chester Hartman (who investigated San Francisco's transformation, see Chapter 14) and sociologist Gregory D. Squires. The title of their edited book suggests that Katrina was a social, not a "natural," disaster: *There is No Such Thing as a Natural Disaster: Race, Class, and Hurricane Katrina* (2006). They argue that Katrina's impact was uneven but for poor African Americans, particularly devastating. It was no accident, they claim, that the poorest

and blackest neighborhoods were hard-hit, even buried under water. Institutional racism, social inequality, and the consequent lack of political clout to get infrastructure (e.g., levees) fixed were key factors that doomed New Orleans's poor and racially segregated African Americans (proportionately more than whites and middle-class residents) to flooding and, worse, death. People with means and/or connections could leave the area, escaping by car to their second homes, hotels, or elsewhere; but those without cars or means were stuck. According to Hartman and Squires and many of their contributors, racialized poverty lies at the heart of the unnatural disaster called Katrina.

Others investigate the other end of the social ladder: the rich, prestigious, and/or powerful. One such account is *Philadelphia Gentlemen* (Baltzell, 1958). This classic study, now two generations old, found two strata of elites in Philadelphia: the social aristocracy, at the very top of the social ladder, and the achieving elite, just below. Together, these two strata made up Philadelphia's upper class. While not completely homogeneous, Philadelphia's upper class contained no African Americans and just a sprinkling of people with southern European or Jewish backgrounds; otherwise, it was mainly white Anglo-Saxon Protestant (WASP).

The finding that Philadelphia's upper class was almost exclusively WASP raises some complicated issues. For instance, now that a poll reveals a declining percentage of people in the United States identifying as Protestant, what might that mean for politics and social life? (See the poll results, published by the Associated Press, later in this chapter.) To what extent do race, ethnicity, and religion affect a person's life chances? Is race or class background a better predictor of a person's position on the social ladder? Are some cities more egalitarian than others? What role does local culture play in determining a person's lifestyle? These are not easy questions to answer. Few researchers have asked questions in this way. Consequently, little data are available. Further, the data that do exist lend themselves to varying interpretations.

In recent times, many scholars and journalists have focused on the richest of the rich in the United States, most of whom live or make their millions or billions of dollars in metropolitan areas. This may reflect enormous changes in the United States in the past generation; more and more wealth is concentrated at the top of the income distribution, making the United States the most unequal (in terms of income distribution) of all so-called advanced, democratic societies (with the exception of Switzerland).

A series of 2007 *New York Times* articles reflects the renewed interest in the very rich. Called the "Age of Riches," the series was written mainly by economic reporter Louis Uchitelle. According to Uchitelle, many of the United States's wealthiest CEOs, entrepreneurs, and financiers "echo an earlier era—the Gilded Age before World War I—when powerful enterprises, dominated by men who grew immensely rich, ushered in the industrialization of the United States." Uchitelle continues, "The new titans [such as Sanford I. Weill, Citigroup's retired head and chair of Carnegie Hall] often see themselves as pillars of a similarly prosperous and expansive age, one in which their successes and their philanthropy have made government less important than it once was." These new tycoons started emerging in the 1970s as constraints on income and taxes receded, constraints their political clout helped to get lifted.

Uchitelle (2007), drawing upon an analysis of tax returns by economists at the University of California at Berkeley and the Paris School of Economics, notes that the share of income going to the top 1 percent of U.S. families doubled from 8 percent in 1980 to 16 percent in 2004. About 15,000 families in the United States have incomes of $9.5 million or more annually. Meanwhile, the average income of people in the United States is falling, while the wealth of the well-to-do grows. Likewise, the U.S. Internal Revenue Service's (IRS) data, based on tax returns, show that people in the United States earned a smaller average income in 2005 than in 2000, for the fifth consecutive year: "the average income in 2005 was $55,238, still nearly 1 percent less than the $55,714 in 2000, after adjusting for inflation" (Johnston, 2007).

IRS data show that the growth in U.S. total incomes was concentrated among those at the top end, notably, those making more than $1 million. The number of such taxpayers grew by more than 26 percent, to 303,817 in 2005 from 239,685 in 2000 (Johnston, 2007). (*Note*: New, since 1988 and 2000, PRIZM

clusters at both the bottom and top of the SER rungs reflect changes in income distribution in the United States [see Chapter 8].)

Such a heavy concentration at the top of the income distribution pyramid occurred in the United States at only two other times: the end of the Gilded Age (1915–1916) and just before the stock market crashed in 1929. Now, Uchitelle notes, it has returned. For one, Sanford Weill, mentioned earlier, is worth over $1 billion—not counting the $500 million he says he has already given away. (He likens himself to Andrew Carnegie, the namesake of Carnegie Hall, of which he is the head, in his philanthropy.)

Some wealthy people in the "new U.S. Gilded Age" credit their fortunes to their talent for business, comparing themselves to baseball players, who have a talent for sport. But critics—often themselves members (or nearly so) of this new elite group—scorn such logic. For one, former Federal Reserve Bank chair Paul A. Volcker says that the very rich are not the driving force of a robust economy, even if they think they are: "I don't see a relationship between the extremes of income now and the performance of the economy" (in Uchitelle, 2007). No doubt, many U.S. (and global) citizens would agree, particularly after a global economic crisis and huge bonuses paid to some traders in risky financial instruments.

Studying the very rich presents problems for researchers. Typically, access is closely guarded. There are other constraints, too, including the subjects' unwillingness to make public statements. Perhaps these are some of the reasons that there are many more studies of the poor than the rich.

GLOBAL SOCIAL STRATIFICATION RESEARCH

Unsurprisingly, researchers all over the world are interested in social inequality. Indeed, social inequality and the questions surrounding it—What are its impacts? Is it "good" or "bad"? Are "modernizing" nations, whatever their economic system, converging in their occupational structures?—are just a few of the issues that researchers of social stratification explore.

Increasingly, social stratification research is comparative. According to Treiman and Ganzeboom (2000), two leading researchers in the field, there have been at least four generations of stratification research.

They say that this research is "increasingly comparative, either over time or cross-nationally or both" (126).

Here, we will take a brief look at some recent work on social stratification in just a few places: a province of Mexico, eastern Europe, and China. Some deal with an entire society, others with a slice of a society in great transition. All are comparative in the sense of comparing one time period to another.

VERACRUZ, MEXICO; CENTRAL AND EASTERN EUROPE; AND CHINA

An ethnography of central Veracruz by anthropologist Hugo G. Nutini (2005) suggests that since the Mexican Revolution of 1910 there has been a transformation of provincial Mexican society. Exploring the Córdoba–Orizaba region in central Veracruz province, he found that the landed aristocracy, formerly empowered by the "hacienda system," lost power. A new ruling class of the very rich and politicians took its place. In addition, a middle class of white-collar professionals has been developing. And importantly, Nutini found, many rural Indians, formerly poor and disenfranchised, went to cities, took advantage of opportunities, and became working class. In sum, Nutini argues that, more and more, Mexico's system of stratification resembles the class system of industrial nations.

Another study, focusing on parts of Central and Eastern Europe, states the author's point of view in the title: *On the Verge of Convergence: Social Stratification in Eastern Europe* (Dománski [1996] 2000). Without referring to Durkheim's theory of convergence, that is what the author, a Polish sociologist, sees happening in Bulgaria, the Czech Republic, Hungary, Poland, Russia, and Slovakia since the dismemberment of the former Soviet Union.

Yet another study focuses on one stratum of society in Eastern Europe: elites in post-Communist Russia. Professor of government and public administration in Sydney, Graeme Gill (1998) notes that Russian elites have long played a crucial role in organizing the society. Despite a transformation toward a market-based society in post-Communist Russia, Gill contends that a dependence on elites continues there today.

And what about stratification in China? Cong Cao (2004) focuses on one group there: the scientific elite. Cao makes no reference to Durkheim in his study of members of the Chinese Academy of Sciences (CAS), but his conclusions echo Durkheim's notions of convergence. Based on interviews with CAS members, Cao finds that Chinese scientists are recognized and promoted by universalistic norms of science. In other words, top Chinese scientists, like top U.S. scientists, largely operate independently of national political and cultural shifts.

In other studies of China, published in *Unemployment, Inequality and Poverty in Urban China* (Li and Sato, 2006), several economists conclude that economic inequality has increased since the mid-1990s. Why? Primarily, they say, marketization and government policies. Editors Shi Li and Hiroshi Sato note that urban income inequality was mainly caused by labor restructuring policies: Millions of workers were forced to leave their work units and thrown into a labor market that did not even exist before the 1980s. Another reason for increased urban poverty, one contributor argues, is that rural poverty was exported to cities (Meng, 2006; also see Chapter 4).

These studies, focusing on modern central Veracruz, Eastern Europe, and China, may or may not be representative of recent research on social stratification. It's hard to know without an exhaustive search. So, without generalizing beyond our data, we can only say this: These studies find occupational status ladders similar to those in Europe and the United States. Durkheimian social scientists would not be surprised. Recall (from earlier in this chapter) that Durkheimians theorize that the relative prestige of an occupation—say, scientist—is basically the same in complex societies—whether in China or the United States—because those societies face similar "functional imperatives."

GLOBALIZATION AND INEQUALITY

Here are a few numbers to ponder: Currently, over 2.7 million people in the world do not have adequate sanitation. More than 830 million suffer serious undernourishment. People in rich countries live, on average, 19 years longer than people in poor countries. The wealthiest 10 percent of people globally control about 50 percent of the world's income. The average CEO listed on Standard & Poor's 500, an index of 500 (mostly U.S.) large corporations, earned 212 times the wages of the average worker in the United States (in Held and Kaya, 2007:1). Pay packages of two top executives at U.S. financial institutions, Bank of America and Regional Financial, totaled almost $28 million and over $29 million—for one year, 2006 (Bauerlein, 2007:A4). In contrast, the pay package of a rural Chinese peasant from January to September 2006 (calculated in U.S. dollars) had grown over 10 percent over the same period in 2005 but still came to less than $358 (US–China Business Council, 2006).

These numbers lead us to ask an important question, particularly when there is a global economic crisis: Does globalization increase or decrease economic and social inequalities? If the integration of global markets, freer trade, and openness to investment boost growth in rich countries, will they do the same for poor countries? These are hard questions to answer. And, as you might guess by now, observers and scholars disagree—not only whether inequalities increase due to globalization but also, if so, whether that's bad, acceptable, or good.

Since the mid-1990s, more and more industrializing, industrial, and postindustrial countries have experienced increased economic inequality. Danish political scientist Gøsta Esping-Andersen (2007:217) notes that globalization is often blamed. But, he thinks, these blame-globalization explanations fail to consider the impacts of two major revolutions with great income impacts: (1) changes in women's economic roles and (2) demographic changes that affect household structures. According to Esping-Andersen, "There is no doubt [that] a strong demographic component [lies] behind the rise of inequality" and that "the risk of poverty declines dramatically when single and coupled mothers work." One of his conclusions: "The conventional male-bread-winner family is losing terrain because young and lower skilled men are the primary losers in the evolving wage distribution" (241).

Figuring out globalization's impacts is not easy. On the one hand, some (e.g., Dollar, 2007) think that globalization furthers economic growth and that growth serves to lessen poverty. This view is common among neoliberals and those who believe in trickle-down economics. Others (e.g., Pogge, 2007) argue that globalization favors the wealthy and that global institutions such as the World Bank and the World Trade Organization do not deliver to the poor. (*Note*: To evaluate many of these intricate and sophisticated arguments, it is helpful to understand statistics, particularly the Gini coefficient, often used to measure income inequality.)

Meantime, political strategists understand that globalization is an important issue. For one, former U.S. Representative and then Obama's Chief of Staff Rahm Emanuel said, "The party that deals with globalization and economic security will win [the presidency in 2008]" (in Toner, 2007). (He said this before various financial crises threatened the world economy in 2008 and beyond.)

Interestingly, few political strategists suggest any links between globalization and immigration. Who, for example, asks what difference it makes—and for whom—between outsourcing goods or services (to poorer countries) and importing labor (from those poor countries) into richer countries?

OTHER VARIABLES INFLUENCING SOCIAL RANK

Social rank is variable from one time and place to another. For example, kings and queens, priests, and warriors once routinely sat atop social ladders. Key differences on who is considered "top dog" or "bottom feeder" depend on a host of factors based in history, culture, religion, and the economy. Here, we limit the discussion to the United States, focusing mainly on modern times.

Historically, U.S. researchers have focused on status as the key dimension of social stratification. Where do such factors as race and ethnicity, religion, sex, and age fit into this model? How are they related to class, power, and status? The answers are far from clear-cut.

RELIGION

As American cities go, Salt Lake City, Utah, is most unusual. Various Native American tribes, including the Shoshone, had lived in Salt Lake Valley for millennia; but the area was settled by Mormons in 1847, and Salt Lake City, as well as the Metropolitan Statistical Area and the state of Utah, remain heavily dominated by Mormon influence. (Yet, the city is far less Mormon than the state of Utah in recent years.)

At least until recently, in no other U.S. city were the lines between church and state less clear. Salt Lake City is the headquarters of the Church of Jesus Christ of Latter-day Saints (popularly called the L.D.S. or the Mormon Church), and the church remains a dominant force; it is a major landowner, business owner, and media controller.

However, in recent years, Salt Lake City has become much less homogeneous, both economically and socially. The Mormon church remains important economically, but it was not the major employer in the region in 2008.

Estimates differ (mainly because the U.S. Census does not collect data about religion), but in 1980 about 60 percent of Salt Lake City's population was Mormon; by 1990 this had decreased to less than 50 percent. According to reporter Matt Canham (2006), the Mormon proportion of Utah's population is steadily shrinking; every county shows a decrease. If current trends continue, Canham notes, Mormon residents in the state will no longer be a majority by 2030. (Newcomers include significant Greek Orthodox and Irish Catholic populations. This religious diversification, some say, has more to do with economic growth than with the Mormon church or its doctrines.)

In the late 1990s, religion reentered the Salt Lake City race for mayor. There was a Mormon vs. "gentile" (i.e., non-Mormon, apparently including lapsed Mormons) mayoral election (Jones in Bernick, 2003). Lapsed Mormon "Rocky" Anderson was elected mayor in 1999 and again in 2003. (He refuses to run for a third term.) Not only is Anderson a former Mormon, but he is divorced and a former lawyer for the American Civil Liberties Union—not the résumé of Salt Lake City mayors who preceded him a generation earlier. During his leadership, Salt Lake City has won several international awards for its environmental programs. And stepping across his city's boundary and into national controversy, Mayor Anderson called for the impeachment of President George W. Bush in 2007.

As mayor, Rocky Anderson leads a city with more than 178,000 residents. These inhabitants include a burgeoning Hispanic population (about 19 percent) and a sizeable gay community.

One of Salt Lake City's most cosmopolitan assets is a high level of literacy in Spanish, Korean, Swedish, and other international languages. This language literacy stems from religious practice backed up by educational opportunity: Mormons send young adults as short-term missionaries throughout the world. When these missionaries return home, they possess conversational ability that serves them well in the global economy. Also, Brigham Young University, a Mormon university in Utah with nearly 30,000 students, offers over 50 languages—from Afrikaans and Hindi to Mayan, Tagalog, and Welsh.

A non-Mormon former mayor of Salt Lake City (an Italian American Catholic and Democrat in Republican, conservative Utah) said years earlier, "We're not quite Greenwich Village, but we've gone from a small-town mentality to a much more cosmopolitan community with a far greater global perspective" (in Johnson, 1991:A13). Salt Lake City's recent history indicates that being part of the global economy can help to forge a new, more cosmopolitan identity—diversity in terms of politics, religion, and culture.

Indeed, much has changed since the late 1970s, when many non-Mormons, particularly the city's handful of African Americans, complained of discrimination. At that time, few modern U.S. cities of its size were so dominated by a single religious group, especially a church that traditionally assigned blacks and women to a separate and lower place in heaven as well as on earth. But by the early 1990s, two non-Mormons, both Democrats and one a Lebanese-born woman, had been elected mayor. In addition, Salt Lake City was named by *Fortune* magazine as the best place in the country for companies to locate in 1990.

In most U.S. cities, the effects of race, religion, and ethnicity on a person's life chances or lifestyle are difficult to assess and disentangle. Religious and ethnic discrimination is often subtle and hard to measure.

How does a researcher gather data on prestigious clubs that refuse admittance to blacks, Jews, or Catholics? How many marriages take place between ethnic group members and WASPs? How often do people in supervisory positions select people from similar ethnic or religious backgrounds when they have a heterogeneous field to choose from? Evidence is scarce.

ETHNICITY, RELIGION, AND REGION

Why is it that people unlike ourselves are not merely different but typically viewed as lower on the status ladder? Is this habit of mind rooted in fear of the unknown? Or ethnocentrism? Is it hard-wired into human brains? I do not know the answer, if indeed there is one. At any rate, most of us rank nearly everything, from neighborhoods and colleges to diet colas and cars, in terms of higher and lower status. Like it or not, people in the United States (and elsewhere) rank ethnic, regional, and religious groups on a status ladder too.

Who ranks at the top of the ladder? When U.S. adults were asked in two polls (1964 and 1989) to rank the social standing of various ethnic, religious, and regional groups in the United States on a scale of 9 (highest rank) to 1 (lowest rank), white Americans born in the United States ranked even higher than "people of my own ethnic background."

People in the United States will rank even a fictitious ethnic group, Wisnians. Although 61 percent of the 1,537 respondents in a national sample survey said that they could not rank the group (because they hadn't heard of them), Wisnians got a relatively low ranking from the 39 percent who did. The director of the survey guesses that "people probably thought that if they were foreign-sounding, and they'd never heard of them, they couldn't be doing too well" (in Lewin, 1992:A10).

The ranking of ethnic, religious, and regional groups can change over time. For example, African Americans, Jews, Japanese, Russians, Chinese, and Latin Americans all climbed the status ladder during the 1964–1989 period. It is unclear why, just as the reasons for ranking some groups above or below others—say, Chinese below Japanese—remain obscure.

Looked at from a different angle, religion (or lack of one) appears to be a fairly good predictor of education and income, two oft-used measures of stratification. The most comprehensive random samples of U.S. religious preferences ever collected, first in 1990 and reported in *One Nation Under God* (Kosmin and Lachman, 1993) and then in 2001 and reported in *Religion in a Free Market: Religious and Non-Religious Americans* (Kosmin and Keysar, 2006), reveal significant differences among denominations. The following

TABLE 11.3 INCOME RANKING BY RELIGIOUS GROUP: MEDIAN ANNUAL HOUSEHOLD INCOME IN 2000 (IN U.S. DOLLARS)

Jewish	$72,000
Unitarian	$58,000
Episcopalian	$55,000
Evangelical/Born Again	$54,000
Hindu	$51,000
Presbyterian	$50,000
Lutheran	$49,000
Methodist	$48,000
Catholic	$47,000
None/no religion (includes atheists, agnostics, humanists)	$46,000
United Church of Christ	$41,000
Mormon	$40,000
Buddhist	$38,000
Baptist	$33,000
Muslim	$31,000
Pentecostal	$31,000
Church of God	$26,000
Jehovah's Witnesses	$24,000

Source: Adapted from Figure 9.4, Barry A. Kosmin and Ariela Keysar, *Religion in a Free Market: Religious and Non-Religious Americans*, 2006, p. 157.

statistics come from these studies. (*Methodological note*: Kosmin and Keysar's 2001 study, published in 2006, represents the best available snapshot of U.S. religious demography. It is based on a random sample of more than 50,000 adults identifying with many religious groups—from Catholics and Evangelicals/Born Agains to Druids, Wiccans, and Sikhs. Still, the study is based completely on self-reports; thus, findings should remain suspect.)

For many decades, members of so-called mainline liberal, Protestant churches such as Episcopalians, Presbyterians, and United Church of Christ/Congregationalists have enjoyed the highest religious social status in the United States. Today, unsurprisingly, they rank high educationally. For example, among Christians, two mainline groups rank highest in terms of college graduates: Episcopalians (56 percent) and Presbyterians (51 percent). But these mainline groups rank below the very most educated groups: Unitarians (72 percent) (note that some Christians do not consider them to be Christian), Hindus (67 percent), and Jews (58 percent). Particularly noteworthy is this finding: In terms of educational achievement, Evangelical/Born Agains rank the same (49 percent) as a high-status mainline group: United Church of Christ.

At the bottom of the educational ranking ladder in the United States are Jehovah's Witnesses (12 percent), members of the Church of God (15 percent), and Pentecostals (16 percent). (In the 1990 survey, much lower percentages of Jehovah's Witnesses and Pentecostals had completed college: 4.7 and 6.9 percent, respectively. Ditto for Catholics: In 1990, 20 percent of Roman Catholics were college graduates, but that increased to 33 percent by 2001.)

There are significant differences in annual median household income too. As Table 11.3 shows, the highest-ranking religious group in the United States is Jews ($72,000), followed by Unitarians ($58,000), Episcopalians ($55,000), and Evangelical/Born Agains ($54,000). At the lowest end of the income ranking are Jehovah's Witnesses ($24,000).

Another noteworthy aspect of religion in the United States is the recent growth of so-called minority and/or previously suppressed religions and groups (Kosmin and Keysar, 2006:29). For example, the Hindu population in the United States probably tripled between 1990 and 2001, and there was a fivefold increase in Evangelical/Born Agains in the same period (Kosmin and Keysar, 2006:15, 25). There was also an increase in numerous other groups, from earth-based and magical ones to Santeria and Scientology. Health professionals, food manufacturers, and greeting card makers are among the many businesses responding to these changes. For instance, since the early 2000s, a variety of holiday cards have become available to mark celebrations from Kwanzaa and Eid al-Fadr to Diwali.

One recent development bears special notice: The Protestant majority seems to be disappearing in the United States (Associated Press, 2004). Between 1993 and 2002, a survey by the National Opinion Research Center showed that respondents who identified as Protestant dropped from 63 to 52 percent.

Meanwhile, the percentages of self-identified U.S. Roman Catholics (about 25 percent of the U.S. population) and Jews (just under 2 percent) remained stable (despite what some feared: increased interfaith marriage). But other shifts were reported: People in the United States who said that they had no religion rose from 9 to almost 14 percent from 1993 to 2002, and people belonging to a host of other religions, including Islam and Buddhism, increased from 3 to 7 percent.

RACE AND ETHNICITY

Long before the United States was the United States, there was a racial hierarchy. Until recently, this hierarchy consisted of a two-tone and unequal color palette: white over black.

Historically, some nonwhites and nonblacks in the United States were forgotten or made invisible; others were redefined. Specifically, most Native Americans, once called "Redskins" by many whites, were living on rural reservations that made them nearly invisible. Then, over time, some "nonwhite" immigrants, including Irish Americans, Italian Americans, and eastern European Jews, were reclassified as "white." A redefinition of one group—the Chinese in the Mississippi Delta—is a story unto itself. During so-called Reconstruction in the South (1865–1877), some white plantation owners imported sharecroppers from China to replace African American slaves. These Chinese workers were first classified as blacks. As they moved from plantations to towns and started small businesses, they were reclassified as essentially white. As Loewen (1988:117) notes, "the Chinese merchant usually enjoys a financial advantage over his working-class neighbor; thus he has economic position to offset caste inferiority."

Referring to both South and North in 1903, renowned social scientist W. E. B. DuBois famously prophesied that the "problem of the twentieth century [in the United States] is the problem of the color line" ([1903] 1997:45). DuBois meant that race relations in the United States were essentially etched in black and white and that blacks were stuck at the bottom of the racial hierarchy by discrimination, prejudice, lack of opportunity, and hate.

One hundred years later, the United States was more diverse racially, ethnically, and religiously (see the previous section). Latinos/Hispanics had displaced African Americans as the single largest "minority" with

13 percent of the population. Asians had increased to 4 percent.

Do these demographic shifts signal a "rainbow coalition" in-the-making? Many observers doubt it. Here is the reasoning of one skeptic, lawyer Nicholas C. Vaca (2004): Increasing tensions between African Americans and Hispanics threaten a potentially powerful coalition. Instead of partnership, there have been increased competition and an uncoupling of Hispanic "interests" from those of African Americans. Further, with increased Latino numbers, many African Americans now see Latinos as a threat to their group's gains in politics and the economy.

A different view of increased Latino numbers is put forth by the late and still controversial Harvard political scientist Samuel P. Huntington (2004). Huntington argued that new immigrants, mainly from Mexico, are changing the U.S. demographic landscape. He predicted a culture clash between Hispanics and Anglos that "will replace the racial division between blacks and whites as the most serious cleavage in American society" (318).

Increased Latino numbers are expected to continue. Some project that by 2050 the U.S. Latino/Hispanic population will reach about 24 percent (and the Asian population will reach about 8 percent; see Lee and Zhou, 2004.) And, as noted, by 2000, African Americans were no longer the largest "minority."

But have increased numbers of Latinos negatively affected African Americans? True, many African Americans have stayed on the bottom rungs of the racial status hierarchy. But scholars disagree on the main reasons why. Some point to new patterns of intermarriage, multiracial identification, and immigration, all with negative impacts on African Americans. Others focus on social and housing segregation. For example, in ethnically-diverse Los Angeles (where the Latino/Hispanic and Asian populations are both relatively recent and large as a result of immigration), the level of African American housing segregation has remained high. "That the level of black segregation remains high even compared to other groups such as Asians and Hispanics," comment two sociologists, "points to the durability of a color line that separates blacks from other groups" (Lee and Bean, 2007:51). Still other social scientists, as noted earlier, focus on employment and education patterns, prejudice, and lack of opportunity to understand or explain why African Americans as a group remain at the bottom of the racial status hierarchy.

Sociologist Herbert J. Gans forecasts an even bleaker future for African Americans than DuBois might have imagined in 1903—and a new color line. Gans (1999a) predicts that the current classification scheme of whites, African Americans (blacks), Asians, and Latinos (Hispanics) may soon morph into a "black–nonblack divide," which would not serve the interests of African Americans. This new hierarchy may happen, Gans thinks, even if more African Americans attain middle-class status. Some evidence supports Gans's views.

If Gans is correct, African Americans in the United States could suffer "disastrous consequences" (Lee and Bean, 2007:59). Gans (1999b) holds out some hope for a U.S. society where race will no longer be used to classify people. But, Gans thinks, this cosmopolitan society is a very far-off possibility. In the meantime, his prognosis is bleak.

Gans is not alone in his bleak forecast for African Americans. In *Who Is White? Latinos, Asians, and the New Black/Nonblack Divide* (2003), George Yancey, a sociologist and an African American, concludes, like Gans, that the United States is moving toward a black/nonblack society: "Instead of evaluating the social acceptance of a group by how 'white' they are, it will be more important to assess the social rejection of a group by how 'black' they are" (15). And, like Gans, he thinks that, like other groups before them (e.g., Irish and Italian Americans), Hispanic and Asian Americans will be socially reconstructed as white. He fears that African Americans as a group will remain in—indeed, will not be able to escape from—a racially-based low-status position resulting in social rejection (158–159). Not surprisingly, Yancey's prognosis about blacks in the future, as well as Gans's speculations, interest scholars in other multiethnic nations, such as Great Britain.

Sociologist James Loewen ([2005] 2006) reminds us about the past (and the continuing present in some cases) of nearly unknown or barely mentioned race-based exclusion in the United States: "sundown towns." Thousands of these towns, established between 1890 and 1968, systematically excluded African Americans from living within their borders; they had to leave by sundown. Located mostly outside the traditional South, sundown towns used (and still use) a variety of methods—from legal formalities to race riots and guns—to keep their cities lily-white. Loewen tells this story about a conversation he had in one such Illinois town:

> "Is it true that 'Anna' stands for 'Ain't No Niggers Allowed'?" I asked at the convenience store in Anna, Illinois, where I had stopped to buy coffee.
>
> "Yes," the clerk replied.... That all happened a long time ago."
>
> "I understand [racial exclusion] is still going on?" I asked.
>
> "Yes," she replied. "That's sad."

Anna, a town of about 7,000 people, including adjoining Jonesboro, is located about 35 miles north of Cairo in southern Illinois. In 1909, after a nearby "spectacle lynching," Anna and Jonesboro expelled African Americans living there. Ever since, both cities have been all white. Almost 100 years later, "Anna" is still considered by its residents and by people nearby towns to mean "Ain't No Niggers Allowed," the acronym the convenience store clerk confirmed in 2001 (Loewen, [2005] 2006).

(*Note*: Sundown towns are not peculiar to the United States. In some former European colonies, including the Ivory Coast, the same restrictions applied postindependence. There, for some years, the Charles de Gaulle Bridge leading from Treichville, a poor African section, into Abidjan, the country's former capital and home to most white Europeans who worked there, was closed after sundown.)

And what of the future? Suggesting, once again, that race is more a social than biological category, Asians in the United States are undergoing what Gans has called **"social whitening."** This is one reason why Gans thinks that a black–nonblack color line will happen. Similarly, historian Gary Gerstle (1999) predicts that Asians and Latinos are both following this pattern of blending in and being accepted by whites (i.e., socially whitened). This has not happened to African Americans.

Another historian envisions a radically different future. In this vision, there is a "postethnic America" where ethnic and racial identifications would be voluntary and floating; that is, individuals would choose to join or leave an ethnic or racial group (Hollinger, 1995). Some commentators (e.g., Mabry, 2008) think that, thanks to popular culture, including hip-hop, this has already occurred, in part (Chapter 10).

What the future holds is murky. The past is more clear. In less than two generations, the U.S. racial status hierarchy has changed enormously for Asians and Latinos/Hispanics—but not for African Americans. Whereas in yesteryear some Asians were called "yellow hordes," they are now often referred to, rightly or wrongly, as "model minorities." Latinos/Hispanics have been rising on the rungs. To the contrary, there remains a persistent pattern of "black exceptionalism," that is, large-scale housing segregation and social separation from other groups. And pessimism among African Americans is on the rise: As of 2007, the majority of African Americans believed that they were becoming worse off in the United States, not better off. A Pew Research Center poll (CBS News, 2007) shows that only 44 percent of African Americans polled expected their prospects to improve in the future (whereas in 1986, 57 percent thought that their futures would be brighter). Many scholars agree with that self-assessment, pointing to—among other things—the persistent disparities of wealth along racial lines (e.g., Shapiro, 2005).

On the other hand, there is some evidence that less strained relations between people of different ethnic and racial backgrounds can occur, and quickly. One study of prejudice, for example, shows that mutual trust between members of different races or ethnicities can spread quickly through a so-called extended-contact effect that travels "like a benign virus through an entire peer group" (Carey, 2008). In addition, it is unclear what impacts the presidency of Barack Obama will have on U.S. ethnic/racial relations.

ETHCLASS

To what degree does ethnicity or religion divide members of the same class? For instance, do upper-class Irish Catholics have more social contacts with lower-class Irish Catholics than with upper-class WASPs? Who knows? Few studies deal with this intersection of ethnicity and social class, called **ethclass**.

Sociologist Milton Gordon, originator of the term "ethclass," wrote years ago that birds of our own feather—the people we can relax with and feel at home with—are "likely to be of the same ethnic group *and* social class" (1978:135).

Yet, ethclass may have limited application. If Herbert Gans is correct, ethnicity becomes mainly symbolic for many whites by the fourth generation in the U.S. How useful, then, is the concept of ethclass?

Clearly, we need much more evidence before we can decide. We might begin by looking more closely at SER neighborhoods, one important place where birds of a feather flock together. For example, in the predominantly white, superrich categories Upper Crust and Blue Blood Estates, does an upper-class Japanese American family feel more at home with its non-Japanese American neighbors than with coethnics who live, say, in SER 17, Bohemian Mix?

There are not much data on these questions, but there is abundant information that African Americans in U.S. cities have different—and unequal—life chances, lifestyles, and power. The Kerner Commission summarized the mountain of data succinctly back in 1968: "Our nation is moving toward two societies, one black, one white—separate and unequal." Decades later, the number of black elected officials had increased dramatically, and high school graduation rates for African Americans had doubled. But, as Harvard University professor Henry Louis Gates, Jr., pointed out in 1994, black America itself consists of at least two societies—separate and unequal: The "black middle class has never been larger." Gates noted back then that "It has quadrupled since 1967, and it doubled during the 1980s alone. Never before have so many blacks done so well. And never before have so many blacks done so poorly." Gates noted that 46 percent of black children lived in poverty. (The figure for white children was about 16 percent.) Further, Gates said that the black underclass had never been larger. His conclusion was that the realities of race no longer affect all blacks in the same way (1994:7–8).

In other words, class disparities *within* the "black community" grew wider in the last generation. While some African Americans made economic advances, many more suffered poverty, unemployment, shorter

life expectancies, and low prestige. (In an economic downturn, I believe, we can expect these intrablack disparities to continue, if not to be magnified.)

These facts are undisputed. But how are we to interpret them? The traditional interpretation has been that racial discrimination is the key factor in limiting African Americans to low-prestige and low-paid work. This interpretation is now under heavy attack. The scholarly work of sociologist William Julius Wilson (at the University of Chicago when he wrote his early books) is indicative of this changing interpretation. (See also Chapters 9 and 10.) When Wilson published the book *Power, Racism and Privilege* in 1973, he paid little attention to class. By 1978, he had changed his mind. In *The Declining Significance of Race* (1978:150), Wilson argued that "class has become more important than race in determining black life-chances in the modern industrial period." Wilson's argument is essentially this: Economic and technological changes (structural factors such as the rapid growth of the corporate and government sectors) have led to a segmented labor market. This has served to solidify class differences between (1) a huge African American underclass (created originally by discrimination and oppression) that is poor and poorly trained and (2) a much smaller group of well-educated, affluent, and privileged African Americans who are experiencing many job opportunities.

One implication of Wilson's work is that the poor underclass—whether they live on Clay Street or hang out at Tally's corner—share a fate. This fate is based on their class position, whether white, black, or brown.

Importantly, Wilson is rethinking his vision of class and race (Chapters 9, 10). His recent work reflects this vision: that both structural factors (e.g., deindustrialization, high levels of unemployment) and cultural factors (e.g., racial discrimination, the lack of two people in the house to share child care), as well as the interaction of these factors, perpetuate inequality in inner-city African American neighborhoods ([1996] 1997, 2009). (Note that Wilson thinks that the concept of ghettoization remains relevant. But, he argues, it should be seen as a set of processes: "segregation, racial stigmatization/domination, economic disadvantage, and state action carried out through policy" [Chaddha and Wilson, 2008:388]).

Wilson's work has stimulated other scholars to investigate the complicated issues concerning the relative importance of race, ethnicity, religion, and class in determining an American urbanite's life chances, lifestyle, and power. No doubt, exploring how these variables interact and contribute to inequalities will be major research topics in this decade and beyond. Hopefully, this will be the case, for much work on these complex and ideologically-loaded issues is sorely needed.

Here is just one example of how issues involving race and class can have enormous impact on policymaking and on individual lives. It concerns school segregation in Cambridge, Massachusetts. In 2002 Cambridge switched from race-based measures to family income as a way of assigning students to schools. It was assumed, or hoped, that these measures would lead to decreased racial segregation. Yet, by 2007, the system had become *more, not less*, racially segregated: almost 60 percent of Cambridge's 12 elementary schools were racially imbalanced compared with less than 40 percent in 2001–2002, before the new policy took effect (January 2007). Cambridge's racial imbalance is especially important because school districts across the United States are considering Cambridge's approach as an alternative to measures aimed at ending racial segregation after a June 2007 Supreme Court ruling that banned the use of race in the desegregation plans of Seattle, Washington, and Jefferson County, Kentucky. (See also the Lacrosse, Wisconsin, class-based school integration plan, discussed earlier in this chapter.)

Whatever policymakers do or say and whatever scholars like Wilson claim, the relative importance of race and class remains much debated in the United States. In the run-up to the 2008 U.S. presidential campaign, for example, candidate Barack Obama commented that his two daughters "have had a pretty good deal" in life (i.e., they are neither poor nor without advantages, no matter what their color) and thus should not benefit from affirmative action assistance. Indeed, Obama told "minority" journalists, "We have to think about affirmative action and craft it in such a way where some of our children who are advantaged aren't getting more favorable treatment than a poor white kid who has struggled more" (in Swarns, 2008:4).

To conclude: Social scientists still ask, Does class matter? If so, how much? The same is true for race: Does race matter? If so, how much? The continuing presence of sundown towns suggests that race still matters in the United States.

James Baldwin's quip about the United States not being a color-blind society—"I'll be black for as long as you tell me that you are white"—remains viable years after his death in 1987. This suggests that race still matters.

But to what extent does race matter? That continues to be a source of disagreement among honest scholars and citizens. Some scholars (e.g., Hertz, 2005) believe that race matters a great deal in explaining earnings immobility, particularly for poor blacks in the United States. As we've noted, many social scientists, including Gans and Yancey, think that race still counts.

So does gender.

GENDER

Abundant statistical data testify to the increasing participation of women in the labor force, declining fertility rates, and many other topics. However, little attention has been paid to women in social stratification studies. There are reasons. Until quite recently, in rich countries women were considered as appendages of their husbands; they were assumed to adopt the status and privileges of the men they married. This remains the case in some rich countries, such as Japan, a country which ranks low on the United Nations Development Program's "gender empowerment measure" (an index of female participation in a nation's political and economic life). In poorer countries, this often remains the case too. (There are many exceptions to the second- or third-class status of women in poor countries, such as the relatively well-off market women of Liberia, who fed their families during wartime when most of their husbands could not find work.)

With singlehood, "hooking up" (typically in big cities), out-of-the-closet relationships, divorce, and full-time paid work becoming a way of life for more and more women, at least in industrial and postindustrial societies, and at different points in their life cycles, this assumption—that women are mere appendages of their mates—is changing. A generation ago, one study concluded that working wives in the United States do not simply borrow their class identity from their husbands; increasingly, women's class identification has to do with such factors as union membership, self-employment, and work in a pink-collar occupation (Simpson et al., 1988).

Also, social scientists themselves didn't pay attention to the variable of gender. For example, like medical research, most studies of urban social stratification in the United States ignored women. In other studies, theorists treated women as a lower-status group, not recognizing the differences among subgroups. Thus, much research and theory are needed on gender stratification and the differential life chances of men and women.

However, there is also much that is known. First, in the United States we know that young women, born after 1990, live in a world different from that of their mothers. Thanks to changes in legislation and societal attitudes, among other factors, young women have greater access to organized sports and colleges, including prestigious colleges and universities. For example, Yale University (which started admitting female undergraduates in 1969) had a first-year class in 2007 that is one-half female. In 2004–2005, women earned 57 percent of all B.A.s awarded in the United States and nearly 60 percent of master's degrees (Deveny and Kelley, 2007:43). Second, in 2007 the U.S. Congress had the highest number of female members in its history: 16 senators and 74 representatives, including Speaker of the House.

We also know that gender stratification and sexual harassment transcend economic and political systems. Sexual harassment against women in the workplace seems to be the norm, not the exception, in some industrial countries. For example, one International Labor Organization study done in the early 1990s reported that 58 percent of Dutch women and 74 percent of British women reported sexual harassment at work.

Women use various strategies to avoid harassment. In Turkey, for instance, young, attractive women try to look older and become desexualized in order to be taken seriously (Shafak, 2007).

Still, gender inequality persists in the workplace, whether women continue to be harassed or not. In the former Soviet countries, the majority of women work at low-paid blue-collar jobs; female professionals tend to be stuck at the lowest levels in their fields. In Israeli collective agricultural settlements (*kibbutzim*), the pioneer women started as equals, but even in this socialist milieu there is gender inequality. (*Note*: Israel had about 230 kibbutzim in 2007; about two-thirds were no longer collectives, having adopted privatization plans. Typically, members voted to privatize as a way to keep their community lifestyle in the midst of global influences. However, the kibbutz movement is not dead. About 20 new kibbutzim, often urban-based, have been started in recent years by young Israelis. Will these new arrangements—nonagricultural, city-based kibbutzim—decrease gender inequality? It's too soon to know.)

Why gender inequality exists in the kibbutz—founded on the ideals of a small, classless society with economic, social, and political equality for all members—is a matter of some debate. But the point here is that sexual stratification exists and is a continuing feature of modern societies, whatever they call their economic–social system—capitalist, welfare state, socialist, or mixed. In other words, *sexism or genderism is an international and intereconomic phenomenon.*

A note on gender and religion: Columnist and writer Vivian Gornick is both Jewish and female. In her view, that makes her doubly an outsider. What does she mean? To her, "Outsiderness is the daily infliction of social invisibility" (1994:123). But which takes precedence—her gender or her religious minority status? Here is what she says, discussing several male Jewish writers, filmmakers, and comedians, including Mel Brooks and Woody Allen (who is Gornick's age): "Every last one of them was trashing women....To them, we weren't friends or comrades. We weren't even Jews or gentiles. We were just girls....I knew that I would never again feel myself more of a Jew than a woman" (122).

WOMEN IN CITIES

As recently as 1975, women in the social science literature of cities were "part of the furniture." In other words, they were there but barely noticed (Lofland, 1975:144).

Since the mid-1970s, however, there has been an explosion of research and action-oriented projects dealing with women in cities. The research deals with a wide range of issues, including why the experience of men and women in cities is quite different. But there seems to be no central focus to this research. Instead, research about women in cities is like the field of urban studies itself, broad and eclectic. In terms of action-oriented projects, there is also a wide range, from Women in Cities International, a Canadian NGO designed to be "an exchange network for various partners concerned with gender equality issues and the place of women in cities on the five continents" (http://www.femmesetvilles.org/english/sets_en/set_intro_en.htm) and host of the first International Seminar on Women's Safety, held in Montreal in 2002, to the promotion of business ownership activities by women.

Since there is no "representative" research about women in U.S. (or other) cities, let's look at a few studies that suggest the broad range. First, works on the intersection of gender, space, and power. Taking Boston as her case study, history professor Sarah Deutsch (2002) argues that women of all classes, ethnicities, and social positions radically transformed the city between 1870 and 1940, so much so that in the latter period women enjoyed much more freedom and some power too. In *Sex Among the Rabble: An Intimate History of Gender and Power in the Age of Revolution, Philadelphia, 1730–1830*, history professor Claire A. Lyons (2006) discovers that in Revolutionary-era Philadelphia, there were women who ran away from their husbands, challenging their patriarchal rights. Her larger argument concerns class and racial divisions in the United States that laid the groundwork in the new nation for common understandings of gender, which, she claims, were part and parcel of subordinating women (and African Americans).

Second, women and work. In *Cleaning Up: The Transformation of Domestic Service in Twentieth Century New York City* (2006), independent scholar Alana Erickson Coble documents changes in one stratum of women's work, suggesting that various forces, including shifts in women's role in society, changes in immigration laws, and the politicization of domestic service, helped to shape the transformation. In addition, she argues, domestic workers themselves took advantage of the times to demand better treatment. In *Nickel and Dimed: On (Not) Getting By in America* ([2002] 2008),

Barbara Ehrenreich describes low-wage work in general; many of the jobs she sought and got for this study attract greater percentages of women.

Third, studies of ethnic women. One study (IANS, 2006) found that the suicide rate in New York City among ethnic women was much higher than that of white women there. For instance, Asian women 65 and older have a suicide rate of 11.6 per 100,000, more than double the rate for non-Hispanic white women in that age group. The biomedical report suggests that young Hispanic women and older Asian women, in particular, are at very high risk of attempting or committing suicide due to "cultural and linguistic isolation, the stress of immigration and a shortage of psychiatric and counselling services." Another study, focusing on political opportunities for ethnic women in London found that they have much more difficulty in becoming elected (and unpaid) local government "councillors" (Women in London, n.d.).

Fourth, divided cities—divided into men's spaces and women's spaces. For example, Dolores Hayden's *The Grand Domestic Revolution* (1981) documents the history of educated, white women's struggles in America to trade mansions for women-centered home design and community planning. Inspired by Susan B. Anthony's call to arms—"Away with your man-visions! Women propose to reject them all, and begin to dream dreams for themselves"—Hayden explores many visionary schemes for emancipating women by transforming individual housework and/or child care into communal activities, including two from the 1860s: Harriet Beecher Stowe's model Christian neighborhood (where 10–12 families would share a laundry and bakehouse) and Melusina Fay Peirce's attempts to organize her neighbors in Cambridge, Massachusetts, into cooperative housekeeping associations and kitchenless houses.

Fifth, residential choice. Because so many U.S. women now work outside the home and have primary responsibility for child care and housework, they seek to minimize their time-wasting commute by living near the workplace. This constrains women's residential—and employment—choices, as several studies show (e.g., Rutherford and Wekerle, 1988).

Sixth, safety. Their safety is a prime concern of women in cities in many countries. Several organizations, including the United Nations, publish newsletters and alerts on this subject.

Seventh, the homeless. Much less attention has been given to homeless women than homeless men in cities. Researchers Cheung and Hwang (2004) studied women who used homeless shelters in Toronto, and for comparison purposes, they analyzed studies conducted in six other cities: Montreal, Copenhagen, Boston, New York, Philadelphia, and Brighton, England. They found that in Toronto mortality rates were highest among homeless women 18–44 years of age. Women in this age group, they found, were 10 times more likely to die than women in Toronto's general population; the major causes of death were drug overdoses and HIV/AIDS. In a study of homeless Korean women, Jesook Song (2006) shows that homeless women in Seoul between 1997 and 2001 were considered the undeserving poor by the government, unlike homeless men.

Eighth, macro-level studies. *Race, Class, and Gender: An Anthology* (2006), edited by Margaret L. Andersen and Patricia Hill Collins, is exemplary. Many selections, often multidisciplinary, have a strong historical and sociological perspective.

Finally, we can predict that a fairly new phenomenon will be the subject of study: the reversal of the wage gap between men and women in major U.S. cities. Between 2000 and 2005, young full-time female workers in New York City and several other large cities earned more than men. Specifically, sociologist Andrew Beveridge shows that young women (21–30 years old) living in New York City earned 117 percent of men's wages between 2000 and 2005. In Dallas, they earned even more: 120 percent of men's wages (in Roberts, 2007:1). Nationwide, the wage gap remains—women earn 89 percent of what men earn.

Why might some women in the United States earn more than men? That, no doubt, will be much studied. A preliminary answer comes from political scientist Andrew Hacker: "Citified college women are more likely to be nonmarried and childless, compared with their suburban sisters, so they can and do devote themselves to their careers" (in Roberts, 2007:1).

AGE

Given the work of Marx, Weber, Bourdieu, and Gans, it is not news that people's tastes differ by class or status

group. But often we forget that age and gender also affect taste.

Take, for example, radio listeners. A comprehensive analysis of NPR listeners in the United States (Liebold, 1988) found that classical music and opera appeal more to women than to men, jazz appeals most to younger men (25–34 years old), and information programs appeal primarily to listeners aged 35–44. More recent surveys, including PRIZM's 2006 data (Chapter 8), suggest that people in the United States aged 55 or above are the highest consumers of talk radio—but not of religious radio.

It is also not news that both sexism and ageism exist in many societies. But structurally, there is an important difference between these two "isms": Sexism seems to surpass the boundaries of economic and social systems; ageism seems to be most prevalent in societies that define human value in terms of economic productive capacity. That is, the more a society believes that "you are what you do," the more the very old and the very young (the economically unproductive) will tend to be devalued.

In the United States, the specter of the old-age home haunts many who see themselves being relegated to the sidelines. Even in Japan, where family obligations traditionally meant taking care of one's parents, many older people face the twilight years bathed in darkness. Over a half-century ago, Japanese moviemaker Yasujiro Ozu sensitively portrayed the plight of an old couple whose children see them as a burden in *Tokyo Story* (1953).

Not hired because they're "too old" or forced to retire, stripped of social roles that give meaning to their lives, and often pushed aside, the old may be called "senior citizens," but they're often treated as less than equal citizens. As the life expectancy in advanced industrial countries continues to increase, what will happen to people in their not-so-golden years?

Some seniors, including Maria Amelia Lopez, age 95 in 2007, have not moved to any old-folks' home. For one, Lopez (known as "the little granny") continues to remain "on top of things" by blogging and corresponding with some of her readers. Lopez received 350,000 hits on her blog (originating in Spain) from December 2006 to September 2007. She says, "I don't want to sit in a corner and take a tablet and sleep all afternoon" (Burnett, 2007:9).

Fig. 11.6 TOO YOUNG OR TOO OLD. Many face age discrimination, but some elders find new careers instead of rocking chairs. Edna W. Newman, for one, started working as a disc jockey in her mid-seventies and became manager of a West Orange, New Jersey, radio station. (Barbara London)

While not alone, Lopez is far from the norm. More regularly, the elderly tend to be hit hardest during hard times, both natural and economic. In 2004 and 2007, it was mainly the aged who died in Japanese earthquakes. Why? One Japanese official put it like this: "Many elderly need help even in normal times. In a natural disaster, they become completely helpless" (in Fackler, 2007:2). In hard economic times, older people can become terrified that they will have less money and longer lives. In the United States, for example, 39 percent of retirees—before Wall Street's turmoil in September 2008 sent confidence and stocks falling—said they expected to outlive their savings; a year before, 10 percent fewer (29 percent) said that they had this fearful expectation (in Leland and Uchitelle, 2008).

Young people also receive unequal treatment. In some cases, American customs or laws presumed to protect children have served to deny them civil rights. In other cases (e.g., widespread exclusion from juries), young adults face discrimination. New York became the first city in the United States to attack discrimination against young people in public places such as restaurants and movie theaters.

The specific consequences of age stratification for young and old alike include economic discrimination, age stereotyping, and territorial segregation. In other words, old and young face some common issues.

ANOTHER LOOK

Scholars and citizens agree that inequality exists. No matter how inequality is defined—by access to money, information, prestige, or power. Most scholars believe

TABLE 11.4 PERCENTAGE OF WEALTH HELD BY THE TOP 10 PERCENT OF ADULTS IN 10 WESTERN COUNTRIES

Country	Wealth Owned by Top 10%
Switzerland	71.3%
United States	69.8%
Denmark	65.0%
France	61.0%
Sweden	58.6%
United Kingdom	56.0%
Canada	53.0%
Norway	50.5%
Germany	44.4%
Finland	42.3%

Source: Table 4 in William Domhoff, 2006 (December) (http://sociology.ucsc.edu/whorulesamerica/power/wealth.html).

that the inequality gap between those who have and don't have is growing wider.

Table 11.4, based on a study by the World Institute for Development Economics Research (in Domhoff, 2006), uses data for the year 2000 (with admittedly spotty information, for which the researchers try to compensate with very sophisticated statistical methods). It shows that wealth in many Western industrial and postindustrial countries is highly concentrated. (Indeed, the top 10 percent of the world's adults control about 85 percent of household wealth globally, where *wealth* is defined broadly as all assets minus debts). Only Switzerland has a higher concentration of wealth among the top 10 percent (71.3 percent) of adults than the United States.

Globally, in just 3 years, 2003–2006, the number of billionaires increased from 476 to 793. By 2007, according to *Forbes*'s annual count, there were 946 global billionaires; their total wealth topped $3.5 trillion. Over half of 2007's billionaires (523) came from just three countries: the United States (415), Germany (55), and Russia (53). For the first time, India had more billionaires (36) than Japan (24) (in Kroll and Fass, 2007). Framed in a very different way, "one hundred millionth of the world's population (1/100,000,000) own[ed] more than over 3 billion people," and income for the lower 55 percent of the world's 6 billion plus declined or stagnated (Petras, 2007).

Why such inequalities exist (and the parts played by gender, race, ethclass, status, power, and religion in perpetuating inequality) is a matter of continuing controversy. At the urban and metropolitan levels, *how* a researcher goes about studying inequalities has less to do with disciplinary background than ideology. And *what* the researcher finds—an open system characterized by social mobility or a more rigid system of small, exclusive elites and social immobility—depends mainly on the theoretical orientation of the researcher. Specifically, those using the concept of status tend to find an open system; those using the concept of class tend to emphasize the rigidity of the social hierarchy. A subtle and immeasurable influence on researchers may also be present: fear of change in the basic nature of the society and the economy. After all, why should we expect urbanists to be free from values about equality and security?

Those desiring to reduce inequality don't agree on how to do it. Programs of equal opportunity, not equal results, have been the liberals' mainstay, together with tax policies and public assistance. Marx had another solution—the creation of a classless society. Weber held out little hope of any solution, believing that even under socialism people would be oppressed and depersonalized by a common enemy: bureaucratic organization. Others have pointed to the rise of a new class, not predicted by Marx: scientists, technicians, intellectuals, and professionals. This new class, it is often argued, shares a more important form of capital than money—culture—and it is increasingly gaining power and demanding autonomy. As noted earlier, Bourdieu called this important badge of distinction "cultural capital."

Unsurprisingly, scholars disagree on who comprises the much talked about "middle class." Weberians see it as an income range that reflects what goods and services a group can buy in the market. Wright see it as a class in the middle—that is both exploiter and exploited. But to many who once thought that they were in it and now wonder, the middle class may represent an attitude or feeling, not an income range—a feeling that members control their economic destiny and can provide for life's necessities as well as for future needs.

Meanwhile, researchers have failed to disentangle the factors that influence collective inequalities, including gender, race, religion, ethnicity, class, religion, and age. Ethnic and gender stratification have been particularly neglected as independent factors that help determine who gets what out of life.

KEY TERMS

American dream The idea, many say "myth," that any individual in the United States can climb the ladder of success if he or she works hard, plays by the rules, and has a pinch of luck. For many, owning a single-family, detached, suburban home symbolizes the realization of the dream.

Bourgeoisie (plural noun) Literally, "people who live in towns or cities" (bourgs). In Marx's analysis of social stratification, the bourgeoisie is the class that owns the means of production and thus controls the social relations of production under capitalism. The class opposing the bourgeoisie is the *proletariat*.

Capital To orthodox economists, there are two types: physical—all useful assets (except unimproved land and natural raw materials) used to produce goods and services—and human—people's knowledge, skills, and energies, which can be used to produce goods and services. To Marx, capital is more than money or machines; it masks a social relation of domination.

Capitalists In Marxist analysis, synonym for *bourgeoisie*.

Castes Rigid social divisions based on status ascribed at birth. A caste system is typified by lack of social mobility; it is a closed class system. The classic example is traditional India, where Brahmins constitute the highest caste and the Harijans (untouchables) constitute the lowest caste.

Class As used by Karl Marx, class position in the social hierarchy is determined by one's relationship to the means of production (ownership or nonownership). As used by Max Weber, class is determined by one's market position. A group of people who share a similar relationship to the means of production (Marx) or market position (Weber) are members of the same class.

Class consciousness Sense of belonging to and identifying with a particular social class. This awareness is accompanied by a sense of solidarity with other individuals in the same class and by the feeling that one's own interests are tied to the position of the class as a whole.

Cultural capital French sociologist Pierre Bourdieu's term for language competencies, attitudes, behaviors, and general familiarity with the culture and symbols of a particular class or status group. Contemporary high-status symbols include a preference for books of poetry over Harlequin novels.

Ethclass Sociologist Milton Gordon's term for the intersection of class and ethnicity in determining a person's identity and assimilation. Example: A middle-class Puerto Rican probably feels more kinship with a middle-class Italian than with a lower-class Puerto Rican.

False consciousness In Marxist analysis, the sense of belonging to or identifying with a social class to which one does not belong objectively.

Forces of production In Marxist analysis, the technological, economic, and knowledge bases of a society. It is one component of the mode of production (together with the social relations of production).

Hegemony A term used by the late Italian Marxist Antonio Gramsci, meaning cultural leadership or domination.

Influence Informal power. Unlike formal power, influence is rooted in such factors as money, guns, organization (e.g., lobby groups, political parties), and personal charisma.

Means of production In Marxist analysis, inputs such as raw materials and tools that produce (or add to) things of value in a society. These inputs include land in feudalism and factory machines in industrial capitalism. Marxists maintain that the dominant class owns or controls the means of production.

Mode of production To Marx, (1) the forces of production plus (2) the social relations of production. Together, these two components shape a society. Thus, the slave mode, the feudal mode, and the capitalist mode of production are different social forms.

Power In Weber's analysis, one dimension of social stratification that can be independent of the economic and prestige orders. Power is the ability to force others, even if they resist, to carry out your policies. The political order consists of administrative–bureaucratic and elected positions in the corporate and governmental spheres.

Proletariat Marx's term for urban propertyless workers who, he felt, stood in opposition to the owners of the means of production (the bourgeoisie or capitalists) who exploited them in industrial capitalist society. One member of this class: a prole (slang) or proletarian.

Social relations of production In Marxist analysis, how people involved in production relate to each other and to the surplus that they collectively produce. Under capitalism, the social relations of production are the relations between the people who produce the surplus (workers) and those who decide how it should be appropriated (capitalists).

Social stratification The process by which individuals and groups rank each other socially and differentiate each other in a hierarchy. From the Latin term *strata* ("layers," singular *stratum*). Caste and class societies are socially stratified.

Social whitening A term first used by U.S. sociologist Herbert Gans to describe the process by which Asian Americans—but not African Americans—blend in and are accepted by whites in the United States. Other social scientists extend the concept to include Hispanics/Latinos but not African Americans.

Socioeconomic status (SES) A composite measure based on income, education, and occupation that combines class and status to determine a person's or group's place on the social ladder.

Status One of Weber's three dimensions for ranking members of a society. Status is based on the prestige or social esteem that others in the society accord a person. It is a position in the social structure that, according to Weber, carries with it a certain lifestyle.

Wealth The total assets a person owns minus debt owed. (The main debt for most adults is home mortgage debt. Other types of debt include auto payments and credit card debt.) Wealth may consist of a house, other real estate, savings accounts, money market funds, stocks, and other securities. Two people with the same income may have very different wealth profiles. Synonym: *net worth*.

World-systems analysis A perspective developed by political sociologist Immanuel Wallerstein, often used by globalization thinkers and antiglobalization activists. This perspective uses the world system as the unit of analysis, not individual nation-states. It stresses the study of interconnected nations and economic systems as the route to better understand modern society and social systems.

PROJECTS

1. **Attitudes on class**. To investigate how some people in your community view the social structure and their place in it, construct a questionnaire and administer it at various sites in the community. You might ask the following questions: Do classes exist in the United States, Canada, China, India, and Mexico? How do you define yourself (upper class, upper-middle class, middle class, lower-middle class, working class)? Does everyone in your town or a nearby town have an equal chance to lead a long life and to get a good job? The questionnaire should be short but include background information on each respondent, including occupation (or job title) or lack of one (retired, unemployed). When examining responses, see how many respondents list themselves as middle class and how many of these are in the U.S. census categories of professional or managerial workers. What attitudes do your respondents hold toward class?

2. **Social status**. Replicate Warner's study of the distribution of housing in Jonesville in your community. Where are the fine houses located? Where do people with high-status occupations live? Is there a concentration of high-status homes in a particular neighborhood or neighborhoods?

3. **Taste differences**. Try to determine who reads and listens to what in your town or area. The first step is to determine if you can get access to data, perhaps from ad agencies or Internet providers, and newspaper circulation departments, that show the ethnicity, gender, age, and income of listeners, readers, and viewers of different media. If you can, choose a few program or article categories (e.g., sports, rap, soap operas, comic strips, video games, pornography, news, classical music) and try to establish differences, if any, in readership, listenership, or viewership. If there are differences, why might these exist?

4. **Wealth: interpreting data on median net worth**. Family wealth (net worth) is based on assets (e.g., cars, stocks, bonds, equity in real estate, bank accounts, antique rugs, rare baseball cards) minus debts (e.g. home mortgage, credit card balances, loans). First, gather the latest data available (from U.S. Census publications) on net worth in the United States. Examine differences by age group, race/ethnicity, and other factors you intuit may be important in determining differences among families. Next, discuss how these data might be interpreted by at least two theorists discussed in this chapter.

5. **Comparing ideas: Marmot and Fuller**. Dr. Michael Marmot and Robert W. Fuller, discussed in this chapter, present critiques of present social stratification ladders in the United States. First, read their two books. Then, state their basic findings, indicating their points of agreement and disagreement. Second, compare their methods of investigation. Finally, speculate why they may agree and disagree on various points.

SUGGESTIONS FOR FURTHER LEARNING

For a very different take on Marx, Weber, and others, see Jack Goody, *The Theft of History* (New York: Cambridge University Press, 2007). Goody, a University of Cambridge emeritus professor of social anthropology, extends his previous critique of what he considers the Eurocentric bias of much of Western history writing and the consequent "theft" by the West of other cultures' achievements, including the invention of capitalism and other -isms and –ocracies.

The late (but ever-controversial) French theorist (some say visionary) Jean Baudrillard (1929–2007) was a postmodernist theorist. He thought that class analysis was unnecessary for understanding *Techno$chaft*. See his *For a Critique of the Political Economy of the Sign* (St. Louis: Telos Press, 1981) and an essay by Dean MacCannell and Juliet Flower MacCannell, "Social Class in Postmodernity," in *Forget Baudrillard?*, edited by Chris Rojek and Bryan S. Turner (London: Routledge, 1993:124–145).

American economist Thorstein Veblen detailed the lifestyles of various status groups in *The Theory of the Leisure Class* (New York: Macmillan, 1899) and popularized the term "conspicuous consumption." Veblen, who taught for a time at the University of Chicago, was concerned, as Weber was, with the growth of rationality in modern life. Veblen advocated a society run by scientists and engineers (technocrats) instead of businesspeople.

More recently, the premier social analyst of French culture, the late Pierre Bourdieu, attempted to rethink Weber's opposition between class and status groups in *Distinction: A Social Critique of the Judgement of Taste* (Cambridge, Mass.: Harvard University Press, [1979] 2002). This important book is "very French," as Bourdieu himself said, in its examples and form. But his examples can be adapted easily to the United States.

Highly readable, Barbara Ehrenreich's *Fear of Falling: The Inner Life of the Middle Class* (New York: Harper Perennial, 1990) looks at the professional middle class (and its cultural capital), which she said is deeply anxious and insecure. Many think that anxiety and insecurity among professionals has only increased since she wrote that book.

Literature dealing with social stratification is varied. It ranges from the classic American-dream tales of upward social mobility by Horatio Alger, including *Ragged Dick* and *Mark, the Match Boy* (New York: Crowell-Collier, 1962), and John P. Marquand's portrait of upper-class life in Boston, *The Late George Apley* (Fort Lee, N.J.: Little, 1937), to Jack London's socialist outrage, expressed in his story of class oppression, *The Iron Heel* (New York: Macmillan, 1907).

For one person's life story, which rekindles the debate over race and class as key factors in the U.S. social ranking system, see *Black Radical: The Education of an American Revolutionary 1946–1968* (New York: New Press, 2007) by Nelson Peery. After fighting in an all-black U.S. infantry division in World War II, Peery asked, "Why am I who never harmed anyone, mistreated, segregated, assigned an unequal place in a country that promises equality?"

In *Cooking, Cuisine and Class: A Study in Comparative Sociology* (New York: Cambridge University Press, 1982), social anthropologist Jack Goody explored why Africa failed to develop what the French call "haute cuisine." Goody discusses the differences in food preparation and consumption in many societies, relating these customs to differences in the society's socioeconomic structures.

For a discussion of the role of women in development since the 1980s, see Amy Lind, *Gendered Paradoxes: Women's Movements, State Restructuring, and Global Development in Ecuador* (University Park: Pennsylvania State University Press, [2005] 2007). In their anthology *Constructing Spanish Womanhood: Female Identity in Modern Spain* (Albany, N.Y.: SUNY Press, 1998), editors Victoria Loree Enders and Pamela Beth Radcliff bring together essays that explore the role of women in nineteenth- and twentieth-century Spain, suggesting, inter alia, that traditional notions of separate spheres between men and women need to be reevaluated.

In *Race, Space, and Riots in Chicago, New York, and Los Angeles*, Professor Emeritus Janet L. Abu-Lughod (New York: Oxford University Press, 2007) compares six major race riots in the United States's three largest metro areas. She explores how space, economics, and politics shape urban rebellions. She analyzes local political cultures as a factor in either defusing or exacerbating urban violence and identifies shared urban issues as well as those unique to each city.

In *Racism: A Very Short Introduction* (New York: Oxford University Press, 2007), Ali Rattansi explores racial prejudices and stereotypes that seem to be embedded in Western culture. These range from very subtle forms of discrimination to cultural imperialism and "ethnic cleansing."

One proposed "solution" to racism is the melding of races. For a look at one multiracial identity, see Kerry Ann Rockquemore and David I. Brunsma, *Beyond Black: Biracial Identity in America* (Lanham, Md.: Rowman & Littlefield, 2007).

Among the scholarly discussions of patterns of racial and ethnic stratification is *Race, Ethnicity, and Inequality in the U.S. Labor Market: Critical Issues in the New Millennium*, a volume of the Annals of the American Academy of Political and Social Science (Thousand Oaks, Calif.: Sage, 2007). The edited volume features several contributions about African Americans and poor whites.

The effects of race on life chances are vividly portrayed in Claude Brown's autobiographical account *Manchild in the Promised Land* (New York: Signet, 1965) and in the novels of Ralph Ellison, Richard Wright, and James Baldwin. Ellison's *Invisible Man* (New York: Signet, 1953) listens to records of Louis Armstrong playing and singing "What Did I Do to Be So Black and Blue?" sitting in his Harlem basement with 1,369 lights—to convince himself that he really exists in a world where people refuse to see him.

For a blistering critique of global capitalism in general and U.S. policy in particular, see Marxist, multidisciplinary social scientist David Harvey, *The New Imperialism* (New York: Oxford University Press, 2005). With his characteristic sharp analysis, Harvey dissects neoliberalism in *A Brief History of Neoliberalism* (New York: Oxford University Press [2005] 2007).

Historically, many novels have dealt with class. Among the recent crop is *The White Tiger* (New York: Free Press, 2008) by Aravind Adiga; this debut novel won the prestigious English Man Booker Prize in 2008. It explores India's class differences (some say "class struggle") through the story of a village boy who becomes the chauffeur to a rich man. Adiga, 33 years old in 2008, is a global shuffler: He lives in Mumbai, was brought up partly in Australia, studied at Columbia and Oxford, and served as a correspondent for *Time* magazine in India. Of his novel, Adiga said that it attempts "to catch the voice of the…colossal underclass" in India.

The concept of class is rarely dealt with head-on by Hollywood. English professor and social critic Benjamin DeMott, author of *The Imperial Middle: Why Americans Can't Think Straight About Class* (New York: Morrow, 1990), says that "class movies" like *Pretty Woman* (1990), *The Bonfire of the Vanities* (1990), and *Driving Miss Daisy* (1989) don't deal responsibly with class because they obfuscate its realities, particularly the power associated with the upper class.

Here is a sampler of older films and video productions, from varying ideological points of view, that deal with the themes of class and status. Oscar-winning Sally Field portrays a southern textile worker in *Norma Rae* (1979), a liberal film based on a real-life event: a successful unionization effort in a southern mill town. Its view of the world is liberal, not radical. Class difference is the driving force of *Pretty in Pink* (1986), a film that asks this old question: Can a young woman from the wrong side of town fall in love and marry the rich kid? (Old-time radio buffs can hear an earlier version of this question on the soap opera *Our Gal Sunday*.)

A feature-length classic from the Marxist perspective is Henry Bieberman's *Salt of the Earth* (1953). Bieberman, one of the "Hollywood Ten" producers blacklisted during the McCarthy era, weaves together themes of class, ethnic, and gender oppression around the incident of a miners' strike in the Southwest. Fritz Lang's classic silent film *Metropolis* (1927) presents a different ideological message: that workers (representing the "hands") and their bosses (representing the "head") each have a distinct place in society but that to work smoothly together both should be joined by human feeling, or "heart"; the film can be interpreted as a defense of rigid social stratification under capitalism. On the other hand, Stanley Kramer's western *High Noon* (1952) can be interpreted as presenting a contrary message. Critic Pauline Kael called *High Noon* a kind of civics lesson in which the frontier Western town represents a "microcosm of the evils of capitalist society" (in *Kiss Kiss Bang Bang* [New York: Bantam, 1969]).

Among the many films that treat topics of racial, ethnic, and/or gender stratification are *Frozen River* (2008), a film by Courtney Hunt. A classic film, Robert Mulligan's *To Kill a Mockingbird* (1962), deals with small-town prejudice against African Americans. Another classic is *Blue Collar* (1978), director Paul Schrader's hard-hitting drama that suggests that autoworkers were divided against one another on the basis of race, ethnicity, and dreams of upward mobility. At the other end of the ideological spectrum is the Oscar-nominated film *The Pursuit of Happyness* (2006), a modern Horatio Alger story starring Will Smith.

One policy initiative trying to deal with matters of class and race in one city is Washington, D.C.'s experiment in paying children in middle schools to come to class, turn in homework assignments on time, and display "good" behavior. In 2008, D.C. Schools Chancellor Michelle A. Rhee announced the pilot program, to be paid for in conjunction with Harvard University's American Inequity Lab, which studies poverty and race issues.

How class-based privilege and racial/ethnic and religious segregation are perpetuated is the subject of *Members Only: Elite Clubs and the Process of Exclusion* (Lanham, Md.: Rowman & Littlefield, 2008) by Diana Kendall. Sociologist Kendall analyzes how patterns of social exclusion heighten social inequality.

Ageism and the loss of roles in old age are sensitively portrayed in Japanese director Yasujiro Ozu's classic film *Tokyo Story* (1953). This film also shows that stratification by age and isolation of older people are international phenomena.

Gender plays a role in many activities, of course. One that is not so obvious is media use. According to the Pew Research Center for the People & the Press (http://people-press.org/report/?pageid=1068, 2006), there is a "news gender gap." For example, men in the United States "dominate the audience not only for sports news but also for news about science and technology, business and finance, and international affairs. More men than women are also found among those who closely follow news events and people in Washington, DC, as well as among those who say they pay close attention to news about local government."

Cross-culturally, researchers find that women are more nurturing and cooperative than men. But are such enduring gender differences due to evolutionary needs or the social roles they play? Here, researchers disagree. See John Tierney's report on current cross-cultural research in "As Barriers Disappear, Some Gender Gaps Widen," *New York Times* (http://www.nytimes.com/2008/09/09/science/09tier.html?_r=1&th&emc=th&oref=slogin; September 8, 2008). Among other findings, research carried out in more than 60 countries suggests that when men and women take personality tests, some of the old Mars–Venus stereotypes reappear: Typically, women are more cautious, emotionally responsive, cooperative, and nurturing than men.

Thanks to the federal government's Works Progress Administration (WPA) in the 1930s, the themes of class, status, and power decorate the walls of many city buildings, including Coit Tower in San Francisco (Chapter 1). Many artists were supported throughout the Depression by WPA projects.

For works about social stratification in poor countries or among low-income people in rich countries, see Lynn Stephen, *Zapotec Women: Gender, Class, and Ethnicity in Globalized Oaxaca* (Durham, N.C.: Duke University Press, 2005), and best-seller *Nickel and Dimed: On (Not) Getting By in America* (New York: Henry Holt [2002] 2008), in which author Barbara

Ehrenreich describes jobs she took at the bottom of the economic ladder, reporting on how hard it is to survive in the United States on the wages of many jobs such as waitress, Wal-Mart "associate," and cleaning woman.

A very influential novel among young Muslims is Islamic convert Michael Muhammed Knight's *The Taqwacores* (originally self-published in a zine format in 2003 and made into a movie in 2008 by director Eyad Zahra; the movie is a Rumanni Filmworks production). It concerns a fictional Islamic punk rock scene. (The title combines *taqwa*, a Muslim concept of love and fear of Allah, plus a punk rock subgenre, hardcore).

REFERENCES

Andersen, Margaret L., and Patricia Hill Collins, eds. 2006. *Race, Class, and Gender: An Anthology*. Belmont, Calif.: Wadsworth Publishing.

Associated Press. 2004. "Protestant majority disappearing in the United States" (July 21): http://www-news.uchicago.edu/citations/04/040721.protestant-nyt.html

Baltzell, E. Digby. 1958. *Philadelphia Gentlemen: The Making of a National Upper Class*. New York: Free Press.

Bauerlein, Valerie. 2007. "Bank of America rewards CEO." *Wall Street Journal* (March 20):A4.

Beller, Emily, and Michael Hout. 2006. "Intergenerational social mobility: The United States in comparative perspective." *Future of Children* 16(2): http://www.futureofchildren.org/pubs-info2825/pubs-info_show.htm?doc_id=388485

Bernick, Bob, Jr. 2003. "Religion re-enters Salt Lake mayoral race: Pollster Jones says it regained dominant role." *Deseret Morning News* (October 31): http://rickross.com/reference/mormon/mormon128.html

Bourdieu, Pierre. [1979] 2002. *Distinction: A Social Critique of the Judgement of Taste*. Trans. Richard Nice. Cambridge, Mass.: Harvard University Press.

Brown, David. 2006. "Wide gaps found in mortality rates among U.S. groups." *Washington Post* (September 12):A1.

Brown, Elaine. 1992. *A Taste of Power: A Black Woman's Story*. New York: Pantheon.

Burnett, Victoria. 2007. "No borders, or age limits, for 'granny' blogger." *International Herald Tribune* (September 10)8+.

Camp, Sharon. 1988. "Poor, powerless and pregnant." Washington, D.C.: Population Crisis Committee.

Canham, Matt. 2006. "Mormon portion of Utah population steadily shrinking." *Salt Lake City Tribune* (June 22): http://www.sltrib.com/ci_2886596

Cao, Cong. 2004. *China's Scientific Elite*. London: Routledge Curzon.

Caplovitz, David. 1963. *The Poor Pay More: Consumer Practices of Low-Income Families*. New York: Free Press.

Carey, Benedict. 2008. "Tolerance over race can spread, studies find." (November 6): http://www.nytimes.com/2008/11/07/us/07race.html?_r=1&th&emc=th&oref=slogin

CBS News. 2007. "Study: Black pessimism on the rise." (November 13): http://www.cbsnews.com/stories/2007/11/13/national/main3496587.shtml?source=RSSattr=U.S._3496587

Chaddha, Anmol, and William Julius Wilson. 2008. "Reconsidering the 'ghetto.'" *City & Community* 7(4):384–388.

Cheung, Angela M., and Stephen W. Hwang. 2004. "Risk of death among homeless women: a cohort study and review of the literature." *Canadian Medical Association Journal:* http://www.cmaj.ca/cgi/content/full/170/8/1243

Clark, Terry Nichols, and Seymour Martin Lipset, eds. 2001. *The Breakdown of Class Politics: A Debate on Post-Industrial Stratification*. Washington, D.C.: Woodrow Wilson Center Press; Baltimore, Md.: Johns Hopkins University Press.

Coffin, Tristam. 1991. "Hard facts on the American economy." *Washington Spectator* (February 1):1–2.

Coble, Alana Erickson. 2006. *Cleaning Up: The Transformation of Domestic Service in Twentieth Century New York City*. New York: Routledge.

Deutsch, Sarah. 2002. *Women and the City: Gender, Space, and Power in Boston, 1870–1940*. New York: Oxford University Press.

Deveny, Kathleen, with Raina Kelley. 2007. "Girls gone bad?" *Newsweek* (February 12):40–47.

DiMaggio, Paul, and John Mohr. 1985. "Cultural capital, educational attainment, and marital selection." *American Journal of Sociology* 90:1231–1257.

Dollar, David. 2007. "Globalization, poverty and inequality since 1980." Pp. 73–103 in David Held and Ayse Kaya, eds., *Global Inequality*. Malden, Mass.: Polity Press.

Dománski, Henryk. [1996] 2000. *On the Verge of Convergence: Social Stratification in Eastern Europe.* Budapest: Central European University Press.

Domhoff, G. William. 2006. "Wealth, income, and power." (December): http://sociology.ucsc.edu/whorulesamerica/power/wealth.html

Ehrenreich, Barbara [2002] 2008. *Nickel and Dimed: On (Not) Getting By in America.* New York: Holt.

Esping-Andersen, Gøsta. 2007. "More inequality and fewer opportunities? Structural determinants and human agency in the dynamics of income distribution." Pp. 216–251 in David Held and Ayse Kaya, eds., *Global Inequality.* Malden, Mass.: Polity Press.

Fackler, Martin. 2007. "In Japanese quake, elderly are hit hardest." *International Herald Tribune* (July 20):2.

Fernandez, Elizabeth. 2008. "Poverty's 'shocking' impact on health." *San Francisco Chronicle* (April 18):A1+.

Fonda, Daren. 2003. "National prosperous radio." *Time* (March 17): http://www.time.com/time/magazine/article/0,9171,433259-2,00.html

Form, William H., and Gregory P. Stone. 1957. "Urbanism, anonymity and status symbolism." *American Journal of Sociology* 62:504–514.

Fox, Maggie. 2008. "Life expectancy falls in poorer U.S. counties: study." Reuters (April 22): http://www.reuters.com/article/scienceNews/idUSN2146521720080422?pageNumber=2&virtualBrandChannel=0

Fuller, Robert W. 2004. *Somebodies and Nobodies: Overcoming the Abuse of Rank.* Gabriola Island, Canada: New Society Publishers.

Gans, Herbert J. 1974. *Popular Culture and High Culture.* New York: Basic Books.

———. 1999a. "The possibility of a new racial hierarchy in the twenty-first century United States." Pp. 371–390 in Michelle Lamont, ed., *The Cultural Territories of Race.* Chicago: University of Chicago Press.

———. 1999b. "An integration scenario or ending the illusion." *Poverty & Race* (November/December): http:"www.prac.org/full_text.php?text.id+1218&item.id=1830&newsletter.id=47&header=Education

Gates, Henry Louis, Jr. 1994. "The black leadership myth." *New Yorker* (October 24):7–8.

Gerstle, Gary. 1999. "Liberty, coercion, and the making of Americans." Pp. 275–293 in Charles Hirschman, Josh Dewind, and Philip Kasinitz, eds., *The Handbook of International Migration: The American Experience.* New York: Russell Sage Foundation.

Gerth, Hans H., and C. Wright Mills, eds. and trans. 1958. *From Max Weber: Essays in Sociology.* New York: Oxford University Press.

Gill, Graeme J. 1998. "Introduction." Pp. 1–6 in Graeme J. Gill, ed., *Elites and Leadership in Russian Politics: Selected Papers from the Fifth World Congress of Central and East European Studies, Warsaw, 1995.* New York: St. Martin's Press.

Gordon, Milton M. 1978. *Human Nature, Class, and Ethnicity.* New York: Oxford University Press.

Gornick, Vivian. 1994. "Twice an outsider: On being Jewish and a woman." Pp. 117–125 in William Vesterman and Josh Ozersky, eds., *Readings for the 21st Century*, 2nd ed. Needham Heights, Mass.: Allyn & Bacon.

Hartman, Chester, and Gregory D. Squires, eds. 2006. *There Is No Such Thing as a Natural Disaster: Race, Class, and Hurricane Katrina.* New York: Routledge.

Hayden, Dolores. 1981. *The Grand Domestic Revolution.* Cambridge, Mass.: MIT Press.

Healy, Melissa. 1994. "U.S. used poor, sick for testing radiation." *San Francisco Examiner* (January 9):1+.

Heilbroner, Robert L. 1978. "Inescapable Marx." *New York Review of Books* (June 29):33–37.

Held, David, and Ayse Kaya. 2007. "Introduction." Pp. 1–25 in David Held and Ayse Kaya, eds., *Global Inequality.* Malden, Mass.: Polity Press.

Herrnstein, Richard J., and Charles Murray. 1994. *The Bell Curve: Intelligence and Class Structure in American Life.* New York: Free Press.

Hertz, Tom. 2005. "Rags, riches, and race: The intergenerational economic mobility of black and white families in the United States." Pp. 16–191 in Samuel Bowles, Herbert Gintis, and Melissa Osborne Groves, eds., *Unequal Chances: Family Background and Economic Success.* Princeton, N.J.: Princeton University Press.

Hollinger, David A. 1995. *Postethnic America: Beyond Multiculturalism.* New York: Basic Books.

Horowitz, Ruth. 1983. *Honor and the American Dream.* New Brunswick, N.J.: Rutgers University Press.

Howell, Joseph T. [1973] 1991. *Hard Living on Clay Street: Portraits of Blue Collar Families.* Garden City, N.Y.: Doubleday, Anchor.

Huntington, Samuel P. 2004. *Who Are We?: The Challenges to America's National Identity.* New York: Simon & Schuster.

IANS. 2006. "Suicide rate among NY's ethnic women is alarming." *Bio-Medicine* (December 9): http://www.

bio-medicine.org/medicine-news/Suicide-Rate-Among-NYs-Ethnic-Women-is-Alarming-16480–1/

Itzkoff, Seymour W. 1994. *The Decline of Intelligence in America: A Strategy for National Renewal.* Westport, Conn.: Praeger.

Jan, Tracy. 2007. "An imbalance grows in Cambridge schools: Placements based on income, not race." *Boston Globe* (July 23): http://www.boston.com/news/education/k_12/articles/2007/07/23/an_imbalance_grows_in_cambridge_schools/s

Johnson, Dirk. 1991. "Prosperity must make room for diversity in Utah." *New York Times* [national edition] (August 25):A13.

Johnston, David Cay. 2007. "Average incomes fell for most in 2000–5." *New York Times* (August 21): http://www.nytimes.com/2007/08/21/business/21tax.html?_r=1&th&emc=th&oref=slogin

Kahlenberg, Richard D. 2001. "Socioeconomic school integration: A reply to the responses: Is class or race the central inequality in education?" *Poverty & Race Research Action Council* (December 1): http://www.equaleducation.org/commentary.asp?opedid=901

Katznelson, Ira. 1992. *Marxism and the City.* New York: Oxford University Press.

Keister, Lisa A. 2004. *Wealth in America: Trends in Wealth Inequality.* New York: Cambridge University Press.

Kempf, Hervé. 2008. "Science looks at the connection between inequalities and ecology." Reprinted and translated from *Le Monde* (April 11) by truthout.org: http://www.truthout.org/docs_2006/042108H.shtml

Kmietowicz, Zosia. 2001. "Health gap between rich and poor in London widens." *British Medical Journal* 323(7317):828: http://www.pubmedcentral.nih.gov/articlerender.fcgi?artid=1172972

Kogevinas, M., N. Pearce, M. Susser, and P. Boffetta, eds. 1997. "Social inequalities and cancer." Lyon, France: *IARC Scientific Publication* 138.

Kornblum, William. 1974. *Blue Collar Community.* Chicago: University of Chicago Press.

———. 1997. *Sociology in a Changing World,* 4th ed. New York: Harcourt Brace College Publishers.

Kosmin, Barry A., and Seymour P. Lachman. 1993. *One Nation Under God: Religion in Contemporary American Society.* New York: Harmony.

Kosmin, Barry A., and Ariela Keysar. 2006. *Religion in a Free Market: Religious and Non-Religious Americans.* Ithaca, N.Y.: Paramount Market Publishing.

Krieger, Nancy, Jarvis T. Chen, Brent A. Coull, and Joe V. Selby. 2005. "Lifetime socioeconomic position and twins' health: An analysis of 308 pairs of United States women twins." *PLOS Medicine* 2(7):e162 (doi:0.1371/journal.pmed.0020162: http://www.pubmedcentral.nih.gov/articlerender.fcgi?artid=1181870

Kroll, Luisa, and Allison Fass, eds. 2007. "The world's richest people." *Forbes* (March 8): http://www.forbes.com/2007/03/06/billionaires-new-richest_07billionaires_cz_lk_af_0308billieintro.html

Lawner, Lynne, ed. [1932] 1975. *Letters from Prison: Antonio Gramsci.* New York: Harper Colophon.

Lee, Jennifer, and Frank D. Bean. 2007. "Redrawing the color line?" *City & Community* (March):49–62.

Lee, Jennifer, and Min Zhou, eds. 2004. *Asian American Youth: Culture, Identity, and Ethnicity.* New York: Routledge.

Leland, John, and Louis Uchitelle. 2008. "Retirees filling the front line in market fears." *New York Times* (September 23): http://www.nytimes.com/2008/09/23/business/23retirees.html

Lewin, Tamar. 1992. "Study points to increase in intolerance of ethnicity." *New York Times* (January 8):A1+.

Li, Shi, and Hiroshi Sato, eds. 2006. *Unemployment, Inequality and Poverty in Urban China.* New York: Routledge.

Liebold, Linda K. 1988. "Audience 88: A comprehensive analysis of public radio listeners." Washington, D.C.: Corporation for Public Broadcasting.

Liebow, Elliot. 1967. *Tally's Corner: A Study of Negro Streetcorner Men.* Boston: Little, Brown.

Loewen, James W. 1988. *The Mississippi Chinese: Between Black and White,* 2nd ed. Prospect Heights, Ill.: Waveland Press.

———. [2005] 2006. *Sundown Towns: A Hidden Dimension of American Racism.* New York: Touchstone.

Lofland, Lyn H. 1975. "The 'thereness' of women: A selective review of urban sociology." Pp. 144–170 in Marcia Millman and Rosabeth Moss Kanter, eds., *Another Voice: Feminist Perspectives on Social Life and Social Science.* Garden City, N.Y.: Doubleday, Anchor.

Lukas, J. Anthony. 1978. "Review of *Chance and Circumstance.*" *New York Times Book Review* (June 11):9+.

Lynd, Robert S., and Helen Merrell Lynd. [1929] 1956. *Middletown.* New York: Harcourt, Brace & World.

Lyons, Claire A. 2006. *Sex Among the Rabble: An Intimate History of Gender and Power in the Age of Revolution,*

Philadelphia, 1730–1830. Chapel Hill: University of North Carolina Press.

Mabry, Marcus. 2008. "Race and politics: Obama tests politics in a changing land." *International Herald Tribune* (June 8):6.

Mackenzie, Suzanne. 1989. "Women in the city." Pp. 109–126 in Richard Peet and Nigel Thrift, eds., *New Models in Geography: The Political-economy Perspective*, vol. 2. London: Unwin Hyman.

Marmot, Michael. [2004] 2005. *The Status Syndrome: How Social Standing Affects Our Health and Longevity.* New York: Owl Books.

Massey, Douglas S. 2007. *Categorically Unequal: The American Stratification System.* New York: Russell Sage Foundation.

McCord, Colin, and Howard P. Freeman. 1990. "Excess mortality in Harlem." *New England Journal of Medicine* 322(3):173–177.

McLellan, David, ed. 1977. *Karl Marx: Selected Writings.* New York: Oxford University Press.

Meng, Xin. 2006. "Economic restructuring and income inequality in urban China." Pp. 65–89 in Shi Li and Hiroshi Sato, eds., *Unemployment, Inequality and Poverty in Urban China.* New York: Routledge.

Miller, Matthew, and Tatiana Serafin. 2006. "The 400 richest Americans." *Forbes* (September 21): http://www.forbes.com/lists/2006/54/biz_06rich400_The-400-Richest-Americans_land.html

Muntaner, Carles, W. C. Hadden, and N. Kravets. 2004. "Social class, race/ethnicity and all-cause mortality in the US: longitudinal results from the 1986–1994 National Health Interview Survey." *European Journal of Epidemiology* 19(8):777–784.

Nasr, Vali. 2008. "Iran and the future of the Middle East." Talk, Fletcher School of Law and Diplomacy's 7th annual Talloires Symposium (May 30–June 1), Tufts European Center at Talloires, France.

Nutini, Hugo G. 2005. *Social Stratification and Mobility in Central Veracruz.* Austin: University of Texas Press.

O'Hagan, Sean. 2005. "A radical returns." *The Observer* (April 3):http://observer.guardian.co.uk/review/story/0,,1450864,00.html

"The Perspectives." 2006. *Newsweek* (November 20):33.

Pace, David. 2005. "AP: More blacks live with pollution." Associated Press, Netscape News (December 13).

Petras, James. 2007. "Global ruling class: Billionaires and how they 'made it'." (March 20): http://www.atlanticfreepress.com/content/view/1212/81/ace

Phillips, Kevin P. 1990. "Reagan's America: A capital offense." *New York Times Magazine* (June 17):26+.

Piazza Tom, senior survey statistician, UC Berkeley's Survey Research Center, Berkeley, CA, 2008. Personal communication: (July 8)

Piketty, Thomas, and Emmanuel Saez. 2006. "Thomas Piketty and Emmanuel Saez respond to Alan Reynolds." (December 20): http://economistsview.typepad.com/economistsview/2007/01/thomas_piketty_.html

Pogge, Thomas W. 2007. "Why inequality matters." Pp. 132–147 in David Held and Ayse Kaya, eds., *Global Inequality.* Malden, Mass.: Polity Press.

Rieder, Jonathan. 1985. *Canarsie: The Jews and Italians of Brooklyn Against Liberalism.* Cambridge, Mass.: Harvard University Press.

Roberts, Sam. 2007. "Reversal in wage gap between sexes." *International Herald Tribune* (August 4–5):1.

Rushton, J. Philippe. 1994. *Race, Evolution, and Behavior: A Life History Perspective.* New Brunswick, N.J.: Transaction Books.

Rutherford, Brent, and Gerda Wekerle. 1988. "Captive rider, captive labor: Spatial constraints and women's employment." *Urban Geography* 9:116–137.

Saunders, Peter. 1981. *Social Theory and the Urban Question.* London: Hutchinson.

Senneker, Harold, with Dolores Lataniotis. 1990. "The richest people in America: The Forbes 400." *Forbes* (October 22).

"Sex harassment a global problem." 1992. *San Francisco Chronicle* (December 1):C1+.

Shafak, Elif. 2007. Interview with Terry Gross, *Fresh Air*, NPR, KALW radio, 9:00 a.m. (February 6).

Shapiro, Thomas M. 2005. *The Hidden Cost of Being African American: How Wealth Perpetuates Inequality.* New York: Oxford University Press.

Simpson, Ida Harper, David Stark, and Robert A. Jackson. 1988. "Class identification processes of married, working men and women." *American Sociological Review* 53:284–293.

Song, Jesook. 2006. "Family breakdown and invisible homeless women: Neoliberal governance during the Asian debt crisis in South Korea, 1997–2001." *East Asia Cultures Critique* 14(1):37–65.

Stern, David Alan. 2007. *Talk of the Nation.* NPR (March 26).

Swarns, Rachel L. 2008. "Obama's careful take on affirmative action: Candidate focuses on class in America." *International Herald Tribune* (August 4):4.

Thernstrom, Stephan. 1965. "'Yankee City' revisited: The perils of historical naiveté." *American Sociological Review* 30:234–242.

Toner, Robin. 2007. "New economic populism spurs Democrats." *New York Times* (July 16): http://www.nytimes.com/2007/07/16/us/politics/16populist.html?th&emc=th

Treiman, Donald J. 1977. *Occupational Prestige in Comparative Perspective.* New York: Academic Press.

Treiman, Donald J., and Harry B. G. Ganzeboom. 2000. "The fourth generation of comparative stratification research." Pp. 123–150 in Stella R. Quah and Arnaud Sales, eds., *The International Handbook of Sociology.* London: Sage.

Uchitelle, Louis. 2007. "Age of riches: The richest of the rich, proud of a new Gilded Age." *New York Times* (July 15): http://www.nytimes.com/2007/07/15/business/15gilded.html?th&emc=th

U.S. Bureau of the Census. 1977. *Social Indicators 1976.* Washington, D.C.: Government Printing Office.

———. 2005. *The 2005 Current Population Survey Annual Social and Economic Supplement.* Washington, D.C.: Government Printing Office.

US–China Business Council. 2006. "China's economy." (October): http://www.uschina.org/info/chops/2006/china-economy.html

"Used cars: The poor get poorer." 1978. *New York Times* (June 18):F17.

Vaca, Nicholas C. 2004. *The Presumed Alliance: The Unspoken Conflict Between Latinos and Blacks and What It Means for America .* New York: Rayo.

Wallerstein, Immanuel. 2004. *World-Systems Analysis: An Introduction.* Durham, N.C.: Duke University Press.

———. [1974] 1980. *The Modern World-System I: Capitalist Agriculture and the Origins of the European World-Economy in the Sixteenth Century.* New York: Academic Press.

Warner, W. Lloyd, et al. [1941] 1963. *Yankee City,* abridged. New Haven, Conn.: Yale University Press.

———. [1949] 1964. *Democracy in Jonesville: A Study in Quality and Inequality.* New York: Harper Torchbooks.

Weber, Max. [1904–1905] 1958. *The Protestant Ethic and the Spirit of Capitalism.* New York: Scribner.

———. [1922] 1958. "Class, status, party." Pp. 180–195 in Hans H. Gerth and C. Wright Mills, eds. and trans. *From Max Weber: Essays in Sociology.* New York: Oxford University Press.

Wheeler, David L. 1994. "An ominous legacy of the atomic age." *Chronicle of Higher Education* (January 12):A6–A7.

Wilson, William Julius. 1973. *Power, Racism and Privilege.* New York: Macmillan.

———. 1978. *The Declining Significance of Race: Blacks and Changing American Institutions.* Chicago: University of Chicago Press.

———. 2009. *More than Just Race: Being Black and Poor in the Inner City.* New York: W.W. Norton.

Wolff, Edward N. [1995] 2002. *Top Heavy: The Increasing Inequality of Wealth in America and What Can Be Done About It,* 2nd ed. New York: New Press.

Women in London. n.d. "Fawcett: Ethnic minority women councillors: Swimming against the tide." http://www.womeninlondon.org.uk/notices/fawcett071029.htm

Wright, Erik Olin. 2000. *Class Counts: Comparative Studies in Class Analysis,* student ed. Cambridge: Cambridge University Press.

———. 1978. "Race, class and income inequality." *American Journal of Sociology* 83:1368–1397.

———. 1985. *Classes.* London: Verso.

Wright, Erik Olin, ed. 2005. *Approaches to Class Analysis.* Cambridge: Cambridge University Press.

Wright, Erik Olin, et al. 1989. *The Debate on Classes.* London: Verso.

Wright, Erik Olin, and Bill Martin. 1987. "The transformation of the American class structure, 1960–80." *American Journal of Sociology* 93:1–29.

Wright, Kai. 2008. "The subprime swindle." *The Nation* (June 26): http://www.thenation.com/doc/20080714/wright

Yancey, George. 2003. *Who Is White?: Latinos, Asians, and the New Black/Nonblack Divide.* Boulder, Colo.: Lynne Rienner.

Ystie, John. 2007. "Does wealth imbalance threaten society's fabric?" *All Things Considered,* NPR, KALW radio (February 5).

CHAPTER 12

DISCOVERING THE RULES

Pedestrians push their way pell-mell through a busy intersection. Subway riders grab the first empty seat they see. Bar patrons sit in a quiet corner to avoid conversation. Automatic teller machine (ATM) users look bored as they await their turn in silence.

Or so it may seem at first glance. But appearances are often deceiving. This is especially the case in face-to-face encounters with urban or suburban strangers.

This chapter looks behind some of those appearances. It focuses on everyday, routine activities of urban life—walking down a busy street in the central business district (CBD), riding public transporta-

tion, meeting people in a bar. Looking closely at such ordinary activities is not easy, precisely because they are so ordinary. We tend to take them for granted and not subject them to analysis. After all, what adult in the United States thinks twice about the proper way to ride a subway or walk down a city street? We know how to accomplish these tasks without thinking! In other words, these actions seem natural.

Here, I treat these "natural" behaviors as curious, problematic, and not at all natural. It is as if we are visitors in a strange, exotic country, prepared to suffer culture shock from exposure to a totally unfamiliar way of life. But geographically, we don't have to move anywhere. Instead, we'll be "traveling" along familiar city streets and perhaps making some startling discoveries.

My aim is to illuminate how routine social interaction takes place and why it happens as it does. This is not as easy as it may seem. As George Orwell famously put it, "To see what is in front of your nose is a constant struggle."

Guiding us on this mystery tour of the familiar will be the insights of a variety of sharp observers. These include social scientists, filmmakers, and tourist guidebook writers.

TAKING A FRESH LOOK AT THE FAMILIAR

In studying urban **social interaction**, we are mostly studying ourselves—our friends and families, workmates, and fellow students—or groups of people about whom we have already formed some opinion. For this reason, it is harder to examine ourselves with detachment than it is to study a foreign culture; we hold fewer preconceived notions and moral judgments about "proper" behavior patterns in faraway lands.

Suspending these assumptions long enough to see our own culture objectively is difficult. That is one reason anthropologists have tended to scrutinize other cultures, not their own. It is also one reason foreigners have provided some of the most astute observations about U.S.culture.

This holds for comic (even if phony) visitors too. Take, for example, Sacha Baron Cohen's 2006 mockumentary, *Borat*. In this politically incorrect send-up of many groups in the United States and in Kazakhstan, British comic Cohen breaks the rules of etiquette, polite conversation, and dress code, among others, making the audience often recognize its own foibles, wince, then laugh.

Indeed, comedians often take a fresh look at the familiar. For one, Jerry Seinfeld's very popular TV series (NBC, 1990–1998 and in syndication) specializes in such comedy. This show "about nothing" ranked number one on *TV Guide*'s 2002 list of "50 Greatest Shows of All Time." (http://www.sonypictures.com/tv/shows/seinfeld/about/).

For most of us, however, it may be difficult (even painful) emotionally to take a fresh look at familiar surroundings. Yet, it can be enlightening.

Anthropologist Horace Miner (1956) and community activist Beverly Slapin (1990) examined parts of their own society using a trained eye, tongue in cheek, and active funnybone (Box 12.1). How many of us could so dispassionately record our own rites, such as the "ritual fasts to make fat people thin and ceremonial feasts to make thin people fat"? It takes discipline and humor to look at ourselves as if *we* are the curious beings.

PEDESTRIAN BEHAVIOR

Since that is our mission—to look closely at the everyday activities of people in urban places—let's begin with an impressive but usually unnoticed feature of city life: the large numbers of total strangers that urbanites encounter daily. Standing on a busy street corner in San Francisco's CBD, for instance, my students counted 4,000 passersby within 1 hour. (Some count many more on one midtown block in Manhattan—about 38,000 pedestrians pass by on an average weekday.)

It is also impressive that pedestrians move in and around the CBD smoothly, with few scuffles or other incidents. But we take this for granted. Does anyone applaud the fact that pedestrians actually reach their destination without knocking each other down or holding up traffic? No, we just expect it.

We in the United States also expect that when we step off a busy street corner, we'll reach the other side of the street without mishap. Upon reflection, however, crossing a busy street is no small accomplishment. Three or four hundred strangers may be marching toward you; armies of unknown people are edging up from behind, all walking at different speeds; cars may be careening into your path; broken glass or dog excrement may be lying in wait. In this potentially dangerous battlefield, crossing the street now seems like a high-risk venture, not a routine activity. And indeed, it can be a high-risk venture: An average of 60 people are killed while trying to cross the street—and hundreds more are injured—in Chicago every year (NBC-TV, 2008).

Still, crossing the street is a routine event. Why? Because in the United States we expect that other pedestrians will follow the "rules of the game" and be competent game players. Like so many everyday activities, street crossing is governed by rules that are widely shared within any culture. These culturally shared rules (**norms**) are often implicit and hidden, but they exist nonetheless. If they didn't, the simple act of crossing a busy street would be impossible.

In the United States, most children learn explicit rules for being good pedestrians: "Cross on the green; wait on the red," "Look both ways before crossing," "Keep your head up," and "Watch out for open

---

BOX 12.1   STRANGE TRIBAL RITES REVEALED!

Body Ritual Among the Nacirema

[The Nacirema] are a North American group living in the territory between the Canadian Cree, the Yaqui and Tarahumare of Mexico, and the Carib and Arawak of the Antilles....

According to Nacirema mythology, their nation was originated by a culture hero, Notgnihsaw, who is otherwise known for two great feats of strength—the throwing of a piece of wampum across the river Pa-To-Mac and the chopping down of a cherry tree in which the Spirit of Truth resided.

Nacirema culture is characterized by a highly developed market economy that has evolved in a rich natural habitat. While much of the people's time is devoted to economic pursuits, a large part of the fruits of these labors and a considerable portion of the day are spent in ritual activity. The focus of this activity is the human body, the appearance and health of which loom as a dominant concern in the ethos of the people....

The fundamental belief underlying the whole system appears to be that the human body is ugly, and that its natural tendency is to debility and disease. Incarcerated in such a body, man's only hope is to avert these characteristics through the use of the powerful influences of ritual and ceremony. Every household has one or more shrines devoted to this purpose. The more powerful individuals in the society have several shrines in their houses, and, in fact, the opulence of a house is often referred to in terms of the number of such ritual centers it possesses.

...The focal point of the shrine is a box or chest, which is built into the wall. In this chest are kept the many charms and magical potions without which no native believes he could live. These preparations are secured from a variety of specialized practitioners. The most powerful of these are the medicine men, whose assistance must be rewarded with substantial gifts....

...In the hierarchy of magical practitioners, and below the medicine men in prestige, are specialists whose designation is best translated "holy-mouth-men." The Nacirema have an almost pathological horror of, and fascination with, the mouth, the condition of which is believed to have a supernatural influence on all social relationships. Were it not for the rituals of the mouth, they believe that their teeth would fall out, their gums bleed, their jaws shrink, their friends desert them, and their lovers reject them....

In conclusion, mention must be made of certain practices that...depend upon the pervasive aversion to the natural body and its functions. There are ritual fasts to make fat people thin and ceremonial feasts to make thin people fat. Still other rites are used to make women's breasts larger if they are small, and smaller if they are large. General dissatisfaction with breast shape is symbolized in the fact that the ideal form is virtually outside the range of human variation. A few women afflicted with almost inhuman hypermammary development are so idolized that they make a handsome living by simply going from village to village and permitting the natives to stare at them for a fee.

...Our review of the ritual life of the Nacirema has certainly shown them to be a magic-ridden people. It is hard to understand how they have managed to exist so long under the burdens they have imposed upon themselves.

Source: Horace Miner, "Body Ritual Among the Nacirema," *American Anthropologist* 58(1956):503–507. Reproduced by permission of the American Anthropological Association from the *American Anthropologist*, 58(3), 1956, and the author. Copyright 1956 by the American Anthropological Association.

Caucasian American Religion, Ceremonies, and Beliefs

There were many different beliefs among the Caucasian American people. Some of them were strange, and some were humorous. Caucasian Americans believed in a supernatural power. They needed it for success in making money and in warfare. For some Caucasian Americans, this supernatural power could be called on in times of great stress. For instance, if a Caucasian American male stubbed his toe or lost in a baseball pool, he was often heard to yell, "Jesus Christ!" (jee'-sus-kryst').

Caucasian American ceremonies were usually of a religious nature. Some ceremonies were for young Caucasian Americans to show their courage by going through torture.

One of the most bizarre of their rituals, the Sacred Yuppie Jogging Ceremony, involved holy footware emblazoned with the legend "Nike" (Ni-kee), assumed to be the name of one of their gods. This legend, along with its symbol, was found on many items of their clothing, mostly footware. These artifacts were involved with their early morning "jogging" (jog'ging) ceremony, thought to be the only ritual in which they attempted to demonstrate their oneness with nature.

Source: Beverley Slapin, *Basic Skills Caucasian American Workbook* (Berkeley, Calif.: Oyate). 1990. Reproduced by permission of Beverly Slapin.

manhole covers." Other rules are not made explicit. For example, how many of us are aware that we follow definite walking patterns? Pedestrians can take any path to get across a busy street, but they don't. Looking at films of people walking down a midtown Manhattan street one block from Times Square, Michael Wolff (1973) found several interesting walking patterns, including the following:

1. In low-density pedestrian traffic, walkers detour from their original path to avoid bumping into another person; after the other person passes, the walkers return to their original path.
2. In high-density pedestrian traffic, there's no room to step completely around an oncoming walker. Thus, to accommodate people coming in the opposite direction, pedestrians use a range of almost imperceptible actions. One maneuver, used especially to avoid bumping into members of the same sex, is the "step-and-slide" (39). Here, a person slightly angles the body, turns the shoulder, and takes a tiny side step.

Now, what happens if a person is a "bad" (incompetent) pedestrian? Usually, dirty looks or sharp words follow. If, for example, a person doesn't execute the step-and-slide maneuver in dense traffic and thus jostles another pedestrian, the jostled party might say something like "Whatsamatter, ya blind?" Such comments suggest that the jostler violated the rules of the game.

To discover people's expectations about routine activities, like walking down the street, researchers try deliberately to break the rules of the game. That's the way Wolff gathered his data. He designed an experiment which aimed at purposefully disrupting routine behaviors. For instance, his experimenters would stay on a straight-line collision course with an oncoming pedestrian. Cameras hidden from view recorded the surprised and shocked reactions of the oncoming pedestrians to this unexpected behavior.

What Wolff concluded from the experiment in New York City is that *cooperation, not competition* (i.e., *not* each person for him- or herself), *is the general rule shared by U.S. pedestrians.* They expect that others will look around and notice who is coming toward them. And they expect that other pedestrians will cooperate

to avoid contact and inconvenience to the other (Wolff, 1973:40).

It turns out, then, that appearances are deceiving; few pedestrians push pell-mell through a busy intersection. Instead, at least in the United States, they avoid collision courses, estimate what moves and countermoves to take, and monitor the immediate environment for problems. And all within a nanosecond!

Few studies of pedestrian behavior exist. Luckily, two are gems, and both come from the late William H. Whyte: "The Skilled Pedestrian" ([1988] 1990) and "New York and Tokyo: A Study in Crowding" (1978). In the first study, Whyte talks about New York walkers the way Hemingway described bullfighters—as people showing grace under pressure: "With the subtlest of motions they signal their intentions to one another—shift of the eyes, a degree or so off axis, a slight move of the hand, a wave of a folded newspaper" (60).

Whyte's comparative study of New York and Tokyo deals with the pedestrian environments of two of the world's largest cities. He concluded that, despite cultural differences, New York and Tokyo pedestrians act a great deal alike:

1. New Yorkers and Tokyoites are highly skilled pedestrians. "They navigate adroitly."
2. Both walk fast. Whyte notes that people in big cities walk faster than people in smaller cities, and this holds true worldwide. The reason is unclear. A social psychologist (Milgram, 1970) thought that the fast pace in very large cities is related to "stimulus overload," a bombardment of stimuli that apparently encourages people to speed up to seek relief. Others maintain that the stimulus overload encourages people in very large cities to walk faster so that they can take advantage of more stimuli that the city offers.
3. Both cooperate to avoid collisions, but "Tokyo's pedestrians are in a class by themselves." The scene that Whyte paints of apparent chaos at a major subway station in Tokyo is instructive:

By all accepted density standards [Shinjuku subway station] is a manifest impossibility....[A]t the rush hours, when the pedestrian traffic reaches an intensity unmatched anywhere, the scene appears chaotic. But it isn't. Somehow, people sort themselves out and for all the density the pedestrian speeds remain quite high; indeed, it is at rush hour that one sees the most running. By rights, people should be bumping into each other all over the place. They don't seem to....

(Whyte, 1978:8–9)

If we think inductively, these micro-observations by Whyte and Wolff suggest certain hypotheses about city life:

1. *Crowding in one's immediate physical presence positively affects how one behaves.*

This hypothesis is all the more interesting because the effects are not in the expected direction.

That is, it is widely believed that crowding is bad for people, that it can debilitate them psychologically. Yet, pedestrians in crowded situations seem to cooperate and, as Whyte's impressions of Tokyo suggest, even to enjoy themselves. (*Note:* Years after Whyte wrote about Shinjuku Station, it was the target of a foiled nerve gas attack. Had it succeeded, real chaos might have ensued; at least 10,000 persons could have died. What impact such terrorism is having on Shinjuku pedestrians is unclear.) Further, in crowded situations urbanites don't seem nearly as indifferent to the needs of others as Wirth implies they should be in "Urbanism as a Way of Life" ([1938] 1969).

Fig. 12.2 WHY DON'T THEY KNOCK EACH OTHER DOWN? The rule of pedestrian behavior in the United States is cooperation, not competition or selfish disregard for others. (Tim Teninty)

2. *Mutual trust—not distrust—is the norm in urban public places.*

That trust, not distrust, is the norm is indicated by people's reactions to violations of trust (e.g., following a collision course while walking down the street): surprise and disbelief. If distrust were the norm, pickpockets could not operate on a busy street. Pedestrians would clutch their valuables. If bumped into, they would assume an evil intent (not incompetence) and call for help.

These hypotheses fit into a larger theoretical framework. According to the late sociologist Erving Goffman, pedestrian traffic codes constitute one of many sets of ground rules that "provide the normative bases of public order" in the United States (1971:5). This means that social order in a crowded city can be maintained only if people don't aggress against one another. Rules (norms) help people adjust to each other's behavior and know what to expect of each other. This allows undisrupted interaction between strangers.

To conclude: Here are two discoveries we have made on this short trip down city streets in the United States:

1. *Routine interaction in public places embodies unspoken but widely shared understandings or rules.* These rules are not usually brought to conscious awareness by members of the culture. If someone violates the rules, others react with disbelief or disapproval.

2. *Shared social understandings are the basis of public order.* Without such rules or norms, other people's actions would be unpredictable and thus frightening or threatening; people would hardly be confident that their own routine goals (like walking to the store) could be reached. If the cement of public order—mutual trust—crumbled, a city would be a battlefield where every stranger constituted a potential threat.

A note on mass violence: Terrorists and revolutionaries understand that distrust can unglue public order. As a founder of The Order (a white racist, Christian organization) told the FBI, he hoped for "anything that would disrupt society in America" so that he would be able to "gather up his army of men and strike against

the system, that being the United States government" (in Ridgeway, 1990:91). Indeed, after the Oklahoma City bombing in 1995, security in all U.S. federal buildings nationwide was beefed up, and Internal Revenue Service employees in the Bay Area, California, were advised to suspend the norm of trust: "Get in the habit of regularly looking around your area for anything suspicious" (Internal Revenue Service, 1995).

In brief, then, terrorist attacks in cities worldwide—whether Mumbai, Baghdad, New York, Madrid, Tokyo, or London—have killed and maimed human beings. And, these acts threatened the norm of trust upon which modern cities everywhere are anchored.

Terrorist violence anywhere is uniquely chilling for several reasons: (1) its targets are often random and (2) it is an attack on social structure as well as individuals. Still, it is important to note that fear and anger may not be the only reactions to mass violence. Many people—far beyond those who have been personally harmed by terrorism, whether in Europe, the United States, Africa, Asia, or elsewhere—share a sense of outrage. This collective outrage, as the eminent sociologist Emile Durkheim ([1895] 1982) wrote long ago, can forge a stronger sense of social solidarity.

SUBWAY BEHAVIOR

On U.S. city streets, it is a common understanding that pedestrians will keep their heads up, scan the environment, and adjust their behavior according to the needs of others. Do the same rules apply below the city streets, on subways?

Just as in the case of walking on the city streets, most of us are unaware that there are rules for riding public transportation—until somebody violates them. That is, riding a bus or subway is such a routine activity that we take it for granted. As ethnomethodologist Harold Garfinkel put it, familiar settings (like subways) are full of "'seen but unnoticed,' expected background features" (1967:36).

Again, our task is to bring these background features into the foreground; our approach, as before, is to treat the familiar as unusual and problematic. In this way we are doing **ethnography**—that is, studying a community's culture by participant-observation. Our job is to decode the verbal and nonverbal messages that people send each other and to describe behavior appropriate to the situation (e.g., riding a subway).

"Appropriate" behavior is culturally relative. What is appropriate in one culture may be out of place in another. Take, for instance, driving and train behavior. For example, rules of the road in Thailand (not in the United States) include transferring hierarchical power to motor vehicles themselves. Big trucks and bulldozers are at the top of the hierarchy; buses are in the middle; cars, motorcycles, and bikes are at the bottom. Thai norms of courtesy (e.g., deference to superiors, conflict avoidance) are often suspended after an accident. Further, as one tourist guidebook puts it, "Driving is on the left, most of the time" (Cooper and Cooper, 1996:205).

Traveling by train (not first class) through Greece, to take another example, is not like train behavior in the United States. In Greece, a passenger can expect some variation on the following scene: passengers sharing whatever food and wine they have with strangers in their compartment, babies nursing at their mothers' breasts, chickens squeezed in the compartment and noisily peeping, smugglers trying to peddle their wares, and people sleeping amid the commotion. In contrast, on U.S. trains, one expects to be casually noticed by other passengers but left alone.

The same is true of American subways. Subway riders expect to be treated with what Erving Goffman called "**civil inattention**." To be civilly inattentive, "one gives to another enough visual notice to demonstrate that one appreciates that the other is present (and that one admits openly to having seen him), while at the next moment withdrawing one's attention from him so as to express that he does not constitute a target of special curiosity or design" (Goffman, 1963:84).

Civil inattention takes various forms. Researchers who conducted participant-observation in Boston and New York City subways found that some riders bury their heads in a newspaper and others stare into space, look straight ahead without expression, or daydream.

Under certain circumstances, the general rule of civil inattention on subways can be suspended. Subway

Fig. 12.3 CIVIL INATTENTION IN THE NEW YORK SUBWAY. In 1938, distinguished photographer Walker Evans started taking surreptitious photos of New York City subway riders. Here, he captures some vacant faces associated with proper behavior on public transport. (*Many Are Called* by Walker Evans, Introduction by James Agee. Copyright © 1966 by Walker Evans. Reprinted by permission of Houghton Mifflin Company)

riders may smile or show openness to others they consider nonthreatening. This category includes children and matronly, middle-aged housewives. That middle-aged women—who look like housewives—constitute no threat is a revealing insight into our culture.

Civil inattention also comes into play when choosing a seatmate in the subway car. People tend to grab the first empty seat they see. But there is another consideration, especially for women: Which potential seatmate looks least threatening? People look for self-contained persons who show civil inattention. When choosing among equally self-contained and civilly inattentive persons, riders tend to sit down next to members of their own sex. This observation qualifies the first impression that subway riders sit in the nearest vacant seat. It also raises fascinating questions about trust levels between the sexes.

What purposes does civil inattention serve? It is one device urbanites use "for immunizing themselves against the personal claims and expectations of others" (Wirth [1938] 1969:153). It may also serve as a mechanism of social control, keeping potentially dangerous situations from happening. When strangers aren't sure of each other's intentions, civil inattention helps to promote privacy and to maintain public order. In other words, the rule of civil inattention protects personal rights and keeps the correct social distance between strangers who are temporarily put together.

What happens if civil inattention fails to sustain proper social distance? Sometimes authorities impose explicit rules. Such is the case in Cairo, Egypt, and Mexico City. Cairo's subway system, completed in 1987, sets aside the first car of each train for women only, to help protect them from the constant peril of male sexual harassment. (*Note*: This policy has its local critics; most fear that gender segregation humiliates women, treating them as weak and subordinate.) In Mexico City, which carries about double the number of passengers as New York City's transit system, "women-only" bus service comes with large pink signs.

EAVESDROPPING: URBANITES AS SPIES

Bystanders may pretend to be civilly inattentive—by reading a newspaper, for example—to cover up a common covert activity: eavesdropping. In a subway car,

elevator, restaurant, gym, or other place where people congregate, a person may appear totally uninvolved, all the while listening intently to strangers' conversations. Why? Perhaps eavesdropping soothes the troubled soul; it allows us to peek into other people's lives and problems without taking any responsibility for them. And it is a low-risk, no-cost activity. Besides, overheard stories can rival soap operas for tantalizing plots. Whatever the reasons for covert listening, the fact is that people do eavesdrop. This suggests that Wirth's ([1938] 1969) "uncaring urbanite" may not be that blasé after all.

Distinguished photographer Walker Evans (1903–1975) (see opening photo in this chapter) once advised us all to engage in relatively safe urban activities that can teach us something, including eavesdropping: "Stare, pry, listen, eavesdrop. Die knowing something. You are not here long" (http://www.photoquotes.com/ShowQuotes.aspx?id=196&name=Evans,Walker).

BAR BEHAVIOR

Within any culture, "proper" social distance varies with the social context. In the United States, strangers keep their distance on subways. But they don't in a bar. The bar is one setting where the proper social distance is considerably less than in a subway.

In a bar, the general rule of civil inattention is suspended. Whereas idle glances on a subway show that a person is closed to social interaction, researchers have found that the same kinds of glances in a bar demonstrate a person's openness. In a bar, almost no patrons bury their heads in a newspaper or book. But if they do, this gesture can serve to open conversation, not close off the possibility, as in a subway. As Sherri Cavan observed while researching her ethnography of bar behavior *Liquor License*: "A middle-aged woman was sitting by herself, thumbing through a large book of Steinberg cartoons. A man sitting at the other end of the bar came over, asked her what she was looking at and then joined her" ([1966] 1973:144). In other words, what might ensure civil inattention in the subway or other settings can be an overture for social interaction in a bar.

If a person enters a tavern alone and wishes to remain alone, he or she will usually sit at the bar, not an empty table, and will sit in a particular way.

According to Cavan, the solitary drinker—who is not open to social interaction—shows the intention to stay closed off by minimizing the physical space he or she occupies. Typically, a man will "sit with his forearms either resting on the edge of the bar, or flat on the bar before him, his upper torso hunched slightly forward over the bar, with all of his drinking accoutrements (drink, cigarettes, change, ashtray, and the like) contained within the area before him" ([1966] 1973:144–145). This posture serves to protect the solitary drinker from eye contact with others (one signal of openness in a bar).

As in many urban settings, what's deemed "proper" behavior differs for males and females. Singles bars, for example, are more open to heterosexual women as participants than more "male-defined" drinking places such as cocktail bars. Yet women in singles bars rarely initiate conversation with a male stranger. Why? Because, according to researcher Mary Jo Deegan, "In general, women who frequent singles bars are generally supportive of traditional male–female relationships....Women uninterested in maintaining these traditional rituals [e.g., responding to male overtures rather than initiating social interaction] do not attend these bars" (1989:44).

Ty Wenzel (2004) saw bar behavior from a different perspective: behind the bar. A former bartender in New York City's East Village for 10 years, she categorizes bar regulars like this:

Expert, Name-Dropper, Snacker (noshes olives and cherries out of the garnish tray)
Babbler chats obliviously through a rush at the bar)
Big Spender (blows cash on everyone except the bartender)
Wall Street types and frat boys ("They act like they're made of money - until the tip")...
(Her favorite) *Floorshows* ("People always try to get them drunk to see what they'll do")

Wenzel does not use the same terms as a trained ethnographer. But her conclusions echo those of sociologist Cavan: Some bar patrons (e.g., "Floorshows") suspend the norm of civil inattention more than others.

To conclude: When people enter a bar in the United States, they are expected to be sociable, not civilly inattentive. If they don't want to be sociable, they have to send body-language signals for privacy (in subways, it's the opposite; people have to send signals for openness). But the solitary drinker is the exception in a bar, for "sociability is the most general rule in the public drinking place. Although the bar is typically populated primarily by strangers, interaction is available to all those who choose to enter" (Cavan, [1966] 1973:143).

Why is it that in most urban public settings in the United States civil inattention serves to limit contact among strangers while sociability is the norm in bars? Cavan thinks this norm is associated with the idea that bars aren't really serious places. Instead, they are considered a setting for a time-out from life's important concerns. Thus, she argues, what might seem threatening or dangerous in a more serious place appears nonthreatening in a bar (Cavan, [1966] 1973:154).

ATM BEHAVIOR

Waiting in line seems to be a quintessentially urban experience, at least in the United States. Sometimes we speak to total strangers. Waiting to see the Chicago Cubs or a hip-hop artist, fans often chat with strangers; shared enthusiasm in a queue that some of my former students (Mimi Gasich, Leslie Hamilton, Jacqueline Leung, Alyson Steele, and Kathryn Van Ploeg)once called an "aficionado line" can create a momentary bond of communality and trust (unpublished data, 1989).

More often, however, people avoid social interaction with strangers in line. This is particularly the case if money is involved. A prime example is ATM behavior.

ATMs are popular in many countries, notably for their convenience. In India, for example, an estimated 60 percent of bank customers use their ATMs at least once a week (BanknetIndia, 2007).

In the United States, cash withdrawal is the primary reason people go to ATMs. And do they go! In one year—1996—there were an estimated 18.2 million+ ATM transactions each month. Since then, an economist at the Federal Reserve Bank in St. Louis estimates that the number of transactions is increasing about 18.6 percent—per *month* (Neely, 1997).

ATMs are not trouble-free. According to a Department of Justice online report (Scott, n.d.), bank

Fig. 12.4 QUEUEING BEHAVIOR. Normally, waiting in line is not fun. But there are exceptions, such as "aficionado lines" (e.g., fans waiting for their favorite singer to appear) and lines where bus riders can lean on sculpture while waiting, as in Seattle's Fremont section (Harvey Bragdon)

surveys suggest that a robbery occurs in every 1 to 3.5 million transactions. The elderly and frail are special targets in the United States.

Sometimes it's easier to walk off with the entire ATM. For instance, in France, an ATM robbery took place a few years ago in St. Cirq Lapopie, a beautifully-preserved medieval village. Robbers didn't just take the money inside; they lifted the entire ATM. It was not replaced.

Globally, most ATM robberies occur between the hours of midnight and 4:00 a.m. Despite such risk, transactions at ATMS worldwide increase at all hours.

Typically, patrons wait in line before transacting business. What do they do while waiting? What they *don't* do is talk to each other. As one observer put it, "What we do at ATMs is engage in a very private act—intercourse with our money in public....Comrades in ATM lines must not speak. In the sidewalk temple of money, it's crude to draw attention to the intimate commercial transaction going on nearby, in plain sight" (Mandel, 1988:A4). Besides, it may be unwise to draw attention as danger and easy money sometimes go hand in hand.

OFFICE BEHAVIOR: A COMPARATIVE LOOK

Imagine that you are an expatriate living and working in Hong Kong. One morning, en route to your office,

you share an elevator with a Chinese colleague. She answers your "Hello" like this, "You've gained weight." Once in the office, another colleague tells you that you're fat. Like Toto in *The Wizard of Oz*, you know you're not in Kansas anymore.

Puzzlement is often what non-Chinese coworkers and managers feel when they work with Chinese colleagues in China. A peek into the workings of a Chinese office highlights deep-seated cultural differences between, say, an office in New York City or Toronto or London and one in Hong Kong.

Here are a few customs that can baffle Western newcomers. (1) *Attitudes toward the company*. Chinese office workers tend to treat their companies like surrogate families. And vice versa. For example, it is customary on Lunar New Year for Chinese bosses—like family elders—to present their employees with red envelopes full of money. Further, employees in Chinese firms are often looked after by a tea lady, a woman who functions as a surrogate nanny, making tea and reheating lunches. (2) *Small-talk topics*. How big is your apartment? What is your salary? Those are questions rarely, if ever, asked of officemates in San Francisco, Toulouse, or Birmingham. On the contrary in Hong Kong. (3) *Sleeping on the job*. Many Chinese nap at their desks at lunchtime. (This is heart-healthy too, according to U.S. medical reports.) (4) *Noise levels*. Chinese workmates expect to be surrounded by loud phone talk, buzzing gadgets, and a "concert of ring tones" (Gallo in Fowler, 2007:B1). (5) *Work and social events.* Official and social events are kept separate. To combine them is considered rude. Thus, a brown bag, working lunch would not happen. (6) *Nonegalitarianism.* Hong Kong offices are hierarchical places where no boss is addressed by his or her first name. Managers do not try to be egalitarian. There is no pretense of equality in the office—or elsewhere: Differences in social position are accepted as normal. (So much for Mao's teachings.) Each position carries a particular measure of interpersonal power. If you ask someone to do something and get a vague response, this nonresponse is typically tied to your lack of *guan-xi* (pronounced goo-an shee, literally *guan-xi* means "connections"; but the word, which has no equivalent in English, refers to a system of mutual obligations). A person's *guan-xi* is all-important in interpersonal relations; it is based on the number and quality of his or her connections and is an important factor in a person's social status. These rules only apply to interpersonal relations, not to strangers or the public. (7) *Gesturing.* Native English-speakers who learn Mandarin Chinese may not grasp subtle differences, particularly in gestures. For example, English-speakers routinely raise their voice to stress a point, making the point strongly and more loudly. In Mandarin, raising your voice means you're angry. If you want to stress a point in Mandarin Chinese, rub your finger aside your nose. (7) *Harmonious relations.* The appearance of smooth social relations is very important in Hong Kong (and China generally). Thus, some behaviors aim to avoid disharmony, such as not saying "no." Chinese workmates may offer reasons a Westerner might think irrelevant, vague, or even hypocritical in order to avoid saying no.

In brief, customs and practices in Hong Kong and U.S. offices differ widely. But rules underlie behaviors in both cases. In the Hong Kong (and, typically, all of China) case, social norms for interpersonal relations help to guard privacy. Formal politeness helps maintain distance, just as civil inattention does between strangers on U.S. subways; this is particularly the case between juniors and superiors. (*Note*: Chinese rules of politeness do not apply to strangers—strangers have no *guan-xi* and thus do not deserve consideration.

Things can change quickly if a stranger—say, on the street—meets a Chinese person face-to-face because the two are no longer strangers.)

EVERYDAY GAMES AND DRAMAS

Looking at people in various public or quasi-public places (e.g., streets, subways, bars, ATMs)—whether in Hong Kong, London, Ottawa, or suburban New York—it is clear that the rules of the game (norms) and the roles people play (e.g., bar patron, subway rider, pedestrian, office worker) help to structure individual behavior, perceptions, even emotions. But to what extent? How much freedom do urbanites have to change the rules of the game? To create new **roles** in the drama of everyday life? Or to play old roles in a new way? Here, social theorists disagree.

WHOSE GAMES DO WE PLAY?

Thus far in Part III, we have drawn connections between what people do and what society expects them to do. We have noted that, whether in a bar or on city streets, people usually follow rules that they didn't construct, although they may be unaware that rules even exist. We also have discussed the impact of macro social structures on individual behavior, particularly noting the effect of class and status on people's actions. For example, various community studies show that what appear to be personal choices—what part of town one lives in, what style of house one has—are heavily influenced by one's social rank in the community.

Most sociologists and anthropologists agree that social structure (including norms, roles, and social ranks) shapes individual identity and behavior. But they debate the *degree* to which people have freedom to invent new games or play by their own rules.

Theorists who focus on the larger patterns of social structure (**macro-level social analysis**) tend to stress the degree to which people follow society's rules. Marxists, for example, maintain that a person's class and class interests are most important in determining attitudes and behavior. Marx thought that what people produce and how they produce it determine a society's norms, morality, ideology, and individual consciousness: "Life is not determined by consciousness, but consciousness by life" ([1859] 1977:164).

Non-Marxists also point to the great impact of social structural variables on individual behavior. For example, Peter L. Berger (1963) wrote that even in the most private games people play—courtship and marriage— the couple doesn't invent the game "or any part of it." The rituals (from dating to meeting the family, from holding hands to making love) are socially set. The two merely decide that they will play the game with each other and not with other possible partners. Sociologist Berger said that people in the United States may believe that love is an "irresistible emotion that strikes where it will." Yet, upon deeper investigation, it turns out that "the lightning shaft of Cupid seems to be guided rather strongly within very definite channels of class, income, education, racial and religious background" (35). In other words, macro theorists of varying orientations point to the *determining role* that social structure plays in molding individual actions and thoughts.

Micro-level social analysis, on the other hand, tends to stress the freedom individuals have to negotiate the rules and improvise new acts. Symbolic interactionists, for example, do not deny that people act within the framework of their society and its rules, but these social psychologists maintain that human beings actively shape their own behavior: Structural features such as social roles and social classes do set conditions for human behavior and interaction but don't "cause" or fully determine behavior and interaction.

Symbolic interactionists see individual behavior as part of a complex process in which people are constantly modifying their own actions in relation to other people's behavior and their interpretations of what's happening. In this view, people are not programmed, mindless robots. Instead, people themselves give meaning to situations and act accordingly. Thus, human behavior—in this view—is an elaborate process of interpreting, choosing, and rejecting possible lines of action, not a mechanical response to external stimuli.

Other social theorists interested in micro processes also stress the active role people play in molding their own behavior. Whatever their theoretical orientation (e.g., **symbolic interactionism, ethnomethodology**), most micro theorists emphasize two points:

1. People have choices about how to act.
2. People bring different meanings to the same event.

Hence, they argue, we must try to understand other people's meanings (i.e., the actors' subjective points of view) if we are to understand their behavior.

This debate over how much freedom people have to make up their own rules is essentially one of degree, not of kind. Both macro and micro theorists acknowledge that social structure and social organization provide the framework within which people act and give meaning to events. The difference is that macro theorists tend to see people as prisoners of society's rules, whereas micro theorists tend to focus on people's ability to push back (or build anew) the prison walls. (*Note*: The simple micro–macro distinction can't capture the variety of approaches to the study of society. For instance, Max Weber examined the development of meaning at the macro level, and commentators on Erving Goffman's work suggest that his micro studies are essentially analyses of social structure.)

Before discussing how micro and macro levels of analysis can be combined to study urban behavior, we turn to several useful concepts developed by micro theorists. These concepts—the **definition of the situation** and the **presentation of self**—deal with the same basic point: that social interaction, customs, and beliefs are often problematic.

"THE DEFINITION OF THE SITUATION" (THOMAS)

Reality, like beauty, exists in the eye of the beholder. The same object or event can have different meanings for different people. And the degree of difference will produce comparable differences in behavior. That is the essence of social psychologist W. I. Thomas's classic statement on the subjective quality of reality: "If men [and women] define situations as real they are real in their consequences" (see Thomas and Thomas, 1928:572).

This statement points out that there are multiple realities, not just one reality. Perhaps this is most evident when cross-cultural social interaction takes place. For instance, as detailed in Chapter 17, North Americans, who converse at a distance of about 12 inches, are considered cold and distant by Latin Americans. Latin Americans, who hold head-to-head conversations, are considered pushy and aggressive by North Americans. The potential consequences are hurt

TABLE 12.1 MULTIPLE REALITIES

Nationwide poll questions, asked of U.S. adults, querying if respondents believed in paranormal phenomena:

Percentage expressing belief in:

	2005	1978
Angels	68%	54%
Devil(s)	61%	39%
Ghosts	40%	11%
UFOs	34%	57%
Witches	28%	10%
Astrology	25%	29%

Sources: (2005 data): "The Religious and Other Beliefs of Americans 2005," Harris Poll® 90, December 14, 2005 (http://www.harrisinteractive.com/harris_poll/index.asp?PID=618) *(1978 data)*: Harris Interactive, Gallup Poll, "Surprising Number of Americans Believe in Paranormal Phenomena" (Princeton, N.J.: Gallup Organization, June 15, 1978) Copyright © Gallup Poll. Reprinted by permission.

feelings, misunderstanding, discomfort, and even prejudice or fistfights.

Here are two examples of multiple realities and their potential consequences.

1. J. J. wines and dines LaDonna at the fanciest restaurant in town for weeks. She fantasizes about marrying him. Then J. J. tells her, "I love you." Before LaDonna reacts to these words, she must decide what they mean—to him. She asks herself, "Is his concept of love the same as mine? Is he just giving me a line? Will his love smother me? How many others does he love?" And so on. How LaDonna reacts to J. J.'s declaration of love (from planning a wedding to saying farewell) depends on what meanings she thinks J. J. attaches to it.

2. Years ago, a civil rights group in Syracuse, New York, showed two photographs to a group of white, suburban, middle-class church members. In each photo, a male teenager, dressed casually, was running down the street. There was only one significant difference between the two teenagers: One was African American and the other was white. Respondents in this experiment were asked to describe what each teenager was doing. The range of responses was as follows, in order of times mentioned:

a. *White teenager running down the street*: (1) Good Samaritan running to help a needy person (perhaps a car accident victim), (2) hurt child running home for help, (3) jogger or Little Leaguer out for exercise.

b. *African American teenager running down the street*: (1) thief running from the police or making a fast getaway, (2) looter during an urban riot running toward a store to rob it, (3) curious spectator running to watch a fire or an accident.

When presented with the profile of their responses, church members were shocked. Because, unbeknownst to them before, most did share a definition of the situation—in this case, one they themselves labeled racist. Yet a few in the group did not attribute negative (indeed, criminal) meanings to the black teenager's behavior. Why did a minority of the group attribute normal behavior (curious spectator) to the black's gesture of running? An interesting research question. But that was not the experimenters' concern. Their concern focused on the potential real-life consequences of the majority's shared understanding: racist stereotypes that can bring psychological—and physical—harm to African Americans. Their goal was to change the majority's definition of the situation.

From the symbolic interactionist point of view, these examples—words of love, gestures of running—show that stimuli have no inherent meaning. By themselves, words, gestures, symbols, and objects are meaningless; people make them meaningful.

Symbolic interactionists do not claim that people are free to attribute any meaning at all to an event or a symbol. To the contrary, they emphasize that meanings are socially derived through interaction. Hence, in the United States, people share the assumption that a star-spangled cloth flying at half-mast means that someone important has died. If they see a white woman in a long white dress with a veil, they assume she is being married. (On the contrary, in traditional Chinese weddings in the United States, the bride wears red; in China and the U.S.–Chinese subculture, white is the color of mourning and death.)

What, then, is the special relevance of this social psychological concept—the definition of the

Fig. 12.5 WHAT'S GOING ON HERE? The answer depends on who's defining the situation. (Lisa Siegel Sullivan)

situation—to urban life? It helps to explain why social order is so much more fragile in the modern metropolis than in traditional rural communities. When groups and individuals share a common definition of the situation, the basis for social order exists. Shared understandings of what is normal, proper, and good behavior characterize *Gemeinschaft* communities. In contrast, *Gesellschaft* and *Techno$chaft* societies are typified by heterogeneous populations with plural belief systems. For instance, people in the United States have different definitions of the situation concerning the supernatural and paranormal (Table 12.1).

More important for human relations, African American and white definitions of the racial situation are worlds apart. Here are just two examples: (1) Polls among African American and white high school students show that the two groups live in different worlds. For instance, for most African American students, affirmative action means opportunity. But to many white students, it symbolizes reverse discrimination. (2) In 2003, at least in one city with a fast-growing His-panic population—Durham, North Carolina—almost 59 percent of Latino immigrant respondents reported feeling that "few or almost no blacks are hard working." One-third said that blacks are "hard to get along with," and 57 percent found that "few or no blacks could be trusted" (Asquith, 2006). Indeed, surveys conducted since 2000 in various U.S. cities, including Los Angeles, Houston, Miami, and New York, generally find that Latinos display more prejudice toward African Americans than African Americans do toward Latinos or than whites display toward African Americans. One scholar's surveys of racial attitudes in Houston, for example, found that when Latino respondents described blacks, they often used such words as "noisy," "loud," "lazy," "dropouts/ uneducated," "hostile," "complainers/whiners," "prejudiced," "aggressive," "angry," "disrespectful/rude," and "violent." The reasons are much disputed, but the conclusions are not: "in general African Americans have more positive views of Hispanics than vice versa" (Mindiola in Judis, 2007). What lies behind such negative stereotypes and racist attitudes? Researchers don't have a single explanation.

Yet, one thing is clear: People do not share a single definition of the situation. It is in the modern metropolis that people are unlikely to share the same definition of the situation and, consequently, are unlikely to react similarly to the same event or stimulus. This situation lends itself to social disruption and conflict.

Let's apply this fairly abstract point to a practical problem: what to teach in a public high school. Imagine that you are a member of a neighborhood group in a large city in the United States; the group is concerned with what teenagers are learning in social studies, courses. Besides yourself, the following neighborhood people show up at the first meeting to discuss what should be taught: astrologers and astrophysicists; gays and straights; Chinese Americans, whites (WASPs and ethnics), Latinos, African Americans, Native Americans, and Sikh Americans; housewives, HIV-positive mothers, and female executives; New Agers and old-timers; a faith-based care provider, car mechanics, lawyers, and a self-proclaimed hippie hedonist; a Marxist community organizer, a libertarian, tax protesters, an advocate of "intelligent design," an ACLU member; an environmentalist and an oil refinery executive; plus atheists, Protestants, Catholics, Jews, Muslims, Buddhists, and Hindus.

Given this diversity, conflicts over what to teach surface immediately. The astrologer insists that students be taught that the position of the stars governs their lives. "Hooey," shouts the astrophysicist, advocating instruction in scientific methods to measure social phenomena. Some Latinos want a bilingual program; others don't. A Marxist community organizer claims that the social science text ignores the key variable in American life—social class—while the libertarian thinks the text is laced with anticapitalist propaganda. A coalition—People United Against Racism—protests that the text is Eurocentric, ignoring all but western European cultural contributions. The environmentalist dislikes the text because it advocates unlimited growth, and the oil company executive says that "kids should learn that without growth, there is no more prosperity." Gays question how the subject of marriage is treated in the required text. Meanwhile, the car mechanic worries that her child can't even spell the word "environment." A feminist castigates the text for its sexist neglect of women in U.S. history, but a lawyer thinks the book gives a "realistic" assessment of American history. And so it goes (Figure 12.5).

SOCIAL ORDER AMID MULTIPLE REALITIES

Given these varied social backgrounds, concerns, ideologies, and stocks of knowledge, it seems a miracle that any collective action can take place. Yet it usually does.

How is social order possible in a milieu of multiple realities? The nineteenth-century sociologist Emile Durkheim answered this important question by taking for granted that people conform to society's rules because they were taught to do so as children and because they benefit from assuming that others will also conform. Durkheim's stance is a structural–functional one, emphasizing the process by which people internalize norms and conform to them.

Other theorists have different answers. Most importantly, philosopher Alfred Schutz (1967) argued that (1) individuals in the same culture share the belief that they can put themselves in one another's shoes and understand how another person could view their behavior, allowing for the development of empathy and understanding, and (2) this empathy and understanding allow people to transcend their personal experience and exchange perspectives through social interaction. Through the exchange of perspectives, Schutz thought, people can question the rules they learned as children. Thus, they can help make or unmake the rules which create social order.

Erving Goffman (1959) might have answered the question "How is social order possible?" like this: People hold different definitions of the situation, but they still have working agreements that help maintain order. This "working consensus" may conceal wide disagreements among participants. But the working consensus is like a contract that states "if you support my act, I'll support yours; and if we cooperate, we'll all get our everyday tasks accomplished."

When people enter the physical presence of others, they take each other's behavior into account (even if no verbal communication occurs). They constantly modify their own behavior in order to act "properly" in a given situation, in a given culture and/or subculture. Acting "properly" reduces vulnerability, risk, and embarrassment. It is also less time-consuming than making up the rules from scratch every time people interact. In this way, social order is upheld.

We now turn to Goffman's ideas on how people try to impose their definitions of reality on others. He contended that we present ourselves in certain ways, trying to control or manage the impressions others have of us.

"THE PRESENTATION OF SELF" (GOFFMAN)

The late Erving Goffman explored "the little interactions that are forgotten about as soon as they occur." He microscopically examined "the little salutations, compliments and apologies" (e.g., smiles and "I'm sorry") that "serious students of society never collect." He found "empty" gestures "perhaps the fullest of all." In short, his domain was "the slop of social life."

Goffman's examples of "the slop of social life" were taken mainly from urban society, but he was not usually classified as an urbanist. And rarely are his micro studies mentioned in the context of urban studies. This is unfortunate, perhaps one casualty of the dubious distinction between things urban and otherwise.

Goffman has been dubbed the "Woody Allen of American sociology" (because he so powerfully unraveled the fragile fabric of everyday life) and the "Kafka

of our time" (because, like the great Czech writer, he communicated the horror, anguish, and some of the absurd comedy of everyday life). His world, like Kafka's, was peopled with ordinary individuals—clerks, bureaucrats, shoppers—doing ordinary things. But in Goffman's hands, this ordinary world became extraordinary and complex.

In Goffman's vision, just getting through the day—standing in a bus line, greeting friends and acknowledging strangers, entering a repair store, and engaging in similar routine activity—is full of ritual, perhaps magic. In his view, this ritual process is worth exploring because it reveals the fragility and complexity of social behavior, particularly urban behavior.

Essentially, Goffman's vision was a theatrical one. He presented the everyday world as a theater in which we all act out roles and give performances in ongoing plays. His imagery is drawn from the stage. Hence, a person (in its first dictionary meaning, from *persona*) is a mask. Brief encounters in urban places are treated as masked rituals. Individuals are always "on" (as in "on stage"), performing and creating their roles. This theatrical model of social behavior recalls Shakespeare: "All the world's a stage and all the men and women merely players."

To Goffman, when we play roles and interpret other people's performances on the stage of everyday life, we wear masks or ritual faces. Our ritual faces aren't who we "really" are—but who we "really" are doesn't much matter. What does matter is the image we want the audience (observers) to have of our performance. Our masks allow us to manipulate our appearances and save face before others. That is what we do, according to Goffman, hundreds of times each day; we have an unspoken understanding with our audience whereby all of us role players agree to conduct ourselves to maintain our own face and the faces of other participants in the scene.

For Goffman, most routine social interaction in urban settings is nothing more than the effort to control the impression we make on others (*impression management*). We manage these impressions to keep up appearances and win acceptance from the audience. We want our audiences to accept our appearance—our performance—because it is on the basis of our appearance (and inferences about it) that they will react to us.

Fig. 12.6 PRESENTATION OF SELF. Ordinary walking down the street may be a put on designed to avoid embrrassment and control the audience's impressions. (Tim Teninty)

An Internet ad is a common way to meet others, particularly in postindustrial society. Here is one person's profile written to attract a partner. How does she present herself? What is not included in her profile? What type of person (e.g., income level, personal traits)does she hope to attract by the way she hope to attract by the way she presents herself:

After teaching high school English in Texas, I came to San Francisco where I had various jobs, including working for BART and Lucasfilm. Later, I went to law school and have been practicing law ever since. I am a partner in my Bay Area firm, and we specialize in construction law. I enjoy my practice and clients, most of whom are engineers—a special breed.

I am the eldest in my family—and the only "girl." Three of my four younger brothers and my mother still live in Texas, where I grew up. My father died recently, but my mother still seems to have all her marbles and enthusiasm. I get a kick out of my family.

After some years, my marriage dissolved. (I remain on friendly terms with my former husband although we are no longer involved in each other's lives.) Now I find myself back in the "dating game."

I live in San Francisco's North Beach neighborhood with a half-Siamese-half-ragdoll cat who is adoring (not a bad quality) but whose conversational skills and sense of humor are limited.

I have been a member of a San Francisco swimming and boating club for many years. Some of my less-athletic friends kid me about swimming with the seals in the cold water, wondering if I am part seal. I assure them NOT—that it's great fun, great exercise, and wonderful for the sense of community. (Many of my close friends are Bay swimmers.) They tell me how disciplined I must be to get up at 4 a.m., readying myself for 3-times-a-week plunges in the brrhish Bay. Recently, I took up golf and road biking, having bought good clubs and an outrageously expensive bicycle to make sure I keep at it!

I love dancing and carousing until 10:00 p.m. (early to work and swimming, I'm afraid). And a good read is always a pleasure for me.
(Courtesy Tommy Knight)

How we present ourselves, Goffman maintained, depends on the impression we want to make on a particular audience. We choose a role from our repertoire of identities. We put on one of our many faces, depending on our intent and our audience. Thus, we don't play the same part in front of all our audiences—family, strangers, colleagues, and so on—because "urban life would become unbearably sticky for some if every contact between two individuals entailed a sharing of personal trials, worries, and secrets. Thus if a man wants to be served a restful dinner, he may seek the service of a waitress rather than a wife" (1959:49).

Con artists are experts in impression management. Take, for example, James Hogue (b. either 1959 or 1960). Over time, he has played a variety of roles, including "Jay Mitchell Huntsman" (when he was a Palo Alto, California, high schooler) and "Alexi Indris-Santana" (a supposed 21-year-old Princeton University sophomore). Princeton admissions officers believed his background to be "unique and impressive": a self-educated ranch hand with a dying mother. Nearly 3 years passed before Alexi was unmasked, by chance. He had performed flawlessly in front of difficult audiences (Barron, 1991:C19). But his repertoire of characters did not end there. Two years later Hogue was accused of stealing more than $50,000 in gems from a Harvard University museum where he worked as a cataloger. After being released from prison in 1997, Hogue became the subject of a documentary film, *Con Man* (Moss, 2001). Ironically, Hogue feared that his Social Security number, shown in *Con Man*, could lead to identity theft.

Hogue's saga continues. In 2006, he was apprehended in Arizona on charges of receiving stolen merchandise. (Capps, 2007). Convicted and sentenced to prison for 10 years, with the possibility of parole in 5 years, who knows where he'll turn up next!

Surely, Hogue understands that demeanor, dress, and speech are important props in managing impressions. Collegians who want to impress teachers as good students avoid appearing inappropriate—say, wearing a bathing suit to class or snoring through a lecture. Likewise, a young lawyer may wear a wedding band and horn-rimmed glasses to give the jury the impression of stability and maturity. A lawyer—female or male—may be rather unorthodox in her or his private life but dress in conservative suits before juries.

How does one dress for a particular result, such as getting a date or being successful at work? This varies from culture to culture (and from subculture to subculture). In the United States, those wishing to go from geek to chic can pay for the service of a professional matchmaker, who will revamp his or her wardrobe (Guynn, 2007:A10).

For those who wish to dress for success, here are a few fashion tips from "image consultants": Men interested in impressing their bosses and clients should not wear bow ties; they give the impression of being unpredictable. Women who want to hide their authority from men could wear an outsized jacket, shirt, and hat with a skirt or slacks. This look, made famous over a generation ago by actress Diane Keaton in Woody Allen's movie *Annie Hall* (1977), exudes the non-threatening charm of helplessness and cuteness. If a woman wishes to flaunt her authority, she might dress like a femme fatale. Looking older or younger can be helped along by wardrobe choice too.

How do we present ourselves in urban public or semipublic places? In ways that will appear proper to those around us, Goffman said. This serves to avert real or potential danger and embarrassment and to get the results we want.

If, however, a person feels that things aren't normal—that "something is up"—he or she may put on a performance to conceal the sense that something is wrong. Sometimes these acts can be pathetic: "Witness the vain and painful effort of someone sitting beside an obstreperous drunk on public transportation; witness the effort of the individual to act as if the drunk were either not there or not a special point of concern, in either case not something to cause his seatmate to appear to be anything but a person in a situation in which all appearances are normal and nothing is up" (Goffman, 1971:271).

For women in cities, ordinary walking may entail a "put-on," a performance designed to show that nothing is up (Figure 12.6). For instance, as a woman walks past a group of men on their lunch hour sitting on the pavement watching the world (and especially women) go by,

> her face becomes contorted into a grimace of self-control and fake unawareness; her walk and carriage become stiff and dehumanized. No matter what they say to her, it will be unbearable. She knows that they

will not physically assault her or hurt her....What they will do is impinge on her. They will use her body with their eyes....They will make her ridiculous, or grotesquely sexual, or hideously ugly. Above all, they will make her feel like a thing.

(Tax in Goffman, 1971:272)

In this urban world of strangers, then, the woman walking down the street is not what she appears to be. She is trying as best she can to avoid embarrassment by managing the impressions that her audience has of her. (Age and past experience may also play key roles too. The twenty-something woman pictured in Figure 12.6, for example, does not seem extremely bothered by the male glances; perhaps she has walked the walk many times before.)

Such everyday encounters—a woman walking by an audience that may not support her act, a man trying to maintain a normal appearance while sitting next to a potentially disruptive drunk, people averting their eyes from each other on subways—were Goffman's primary focus. More precisely, he was concerned with how these social encounters are structured. And Goffman thought that the most significant factor in this pattern of social interaction is "the maintenance of a single definition of the situation...expressed...and sustained in the face of a multitude of potential disruptions" (1959:254).

At this point, we return to some shared definitions of the situation—those working agreements, usually unspoken, that hold in a milieu of multiple realities—urban society.

WALKING THE TIGHTROPE

MINIMIZING INVOLVEMENT, MAXIMIZING SOCIAL ORDER

Urban society presents a Janus-like face: freedom and anarchy. One side offers freedom for individuals to choose from among alternative realities. The other portends danger: that the social order will break down from conflict over what's proper or right (normative conflict). That urbanites do take collective action and are not in constant conflict with each other suggests that some rules or norms, some shared definitions of the situation, still hold in this milieu of multiple realities. Throughout this chapter, we have seen indications that such norms exist. On the city streets, for instance,

pedestrians cooperate so that they can all reach their destinations.

Below city streets, people appear civilly inattentive while they ride the subway. But here again, the implications are two-sided. The very norms that protect personal privacy and limit involvement with strangers (e.g., civil inattention) also promote the indifference so often attributed to urbanites. "I didn't want to get involved" is a common reason given by people who walk away from fellow human beings in trouble in urban public places. Yet the norm of noninvolvement may be highly situational. According to experiments conducted by social psychologists in several countries, urbanites are less likely to intervene in emergency situations if a crowd is nearby.

Arguably the most famous bystander study in the United States, by Latané and Darley (1970), found that, in a crowd, each individual assumes that someone else will take responsibility. Thus, what appears to be indifference is really something else: a "diffusion of responsibility."

Bystander behavior in the United States may not have changed much over the decades (but technologies, such as cameras in cell phones, certainly have had many impacts, including identifying culprits). For example, in Hartford, Connecticut, an elderly man was hit by a car in May 2008; he was left alone—injured—in the street by many bystanders and passing cars who witnessed the hit-and-run. Similarly, in late January 2009, a homeless man lay unconscious on a busy D.C. street for 20 minutes before anyone called for help. He later died (Aol.com, 2009). Yet, the same principle obtains: diffused responsibility.

This notion of diffused responsibility again points to *numbers* as a variable in urban social behavior. Further, it calls into question Wirth's notion that urbanites are indifferent, blasé, and uncaring.

To conclude: Urbanites seem to walk a tightrope. On the one hand, to get through the day, they cooperate with strangers. On the other, they maintain distance from them. Norms of behavior in public places provide guidelines on the proper degree of intimacy or noninvolvement (not the specific behaviors) expected there.

Most urbanites follow a mini–maxi strategy: They try to *minimize involvement* and to *maximize social order*. They have a common understanding that permits routine social interaction to take place. They agree to cooperate to the extent that daily public life can go on. At the same time, they agree to protect their personal space by limiting the intensity of their involvement with strangers.

The mini-maxi notion suggests that the quality of urban social behavior can best be understood by combining seemingly opposite ideas: "intimate anonymity," "public privacy," and "involved indifference." These descriptions seem schizoid. Yet they indicate the precarious balancing act that urbanites perform many times daily.

CONSTRUCTING SOCIAL REALITY

Some norms of public behavior, such as civil inattention, seem to work to everyone's benefit. But this doesn't mean that all such rules are so mutually beneficial. A question posed by Erving Goffman focuses on this point.

In *Relations in Public*, Goffman commented that people's immediate surroundings—their homes and offices, for example—are viewed as their possessions, as part of their "fixed territory" (1971:288). People assume that these fixed territories will be free of danger, like a safe haven, for "the individual's sense of privacy, control and self-respect is tied to the dominion he exerts over his fixed territories."

What happens when someone's fixed territory is damaged by people who don't share the same standards of care? That is what occurred to the president of Columbia University, Grayson Kirk, when 150 student demonstrators occupied his office for 6 days in 1969. When Kirk returned to his office, he found cigarette butts and orange peels covering his rug, plus other remnants of the occupation. Looking around at this sight, he turned to reporters and asked, "My God, how could human beings do a thing like this?" (*Note*: A generation later, strewing orange peels and cigarette butts may seem rather innocuous next to other courses of possible action—say, bomb blasts. But the university president treated his office as sacred space, as his "fixed territory"; and as an authority figure, he was not used to having his space disrespected.)

Kirk may have asked how human beings could do such a thing. But Goffman asked different questions:

The great sociological question, of course, is not how could it be that human beings would do a thing like this, but rather how is it that human beings do this sort of thing so rarely. *How come persons in authority have been so overwhelmingly successful in conning those beneath them?*

(1971:288n, italics mine)

With these questions, Goffman hinted that we can't really understand how the rules work without looking at both the process (micro focus) and the structure (macro focus) of social interaction. That is, people may be active agents in creating new performances, but they create them within a cultural, political, and historical context.

THE PUBLIC DEFINITION OF REALITY

In urban society—characterized by multiple realities—competing individuals and groups are constantly struggling to transform their own definition of reality into the public definition of reality: a world of ready-made, taken-for-granted meanings, attitudes, feelings, and thoughts. As the student demonstrators' behavior indicates, this ready-made world of meanings is neither unchanging nor unchangeable. Meanings are open to constant negotiation and reinterpretation.

TABLE 12.2 SOME WIDELY-SHARED DEFINITIONS OF REALITY IN THE UNITED STATES

Economic sector	Competition is a good thing. Owners of firms have the right to decide what products or services to offer and how much to pay their workers (with a minimum age floor).
Political sector	Government and politics are so complicated that most people in this country can't understand what's going on.
Aesthetic sector	Men and women who weigh 350 pounds are not physically attractive.
Social sector	Having a large family—10 children—is a strain on the parents and a burden on society.
Health sector	Smoking is bad. Daily exercise and eating fruits and vegetables daily are good.

Still, at the same time, there are widely shared assumptions about how social interaction should take place at a particular historical moment. These shared assumptions (definitions of reality) are not simply there; they are generated by social processes and molded by power relations, class structures, and other social structural features.

We don't all have an equal chance of getting others to accept our definition of reality. As two sociologists of knowledge wrote a generation or so ago: "He who has the bigger stick has a better chance of imposing his definitions of reality" (Berger and Luckmann, 1967:109).

Now we turn to a discussion of African American street corner men, one group of people in the United States who don't have big sticks (power, authority, wealth, high status, control over or access to mass media). Consequently, they have less chance of imposing their definitions of reality on other groups. In telling their story, Elliot Liebow demonstrated the power of applying both micro and macro levels of analysis to the study of urban social behavior.

COMBINING MICRO- AND MACROANALYSIS TO STUDY SOCIAL BEHAVIOR

CASE STUDY: *TALLY'S CORNER*

Anthropologist Liebow (1967) recorded the daily, routine activities of 24 black men who hung out around a corner, Tally's corner, near a carry-out restaurant in Washington, D.C. He talked with them on the street and accompanied them to their haunts: their homes, pool halls, neighborhood stores, and sometimes courtrooms.

Liebow was an outsider for many reasons (race, religion, occupation, residence, manner of speech), but he participated in their lives as well as observing them. (Indeed, he reported that his marginality was disadvantageous in some ways but partially offset by the fact that "as an outsider, I was not a competitor" [1967:251]). His data were drawn from observing the actions of the men—unskilled construction workers, busboys, menial workers, and the unemployed, from their early twenties to their mid-forties.

A casual observer might think that the street-corner men hang out because they're lazy, irresponsible, seeking instant gratification, or present time–oriented. They are wrong, said Liebow. And here is how he came to this conclusion.

To understand why the men hung out on the street corner, why they worked at the jobs they did—or quit—and why they held the attitudes they did, Liebow moved from the micro level (the street corner) to analyze larger social patterns that shaped their lives (macro level). In so doing, he demonstrated that the men's jobs and self-concepts were molded by their place in the class and status system.

To begin with, the jobs the street-corner men could get—parking attendant, janitor, counterman, stock clerk, and the like—were generally dead ends. What janitor ends up at a white-collar job in the building he or she cleans? More important, all available work was low-paid and low-status. Liebow noted that neither society nor the street-corner man who performed these jobs thought they're worth doing and worth doing well: "Both employee and employer are contemptuous of the job. The employee shows his contempt by his reluctance to accept it or keep it, the employer by paying less than is required to support a family" (1967:58).

Thus, these men were trapped in work that offered no prestige, little money, no chance for advancement or interesting opportunities, and little else. More prestigious work was closed to them. They lacked the education (most went to inferior schools), and they didn't have a network of friends and contacts that upper middle-class people routinely develop by going to the right schools and/or networking. Finally, they belonged to a minority group, one that experienced racial discrimination in employment and opportunities for training in highly paid trades.

In short, these were men without a future. And they knew it.

Not having a future affected even the most intimate sphere of their lives: relationships with friends and lovers. Given the street-corner men's structural situation, "friendship is easily uprooted by the tug of economic or psychological self-interest or by external forces acting against it." Friendships were very meaningful to the street-corner men, but they were often threatened by routine crises that more affluent people don't face constantly.

Only by looking at the ways social structure impinges on the street-corner men's lives, Liebow implied, can we make sense of their seeming refusal to work and their treatment of friends and lovers.

Liebow concluded that the key factor in these men's lives was not psychological but rather social structural: the inability to earn a living and support their families. Behind their attitude toward their work and themselves was society's evaluation that they were worthless.

If Liebow had stopped his analysis at the micro level of face-to-face interaction on the street corner, he could not have made the connections between personality and social structure. Nor could he have shown that the way these men define their situations grows out of the values, sentiments, and opportunities provided by the larger society.

ANOTHER LOOK

Being urban involves playing games and following rules we didn't create. Yet, as the symbolic interactionists emphasize, urbanites can break the rules or help create new ones.

Breaking the rules entails taking risks. These risks can be minor or life-endangering. To break the unspoken rule of sociability in a bar by slighting a stranger may earn a person nothing more than a dirty look. But who knows? Perhaps this anonymous person believes himself or herself to be the Devil and responds with a stab of a pocket knife. Similarly, college students who stage a live-in at the president's office may risk jail, expulsion from school, or long-term surveillance as "troublemakers."

The other side of this coin is that rule-breaking behavior (deviance from norms) can lead to new definitions of reality and social change. In the students' case, their actions could have contributed to a general reconsideration of the proper relationship between students and authority figures.

People seem to accept injustice as long as they think it is inevitable or grant it moral authority. India's untouchables (*Dalits*), for instance, have accepted their low status because they assume they are being punished for acts committed in previous reincarnations. If, however, people think that an injustice is unnatural, they often rise up against it. Once again, this illustrates W. I. Thomas's dictum and demonstrates the link between beliefs and social action.

Most of the time, most of us don't break the rules. The rules provide comfort and security. They serve to reduce potential risk, physical or psychic. This is especially true in urban public life. Urbanites are surrounded by people whom they know nothing about— where they are coming from or where they are going, literally and figuratively. It's easier to conform, and we expect others to do the same.

This is what many general rules—civil inattention, for instance—are all about: risk avoidance. Of course, avoiding risk in some places, such as war-zone cities, requires other rules—but rules there are!

Indeed, much of urban public behavior everywhere can be understood as attempts to avoid risk. This stands in contrast to everyday encounters in rural, small-scale societies. In Greek *poleis*, citizens knew each other on sight. There was no wide diversity in their definitions of the situation. They could reasonably predict one another's behavior. In this milieu, urban public life could thrive.

Can urban public life survive, let alone thrive, in postindustrial society? That seems to be *the* question. Particularly in a post-9/11 world, have we put such a high premium on maintaining social order and personal privacy that we avoid the promise of city life: new experiences, learning from people unlike ourselves? Will those who can afford it retreat to private spaces (e.g., a home with a room-sized television) or gated-up, moat-like separation, well protected from the risky arena of urban streets and gatherings? Or can we create a new urban public life that offers growth opportunities for all?

Numerous visionaries think they know the way to enrich city life. Their solutions depend mainly on their ideologies and levels of analysis: radical changes in the rules of the game, transforming lower-class individuals into middle-class citizens, or decentralizing public institutions and promoting community control.

However we evaluate such proposals to enrich urban public life, one point is clear: The way people interact at the face-to-face level cannot be divorced from larger patterns of social structure. Micro meets macro, intersecting at the carry-out street corner and every other urban public place.

KEY TERMS

Civil inattention Erving Goffman's term, referring to a general rule (**norm**) of urban social interaction. It occurs when "one gives to another enough visual notice to demonstrate that one appreciates that the other is present (and that one admits openly to having seen him), while at the next moment withdrawing one's attention from him so as to express that he does not constitute a target of special curiosity or design."

Definition of the situation W. I. Thomas's term, referring to the idea that objective reality is less important than people's subjective interpretation of events, objects, and actions. His famous statement "If men define situations as real they are real in their consequences" suggests that the same action or event can hold various meanings for various people and that people will respond differently to the same action or event, depending on the meaning they attach to it.

Ethnography A study of a group of people or a community using fieldwork methods (participant-observation, in-depth interviewing) to describe behavior and attitudes. Ethnographers focus on actors' subjective meanings and definitions of the situation.

Ethnomethodology A movement or "school" in sociology led by Harold Garfinkel. Ethnomethodologists (from the Greek *ethno*, "people"; *meth*, "a way of doing things") study the unspoken, tacit rules and agreements that govern ordinary, everyday activities. Often, their method is to break the rules, making background expectancies inoperative, to understand commonsense knowledge.

Macro-level social analysis Analysis of social structural features (class structure, discrimination patterns, educational institutions, etc.) that mold an entire society.

Micro-level social analysis Analysis of interpersonal processes that mold everyday social interaction.

Norms Rules of the game; standards of right and wrong behavior that are shared by a group or society. Norms change over time and vary from culture to culture.

Presentation of self Erving Goffman's term, referring to the self-conscious attempt a person makes to control the impressions that other people have of her or him.

Role The performance of expected rights, obligations, and behaviors associated with a person's status.

To "play a role" is to act according to expected, preestablished behavior patterns. Role is inseparable from status; status is a collection of rights and duties, and role is the performance of those rights and duties.

Social interaction (face-to-face) Encounters that happen any time two or more people come into each other's physical presence, thereby exerting reciprocal influence on each other's behavior. Verbal communication is not necessary for social interaction to take place.

Symbolic interactionism A theoretical perspective within sociology that focuses on micro-level processes of social interaction. Symbolic interactionists pay special attention to the meanings people attach to events and behavior and the ways in which they communicate meanings (via words, gestures, and other symbols).

PROJECTS

1. **Classroom behavior, micro level.** Few students subject what goes on in the classroom to objective analysis because it is such a routine, familiar activity. That is the goal of this project: to analyze the rules of the classroom game. Observe three classes with different teachers and examine such features as the following: Who sits where? Who initiates discussion? What do people wear? What are they talking about? What is the manner and style of speech used (vocabulary, tone, loudness)? Who negotiates possible disagreements? What happens if some disruption occurs? On the basis of your preliminary observations, formulate at least two hypotheses about classroom behavior.

Now, do a second round of observations. This time, test your hypotheses. If, for instance, you posit that teachers tend to pay more attention to students sitting near them than to students farther away (e.g., in the back of a large classroom), count the number of times eye contact is maintained with each group, as well as other indicators of attentiveness (e.g., responsiveness to questions from each group). If you hypothesize that female students are more likely to speak up in class than male students if the teacher is female, then compare and contrast the number of times women speak in various classes taught by males and females. Depending on your hypotheses, you may want to note indicators of restlessness (coughs, slouched body posture), lack of interest in the class (side conversations, newspaper reading, falling asleep), or control mechanisms (assigned seat arrangements, attendance taking, etc.). Reexamining your data, what general rules for classroom behavior do you find?

2. **Classroom behavior, macro level.** The purpose of this project is to reexamine the data collected in project 1 in light of larger social contexts. For example, do the class size, teaching format, and interpersonal dynamics of the class reflect the power and status patterns of the larger society? Do the age, sex, race, and academic rank of the professor seem to affect students' response or teacher's style? Is the classroom a setting for democratic participation or a training ground for hierarchical organization? What authority relationships do students take for granted?

3. **Breaking the rules: making the background expectancies inoperative.** U.S. urbanites generally display trust—not distrust—to strangers. If in the United States, test the existence of this norm by the following experiment: Board a city bus and ask the driver if this bus passes a certain street that you want. After receiving an answer, ask again, "Does it really pass this street?" Continue this line of questioning (e.g., "Are you sure?"). What is the bus driver's reaction? (And your own?) If outside the United States, does the norm of trust hold where you are located?

4. **Presentation of self.** Think about a social occasion that you attended recently (say, a party) at which there were people previously unknown to you. How did you present yourself? What clothes did you wear? What information did you reveal about yourself to these strangers? What impressions did you want them to have of you? How did you go about managing these impressions? Finally, in your terms, was it a successful performance?

5. **Definitions of the situation.** Pick a contemporary issue with wide-ranging consequences (e.g., immigration). Using archival materials, interviews, and media resources (e.g., Internet blogs), try to better understand the range of attitudes and feelings about the issue and the bases on which people or groups disagree (e.g., religion, rural or urban residence, political ideology, years of education, gender, marital status, race and/or ethnicity).

6. **Supermarket behavior, a comparative analysis.** Visit supermarkets in several (and distinct) sections of a city or, if possible, in two countries. What differences in behavior do you observe? For example, do customers in both settings routinely perform the slip'n slide maneuver to avoid shopping carts or people, or do they stand their ground, making passersby change course? Is there any conversation between strangers in either setting? If so, where and what seems to instigate conversation? What makes customers grumble or be impatient in both settings? How are children's temper tantrums handled by staff and other customers—ignored, frowned upon visibly, commented upon? After you conduct your participant-observation, write up a few pages detailing the commonalities and differences you've observed. Finally, offer at least one hypothesis about why differences may exist.

7. **Netiquette.** Rules for Internet behavior are evolving, quickly. What are several current rules for communicating with someone you do not know face-to-face? For example, is deception acceptable? First, analyze your own Internet behavior. Next, construct a survey and administer the survey to classmates, workmates, family, etc. Then, explore what others have written on this subject. Lastly, sum up your results—with proper citations.

8. **Culturally (and subculturally) based norms.** If you spend time regularly in another nation, say, Mexico or Japan, or in a subculture, such as Goths or an occupational subculture, observe how "inside pedestrians," for example, shoppers walking down supermarket aisles, respond to those coming toward them. Do they automatically do the slip'n slide maneuver, or do they wait until the person who wishes to pass signals his or her intention and then move out of the way? What differences that seem to be culturally based or subculturally based (rather than personal idiosyncrasies) do you observe? What might account for such differences?

SUGGESTIONS FOR FURTHER LEARNING

Social psychologist Philip Zimbardo, the creator of the "Stanford prison experiment" in 1971, turned his attention to nonexperimental examples of atrocities and bad behavior, including the U.S. military's treatment of prisoners at Abu Ghraib, the infamous Iraqi prison, in *The Lucifer Effect: Understanding How Good*

People Turn Evil (New York: Random House, 2007). Zimbardo found that, like in the Stanford "prison," even "normal" people, given the right situation, will cooperate in violence, abandoning deeply held moral codes.

Erving Goffman, who stressed the impact of roles on human behavior, would not have been surprised at Zimbardo's findings. Goffman's work challenges most of our assumptions about the role of "personality" in human action.

Micro studies in urban social interaction include several works by Canadian-born sociologist Erving Goffman. See especially the "weird but brilliant light," as one reviewer called it, that he sheds on "normal appearances" in *Relations in Public: Microstudies of the Public Order* (New York: Basic Books, 1971).

Interest in pedestrian behavior seems to be increasing. Perhaps, in part, this increased interest reflects concerns about energy conservation. At the University of Washington, for example, a graduate seminar (Pedestrian Travel, Land Use, and Urban Form) concentrates on "walking as a mode of transportation in cities and city-regions, including social, cognitive, and perceptual dimensions of pedestrian movement and behavior theory." A scholarly paper by Megan Hoyt at the University of Washington explores pedestrian behavior in Trondheim, Norway; she found, inter alia, that time of day and day of the week affected walking choices more than weather or levels of darkness (*Valle Review*, August Report, March 2001; http://www.engr.washington.edu/valle/valle_review/01_valle_review.pdf). "Artificial Societies of Intelligent Agents," a 2001 unpublished thesis by Carlos Gershenson at the Fundación Arturo Rosenblueth in Mexico City, discusses pedestrian behavior from a variety of approaches, including social science, artificial intelligence, and engineering.

Seeing ourselves reflected through the eyes of an outsider (and a good observer) is often instructive. British author Adam Nicholson offers this advice to his compatriots in "Shopping Around" the Trumbull Shopping Park in Connecticut: "Always have a guide in the United States; it's a much more foreign place than you think." In his book of essays *On Foot* (New York: Harmony Books, 1990), Nicholson remarks that the shopping mall, "a climate-controlled cocoon," is "the new heart of the New World (there are now more shopping malls in the States than either post offices or secondary schools)" where "occupants turn away from the world outside towards a neat and unfrightening vacuum . . . where people go for long walks in the most comforting landscape they know" (89).

The environmental characteristics of bars, as well as women's behavior in bars, are tied to women's risk for bar-related aggression. Those are findings by researchers at the University of Buffalo (New York) Research Institute on Addictions. The study, "The Role of the Bar Context and Social Behaviors on Women's Risk for Aggression" by Amy M. Buddie and Kathleen A. Parks (*Journal of Interpersonal Violence*, December 2003, 18, 1378–1393), shows that heavy drinking, going to (and leaving) a bar with strangers or individuals not well known to the women, and talking to a greater number of individuals while in the bar are associated with bar-related aggression. Pool-playing and illegal activities (involving drug sales or prostitution) in a bar, they found, increase the risk of severe physical aggression.

Paul Ekman provides some clues on how people maintain normal appearances while acting deceitfully in his highly readable book *Emotions Revealed: Recognizing Faces and Feelings to Improve Communication and Emotional Life*, 2nd ed. (New York: Holt, [2003] 2007). He describes how to spot a liar, inter alia.

For a vision of the world as nearly nothing but appearances—the world as masked ball—see Tom Wolfe's cynical novel *The Bonfire of the Vanities* (New York: Farrar, Straus & Giroux, 1987).

Globe-trotting novelist and essayist Paul Theroux discovered an alien land on his New York City "Subway Odyssey," *New York Times Magazine*, January 31, 1982, pp. 20+. He noted that it is "beat up with patches of beauty, like a cityscape in China or India." Theroux wrote that "as a New York City subway passenger, you are like [T. S. Eliot's] J. Alfred Prufrock—you prepare a face to meet the faces that you meet."

Psychologist Ervin Staub has made a life's work of studying the role of the bystander. Inspired by people who intervened to save him from the Nazis, Hungarian-born Staub studied factors that make people more likely to come to someone's aid.

New York University's Department of Performance Studies offers "Aesthetics of Everyday Life," a course that helps students to look at New York City through the eyes of an anthropologist. The course description notes that, among other topics, students "will examine the phantasmagoria of New York city streets and open spaces (Washington Square, Times Square); the vernacular imprint on the built environment (graffiti, sidewalk altars, casitas, vendors, Christmas lights); the festivalizing of the city (Easter Parade, and Hasidic Purim in Brooklyn); home and homelessness; death in the vernacular, including memorial walls in various New York City neighborhoods, and the role of tourism, museums, and performance artists in constituting the quotidian."

Akira Kurosawa's great, enigmatic film *Rashomon* (1951) gives an acquaintance with multiple realities. This Japanese film (later copied in Hollywood, with an American setting, and called *The Outrage*) portrays a double crime, variously interpreted by three participants and a witness. What really happened? Kurosawa doesn't say.

Numerous visions of urban encounters are found in art. Franz Kafka's story "The Metamorphosis" (of Gregor Samsa from a clerk to a gigantic insect) deals with the alienation and anonymity of urban life. Gritty movies often present a vision of mean city streets. This mood is exemplified in *Taxi Driver* (1976): An angry cabbie, embittered by what he sees of human cruelty in New York City, buys a gun and begins to kill the crooks and pimps he despises. In *Children of Men* (2006), Mexican director Alfonso Cuarón creates a gray-toned, violent British police state where urban places are war zones, typified by terror.

In contrast, some movies depict the big city as a place where strangers can connect and partake of a rich cultural heritage. The French hit *Amélie* (2001) features a shy, innocent waitress in Montmartre (Audrey Tautou) whose mission is to make others happy, which, in so doing, brings her love.

A classic work combining macro and micro approaches to the study of urban social interaction is Elliot Liebow's *Tally's Corner: A Study of Negro Streetcorner Men* (Boston: Little, Brown, 1967). Although written decades ago, it remains a model of doing social science. It was reprinted, in a second edition, in 2003 by Rowman & Littlefield (Lanham, Md.).

REFERENCES

Aol.com. 2009. "People ignore dying man on street." (February 2): http://news.aol.com/article/people-ignore-dying-man-on-street/325776

Asquith, Christina. 2006. "Scholars ask why Latinos view blacks poorly." (July 12): http://www.diverseeducation.com/artman/publish/article_6086.shtml

BanknetIndia. 2007. "Indian ATM Industry." (May 31): http://www.banknetindia.com/atm_press1.htm

Barron, James. 1991. "Princeton says 'con artist' is foiled." *New York Times* (national edition) (February 28):C19.

Berger, Peter L. 1963. *Invitation to Sociology: A Humanistic Perspective*. Garden City, N.Y.: Doubleday, Anchor.

Berger, Peter L., and Thomas Luckmann. 1967. *The Social Construction of Reality*. Garden City, N.Y.: Doubleday, Anchor.

Capps, Reilly. 2007. "Con artist James Hogue pleads guilty to theft." (March 15): http://www.telluridegateway.com/articles/2007/03/15/news/news03.txt

Cavan, Sherri. [1966] 1973. "Bar sociability." Pp. 143–154 in Arnold Birenbaum and Edward Sagarin, eds., *People in Places: The Sociology of the Familiar*. New York: Praeger.

Cooper, Robert, and Nanthapa Cooper. 1996. *Culture Shock: Thailand*. Singapore: Times Editions.

Deegan, Mary Jo. 1989. "The meet/meat market ritual." Pp. 31–50 in *American Ritual Dramas: Social Rules and Cultural Meanings*. New York: Greenwood Press.

Durkheim, Emile. [1895] 1982. *Rules of Sociological Method*. New York: Free Press.

Evans, Walker. [1966] 2004.*Many are Called*. New Haven, Conn.: Yale University Press.

Fowler, Geoffrey A. 2007. "Cubicle culture: In China's offices, foreign colleagues might get an earful." *Wall Street Journal* (February 13):B1.

Harris Interactive. 2005. "The religious and other beliefs of American, 2005." Harris Poll 90 (December 14): http://www.harrisinteractive.com harris_poll/index.asp?PIO=618.

Gallup Organization. 1978. "Surprising number of Americans believe in paranormal phenomena." (June 15). Ginaton, N. J.: Gallup organization.

Garfinkel, Harold. 1967. *Studies in Ethnomethodology*. Englewood Cliffs, N.J.: Prentice Hall.

Goffman, Erving. 1959. *The Presentation of Self in Everyday Life*. Garden City, N.Y.: Doubleday, Anchor.

———. 1963. *Behavior in Public Places*. New York: Free Press.

———. 1971. *Relations in Public: Microstudies of the Public Order*. New York: Basic Books. Guynn, Jessica. 2007. "Love 2.0." *San Francisco Chronicle* (February 14):A1+.

Internal Revenue Service. 1995. "San Francisco District Safety Bulletin—Bomb Threats." (May 4) San Francisco: IRS.

Judis, John B. 2007. "Hillary Clinton's firewall." *New Republic* (December 18) (http://www.tnr.com/politics/story.html?id=314e8fae-3fd3-4af2-bfde-f0f8e069c1fe).

Latané, Bibb, and John Darley. 1970. *The Unresponsive Bystander: Why Doesn't He Help?* New York: Appleton-Century-Crofts.

Liebow, Elliot. 1967. *Tally's Corner: A Study of Negro Streetcorner Men*. Boston: Little, Brown.

Mandel, Bill. 1988. "ATM rites and rituals for our time." *San Francisco Examiner* (October 14):A4.

Marx, Karl. [1859] 1977. "The German ideology." Pp. 159–191 in David McLellan, ed., *Karl Marx: Selected Writings*. New York: Oxford University Press.

Milgram, Stanley. 1970. "The experience of living in cities." *Science* 167:1461–1468.

Miner, Horace. 1956. "Body ritual among the Nacirema." *American Anthropologist* 58:503–507.

Moss, Jesse, director/producer. 2001. *Con Man*. New York: Mile End Films.

NBC-TV. 2008. "Don't walk: Study finds city's most dangerous intersections." (August 4): http://www.nbc5.com/traffic/17092309/detail.html?rss=chi&psp=news

Neely, Michelle Clark. 1997. "The ATM surcharge debate." *Regional Economist* (July): http://stlouisfed.org/docs/publications/re/1997/c/re1997c3.pdf

Ridgeway, James. 1990. *Blood in the Face*. New York: Thunder's Mouth Press.

Schutz, Alfred. 1967. *Collected Papers*. Maurice Natanson, ed. The Hague: Martinus Nijhoff.

Scott, Michael S. n.d. Department of Justice. "Robberies at automated teller machines." (http://www.cops.usdoj.gov/pdf/e05021551.pdf).

Slapin, Beverly. 1990. *Basic Skills Caucasian Americans Workbook*. Berkeley, Calif.: Oyate.

Thomas, William I., and Dorothy Swaine Thomas. 1928. *The Child in America*. New York: Knopf.

Wenzel, Ty. 2004. *Behind Bars: The Straight-Up Tales of a Big-City Bartender*. New York: St. Martin's Griffin Press.

Whyte, William H. [1988] 1990. "The skilled pedestrian." Pp. 56–67 in *City: Rediscovering the Center*. New York: Doubleday, Anchor.

Whyte, William H., assisted by Margaret Bemiss. 1978. "New York and Tokyo: A study in crowding." Pp. 1–18 in Hidetoshi Kato, ed., *A Comparative Study of Street Life*. Tokyo: Research Institute for Oriental Cultures, Gukushuin University.

Wirth, Louis. [1938] 1969. "Urbanism as a way of life." Pp. 143–164 in Richard Sennett, ed., *Classic Essays on the Culture of Cities*. New York: Appleton-Century-Crofts.

Wolff, Michael. 1973. "Notes on the behavior of pedestrians." Pp. 35–48 in Arnold Birenbaum and Edward Sagarin, eds., *People in Places: The Sociology of the Familiar*. New York: Praeger.

WHO RUNS THIS TOWN?

Tim Teninty

Tim Teninty

CHAPTER 13

THE SKELETON OF POWER

"WHO RUNS THIS TOWN?"

That sounds like a simple question, but it's deceptive. And as with most questions worth asking, serious observers answer in different ways.

Political scientists, lawyers, and public administrators often approach this question by examining a city's legal structure. This is because, as President Franklin D. Roosevelt once said, "structure is government." Knowing what cities and city officials can do legally is vital to understanding who runs any town.

But a city's legal structure reveals only a small part of the story. Local politics now takes place within a larger, often global, context of public and private institutions.

In the United States, knowing how a city fits into the web of intergovernmental and corporate relations—spinning out from, say, Beijing or other international capitals to Washington, D.C., sometimes bypassing the state capital, and weaving its way down to city hall—is important for understanding who and what run U.S. towns. But understanding the networks of informal power and influence may be more important, perhaps crucial, in figuring out who has the ability to get things done. For instance, Chicago's city charter contains no mention of party bosses or ethnic voting blocs. Nor does it refer to the influence of global corporations, Internet-based businesses (e.g., eBay, gambling sites), "body shops" (government contractors, such as the very profitable Science Applications International Corporation [SAIC], a San Diego–based private corporation with 44,000 employees—more than the U.S. Departments of Labor, Energy, and Housing and Urban Development combined), nationwide religious groups, organized crime, street gangs, and other interest groups on public policy. Yet these individuals and organizations can be key actors in city politics. Thus, both formal and informal power structures—at both the micro and macro levels—need to be examined before any conclusions are reached about who runs any town.

This chapter looks at the public institutional framework of local government in the United States—only. Why *only* the United States? Because globally local governments differ so widely that justice cannot be done to their range in one chapter. Further, the organization of local government can be dizzyingly confusing. Even to the locals! Take towns in Great Britain, for example.

One British guidebook notes, "The set-up of UK Local Government is extremely confusing even to those of us who live here" (Edkins, n.d.).

This chapter investigates questions such as these: How are U.S. cities legally organized? What power and formal authority do city officials have? How do cities interact with other units of government in the U.S. federal system? Chapter 14 deals with the other aspect of power: extralegal structures. It examines informal networks of power and influence, mainly from a historical perspective. Then, Chapter 15 examines contending views of how community power and influence have worked in U.S. cities since World War II.

First, a word about the name of the game: power. Like love, truth, beauty, and other abstract concepts, power can be defined in at least 100 ways. Here, *power* means the ability to force an individual or group to do something, even if they resist.

Ultimately, power is rooted in the threat of force or its actual use. People in many cities across the globe, from Port-au-Prince, Haiti, to Kigali, Rwanda, and Monrovia, Liberia, to New York City, Madrid, Najaf, and Kabul understand that the accepted balance of power can be upset by anyone brandishing a lethal weapon. Even a 10-year-old with a gun, stones, brick, or machete can become powerful.

Power can be distinguished from authority and influence. By **authority**, we mean legitimate power, power used in such a way that people see it as legitimate. By *influence*, we mean informal power, sometimes based on persuasion. Chicago gangster Al Capone, both powerful and influential (but lacking in authority), understood the difference: He once said, "You can get much farther with a kind word and a gun than you can with a kind word alone (in http://www.quotemountain.com/famous_quote_author/al_capone_famous_quotations/)."

We begin with an overview of governmental power and authority. In particular, we examine the role that citizens think government should play in their lives.

THE SCOPE OF GOVERNMENT

"That government which governs least governs best." Jefferson's saying reflects the deep distrust many people in the United States feel toward government at any level, no matter who runs it. Fear of excessive government and centralized, faraway authority is a recurrent theme in U.S. history, rooted in the Jeffersonian ideals of liberty and small government.

GOVERNMENT'S LIMITED SCOPE IN THE UNITED STATES

For ideological reasons, the scope of government in the United States is smaller and weaker than that of any other major country in the world today. In France, England, and Sweden, for instance, government is expected to regulate the extent and nature of physical growth and to oversee the general health and welfare of its citizenry. And, as Table 13.1 shows, many countries collect much more revenue per capita to pay for such services. But the dominant ideology in the United

TABLE 13.1   GROSS DOMESTIC PRODUCT (GDP), TAX REVENUES, AND POPULATION FOR SELECTED COUNTRIES, 2003

	Gross Domestic Product, Tax Revenue & Population, 2003				
	GDP millions of US $	GDP per capita	Tax Revenue millions of US $	Tax Revenue per capita	Population thousands
Australia	527,975	$ 26,402	166,840	$ 8,343	19,998
Austria	255,146	$ 31,432	109,968	$ 13,547	8,118
Belgium	304,352	$ 29,337	138,176	$ 13,319	10,374
Canada	873,914	$ 27,630	295,383	$ 9,339	31,629
Czech Republic	90,488	$ 8,870	34,114	$ 3,344	10,202
Denmark	211,238	$ 39,190	102,028	$ 18,929	5,390
Finland	161,703	$ 31,020	72,443	$ 13,897	5,213
France	1,788,032	$ 28,933	776,006	$ 12,557	61,799
Germany	2,442,915	$ 29,603	867,235	$ 10,509	82,523
Greece	173,022	$ 15,720	61,769	$ 5,612	11,007
Hungary	82,158	$ 8,112	31,631	$ 3,123	10,128
Iceland	10,387	$ 35,907	4,134	$ 14,291	289
Ireland	152,098	$ 38,111	45,173	$ 11,319	3,991
Italy	1,467,747	$ 25,265	632,599	$ 10,889	58,095
Japan	4,326,747	$ 33,905	1,094,667	$ 8,578	127,613
Korea	609,221	$ 12,731	154,133	$ 3,221	47,853
Luxembourg	27,005	$ 60,012	11,153	$ 24,785	450
Mexico	640,147	$ 6,232	121,628	$ 1,184	102,726
Netherlands	512,142	$ 31,567	198,711	$ 12,248	16,224
New Zealand	81,398	$ 20,152	28,408	$ 7,033	4,039
Norway	220,664	$ 48,339	95,768	$ 20,979	4,565
Poland	209,360	$ 5,482	71,601	$ 1,875	38,187
Portugal	147,205	$ 14,100	54,613	$ 5,231	10,440
Slovak Republic	32,614	$ 6,064	10,143	$ 1,886	5,378
Spain	879,951	$ 20,948	307,103	$ 7,311	42,006
Sweden	301,385	$ 33,644	152,501	$ 17,024	8,958
Switzerland	321,881	$ 43,468	94,955	$ 12,823	7,405
Turkey	239,442	$ 3,387	78,537	$ 1,111	70,690
United Kingdom	1,795,848	$ 30,154	639,322	$ 10,735	59,555
United States	10,942,668	$ 37,594	2,801,323	$ 9,624	291,077
OECD Average		$ 25,805		$ 8,004	

Source: OECD Revenue Statistics 1965–2004, OECD, Paris, 2004. © Urban Institute, Brookings Institution, 1439

States assigns as much responsibility as possible to the private, rather than the public, sector.

The scope of the public sector at all levels—federal, state, and local—increased dramatically in the twentieth century as the United States changed from a country of farms and small towns to a metropolitan nation. Yet, governments still operate in a climate generally hostile to them.

Particularly after a series of widely reported scandals in high places—from Watergate in the 1970s to reports in the 2000s of corruption, payoffs, cover-ups, lying to the public, and sexual no-nos, not to mention shameless lobbying—an atmosphere of public cynicism prevails. Trust in both national government and corporate America has declined in recent years. Scandals at Enron, WorldCom, and other major corporations did not help restore confidence in big business. According to a 2002 CBS poll, only one in four people in the United States thought that corporate executives were honest. Further, only 6 percent expressed high levels of confidence in major companies (Roberts, 2002).

In the United States, trust in government has been steadily eroding for decades (see NPR–Kaiser–Kennedy School Poll, 2000). This mood is captured in one reporter's comment about Congress over a generation ago, which remains apt: "The crime rate in Congress is probably higher than in downtown Detroit (Newfield in Bogart, 1980:5r)."

For decades, conservative and libertarian groups have attacked big government and big spending. (Although the rhetoric of so-called conservatives at the national level did not match their actions, such as government bailouts of struggling financial institutions.)

At the local–state level, California's Proposition 13 (the Jarvis–Gann initiative), passed in 1978, is often named as the harbinger of a nationwide revolt against "tax-and-spend" government. This initiative amended the state's constitution in a way that reduced county property taxes, by nearly one-half, and restricted their future growth. Since many local government services are funded by the property tax, Proposition 13 effectively limited the expansion of local government service.

Why did the tax revolt happen first in California? Analysts point to one specific demographic reason—

suburban growth (which provided a base for an expanding conservatism)—plus the state's involvement in trade with Asia's industrial–technological sector. Sociologist Harvey Molotch added an often overlooked factor: then skyrocketing property values. Molotch (1990:183) says that California's rising property values fueled rising property taxes: "the cutbacks blamed on Proposition 13 (including draconian budget decreases for public hospitals, paramedics, coastal protection and a proliferation of user fees for services formerly free) were due to wealth creation, rather than wealth erosion." Still, it didn't feel that way to homeowners, especially older ones on fixed incomes. On paper, their homes had increased in value. But homeowners couldn't eat or spend the profits unless they sold their homes. Thus, older homeowners, not corporate business, spearheaded Proposition 13 as a security blanket for their future.

California's cities were only the first to feel the fiscal pinch. Taxpayers' rebellions soon occurred in many states. (Joblessness played a part too: Nationwide, nearly one in seven manufacturing jobs had disappeared in the private manufacturing sector in about 3.5 years from mid-1979 to the end of 1982.)

In this economic climate, voters elected conservative political leaders. No new taxes! Reduce government spending! Privatize! These messages became rallying cries. They were the centerpiece of Margaret Thatcher's Conservative government in Great Britain (1978–1990) as well as the Reagan and George Herbert Walker Bush administrations (1980–1992).

Shortly, we will look at how federal policies affect cities. First, let's examine the impact of state policies on local government.

To begin with, starting more than a generation ago, the fiscal pinch became the fiscal crisis in many states. From the late 1970s on, downsizing was in. Due to circumstances beyond their borders (e.g., economic recession that cut into tax receipts, the credit crisis in 2007 and beyond), local governments in many states faced agonizing choices in "cutback management."

PARADOXICAL ATTITUDES TOWARD GOVERNMENT

Attitudes toward government in the United States are often paradoxical. On the one hand, voters may desire limits on government's growth. On the other, they look to government to solve many issues of collective concern. In other words, people may wish that government's powers were less, but they expect it to do more. In the case of California, some analysts of Proposition 13 concluded that what the voters wanted was something for nothing: lower taxes and more public services—simultaneously.

PUBLIC-PRIVATE SECTOR RELATIONSHIPS

Even in spheres where the U.S. government is expected to act (either as problem solver, distributor of resources and benefits, or regulator), it is assumed that public policy will be made in conjunction with private group interests.

Often, private interests play a significant, some say dominant, role in public decision making. At the local level, for example, real estate brokers and large land developers have a significant impact on zoning decisions and private business influences urban redevelopment plans. Similarly, professional organizations, unions, and corporate officials are generally consulted on policies affecting their interests. Often, such groups initiate policy proposals.

The political philosophy that underlies these public–private sector relations is rooted in classical liberalism and pluralist democracy. The dominant ideology in the United States holds that government reflects the individual citizens' wishes through group representation, and that government does not serve any one group's interest more than another's. Hence, under the theory of pluralism or interest-group democracy, government *should* act as a broker, balancing private interests.

THE "PROPER" ROLE OF LOCAL GOVERNMENT

The dominant U.S. ideology holds that local government should act as a forum in which competing private interests negotiate and come to an accommodation that serves the entire community's interest. In this view, government is supposed to be a facilitator of private economic activity, not an obstacle. Thus, private enterprise expects local government to set the stage for its activities by providing infrastructure (e.g., streets and sewers), maintaining police and fire protection, supporting a "good business climate" (e.g., keeping business taxes low, assuring the absence of

"inappropriate" street people outside tourist hotels), and regulating certain activities to prevent chaos and quackery (e.g., land-use regulations, public-health standards).

To protect their citizens' welfare and to prevent untrammeled competition, local governments today have varying degrees of authority to intervene and regulate private business—by granting health permits to restaurants, construction permits to builders, and so forth. Clearly, the granting or withholding of such benefits can mean economic life or death to private entrepreneurs. Given these economic stakes, we could predict that local politics cannot be separated from economics. This close connection between political power and potential profit should be kept in mind when analyzing who runs any town.

To conclude: As of 2002, there were 87,525 local governments in the United States (see Table 13.2). These local governments provide a number of services and goods for collective consumption and individual betterment, ranging from well-maintained roads to legal entitlements to make money. Various groups are concerned when their interests are at stake, whether they involve getting sewer hook-ups for a suburban housing development or a neighborhood day-care center.

Local government is at the center of competing demands for its scarce resources. It can't fund all projects proposed. It can't award more than one contract to build a new school or give everyone a license to operate a taxi. And in hard economic times, such as the recessionary 2000s, it may not be able to pay both its police officers and its paramedics. In this milieu, there are bound to be conflicts of interest, opportunities for corruption, and attempts to manipulate or persuade the public via the mass media.

LOCAL POLITICAL ENVIRONMENTS

Local communities don't answer the normative question "What should government do?" in the same way. Some communities expect—and expect to pay for—only minimal public services. (Some communities want top-notch services, such as schools and police protection, but prefer that the services be provided by private companies.) Others demand a higher level of services and more of them. Thus, the local political

TABLE 13.2   U.S. LOCAL GOVERNMENTS, 1952–2002

Type of Government	U.S. Government Units: 1952–2002										
	2002	1997	1992	1987	1982	1977	1972	1967	1962	1957	1952
Total	87,900	87,504	86,743	83,237	81,831	79,913	78,269	81,299	91,236	102,392	116,805
Federal government	1	1	1	1	1	1	1	1	1	1	1
State governments	50	50	50	50	50	50	50	50	50	48	48
Local governments	87,849	87,453	86,692	83,186	81,780	79,862	78,218	81,248	91,185	102,343	116,756
General purpose	3,034	3,043	3,043	3,042	3,041	3,042	3,044	3,049	3,043	3,050	3,052
County	35,937	36,001	35,962	35,891	35,810	35,684	35,508	35,153	35,141	34,415	34,009
Municipal	19,431	19,372	19,296	19,200	19,076	18,862	18,517	18,048	17,217	16,807	
Township (school districts)	13,522	13,726	14,556	14,721	14,851	15,174	15,781	21,782	34,678	50,454	67,355
Special districts	35,356	34,683	33,131	29,532	28,078	25,962	23,885	21,264	18,323	14,424	12,340

Source: Adapted from U.S. Census Bureau, Table A, p. 5 , July 2002 (http://ftp2.census.gov/govs/cog/2002COGprelim_report.pdf).

environment is a key factor in analyzing the scope of local government.

According to neoconservative "public choice" theorists, people rationally choose a local political environment. For instance, when a woman chooses a particular place to live, she chooses one bundle of services over another. If she doesn't like the particular service bundle, she can vote with her car. Others disagree, saying that residential choices are due either to "forced choice," "dumb happenstance" (Molotch, 1990:195), or shared lifestyles (e.g., Weiss, 1988). Whatever their motivation for choosing one community over another, people do live in cities and suburbs that offer different services.

The following typology applies only to U.S. suburbs, classifying them according to their attitude toward economic development:

1. *Aggressive*. Suburbs that aggressively compete for business or industrial activities. Types pursuing this strategy: (1) older, close-in suburbs suffering from problems similar to those of their central city (e.g., fiscal pressure, stagnating income) and (2) newer, more prosperous suburbs.

2. *Regulatory*. Suburbs that adhere to regulations believed to be in the public interest and that are considered more important than development per se. Type pursuing this strategy: those with attractive land that can choose which development they want.

3. *Cooperative*. Suburbs that are moderately prodevelopment. Type pursuing this strategy: stable, established communities.

4. *Retentive*. Suburbs that want to retain existing businesses and industries. Type pursuing this strategy: old, stable suburbs of mixed residential–commercial activity.

5. *Reactive*. Suburbs that have no formal policy on economic development but react case by case. Type pursuing this strategy: developed suburbs (Pelissero and Fasenfest, 1988).

6. *Antidevelopment*. Suburbs that oppose economic development. Type pursuing this strategy: ecology-minded and/or upper-income suburbs.

According to the developers of this five ideal-type classification (I added the sixth type), the values of local elected officials in the suburbs they studied "shaped the particular mix of policies followed in each suburb" and "determined the suburban community's approach to development" (Pelissero and Fasenfest, 1988:11).

Whether city or suburb, the population size and mix, the values of local elected officials, and the attitudes toward economic growth influence the local political environment. So does the level of tax resources available. For instance, relatively homogeneous, residential, upper-status suburbs (e.g., PRIZM's Upper Crust) do not need to promote economic growth or mediate among conflicting interests. Large, heterogeneous cities, on the other hand, often seek to juggle conflicting interests.

CITIES AS CREATURES OF THEIR STATE

In the United States, cities are entirely creatures of their state governments. This stems from a decision made by the republic's founding fathers; they made no mention of cities in the U.S. Constitution. Instead, they granted the states the right to create or not to create all local jurisdictions, including cities.

When the states did create cities, they kept legal power over them. Hence, it is the 50 state legislatures that decide how city governments are structured.

GENERAL-LAW CITIES AND CHARTER CITIES

States grant legal powers to their creatures—the cities—in two different ways. Some states establish the general powers of city governments in state law; these are called **general-law cities**. Other states spell out the powers of a city in a charter approved by the legislature; these are called **charter cities**.

Charters granted to cities by their states vary in content, but most describe the form, composition, powers, and limitations of city officials. To illustrate, a city **charter** might state that the **city council** will be elected every 4 years, have one representative from each of 10 districts, and have authority over personnel, zoning, parks, and budgeting.

An important variation is the **home-rule** charter. Under home-rule provisions in a state constitution, the precise definition of city powers is left up to the city voters, within limits set by the state constitution. About 75 percent of large U.S. cities operate under home-rule provisions. About half of the states provide for home rule in their state constitutions, and about a dozen more allow home rule through legislation.

Charters can be revised. However, voters usually greet revision with yawns.

New York City was forced to revise its charter in 1989 after the U.S. Supreme Court ruled that the city's top government body, the Board of Estimate, was unconstitutional (because it violated the principle of one person, one vote). New Yorkers approved a complete overhaul of municipal government, eliminating the Board of Estimate, a unique legislative–executive hybrid that exercised more power than the city council.

DILLON'S RULE

When a legal question arises concerning the extent of power granted by a state to a city, the courts have traditionally ruled against cities. In other words, the courts narrowly construe city powers. This narrow construction of city powers is based on **Dillon's rule**, named for Iowa State Judge John F. Dillon, who presided over a court decision in 1868 (see National League of Cities, n.d.).

What difference does it make if states legally control cities and if the courts narrowly interpret city powers? A great deal. Dillon's rule means that a city cannot operate a hot dog stand at the city park without first getting the state legislature to pass an enabling law, unless, by chance, the city's charter or some previously enacted law clearly covers the sale of hot dogs.

Because cities can do only what state legislatures expressly permit them to do (or what is "fairly implied" or "indispensable"), city charters often describe city powers in painstaking detail. For example, in the former city charter of Nashville, Tennessee, the replacement of regular members of the fire department above the rank of "pipeman" or "ladderman" (due to illness or disability) was spelled out so that there could be no mistake concerning the chain of command: the fire chief, subject to the mayor's approval, was to designate any regular member of the fire department from a lower rank to perform the duties of such member during his (or her) absence.

Even under home-rule charters (whereby cities can amend charters without going back to the legislature), cities are far from independent. They are still bound by the law of their state. And the state is omnipotent. In a 1923 case involving the city of Trenton and the state of New Jersey, the U.S. Supreme Court ruled that a state has the legal power to eliminate cities altogether, even against the will of the city's residents.

CHANGING RELATIONSHIPS

STATE LEGISLATURES AND CITY INTERESTS

The posture of a state legislature is important to the cities of that state. Unfortunately for cities, historically, state legislatures generally adopted negative stances toward their cities—boxing them in with narrow grants of legal power and voting new power grudgingly.

City politicians have long felt victimized by their state legislatures. But the villains in the piece changed as the nation's population shifted from rural to urban to suburban locations. Specifically, before 1962, U.S. cities faced state legislatures dominated by rural, and usually antiurban, interests. By 1960, almost 70 percent of the U.S. population was urban, but about one-third of the states still had very large proportions of their population in rural areas. Further, before 1962, most state legislatures did not have the one person, one vote rule. Usually, state legislative districts were drawn so that rural voters could elect more than their proportional share of representatives. Before 1962, for example, only 11 percent of Californians (mainly from rural areas) could elect a majority of members of the California State Senate.

Beginning with a landmark Supreme Court case in 1962, *Baker v. Carr*, an ongoing process of **reapportionment** has been under way. This court decision required one person, one vote. It led to a redrawing of electoral district lines so that the population in all legislative districts is substantially equal.

Since *Baker v. Carr* in 1962, rural domination of state legislatures has generally been reduced. But suburbs, not cities, have been the major benefactors. Demographics helps to explain why. By 1970, the U.S. population was roughly one-third urban, one-third suburban, and one-third rural or small town, with a slight suburban dominance. (*The share of the U.S. population living in suburbs doubled from 1900 to 1950. From 1950 to 2000, it doubled again. By 2000, the majority, 52 percent, of the U.S. population lived in suburbs.*)

The irony is this: State legislatures were reapportioned to ensure one person, one vote at the very time that population was shifting to the suburbs. Thus, reapportionment generally did not significantly benefit big cities. It did benefit suburbs and hurt rural areas.

In many states, a suburban–rural—antiurban coalition emerged in the 1970s, replacing the historic rural–antiurban coalition. This post-1970 antiurban coalition often voted (and continues to vote) against legislation designed to meet "big-city problems."

Antiurbanism escalated in the 1980s (and later, under a new name: "prosuburbanism"). By 1990, mounting budget deficits in state capitals forced many populous and suburban states, including California and Ohio, to make drastic cutbacks in welfare and education; these program cuts adversely affected more urbanites than suburbanites.

By the early 2000s, antiurbanism morphed into prosuburbanism. As discussed below, some members of the U.S. House of Representatives organized a "suburban agenda." Implicitly, this agenda pit the concerns of suburbanites against urbanites.

SUBURBS VERSUS CITIES

More than a generation ago, distinguished urban historian Richard C. Wade called suburbanization "the most important fact of American social and political life" since 1945 (1982:20). A number of analysts agree, noting a related fact: the emergence of two separate—and unequal—communities in the United States, suburbs and cities. (But, as we shall see, this clear separation has broken down in many U.S. metro areas, particularly when many inner suburbs suffer high poverty rates.)

Many suburbanites feel disconnected from (and fearful of) urban poverty, street crime, and other conditions facing their city neighbors—and more and more their *suburban* neighbors. Perhaps that is one reason more and more people are choosing gated communities, both in suburbs and in cities. (Suburban fear of urban poverty is rather ironic in the United States as, since 2005, the poverty rate in many close-in suburbs rivals or bests city rates.)

This emotional apartheid, based on suburban fear of city folk, can start very young. Student research teams in my classes at San Francisco State found, for instance, that children in suburban San Francisco held extremely negative views of the city. Although over 80 percent of the preteenage respondents had never visited San Francisco, they characterized the city as the home of crime, grime, and slime. The vast majority had nothing positive to say about San Francisco, the city voted— 16 years in a row—by readers of a U.S. travel magazine as their top destination (Thousman, 2008).

Perhaps it is no accident, then, that Orlando, Florida, home of Disney World's Magic Kingdom (claiming 15.4 million visitors in 2000)—not San Francisco, "everyone's favorite city," or any national park or New York City or Los Angeles—is the most popular vacation destination in the United States. It is also noteworthy that the top destination in the United States by motorcoach in one post-millennium year, 2001, was Branson, Missouri. As a *New York Times* reporter put it years earlier when Branson started its rise, "the astounding growth of this squeaky-clean, virtually all-white, middle-of-nowhere Mecca is a revealing slice of America." One tourist at Branson's Elvis-A-Rama and glitzy country music theaters revealed why he vacationed there rather than in Los Angeles: "There's no smog blowing down from the hillsides. There's no graffiti. There are no gangs. I'm not prejudiced, but it's nice to be someplace where everyone speaks English" (in Applebome, 1993:B1).

Recent Suburban Antiurbanism in the United States
Suburban–city antipathy remains, despite the suburbanization of poverty and other so-called urban problems that now are part of suburban life. Indeed, months before they lost control of the U.S. House of Representatives in 2006, Republicans organized a "suburban agenda." Fifty members of the House of Representatives, all representing suburbs and all Republican, joined the Suburban Agenda Caucus. Here is what one Caucus member, Congressperson Mike Castle (R-Del.), wrote on his blog in May 2006:

> Delaware communities are often considered suburbs of the major cities that surround us—such as Wilmington, Baltimore and Philadelphia. It is where many families reside and where concerns about open space, education and health care are top on residents' minds. Because of this, I joined the Suburban Agenda Caucus in the House of Representatives, comprised of 50 Members representing suburban areas, from Washington State to Florida. We recently unveiled a new family agenda for Congress that will focus on addressing the needs and priorities of suburban communities throughout the United States. The Caucus is pushing individual bills backed by voters in suburban areas including 401 Kids Savings Accounts, Health Information Technology, Open Space Conservation and Internet Protection for Kids.
>
> *(Castle, 2006)*

Was Congressperson Castle asserting that city folk are *not* concerned with such "family agenda" issues as open space, education, and health care? Or was this suburban agenda, poll-tested in 22 suburban counties, more about winning elections in mainly formerly Republican districts on the edge of big cities?

The head of the Suburban Caucus, a Republican from Chicago's northern suburbs, argued that the suburban agenda was neither Democratic nor Republican: "It comes out of suburban thinking" (in James, 2006). Some close observers disagreed. Two *Chicago Tribune* reporters called the suburban agenda an election ploy by Republicans to appeal to suburban voters, many of whom were Democratic voters who had left cities for inner suburbs (Zeleny and Kuzcka in James, 2006). If so, the ploy didn't work very well: Republicans lost control of the House, and the losses included six caucus members. (The losses had less to do with the suburban agenda than with other issues, including the Iraq War, inappropriate sexual behavior with underage boys [Mark Foley, R-Fla.], and an FBI investigation [Curt Weld, R–Pa.].)

In the past generation, so many urbanites moved to the suburbs that, by 2000, the *majority* of people in the United States lived around central cities, not in them. Movers' reasons varied widely. One key reason concerned a desire to flee—from city people, from city "problems," and/or from paying for public programs to address those problems. Radical observer Mike Davis (1993) calls this attitude "the War against the Cities." I call it the "moating and gating of suburban America" or the "Yes, you *can* run and hide" syndrome. Whatever it's called, it describes suburban antiurbanism.

What lies behind this suburban antiurbanism? Analysts disagree. *Chicago Tribune* Washington bureau chief Frank James (2006) implies that race—whites vs. people of color—is all-important. James points to the thinly veiled "us" vs. "them" comments by a member of the Republican Suburban Caucus:

> You know, the federal government has all kinds of programs for our cities....We devote tons of resources to our cities as well we should....But oftentimes it seems to the people who live in the suburbs that it is done at their expense.
>
> *(James, 2006)*

Reporter James comments that this congressperson's words could easily be seen as an appeal to white voters: "Since cities tend to have higher percentages of African Americans and other minorities than many suburbs, [the Caucus Congressperson's] comments could certainly be interpreted as an attempt to capitalize on white voters' flawed perceptions that blacks and other minorities receive most federal funding."

Radical iconoclast Mike Davis (1993) sees race and conservative politics as the keys to suburban antiurbanism. According to Davis, a conservative coalition in Congress united suburban and rural representatives in both major political parties against any federal reinvestment in big cities dominated by minorities. Indeed, he charges that all major candidates for president in 1992 may have acted "in cynical concert to exclude a subject [from their debates] that had become mutually embarrassing—cities": "The word 'city' now color-coded and worrisome to the candidates' common suburban heartland—was expunged from the exchanges. Thus the elephant of the urban crisis was simply...conjured out of sight" (3). Davis concludes that the 1992 presidential election showed that "the big cities, once the very fulcrum of the political universe during Franklin Roosevelt's presidency, have been demoted to the status of a scorned and impotent electoral periphery" (3).

(Bringing Davis's argument forward, cities have remained a non-issue in all U.S. presidential elections since. However, some think—or hope—that postelection "realities" of President Obama's United States, such as the desire to decrease unemployment in part by fixing infrastructure, may change that.)

Public-opinion analyst William Schneider also attributes suburban antiurbanism to conservative ideology. Schneider claims that "a major reason people move out to the suburbs is simply to be able to buy their own government. These people resent it when politicians take their money and use it to solve other people's problems, especially when they don't believe that government can actually solve those problems" (1992:38).

"URBANIZATION OF THE SUBURBS"

Yet, ironies abound. First, some U.S. suburbs *look* more like inner cities than stereotypical, upper middle- and upper-class, pale-faced suburbs, such as the one depicted in the film *American Beauty* (1999). Second, suburban poverty is not an oxymoron. Indeed, in 2005, for the first time in U.S. history, poor suburbanites outnumbered poor urbanites in the nation's 100 biggest metro areas. According to Brookings Institution analysts Berube and Kneebone (2006), *over 12 million people in U.S. suburbs of the 100 most populated metropolitan areas were defined as poor while fewer—11 million—urbanites in those same metro areas were defined as poor.*

This new reality of more suburban than urban poor in the largest U.S. metro areas could/should change stereotypes: Big cities are usually seen as home to the nation's poor, surrounded by suburbs populated by middle- and upper-income residents. Yet, U.S. suburbs are more diverse in terms of race and class than ever before. One reason: Increasing numbers of recent immigrants (whose incomes tend to be lower than native-born U.S. residents) are settling in suburbs, not cities—particularly in the South and the West.

In addition, many suburbs now face so-called big-city problems, such as rising crime, low-paying jobs, and low-performing schools. In 2006, the president of the National Urban League (Morial in Associated Press, 2006) called it "the urbanization of the suburbs." (Surely, he was referring to this sense of the word "urbanization," as discussed in Chapter 5: urbanization may refer to the process of becoming urban in terms of social, technological, political, and spatial organization.)

I think there is another important factor behind antiurbanism: widespread pessimism about the future. Citizens seem resigned to diminishing expectations and urban (and suburban) decline. This feeling is rooted in global shifts that affect people in suburbs, cities, and rural areas, albeit differently.

Historically, and for good reason, people in the United States were optimistic after World War II: They had rising expectations for the national economy and their own fortunes. Especially if they were white, they expected that their children would live with more, not less, than they had. Even without having heard of Burgess's hypothesis, they understood that moving *out* to the suburbs meant moving *up*. Literally millions of white middle-class and working-class people in the United States left town in the 1950s and beyond.

But by the 1970s and early 1980s, global economic restructuring hit home. Once secure and relatively high-paid jobs in manufacturing moved to cheaper labor areas. Few high-paid jobs replaced them. White-collar and no-collar (digirati) workers, including top managers, also felt insecure as companies merged or went "offshore," and they found themselves unemployed or "rightsized" out of work. Consequently, for ever-increasing numbers, future prosperity seemed dreamlike.

By the early 1990s, people in the United States were wondering what had gone wrong. Increasingly, many were satisfied if they could keep their income and living standards from declining.

In sum, downward mobility was knocking at the door. What does this have to do with suburban anti-urbanism? Probably a great deal. During boom times, it is easier to have compassion for—or at least neutrality toward—strangers and people unlike oneself (or assumed to be different). During gloomy economic times, the politics of resentment can grip the heart and purse, widening the gulf between "us" and "them." The newly-insecure often assign blame to someone or something for their falling fortunes, not to global processes beyond their control. In this milieu, many fled to gated communities or "safer" suburbs rather than fight what they saw as irreversible urban decline, especially dangerous streets.

Liberals would say that the well-off blame the victims. Conservatives would say that the well-off rightly blame those who have not helped themselves but prefer to live off government giveaways. Marxist radicals would say that it is ironic: A group of better-off people blame those at the bottom of the social ladder instead of the structures of capitalism that tend to impoverish them both.

Meantime, we should remember that the term "suburb" covers many types of communities (Chapter 8). In Europe, many inner suburbs are populated by lower-income immigrants, including large percentages of underemployed or unemployed who live in high-rise tenements. And, as Table 13.3a and b show, many global "suburbs" have more residents than cities considered large in the United States (even if scholars disagree on exactly which suburbs are the largest in the world).

In the United States, the *stereotypical* suburb is a bedroom community of upper-income, mainly or all-white areas beyond the city limits. It features well-manicured lawns and single-family homes, such as those on Wisteria Lane, the home of TV's *Desperate Housewives*.

Yet, U.S. suburbs are much more diverse racially, socially, and economically. The range of suburbs in the United States is considerable: from poor white suburbs; predominantly middle-class African American suburbs; older, shabby industrial suburbs; mixed-use suburbs; rich residential suburbs, and lower-income Latino suburbs (e.g., Huntington Park outside Los Angeles, Berwyn and Stone Park in suburban Chicago) to Asian-dominant suburbs such as Los Angeles's Monterey Park, whose 2000 population was more than 40 percent Chinese American and over 60 percent Asian and Asian American, including Vietnamese and Korean, with a substantial number living in poverty.

In the past two decades or so, particularly in larger metro areas, there has been an upsurge of new ethnic, suburban residents. Activities to serve them often follow but not at the expense of non-ethnicity-based activities. For example, in one upscale Boston suburb with increased numbers of Chinese Americans, in recent years it has not been unusual to come upon a scene like this: "Between reciting Chinese poetry and performing traditional dance routines, [Chinese American] kids munched on McDonald's fries and hunched over Game Boy consoles" (Noonan, 2007).

In the past two decades or so, there have been other momentous city–suburban changes. Importantly,

TABLE 13.3A, B   THE WORLD'S LARGEST INCORPORATED SUBURBS, TWO VIEWS

Table 13.3a.*

Rank	City	Population	Metropolitan Area	Nation	Source
1	Giza	2,221,868	Greater Cairo	Egypt	Egypt Census, 1996
2	Quezon City	2,173,831	Metro Manila	Philippines	Philippines Census 2002
3	Bekasi	1,931,976	Greater Jakarta	Indonesia	Indonesia Census 2000
4	Ecatepec de Morelos	1,688,258	Greater Mexico City	Mexico	Mexico Census 2005 CONAPO
5	Kobe	1,528,940	Greater Osaka	Japan	Japan Oct. 2006
6	Tangerang	1,488,666	Greater Jakarta	Indonesia	Indonesia Census 2000
7	Depok	1,353,249	Greater Jakarta	Indonesia	Indonesia Census 2000
8	Kawasaki	1,342,232	Greater Tokyo	Japan	Japan Oct. 2006
9	Guarulhos	1,283,253	Greater São Paulo	Brazil	Brazil IBGE Estimate 2006
10	Thana	1,261,517	Greater Mumbai	India	India Census 2001

*Does not include cities that require exact records of birth, death, and moving, such as in Japan and Brazil, which estimate city populations annually.

Table 13.3b

Rank	City	Population	Metropolitan Area	Nation	Source
1	Bekasi	1,931,976	Greater Jakarta, Jabotabek	Indonesia	Indonesia Census 2000
2	Ecatepec de Morelos	1,688,258	Greater Mexico City	Mexico	Mexico Census 2005 CONAPO
3	Tangerang	1,488,666	Greater Jakarta, Jabotabek	Indonesia	Indonesia Census 2000
4	Depok	1,353,249	Greater Jakarta, Jabotabek	Indonesia	Indonesia Census 2000
5	Kawasaki	1,342,232	Greater Tokyo Area	Japan	Japan Oct. 2006
6	Guarulhos	1,283,253	Greater São Paulo	Brazil	Brazil IBGE Estimate 2006
7	Thana	1,261,517	Greater Mumbai	India	India Census 2001
8	Kalyan	1,193,266	Greater Mumbai	India	India Census 2001
9	Saitama	1,182,000	Greater Tokyo	Japan	Japan Census 2005
10	Caloocan	1,177,604	Metro Manila	Philippines	Philippines Census 2002

Source of Indonesian and Indian population data is citypopulation.de.

poverty has moved into the suburbs in a big way. In the 100 biggest U.S. metro areas, suburban poverty now outranks urban poverty in terms of numbers of people affected. (Note, however, that the poverty *rate* in U.S. big cities [18.4 percent] remains higher than in their close-in suburbs [9.4 percent].)

Given that many feel that the future portends fewer, not more, property owners, U.S. suburbanites seek to hold the line economically. This condition makes them very tax-sensitive. The upshot is often suburban hostility, particularly in suburbs farther from the urban core, to both government and cities. This hostility coincides with two recent sociospatial developments that have important political consequences:

1. Since 1990, suburban residents are a majority in many states, including the nation's largest, California.
2. Many suburbanites live in edge cities or post-suburbia, settlements that are no longer dependent economically and socially on the urban core.

In brief, scarcity—not familiarity—can breed contempt. Fear can also breed secession from the union—not of South or Sunbelt from North and Rustbelt but of outer suburbs from the urban core. With little hope for a more prosperous future and no sense of community with their urban neighbors, suburbanites are not anxious to share their tax dollars with urban strangers.

Yet, ironically, many suburbs share city-type problems, including poverty, as already noted. As many Big City mayors have long held, a city's problems cannot be walled in. For example, affluent suburban counties around New York City face congestion, drugs, crime, expensive housing, garbage mounds, air pollution, and other so-called urban problems. Further, according to the U.S. Bureau of Justice Statistics, in 2005, urbanites did have the highest violent victimization rates, but suburbanites were far from crime-free. For example, six urbanites, four suburbanites, and four rural residents per 1,000 were victims of aggravated assault (Bureau of Justice Statistics, 2009).

Nonetheless, few suburbanites apparently see a common future with their urban neighbors. Nor do those seeking high political office. For more than a

quarter-century, perhaps reflecting the demographic shift to the suburbs, no U.S. presidential candidate has addressed specifically urban issues.

So, if you mix economic insecurity, fear for personal safety on city streets, and tense race relations with long-standing cynicism about government, what have you got? A recipe for a volatile brew. Depending on your ideology and optimism–pessimism quotient, you see either (1) the new survival of the fittest, (2) creative challenges, or (3) the war of all against all.

It is noteworthy that when issues are not framed as urban–suburban, U.S. suburbanites seem to follow the Golden Rule. Take health care, for example. One national random sample poll in 2007 (Roberts, 2007) revealed that a vast majority of respondents favored coverage for everyone, presumably urbanites as well as suburbanites and rural dwellers. Similarly, a 2008 poll (*Rasmussen Reports*, 2008) found that 67 percent of respondents thought that the same level of insurance coverage available to members of Congress should be available to everyone. (Note that neither poll asked respondents if they were willing to pay more money to cover insurance for everyone. A poll years earlier did find that suburbanites said they would pay for urban dwellers to be insured.)

To summarize: U.S. cities are creatures of state law. States can grant or take away powers from cities at will. State legislatures spell out city powers in general laws or charters. In some states, cities are granted considerable discretion to determine their own structures and powers under home-rule charters, but even home-rule cities are far from independent. Furthermore, cities have been under the domination of state legislatures, historically controlled by rural interests and antiurban attitudes.

Demographic shifts and reapportionment reduced rural domination. But ironically, suburbs—not cities—gained the most influence and power from these changes. Unhappily for cities, suburban dominance, combined with economic hard times and fiscal austerity, led to a new and grimmer round of antiurbanism.

LOCAL GOVERNMENTS IN A GLOBAL SOCIETY: "TAKING RESPONSIBILITY FOR THE SKY"

"All politics is local." This maxim, often attributed to the late speaker of the U.S. House of Representatives

436 WHO RUNS THIS TOWN?

Tip O'Neill, means that local interests mold national political issues. Closing a naval base, for example, may be influenced by the local unemployment rate and the clout of the district's congressperson.

But there is another sort of local politics, and it works in reverse: It starts locally and spreads. For instance, the city council of Irvine, a city in postsuburban Orange County, California, passed legislation restricting chlorofluorocarbons (CFCs) in the city. The anti-CFC ordinance raised the cost of some goods for local residents and caused hardships for some businesses. Indeed, it seemed idealistic, even quixotic, for one city council to try to solve the ozone depletion situation and to take responsibility for the sky. So why did they do it? Perhaps the idea of locality takes on renewed importance as global problems feel overwhelming, and political awareness can lead to a feeling of helplessness if some action isn't taken. Perhaps they asked themselves, "If not us, who?" and refused to accept the answer of "Nobody."

Not a prairie fire but at least a flashlight, the action of one city, Irvine, illuminated the actions of other localities. Indeed, many other places, from California and New York to Japan's Shiga Prefecture, have taken responsibility for the sky...and the earth...and the water...and their fellow beings. In Detroit, 125 teenagers and young adults worked with local residents to rehabilitate houses and march against crack houses as part of a Green Cities project. Two communities, one in Japan and the other in Siberia, have a "sister lake" relationship; they jointly study the flight of birds that migrate to and from their areas. And so on.

To conclude: Local actions—from passing antipollution and gun-control ordinances to conducting municipal foreign policy—have wider political significance. Such local deeds not only encourage collective action but also signal local resistance to the power of the nation-state.

FORMS OF CITY GOVERNMENT

Globally, forms and functions of municipal government differ widely—from Bolivia's elected mayors and councils and Bangladesh's (proposed) four-tier system to the (mega)city-state of Singapore, with its three-tiered local system. Since 1990, many sub-national governments have undergone fundamental transfor-

mation. For example, before 1990, most countries in East Asia were highly centralized, but now local or regional governments from China to Thailand are responsible for delivering some critical services and economic development.

Some comments and concepts we will discuss (e.g., know-who) may or may not apply to local governments globally. Given space constraints, here we will discuss only forms of city government in the United States.

As suggested, the first step in understanding how U.S. cities (including suburban cities) work is to clarify the city–state relationship. The second step entails understanding how a city's internal government is structured.

Getting something done in a city takes know-how and *know-who*. Who has the authority to condemn an unsafe building? What bureaucrat can grant a permit to hold a rally in the park? Can the mayor fire the school superintendent who has ordered the closing of the high school for his own birthday? Knowing whom to go to and how to get something done begins with an understanding of a city's governmental form.

Most U.S. city governments fall into one of three categories: the mayor–council form, the council–manager form, and the commission form. (In New England, town meetings also exist; they are used mainly by cities with less than 10,000 population and exclusively by cities with fewer than 100,000 inhabitants.) Large U.S. cities generally have a mayor–council form. Some smaller cities also follow this model.

However, many smaller and medium-sized communities, particularly metropolitan suburbs that grew up in this century, have a city council–manager form. Here, a city manager, appointed by the city council and accountable to that legislative body, plays a key leadership role, and the elected mayor is less important.

Finally, some cities have a commission form of government. Here, elected commissioners act collectively as the city council and individually as heads of city departments.

MAYOR–COUNCIL FORM

The **mayor–council form** is the most common form of city government in the United States. It is also the predominant form in large cities. The organization

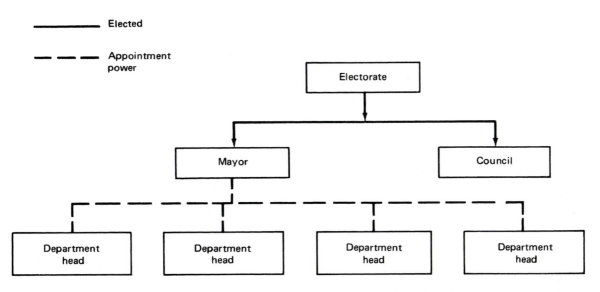

Elected
Appointment power

Fig. 13.2 THE MAYOR–COUNCIL FORM OF LOCAL GOVERNMENT IN THE UNITED STATES.

chart in Figure 13.2 shows that under this form of government mayors typically have appointment power—that is, they can appoint department heads. They do not have this power in council–manager cities.

The organization chart also shows that the mayor and city council are elected independently. The mayor's independent elected status and significant appointment power indicate that under the mayor–council form mayors have important executive powers. Other factors, not revealed on the organization chart, contribute to the mayor's role as executive leader. These may include the ability to intervene directly in the conduct of city government operations, to veto the city's budget, and to initiate legislation.

COUNCIL–MANAGER FORM

Consider Figure 13.3. The fact that the mayor is in a box, somewhere off in left field, is a significant feature of the **council–manager form of government**. Under this form, which is common in many medium-sized U.S. communities, the mayor has much less power and authority than in a mayor–council government. The important actor in this fairly recent form of government is the **city manager**, appointed by the city council, as Figure 13.3 indicates. Usually, the manager serves at the pleasure of the elected city council and

can be removed at any time if a majority of councillors so decide. The city manager, in turn, typically has the power to hire and fire heads of city departments. He or she is also responsible for preparing the city budget, developing policy recommendations for the council's action, and overseeing city government.

In many cities, the city manager draws a bigger salary than the mayor or council members (who may be part-time or amateur administrators). Further, the city manager has a larger personal staff and more control over the flow of information than the mayor or councillors. This combination of professional expertise and access to and control over information gives city managers informal power beyond what is revealed in organization charts.

COMMISSION FORM

Under the **commission form of government**, voters elect a relatively small number of commissioners, who play a dual role as legislators and executives. Commissioners approve legislation and also head the city's departments.

The commission form was introduced in Galveston, Texas, following a flood in 1900 that left the city and its finances under water. Today, no U.S. city with a population over 500,000 operates under this form—for

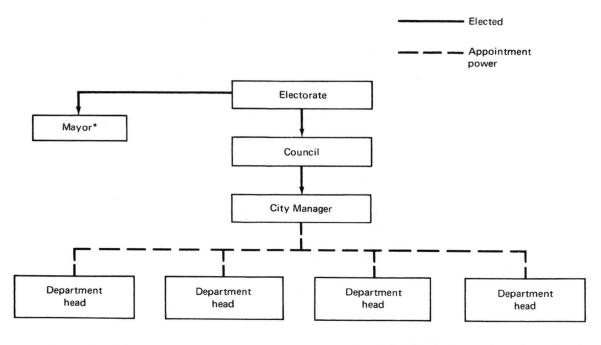

* Independently elected or appointed from among the council members

Fig. 13.3 THE COUNCIL–MANAGER FORM OF LOCAL GOVERNMENT IN THE UNITED STATES.

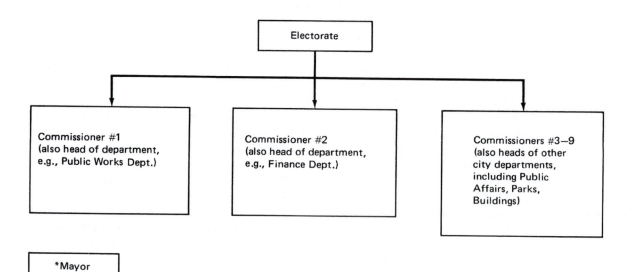

* Usually appointed from among commissioners.

Fig. 13.4 THE COMMISSION FORM OF LOCAL GOVERNMENT IN THE UNITED STATES.

good reasons. As Figure 13.4 shows, there is no strong executive leader. Power is exercised collectively by the city commissioners—the parks commissioner, police commissioner, and so on. Historically, this ideal of collective leadership has resulted in lack of coordination and government by amateurs.

To conclude: Few cities today use the commission form, the mayor–council structure predominates in larger cities, and council–manager governments are most commonly found in medium-sized cities and suburbs. Why is the council–manager form so attractive to medium-sized communities and so unattractive to large cities? To understand this, some background is necessary.

The city manager plan was initiated in Staunton, Virginia, in 1908. It spread slowly throughout the nation up to the 1940s. After World War II, the council–manager form became widespread in medium-sized communities, especially upper-income, white suburbs. Generally speaking, these suburbanites thought that the council–manager form would ensure professional, businesslike government and guard against something defined as inefficient, unprofessional, and corrupt: big-city politics. Many observers think that council–manager governments are best suited to relatively homogeneous white-collar communities. Why? Because there the political representation of diverse interests is not important. Thus, ordinarily we shouldn't expect to find a city manager running a city composed of various ethnic groups and a significant blue-collar population. Typically, mayors operate in cities that mediate among diverse interests, not cities that seek primarily to create pleasant living conditions.

ORGANIZATION OF CITY GOVERNMENTS

MAYORS, STRONG OR WEAK

In U.S. cities with mayor–council governments, the **mayor** is popularly considered to be the head of city government, the responsible official with whom the local buck stops. But as the song says, "It ain't necessarily so." Often, a mayor is powerless to improve bus service, create jobs for the unemployed, or reorganize the delivery of city services. Although decades old, the following exchange before a congressional committee between then U.S. Senator Abraham Ribicoff

(D.-Conn.) and then mayor of Los Angeles, Sam Yorty, is instructive:

Senator Ribicoff: As I listened to your testimony, Mayor Yorty, I made some notes. This morning you have really waived authority and responsibility in the following areas: schools, welfare, transportation, employment, health, and housing, which leaves you as head of a city with a ceremonial function, police, and recreation.

Mayor Yorty: That is right, and fire.

Senator Ribicoff: And fire.

Mayor Yorty: Yes.

Senator Ribicoff: Collecting sewage?

Mayor Yorty: Sanitation; that is right.

Senator Ribicoff: In other words, basically you lack jurisdiction, authority, responsibility for what makes a city move?

Mayor Yorty: That is exactly it. (U.S. Senate, 1966–1967:774)

In this exchange, Senator Ribicoff seems to blame Mayor Yorty for "waiving" responsibility. But in fact, Yorty never had the responsibility. Then, as now, in Los Angeles (and many other cities), mayors have limited powers, making them weak chief executives. Nonetheless, as outgoing San Francisco Mayor Dianne Feinstein (and later U.S. senator) warned her successor, "Anytime there's trouble, whether [the] Muni[cipal railway] breaks down or someone is cited for double parking, they all come to you. There is no Teflon with this job" (1988:5).

Under the weak mayor–council arrangement, the city council or independent administrative boards dominate city decision making. Further, mayors (either strong or weak) have no authority to control many independent units of government within their political boundaries (e.g., school districts), as we shall soon see.

In weak-mayor governments, administrative boards or commissions exercise power independently of the mayor (who typically appoints members and can remove them). This arrangement serves to broaden the base of political participation. Indeed, city boards are often appointed with a keen eye on local power blocs. In San Francisco, for example, members of appointed boards reflect the city's ethnic and cultural pluralism.

They are composed of a mix of African Americans, whites, Latinos, Asian Americans, single parents, labor unionists, real estate brokers, gays and lesbians, environmentalists, and so forth.

Weak or strong, mayors often have little discretion over city money. In San Francisco, for example, the mayor controls only about 30 cents out of every budget dollar. The rest has to be spent on programs mandated by federal and state government, such as health care and jails.

HYPERPLURALISM AND GOVERNMENT BY BUREAUCRATS

A weak-mayor form of government is attractive to many citizens because it can lead to a government that is responsive to diverse interest groups. But does it lead to responsible government? No, say many political scientists. Years ago, Frederick Wirt made a strong case for the idea that the costs of the weak-mayor form outweigh its benefits.

Political scientist Wirt (1971:114) argued that the price paid for decentralized, fractionated power in a pluralistic city is an inability to formulate and implement long-range public policy. Wirt argued that if successful policy outcomes rest on the agreement of many disparate private groups and public authorities, the power of one component to block any action is magnified. The result, he said, is that over time only minor policy adjustments are possible.

According to Wirt, the result of so many disparate actors playing the political game is **hyperpluralism**. Having too many (*hyper*) different decision points and too many groups with veto power (*pluralism*) paralyzes public policymaking. The result, Wirt said, is non–decision making.

In the absence of strong executive leadership and the presence of disparate competing factions, who runs a heterogeneous U.S. city? According to Wirt, the bureaucrats take over. He claimed that the result is a "government by clerks": long-staying, professional civil servants who were never elected and thus can't be recalled. They may be regulated by professional norms of service and efficiency, but they're not accountable to the citizenry. (*Note*: Unlike Wirt, some think that a "government by clerks"—composed of a competent and loyal bureaucracy—is not such a bad option.)

The growing strength of municipal unions further erodes city executives' power and authority. Max Weber (Chapter 11) predicted what some call the *bureaucratic phenomenon*—the rise and expansion of rational but fearsome bureaucratic administration and politics.

Decades ago, many studies of big-city politics found decision making there to be hopelessly fractionated (e.g., Sayre and Kaufman, 1960). Today, some wonder if cities are ungovernable; they ask whether or not there are any solutions to unresponsive bureaucracies, proliferating and competing interest groups, weak control over public employees, and dwindling fiscal resources. But others argue that bureaucracies can become responsive, and communities can be empowered if only the entrepreneurial spirit is introduced. And still others, as we shall see in Chapter 14, have a different slant altogether. They claim that it doesn't matter if bureaucrats or bosses run the town; neither is accountable to the citizens, and neither has the interests of most citizens in mind. Among other things, what is needed, they say, is more citizen participation and grassroots organizing.

To conclude: The formal structure of government limits leadership. Weak mayors have a hard time providing executive leadership and gathering resources to meet urban needs. Even strong mayors, who have more authority to meet some urban needs, can't control many key policy areas that have an impact on the quality of life in their cities. Nonetheless, mayors—weak or strong—bear the brunt of public dismay when trouble occurs.

Given their limited legal power, weak mayors must use informal powers to push through their programs. These include the power to persuade, the support of public opinion, and, in some cases, the influence that comes from controlling a well-oiled political machine. (Box 13.1 outlines some factors that make a mayor weak or strong.)

THE CONTEXT OF LOCAL GOVERNMENT

I have hinted at one reason that U.S. mayors are unable to govern effectively: They can't control other units of government. Both strong and weak mayors operate in the context of a fragmented metropolis and a global economy.

BOX 13.1 WHAT MAKES A MAYOR STRONG OR WEAK

Legal Structure

Strong

1. Mayor–council plan, which grants the mayor the following powers in the city charter:
   a. A 4-year term of office with possible reelection for many terms
   b. Power to appoint and remove city commissioners and/or department heads at will
   c. Power over the city budget (e.g., the right to submit an executive budget or have veto power over items in the budget)

Weak

1. Council–manager or commission form of government, with only a ceremonial role for the mayor
2. Mayor–council plan, in which the city charter limits the mayor's power in the following ways:
   a. A short term of office (e.g., 2 years)
   b. Commissioners and department heads not subject to the mayor's authority (e.g., commissioners appointed by the city council, agency heads protected by civil service)
   c. Little or no authority over budget matters

Local Government Context

1. State constitution and/or general laws and/or city charter provisions do not significantly limit city authority
2. City performs many important local government functions

1. State constitution and/or general law and/or city charter provisions limit city authority significantly
2. Other layers of government (county, special districts, etc.)

Personal Power and Influence

1. An effective political organization (e.g., a well-oiled political machine)
2. Strong support from powerful local interests, such as the financial/business community or labor

1. A weak or substantially nonexistent political organization
2. Lack of support from powerful local interests

FRAGMENTATION OF THE METROPOLIS

To paraphrase Abraham Lincoln (who once commented that "God must love the common man, he made so many of them"(see Cyber National International, 1997–2003), we could say that God must have loved cities too because She or He made so many of them. Over the decades this has remained the case. Indeed, there are more, not fewer, units of most local government in the United States now than 20 or 30 years ago. (The big exception is school districts, greatly consolidated since the 1950s.) By July 30, 2002, there were 87,849 units of local government. Of these, 38,971 were general-purpose local governments—3,034 county governments and 35,937 subcounty governments, including 19,431 municipal governments. The rest, over 50 percent of the total, were "special-purpose" local governments, including 13,522 school districts (a significant drop from 67,355 in 1952) and 35,356 special districts (see Table 13.4).

To further complicate matters, local government is organized in a crazy quilt pattern of separate and often overlapping types. To unravel the intricacies of this crazy quilt, some basic vocabulary is necessary. **Municipality** is the U.S. Census Bureau's term for general-purpose units of local government. Cities are general-purpose governments; that is, they undertake a variety of functions and provide a range of services. Hence, by definition, *cities are municipalities. Towns, townships, and boroughs are also municipalities.* Other units of local government—separate from municipalities—include school districts, other special districts, and counties. *Fragmentation, proliferation,* and *Balkanization* are terms often used to refer to this pattern of local government.

This is the way the crazy quilt of local government is patterned within a Metropolitan Statistical Area (MSA): Cities and other municipalities lie within the boundaries of a county. Within city boundaries (and often extending beyond them) are school districts and various other special districts that are independent of the city. Each unit of government—county, city, special district, school district—is a separate legal entity. This is important for analyzing how local government operates.

TABLE. 13.4 SPECIAL DISTRICTS, BY FUNCTION, 2002.

Function	Number
Total	35,356
Total single-function districts	32,157
Natural resources	7,026
Fire protection	5,743
Water supply	3,423
Housing and community development	3,413
Sewerage	2,020
Cemeteries	1,670
Libraries	1,582
Parks and recreation	1,314
Highways	767
Health	743
Hospitals	735
Education	530
Airports	512
Utilities other than water supply	485
Other	2,194
Multiple-function districts	3,199

Source: Adapted from Table D, p. 7, U.S. Census Bureau, July 2002 (http://ftp2.census.gov/govs/cog/2002COGprelim_report.pdf).

SPECIAL DISTRICTS

Special districts are the most widespread type of local government in the United States, and their number keeps growing. As of 2002, there were 35,356 special-district governments; in 1942, there were only 8,299.

One of three types of "special-purpose governments" (the others are corporations and authorities) in the United States, they are set up to serve either a single purpose (e.g., sewage treatment, housing–community development, hospital services, or fire protection) or several purposes, such as sewage and water provision.

Directors of special districts are not accountable to city or county government officials because special districts are totally separate legal entities. Their boundaries do not necessarily conform to those of any other local government unit. Often, they overlap the boundaries of the city and each other.

The existence of independent, overlapping special districts can create problems for the coordination of public services. In one unincorporated area of Portland, Oregon, for example, 11 separate special districts provide various services to area residents. No boundaries of these 11 special districts are contiguous. Some residents live within the borders of one district but just outside the borders of another. Further, each of the 11 districts has its own governing body, which is totally separate from all other local government units. Uncoordinated services can result if sewer district supervisors use plan A for digging ditches while water district supervisors use plan B for supplying water.

Many states have attempted to limit the proliferation of special districts and to consolidate existing ones. These efforts have met with only limited success.

Why are special districts so popular? The main reason is that special districts are separate from other local governments and, thus, not subject to their debt limits. Special districts can issue bonds or borrow money after other local governments have reached the legal limits of their borrowing authority. For example, residents who want more sewers in a city that has already reached its debt limit might form an independent sewer district. The new special district could sell bonds to finance the sewer construction, unrestricted by the city debt limit. Also, districts can be drawn around a functional area, regardless of local government boundaries. A mosquito-abatement district may cover the swampy part of three cities.

COUNTIES (INCLUDING URBAN COUNTIES)

Historically, the **county** has proved to be a very stable unit of government; its boundaries have generally remained unchanged for decades. For this reason, the county is used by the U.S. Census Bureau as the basic unit of the MSA.

In rural areas where there are no incorporated cities, county government acts as the general-purpose local government; typically, it regulates land use, licenses businesses, and provides police and fire protection. In urban areas, cities usually take over the basic general-purpose local government functions for their residents. In urban areas, counties serve as the general-purpose local government only for the unincorporated territory that lies within them. Counties also may provide some services to the residents of cities within their boundaries. For example, frequently the county operates libraries within both cities and unincorporated areas.

In recent times, a new spatial–demographic entity has emerged: the **urban county**. This term is used in various ways. It may refer to (1) a county that has assumed comprehensive authority over governmental functions, as in the case of Miami-Dade County, Florida; (2) any county with a large, dense population, giving it the characteristics of a city; or (3) a county that meets specified population size and legal power requirements to be eligible for certain federal funds.

Urban counties will probably become increasingly important. Recognizing this, some states have passed legislation that treats urban counties essentially as cities.

THE STATE'S ROLE IN URBAN AFFAIRS

Apart from their formal legal power, states exert power and authority over cities in many ways. For example, state programs operate within a city's boundaries, and cities may have little or no influence on these programs. Highway construction is illustrative. A state-funded highway can dramatically affect local land use, industrial location, and housing. Yet those cities through which it passes have no voice in determining its route.

The level of state involvement with urban issues varies widely. After the War on Poverty and other Great Society programs of the 1960s, U.S. statehouses were often bypassed by federal grants directly to city halls or neighborhood groups, thus decreasing state clout over their cities. However, some states have taken an active role, creating institutions to deal with their cities.

To summarize: City governments are only one of several units of local government in the United States. Counties, school districts, and other special districts also exist, often performing city-like functions. In MSAs, there is a crazy quilt of fragmented and overlapping municipalities, counties, school districts, and other special districts. Some states also play a significant role in local affairs.

AREAWIDE PLANNING EFFORTS

In theory, the variety and vast array of decentralized local governments ensure citizens a democratic voice in matters that directly affect their lives. In practice, however, things are quite different.

For one thing, voters have little or no control over the most widespread of all local governments: the special district. Critics charge that supervisors of special districts often put special interests, particularly private business, or technical concerns above the public interest. Influential labor negotiator Theodore W. Kheel, for one argued that the Port Authority of New York and New Jersey (a multistate special district which owned the World Trade Center) is dominated by the interests of its corporate bondholders. In effect, Kheel said, the Port Authority serves the rich and is indifferent to the needs of people in the New York City area (Kheel, [1969] 1971:443–449).

For another thing, many local issues, particularly land-use and economic growth policies, have areawide effects. If city A permits a large chemical factory to locate there, nearby cities can be affected (by pollution, new transport patterns, etc.). But the affected cities have no say in the matter. Thus, the crazy-quilt pattern of fragmented local government appears to give metropolitan residents the worst of both worlds: little democratic control and lack of coordinated policies.

Pushed largely by federal government requirements or incentives, most MSAs have established some kind of metropolitanwide planning organization. These organizations, called either a **council of governments (COG)** or an **areawide planning organization**, are strictly voluntary and advisory. Local governments are not legally required to follow their recommendations. Consequently, COGs operate on good will. And sometimes good will runs smack into a fiscal crunch or serious political disagreement. The case of a large COG, the Association of Bay Area Governments (ABAG), is instructive. ABAG is the land-use planning agency for the nine-county San Francisco Bay Area, and by some accounts, it is a powerful lobbying group. Besides conducting research and advising on water quality and other matters, ABAG sets mandates for low-income housing.

Do COGs represent the wave of the future for interlocal cooperation and areawide coordination? Not likely. To date, most have been little more than intergovernmental talk shows: Views are expressed, but nothing much happens—unless the going gets rough. Then, cities and other local governments walk out. (Example: Years ago, three cities, claiming lack of resources to comply with the housing guidelines, pulled out of ABAG.)

CHANGING GOVERNMENTAL STRUCTURES AND PATTERNS

BROAD REGIONAL GOVERNMENT?

Decades ago, a leading population analyst wondered how the fragmentation of local government could handle enormous webs of urbanization that were the United States's future. He advised that the best way to deal with urban regions that were politically fragmented, socially atomized, and economically complex would be broad regional government.

In the intervening years, broad regional government has often been viewed as a rational response to governmental fragmentation. And it has been adopted by some cities globally, notably Barcelona, Spain.

But regional government has not been politically acceptable in the United States. Indeed, even regional agencies for one function—say, public transit—can be suspect. Anyone who thinks politicians in Oakland, San Francisco, and the surrounding suburban cities will agree to unify the Bay Area's competing transit systems, for example, is under the influence of a legal or illegal substance.

Is small, fragmented government, and a great deal of it, more or less democratic than other options? Here, ideology determines one's views. Neoconservatives assume that small governments are more responsive to citizens' preferences than big, bureaucratic ones. Thus, they prefer fragmentation to centralized governments. Others hold diametrically opposed views. Some years ago political scientist Gregory R. Weiher (1991:195), one dissenting voice, wrote that fragmented local government is *anti*democratic: "The American model of democracy," Weiher wrote, "requires a citizenry in which social groups are not radically isolated from one another"; but "the system of urban jurisdictional boundaries" sponsors segregation of many kinds:

"whites from blacks, lower income groups from the middle class, religious groups from one another." Thus, in his view, fragmentation is an instrument of antidemocracy.

There are some strong regional agencies in the United States as well as regional land-use planning organizations. There is even one umbrella-type agency that is essentially an areawide planning and coordinating agency: the Metropolitan Council of the Twin Cities, Minneapolis–St. Paul, area. It has a tax-sharing formula whereby the region shares some of the tax revenue from new development. It serves a seven-county metro area, providing some essential services to the region, including the region's largest bus system.

As of the late 2000s however, there is no broad-based regional government in the United States. It has proved to be too hard of a sell politically.

How, then, are—and will—public services be delivered to metropolitan and megalopolitan residents? Probably, mostly by muddling through. Thus far, public services have been provided via a combination of traditional responses, minor adaptations, and innovative experiments. (It is noteworthy that in some areas, typically upscale, some formerly public services have been replaced or supplemented by private guards, private schools, and private police.)

TRADITIONAL RESPONSES AND MINOR ADAPTATIONS

On the more traditional side, residents of the urban fringe (unincorporated areas near a municipality that have urban service needs) are getting such urban services as police and fire protection in various ways: (1) by incorporation, thus creating a new municipality; (2) by contracting with the county or a nearby municipality for services; (3) by annexation; and (4) by forming special districts. Each of these techniques has its own problems and prospects.

Incorporation creates yet another local government, thereby adding to local fragmentation. Further, if its county is already financially strapped, the newly incorporated city can deprive the county of needed revenue. Contracting for services allows urban fringe residents to keep their highly valued rural environment, but at whose expense? Some observers feel that under contracting arrangements, city residents pay more than their fair share because residents of unincorporated areas don't pay for large capital investments (jails, firehouses, etc.) or for training city employees.

The problem of coordinating special districts has already been noted. Recall also that the number of special districts has grown enormously since the 1950s, resulting in even more fragmentation of the metropolis.

Annexation is the only traditional response that doesn't lead to an increased number of local governments. Annexation results in political integration rather than metropolitan government. However, since it requires boundary changes, annexation is not feasible in many MSAs, where most land is already incorporated into municipalities.

To cope with disputes over annexation, incorporation, and special district formation, some states have set up boundary commissions. So far, they have helped somewhat to check the further proliferation of local governments, but they have had little success in reforming the existing crazy quilt of local governments in the metropolis.

INNOVATIVE EXPERIMENTS

In France, Canada, and West Bengal, to take just a few examples, politicians have successfully forged innovations in sub-national governments in recent decades. This has not been the case in the United States. From after World War II until the 1970s, a few scholars and politicians in the United States touted innovative experiments in regional and metropolitan government, but attempts at structural innovation sputtered by the 1990s.

Since 2000, there has been almost none in the United States (the exception: Louisville's consolidation with suburban Jefferson County in 2000). Further, scholarly as well as citizen interest in structural changes at the local and regional levels of government became like the Spice Girls, grunge, and fluorescent T-shirts: out of style.

In the United States, the most ambitious proposals—broad regional government and a single, unified metropolitan government (called a "one-tier" or "one-level" government)—remain mere plans on a drawing board. But in North America, there are four models of structural change currently in operation plus one entrepreneurial framework for delivering public services.

Metro: To date, the most ambitious effort at structural change in North America is the metropolitan government of Toronto, Canada. Metropolitan Toronto first established a "two-tier" **federation** in 1953; Metro operated until 1997 when it was again transformed.

The original Metro consisted of a single, areawide government as the first tier and the preexisting local governments as the second tier. The newly created metropolitanwide first tier, called the Municipality of Metropolitan Toronto (or Metro), was governed by representatives from the preexisting governments: Toronto's municipal government plus 12 suburban governments. Metro had jurisdiction over the entire metropolitan area. It had power over many important urban functions: property assessment, water supply, sewage disposal, mass transit, health services, welfare, administration of justice, arterial roads, parks, public housing, redevelopment, and planning.

Under Toronto's two-tier plan, some functions were retained by local governments while others were shared with Metro. For instance, Metro maintained reservoirs and pumping stations, but the second tier of local governments handled the distribution of water to their residents. By the 1990s, the population of the Greater Toronto area had grown enormously, and the area had become, according to the United Nations, "the most multicultural city [*sic*] in the world" (in MOST Clearing House, n.d.).

By the end of the twentieth century, many believed that Metro had become irrelevant because it no longer covered most of the population in the ever-growing urban area. (In 2005, the Greater Toronto area had a population of about 5.8 million residents.) After a referendum, which failed to win voter support in all six municipalities involved, an amalgamation was pushed through by the ruling Ontario political party. Thus, in 1998 Metro morphed into a regional municipality formed of smaller municipalities. The larger Metro government was retained, and the existing city of Toronto and five other smaller municipalities became a new city of Toronto.

Note that a Toronto-like framework was adapted in Montreal, Canada, in 2002. However, many suburbanites, particularly English-speaking and rich ones, protested the annexations of their suburbs into the proposed federated system; they viewed a federation as a power grab by larger cities, particularly French-identified Montreal. The Montreal Urban Community was transformed into a federated system, but as of 2006, 32 out of the 89 constituent communities voted to "demerge" or de-amalgamate.

The comprehensive urban county: Short of federation or amalgamation, there is another model of structural change: the comprehensive urban county plan. Operating in Miami-Dade County, Florida, since 1957, a two-tier government gives the county government a powerful and integrating role over an area of 2,054 square miles and 27 municipalities.

Among its functions, the comprehensive urban county government (Figure 13.5) is authorized to promote the entire area's economy, own and operate mass-transit systems, construct expressways, provide uniform health and welfare services, and maintain central records and communication for fire and police protection.

Consolidation: City–county consolidation is another technique. It is a one-government, not a two-tier, approach.

Usually, this type of governmental reorganization consists of the total or substantial merging of the county government with the largest city (or all municipalities) within its boundaries. From World War II to the 1990s, there were four major city–county consolidations, three of which remain: Jacksonville–Duval County, Florida (1967), which in 1992 became a *former* consolidation; Baton Rouge–East Baton Rouge Parish (the parish is Louisiana's equivalent of the county) in 1947; Nashville–Davidson County, Tennessee (1962); and Indianapolis–Marion County, Indiana (1969).

In the 1990s, two Georgia city–county consolidations took place: Athens-Clarke County and Augusta-Richmond County.

Special districts: A more moderate type of institutional change is the formation of metropolitanwide special districts, either single- or multipurpose in nature. The former owner of the long-gone World Trade Center in New York City, the Port Authority of New York and New Jersey, is such a special district, one that crosses state as well as municipal boundaries.

PRIVATIZATION OF PUBLIC SERVICES

The U.S. government's contracting out to private firms is neither new nor experimental. Wells Fargo Bank horseback riders, known as the Pony Express, delivered the mail west of the Mississippi on contract to the U.S. government. Later, starting in World War II, millions of private employees worked in defense-connected industries on government contracts.

More recently, private soldiers working for contractor Blackwater (better known for assignments in war zones such as Iraq) patrolled post-Katrina streets in New Orleans (Scahill, 2007). (Some claim that the U.S. government "outsources" intelligence work to private contractors, including Lockheed Martin and General Dynamics. They estimate that between 50 and 70 percent of U.S. intelligence work, training, and technology are handled by private firms, making it a sector of at least $20 billion [Chaterjee in Sunnucks, 2007; Shorrock, 2008a]).

What is new at the local level is the growth and range of privatization (also called "privatism"). In the Reagan era, many U.S. communities faced tax revolts, cutbacks in federal funds, shrinking tax collections due to economic recession, and fiscal austerity with continuing demands for services—all at the same time! Localities turned to "entrepreneurial government" as a way to meet the challenges. Local governments contracted with private firms for services or entered partnerships with businesses. At least 75 communities in 15 states, mainly new suburbs and cities hard pressed for revenue, contracted with private companies to provide protection against fire.

Contracting out to private companies or nonprofit organizations became widespread in many U.S. cities.

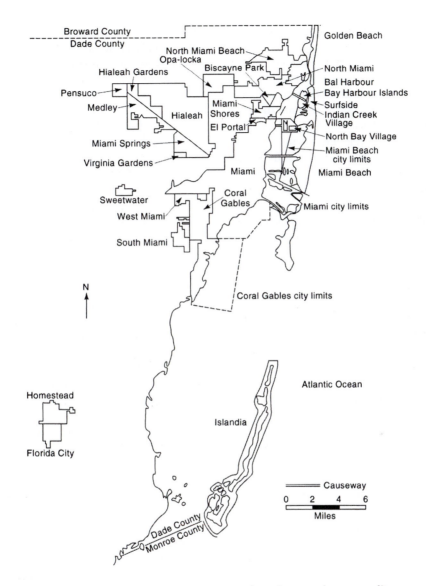

Broward County
Dade County
North Miami Beach
Opa-locka
Biscayne Park
Hialeah Gardens
Pensuco
Medley
Hialeah
Miami Shores
El Portal
Miami Springs
Virginia Gardens
Golden Beach
North Miami
Bal Harbour
Bay Harbour Islands
Surfside
Indian Creek Village
North Bay Village
Miami Beach city limits
Miami Beach
Miami
Sweetwater
Coral Gables
West Miami
Miami city limits
South Miami
N
Coral Gables city limits
Atlantic Ocean
Homestead
Islandia
Florida City
Dade County
Monroe County
Causeway
0   2   4   6
Miles

Fig. 13.5 METROPOLITAN MIAMI-DADE COUNTY, FLORIDA. In its early years, the metropolitan government in Miami-Dade County (formerly Dade County), faced opposition and a continuing struggle between the county and municipalities, the two levels of government that composed it. Later, however, residents turned their attention from government structure to less abstract issues, such as racial and ethnic tension, changing demographics, hurricane disaster relief, high crime rates, and poverty. By 2005, poverty rates had remained essentially unchanged since 1979 (although the county's population doubled between 1960 and 1990). Those affected disproportionately by high poverty rates as of 2007 were Hispanics, the majority group in the county (61 percent of the total population with about 17 percent living in poverty), and African Americans, with about 29 percent below the poverty line (Miami-Dade County's Planning and Zoning Department, 2007, http://www.co.miami-dade.fl.us/planzone/pdf/Overview%20of%20the%20Socio-Economic.pdf). Also by 2007, Miami-Dade's county manager presided over 30,000 employees, 60 departments serving over 2.3 million residents, and a budget of $6.9 billion.

The range includes Philadelphia's operation of golf courses, homeless shelters, and parking enforcement to private enterprises in Phoenix, Arizona, running building and grounds maintenance, landfill operations, the bus system, garbage collection, and street maintenance. Other cities sold museums to private businesses under leaseback arrangements or contracted out the running of jails and prisons.

The story of Ecorse, Michigan, is instructive. In the 1950s, this small industrial town downriver from Detroit boomed. By the early 1980s, plant closings around Detroit plus cutbacks threatened to nearly sink Ecorse. Indeed, Ecorse became the first U.S. city to go into receivership. The court told an expert on city finance to close Ecorse's gap between revenue and expenditures. What the expert did was to privatize. He contracted out garbage pickups, public works, animal control, and other services. From 1986 to 1991, the $6-million city deficit had been turned into a $100,000 surplus.

Privatization boosters in the United States included Bill Clinton when he was president and many so-called New Democrats. This suggests that in less than a generation people in the United States had changed their expectations of government. In 1968, Robert Kennedy ran for president on a liberal platform, arguing that government was an instrument for the public good. By 1992, the three major candidates for president—Republican, Democrat, and United We Stand—seemed to share the belief that government was the enemy. Even in recent years, U.S. presidential candidates (including sitting senators) have run campaigns as "outsiders" or platforms vowing to "change Washington."

Candidates' running away from identification with government coincided with calls to "reinvent government" and to privatize public services. One best-selling book, *Reinventing Government* (1992), had great impact. (Some, including Shorrock [2008b], claim that Vice President Al Gore was particularly taken with the efficiency claims of privatization.) Written by privatization's leading U.S. advocate, David Osborne, and his coauthor Ted Gaebler, a former city manager in California, it argued that local government bureaucracy had outlived its mission (to fight corruption) and usefulness. Their fix: more market-oriented government to meet declining revenues

and increasing demands for consumer services. Subsequently, Osborne and Peter Plastrik offered strategies for *Banishing Bureaucracy* (1998) and suggested tools for transforming government (2001).

THE REPORT CARD

Have these innovations been success stories or not? Opinions differ widely. Most observers think that Toronto's two-tier government has made substantial strides toward rational policymaking for the metropolis.

Comprehensive urban counties: Scholars give only a C or C+ to Miami-Dade County's comprehensive urban county plan. One assessment points to considerable instability in the relationship between the urban county government and preexisting municipal governments, as well as continuing fiscal and administrative problems. And some say that the Miami-Dade County's two-tier arrangement suffered from continuing rivalry between the county and cities for the allegiance and control of their citizenry. Meanwhile, government structure is not a burning issue for Miami-Dade residents; they are more interested in less abstract issues such as jobs, crime, and racial–ethnic tension.

Consolidations: City–county consolidations face great opposition, usually from outlying residents who must approve the consolidation by popular vote. But sometimes opposition comes from central city residents (who also must approve the change).

Special districts: As for the most moderate structural reform, the metropolitanwide special district, it has made significant gains in dealing with pressing metropolitan needs but is limited to one or a few functions. Further, like special districts that are not metropolitanwide, it is criticized for its nonaccountability to the people it serves.

Privatization: Privatization has vocal supporters and detractors. Boosters praise its cost savings, efficiency, and accountability. Libertarians tend to be its biggest cheerleader. Osborne and Plastrik (1998) claim that Indianapolis saved more than $1 million over 7 years by privatizing. Detractors disagree for a host of reasons. Neoconservative thinkers don't want to *re*invent government; they want to *dis*invent government—at least until recently, they said they did. Some wanted less bureaucracy, which meant less government. But some liberal critics call contracting out a union-busting strategy designed to weaken or destroy public employee unions by wringing concessions from them. Further, they note, governments are a major employer of so-called minorities; reducing government jobs has a disproportionately negative impact on people of color and women. Others fear that if public schools and prisons are turned over to for-profit agencies, there will be less accountability to all citizens or, they warn, private prisons and private jails threaten civil rights, leaving prisoners with less protection against brutality and arbitrary discipline and not guaranteeing "customers" the rights of citizens.

Other criticisms of privatization abound. One concerns the privatized services' ability to serve everyone equally. For example, they claim that private fire departments left nonsubscribers' homes burning while fighting fires at subscribers' homes. Meantime, some critics warn of opportunities for a new kind of bossism; they fear that the contract bidding process could degenerate into patronage in pinstripes.

Finally, radical scholars and activists wonder who wins the most under privatization. Some think that the profit motive may be a powerful incentive but ill-suited to achieving public-policy objectives because the payoffs serve narrow, private interests. Sometime ago, Harvard scholar Elaine Bernard (1993) offered a more blistering critique, saying that privatism is part of a conscious effort by business to decrease public expectations of government and thereby limit more progressive options.

To conclude: It appears that the current crazy quilt of local government is being patched up with bits and pieces. There is no whole new cloth.

Why have efforts to reform local government structure met with so little success? First, many interest groups correctly perceive that major structural changes would not be in their narrowly defined

self-interest. Suburbanites, for example, tend to oppose any reform that links their future to the fiscal and political problems of their nearby city. African American and Latino leaders in big cities often oppose metropolitanwide government because they could lose their recently won power in some central cities. Northern Democrats tend to resist metropolitanwide government if Republicans form a numerical majority in the metro area as a whole but not in the central city.

Second, structural reform is hard to sell to voters. By contrast, metropolitanwide special districts can be established either without a popular vote or by state law requiring a popular majority in the entire area. Federation, comprehensive urban counties, and city–county consolidations usually require popular majorities in all of the municipalities involved, a very difficult consensus to obtain.

Scholars don't agree on how metropolitan politics should be structured. One group, the centralists or consolidationists, claims that there are too many local governmental units to provide efficient, effective, and responsible government. Their solutions: centralized metropolitan or even broad regional government. Another group holds that government is not decentralized enough to provide responsive government. Their solutions: community control or neighborhood government. Finally, still another group thinks that the present system works well and is highly desirable because it allows citizens to maximize their choices in the consumption of public goods (e.g., through choice in housing location). This group has no proposed solutions because it doesn't define fragmentation as a problem.

Whatever scholars propose about metropolitan politics, citizens dispose in the end. Proposed reforms of any sort inspire yawns or fear—fear of more bureaucracy, more expense, less control, or changes in the balance of local power. And yawns because the connections between structure and policy outcomes, too often, remain unexplained or seemingly too boring for citizens to care about. Thus, the chances of reshaping U.S. local government seem dim.

THE FEDERAL ROLE IN URBAN AFFAIRS

Even without structural reorganization, local government priorities and programs in the United States have changed dramatically since the New Deal in the 1930s. Corporate business decisions have had significant impacts on localities, such as where to locate a new office or where to invest or disinvest. (Chapters 14 and 15).

Here, let's focus on another important external agent of change: the federal government. Federal officials have pushed (critics say forced) cities to rethink their programs with a variety of incentives, penalties, and mandated duties.

We now turn to a brief history of federal expansion in local life. It is divided into three eras: 1930s–1950s, 1960s–1992, and 1992–summer 2008.

EXPANSION OF FEDERAL INVOLVEMENT IN U.S. LIFE, 1930s–1950s

Since the 1930s, the federal government has been playing a larger role in U.S. life. The expansion of federal involvement in the economic and social life of the country has significantly affected metropolitan politics, both directly and indirectly. This means that the question "Who runs this town?" can't be answered without reference to the federal government.

It was during the Great Depression of the 1930s that the role of the federal government in U.S. life began to grow. Amid the bread lines and competing ideologies of the time (ranging from radical proposals to redistribute wealth and power, technocratic manifestos to let scientists and engineers run government, and hate campaigns blaming African Americans and Jews for economic distress to demagogic appeals for fascist-type rule), President Franklin D. Roosevelt's New Deal administration moved decisively to maintain social order and economic security. (Radical critics say that it worked to *save* capitalism; conservative critics, to *end* capitalism.) Millions of people in the United States, assumed to be "temporarily poor" during the Depression, were provided some form of social security through New Deal programs. Many functions once handled privately (by family, charities, etc.) or not at all were assumed by the federal government.

According to urban historian Richard C. Wade, the growth of federal power under the New Deal "developed out of the intractability of 25 percent unemployment, a stagnating economy and the desperation of

millions" (1982:21). New Deal programs did not take over state and local rights: "Those governments simply had no capacity to meet even the most immediate relief needs, much less to plan for the future." The New Deal added programs that provided a safety net, such as a minimum wage, unemployment insurance, and Social Security. It also offered major assistance to middle-class citizens via such programs as the Federal Housing Administration's below-market-rate mortgages and the Federal Deposit Insurance Corporation, guaranteeing some bank savings.

Subsequently, during World War II and after, the role of the federal government kept growing. (As might be predicted, so did the role of private interests that sought some of the growing state's resources.) Most citizens accepted the centralized system in Washington, D.C., and new programs served new needs, such as the GI Bill of Rights for returning service personnel.

Meanwhile, the "temporarily poor" didn't disappear, and the national interest of a world power was translated into the need for defense industries located throughout the country and efficient transport links. Soon federal funds flowed into and around the nation's small towns as well as big cities. At the same time, modern technology and corporate business organization expanded significantly, and the Springdales of the nation—small towns and hamlets—found themselves in the midst of a mass society (Vidich and Bensman, [1958] 1968). As a result, decisions made in faraway federal agencies and corporate headquarters affected the lives of Americans in cities and rural areas, whether they realized it or not (see Introduction, Figure C).

Federal policies don't have to be labeled "urban" to affect urban life. Indeed, many federal programs not so designated have changed the fabric of the metropolis as much as, or more than, funds earmarked for cities. Let's take a look at two such post–World War II programs: housing and transportation.

HOW FEDERAL POLICY AFFECTED POSTWAR HOUSING AND TRANSPORTATION

Housing

Beginning with the New Deal, the U.S. federal government has pursued policies intended to strengthen financial institutions that provide mortgage money for housing, particularly single-family, detached houses. For instance, the Federal Housing Administration (FHA) was created in the midst of the Depression, when millions of homeowners were defaulting on mortgage payments because they were out of work, housing construction was at a virtual standstill, and banks were going bankrupt. The FHA was established to provide mortgage insurance to protect lenders (banks) against the risk of default on long-term, low-down-payment mortgage loans. The FHA contributed to a gradual recovery of the home finance industry during the 1930s, and then it spurred the massive post–World War II suburban housing boom.

Other federal housing credit institutions in the United States (e.g., the Federal National Mortgage Association, popularly called Fannie Mae) helped to create a national secondary mortgage market so that housing construction funds could flow freely into growth areas. (Since then, a private market for poor credit risks developed: the so-called subprime mortgage sector. "Subprime" borrowers are less than creditworthy risks.) Most blame failures in the housing sector—at least to a significant degree—for the faltering of the U.S. economy in 2007 and beyond. (It is noteworthy that the Republican George W. Bush administration—led by Secretary of the Treasury Hank Paulson, one-time head of a major Wall Street securities firm—sponsored financial aid to Fannie Mae and Freddie Mac, another big, government-sponsored housing credit institution, in 2008.)

What impact did these post–World War II federal housing policies have on cities and suburbs? An enormous impact. By stimulating suburban growth, federal programs underwrote the exodus of white middle-class residents from central cities. In so doing, they helped to cement metropolitanwide housing patterns of economic and racial segregation.

Transportation

Similarly, the billions of dollars poured into highway construction by Congress after World War II had a broad impact on the metropolis. The new interstate highway system, funded 90 percent with federal money, allowed commercial and industrial enterprises to move out of their central city locations and relocate in the suburbs. These location decisions by private business contributed to the erosion of the central city's tax base and to its financial stagnation.

To conclude: Whether intended or not, national policies—not specifically deemed urban—have helped to change the shape and character of U.S. cities since World War II. In particular, federal policies opened up the suburbs, spurred regional growth in Sunbelt cities where new defense-related industries were generously supported, and provided the infrastructure (roads, airports) for private business to serve a national and global mass market. Cities, legal creatures of the state, increasingly became economically and socially tied to the national and international political economy.

FROM FEDERALISM TO THE NEW FEDERALISM, 1960s–1992

In the 1960s, the number of federal programs aimed specifically at the metropolis rose dramatically. So did funding levels. Not surprisingly, the size and number of federal agencies that implement urban-oriented programs followed suit.

A cabinet-level agency, the Department of Housing and Urban Development (HUD), was established by President Lyndon B. Johnson in 1965 specifically to address urban needs. A year later, the Department of Transportation (DOT) was set up, increasing the national government's already-active role in financing urban transit. Other cabinet-level departments expanded their urban programs as part of LBJ's Great Society. New programs, including the controversial War on Poverty, channeled funds directly to cities or urban community groups.

Those were the heady days of Head Start, Job Corps, Model Cities, Foster Grandparents, Legal Services, Community Action, and so on. To liberals, these 1960s Great-Society programs represented a step in the right direction: government intervention to provide equal opportunity for all citizens. To radicals, these programs represented government's attempt to keep cities calm and co-opt the poor by throwing out a few crumbs instead of attacking the capitalist structures that put people in poverty. To conservatives, these programs represented "a ragbag."

When President Richard M. Nixon started his second term in 1972, he proposed a New Federalism. He promised to take powers away from the federal government and give authority and flexibility to the state and local governments. The showpiece of Nixon's New Federalism was **general revenue sharing**, a program with few strings attached. Funds could be used to finance nearly any local government program. (Before the 15-year revenue-sharing program ended in 1987, $85 billion was distributed to 39,000 cities and towns, where the money was spent to purchase a variety of products and services, from flowers to fire trucks.)

President Nixon and his successor, the late Gerald Ford, did not destroy LBJ's Great Society, but they did change its course. While keeping up the level of federal spending for local programs, they redirected funds away from big cities in the Northeast, considered Democratic strongholds, to the urban South and West.

The numbers tell the story of federal expansion. In one decade, 1969–1979, federal outlays to state and local governments quadrupled to $85 billion, much of it being spent in cities (U.S. Office of Management and Budget, 1978:175). In percentage terms, cities' dependence on federal aid for their general revenue grew from 4 percent to 14 percent from 1965 to 1980.

Then, the Reagan–George H. W. Bush "revolution" changed all that. President Ronald Reagan introduced his New Federalism in his 1981 State of the Union message. Underpinned by the conservative/libertarian ideas of Milton Friedman, Reagan's New Federalism decentralized many federal activities to states and local governments, assuring that such decentralized programs would be more responsive to the two most interested groups: the people they were meant to help and the people who were paying for them.

New Tasks, Less Money

However, instead of sustaining the level of federal funds flowing to states and cities, the Reagan and George H. W. Bush administrations slashed the funding of federally-financed, locally-administered programs. Many federal grants-in-aid for education, public works, mass transit, and housing were cut or cut out. From 1980 to 1992, federal dollars spent on U.S. cities declined by 59 percent. Briefly put, the federal government gave the states new tasks but less money.

Cutbacks in federal aid were accompanied by stagflation, high interest rates, and bad economic times. This combination of hard times and budget cuts left localities tax-starved and defunded. Which is what many conservatives wanted: Governments could do less with less money.

More than half of the state and city governments in the United States faced serious financial shortfalls by 1990. Liberals complained. Urbanist George Sternlieb of Rutgers University opined, "We don't have New Federalism, we have New Feudalism, where every community fends for itself with a hodgepodge of responsibilities and taxing powers" (in Hinds and Eckholm, 1990:A11). Worst-case budget scenarios became common. For example, hundreds of patients and doctors jammed into San Francisco's City Hall to complain that more cuts to health clinics would endanger lives. The next day, hundreds of children and parents went to City Hall to complain that more library cuts would endanger the literacy of the next generation. Competition for scarce funds between libraries and health clinics was so fierce that one advocate for health care drove home his cause like this: "Dead people can't read books" (in Sandalow, 1993:1).

Severe cutting, even gutting, of cities' social programs raised critical voices to a fever pitch. Reporter Bob Scheer called local government the "garbage can of American politics," left to pick up the pieces of "problems (e.g., crime, drugs, disoriented vets) that the federal and state governments have failed to adequately deal with" while "their tax base is pared to the bone" (1993:1).

To conclude: Starting with the New Deal, the federal government became heavily involved in a wide range of urban programs, from child nutrition and law enforcement to community development. Cities lobby Congress intensely for programs through both nationwide organizations and individual lobbyists.

Long ago, political scientist John Mollenkopf (1983) pointed out that which political party controls Congress does make a difference to cities. In his study of urban legislation from 1933 to 1980, Mollenkopf argued that when Republicans had national control, they redirected money away from central cities to the suburbs and newer metropolitan areas of the Sunbelt. Further, Republicans restructured intergovernmental aid—by channeling it through states and block grants, for instance—to ensure that voters in central cities had the least possible influence.

The balance between city and suburban political power started shifting mightily to the suburbs in 1972 with Nixon's general revenue sharing. By 1992, more than one-half of U.S. cities were saddled with major service burdens and limited options. In a time of economic decline, they faced decreased federal and state aid, state prohibitions against raising local taxes, and widespread suburban antiurbanism.

From 1992 to summer 2008, no major presidential candidate specifically addressed urban issues such as crushing service burdens or homelessness. This neglect would not have surprised urban historian Richard C. Wade. A generation earlier, he noted that the country's political and social power had been permanently reallocated, completing the "suburban captivity of American politics" (1982:21). Of course, Wade could not see the future except through a glass darkly. He did not predict that, by 2005, the percentage of poor in many suburbs around the largest U.S. cities would outnumber the percentage of poor inside central cities. Neither did Wade foresee that the rising cost of energy might push some suburbanites back to U.S. cities, thus changing the urban–suburban mix in the United States.

A NAMELESS PERIOD, 1992–SUMMER 2008

Unlike previous administrations, neither President Bill Clinton nor President George W. Bush stamped a name, such as the New Federalism, on his urban program. (Some critics, however, called these policies "fend for yourself federalism.") During their tenures, there was no easily identifiable urban policy. Perhaps on purpose. That is, political purpose. Even so, federal programs (or the lack of them) aimed at cities and suburbs continue to have serious impacts.

Clinton's Urban Policies

During the Clinton years (1993–2001), unemployment dropped to record lows. So did inflation. The federal budget was in surplus. Crime rates dropped in many places. These greatly affected cities.

Under Clinton, several policies and laws also had great impacts on cities and cityfolk. For exam-

ple, Clinton expanded the Earned Income Tax Credit (EITC), which proved to be the Clinton's most effective antipoverty measure; it provided the working poor with more income than any other program. Further, Clinton's Department of Housing and Urban Development promoted community development corporations as a way to revitalize poor urban neighborhoods; in Los Angeles (and other cities), community development corporations built most of the affordable housing that was added to the city's inventory in over 10 years.

However, critics hold that Clinton's policies had little to do with improved urban conditions. They argue that cities improved basically because of an unprecedented national economic expansion. Others think that this economic expansion was reinforced by federal policies sponsored by Clinton, particularly those that reduced joblessness.

Clinton's most controversial urban-oriented legislation was the welfare reform bill of 1996: the Personal Responsibility and Work Opportunity Reconciliation Act (PRWORA). The day it passed in August 1996, Clinton announced that PRWORA would end welfare "as we know it." The day after, a *Washington Post* reporter hailed Clinton's bill as "historic," rewriting 60 years of social policy, "ending the federal guarantee of cash assistance to the poor and turning welfare programs over to the states" (Vobedja, 1996). The bill required recipients to work (so-called workfare rather than welfare) and limited benefits to 5 years.

Clinton's PRWORA was intensely disliked in many quarters, particularly by noncentrist Democrats. Some believed it pulled the "safety net" out from under the nation's least fortunate. Others dubbed it "forced labor," not "workfare" (e.g., Dunlea, 1997). The National Organization of Women called it "punitive" (Lee and Weinstein, 1996). But by spring 2007 no one in the mainstream media or in national politics seemed to care one way or the other.

George W. Bush's Urban Policies

During George W. Bush's presidency, the focus shifted. Bush preferred private answers to public challenges. Thus, he favored cutting taxes, particularly for those at the top of the income ladder; reducing government regulations on business; and privatizing previously government-funded public services such as drug counseling. These measures were aimed, his administration said, at increasing investment and jobs and saving taxpayers' dollars. Conservatives and libertarians were pleased with such measures, assumed to stimulate the economy and promote the "trickle-down" effect. (The other major Bush initiative in terms of funding—U.S. military spending for wars in Iraq and Afghanistan—did not get widespread support from libertarians.)

A U.S. economic recession ended in late 2001. But the recovery over the following 2 years was mainly jobless as U.S. firms shipped white- and blue-collar jobs overseas. Thus, during Bush's first 3 years as president, unemployment *increased* (from 4 to 6 percent). Between 2000 and 2003, median household income fell, and the poverty rate rose (from 11.3 percent to 12.5 percent or, otherwise put, from 31.1 million to 35.9 million). After 9/11, funds for a domestic "war on terrorism," together with big tax cuts for some and big military spending, led to spiraling budget deficits. Discretionary funds for social or antipoverty programs dried up, which is what many conservatives thought prudent. Later during his administration, bank bailouts and credit infusions into the banking system—designed to stem financial crises that began in 2007—would increase the deficit more.

Critics say that the Bush administration's "war on terrorism" and "homeland security" programs have had a disproportionate and negative impact on U.S. cities. They claim that the federal government has required cities to dramatically increase security (e.g., at airports, ports, and sporting events) and to improve emergency preparations but that the cities were not given adequate funds to pay for these programs. According to sociologist Peter Dreier (2004), cities were spending $70 million a week out of their own coffers just to comply with each "orange alert" security threat from the federal Department of Homeland Security. Similarly, others argue that cities were asked to comply with expensive federal mandates, especially homeland security and antiterrorism initiatives, but that federal funds were not provided to help pay for the mandated programs.

Aside from responses to financial crises, such as federal intervention in the banking and credit mar-

kets, two Bush initiatives have had the most impact on metro areas. They are the following: (1) No Child Left Behind and (2) Faith-Based Initiatives.

No Child Left Behind

The No Child Left Behind Act of 2001 requires local schools to raise standards via testing and to issue annual report cards on students' improvements. The bill requires federal and state governments to punish schools that don't meet the standards. Critics say that Bush failed to ask for enough funds that could pay for hiring more teachers, reducing class sizes, and improving facilities that could help low-achieving students, especially students in inner-city schools. They also claim that there is a mismatch: Needy inner-city schools may be the most likely to lack the resources and funds to comply with the act and thrive.

Critics also point out that there may be widespread cheating in the program to obtain better results. Teachers at 123 schools in California, for example, admitted to helping students cheat on exams given to meet the requirements of No Child Left Behind. According to *San Francisco Chronicle* reporters, "Incentives to bend the rules are strong in the No Child Left Behind era, when persistently low scores can shut down a school, trigger a takeover or force teacher transfers, experts say" (Asimov et al., 2007:A1).

Faith-Based Initiatives

Under President Bush, Congress increased funds to private religious organizations to provide social services such as prisoner reentry programs, drug counseling, homeless shelters, and food banks. How was this done? In part by "earmarks." A *New York Times* analysis (in Henriques and Lehren, 2007:A7) observes that the number of earmarks (narrowly-tailored appropriations that bypass the normal appropriations and competitive bidding processes) increased sharply in recent years: From 1989 to January 2007, Congress approved about 900 earmarks to religious groups, totaling $318 million. In comparison, fewer than 60 earmarks for faith-based groups were passed in the 1997–1998 congressional session.

Aside from earmarks, Bush bypassed Congress and operated instead through executive orders and regulatory changes at the cabinet level to insure faith-based programs. In 2002, Bush created the Faith-Based and Community Initiative (WHOFBCI) in the White House, which, according to its press release (White House, 2006), awarded more than $2.1 million in grants to religious organizations in fiscal year 2005 by seven federal agencies. Again bypassing Congress, in 2006 Bush created, by executive order, the Center for Faith-Based and Community Initiatives at the U.S. Department of Homeland Security. The center is charged with coordinating Homeland Security's efforts to remove obstacles to faith-based and community organizations in providing disaster relief services.

Typically, faith-based initiatives are popular with groups considered part of the base of the Republican Party, including evangelical Christians. Many others question their constitutionality and/or their effectiveness. Others question the use of executive orders and other devices to bypass Congress. Indeed, some called him an imperial president.

To conclude: During Clinton's presidency, the U.S. economy surged, a not-unimportant factor in promoting more jobs and more livable cities. During this strong economy, Clinton fulfilled his promise as a centrist Democrat, getting a welfare-reform bill passed (that enraged "progressives" and those called "leftists" by those who weren't).

Later, George W. Bush ran for U.S. president as a "compassionate conservative." Whether his administrations lived up to the compassionate part is a matter of great dispute. However, most agree that his nonfiscal policies (not his second administration's bailouts of private firms, for example, part of his fiscal policy) were more conservative than those of any other administration in living memory.

With what some call "fend for yourself federalism" (Morgan et al., 2006) under Bush, federally funded urban programs were slashed, thanks to a combination of factors, including ideology (a preference for privatization, including faith-based social programs and its view of poverty as being due primarily to personal character flaws), war spending, a budget deficit, tax cuts of about $1.3 trillion, and perhaps politics: Gore beat Bush among urban voters, and two groups long defined as urban voters—African Americans and Hispanics—did not vote overwhelmingly for Bush.

THE QUESTION RECONSIDERED: WHO RUNS THIS TOWN?

Federal regulations, state laws, areawide planning suggestions, special-district decisions, county legislation, neighborhood requests. This list suggests that cities are not masters of their own fate. Instead, they are just one layer of government operating within a web of government—some call it a marble cake—of overlapping and intersecting layers.

To attain one's political goals, knowledge of the formal structures of government is essential. Knowing who's in charge in this governmental maze—who to blame, where to go for an authorization, where to protest a decision—is the first step in getting something done in city politics.

Here is a case study of one citizens' group, Bananas, that successfully worked its way through the maze of political structures. It highlights the necessity of appreciating the complexities of government's formal organization. It also shows that, in the United States, any meaningful response to the question "Who runs this town?" must take into account the web of government reaching from Washington, D.C. (and beyond), to the neighborhood day-care center.

CASE STUDY: WHAT BANANAS LEARNED ABOUT THE FORMAL STRUCTURE OF GOVERNMENT

The sign over a small building in north Oakland, California, reads BANANAS. No fruit is for sale there. Instead, on the front porch lie ice-cream containers, fabric remnants, and wood scraps—all ingredients for children's play projects.

Inside the building, organized chaos prevails. A dozen women are answering phones and giving information about day care as actively as stockbrokers tell their clients about hot prospects. Parents and children stream into and out of the information area. A social service worker answers the "Warm Line," a pre—crisis counseling service for parents with day-care needs.

What's going on here? The name says it all: Bananas, a multipurpose community service, helps to prevent parents from "going bananas" by providing various kinds of assistance with their preschool children. It does all this in 11 languages, including English, Mien, Thai, and French.

Fig. 13.6 BANANAS. This group of women in San Francisco's East Bay learned their way around governmental structures. After years of hard work, they got what they wanted. (Cathy Cade)

Bananas didn't happen overnight. It grew out of years of frustration, organizing, and political struggle. The program director had gained some prior political experience during her fight to organize an employees' union on the University of California at Berkeley campus. Staff members learned by personal experience. Their first lesson was how to deal with and through governmental structures. To a significant degree, Bananas exists today because it learned this lesson.

In 1972, a small group of women—Bananas—became concerned that Berkeley had no place where parents could get information to help to set up play groups for preschool children. (Later, the group moved to nearby north Oakland; Bananas now serves the northern part of its county, Alameda.) This nonhierarchical group had no money or community support, but the members did have energy and commitment to their cause. They began to organize information assistance to parents, children, and day-care providers. After 4 years of hard work, they began to deal with city officials, trying to get government support for their activities.

In the process, they discovered whom to approach ("know-who") to get their project moving. Here are some of the lessons they learned.

1. *Find out who makes the decisions in city government.* Berkeley has a council–manager form of government. The city manager has the final word under this system, and negotiations for funding were carried out directly with him. Bananas didn't deal with the mayor. The specific budget recommendation came from the city manager since his office prepares the city budget.

2. *Find out what the city is authorized to fund.* There is no prohibition in Berkeley against using taxpayers' money for day-care activities. If there were, Bananas would have had to seek funding elsewhere.

3. *Find out what government agencies have an interest in the activity (and how they relate to city government).* Berkeley, like other towns, exists in a web of governments. Bananas had to learn the structure regarding child care. At the level closest to home is the Berkeley Unified School District, a special district run by an elected school board. The board, which is not accountable to city government, was often in disagreement with city officials. The school district provides child care for preschool children in the schools. Thus, it is an interested party regarding other day-care activities in the community. Bananas dealt with the school board, not the Berkeley City Council, to coordinate information and referral activities.

Bananas also dealt with another interested party: the Berkeley Parks and Recreation Department. This city department administered a voucher system, paying low-income and working mothers a stipend for day care. Bananas' staff members worked with the Parks and Recreation Department on a daily basis to refer voucher recipients to appropriate day-care centers.

Yet another interested party was the county. Alameda County, in which Berkeley is located, operated day care–related programs. The county's Social Services Department administered a federal program giving child-care vouchers to eligible recipients. When Bananas felt that the county was not taking full advantage of the voucher program, they pressed for wider benefits. To accomplish this, they went to the County Board of Supervisors, not the Berkeley City Council.

Bananas also dealt with a state-mandated regional center for child care, a clearinghouse for so-called special-needs children. To provide clear guidance to parents, Bananas had to go to this regional planning organization for information.

Then there was the state of California. It, too, was (and is) involved in child care. (The state subsidizes certain types of day care for children with special needs.) Bananas learned about the direct aid the state could provide to their clients.

Indirectly, through the county programs, Bananas was involved with federal funding. They also found out that the-then Department of Health, Education and Welfare (later divided into two cabinet-level departments, Health and Human Services and Education) provided direct funding to a few special day-care operations.

So, who runs this town? Bananas moved through the governmental maze to find out. At the level of formal structure, they discovered, often the hard way, that power and authority in their area of concern, child care, were shared by different layers of government and several city bureaucracies.

Eventually, Bananas got what they wanted but not before they learned how informal networks of power operate. That is a theme continued in Chapters 14 and 15.

ANOTHER LOOK

U.S. citizens and scholars agree that the role of government at all levels has increased dramatically since the 1930s. They disagree on whether this is desirable, necessary, or inevitable in mass society. (Yet, most think that this trend will likely continue.)

Concerning local government, U.S. traditions favor fragmented authority and power. While many political scientists (particularly liberals) describe the current crazy quilt of local government as "irrational" and "inefficient," voters have not supported major structural change. Particularly in gloomy economic times, voters have turned their attention elsewhere: how to get more (or the same services) for less (taxes)—at the same time. Some hope that contracting out public services will be an answer to the tax crunch, but critics think that privatization is fraught with possibilities for inequity, corruption, and even a new sort of bossism.

Meanwhile, observers wonder if local governments—whatever their structure—matter much in a global society. To public choice theorists (e.g., Tiebout, 1956), locality does remain important because people choose a particular place to live so that they can choose among bundles of services. But others say that people's residential choice is not dictated by such market logic (Chapter 8). Further, critics argue that local politics can no longer meet the burdens that citizens place upon it because a series of factors, including the powers of higher levels of government which combine to hem in local governments and render them powerless to manage the quality of community life.

Perhaps. But at the same time there are local officials and ordinary citizens who reject powerlessness. Some practice spirited acts of nonviolent resistance by taking responsibility for their fellow beings and a small piece of the sky. Others, using the rhetoric of populist rebellion, form private armies and stockpile weapons against what they fear or hate: faraway, big government and urbanism as a way of life. Between these two reactions to powerlessness lies a chasm of difference—and direction. In my view, one looks backward to the values of a (real or romanticized) frontier past and the other accepts (for better and worse) the urban present and the global urban future.

Long ago, two social scientists predicted that there would be an enduring battle between these two orientations. In *Small Town in Mass Society* ([1958] 1968), sociologists Arthur J. Vidich and Joseph Bensman observed that some small farmers and rural town dwellers resisted "perhaps irreversible" trends toward *Gesellschaft* values. They cautioned that the defeat of ruralism in the United States could lead to a populist backlash based on rural hostility and defensiveness:

> Populist democracy [identified with grassroots democracy and "Americanism"] may become the basis for new social movements which could subvert the foundations of the present by holding to romanticized images of the past. An organized nativistic movement based partly on a xenophobic isolationism could shelter…defensive populists [and] a variety of other groups whose resentments are less crystallized but which could find a focus in some form of nativism.
>
> *([1958] 1968:346)*

This populism had its origins in an earlier democratic ideology, but as Vidich and Bensman warned, it could go sour and become nativistic, antidemocratic, and quasi-totalitarian.

If some accommodation is not worked out between populist patriots (and other groups that have become influential since *Small Town in Mass Society* was published, such as religious conservatives and angry, unemployed people) who uphold "traditional" values and modernists who uphold urbane values of heterogeneity, tolerance, and cosmopolitanism, we can predict that power—not authority—will prevail. Perhaps that is why Vidich and Bensman ended their community study with a plea to avoid a direct confrontation between the opposing orientations.

KEY TERMS

Annexation The addition of territory to a unit of government. Annexation usually involves a city's adding adjacent land to meet the problems of metropolitan expansion.

Areawide planning organization See council of governments.

Authority Power used in such a way that people see it as legitimate.

Charter The basic law of a local governmental unit that defines its powers, responsibilities, and organization. State constitutional or statutory provisions specify the conditions under which charters will be granted.

Charter city A city whose powers are defined by a charter from the state. Contrast: *general-law city.*

City council The policymaking and, in some instances, administrative board of a city. City councils are typically unicameral bodies.

City manager A professional administrator, appointed by the city council, in a council–manager form of government.

Commission form of government A form of city government in which both legislative and executive powers are exercised by commissioners. Not to be confused with a city commission. Features include (1) the concentration of legislative and executive power in a small group of commissioners elected at large on a nonpartisan ballot; (2) the collective responsibility of the commission to pass ordinances and control city finances; (3) the individual responsibility of each commissioner to head a city department; and (4) the selection of a mayor from among the commissioners, effectively reducing that office to one of largely ceremonial functions.

Council–manager form of government A form of city government in which the city council appoints a professional administrator, the city manager, to act as the chief executive. With variations from city to city, the essentials of this plan are (1) a small council of five or seven members elected at-large on a nonpartisan ballot, with power to make policy and hire and fire the manager; (2) a professionally-trained manager, with authority to hire and fire subordinates, who is responsible to the council for efficient administration of the city; and (3) a mayor chosen separately or from within the council but with no executive functions.

Council of governments (COG) A voluntary organization of municipalities and counties concerned with areawide problems in a metropolitan area.

County A major local government subdivision in the United States. Counties may perform a variety of local government functions, including provision of welfare and social services, administration of libraries, and road repair. Counties are typically governed by boards of supervisors or county commissioners. In rural areas, counties usually act as the general-purpose local government. In urban areas, they act as the general-purpose government for unincorporated territory and provide some services to residents of both unincorporated and incorporated areas within them.

Dillon's rule A rule (not a law) enunciated by Iowa Judge John F. Dillon, a nineteenth-century authority on municipal corporations, stating that a municipal corporation (such as a city) can exercise only those powers expressly granted to it by state law, those necessarily implied by the granted powers, and those essential for the purposes of the organization. If any doubt exists, it is to be resolved against the local unit in favor of the state.

Federation An approach to municipal governmental reorganization that assigns areawide functions to an areawide or metropolitan government and leaves local functions to existing municipalities. Example: Toronto's Metro government.

General-law city A city created pursuant to the general law of the state in which it is located rather than under a charter.

General revenue sharing An approach to the transfer of federal funds to lower levels of government—states and general-purpose local governments. Under general revenue sharing, states and local governments may use federal monies as they decide; there are no strings attached. This contrasts with program-related monies.

Home rule Power vested in a local government, such as a city, to craft or change its charter and manage its own affairs, subject to the state constitution and the general law of the state. Under home rule, state legislative interference in local affairs is limited.

Hyperpluralism The belief of some political scientists that city governments suffer from too many (*hyper*) private groups and public authorities playing the political game, which results in the paralysis of urban policymaking and the consequent bureaucratic takeover of political functions.

Incorporation The formation of a new city from previously unincorporated territory. State law specifies how new cities are to be incorporated.

Mayor The titular head of city government. The degree of a mayor's legal authority varies. In mayor–council governments, there are strong and weak mayors. In council–manager governments, the city manager runs the city's day-to-day affairs.

Mayor–council form of government A form of city government in which the mayor is elected to serve as the executive officer of the city and an elected council serves as the legislative body.

Municipality The U.S. Census Bureau's term for general-purpose units of local government other than counties. Municipalities include cities, towns and townships, and boroughs.

Reapportionment Redrawing of legislative district lines so that representation in elected government bodies is proportional to the actual population. In 1962 the U.S. Supreme Court ruled in *Baker v. Carr* that representation had to be on a one person, one vote basis.

Special district An independent unit of local government established to provide one or more limited functions, such as water. Special districts are usually created to meet problems that transcend local government boundaries or to bypass taxation and debt restrictions imposed upon local units of government by state law.

Urban county (1) A county with responsibility for providing urban services for incorporated or unincorporated areas within its borders; (2) a county where there is a substantial and densely settled population, giving it the character of a city; or (3) a county that meets specific criteria enabling it to receive certain federal funds.

PROJECTS

1. **City government**. Determine the legal structure of the city in which you live or that of one nearby. Is it a general-law or a charter city? If a charter city, is it a home-rule charter city? Next, determine the form of the city government: mayor–council, council–manager, or commission. What are the major commissions, boards, departments, and agencies of the city?

2. **Local government context**. Examine the various layers of government, of which your city (or a nearby one) is just one. For instance, what kind and how many special districts lie within the city? What are significant state and federal involvements in the city? How have cutbacks at the federal and/or state levels in the past decade affected local services?

3. **Privatization**. If a nearby city has turned over public services to private contractors, analyze the impacts. Has privatization been cost-effective and efficient? Are customers happy with the service providers? Are there complaints, and if so, what kinds?

4. **Public–private sector relations**. Compare and contrast U.S. public–private sector relationships with those in at least two European and one Latin American country. How does each nation deal with the interests of various groups, including labor unions, nonprofit associations, groups representing professionals (e.g., doctors, professors)? Are there structural mechanisms to deal with possible conflicts among these groups— say, on regional or national policy matters affecting them?

SUGGESTIONS FOR FURTHER LEARNING

For a hopeful view of the state of U.S. cities, see *Comeback Cities: A Blueprint for Urban Neighborhood Revival* (Boulder, Colo.: Westview, 2001) by Paul S. Grogan and Tony Proscio. Trumpeting a post-2000 urban renaissance, they point out that by 2000 the nation's overall poverty rate (11.3 percent)–and that of central cities (16.1 percent)–was lower than it had been in 25 years. Even air quality had improved in some cities. (Note: "Comeback cities" can suffer setbacks in short order. Events and processes beyond cities' control, such as the rising price of key food commodities, the continued outsourcing of middle-class jobs, and the subprime mortgage meltdown starting in 2007, negatively affected many U.S. cities.)

Sociologist Peter Dreier (2004), among others, has a darker view than Grogan and Proscio. He claims that President Bush's administration neglected cities, that the economic recovery of the 1990s bypassed the nation's most troubled and poor urban and suburban neighborhoods, and that income inequality increased.

Neoconservatives Edward Banfield and James Q. Wilson wrote *City Politics* in 1963 (New York: Vintage). although decades old, it contains a clear and readable explanation of state–city relations and formal city structure.

M. Gottdiener's *The Decline of Urban Politics: Political Theory and the Crisis of the Local State* (Newbury Park, Calif.: Sage, 1987) argued against neoconservative definitions and explanations. The book, written a generation ago, still signals a view long held by some social scientists.

In *The Fractured Metropolis: Political Fragmentation and Metropolitan Segregation* (Albany: State University of New York Press, 1991), Gregory R. Weiher argued that local government is far from democratic. In his view, it serves mainly parochial interests and is meant to avoid diversity in order to protect local advantage.

Do privatization and public–private partnerships work? For a ringing endorsement , see David Osborne and Ted Gaebler's *Reinventing Government: How the Entrepreneurial Spirit Is Transforming the Public Sector*, published in 1992 and discussed in this chapter. For a critique, see law professor Paul R. Verkuil,

Outsourcing Sovereignty: Why Privatization of Government Functions Threatens Democracy and What We Can Do About It (New York: Cambridge University Press, 2007). For a brief assessment of privatization efforts, see Mildred Warner's 2006 report, "Restructuring Local Government," http://government.cce.cornell.edu/default.asphttp://tgovernment.cce.cornell.edu/coc/viewpage_r.asp?ID=Privatization.

Some political scientists think that the nation-state and the city became interdependent decades ago. See, for example, Ted Robert Gurr and Desmond S. King, *The State and the City* (Chicago: University of Chicago Press, 1987).

Several organizations conduct urban policy research. Most notable is the National League of Cities, established in 1924 by and for reform-minded state municipal leagues; it represents more than 1,300 cities. It keeps member cities informed on national policies that have local impact and undertakes research and analysis on policy issues that affect cities.

The Washington, D.C.–based Conference on Alternative State and Local Policies, founded in 1975, provides, in its own words, "a national forum to assist progressives in developing strategies for change." Its publications range from books on state and local tax reform to legislative briefs and policy memos.

REFERENCES

Applebome, Peter. 1993. "Heedless of scorners, a G-rated Las Vegas booms in the Ozarks." *New York Times* (national edition) (June 1):B1+.

Asimov, Nanette, et al. 2007. "Teachers who cheat: Some help students during standards test—or fix answers later–and California's safeguards may leave more breaches unreported." *San Francisco Chronicle* (May 13):A1.

Associated Press. 2006. "Suburban poverty rising in U.S.: Report: More than 12 million in suburbs considered poor, outnumbers inner-city figures." CBS News (December 7): http://www.cbsnews.com/stories/2006/12/07/national/main2237136.shtml

Bernard, Elaine. 1993. "On creating a new party." Alternative Radio, Boulder, Colo. (April 2).

Berube, Alan, and Elizabeth Kneebone. 2006. "Two steps back: City and suburban poverty trends 1999–2005." Washington, D.C.: Brookings Institution (December): http://www.brookings.edu/metro/pubs/20061205_citysuburban.htm

Bogart, Beth. "Corruption ia in rhe system!: *In These Times* (February 20–26):5.

Capone, Al. n. d. "Al Capone famous quotes." http://www.quotemountain.com/famous_quote_author/al_capone_famous_quotations/

Castle, Mike. 2006. "Delaware would benefit from pro-family, suburban agenda." (May): http://www.castle.house.gov/index.php?option=com_content&task=view&id=249

Cyber National International, Ltd. 1997–2003."Abraham Lincoln." http://www.cybernation.com/victory/quotations/authors/quotes_lincoln_abraham.html

Davis, Mike. 1993. "Who killed L.A.: The war against the cities." *CrossRoads* 32:2–19.

Dillon, John F. 1911. *Commentaries on the Law of Municipal Corporations*, 5th ed., vol. 1, sec. 237. Boston: Little, Brown.

Dreier, Peter. 2004. "Urban neglect: George W. Bush and the cities: The damage done and the struggle ahead." *Shelterforce Online* (September/October, 137): http://www.nhi.org/online/issues/137/urbanneglect.html

Dunlea, Mark. 1997. "'Welfare reform:' Clinton kills safety net." *Synthesis/Regeneration* 12: http://www.greens.org/s-r/12/12–15.html

Edkins, Keith. n.d. What is the structure of UK local government? http://www.gwydir.demon.co.uk/uklocal-gov/structure.htm

Feinstein, Dianne. 1988. "Mayors' tips for the new mayor." *San Francisco Chronicle* (January 9):A5.

Henriques, Diana B., and Andrew Lehren. 2007. "Religious groups reap share of federal aid." *San Francisco Chronicle* (May 13):A7.

Hinds, Michael de Courcy, with Erik Eckholm. 1990. "80's leave state and cities in need." *New York Times* (national edition) (December 30):A1+.

James, Frank. 2006. "Congress' suburbanites vow to fight for suburbs." *The Swamp, Chicago Tribune* Washington Bureau blog: http://weblogs.chicagotribune.com/news/politics/blog/2006/05/congress_suburbanites_vow_to_f.html

Kheel, Theodore W. [1969] 1971. "The Port Authority strangles New York." Pp. 443–449 in David M. Gordon, ed., *Problems in Political Economy: An Urban Perspective*. Lexington, Mass.: Heath.

Lee, Andrea, and Mira Weinstein. 1996. "Clinton veto needed on punitive welfare legislation." *National NOW Times:* http://www.now.org/nnt/01–96/welfare.html

Mollenkopf, John. 1983. *The Contested City*. Princeton, N.J.: Princeton University Press.

Molotch Harvey. 1990. "Urban deals in comparative perspective." Pp. 175–198 in John R. Logan and Todd Swanstrom, eds., *Beyond the City Limits: Urban Policy and Economic Restructuring in Comparative Perspective.* Philadelphia: Temple University Press.

Morgan, David R., Robert E. England, and John P. Pelissero. 2006. *Managing Urban America*, 6th ed. Washington, D.C.: CQ Press.

MOST Clearing House. n.d. "Best Practices. Metro Toronto's changing communities: Innovative responses." http://www.vcn.bc.ca/citizens-handbook/unesco/most/usa9.html

National League of Cities. n.d. "About cities: Cities 101."ithttp://www.nlc.org/about_cities/cities_101/154.aspx

Noonan, Erica. 2007. "New year, old ways: Chinese school grows as parents keep traditions alive." *Boston Globe* (February 15): http://www.boston.com/news/local/articles/2007/02/15/new_year_old_ways/

NPR–Kaiser–Kennedy School Poll. 2002. "Attitudes toward government." http://www.npr.org/programs/specials/poll/govt/gov.toplines.pdf

Osborne, David, and Ted Gaebler. 1992. *Reinventing Government: How the Entrepreneurial Spirit Is Transforming the Public Sector.* Reading, Mass.: Addison-Wesley.

Osborne, David, and Peter Plastrik. 2001. *The Reinventor's Fieldbook: Tools for Transforming Your Government.* New York: John Wiley & Sons.

———. 1998. *Banishing Bureaucracy: The Five Strategies for Reinventing Government.* New York: Plume.

Pelissero, John P., and David Fasenfest. 1988. "A typology of suburban economic development policy." Paper delivered at the annual meeting of the American Political Science Association, Boston, MA, September 3–6.

Rasmussen Reports. 2008. "Americans give low marks to U.S. health care, but 69% rate their health insurance good or excellent." (July 7): www.rasmussenreports.com/public_content/politics/issues2/articles/americans_give_low_marks_to_u_s_health_care_but_69_rate_their_health_insurance_good_or_excellent

Roberts, Joel. 2002. "Poll: Little faith in big biz." CBS News (July 10): http://www.cbsnews.com/stories/2002/07/10/opinion/polls/main514732.shtml

———.2007. "Poll: The politics of health care." CBS News (March 1): http://www.cbsnews.com/stories/2007/03/01/opinion/polls/main2528357.shtml

Sandalow, Marc. 1993. "S.F.'s $188 million deficit will force tough choices." *San Francisco Chronicle* (May 17):A1.

Sayre, Wallace, and Herbert Kaufman. 1960. *Governing New York City: Politics in the Metropolis.* New York: Russell Sage.

Scahill, Jeremy. 2007. *Blackwater: The Rise of the World's Most Powerful Mercenary Army* . New York: Nation Books.

Scheer, Bob. 1993. "S.F. soaking up nation's troubles." *San Francisco Examiner* (June 27):A1.

Schneider, William. 1992. "The suburban century begins." *Atlantic Monthly* (July):33–44.

Shorrock, Tim. 2008a. *Spies for Hire: The Secret World of Intelligence Outsourcing.* New York: Simon & Schuster.

———. 2008b. Interview on NPR's *Fresh Air* with Terry Gross (May 14).

Sunnucks, Mike. 2007. "Fort Huachuca intelligence center draws private contractors." *Business Journal of Phoenix* (November 7): http://www.bizjournals.com/phoenix/stories/2007/11/05/daily27.html

Thousman. 2008. "San Francisco voted #1 U.S. city by Conde Nast Traveler readers for 16th consecutive year." (October): http://www.onlyinsanfrancisco.com/sfnews/?p=73

Tiebout, Charles. 1956. "A pure theory of local expenditures." *Journal of Political Economy* 64:416–424.

U.S. Bureau of Justice. 2009. "Crime characteristics." (April 21): http://www.ojp.usdoj.gov/bjs/cvict_c.htm

U.S. Bureau of the Census. 2002. 2002 Census of governments. GC01–1P: http://ftp2.census.gov/govs/cog/2002COGprelim_report.pdf

U.S. Office of Management and Budget. 1978. *Special Analyses of the Budget of the United States Fiscal Year 1979.* Washington, D.C.: Government Printing Office.

U.S. Senate. 1966–1967. *Federal Role in Urban Affairs.* Hearings before the Subcommittee on Executive Reorganization of the Committee on Governmental Operations, 89th and 90th Cong., 2nd sess.

Vidich, Arthur J., and Joseph Bensman. [1958] 1968. *Small Town in Mass Society: Class, Power and Religion in a Rural Community.* Princeton, N.J.: Princeton University Press.

Vobedja, Barbara. 1996. "Clinton signs welfare reform, turns programs over to states." *The Tech* 116(31): http://www-tech.mit.edu/V116/N31/clinton.31w.html

Wade, Richard C. 1982. "The suburban roots of the new federalism." *New York Times Magazine* (August 1):20+.

Weiher, Gregory R. 1991. *The Fractured Metropolis: Political Fragmentation and Metropolitan Segregation*. Albany: State University of New York Press.

Weiss, Michael J. 1988. *The Clustering of America*. New York: Harper & Row.

White House. 2006. "WHOFBCI accomplishments in 2006." http://www.whitehouse.gov/government/fbci/2006_accomplishments.html

Wirt, Frederick M. 1971. "The politics of hyperpluralism." Pp. 101–125 in Howard S. Becker, ed., *Culture and Civility in San Francisco*. New Brunswick, N.J.: Transaction Books.

Thomas Nast

CHAPTER 14

BOSSES, BOODLERS, AND REFORMERS

Urban politics is a drama. It is played out against a backdrop of legal, institutional structures. A tidy U.S. organization chart would show these structures in a series of boxes: the mayor or city manager, followed by the city council and department heads, boxed in at the center of a mosaic of governments from Washington, D.C., down to the local board of education.

But what the organization chart doesn't show lies at the heart of the drama—patterns of influence. The two are inseparable. Formal structure is the skeleton of politics. Informal structures breathe life into the body politic. Getting something done in a city, whether having an ordinance passed or starting a government-funded program, requires *acquaintance with* structures of influence as well as *knowledge about government*.

Influential private institutions, from multinational corporations to local banks, make critical decisions that affect, even determine, the well-being of urban communities. For example, they provide jobs and housing, influence land-use patterns, and affect air and water pollution.

Structures of influence can operate *extra*legally or *il*legally. Political action committees (PACs), parent–teacher associations (PTAs), and police benevolent associations (PBAs) exemplify legal organizations

464

Fig. 14.2 ORGANIZATION CHART. Charts show only how formal structures operate. They can't reveal how informal influences affect city politics. (Richard Hedman)

seeking to influence public policy *extralegally*. In the United States, and in many other places, such groups hire paid staff (strategists and lobbyists) to advance their point of view or to write legislation (or rules) that concern their interests.

In the United States, citizens accept such groups and their lobbyists as legitimate actors in the political process. But they are not mentioned in city charters, the U.S. Constitution, or indeed most anywhere else; that is why they are called *extra*legal. (By contrast, in most European Union countries, there is a legal, not extralegal, institution based on the French model, the Conseil Économique et Social. It includes representatives from a variety of backgrounds, including labor, the professions, and nongovernmental organizations; it acts as an advisory council to the bodies to which it is attached, often a regional government).

Other organizations operate illegally, sometimes in opposition to elected officials, sometimes in tandem. For example, Mexican and Afghani drug lords' private armies represent powerful, illegal groups that influence through intimidation and violence. Organized crime holds sway across the world, from the *yakuza* in

Tokyo and drug cartels in Asia and Latin America to the so-called Russian mafia in the Ukraine and New York City.

Perhaps the most notorious structure of influence operating in tandem with government officials is (or perhaps was) Sicily's *sistema del potere*: the power structure or system. In the towns of Sicily, "almost everything is explained with the phrase 'sistema del potere'. . . . According to law enforcement authorities in Rome and Palermo, the public purse was one of the largest sources of income for the Mafia in the early '90s" (Viviano, 1993:A1, A10). Journalist and author Frank Viviano (born in Detroit as Francesco Paolo Viviano) wrote in 1995: "The 'sistema,' which has ruled Sicily since my great-grandparents were children, has grown into a transnational empire of crime, and a trading power of phenomenal reach." Few public governments command such vast resources—or loyalty.

Thankfully, history is not destiny. Yesterday's institutions need not be tomorrow's fate. In western Sicilian towns, for example, citizens' groups organized the Anti-Mafia Coordinating Association. In Italy, a web of scandals implicating the nation's political elite brought widespread demands to stop politicians from running the country as if it were a collection of medieval fiefdoms.

Still, today's systems of influence can, in part, be understood by looking at the historical context. Here, we focus on extralegal influences on U.S. urban politics.

Let's begin by looking back to a time when bosses and **machine** politics ran most U.S. cities. Over time, most old-style machines ran out of steam, but newer-style machines are still alive.

This chapter traces these changes in local politics and suggests reasons for the changes. It begins with a discussion of a uniquely American institution: the city political machine. For decades, bosses and their machines provided the power and energy to get things done.

THE CITY POLITICAL MACHINE

Beginning after the Civil War, virtually all U.S. cities at one time or another were dominated by a political machine. In some cities, machines rose and fell in a few years, succeeded by other machines or reform governments. In others, a machine retained power for generations. Today, with some notable exceptions such as Chicago, only fragments of the great old machines remain. So-called reform governments replaced most of them, and new forms of coalition politics arose.

Yet, the old machine, which generally ran out of steam, is a political model that has present-day applications. In many large and small U.S. cities, politics is organized on a machinelike basis or has surviving elements of party machinery. For instance, many cities have ward-sized bosses who act like the old machine bosses.

A colorful cast of characters revved up the old machines and kept them oiled: men like cigar-chomping Tammany leader George Washington Plunkitt in New York City and Chicago's Richard J. Daley, a man of many malapropisms. Another set of actors and actresses helped to smash the machines: reformers or, as the bosses called them, "goo-goos."

A BUNCH OF CROOKS OR FRIEND OF THE POOR?

In the 1870s, political satirist Thomas Nast drew devastating cartoons depicting New York City's Boss Tweed and his Tammany Hall (the Democratic Party machine) ring of machine operatives. One cartoon (shown at the beginning of this chapter) shows the Tweed Ring feasting on the corpse of New York City, strewn with the bones of law, liberty, justice, and the city treasury. Standing on a cliff crumbling in a political storm, the Tammany "vultures" intone pseudo-prayerfully, "Let us prey." Nast's cartoons helped to fix one image of machine bosses that persists in the U.S. mind: corrupt, incompetent characters concerned primarily with taking money from the public treasury to feather their own nests.

There is also a contradictory image that remains in the U.S. imagination: the city machine as friend, even family, to the poor and powerless, particularly lower-class white ethnics. This vision can be found in popular literature that romanticizes the city boss. In Edwin O'Connor's novel *The Last Hurrah* (1956), for instance, Boston's Mayor Jim Curley is portrayed as the warm-hearted protector of the city's Irish in the late nineteenth century.

Which image more nearly approximates the reality? Before deciding, let's look at how machines work(ed), what services the old machines provided, and what forces led to their general extinction.

HOW CITY MACHINES WORK(ED)

Whether past or present, city machines are highly structured, hierarchical organizations with no pretense to an individualistic mentality. In fact, party discipline and organizational loyalty fuel the machine.

Controlling votes is the name of the machine game. The machine is goal-oriented: Its goal is getting nominees elected to public office.

Machines are organized to achieve their goal of electing nominees. A cadre of loyal party workers (and a core of voters) is held together by a mixture of material rewards and psychic benefits, including personal recognition, jobs, and a sense of community. This loyal cadre is part of a highly-disciplined party hierarchy headed by a single executive or board of directors.

Typically, the hierarchically-structured machine has (or had) a bottom rung in charge of mobilizing the votes of a single **precinct** (the basic unit of voting and party organization in the United States; in recent years arguably the best-known precinct captain on

Chicago's South Side was Michelle Obama's late father, Frasier Robinson, a city employee). Precinct captains are responsible to **ward** captains or bosses. At the top is a central committee composed of ward bosses and the central boss. Loyalty, trust, and discipline bind the machine's lower and upper levels together.

At the street level, where voters deal with machine operatives, contacts were (and are) face-to-face and unbureaucratic. This lack of red tape and freedom from bureaucratic rigidity were appealing features to nineteenth- and twentieth-century immigrants. These newcomers feared or could not understand city hall, settlement houses, and private charities that were supposed to be tending to their needs. Tammany Hall leader George Washington Plunkitt boasted that he could get clothing and temporary shelter to fire victims in his New York City ward very quickly—before they froze to death—while the city and private organizations could not.

In dealing with constituents, machines are (and were) informal. But internally, they run like an army or a business. Here is a British scholar's comment about late nineteenth-century city machines:

> An army led by a council seldom conquers: it must have a commander-in-chief, who settles disputes, decides in emergencies, inspires fear or attachment. The head of [the machine] is such a commander. He dispenses places, rewards the loyal, punishes the mutinous, concocts schemes, negotiates treaties. He generally avoids publicity, preferring the substance to the pomp of power.... He is a Boss.
>
> *(Bryce, 1889:109)*

Sitting "like a spider, hidden in the midst of his web," the boss recalls another publicity-shy figure: the godfather. The fictional Don Corleone in the book *The Godfather* (Puzo, [1969] 1973), subsequent movies (1972, 1974, 1990), and a 2006 video game is a commander-in-chief, running an organization resembling an old-style machine.

Once in control of a city, a machine fueled its engine in numerous ways:

1. It gained control of *patronage* jobs. Chicago's Mayor Richard Daley (head of the Cook County Democratic machine) personally controlled at least 25,000 jobs.

2. It decided who got *city contracts*, often padded to permit healthy profits for machine supporters.

3. It gave *insiders a chance to speculate* in real estate by profiting from advance tips on city action (Box 14.1).

4. Like Don Vito Corleone (Marlon Brando in the movie trilogy of *The Godfather*), it *granted requests* to loyalists. It also granted special favors (e.g., zoning variances) for a bribe to the machine.

5. It got *kickbacks* from recipients of city contracts.

6. Sometimes it got *pocket money from blackmail* of persons threatened with criminal prosecution by machine-controlled city attorneys.

To summarize: The city machine is an informal structure of influence and power that never appears in a city's charter or organization chart. It mobilizes votes and distributes the benefits of office to supporters. Internally, the city machine is held together by trust and discipline. It combines rational goals with brotherly loyalty. Like an army or a business, it is based on strict discipline and hierarchy. But a machine deals with its constituents in a nonbureaucratic, personal manner. Its power and influence in the city are based on the services it provides.

WHAT SERVICES MACHINES PROVIDE(D)

Getting some help with the rent or a job at city hall. Maybe some graft (what Plunkitt called "honest" or otherwise). These don't seem to be big benefits to get from a city machine. Yet when all the thousands of small favors and economic assists are totaled, they add up to a major urban social service: an informal welfare system.

Remember that city machines rose to prominence in the nineteenth century as hundreds of thousands of European immigrants, mostly poor and unskilled, poured into the nation's cities. These immigrants had few support networks. Family members and friends were frequently left behind in the old country. Private charities and churches were ill-equipped to deal with all the immigrants' daily needs, and there were almost no government welfare programs. In this context, the old machine functioned as a personal deliverer of services, without layers of bureaucracy.

Like family, the machine could be counted on. It could bail you out of jail, get you a job when work was hard to find, give you free railroad passes, remember you with a gift for your wedding, and generally help you when you needed help. And at Christmas time, there was food. Chicago's renowned social reformer and Hull House director Jane Addams records that the alderman from her ward, Johnny Powers, the famed "Prince of Boodlers" (grafters), personally delivered 10 tons of turkeys and ducks, shaking each voter's hand as he greeted them with a "Merry Christmas" (Addams, [1898] 1972:14).

The old machine also served as a vehicle of economic assimilation for immigrants. This kind of assimilation promoted upward mobility, but it allowed white ethnic immigrants to keep their ethnic identities. Indeed, city machines fostered ethnic identity, not cultural assimilation. This is ironic, for even opponents of machine corruption thought that at least machines were doing something good: ladling the immigrants into the melting pot (Stead, 1894).

But to the contrary, machines encouraged the stewpot. They used a variety of techniques to capitalize on ethnic and racial differences. One technique involved settlement patterns. In Chicago, for example, the Irish tended to reside on the South Side. This housing pattern was encouraged by the machine, for the Irish could then be controlled by a ward boss of their own ethnic background and become a voting bloc.

To most people in a city ward, machine politics meant ethnic politics. And ethnic politics provided a way to climb the economic ladder for white ethnics, who were generally barred by class and ethnic prejudice from advancing through jobs in commerce and industry.

The career of George Washington Plunkitt, longtime Tammany boss in New York City, shows how the machine provided opportunities for at least a few lower-class white ethnic males. Plunkitt started out as a butcher's assistant in a working-class Irish ward. He rose through the ranks of the Tammany machine, becoming the master of "honest graft" (Box 14.1).

BOX 14.1 HOW THE MACHINE WORKED

"Practical" Advice from George Washington Plunkitt, Tammany Hall Politician

On Controlling Votes

There's only one way to hold a district; you must study human nature and act accordin'. You can't study human nature in books....If you have been to college, so much the worse for you....To learn real human nature, you have to go among the people, see them and be seen. I know every man, woman, and child in the Fifteenth District, except them that's been born this summer—and I know some of them, too. I know what they like and what they don't like, what they are strong at and what they are weak in, and I reach them by approachin' at their right side....For instance, here's how I gather in the young men. I hear of a young feller that's proud of his voice....I ask him to come around to Washington Hall and join our Glee Club. He comes and sings, and he's a follower of Plunkitt for life.

What tells in holdin' your grip on your district is to go right down among the poor families and help them in the different ways they need help. I've got a regular system for this. If there's a fire in Ninth, Tenth, or Eleventh Avenue, for example, any hour of the day or night, I'm usually there with some of my election district captains as soon as the fire-engines. If a family is burned out I don't ask whether they are Republicans or Democrats, and I don't refer them to the Charity Organization Society, which would investigate their case in a month or two and decide they were worthy of help about the time they are dead from starvation. I just get quarters for them, buy clothes for them...and fix them up till they get things runnin' again.

Another thing. I can always get a job for a deservin' man. I make it a point to keep on the track of jobs, and it seldom happens that I don't have a few up my sleeve ready for use.

On "Honest Graft"

There's an honest graft, and I'm an example of how it works. I might sum up the whole thing by sayin': I seen my opportunities and I took 'em. Just let me explain by examples. My party's [the Democrats] in power in the city, and it's goin' to undertake a lot of public improvements. Well, I'm tipped off, say, that they're going to lay out a new park at a certain place. I see my opportunity and I take it. I go to that place and I buy up all the land I can in the neighborhood....Ain't it perfectly honest to charge a good price and make a profit on my investment and foresight? Of course, it is. Well, that's honest graft.

Source: William L. Riordan, *Plunkitt of Tammany Hall* (New York: Dutton, [1906], 1963), pp. 3–4, 91–92; subheads mine. First published 1963 by E. P. Dutton and Co., Inc., and reprinted with permission. All rights reserved.

Now, let's look at two well-oiled, efficient machines. Operating almost 100 years apart, the Tweed Ring controlled New York City from 1866 to 1871, and the Daley machine controlled Chicago politics from 1955 until Daley's death in 1976—and beyond; his son, Richard M. Daley was elected mayor in 1989 and reelected in 2007 for his sixth term. In 2005, *Time* magazine named Rich Daley the best of the United States's five big-city mayors. And despite a city hall corruption scandal, a federal bribery probe of some city officials, and the illegal demolition of a city airport during his fifth term, Daley was easily reelected in 2007.

These brief case studies give a flavor of the bosses and the forces that promoted them. First, Boss Tweed.

CASE STUDY: NEW YORK CITY'S TWEED RING, 1866–1871

Most often, political scientists point to Tammany Hall boss William Tweed and his Tweed Ring as exemplars of corrupt machine rule. Some assert that Tweed (who never ran for mayor) and his ring (the mayor, city controller, some aldermen, numerous operatives) stole as much as $200 million from the public treasury in 5 years.

Tweed was a huge man with uncouth manners, and he spent money conspicuously. Since he had been a man of modest means before rising through Tammany's ranks, he was often attacked as a vulgar crook, a plunderer. Cartoonist Thomas Nast was a particularly effective and vicious assailant, depicting Tweed as a vulture (see cartoon opening this chapter).

There is little doubt that Tweed was corrupt. It is also true that New York City's debt rose rapidly under Tweed, about $31 million in 2 years. And construction projects sponsored by Tweed—particularly the ornate courthouse near City Hall (the setting for many movie trials)—were scandalously expensive.

But before passing judgment on Tweed, consider his social context and the sources of contemporary criticism. First, many of Tweed's critics came from educated, wealthy, white Anglo-Saxon Protestant (WASP) backgrounds. Thomas Nast is a case in point. In his cartoons, Nast often depicted lower-class Irish as apes. He was distressed to see power in "his" city pass into the hands of people he considered ill-mannered and

unpolished: Irish Catholic immigrants, mainly poor and uneducated. (It is noteworthy that Nast did not use his poison pencil to caricature WASP robber barons like John Jacob Astor, who enjoyed warm working relationships with the bosses and who were hardly paragons of virtue. Indeed, the robber barons' unscrupulous wealth-getting techniques—stock manipulation, price fixing, false advertising—and profits from political corruption—made the taking of public boodle pale by comparison. Thus, Nast's attacks on the Tweed Ring seem to be based more on class, ethnic, and religious bias than on righteous indignation against corruption per se.

Second, it isn't clear that the Tweed Ring was really a machine at all. The standard interpretation of the machine depicts it as a tight-knit organization based on greed and personal gain, with little regard for the public interest. Those who interpret the machine in this way, seeing it essentially as a system of organized bribery operating without a sense of the public good, point to the Tweed Ring's ability to dominate virtually every aspect of New York City's political life.

But an alternative view of the Tweed Ring holds that tight-knit machines didn't emerge until much later in the nineteenth century. Then, it is argued, business entrepreneurs needed stable city governments to provide the proper climate for long-term business investments.

Whether or not it was a tight-knit machine, the Tweed Ring did have a substantial impact on New York City, then undergoing rapid change. It pressed a range of school, hospital, and public works projects; obtained reforms to protect city teachers' job security; and established much needed public baths. The Ring provided jobs for lower-class laborers before government employment or unemployment programs existed. It changed the bias of the New York City Parks Commission, which had previously concentrated funds in Central Park to benefit upper-class residents, diverting funds to smaller parks that better met the needs of lower-class immigrants. It secured a new city charter in 1871 that centralized city government and reduced government fragmentation (and, not incidentally, made the machine's work easier). This charter reform represented a more efficient way of reviewing budgets than the former structure, in which each city department presented an independent budget to the state legislature.

Finally, Tweed, who died in jail a broken man in 1878, may have been much maligned by history. In the past generation, scholarship suggests that the extent of the Tweed Ring's corruption was far less than was previously believed.

Thus, the ledger sheet shows that Tweed and his ring were both *a bunch of crooks and a friend to the poor*. They were something else too: *a friend of the rich*, especially the rising class of entrepreneurs, whose fortunes grew during the post–Civil War period of rapid industrialization and urbanization. The Tweed Ring didn't challenge the fundamental interests of the new entrepreneurs.

Nast and other patricians may have hated Tweed and his lower-class ilk, but the machine bosses weren't antibusiness. Nor were they radical in their politics. Tweed's Ring worked comfortably and often closely with the robber barons. In fact, when Tweed was being prosecuted in 1871 for corruption, John Jacob Astor and five other millionaires signed an affidavit attesting to Tweed's good character, swearing that he never stole a cent from the New York City treasury. Financier Jay Gould (who once boasted that he could hire one-half of the working class to kill the other half) paid Tweed's $1-million bail.

CASE STUDY: THE RICHARD J. DALEY MACHINE IN CHICAGO, 1955–1976—AND WAY BEYOND

People called Chicago Mayor Richard J. Daley many names: king maker (for his support of John F. Kennedy for president in 1960), fascist pig (for his role at the Democratic National Convention in 1968), a damn good mayor (even the beacon of Republican sentiments, *The Chicago Tribune*, supported his later mayoral campaigns), last of the big-city bosses, or simply "Boss." Observers dispute the wisdom of his policies, but they agree that Mayor Daley had clout. And Daley's clout, extending far beyond Chicago, was based on his leadership and control of the Cook County (Chicago) Democratic Party machine, the nation's last full-blown, old-style machine.

In many ways, Dick Daley resembled the bosses of the nineteenth century more than most of his urban contemporaries. Like so many Chicago machine politicians before him, Daley came from a lower-class, Irish immigrant family. He grew up in the Bridgeport section of Chicago, an Irish American neighborhood, and he never moved away. A devoutly religious and old-fashioned family man, Daley didn't try to be refined or polished. Chicagoans delighted in his malapropisms (e.g., "Together we must rise to ever higher and higher platitudes").

Yet despite his rough edges, Harvard-educated presidential nominee JFK and corporate business executives paid him court at city hall. The reason: He had clout, power, and influence based in a well-oiled machine.

Daley didn't create Chicago's machine. It grew out of the economic crisis of the 1930s (Gosnell, [1937] 1968:8). The machine was consolidated during the 1930s and 1940s but weakened by Daley's predecessor. In the 1950s, at a time when machines in New York City and other places were withering away, Daley refueled the machine by making adaptations, promoting internal reforms, and attracting federal funds to the city.

Under his leadership, the day-to-day activities of Chicago's ward bosses remained much as they had been for decades. A ward boss's typical evening consisted of the following types of work: talking to a black building manager seeking a reduction in the $20 per month rodent-extermination charge in his building; listening to two precinct captains who were asking for 42 garbage cans; counseling a female computer programmer who thought she was being mistreated by her supervisor; and speaking to a Polish American truck driver who was looking for work. In each case, the ward boss said that he would see what he could do (Rakove, 1975:122).

The following story, recounted by a *New York Times* reporter, exemplifies how the Daley machine worked at the street level: A secretary was robbed at knifepoint en route home. The next day, she returned to the crime scene, hoping to retrieve her beloved red suede purse. She asked a city garbage crew that was passing by if they had seen the purse. The crew chief said yes, it was in the truck—along with several tons of garbage. The crew chief phoned his foreman, who phoned the precinct captain, who ordered the truck driven to a vacant lot. There, the entire load of garbage was dumped out

Bosses, Boodlers, and Reformers

until the purse was found. Then, the precinct captain took the woman and her leather purse to a friend's dry-cleaning shop, where the purse was cleaned without charge. After all this, the secretary was driven to her place of work. Two years later, in 1975, she voted to reelect Richard J. Daley as her mayor (Malcolm, 1986:20).

As central boss, Daley spent part of each workday in activities that helped his reelection and ensured machine control. One observer reported the following:

> By two o'clock [Daley's] back behind his desk and working. One of his visitors will be a city official unique to Chicago city government: the director of patronage. He brings a list of all new city employees for the day. The list isn't limited to the key employees, the professional people. All new employees are there—down to the window washer, the ditch digger, the garbage collector. After each person's name will be an extract of his background, the job, and most important his political sponsor. Nobody goes to work for the city, and that includes governmental bodies that are not directly under the mayor, without Daley's knowing about it.
>
> *(Royko, 1971:23)*

Daley wanted to see every name on the list because the individual became much more than an employee: "he joins the political Machine, part of the army numbering in the thousands who will help win elections. They damn well better, or they won't keep their jobs" (Royko, 1971:23).

What drove Daley and his ward bosses to devote so much time and energy to people's personal problems? To larger issues affecting city life? For many, the motive was payoffs and jobs. Daley himself was never accused of enriching himself at the public trough, but relatives and friends were found on the city payroll. For others, there were some of the same motives that impel people in other walks of life: ego satisfaction, power, success. But not fame—for most ward bosses remain unknown to the public. Nor ideology—Chicago's machine operatives are essentially pragmatists, not ideologues. They may share many concerns of the liberal wing of the Democratic Party, but they don't seek to implement a particular political platform. Instead, they seek to win elections, provide services, and act as

power brokers between conflicting ethnic and interest groups. One ward boss summarized his philosophy as follows: "Don't make no waves" and "Don't back no losers" (Neistein in Rakove, 1975:11).

In terms of substantive policies, the Daley machine encouraged large-scale business in the city. For example, to sweeten the pot for the giant Sears corporation, seeking to build a headquarters, the city agreed to pay more than $1 million to relocate sewer lines for the proposed building (O'Connor, 1975:139). The Sears building, one of the world's tallest (and, since 2009, renamed for its key tenant, an English-based company) is only one of many built during Daley's rule.

"Boss" Daley's record on housing construction, however, is another and controversial story. Daley's machine effectively blocked dispersal of low-income, racially integrated housing. This led to an even higher concentration of African Americans in virtually segregated neighborhoods. Chicago remains one of the North's most racially segregated cities to this day. (Under Daley's son, Chicago's multiterm Mayor Richard M. Daley, African American residential segregation remains high. It remains even higher than the housing segregation of Latinos, which, in the late 1990s, was greater in "Chicagoland" than in any other major metropolitan region in the United States.)

In terms of internal organization, the Daley machine adjusted to the city's changing ethnic composition, in particular to the increase in African American and Hispanic communities. Widening the patronage net from old-line ethnic group supporters, the Daley machine reached political accommodation with the late William Dawson, a member of Congress who ran a tight-knit black submachine on Chicago's South Side.

But the era of the African American tight-knit submachine was short-lived. African Americans had long cooperated with (or were co-opted by) the machine, seeing no viable alternative. But President Reagan's commitment to cut back the welfare state plus changing demographics in Cook County rewrote the rules of the game. Then, a remarkable grassroots movement of over 200 organizations—from church groups to People Organized for Welfare and Employment Rights (POWER, a coalition of African Americans, whites, and

Fig. 14.3 MAYOR RICHARD J. DALEY. Chicago's late mayor was largely responsible for reviving the city's central business district in an era of suburban decentralization. Under his aegis, Sears built what was, at the time, the world's tallest building on the central business district's fringe: the Sears Tower. (Ironically, Sears Roebuck's business fortunes later declined. By 1995, their tower offices were moved to Hoffman Estates, a suburb and, as of 2009, its name is off the Tower.) (*Chicago Tribune* photo)

Latinos)—focused African American disaffection from the machine. By 1982, a voter registration drive in the African American community (one slogan: "Praise the Lord, and Register") signaled a growing political consciousness and nonmachine participation in the political life of the city.

Meanwhile, for many reasons, the citywide machine was creaky. Daley's political machine started declining before his death in 1976. In 1983, anti-machine candidate Harold Washington (originally a product of the Dawson submachine) was elected the city's first African American mayor and the city's first

reform mayor in 50 years. Some observers sounded the death knell of the machine.

Is the Chicago machine dead? Observers disagree, but—to date—no one has written its total obituary.

In 1987, reform mayor Harold Washington died at his City Hall desk during his second term. He wasn't mayor long, but his influence was widespread. For one, President Barack Obama credits Harold Washington as an inspiration during his run for the Senate. (Hear Ira Glass's radio program on National Public Radio, *This American Life*, 2007, for a 20-year celebration of Washington's life.)

After Washington's death, Daley's son, Richard M. Daley, was elected—and reelected—mayor. *Newsweek* called young Daley a "genius at creating [his] own dynasty" ("Conventional Wisdom," 1990:4). Even so, the future of Chicago's machine was far from assured.

When son Rich Daley took over the city, it was not the growing, prosperous city that his father ruled. Indeed, by the early 1980s, the "city that works" didn't. As a *Chicago Tribune* headline trumpeted, there were "Fewer Firms, Fewer Jobs, Less Revenue" (Longworth, 1981:1). Chicago had experienced disinvestment, deindustrialization, and a net loss of 123,500 jobs between 1972 and 1981. In addition, fiscal crises affected virtually all public services, and tensions along racial, ethnic, and class lines that historically divided Chicago, a city of neighborhoods, got worse. Some business leaders spoke fondly of the "good old days" under Mayor Daley (the city's central power broker), but no amount of patronage or turkeys—the kinds of goodies that machines can offer their loyal followers—could make such structural challenges disappear.

By the early 1990s, the times were changing, even in Chicago. Taxpayers demanded higher-quality services and lower tax bills. City officials feared the out-migration of working-class homeowners. Mayor Rich Daley, "Son of Boss," privatized a range of former patronage jobs, including janitorial services, tree stump removal, and parking ticket enforcement. (Critics of privatization claim that African American city workers were hardest hit because they held a disproportionately large number of jobs amenable to privatization: service and maintenance.) Daley's privatization efforts confirmed that "the taxpayer is more important than the payroller" (Green in Mahtesian, 1994:A3). Once again, some sounded the death knell for old-style bossism.

By the late 1990s, the city worked again. With Daley's son as mayor, Chicago worked better—at least for some and in some ways. Yes, racial and ethnic segregation remained very high. Yes, Chicago's facelift was concentrated in or near downtown with the splendor of Millennium Park (opened in 2004) and renovations at Museum Park (1998). Yes, certain neighborhoods prospered more than others, particularly lakefront, riverfront, and North Side communities. Yes, the South Side and the West Side suffered high crime and poverty rates. Yes, bribery and corruption scandals marked his tenure as mayor. Nonetheless, under Rich Daley retail areas were revitalized and infrastructure investments made. Some shabby neighborhoods started showing signs of renewed life. Chicago became known as a "green city" for its eco-friendly policies, including 10,000 bike racks, the absorption of combustion emissions by extensive gardens from the ground to the rooftops, and a Green Alley initiative (where alleys were retrofitted with environmentally sustainable road-building materials).

In addition, Daley, the son, presided over a diversified, balanced economy with large numbers of new corporate headquarters attracted to the city or metro area. Tourism increased, and the transit authority was modernized. For all these efforts, Rich Daley was picked by *Time* magazine in 2005 as the best mayor of U.S. large cities.

Critics accuse "Son of Boss" of using machine politics to remain mayor. Perhaps, but Daley is very popular with Chicago's citizenry. As of this writing, he has won the mayor's office six times, often by large margins. In 2007, running against two African American candidates (in a city with a population of about 37 percent African Americans), Daley won by a landslide.

In February 2007, just before he was reelected by over 70 percent of the vote, here was the scene in Rich Daley's city: A mayor overseeing an administration, including top aides, being investigated by the FBI for bribery and corruption. An alderman (a woman but all city councilors are called "aldermen") facing a federal bribery charge ran to keep her seat. (She lost.) Four former aldermen who had served jail time for corruption were running for their old jobs. (They lost.) In other words, Chicago's city elections, as recently as 2007, took place in a city legendary for bossism and graft (Associated Press, 2007)—in legendary Chicago style.

Conventional wisdom is that in many cities this mismatch—between goodies available and goodies needed—did the bosses in years before: during FDR's New Deal in the 1930s. But not in Chicago. As one wag commented years ago, and his comment is no doubt still relevant: "Chicago is America's museum, where old ways are on display" (Will, 1984:92).

Fig. 14.4   MAYOR RICHARD M. DALEY. Daley's son, Richard M. Daley, has been elected mayor six times thus far, from 1989. Under his aegis, the Windy City has built eco-friendly buildings and pioneered urban standards in renewable energy, among other "green" initiatives. He also initiated the grandest building projects since the Columbian Exposition, including Millennium Park (*pictured here*), which opened in 2004. Here, Mayor Daley (*far left*) is pictured with architect Frank Gehry (*third from left*) and city officials. (Courtesy, City of Chicago)

Goodies, often called "pork," still have a place in Chicago—as elsewhere. In March 2007, the Twelfth Ward alderman (city councillor) who represented the Douglas Park neighborhood voted for a $500-million city-backed guarantee in order to be considered for the 2016 Summer Olympic games; he put his vote in the context of pork: "Listen, Douglas Park is going to get the aquatic center, so, I can't complain" (in NBC5.com, 2007).

To conclude: Under "Son of Boss," Mayor Richard M. Daley, Chicago morphed from Rustbelt metropolis to shiny green giant of the heartland. How much is his success due to a well-oiled machine? That's unclear. Observers don't agree how much of this Daley's success is due to machine politics.

What most observers would agree upon, no doubt, is this: Sandberg's poem "Chicago" still works to describe the City of the Big Shoulders, at least in part. No longer Hog Butcher for the World (most of the meatpacking industry left Chicago years ago), Chicago remains a Player with Railroads; it is a major transport and distribution center. Like other global cities, it is less a Tool Maker and more a major financial center. By 2008, Chicago placed thirteenth on UBS(a Swiss bank)'s list of the world's richest cities in terms of purchasing power.

Observers would probably agree on two more points. First, if Rich Daley's regime is a machine, it does not run like machines of yesteryear. And second, clout remains important in Chicago. The *Chicago Tribune*'s blog about local politics, called Clout Street, explains its name like this: "Clout has a special meaning in Chicago, where it can be a noun, a verb or an adjective." Clout, the blog states, is an exercise of political influence that is "a uniquely Chicago style" (2007).

Shortly, I'll discuss why most U.S. city machines fell decades ago. First, let's explore why they rose.

WHY MACHINES RISE

Muckraking journalist Lincoln Steffens once asked a New York City boss, "Why must there be a boss, when we've got a Mayor and a council…?" The boss broke in, "That's why. It's because there's a mayor and a council and judges and a hundred other men to deal with" (Steffens, 1931:187).

Sociologist Robert Merton ([1958] 1968) offered a more theoretical approach to the reasons behind the machine's existence, one from the structural–functional perspective. Merton held that a persistent social structure must perform some positive functions inadequately fulfilled by other structures or else it would cease to exist. He argued that machines fulfill latent functions unmet by other institutions, including the following: humanized, personalized welfare for the poor; direct, centralized contact for big-business interests; jobs and social mobility for ethnic newcomers and others who cannot move up (socioeconomically) in business and industry; and protection for various illegal activities run by those excluded from legal opportunity structures. In brief, it serves the needs of the poor and certain interest groups, especially business.

Conflict-oriented theorists hold a different view. They agree that machines provided services to the poor—and to wealthy entrepreneurs—but they argue that these needs could have been met in other ways with more radical consequences. According to this perspective, the Tammany Hall machine in the nineteenth century was a conservative force, preying on the poor and helping to preserve the structure of poverty inherent in capitalist enterprise. That is, the machine diffused or co-opted the energies of the lower class—which, in European countries, was calling for revolutionary answers to poverty, not help with the rent. In this view, the Daley machine is comparable to a colonial empire, ruling white ethnic groups by a combination of divide-and-rule tactics and relegating most Irish Americans, as well as African Americans and Spanish-speaking people, to the position of a submerged majority.

These two interpretations do not stand in total contradiction. Rather, their emphases differ. So do their assumptions about the nature of politics in the United States. Both note the machine's latent functions but disagree on who really benefited from their rule.

WHY MACHINES FALL

The logical extension of the structural–functionalist argument on the rise of machines is this: Machines fall when they no longer serve needed functions or when other institutions evolve to fulfill the same functions. Thus, according to this analytic framework, machines have gradually withered away because of long-term macro-level changes affecting cities. The following reasons are usually advanced for the old machine's widespread demise in the twentieth century:

1. *The scope of government increased.* Fewer people depended on city machines for favors and rewards as government began supplying welfare services. Also, party machines couldn't offer as many goodies when various reforms took hold (e.g., the rise of a civil service, merit-based bureaucracy that cut into patronage jobs).

2. *Competing institutions (besides government) grew in strength.* Labor unions and single-issue groups gained influence and power at the expense of political parties and their machines.

3. *Business interests no longer found the machine useful.* As the scope of the federal government expanded in the twentieth century and as corporate business expanded its operations throughout the nation's cities, big business could deal with the centralized federal regulatory commissions (such as the Interstate Commerce Commission), many of which they helped to establish. At the city level, some local business leaders were in the forefront of government reform, realizing that good-government reformers would sponsor policies in their interests (e.g., efficient government) and that the bosses had become a liability to them.

To summarize: Old-style machines withered away because of macro-level changes in U.S. society that affected cities: the growth of big government, which supplied social services, and the expansion of big business, which wanted to deal with centralized control at the federal level. In brief, the machine's unique functions were gradually taken over by rival institutions. In most cities, old machines were replaced by newer, more streamlined models of government.

LOCAL GOVERNMENT REFORM

Long-term societal changes in U.S. life, especially the growth of corporate business and the expanded role of the federal government, were accompanied by vigorous municipal reform efforts that contributed to the fall of machines. It is unlikely that reformers could have smashed city machines on the strength of their ideas alone, but the combination of historical forces undermining the machine and articulate, organized reformers desiring its demise led to a reform agenda.

So-called goo-goos (good-government reformers) emerged in the latter part of the nineteenth century as a response to machine politics, immigration, industrialism, and rapid urbanization. The successes and failures of these reformers explain much of the variation in local government forms today. For example, before the reform movement, virtually all local governments had a mayor–council form. The widespread council–manager form in medium-sized and smaller communities today is a direct outgrowth of the goo-goos' efforts.

THE GOO-GOOS: A DISPARATE LOT

Leaders in the U.S. movement to reform municipal government, a movement dating roughly from the 1890s through the Progressive Era to 1917, had motives as mixed as their backgrounds. Some were like college-educated Jane Addams, a settlement-house worker distressed by urban poverty and social isolation in the city. Addams viewed reform as one way to get city government to meet the desperate needs of the people who came to her Hull House in Chicago. There were muckraking journalists too, like Lincoln Steffens, who exposed *The Shame of the Cities* (1904); they sought to control urban crime, graft, vice, and political corruption. There were professors of political science and

public administration who wanted to extend administrative norms of behavior (rationality and efficiency) to the political sector, particularly to the executive branch. And there were other academics, including sociologists at the University of Chicago, who wanted to recreate the conditions of a small-town community within the metropolis and to stem what they considered social "disorganization."

What groups provided the good-government movement with its principal strength and fundamental purpose—middle-class reformers, professionals, or business groups? This has been a subject of lively debate among scholars.

Since the thoughts of the reformers are preserved in their writings, it's possible to get a sense of what they believed they were doing. But many scholars advise going beyond the reformers' words and focusing instead on the *practice* of reform to get a better perspective.

Reformers may have described themselves as just plain folks interested in morality, rationality, and efficiency in city government; but one historian claims this was hardly the case. According to Samuel P. Hays (1964), most reformers were WASPs from upper-income business or professional backgrounds.

In Hays's view, the disparate lot of reformers had a rather self-serving purpose that united them, whether they were conscious of it or not: the centralization of decision making. Doing business at the ward level was simply not what the business and professional people wanted; their world was cosmopolitan, not based in their neighborhood community.

Furthermore, Hays contended, the reformers' manifest goal—government by trained professionals—meant that nonprofessionals would be shut out of city government. In effect, this meant that minorities, immigrants, and members of the lower class would be excluded from city politics. In other words, Hays contends, the latent function of the reform thrust for businesslike, efficient government was to consolidate power in the hands of upper middle- and upper-class WASP elites.

THRUSTS OF THE REFORM MOVEMENT

The municipal reform movement had several interconnected thrusts. First, it attempted to make machine government difficult or impossible. Second, it tried to make elected officials more accountable to voters. Third, it sought to make government less political and more businesslike. Fourth, it tried to stamp out industrial disorder and movements considered dangerous and "anti-American." Each thrust led to a set of specific measures.

To make machine politics more difficult, reformers supported **direct primaries** (in which voters, not the machine bosses, select candidates); nonpartisan elections; and citywide, at-large elections (rather than ward or district elections, which, in theory, increase the clout of ward bosses). To make local government officials more responsive to citizen demands, reformers pushed the **initiative**, **referendum**, and **recall**—measures aimed at giving citizens more direct say either in proposing and deciding on legislation or in removing officials thought to be insensitive or corrupt.

To "take politics out of government" and make it more "efficient" (i.e., more businesslike), reformers sponsored measures to change the form of local government and to professionalize government. To separate politics from administration, they pushed the council–manager form of government. To take the "spoils" out of office, they wanted civil service merit examinations for local government service. This would not only cut patronage possibilities but also provide job security for bureaucrats, who couldn't be dismissed when a new faction gained control of city hall. To increase the efficiency of city government, they supported professional education in public administration and city planning.

Finally, reformers founded a number of private institutions aimed at "Americanizing" the children of immigrants. These included settlement houses, the YMCA, and the Playground Association of America. Reformers also used the public schools to inculcate values of patriotism, obedience, and duty. It was in the 1880s, for instance, that saluting the flag was introduced into grammar schools. These reform efforts at citizenship training and patriotism grew out of mixed motives: humanitarianism and/or an urge to turn "them" into "us," thus preserving the dominant WASP culture in the face of immigrant, non-Protestant religious beliefs and southern and eastern European cultural traditions (see Chapter 10).

That many reformers acted out of ethnic prejudice and class interests is suggested in the comments of Andrew D. White, a Progressive reformer and the first president of Cornell University, in 1890:

> ...a city...should logically be managed as a piece of property by those who have created it...or a real substantial part in it [and not by] a crowd of illiterate peasants, freshly raked in from the Irish bogs, or Bohemian mines, or Italian robber nests....
>
> *(in Banfield and Wilson, 1963:153)*

What White and many other Progressive reformers sought to prevent was a city ruled by a "proletariat mob" (in Banfield, 1961:213). They also wanted to prevent the rise of anti-American "isms," particularly socialism, anarchism, and syndicalism.

It is an almost forgotten fact that one "ism"—municipal socialism—was a serious competitor to the reform movement. Between 1900 and the start of World War II, Milwaukee, Berkeley, and other cities elected socialists to the city council or the mayoralty. The Industrial Workers of the World (the Wobblies [Chapter 1]) also presented radical alternatives to good-government reform measures.

To summarize: Beginning at the end of the nineteenth century and gathering momentum in the early twentieth century, a disparate lot of reformers—ranging from settlement-house workers and journalists to professors of public administration and businesspeople—called for reforms in city politics. Their major goals were (1) to make machine politics difficult or impossible, (2) to make elected officials more accountable to voters, and (3) to make government more businesslike and less political. This group of reformers, mainly members of the new middle and upper classes (professionals and expansionists from business, labor, and agriculture) wanted to adapt the new urban-industrial society to meet their own needs. They chose government reform to do it. In place of the personalized, ward-level, somewhat representative government under the machine, they urged efficiency-minded, professional, centralized city government. One latent function of their agenda was to wrest control of the nation's cities from those they considered unprofessional and uncouth: lower-class, white ethnics.

HOW SUCCESSFUL WERE THE REFORMERS?

Many structural changes desired by the good-government reformers were instituted in U.S. cities, particularly medium-sized and smaller cities. For instance, the council–manager form of government is a direct outcome of the goo-goos' efforts. But reformers never completely gained control over city governments, and the larger, more heterogeneous cities were especially difficult for reformers to reshape.

At this point, we should ask, What difference did reform make in the actual day-to-day operations and policies of city governments? Scholars don't agree. Some say that, in general, the more a city government was reformed, the less responsive it became to the needs of different racial and income group constituencies in the city. And some argue that the machine controlled and manipulated the lower-class vote, but the reformers reduced and trivialized it. Others find that, in the long run, government structure matters very little when it comes to city taxing and spending policies.

What does most research show? Most assessments conclude that good-government reform led to *lower* voter turnouts, *less* diversity in the class and ethnic composition of city government, and *less* responsive and representative government.

Only the most naive goo-goos thought that municipal reform would end patterns of influence, and indeed it has not. Even in completely reformed governments, trained professionals do not develop value-neutral policies without regard to their political consequences.

A note about reformed governments and their critics: A reevaluation of Progressive Era reforms came from two would-be reformers who have since faded from view: David Osborne and Ted Gaebler, authors of *Reinventing Government* (1992). They wrote that municipal reforms (e.g., civil service merit systems, criteria for awarding government contracts) did limit graft and corruption. But, they said, these reforms resulted in government bureaucracies that undermined effective government: "In making it difficult to steal the public's money, we made it virtually impossible to manage the public's money." The result: slow, inefficient, and impersonal government (14).

Osborne and Gaebler's alternative? Entrepreneurial government at all levels of government—"from school-house to statehouse, city hall to the Pentagon." This new type of government, they argued, would encourage competition rather than monopoly; emphasize mission, not rules; decentralize authority; meet customers' needs; and "steer more than row." (We can guess, correctly, that libertarians were big supporters of "entrepreneurial government.")

Max Weber (Chapter 11) thought that bureaucracy was deadly but efficient. Osborne and Gaebler, by contrast, saw it as deadly and *in*efficient. They claimed that bureaucratic governments just don't fit a fast-paced, postindustrial world where "customers" demand high quality and choice in a marketplace of niches, not mass markets.

Critics, however, feared (and still fear) that government *by* entrepreneurs could easily become government *for* entrepreneurs. (At the federal level, critics in the 2000s raised this concern when the government bailed out some financial institutions, particularly those that gave big cash bonuses to some employees, such as AIG.) Without rules and professionalization, how can "honest graft," as Plunkitt called it, and the plunder of public funds be controlled?

BOSSES AND MACHINES: AN UPDATE

With notable exceptions like Chicago, the old machines were broken by a combination of the goo-goos' reform efforts and macro-societal factors such as the rise of rival institutions. But fragments of the machines remain. In many cities, a hundred little amenities of life can depend on the clout of ward-level bosses: how many times each week garbage is collected, who gets a new construction job, or how brightly the streetlights shine.

However, political patronage suffered a sharp blow in 1990: The Supreme Court ruled 5 to 4 that the use of partisan political considerations as the basis for hiring, promoting, or transferring most public employees was unconstitutional. This ruling prevents a mayor from reserving camp counselor jobs in the park system or nonpolicy jobs in the sanitation department, for example, for his or her supporters.

In short, good-government reform didn't completely do away with time-honored patronage jobs or other benefits that politicians can dispense to supporters. Despite civil service merit exams, nonpartisan elections, and other reforms, who you know—or who you can get to—still counts in city politics.

One modern development is noteworthy: the newer machine. The newer machine derives its power base from nonelected office—the city's bureaucratic administration. It doesn't depend on loyal ward bosses or city councillors who deliver votes or give out turkeys at Christmas.

ROBERT MOSES, NEWER-STYLE BOSS

The newer machine and how it works are best exemplified by one man and the empire he built: Robert Moses's New York City. A lifelong bureaucrat and appointed official, Moses never served as mayor of the nation's largest city. Yet it was Moses—not the mayors, city planners, professorial consultants, or Democratic Party heads—who shaped modern New York City's urban environment. From the 1930s to the late 1960s, Moses molded a city and its sprawling suburbs. And his influence didn't stop there: In the twentieth century, "the influence of Robert Moses on the cities of [the United States] was greater than that of any other person" (Mumford in Caro, 1975:12).

How Moses, hardly a household name, built his empire and used his power to shape a city in his own vision is a tale well told by Robert A. Caro in *The Power Broker: Robert Moses and the Fall of New York* (1975). The following quick study of Moses is based on Caro's Pulitzer Prize–winning book.

Robert Moses (1888–1981) started his long career in 1909, during the era of municipal reform. A passionate idealist with imagination, iron will, determination, arrogance, and dreams, he worked for the good-government organization in New York City as a specialist in civil service reorganization. He argued for the idea that jobs and promotions should be awarded on the basis of merit, not patronage. He spent the years 1914–1918 in the administration of New York City's reforming mayor: 1 year devising a public personnel system and another 3 years fighting to get it adopted. He battled with the city's appropriations unit, the Board of Estimate, which was "dominated by one of the most corrupt political machines the United States had ever known" (Caro, 1975:4), to replace patronage with civil service.

By 1918, Moses had made such a nuisance of himself that Tammany Hall decided to crush him—and it did. Caro reports that at the age of 30, with his civil service personnel system papers being used as scrap paper, "Robert Moses, Phi Beta Kappa at Yale, honors man at Oxford, lover of the Good, the True and the Beautiful, was out of work and, with a wife and two small daughters to support, was standing on a line in the Cleveland, Ohio, City Hall, applying for a minor municipal job" (1975:5).

According to Caro, Robert Moses spent the rest of his life using that same iron will, determination, and imagination in another way: to amass power. He wanted power to transform his ideas into reality. And he was successful.

Moses sat atop an empire built on the bureaucracies of New York City parks, urban renewal, and highway programs. The immensity of his power and his empire is suggested by a few statistics: seven bridges linking the island boroughs of New York were built from 1931 to the early 1960s, and Robert Moses built every one of them. Between 1945 and 1958, not one of over 1,000 public housing sites was selected without Moses's OK. Moses built every superhighway in New York City except one. He built Shea Stadium and decided what factories, stores, and tenements would be razed for urban renewal. He was the dominant force behind two huge private housing developments in Manhattan and the Bronx.

More important, for over 30 years, Moses established the priorities of what got built in the New York metropolitan region. This had a vast impact on "not only the physical but also the social fabric of the cities, on the quality of life their inhabitants led" (Caro, 1975:7–8).

How did Robert Moses become the United States's greatest builder—of roads, parks, hospitals, schools, urban renewal sites, and even sewers (whose design and site he approved)? He used an institution still in its infancy when he came to it in the 1930s: the public authority. Public authorities supposedly are entities outside governmental bureaucracies. Their members are appointed for long terms, which, in theory, insulates them from politics. They were institutions thought to be not only outside but *above* politics. But under Moses, public authorities—the Triborough

Fig. 14.5 ROBERT MOSES, POWER BROKER. Operating behind the scenes, Moses shaped most of the development of highways, bridges, parks, beaches, and related infrastructure for the New York City area, as well as massive redevelopment projects and housing construction. (Arnold Newman, courtesy of Robert Moses)

Bridge Authority, New York's Housing Authority, and so on—were political machines "oiled by the lubricant of political machines: money. Their wealth enabled Moses…to exert a power that few political bosses in the more conventional mold ever attain" (Caro, 1975:17).

To conclude: Robert Moses was a political boss, newer style. Using the public authorities as his power base, he became "the locus of corruption in New York City" (although personally, he was honest in financial matters). Giving out contracts and commissions (for public relations, insurance, building contracts, etc.), Moses replaced graft with legal benefits.

THE LOCAL-NATIONAL CONNECTION

Act locally. Fund nationally. The Internet has been playing a major role in candidates' ability to fund-raise and organize. Candidates of all political stripes have used the Internet to raise money from donors, sometimes raising more from out-of-state donors than from in-district contributors. Ironically, while advocating county-level government, some ultraright local leaders use the Internet to organize and fund-raise across state lines.

Here are two illustrations of the impact of national groups on local politics: (1) the Christian Coalition and (2) EMILY's List. Both are media-savvy and, unlike city political machines, very ideologically committed.

(1) The conservative Christian Coalition was created in 1989 from mailing lists used by the 1988 presidential candidate and televangelist Pat Robertson. By 1993, it claimed 350,000 members with 750 local chapters and an annual budget of $8–10 million (Sullivan, 1993:34). (By the 2000s, many think it is a shadow of its former self.)

The coalition is (or was) cemented by a desire to halt what supporters perceive to be the decline of Christian "traditional" and "profamily" values. According to the late Jerry Falwell, long associated with Christian conservative causes, "We [the Christian Coalition] don't tell [voters] to vote Republican or Democrat....We instruct them to vote Christian. Christian is simple. That's a buzzword for pro-life, profamily, strong national defense" (in Boston, 2004).

By 2007, there was trouble inside the Christian Coalition. Pat Robertson had long since stepped down as president; several state organizations had opted out of the coalition, and the first executive head, Ralph Reed, had been implicated in the Jack Abramoff payoff scandal. In addition, membership had probably dropped considerably. The Christian Coalition claimed to represent "a growing group of over 2 million people of faith all across America" (Christian Coalition of America, n.d.), but some say that its membership numbers no more than 300,000. Further, some (e.g., Gilgoff, 2007) argue that the Christian Coalition's influence has waned as other groups, particularly James Dobson's Focus on the Family, have taken over political influence from it.

When the Christian Coalition began, it used grassroots tactics—combined with national fund-raising—to organize "an army who cares." Its motto: "Think like Jesus. Lead like Moses. Fight like David. Run like Lincoln" ("Perspectives," 1993:23). At political-activism sessions they trained people to be effective—to get elected to school boards, city councils, state legislatures, and key positions in political parties. Robertson's goal when he organized the coalition? In his own words, to be "the most powerful political organization in America" by the year 2000 (in Sullivan, 1993:34).

Robertson's goal may or may not have been reached. But in 2004, then Christian Coalition president Roberta Combs said the group (which she called "the *new* Christian Coalition") would be a permanent fixture on the political scene (in Boston, 2004).

Time will tell if Coombs was right. Meantime, the Christian Coalition has many fewer members than just a few years ago. Yet, it does remain a political force with a national legislative agenda. In 2007, for example, their agenda for the 110th Congress, First Session, included confirming as many conservative judges as possible and trying to get a vote on a federal marriage amendment to the Constitution (Christian Coalition, 2007).

The language of the coalition often includes fighting words. For instance, the group's field director told supporters at a training session in 2004 that "the enemy" (i.e., the "extreme Left") should be destroyed:

> You're going to run over them. Get around them, run over the top of them, destroy them—whatever you need to do so that God's word is the word that is being practiced in Congress, town halls and state legislatures. That's your job.
>
> *(in Theocracywatch, November 2006).*

Has the Christian Coalition been successful? Many elected officials think so. For one, U.S. Senator (and short-time presidential candidate in 2007) Sam Brownback (R-Kan.) credited the Christian Coalition's voter guides, passed out in Kansas churches (and, when some churches balked at distributing the guides, in Wal-Marts and gas stations), for his electoral success to the House of Representatives and to the Senate.

As noted, whether the coalition's influence will continue is up in the air. By 2007, the coalition seemed in disarray. It had fewer members. Ralph Reed, a former bigwig, had been discredited; and there was a lack of unanimity (e.g., former coalition head Robertson and others backed different Republicans as presidential candidates.)

(2) Also ideologically based, but in direct ideological opposition to the Christian Coalition, is a group dedicated to helping Democratic, pro-choice women win political office: EMILY's List (an acronym for *Early Money Is Like Yeast; it makes the dough rise*). Ellen Malcolm founded this organization in 1985. According to its Web site,

> EMILY's List, is dedicated to building a progressive America by electing pro-choice Democratic women to federal, state, and local office. We are a network of more than 100,000 Americans—from all across the country—committed to recruiting and funding viable women candidates; helping them build and run effective campaign organizations; training the next generation of activists; and mobilizing women voters to help elect progressive candidates across the nation.
>
> *(EMILY's List, n.d.)*

In 1992, the group had 24,000 members and gave $200,000 from its campaign chest to 171 state and local candidates. By 2006, it claimed 100,000 members (Emily's List, 2006).

According to founder Malcolm, EMILY's List pays close attention to local races. Why? Because, Malcolm says, "this is exactly what the Christian Coalition is doing" (in Friedman, 1993:65).

Has EMILY's list been effective? Their leaders think so. They take credit for helping "to change the face of power in America." They claim to have helped elect 67 members of Congress, 13 senators, and eight governors, all Democrats and all pro-choice. In addition, they claim to be the largest financial resource for "minority" women running for federal office.

Do Robertson's successors and Malcolm represent a new kind of boss, one suited to the electronic superhighway? Have other organizations with a big Web presence, such as the liberal-identified MoveOn.org, changed the political game? All seem to wield influence over armies of workers. But if they do run machines, Boss Tweed and Boss Richard J. Daley would hardly recognize their style and ideological commitment.

ANOTHER LOOK

The U.S. made a unique contribution to urban politics: the city machine. In general, theorists agree that the machine was a product of its times, rising in an era of rapid industrialization and urbanization and falling in an era of national expansion.

But theorists disagree on the costs and benefits of the city machine, which was based on networks of influence and power rather than legitimate authority. Disagreements center on who benefited most, and the answers depend on the scholar's theoretical orientation.

Social scientists who stress the idea of harmony in the social system (structural–functionalists) say that the city machine served the needs of various social groups. When the machine stopped serving those needs, they argue, the machines sputtered.

Conflict theorists have a different interpretation. They say that the old machines served the interests of the rising class of businesspeople more than it served the poor, and it ran out of steam when the business interests found new and better ways to serve their needs. Further, conflict-oriented scholars argue that the city machines served an important latent function: By providing some benefits to a few ethnics, they diverted the lower classes from seeking more radical alternatives to their plight.

The U.S. good-government reform movement is also variously interpreted. Some scholars see it as a progressive step toward efficiency and rationality in local government. Others view it as a power grab by professionals and entrepreneurs to control the cities, preventing the "unwashed proletarian mob" from taking power.

On one point scholars agree, whatever their theoretical orientation, discipline, or political ideology: No type of structural reform has succeeded in doing away with informal networks of influence. Neoconservatives like Nathan Glazer and the late Daniel Patrick Moynihan pointed to whole bureaucracies in New York City's reform government that exist mainly to serve ethnic interests. In an update to *Beyond the Melting Pot* (1979:ix), they wrote that "ethnicity and race dominate the city, more than ever seemed possible in 1963." Liberal scholars often point to the widening net of influence, as Chapter 15 details. Radicals tend to focus on behind-the-scenes dealings by elites that influence city policymaking and on arrangements in capitalist cities that serve the interests of land developers and corporate business more than those of poor ethnic groups. Once again, while they agree that informal networks count in city politics, they disagree on *how* these networks operate and *who* they benefit most. That is the subject to which we now turn.

KEY TERMS

Direct primary Selection of candidates to run in an election by direct vote of the electorate rather than selection by a party committee or another backroom method.

Initiative An electoral device by which interested citizens can propose legislation through petitions signed by a specified number of registered voters (usually 5–15 percent). The initiative process bypasses local elected officials. If passed, an initiative becomes law without being considered by the local governing body.

Machine A political organization to mobilize votes and distribute the benefits of office to its members.

Precinct The basic unit of city-level, political party organization in the United States. Cities and counties are divided into precinct polling districts, each containing from 200 to 1,000 voters.

Recall A provision permitting removal of elected officials before the expiration of their terms if the electorate so votes in a special recall election. It was introduced by reformers as a device to increase the accountability of local elected officials.

Referendum An electoral device that permits citizens to decide directly upon proposed legislation. A proposed bill is placed on the ballot and voted on directly by the electorate. Their decision is binding on the local governing body of the jurisdiction in which the referendum took place.

Ward The political division of a city for the purpose of electing members to the city council (or board of aldermen). In cities where there are district elections, each ward elects one representative to the local governing body.

PROJECTS

1. **Biography of a boss**. What kind of people were the bosses—for example, were they professional politicians, young, WASPs, lower middle-class by birth? Were there any women among them? Select a famous (or infamous) U.S. city boss and do a biographical sketch. What social and economic context set the stage for the boss's reign? What was his or her ethnic identity and power base? Can you determine the sources of his or her money and power? With what concrete activities is the boss associated? What finally happened to her or him? Relate the facts of the boss's life to some of the theoretical material in this chapter on how machines worked and the functions they served.

2. **Machines**. The shadow of old machines lives on in more subtle forms today. One area in which machinelike structures are likely to exist is the delivery of social services to low-income groups. Is this the case in a community near you? Examine a social service program, and see if you can identify a strong, boss-like figure (or figures) in the program who dominates decision making (e.g., who is hired and where grant money goes). Is there an ethnic basis of power in the system? What latent and manifest functions does the program(s) serve?

3. **Reformers**. Examine local political reform movements in one U.S. city. Examine political histories to determine what group(s) was active in charter revision or other political reform activities. What groups are currently active in local government reform? Determine the social bases of the groups—past and present—and their agendas. What do they say about their own motives? Are there alternative explanations for their political behavior?

4. **City reform outside the United States.** What have cities outside the United States done to reform their local governments? When? And why? Compare and contrast at least two cities, on two continents, trying to determine who led the reform movements and under what conditions. Were the movements successful? If not, why?

SUGGESTIONS FOR FURTHER LEARNING

The scholarly literature about urban politics has changed greatly in the past several decades, so much so that many texts are being totally rewritten rather than revised. Yet few of the new texts mention, let alone discuss at length, global influences on local decisions (e.g., location decisions by multinational corporations, international trade agreements).

A vast literature on comparative local governments exists, but much of it is dated. Some more recent studies include Alistair Cole, *Local Governance in England and France*, Routledge Studies in Governance and Public Policy (New York: Routledge, 2001), which lists policy reforms in the two countries since the early 1980s.

Newer studies often focus on a particular aspect of local governments. Helmet Druke's study of "e-government," *Local Electronic Government: A Comparative Study* (New York: Routledge, 2005), typifies the genre. This scholarly work, not for beginners, includes empirical research on e-government in the United States, the United Kingdom, Finland, France, Germany, the Netherlands, and Japan.

For a historical look at U.S. urban bosses and the way they operated, see Harold Zinc's *City Bosses in the United States* (Durham, N.C.: Duke University Press, 1930). It remains a classic.

A standard negative interpretation of Boss Tweed and the Tweed Ring can be found in Seymour Mandelbaum, *Boss Tweed's New York* (New York: Wiley, 1965). In contrast, Leo Hershkowitz, in *Tweed's New York* (Garden City, N.Y.: Doubleday, Anchor, 1978), depicts Tweed as a victim of the older New York City elite, which disliked him as much for his involvement with Catholic (largely Irish) voters and politicians as for his graft.

E. L. Doctorow's *The Waterworks* (New York: Random House, 1994) takes place in New York City just as the Tweed Ring starts to come apart in 1871. McIlvaine, Doctorow's journalist narrator in the novel, says this about the ring: "They were nothing if not absurd—ridiculous, simple-minded, stupid, self-aggrandizing. And murderous. All the qualities of men who prevail in our Republic." The amoral spirit of New York City pervades the novel. According to historian Simon Schama, Doctorow's "New York of then and now and ever is a place imprisoned in thuggish corruption, where the police conspire with, rather than against, crime; a lair of vampire capitalism, a warren of alleys crawling with the urchin 'street rats' who subsist on the refuse of the city's wants and needs, darting beneath the wheels of indifferent carriages, vending the news, loitering at the edge of scummy saloons" ("New York, Gaslight Necropolis," *New York Times Book Review*, June 19, 1994, p. 31).

Machinelike organizations have suffered in recent decades. For example, in San Francisco's Chinatown, the once dominant Chinese Six Companies (Chinese Consolidated Benevolent Association) had great influence from 1882 to the 1970s. Its influence waned by the 1980s, in part due to the rise of governmental social service agencies.

Mayor Richard J. Daley and his machine are best described in Milton Rakove, *Don't Make No Waves . . . Don't Back No Losers* (Bloomington: Indiana University Press, 1975). Rakove, a political scientist who spent years as a participant-observer of the Chicago machine, shows how the machine was organized, what values its members held, and what it did.

Robert Moses remains a controversial figure long after his death in 1981. San Francisco architecture critic Allan Temko called him a "brilliant and ruthless czar of public works, who for 40 years was virtually a law unto himself." Some do not share such rosy evaluations. "Unfortunately, [Robert Moses] will have a double epitaph: 'He was the man who built New York' and 'He was the man who strangled Red Hook and killed substantial parts of the Bronx.'" That was the assessment of the president of the Triborough Bridge and Tunnel Authority, Robert Moses's last power base, on the occasion of Moses's birth centenary in 1988. Robert A. Caro's *The Power Broker: Robert Moses and the Fall of New York* (New York: Vintage, 1975) is a massive dissection of how Robert Moses masterminded much of the physical development in New York City—bridges, beaches, parks, housing projects, and such colossal developments as the United Nations building and Rockefeller Center.

In *All that Is Solid Melts into Air: The Experience of Modernity* (New York: Simon and Schuster, 1981), Marshall Berman puts Robert Moses's construction of the Cross-Bronx Expressway into a macro context: "So often the price of ongoing and expanding modernity is the destruction not merely of 'traditional' and 'pre-modern' institutions and environments but—and here is the real tragedy—of everything most vital and beautiful in the modern world itself. Here in the Bronx, thanks to Robert Moses, the modernity of the urban boulevard was being condemned as obsolete and blown to pieces, by the modernity of the interstate highway" (295).

One of Frank Capra's social-message films, the classic *Mr. Smith Goes to Washington* (1939), depicts a back-room political boss and businessman at the federal level, Jim Taylor (head of the Taylor machine in the U.S. Senate), being countered, somewhat unsuccessfully, by a righteous and moral opponent. Movie critic Robert Sklar comments in *Movie-Made America* (New York: Random House, 1975) that "once Capra's heroes begin their open struggles with wealth and power, they find themselves unable to triumph by asserting their strength and involving their alliances. [The political bosses] are simply too wealthy and powerful" (211).

For an investigative reporter's take on the rise of the U.S. Christian Right, see *The Jesus Machine* (New York: St. Martin's Press, 2007) by Dan Gilgoff. Gilgoff argues that in 2007 James Dobson, head of Focus on the Family and the Family Research Council, was the most powerful evangelical leader in the United States. Gilgoff traces the rise of evangelical influence in politics from the Moral Majority and Christian Coalition in the 1970s and 1980s to Focus on the Family in the 1990s and 2000s.

REFERENCES

Addams, Jane. [1898] 1972. "Why the ward boss rules." Pp. 10–15 in Bruce M. Stave, ed., *Urban Bosses, Machines, and Progressive Reformers.* Lexington, Mass: Heath.

Associated Press. 2007. "Chicago election features allegations, ex-cons: Four politicians who served time for corruption want their jobs back." (February 14): http://www.msnbc.msn.com/id/16650706/

Banfield, Edward C. 1961. *Urban Government.* New York: Free Press.

Banfield, Edward C., and James Q. Wilson. 1963. *City Politics.* New York: Vintage.

Boston, Rob. 2004. "Inside the Christian Coalition: Religious Right group finds Americans United obstacles blocking its 'road to victory'."*Americans United for Separation of Church and State* (November): http://www.au.org/site/News2?page=NewsArticle&id=7007&abbr=cs_

Bryce, James. 1889. *The American Commonwealth.* New York: Macmillan.

Caro, Robert A. 1975. *The Power Broker: Robert Moses and the Fall of New York.* New York: Vintage.

Christian Coalition of America. 2007. "Christian Coalition of America." (February 28): http://www.cc.org/issues.cfm);—n.d. (http://www.cc.org/about.cfm

Clout Street. 2007. *The Chicago Tribune* blog (February 27): http://newsblogs.chicagotribune.com/clout_st/

"Conventional Wisdom." 1990. *Newsweek* (April 2):4.

EMILY's List. n.d. "About Emily's List:" http://www.emilyslist.org/about/

———. 2006. http://www.emilyslist.org/newsroom/releases/2006elections.pdf

Friedman, Jon. 1993. "The founding mother." *New York Times Magazine* (May 2):50+.

Gilgoff, Dan. 2007. *The Jesus Machine: How James Dobson, Focus on the Family, and Evangelical America Are Winning the Culture War.* New York: St. Martin's Press.

Glass, Ira. 2007. *This American Life.* (November 11). KALW-radio.

Glazer, Nathan, and Daniel Patrick Moynihan. 1979. *Beyond the Melting Pot: The Negroes, Puerto Ricans, Jews, Italians, and Irish of New York City,* 2nd ed. Cambridge, Mass.: MIT Press.

Gosnell, Harold F. [1937] 1968. *Machine Politics: Chicago Model.* Chicago: University of Chicago Press.

Hays, Samuel P. 1964. "The politics of reform in municipal government in the Progressive era." *Pacific Northwest Quarterly* 55:157–169.

Longworth, R. C. 1981. "Fewer firms, fewer jobs, less revenue." *Chicago Tribune* (May 11):1.

Mahtesian, Charles. 1994. "No room for patronage in new Chicago." *San Francisco Sunday Examiner and Chronicle* (May 8):A3.

Malcolm, Andrew H. 1986. "Study sees Chicago as a divided city," *New York Times* [National edition] (October) A16.

———. 1986. "Daley, 10 years gone, remains 'the mayor'." *New York Times* (national edition) (December 21):A20.

Merton, Robert. [1958] 1968. "Manifest and latent functions." Pp. 731–738 in *Social Theory and Social Structure.* New York: Free Press.

NBC5.com. 2007. "City Council Approves $500 million Olympic financial guarantee." (March 12): http://www.nbc5.com/news/11235030/detail.html?treets=chi&tid=2658514308813&tml=chi_7am&tmi=chi_7am_1_07200303132007&ts=H

O'Connor, Edwin. 1956. *The Last Hurrah.* Boston: Little, Brown.

O'Connor, Len. 1975. *Clout.* New York: Avon.

Osborne, David, and Ted Gaebler. 1992. *Reinventing Government: How the Entrepreneurial Spirit Is Transforming the Public Sector.* Reading, Mass.: Addison-Wesley.

"Perspectives." 1993. *Newsweek* (May 17):23.

Puzo, Mario. [1969] 1973. *The Godfather.* New York: Fawcett World.

Rakove, Milton. 1975. *Don't Make No Waves...Don't Back No Losers.* Bloomington: Indiana University Press.

Riordan, William L. [1906] 1963. *Plunkitt of Tammany Hall.* New York: Dutton.

Royko, Mike. 1971. *Boss.* New York: Signet.

Sharlet, Jeff, [2008] 2009. *The Family: The Secret Fund amentalis at the Heart of American Power.* New York: Harper Perennial.

Stead, W. T. 1894. *If Christ Came to Chicago: A Plea for the Union of All Who Love in the Service of All Who Suffer.* Chicago: Laird & Lee.

Steffens, Lincoln. [1903] 1904. *The Shame of the Cities.* New York: P. Smith.

———. 1931. *The Autobiography of Lincoln Steffens.* New York: Harcourt, Brace.

Sullivan, Robert. 1993. "An army of the faithful." *New York Times Magazine* (April 25):32+.

Theocracy Watch. 2006 (November): http://www.theocracywatch.org/index_before_nov_06.htm

UBS, 2008. "London is the most expensive city in the world while Zurich is home to highest wage earners." (June): http://www.citymayors.com/economics/usb-purchasing-power.html

Viviano, Frank. 1993. "How Mafia rules its empire." *San Francisco Chronicle* (May 20):A1+.

———. 1995. "The new Mafia order." *Mother Jones* (May/June): http://www.motherjones.com/news/feature/1995/05/viviano.html

Will, George F. 1984. "A devil of a town." *Newsweek* (February 13):92.

Bernhard Knierim

If Boss Tweed or Boss Daley were alive today, he would find a much expanded political arena. Typically, old-style machines were based on coalitions of white ethnic immigrants, business interests, and boodlers. Today, the range of political players is broader.

On the local scene are such additional players as municipal employee unions, lesbians, transgender activists, feminists, race- and ethnicity-based organizations, corporations, and a host of single-issue lobbyists (tax revolters, environmentalists, pro-lifers, nude-beach proponents, historic preservationists, and so forth). All represent legal, private, or nonprofit organizations, acting informally and extralegally—that is, without specific mention in the city charter.

And let us not forget influential private players. That they play a key role in policymaking (at all levels of government) is inferred by the comment of Jim

Rogers, the chief executive of Duke Energy, an energy supplier to three continents, noting why utility companies should help draft laws on emissions control: "If you're not at the table, you're probably on the menu" ("On the Record," 2008).

In addition, another set of players makes its will known without a vote on the city council: people and groups engaged in illegal activities. These include street gangs, organized crime, terrorists or freedom fighters (depending on where you stand), and international drug cartels. Many have muscle. All have their own agendas.

Journalist–historian Misha Glenny claims that some of these groups, which he calls "McMafia" (2008a), operate worldwide and control about 20 percent of the world's gross national product. According to Glenny, McMafia is the darker side of the global economy, with activities ranging from caviar smuggling in Kazakhstan and Nigerian Internet scams to the marijuana trade in British Columbia and trafficking women in many cities globally. (We might add that Latin American drug cartels operate in many U.S. cities, not only in border cities.)

Nationalism and religious hatred do not prevent warring parties or enemies (e.g., Serbs and Albanians, Israelis and Russians) from cooperating in criminal endeavors (Glenny, 2008b). Why? In a phrase, huge profits.

Criminal gangs can also terrify (or worse) others with weapons, such as knives and guns. For one, the MS13 transnational gang, which started in Los Angeles and spread to Central America (often via deportees), is known for such violence.

Throughout the world, few (if any) places seem to be exempt from corruption. But some nations, cities, and neighborhoods operate in a culture of corruption. For example, Haiti under the Duvaliers was known as one of the world's great "kleptocracies." Under President Robert Mugabe, Zimbabwe gained a similar reputation. In 2007, China's chief of food safety was executed for taking massive bribes which permitted tainted food to be exported (and the consequent deaths of both humans and animals on several continents). To get something done in Lagos, Nigeria, presumes an understanding of the widespread system of payoffs and "dash" (tips or bribes).

Corruption and bribery scandals have long been common in the United States at all levels. At the local level, residents and small business owners in some neighborhoods get protection from gang members or racketeers, not the police (although in some cities police routinely take their cut of protection or other rackets). Kickbacks from government contracts, although illegal, remain standard operating procedure in countless city halls and statehouses. At the national level, one postmillennium scandal had unusually high-level repercussions: Payoffs by Republican lobbyist Jack Abramoff culminated in the resignation of some federal officials and Abramoff's imprisonment for various crimes, including conspiracy to bribe lawmakers.

How do people figure out whom to trust in this jam-packed scene of extralegal and illegal groups, not to mention civil servants and elected officials? How do they find one another, let alone work together, for mutual benefit? How can ordinary citizens participate in public decision making? What impact are these varied new players having on community power relations? And how can any group get what it wants without going bananas? We now turn to these questions.

COALITION POLITICS

Past or present, people representing varied interest groups in the city join together in alliances, trying to secure benefits that local government can dispense. What contractor will get the bid for a new building? Which neighborhood will get the building? What kinds of services will be dispensed there? Which people will get the jobs created by the new building? Such specific concerns are often the objects of intense political struggle fought out in the arena of coalition politics. In this arena, several rules of the game are commonly understood: "you help me and I'll help you" and "politics makes strange bedfellows."

In Tweed's New York City, political battles were fought over which neighborhoods got public baths, what jobs went to the Irish or other ethnic groups, and who got the lucrative contract to plaster the new courthouse. Graft and ethnic politics played a major role in determining who got what from the city treasury.

Today, ethnic politics remains a factor and graft has not been eliminated—even in the most reformed governments. But now groups and individuals also seek a bigger share of the legal benefits available from municipal government. And single-issue groups seek government's help in furthering their aims, whether they be banning trans fats in local restaurants or setting up a women's health center.

From Tweed's day to the present, the players and issues may have changed, but the game remains the same: coalition building. Whether old machine, reform government, or issue-oriented politics in a reform context, groups compete for scarce resources by organizing coalitions. These coalitions are informal and extralegal; that is, they have no formal standing in the city's legal structure.

U.S. CASE STUDY: THE FIGHT OVER YERBA BUENA

One battle in San Francisco over who got what—and what share—of public resources illustrates the nature of coalition politics. This battle is meticulously described in *Yerba Buena: Land Grab and Community Resistance in San Francisco* (1973) by city planner Chester Hartman (and updated by others). Hartman's book is a prime source of the following discussion. Although written over a generation ago, it details the ever-current and complex nature of coalition building and the stakes involved in the bitter contest over land use.

Two other works are key to understanding the politics of Yerba Buena from the beginning: (1) Rich DeLeon's study *Left Coast City: Progressive Politics in San Francisco 1975–1991* (1992) and G. William Domhoff 2005's blog updating the Yerba Buena story. Political scientist DeLeon (who is working on a sequel to his early 1990s study) draws a contrast between the city's progrowth coalition of real estate developers and labor unions that first pushed Yerba Buena forward and the city's more recent (and atypical) slow-growth coalition of "three Lefts"—liberalism, environmentalism, and populism—that came together in the mid-1980s to limit physical development of the city.

Here, let's first focus on the progrowth coalition that put together the Yerba Buena project. Then, we'll take a brief look at what's happened since then.

Background

Yerba Buena is an 80-acre parcel of land adjacent to San Francisco's central business district (CBD). (In Burgess's model, it is—or was—part of the zone-in-transition.) It was the focus of an intense political struggle in the late 1960s and 1970s, for it was the proposed site of a comprehensive redevelopment program.

Once, Yerba Buena thrived. After the San Francisco earthquake in 1906, the Southern Pacific Railroad located its main terminal there, bringing with it a cluster of luxury hotels, warehouses, and light manufacturing plants.

But by the mid-1960s, Yerba Buena was in decline. As Chapters 5 and 16 describe in detail, macrosocietal trends changed the face of the city. Manufacturing activity declined, white-collar work increased, new technologies made the railroad obsolete for many purposes, and the composition of the city's population was changing.

These economic and demographic forces took their toll on Yerba Buena. By the 1960s, most of its warehouses had been abandoned for new ones near port, airport, or suburban locations. Manufacturing had declined. Few goods and people came into the city by train. The residential population of the area consisted of elderly, single, lower-class men and a mixture of ethnic families. Most residents were poor, without power or prestige. They lived in the old luxury hotels, which had long since become residential hotels, offering cheap accommodations in very faded elegance. Many were clients of welfare and social service agencies.

Change for the area seemed inevitable. But what kind? In whose interests?

One answer was aggressively pursued by the local public agency responsible for urban renewal and redevelopment, the San Francisco Redevelopment Agency (SFRA), and a coalition of interest groups it helped to put together. This constellation of interests proposed a convention center complex—the Yerba Buena Center. Their plan included a convention center, tourist hotels, a sports arena, office buildings, and a parking garage. It was to be a joint venture of private and public resources. The SFRA would clear the land, the city and private developers would build the center, and city bonds would underwrite some publicly-owned parts of the center.

The Pro-Yerba Buena Center Coalition

Private business groups formed the backbone of the coalition put together by the SFRA. Why did they

Fig. 15.2 REDEVELOPMENT: FOR WHAT? FOR WHOM? These were concerns underlying the struggle between competing coalitions for or against San Francisco's Yerba Buena Center when it was proposed. (Michael Schwartz)

support it? Traditional political stakes were involved: economic gain, jobs, and a variety of other benefits.

First, private economic gain. Several long-established local business groups viewed the proposed Yerba Buena Center as a boon. The San Francisco Convention and Visitors' Bureau was in the forefront of the pro–Yerba Buena forces. Composed of tourist-oriented businesses, the bureau wanted a convention complex for obvious reasons. Visiting conventioneers would eat in their restaurants, patronize their clubs and bars, and buy "I Got My Crabs at Fisherman's Wharf" T-shirts in their stores. Likewise, the local Hotel Owners' Association envisioned conventioneers packing their hotels. The Chamber of Commerce thought a convention center would be generally good for business. These pro–Yerba Buena

Center commercial interests did not just make rhetorical statements about the benefits to the city from such a project. They funded studies "proving" how much San Francisco would benefit from the proposed center. In addition, they lobbied elected city officials to give necessary approvals and actively intervened in project planning.

Second, jobs. The proposed construction of a massive new physical complex was attractive to the building trades unions, and thus, they joined the pro–Yerba Buena coalition. At times, when the project was stalled, they mobilized support in the form of street demonstrations.

Third, a host of other benefits. Different versions of the Yerba Buena plan reflected efforts to woo a wide range of interest groups. An Italian cultural center was proposed by the city's Italian American mayor to get support from San Francisco's influential Italian American community. A civic light-opera center was added to the plan in an attempt to appeal to the local social elite, who wanted such a cultural facility. Plans for parking garages were expanded and shifted closer to a nearby department store; a high-level executive of the store served as head of the Redevelopment Commission (the appointed body in charge of the SFRA) and as a member of the corporate board that would run the parking garages.

In short, a pro–Yerba Buena Center coalition came together around self-interest. Members of the alliance sought different resources and benefits: money, jobs, cultural facilities, and other perquisites for themselves. They didn't define this as selfish. In their minds, what they wanted for themselves made a good, livable city.

This pro–Yerba Buena Center coalition had enough clout to move ahead with the project. The local mass media added their influence in the form of editorials and news stories, stressing the benefits to the city as a whole from a convention site. By 1966, the SFRA had obtained a federal grant to acquire land, relocate the residential occupants, and demolish buildings.

Opponents and an Improbable Anti Coalition

Then, a reaction set in. Neighborhood residents, mostly poor and elderly, fought to stop what they saw as a land grab. Some residents, seasoned in the labor struggles of the 1930s, established an organization called Tenants and Owners in Opposition to Redevelopment (TOOR) to represent and protect neighborhood interests. TOOR demonstrated against the proposed convention center, appealed to the city government to stop it, and filed a lawsuit to block the project. In their view, the Yerba Buena Center would destroy the neighborhood they had long called home. If development did take place, they demanded fair treatment: construction of subsidized housing they could afford, located in the same neighborhood or nearby; social services and open space; and a voice in planning how their future neighborhood would be built.

When it started, TOOR hardly seemed a threat. It had little clout, especially against the well-staffed pro–convention center coalition. About all it did have,

according to grizzled ex-labor leader George Wolff, who led TOOR, was a sense of injustice. It was a good issue or beef. Armed with a good beef, neighborhood residents fought hard to preserve their turf. But alone, without allies, a sense of moral outrage was a weak weapon.

TOOR, staffed by several politically-astute radicals who lived in the neighborhood and representing a group of ethnically-diverse poor and elderly persons, initially found an ally in a very different group: environmentalists. These people (mainly young professionals who lived far from Yerba Buena) opposed the project on ecological and aesthetic grounds. They feared that high-rise buildings in Yerba Buena would destroy the city's low-density land use and offbeat charm. They didn't want more cars to come into the city and add to air pollution. Housing and social services—the Yerba Buena residents' main concern—were not the environmentalists' key issues. But since both the environmentalists and TOOR wanted to stop the Yerba Buena project, they made common cause.

This improbable coalition between the poor and elderly and the affluent and young was joined at one point by another group: disgruntled taxpayers. The proposed Yerba Buena project was going to be very expensive, and a portion of the development was to be financed by city-backed bonds. City officials, with rosy projections, told taxpayers that the bonds would be paid off at no cost to the city. But the taxpayers' group feared that the convention center could be a financial disaster and that the city would have to raise property taxes in order to repay its bonds. Moreover, the taxpayers' group resented the fact that the city had not submitted the bond issue to voter approval. They felt that this was illegal as well as immoral. So another temporary alliance was struck with the neighborhood residents by yet another group that opposed the convention center (some taxpayers)—but for very different reasons.

Eventually, the original pro–Yerba Buena coalition found itself under attack on several fronts. Sued in federal court for illegal displacement of the residents, vilified before officials of the Department of Housing and Urban Development, and lambasted at city hall, they came to a standstill. For a while.

Then, a complex deal was struck between the city and TOOR. Essentially, TOOR obtained funding for housing projects in exchange for an end to litigation. Thereafter, TOOR sided with the city against its former allies, the environmentalists and fiscal opponents of the convention center.

The Outcome

What was the eventual outcome of the struggle? As is so frequently the case in politics, neither TOOR and its sometime allies nor its opponents totally won or lost. The pro–Yerba Buena Center coalition won to the extent that the major outlines of its proposal were kept intact. However, TOOR won significant accommodations. New, low-rent housing units had been built by the late 1970s, including Wolff House (named for TOOR's leader, who died during the struggle), which now houses former residents of the Yerba Buena area. Relocation benefits and social services were improved too.

TOOR's sometime allies got the city to undertake environmental-impact analyses, scale down the size of the parking garages, and increase the amount of public open space in the project area. And the taxpayers' group won in the sense that it persuaded the city to reduce the amount of the bond issue and, hence, the city's potential fiscal liability.

Larger Issues

From another angle, Yerba Buena's story is part of a larger saga: economic restructuring in central cities, global economic recession, and competition in the global marketplace. In the late 1980s, property values for luxury office space in San Francisco had plummeted. Again and again, Yerba Buena's chief developer, Olympia & York (O&Y, a Toronto-based real estate builder—it became the largest property development firm in the world by the 1980s and went bankrupt in the 1990s) downscaled its deal with the SFRA. In the end, O&Y committed to build only one, instead of three, office towers. (The city had counted on O&Y's building three office towers and collecting $68 million from them; the money was to be spent on a state-of-the-art arts center, a park, a children's center, etc.) By 1992, O&Y was struggling to survive under bankruptcy protection. Meanwhile, the project was unfinished.

Morals of the Story

This case study illustrates some important points about urban politics. First, informal power arrangements are key to understanding how things get done. *Nothing in the city charter of San Francisco or any other city deals with the role that private interest groups or citizens' action associations plays in policymaking. Yet such groups are leading actors in the process of policy formation.* Nor does the city charter or the organizational chart of city government indicate the relative influence of neighborhood residents versus opposing groups or the possibility of increasing that influence by coalition building. These are matters of informal power and influence.

Second, the Yerba Buena struggle illustrates that in U.S. cities, by and large, it is *private* interests that mold the plans of proposed projects. *Government units, such as redevelopment agencies, act as power brokers* to resolve conflicts among competing private groups.

Third, *successful political outcomes can result from effective coalition-building efforts.* In most cases, a rather strange mix of political actors can find themselves making common cause. In Yerba Buena, for a time, labor unions and business interests joined forces to promote the proposed convention center; the elderly poor, led by neighborhood radicals, were aligned for a while with liberal, socially-esteemed environmentalists and fiscal conservatives. This array of forces on both sides came together on a single issue; it was not a broad-based coalition of a multi-issue nature, which is much more difficult to put together or sustain.

Finally, the Yerba Buena case shows that *in politics, few things happen overnight.* Participation in coalition politics can lead to anxiety for people with short time lines, low frustration levels, and a distaste for conflict. Moving a project forward or trying to stop it takes patience, wits, organizational talent, energy, imagination, and perseverance. Often, it also takes money, access to the mass media, endless strategy meetings, and hard bargaining. Some players in the game of politics command more resources than others by virtue of their social and economic position, their personal characteristics, and their occupational role. However, while players don't start with equal resources, even the most well-organized and powerful groups (in the Yerba Buena case, economic elites and government officials) sometimes reach political accommodation with less powerful groups having fewer resources.

Updates

In 1971, TOOR became TODCO (Tenants and Owners Development Corporation), a nonprofit, community-based housing development corporation. By 1984, there were several community-development corporations in the city, including TODCO, and they "were receiving more housing funds than the Redevelopment Agency, making them the single largest conduit for low-income housing production in the city" (Beitel, 2004:102).

After TODCO signed a contract with the SFRA in the early 1970s, office buildings started going up in Yerba Buena. But long, drawn-out lawsuits plus issues of finance and design delayed the completion of one anchor of the new Yerba Buena—the Moscone convention center. It was completed in 1981. Later, in 1993, Yerba Buena's Cultural Center and Yerba Buena Gardens opened.

By 2006, TODCO claimed to have developed housing for more than 1,200 community members. The entire area of SoMa (South of Market Street), including Yerba Buena, had been transformed into a vibrant neighborhood of art, culture, green space, office blocks, expensive high-rise apartments, and low-income housing.

According to sociologist G. William Domhoff (2005), Yerba Buena accomplished its purpose, which, in his view, was to create a larger downtown, complete with office buildings as well as cultural and tourist attractions. But, perhaps more importantly, Domhoff thinks, is the role that TOOR/TODCO and other "tenacious" opponents played in influencing local politics: "because of the tenacity of the opponents, you've also got a lot of nice low-income housing, plus more cultural institutions than would have happened otherwise." According to Domhoff, Yerba Buena had much wider implications for citizen activism, not only in San Francisco:

> The 40-year-plus battle carried out by a determined band of progressive activists and neighborhoods in San Francisco has led to many major successes that have put real limits on the worst excesses of the "local growth coalition" [Molotch and Logan's term, discussed later in this chapter]. These victories show

what is possible under the right conditions with patience, sound strategies based on experience, and committed leadership, and they have made San Francisco a more livable city. The activists forced the city to deal with them, and they have become the voice for low-income communities through community development corporations and other community-based organizations.

(2005)

To Domhoff, then, citizen activists played a major role in Yerba Buena's development.

Officials of Yerba Buena Gardens (owned by the SFRA) have a different take. On their Web site they claim a key role for art and artists in Yerba Buena's development:

> The vision for Yerba Buena was built on three firm legs. The first was the idea of *bringing art and artists into the area initially with the understanding that community development would follow* [italics mine]. Whether it's SoHo in New York or the Left Bank in Paris, artists have often played the role of explorer, homesteader, and developer for future urban growth. The second idea was the concept of diversity.... Diversity brings durability and healthy development to both the evolving garden and the growing community. The third idea was sustainability. (http://www.yerbabuenagardens.com/history.html)

Comparing these few accounts concerning who and what were key to Yerba Buena's redevelopment, it is clear that there is no consensus. This lack of unanimity about Yerba Buena leads us to consider broader questions about the nature of community power. As you might imagine, keen observers do not agree. We now turn to this ideologically-loaded issue.

COMMUNITY POWER

According to most U.S. civics texts, local decision making is a broadly participatory effort. Almost everyone, the texts imply, has a chance to express strongly-held views; then consensus emerges, reflecting the public interest. The Yerba Buena case study suggests that this conventional textbook version of how decisions are made is idealized. How can we better understand the local decision-making process? What theoretical framework best fits the actual practice? Researchers have been investigating these questions for decades, and they don't agree.

Community power research in America began with a few participant-observer studies in the 1920s and 1930s, after the reform movement had gained a foothold in many U.S. cities. The most influential work of this period was produced by Robert S. and Helen M. Lynd, professors of sociology and social philosophy. Their landmark studies *Middletown* ([1929] 1956) and *Middletown in Transition* (1937) traced the day-to-day life of a typical small Midwestern urban community (Muncie, Indiana, never identified by name by the Lynds). In Middletown, the Lynds found that government was "enmeshed in undercover intrigue and personalities" (1937:322) that operated mainly behind the scenes. The Lynds concluded that voters were apathetic and that "experts" (doctors, intelligence testers, etc.) were starting to displace the authority of the judicial system. Further, according to the Lynds, government in Middletown was becoming an "adjunct to the city's dominant interests," particularly business (1937:chapter 24).

After World War II, community power research attracted numerous investigators, mainly those working in the sociological and social anthropological traditions. Later, starting in the 1960s, a new spate of studies appeared, largely in response to those in the 1950s. These studies, mainly conducted by political scientists, challenged both the methodologies and the findings of the earlier studies. By the mid-1970s, researchers turned their attention to one issue they considered crucial: the physical restructuring of communities, or "urban renewal."

Since the mid-1970s, theorists have been trying to join micro to macro concerns. For instance, they asked, Do macro-economic processes determine urban policies or merely constrain them? What is the connection between the attempt to control urban space and the attempt to dominate the larger society? What is the role of the nation-state in urban growth or decline? How do public government and private business decisions interact to affect cities? Given national politics and the international mobility of capital, do local political leaders have some room to move or are they essentially powerless in the struggle to shape the future of their cities?

From the mid-1970s to the early 1980s, there was a boom in community power research among U.S. political scientists. Then, it suffered a quick decline, so much so that community power research was called an "intellectual fad" (Peng, 1994).

Why did most U.S. political scientists turn to other research topics? An interesting question but not central to our present concerns. In any event, interest and research in community power waned, and a comeback does not seem to be in its future.

Even so, it is worth exploring the ways community power researchers answered the question "Who runs this town?" and the reasons these researchers disagree. We pay special attention to competing models of community power: the elitist versus the pluralist model plus newer models of urban political economy, the city-as-growth-machine and the urban regime model.

THE ELITIST MODEL

"Who runs this town?" According to Floyd Hunter, a relatively small, cohesive economic elite. Hunter's seminal study *Community Power Structure* ([1953] 1963) found that in "Regional City" (Atlanta, Georgia) a rather small group of rich and/or socially prestigious local influentials controlled the city's decision making. These influentials, Hunter said, shared similar values and weren't, for the most part, accountable to the public.

How did Hunter arrive at his conclusions? To identify Regional City's influentials, Hunter used the method of **reputational analysis**. First, he compiled a long list of people who might exercise power in Atlanta. From various sources, Hunter constructed a preliminary list of 175 names. Second, he selected a panel of people to judge the names on the list; these judges were balanced in terms of ethnicity, religion, age, occupation, and sex. Those people receiving top ratings from the judges left Hunter with a short list of 40 names. Finally, he conducted personal interviews with all those on the short list accessible to him (27 persons), asking them to identify the most influential people in the city. From their replies, Hunter reached this conclusion: The community power structure of Atlanta was dominated by top executives in banking, finance, commerce, and insurance. There were also some lawyers, industry executives, and

Fig. 15.3 ELITIST MODEL. According to Floyd Hunter, a small elite makes virtually all the important decisions in urban politics. (Richard Hedman)

socially prominent persons; but they were far fewer in number. Interestingly, the smallest number of influentials came from the sectors of government and labor.

After establishing that Atlanta was run by a small group of business and professional people, Hunter explored the interaction among these elites. Here, he used another research technique: **sociometry**, a method for studying small-group interaction—who interacts with whom. By tracing what committees the top 40 participated in, what corporate boards they sat on, and what social clubs they belonged to, Hunter concluded that the most influential people in Atlanta interacted very closely. As one interviewee told Hunter: "there are 'crowds' in Regional City—several of them— that pretty well make the big decisions. There is the crowd I belong to [the Homer Chemical crowd]; then there is the First State Bank crowd, the Regional Gas crowd, the Mercantile crowd, the Growers Bank crowd, and the like" (in Hunter, [1953] 1963:77).

These "crowds," according to the people Hunter interviewed, were primarily responsible for making fundamental city decisions, such as the decision to undertake urban renewal in the downtown area. These decisions were made by informal consensus of the economic elites. Formal government decision makers, including the mayor, were only peripheral actors until the stage of implementation was reached.

In general, subsequent studies of community power using Hunter's reputational method have come to the same conclusion. In brief, the elitist model using Hunter's methods finds that community power is held by elites or "crowds."

Many sociologists agreed with this **elitist model**, but the implications of Hunter's research were upsetting to those who saw city political processes (and U.S. politics in general) as a participatory process that promoted the public interest rather than narrow private interests. Hunter's model—that elites ran the city of Atlanta and largely determined the fate of over 300,000 inhabitants (the city's population when he studied it)—led to more studies of community power and a competing model: the **pluralist model**.

THE PLURALIST MODEL

"Who runs this town?" According to a Yale political scientist's influential study, published in 1961, community power is *not* held by a small, cohesive economic elite. Rather, power is shared among different local elites. Investigating *Who Governs?* (1961) in New Haven, Connecticut (population then 150,000), Robert Dahl found that power was broadly diffused. Decision makers in one issue area, such as education, weren't influential in another, such as urban redevel-

opment. Thus, Dahl concluded that pluralist democracy works at the urban level.

How did Dahl arrive at his findings? To identify community influentials, he employed **decision analysis**: observation and analysis of a political system (also termed "issue" or "event analysis"). This technique focuses on the actual decision-making process. Dahl chose three key local areas—education, urban redevelopment, and nominations for political office—and looked at decisions in each made over a period of about a decade. From interviews with participants in the decisions, news accounts, written records, and observations, Dahl determined who initiated successful proposals or who successfully vetoed someone else's policy alternative. Then, Dahl judged that those

Fig. 15.4   PLURALIST MODEL. Pluralists argue that urban politics is characterized by the representation of various interests in the community, not the domination of a cohesive elite. (© 1976 Richard Hedman)

with the greatest proportion of successes in making public policy were the most influential leaders in New Haven.

Dahl determined that leadership in New Haven was more specialized than Hunter had found in Regional City. In Hunter's Atlanta, there was a set of interlocking relationships between a small financial–commercial elite that was influential in essentially all major decisions. That is, the banker or manufacturer who had a major say in redevelopment decisions also influenced education and party nomination decisions. By contrast, in New Haven, Dahl found a specialization of influence: "With few exceptions any particular individual exerts a significant amount of direct influence in no more than one of the three issue areas studied" (1961:181). Thus, he deduced that New Haven was not monolithic in its power structure. Rather, it was pluralistic. Diverse groups, each with its own sphere of influence, ran New Haven.

Dahl also found diversity among the leaders. They came from various class, white ethnic, and religious backgrounds. (Dahl didn't describe their race; presumably all were white.) No one stratum of society, he argued, produced leaders in different issue areas.

Yet Dahl did not claim that the groups in New Haven shared power equally. Still, in his view, "New Haven [was] a republic of unequal citizens—but for all that a republic" (1961:220).

THE CITY-AS-A-GROWTH-MACHINE MODEL

Dahl recognized land development as one important area of urban politics. Indeed, he celebrated New Haven's mayor as an entrepreneur of redevelopment. But Dahl did not make urban growth central to his analysis. By contrast, Hunter did; he noted that, among Atlanta's top leaders and underprofessionals, the highest-priority issue in 1950 and 1951 concerned land use: the Plan of Development (a plan for annexing unincorporated areas to Atlanta).

Starting in the mid-1970s, community power research shifted away from Dahl's pluralist model and Hunter's elitist model to urban political economy models. Yet in the tradition of Hunter, these models put urban growth politics at center stage.

Community power studies in the newer urban political economy tradition constitute variations on a general theme: *growth-oriented urban alliances*. Some theorists think that the private sector forms the basis of urban renewal support. Others think that "political entrepreneurs" build progrowth coalitions out of conflicting interests. Some analysts argue that business elites are internally divided and depend on the state to coordinate their various interests. Others think that large businesses work together to ensure their general prosperity.

Some use the concept of "urban regime" (e.g., Stone, 1989; DeLeon, 1992), acknowledging that U.S. local governments alone can't mobilize and coordinate the necessary resources to govern and bring about results. Therefore, business leaders typically play a vital role in a city's informal governing coalition: Local officials want business investment, but, conversely, businesses also want government cooperation.

In general, theorists of growth-oriented urban alliances share the following premises: (1) local government officials must sustain growth to maintain local services and fiscal well-being and (2) local business firms get involved in local politics to help their profitability, such as increasing the value of their property. So, both local officials and business have an interest in urban growth, and this mutual interest leads to their working together in a progrowth coalition (Fleischmann and Feagin, 1987:208). In addition, these theorists think that (3) local politics counts—it is not merely a reflection of larger macro-economic forces—and (4) local political leadership makes a difference in determining which cities get what.

Now, let's look more closely at one variant of the general model: the **growth machine model**. Sociologist Harvey Molotch first published his model in 1976. It was later amplified in *Urban Fortunes*, a prize-winning book by fellow sociologist John R. Logan and Molotch (1987).

First, research methods. Unlike Hunter or Dahl, Logan and Molotch rely primarily on historical and social science research studies. Instead of conducting original research, they use other people's case studies, often reanalyzing the original data and offering new interpretations.

Now, substance. According to the city-as-a-growth-machine model, "The desire for growth creates consensus among a wide range of elite groups, no matter how split they might be on other issues" (Logan and Molotch, 1987:50–51). Logan and Molotch note that even pluralist studies of community power, such as Banfield's (1961) study of Chicago, also find that elites agree on one central issue: Urban growth is good. Numerous community power studies from a host of perspectives, including studies of U.S. southern border cities, Dallas and Fort Worth (Melosi, 1983), and Atlanta at two points in time (Hunter, 1953, 1980), also find that elites were united on growth policy.

Logan and Molotch reject both pure economic logic and natural geographic factors as key shapers of cities. Instead, they say that "the activism of entrepreneurs is, and always has been, a critical force in shaping the urban system, including the rise and fall of given places" (1987:52). In the nineteenth century, U.S. communities—or primarily their development elites—competed among themselves for growth stimuli, particularly government-funded transportation infrastructure (e.g., railroad routes) and government-supported institutions such as colleges and prisons. In frontier towns, "growth entrepreneurs" were mainly professionals but law, medicine, and pharmacy quickly became sidelines. These individuals made their money as town developers.

Chicago's William Ogden was "perhaps the most spectacular case of urban ingenuity." Ogden came to the Windy City in 1835 and succeeded in becoming Chicago's mayor, great railway developer, and owner of much of its finest real estate. He was also the organizer and first president of the Union Pacific Railroad. Using his business and civic roles, Ogden was able to make Chicago "the crossroads of America, and hence the dominant metropolis of the Midwest. Chicago became a crossroads not only because it was 'central' (other places were also in the 'middle') but because a small group of people (led by Ogden) had the power to literally have the roads cross in the spot they chose." Ogden himself became wealthy out of the deals that resulted from this marriage of government activity and land sales (Logan and Molotch, 1987:53–54).

Fig. 15.5 CITY-AS-A-GROWTH-MACHINE MODEL. According to Logan and Molotch, local entrepreneurs, not economic imperatives or a wide variety of interest groups, are primarily responsible for the shape of cities. In this model, businesspeople actively promote growth in their own interest. (Lisa Siegel Sullivan)

In more recent times, Logan and Molotch note, entrepreneurs still make a difference. For instance, in 1956, Colorado leaders convinced President Eisenhower to link Denver to Salt Lake City by an expensive mountain road, thus removing the threat that Cheyenne, Wyoming, would become the Western crossroads.

In short, Logan and Molotch reject deterministic economic or geographic explanations of how cities rise in the nation's hierarchy. Rather, they point to the all-important role of a city's entrepreneurs who make things happen.

To make things happen, cities try to create a "good business climate." A first-rate opera or ballet company may subtly enhance a city's growth potential. Low taxation and "cooperative" government set a good mood. But some ingredients are crucial for a good business climate: "There should be no violent class or ethnic conflict" (Logan and Molotch, 1987:60). And perhaps most important, the local public attitude should be progrowth.

In terms of the organization of the growth coalition, Logan and Molotch (1987:62) comment that those who spend their time and money participating in local affairs are those who have the most to gain or lose in land-use decisions: "Local business people are the major participants in urban politics, particularly business people in property investing, development, and real estate financing." Businesspeople's interaction with public officials, including their financial support of campaigns, gives them what others call "systemic" power. Local newspapers and other monopolitic business enterprises are also tied to metropolitan growth, although they are not directly involved in land use.

Since much of the private sector's effort to achieve growth involves government, "local growth elites play a major role in electing local politicians, 'watch dogging' their activities" (Logan and Molotch, 1987:63). Key players include politicians, the local newspaper publisher, leaders of utilities, and transportation bureaucrats, both public and private. Auxiliary players have less of a stake in growth but still play a role in promoting or maintaining it: universities, symphony orchestras, professional sports teams, organized labor, self-employed professionals and small retailers, and corporate capitalists. Some of these groups support growth because of what they will gain in rent; some stand to receive other financial profits.

Local growth is sold to different groups on different grounds—jobs, attraction of tourist dollars, enhancement of civic pride, and so on. But, Logan and Molotch argue, many of these claims are phony. Take, for instance, the appeal to workers that growth "makes jobs." In their view, growth in one city does not make jobs. Instead, the city "competes with other cities for its share of newly-created U.S. jobs" (89). (We can update Logan and Molotch here, noting that since their important book was published, competition has expanded to include intercity competition across national borders.)

Who actually wins the most from urban growth? Logan and Molotch say that governments are mobilized to intensify land uses for private gain—rent and other profit. In most cases, they say, local growth is "a transfer of wealth and life chances from the general public" to what they call the "rentier groups" (a term generally used to mean groups that live off of government securities or other dividends but used by Logan and Molotch to specify people who profit from rents of buildings and land) and their associates (1987:98).

Wider application? Does this model work outside the United States? Good question. With some variation, many think so (e.g., Ren, 2008).

COMPARING THE MODELS

Logan and Molotch, Dahl, and Hunter disagreed on the role and degree of involvement of the business community in U.S. local government. For Dahl, professional politicians determined government decisions, while business executives and professionals made their mark in civic organizations. For Hunter, a commercial–financial elite informally set basic policy, later implemented by government officials. For Logan and Molotch, local business was the major participant in urban politics, but local business and local government made good marriage partners because both were interested in growth and needed one another.

All the model makers are trained social scientists committed to scientific rigor, accuracy, and honesty. How, then, could they arrive at such different conclusions about who runs this town?

WHY THE THEORISTS DISAGREE

In the case of Dahl and Hunter, one possibility is that the towns themselves are different and that their findings reflect significant variations between Atlanta and New Haven. However, this explanation falls apart in light of subsequent restudies of the two towns. On the one hand, a restudy of New Haven found that a big-business ruling elite controlled the city (Domhoff, 1977). A restudy of Atlanta found that a series of competing coalitions existed (Jennings, 1964). Evidently, the power structures of Atlanta and New Haven aren't as different as scholars' perceptions of them.

In other words, *what you see depends on how you look at it.* Here are the bases for the researchers' disagreements:

1. *Differences in disciplinary perspectives.* Logan and Molotch are trained in sociology but draw freely on ideas rooted in geography, economics, and history. Their focus on informal elites and big winners and losers in urban growth (in terms of race and class) reflects their sociological perspective. Hunter was trained in sociology and anthropology; he emphasized social structure and social class in his analysis of community power. Instead of giving weight to the formal machinery of government, he focused on informal social networks (crowds). In fact, he argued that formal decision makers were brought into policymaking only after the real decisions had been made in the private sector. In contrast, political scientist Dahl emphasized the importance of formal government structure. He did not take a close look at informal decision making. Consequently, official position (e.g., mayor) plays a much more important part in Dahl's analysis of power structures than in Hunter's work.

2. *Differences in research methods.* Logan and Molotch rely on other researchers' empirical studies, which employed a variety of research methods. Thus, their differences with Hunter and Dahl do not lie here.

   The elitist–pluralist debate has centered largely on this issue. Hunter's critics charged that his reputational method leads to the identification of a relatively small economic elite.

Critics say that if you ask "Who are the top leaders in this town?" you are sure to find a small, cohesive leadership. In addition, critics charge that Hunter confused the reputation for having power with the *substance* of power. The fact that knowledgeable people think an individual exercises power is not proof; it is only hearsay. Thus, Hunter and those who hold an elitist model of power are accused of lack of rigor in their methods of research.

By the same token, Dahl's critics charge that decision (or event) analysis is misleading. They claim that it leads to the identification of a pattern of broader participation in decision making than actually exists.

Critics of pluralism argue that Dahl's decision analysis neglects a whole dimension of power: the ability to keep issues out of the decision-making arena altogether. For example, a study that defines the issue as the decision makers did might conclude that, in the 1940s, the major issue in a southern town in the United States was fluoridation of the water supply— that is what decision makers there might have said. (Of course, this would overlook the fact that schools in that town were entirely segregated or that racial discrimination existed; these were not issues for the local policymakers.) In other words, *decision analysis can't investigate nondecisions,* those that never reach the public stage (e.g., the nondecision to keep schools segregated).

Further, Dahl's critics disputed the choice of decisions he investigated—political nominations, public education, and urban redevelopment—arguing that such decisions narrowed the field of political activity and neglected broader, private sector decisions. Finally, critics pointed out that Dahl gave little specific information on the decisions he studied, so readers must take his conclusions on faith.

It is noteworthy that subsequent community power studies using Hunter's reputational technique tended to find elitist patterns of local power, while studies using Dahl's decision analysis tended to find pluralist patterns of local power. This suggests an implicit bias in the research techniques.

Logan and Molotch use neither the case study approach nor reputational or decision analysis. Instead, they draw on a range of research studies from various perspectives and disciplines, often reinterpreting the authors' findings.

3. *Differences in theoretical orientation.* Logan and Molotch start from a viewpoint that puts individuals, not abstract market forces or macroeconomic imperatives of the larger system, at center stage: "All capitalist places are the creations of activists who push hard to alter how markets function, how prices are set, and how lives are affected." This point of view distinguishes them from both the mainstream ecological paradigm of Burgess and the structuralism of neo-Marxian urbanists, which, in their view, are too deterministic. They also reject Dahl's pluralism. Focusing on local elites who try to make money from urban development, Logan and Molotch argue that growth is often portrayed falsely by these elites as beneficial to all when, in actuality, both the advantages and disadvantages are unevenly distributed. In tone, they are close to Hunter.

Hunter assumed that inherent conflict exists between social classes, that the interests of the few (the crowds of economic elites) run counter to the interests of the many. It follows, then, that the elites rule in their own interest against the interests of the citizenry. Hunter rejected the notion that government is neutral, a mere negotiator among interest groups representing a wide spectrum of the population. By contrast, in *Who Governs?* Dahl took social stability for granted. Consequently, he does not explore the measures that ensure social continuity (e.g., lack of information, threats of coercion).

Conflict-oriented theorists criticize Dahl and pluralists generally for assuming that a political consensus exists and that this consensus works to everyone's benefit. This assumption of social harmony, critics say, prevented pluralists from studying how and in whose interests this alleged consensus is maintained. On

the other hand, pluralists attacked Hunter and conflict-oriented theorists generally for looking for conflict based on social class differences and therefore finding it.

4. *Differences in levels of analysis.* Both Dahl and Hunter dealt with cities as cities, not as centers of larger metropolitan areas. Hunter did discuss the ties of Atlanta's influentials to the federal government and foreign interests, but both Hunter and Dahl focused on the city level. Thus, their differences cannot be accounted for by the level of analysis they used.

Indeed, both scholars have been criticized for restricting their discussion of community power to the micro level. In his classic restudy of New Haven, sociologist Domhoff (1977) argued that community power in that city cannot be understood if it is not placed in a macro-political context. Domhoff believed that New Haven's suburban ruling class (which Dahl thought had withdrawn from city politics) had become part of a national network of urban planning, dominating the politics and culture of the central city via decision making at the national level.

Sociologists Vidich and Bensman came to similar conclusions. They insisted that community politics cannot be understood except in the context of national life. In their seminal (and now-classic) study, *Small Town in Mass Society* ([1958] 1971:320), Vidich and Bensman claimed that as early as the late 1950s "almost all aspects of [small-town life in upstate New York] were controlled by external forces over which [townspeople] had little control; the idea of democratic self-determination had no basis in fact." A case study of Caliente, a U.S. small town in the western desert (Chapter 18), also concludes that life-and-death community decisions are often made in places far from the community (Cottrell, 1951).

Logan and Molotch focused on "place-based" (local) elites, but unlike both Hunter and Dahl, they consistently linked local development to national policy. Their macro–micro linkage resulted from their theoretical orientation: non-Marxist urban political economy.

5. *Differences in political ideology.* Logan and Molotch attempted to construct a "sociology of urban property relations" (1987:13). Paying great attention to human agents in urban growth, they rejected various forms of what they deemed determinism. Specifically, they rejected the notion that city space is a mere reflection of larger processes under capitalism, particularly capital accumulation and the reproduction of social classes.

Logan and Molotch inferred that meaningful participation is extremely limited. Here, they would agree with both Dahl and Hunter. Dahl and Hunter found relatively small numbers of people participating in community decision making. In both cases, the top leadership represented about one-one hundredth of the city's population. Also, they agreed that the top leaders work with a second level of minor decision makers (Dahl called them "subleaders" and Hunter called them the "understructure") but that a very small group effectively made major decisions. Thus, their findings do not seem too different. The *major difference between Hunter and Dahl lies in the interpretation of their data.* And their interpretations stem from normative assumptions about how democracy *should* work.

Hunter implied that something was rotten in Atlanta; local government practice didn't live up to democratic ideals. In his view, it was not proper for a small economic elite to make decisions, for he assumed that the interests of elites are not the interests of the citizenry as a whole. Hunter ([1953] 1963:239) found that most people are apathetic about politics because they're not consulted about decisions that affect their lives. Further, he found that people disadvantaged by the status quo are not an articulate group and can't make their demands known. (Echoes of this argument, from a different angle, can be found in the work of political scientist Claus Mueller; see Chapter 2.) However, Hunter didn't accept the elitist community power structure as inevitable or legitimate. He offered proposals, based on his community organization background, to bring about wider participation in local politics and to make pluralism really work.

Dahl was more pessimistic. When he wrote his New Haven study, Dahl thought that the masses should not be full participants in the political process because they are the "apolitical clay" of the system (1961:227). At that time (see next paragraph), he believed that it was better for this inert mass of clay to remain inert.

Note: People, including scholars, can change their minds. A generation ago, Dahl became a member of the Democratic Socialist Organizing Committee, an organization committed to ideals closer to Hunter's proposals than to interest-group pluralism. Much later, after becoming professor emeritus of political science and the senior research scientist in sociology at Yale, Dahl wrote *On Political Equality* (2006), asking whether or not more political equality is a worthwhile future goal for the United States. Quite unlike the Dahl who wrote *Who Governs?* in 1961 (reissued in 2005), Dahl answered with an unqualified yes: More political equality is a worthwhile goal.

But back in the 1950s, Dahl thought that democracy's health was best preserved by depending on the competence and standards of political elites. For this reason, some observers claim that pluralism was misnamed; it should have been called "democratic elitism" (Bachrach, 1967).

Some critics suggested that by putting his stamp of approval on New Haven's power structure, Dahl wrote off the mass of citizens without examining why they're apathetic or ill-informed. Others charged that Hunter was too optimistic about the common people ever being full participants in the political process.

To (former) pluralists like Dahl, government promotes the general welfare, not special interests, and market forces primarily shape cities. To followers of Hunter's elitist model, business elites are the prime mover; government follows their lead. To Logan and Molotch, entrepreneurs primarily shape cities in their own interest, within a context of economic and political forces; local government also seeks growth, for different reasons, so business and government are natural allies.

Interestingly, conservative and liberal social scientists who look at cities tend to see pluralistic power structures, whereas radical social scientists tend to see elitist systems of power. Similarly, decentralists tend to view community power as highly concentrated; centralists tend to see a dispersion of power.

To conclude: Over the decades, the study of community power has attracted a variety of scholars, including those not often considered urbanists (e.g., Dahl, Hunter). Why? The microcosm of the city provides a testing ground for democratic theory in general. Or so the theorists thought. Perhaps this is the key to understanding the long-standing (but now moribund) debate between elitists and pluralists.

Scholars engaged in the debate over the nature of community power were dealing with an age-old normative question: "Who should govern?" Pluralists found that decision makers—professionals, experts, members of the well-educated upper middle class, and a few lower-status people—run things in a rational, efficient, and evenhanded manner. Their rule ensures social order. Critics of pluralism, on the contrary, found that local decision makers were members of elite groups who make decisions with their own interests in mind, interests that conflicted with those of groups denied access to policymaking, particularly lower-class and lower-status people. Hunter and those using the elitist model were far less concerned with questions of efficiency and rationality in government than were the pluralists; the elitists stressed issues of equality and equal representation of everyone's interests. Between these two perspectives lies a chasm of difference.

Although community power research in the United States nearly expired in the 1980s and has not been revived, the topic of power—at the levels of the nation and the globe—remains a key concern of social scientists. As we

might guess, who should govern and how we are actually governed are both highly disputed questions.

APPLYING THESE MODELS ELSEWHERE

What results do we find if these models are applied to cities with different histories? It all depends. But many scholars believe that the growth machine model—possibly with some modifications—is a better fit to postindustrial cities when examining urban transformation. For example, in his case study of Shanghai, China's, recent historical preservation efforts in a hip, inner-city area, Xuefei Ren (2008), a sociologist at Michigan State University, concludes that both private and public actors (chiefly international architectural firms, private business developers, the media, and local universities) play crucial roles in Shanghai's growth machine.

CITIZEN POLITICS

CITIZEN PARTICIPATION

In a few Swiss cantons; a town in Basque country, Spain; and parts of the United States there is another model of local power: the town meeting. It is not included here for several reasons, mainly because it is so limited. (In the United States, Vermont, New Hampshire, Maine, Connecticut, Massachusetts, and a few other places, including parts of Wisconsin and Minnesota, have town meetings. Often touted as direct democracy [e.g., Zimmerman, 1999], annual town meetings—which often serve more as a place to exchange news than a decision point for weighty matters—may be an endangered species. In addition, state governments have taken over many decisions formerly left to the towns.) So, back to our three models of community power.

The late European social scientist Stein Rokkan once said that "votes count but resources decide (Rokkan, 1966:105)." All three models of U.S. community power support this view. Neither Logan and Molotch, Dahl, nor Hunter give much attention to voters' choices as determinants of local politics.

Likewise, neither the pluralist, elitist, nor city-as-a-growth-machine model finds that great numbers of local citizens participate in U.S. decision making. In fact, even though the political arena may seem infinitely more crowded than in Boss Tweed's day, community power researchers of all ideological stripes find that *only tiny minorities of the population play the game of city politics.*

Pluralists assume that these actors, while small in number, represent a diversity of groups and interests. Further, they assume that political leaders don't serve the interests of one group more than those of another. Pluralists point to the following individuals or groups as participants in the political process, either formally or informally: (1) government officials, both elected and appointed; (2) government bureaucrats; (3) business executives and business-oriented organizations (e.g., chamber of commerce); (4) organized labor; (5) political parties; and (6) special-interest groups and single-issue groups (e.g., the Association for the Education of the Mentally Retarded, local garden clubs).

Radical critics of pluralism reject the idea that the power of the local garden club can be equated with the power of corporate institutions. They say that, for example, to equate the PTA with Mobil or Microsoft is to ignore the message of George Orwell's *Animal Farm* ([1954] 2004): "All animals are equal...but some are more equal than others." Further, they point to the millions of dollars that big lobbies spend annually,

Fig. 15.6 STARTING YOUNG. Citizen participation can mean attending a political rally, voting, lobbying, bringing a lawsuit, e-mailing a comment to city hall, rioting, protesting, and/or running for office. (Deborah Mosca)

dollars that ensure access to policymakers at the very least and serve to make the "level playing field" a myth (see Table 15.1).

Amid race riots and other urban conflagrations in the 1960s, a number of activists and political theorists tried to change the rules of the political game. Their goal: to make the less equal a bit more equal, to bring new players into the arena of politics. Specifically, they sought to broaden the structures of influence and power to include those whom Dahl and Hunter agreed didn't participate in local policymaking: the poor and near-poor, the powerless, racial minorities, and the socially unesteemed. What they called for was *citizen participation*.

But exactly who should participate? How much power should people long excluded from politics now have in making public policy? What would the stirring slogan "Power to the People" mean in practice? These questions stirred controversy and fear in the 1960s. And, to a debated degree, memories of those days still haunt or inform U.S. politics.

Since that time, the focus of citizen participation has shifted, suggesting that the stakes are big when there is

TABLE 15.1 TOP 10 POLITICAL ACTION COMMITTEE (PAC) CONTRIBUTORS TO U.S. FEDERAL CANDIDATES, 2005–2006*

PAC Name	Total Amount
National Association of Realtors	$ 3,756,005
National Beer Wholesalers Association	$ 2,946,500
National Association of Home Builders	$ 2,900,000
National Auto Dealers Association	$ 2,821,600
Operating Engineers Union	$ 2,784,435
International Brotherhood of Electrical Workers	$ 2,782,875
American Bankers Association	$ 2,747,299
Laborers Union	$ 2,680,650
American Association for Justice	$ 2,558,000

*Totals include subsidiaries and affiliated PACs, if any. The names are those of the organization connected with the PAC, e.g., the Coca-Cola Company Nonpartisan Committee for Good Government would be listed as Coca-Cola Co.

Source: Federal Elections Commission, based on data released on February 19, 2007 (http://usgovinfo.about.com/od/thepoliticalsystem/a/aboutpacs.htm); from Robert Longley, *Your Guide to U.S. Gov Info/ Resources.*

a proposed change in the political rules. Here is a brief history of events and movements in the 1960s (and beyond) that had an impact on U.S. urban politics.

In the early 1960s, the civil rights movement mobilized large numbers of African Americans, many of whom had never before voted or participated in more active forms of public policymaking. Typically, these new political players came from lower-class backgrounds and had lifestyles that differed from those of traditional decision makers. Many people wondered how these new players would use their potential for political power.

"Maxfeas"

In 1964, Congress passed the War on Poverty program put forward by then president Lyndon B. Johnson. The debate over how "the people" would exercise their power heated up, for no one could predict how newly politicized African Americans (and others long excluded from the political process) would use their resources. Under the War on Poverty program, the federal government mandated a rather vague provision for the "maximum feasible participation of the poor" in community action programs ("maxfeas" for short). This meant that poor people were supposed to participate in the planning and execution of community action programs. However, members of Congress and mayors alike had few hints that maxfeas would be taken seriously. When there was a surge of energy and militant action by the poor in many cities, mayors and other traditional political actors were taken by surprise. And they were not happy. Some local officials developed ingenious methods of dealing with citizen participants, especially militant ones. Often, they sent out what novelist–journalist Tom Wolfe (1971) called the "flak catchers," low-level bureaucrats whose job entailed calming the militants down and catching their flak. Meanwhile, when the new political participants tried to secure social changes in their own interests, they were called a host of names, including "un-American."

Congress did not intend that the opportunity extended to the poor and powerless should upset the traditional balance of power at the urban level. Big-city Democratic mayors complained to the national Democratic administration, threatening to do something if funds weren't redirected away from community groups and funneled back to them.

By the late 1960s, the War on Poverty had been reduced to a holding action. Vietnam gripped the nation and the federal purse. Some activists switched from antipoverty to antiwar efforts, and critics raged against the program. Mayors and members of Congress had been stung by the unintended consequences of the maxfeas provision for citizen participation. Even the War on Poverty's sponsor, President Johnson, accused the program of being run by "sociologists and kooks." And Daniel Patrick Moynihan, wearing his professorial hat, argued that maxfeas was based on *Maximum Feasible Misunderstanding* (1969). The political backlash against "too much participation" by the "wrong kinds of people" emasculated the antipoverty program, and President Richard M. Nixon dismantled most of the War on Poverty programs during the early 1970s.

Looking back, people involved in the 1960s attempts at citizen participation have mixed feelings. Some feel that it was a time of exciting social change. Others wonder if it was a cruel hoax, perpetuating political and economic inequality under the guise of equal opportunity.

Today, participation in politics for some citizens is a spectator activity (voting, putting a bumper sticker on the car). For others, it is more involving: e-mailing the mayor, giving money to a candidate, signing an Internet petition, joining a group with political goals, and/or blogging. And for a very few, participation means running for political office, leading a protest, or sponsoring a recall campaign. And for a handful, it is much more dangerous: committing an act of civil disobedience or terrorism.

DARK SHADOWS

Aside from a possible (say some probable) economic meltdown, at least two dark shadows cloud the U.S. horizon: (1) terrorism and (2) disdain and/or hatred of "them." Many, including myself, believe these two threatening shadows are connected—by various strands of fear. Let us begin with terrorism.

Most people in the United States associate terror with attacks by "them," that is, people who dislike or hate the United States, whether their feelings

are rooted in anticapitalism, antimodernism, or other isms that the United States has come to symbolize. Long security lines at airports are one response to fears of terrorism.

Yet, many—both in the United States and globally—associate terror with the U.S. government itself. For example, media critic Norman Solomon claimed that the United States is a "warfare state" (2007) where people do not resist governmental actions. Political scientist Chalmers Johnson (2004, 2007) was once a strong conservative voice; now the East Asian expert believes that military spending and bases have turned the United States into a new kind of empire.

How might fear and trembling of terrorism be connected to fear of "them"? Here is one analysis: By the mid-1990s, many people in the United States felt left behind to wallow in a swamp of discontent. Momentous changes had touched people's daily lives—the reorganization of the economy with a loss of jobs for many, deindustrialization, a communications revolution, transnational interdependence, social movements, and so on. Starting earlier and continuing with warp speed after 9/11/2001, there was a range of responses in the United States to a time of terror and change. Widespread fear of "them" together with fear of both personal and national decline were common.

But instead of a reasoned, modulated public conversation over choices, there were loud noises: the fever-pitched voice of snarling citizens, cocked guns of a paramilitary counterculture, and hate-filled speeches, sermons, and blogs blaming "them" for personal and national ills. Alienated, some stopped voting. Facing postmodern society, some looked back to a romanticized rural past, just as Tönnies had done in his dislike for modern society. Others used the airwaves or the Internet, blaming "them" (female executives, people of color, gays, environmentalists, animal-rights supporters, politicians, Jews, etc.) for their own loss of affluence, status, and hope. And a few, perhaps inspired by Travis Bickel, the fictional Vietnam vet in Martin Scorsese's *Taxi Driver* (1976), used violence to cleanse the cities of "scum."

By September 11, 2001, it was clear that some zealots were ready and able to use violence to attain their goal: cleansing cities—and indeed whole societies—of what they considered "scum." Globally, the best-known zealot group remains al-Qaeda ("the base" in Arabic), an alliance of Sunni Muslims put together in 1988 by Osama bin Laden. Bin Laden's vision of "the good society" is rooted in a puritanical Islamic creed: Wahhabism. This sect, begun in the eighteenth century by Arabian preacher Abd al-Wahhab, was "designed to shape a puritanical Muslim society" (Burama and Margalit, 2004:135). Current followers of Wahhabism seek to create a society based on religious purity ruled by divine law and free of Western behavior (considered barbaric and immoral) and material greed. Followers seek clear rules governing politics, family life, and male–female relationships. Citizen participation in decision making is implicitly an enemy, for Wahhabis believe that only God (Allah) can provide guidance.

Globalization is also an enemy to Wahhabis. Perhaps surprisingly, in the United States many, including some radicals, ultrarightists, conservatives, and liberals, agree. But for very different reasons. Some fear that globalization is an enemy of citizen participation. Others fear that globalization is an enemy of the nation-state. Not surprisingly, critics of globalization disagree on how to respond to its challenge.

Some suggest that effective citizen participation has become meaningless in a global economy. In particular, some liberals and some radicals fear that the World Trade Organization (WTO) and other organizations, including the World Bank, govern world trade without input from local or state governments, let alone citizen groups. One of their chief concerns is that citizen participation is being replaced by faceless, unelected bureaucrats who sit in secret administrative tribunals in faraway places, deciding key issues.

Radicals are divided. Some stress the importance of nonviolent local action. Others call for massive resistance to what they consider murderous, imperialist policies. (In 2008, some radicals called for citizen input of some kind when the U.S. government intervened in financial markets.)

Ultrarightists put a different spin on globalization. Many fear a "satanic" conspiracy aimed at establishing a one-world government that, they claim, is run by evil Jewish bankers, Bolsheviks, the Federal Emergency Management Agency, and the United Nations. Their solution: the primacy of county-level government, property rights, and the right to bear arms. Critics denounce them as paranoids seeking easy answers to complex processes that serve to lower their social position.

Meanwhile, economic conservatives are not much concerned with the possible ramifications for citizen participation in the global economy. Why? Traditionally, they have preferred the market to decide who gets what. (It is noteworthy that, in 2008, some leading economic conservatives led the charge for U.S. government intervention in previously-private financial institutions in order to stabilize global markets. They did not ask for citizen participation in decision making.)

Aside from those who prefer market decisions, people of varying stripes have been looking to new forms of citizen participation. One tool with enormous potential is electronic communication.

ELECTRONIC DEMOCRACY?

By the 1970s, the term "citizen participation" had vanished from the political vocabulary in the United States. Recently, this term resurfaced—with a twist. Now, as often as not, it refers to electronic participation, sometimes called "e-democracy."

Many cities worldwide now have interactive Web sites. And globally, from Brazil and Spain to Korea and beyond, some have high hopes for citizens' media and "wired democracy" (e.g., Clift, 1999).

Indeed, the Internet has been hailed as *the* tool that would revolutionize political systems at all levels. Ward and Vedel (2006) note that the Net could become a major tool for democracy "by allowing anyone anywhere access to information and opinions of anyone else, anywhere else." In this vein, Andrea Slane (2007) wrote hopefully that

> All individuals can soon, if we take the necessary actions, together build a new Information Society based on shared knowledge and founded on global solidarity and a better mutual understanding between peoples and nations.

Building a "new Information Society" can also mean organizing protests online. Such were the 2008 cases in Seoul, Korea and Egypt. In Korea, students—using

BOX 15.1   HOW TO SUCCEED AS AN ELECTED OFFICIAL

According to Comedy Central's "news"caster Jon Stewart, politicians need more than intelligence, dedication, and a grasp of the issues. To succeed in public office, Stewart says, a person needs that indefinable quality of "it."

Here is an adapted version of Stewart's original quiz. It may help you decide whether you have "it" or not. Answer honestly!

1. Do folks from various ethnic/socioeconomic backgrounds feel comfortable with you, even when you don't know them or care about them?
2. Is it possible for you to cry or express strong emotions on cue?
3. Do you have followers?
4. Does your portrait look good hanging on a government wall?
5. In school, did you have many campaign volunteers when you ran for student council but very few "true" friends?
6. If you have children, have they written articles about you as a puzzling person?
7. Do you put people so at ease that, in a crowded room, they feel they are alone with you?
8. Do you fill up any room in a house?
9. Can your character defects be passed off as lovable quirks?
10. Are you often "it" when you play tag?
11. Do you have enough gray hair to show that you have experience but not enough to make you look ready for Medicare?

Scoring: If you answered yes one to four times, you don't have enough "it" to run for office. If you answered yes five to eight times, you might be moderately successful at the city level or as a local news anchorperson. If you answered yes more than nine times, start preparing your campaign slogans!

Source: Stewart and the writers of the *Daily Show*, 2006, p. 127.

---

the Internet—organized significant political protests against lifting a ban against U.S. beef) (see Sang-Hun, 2008), and in Egypt, a protest against rising food prices and the national government began on a Facebook page. The Egyptian government response was quick and severe; the main organizer was arrested and beaten, and another organizer was arrested (Cohen, 2008:12), showing just how seriously the government took this threat.

Quickly—in just over a decade—the Internet moved from a tool of a relatively few computer nerds and academics to become a global medium of central concern to political actors. What's behind this burst of what some call "techno-enthusiasm" (Ward and Vedel, 2006)? Some say that it is partially based on the belief that the Internet is unique among communications media because it is decentralized, lacks editorial control, and is so fast that volumes of information can be transferred worldwide quickly.

So, we might (and should) ask, does the Internet constitute a step toward electronic democracy? Do wired city halls and electronic town meetings signal wider citizen participation? Or are they just new ways of fooling Jane and John Q. Public into believing they have a real voice—when they have but a faint whimper? Assessments and hopes differ.

There are other ways that electronic networks facilitate citizen action. First, organizing has become easier. In South Korea, for one example, thousands of teens, networking via the Internet and coordinating via text messages in spring 2008 protested in the streets of Seoul (chanting "No to mad cow"; the country's president had agreed to lift a ban on U.S. beef). This phenomenon is called "digital populism" or "Web 2.0 protest" locally (Sang-Hun, 2008).

Second, the Internet has facilitated money-raising, quick dissemination of information, and the possibility of citizen participation in Internet-based forums. The presidential campaign of Barack Obama raised millions of dollars, much from small donors, via the Internet. Indeed, some analysts think that the Internet's function of raising campaign money has done more to curb the influence of big donors and special interests than over a decade of federal restrictions on campaign contributions (in Wayne, 2008:4). In terms of quickly responding to rumors, the staffs of political candidates at all levels now routinely use the Net to put their own spin on information. And, as we know, the Web carries scads of information, including political gaffes that show up on YouTube within hours, if not minutes. Indeed, many observers feel that such "new media" have changed the rules of the political game forever.

To conclude: Can a superhighway be a vehicle for all sorts of citizen participation? Perhaps, if the highway is electronic. But the evidence is not yet in. Some researchers do not think the Internet increases meaningful, wider citizen participation. For example, two students in a Duke University course, The Internet and Politics, concluded that while teleconferencing, wired city halls, and interactive campaign Web sites may affect *how* citizens participate in politics, "they will not necessarily change *who* participates" (Kennedy and Stempel, 2006 [italics mine]). Yet, others point to the ease of organizing protests (such as the one in Seoul, which brought new political participants into the arena) and the possibility of hearing new voices via such vehicles as Internet forums.

Some scholars think that the Internet will perpetuate existing patterns of participatory inequality in the United States (Krueger, 2002: 476). The technology for widespread citizen participation is not in question: Interactive video, text messaging, e-mail, blogs, vlogs, computer conferencing, and other means for citizen input already exist.

What remains problematic are the ends to which this powerful technology will be put. Yes, Internet organizing and informing has been highly effective. From raising money for political campaigns in the United States and organizing student protests in France to tracking transportation use in Singapore and speedily exchanging data among scientific peers worldwide, the Internet has—in a very short time—become invaluable. Yes, the Internet has enabled strangers to meet, greet, and organize, as in the case of South Korea. Yes, there are possibilities for bottom–up (instead of top–down) politics and change via YouTube and citizen-produced political ads. Indeed, citizen-produced ads may change a great deal.

At the same time, various issues bear close watch. These include the spread of pseudoparticipation, government or private group snooping, and manipulation of the many by the few via electronic means.

A turbo-account of citizen participation in U.S. politics since the 1950s: Starting after World War II and continuing on, a variety of movements and events changed political participation in the United States at all levels of government and private organizations. Most notably, so-called minorities spoke up and out. This includes African Americans, gays, and women (a numerical majority in the United States).

Since World War II, numerous subcommunities around the globe have organized. These include subcommunities based on ethnicity, religion, age, medical status, gender identity, or a single issue, such as environmental protection.

In other words, new players entered the political arena at all levels. Rarely were these new game players greeted with enthusiasm or grace by traditional decision makers. In some cases, repression, threats, and murder accompanied the struggle for citizen politics. But so did political accommodation. Voting rights were made secure for African Americans through grassroots organizing. The number of African Americans and Latinos who held elected office in cities grew. (By 2000, there were 9,040 African Americans elected officials in the United States, a sixfold increase since 1970. In California, where the 2000 Census showed that nearly one-third of the state's residents [32.4 percent] were Hispanic, 25 percent of the state's assembly members were Hispanic.)

David Bostitis of the Joint Center for Political and Economic Studies (2002) found that the number of African American mayors being elected in U.S. cities with over 50,000 residents, where the majority of the population is *not* African American, is increasing. Interestingly, Bostitis also found that the sixfold increase of African Americans elected between 1970 and 2000—quite a jump—was due primarily to African American *women*.

Women in general have been running successfully for political office at the local level in the U.S.: by 2009, of the 1,142 mayors of U.S. cities with populations over 30,000, 193 (16.9 percent) were women (Rutgers Center for American Women and Politics, 2009).

For some, serving in office or supporting those who do brings desired political goals. Other methods people use in the game of local politics to get what they want include the following: picketing the mayor's office, e-mailing the city manager, starting an Internet blog, signing an online petition, filing a lawsuit in federal court, circulating a video on YouTube, lobbying the bureaucrats, bad-mouthing the opposition, going on a hunger strike, convincing the chamber of commerce, taking out an ad in the newspaper, flaming an official on the Internet, leaking a juicy tale to the press, bribing a housing inspector, seizing the bulletin boards, mau-mauing the flak catchers, organizing the grass roots, building a coalition, terrorizing a neighborhood, rioting, asking the ward boss, and threatening to move a factory out of town or out of the country to a place with cheaper taxes.

What methods work best? That depends on the circumstances. There is no single answer. Moreover, the methods people use to reach their political goals depend on who they think runs the town. (For example, followers of pluralist Dahl might lobby functional experts on a particular issue, while followers of the growth machine model might figure out how their project fits in with the community's economic development and then rally support from members of a progrowth coalition.)

Most people in the United States work within the existing political system, by either lobbying, organizing, bringing lawsuits, or finding—and pushing—the levers of power. This brings us back to Bananas, the day-care service group encountered in Chapter 13.

CASE STUDY CONTINUED: HOW BANANAS
LEARNED WHO RUNS THIS TOWN AND
GOT SOME THINGS DONE

Terrorists play by their own rules. Others, who think they're all-powerful, may try. But groups trying to reach their political goals have to understand the rules of the game. Bananas had to learn about formal government structure before they knew whom to approach. That learning process was accompanied by some important lessons in the structure of influence. Here is a summary of what Bananas learned.

Over the course of several years, as Bananas provided services welcomed by the community and built credibility, they found that they could work with members of the so-called machine of Ron Dellums (a member of Congress at the time, later elected mayor of Oakland, California).

And Bananas found that things got done when then congressperson Dellums called a state assemblyman, who in turn talked to a Berkeley City Council member and a county supervisor about space for a day-care center. In the past, Bananas had asked, written memos, talked, demonstrated, and lobbied. Now, it took only a few phone calls from the right people to bring action. According to Bananas' first program director, the group could never have gotten funding from the city of Berkeley or accomplished many of its goals without the backing of the Dellums machine (Curry, 1978).

Political lesson 1. The city machine (or at least its shadow) lives on, even in the most reformed and progressive governments. Not the Tweed Ring of yesteryear or a Richard J. Daley–like version but a shadow model. In Berkeley, California (population about 120,000), there was a shadow machine that included elected officials in the city of Berkeley, the neighboring city of Oakland, the county government, the state assembly, and the U.S. House of Representatives. That is, a group of Democratic Party politicians—ranging from the city and county to the state and national levels—worked closely together on issues of common concern. Then congressperson Ronald Dellums (D-Calif., 1971–1998; elected mayor of Oakland 2007) was an influential member of this group, often referred to locally as the "Dellums machine." The so-called Dellums machine didn't look much like the old machine near and dear to Boss Tweed and his ilk. It lacked strict discipline and hierarchical structure. Its goal was not spoils; its members pressed a particular political agenda and shared an ideological perspective. But it did work to mobilize votes and dispense benefits.

Political lesson 2. In local government, there is usually more than one coalition; a group trying to obtain something can work with several coalitions. As in many cities, Berkeley politics had various coalitions. Aside from the Dellums group, there was the Berkeley Democratic Club (a group of more middle-of-the-road liberals than members of the Dellums machine). Bananas didn't deal with the Democratic Club for several years. But as this group gained more seats on the city council (and the Dellums-supported group lost seats), Bananas found that it had to work with another ally.

Political lesson 3. Ethnicity and race remain important factors in city politics; compromise among different ethnic groups often entails conflict. Today, Bananas is a multiracial group. But it began as a mainly white group that splintered from a biracial day-care organization. The split between African Americans and whites centered on jobs and services: who would work at the day-care centers and which community (African American or white) would receive more services. For some time, tempers ran high as the African American–dominated group charged racism and Bananas' staff accused them of racial power plays. Meanwhile, the African American–dominated group received city funds for day care and Bananas didn't. As Bananas appealed to a broader constituency and became known as a resource for other day-care groups (including a Chicano group that Bananas helped to obtain city space), it gained credibility. Finally, after 5 years of grassroots organizing, a new Berkeley city manager, himself an African American, decided to mediate between the two groups. After about 6 months of negotiations, the city's day-care budget was split, half going to the African American–dominated group and half to Bananas. Later, Bananas expanded its membership and became a multiracial group.

Political lesson 4. Never underestimate the power of goodwill and mutual aid. Bananas alone was weaker than Bananas supported by a range of community interests: single parents, feminists, day-care center operators, and community service agencies.

Political lesson 5. Adaptability increases the chances of survival in changing times. In times of recession and near-broke local government, funding from private and nonprofit sources becomes crucial. As government funding cutbacks hit hard, Bananas scrambled for funds to keep its doors open. Along with nearly 200 other groups, Bananas applied to the Gulf & Western Foundation, a nonprofit foundation, for financial aid. It won a 3-year, $135,000 grant to strengthen its resources and add staff in 1983. Decades later, Bananas was still alive and very active.

To conclude: Bananas learned the facts of community political life by personal experience. Members of the group spent years of hard work learning how to accomplish their goals. Understanding the informal power structure of the city was a major element in their eventual success.

ANOTHER LOOK

Urban politics, using either peaceful methods of compromise, negotiation, and back-room deals or more militant techniques of confrontation and intimidation, is a process that determines who gets what from the public purse. The history of U.S. cities shows that both formal and informal power structures are used and manipulated by people seeking public resources. (While there are national differences—for example, some countries lean more heavily on technocrats and/or bureaucracies and have no history of citywide machines—the manipulation of both formal and informal power structures is common worldwide.)

The way groups play the political game depends on how they think it works. And the way scholars describe the structure of community power depends on their research methods, political ideology, level of analysis, theoretical orientation, and intellectual discipline. The debate between pluralists and elitists illustrates once again that what you see depends on how you look at it.

It is also noteworthy that—at least until blogs, vlogs, text messaging, and Internet petitions became widespread—scholars agreed on one point: The number of people involved in making key decisions affecting a city's distribution of resources is very few, relatively speaking. Is this good or bad? Here, scholars disagree. Some fear hyperpluralism and the consequent government by bureaucrats. Others are more frightened by the notion that small elites control the quality of urban life. Some libertarians would like to turn most government functions over to private institutions. Still others suggest that the issue is essentially false, for the whole idea of local control is a mere illusion—key decisions affecting cities are no longer made there, for the growth of big business and big government has changed the nature of politics. In this view, significant decisions with political impact—where a new company will locate and pay taxes, how much federal aid the city will get, and so on—are made far away from the city, with little citizen participation.

KEY TERMS

Decision analysis A research technique, associated with Robert Dahl, used to gain an understanding of how a political system works. It involves the observation and analysis of decision making and the actors involved in making decisions. The decision analyst attempts to find out who made important decisions and how they were made by observing events directly, analyzing historical records, and interviewing participants in the decision (e.g., urban renewal project sites).

Elitist model of community power A model, associated with Floyd Hunter, that describes urban politics as dominated by a relatively small, cohesive elite, primarily from the private business sphere.

Growth machine model A model, associated with sociologists Harvey Molotch and John Logan, that describes urban politics as dominated by a local progrowth coalition of businesses, commercial landowners, and rentiers (persons with a fixed income from stocks and bonds or persons who profit from rents); government agencies are also key actors in the politics of growth.

Pluralist model of community power A model, associated with political scientist Robert Dahl, that describes urban politics as pluralistic in terms of the individuals or groups represented in decision making, with no one dominant group.

Reputational analysis A research technique, associated with Floyd Hunter, used to gain an understanding of how a political system works. It involves surveying the opinions of knowledgeable persons in the community about who makes key decisions.

Sociometry The study of the network of relationships among members of a group. The patterns of interaction in a group can be presented diagrammatically, using a sociogram.

PROJECTS

1. **Community power**. Do a reputational study of power in your community. The simplest form might consist of having professors at your college or university list the most influential people in the community. More time-consuming and more valuable studies would involve surveys of several different types of "knowledgeables" and/or use of an expert panel with follow-up interviews, asking those who score high on the list to identify powerful actors in the community.

2. **Community power**. Do a decisional study in your community. A simple approach would be to analyze who participated in two or more issues, based on newspaper coverage of the issues. Content analysis of news articles could be supplemented by one or more of the techniques used by Dahl: interviews, direct observation (e.g., attending sessions of formal decision-making bodies), and examination of historical records.

3. **Community power**. The recent destruction of squatter apartment houses ("squats") in Germany, Denmark, and the Netherlands offers material for a case study in community power. Here is a brief outline of urban spatial change in Berlin: In the 1970s and 1980s, there were many "alternative" living projects and "squats" throughout German cities, including Berlin. Many squats were dilapidated, but residents slowly fixed them up. According to many observers, such squats—populated by a mix of tenants from anarchists to utopian artists—were the scene of creative uses, including reasonably priced concerts by European rock bands. But lately, the Berlin real estate market heated up, and global investors are now buying up Berlin real estate. Already at least one Berlin squat has been transformed into luxury lofts. Discuss which theoretical perspective best explains this transformation.

4. **Local citizen participation**. In what ways do people in your community participate in local politics? Construct a questionnaire that asks respondents about any and all activities that might have political implications, including signing Internet petitions, acting as a block captain, heading a renters' or homeowners' association, attending political meetings, voting, etc. Try to get responses from a broad cross section of residents. After collecting these data, what do you conclude about the level of (legal) local political participation?

5. **Local citizen participation**. Attend several meetings of a city government, including local commissions. Focus on two controversial issues. If controversies—say, over placement of cell phone antennae and raising taxes—are discussed, how many people, representing what interests, attend and speak out? Do both issues attract the same proponents and opponents? How long have participants, representing various views, been vocal about the issue or issues? What costs, if any, have interested parties incurred (e.g., cash paid to retain lawyers, workdays missed to research the issue, family events unattended due to work on the issue)? What are the characteristics of the participants in terms of age, gender, work status, and race/ethnicity? What generalizations can you make concerning community power based on your attendance at these meetings?

SUGGESTIONS FOR FURTHER LEARNING

Few texts discuss the role of the ever-growing global illicit trade on local politics. Luckily, some studies do, including *Illicit* (Garden City, N.Y.: Anchor Books, 2006) by Moisés Naím, former Venezuelan minister of industry and trade. Naím examines the global reach of government-corrupting illicit trade (drug smuggling, organized crime, money laundering, etc.) and suggests that local governments can be seriously impacted by a wide range of illegal activities. He mentions, for example, a New York City banker's avoidance of taxes by sending money to offshore tax havens and a Chinese market vendor's selling counterfeit DVDs.

Like the illicit drug trade, few U.S. history books tell the story of a terrorist incident in the "first wave of terror" in the country. In 1920 a bomb was detonated on Wall Street, killing 39 people and injuring hundreds. For the full story, see Beverly Gage, *The Day Wall Street Exploded: A Story of America in Its First Age of Terror* (New York: Oxford University Press, 2009).

The classic statement of the elitist model of community power is Floyd Hunter's *Community Power Structure* (New York: Anchor, [1953] 1963). The classic opposing statement from the pluralist perspective is Robert Dahl's *Who Governs?* (New Haven, Conn.: Yale University Press, 1961).

For case studies of community power in the pluralist tradition, see Roscoe C. Martin, Frank Munger, et al., *Decisions in Syracuse: A Metropolitan Action Study* (Bloomington: Indiana University Press, 1961), and Wallace S. Sayre and Herbert Kaufman, *Governing New York City* (New York: Russell Sage, 1960).

For case studies in the elitist tradition, see Ritchie P. Lowry's study of "Micro City" (Chico, California), *Who's Running This Town?* (New York: Harper & Row, 1965), and August E. Hollingshead's study of Morris, Illinois (studied also by W. Lloyd Warner and named "Jonesville"), *Elmstown's Youth* (New York: Wiley, 1949).

For a critique of pluralist politics from a different point of view, see Charles Blattberg, *From Pluralist to Patriotic Politics: Putting Practice First* (New York: Oxford University Press, 2000). Blattberg, a Canadian political philosopher, argues essentially that reconciliation and conversation, not negotiation, is possible so that there are no winners or losers in politics.

For theories underlying community power models, see Harvey Molotch, "The City as a Growth Machine: Toward a Political Economy of Place," *American Journal of Sociology* 82(1976):309–330; Clarence N. Stone, *Regime Politics: Governing Atlanta, 1946–1988* (Lawrence: University Press of Kansas, 1989); and William G. Domhoff, *Who Rules America Now? A View for the '80s* (Englewood Cliffs, N.J.: Prentice Hall, 1983). (Note that these studies are decades old, reflecting the current lack of interest in the topic.) One recent assessment of Stone's work, *Power in the City: Clarence Stone and the Politics of Inequality* by Marion Orr and Valerie C. Johnson (Lawrence: University Press of Kansas, 2008), includes Stone's original article, "Urban Politics Then and Now." The collection not only serves as a primer on Stone's work but also includes the scholarly debates about power and inequality since the 1950s.

Nearly a generation ago, M. Gottdiener addressed what he considered to be *The Decline of Urban Politics* (Newbury Park, Calif.: Sage, 1987). He focused on the role of the "local state."

New York is not only the largest U.S. city; it is also a global city. No surprise, then, that the Big Apple has inspired a spate of studies. For a look at New York City in the 1980s and early 1990s, see John Hull Mollenkopf, *A Phoenix in the Ashes: The Rise and Fall of the Koch Coalition* (Princeton, N.J.: Princeton

University Press, 1993). Another study of a very different kind, first published in 1966, was republished in 2006: William Labov's foundational work of sociolinguistics, *The Social Stratification of English in New York City*, 2nd edition (New York: Cambridge University Press). In this pioneering work, brought up to date by Labov 40 years later, the Lower East Side, an area of great complexity and variability, remains the focus.

In their introduction to *The Urban Politics Reader* (New York: Routledge, 2006), authors and editors Elizabeth A. Strom and John H. Mollenkopf note various constraints on big-city mayors' decision making (e.g., the relocation of people and economic resources in a global economy) but still think that city officials have the "ultimate responsibility" to meet such challenges. In *The Restless City: A Short History of New York from Colonial Times to the Present* (New York: Routledge, 2006), history professor Joanne Reitano notes that New York City has long been a bastion of provocative figures and leaders from 1609 to 2001. She includes Mayor Rudy Giuliani in that group.

A conference on citizen participation and technology sponsored by the Korean Web site OhmyNews differentiated between "traditional" and "citizen's" media. According to reporter Gregory Daigle (March 6, 2007), here are some contrasts: traditional media lecture, citizen's media promote conversations; traditional media are one to many, citizen's media are many to many; traditional media are corporate/autocratic, citizen's media are democratic/collaborative; traditional media are run by elite professionals, citizen's media are consumer-driven (OhmyNews International Citizen Reporters' Forum, session 1, http://english.ohmynews.com/articleview/article_view.asp?article_class=11&no=305075&rel_no=1).

REFERENCES

Bachrach, Peter. 1967. *The Theory of Democratic Elitism: A Critique*. Boston: Little, Brown.

Banfield, Edward C. 1961. *Political Influence: A New Theory of Urban Politics*. New York: Free Press.

Beitel, K. E. 2004. "Transforming San Francisco: Community, capital, and the local state in the era of globalization, 1956–2001." Ph.D. diss. Department of Sociology, University of California, Davis.

Bostitis, David. 2002. "Black elected officials: A statistical summary, 2000." *Joint Center for Political and Economic Studies* (March 28): http://www.findarticles.com/p/articles/mi_qa3812/is_200205/ai_n9058139

Burama, Ian, and Avishai Margalit. 2004. *Occidentalism: The West in the Eyes of Its Enemies*. New York: Penguin.

Clift, Steven. 1999. "A wired agora: Minneapolis, citizen participation, the Internet and squirrels." http://www.publicus.net/present/agora.html

Cohen, Noam. 2008. "In Egypt, Wikipedia more than a hobby." *International Herald Tribune* (July 21):12.

Cottrell, William Fred. 1951. "Death by dieselization: A case study in the reaction to technological change." *American Sociological Review* 16:358–385.

Curry, Arlyce. 1978. Personal interview with Dick LeGates, Berkeley, Calif. (July 21).

Dahl, Robert. 1961. *Who Governs? Democracy and Power in an American City*. New Haven, Conn.: Yale University Press.

———. 2006. *On Political Equality*. New Haven, Conn.: Yale University Press.

DeLeon, Richard Edward. 1992. *Left Coast City: Progressive Politics in San Francisco, 1975–1991*. Lawrence: University Press of Kansas.

Domhoff, G. William. 1977. *Who Really Rules? New Haven and Community Power Reexamined*. New Brunswick, N.J.: Transaction Books.

———. 2005. "Why San Francisco is different: Progressive activists and neighborhoods have had a big impact." (September): http://plebe.ucsc.edu/sociology-twentieth new/whorulesamerica/power/san_francisco.html

Fleischmann, Arnold, and Joe R. Feagin. 1987. "The politics of growth-oriented urban alliances: Comparing old industrial and new Sunbelt cites." *Urban Affairs Quarterly* 23:207–232.

Glenny, Misha. 2008a. *McMafia: A Journey Through the Global Criminal Underworld*. New York: Alfred Knopf.

———. 2008b. Interview with Terry Gross, *Fresh Air*, NPR (April 17).

Hartman, Chester. 1973. *Yerba Buena: Land Grab and Community Resistance in San Francisco*. San Francisco: Glide.

Hunter, Floyd. [1953] 1963. *Community Power Structure: A Study of Decision Makers*. New York: Doubleday, Anchor.

————. 1980. *Community Power Succession.* Chapel Hill: University of North Carolina Press.

Jennings, M. Kent. 1964. *Community Influentials: The Elites of Atlanta.* Glencoe, Ill.: Free Press.

Johnson, Chalmers. 2004. *The Sorrows of Empire: Militarism, Secrecy, and the End of the Republic.* New York: Metropolitan Books.

————. 2007. *Nemesis: The Last Days of the American Republic.* New York: Metropolitan Books.

Kennedy, Ben, and Brian Stempel, 2006. Paper written for Duke University course, "The Internet and politics." http://www.reed.edu/~gronkep/webofpolitics/projects/techandparticipation/index.html

Krueger, Brian S., 2002. "Assessing the potential of Internet political participation in the United States: A resource approach." *American Politics Research,* 30(5):476–498.

Logan, John R., and Harvey Molotch. 1987. *Urban Fortunes: The Political Economy.* Berkeley: University of California Press.

Lynd, Robert S., and Helen M. Lynd. [1929] 1956. *Middletown.* New York: Harcourt, Brace & World.

————. 1937. *Middletown in Transition.* New York: Harcourt, Brace & World.

Melosi, Martin. "Dallas-Forth Worth: Marketing the metroplex." Pp. 162–195 in Richard M. Bernard and Bradley R. Rice, eds., *Sunbelt Cities: Politics and Growth since World War II.* Austin: University of Texas Press.

Moynihan, Daniel Patrick. 1969. *Maximum Feasible Misunderstanding.* New York: Free Press.

"On the record." 2008. *International Herald Tribune* (June 28–29):16.

Orwell, George. [1954] 2004. *Animal Farm.* London: Nick Hern Books.

Peng, Yali. 1994. "Intellectual fads in political science: The cases of political socialization and community power studies." *PS: Political Science and Politics* (March):100–108: http://www.jstor.org/view/10490965/ap020026/02a00220/3?frame=noframe&userID=a9e52087@berkeley.edu/01cc99331300501b88e85&dpi=3&config=jstor

Ren, Xuefei. 2008. "Forward to the past: Historical preservation in globalizing Shanghai." *City & Community* 7(1):23–43.

Rokkan, Stein. 1966. "Norway: numerical democracy and corporate pluralism." Pp. 70–115 in Robert A. Dahl, ed., *Political Oppositions in Western Democracies.* New Haven, Conn.:Yale University Press.

Rutgers Center for American Women and Politics, Eagleton Institute of Politics. 2009. "Fast facts." http://www.cawp.rutgers.edu/fast/levels_of_office/local-women

Sang-Hun, Choe. 2008. "Korean leader considers ways to rework government.". *New York Times:* http://www.nytimes.com/2008/06/11/world/asia/11korea.html?scp=3&sq=,%20Sang-Hun%20Choe%202008/,%20Korean%20Beef%20protesters%20and%20Internet&st=cse

Slane, Andrea. 2007. "Democracy, social space, and the Internet." *University of Toronto Law Journal* 57(1):81–105.

Soloman, Norman. 2007. "Let's face it: The warfare state is part of us." *Media Channel* (August 22): http://www.mediachannel.org/wordpress/2007/08/22/lets-face-it-the-warfare-state-is-part-of-us/

Stewart, Jon, and the writers of the *Daily Show.* 2006. *America (the Book): A Citizen's Guide to Democracy Inaction,* teacher's ed. New York: Warner Books.

Stone, Clarence N. 1989. *Regime Politics: Governing Atlanta, 1946–1988.* Lawrence: University Press of Kansas.

Vidich, Arthur, and Joseph Bensman. [1958] 1971. *Small Town in Mass Society: Class, Power, and Religion in a Rural Community.* Garden City, N.Y.: Doubleday.

Ward, Stephen, and Thierry Vedel. 2006. "Introduction: The potential of the Internet Revisited." *Parliamentary Affairs* 59(2):210–225: http://www.esri.salford.ac.uk/ESRCResearchproject/abstracts.php#paintro2006

Wayne, Leslie. 2008. "Obama sounds dirge for public financing." *International Herald Tribune* (June 21–22):4.

Wolfe, Tom. 1971. "Mau-mauing the flak catchers." Pp. 117–184 in *Radical Chic and Mau-Mauing the Flak Catchers.* New York: Bantam.

Zimmerman, Joseph F. Zimmerman, 1999. *The New England Town Meeting: Democracy in Action.* New York: Praeger.

SPACE AND PLACE

PART VI

Allan Jacobs

METROPOLITAN FORM AND SPACE

For the tourist, a city proudly presents its unique and shiny face—its Fisherman's Wharf, Empire State Building, or Eiffel Tower (called a "metal asparagus" when it opened in 1889; see http://fastrider.net/ France/EiffelTower/EiffelTower/htm, n.d.)). Typically, tour buses with oversized windows bypass a city's black eyes, such as the South Bronx or the waste-disposal center, popularly called a "garbage dump."

Geographers may be interested in the unique features of a city, asking how and why they happen to be there. David Harvey's inquiry (1989b) into the building of Sacré-Coeur, the grandiose church atop Paris's

Montmartre, is exemplary. But, in addition, geographers look for patterns in city form and space.

Walking around Big City, USA, and its edges, an astute observer might notice the following spatial features:

1. Residences of affluent and poor people segregated in different areas.
2. Lumberyards located outside the **central business district (CBD)**.
3. Shops offering specialty items or services, ranging from Nigerian wood carvings and evangelical religious books to income tax assistance, all situated in commercial areas.
4. Sprawling shopping malls, with hundreds of parking spaces, set in edge cities or postsuburbia.

These observations can be used to generate hypotheses (scientifically testable statements of relationship) about metropolitan form and space. Here is one hypothesis: People and activities are not randomly distributed throughout a city or metropolis; specific spatial patterns exist, influenced by such factors as the mix of commodities and services produced there. This hypothesis is confirmed by geographers who measure spatial patterns and theorize about why they take the forms they do.

But the concept of space is not the exclusive province of geographers. Indeed, after years of neglect, space is a hot topic in social theory and philosophy.

BRINGING SPACE BACK IN

In terms of its theoretical importance, space rivaled the spotted owl: It was almost extinct by the mid-twentieth century. Practical, political, and theoretical concerns—the seeming annihilation of space by time and a global economic system, to name just two—had marginalized the concept of space.

Then, starting in the 1970s, space was brought back into social theory in a big way. Likewise, it returned to popular consciousness, thanks to Earth Day and Google maps, among other events and sites.

Now, influential thinkers in a range of disciplines and hybrids (e.g., geography, city planning, economic sociology, and cultural theory) point to space as a key to understanding modern social, political, and economic life. As one book title succinctly put it, *Place Matters* (Dreier et al., 2004).

At the same time, however, some point to space's *decreasing* importance. In this view, the borderless Internet plus multilocational and multinational corporations make space less and less important.

HENRI LEFEBVRE'S INFLUENCE

The late Henri Lefebvre, a major intellectual figure in Europe (and a one-time Parisian taxi driver), played a key role in reviving the interest in space. A daring and creative thinker, Lefebvre developed a theory of space, and he introduced the role of politics in shaping people's attitudes about the city. His work influenced David Harvey and Manuel Castells, major contributors to what was (and is still) called the "new" urban paradigm. (*Note:* Hardly new, it is still called that. Joe R. Feagin published a book with "new" urban paradigm in the title in 1998, but most of the writings dated from 1982–1992.)

According to Lefebvre (1901–1991), space plays a preeminent role in modern societies. In his influential and demanding book *The Production of Space* ([1974] 1991), philosopher–urbanist–activist Lefebvre said that the effects of space may be observed on all planes—from the "arrangement of surfaces in a supermarket" to the "ordering of 'flows' within nations or continents" (412). Most important, Lefebvre said, we should be concerned "with space on a world scale." In his view, only by generating or producing a space can groups, classes, ideas, values, and political systems be recognized. For Lefebvre, space was much more than a built environment; it was also a force of production and an object of both consumption and political struggle.

This chapter draws on a number of disciplines and hybrids to better understand spatial patterns among and within cities. It begins with a discussion of the system of cities: how cities are arranged in relation to each other. Then, it examines the internal structure of the city: how spatial patterns are arranged within the modern U.S. city and its surrounding area.

THE SYSTEM OF CITIES

CENTRAL PLACE THEORY

Why is a city located at point A rather than at point B? Why are there so few big cities and so many small towns in a regional landscape?

Geographers have been asking such questions at least since 1826, when a German economic geographer, Johann von Thunen, published *Isolated State* ([1826] 1966). More than 100 years later, another German geographer, Walter Christaller, developed a comprehensive model: **central place theory** (Figure 16.2). This model suggests that, over space, a hierarchy of places develops in which a few large cities dominate bigger numbers of smaller cities. The upshot: "a dense network of evenly-spaced trade center towns that serve the local population" (Hudson, 1985:11).

Christaller's theory attempts to demonstrate a relationship between the number, importance, and distance of cities from one another within a geographical area or region. It deals with two key

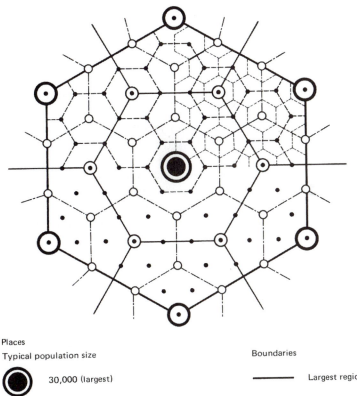

Places

Typical population size

- 30,000 (largest)
- 10,000 (large)
- 4,000 (medium)
- 2,000 (small)
- 1,000 (smallest)

Boundaries

- —— Largest region
- —— large region
- —·—· medium–size region
- —··—·· small region
- ----- smallest region

Fig. 16.2 CHRISTALLER'S CENTRAL PLACE THEORY. According to economic geographer Walter Christaller, the largest central place in the region illustrated (population 30,000) is the most important market center for a large, hexagonal region around it. Progresssively smaller central places lie at the center of a system of smaller, hexagonal market regions within the main market region. *Source:* Walter Christaller, *Central Places in Southern Germany* (Englewood Cliffs, N.J.: Prentice Hall, 1966), p. 66. Copyright 1933 by Gustav Fisher Verlag Jena. Reprinted by permission.

variables: city *importance* (roughly measured by population size) and *distance* to other cities and urban communities.

Briefly, Christaller's theory goes like this: A *central place* (a centrally located city or urban community) provides goods and services to people living in the surrounding region, commonly called a hinterland. A hierarchy of goods and services is available (ranging from the lowest to the highest order of services available), depending on the importance or population size of the city. Central places of the lowest order (small towns) serve only a nearby area. Central places of a higher order (larger towns and cities) serve a roughly hexagonal area covering a larger surrounding region; this region might contain several lower-order central places.

Central place theory conceives of cities as part of a regional landscape, not as self-sufficient economic entities. Various commodities and services must be exchanged. Some items will be "exported" from the city, such as banking services or manufactured goods. These will be exchanged for food and other things that the city "imports."

Traditionally, central place theorists use two measures to determine the level of economic interchange between a city and its outside world—**hinterland** and **range**. A city's hinterland is the surrounding area to which a city (central place) provides goods and services. A city's range is conceptualized as the area from which persons travel to the central place to purchase a service or merchandise, such as a baseball game or gasoline, offered there.

DOES CENTRAL PLACE THEORY WORK TODAY?

Unsurprisingly, Christaller's theory works best under the conditions that his model assumes: flat land areas with a uniformly distributed population and a relatively unspecialized economy. Thus, in places like Iowa in the 1930s, where these conditions existed, there was an observable hierarchy of cities: many hamlets, fewer villages, and many fewer towns.

Central place theory may have been correct in its basic predictions—for its time and place, such as a relatively unspecialized economy (Iowa in the 1930s). But the theory is silent on how such a system might have come about.

A generation ago, geographer John C. Hudson (1985) broke the silence in terms of the United States. Starting in the 1850s, Hudson said, railroad companies played an important role as deliberate designers of the settlement system on the prairies and plains of North America. For instance, in North Dakota, Hudson found that line-chains of towns were planned deliberately by those—with influence and money—able to realize their plans. Thus, the system of cities on the Great Plains resulted primarily from the railroads' actions to serve their own interests—not from natural evolution or chance. Nonetheless, the Plains' settlement pattern does match the predictions of central place theory.

But does central place theory predict settlement patterns *outside* agricultural regions? Does it explain where cities will be located in postindustrial society? In a word, no.

Central place theory does not explain the urban hierarchy in a global economy. To understand why, let's look at Iowa again, this time in the late 2000s, not the 1930s. First, the state's economy is no longer unspecialized; its top exports were not agricultural products but rather industrial machinery, computer equipment, and scrap. Second, Iowa's hinterland is the world. Iowa's products are exported widely, from Canada to China (United States–China Business Council, 2008).

Now, Iowa is typical, not an exception. Throughout the United States, millions of metropolitan and post-suburban jobs depend on exports to places outside the United States. For example, California's economy is deeply tied to world markets (U.S. Department of Commerce, 2007). Nearly one-fifth of all manufacturing workers in the state depended on exports for their jobs in 2003, and exports sustain thousands of California businesses. In one year (2006), California's export shipments of merchandise totaled $128 billion, ranking it second only to Texas ($151 billion) among the states in terms of total exports.

But the impact of exports on state economies is variable. In other words, some states are export-job winners, while others are losers. Ohio is one of the losers: Between 1999 and 2003, Ohio lost 191,000 jobs, mainly in the manufacturing sector and particularly in electronics-related industries (Honeck, 2004:4).

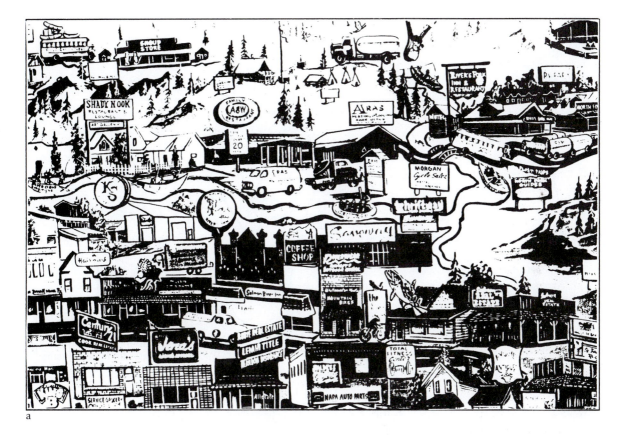

a

Fig. 16.3 ELECTRONIC RETAILING. Internet-based retailers (e.g., Amazon.com) play havoc with the concept of range. Instead of shopping nearby, (*a*) a consumer in Salmon, Idaho (a rural town of less than 3,000), where big department stores or discount stores don't exist, as this poster by Jerry Grusell shows, (*b*) or a consumer in Chicago, Illinois, can order many goods and services—from exercise equipment and specialized books to high-fashion outfits and psychic advice—sitting at home, in front of a computer screen. (Tim Teninty)

In brief, city systems in postindustrial economies like the United States are unlike those in southern Germany in the 1930s when Christaller conducted his research. One big difference is that *the U.S. economy today is dominated by large, multilocational firms*. Take the big-box store Costco. In the early 2000s, the multilocational Costco, headquartered in Issaquah, Washington, had 432 stories in the United States, Canada, the United Kingdom, Taiwan, Korea, Japan, and Mexico with sales of $41.7 billion and 102,000 employees worldwide (*Confectioner Magazine*, 2004).

A second difference concerns the *internationalization of hinterlands*. Christaller's model assumes regional hinterlands. Today, firms cross national boundaries so often that many sectors in the "U.S. economy" are not North American anymore. Fast-food franchisers like McDonald's are the most visible planetary enterprises. But many businesses have a global reach. For example, Baker & McKenzie was the world's largest law firm in 2000, employing 2,800 attorneys in 35 countries (Business Wire, 2000). This group, nicknamed "McFirm," is not a U.S. firm with foreign offices; it is an international firm with attorneys from at least 60 nations. Over 80 percent of the firm's lawyers practice outside the United States (Baker & McKenzie has served as a training ground for

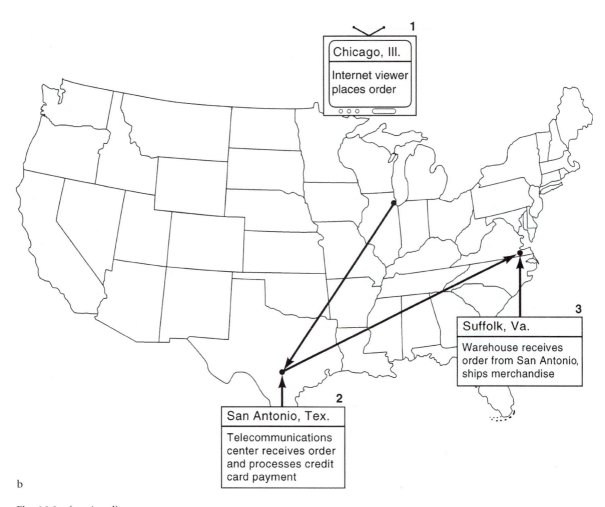

1 Chicago, Ill. — Internet viewer places order

2 San Antonio, Tex. — Telecommunications center receives order and processes credit card payment

3 Suffolk, Va. — Warehouse receives order from San Antonio, ships merchandise

b

Fig. 16.3 *(continued)*

future notables such as Christine Lagarde, former head of the firm, later appointed French minister of the economy and finance by President Sarkozy.)

The Internet has played a key role in extending business's global reach, thus changing the nature of the hinterland. And seemingly overnight. The Worldwide Web has become a vast marketplace that makes all physical boundaries—national as well as city, suburban, and state—easy to ignore. Companies big and small as well as individuals (including spammers from everywhere) troll the Internet for new customers (or marks).

Here is an indication of the Internet's swift, global commercial growth: In April 1993 there were 6,545 commercial users on the Net. One year later, the number had more than doubled—to 14,154 commercial users (in Lewis, 1994:3–6).

Since 1994, the number has grown exponentially. So has general use, which means there are many more potential customers everywhere! One market research firm found that 747 million people aged 15 and older used the Internet worldwide in January 2007, a 10 percent increase from January 2006. The United States had the largest number of users, with 153 million. In descending order, the next top users were located in the following countries: China, Japan, Germany, Britain, South Korea, France, India, Canada, and Italy (comScore Networks, 2007).

A third difference concerns *the growth of government intervention*. Christaller's model assumes relatively little government influence on business's location decisions. Now, however, state and local officials often play important roles, lobbying private corporations to locate in their state or city. For example, after California's governor personally phoned the president of a toy company in Denmark, the state legislature changed tax laws affecting non-U.S. companies, and a team of state–local, private–public officials promised over $7 million in assistance with marketing and roads if the company located outside San Diego. It did.

Lastly, *Christaller's model wrongly predicts the role of the biggest city, populationwise, in a system of cities*. If the model were correct, the largest city in a system of cities—in the United States, New York City—would contain the headquarters of the nation's largest business corporations. But in the 1970s only one-quarter of the 500 largest U.S. corporations were headquartered in New York City (Pred, 1977). By 1989, New York City had only 59 headquarters of the top 500 (Sassen, 1991:171). By 2007, the number had again declined: It had only 45 of the nation's largest corporations headquartered there (*Forbes*, 2007).

To conclude: In the national or global economy, central place theory neither explains nor predicts how the system of cities works. Briefly, the national economy has been reorganized by multilocational corporations, which have redefined the economic functions of cities and brought new patterns of urban development. From the viewpoint of corporate managers, postindustrial cities are interchangeable.

Christaller's hierarchy of cities, developed for a different time and place (one dominated by small towns and farms) no longer describes the urban hierarchy in postindustrial society. According to most social scientists today, the global urban system has been deeply influenced by increasing globalization and the economy's "informationalization."

THE U.S. SYSTEM OF CITIES

Looking at what he terms the "U.S. urban system," Ingolf Ivogeler, a professor of geography, argues that U.S. urban history can be divided into five phases, each characterized by its energy sources and transportation modes (Table 16.1). Ivogeler (2005)asserts that differences in energy sources and transportation modes result in distinctive critical locations and spatial patterns. Like many scholars, he credits information via the Internet and electronics as the key to recent city placement or growth.

Note that neither Ivogeler's schema nor Pred et al.'s (1977) evidence invalidates a key assumption underpinning central place theory: *Cities can't exist if residents do nothing but take in each other's laundry.* That is, for a city to stay viable, there must be economic exchange between it and the world outside. This remains the case for twenty-first century supercities just as it did for urban specks in a rural world some 5,000 years ago.

To paraphrase poet John Donne, no city is an island. Cities and their hinterlands are interdependent in terms of economic functions. Christaller, of course, assumed that hinterlands would depend essentially on a nearby central place. In recent years, other theorists reconceptualized the notion of hinterland, suggesting that the nation and the world can be a central place's hinterland.

CLASSIFYING CITIES BY FUNCTION

Two geographers, Chauncy Harris and Edward Ullman (1945:7), pioneered the effort to classify cities by function. They reasoned that cities fall into three types:

1. Cities as *central places* (performing comprehensive services for a surrounding area; these cities tend to be evenly spaced throughout the region).
2. *Transport cities* (performing "break-of-bulk" services; these cities tend to be arranged in linear patterns along rail lines and at seacoasts).
3. *Specialized function cities* (performing one service, such as mining or recreation, for large areas).

Harris and Ullman did not think that U.S. cities were unifunctional. Rather, most cities would perform a combination of functions, and the relative importance of each factor would vary from city to city. New York City, for instance, was seen as a principal center for wholesaling and retailing (central place type), a great

TABLE 16.1 DEVELOPMENT OF THE U.S. URBAN SYSTEM

Time Line	Energy Sources	Transport	City Location	Spatial Pattern	Typical cities
Pre-1820	Humans, animals, wind, water	Horses and wagons on dirt roads; flatboats on rivers, and sailing ships on oceans	Seaports on river mouths; agricultural villages	Dispersed in agricultural areas; linear dispersion along transshipment points	Boston, New York, Philadelphia, Hartford, Charleston
1820–1840s	Water power, wooden steam engines	Steamboats on rivers and canals	Interior ports on rivers, lakes, canals	Linear dispersion along major waterways	Cleveland, Buffalo, Pittsburgh
1850–1860s	Coal-burning steam engines	Iron railroads connect nodes— but not the nation	Interior rail nodes at lake, sea, and river ports	Connected to national markets	Chicago
1870–1920s	Coal, steam, and electricity	Steel railroads connect the nation, and quickly	Rail centers without regard to water sites	Dispersed in West and South, near natural resources	Dallas, San Francisco
1930s to present	Internal combustion engines, natural gas and oil	Various kinds. Since the 1980s, particularly information via electronics and the Internet	Highways, airports	Major new metropolitan centers in the periphery.	Los Angeles, Miami

Source: Adapted from http://www.uwec.edu/geography/Ivogeler/w111/metro1.htm.

port (transport type), and a manufacturing center (specialized function type).

NEWER SPATIAL MODELS

Essentially, central place theory and functional classification sought to answer these questions: What types of economic functions will occur in a city of a given size? How does this city relate to its hinterland?

More recent theory addresses a different question: Where does a city (or metropolitan region) with a particular production–consumption profile fit into a national or world system of cities?

Starting in the 1970s, social theorists have tried to understand the impact of large-scale changes on the organization of metropolitan space. Generally, theorists point to the following shifts to explain why a world urban system exists: (1) *economic restructuring*, the transformation from manufacturing to services-information and deindustrialization in so-called advanced economies; (2) *the new international division of labor* ("Needle," see Chapter 5); and (3) *the internationalization of capital*. A variety of social scientists— geographers, urban planners, political scientists,

political sociologists—have been writing about the world urban system in recent decades.

Theorists do not always agree on major issues, including this key question: Is space a mere reflection of social forces or an independent element of social life? Nevertheless, these urban theorists tend to share a vocabulary and a multidisciplinary approach called the "political economy perspective" or the "new urban paradigm." (As mentioned earlier, the "new" urban paradigm is not so new anymore. But it has not been renamed.)

Two models based on this new urban paradigm were reviewed in Chapter 5: the new international division of labor (Needle) and Logan and Molotch's typology of U.S. cities. Now, let's consider a composite model that focuses on the global network of cities. This composite model parallels the work of Manuel Castells and John Mollenkopf, discussed at some length in Chapter 19.

THE GLOBAL NETWORK OF CITIES

What follows is, first, a brief summary of the political economy model of the global network of cities and, second, one group's attempt to rank world cities according to four key functions: accountancy, advertising, banking/finance, and law. First, a summary of the political economy model.

The Political Economy Model

This summary is based primarily on ideas from these sources: Michael Peter Smith and Joe R. Feagin's introduction to *The Capitalist City* ([1987] 1989) and Saskia Sassen's work, including *The Global City: New York, London, Tokyo* (1991), a book widely praised as being "central" to understanding the postindustrial world, and her article "Sharp-Elbowed Cities" (2008). (Sassen is widely respected. Another book, *Territory, Authority, Rights: From Medieval to Global Assemblages* [2006a], has garnered similar praise. One academic reviewer called it "brilliant and pioneering," "a stunning achievement." She writes for a wider audience too, including *Newsweek International* readers.)

First, a note about authors who focus on global systems of cities. Scholars who think about global **systems of cities** tend to criss-cross disciplinary lines. Feagin is exemplary, as noted in Chapter 2. But Sassen is in a class by herself. She is a one-person model of globalism and interdisciplinarity: Now a U.S. citizen, Sassen has held university professorships in several disciplines or fields (sociology, urban planning) in the United States, and she has also taught at the London School of Economics. She was born in Holland, grew up in Buenos Aires, studied in Rome, earned a Ph.D. in economics and sociology in the United States, served as a postdoctoral fellow at the Center for International Affairs at Harvard University, and then studied philosophy in France. She grew up speaking five languages.

We now turn from Sassen's global-interdisciplinary background to her global-interdisciplinary perspective on cities. Although her personal history and interdisciplinary background may differ from theirs, she essentially shares a perspective with theorists Smith and Feagin.

According to Sassen, Smith, and Feagin, modern capitalism is a global network of both corporations and cities. At the top of the global urban hierarchy are *first-tier* cities (also called "world command" or "global" cities). These include Tokyo, London, and New York. First-tier cities have "extraordinary concentrations of top corporate decision-makers representing financial, industrial, commercial, law and media corporations" (Smith and Feagin, [1987] 1989:3), and they perform central place functions at the global level (Sassen, 1991:169). Otherwise stated, first-tier cities are the brains of the global economy.

Spatially, the transnational corporate web is grounded in global cities. Global cities themselves constitute a system, particularly in terms of international finance, investment, and real estate markets. This means that what Sassen calls "transnational spaces" (spaces outside the control of any state or national government) exist within first-tier cities. For example, neither the state of New York nor the U.S. government can control the wages or working conditions of the employees of New York City–based multinational corporations who work in Mexico, China, or other offshore locations.

Socially, it means that *the world economy has created a two-tier class structure inside global cities*: People who live there are almost exclusively highly paid professionals in financial and "producer services" (e.g., lawyers, accountants, ad executives) or low-wage workers (e.g., janitors and truck drivers) who ensure the smooth functioning of the financial and producer service sectors.

Only a handful of cities rate first-tier status. Most occupy niches lower down in the world urban hierarchy.

Non-first tier cities can be of several types. These types range from *specialized command cities* (which concentrate the headquarters of a particular industry, e.g., rubber companies in Akron, Ohio), *divisional command cities* (which concentrate major divisions of top firms, e.g., oil companies in Houston), *specialized manufacturing cities* (e.g., car manufacturing in Birmingham, England), *state command cities* (e.g., Brasilia, Washington, D.C.), to many *difficult-to-classify cities* that perform diverse economic and state functions (e.g., Mexico City, Singapore, and São Paulo). All types are interconnected through an organizational web of transnational corporations and their suppliers. (See also Chapter 5.)

In 2008 Sassen noted that the network of global cities had expanded dramatically from the 1980s when globalization took off. Then, only three cities—New

York, London, and Tokyo—acted like "global cities," that is, as bridges between "vast emerging global markets and national economies" (2008:27). By 2008, she says, there were more than 20 major global cities and 50 minor ones: "the biggest shift is the ascendancy of Asia and Europe relative to [the United States]" (2008:27). She notes that between 2006 and 2008 new cities rose alongside traditional powerhouses such as London and Paris, so much so that several U.S. rivals (e.g., Los Angeles) were displaced out of the top 15 cities. Meantime, Madrid, Amsterdam, Copenhagen, Sydney, Hong Kong, and Singapore rose to greater heights on a scale measuring cities' fitness to thrive in the global economy. She concludes that "The loss of position of U.S. cities is part of a systemic evolution as diverse parts of the world rise." She concludes that "the new urban order is not a zero-sum game" (2008:27).

To conclude: The political economy model or "new" (in quotes because it is no longer new) urban paradigm assumes that corporate and city networks are inextricably intertwined in a capitalist world market. In this model, theorists wrote (a generation ago) that the top 500–1,000 multinational corporations "have created an integrated, worldwide network of production, exchange, finance and corporate services arranged in a complex hierarchical system of cities" (Smith and Feagin, [1987] 1989:6).

Sassen ([1994] 2006b:2) argues that analysts and politicians who proclaimed the end of cities in the late twentieth century, due to "massive developments in telecommunications and the ascendance of information industries," were wrong. She thinks that in the information economy cities have not been made obsolete. Rather, some have added new economic functions and revivified their CBDs.

A Related, Functional Approach to Ranking World Cities

According to Sir Peter Hall, a preeminent contemporary geographer and urbanist (b. 1932), by 1991 so-called developed countries had economies based on the shift from manufacturing to services and information handling. This shift, Hall thinks, increased the importance of cities at the top of the urban hierarchy—the so-called world or global cities. (Ranking

cities is not new. It dates at least to city planner Patrick Geddes's 1915 book *Cities in Evolution*.)

With echoes of Harris and Ullman's functional approach to the internal structure of cities (discussed later in this chapter), Hall wrote that *The World Cities* ([1966] 1967) are cities that perform multiple roles, including being centers of international and national political power; international and national trade; banking, insurance, and finance; "advanced" professional activity such as medicine, law, and higher education; information gathering and diffusion (notably by publishing and the mass media); and arts, culture, and entertainment.

Many scholars credit Hall's analysis ([1966] 1997) of London, Paris, Randstad (in Holland), the Rhine-Ruhr, Moscow, New York, and Tokyo as the starting point for studying the global urban hierarchy. Although he did not pioneer the concept of the world city, Sir Peter Hall put the concept of "world city" on the agenda of contemporary urban studies (Beaverstock et al., 1999).

As noted, many scholars think that Hall's work on world cities was seminal. Building on Hall's work, plus the work of others, particularly the aforementioned Saskia Sassen (1991, [1994] 2006b), members of the Globalization and World Cities Study Group and Network (GaWC) in England have ranked world cities on the basis of four key functions: accounting, advertising, banking, and law. Cities are then scored on the basis of these key services, considered "advanced producer services." The total score provides a measure of a city's "world city-ness."

At the top of the global urban hierarchy, the GaWC geographers say, are 10 "alpha" world cities. These are followed by 10 second-tier, or "beta," world cities. On the third-tier are 35 "gamma" world cities (Beaverstock et al., 1999).

In 1999, GaWC found 55 world cities, mainly in three geographical areas: northern America, western Europe, and pacific Asia. In addition, they found another 68 cities showing evidence of world city formation (see Table 16.2).

Arguably, the biggest contribution of the GaWC group thus far is their inventory of cities below the highest level, that is, beta and gamma cities. Combined, the alpha, beta, and gamma inventory

TABLE 16.2   THE GaWC INVENTORY OF WORLD CITIES

A. Alpha world cities (prime cities)

12: London, Paris, New York, Tokyo

10: Chicago, Frankfurt, Hong Kong, Los Angeles, Milan, Singapore

B. Beta world cities (second-tier, major world cities)

9: San Francisco, Sydney, Toronto, Zurich

8: Brussels, Madrid, Mexico City, São Paulo

7: Moscow, Seoul

C. Gamma world cities (third-tier, minor world cities)

6: Amsterdam, Boston, Caracas, Dallas, Dusseldorf, Geneva, Houston, Jakarta, Johannesburg, Melbourne, Osaka, Prague, Santiago, Taipei, Washington

5: Bangkok, Beijing, Montreal, Rome, Stockholm, Warsaw

4: Atlanta, Barcelona, Berlin, Buenos Aires, Budapest, Copenhagen, Hamburg, Istanbul, Kuala Lumpur, Manila, Miami, Minneapolis, Munich, Shanghai

Note: Cities are ordered in terms of "world city-ness" with values ranging from 1–12 with 12 being the highest rating.

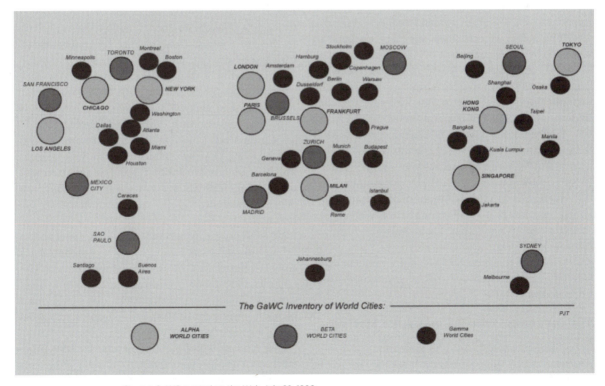

Source: GaWC, posted on the Web July 28, 1999.

presents a world geography of global service centers. The researchers find a "remarkable, regional concentration," which they take as an expression of "uneven globalization."

Note that in the GaWC schema, population size of a world city is not key. What is key is that it is (or is not) a "postindustrial production site." In other words, *a world city* (Sassen's term) *has global competence in advanced producer services*.

We now move from the political economy model of how cities relate to one another in a world system and the related GaWC approach (one that stresses functions, not population size) to world city ranking to another topic: spatial patterns *within* cities. Here, we focus on U.S. cities.

Why not discuss cities all over the globe? Because internal city structure varies enormously. For example, Kyoto's spatial pattern is modeled on a grid from imperial China (Chapter 4), and European cities created long before industrialism, such as Paris, tend to be ringed by poorer suburbs.

Note: The "geography of recession" may be reshaping city patterns. So thinks urban theorist Richard Florida. He projects, for example, the continued rise of mega-regions and the demise of many U.S. Rustbelt cities. Florida writes that the recession marks not only the end of a chapter in U.S. economic history but "the end of a whole way of life" (2009). He concludes that whatever the U.S. government may do, "there will be a concentration of output, jobs, and innovation in a smaller number of bigger cities and city-regions" and that "Band-Aids and bailouts cannot change that."

Here, we'll focus on two key questions: How are U.S. cities internally structured? Why are they structured that way?

THE INTERNAL STRUCTURE OF U.S. CITIES

Fancy houses, skyscrapers, public housing, factories, and warehouses. What part of town are they in? As we hypothesized at the beginning of this chapter, they are not located just anywhere by chance.

To determine exactly where they are located requires empirical investigation. It means, first of all, going out and observing what facilities do or do not exist in different locations.

In our effort to understand how people and their various activities are distributed over space, we do not have to start from scratch. Since the 1920s, North American social scientists have collected data and constructed models that attempt to describe and explain patterns of urban space. First, let's look at the three classic models of the **internal structure** of the U.S. industrial-capitalist city: the concentric zone model, the sectoral model, and the multiple nuclei model.

CLASSIC MODELS

Burgess's Concentric Zone Model

University of Chicago sociologist Ernest W. Burgess pioneered the systematic study of the North American city's internal structure. In the 1920s, he developed a model of internal city structure and urban growth: the so-called Burgess **concentric zone model** or hypothesis. This model grew out of Burgess's fascination with Chicago, a remarkable city at a remarkable time. Early in the last century, Chicago—the laboratory for the **Chicago school of sociology**—was a city in transition. The population change in the city over a very short period of time was noteworthy. In 1880 the emerging metropolis had about 500,000 inhabitants. Ten years later, the population had more than doubled.

Chicago was (and remains) a city of ethnic diversity. By 1920, there were large communities of Czechs, Italians, eastern European Jews, Swedes, Germans, Irish, Italians, Lithuanians, Poles, and increasing numbers of African Americans (4.1 percent of the population at that time).

The Windy City resembled a vast collection of urban villages, each having its own churches, social clubs, politicians, newspapers, welfare stations, schools, and restaurants. Alongside this ethnic diversity was prejudice, especially against the newer immigrants from southern and eastern Europe, and a desire to residentially segregate the foreign stock.

As Chicago's population increased, these urban villages or *enclaves* (enclosed territories) grew, contracted, or shifted. Burgess was impressed with the great differences among various city neighborhoods and tried to make sense of the spatial patterns and cultural life in these communities. He speculated that there was a pattern to the way these neighborhoods grew or shifted, just as there was in plant and animal communities (Park et al., 1925:47–62). This theoretical framework—that cities, like plant and animal communities, have a characteristic organization and develop territorially as a result of competition for space—is called "**urban ecology**" or, more broadly, "human ecology."

Urban ecologists are concerned with the study of the spatial distribution of people and institutions in cities. This distinctive perspective originated with members of the Chicago school, particularly Robert Park and Ernest W. Burgess. It was continued by such researchers as geographer Brian J. L. Berry and sociologist John Kasarda (1977). (In recent years, both turned their attention to other topics not traditionally covered by urban ecology, particularly globalization. Kasarda is perhaps best known for pioneering the concept of "aerotropolis" or airport cities, that is, cities that take advantage of major airports which act as key nodes for global production and business.)

Key concepts in this perspective include competition for a place in urban space, residential segregation, **invasion**, and **succession**. Implicit hypotheses in urban ecology include the following:

1. Cultural changes in a city are correlated and reflected in changes in spatial, territorial organization.
2. There is an intimate relationship between the social and moral order in a city and physical space, between physical distance and social distance, and between residential proximity and social equality.

Urban ecologists investigate the interrelationships between physical space and the social order at three levels: neighborhood, city, and region.

Working from the perspective of urban ecology, Burgess developed and refined a zonal model. The city can be conceived as a series of concentric circular zones of typical combinations of land use (Figure 16.4). This model was derived from empirical research through inductive reasoning processes. Yet, as noted in Chapter 3, Burgess worked from a theoretical framework (urban ecology) so that the concentric zone model is a product of both inductive and deductive reasoning processes.

Here is what Burgess says about his model: "In the growth of the city we have differentiated the series of

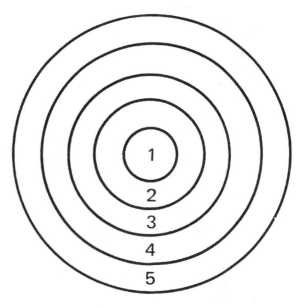

Fig. 16.4 BURGESS'S CONCENTRIC ZONE MODEL OF THE U.S. INDUSTRIAL CITY. In this dartboard, zone 1 = the CBD, 2 = wholesale and light manufacturing and lower-class residential, 3 = working-class residential, 4 = middle-class residential, and 5 = commuter's zone.

concentric zones which is one way of indicating as the city expands outward from its center, how each successive zone tends to encroach upon the further outlying zones" (Burgess and Bogue, 1964:11).

Burgess saw the city as containing five successive zones. Zone I is the center of business and civic life. Zone II surrounds zone I; it is the zone-in-transition, where "areas of residential deterioration caused by the encroaching of business and industry from Zone I" are found. It is a district of rooming houses, slums, and artists' colonies. Zone III contains duplexes or two-family housing where immigrants and second-generation families (the children of immigrants) live. Zone IV houses "small businessmen, professional people, clerks, and salesmen," who live in apartments and shop at neighborhood shopping centers. Zone V consists of a ring of bedroom suburbs (Burgess, [1923] 1925:114–123).

This zonal model doesn't just describe spatial patterns; it contains an implicit hypothesis on the relationship of urban space to social order. Burgess thought that physical location and people's social background are connected in city space. Taking one example—family type—Burgess noted that zone I (the CBD) is mostly a "homeless men's region", zone II is "the habitat of the emancipated family", zone III is "the natural soil of the patriarchal family transplanted from Europe", zone IV provides "the favorable environment for the equalitarian family", and zone V is "without question the domain of the [female-centered] family" ([1923] 1925:114–123).

What, then, is the relationship between physical location and social background? The model postulates an inverse relationship between central location and an urbanite's socioeconomic status (SES). That is, the higher up on the social ladder, the farther the person lives from zone I.

In brief, then, *the zonal model hypothesizes that where people live depends on their position on the social ladder.* If this is correct, we should be able to predict changes in urban residence patterns. For instance, we should expect a relationship between social mobility and physical space. Thus, we could predict that as people move up the social ladder, they move out from the city center. And many urban ecology studies conducted in the 1920s showed that this was indeed the case. Immigrant groups first settled in zone II, the zone-in-transition, and moved to outlying zones as they moved up socioeconomically. Then, other new migrants to the city would replace the groups that moved up—and out. Such was the succession of residential movements in the city.

A classic illustration of succession is found in Lowell and other textile mill towns of nineteenth-century Massachusetts. First the English, then the Irish after them, then the Czechs and central Europeans, and finally the Italians, Poles, and other southern and eastern European immigrants resided near the CBD. Over the generations, as each group moved up the SES ladder (say, from unskilled worker to skilled laborer to first-line supervisor and perhaps to manager), its residence moved farther out. As one group moved up and out, its homes were sold or rented to a group below it on the social ladder. Thus, various groups succeeded one another on the same plots of ground. (*Update*: From the 1980s to 2000, Lowell went from former mill town to former technology center to former high-unemployment center to newly prosperous tech-service center. In the 1980s, new groups, including 20,000 Cambodians, were living near the CBD. By 2000, Lowell also had significant numbers of Laotians, Vietnamese, and Hispanics, particularly Puerto Ricans).

The zonal model contains another hypothesis that concerns urban growth. It postulates that cities and towns tend to expand radially from their CBD.

All hypotheses in the zonal model grow out of one basic assumption: that economic competition is the chief organizing agent of human communities. Darwin thought that competition in the struggle for existence is the key variable in the organization of animal communities. *Burgess thought that economic competition played a similar role in human affairs and believed that it was expressed in terms of a struggle over space.*

According to Burgess, people and business activities tend to be separated into rather homogeneous subareas of a city, and this segregation into so-called natural areas is part of the competition for space. That is, these homogeneous natural areas are not planned but result from the workings of the self-regulating economic market (Adam Smith's "invisible hand," Chapter 3).

To Burgess, then, market forces are the key determinants of a city's internal structure. On this point, most urban land economists and urban geographers agreed with Burgess. Many still do. Others developed different models of city structure, however, including two competing models.

Hoyt's Sectoral Model

In the 1930s, real estate economist Homer Hoyt looked at the residential patterns of 142 U.S. cities. As Hoyt organized his data, he observed spatial patterns that didn't fit Burgess's model. Here were Hoyt's main criticisms of the concentric zone model:

1. The retail shopping center, not the financial center, is the central point in most cities.
2. The wholesale and light manufacturing zone adjoins the CBD but does not encircle it.
3. Heavy industry tends to follow river valleys and riverfronts, bays or deep tidal basins, or outer belts. New transportation technology is the

key factor here, for it is no longer necessary for industry to locate in a concentric pattern close to the center of the city.

4. Working-class people tend to locate near industry. However, factories *do not* form a concentric circle around the CBD; neither do the workers' homes.

5. High-rent areas do not form a complete circle around the outer edge of the city.

6. Commuter housing takes the form of scattered, isolated communities; it is not a zone at all. (1939:17–23).

Hoyt's data did more than conflict with Burgess's hypothesis. They suggested an alternative model of the industrial city: a **sectoral model**. This model, pictured in Figure 16.5, describes U.S. cities as organized in wedges of activity moving outward from the city center, particularly along rail lines, roads, trolley tracks, and other transportation corridors.

Hoyt found that the rent structure of housing also tended to be organized by sectors, not zones. Thus, rents along a transport line moving out from the center of the city were often similar. A high-rent wedge might start near the center of the city and follow an exclusive boulevard out to the city's edge. A low-rent wedge might follow the railroad corridor.

Harris and Ullman's Multiple Nuclei Model

Geographers Chauncy Harris and Edward L. Ullman (1945) developed another model of urban form that departs significantly from both the concentric zone and sectoral models. They based their **multiple nuclei model** on the idea that cities develop not one but many nuclei (centers) of activity (Figure 16.6).

According to Harris and Ullman, four factors cause the development of multiple nuclei:

1. Certain activities need specialized facilities (e.g., a port needs a waterfront).

2. Similar activities tend to cluster together (e.g., financial institutions group together on Wall Street in New York City).

3. Some unlike activities are incompatible (e.g., an auto-assembly plant and an entertainment district would not be good neighbors).

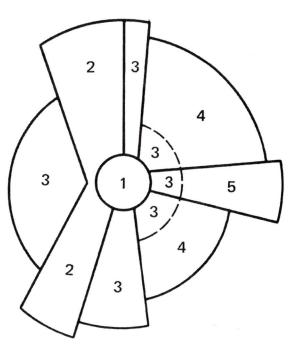

Fig. 16.5 HOYT'S SECTORAL MODEL OF THE U.S. INDUSTRIAL CITY. Zone 1 = CBD, 2 = wholesale and light manufacturing, 3 = lower-class residential, 4 = middle-class residential, 5 = upper-class residential. (Adapted from Chauncy Harris and Edward L. Ullman, "The nature of cities." *Annals of the American Academy of Political and Social Science* 242:13, fig. 5. Copyright by the American Academy of Political and Social Science, 1945. Reprinted by permission of the publisher and Chauncy Harris.

4. Certain activities cannot compete financially for the most desirable sites (e.g., lower-class housing and warehousing cannot afford to locate in high-rent districts).

HOW USEFUL ARE THE CLASSIC MODELS?

The three models of urban form and growth may shed some light on spatial patterns in some U.S. cities. But over the years, critics have raised the following criticisms of their usefulness in understanding U.S. cities:

1. *No general model is possible.* No city is so neatly organized that it totally fits some theoretical model. Physical features such as hills and lakes serve to distort expected spatial patterns.

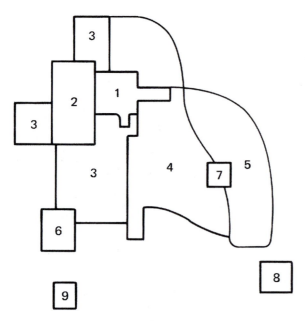

Fig. 16.6 HARRIS AND ULLMAN'S MULTIPLE NUCLEI MODEL OF THE U.S. INDUSTRIAL CITY. Zone 1 = CBD, 2 = wholesale and light manufacturing, 3 = lower-class residential, 4 = middle-class residential, 5 = upper-class residential, 6 = heavy manufacturing, 7 = outlying business district, 8 = dormitory suburb, 9 = industrial suburb. (Adapted from Chauncy Harris and Edward L. Ullman, "The nature of cities." *Annals of the American Academy of Political and Social Science* 242:13, fig. 5. Copyright by the American Academy of Political and Social Science, 1945. Reprinted by permission of the publisher and Chauncy Harris.

2. *The models are time- and place-bound.* The models, constructed between the early 1920s and mid-1940s, apply to only some North American cities in the era of industrial capitalism. They cannot explain or predict spatial patterns in postindustrialism. Nor do they explain or predict urban land use outside of western Europe and North America, which evolved in ways that have little to do with market forces. For example, the spatial development of Lagos, Nigeria; Brasilia, Brazil; and New Delhi, India, was influenced by political, military, and symbolic factors (e.g., colonialists' desire for social control, imperial or nationalist pride).

3. *The models neglect noneconomic values.* The classic models are based on economic logic; they

overlook sentiment, local culture, social movements, and politics as influences on spatial patterns. (Also, see 2 above.)

First, let's focus on the last major criticism: the models' economic bias. From different angles, Walter Firey, Gerald Suttles, and Mike Davis all argue that the models are economistic. Other critics say that politics affects land use and that this major factor is missing from the models. Next, let's look at two other possible paths to understanding city space: (1) social area analysis, an approach to studying urban growth and differentiation that implies a critique of the classic models, and (2) computer modeling as a method of describing and generalizing about urban space. Finally, let's look at a recent spatial model of metropolitan space.

Firey's Critique: The Classic Models Are Too Deterministic

An important critic of the classic models, sociologist Walter Firey (1947), argued long ago that city land-use patterns are not based purely on deterministic, economic considerations. He claims that such nonrational factors as *sentiment* and *symbolism* influence city shape.

Looking around Boston, Firey noted that actual land use didn't fit the patterns predicted by any of the classic models. For instance, old churches and the Boston Common (a public park) are located on very expensive land, and low-density eighteenth-century redbrick buildings stand on Beacon Hill, a high-status, high-rent residential district. If the models were correct, none of these should have been standing; they would have been torn down to make way for higher-density uses in the economic competition for space.

Firey concluded that the classic models couldn't account for noneconomic considerations: people's sentimental attachment to urban landmarks, whether their existence made economic sense or not. He rejected several notions inherent in the classic models: (1) that physical space can be divorced from cultural values, (2) that land use blindly follows some sort of Darwinian economic imperative, and (3) that people passively accept whatever the market dictates. Many events offer support for Firey's views. Consider, for example, the numerous instances where

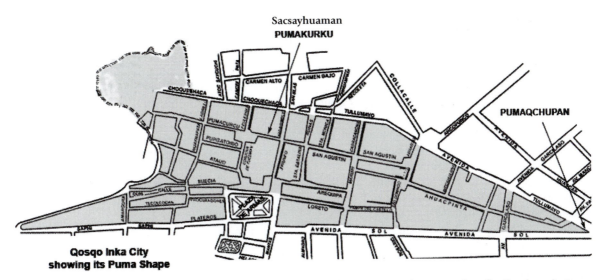

Fig. 16.7 A RARE CITY SHAPE. Rarely is a city shaped like an animal. Cuzco, Peru, is an exception. (In Quechua, the Incan language still spoken by many Peruvians today, Qosqo [Cuzco] means "navel of the world." The city was once the capital of the Inca Empire, located at the empire's center.) In the early 1400s, Pachucutec, an Incan politician and urban developer, designed Cuzco in the shape of the body of a puma (a mountain lion). The puma's "head" (added here) may have been a temple to the sun god at nearby Sacsayhuaman. Spanish conquistadors conquered Cuzco in 1534, razing Incan temples and using their stones to build Catholic churches and mansions for themselves. Today, the puma shape remains intact. (Tim Teninty)

historic-preservation societies have saved buildings from the wrecker's ball.

To correct for the economic determinism of the human ecologists' classic models, Firey called for an approach he termed "cultural ecology." This approach, in contrast to urban ecology, would take into account specific cultural and historical factors that influence a city's land-use patterns.

Local Culture Counts!

Sociologist Gerald D. Suttles (1984) agreed with Firey: The classic models left cultural values out. But Suttles thought that Firey himself didn't give culture its due. According to Suttles, Firey treated culture as a kind of leftover—an intangible residue. By contrast, Suttles suggested making local culture an integral element of cultural ecology, not a mere residual factor.

By "culture," Suttles meant everything from what people put in their museums to what they write on their T-shirts. And, Suttles wrote, some cities have "alot of local culture":

> songs that memorialize their great streets or side streets, homes once occupied by the famous or infamous, a distinctive dialect or vocabulary, routine festivals and parades that selectively dramatize the past, novels, dirty lyrics, pejorative nicknames, special holidays, dead heroes, evangelical moralists, celebrated wastrels, and so on.
>
> *(1984:284)*

According to Suttles, cities with a great deal of local culture tend to have a strong self-image, replete with icons of entrepreneurial success and ethnic mobility, historic districts, corporate images, and representations of civic life. We might add that a city's sports team and its larger-than-life players bestow identity.

Other researchers also conclude that local culture counts. For example, Molotch et al. (2000) studied Santa Barbara and Ventura, two California towns that confronted "big events and mundane happenings" with very different results. They found that local history helps to produce a particular "character," which over time constitutes a local "tradition."

At the same time, quick shifts in city identity can occur. Take, for example, Bilbao, Spain. Less than a generation ago, Bilbao was a grimy industrial town. Now, it is a destination. What sparked the change?

One building—its Frank Gehry-designed Guggenheim Museum. Next may be cities in the oil-rich United Arab Emirates (UAE): spectacular buildings planned for the city-state of Dubai; a second Louvre to be built in Abu Dhabi, the UAE's capital and the richest city in the world. Imported art treasures will no doubt change these city identities, bringing glory to once-barren desert outposts. Local governments may also hope that these buildings are investments in tourism, bringing planeloads of high-end tourists.

It may seem bizarre, but urban traffic accidents can be a mark of local culture too. New York City, for instance, has a highly unusual pattern of car victims: In the United States as a whole, the fatal victim of a city traffic accident is six times more likely to be a driver or a passenger than a pedestrian. But in New York City, about 50 percent of the victims are pedestrians. Why? Perhaps because pedestrians and drivers challenge one another more often than in other cities. That is, New York City has a local culture of challenge. Typically, cars "win" in New York City. In other words, one of New York City's traffic problems may be "that it is filled with New Yorkers" (Wald, 1993:1).

For a variety of reasons, including newness, many cities remain "nonentities." Suttles does not name any such nonentity, but Gertrude Stein did. In a famous putdown of Oakland, California, her onetime hometown, she remarked, "There is no there there" (Stein [1937] 2004, Ch.4).

Recognizing local culture as part of the objective realm and integrating it into the ecological approach, Suttles argues, may help to explain some aspects of city life. For one thing, he suggests, we can better understand why some places resist land redevelopment while others do not.

Mike Davis's Update: The Ecology of Fear

Mike Davis (1992a) sees Burgess's ecological model as a tribute to social Darwinism. To Davis, author of *City of Quartz: Excavating the Future in L.A.* ([1990] 1992b), Burgess's model is a "combination of half-moon and dart board...[that] represents the five concentric zones into which the struggle for the survival of the fittest (as imagined by Social Darwinists) supposedly sorts urban social classes and housing types" (3).

Davis offered his own zonal model, remapping the zones not of Chicago but of Los Angeles after the so-called Rodney King riots in 1992. Davis kept such factors as class and race, but he added what he calls a "decisive new factor" in understanding the ecology of Los Angeles: *fear*. Fear, he wrote a decade before 9/11, was eating the soul of the city, and different groups coped by adopting "security strategies and technologies according to their means (1992a).

In the early 1990s, Davis wrote that a new species of spatial enclave was emerging in Los Angeles: *social control districts*. These districts, found in Burgess's zones I and II, included *abatement districts* (e.g., a prostitution abatement zone), which extend traditional police power over industries and behaviors deemed "noxious"; *containment districts* (e.g., the core's "homeless containment district"), which "quarantine potentially epidemic social problems"); and *enhancement districts* (e.g., drug-free zones), which add legal penalties to crimes committed near public institutions.

Outside the inner rings, Davis suggested that some "overclass" Los Angeles neighborhoods were moving to exclude the underclass. He foresaw that "electronic guardian angels" would protect upwardly mobile Anglos while consigning the underclass to "community imprisonment."

What does this add up to? In Davis's view, the militarization of the landscape. Zone I, the downtown core, becomes a fortress comprehensively monitored by video. This surveillance constitutes "a virtual scanscape—a space of protective visibility that increasingly defines where white-collar office workers and middle-class tourists feel safe Downtown" (Davis, 1992a:5). Davis predicted that video monitoring of Zone I workplaces would become "linked with home security systems, personal 'panic buttons,' car alarms, cellular phones, and the like, in a seamless continuity of surveillance over daily routine" (5).

Zone II in Burgess's model, inspired by Chicago, was the zone-in-transition. In Davis's model, it is the "halo of barrios and ghettos" that surrounds Los Angeles's fortified core. This tenement zone is "the most dangerous zone" of Los Angeles. Nearby MacArthur Park, once the crown jewel of the city park system, was, when Davis wrote his book, a "free-fire zone where crack dealers and street gangs settle their scores with shotguns and uzis" (Davis, 1992a:6), Many bungalows in the zone looked like prison cells—or cages—where "working-class families must now lock themselves in every night" (7).

In Zone III (Burgess's zone of working men's homes), Davis saw a vast network of watchful neighbors providing a "security system that is midway between the besieged, gun-toting anomie of the inner ring and the private police forces of more affluent, gated suburbs" (1992a:13). The danger here, he said, is that thousands of citizens become police informers under the official slogan "Be on the Lookout for Strangers," and this "inevitably stigmatizes innocent groups." In Zone IV of Davis's Los Angeles, there were many gated communities resembling a "fortified honeycomb, with each residential neighborhood now encased in its own walled cell" (15). Here, as in Zone V (wealthy neighborhoods on the distant metropolitan frontier, Burgess's commuter zone), "mini-citadels" are inhabited by more and more "geron[to]crats," the "ruling class of aged, Anglo Baby-boomers, living in 'security-patrolled villages.'" Beyond Zone V lies the "toxic rim," a "zone of extinction," where polluting industries and disasters waiting to happen are being located.

Did Davis see a way out of this "bad dream"? Maybe. He thought it was theoretically possible—but practically difficult—to avoid "mega-city apocalypse" by reversing U.S. urban decay with massive new public works (Davis, 1992a:20).

Global update: The United States is hardly alone in developing what Davis calls the "scanscape." Many nations have already added widespread surveillance capabilities. China may be the most advanced in this effort. In Shenzen, a city of over 12.4 million, the national government has put 20,000 surveillance cameras in the city and has issued residency cards with powerful computer chips that include a person's police record, work history, ethnicity, and many other traits. (In theory, such cards will allow the police to catch criminals and better control a very mobile rural population, including about 10 million peasants who move to big cities annually. But, as a reporter put it, these cards and cameras could "help the Communist Party retain power by maintaining tight controls on an increasingly prosperous population at a time

when street protests are becoming more common" [Bradsher, 2007]). Some journalists reported that during the 2008 Olympic Games in Beijing, the Chinese government placed over 300,000 surveillance cameras throughout the city.

Although China may be the most advanced in surveillance techniques, it is not alone. Great Britain is often called "the most watched society in the world." According to one reporter, "The country boasts 4.2 million security cameras (one for every 14 people), a number expected to double by 2018" (Werth, 2008:10). And in Chicago—the city that Burgess described—a plan was put forward in summer 2008 (and imagined by Davis in 1992) to link private cameras, already in place in banks, bakeries, and many other businesses as well as private homes, with the city's own surveillance cameras run by the city.

To conclude: Davis, Firey, and Suttles all rejected the purely economic logic of the classic models. Firey and Suttles added sentiment and local culture as influences on city space. Davis added political and social factors, particularly repression, fear, and monitoring by the overclass of the underclass.

In his theorizing about unplanned city growth, Burgess shared an evolutionary bias with conservative thinkers. Yet Burgess and his University of Chicago sociology colleagues were concerned with social reform too. In the 1930s, the Department of Sociology at the University of Chicago organized a project to bring "community development" to Chicago's near North Side slums. Decades later, Mike Davis rejected Burgess's conservative theoretical bias but shared Burgess's hope that nonviolent urban reform can stop "dystopic tendencies" operating in cities.

Note that time can change how a theorist is viewed. Mike Davis, for example, has become less "way out" as decades pass. Indeed, in recent years, many urban observers have come to agree with Davis (a professor in the University of California system in 2009).

Other Critiques: Politics Counts

In Davis's Los Angeles, the "natural order" is far from natural: Social control and surveillance stabilize class and race relations; inequality and fear become accepted as natural; razor-wire substitutes for white picket fences and electronic cameras replace dogs named Spot. Ideologically, then, there is a chasm between Burgess's model and Davis's update.

In large part, this ideological chasm reflects political changes in the United States. When Burgess first published his zonal model in 1923, market forces played a larger role than now in determining what was located where in U.S. metropolitan space. So, it is no wonder that he viewed city form as a result of Darwinian struggles for space.

But since the 1920s, the so-called invisible hand of the market has been greatly mitigated by government intervention. As in many places globally, governments in the United States affect the price and use of land in metropolitan space through a variety of programs and policies, including local zoning laws, housing subsidies, tax write-offs for certain types of construction, local rent control, federal and state investment in infrastructure, the placement of a city garbage dump, and the closing of a military base.

To conclude: Burgess published his concentric zone model in a time of limited government. This may account for his neglect of political factors in the struggle for urban space. (The two other classic U.S. models—Hoyt's sectoral model and Harris and Ullman's multiple nuclei model—came later, but they too pay no attention to politics as a force in city shape.)

There were individuals, as much as 20 years before Burgess published his model, suggesting that politics affected land use. Muckraking journalist Lincoln Steffens, for one, exposed the corruption of local government by business, calling it *The Shame of the Cities* ([1903] 1904). To Steffens, local business meddled with the "self-regulating" market because "in a country where business is dominant, businessmen must and will corrupt a government which can pass laws to hinder or help business" ([1931] 1937:299).

By the time Burgess published his model, the U.S. municipal reform movement had often succeeded in limiting the influence of urban political machine bosses. (Ironically, the machine's influence remained in Chicago, the city that Burgess studied and used as his model.) These bosses, like Boss Tweed, had regularly intervened in the market of supply and demand for political ends (Chapter 15).

Today, most urban theorists recognize that a variety of players can influence governmental land-use decisions. In the United States, this recognition, together with the expansion of government's role in urban life, underlies a newer model of urban land use. Before turning to this newer model, however, let's look briefly at two other approaches to investigating urban growth: (1) social area analysis and (2) computer modeling.

SOCIAL AREA ANALYSIS: A METHOD OF INVESTIGATING URBAN GROWTH AND DIFFERENTIATION

Some, including Firey and Suttles, faulted the classic models for leaving out cultural variables. Others criticized Burgess, Hoyt, and Harris and Ullman for neglecting societal variables. These critics pointed out that the classic models treat the city as if it were an island, adrift from its larger society.

One approach, social area analysis, looks at city form and space as a product of societal forces. Social area analysis (technically, the term refers to a method of investigation developed by sociologists Eshref Shevky and Wendell Bell [1955]) starts from a basic premise: Urban growth and differentiation result from changes in the organization of society. Specifically, they argued that groups in society tend to segregate themselves on the basis of social rank, family type, and ethnicity and race.

According to social area analysis, as a city becomes more complex and heterogeneous, areas within it become more homogeneous in terms of social rank, family status, and ethnicity. One study of the Chicago metropolitan area using Shevky and Bell's basic approach found this generally to be the case. (Note that Neilsen Claritas's PRIZM system is based more on status rank, not class or ethnicity. See Chapter 8.)

Few disagree with the underlying premise of social area analysis: Changes in the socioeconomic organization of society have spatial effects. But the Shevky-Bell model has been questioned on both theoretical and empirical grounds.

COMPUTER MODELS OF URBAN STRUCTURE

No computer model of urban structure has yet gained wide acceptance. Still, computer models are being used to map a variety of projects, including alternative urban futures.

PERSPECTIVES ON METROPOLITAN SPACE SINCE THE 1970s

Perhaps we live at "dusk" (the historical moment between the end of one era and the beginning of another), a moment that Hegel thought would encourage clear vision, even wisdom. That may explain the burst of urban theory in the United States and western Europe starting in the 1970s.

THE POLITICAL ECONOMY MODEL OR THE "NEW" URBAN PARADIGM

One newer approach to city spatial structure, referred to in earlier chapters, is the new urban paradigm or, alternatively, the political economy model. It stresses the role of power in the allocation of urban land.

Unlike Burgess's model, the "new" paradigm assumes that both economic and political power, not economic competition in a "free-enterprise market," are key determinants of who gets what in city space. It assumes that such factors as the social class system, social conflict, and the non-neutral role of government influence the spatial patterns of U.S. cities.

This so-called new paradigm is rooted in Marxist thought. Initially, the model was championed by neo-Marxists. Geographer David Harvey's *Social Justice and the City* (1973) and urbanist Manuel Castells's *The Urban Question: A Marxist Approach* ([1972] 1977) are usually credited as seminal studies.

Very quickly—by the early 1980s—more and more mainstream social scientists began to see the urban world through the lens of the political economy model. For example, Logan and Molotch are not Marxists, but they share some of the model's basic assumptions and apply them in their prize-winning and still influential 1987 book *Urban Fortunes*.

Now let's take a brief look at the ideas of David Harvey and Manuel Castells, two contributors to the new urban paradigm. Although they disagree with one other on some key points, both link the city to broader patterns of global restructuring and both draw on Marx's ideas. In addition, both are international figures whose ideas, teaching, research, and personal identities cross many borders.

David Harvey

In a time when many, if not most, academics inhabit disciplinary cubbyholes, British scholar David Harvey stands out in contrast as a transnational, Renaissance-like person. Formerly a professor in the United States and holder of the distinguished chair of geography at Oxford University, he has written about topics as far afield as Nietzsche's images of destruction and creation (1989a), neoliberalism (2006), the United States and the "new imperialism" (2005), and the history of the Sacré-Coeur Basilica in Paris (1989b). Here, we'll focus on just a few of his ideas, mostly developed in his groundbreaking book *Social Justice and the City* (1973).

Working within the framework of Marx's work on capitalist accumulation, Harvey asks how any particular urban spatial pattern came to exist. Unlike Burgess, Harvey rejects benign biotic processes and Darwinian competition as determinants of city space. Rather, he says, capitalist city spatial patterns result from social conflict, class struggle, political–economic competition, and capitalism's need to accelerate development.

The key element in shaping and reshaping capitalist cities, according to Harvey, is capitalist production. In his view, urban space is constantly being restructured under capitalism as a joint result of government policies (e.g., tax rates set by localities) and private firms' location decisions (influenced by capitalism's need for accelerated development).

Some mainstream theories, Harvey notes, do describe and predict land use in the Western capitalist city. For example, Alonso's bid rent theory (Chapter 2) correctly predicts what happens to poor folks: They end up in slums on high-priced land near the city center, where they can least afford to live.

But Harvey wants more than *description*. He calls for change—change in the underlying conditions that promote such unjust (in his view) outcomes. His *prescription*: Eliminate ghettos. How? By doing away with "competitive bidding for land use" and replacing it with a "socially controlled urban land market and socialized control of the housing sector" (Harvey, 1973:127). In other words, Harvey thinks that people made up the political rules for the economic system (including the rules determining land rents and values) in the first place and that people can change them.

As Harvey sees it, people can remake the political–economic rules, but capitalism's circulation process frames the rules and affects urban spatial processes. Here is his logic: The capitalist system produces more commodities than can be used or consumed. Faced with these crises of overproduction, capitalists prefer investing in commodities than in fixed capital (e.g., office buildings) because they stand to earn higher profits. But they will invest in fixed capital when there is an overaccumulation or surplus of capital.

After World War II, a time of overaccumulation in the United States, capitalists (buoyed by government policies such as road building and Veterans Administration loans to home buyers) used their surplus capital to fund suburban development. According to Harvey, this illustrates the circle that capitalists seek to complete: putting money into circulation as investment and returning this money as money *plus profit*.

Suburbanization, deindustrialization, gentrification, urban redevelopment, and reorganization of the urban hierarchy are a few of the processes that occur as "part of a continuous reshaping of geographical landscapes" by capitalist forces. According to Harvey, the built—and rebuilt—landscape of cities and suburbs thus has more to do with capitalist profitability than with efficiency or people's needs.

Manuel Castells

Manuel Castells shares one of Harvey's views: People can change the rules of the game. In fact, Castells sees the city as a theater of action where organized groups and social movements try, often successfully, to change the rules in their own interest. As an example, Castells notes the gay movement's success in reorganizing neighborhood space in San Francisco. Not only was the gay social movement successful in reallocating physical and social space, but it also changed the political landscape, becoming an important force in San Francisco (Castells, 1983:337).

But, like Harvey, Castells see urban land allocation as much more than an expression of local political action. Both look to broad societal forces, particularly market forces, class struggles, and government policies, as key influences on spatial patterns in capitalist cities.

According to Castells, cities and world regions are being transformed by the combined impact of a technological revolution and the restructuring of capitalism. In addition, he says, the transformation of the modern state plays a role in changing spatial patterns. For example, in Castells's view, the

> rise of a technologically-oriented warfare state has a definite suburban form on the fringes of the large metropolitan areas in expanding regions.... Militarization, high-technology development, and suburbanization seem to be closely related processes, in the specific conditions of the United States, and as a consequence of the policies associated with the rise of the warfare state.
>
> *(1989:306)*

In the warfare state, Castells expects cities to become more internally segregated, not only socially but also culturally and functionally (306).

Castells calls his theorizing part of a technoeconomic paradigm (1989:350). Yet the name may mislead, for Castells is not a determinist; he believes that human actions—setting up a worldwide network of local governments, active citizen participation, for example—can "master the formidable forces unleashed by the revolution in information technologies" and lead to new sociospatial structures, reintegrating time and social space.

To conclude: The acceptance of the political economy model by mainstream social science is ironic—indeed, doubly so. First, mainstream social scientists in the United States had not even discussed Marx's ideas for decades, let alone embraced them. In the 1920s, Park and Burgess dismissed Marx's ideas as either wrong or irrelevant. At the height of the cold war in the 1950s, only the rarest, most deviant social scientist assigned Marx to college students.

Yet acceptance of the political economy model came very quickly in the late 1970s and early 1980s, when the cold war was still hot enough to make Marxist ideas suspect.

Second, and perhaps even more ironic, growing acceptance within academia of the Marxist-inspired political economy model started in the early 1980s. That is the same time that U.S. and British voters veered toward Reaganomics and Thatcherism plus conservative calls for a return to "free-market" economics (often used as a synonym for capitalism).

The upshot: In at least two postindustrial nations, there was a mismatch between popular consciousness and theoretical understanding: Just as urbanists revised or rejected Burgess's views of the free market, national administrations in the United States and Great Britain revived those very ideas.

Competing models? True, as some point out, the political economy model is not comprehensive. For example, it does not account for conflicts over multicultural curricula or other conflicts based on identity and culture, not economics. But currently, there is no competing model that liberal or conservative social scientists offer for understanding urban spatial structure in postindustrial society.

The model described below of the multinucleated region is not an ideological competitor; it lies squarely in the radical tradition. For the moment, then, this no longer-new-urban paradigm still has the ideological field all to itself.

THE MULTINUCLEATED METROPOLITAN REGION MODEL (OR "POLYCENTRIC URBAN REGION")

Dissatisfied with existing approaches to spatial restructuring, M. Gottdiener set out in the 1970s to study the relationship between *Late Capitalism* (Mandel, [1972] 1987) and *deconcentration*: the absolute increase of population and density of social activities in areas outside traditional city regions and population centers (Gottdiener, 1985:9). His goal was to better understand modern patterns of spatial restructuring and urban deconcentration in the United States.

Although Gottdiener distanced himself from the models of Lefebvre, Castells, and Harvey, he was influenced by their work. Indeed, his model can be viewed as a modification, not a rejection, of the political economy approach. We need not detail the differences among the models here, except to point out that Gottdiener's vision is more oriented to the "transformation of social relations" and the role that the state (government) plays in sociospatial patterns.

In a nutshell, here is Gottdiener's thinking: Besides people, so much industry and banking and so many corporate headquarters had moved to U.S. suburban areas by the 1970s that these areas were transformed into

centers of metropolitanwide activities. This process of becoming an urbanized region is called "deconcentration," and the new space it produces is called a "**multinucleated** (or "polynucleated") **metropolitan region**."

Orange County in southern California is an example of this qualitatively new form of settlement space (Gottdiener, 1985; Gottdiener and Kephart, 1991). Nothing like Orange County had ever happened. According to sociologists Gottdiener and George Kephart, this new spatial form meant that the traditional concept of the city had become obsolete: "urban life is now organized in metropolitan regions composed of polynucleated and functionally differentiated spaces...that are neither suburbs nor satellite cities; rather, they are fully urbanized and independent spaces that are not dominated by any central city" (1991:34). Yet, these new decentralized counties have the "economic vitality and cultural diversity formerly associated with the traditional central city" (Kling et al., 1991:9).

In the last decade or so, European researchers have been particularly prolific in their studies of multinucleated regions, called "polycentric urban regions," or PURs. (For example, Bailey and Turok [2001] studied central Scotland as a PUR, noting that planners often think that PURs in northwest Europe both safeguard environmental objectives and promote economic competitiveness. But they concluded that central Scotland may not even be a PUR.)

Postsuburban Orange County is one of over 20 such polynucleated regions in the United States. In Orange County, there is no dominant urban center: About 70 percent of its population live outside its three largest cities. Indeed, the nickname of the county, the "O.C.," is better known than the names of cities it contains. In 2007 Orange County employed over 1.5 million people, many in the information sector. Once viewed as a lily-white, upper-class bastion, its population had greatly changed by the 2000s: Its 3 million+ residents were ethnically mixed, including large numbers of Hispanics and Vietnamese Americans. (One longtime characteristic remained: The O.C. remains a Republican stronghold.)

Orange County offers the full array of services associated with urban life, but it is not an urban center. Rather, according to Gottdiener and Kephart (1991:34), it is "a sociospatial form of late capitalism."

Using a sample of 21 counties like Orange County (i.e., multinucleated, highly urbanized counties adjacent to traditional urban centers), Gottdiener and Kephart tried to assess what factors account for the growth of such postsuburban centers. They concluded that high technology is the primary base of economic growth in many counties—but not all. Nor can the growth in services alone account for the emergence of the multinucleated economy. In their view, many social forces—"military-related spending in the permanent war economy, the growth in high technology, the [then] robust real estate market, racism, the flight of the white industrial working class to the hinterland, the construction of traditional [non-high-technology] manufacturing plants, the hypertrophic expansion of service-related industries, and new arrangements in the corporate business structure—have all combined" to produce this new settlement space (52).

Retail life in Orange County and other multinucleated metropolitan regions is dominated by enclosed shopping malls, highlighting the "core cultural value of consumerism" (Kling et al., 1991:9). (*Irony*: The man who pioneered the design of shopping malls in the early 1940s, Austrian-born architect Victor Gruen [1903–1980], included public cultural facilities as well as retail stores in his original plans. Developers perverted his plans, and later Gruen denied that he was the father of the malling of the U.S. (see Kowinski [1985] 2002).

To conclude: The multinucleated metropolitan region model in the United States and PUR models in Europe attempt to rethink urban spatial patterns in light of macro-level changes. These include shifts in the organization and structure of information technology, the economy, and the political system. Like the political economy model which they complement, they reject the premises of the classic models.

WHERE PEOPLE LIVE

HOW RACE AND ETHNICITY AFFECT HOUSING PATTERNS

Melting pot? Salad bowl? Stewpot? Witches' brew?

Which food metaphor best symbolizes the situation of multiethnic U.S. cities? The answer depends on many factors, including the ethnic/racial composition of the city.

As noted earlier (Chapters 10, 11), some groups did melt into the dominant culture, others were partially assimilated, some rejected the dominant culture altogether as a matter of choice, some were rejected by the dominant culture, and still others were hardly affected.

One way of measuring the degree to which an ethnic or racial group has blended into the dominant culture is to examine that group's housing pattern over time. Housing patterns—segregation or dispersion, for example—are not the only measure of assimilation. (Intermarriage rates are another key measure.) But residential patterns often indicate larger patterns of social mobility and/or lack of social mobility and acceptance.

Before moving on, a few words about the measurement of residential segregation are appropriate. Researchers use various indexes to measure racial segregation, and unsurprisingly, different measures yield different results.

One widely used measure is the **index of dissimilarity**. This measures the distribution of white and nonwhite (synonymous with "Negro" when used in a landmark 1965 study by the Taeubers) households among census blocks. (Importantly, this measure based on black–white housing segregation indicates both how much the racial/ethnic composition of the United States has broadened since the 1960s and how much the key issue has remained the same over the decades—that is, a question of African American/ white segregation.) A census block (not census tract, which tends to have a lower score for similarity) can have a score from 0 to 100: The higher the number, the higher the level of racial segregation. The index of dissimilarity looks at the population of a racial group in an entire city and asks this question: To make every census block in the city mirror the racial makeup of the city as a whole, what percentage of each group would have to move to another block?

In 2000, more than 74 U.S. metro areas had scores higher than 0.60. Williams and Collins (2001:2) point out that scores of 0.60 (meaning that 60 percent of African Americans would have to move to another block in order to eliminate racial segregation) are very high. The index of dissimilarity is a measure of *absolute* segregation.

Another index, the **index of exposure**, measures *relative* segregation. This index measures the proportion of people in a neighborhood sharing the same ethnic/racial background. Often, it is used as a stand-in for measuring positive interaction between racial groups; the assumption here is that physical proximity to people from other racial/ethnic groups promotes positive interaction and empathy. (This is an iffy assumption. Anecdotal evidence from several racially mixed high schools and colleges in the Bay Area suggests the opposite: Physical closeness by itself is no guarantee of positive interaction. Indeed, without attention to stereotypes and deep-seated feelings, familiarity can lead to contempt.)

Now, let's consider the contrast between the housing patterns of white, Dutch immigrants and their families in Kalamazoo, Michigan, and African American migrants to Chicago over time. Families with Dutch surnames spread throughout Kalamazoo between 1873 and 1965. They did not stay grouped together in one area (Jakle and Wheeler [1969] 1972).

Contrast the Dutch pattern of housing dispersion in Kalamazoo to the pattern of African American housing segregation and concentration in Chicago. Dutch immigrants in Kalamazoo dispersed as they moved up the socioeconomic ladder and became "Americanized." There was no residential area of the city from which they were systematically excluded.

Conversely, Chicago's African Americans were systematically excluded from some sections of the city and did not, as a group, climb the socioeconomic ladder. Thus, in 1970, Chicago's African Americans remained highly segregated and concentrated in a small **ghetto** area near the center of the city (as predicted by Alonso's bid rent theory).

Moreover, this pattern of African American segregation and concentration extended to metropolitan Chicago. In 1970, almost 50 percent of Chicago's suburbs with more than 2,500 inhabitants had no black residents; only two had more than 50 black residents. By 1980, the total African American population of Chicagoland's suburbs had increased a small percentage: from 3.6 percent in 1970 to 5.6 percent in 1980 (Herbers, 1981:1). Interpreting this small increase is problematic, for much of the suburbanization increase occurred in older, close-in industrial

areas, not in high-status areas such as PRIZM'S SER 01 Upper Crust or 02 Blue Blood Estates. In farther-out suburban counties, such as McHenry County (which experienced a population growth of over 32 percent during the decade), African Americans constituted a minuscule presence, 0.1 percent of the population in 1980. Similarly, in farther-out suburban DuPage County, African Americans made up 1.6 percent of the population.

By the 2000 Census, there had been some changes. According to an analysis of U.S. Census data by Guy Stuart (2002) of Harvard University's Kennedy Center, 27 percent of African Americans (up from 19 percent in 1990), 39 percent of all Latinos (up from 29 percent in 1990), and 61 percent of Asian Americans lived in the suburbs of Chicago and its six-county metro area (excluding five so-called satellite cities such as Evanston and Joliet). By 2000, 75 percent of whites (up from 67 percent in 1990) lived in Chicago's suburbs. Some neighborhoods of Chicago (e.g., Hyde Park) and some close-in suburbs (e.g., Oak Park) did show that racial integration was possible.

But, in general, in 2000, segregation of African Americans and Latinos persisted throughout the Chicago metro area. For example, 67 percent of all African Americans in incorporated suburbs would have to live in another suburb to achieve integration with white suburbanites (Stuart, 2002:3), and African Americans and whites shared only one Chicago suburb. Whites and Latinos shared only three suburbs. In contrast, Asian Americans and whites shared 10 suburbs (5).

What we have in Chicagoland, then, is the continuation of a metropolitanwide pattern identified by Berry and Kasarda decades earlier (1977:21–52): the segregation and concentration of African Americans. But, in the 1970s, there was a color line between city and suburb. Now, that line has shifted. The new color line is between suburb and suburb, where segregation in terms of race/ethnicity remains high for African Americans and Latinos.

In one decade, 1990–2000, housing segregation (between white and African American and Latinos) *increased* in almost every U.S. large suburban area. Across the nation, about 80 percent of whites lived outside of cities. (In contrast, 70 percent of African

Americans and Latinos lived in cities or inner-ring suburbs.) Even more telling is this statistic: As of 2000, *86 percent of whites in the United States lived in neighborhoods where minorities made up less than 1 percent of the population.*

Earlier, there was a pattern of "chocolate cities and vanilla suburbs" (Farley et al., 1978, 1994) in the United States. No longer. Yet, a pattern of African American—and Latino—segregation is nationwide. Stuart (2002) concludes that, for the most part, U.S. neighborhoods remain highly segregated. Only cities with small numbers of so-called minorities have become more integrated since 1970.

One of the most segregated areas in the United States can be found along muddy roads in south Texas. Not visible from the road, some 400,000 Latino families live in this six-county area, crowded into rundown trailers and hobbled-together dwellings in subdivisions called *colonias*. To the outsider, these *colonias* appear to be slums, disorganized and disheveled. But dwellers there (mainly legal immigrants)—through determination, hard work, protests, and savings—have improved their dwellings and gained access to water and safe sewage disposal (Eckholm, 2007:5).

If sociologists Gans and Yancey (Chapters 10 and 11) are correct, Latinos and Asians will be "socially whitened" and thus integrated into U.S. city and suburban neighborhoods. But segregated housing patterns for African Americans may well persist.

Why? Is this continuing pattern of African American housing segregation and concentration mainly a matter of racial discrimination? Many think so. Population researchers Massey and Denton, for instance, say that their research shows that "black suburbanization is completely unrelated" to socioeconomic factors (e.g., occupational status, household income), contextual factors in the metropolitan area (e.g., housing inflation, employment growth), or compositional factors (e.g., population characteristics of the central city and suburbs). In other words, a generation ago Massey and Denton (1988:622) concluded that, long after the Civil Rights Act of 1968, there are "strong penalties for being black" in the process of spatial assimilation and that African Americans do not have equal access to housing in either suburbs or cities.

In the case of Chicago, the late Mayor Richard J. Daley did not hide his racism. He believed that it was right to keep blacks out of established white ethnic neighborhoods because they "didn't keep their yards clean, and the neighborhoods went to hell and that kind of thing" (Erlichman in Scheer, 1979:8).

But many observers think housing segregation is much more complicated, involving issues of social rank as well as race. For some (e.g., Berry and Kasarda, 1977:22), the key to understanding the virtual isolation of metropolitan Chicago's African Americans is neighborhood status:

> Since blacks as a group are considered of lower status by many whites and, in large concentrations, are associated with residentially undesirable areas, the arrival of large numbers of blacks reduces a neighborhood's rank in residential status hierarchy for whites.... Because neighborhood status is so affected by racial change, areas that attract large concentrations of blacks are typically unable to retain white residents...

Berry and Kasarda's findings of decades ago in Chicago support what other researchers have found in many U.S. cities: If whites can possibly afford to do it, they will live with those of their own social rank and race. (PRIZM focuses on social rank, not race. But its basic premise is that birds of a feather flock together [see Chapter 8]. If so, people of the same social rank—irrespective of race—should prefer to be neighbors. This may be the case for some groups, say, Asian Americans and whites, but not whites and African Americans; in the United States most whites choose not to live with African Americans of similar social rank.)

Those familiar with the Burgess model and social area analysis should not be surprised by white preferences in the United States to live near people "like themselves" (at least in terms of color—not class as either Weber or Marx defined class). Both the Burgess model and social area analysis hypothesize that in urban society people will sort themselves out by social background variables. Burgess and Park thought this sorting-out process happened in an unplanned fashion, creating "natural" areas. And before the Great Depression, they charted the shift of ethnic neighborhoods in Chicago, using the terms "invasion" and "succession" to describe some of the sorting and sifting.

Since the University of Chicago researchers first used these terms to describe residential urban change, studies in Chicago and elsewhere have documented the process. They tend to find a period of "penetration," in which a few minority families buy into a residential area. This period is followed by the "invasion," in which a substantial number of their group follows.

Neighborhood invasion is sometimes accompanied by block-busting, a tactic practiced by unscrupulous real estate speculators. In a typical block-busting situation, the speculator comes into a white neighborhood and warns residents that "they" (African Americans, typically) are going to move in very quickly. White residents are led to believe that their property values will drop sharply as the area becomes "undesirable." These scare tactics may stimulate panic selling at artificially low prices. Then, the block-buster can purchase the houses cheaply and resell them to minority buyers at inflated prices.

As this scenario suggests, invasion and succession are not always natural processes. Race baiting, rezoning, and bank *redlining* (refusal to grant loans in areas around which red lines have been drawn) are examples of conscious, planned responses by individuals and institutions that often intervene in the trickle-down, invasion–succession model.

To conclude: "American apartheid" is what Douglas Massey (1990), a leading population researcher, once called the pattern of racial separation between whites and African Americans in the United States. Massey's 1990 study uses older data, but in terms of racial separation and segregation, not much has changed in the intervening years despite other changes (e.g., Barack Obama's successful presidential bid).

If the United States is typified by residential "apartheid," how did this pattern evolve? Here, there is disagreement. Some think that race (and class) segregation in the United States is a by-product of conscious policy decisions by local political actors who engage in local protectionism. Others, including most African Americans (67 percent), think that discrimination is pervasive when buying a house; but they tend to blame racial bias, not conscious policy decisions (in Yen, 2007:A13).

Scholars estimate that economic factors (e.g., low social class or SES) account for only 10 percent of African American residential racial segregation in U.S. cities. So, what accounts for the other 90 percent? One respected sociologist wrote some years ago that the rest is linked to negative racial attitudes in the United States (Abu-Lughod, 1991:260).

In Chicago, one of the most black–white segregated big cities in the United States, these patterns date back at least to World War I. In 1917, for instance, the Chicago Real Estate Board asked for the cooperation of "influential colored citizens" to ensure that the great immigration of African Americans into the city did not lead to housing throughout the city for them. The realtors advised, for business reasons—not racial prejudice—that the newcomers stay in continuous blocks rather than dispersing widely (in Helper, 1969:25).

Ironically, then, at the very time that Burgess theorized that economic competition underpinned urban growth and that "natural" areas resulted from urban differentiation, realtors openly sponsored policies that foiled the market's so-called natural processes. Later, after World War II, it was federal policy that foiled the market. As mentioned earlier, billions of U.S. tax dollars supported highway construction and suburban home loans. Whether intended or not, these popular government programs—paid for by white and nonwhite taxpayers alike—hardened the pattern of residential apartheid: Large numbers of returning non-Hispanic white vets took advantage of Veterans Administration loans, buying homes in the new suburbs. Meanwhile, other vets were discouraged or prevented (by covenants or negative attitudes) from buying suburban homes.

Once again, private and public policies intervened in natural processes, helping to shape local character. Times have changed since theorists wrote about "natural" processes. And so have citizens' attitudes about "natural" processes.

WHAT PEOPLE LIVE IN

For decades, mobile homes suffered from a bad rep and a bad rap. Typically, mobile homes were portrayed as ticky-tacky housing for lower-income people of questionable taste and habits, so-called "trailer trash."

By the 1980s, both the name and the image had changed. Renamed and repackaged as "manufactured housing," the homes appealed to a broad spectrum of buyers—retired folks, middle-income families, and others. Whereas years ago trailer parks down by the railroad tracks were common, now, more often than not, they are well-kept subdivisions with names like "Forest Crest Estates." (The vast majority were not mobile at all; 90 percent had no wheels.)

The 1990s were a decade of enormous growth for manufactured homes in the United States. But by 2000 shipments had declined 28 percent to 250,550 homes. In 2001, there was an even steeper decline.

The steep decline of manufactured homes is probably related to another kind of housing being manufactured in the United States: modular homes. Unlike manufactured homes, constructed on a steel chassis and towed on their own wheels to home sites, modular homes are taken to a home site on a flatbed truck or on a removable chassis. Then, sections are put on a foundation and attached with bolts and straps. The cost of a modular home in 2007 could be much cheaper than that of a traditional home; they started at about $47,000 for a little over 2,000 square feet, not counting the site, the setup, and the foundation (Stark, 2007:G5).

HOW AGE AFFECTS HOUSING PATTERNS

At different points in their life cycle, individuals may seek out different neighborhoods For instance, as a middle-income woman goes through life, in her 20s she may reside in a singles area near the heart of the city, later move to a suburban house to raise children and commute to work, and, after the children grow up, move to a city apartment. In Nielsen Claritas's 2006 terms, she may have started in SER 16 Bohemian Mix, moved to SER 12 Bright Lites, L'il City or SER 11 God's Country or SER 18 Kids & Cul-de-Sacs, then back to the city to SER 07 Money & Brains. Years later, she may move again, perhaps to SER 21 Gray Power.

Understanding the population characteristics of neighborhoods and towns in terms of age (and family structure) is essential to informed policymaking. It would make no sense to locate day-care centers in the heart of a retirement colony or playgrounds where there are no children.

The population pyramid is a convenient device for presenting information about a community's age composition. Figure 16.8 shows pyramids for two different kinds of communities in terms of age. Pyramid A is top-heavy, illustrating that most neighborhood residents are middle-aged or older. Pyramid B bulges out at the bottom, revealing the relatively large number of children in the neighborhood.

Pyramid-type diagrams can be used to display various characteristics of a population, including sex, income, family composition, occupation, and marital status. These pyramids are useful for looking at a given population at one moment in time—say, 2008. But they are static; they don't reveal how the population characteristics of a community may change over time. For this kind of data analysis, a dynamic study is required.

GENTRIFICATION

A dynamic study of a neighborhood located in Burgess's Zone III might show the following breakdown by social rank over time: 1995: 80 percent working class, 5 percent middle class, 25 percent upper middle class; 2005: 40 percent working class, 10 percent middle class, and 50 percent upper middle class. These data indicate that the neighborhood is undergoing **gentrification** (from the English *gentry*, the class immediately below the nobility). That is, people of higher class and status "invaded" a working-class area, renovating existing homes. This is not what the invasion–succession model predicted. In fact, gentrification represents the opposite process, one we might call "trickle-up." Some theorists call this process "reinvasion."

Gentrification has occurred in many U.S. cities that have charming inner-city homes. In Washington, D.C., for instance, the now fashionable and expensive Georgetown section was primarily a lower-status area until World War II.

Some observers applaud this development. They say that gentrification brings back the white middle and upper middle classes to the city, thereby upgrading the housing stock and increasing the tax base.

But an important question remains: Where will those gentrified out of their homes go? Those who can no longer afford to live in their longtime home neighborhoods must move somewhere.

To illustrate the population and demographic trends associated with gentrification, let's look at one

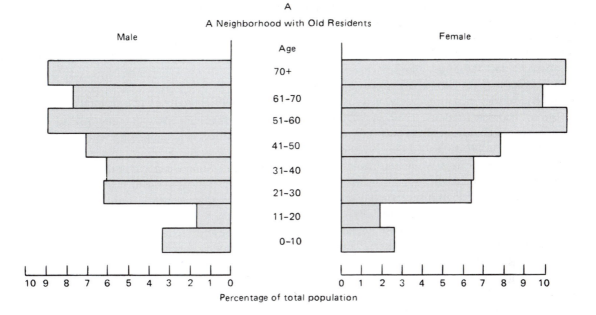

A

A Neighborhood with Old Residents

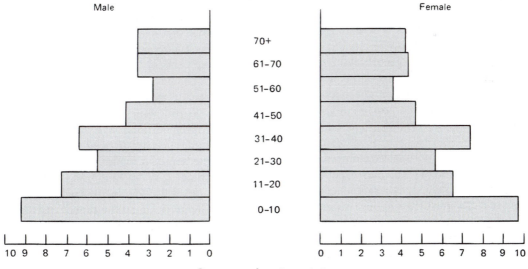

B

A Neighborhood with Younger Residents

Fig. 16.8 POPULATION PYRAMIDS OF TWO NEIGTHBORHOODS WITH DIFFERING AGE STRUCTURES, DISAGGREGATED BY GENDER.

census tract, 708, in Boston's South End and its gentri-fication over time. This tract consists of 13 city blocks about 1 mile from Boston's CBD. It reached its popu-lation high in 1950 with almost 6,000 residents. Then, for about 20 years, it shrunk—about 50 percent. "White flight" seems to have been a key reason: The tract's white residents declined from over 40 percent to under 10 percent between 1940 and 1960. By 1970, almost one-quarter of all housing units in tract 708 were vacant (Vigdor, 2002:136). Then, in the 1960–1970 decade, the situation started to change. White households stopped leaving, and the share of the residents who graduated college or who worked in a professional occupation mushroomed. Gentrification continued. By 2000, the tract's population increased more than 50 percent (but it was still lower than it was at its peak in 1950). Vigdor (2002:137) says that "Non-Hispanic whites reclaimed the racial majority in the tract in 1990, while blacks declined from five-sixths to roughly one-quarter of the population between 1970 and 2000."

One way to understand the changes in Boston's tract 708 is this: Richer whites, paying higher taxes, "reclaimed" and revivified a shabby neighborhood. A different spin is this: Poor and low-income residents, many of color, were displaced by affluent, well-edu-cated whites. This displacement is often one outcome of gentrification.

A less obvious effect of gentrification concerns jobs. Often, gentrification can mean that housing for the well-off displaces jobs for the poor. This is what occurred in Manhattan a generation ago: Many manufacturing industries were squeezed out by resi-dential lofts.

Theorists using the political economy paradigm (the "new" urban theory) approach gentrification from another angle. They say that investment capital moved out of U.S. central cities in the 1950s and into suburbs, where profit rates were higher. Later, when inner cities deteriorated, a "rent gap" resulted, and capital returned to earn higher profits. The big winners in this process, they say, are the owners of capital; the big losers are the displaced urban poor.

So, what is to be done? Should public policy slow down or speed up gentrification? That is a normative issue, a question of values—not a question that can be answered by looking at data.

Up to this point, we have treated housing patterns as if they existed in isolation. Now, we will examine patterns of industrial and commercial activity in cities and suburbs that influence housing and many other land uses.

Government-Sponsored Gentrification

The process is happening in many cities globally. But in some cities, it is happening with the great assis-tance of the local or national government. In Beijing, for example, slum-clearance projects accelerated after 2001 when the city's bid to host the 2008 Olympic Games was accepted. Many residents were displaced, and some poor, vibrant neighborhoods were demol-ished in the effort to rebuild for the Olympics. (Other neighborhoods were also destroyed. For one, "hutong neighborhoods" feature—or featured before the urban renewal and gentrification—courtyard houses dating to the thirteenth century in the city's narrow alleyways or *hutongs*; few survived the building boom that transformed the capital city since the mid-1990s. The city's expansion also meant that the ancient stone walls encircling old Beijing were destroyed and new housing ringed the city.) The Qianmen area, for exam-ple, was a poor but thriving area south of Tiananmen Square, which housed many of Beijing's teahouses and theaters (Ouroussoff, 2008:2). Now, shopping malls and ugly office blocks stand where the hutongs once were.

One blatant example of forced, government-sponsored gentrification has been taking place in Cambodia. Neighborhood land, filled with shanties, is being seized, often in late-night raids by police and soldiers, who sometimes burn down whole areas. If the Cambodian economy continues to heat up, such forced seizures will undoubtedly continue as "mod-ernization" requires land. (The capital city of Phnom Penh is starting to transform itself with modern build-ings; this process has meant expropriating the land of Cambodia's poor: Between 1998 and 2003, the city government there forcibly evicted 11,000 fam-ilies [World Bank in Mydans, 2008:8]). In a recent report, Amnesty International estimated that 150,000 Cambodians all over the country risked forcible evic-tion as a result of new development projects, land dis-putes, and land seizures (Mydans, 2008:8).

Ghettoes, Enclaves, and Barrios

Many trace the creation of the modern ghetto to sixteenth-century Venice. Most agree that its aim, then as now, is involuntary segregation.

Today, the word "ghetto" is often used to describe poor African American neighborhoods in the United States. But the phenomenon exists nearly worldwide. A few examples: segregated areas for the Roma in middle Europe and Italy, Burakumin in Japan, and Aborigines in Australia.

Diego Vigil suggests that the ghetto resembles low-income, Latino barrios (neighborhoods). There, Professor Vigil says, most Mexican immigrants "are subjected to spatial and social isolation from the opportunities afforded to others residing beyond the barrio boundaries" (2008:366).

Is "ghetto" merely a descriptive term of a geographical site? Many think not. For one, Talja Blokland (2008) thinks that the word "ghetto" carries a "negative moral connotation" because it is "a label for spatial expressions of forms of exclusion" (375). By contrast, the world "enclave" is used by many to describe voluntary or self-segregation.

Is deghettoization or debarrioization possible? Renowned urbanist Herbert J. Gans (2008) thinks that deghettoization today is very difficult. Gentrification, Gans says (355), can lead to deghettoization; but most people gentrified out of their homes move to other ghettoes. Further, Gans doubts that ghettoes—of either the very rich or poor—can be eliminated via local policy.

Yet, some think it's time to abandon use of the terms "ghetto" and "hyperghetto" (a word used by Loic Wacquant [2008] to describe socially-isolated, hyperpoor, African American areas in the United States) for a neighborhood or an institution. Why? In part because ghettoes they say, are maintained through constrained choice, not involuntary segregation.

ECONOMIC ACTIVITIES IN U.S. METROPOLITAN SPACE

After streets and roads (which consume the largest amount of a city's space), housing is usually the most widespread land use. Commercial and industrial activities take up far less space, about 10 percent combined;

and, as some businesses switch from place-based to Internet-based operations, the percentage may drop more.

Although economic activities don't take up much room, relatively speaking, they greatly influence what kinds of housing exist in a city (rooming houses, McMansions, slums, etc.). They also influence what kinds of people live there.

CENTRAL BUSINESS DISTRICT

The CBD is the key commercial area in most modern U.S. cities (but not necessarily metro areas—see the discussion earlier in this chapter of the O.C., e.g.).

The CBD is much more than a physical place. It is a symbol of a city's cultural vitality as well as of its economic well-being. It may evoke numerous images: skyscrapers, hustle-bustle, street musicians, homeless panhandlers, high fashion, litter, big department stores and small boutiques, and/or empty streets after the offices close. And, especially since 9/11, fear and trembling.

It is worth nothing that some of the CBD's symbolic sparkle means less and less to more and more U.S. metropolitanites these days. Why? Because with the shifts of people, jobs, cultural venues, and retail trade to U.S. suburban and postsuburban areas, fewer people need to go "downtown" for jobs, goods, services, or entertainment. Indeed, the U.S. Census of Retail Trade stopped publishing CBD-specific data by 1982, reasoning that the migration of retail trade to the suburbs appeared "complete" by that time (U.S. Bureau of the Census, 2000:150). Further, many (exact numbers are unavailable) now shop online, avoiding trips downtown or to suburban malls. Still, for untold numbers, pride and emotional attachment to a downtown remains.

Following Walter Firey's remarks about people's sentimental attachment to landmarks, we could hypothesize that a rundown or terrorized CBD has subtle psychological effects on urbanites. But beyond these difficult-to-measure effects, the CBD in the United States serves (or served) basic economic functions. Its major functions are (or were, in some cases) (1) the retail selling of goods and services for profit and (2) the performance of office and financial activities for a city and its hinterland, which, particularly in global cities, could be the world.

As in central place theory, exchange plays a key role in understanding the importance of the CBD in the United States. Exchange of goods, services, and information requires social interaction; and intensely developed areas like the CBD permit convenient, face-to-face interaction. For example, tens of thousands of corporate and financial workers are concentrated in a small physical area on New York City's Wall Street.

In the Internet era, the exchange of goods, services, and information no longer requires face-to-face interaction. What this means for the CBD remains murky. Yet, Saskia Sassen ([1994] 2006b) points out that CBDs in global cities, such as New York City, remain vibrant.

How can a CBD be precisely defined and delimited? Decades ago, the U.S. Census of Retail Trade (U.S. Bureau of the Census, 1976:introduction) provided some guidelines: The CBD is "an area of very high land valuation; an area characterized by a high concentration of retail businesses, offices, theatres, hotels, and 'service' businesses; and an area of high traffic flow." Ordinarily, the CBD follows existing census tract boundaries, consisting of one or more whole census tracts.

To delimit CBDs more precisely, geographers map and measure a variety of things: building heights, traffic flows, employment in retail trade, land values, and residents' perceptions of the CBD. Older studies found that land values peak close to the center of the CBD and that land uses within the CBD change as distance from this point of peak land value increases. For example, the proportion of land devoted to retailing declines as one moves out from the point of highest land value. (See Alonso's bid rent curve, Chapter 2.)

Land uses vary in vertical space too. Moving upward from the ground floor of buildings in the CBD through successive stories, offices increase while retailing declines.

CBDs changed with newer, faster communications technologies and the advent of the postindustrial economy. Specifically, in the postindustrial economy, white-collar and service industries gained in importance as retail sales activities in the U.S. CBD declined; suburbs drew downtown department store customers, and big stores tended to decentralize rather than expand in the CBD. New communications technologies made it possible to communicate quickly without face-to-face interaction.

These changes meant that firms once clustered in the CBD became free to move, even to offshore locations. Thus, an insurance company in Boston can maintain a symbolic presence downtown but also have back offices in far-flung suburbs or in India. The company can interact with customers and companies by the Internet, fax, and/or telephone instead of face-to-face. Plus, it can store and retrieve its data anywhere, presumably in cheaper locations, rather than in the CBD.

Time was when a fancy downtown address meant a great deal status-wise. This was particularly true for stockbrokers. America's best-known street, Wall Street, was the quintessential "good" address. But now, with global finance and the Internet, brokers do business from St. Louis to the corner of Last Chance Gulch and Sixth Street in Helena, Montana. Besides, Wall Street's name may have been tarnished since various publicly discredited actions in the 2000s.

The roller coaster: From the 1950s to the 2000s, many CBDs in the United States have been on a roller-coaster ride, surging with expansion, dipping with vacant buildings in an overbuilt downtown, and (less often) resurging. By the mid-1980s, new office buildings, retail stores, and people poured into many downtowns. Even in some U.S. Rustbelt cities like Cleveland, the CBD comeback was phenomenal. But this expansion was short-lived in some places: By the early 1990s, increased white-collar unemployment, new federal tax laws, a worldwide economic slowdown, and a sagging national economy spelled trouble for many CBDs. Then, in some cities, CBDs rebounded, for a short while, after the millennium. By the late 2000s, however, vacancy rates in many CBDs increased as bankruptcies or store closings in the CBD (e.g., The Sharper Image)reflected an economic recession and a significant downturn in consumerism.

Even in the best of times, however, a vibrant CBD is not an equal-opportunity employer. CBD jobs tend to be white-collar and pink-collar (female-dominated jobs such as secretarial work). Meanwhile, many urbanites needing work are qualified for blue-collar work—and most of that work has moved outside of town to suburban locations or outside of the country. So, there is often a bad fit in the CBD (and the entire central city) between workers wanted (white-collar) and workers available (blue-collar). Typically, the hardest hit by this mismatch are low-income African Americans.

Now, CBDs face newer challenges. What impacts, for example, are e-business and e-cbds (electronic central business districts) having on brick-and-concrete CBDs? The answers are far from clear. And what impacts are terrorism, or fear of terrorism, having on CBDs? One study suggests that since 9/11 the perception of terrorism has had serious impacts. In their study of post-9/11 Chicago, Abadie and Dermisa (2006) suggest that Chicago's CBD, which includes possible terrorist targets such as the landmark Sears Tower (the tallest building in the United States since 1973; renamed Willis Tower in 2009 after its key tenant, a London-based insurance company), experienced more increases in vacancy rates than other areas of the city. They conclude that economic activity in CBDs, particularly office real estate markets, can be greatly affected by the perceived level of terrorism.

Yet another challenge for CBDs is an economic downturn in the United States and way beyond. As consumer spending slowed and credit markets tightened in 2008 and afterward, many U.S. retailers declared bankruptcy and closed their CBD stores. Such store closings are expected to remake CBDs as well as suburban shopping malls (where CompUSA and Circuit City, for two, closed their doors in 2008 and 2009) across the country.

DECENTRALIZED AND MULTICENTERED COMMERCIAL ACTIVITIES

Starting after World War II, commercial activities in the United States were increasingly located outside the central city. By the 1970s, a new spatial entity took form: a postsuburban zone. As detailed earlier in this chapter, Orange County, California, exemplifies this entity; it is organized around "many distinct, specialized centers rather than a traditional city center surrounded by industrial and residential areas (Kling et al., 1991:6).

More recently, decentralization has gone global. Practically, this means that employees answering an 800 helpline number (in English) or processing claims for an insurance company in Iowa might be in India or the Philippines.

MANUFACTURING

Manufacturing consists of (1) transforming raw materials into new products and (2) assembling component parts into new products such as cars. This transformation usually takes place in a factory or mill. Indeed, the "dark satanic mill" and factory smokestack once symbolized a city's economic lifeblood.

In the postindustrial economy, manufacturing in the United States has declined relative to the service and information sectors. A few statistics tell the story succinctly: In the 1950s, about 33 percent of all U.S. workers held manufacturing jobs. With deindustrialization, the proportion plummeted to 17 percent by 1991 (Barlett and Steele, 1992:18) and 13 percent by 2002 (Hagenbaugh, 2002).

With economic restructuring, a global assembly line now exists. It stretches from the *maquiladoras* near the U.S.–Mexican border to the prison workshops of China and from the sweatshops of Los Angeles to the redesigned auto plants in Tennessee.

ANOTHER LOOK

"Have economic logic. Will travel." That could be the motto for early theorists concerned with the shape of urban space in Europe and North America. Economic assumptions underlie the classic models of urban form and space, and they cross-cut disciplines and political ideologies.

Central place theorists used economic logic to deduce that there is a system of cities, a functionally interdependent urban hierarchy. Theorists who classify cities by function also assumed economic interdependence. Durkheim (Chapter 6) did the same. The U.S. government bases its definition of the metropolitan statistical area on the notion of an integrated labor market (Chapter 7). Urban ecologists built a theoretical framework around the idea that human communities develop spatially as a result of economic competition and that industrial cities are structured internally by market forces.

Even critiques of central place theory and the classic models assign a major role to economic forces in shaping the modern city. For example, in Walter Firey's critique of Burgess's, Hoyt's, and Harris and Ullman's models of city structure, economic factors are not denied. (However, Firey says that people do not live by the exchange of bread alone, and that noneconomic factors such as sentiment and symbolism should be added to the models.) And even those like Lewis Mumford (Chapter 4) who think that religion and art have historically determined human settlement patterns say that unrestricted economic competition has shaped the modern U.S. city.

Newer models and perspectives on urban and metropolitan space—the political economy model, the multinucleated metropolitan region model, Davis's ecological update—add such factors as state intervention, grassroots social movements, and overwhelming fear to the mix of influences on space. But all modelers respect the role that money and investment capital play in spatial patterns.

In sum, theorists from many disciplines agree that macro-level economic factors have influenced, even determined, the shape and form of metropolitan space. But they do not agree on whether or not this growth of modern cities has been "good" or "bad" for people who live in them. That is, theorists of urban form *de*scribe the same processes affecting urban spatial growth and differentiation but *pre*scribe varied solutions for changing the modern metropolis. This situation should sound familiar: Nineteenth-century theorists (Marx, Tönnies, Durkheim) described the rural–urban shift in similar ways. But they too prescribed different solutions to what they viewed as the ill effects accompanying that shift.

The design of new cities, of course, depends on what people think is wrong with the old ones. In part, Chapter 17 deals with this issue. It also suggests how micro-level factors affect urban space and how micro- and macro-level forces together shape urban space.

Generally speaking, the "new" urban paradigm, not so new any longer, is based on radical theory. Joe R. Feagin, for one, draws inspiration from radical sources. But the Manhattan Institute, a nonprofit think tank in New York City associated with conservative thought, uses the same term with a very different meaning.

KEY TERMS

Central business district (CBD) A North American term indicating the heart of the industrial city, commonly referred to as "downtown." The U.S. Census Bureau defines the CBD as an area of very high land valuation characterized by a high concentration of retail businesses, offices, theaters, hotels, and service businesses, as well as high traffic flow.

Central place theory Economic geographer Walter Christaller's 1933 theory, which holds that a hierarchy of central places (cities) evolves to serve surrounding hinterlands. The smallest central places, offering a limited range of goods and services, serve relatively small, hexagon-shaped areas, while the largest central place in a region has a wide range of goods and services available and a much larger hinterland containing many smaller and intermediate central places.

Chicago school of sociology A school of thought developed at the University of Chicago that attained its greatest prestige in the late 1920s and early 1930s. Sociologists Ernest W. Burgess and Robert E. Park were leading members of the school. The urban ecology perspective developed by the Chicago school shaped subsequent thinking about cities.

Concentric zone model A model of the internal structure of the city, developed by Chicago sociologist Ernest W. Burgess in the 1920s, that conceptualized cities as organized in a series of concentric zones radiating out from the center. Each zone tended to have a different population type and a different set of land uses and functions. Immigrant ethnic groups, according to Burgess, initially tended to settle close to the center of the city and gradually moved out toward the periphery as they became assimilated.

Gentrification The process whereby members of a higher-income and higher-status group move into a neighborhood occupied by lower-income, lower-status persons. When this "trickling up" occurs, the neighborhood will be physically improved but many of the former residents displaced. This process reverses the filtering-down process whereby one group moves up the socioeconomic ladder and another group, lower on the ladder, moves into the housing left behind.

Ghetto A section of a city, often rundown and/or over-crowded, inhabited chiefly by a minority group that is effectively prevented from living in other areas because of prejudice or economic barriers. Historically, the word was first used in medieval Venice to refer to the place where armaments were kept; later, this arsenal area became the Jewish quarter of Venice. Over time, "ghetto" became a synonym for the area where Jews were forced to live in isolation by law or custom. Over the centuries, its meaning became more inclusive. In the United States, it now denotes a section of the city where certain groups (generally poor, often people of color or new immigrants) are forced to live for economic, if not social, reasons.

Hinterland In central place theory, the area adjacent to and dependent on an urban center. This term once referred to the backcountry or the area in back of the coastal region. Today, it refers to the urban sphere of influence or trade area—which may be global in scope.

Index of dissimilarity A measure of *absolute* racial segregation in housing citywide. It measures the distribution of white and nonwhite households among census blocks. Each census block can have a score from 0 to 100; the higher the number, the higher the level of racial segregation. The index looks at the population of a racial group in an entire city, asking this question: To make every census block in the city mirror the racial makeup of the city as a whole, what percentage of each group would have to move to another block?

Index of exposure A measure of *relative* racial segregation in housing. It measures the proportion of people sharing the same ethnic/racial background in a neighborhood. Often, it is used as a stand-in for measuring positive interaction between racial groups, the assumption being that physical proximity to people from other racial/ethnic groups promotes positive interaction and empathy.

Internal structure of the city The location, arrangement, and interrelationships between social and physical elements within a city.

Invasion and succession Terms that describe the process of social change in cities. These terms fit into a theoretical model that sees successive social groups competing for and succeeding one another in a given physical area. "Invasion" describes the entrance into an area of a new class or group and the resulting displacement of certain other classes or groups of existing residents. The process may, however, involve an amalgamation of the invasion types with the resident types. "Succession" describes the order, in a series of territorial occupations, as one group in an area is forced out or replaced by another.

Manufacturing Transforming a substance into a new product. Assembly of component parts is also considered manufacturing if the new product is not a building (a structure or other fixed improvement).

Multinucleated metropolitan region Neither city nor suburb, a new spatial form with many specialized centers characterized by enclosed shopping malls, usually a conglomeration of hi-tech industry, services, and information processing. Examples include Orange County, California, and Suffolk County, New York.

Multiple nuclei model A model of the internal structure of the city developed by geographers Chauncy Harris and Edward L. Ullman in 1945. In their view, a city has more than one nucleus. Thus, not only the CBD but also a port, a university, or an industrial area may act as the center around which activities are organized.

Range A term in central place theory referring to the zone or tributary area around a central place from which persons travel to the center to purchase the good (service or merchandise) offered at that place. Theoretically, the upper limit of this range is the maximum possible radius of sales. The lower limit of the range is the radius that encloses the minimum number of consumers necessary to provide a sales volume adequate for the good to be supplied profitably from the central place. Today, electronic retailing and catalog shopping make the concept obsolete for many goods and services.

Sectoral model A model of urban growth developed by real estate economist Homer Hoyt in the 1930s. The model holds that classes of land use tend to be arranged in wedge-shaped sectors radiating from the CBD along major transportation corridors.

System of cities A term describing how cities of different sizes and functional types are interdependent and economically interrelated in systematic ways. Pre-1970s literature on the system of cities describes the specialization of functions among cities (in Europe and North America mainly) and how they interact; post-1970s literature focuses on the global urban hierarchy.

Urban ecology The study of the spatial distribution of people and institutions in cities from a distinctive perspective, originated by members of the Chicago school of sociology, particularly Ernest W. Burgess and Robert E. Park.

PROJECTS

1. **Postsuburbia**. Compare and contrast any three postsuburban counties in the United States (e.g., Prince Georges, Maryland; Fairfax, Virginia; Gwinnett/De Kalb, Georgia; Orange, California; Du Page, Illinois; Contra Costa, California; Oakland, Michigan; Montgomery, Pennsylvania; San Mateo, California; Fairfield, Connecticut; Norfolk, Massachusetts; Broward, Florida; Monmouth, New Jersey; Santa Clara, California) with three industrial or postindustrial cities. Using U.S. Census data, look for the annual county employment growth by sector (e.g., manufacturing, land development, finance, service), demographic data (e.g., total population, size of the largest place in 1990 and 2000), and socioeconomic characteristics (e.g., race/ethnicity, median family income, poverty rate, unemployment rate). What features do the postsuburban counties share? Are some more like industrial or postindustrial cities than bedroom communities, the old stereotypical suburb?

2. **Age–gender pyramids**. Review Figure 16.8 and the discussion of age–gender pyramids. Obtain the most recent volume of *U.S. Census of Population and Housing*, which contains census tract information for your community. Select one census tract with a high concentration of older residents and one that has a high concentration of young children. (If any other census tracts stand out as having unusually nonuniform distributions of population by age or gender, you may want to include them as well.) Construct age–gender pyramids for each census tract. Construct some plausible hypotheses about the areas based on the census data alone. Finally, visit the two census tracts. Do your personal observations seem to support your hypotheses?

3. **ZIP CODE clusters and social area analysis**. Is the thinking behind the lifestyle clusters of Nielsen Claritas (Chapter 8) similar to the underlying principles of social area analysis? If yes, what are the commonalities. If not, what are the key differences?

SUGGESTIONS FOR FURTHER LEARNING

Take a look at recent urban geography texts to see the discipline's boundaries or lack of same. Note the range of topics covered.

A spate of recent books deal with various aspects of neighborhood change in the United States. Two dealing with immigration and neighborhood change are a volume edited by sociologist Douglas Massey, mentioned in this chapter for his various studies of U.S. housing segregation, *New Places: the Changing Geography of American Immigration* (New York: Russell Sage Foundation, 2008), and *Where We Live Now: Immigration and Race in the United States* (Berkeley: University of California Press, 2009) by sociologist–demographer John Iceland. Iceland finds that, while the future remains uncertain, evidence suggests that U.S. metro areas are not splintering irrevocably into homogeneous, ethnically-based areas. Indeed, he finds that U.S. neighborhoods may become less, not more, segregated.

Globalization has become a hot topic in recent years. For a detailed discussion of the various streams of scholarly globalization research, see Jon P. Beaverstock, Richard G. Smith, and Peter. J. Taylor's 1999 article "A Roster of World Cities," in *Cities* 16(6):445–458. They give Peter Hall and Saskia Sassen the credit they both deserve as original thinkers on this important topic. Also see the spate of books by one of globalization's leading theorists, Saskia Sassen (e.g., *A Sociology of Globalization* [New York: W.W. Norton, 2007]), writing on the topic since the early 1990s.

Unfortunately, the works of many important social theorists are not easily accessible. Foremost in this category is Marx's *Capital* (*Das Kapital*). The profound (but dense and difficult) category includes the shapers of the political economy paradigm, Henri Lefebvre, *The Production of Space* (Cambridge, Mass.: Blackwell, [1974] 1991); and Manuel Castells' writings.

The "new" urban paradigm is most often associated with thinkers drawing on Marx's ideas. For an exception, see articles collected from *City Journal*, a quarterly magazine of urban affairs published by the conservative think tank, the Manhattan Institute, in *The Millennial City: A New Urban Paradigm for 21st-Century America*, edited by Myron Magnet (Chicago: Ivan R. Dee, 2000). Contributors, including Nathan Glazer, reject what they call "municipal welfare ideology" and suggest alternative ways to educate children, lower crime rates, and improve the quality of urban life, among other issues.

For a discussion of ideas that underpin the multinucleated metropolitan region model of space, see Rob Kling, Spencer Olin, and Mark Poster, eds., *Postsuburban California: The Transformation of Orange County Since World War II* (Berkeley: University of California Press, 1991).

In *Tompkins Square Park* (New York: Powerhouse Books, 2008), Q. Sakamaki, a Japanese photographer living in New York City, and Bill Weinberg document the gentrification and antigentrification movements of one part of New York City. The book pays tribute to the culture in the 1980s in the park and its environs. Although poor and riddled with homelessness, addiction, AIDS, and dangerous streets, this East Village neighborhood was also life-affirming and full of camaraderie. Now, Sakamaki says, "We lost our culture."

Starting before World War I, Chicago was the lab for urban sociology and geography in the United States, and the literature on the city's sociospatial structure continues to be rich. For a historical analysis of its residential segregation, see Arnold R. Hirsch, *Making the Second Ghetto: Race and Housing in Chicago, 1940–1960* (New York: Cambridge University Press, 1985). Hirsch looks at various ways that racial integration was blocked in the city, ending in a ghetto supported by government action.

For discussions of economic recession and city importance, see Richard Florida's *Atlantic Monthly* article "How the Crash will Reshape America" (March 2009) (http://www.theatlantic.com/doc/200903/meltdown-geography/6). Florida discusses the book of his colleague Chris Kennedy at the University of Toronto, *The Wealth of Cities* (forthcoming as of April 2009). According to Florida, it shows that only

> wholesale structural changes, from major upgrades in infrastructure to new housing patterns to big shifts in consumption, allow places to recover from severe economic crises and to resume rapid expansion. London laid the groundwork for its later commercial dominance by changing its building code and widening its streets after the catastrophic fire of 1666. The United States rose to economic preeminence by periodically developing entirely new systems of infrastructure—from canals and railroads to modern water-and-sewer systems to federal highways. Each played a major role in shaping and enabling whole eras of growth.

REFERENCES

Abadie, Alberto, and Sofia Dermisa. 2006. "Is terrorism eroding agglomeration economies in central business districts? Lessons from the office real estate market in downtown Chicago." *National Bureau of Economic Research Working Paper W12678* (November): http://papers.ssrn.com/sol3/papers.cfm?abstract_id=942973

Abu-Lughod, Janet L. 1991. *Changing Cities: Urban Sociology*. New York: HarperCollins.

Bailey, Nick, and Ivan Turok. 2001. "Central Scotland as a polycentric urban region: Useful planning concept or chimera?" *Urban Studies* 38(4):697–715.

Barlett, Donald L., and James B. Steele. 1992. *America: What Went Wrong?* Kansas City: Andrews and McMeel.

Beaverstock, Jon P., Richard G. Smith, and Peter J. Taylor. 1999. "A roster of world cities." *Cities* 16(6):445–458.

Berry, Brian J. L., and John D. Kasarda. 1977. *Contemporary Urban Ecology*. New York: Macmillan.

Blokland, Talja. 2008. "From the outside looking in: A 'European' perspective on the *Ghetto*." *City & Community* 7(4):372–377.

Bradsher, Keith. 2007. "Big Brother gets high-tech help in Shenzhen." *International Herald Tribune* (August 12): (http://www.iht.com/articles/2007/08/12/asia/china.1-113312.php

Burgess, Ernest W. [1923] 1925. "Growth of the city." Pp. 47–62 in Robert E. Park, Ernest W. Burgess, and Roderick McKenzie, eds., *The City*. Chicago: University of Chicago Press.

Burgess, Ernest W., and Donald J. Bogue, eds.*Contributions to Urban Sociology*. Chicago: University of Chicago Press.

Business Wire. 2000. "Baker & McKenzie selects Next-Page technology to improve attorney productivity." (September 19): http://www.encyclopedia.com/doc/1G1-65310280.html

Castells, Manuel. [1972] 1977. *The Urban Question: A Marxist Approach*. Cambridge, Mass.: MIT Press.

—— 1983. *The City and the Grassroots: A Cross-Cultural Theory of Urban Social Movements*. Berkeley: University of California Press.

—— 1989. *The Informational City: Information Technology, Economic Restructuring and the Urban–Regional Process*. Cambridge, Mass.: Blackwell.

Christaller, Walter. [1933] 1966. *Central Places in Southern Germany*. Trans. C. W. Baskin. Englewood Cliffs, N.J.: Prentice Hall.

comScore Networks. 2007. "Worldwide Internet audience has grown 10 percent in last year, according to comScore Networks." (March 6): http://www.comscore.com/press/release.asp?press=1242

Confectioner Magazine. 2004. "Special report, top 25." http://www.confectioner.com/content.php?s=CO/2004/05&p=7

Davis, Mike. 1992a. *Beyond* Blade Runner: *Urban Control, the Ecology of Fear*. Open Magazine Pamphlet 23. Westfield, N.J.: Open Media.

—— [1990] 1992b. *City of Quartz: Excavating the Future in L.A.* New York: Vintage.

Dreier, Peter, John Mollenkopf, and Todd Swanstrom. 2004. *Place Matters: Metropolitics for the Twenty-First Century*. Lawrence: University of Kansas Press.

Eckholm, Erik. 2007. "Crude shacks mask high hopes in south Texas shantytowns." *International Herald Tribune* (August 27):5.

Farley, Reynolds, Howard Schuman, Suzanne Bianchi, Diane Colasanto, and Shirley Hatchett. 1978. "Chocolate city, vanilla suburbs: Will the trend toward racially separate communities continue?" *Social Science Research* 7:319–344.

Farley, Reynolds, Charlotte Steeh, Tara Jackson, Maria Krysan, and Keith Reeves. 1994. "The causes of continued racial residential segregation: Chocolate city, vanilla suburbs revisited." *Journal of Housing Research* 4:1–38.

Feagin, Joe R. 1998. *The New Urban Paradigm: Critical Perspectives on the City*. Lanham, Md.: Rowman and Littlefield.

Firey, Walter. 1947. *Land Use in Central Boston*. Cambridge, Mass.: Harvard University Press.

Florida, Richard. 2009. "How the crash will reshape America." *Atlantic Monthly*: http://www.theatlantic.com/doc/200903/meltdown-geography/6

Forbes. 2007. "Our annual ranking of America's largest corporations." (April 30): http://money.cnn.com/magazines/fortune/fortune500/2007/cities/

Gans, Herbert J. 2008. "Involuntary segregation and the *Ghetto*: Disconnecting process and place." *City & Community* 7(4):353–357.

Geddes, Patrick. [1915]1968. *Cities in Evolution: An Introduction to the Town Planning Movement and to the Study of Civics.* New York: Harper & Row.

Gottdiener, M. 1985. *The Social Production of Urban Space*. Austin: University of Texas Press.

Gottdiener, M., and George Kephart. 1991. "The multi-nucleated metropolitan region: A comparative analysis." Pp. 31–54 in Rob Kling et al., eds., *Postsuburban California: The Transformation of Orange County Since World War II*. Berkeley: University of California Press.

Hagenbaugh, Barbara. 2002. "U.S. manufacturing jobs fading away fast." *USA Today* (December 12): http://www.usatoday.com/money/economy/2002-12-12-manufacture_x.htm

Hall, Peter. [1966] 1967. *The World Cities*. New York: McGraw-Hill.

Harris, Chauncy, and Edward L. Ullman. 1945. "The nature of cities." *Annals of the American Academy of Political and Social Science* 242:7–17.

Harvey, David. 1973. *Social Justice and the City*. Baltimore, Md.: Johns Hopkins University Press.

—— 1989a. *The Condition of Postmodernity*. Cambridge, Mass.: Blackwell.

—— 1989b. "Monument and myth: The building of the basilica of the Sacred Heart." Pp. 200–228 in David Harvey, ed., *The Urban Experience*. Baltimore, Md.: Johns Hopkins University Press.

—— 2005. *The New Imperialism*. New York: Oxford University Press.

—— 2006. *A Brief History of Neoliberalism*. New York: Oxford University Press.

Helper, Rose. 1969. *Racial Policies and Practices of Real Estate Brokers*. Minneapolis: University of Minnesota Press.

Herbers, John. 1981. "Census finds more blacks living in suburbs of nation's largest cities." *New York Times* (national edition) (May 31):1+.

Honeck, Jon. 2004. "International trade and job loss in Ohio." *Policy Matters Ohio* (February): http://www.policymattersohio.org/pdf/trade_report.pdf

Hoyt, Homer. 1939. *The Structure and Growth of Residential Neighborhoods in American Cities.* Washington, D.C.: Federal Housing Administration.

Hudson, John C. 1985. "Plains country towns." *Mosaic* (Fall):11–15.

Ivogeler, Ingolf 2005. (March 7): http://www.uwec.edu/geography/Ivogeler/w111/metro1.htm.</

Jakle, John, and J. A. Wheeler. [1969] 1972. "The Dutch and Kalamazoo, Michigan: A study of spatial barriers to acculturation." *Tijdschrift Voor Economische en Sociale Geografie* 60:249–254.

Kling, Rob, Spencer Olin, and Mark Poster, eds. 1991. *Postsuburban California: The Transformation of Orange County Since World War II.* Berkeley: University of California Press.

Kowinski, William S. [1985] 2002). *The Malling of America.* Bloomington, IN: Xlibris Corporation.

Lefebvre, Henri. [1974] 1991. *The Production of Space.* Trans. Donald Nicholson-Smith. Oxford: Blackwell.

Lewis, Peter H. 1994. "Getting down to business on the net." *New York Times* (national edition) (June 19):sec. 3, 1+.

Logan, John R. and Harvey L.Molotch, 1987. *Urban Fortunes: the Polical Economy of Place.* Berkeley: University of California Press.

Mandel, Ernest. [1972] 1987. *Late Capitalism.* Trans. Joris DeBres. London: Verso.

Massey, Douglas S. 1990. "American apartheid: Segregation and the making of the underclass." *American Journal of Sociology* 96:329–357.

Massey, Douglas S., and Nancy A. Denton. 1988. "Suburbanization and segregation in U.S. metropolitan areas." *American Journal of Sociology* 94:592–626.

Mydans, Seth. 2008. "In land seizures in Cambodia, the poor lose again." *International Herald Tribune* (July 18):8.

Ouroussoff, Nicolai. 2008. "Renewal drains Beijing neighborhoods of life." *International Herald Tribune* (July 24):2.

Park, Robert E., Ernest W. Burgess, and Roderick McKenzie. 1925. *The City.* Chicago: University of Chicago Press.

Pred, Allen. 1977. *City Systems in Advanced Economies.* New York: Wiley.

Sassen, Saskia. 1991. *The Global City: New York, London, Tokyo.* Princeton, N.J.: Princeton University Press.

———. 2006a. *Territory, Authority, Rights: From Medieval to Global Assemblages.* Princeton, N.J.: Princeton University Press.

———. [1994] 2006b. *Cities in a World Economy,* 3rd ed. Thousand Oaks, Calif.: Pine Forge Press.

———. 2008. "Sharp-elbowed cities." *Newsweek International* (September 15):27.

Scheer, Robert. 1979. "Ehrlichman talks about Nixon." *San Francisco Chronicle* (May 30):8.

Shevky, Eshref, and Wendell Bell. 1955. *Social Area Analysis.* Berkeley: University of California Press.

Smith, Michael Peter, and Joe R. Feagin, eds. [1987] 1989. *The Capitalist City: Global Restructuring and Community Politics.* Cambridge, Mass.: Blackwell.

Stark, Judy. 2007. "The latest modular homes sparkle with upgrades, options, lots of room." *San Francisco Chronicle* (March 28):G5.

Steffens, Lincoln. [1903] 1904. *The Shame of the Cities.* New York: McClure Phillips. (Originally published in 1903 as seven articles in *McClure's Magazine.*)

———. [1931] 1937. *The Autobiography of Lincoln Steffens.* New York: Harcourt, Brace.

Stein, Gertrude. [1937] 2004. *Everybody's Autobiography.* Brooklyn, N.Y.: Exact Change.

Stuart, Guy. 2002. "Integration or resegregation: Metropolitan Chicago at the turn of the century." http://www.civilrightsproject.harvard.edu/research/metro/Chicago%20Study4.pdf

Suttles, Gerald D. 1984. "The cumulative texture of local urban culture." *American Journal of Sociology* 90:283–304.

Taeuber, Karl, and Alma Taeuber. 1965. *Negroes in Cities.* Chicago: Aldine.

United States–China Business Council. 2008. "Iowa exports to China." http://www.uschina.org/public/exports/states/individual/iowa_2007.pdf

U.S. Bureau of the Census. 1976. *Census of Retail Trade, 1972.* Vol. 2, *Area Statistics.* Washington, D.C.: Government Printing Office.

———. 2000. "History of the United States Census." http://www.census.gov/prod/ec97/pol00-hec.pdf

U.S. Department of Commerce, Office of Trade and Industry Information, International Trade Administration. 2007. "California: Exports, jobs, and Foreign Investment." (March 12): http://www.ita.doc.gov/td/industry/otea/state_reports/california.html

Vigdor, Jacob L. 2002. "Does gentrification harm the poor?" *Brookings-Wharton Papers on Urban Affairs* 133–182.

Vigil, Diego. 2008. "Barrio genealogy." *City & Community* 7(4):366–371.

von Thunen, Johann Heinrich. [1826] 1966. *Isolated State*. Trans. Carla M. Wartenberg, Peter Hall, ed. Oxford: Pergamon.

Wacquant, Loic. 2008. *Urban Outcasts: A Comparative Sociology of Advanced Marginality*. Cambridge: Polity.

Wald, Matthew L. 1993. "Traffic deaths in New York say a lot about New Yorkers." *New York Times* (national edition) (May 9):1.

Werth, Christopher. 2008. "The technologist: Watching the watchers." *Newsweek International* (September 8):10.

Williams, David R., and Chiquita Collins. 2001. "Racial residential segregation: A fundamental cause of racial disparities in health." *Public Health Reports* (September–October, 116): http://www.publichealthreports.org/userfiles/116_5/116404.pdf

Yen, Hope. 2007. "U.S. blacks pessimistic about racial progress, study finds." *San Francisco Chronicle* (November 14):A13.

CHAPTER 17

A SENSE OF PLACE

Stephen Hender

How important is a sense of place? Important enough for U.S. presidents to evoke it. President George W. Bush chose his place carefully when he gave a televised speech announcing (prematurely, as it turned out) on May 1, 2003, that "the United States and our allies have prevailed" in Iraq: Bush gave this speech aboard the deck of the aircraft carrier USS *Abraham Lincoln*, a symbol of war heroes, power, and glory.

U.S. presidents are not alone. Queens, self-anointed leaders, and officials almost everywhere know that identification with place can have a subtle emotional impact on citizens.

Physical settings can have mind-boggling effects as well. Consider the case of Carlos Castaneda. (Note that he remains controversial). Margaret Mead and some anthropologists praised his work, but many called Castaneda a fraud or pseudoanthropologist. Castaneda claimed many paranormal events, including his becoming a live crow. He died in 1998, a year before the University of California press issued the thirtieth anniversary edition of his first book, discussed in part in this chapter. Sociologist Marcello Truzzi was among the first to say that his books were a hoax. One writer said that "His only real sorcery was turning the University of California [his publisher] into an ass." [Lindskoog in Gardner, 2000:164]). As an anthropology graduate student at UCLA, Castaneda set out to do fieldwork among the Yaqui Indians. Once there, he became drawn into the mystical reality of his informant, a sorcerer named Don Juan. At one point, Don Juan suggested that he find his "own spot" on the floor of the cabin where they were staying. Puzzled, Castaneda tried to respond to this strange request. He felt around and "saw" two spots on the floor that appeared to glow and shimmer. When he approached one spot, he felt nauseous and afraid; the other one made him feel exhausted. Later, he heard Don Juan talking and laughing above his head and woke up. "You have found the spot," Don Juan told him (Castaneda, 1968:29–30, 34).

Castaneda's extraordinary experience, whether actual or mere figment of a vivid imagination, illustrates two themes that run throughout this chapter:

1. The sense of place can have a powerful, even magical, impact on us—often at the unconscious level.

2. People perceive and attach meaning to physical space in various ways.

These themes complement a macro-level theme of Chapter 16—namely, that city form and space reflect a society's economic and social structures.

This chapter, then, is about how people perceive and use space. It begins with a discussion of general perception and spatial perception. Next, it examines views about the effects of the physical environment on human behavior. Then, it moves to close encounters in space: What happens if a man tries to invade a woman's personal space or if outsiders enter your turf? After reviewing the findings of environmental psychology—a subdiscipline devoted to the study of behavior/environment—the chapter considers the principles that architects, landscape architects, urban designers, and planners use to shape urban space. Finally, it turns to dreams, grand dreams of creating new cities.

PERCEPTION: FILTERING REALITY

One person's reality is another's fantasy (see Introduction). People in the same city depend on differing cognitive maps (Chapter 2). Radicals, liberals, and conservatives look at the political economy and see very different realities (Chapter 3).

Figure 17.2 indicates why people disagree on what's real. It shows that perceptual data are processed through three reality filters: cultural, social, and psychological. It implies that the way we filter perceptual data determines how we construct "objective" reality.

CULTURAL FILTERS

Reflecting on how culture transforms physical reality (what is there) into experienced reality, U.S. anthropologist Dorothy Lee wrote the following:

> [T]he universe as I know it or imagine it in the Western world is different from the universe of the Tikopia, in Polynesia. It follows…that I feel differently about what I see. As I look out of my window now, I see trees, some of which I like to be there, and some of which I intend to cut down…the Dakota Black Elk Indian, however, saw trees as having rights to the land, equal to his own.

(1959:1)

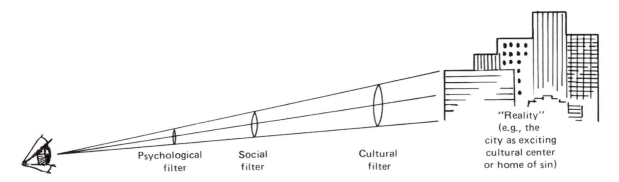

Fig. 17.2 THREE FILTERS OF REALITY. Sense data pass through cultural, social, and psychological filters before becoming "objective" reality in our minds.

In other words, people feel differently about a tree or another object because they perceive them within the conceptual framework of their own culture. The same is the case with behavior: "When I throw a ball, do I perform an aggressive causal act, as my culture predisposes me to believe? Or does the ball leave my hand, as the Greenland Eskimo puts it, or do I merely actualize the ball's potential to move, as the Navaho would have it?" (Lee, 1959:2).

Others suggest that what we see and feel depends on what language we speak. According to the Sapir–Whorf hypothesis (named for its developers, anthropologist Edward Sapir and amateur language-fancier Benjamin Whorf), language does much more than reflect culture; it molds our worldview and thoughts. In this view (called "determinist" by some, "culturally relativist" by others, and "unprovable" by yet others), a group's conception of reality is significantly determined by the categories available to its members in their language. For instance, Hopi Indians have no tenses in their language, nor do they have nouns for times or days. The Sapir–Whorf hypothesis suggests that, as a result, Hopis see the world in terms of dynamic, ever-changing motion. By contrast, English speakers see the world in terms of nouns and linear progression; for them, seconds, hours, and years mark the "reality" of time passing by. English speakers also tend to see events as having a beginning, a middle, and an end; they define things as past, present, or future. This way of viewing the world is foreign to a Hopi speaker. (*Note*: The intellectual history of this

"hypothesis" is tangled but instructive. Many linguistic anthropologists abandoned the Sapir-Whorf hypothesis long ago. Naysayers point to various problems, including the difficulty of testing the so-called hypothesis and the difficulty of sifting the effects of factors influencing culture, such as history, from language itself. In addition, to some, the hypothesis is politically incorrect; it has been used by some to justify racist or ethnicist ideas regarding the supposed superiority [or inferiority] of specific cultures. Experiments with deaf children raised by hearing parents have tried to test the hypothesis. Still controversial, the Sapir-Whorf hypothesis is far from universally accepted now.)

Language and other elements of culture (including the objects we produce and the beliefs we hold) provide the context in which we perceive reality. Within that broad cultural context, there are often subcultural meanings too. For instance, gyrating wildly on a disco dance floor may be perceived as harmless fun by many, if not most, people in the United States or Canada but not by members of a religious community which equates dancing with evil.

Who is to say which cultural or subcultural reality is "true"? Or, as anthropologist Lee (1959:2) asked, "Are they all true, all different facets of the same truth?"

SOCIAL FILTERS

Social identity also helps to shape the reality people perceive. Consider, for example, a common scene of pedestrians and shoppers along Chicago's opulent

"Magnificent Mile" at Christmas. The meanings observers attach to this bustling scene—and what they actually see—can differ with social background. A child might notice only one item in this morass of sense data: the stuffed toys in the store windows. A journalist might see an unusual or a paradoxical event, perhaps a bag lady sifting through the garbage amid the affluence. Meanwhile, the bag lady sees none of this as she searches through the garbage for something to eat.

It follows that *what we see and how we distort features of the urban environment are conditioned by who we are.* One classic study, "They Saw a Game" (Hastorf and Cantril, 1954), documents the importance of the perceivers' social and academic affiliations in the selective perception of a college football game. Surveying fans of both teams, researchers found that they actually "saw" very different games.

PSYCHOLOGICAL FILTERS

Finally, we filter information through our own particular needs, memories, feelings, past experiences, and present concerns. A starving person in Darfur might focus on food scraps lying on the ground, whereas a well-fed congressperson, touring refugee camps, might not notice them.

Psychoanalysts also point to the role that fantasies, myths, and long-forgotten experiences play in perceiving reality. How these operate is a matter of debate, but it is generally acknowledged that the unconscious mind can have powerful effects on a person's thoughts and acts. Sigmund Freud first became aware of the power of the unconscious in 1882; later he called this "psychic reality."

To conclude: How we construct reality depends partially on chance—the culture and times into which we're born and raised and, perhaps, the language we speak—partially on our social location and identity; and partially on our psychic history and present concerns. Thus, what our senses pick up from the environment and translate into "objective reality" constitutes a highly selective process of perception.

PERCEIVING THE BUILT ENVIRONMENT

Billboards, tombstones, buildings, highways, and everything else people construct form the **built environment**. The built environment serves both functional and symbolic purposes. For instance, an apartment building at a "good address" is more than a shelter; it is a symbol of the residents' status. As an essayist of metropolitan life put it long ago, "Nothing succeeds like address" (Lebowitz, [1974] 1978). Echoes of Nielsen Claritas (Chapter 8)!

According to architecture professor Beatriz Colomina (1996), technology has changed the way people perceive space. Pointing particularly to visual technologies such as photos, films, and exhibits, Colomina says that people now define space by images, not walls.

ARCHITECTURE AS SYMBOLIC POLITICS

Buildings offer clues to the values of the people who built them. Years ago, political scientist Harold Lasswell (1979) argued that many U.S. buildings reflect one of the society's central concerns: power. In Lasswell's view, architecture makes a political statement, expressing the values of a society's dominant elites.

Normally, the built environment sends another message, one of social order. But order can quickly turn into disorder—or chaos. For example, when the Twin Towers of the World Trade Center were felled by terrorists on September 11, 2001, there was a sense of things gone wrong in the universe, not only in New York City.

Globally, it is noteworthy that, in some places and for some people, attacks on the built environment can carry a very different meaning. For example, to some, 9/11 symbolizes things gone *right* in the universe: empowerment against capitalism, the United States, and/or modernism.

Architecture speaks in different voices, depending on who's listening. When French radicals occupied the Basilica of Sacré-Coeur in Paris in 1971—100 years after the Paris Commune's attempt at self-government—they attacked the church atop Montmartre as a symbol: the betrayal of revolutionary ideals and the rise of reactionary movements (Harvey, 1989). Similarly, when suicide bombers attacked architect Minoru Yamasaki's World Trade Center in New York City on September 11, 2001, they were not commenting on the buildings' artistic merit. Rather, the buildings were attacked as symbols of U.S. power.

Fig. 17.3 FORTRESS AMERICA. The fortress-like Pentagon in suburban Washington, D.C. symbolizes U.S. military might. The almost worldwide phenomenon of "forting up" in gated communities symbolizes, inter alia, the wish to separate "them" from "us." (U.S. Army photo)

Embassies of any country are particularly symbolic. As reporter Jane Loeffler put it, "Public architecture is inherently political, and all the more so for embassies" (2008). A new U.S. embassy in Berlin opened on July 4, 2008. Scorned by critics who called it "banal," "monstrous," and Fort Knox–like (not a compliment), it was disliked perhaps more symbolically than architecturally. According to Loeffler, "It was meant to be an example of design excellence that would illustrate [the United States's] commitment to the newly reunified Germany . . . it expresses optimism and trust . . ." (41), but one reason it is so disliked by

the German public at large is that it is "little more than a memento from the despised George W. Bush administration" (Loeffler, 2008:39).

The symbolic nature of diplomatic missions, both embassies and consulates, makes them targets for terrorists. In Istanbul, Turkey, for example, the British consulate was the scene of murders by terrorists in 2003, and the U.S. consulate there, called a "fortress" by many, underwent a lethal attack in July 2008.

Most often, architecture reflects the voices of the powerful. In the United States this means that big cities reflect the look of the corporate culture, not

a

b

Fig. 17.4 HOW BUILDINGS SPEAK TO US. "Our architecture reflects us, as truly as a mirror," said the inventor of the skyscraper, Louis Sullivan. As objects, buildings can represent the values of a culture—in tall church spires, factory smokestacks, or skyscrapers housing corporate headquarters and banks. Buildings send different messages to different audiences too. (*a*) Once part of the Forbidden City in Beijing, this former temple, a symbol of grace and imperial power under China's former rulers, is now a people's museum. (*b*) Downtown Chicago, with its steely majesty and (former) industrial power, combined with a curlicue bit of fantasy, a parking garage. (Galen Cranz)

of local cultures. Indeed, the then *New York Times* architecture critic Herbert Muschamp argued that the 1992 riots in South Central Los Angeles were caused in large part by "the lack of integration between the homogenized culture of corporations and developers and the culture of minority neighborhoods." Then, Muschamp (1993b:30) asked whether or not inner city neighborhoods *wanted* to be remade in the image of corporate culture: "Must success always look like a Marriott Hotel? A Kmart? A cluster of glass high-rises?"

Muschamp raised issues of power and culture. Not surprisingly, when the weak become more powerful, meanings attached to buildings often change. And this is probably the case globally. Before the Chinese Revolution in 1949, for example, pagoda-like buildings in Beijing's Forbidden City symbolized the grace and power of China's ruling dynasties. Later, the same buildings came to represent the former rulers' exploitation of the peasants' resources and labor. (And in future, as tourism to China grows, we might expect yet another change of meaning attached to the Forbidden City buildings.)

If large-scale economic change occurs, buildings can reflect the transformation. An industrial wasteland can become a postindustrial workplace of media-based industries. Architects and planners—"symbolic analysts," to use Robert Reich's term ([1991] 1992, see Chapter 7)—shape visions of change, and their buildings can document the shift from manufacturing to information and services.

Symbolically, the contemporary architecture of metropolitan Washington, D.C., reflects a new capitalist order. That is the assessment of professor of urban planning Paul Knox (1991). In his opinion, the postmodern built environment of recent years is a decentralized arena of production, linked by global communication networks and marked by a postmodern aesthetic of playfulness, combinations of styles, and designs that differentiate social classes (as predicted by Bourdieu, see Chapter 11).

And sometimes buildings are shaped as monuments to the past. The U.S. Holocaust Memorial Museum in Washington, D.C., which opened in 1993, is one such monument to memory (Figure 17.5). According to Muschamp, the building itself and the exhibits inside are so compelling that their emotional impact is shattering. Muschamp (1993a:sec. 2:1) said that "a place is a form of knowledge. James Freed's design arises from that pivotal idea." Architect Freed immersed himself in the built environment of Hitler's Final Solution, and some images remained unforgettable, particularly the observation towers (reminding prisoners of their total lack of control) and the brick ovens with steel bands placed around them "when the ovens threatened to explode from overuse." Freed absorbed these forms into his building "as if he could distill their meaning in a ritual of recollection." The result: "an architectural vocabulary that is partly symbolic, partly abstract." "Images of confinement, observation, atrocity and denial surface and recede within the building's hard industrial forms: expanses of brick wall bolted with steel, floating glass bridges engraved with the names of devastated cities, lead pyramids clustered into sentry-box rooflines" (1993b:32). This museum, Muschamp concluded, is "a place quarried from the memory of other places."

Building a monument to memory is often fraught with controversy. Quarrels over "proper" memorials to (1) the Rev. Martin Luther King, Jr., and (2) those killed at the World Trade Center's Twin Towers on 9/11 are illustrative.

In 2006, 38 years after Dr. King was assassinated, ground was broken for his memorial about one half-mile from the Lincoln Memorial on the National Mall in Washington, D.C. Why did it take so long? Because the memorial's design, placement, and cost were contentious.

Not one but several architectural competitions were held for a memorial to commemorate those who perished on September 11, 2001, at "ground zero" in New York City. Fund-raising efforts were started, stopped, and restarted. The space—considered hallowed ground by many and commercially desirable by others—remained empty for over 5 years. Despite continuing disagreement on the project's design, ground was broken in summer 2006.

A final word about the symbolic nature of buildings: Although he could not have predicted it, the fleeting nature of symbols is perhaps best expressed by an architect whose own work's meaning changed with time and events. It comes from Japanese architect

Fig. 17.5 MONUMENT TO MEMORY. The U.S. Holocaust Memorial Museum in Washington, D.C., evokes the horror of the Nazi death camps of the 1940s where 11 million human beings—6 million Jews and 5 million others, including people deemed "handicapped," Jehovah's Witnesses, gays, Polish intellectuals, and Roma (Gypsies)—were killed in a cold, systematic way. On April 19, 1993, during the week of the museum's opening, a Roper poll revealed that memory can be faulty: *Over one-third of U.S. adults in the random sample survey thought the Holocaust may not have happened* (22 percent thought that it was possible that the Holocaust never happened; another 12 percent did not know if it was possible that it happened). A follow-up poll by Roper's rival, the Gallup Organization, found that asking the question in a different way (specifically, without a double negative) may have led to different responses. Even so, nearly one out of five respondents indicated some doubt that the Holocaust occurred. (Alan Gilbert, Courtesy of the U.S. Holocaust Memorial Museum)

Minoru Yamasaki, chosen over 10 U.S. architects in a competition to build the World Trade Center:

> The World Trade Center is a living symbol of man's dedication to world peace...beyond the compelling need to make this a monument to world peace, the World Trade Center should, because of its importance, become a representation of man's belief in humanity, his need for individual dignity, his beliefs in the cooperation of men, and through cooperation, his ability to find greatness.
>
> *(Yamasaki, n.d.)*

LAS VEGAS, NEVADA

Sometimes the built environment sends messages that are far from subtle. Such is the case of Las Vegas (Figure 17.6). In 2000, this U.S. city, a gambling (or "gaming") and pleasure spot supreme, was the center of the fastest-growing U.S. metro area for the fourth decade in a row. Indeed, in just one decade, 1990–2000, the metro area gained 83.3 percent population. (*Note*: By summer 2007, the Las Vegas metro area had a more dubious distinction: It ranked among the top three metro areas in the United States for mortgage foreclosures [RealtyTrac, 2007].)

The city of Las Vegas itself gained enormous population in recent decades. It mushroomed from under 26,000 in 1950 to almost 576,000 in 2005 (City of Las Vegas, 2006).

To journalist–novelist Tom Wolfe, Las Vegas is "the only town in the world whose skyline is made up neither of buildings, like New York, nor of trees, like Wilbraham, Massachusetts, but signs" (1977:7). Time has passed since Wolfe wrote that, but a skyline of signs remains a signature of Las Vegas.

In the 1970s, when Wolfe and architect Robert Venturi and his colleagues wrote about Las Vegas, its buildings were little more than concrete sheds with neon signs, including a restaurant shaped like a duck—which is actually one huge sign. Venturi and his colleagues ([1972] 1977) called this "duck and shed" architecture. They wrote that these extreme forms of advertisement are functional to the local economy.

Still today, the Las Vegas Strip depends on persuading transient consumers to stop and spend money. In addition, the unlikely blend of architectural styles at gambling casino–hotels like the 50-storey replica of the

Fig. 17.6 FANTASYLAND. Las Vegas appeals to fantasies of fortune, fun, and folly by lifting visitors out of everyday reality. (Tim Teninty)

Eiffel Tower and Caesar's Palace—Italian Renaissance, neoclassical, modern, and early Christian tomb—are very functional, for they appeal to the fantasies of a diverse clientele.

In Las Vegas, the built environment doesn't let you forget where you are. True, building and population booms in past decades attracted a number of financial-service companies and nongambling businesses to the city of Las Vegas and its metro area, both greatly diversified economically and socially in the past half-century. Still, no one familiar with U.S. urban culture could mistake its pleasure domes for a center of manufacturing or high finance. "The Strip," as part of Route 91 in Las Vegas is called, is legendary for its glitzy gambling casinos and its very own Egyptian sphinxes, Venetian Grand Canal, Eiffel Tower, and New York City streets.

In 2007, the *New York Times* headlined that "In Las Vegas, Too Many Hotels Are Never Enough," citing the hotel building frenzy from about 35,000 guest rooms in the mid-1970s to about 151,000 by the mid-2000s (Rivlin, 2007). CityCenter, billing itself as the most expensive privately funded project in U.S. history when completed (target date 2010) will be a minicity of 66 acres bordering the Las Vegas Strip. It will feature six towers that reach as high as 61 stories, including a 4,000-room hotel. (Whether CityCenter turns out to be recession-proof remains an open question.)

BOX 17.1 SIGNS, SEX, AND SHOW BUSINESS

The Las Vegas Story

Las Vegas is the only town in the world whose skyline is made up neither of buildings, like New York, nor of trees, like Wilbraham, Massachusetts, but signs. One can look at Las Vegas from a mile away on Route 91 and see no buildings, no trees, only signs. But such signs! They tower. They revolve, they oscillate, they soar in shapes before which the existing vocabulary of art history is helpless. I can only attempt to supply names—Boomerang Modern, Palette Curvilinear, Flash Gordon Ming-Alert Spiral, McDonald's Hamburger Parabola, Mint Casino Elliptical, Miami Beach Kidney. Las Vegas' sign makers work so far out beyond the frontiers of conventional studio art that they have no names themselves for the forms they create....

In Las Vegas no farseeing entrepreneur buys a sign to fit a building he owns. He rebuilds the building to support the biggest sign he can get up the money for and, if necessary, changes the name....In the Young Electric Sign Co. era signs have become the architecture of Las Vegas....Men like...Jack Larsen, formerly an artist for Walt Disney, are the designer–sculptor geniuses of Las Vegas, but their motifs have been carried faithfully throughout the town by lesser men, for gasoline stations, motels, funeral parlors, churches, public buildings, flophouses and sauna baths.

Then there is a stimulus that is both visual and sexual—the Las Vegas buttocks decolletage. This is a form of sexually provocative dress seen more and more in the United States, but avoided like Broadway message–embroidered ("Kiss Me, I'm Cold") underwear in the fashion pages, so that the euphemisms have not been established and I have no choice but clinical terms. To achieve buttocks decolletage a woman wears bikini-style shorts that cut across the round fatty masses of the buttocks rather than cupping them from below, so that the outer-lower edges of these fatty masses, or "cheeks," are exposed. I am in the cocktail lounge of the Hacienda Hotel, talking to managing director Dick Taylor about the great success his place has had in attracting family and tour groups, and all around me the waitresses are bobbing on their high heels, bare legs and decolletage-bare backsides, set off by pelvis-length lingerie of an uncertain denomination....On the streets of Las Vegas, not only the show girls, of which the town has about two hundred fifty, bona fide, in residence, but girls of every sort, including, especially, Las Vegas' little high-school buds, who adorn what locals seeking roots in the sand call "our city of churches and schools," have taken up the chic of wearing buttocks decolletage step-ins under flesh-tight slacks. with the outline of the undergarment showing through fashionably.

Source: Tom Wolfe, *The Kandy-Kolored Tangerine Flake Streamline Baby* (New York: Bantam, 1977), p. 8. Copyright © 1963, 1964, 1965 by Thomas K. Wolfe, Jr. Copyright © 1963, 1964, 1965 by New York Herald Tribune, Inc. Reprinted by permission of Farrar, Straus and Giroux, Inc.

What's behind the building boom? A reporter thinks that it is founded on one-upping the competition: "Ever since the mobster Bugsy Siegel opened the first modern hotel casino here in 1946, the surest means for gaining attention has been to one-up the competition by building an even more monstrously immense pleasure palace" (Rivlin, 2007).

Apparently, people never tire of Las Vegas. The "over-the-top expansion," in the words of Las Vegas hotel magnate Steve Wynn, whose MGM Mirage group is building CityCenter (in Rivlin, 2007), is fueled by a 95 percent weekend occupancy rate, partly due to the city's success in advertising itself as a convention venue. (With 5,000 rooms, Wynn's MGM Mirage was, as of 2007, the largest hotel in the world.)

Adding to the boom is Las Vegas's marketing itself to a new type of visitor: aging "boomers" in the United States entering the empty-nest phase of their lives with money to spend. (Contrary to what some predicted, Native American casinos in more than 30 states have not had a negative impact on Las Vegas.

At least not at this writing. However, a weak economy and soaring fuel prices may serve to lessen the number of visitors.) Boomer visitors come for celebrity shows and good food, whether they gamble or not. Thus, Vegas's old appeal—cheap hotel rooms and all-you-can-eat-buffets—disappeared as hoteliers themselves gambled a generation ago; they targeted families and more upscale guests. Their gamble paid off.

Las Vegas has a distinctive sense of place. Indeed, its buildings have been called many names—not all complimentary—ranging from "pleasure zone architecture," "commercial vernacular," to "destructive extravaganza."

Some voice quite another view about Las Vegas's distinctive personality. Columnist Bob Herbert, for one, writes that "There is probably no city in...[the United States] where women are treated worse than in Las Vegas" (2007:7). Herbert decries the "tone of systematic, institutionalized degradation" that prostitution, legal or illegal, puts on women in Las Vegas. One researcher goes further, claiming that Las Vegas is "the epicenter of North American prostitution and sex trafficking" (Farley in Herbert, 2007).

Most cities anywhere are far less distinctive or bizarre, depending on your taste. Nonetheless, most people feel a sense of place wherever they live because they invest the natural and built environment with meaning and sentiment.

There is only one Las Vegas worldwide. But there are copies or homages, unplanned or not. A prime example: Ashgabat formerly Ashkabad), the capital of Turkmenistan. Fueled by oil and gas wealth, the capital was formerly part of the steppe but now features an urban landscape that somewhat rivals Las Vegas. Its architecture has been called "Stalin-Vegas" (not a compliment) because it features white marble and green-tinted glass "as if the city was designed by a warden who thought public spaces should look like mausoleums viewed through sunglasses" (Chivers, 2007:2). Golden statues, busts, and placards of the designer himself—the president for life, Saparmurat Niyazov (who died in 2006)—decorate the monuments in Ashgabat, whose estimated population is about 600,000.

CHINA: SHAPING AN EMERGING NATIONAL IDENTITY

According to a leading architectural critic, stepping out of Beijing's glittering airport, built in time to welcome visitors to the 2008 Summer Olympics, is comparable to the epiphany that Adolf Loos experienced when he stepped off a steamship in New York Harbor more than a century ago: Viennese architect Loos crossed a threshold into the future, out of culturally obsolete Europe. New Beijing gives visitors the very same feeling, says Nikolai Ouroussoff (2008): "It's the inescapable feeling that you're passing through a portal to another world, one whose fierce embrace of change has left Western nations in the dust."

Beijing had an extreme make-over in preparation for the 2008 Olympics. A number of remarkable buildings by renowned Western architects were constructed, including Norman Foster's air terminal, a national stadium ("the bird's nest," designed by Herzog & de Meuron), an egg-shaped national theater by Paul Andreu, and Rem Koolhaas's imaginative, slanting headquarters for the Chinese TV authority.

According to Ouroussoff (2008), these buildings may be expressions of China's budding global primacy. But, in his view, they are much more: "China's new architecture exudes an aura that has as much to do with intellectual ferment as economic clout."

The drive from the Beijing airport passes by a "banal landscape of ugly new towers," many of which are located in gated communities which, Ouroussoff argues, reflect "the widening disparity between affluent and poor." These shoddily built apartment blocks, constructed in the run-up to the Olympics, are so poorly constructed that, he says, they look "decrepit and decades old."

What messages are being sent by Beijing's newly constructed buildings? Modernist symbols such as the airport and the national theater, Ouroussoff (2008) says, reflect China's effort to give shape to an emerging national identity.

But, taken together, the ugly, shoddily built towers and the modernist landmarks suggest two very different faces of modern China. In Ouroussoff's words (2008), "Everything, it seems, is possible here [in China], from utopian triumphs of the imagination to soul-sapping expressions of a disregard for individual lives."

Update: Less than a year after the Olympics, some architect-designed buildings in Beijing looked desolate or worse. Indeed, in 2009 one building burned: a 31-storey building designed by Rem Koolhaas's group (next to the iconic headquarters of China Central TV, also designed by Koolhaas's group). In addition, fewer than the expected number of tourists were paying to visit buildings designed by famous Western architects. So, as of this writing, local officials are trying to find new uses, including shopping malls, for several buildings.

DOES ENVIRONMENT DETERMINE BEHAVIOR?

Will youngsters growing up amid the glitzy signs and desert sands of Las Vegas be significantly different from those raised in snowy, tree-lined Wilbraham, Massachusetts? Does bad housing produce bad people?

The extent to which the natural and built environments affect behavior is a subject of persistent debate. One view maintains that environment determines behavior. At the very least, it holds, the natural and built environments play a key role in determining behavior. Britain's late Lord Manny Shinwell spoke eloquently for (or against, given his own life experience) this point of view: **environmental determinism**.

Shinwell (1884–1986), according to R.W. Apple, Jr, then a *New York Times* reporter (1979) grew up in Glasgow, Scotland's, notoriously squalid Gorbals slum, where there was "every opportunity to become a criminal, and even the best of us emerged from it as hardened agitators and rebels." Shinwell did not become a criminal. He did get out of the Gorbals and became a combative orator in the British Parliament for 48 years.

Shinwell's story raises difficult questions. Was it the filthy smoke pouring in and the crowding or was it the poverty and social conditions in the Gorbals that influenced residents' behavior? This is hard to sort out, for bad physical conditions often go hand in hand with low income and low status. If a teenager living in a deteriorated tenement commits robbery or murder, we can't conclude that the physical environment determined such behavior.

Another, more recent, true story raises similar questions. This one concerns two soccer players from Liverpool, England, who share the same background—unstable homes in Liverpool's tough neighborhoods—but went in different directions. The first Liverpudlian, Steven Gerrard, was honored with a fellowship from a hometown university. The second, professional athlete Joey Barton, served prison time for assault; he is known as a violent man who beat up a teammate severely (Hughes, 2008:16).

So, not all people who live in the same physical environment, like the Gorbals or a tough Liverpool neighborhood, become criminals. Indeed, Shinwell and Gerrard did not. These facts support critics of physical environmental determinism. Critics argue that cultural and psychological variables have more influence on behavior than does physical environment.

This dilemma of interpretation can be illustrated by examining two notoriously bad physical environments, both public housing projects: Pruitt-Igoe and Cabrini-Green. Neither still exists.

CASE STUDY 1: PRUITT-IGOE, ST. LOUIS

Before its demolition in 1974, Pruitt-Igoe in St. Louis, Missouri, symbolized the worst kind of urban envir-

onment. The massive public housing project covered 57 acres and contained 33 slab construction buildings, each with 2,762 apartments on 11 stories. It was designed originally to house about 10,000 people, whites living in the Igoe portion and African Americans living in the Pruitt portion. A Supreme Court decision barred this racial segregation, and the project became racially integrated.

When Pruitt-Igoe opened in 1954, it won praise as an exciting advance in low-income housing. A decade later, it was the subject of worried commission reports as a social disaster. By the mid-1960s, it was occupied entirely by poor blacks, mainly on welfare and disproportionately living in large, female-headed households. By the early 1970s, federal officials gave up on Pruitt-Igoe. The entire project was dynamited and demolished in 1974 (Figure 17.7).

Reviewing the sad history of Pruitt-Igoe, an environmental determinist would have a ready explanation for its failure: bad physical design. Pruitt-Igoe was large and densely settled. Each high-rise was identical to the next. The project had virtually no open space, elevators that stopped only on some floors, easily broken windows, and other poor design features. To a physical determinist, social disaster was predictable, for the project design spelled trouble.

In contrast, a critic of physical determinism would point out that physical design (which had won many architectural kudos) was the least of the problems at Pruitt-Igoe. In a housing project with a large number of poor children, juvenile delinquency and vandalism could be anticipated—no matter how well designed. Further, as long as tenants were unemployed, without ownership rights in their residence, and conscious of their "bad address," hopelessness and hostility could be expected.

Who's right? Perhaps no one. One perceptive commentator argues that there is no right answer because it is based on faulty assumptions. Galen Cranz, a sociologist of spatial behavior, believes that both environmental determinists and their critics are on the wrong track. Cranz (unpublished study) says that there is a reciprocal relationship between the built environment and human behavior. The built environment affects behavior but, at the same time, reflects broader social, economic, and political forces. In her view, people receive messages about the social

Fig. 17.7 PRUITT-IGOE HOUSING PROJECT. St. Louis, Missouri's, vast low-income residential complex was praised initially for its architecture but came to symbolize bad design and social disaster. Built in 1954, it was demolished just 20 years later by the U.S. Department of Housing and Urban Development. (U.S. Department of Housing and Urban Development)

meaning of their world from many sources—verbal, nonverbal, and environmental. Usually, these varied sources transmit similar messages, only in different symbolic forms. Cranz calls this "redundancy."

Applying the redundancy concept to the Pruitt-Igoe case, we note how verbal, nonverbal, and environmental sources sent the same message to poor African American residents: You are inferior. This message was reinforced in subtle and not-so-subtle ways—waiting in line for welfare checks, being subjected to police surveillance, and so forth. Residents could hardly avoid knowing that the larger society devalued them as low-status, low-income persons. The message was all around them—for example, in the mass media, the only visible African Americans were most often cast as bad people or losers when the project was standing. So Pruitt-Igoe's prison-like physical design merely confirmed and reinforced the larger society's negative attitude toward them. Over and over, in various forms, the message of inferiority went out. Redundancy.

CASE STUDY 2: CABRINI-GREEN, CHICAGO

More heavily populated than Pruitt-Igoe, Chicago's Cabrini-Green was synonymous with the worst of the worst of U.S. public housing. Named for Italian American nun Mother Cabrini, the first North American to be canonized, and William J. Green, a Great-Society congressperson, the project reflected U.S. planning ideas current at the time it was built: between 1942 and 1962.

At its peak, Cabrini-Green was home to 20,000 residents in 28 high-, mid-, and low-rises on 70 acres of land. But, in 1996, the federal government mandated the destruction of 18,000 units of public housing in Chicago (together with tens of thousands of public housing units nationwide). Chicago's housing authority planned to raze most high-rise public housing in the city, including much of Cabrini-Green except the original row houses. By 2005, the majority of residents had lost their apartments to demolition. New market-rate housing was built, almost completely surrounding the remaining public housing.

Early residents of the row houses, one of the project's four sections, were primarily Italian Americans. By 1962 the majority of residents in the total project were African American.

By the 1990s, Cabrini-Green was so infamous that its name was short-hand for all that was wrong with public housing in the United States. Among the printable adjectives used to describe it: "crime-ridden," "drug-infested," and "gang-controlled." Fearing for their lives, many Chicago police refused to go inside after several officers had been shot and killed there. Chicago's Mayor Jane Byrne moved in—with police and bodyguards—to show how safe it was in 1981; she left after only 3 weeks. (Chicagoans considered her move-in to be essentially a publicity stunt.)

Mayor Byrne's move-in and quick move-out did bring attention to the project, reinforcing the judgment that Cabrini-Green was the worst of the worst. Many residents feared for their safety there and reasonably so. A 7-year-old boy was killed by a stray bullet while walking to school with his mom in 1992. In 1997, a 9-year-old girl was brutally raped and poisoned in a stairwell, rendering her blind, paralyzed, and unable to speak.

Aside from psychic fear, Cabrini-Green's residents suffered decay and city neglect. These included infestations of rats and cockroaches, rotting garbage, and hallway stench.

The setting for several movies and TV sitcoms, Cabrini-Green was almost always portrayed as a very bad place. One TV sitcom, *The Bernie Mac Show* (FOX, 2001–2006), implied that Cabrini-Green was a place to escape from: Two nieces lived there before going to live with Bernie. Several movies, including *Whiteboyz* (1999), used it as a backdrop for drug use and gang violence. A graphic novel series, *Give Me Liberty* by Dave Gibbons and illustrator Frank Miller ([1990] 2008), showed the Cabrini-Green neighborhood in the short-term future as a gigantic walled prison for its poor residents. In another futuristic comic book series, *Kingdom Come* ([1996]2008) by Mark Waid and illustrator Alex Ross, there is a green monster character named Kabrini. Some nonresidents identified Cabrini-Green with Kabrini, that is, with horror and fear. These included some near-neighbors who could hear drug deals and gunshots at Cabrini-Green from their upscale apartments on Chicago's toney North Side.

However, negative feelings toward Cabrini-Green were not universal. In the documentary film, "Voices of Cabrini: Rebuilding Chicago's Public Housing," (Bezelel and Ferrera, 1999) some longtime residents voice upset at the loss of community that they predicted would result when Cabrini-Green was torn down.

Aside from its notoriety, Cabrini-Green and its neighborhood are very familiar to social scientists, developers, and locals—for different reasons. Historians and social scientists may recognize the area because it was described (not as the "Gold Coast") by Harvey Warren Zorbaugh in his University of Chicago dissertation (under sociologist Robert Park) and published as *The Gold Coast and the Slum* in 1929. Zorbaugh described "Little Sicily" as a slum whose Sicilian "peasants" occupied the area. (The original row houses in Cabrini-Green were once inhabited by Sicilian Americans.)

Developers and locals knew that Cabrini-Green was surrounded by affluent areas, notably the Gold Coast, also described by Zorbaugh, and upscale Lincoln Park, nationally famous for its zoo and views of Lake Michigan. Chicago's Gold Coast and Lincoln Park (SER 04 in PRIZM'S 2006 data) cater to white and Asian, high-income, hip singles and families; their consumption and eating habits could not be more different from those of former Cabrini-Green residents. One securities lawyer living near Cabrini-Green described his eating habits like this: "The staples around here are coffee, bagels, and sushi" (Singer in Weiss, 2000:185). What a stark contrast to a neighborhood like Cabrini-Green, where preferred products included malt liquor and Kentucky Fried Chicken (Weiss, 2000:300–301).

By the 1990s, speculators gambled that property near Cabrini-Green would increase in value as the project would eventually be razed, and thus they bought property nearby. They guessed right. Since the mid-1990s, developers converted vast industrial land tracts surrounding Cabrini-Green into market-rate homes, offices, and retail stores.

Cabrini-Green's redevelopment and relocation of residents remain controversial and legally questioned. Some "workfare affordable" and "replacement" housing was planned in the redevelopment of the site. But there was also much gentrification because the area is so desirable; housing built nearby was destined almost totally for very affluent buyers.

By 2006, the neighborhood had greatly changed. Affluent whites, not poor African Americans, dominated the area. Most of Cabrini-Green had disappeared.

With it, some say, went a sense of community and the occasional triumph. Most movies showing Cabrini-Green were like the older film, *Cooley High* (1975), showing the project in a grim light. Yet, one Hollywood film suggested that there was an occasional victory: *Hardball* (2001). This film, set in Cabrini-Green, features Keanu Reeves as an aimless guy whose life is turned around by coaching Cabrini-Green's Little League team. Critics panned it. But it showed how poor African Americans lived with hardship on a daily basis and even managed to find meaning and love. And, once in a while, victory. (*Note*: *Hardball* opened in Chicago on the weekend after 9/11. *Chicago Tribune* reporter Mary Schmich [2001] acknowledges how popular it was among Cabrini-Green youth.) Thus, at least in the film, even in notoriously squalid and dangerous environments like Cabrini-Green, some managed to be victorious.

To conclude: In Europe, at least since the mid-eighteenth century, some philosophers have claimed that human beings could be changed by changing the environment they live in. Philosopher–psychologists David Hartley (1749) in England (who influenced early English socialist Robert Owen, discussed later in this chapter) and Claude Adrien Helvétius ([1758] 2004) in France represent this idea. Others thought them eccentric, at the very least.

To this day, social scientists and citizens continue to disagree about the environment–behavior interaction. So, how do environment, particularly housing, and behavior interact?

Perhaps Winston Churchill had the final word. When he reopened the House of Commons after World War II, he said, "We shape our buildings and then they shape us" (1943).

THE SPIRIT AND ENERGY OF PLACE

GENIUS LOCI

Novelist Lawrence Durrell once wrote that it is not buildings that shape human identity. Rather, it is the "spirit of place" ([1969], 1997).

What is the *spirit* of place? According to philosopher and architectural historian Christian Norberg-Schulz ([1979] 1984:5), ancient Romans thought that there is a "spirit of place" or guardian spirit of the locality (genius loci) that gives life to people and places, accompanying them from birth to death and determining their character. These Romans, Norberg-Schulz wrote, believed that they should come to terms with the guardian spirit of the locality because survival depended on having a good relationship with the place in both the physical and the psychic senses.

FENG SHUI

In some cultures, a good relationship with place is all-important. Such is the case in traditional Chinese culture. Today, many home builders, business owners, city planners, and interior decorators are influenced by feng shui—that is, the "feel of a place."

Literally, the words "feng" and "shui" (pronounced "fěng shwā",) mean "wind" and "water." Figuratively, the technique is based on the idea that there are currents of invisible energy that flow in certain directions, just like the energy flows of wind and water.

Feng shui aims at ensuring that all things are in harmony with their surroundings. Ninth-century scholar Yang Yun-sung originally codified the principles of feng shui. He drew inspiration from the harmonious, undulating hills and meandering rivers around Gwelin in southwest China, a spectacularly scenic region celebrated by centuries of Chinese poets and painters.

Today, many people dismiss feng shui as mere superstition. But others, particularly in Hong Kong, Viet Nam, and other parts of the world where the Chinese have been influential, still plan houses and villages based on its principles. In the San Francisco Bay Area, for example, it is not unusual for a feng shui expert to suggest the "perfect direction" of a business (ensuring prosperity) or the "perfect arrangement" of a home (creating happiness and tranquility).

According to feng shui principles, a bend in the river outside a hotel might help the hotel's financial success. A house's entrance door must open inward in order to attract good energy, or ch'i (the same term used by acupuncturists to describe the body's flow of vital energies).

To conclude: Do the spirit and energy of place remain defining elements of human experience? Or have technology and social reorganization destroyed the traditional importance of place? There is no one answer.

Years ago some touted TV as a "19-inch neighborhood," claiming that it had replaced a sense of place for many people. We might update that observation, arguing that many global citizens surmount space and place (and time zone differences) by meeting friends in cyberspace: For uncountable millions, e-mail, text messaging, and MySpace, Facebook, or Linked-in bonding replace coffee klatschs and pickup basketball. At the same historical moment, however, others, from Darfur to the Middle East and Sri Lanka, are sacrificing their lives for inches of ancestral land invested with political, religious, tribal, or ethnic significance.

It is safe to say that in *Techno$chaft*, the spirit of place does not play a defining role in most people's lives. Indeed, there may be much less of a spirit of place, particularly for members of electronic networks. Why? Because computers, faxes, and other "instruments of instant artificial adjacency" are creating "Cyberbia": an "ageographical city" that is "visible in clumps of skyscrapers rising from well-wired fields next to the Interstate; in huge shopping malls...in the clouds of satellite dishes pointed at the same geosynchronous blip" (Sorkin, 1992:xi).

Still, tourism is (at least until soaring gas prices and a global economic recession began in the 2000s) arguably the biggest legal business in the world. This suggests that the experience of place remains of keen interest.

For some, place can translate into shopping opportunities. In mid-2008, for example, a record number of tourists from abroad came to New York City and outspent tourists in Las Vegas and Orlando (Williams, 2008:1).

Of course, some areas are more tourist-dependent than others. Relatively cheap organ transplants ("transplant tourism"), good weather, superb music, and/or historic sites can be big draws for international visitors. Tourism in Oaxaca, Mexico, for example, accounts for about 80 percent of the poor state's economy; hoteliers, shop owners, restauranteurs, and handicraft sellers depend on the estimated 1.4 million yearly visitors for their livelihoods. (In 2006, political unrest in Oaxaca caused several countries, including the United States, Canada, and France, to issue travel warnings to avoid the city. The consequent loss of income resulted in more than 3,000 tourist-dependent workers' unemployment [Campbell, 2007:A17]).

Tourism is often viewed by locals as a mixed blessing. It brings hard currency—and sometimes trouble. As the mayor of Malia, Crete, opined about young British tourists in 2008, "They scream, they sing, they fall down, they take their clothes off, they cross-dress, they vomit" (in Lyall, 2008)—clearly actions of which the mayor disapproved. Malia is just one European resort full of young tourists on packaged tours "offering cheap alcohol and a license to behave badly" (Lyall, 2008).

Yet, when tourism falls as a result of economic downturns, people and businesses can suffer. In the first half of 2008, Spain, competing with cheaper vacation spots like Turkey (and feeling the slide of the British pound plus the weakened dollar vis-à-vis the euro) had perhaps the worst tourist season in 48 years: The biggest hotel group in Spain reported a 41 percent decline in revenues (Reuters, 2008:20).

EXPERIENCING PERSONAL SPACE

Has someone recently gotten "too" close to you, playing an iPod in "your" space? Did a "close talker" make you feel hostile? ("Close talker" is a term used on the long-running *Seinfeld* TV show, now in syndication, to describe a person who gets in your face while talking to you.)

People experience space very differently. How we encounter space depends on our reality filters and on the kind of space we occupy. Here, we focus on two types of occupied space: personal and social.

An environmental psychologist and author of a seminal study on the topic, Robert Sommer (1969:viii), used the term **personal space** in two ways: to describe (1) "the emotionally charged zone around each person, sometimes described as a soap bubble or aura, which helps to regulate the spacing of individuals" ("the invisible force field around your body" is the way Rosenbloom [2006] put it) and (2) "the processes by which people mark out and personalize the spaces they inhabit." Personal spaces are those we consider ours.

How deep is our experience of space? One study found that the (unwritten) "rules" of personal space are so powerful that humans even impose them on avatars (digital representations of the humans controlling them) in a cyber game (in Rosenbloom, 2006).

How important is our experience of space? One online TripAdvisor survey on airplane preferences in 2007 suggests that it is very important. Respondents put a higher premium on more personal space than some tantalizing goodies, voting for more legroom and larger seats over great food and massages. Before soaring jet fuel costs, one airline picked up on this, promoting its New York–London hop as giving passengers "21 square feet of personal space."

PERSONAL SPACE AS PROTECTIVE BUBBLE

We treat our bodies and the invisible bubble surrounding our bodies as the most private, inviolate territory. It is ours; we own it. All societies have rules about touching the bodies or invading the body territories of others. In the United States, for instance, affectionate body contact between heterosexual males is nearly taboo—except in special circumstances, such as on the football field.

What happens if another person tries to break our bubble by invading it? That depends. We may withdraw and move away, we may get hostile, or we may do nothing.

Researchers find that gender is a key variable in people's reactions to the invasion of personal space. One experiment, performed in a college library, found that female students—much more than male students—tried to protect themselves against unwanted spatial invasions (Klinge, [1999] 2008). Earlier studies, including one conducted on Los Angeles beaches, found that men routinely invade women's personal space but the reverse is not acceptable. Why? Either women are simply more sociable than men or women can't prevent their space from being invaded because, in general, their social status is lower than that of men and/or they are socialized differently. The reasons remain unclear.

Even in cyberspace, U.S. women's gender roles may remain traditional, particularly a dependence (much more so than men) on others for a sense of self. This may suggest that women's space is invaded more from lack of control and/or acceptance of societal expectations than from some innate sociability (see Magnuson and Dundes, 2008).

How big is a person's bubble? That depends too. Bubble sizes vary from culture to culture. Not knowing this could lead to misunderstanding, even trouble. That is one reason U.S. embassy officials receive training in what anthropologist Edward T. Hall (1959) called **proxemics**: the study of how people in different cultures use intimate space, particularly for social interaction such as conversation.

Hall, a pioneer in the study of personal space, illustrated why proxemics is important for cross-cultural understanding: "In Latin America the interaction distance is much less than it is in the United States. Indeed, people cannot talk comfortably with one another unless they are very close to the distance that evokes either sexual or hostile feelings in the North American." The result, Hall said, is that "when they move close, we withdraw and back away. As a consequence they think we are distant or cold, withdrawn

and unfriendly. We, on the other hand, are constantly accusing them of breathing down our necks, crowding us, and spraying our faces" (1959:164).

Nonverbal communication may be equally misunderstood. In the 1960s, Hall recounted a personal experience that illustrates the point. While waiting for a friend in an empty hotel lobby in Washington, D.C., Hall seated himself in a solitary chair. He expected any stranger to leave him alone. Yet, a stranger entered the lobby and stood so close to Hall that he could hear him breathe. Hall moved slightly to signal his annoyance with body language. The stranger only moved closer. But Hall would not abandon his post. He thought, "Why should I move? I was here first." Moments later, a group arrived to join his "tormentor." It was then that Hall realized, from gestures and language, that the stranger was an Arab. Later, Hall described the scene to an Arab colleague, who helped him understand what had happened: "In Arab thought I had no rights whatsoever by virtue of occupying a given spot; neither my place nor my body was inviolate! For the Arab, there is no such thing as an intrusion in public. Public means public" (1966).

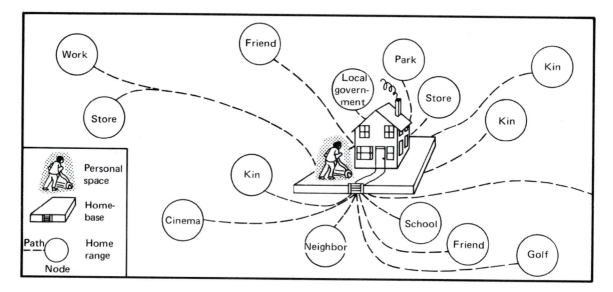

Fig. 17.8 IMMEDIATE PHYSICAL ENVIRONMENT. People tend to see their personal space, home base, and home range as inviolate territories or "defensible space." (J. D. Porteous, "An Organizing Model of Territoriality in an Urban Setting," in *Environment and Behavior: Planning and Everyday Urban Life* [Reading, Mass. Addison-Wesley, 1977], p. 29. Copyright © by J. Douglas Porteous. Reprinted by permission.)

The size of a person's inviolate sphere of privacy varies with the surroundings, the social importance of the person, and other characteristics such as age. Each culture has implicit rules about the proper spatial distance in particular situations. In the United States, a person who invades another's body territory—even for a specific purpose, such as asking directions—usually acknowledges the intrusion by saying "Excuse me."

PERSONALIZING OUR SPACE: HOME TERRITORIES

Home territories are areas where participants have relative freedom to act as they want plus a sense of intimacy and control over the area. In other words, they are spaces in which we feel safe and comfortable. Home territories consist of *home base* (the home and its immediate surroundings) and *home range* (places where a person feels safe and a sense of belonging).

Increasingly, some argue, feelings of danger and fear are changing the notion of "home." For example, architecture professor Beatriz Colomina (2007) suggests that home is like a battlefield—with its use of technology designed originally for military ends.

Others look at new technologies with a skeptical eye, particularly for their role in changing human

Fig. 17.9 HOUSE AS SYMBOL. A residence is often sold on the basis of status appeal, not function. In this ad, which appeared in the *New York Times*, the high status of a former occupant and famous entertainers, seclusion, and ZIP code are the selling points of this property.

interaction and concepts of home. Paul Virilio, best known for his "dromology" or study of speed ([1977] 2007), is exemplary. French urbanist and theorist Virilio (b. 1932) emphasizes the role of technology in changing much of contemporary life, including home. (Indeed, Virilio sees speed—not class or status or power—as the prime shaper of civilization.) He thinks that new technologies will transform the home into a place of domestic simulators and virtual space rooms (in Sans, n.d.).

Home Base

Home in the United States, for some (most?) is a safe haven amidst the turbulent seas of life. Home embodies the familiar, and it is the place many feel most comfortable.

Perhaps because home is bound up with our identity, most of us rise—instinctively—to its defense when it is threatened. Or as the English say, "A person's home is his (or her) castle."

Meanings attached to home pass through cultural, social, and psychological filters. In the United States, the meaning of home base varies with social class and status. For example, a study of Pruitt-Igoe, before it was demolished (see the extended discussion of this project earlier), found that the most important function of home to tenants there was house-as-safe-haven (Rainwater, 1966). The study suggested that lower-class, low-status tenants lived in a world of perceived threat: crime and vandalism, health hazards, verbal abuse, and so on. To them, home represented a retreat.

By contrast, to upper-class, high-status groups— say, those who live in PRIZM's top-ranked lifestyle clusters–home symbolizes their high social rank too (Chapter 8). Striving younger executives, for instance, may choose mock colonial homes that conspicuously display their stability and wealth; more established professionals may prefer less showy homes.

Living spaces are more than devices for sending messages to others about who we are—or wish to be. Homes are also symbols of the way we perceive ourselves. According to Claire Cooper Marcus, the way we arrange furniture and pictures as well as the plants we buy are forms of self-expression, messages we want to tell ourselves. She calls this "house-as-symbol of self" ([1995] 2006).

Fig. 17.10 LOW-COST SHELTER FOR THE HOMELESS. Worldwide, homeless and poor people construct shelters out of oddments. San Francisco architect Donald Macdonald has another idea: building compact, low-cost shelters called "city sleepers." (Josh Freiwald)

Through their homes, people often tell themselves one thing and outsiders another. In most U.S. homes, for instance, the living room doesn't look lived in. No cookie jars, coats lying around, or papers strewn about. If guests are expected, it is usually the living room that is cleaned up, while unkempt bedrooms or other private spaces are left as is. In France, upper-status families often have a special room for entertaining—the parlor, whose perfect appearance usually contrasts with the messier private spaces. Similarly, Japanese American families in northern California often present a conventional image to their neighbors by their front-yard landscaping; for their own enjoyment, they use a rear, hidden-from-view Japanese garden.

What do U.S. home buyers want? According to a 2007 National Association of Realtors survey (in Miller, 2007:B8), prospective U.S. home buyers sought bigger, more energy-efficient, technology-equipped, and younger homes than they did just a few years before, in 2004. The most cherished features were neither a kitchen nor a family room; they were central air conditioning (especially in the Midwest and the South), an oversized garage (in the West), and a backyard or play area (in the Northeast).

(By 2009, many home buyers sought very different kinds of houses, the kind which didn't lose value and the kind that would not be foreclosed upon!)

"THE ARCHITECTURE OF DESPAIR"

At the same time that many in the United States want larger, technologically "smart" homes, another type of housing—makeshift homes—is becoming more common. These makeshift homes are symbols of something very different: permanent homelessness.

Although it may seem to be an oxymoron, increasing numbers of homeless persons are constructing homes or home-like boxes and shacks. These structures—made of orange crates, refrigerator shelving, or other leftovers—have been called the "architecture of despair." Some think they reflect the need to create a sense of home, no matter how extreme the circumstances. Such spontaneous settlements are reminiscent of the no-tech shantytowns in poor countries, such as Rio de Janeiro's *favelas* and bamboo riverside huts in Dhaka, Bangladesh.

Makeshift dwellings may or may not qualify as examples of what J. B. Jackson (1984:85) called "vernacular architecture." (Jackson, an influential voice in landscape studies, wrote that vernacular dwellings suggest something "traditional": "the dwelling of the farmer or craftsman or wage earner.") Makeshift street architecture is constructed with local techniques, local materials, and the local environment in mind, all characteristics of vernacular architecture.

Whether or not vernacular, makeshift street dwellings are more than mere shelter. They are symbols of people's inventiveness and, at the same time, seemingly permanent poverty.

Home Range

Beyond home base lies home range, where a person feels like he or she belongs. As noted in the next section, public territories (social space) are often converted into the home range of individuals or social groups.

The extent of a person's home range varies with age, social standing, background, and personal disposition. Children tend to have the narrowest home ranges. Very young children may perceive a one-block area around home as home range. For older children, home range is often equated with their neighborhood.

For some adults, too, home range consists of little more than their neighborhoods. This is often the case with new, non-English-speaking immigrants. One student told me that his mother had not left San Francisco's Chinatown since her arrival from China some 40 years earlier. This anecdote is not evidence, but it does suggest that residents of homogeneous ethnic neighborhoods have a stronger sense of home range than residents of more heterogeneous neighborhoods and/or more fear of the world beyond the neighborhood. (A research project perhaps!)

For other adults, the workplace is a home territory. A person can invest his or her office with the symbolic meaning of home base—inviolate territory and safe haven. For instance, when a TV sportscaster in Fresno, California, was interrupted (on air) in the TV studio by a (toy) gun-toting man, he was first petrified and then angry because it was a violation of privacy, just as if a person had entered his home.

The most dramatic example of workplace-as-safe-haven is a government's embassy building. Traditionally and by international accord, any government's embassy anywhere in the world is considered inviolate territory; an embassy building symbolizes the honor and security of a nation. Thus, it is no accident that terrorists have chosen embassies as their targets.

And it is no accident that the United States has built its largest embassy in the world in Baghdad, Iraq. What does this building, opened in May 2008, symbolize? That depends whom you ask! To one Iraqi graduate student, it is "a symbol of occupation for the Iraqi people." She continued, "We see the size of this embassy [104 acres, 21 buildings in a protected enclave] and we think we will be part of the American plan for our country and our region for many, many years" (in LaFranchi, 2008). But to people serving in U.S. government positions in Baghdad, the fortress embassy may symbolize safety.

The giant U.S. Embassy in Iraq, the death and destruction at the Twin Towers, and the little everyday experiences of discomfort when someone moves "too close" indicate that people invest physical space with symbolic meaning and that these meanings can have a powerful impact on our feelings and actions. This impact may be intensified when territorial encroachment occurs. For many others, particularly Asians who practice feng shui and/or who live in cities built on symbolic grids (Chapter 4), the symbolism of place and space is a cultural given.

PRIVATIZATION OF DOMESTIC PUBLIC SPACE

Before industrialization and urbanization in western Europe, there was little distinction between domestic public and private space. In medieval France, for example, in all dwellings—aristocratic to peasant—all-purpose rooms were the rule. Then, first among noble households and gradually among households lower on the social ladder came "privacy in sleep; privacy in eating; privacy in religious and social ritual; finally, privacy in thought" (Mumford, 1961:285). In other words, domestic privacy largely replaced communality.

In terms of privacy, many observers draw a parallel between the home and the city, suggesting that the city is the home writ large. That is, instead of using public space, urbanites (at least those who can afford to do so) retreat into their safe havens called home.

PRIVATIZATION OF ONCE-PUBLIC SPACE

Housing developers often use their political clout to gain local permission to privatize beaches, scenic areas, or other parts of the natural environment previously enjoyed by the public (Sullivan, 2003). One example is Hokulia, a 1,550-acre golf resort located oceanside in Hawaii. Although state law forbids dense housing construction on farmland, in 2001 a developer cleared a large section of land zoned for farming in order to build a multimillion-dollar, residential, gated community (GC). The project was challenged legally in 2003. Then, lobbyists working for the developer succeeded in getting Hawaii state law amended to allow Hokulia to be developed (and to change decision-making state law to allow local—not state—officials to make future decisions about the transformation of farmland).

The Hokulia case would not surprise social scientists Molotch and Logan. As detailed in Chapter 15, they coined the concept and the term "the growth machine" to discuss the political economy of place. Others have since expanded this concept, calling it "the gating machine." This term has been applied to Hokulia and other places (e.g., the Stoney Hill GC in the Santa Monica Mountains near Los Angeles, which allowed the privatization of public streets). According to the coiners of the phrase "the gating machine," social scientists Elena Vesselinov et al. (2007), it is "the combination of the interests and actions of local government, of real estate developers, of the media and the consumers."

What produces this gating machine? In Vesselinov et al.'s view (2007), it is urbanites' fears combined with the interests of local governments (e.g., maintaining a healthy tax base), local governing elites, and developers.

In the United States GCs are proliferating (Vesselinov et al., 2007). An estimated 50 percent of all new housing being built in major U.S. metropolitan areas lies within GCs and other planned, collective developments (Nelson, 2005).

Vesselinov et al. (2007) conclude that GCs in the United States are likely to permanently contribute to the continuous fragmentation of cities, increased urban residential segregation, and more urban inequality. Other researchers reach similar conclusions (e.g., Low, 2003).

Meanwhile, GCs remain a fast-growing phenomenon globally, from Argentina and Canada to Asia and beyond (Atkinson, 2006). In the process, more and more once-public space is being transformed into private spaces with such signs as "Private Beach—Keep Out" warning outsiders to stay away.

Let us also remember that GCs are not new. Indeed, they are ancient. Take the case of China. As Ryszard Kapuściński points out in *Travels with Herodotus* (2007:58), China was a "nation of walls" for centuries, starting with the Great Wall (which demarcated the empire's northern borders) and extending to walls that were erected between "warring principalities, between regions and even neighborhoods." Walls guarded palaces and markets. And "walls encircled private homes," separating neighbor from neighbor, family from family.Kapuściński decries the use of walls as "evidence of a historical inability of people...to communicate, to confer and jointly determine how best to deploy enormous reserves of human energy and intellect." The late journalist–author Kapuściński seemed sad that "the very first reflex in the face of potential trouble [in ancient China] was to build a wall. To shut oneself in, fence oneself off" (59). We might ask whether today's GCs result from similar human impulses.

EXPERIENCING SOCIAL SPACE

Social space consists of public territories that, officially at least, offer equal access to all. Individuals generally feel that they do not control the use of social space, although they have free access to it. People in the United States tend to maximize their privacy and minimize their involvement with strangers in social space (Chapter 12).

PUBLIC AND PRIVATE SPACE AS SYMBOL

Tiananmen Square in Beijing, China, is the largest public space on earth. On one corner stands the fast-food restaurant Kentucky Fried Chicken, reputedly the largest in the world in terms of sales. But for those of us old enough to remember, neither of these factoids defines Tiananmen Square. Instead, thanks to electronic media, most people born after 1980—wherever they live—associate this monumental public space with the events of June 3–4, 1989: the Chinese army's lethal attack on peaceful dissidents.

To China's leaders, Tiananmen Square symbolizes the smashing of a "serious counterrevolutionary rebellion." To many others, the square symbolizes the crushing of the spirit of democracy. Either way, the world's largest social space is much more than 100 acres of land; it is a place full of meaning—even for most of us who have never been there.

Similarly, the Twin Towers in New York City was once an architectural showpiece and a "good" address for lawyers, among others. After 9/11, the ground upon which the towers once stood has come to symbolize terror and vulnerability to most people in the United States.

COLONIZING SOCIAL SPACE

Officially, streets, public beaches and parks, and other public territories are open to all. In practice, these social spaces often become colonized or expropriated into some group's home territory. At that point, the invisible borders of this private "turf" may be defended against invaders.

Sometimes the transformation of public territory into private turf reflects a strong sense of community. If so, rigid divisions between insiders and outsiders—"us" and "them"—can occur, resulting in hostility or territorial terror. In Boston, Chicago, San Francisco, and other big U.S. cities, this is often the case. Woe to the tourist who makes a wrong turn and finds herself or himself in a part of town that is hostile turf.

Even a small urban space can become privatized, sometimes with deadly consequences. Some years ago, a man was shot to death in San Francisco over a parking space; it had been "reserved" by members of a local gang as a sacred shrine to a murdered gang member.

Moscow's "summer cafés exemplify people's ingenuity in turning even postage-stamp spots into much-sought-after places. In Moscow, summers are short, and the rest of the year offers little possibility for enjoying life outside. So, summer outdoor cafés have taken on a special importance: over the last decade or so, people have colonized street spaces that once offered little in the way of coziness" (Bernard, 2008). Sidewalk cafés offer a few minutes in the sun and tranquility. Prices for a cappuccino are not cheap, but patrons (mainly urban professionals) are happy to sip their coffee while basking in the sun.

STREET PEOPLE'S TURF

Panhandlers and the homeless stake out a sidewalk or doorway in many cities. Then, they privatize or colonize their territory, discouraging spatial invasion by other street people or "respectable types."

Generally speaking, street musicians, pretzel peddlers, and newspaper hawkers add liveliness and color to urban space. So, few complain about their privatizing public space.

But public reaction to the homeless is another story. The homeless can make passersby uncomfortable, either because their presence reminds "respectable types" of the existence of poverty in the midst of affluence or because their appearance and/or behavior can be unpredictable or frightening. A nonthreatening

Fig. 17.11 PRIVATIZING PUBLIC SPACE. Animals often serve as props for the homeless. Dogs, in particular, seem to encourage contributions from passersby in the United States and discourage spatial invasion by other street people. (Brack Brown)

dog or another companion animal may cut through a passerby's fear, guilt, or disgust, thus narrowing the social and physical distance between passerby and homeless and reestablishing a sense of humane and human encounter (Figure 17.11).

Not all storeowners complain about the homeless hanging around. For one, a bookstore owner in northern California encourages a homeless man to stay in front of his store's door at night. Why? Because "he keeps away the others who piss there" (Thomas Sherman Whitmore, personal communication, Berkeley, Calif., March 24, 2007).

One group—homeless women—tend to be barely visible to mainstream society. Thanks to Elliot Liebow, however, we can gain insight into some of their lives. In *Tell Them Who I Am* (1993), Liebow introduced us to about 20 homeless women (mainly white and middle-aged or older)in suburban Washington, D.C. His ethnography permits us a window into their desolation, pain, and moments of grace.

As noted earlier, urban anthropologist Liebow illuminated another nearly invisible segment of society, invisible at least to middle-class whites: poor African American males congregating at *Tally's Corner* ([1967] 2003) in Washington, D.C. While Leibow's books may have been written a generation ago, they remain most insightful and astute; indeed, *Tally's Corner*'s second edition was published in 2003.

STREETS

All over the world, "cool" or "hot" streets (fashionable and trendy avenues) come and go. What makes some work and others fail? No one knows exactly. Sometimes it's a synergy or mix of uses that attracts a crowd. Other times it's word of mouth about a reasonably priced and yummy restaurant located amidst places to browse. Or sometimes it's the specialization of one item, like London's Savile Row for men's tailored suits.

A city street can change its character radically—and quickly. Here is a colorful description of the transformation of one Paris street: "Rue Bagnolet's metamorphosis is going to make Extreme Makeover look like a do-it-yourself eyebrow pluck" (Stehli, 2007).

For urbanites, the city street—trendy or not—is the most commonly used social space. Why? Because most walk, wheel, or ride down city streets almost daily.

Years ago, after observing street behavior in New York City and Tokyo, William H. Whyte (1978:14–16, [1988] 1990) concluded that people like somewhat crowded streets. This observation still flies in the face of assumptions made by many planners and architects who, in Whyte's view, "overscale" and bury streets in underground concourses or put streets "up in the air in glass-enclosed walkways." According to Whyte, the result is loss of the vital friction of social space plus a loss of activity and liveliness.

To conclude: Whether human territoriality is genetically programmed or culturally learned is a matter of much debate. In either case, people do display a sense of territoriality. Human ecologists have long used the concept of territoriality in their analysis of urban communities (e.g., Park et al., 1925). They pay particular attention to territorial invasion of one ethnic group by another.

In the past generation or so, social scientists, as well as philosophers and literary theorists, in the United States and elsewhere (France in particular) have focused on the symbolic (and thus *non*rational) meanings of space. This focus can be viewed as an implicit critique of the classic models of urban space. The work of Robert Sommer, Edward T. Hall, William H. Whyte, and Jean Baudrillard, to name just a few theorists, suggests that nonrational, noneconomic factors influence people's perception and use of space. Shades of Walter Firey, Gerald Suttles, and Mike Davis!

GLOBALIZATION AND THE EXPERIENCE OF "SOMEWHERE"

Why are visitors from postindustrial nations so attracted to small, rural places? Barry Bartman and Tom Baum (1998) think they know. These tourism researchers claim that rural communities are attractive because they assert their distinctive character in the face of a movement toward global uniformity. Looking for "distinctive character" in rural hamlets, however, could be an expression of nostalgia for the romanticized past. (Of course, those living in such hamlets today may not agree that social relations are any less complicated there than in big cities.)

The flip side is this: Some fear that globalization is turning Somewhere into Nowhere—or Everywhere. These critics say that globalization leads to a loss of the sense of place. For one, author–critic John Berger (b. 1923) believes that "delocalization" refers not only to moving production "wherever labor is cheapest and regulations minimal" but also to the loss of a sense of place. Why? Berger says that it undermines "the status of and confidence in all previous fixed places, so that the entire world becomes a single fluid market." The upshot, according to Oxford-trained Berger, who himself moved from a cosmopolis to a rural village in the mid-1970s: "The consumer is essentially somebody who feels or is made to feel lost unless he or she is consuming. Brand names and logos become the place names of the Nowhere" (2007).

Others laud the possibility of traveling to the proverbial Timbuktu and finding the familiar, particularly at mealtime. Often, these searchers hail from rich countries; they seek new experiences—within the limits of a safe adventure. (If a person has food allergies or is traveling with finicky tots, the perceived need for the familiar and safe that accompanies globalization, such as finding food without peanuts or beloved peanut butter, can be especially comforting.) Perhaps this search-for-the-new-within-safe-boundaries is one reason for the ever-increasing popularity of cruises, particularly among older passengers from rich countries such as the United States and Canada.

POLICY IMPLICATIONS

What are some policy implications that follow from these insights about human spatial behavior? About two generations ago, psychologist Bob Sommer (1969) argued that an understanding of how people perceive and use space is fundamental to intelligent design of the built environment. (To my knowledge, Sommer's argument has not been successfully challenged in the intervening years.)

Sommer's studies of various intimate and public environments—from homes for the elderly to the Los Angeles airport—suggest that even very minor rearrangements of things in space can affect people's behavior. For instance, he visited a hospital where the chairs were arranged in such a way as to make cleaning the floors easy but conversation among patients impossible. A slight shift of the furniture gave patients a chance to converse freely.

Sommer's ideas about space have had particular significance for those displaced from their home base and home range: people who live in total institutions, such as hospitals and jails. Institutionalized people have little control over their personal space. The psychological implications of feeling powerless to control one's immediate environment are suggested in the following account of a schizophrenic as she neared recovery in a hospital: "To the stupefaction of the nurse, for the first time I dared to handle the chairs and change the arrangement of the furniture. What unknown joy to have an influence on things; to do with them what I liked" (in Sommer, 1969:83).

Increasingly, design professionals draw on the work of Sommer and other students of the environment to better shape the spaces in which we live, work, and play. For example, long ago Apple Computer in Silicon Valley, California, redesigned its work spaces, replacing the open-plan cubicles with private spaces for computer designers and common areas for informal meetings. This arrangement reflects what some call the spirit of Silicon Valley: an informality together with an intense commitment to work.

Design professionals are also becoming aware that what is important to them, such as subtle nuances in building design, may be relatively unimportant to people who have to use those spaces. For instance, tenants in low-income housing may prefer better maintenance service and less subtle architecture. And larger kitchens—the typical social gathering place for residents—but smaller living rooms.

In brief, then, there can be a wide gap between what planners think people want/need and what people actually want. William Whyte's caustic comments about the planned disappearance of lively streets suggest this gap. Other defenders of the lively street, particularly the late Jane Jacobs (1961), may have had a large popular following; but to date, their impact on planning and public policy has been limited.

ENVIRONMENTAL PSYCHOLOGY

Environmental psychology deals with the relationships between human behavior and the physical environment, both natural and built. Theorists and researchers in this subdiscipline commonly are trained as psychologists, but other behavioral scientists call themselves environmental psychologists too. Researchers tend to focus on limited kinds of human behavior, particularly people's perception of the environment and the environment's impact on their actions and emotional states.

KEY CONCEPTS AND RESEARCH THRUSTS

Environmental psychologists have no single model for studying behavior–environment relationships (see Bell et al., 2005). But researchers do share a vocabulary, including the following concepts:

1. *Cognition.* How people assign meaning to the world around them and make sense out of their environment or personal space: (a) the moving bubble around our bodies and (b) the process of personalizing immediate space.
2. *Crowding and overcrowding.* A large number of persons gathered closely together in limited space.
3. *Dominance behavior.* How people react in situations of inequality.
4. *Perception.* How people perceive or become aware of their environment.
5. *Privacy.* Freedom from the presence or demands of others.
6. *Sensory adaptation.* How people adapt to the environment, particularly under conditions of stress or sensory overload.
7. *Territoriality.* How people identify, possess, feel safe in, and/or defend space.

Long before researchers called themselves environmental psychologists, they conducted behavior–environment studies. But such studies were rather haphazard, proceeding "in fits and starts depending upon local interest and the availability of funds" (Sommer, 1969:8).

Over time, large corporations funded basic research on people's reactions to temperature, light, color, and sound. They also supported applied research, including studies of light intensity in factories, carpeting in hospitals, and background music in offices. One landmark in applied research, funded by plumbing suppliers, is the work of Alexander Kira and his Cornell colleagues, *The Bathroom: Criteria for Design* ([1966] 1976). This 8-year study may evoke snickers, but Kira's

findings have serious implications for environmental design. For example, Kira's work shows that most standard bathroom equipment is difficult for the disabled and elderly to use with ease. This leads to a sense of helplessness and frustration. The implication here is that redesign of basic household equipment could decrease their feeling of powerlessness.

One particularly important area of applied research concerns institutional settings, such as hospitals, offices, schools, and college dorms. Sommer's research suggests that institutional decisions about space are often made with little knowledge of users' behavior. Environmental studies can make clear the impacts of various alternatives—open or partitioned offices, secluded or centrally located nurses' stations, movable or stationary school desks—on people's emotional states and patterns of social interaction.

We should remember, however, a basic point sometimes downplayed or overlooked by environmental psychologists: *Spatial arrangements reflect power arrangements.* This means that users' needs and institutional needs may be in direct conflict. How space is arranged may reflect the need of people in charge to maintain control or to provide services efficiently rather than humanely. Schoolchildren, for instance, may prefer to have movable rather than stationary desks. But teachers may find the constant rearrangement of their pupils disconcerting. Similarly, secluded nurses' stations in hospitals may isolate nurses from one another, patients, and visitors; yet this arrangement may be considered functional by hospital administrators because it makes "time-wasting" chit-chat difficult. Even minor rearrangements of space, then, may entail changes in the structures of power and authority.

RATS, CHICKENS, AND PEOPLE

Sommer argued "that more is known about animal than about human spatial behavior" (1969:12). Not much has changed since Sommer wrote that.

On the one hand, much research has been conducted on the way animals adapt to shared space. (One of my favorites: why cats spray!) We know, for instance, a great deal about the connections between the crowding of rats and their disoriented behavior, about the crowding of chickens and their decreased egg laying, about the territoriality of captive animals and their strengthened dominance orders. Laboratory animals do react to crowded conditions by competing for space and by developing certain pathologies. But less is known about the human animal. How do high density and crowding affect us? And what about people in captive spaces like total institutions: Do they develop a stronger sense of territoriality?

Reviewing studies of human crowding in various environments—prisoner-of-war camps, slave ships, densely populated cities such as Hong Kong, and housing units with more than 1.01 persons per room—what do we find? Mixed and ambiguous conclusions. Why? Because, in brief, crowding tends to go hand in hand with other factors, such as powerlessness and low status. If, for instance, prisoners of war are psychologically disoriented, how can it be shown that crowding is the key variable leading to their disorientation?

Perhaps other factors—isolation from the familiar, lack of control over space, and so on—may be more important than density. Some studies suggest, for instance, that crowding has no measurable impact on residential well-being and minimal effects on social interaction.

An important note: Those who lack the social power to control their space, such as the disabled, the poor, and children, may be more affected by residential crowding, not crowding per se. For example, schoolchildren who live in crowded housing may indeed learn less well than those who don't. But, the key factor here may have little to do with crowding; it may be the presence or absence of someone in the room.

(Some studies, however, do suggest that noise—say, from nearby airports as well as background music—and high density in the classroom itself play key roles in children's learning. See Maxwell, 2007.)

Cultural differences may play important roles too. For example, Japanese researcher Osamu Wata (1992) explored crowding and behavior in Japanese public and semipublic spaces. He suggests that cultural variables, including a noncontact culture, might encourage the experience of crowding.

Concerning territoriality, caged people may react like other caged animals. In a classic study of schizophrenic patients on a psychiatric ward, psychologists found that territoriality was important in the patients'

behavior and helped to define the social hierarchy of the ward (Esser et al., 1970).

In terms of high-density cities, some conclude that living in such cities does not cause social pathology. For one thing, studies that link cities to social pathology overlook the possibility that many urban dwellers, including "type A" personalities, may prefer high input levels. Further, some studies find that villages and small towns—not cities—were often the scenes of great stress and violence, particularly during the Middle Ages in Europe and in the early nineteenth century in the United States. In *Wisconsin Death Trip*, for example, historian Michael Lesy ([1973] 2000) documents barn burnings, attacks by gangs of armed tramps, alcoholism, madness, and more (e.g., witchcraft) in one county of rural Wisconsin before the turn of the twentieth century.

Such findings contradict the view that violence is part and parcel of dense, urban-industrial centers. Indeed, such findings may undermine the basic claim that the city, with its anonymity and crowding, is—in and of itself—a key factor in causing violence and stress.

To conclude: Behavior–environment studies are problematic for several reasons. In most cases, people are not captive animals like lab rats. Leaping from conclusions about rats, cats, or chickens to the way humans react is unjustified.

Further, the notion that persons in authority (e.g., hospital administrators and office managers) are unaware of users' needs may be naive. Ken Kesey's now classic portrayal of Nurse Ratched (Louise Fletcher in the 1975 movie version) in *One Flew Over the Cuckoo's Nest* (1962) illustrates the point. Consciously or unconsciously, Nurse Ratched manipulated mental patients by exercising control over their space. Her desire to maintain authority conflicted with some of her patients' needs to control their space. Guess who won out? Like so much else in urban life, those with power, authority, or high status have more ability to control their space than those without these resources.

This brings us to a more thorough exploration of the design of urban spaces. What assumptions or theories underlie the thinking of those who shape the spaces we live in: building architects, landscape architects, planners, interior decorators, and other design professionals?

SHAPING SPACE

DESIGN PRINCIPLES

When men and women receive their degree in architecture from Harvard University, a university official pronounces them qualified "to shape the space in which we live." This pronouncement makes design professionals sound like value-free technicians, which, of course, they are not.

Those deemed qualified to shape urban space—architects, landscape architects, licensed interior decorators, planners, and other design professionals—learn to think in a certain way about the physical world. This way of thinking is called design.

What is design? Many definitions of this word, both a noun and a verb, have been put forward (see Rawsthorn, 2008:8). Here, we concentrate on only one: according to architect–designer Christopher Alexander, design is "the process of inventing physical things which display new physical order, organization, form in response to function" (1964:1). In his early theoretical work *Notes on the Synthesis of Form*, Alexander stated that "every design problem begins with an effort to achieve fitness between two entities: the form in question and its context" (1964:15). However, a physical form is part of a whole ensemble of components, and one design objective (e.g., using the most appropriate material for each part of a building) may conflict with another design principle (e.g., using uniform materials for an entire project).

Achieving "fitness" between form and context is particularly difficult when the context is obscure. This is the case when architects and planners try to design an entire new city.

What constitutes a good fit between form and context? That's hard to define. Perhaps it is easier to see what constitutes a bad fit. For instance, we know there is a bad fit if a seesaw in a children's playground is designed with dangerously sharp edges.

Of course, design questions involve value judgments. Most important, whose values will be served? Consider, for example, one of eight purposes of urban design outlined by Paul D. Spreiregen: "To make the city humane" (1965:68–69). That seems a noble

purpose, but what does it actually mean? To urban designers (who are usually trained as architects initially but concentrate on large-scale design issues), it may mean the razing of a densely settled area they consider a slum. This may seem inhumane, however, to residents of such a neighborhood who happen to like it there. Such was the case with Boston's West End, as Herbert Gans fully describes in *The Urban Villagers* ([1962] 1982).

In other words, *designing urban spaces is not a value-neutral process*. Perhaps it was the growing awareness of this fact that led Christopher Alexander to depart from his original scientific–rational approach to design and to embark on a new course, one that rejects many established design principles and does not pretend to be value-free. (Alexander's work dates back decades, but it remains controversial.)

Modern city planning and urban design, Alexander maintains, are based on an unfortunate model—the city as a tree: a rigid, abstract structure that lacks complexity and contains no overlapping structures. He argues that "it is this lack of structural complexity, characteristic of trees, which is crippling our conceptions of the city" ([1965] 1978:382). In his view, a city is not a tree; a city should be designed with ambiguity, overlap, and multiplicity of aspect.

In 1977, Alexander and his colleagues published a seminal work on city design, calling for a new way to design for complex social systems. They developed what they call *A Pattern Language* (Alexander et al., 1977). The "language" consists of some 250 elements that the authors thought should be considered in the design process.

Alexander and his colleagues didn't pretend to be value-free. Instead, they called for a participatory, process-oriented, dynamic structuring of symbolic and functional patterns in environmental design. Here is a small sample of their design principles:

1. *On home and work.* "The artificial separation of home and work creates intolerable rifts in people's inner lives....Concentration and segregation of work leads to dead neighborhoods" (1977:52).
2. *On communal space.* "Give every institution and social group a place where people can eat together [because] without communal eating,

no human group can hold together" (699, 697).

3. *On institutional scale.* "To make the political control of local functions real, establish a small town hall for each community of 7000, and even for each neighborhood" (240).

4. *On access to ideas and services.* "Allow the growth of shop-size spaces around the local town hall, and any other appropriate community building. Front these shops on a busy path, and lease them for a minimum rent to ad hoc community groups for political work, trial services, research, and advocate groups. No ideological restrictions" (244).

5. *On the importance of multipurpose, communal places.* "Somewhere in the community [create] at least one big place where a few hundred people can gather, with beer and wine, music, and perhaps a half-dozen activities, so that people are continuously criss-crossing from one to another (446).

Although this classic work is more than a generation old, the sample above reveals that Alexander and his colleagues represented—and still do—an alternative to mainstream ideas and practices of architecture and planning that stresses functional order and the separation of contexts within city space.

Clearly, Alexander is a decentralist, trying to mold the physical environment to meet what he considers "human needs" for small-scale community and activity. He is also an integrator, trying to bring together in space various activities that people enjoy or need for survival.

In more recent times, Alexander has explored the underlying nature of order in the built and human environments (2003–2004). Whatever one thinks of this later work (deemed controversial for other reasons, including his spirituality), Alexander's earlier work remains controversial, particularly his insistence on what might be called "messy order," such as criss-crossing functions in space.

Years ago, *A Pattern Language* sent ripples through many architectural and design schools. But since then it hasn't had much impact on the built environment. Given the radical restructuring of social life that it implies, this is not surprising.

Designing an attractive, functional city is the goal of many a planner or designer, even if few get the chance. Architects, on the other hand, design buildings. What are their goals? Architects try to design buildings that are orderly, economical, and aesthetically pleasing. Of course, what is orderly, economical, or pleasing depends on one's taste and values.

To architect–designer Alexander, tree-like order in a building or city is deadly. Large-scale environments, which might be economical, bring high social costs in the long run. And aesthetic pleasure, Alexander would argue, comes not from having everything in its separate place but from interlacing varied human activities.

To conclude: Most design professionals do not make explicit the values underlying their work. Christopher Alexander is an exception. He has made numerous unsubstantiated statements about the nature of human beings (e.g., "All people have the instinct to decorate their surroundings" [Alexander et al., 1977:1147]). Yet he has never hidden his ideology. He continues to stress the need for community and communalism, the need for people to create and recreate their own environments, and the need to learn from various aspects of the city. He prefers small, family-owned grocery stores, places where urbanites can watch the world go by, and elevated places as city landmarks. Most of all, he has sought to enrich the city by breaking it into "a vast mosaic of small and different subcultures, each with its own spatial territory, and each with the power to create its own distinct life style...so that each person has access to the full variety of life styles in the subcultures near his [or her] own" (Alexander et al., 1977:50).

Alexander's vision of decentralized subcommunities is not widely shared in the design professions. Nor is it economically probable if current dominant values don't change. And his recent writings—a four-volume series (2003–2004) on the nature of order—may seem idiosyncratic at the very least and too spiritual and cosmological for many. But his ideas may have had an impact on the postindustrial cities of North America. And his explicit ideology is a refreshing antidote to the falsely value-free rhetoric of so many design professionals.

DESIGNING THE NATURAL ENVIRONMENT

Landscape and architecture may seem contradictory, but together they reflect the goal of landscape architecture: to shape the natural environment just as the architect molds the built environment. Together with his working partner, Calvert Vaux, Frederick Law Olmsted, the profession's pioneer, coined the term "landscape architecture" (*US History Encyclopedia*, n.d.) in 1858.

Olmsted, the developer of Central Park in New York City, had specific ideas about parks. He wanted to keep rural nature in a close relationship to the industrial cities growing up in post–Civil War America. This would relieve the anxiety of urban life, Olmsted thought. Parks would also strengthen the sense of community within large cities. Where else, he asked, could over 50,000 people come together "with an evident glee in the prospect of coming together, all classes represented…each individual adding by his mere presence to the pleasure of all others?" (in Glaab and Brown, 1976:234).

Olmsted's influence stretched from New York City's Central Park and the boulevards of Chicago to San Francisco's Golden Gate Park. He inspired a park and boulevard movement in the late nineteenth century, and he provided the ideology for reshaping the industrial city.

Assessments of Olmsted's work vary. To some, Olmsted was more instrumental than anyone else in reshaping—for the better—the way in which American cities were to grow. But critics argue that Olmsted, and the designers and planners he inspired, were antiurban and aristocratic in their approach to parks. Their aesthetically pleasing, grand getaways from soot and noise, it is argued, did nothing to relieve the urban anxiety rooted in poverty and social conflict.

However Olmsted's work is judged, he left an indelible stamp on the natural environment of U.S. cities. Indeed, one could reasonably claim that the natural and built environments of U.S. cities today are, to a significant degree, the handiwork of two impassioned men: Olmsted, who developed Central Park in the nineteenth century, and Robert Moses (master builder or destroyer of living communities, depending on your viewpoint), who controlled Central Park and much else in mid-twentieth-century New York City (Chapter 14). Neither was an elected political official.

Today, landscape architects rarely have a chance to reshape huge pieces of urban space or to impose their ideologies on an entire city, let alone a nation. Instead, most do the following kinds of work: landscape planning and assessment (e.g., evaluating the suitability of land for a new national park), site planning (e.g., analyzing a proposed hospital site to assess the fit between the form of the natural environment and the building), and/or landscape design (i.e., supergardening—selecting plants and materials).

Landscape architects (almost named "rural embellishers" by Olmsted) are not the only professionals concerned with the natural environment. Increasingly, urban designers and city planners are devoting attention to working with, rather than against, nature.

THE IMAGE OF THE CITY

MAKING THE CITY OBSERVABLE

Urban designers try to make the city observable. What does that mean? It means making clear visually the patterns of the city.

Kevin Lynch developed specific ideas about the visual image of the city (Figure 17.13). Decades ago Lynch, in a classic study (1960), classified the contents of a city's image that are associated with physical forms into five main elements: paths, edges, nodes, districts, and landmarks. In Lynch's scheme, *paths* are the channels along which an observer moves: streets, transit lines, railroads, canals. *Edges* are linear breaks in the continuity of the city: shores, walls, railroad cuts, edges of development. *Districts* are the medium-to-large sections of the city having some common identifiable character that an observer may mentally enter. *Nodes* are strategic spots in a city: intensive loci to and from which people travel. *Landmarks* are reference points that the observer does not enter.

One of Lynch's main interests was the **imageability** of a city: that quality of the urban landscape that evokes a strong image in the mind of anyone who observes it. Imageability is "that shape, color, or arrangement which facilitates the making of vividly identified, powerfully structured, highly useful mental images of the environment" (Lynch, 1960:9).

Lynch was concerned with a city's imageability, or heightened visibility, because he found in his research that people feel most comfortable in city space when they can recognize its overall patterns. Lynch's work has influenced urban designers throughout the world.

Fig. 17.12 IMAGEABILITY. Built to mark the centennial of the French Revolution, Gustav Eiffel's Tower in Paris is perhaps *the* most recognizable structure in the world. Although widely disliked and called uncomplimentary names when first built, including "metal asparagus," over 200 million people have visited since it opened in 1889. This photo, taken from the North Tower of Notre Dame, shows other recognizable landmarks (e.g., the St. Germain-des-Prés Church) that give Paris a sense of heightened visibility. In Lynch's scheme, Paris is very imageable; that is, it evokes a strong image in the mind of all who observe it. (Dave Hildebrandt)

The design of Ciudad Guyana in Venezuela, for example, was inspired by his ideas.

To conclude: Apparently, people need to recognize and make coherent patterns out of their physical surroundings. To Kevin Lynch, it is the job of city planners and urban designers to make the city's image more recognizable, vivid, and memorable to the city dweller. Clear images, Lynch believed, give people emotional satisfaction, an easy framework for communication, and personal security. To architect–designer Christopher Alexander, coherent patterns

of environmental structure are also crucial, but he would design them in a more complex, subtle way: via overlapping and criss-crossing functions in space. Both design theorists emphasize the social and psychological impact of urban forms on city dwellers' well-being.

DESIGNERS, GRAND AND LESS GRAND

A city can be considered an art form—a special art form that reflects the builders' belief system and values. Villages constructed by the Dogon Tribe in West

Africa reflect their values and cosmology. The tribe feels indissolubly connected with the cosmos and its timeless rhythms, and the physical layout of the Dogon village reflects this belief. Each building stands in a particular relation to the sun, and the granary building (symbol of the world system) is constructed with invariant male–female parts (Griaule, 1965). A Dogon community is a work of artistic symmetry and cosmic vision; it is a symbolic representation of the tribal universe. Similarly, the ancient city of Babylon was more than a city; it was a vision of heaven on earth.

Heaven on earth—or at least a better society—has been a perennial interest of philosophers, artists, and city planners everywhere. Often, the ideal city transcends the dominant ideas of the society that produced it. Like artists, visionary planners suggest solutions to problems only dimly understood in their own time. Thus, in the twelfth century, European visionaries designed cities of God on earth amid war and strife. In the nineteenth century, utopian socialists designed classless communities amid the evolution of industrial capitalism.

Here, I focus on only a few designers and design movements. This brief survey is intended to indicate the range of visions and the sources from which they sprang: patriotism, profit, philanthropy, paternalism, pure aesthetics, political and social control, ideology, religious ardor, and utopian dreams.

PIERRE-CHARLES L'ENFANT'S WASHINGTON, D.C.

Major Pierre-Charles L'Enfant was a grand designer inspired by the vision of America as a new society. L'Enfant, a young French infantryman, came to the colonies to fight in the Revolutionary War.

For several years after the war, the new national government moved from place to place, debating alternative sites for the nation's capital. Badly divided, Congress finally decided on a new location on the Potomac River, and George Washington himself rode along the wild, swampy 80-mile general location, choosing the precise site where Washington, D.C., now stands. Meanwhile, L'Enfant was instructed to do general survey work on the new site. Interpreting this charge very liberally, he plunged ahead, with remarkable results.

Fig. 17.13 LYNCH'S ELEMENTS OF THE CITY IMAGE. (Paul D. Spreiregen, *Urban Design: The Architecture of Towns and Cities* [New York: McGraw-Hill, 1965], pp. 50–51. Copyright © 1965 by the American Institute of Architects. Reprinted by permission.)

On one design point, L'Enfant was adamant. The new capital was not to be a grid city, with parallel streets running at right angles to one another. While practical, the grid lacked the grandeur L'Enfant thought appropriate to a capital city. Thomas Jefferson, a designer as well as a philosopher and future president, approached L'Enfant with his own proposal: a checkerboard city with alternate squares left in open space. L'Enfant responded that such a grid concept was "tiresome and insipid." L'Enfant won.

Today, Washington reflects L'Enfant's grand design. There is a wheel-like arrangement of streets running off a central spoke, long malls with vistas, broad diagonal avenues bearing the names of the original 13 colonies, and major public buildings arranged in a federal triangle.

UTOPIAN VISIONARIES

In the United States, utopian visions existed from the very beginning. Indeed, to some, the United States itself was utopia: the New World, a chance to create paradise on earth. The names of colonial towns—New Haven, Connecticut, and New Hope, Pennsylvania, to name only two—convey this idealism.

Early utopians were inspired by religious visions. Generally, they set up small, intentional communities. Most often, they were Protestant separatists breaking away from established sects, such as the United Society of Believers, popularly called Shakers. The oldest communistic society in the United States, the Shakers, set up a parent community in 1792 at Mount Lebanon on the border of Massachusetts and Connecticut.

In the nineteenth century, religiously inspired utopian communities flourished from Oneida, New York, to the frontier of the Midwest. But there was also a new development: the growth of *secular* utopian visions. Some were translated from paper blueprints into actuality.

One of the most famous is Robert Owen's experiment at New Harmony, Indiana. Owen, a rich industrialist-turned-utopian-entrepreneur, came to the United States from Scotland in the 1820s to introduce a new system of society that would remove the reasons for conflict among individuals. Utopian socialist Owen (like his French contemporary Charles Fourier) believed that large cities around industrial areas were unhealthy and that the best alternative was a small, self-sufficient community. In such a community Owen hoped to promote a noncompetitive, wholesome way of life based on socialism and education.

Owen designed an architectural model of his ideal community: a square-shaped arrangement that would contain between 800 and 1,200 people. Inside the square were to be public buildings, while families would live on three sides and children over 3 years of age would live on the fourth side. Outside the square were to be manufacturing facilities, stables, farm buildings, and agricultural land Podmore. ([1907] 2004)

The design plan of New Harmony was never realized. Instead, Owen and his followers moved into a village formerly occupied by another utopian sect. The hopes for New Harmony were not realized either. The dream of utopian socialism was quickly shattered by internal dissent.

Still, the failure of New Harmony did little to dampen the spirits of other communitarian experiments in the mid-nineteenth century. Dozens of other communities, both religious and secular, were established. One of the longest-lived was John Humphrey Noyes's community of radical Protestants in Oneida, New York. Their imposing Mansion House still stands, and descendants of the original Oneida community still conduct tours, explaining to visitors how the system worked. Of special interest, guides say, is the Oneida community's theory and practice of communism in human relationships as well as material goods (via "complex marriage" and the dissolution of the nuclear family).

COMPANY TOWNS: LOWELL, MASSACHUSETTS, AND PULLMAN, ILLINOIS

New Harmony and Oneida exemplify the search for a radically new and better social order through communitarian socialist ideals. Planned manufacturing towns were inspired by different motives: profit, paternalism, and/or reform in the interest of softening class antagonism.

Lowell, Massachusetts, is the most famous example of early planned manufacturing towns. Built by Frances Cabot Lowell in the early nineteenth century, it was the model for dozens of other New England mill towns.

Realizing that he would need abundant cheap labor to run his water-powered textile mills, Lowell set out to attract workers, mainly New England farm girls, to his town. And disturbed at the horrific social conditions in English factory towns that he had visited, Lowell set out to improve the workers' lot. The result: Lowell, Massachusetts, a planned town. It was laid out physically to fit the social order Lowell envisioned. Textile mills lined the river, flanked by a canal. Between them was housing for the United States's first female labor force—boarding houses operated much like convents (see Eisler, 1997). A main road linked the manufacturing and housing areas to other urban activities.

About a half-century later, cities privately built by industrialists reached their zenith in Pullman, Illinois. George M. Pullman, the railroad sleeping-car magnate, decided to consolidate his manufacturing activities and housing for his workers at a 4,000-acre site about 12 miles south of Chicago.

Designed by an architect and a landscape engineer, the town of Pullman was meant to be a model industrial community. When it went into operation in 1881, the town presented a strong contrast to the crowded, unsanitary tenements of industrial cities. There were neat row houses, a shopping center, an elegant theater, a hotel, a church, a school, and a host of cultural institutions (excluding bars and brothels). By the early 1890s, the population had reached about 12,000 Pullman workers and their families—living in Pullman-owned homes (Papke, 1999).

Why did George Pullman build such a town? In part, he had a great deal of imagination. And he was an environmental determinist of sorts and thought that miserable urban conditions led to workers' "costly vices." In part, he also hoped his planned community "would soften the bitter antagonism which wage earners often felt toward their employers, and would enable him to attract a stable and highly competent labor force; it would also earn 6 per cent on the money invested in it" (Glaab and Brown, 1976:237).

Did the town serve Pullman's ends? No. Paternalism or "benevolent, well-wishing feudalism," as it was often called in its own day, went against U.S. democratic ideals. Labor violence, culminating in the Pullman strike of 1894, showed that workers' hostility

toward their benevolent boss was not softened by decent housing or terraced front yards. Shortly after the strike, an Illinois court ruled that Pullman's company had no legal right to run the town. Eventually, Pullman got rid of the town, and it was annexed to Chicago.

Lowell and Pullman are striking examples of company towns with pretensions to design excellence. But they are part of a broader pattern. Similar experiments, much less grand in scale, include Kohler, Wisconsin (plumbing fixtures); Hershey, Pennsylvania (candy bars); and Gary, Indiana (steel).

BARON HAUSSMANN'S PARIS

What is the world's most visited city? What is the world's most beautiful city in the eyes of European and U.S. tourists? The answer to both questions: Paris. France hosts the most tourists of any country globally and Paris's monuments, including the Louvre, Disneyland (in suburban Paris), and the Eiffel Tower (widely ridiculed when it opened in 1889) are top draws. (*Note*: China is expected to supplant France as the top tourist destination in future decades.)

It has not always been so. What visitors now think of as Paris, "the City of Lights," is not very old. The city may date to the Parisii Gauls, then the Romans, but today's Paris of wide boulevards and stately monuments was born only in the 1860s when Napoleon III and high-ranking public official Baron Georges-Eugène Haussmann (1809–1891) transformed the city.

Emperor Louis Napoleon, head of the Second Empire, appointed Haussmann to be the equivalent of a planning czar. His mission: to transform and modernize Paris.

Probably an authoritarian and undoubtedly a technocrat, Haussmann left his indelible stamp on Paris. He tore down much of the congested, decaying old city, leaving countless thousands homeless. He built broad boulevards, parks, squares, new neighborhoods, and a new sewer system for the city.

Scholars agree that Haussmann transformed Paris. They disagree on whether his redo was "good" or "bad." Some depict him as the destroyer of low-income and working-class Paris, responsible for the "bourgeoisification" of old Paris. Others see Haussmann as the great city planner of modern Paris,

Fig. 17.14 BOULEVARD HAUSSMANN, PARIS. This grand boulevard is named for Baron Georges-Eugène Haussmann, the official who directed the nineteenth-century transformation of Paris, including the grand boulevards. (Gesche Würfel)

the person responsible for the modernization and beautification of the city. Ironically, novelist Victor Hugo despised the Second Empire and Haussmann, but his *Les Misérables* ([1862] 1987), like much popular literature of the day, contributed to upper- and middle-class acceptance of the need to transform dirty, unsanitary sections of Paris.

Why did the Emperor and Haussmann want to transform Paris? Most likely, for mixed motives: to provide better sanitation in a crowded, unhealthy city with a grossly inadequate waste-disposal system; to control what bourgeois inhabitants considered the "dangerous" class (the working class) and

their "moral decline" in the new industrial age; to glorify the reputation of Napoleon III; to control traffic flows; to foster economic growth; to beautify dingy, working-class areas by razing them and building anew; to construct new tree-lined grand boulevards and large gardens of great beauty; and last, but probably not least, to ensure that Paris would be less prone to revolutions by making the people's barricades harder to construct.

In 1867, about 200,000 visitors came to an international exposition in Paris which boasted over 50,000 exhibitors, including hundreds from Great Britain, Ireland, Canada, and the United States. This was the moment that Baron Haussmann's new, modern Paris was shown off.

Over the decades, many planners were influenced by Haussmann's vision. In the United States, Chicago's Daniel Burnham, the soul of the "City Beautiful" movement, was among Haussmann's admirers.

In Beijing, a giant redo for the 2008 Olympic Games is surpassing, in scale, Haussmann's transformation of Paris. However, no serious observer has yet called the Chinese capital's make-over part of a City Beautiful movement.

THE CITY BEAUTIFUL MOVEMENT

Industrial and cultural expositions were popular in the United States as well as in Europe in the nineteenth century. Chicago, the symbol of the rising industrial city, was chosen to host the quatercentenary of Columbus's "discovery" of America. This World's Fair of 1893–1894 (called the Columbian Exposition, Chapter 1) marked the beginning of great interest in city planning and landscape architecture in the United States.

The Columbian Exposition was not a typical fair. It was a brand new city. Working from a design by Frederick Law Olmsted, Chicago architect–planner Daniel H. Burnham supervised the construction of what came to be called the "White City" (See Chapter 1). This monumental group of buildings, constructed on a plan, was set in an environment of green open space, grand boulevards, and an artificial lagoon on Chicago's South Side.

By the time the Chicago fair closed in 1894, about 27 million people had attended. What they saw, and the memories they took back to their dreary mill towns and lackluster cities, was a mix of classical Greece, imperial Rome, Renaissance Italy, and Bourbon Paris. This mixture expressed the explosive energy and optimism of the industrial United States. Millions had admired the beauty and splendor in Chicago, previously better known for its crime and grime and its grain, not its stupendous statues and civic beauty.

After the Columbian Exposition, civic beautification organizations sprang up in many cities and the City Beautiful movement took hold. "Make no little plans," Burnham advised in 1912, for "they have no magic to stir men's blood. Make big plans; aim high in hope and work."

While the near-evangelical fervor of Burnham and his followers didn't lead to the total reshaping of U.S. cities, his bold vision did have an impact. Today, touches of City Beautiful architecture and landscaping can be found throughout the United States, from Omaha and Buffalo to St. Louis, Seattle, and San Francisco. Perhaps even more important, Burnham and Olmsted's White City and Burnham's subsequent plan for Chicago's urban growth in 1909 signaled a new era: the growing acceptance of city planning as a legitimate tool for the urban-industrial United States.

EBENEZER HOWARD'S GARDEN CITY

Visionary Ebenezer Howard (1898) combined socialist principles with romantic ideals to propose a new kind of planned community: the garden city. In the English reformer's vision, the best of the countryside and city could be combined by building small, rather self-sufficient communities limited to about 30,000 people, surrounded by permanent green belts.

Around the turn of the twentieth century, Howard proposed that London be surrounded with cooperative communities where slum dwellers and people of all income groups would live and collectively own the land. The aim of these new towns was to motivate London slum dwellers to resettle willingly—without being forcibly displaced, as urban renewal in the United States has so often done—and to provide standard housing, as well as to "save" London by providing new parks, sewers, and so forth.

When two garden cities were actually built in England, planners throughout the world became interested. Garden cities became fashionable in the United States after 1910. But many, like Forest Hills Gardens, New York (financed by the Russell Sage Foundation and designed by Frederick Law Olmsted, Jr.), became bedroom communities for affluent commuters, not cooperatively-owned communities for all income groups, as Howard had proposed.

The garden city movement in the United States attracted noted urbanists, including Lewis Mumford. Yet Howard's ideas for stemming the slums and sprawl of industrial cities did not progress very far in the United States, given its traditions of private enterprise.

Despite Daniel Burnham's memorable phrase, big plans have never really stirred American blood—at least, not enough to totally rebuild or redesign cities. Instead, city planning has proceeded piecemeal. Private master builders (e.g. the Levitts of Levittown), and a few public builders (headed by the master builder—or destroyer, depending on your perspective—Robert Moses in New York City) did change the face of the metropolis in the twentieth century, but such efforts followed no overall plan. Why? Some observers point to deep-rooted American traditions of localism and the fear of federal government intervention as destructive of democratic ideals. A generation ago, this view was expressed by then Wisconsin governor Lee Dreyfus (governor from January, 1979 to January, 1983, when he advised that the federal government should only defend the shore, deliver the mail, and stay out of everyone's lives.

Some Marxists have a different explanation. They claim that modern American cities grew in an unplanned way as a result of capitalism. They start from the basic assumption that the mode of production (i.e., the sum of productive forces and relations of production) influences the spatial and temporal organization of any environment indirectly (through specific kinds of relationships that dominate a given society). In their view, "primitive society" is characterized by structures based on a kinship system of houses branched around families. By contrast, in feudalism there is a closed circle of class-based relationships: Lords and ladies live in their castles, serfs work and live in their fields and villages, and merchants and artisans inhabit the towns. And in monopoly capitalism, private property and corporate investment set the broad parameters within which land and housing patterns emerge.

In this view, one such land-use pattern in monopoly capitalism is "corporate centralization." It has brought office development to major central cities and a "bimodal distribution of development, in the center and in the outlying ring" of many U.S. cities such as Houston (Feagin and Smith, [1987] 1989:28, 29).

MEGASTRUCTURES OR MINISTRUCTURES?

The tradition of grand design is alive and well in many parts of the world. The range of innovative ideas—from satellites in the sky to underwater structures—is suggested in Chapter 8.

Interestingly, some of the most critically acclaimed designers transcend borders with ease. For example, when Japanese-born, U.S. trained architect Fumihiko Maki (who invented the term "megastructure" in the 1960s—he designed San Francisco's Yerba Buena Center for the Arts in 1993) won the Pritzker Prize, the equivalent of a Nobel Prize in architecture, he was cited by the jury for his fusion of East and West, as well as traditional and modern cultures. Jurors said that Maki blended an architecture representing the age-old qualities of Japan while juxtaposing contemporary construction methods and materials.

Here, we focus on just a few architect–visionaries. First, the ideas of Paolo Soleri, an architect–planner who has crossed both national and disciplinary boundaries. We also examine a key criticism of Soleri's work: For all his futurism, he is reinventing not the wheel but the tree. Then, we take flight with the fantasies of Lebbeus Woods. Then, we look briefly at some ideas of Buckminster Fuller, a polymath who called himself a "comprehensive anticipatory design scientist and "astronaut from Spaceship Earth." Next, we examine a building boom 80 feet underwater, at Red Bird Reef off the Delaware Coast. Made of retired New York City subway cars, it is basically "luxury condominiums for fish" (Tinsman in Urbina, 2008). This is not (yet) being used for human condos, but who knows what the future holds? Finally, we consider a building—only on the drawing board as of this writing—by David Fisher, an Italian Israeli architect (whose claim to previous fame is the development of the "Leonardo da Vinci Smart Bathroom," a prefab system for hotels under construction). Fisher dreamed up a controversial, rotating, 68-storey combination hotel, office tower, and apartment building for an oil-rich emirate that some call a playpen for architects. (As of 2008, the world's tallest building was located there, and a variety of new buildings are in process.) As a headline put it, "Dubai Puts a New Spin on Skyscrapers" (Frangos, 2007:B1). (*Sidenote*: About 85 percent of Dubai's population and 99 percent of its private labor, including over a million construction workers, is composed of "guest workers" from various countries, including Pakistan and India.

The workers earn little and are notoriously mistreated. They live in conditions that critics compare to indentured servitude.)

A Blend of Architecture and Ecology

Paolo Soleri has long advocated a new kind of city for the future. Soleri's dream is not easy to describe in words; linear, analytical thought is not his forte. Perhaps the best way to understand his vision is by looking at the plans for a Soleri-designed community, which he calls an **arcology** (1969): the blend of architecture and ecology. An arcology is intended to place people in megastructures, making the land available for agriculture, work, and leisure.

In terms of design, Soleri's arcologies have one surface but many levels. Most extend below the ground and high in the air. They range from a massive arcology holding 500,000 residents on less than 2 square miles of land to an offshore community anchored to the continental shelf.

Despite their massive scale, Soleri says, his arcologies are "about miniaturization": creating a more intimate and less wasteful form of human spatial organization. The large spaces of the arcologies would be divided into large and small spaces to give inhabitants a sense of human scale.

Decades ago, Soleri and some of his followers began construction of an arcology for about 3,000 inhabitants at a remote desert site about 70 miles north of Phoenix, Arizona. Named Arcosanti, it is a prototype of futurist Soleri's vision.

As of 2007, however, the plan to draw an initial 5,000 to Arcosanti lagged; the population was fewer than 100 people. The arcological tower that was to house 100,000 residents, the Hyper Building, is yet to be started. Mr. Soleri, who lives near Phoenix and spends one or two nights weekly at Arcosanti, told a reporter that tourism and the sale of bells isn't quite enough to finance his projects, suggesting that another $50 million might help (Colin, 2007).

Like most visionaries, Soleri has both devoted followers and vocal detractors. One of the most interesting critiques of his work comes from Christopher Alexander. He finds the organic shapes of Soleri's futuristic cities to be organized on the old principle of the tree, complete with its rigid structure.

Alexander rejects the city-as-tree plan as artificial. More important, Alexander makes a connection between city form and human personality. In his view, cities rigidly structured like trees help to create rigid, disciplined people. The city-as-tree may have been suitable for ancient Roman military camps, Alexander thinks, because discipline and order were the values of those in charge. But the tree is not suitable for modern, pluralistic societies. In other words, Alexander finds a bad fit between tree-like cities and democratic contexts.

A Synthesis of High Tech and Nature

The models of architect Lebbeus Woods create a fanciful world existing somewhere between the visions of Aldous Huxley and the Brothers Grimm. It is a world where high technology and nature—not normally considered a good couple—come together. In Woods's drawings, pod-like structures float over Paris streets, trailing nets that shift with the wind. Buildings envisioned for underground Berlin shift with the earth's tectonic plates.

Woods, founder of the Research Institute for Experimental Architecture, wants to reinvent the world in all of its complexity. And he wants to replace hierarchy with *heterarchy*, a cybernetics concept referring to systems composed of networks of independent, autonomous parts. (In his view, hierarchical systems are composed of interdependent parts, and this interdependence robs the parts of their autonomy.) Practically, this means he highly values individualism, and he designs with this value in mind.

How does Woods concretize individualism? He makes the home a live–work lab where advanced electronic machines (computers, faxes, electronic musical instruments, etc.) are a focal point. By embracing these machines, he thinks, people can interact with other people, develop themselves, and understand the changing forces that animate the natural world.

Since 9/11, Woods has been designing installations which critique the form of the geometric box, a form that he says rules most building designs. To replace these structures, Woods (2004) proposes a dynamic field of potential energy. Further, Woods imagines a built space in the midst of collapse; it lives solely in imagination.

Bucky Fuller, Visionary of Change Buckminster (widely called "Bucky")

Fuller once said that his simple aim in life was "to remake the world." He tried. His most widely known project, the geodesic dome, has given emergency shelter to thousands of homeless people, including some displaced by Hurricane Katrina. But he never completed many of his designs, including a floating city and a flying car. Nor did he ever finish a long-promised book on his theory of energetic–synergetic geometry.

During his lifetime, Fuller (1895–1983) was adopted by hippies in the 1960s as a visionary thinker. But the design and architecture establishments basically dismissed him as an eccentric nut.

Some of his ideas are now getting a rethink. As the curator for "Buckminster Fuller: Starting with the Universe," a 2008 show at the Whitney Museum of American Art in New York City, put it: "In some ways his 'comprehensive, anticipatory design science' is more relevant for design today than it was even in his own time" (Hays in Rawsthorn, 2008:19). Fuller's vision, for example, that the designer is a change agent, working to solve global problems by translating science and technology into useful innovations, has recently gained admirers. Also, in recent years, Fuller's insistence (dating to 1928) on humanitarian and sustainable design has influenced builders from India and Africa in their use of alternative materials, construction methods, and designs for sustaining the environment.

Underwater Subway

Cars Starting in 2001, hundreds of retired New York City subway cars have been thrown off a barge into 80-foot waters off the Delaware coast. These old subway cars have not only created a deep-sea building boom; they have transformed a formerly empty stretch of ocean floor into a "bountiful oasis" of teeming fish (Urbina, 2008).

Carpeted in sea grasses, this thriving community of teeming fish living in and above the subway cars shares problems with some aboveground cities: overcrowding, crime, and traffic. Why? Apparently, the flounder and bass like their new home so much that they have an overcrowding problem. In addition, there are human issues: Theft and sabotage of fishing pots have doubled in recent years. Critics point to more costly materials, such as rock and concrete, as safer, more durable materials for artificial reefs. Others oppose the use of subway cars because they contain asbestos.

As of now, no voices have suggested that such an artificial reef could house humans. But who knows what ingenious, imaginative planners may try!

Building Tall and Spinning—Architect, Visionary, and/or Nutcase?

David Fisher's design for a 68-storey spinning tower in Dubai has been dubbed "outlandish," a "sign of architectural apocalypse," and "absurd." But the ruler of oil-rich Dubai, whose government is sponsoring the building, sees this not-yet-built skyscraper as a unique landmark for his emirate.

Fisher's spinning skyscraper, if built, will not seem out of place in Dubai. Already there are other unusual (to say the least) creations, including an artificial archipelago shaped like a world map, a luxury hotel built under water, an indoor ski slope, and private residences dotting a phony island chain, shaped like a palm frond.

In Fisher's design, each of the 68 stories of the rotating tower would be (the verb tense is important here as some think the building will never leave the drawing board, particularly in times of global recession) doughnut-shaped and attached to a central core. According to a high-rise engineer on Fisher's design team, the building's structure will be a "concrete silo" with doughnuts (Robertson in Frangos, 2007:B8). The doughnuts will rotate but not fast. One rotation would take about 90 minutes. Each floor would rotate independently. The result: a constantly shifting architectural shape.

Fisher's rotating skyscraper would fit right into Dubai's skyline. (Another spinning tower may also be built. This second skyscraper, designed by James Abbott of a Hong Kong–based group, would spin just once a week, giving people 360-degree views.) Called "eccentric" by some, "inventive" by others, Dubai's skyline is "powered by oil money, big ambitions, and architectural whimsy" (Frangos, 2007:B8). Oil-rich Dubai and Abu Dhabi, the nearby United Arab Emirates capital, seem destined to splurge on controversial structures.

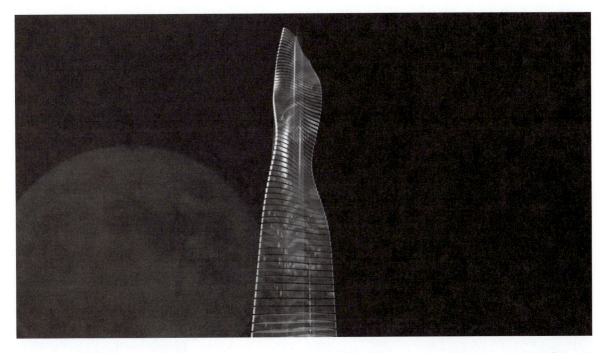

Fig. 17.15 SPINNING TOWER FOR DUBAI. "Inventive" or "eccentric" architecture, depending on your point of view, is defining oil-rich cities in the United Arab Emirates. (David Fischer)

POSTNATIONALIST ARCHITECTURE

Lille, France, is near the French entrance to the Channel Tunnel or "Chunnel." It is also the site of Euralille, an impressive postnationalist project of public architecture financed by the European Union (EU). This mega-project celebrates cyberspace, not nationalism. In the words of a short-story writer, Euralille "looks and feels as if a lunar research station has crash-landed onto a small, respectable French market town. This is meant as a compliment" (Coupland, 1994:H45).

According to Euralille's master planner, the Dutch-born architect and Eurocitizen Rem Koolhaas (pronounced "cool house"), "architecture reveals the deepest and sometimes most shocking secrets of how the values of a society are organized" (in Coupland, 1994:H45). Koolhaas (whose firm designed iconic buildings in Beijing before the Olympic Games) incorporates into his work the structural processes that he feels inform postmodern society and creates architectural metaphors for these processes, including the following: transnationalism, diversity, the obsolescence of physical space, centerless cities, deregionalization, deindustrialization, fragmentation, fluidity, and "drive-thru-ness" (Coupland, 1994:H45). For instance, in Koolhaas's project, walls turn into doors, doors and walls disappear, and roads flow through structures.

THE NEW URBANISM

Husband-and-wife planning team Andrés Duany and Elizabeth Plater-Zyberk are two founding figures in the new urbanism movement. Designer–architect Peter Calthorpe has long been associated with new urbanism too. For decades, he has worked toward the key principles of new urbanism: "that successful places—whether neighborhoods, villages, or urban centers—must be diverse in use...walkable...and environmentally sustainable" (Calthorpe, n.d.).

According to Duany and Plater-Zyberk, neighborhood design is the key to new urbanism. Here are some essential design elements: a mixed-use town center where most dwellings lie within a 5-minute walk; a mix of housing types, including apartments

Fig. 17.16 NEW URBANISM IN COLORADO. Prospect is a housing development in Boulder County designed by Duany Plater-Zyberk & Company, who also designed the new urbanist community of Seaside, Florida. It was started in the mid-1990s. (Bronwyn Fargo)

and houses so that people at different stages in the life cycle and income groups can live together; shops and offices at the edge of the neighborhood; a close-enough school so children can walk there; parking spaces that are nearly hidden from view; tree-lined, narrow streets that favor walkers and bike riders and slow down auto traffic; sites for community activities; and a self-governing neighborhood association. In brief, the new urbanism favors walkable, modern, human-scale neighborhoods which offer an alternative to conventional U.S. suburbs and suburban sprawl.

The most famous example of the new urbanism is Seaside, Florida. It is a planned community designed by Duany and Plater-Zyberk and built between 1984 and 1991.

CELEBRATION, FLORIDA: WALT DISNEY MEETS NORMAN ROCKWELL?

Celebration, Florida, is a planned community constructed by the Walt Disney Company next door to Disney World in Orlando, Florida. Started in 1994, Celebration has the flavor of a 1930s village in the U.S. South with a Caribbean flourish: brightly colored, stucco buildings. About 2,500 homes cluster around a small, pedestrian-friendly shopping center.

Celebration is often cited as an example of new urbanism. But it does not (or did not—Disney sold the town center in 2004 to a private group) meet one important criterion of new urbanist ideals: self-governance. Under Disney's stewardship, the Disney Company (not the residents) made major decisions concerning the town.

Some critics heap scorn on Celebration. For one, Ada Louise Huxtable (1997), former *New York Times* architectural critic, abhors ersatz urbanity and a spurious sense of place in places like Celebration. According to Huxtable, Celebration is an attempt to build an artificial and sanitized "surrogate environment," a created world detached from everyday experience. A town like Celebration, built in the twentieth century but standing in a timeless era, disturbs Huxtable.

Others say that Celebration is a romanticized vision of a U.S. small town where children say their prayers and families say grace before a meal and everyone knows his or her neighbors. That is, it's a tribute to the clean, simple, rural life that may never have existed except in nostalgic Norman Rockwell paintings. (Interestingly, Rockwell spent his youth and went to art school in New York City, not the kinds of places he later painted, most famously for the covers of the *Saturday Evening Post*.) One scholar–critic put it like this: Celebration is a Disneyesque "crossroads of nostalgia and consumerism, the Disney [Company's] celebration of the American past, a two and one half billion dollar nostalgic look backward at the American small town..." (Hogan, 2003).

But some observers are kinder. For one, sociologist Andrew Ross. Ross lived in Celebration for a year and then wrote *The Celebration Chronicles: Life, Liberty, and the Pursuit of Property Value in Disney's New Town* (2000). What he found in Celebration was not only a picture-book town but also a real place, with real problems.

OTHER ALTERNATIVES

"GREEN" STRUCTURES

Before the 2000s, some nations tried to become "green"; that is, they became concerned and actively tried to improve their own and the planet's environment. But even in an age of information and perhaps data overload, there were no common performance measures. In early 2008, staffs at centers located at two U.S. universities (Yale and Columbia) released an index which attempts to remedy the data problem. Called the Environmental Performance Index (EPI), its purpose is to assess the globe's environmental challenges and the responses of individual countries. Although far from accurate, it contains the best available data

to date in 25 categories, including carbon emissions and water quality. Perhaps surprisingly, some big and some small nations occupy ranks at both the top and bottom; the same is true for rich and poor countries.

Efforts to be greener did not stop at national borders. U.S. states passed bills with various names such as Massachusetts's Green Communities Act of 2008, aimed at reducing dependence on fossil fuels and encouraging the use of clean technologies.

By the early 2000s, many cities were touting their efforts to be more environmentally sensitive. For example, London restricted driving in a key central area, and Paris introduced nonpolluting bikes to borrow throughout the city. Meanwhile, "green" buildings were proudly announced in San Francisco and Chicago, among other cities.

Various architects and designers have been involved with efforts to construct environmentally friendly buildings. Here, only one of many is discussed: Shigeru Ban, a Japanese architect who lives in Paris but spends several days a month in Tokyo and New York, where he has offices.

Globe-trotting Ban leads a nomadic life, and perhaps very appropriately, one of his "green" projects (although he rejects the word "green" as vague) is the Nomadic Museum. This structure is made from cargo containers, stacked grid-like. It is a temporary structure that can be reassembled almost anywhere. Inside, there are colonnades of recycled paper tubes, which create the feeling of twin church naves. Decorating the entrance and exit are huge hanging curtains, looking like gorgeous Indian silk but made from recycled teabags.

Ban has been active in many places, including post-atrocity Rwanda and post-earthquake western Turkey. Everywhere he works, Ban tries "to give comfort to people" (in Kimmelman, 2007:20), using materials that "don't require more energy to take down than they did to put up." Some buildings, Ban thinks, should be built *not* to last.

CAR-LESS COMMUNITIES?

Part of a movement called "smart planning," Vauban is a German upscale community near the Swiss and French borders, that has gone essentially carless. Except for the community's main street (where a tram runs to downtown Freiburg) and a few avenues on the edge of Vauban, the streets of the community (completed in 2006) are car-free. (Car ownership is allowed in Vauban, but there are only two very expensive garages—at the edge of the development—to park. About 70 percent of Vauban's families do not own cars, and 57 percent sold a car to move here (in Rosenthal, 2009).

In the U.S., there are plans to develop similar communities. In California,for example, a Vauban-like community, called Quarry Village, is being planned on the outskirts of Oakland. It will be accessible via mass transit to the Bay Area Rapid Transit (BART) and to the California State University's campus in Hayward.

Whether or not car-less communities will have mass appeal, of course, is another issue. So far, they appeal to more affluent Europeans and people in the United States.

ANOTHER LOOK

Whatever grand designers dream up, people will undoubtedly continue to personalize their space. A spot of color here, a sentimental remembrance there, status symbols and territorial markings all around.

Still, no matter how creative we are in trying to control and personalize our space, we are limited by the larger social context. People who want to live in large communal groups, for example, can't do so if the housing stock is composed of small apartments. Social facts constrain individual action.

Theorists disagree on this: How much does the built environment influence human behavior? Does the physical environment merely reflect, or can it also create, social reality? Social scientist Harold Lasswell views architecture as a symbolic expression of a society's dominant values. So do architect Christopher Alexander, novelist Lawrence Durrell, and neo-Marxist geographer David Harvey.

But design theorist Alexander goes a step further; he wants to create new physical forms in order to create new social patterns. Alexander argues that city form and space not only reflect values but also shape human action. In his view, a new society cannot be constructed on the cornerstones of old buildings. In fact, many visionaries share that idea.

Sociologists of the Chicago school (Park, Burgess) had a different perspective. As sociologists, they didn't focus on the design of buildings, but they did insist on the interrelationship of spatial forms and social processes, notably economic competition. Moreover, Park and Burgess were interested in reforming the industrial city, not remaking it. Their hope was to improve the physical environment in order to decrease what they considered "social disorganization." A strong emphasis on determinism, whether physical (Alexander) or socioeconomic (Park and Burgess), underlies much of this thought.

Meanwhile, other theorists implicitly reject physical determinism and the idea that bad physical environments produce social disorganization. Herbert Gans's work is illustrative. Gans says that living in what others might call a slum—such as Boston's West End—does not lead to social disorganization. Nor does moving to and living in suburban Levittown change people's behavior. Creating new buildings, even new institutions at the community level, had little impact on how Levittowners acted or felt (Chapter 8). In other words, the extent to which space and place influence or mold behavior remains controversial. As on many other key issues, theorists do not share a vision.

Finally, micro meets macro in metropolitan space. The way people perceive, use, and interpret their environment is linked to their social–cultural being. And there is another important connection: Just as the command over space in a classroom or hospital reflects micro–power relationships, the command over urban–suburban–postsuburban space reflects macro–power relationships.

KEY TERMS

Arcology Architect Paolo Soleri's term, blending elements of architecture and ecology, to describe compact, self-contained futuristic cities, which he compares with the design of great ocean liners. Soleri's arcologies range from small projects like Arcosanti, an experimental community still (after decades of money and other problems) under construction in Arizona, to megastructures to replace New York City.

Fig. 17.17   A SPECIAL SENSE OF PLACE. Inventor of a nonexplosive gas lamp Charles Pigeon and his wife are immortalized in their bed, located in the Montparnasse Cemetery in Paris. (Carite Massot)

Built environment As distinguished from the natural environment, it is everything that people have constructed.

Environmental determinism The view that the built environment plays a determining, or at least crucial, role in shaping human behavior.

Imageability Kevin Lynch's term describing the degree to which a city is visually legible or evokes a strong image in any observer's mind.

Personal space As used by Robert Sommer, both the bubble around each person and the processes by which people demarcate and personalize the spaces they inhabit.

Proxemics The study of how people in various cultures use space, especially for social interaction. Edward T. Hall pioneered proxemics.

PROJECTS

1. **Personal space**. How large are various people's protective bubbles? Test the size of their bubbles by breaking them—that is, by invading their space. Be sure to choose a range of people whose space you can invade: older and younger, authority figures, family and friends, men and women. If possible, also pick non-North Americans in your nonrandom sample. At what distance do these various people seem to feel uncomfortable when you engage in a conversation?

2. **Uses of social space**. Observe how people use space. For example, select a social space, such as a park, and identify users and their behavior. Are there any instances of expropriation or personalizing of social space?

3. **City planning**. What is the general design of the community where you live? Is it what Christopher Alexander would call a tree? Are there subtle, complex, overlapping functions in space? Or does it fit more into the model of the new urbanism?

4. **Utopia**. Design a city (in physical terms) that reflects your particular notion of a social–political–economic ideal way to live. Include the location of major institutions, living quarters, and basic economic activities. Then, have others—unlike yourself in terms of age, racial/ethnic background, religious beliefs etc.—comment on what's missing from your Utopia, if anything, from their viewpoint. What might they add or substitute?

5. **House as projected symbol of self**. Interview women, men, and children living in different ZIP code neighborhoods, trying to better understand what kinds of *dream residences* they choose. Develop an interview schedule so that you ask each respondent the same questions. A few possible questions: What type of home do you prefer—a single-family, detached dwelling; an apartment; a condo; a cohousing arrangement; or something else (please specify)? What should be the largest room—kitchen, living room, den, other (please specify)? Do you prefer a feeling of formality or informality? What colors would you choose for the kitchen? Then analyze the responses, paying special attention to possible patterns of difference.

6. **Defining home**. Using a combination of archival research and interviews, determine how various age-based, income and/or status, religious, ethnic, and regional groups define "home."

SUGGESTIONS FOR FURTHER LEARNING

Some classics in the field of personal and social space are cited in the chapter itself (e.g., Robert Sommer's studies on personal space; Edward T. Hall's studies of proxemics). To these should be added, in my view, the collected works of Erving Goffman, particularly *Relations in Public* (New York: Basic Books, 1971), *Encounters* (Indianapolis: Bobbs-Merrill, 1961), and *Asylums* (Garden City, N.Y.: Doubleday, 1961). These studies may have been conducted decades ago, but they are not dated.

Geographers Richard Peet and Nigel Thrift suggest that some nineteenth-century geographers justified Euro-American hegemony as the "natural, even god-given consequence of the superior physical environments of Western Europe and North America." See their *New Models in Geography*, vol. 2 (London: Unwin Hyman, 1989) for a discussion of the possible relationship between environmental determinism, social Darwinism, and nineteenth-century imperial expansion.

The symbolism of physical settings concerns a wide range of scholars. For instance, the late and globally—recognized professor of the history of religions Mircea Eliade discussed the religious meaning of dwellings, which he saw not only as "machines for living" but also as "the universe that man constructs for himself by imitating the paradigmatic creation of the gods, the cosmogony," in his essay "The World, the City, the House," in *Occultism, Witchcraft and Cultural Fashions* (Chicago: University of Chicago Press, 1975).

Can people be happy and really human without green spaces and nature? No, according to sociobiologist Edward O. Wilson's biophilia hypothesis presented in *Biophilia* (Cambridge, Mass.: Harvard University Press, 1986). For Wilson, *biophilia* is people's "innate tendency" to focus on life and lifelike processes. Wilson thinks that human existence depends on this propensity. His "hypothesis" (in quotation marks here because it is unclear whether or how it might be tested) holds that humans have a genetically based need to affiliate with the natural world.

For the story of the first substantial green building to be built on a college campus, see David W. Orr's *Design on the Edge: The Making of a High-Performance Building* (Cambridge, Mass.: MIT Press, 2008). Orr describes how the original idea was translated into a building on the Oberlin (Ohio) campus.

The evocation of a sense of place is commonly the forte of visual and literary artists. In the film *Mystic River* (2003), director Clint Eastwood offers a close-up look at an Irish American, blue-collar neighborhood in Boston. In *Look Homeward, Angel* (New York: Scribner, 1929), novelist Thomas Wolfe exalts Asheville, North Carolina, while Sinclair Lewis satirizes small-town American life in *Babbitt* (New York: Harcourt, Brace, 1949).

A documentary which focuses on one woman's sense of place—Varaire, her village in southwest France—is Parisian filmmaker Guillaume Dreyfus's *Lia* (2008). In her nearly 100 years, Lia seems content to have stayed almost her entire life in Varaire and its surrounding farms; she never visited Paris, for example. At the turn of the twentieth century, many villagers, including Lia's kinfolk, migrated to California for work, but Lia had no desire to visit them. She lives simply in the house where she raised her children. In the movie, a sense of place is linked to what others might call "the peasant soul."

A sense of place is sometimes evoked by social scientists and historians. See, in particular, Jane Jacobs's description of New York City's Hudson Street in *The Death and Life of Great American Cities* (New York: Vintage, 1961).

New Yorker critic Brendan Gill believed that America's leading authorities on urban life nearly always turn out to be learned amateurs, people like Frederick Law Olmsted and Jane Jacobs. If so, a worthy addition to this list is the late William H. Whyte. His years of scholarly labor about cities are published in *City: Rediscovering the Center* (New York: Doubleday, Anchor, [1988] 1990).

But beware: Amateurs, like experts, can make serious mistakes. In the case of the Sapir–Whorf hypothesis, linguistics professor Geoffrey K. Pullum argues that Benjamin Lee Whorf, a Connecticut fire-prevention inspector, published an amateur linguistics article in an MIT alumni publication, which was reprinted widely, replete with its false claims intact. See Pullam's *The Great Eskimo Vocabulary Hoax and Other Irreverent Essays on the Study of Language* (Chicago: University of Chicago Press, 1991).

For an insider's look on an infamous housing environment, see *Voices of Cabrini: Rebuilding Chicago's Public Housing*, a 1999 documentary by Ronit Bezalel and Antonio Ferrera. More information can be found at http://www.voicesofcabrini.com.

Hoop Dreams (1994), named best documentary of the 1990s by TV/newspaper film critic Roger Ebert, follows William Gates, a Cabrini-Green resident, and fellow hopeful Arthur Agee, not from this project. Both young men dreamed of becoming pro basketball players. Ten years later, Gates was a senior pastor at the Living Faith Community Center in Cabrini-Green, and his older brother Curtis, who had lived vicariously through his younger brother, had been murdered at age 36.

A series of essays, ranging from Margaret Crawford's "The World in a Shopping Mall" to Michael Sorkin's "See You in Disneyland," are brought together in Michael Sorkin, ed., *Variations on a Theme Park: The New American City and the End of Public Space* (New York: Hill and Wang, Noonday, 1992). The authors see megamalls, zones of gentrification, pseudohistoric markets, and corporate enclaves as forms of a new sort of cityscape. The paradigm for all these places, they argue, is the theme park.

Utopian visions and some historical attempts to actualize them in the United States are detailed in Charles Nordhoff, *The Communistic Societies of the*

United States (New York: Dover, [1875] 1966). He includes a variety of religious and secular groups, including the Oneida community, the Amana Society, and noncommunistic colonies.

Part utopian, part pragmatic, cohousing is one response to single-parent families and two-income households. Pioneered in Denmark, a cohousing development, typically of 20 units, groups private houses around a central commons and shared kitchen, dining, and child-care facilities. See Jo Williams, "Designing Neighbourhoods for Social Interaction: The Case of Cohousing," *Journal of Urban Design* 10:195–227 (June 2005).

J. B. (John Brinckerhoff) Jackson has been called America's most distinguished landscape historian. The late Herbert Muschamp, a former architectural critic for the *New York Times*, wrote that Jackson was the United States's "greatest living writer on the forces that have shaped the land this nation occupies." In *Discovering the Vernacular Landscape* (New Haven, Conn.: Yale University Press, 1984), Jackson drew a distinction between the established landscape ("maintained and governed by law and political institutions, dedicated to permanence and planned evolution") and the vernacular landscape ("identified with local custom, pragmatic adaptation to circumstances, and unpredictable mobility"). For a collection of his essays, some from *Landscape* magazine, which he long edited (and collected by editor Helen Lefkowitz Horowitz), see John Brickerhoff Jackson, *Landscape in Sight: Looking at America* (New Haven, Conn.: Yale University Press, 2000).

Edward T. Hall, founder of proxemics, describes his own work as paralleling Jackson's studies on vernacular landscape. In *An Anthropology of Everyday Life: An Autobiography* (New York: Doubleday Anchor, 1992), Hall recalls architect Mies van der Rohe's comment—"God is in the details"—and says that he concentrates on understanding the details of everyday life.

See *Robert Venturi: Complexity and Contradiction in Architecture* (New York: Museum of Modern Art, 2002) for Venturi's "gentle manifesto for a nonstraightforward architecture." This edition is introduced by Vincent Scully, an influential Yale teacher and early proponent of Venturi's work. For an interview featuring Robert Venturi and Denise Scott Brown, see *Charlie Rose*, December 17, 2001, on DVD, released by Charlie Rose, Inc., in 2006.

From globalization to cognitive maps, *Spatial Behavior: A Geographic Perspective*, by Reginald G. Golledge and Robert J. Stimson (New York: Guildford Press, 1996) presents a comprehensive survey of the field. There's an innovative chapter on geography and "the other," which asks students to think critically about power relationships.

In *Space and Place: The Perspective of Experience* (Minneapolis: University of Minnesota Press [1977] 2001), Chinese American geographer Yi-Fu Tuan explores how people think about space, how they form attachments to home and neighborhood (and country), and how a sense of time affects feelings about space and place. Tuan suggests that the key distinction is this: Place is security, and space is freedom; people are attached to place and long for space. He discusses sacred versus "biased" space, mythical space and place, time in experiential space, and cultural attachments to space. Love of place (or people's emotional bonds to place) is a theme of Tuan's *Topophilia: A Study of Environmental Perceptions, Attitudes, and Values* (New York: Columbia University Press Morningside Edition, [1974] 1990). In this book, Professor Tuan explores the links between environment and worldview and examines the search for environment in the city, suburb, countryside, and wilderness.

Wearing another hat, Tuan was a founding director of the Center for American Places (CAP) in 1990. CAP publishes books that "enhance the public's understanding of, appreciation for, and affection for the places of America—whether urban, suburban, rural, or wild." It also publishes some books on the international scene. (For more information, see CAP's Web site, www.americanplaces.org.)

In *The Poetics of Space* (Boston: Beacon Press [1960 in French; 1964 in English], 1994), Gaston Bachelard muses about space, how we live in houses, and how domestic space and place affect us psychologically. Some hail this study as "classic" and "magical." Mainly known as a philosopher, Bachelard held degrees in physics, mathematics, and philosophy.

In *The House: Its Origins and Evolution* (London: Constable & Robinson, 2002), architect Stephen Gardiner says that the house has always been inspired by natural forms. Originally, he says, these forms were made from "the materials of the land—mud and reeds" and were rounded (4). He notes that the development of the rectangular house plan is a theme running through the long history of the house (6). In his view, three remarkable architects dominated the twentieth century: Frank Lloyd Wright, Le Corbusier, and Mies van der Rohe (233).

According to reporter–novelist James Howard Kunstler, almost everything built in the half-century before the turn of the twenty-first century in the United States is "depressing, brutal, ugly, unhealthy and spiritually degrading...." Kunstler has a gift for strong images but questionable generalizations. See his *The Geography of Nowhere: The Rise and Decline of America's Man-Made Landscape* (New York: Simon and Schuster, 1993).

New urbanist architects would disagree with Kunstler. For one, architect Peter Calthorpe in *The Next American Metropolis* (Princeton, N.J.: Princeton Architecture Press, 1993), argues against suburbs but for "neotraditional," small-town grids. Laguna West, a master-planned community outside Sacramento, California, uses his neotraditional principles.

In *Paris, Capital of Modernity* (New York: Routledge, 2003), urbanist David Harvey discusses Baron Haussmann's redo of the city. This book is not a breezy history of the City of Light. Rather, it is a very serious and interdisciplinary investigation into the complicated and turbulent era of France's Second Empire (1852–1870).

Called by some the "master builder," Louis Sullivan believed that architecture is the true mirror of a nation's values: "As you are, so are your buildings. And, as your buildings, so are you." For an insight into Sullivan's work, see a classic work, *Louis Sullivan: Prophet of Modern Architecture* (New York: W.W. Norton, 2005). The newer edition updates Hugh Morrison's original of 1935.

My Architect, a 2003 documentary film about acclaimed U.S. architect Louis Kahn, written and directed by his son Nathaniel, features Kahn's philosophy of building as well as the buildings themselves. Very spiritual and influenced by ancient structures, Kahn influenced many other architects, including Frank Gehry. The film, in part a son's quest to know his father, features interviews with I. M. Pei, Philip Johnson, and other architects.

For an architectural critic's view of Kahn, see Martin Filler's *Makers of Modern Architecture: From Frank Lloyd Wright to Frank Gehry* (New York: New York Review Books, 2007). Filler devotes short, readable essays to over 20 architectural giants, including Kahn, Calatrava, and Piano.

Professor Clare Cooper Marcus discusses the importance of some nonbuildings in helping people to get better in "Healing Gardens in Hospitals" (http://www.idrp.wsu.edu/). Her research, reflected in this 2005 online article, shows that patients, visitors, and staff members of hospitals can all experience reduced stress when gardens are present.

The late urban guru Jane Jacobs sparkled with insight on how city space might be used humanely. She liked the creative disorder of older neighborhoods, active streets, and well-used odds and ends of city space. Her book *The Death and Life of Great American Cities* (New York: Random House, Modern Library, [1961] 1992) was a seminal work and a bestseller.

For a range of perspectives within the social sciences on space and place, see the journals published by professional associations, such as the American Sociological Association's *American Sociological Review.* Also see recent issues of various journals specializing in a topic connected to space and place, such as the Czech-based *Cyberpsychology*, which began publication in 2008.

Among the many works that deal with racial/ethnic aspects of place is *The Black Metropolis in the Twenty-first Century: Race, Power, and Politics of Place* (Lanham, Md.: Rowman & Littlefield, 2007), edited by Robert C. Bullard, a sociologist widely acclaimed for his studies of environmental justice. Various essays deal with government's role in shaping metro regions and the connections between place, space, and race.

Novelist Toni Morrison often writes with an epic sense of place. See, for example, *Sula* (New York: Vintage, [1974] 2004) and *A Mercy* (New York: Knopf, 2008).

REFERENCES

Alexander, Christopher. 1964. *Notes on the Synthesis of Form.* Cambridge, Mass.: Harvard University Press.

Alexander, Christopher. [1965] 1978. "A city is not a tree." Pp. 377–402 in Stephen Kaplan and Rachel Kaplan, eds., *Humanscape: Environments for People.* North Scituate, Mass.: Duxbury.

———. 2003–2004. *The Nature of Order.* Vol. 3, *A Vision of a Living World.* Berkeley, Calif.: Center for Environmental Structure.

Alexander, Christopher, Sara Ishikawa, and Murray Silverstein, with Max Jacobson, Ingrid Fiksdahl-Kins, and Shlomo Angel. 1977. *A Pattern Language: Towns, Buildings, Construction.* New York: Oxford University Press.

Apple, R. W., Jr. 1979. "Britain's notable nonagenarians." *New York Times Magazine* (November 11):50.

Atkinson, Bland. 2006. *Gated Communities: International Perspectives.* New York: Routledge.

Bartman, Barry, and Tom Baum. 1998. "Promoting the particular as a niche cultural strategy in small jurisdictions." In W. Faulkner, ed., *Proceedings, Progress in Tourism and Hospitality Research.* Australian Tourism and Hospitality Research Conference. Gold Coast.

Bell, Paul A., et al. 2005. *Environmental Psychology,* 5th ed. Mahwah, N.J.: Lawrence Erlbaum.

Berger, John. 2007. "Ten dispatches about place." *Orion Magazine* (July/August): http://www.orionmagazine.org/index.php/articles/article/307

Bernard, Anne. 2008. "Moscow journal: With some construction ingenuity, cafés for one season." *New York Times* (July 14): http://www.nytimes.com/2008/07/14/world/europe/14moscow.html?_r=1&th&emc=th&oref=slogin

Bezalel, Ronit, and Antonio Ferrera. 1999. "Voices of Cabrini: Rebuilding Chicago's Public Housing." (documentary film produced by Judy Hoffman.)

Calthorpe, Peter. n.d. (http://www.calthorpe.com/bios/pcbio.htm

Campbell, Monica. 2007. "Refurbished Oaxaca beseeches tourists to return." *San Francisco Chronicle* (April 5):A17.

Castaneda, Carlos. 1968. *The Teachings of Don Juan: A Yaqui Way of Knowledge.* New York: Pocket Books.

Chivers, C. J. 2007. "Letter from Turkmenistan. 'Stalin-Vegas' rises from the desert floor." *International Herald Tribune* (July 19):2.

Churcfhill, Winston. 1943. "Famous quotations and stories." The Churchill Centre and Museum at the Cabinet War Rooms, London. (October 28): http://www.winstonchurchill.org/learn/speeches/quotations.

City of Las Vegas, Planning and Development Department. 2006. "….and another thing." http://www.lasvegas-nevada.gov/files/And_Another_Thing_2nd_Qtr_06.pdf]

Colin, Chris. 2007. "Sipping from a utopian well in the desert." *New York Times* (September 16): http://travel.nytimes.com/2007/09/16/travel/16next.html?th&emc=th

Colomina, Beatriz. 2007. *Domesticity at War.* Cambridge, Mass.: MIT Press.

———. 1996. *Privacy and Publicity: Modern Architecture as Mass Media.* Cambridge, Mass.: MIT Press.

Coupland, Douglas. 1994. "Rem Koolhaas, post-nationalist architect." *New York Times* (national edition) (September 11):H45.

Durrell, Lawrence.[1969] 1997 *Spirit of Place.* New York: Da Capo Press.

Eisler, Benita, ed. 1997. *The Lowell Offering: Writings by New England Mill Women (1840–1945).* New York: W.W. Norton.

Esser, A. H., et al. 1970. "Interactional hierarchies and power structure in a psychiatric ward: Ethological studies of dominance in a total institution." Pp. 25–61 in S. J. Hutt and C. Hutt eds., *Behavioural Studies in Psychiatry.* Oxford: Pergamon Press.

Feagin, Joe R., and Michael Peter Smith. [1987] 1989. "Cities and the new international division of labor: An overview." Pp. 3–34 in Michael Peter Smith and Joe R. Feagin, eds., *The Capitalist City: Global Restructuring and Community Politics.* Cambridge, Mass.: Blackwell.

Frangos, Alex. 2007. "Dubai puts a new spin on skyscrapers." *Wall Street Journal* (April 11):B1+.

Gans, Herbert. [1962] 1982. *The Urban Villagers,* updated and rev. ed. New York: Free Press.

Gardner, Martin. 2000. *Did Adam and Eve Have Navels? Discourses on Reflexology, Numerology, Urine Therapy, and Other Dubious Subjects.* New York: W.W. Norton.

Gibbons, Dave, and Frank Miller (illustrator). [1990] 2008. *Give Me Liberty.* Milwaukie, OR: Dark Horse Comics.

Glaab, Charles N., and A. Theodore Brown. 1976. *A History of Urban America,* 2nd ed. New York: Macmillan.

Griaule, Marcel. 1965. *Conversations with Ogotemmeli.* London: Oxford University Press.

Hall, Edward T. 1959. *The Silent Language.* Garden City, N.Y.: Doubleday.

———. 1966. *The Hidden Dimension.* Garden City, N.Y.: Doubleday.

Hartley, David. 1749. *Observations on Man, His Frame, His Duty, and His Expectations*. London: Samuel Richardson.

Harvey, David. 1989. "Monument and myth: The building of the Basilica of the Sacred Heart." Pp. 200–228 in *The Urban Experience*. Baltimore, Md.: Johns Hopkins University Press.

Hastorf, Albert H., and Hadley Cantril. 1954. "They saw a game: A case study." *Journal of Abnormal and Social Psychology* 49:129–134.

Helvétius, Claude Adrien. [1758] 2004. *De L'Esprit or Essays on the Mind and Its Several Faculties*. Kila, Mont.: Kessinger Publishing.

Herbert, Bob. 2007. "Living off women." *International Herald Tribune* (September 5):7.

Hogan, Kathleen M. 2003. "Parson Disney's fable." *Cyberbia Forums:* http://xroads.virginia.edu/~MA98/hogan/celebration/front.html

Howard, Ebenezer. 1898. *Tomorrow: A Peaceful Path to Real Reform*. London: Sonnenschein.

Hughes, Rob. 2008. "Soccer: From the same streets, in opposite directions." *International Herald Tribune* (July 30):16.

Hugo, Victor. [1862] 1987. *Les Misérables*. Trans. Lee Fahnestock and Norman MacAfee. New York: Signet.

Huxtable, Ada Louise. 1997. *The Unreal America: Architecture and Illusion*. New York: New Press.

Jackson, John Brinckerhoff. 1984. *Discovering the Vernacular Landscape*. New Haven, Conn.: Yale University Press.

Jacobs, Jane. 1961. *The Death and Life of Great American Cities*. New York: Vintage.

Kapuściński, Ryszard. 2007. *Travels with Herodotus*. Trans. Klara Glowczewska. New York: Alfred A. Knopf.

Kesey, Ken. 1962. *One Flew over the Cuckoo's Nest*. New York: Viking.

Kimmelman, Michael. 2007. "Building to last, just long enough." *International Herald Tribune* (May 23):20.

Kira, Alexander. [1966] 1976. *The Bathroom: Criteria for Design*. New York: Viking.

Klinge, J. William. [1999] 2008. "How different areas of personal space are protected: A look at gender differences." http://clearinghouse.missouriwestern.edu/manuscripts/125.asps

Knox, Paul L. 1991. "The restless urban landscape: Economic and sociocultural change in the transformation of metropolitan Washington, D.C." *Annals of the Association of American Geographers* 81:181–209.

LaFranchi, Howard. 2008. "Iraqis see red as US opens world's biggest embassy." *Christian Science Monitor* (April 24): http://www.csmonitor.com/2008/0424/p01s04-wome.html

Lasswell, Harold. 1979. *The Signature of Power*. New Brunswick, N.J.: Transaction Books.

Lebowitz, Fran. [1974] 1978. *Metropolitan Life*. New York: Fawcett Crest.

Lee, Dorothy. 1959. *Freedom and Culture*. Englewood Cliffs, N.J.: Prentice Hall.

Lesy, Michael. [1973] 2000. *Wisconsin Death Trip*. Albuquerque: University of New Mexico Press.

Liebow, Elliot. [1967] 2003. *Tally's Corner: A Study of Negro Streetcorner Men*, 2nd ed. Lanham, Md.: Rowman & Littlefield.

———. 1993. *Tell Them Who I Am*. New York: Free Press.

Loeffler, Jane. 2008. "The rows on embassy rows." *Newsweek* (international edition) (July 7–14):39–41.

Low, Setha. 2003. *Behind the Gates: Life, Security, and the Pursuit of Happiness in Fortress America*. New York: Routledge.

Lyall, Sarah. 2008. "Some Britons too unruly for resorts in Europe." *New York Times* (August 24): http://www.nytimes.com/2008/08/24/world/europe/24crete.html?_r=1&th&emc=th&oref=slogin

Lynch, Kevin. 1960. *The Image of the City*. Cambridge, Mass.: MIT Press.

Magnuson, Melissa Joy, and Lauren Dundes. 2008. "Gender differences in 'social portraits' reflected in MySpace profiles." *CyberPsychology & Behavior* 11(2):239–241.

Marcus, Claire Cooper. [1995] 2006. *House As a Mirror of Self: Exploring the Deeper Meaning of Home*. York Beach, Maine: Nicholas-Hays.

Maxwell, Lorraine. 2007. "The role of noise and density in school health and safety." www.iceh.org/pdfs/LDDI/2007Series/Maxwell.pdf

Miller, Adam. 2007. "Sellers, get to know home buyer's preferences." *Epoch Times* (northern California edition) October 18–24:B8.

Mumford, Lewis. 1961. *The City in History*. New York: Harcourt, Brace & World.

Muschamp, Herbert. 1993a. "Shaping a monument to memory." *New York Times* (national edition) (April 11):sec. 2, 1+.

———. 1993b. "Things generally wrong in the universe." *New York Times* (national edition) (May 30):sec. 2, 30.

Nelson, Robert H. 2005. *Private Neighborhoods and the Transformation of Local Government*. Baltimore, Md.: Urban Institute Press.

Norberg-Schulz, Christian [1979] 1984. *Genius Loci: Towards a Phenomenology of Architecture*. New York: Rizzoli.

Ouroussoff, Nicolai. 2008. "In changing face of Beijing, a look at the new China." *International Herald Tribune* (July 12): 13.

Papke, David Ray. 1999. *The Pullman Case: The Clash of Labor and Capital in Industrial America*. Lawrence, KS: University of Kansas Press.

Park, Robert E., Ernest W. Burgess, and R. D. McKenzie. 1925. *The City*. Chicago: University of Chicago Press.

Podmore, Frank. [1907] 2004. *Robert Owen: A Biography*. Stockton, CA: University of the Pacific Press

Porteous, John Douglas. 1977. *Environment and Behavior: Planning and Everyday Urban Life*. Reading, Mass. Addison-Wesley.

Rainwater, Lee. 1966. "Fear and the house-as-haven in the lower class." *Journal of the American Institute of Planners* 32:23–31.

Rawsthorn, Alice. 2008. "What defies defining, but exists everywhere?" *International Herald Tribune* (August 18):8.

Realtytrac. 2007. "Stockton, Detroit, Las Vegas post top foreclosure rates." (August 14): http://www.realtytrac.com/ContentManagement/pressrelease.aspx?ChannelID=9&ItemID=773&accnt=64847

Reich, Robert B. [1991] 1992. *The Work of Nations: Preparing Ourselves for 21st-Century Capitalism*. New York: Vintage.

Reuters. 2008. "Shops and restaurants ask where tourists went." *International Herald Tribune* (September 5):20.

Rivlin, Gary. 2007. "In Las Vegas, too many hotels are never enough." *New York Times* (April 24): http://www.nytimes.com/2007/04/24/business/24vegas.html?th&emc=th

Rosenbloom, Stephanie. 2006. "In certain circles, two is a crowd." *New York Times* (November 16): http://www.nytimes.com/2006/11/16/fashion/16space.html?ex=1321333200&en=2d57a58460696fe0&ei=5088&partner=rssnyt&emc=rss

Rosenthal, Elizabeth. 2009. "In German suburb, life goes on without cars." *New York Times* (May 12): A1.

Ross, Andrew. 2000. *The Celebration Chronicles: Life, Liberty, and the Pursuit of Property Value in Disney's New Town*. New York: Ballantine Books.

Sans, Jérôme. n.d. "Dialogues: A discussion of love and chance with Paul Virilio." http://www.watsoninstitute.org/infopeace/vy2k/sans.cfm

Schmich, Mary. 2001. "'Hardball' hits 9 tough critics where they live." *Chicago Tribune* (September 21): http://www.chicagotribune.com/news/columnists/chi-010921schmich,0,7079140.column

Soleri, Paolo. 1969. *Arcology: The City in the Image of Man*. Cambridge, Mass.: MIT Press.

Sommer, Robert. 1969. *Personal Space*. Englewood Cliffs, N.J.: Prentice Hall.

Sorkin, Michael, ed. 1992. *Variations on a Theme Park: The New American City and the End of Public Space*. New York: Hill and Wang, Noonday Press.

Spreiregen, Paul D. 1965. *Urban Design: The Architecture of Towns and Cities*. New York: McGraw-Hill.

Stehli, Jean-Sébastien. 2007. "Hot blocks." *France Today* (August): http://www.francetoday.com/features/hot_blocks.php

Sullivan, Jennifer A. 2003. "Laying out an 'unwelcome mat' to public beach access." *Journal of Land Use and Environmental Law* 18(2):331–354.

TripAdvisor. 2007. "TripAdvisorhttp://www.breakingtravel/news.com/news/article/btn20070405103415422/

Urbina, Ian. 2008. "Growing pains for a deep-sea home built of subway cars." *New York Times* (April 8): http://www.nytimes.com/2008/04/08/us/08reef.html?th&emc=th

US History Encyclopedia:, n.d. "Landscape architecture." http://www.answers.com/topic/landscape-architecture

Venturi, Robert, Denise Scott Brown, and Steven Izenour. [1972] 1977. *Learning from Las Vegas*. Cambridge, Mass.: MIT Press.

Vesselinov, Elena, et al. 2007. "Gated communities and spatial inequality." *Journal of Urban Affairs* 29(2):109–127.

Virilio, Paul. [1977] 2007. *Speed and Politics*, 2nd rev. ed. Los Angeles: Semiotext(e).

Waid, Mark, and Alex Ross (illustrator).[1996]2008. *Kingdom Come*. New York: DC Comics.

Wata, Osamu I. 1992. "Crowding and behavior in Japanese public spaces: Some observations and speculations." *Social Behavior and Personality: An International Journal* 20(1):57–70.

Weiss, Michael J. 2000. *The Clustered World: How We Live, What We Buy, and What It All Means About Who We Are*. Boston: Little, Brown.

Whyte, William H. 1978. "New York and Tokyo: A study in crowding." Pp. 1–18 in Hidetoshi Kato, ed., *A Comparative Study of Street Life: Tokyo, Manila, New York*. Tokyo: Research Institute for Oriental Cultures, Gakushuin University.

———. [1988] 1990. *City: Rediscovering the Center*. New York: Doubleday, Anchor.

Williams, Alex. 2008. "New York switcheroo." *International Herald Tribune* (August 2–3):1+.

Wolfe, Tom. 1977. *The Kandy-Kolored Tangerine-Flake Streamline Baby*. New York: Bantam.

Woods, Lebbeus. 2004. *The Storm and the Fall*. Princeton, N.J.: Princeton University Press.

Yamasaki, Minoru. n.d. http://www.greatbuildings.com/buildings/World_Trade_Center.html

Zorbaugh, Harvey Warren. 1929. *The Gold Coast and the Slum: A Sociological Study of Chicago's Near North Side*. Chicago: University of Chicago Press.

PAYING THEIR WAY

PART VII

Lucy Hilmer

CHAPTER 18

PRODUCING, CONSUMING, EXCHANGING, TAXING, AND SPENDING

John N. Ballator

Social theorists rank economic activities high on their list of factors that influence, perhaps determine, the fate of cities and nations. Recall, for example, the debate over the earliest cities: Economic assumptions underlie both the Childe thesis and the trade thesis of Jane Jacobs (Chapter 4); both assume that what people produce and exchange are prime determinants of human settlement patterns. Burgess's concentric zone hypothesis rests on another economic assumption, namely, that economic competition is the key determinant of land use. Although not spelled out explicitly, Mike Davis's analysis of global slums

(Chapter 2) is rooted in economics too. Further, the U.S. government's Metropolitan Statistical Area (MSA) concept grew out of economic reasoning; it uses the integrated labor market as the leading indicator of interdependence within a geographical area. Likewise, Logan and Molotch's typology of contemporary cities (Chapter 5) is based on socioeconomic logic—specifically, that cities play varied roles in the international division of labor. So is the concept of a "global city," put forward by Saskia Sassen and others.

Scholars from many fields and interdisciplines agree with the observation that, fundamentally, the metropolis can (and should be) seen as a focus of production. Thus, this chapter focuses on some basic, metropolitan economic functions. It pays special attention to what most theorists think is the single most important factor in the growth or decline of metropolitan economies: the health of the global and national economies. (The late Jane Jacobs was a dissenter on this key point. Just as she turned conventional wisdom on its head about early cities, [Chapter 4], iconoclast Jacobs reversed the taken-for-granted economic relationship of cities to nations. Essentially, she argued [1984] that strong urban economies are the backbone and motor of the wealth of nations, not vice versa.)

At the outset, we should note two different phenomena related to economics and metropolitan life. First, there appears to be a serious mismatch between theorists' high ranking of economics as an influence on our fates and the general public's economic literacy. Typically, in the United States, courses in economics are not required by secondary schools or colleges. Bookstores devote more space to self-help and mysticism than to economics, with some notable exceptions such as *Freakonomics* (Chapter 2 and discussed later in this chapter).

In general, mass media do not provide in-depth debates on economic issues such as tax policy, roots of the global economic recession, or international trade agreements, perhaps because economics seems so complicated or boring. This mismatch—between theorists' agreed-upon assumption of the importance of economics and the U.S. public's understanding of the economy—does not bode well for democratic participation.

However, some help may be on the way. *Freakonomics: A Rogue Economist Explores the Hidden Side of Everything* (2005), a book by economist Steven D. Levitt and journalist Stephen J. Dubner, was such a best-seller that it was revised and expanded from its original edition shortly after its original publication. It sold 3 million copies worldwide by 2008, and its authors established a blog shortly after publication. This suggests that a larger public is interested in economics when it's presented in readable, nonjargony prose. Hopefully, other academics will take the point.

Help may come from quite another direction too: fear. When, in 2007–2008, after so-called NINJA loans (NINJA = No income, No jobs, No assets), subprime mortgage foreclosures and shocks to the global financial system (a "financial tsunami" to use former Federal Reserve chair Alan Greenspan's term) brought financial loss to many far from Wall Street, some tried to figure out their own financial situation. This leads to the next point.

Here is the second phenomenon to think about: "the future is happening far faster than anybody ever thought it would" (Coupland, 1994:H45). Alan Greenspan, for one, said that he certainly didn't predict the "financial tsunami" and indeed was shocked at the near-global collapse of the stock market in fall 2008.

Consider, also, that urban economics did not even exist until 1965, when the first urban economics text appeared. Just one generation later, the subdiscipline of urban economics seemed woefully outdated. What changed? The economic landscape—and an appreciation that cities are part of a global economic system of producers, consumers, and exchangers.

Today, to a significant degree, mayors cannot direct their economies. Neither can nations. Iceland's announcement in 2008 of bankruptcy due to global financial crisis is indicative.

Many observers say that the nature of global challenges, including credit crises and energy availability and price, defy quick or one-nation fixes. In part, commentators note, this reflects the power of multinational corporations (MNCs). The U.S. government, for example, may outlaw trading with nations defined as "enemies," but it cannot stop U.S.-identified MNCs from trading illegally with presumed "enemies" through non-U.S. subsidiaries.

POLITICAL ECONOMY: A BEGINNING VOCABULARY

Let's begin with a basic vocabulary of political economy. Of course, all economists don't agree; differing ideological assumptions play a key role in their disagreements. Consider the concept of "the market" of supply and demand. The self-regulating market mechanism is central to classical liberal economics. Most introductory textbooks look at the world through the filter of the "competitive" market. Yet many economists reject this basic assumption about how the world works. Indeed, some influential modern liberals view the market mechanism with suspicion or even disdain. For one, the late John Kenneth Galbraith long (and long ago) argued that supply and demand no longer work to regulate the economy. In general, Galbraith (1968) said that business corporations manipulate the market to suit their own needs. In particular, the free market doesn't work at all to regulate oil prices, according to Galbraith. Further, he wrote (1979:3), the Organization of Petroleum Exporting Countries (OPEC) oil cartel has proved "inconveniently resistant to free market doctrine."

Decades later, Galbraith's son, James, an economics and public policy professor (also not known as a conservative) went farther. In 2008 he wrote that, instead of depending upon the market, President George W. Bush and his administration turned the United States into a "corporate republic." Galbraith argues that the Bush administration brought both the methods and mentality of big business to public life, turning the United States into a "predator state," which did not try to reduce government but instead tried to divert public money into private hands (see Chapter 3).

Other voices, from some unexpected corners, echo Galbraith's words. We might predict that Marxist economists would repudiate the market mechanism, and indeed they do. They argue that the U.S. economy (and its subsystems of urban economies) is best understood in the framework of monopoly capitalism, not the competitive market system. But we might be surprised to find that some conservatives question free-market theory. Respected scholar Charles Lindblom, a professor emeritus of politics and economics at Yale, considered a conservative, stirred great controversy a generation ago with his 1978 book *Politics and Markets*. (A major U.S. corporation was so upset that it paid for a full-page ad in a leading newspaper to counter Lindblom's arguments.) He maintained that the emergence of large private corporations renders market doctrine obsolete. Essentially, Lindblom concurred with J. K. Galbraith: Markets are necessarily manipulated by big business corporations in order to ensure economic stability and growth.

More recently, market doctrine in the United States has come under serious reconsideration. Indeed, some say that the policy of Hank Paulson (secretary of the U.S. Department of the Treasury and former chair of one of the world's biggest investment banks) of putting taxpayer money directly into banks smacked of socialism, not free-market doctrine. Others snapped that the joining of big business with big government was akin to fascism. Without calling it by any name, one blogger predicted that, by 2018, the U.S. financial system will exist entirely under the ownership of the Treasury and Federal Reserve. The blogger, grad student Neil Abrams (2008), concludes that this would place "finance in the same league as national security as a government-provided public good...."

Yet market doctrine continues to enjoy widespread support, not only among U.S. libertarians but also among U.S. mainstream economists. Indeed, in *Economics*, the best-selling-ever introductory economics text in numerous editions (as of 2006, the eighteenth, in paperback), Nobel laureate Paul Samuelson, joined, since 1985, by coauthor William D. Nordhaus, contend that while markets are far from perfect, generally they work effectively to answer the questions of who gets what and what goods are produced (Samuelson, 1964; Samuelson and and Nordhaus 1992).

Once again, this shows that what you see depends on how you look at it. With this in mind, let's consider some concepts—first mainstream (classical and neoclassical), then alternative—that political economists use to explain how the world works.

SUPPLY, DEMAND, PRICE, AND THE MARKET MECHANISM

Twin concepts—supply and demand—provide the cornerstones of classical and neoclassical economics; this branch of economic thought is associated with Adam Smith ([1776] 1970). More recently, one spokesperson for neoclassical economics was the late Nobel laureate Milton Friedman. The economics department at the university where Friedman taught, the University of Chicago, is associated with this branch of thought.

The logic of supply and demand is as follows. In a market, or "free-enterprise," economy, the **supply** of a particular good, such as automobiles, is assumed to be related to consumer demand. Why produce a car if no one will buy one? (An advertising campaign might, of course, persuade consumers that they need a car or a second car, thus stimulating demand for the product.) **Demand** for a product implies that consumers both want and will pay for it. The number of cars that will be produced, the logic goes, depends on their cost. At $18,000, the demand for a new car will be great, assuming there is gas to power it. As the **price** rises to $48,000, demand falls. A demand curve shows that the lower the price, the greater the demand. (see Figure 18.2)

Now, let's look at the supply side. How many cars will be produced at different prices? This information can be charted with a supply curve. Suppose, for example, that new compact cars are selling for $20,000. But at that price, manufacturers do not want to supply any cars to the market because instead of making a profit, they would lose money. Car manufacturers would produce something else that yielded a higher profit. But they would be willing to produce about 5 million cars if the price were $25,000. As the price keeps rising, manufacturers are willing to supply increasing numbers of cars. A supply curve indicates that the higher the price, the more cars will roll off the assembly lines. (see Figure 18.3)

At some point, classical economic theory continues, a point of equilibrium between supply and demand will be reached. That is, there will be a price that satisfies both consumers and producers. In the case of cars, this equilibrium point can be found by putting the demand and supply curves together and noting the point at which they intersect.

Above the equilibrium point, the theory states, there will tend to be a surplus of cars on the market and, hence, a downward pressure on the price. Below the equilibrium price, there will tend to be a shortage of cars and, hence, an upward pressure on the price. According to Samuelson and Nordhaus (1964:63), the equilibrium price is the only price that can last for any length of time. This is because the equilibrium price "is that at which the amount willingly supplied and the amount willingly demanded are equal." (see Figure 18.4)

PROFIT

A basic assumption underlies this discussion of supply and demand: Suppliers attempt to maximize their profit, while consumers attempt to maximize their well-being (utility).

What exactly is profit? According to Samuelson and Nordhaus, **profit** is what "you have left over from the sale of product (your oranges, apples, bread, and manicures) after you have paid the other factor costs" (wages, interest, rent) (1964:181). Firms pursue different strategies to maximize profit. They may hire cheaper labor, employ more efficient managers, increase advertising, buy less expensive raw materials, expand markets, and so forth. Or they may relocate to areas, either at home or offshore, where labor and taxes are lower or antipollution regulations are minimal.

Is profit the only goal of private business firms? Here, economists disagree. Some argue that business has a social responsibility to the community in which it operates. Nonsense, retorted the dean of economic conservatives (and libertarians) Milton Friedman. He maintained that the business of business is business: the "Social Responsibility of Business Is to Increase Its Profits" (1970)—nothing else. Other economists (e.g., Lindblom and Galbraith) disagree, contending that modern corporations seek stability and growth as well as profit.

UTILITY

Do individuals and households also try to maximize their gain? Yes, according to free-market doctrine. Indeed, the "rational, self-interested economic individual" (maximizing utility or well-being) is a key psychological assumption underlying classical liberal economics. As detailed in Chapter 3, liberal philosophers and political economists base their view of how the world works on this vision of human nature.

But this basic assumption has been under suspicion, even attack, for decades. One critic, Harvey Leibenstein (1976), argued that market doctrine is wrong; people

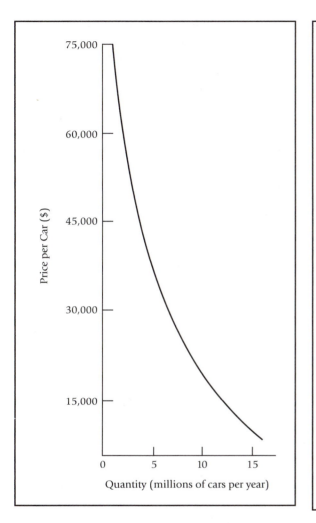

Fig. 18.2 DEMAND CURVE. This curve for cars slopes downward, indicating that as the price increases, demand decreases.

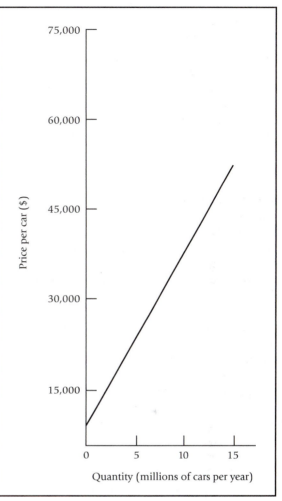

Fig. 18.3 SUPPLY CURVE. This curve shows that the higher the price for cars, the more will be supplied to the market.

don't follow the model of rationality attributed to them. Many feminist economists agree (Chapter 2).

Despite such criticism, the model of rational economic behavior underlies conservative, libertarian, and liberal thought. Meanwhile, Marxists have a different perspective. They tend to emphasize the deception (via advertising, mass media, political rhetoric, etc.) used by dominant elites to control and confound members of the working class, making it difficult for them to even know what's in their best interest.

EXTERNALITIES

When something is produced—bits of information, bottled water, microchips—the production process can have external effects. These effects may benefit or penalize innocent bystanders. For example, if a chemical plant dumps waste into a river, the waste contaminates the river for everyone. This is called a "negative externality." On the other hand, a "positive externality" can bring social benefits to members of the community. A new Metro station in

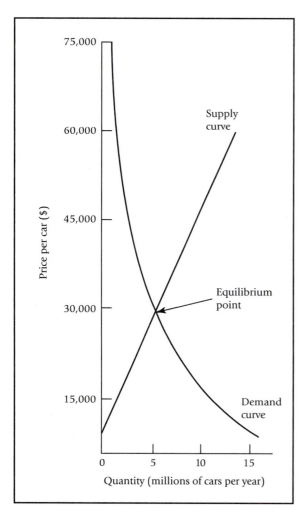

Fig. 18.4 EQUILIBRIUM PRICE. The point at which the supply curve intersects with the demand curve is called the "equilibrium price" or "point." This is the point at which the amount of a product produced and the amount demanded are the same.

or benefits do not equal social costs or benefits" (Samuelson and Nordhaus, 1992:736).

Even the most rational, self-interested person may not be able to calculate the effect of externalities. What, for instance, is the impact of toxic wastes entering the groundwater of border towns in Mexico and the United States? Or consider the case of gambling in Atlantic City, New Jersey. The majority of urbanites there, including one pastor of a downtown church, voted for casino gambling in the 1970s. They reasoned that new hotels and gambling would bring jobs and an economic boost to the city's lagging economy. However, many have since changed their minds. Gambling brought an influx of prostitutes and purse snatchers to the downtown area. One result was a sharp decline in membership and attendance at central city churches.

Either positive or negative, externalities are not distributed equitably. Indeed, many observers argue that negative externalities affect the powerless much more than the powerful. In *Unequal Protection: Environmental Justice and Communities of Color* (1994), sociologist Robert D. Bullard and others document toxic racism in many American cities. For example, in a 1-square-mile area of Los Angeles (with a majority population of African Americans and Latinos), there are waste dumps, smokestacks, and toxic wastewater pipes. In the industrial corridor of Louisiana, which is home to a largely African American population, there is a "toxic gumbo" of carcinogens. In Carver Terrace, an African American subdivision in Texarkana, Arkansas, there are homes built on a toxic waste site of pentachlorophenol (PCP), arsenic, and creosote.

Years after Bullard published his book, others noted toxic racism in New Orleans: Federal Emergency Management Agency (FEMA) trailers given to survivors of Hurricane Katrina. Many trailers, housing African Americans, were so toxic that FEMA officials counseled their employees not to enter them.

In many cases, contemporary governments intervene to control negative externalities such as toxic gumbo. Liberal economists say—rightly or wrongly—that "most people today agree that government is needed to curb some of the worst externalities created by the market mechanism" (Samuelson and Nordhaus, 1992:42).

Washington, D.C., may give an economic boost to surrounding shops. The bees from a flower nursery may pollinate the neighbors' gardens—all without cost to the neighbors.

Externalities (also called "spillover effects") occur outside the market. An individual or a firm can benefit or hurt people without economic compensation or payment: "Externalities exist when private costs

EQUITY

Equity refers to the fair or just allocation of something. What's considered fair, of course, is a matter of perspective. Consider the case of a gas shortage. Pure market theorists think it fair to allocate available gas by the price system: Those who can afford the product will pay the higher price; others will make substitutions or do without. Liberals think this unfair, preferring some kind of rationing system.

What's fair or equitable is filtered through a larger framework of justice, a normative theory. Take income distribution, for example. A market system often generates great income inequality. Is this situation fair? According to liberal economists Samuelson and Nordhaus, this is a question for politics and ethics, not economics: "Economics cannot answer questions of how much poverty is acceptable and fair" (1992:44). As we shall see shortly, Marxist economic thought makes no such sharp distinction between politics and economics.

EFFICIENCY

In mainstream economics, **efficiency** refers to "the absence of waste, or the use of economic resources that produces the maximum level of satisfaction possible with the given inputs and technology" (Samuelson and Nordhaus, 1992:735). Classical and neoclassical theory holds that the market works—and works better than other economic systems—to produce efficiency: In a competitive market, a business firm will find the cheapest way to produce a product—say, a gas range—by efficiently using land, labor, and other factors of production. If it doesn't, the theory holds, the company will not survive the competition.

Efficiency is usually measured by cost per unit of production. Thus, if the GeeWhiz Company produces a stove at a cost of $5,000 while the Flamethrower Company produces a comparable stove at a cost of $2,500, Flamethrower is considered to be twice as efficient as GeeWhiz.

However, efficiency is not always easy to measure, particularly in the postindustrial economy. More and more people are working in the service and information sectors, where efficiency is no longer a matter of producing cheaper stoves. How can a public schoolteacher's or public administrator's efficiency be measured when profit is not a goal and social benefit is hard to gauge with precision?

Today, governments intervene to remedy market inefficiencies. For instance, in the United States, the federal government subsidizes public goods (e.g., national defense), counters monopolies (via antitrust law), regulates negative externalities (e.g., antipollution laws), and intervenes in the marketplace (e.g., bank bailouts during the "mortgage meltdown crisis" and the "credit crunch"). Local governments also intervene in markets; they provide public goods (e.g., community swimming pools) and regulate negative externalities (e.g., antismoking ordinances).

Mainstream economists do acknowledge that efficiency can conflict with equity. According to Samuelson and Nordhaus, "Even the most efficient market system may generate great inequality" (1992:43). They cite the example of the Irish potato famine of 1848 and 1849: "Queen Victoria's laissez-faire government let millions of Irish children, women, and men starve ... when a fungus suddenly destroyed the potato crop." Similarly, economists Robert Heilbroner and Lester Thurow say that markets "allocate goods and services more effectively than other systems of rationing, particularly planning in one form or another," but they note that "the underlying distribution (or maldistribution) of income clashes with other standards of the public interest that we value more highly than efficiency" (1994:181).

AN ALTERNATIVE VOCABULARY

Today, a wide range of people in the United States reject both liberal and conservative perspectives on how the political economy does and should work. These range from former Dominican priest Matthew Fox (2006) and goddess worshipper Starhawk (2005) to the Hopi in the Southwest (McLeod, 2001), all of whom reject notions of profit, efficiency, and utility, embracing instead a global reverence for the earth.

Here, let's focus on one alternative to conservative and liberal visions: Marxist political economy. Generally, Marxists argue that consumer sovereignty is a sham and that the public good can't result from each individual's pursuit of self-interest. Most neo-Marxists agree that globally, unregulated MNCs or transnational corporations are the world's most powerful economic actors.

Now, let's examine several concepts that are central to the Marxist critique of the market mechanism and capitalism. Although brief, this discussion will indicate why Marxist analyses of the economy are so at odds with mainstream studies.

CAPITAL

To non-Marxists like Paul Samuelson and William D. Nordhaus (1992), **capital** is simply one input of production. (The other two are land and labor.) It consists of "durable produced goods that are in turn used in production. The major components of capital are equipment, structures, and inventory" (730). Capital goods include "machines, roads, computers, hammers, trucks, steel mills, automobiles, washing machines, and buildings" (20). The U.S. economy exemplifies **capitalism** because (1) capital, or *wealth*, is primarily the private property of the capitalist and (2) private markets are the prime vehicles used to allocate resources and generate incomes.

By contrast, to a Marxist, capital is not just a thing, like machines. It is much more. It is a social relation. Marxists think that the means of production in society, like machines, become capital when "they have been monopolized by a certain sector of society and used by that class to produce surplus value—that is, the income of the capitalist class (generally, profits, interest, and rent) that comes from the exploitation of another class" (Gurley, 1975:32). Thus, for Marxists, capital is more than the means of production in society; it is the way in which these means are used. In this way, Marxist thought links economics to politics and social order. To a Marxist, capitalism is not only an economic system based on private property; it is also a political and social system based on the domination and exploitation by capitalists of nonpropertied workers.

SURPLUS VALUE

Business firms make a profit because they are efficient and compete successfully in the marketplace. Often, firms buy something (raw materials), fashion it into a manufactured good, and resell it for profit.

Or they exchange goods for profit. Or they increase prices, which provides profits. That is how free-market theorists explain profitability. Marxists have a different explanation.

To a Marxist, a key source of profit in capitalist economies derives from **surplus value**. What is surplus value and when does it arise? Marx's concept of surplus value may be explained in this way: "Surplus value arises when a capitalist purchases labor-power (the capacity for labor) at its value, employs the labor-power in a work process that he controls, and then appropriates the commodities produced. Surplus value is the difference between the net value of these commodities and the value of labor-power itself" (Gurley, 1975:33).

In this view, the secret of profit is human labor-power. Specifically, a worker sells his or her labor-power (mental and physical capabilities) to a capitalist and then the capitalist uses the labor-power to get commodities which have a value higher than that of the labor-power bought. Thus, in this view, profit results from the exploitation of labor in the production sphere.

MONOPOLY CAPITALISM

In nineteenth-century Great Britain and the United States, the characteristic economic unit was the small firm. Typically, many textile firms (like Lowell's factory in Massachusetts) or bakeries produced a small share of the total product available in the marketplace. Such firms often faced stiff competition from one another. This situation typified competitive capitalism.

Marxist scholars emphasize how much this situation has changed since the nineteenth century. The typical economic unit now—and since the 1960s—Paul Baran and Paul Sweezy wrote, is "a large-scale enterprise" which produces a significant share of an industry's output and can control its "prices, the volume of production, and the types and amounts of its investments" (1966:6). In other words, they contended, the typical economic unit in capitalist countries has taken on the attributes of a monopoly.

In their classic book *Monopoly Capital: An Essay on the American Social and Economic Order* (1966), Baran and Sweezy focused on one major theme: the ways in which profit or surplus—"the difference between what a society produces and the costs of producing it"—is generated and absorbed under monopoly capitalism. (*Note*: Marxist theorists don't equate profit and surplus. However, one form of profit, in their view, results from the private appropriation of surplus value.) They stressed the critical role that technological innovation played in the development of a system composed of giant corporations that maximize profit and accumulate capital: **monopoly capitalism**.

These corporate giants, Baran and Sweezy argued, are price-makers: "they can and do choose what prices to charge for their products" (57). Price-makers ban price-cutting to reduce competition and remove "the dangerous uncertainties from the rationalized pursuit of maximum profits" (59). Often, this takes the form of cartels that regulate prices and output. Or it takes the form of tacit collusion among business firms. In either case, the result, they claimed, is clear: Competitive capitalism has faded away, replaced by monopoly capitalism. And they argued that the capitalist state (e.g., the U.S. government) actually functions to strengthen monopoly and regularize its operations.

The implications of Baran and Sweezy's critique of market doctrine are wide-ranging. For example, they contended that the Great Depression of the 1930s was not "the Great Exception" but rather the "normal outcome of the workings of the American [read 'U.S.'] economic system" (1966:240).

Without going into their complex analysis of capitalist crises, let us examine one issue of special relevance to U.S. urban areas (and, increasingly, urban everywhere): automobilization. Writing over a generation ago, Baran and Sweezy (1966:244–245) posed an interesting question: Why did the second wave of auto production in the United States occur after World War II and not in the 1930s, when it would have led to a needed economic boom? After all, the technology existed. And people presumably needed more cars as much in the 1930s as in the 1940s. The answer, they wrote, "is that in 1937 people did not have the required purchasing and borrowing power to get things started, while after 1945 they did. . . . We have here a classic case of quantity turning into quality." What they meant is that the post–World War II suburban boom generated a snowball effect, making shopping centers and other facilities either necessary or

profitable. But even with these powerful stimuli and with defense spending increases, Baran and Sweezy (1966:246) said, unemployment grew. Their conclusion: "Surely, an economy in which unemployment grows even during the expansion phase of the business cycle is in deep trouble" (248).

LATE CAPITALISM

To economist Ernest Mandel ([1972] 1987:9), late capitalism is a further phase of monopoly capitalism (which he equated with imperialism) that started after World War II. More than a generation ago, Mandel said that late capitalism is typified by a centralization of capital: A few very large financial groups "dominate the economy of each capitalist country," and "these giant monopolies divide the world markets of key commodities between themselves" (594–595). In late capitalism, the MNC becomes the main form of capital.

SOCIAL STRUCTURES OF ACCUMULATION

Starting in the late 1970s, a group of U.S. economists working in the Marxian tradition put forward a new approach to analyze the structure and development of capitalist economies and societies: the *social structure of accumulation* (SSA). SSA refers to "the complex of institutions which support the process of capital accumulation. The central idea of the SSA approach is that a long period of relatively rapid and stable economic expansion requires an effective SSA" (Kotz et al., 1994:1).

For our discussion, what is most important about this approach is that it includes political and cultural institutions as well as economic ones. At the domestic level, these institutions may include such arrangements as the organization of work, the role of the state in the economy, and the type of race and gender relations. At the international level, these institutions may include financial, trade, and political environments.

To conclude: The view that economic life is inseparable from political and cultural life is a key assumption of Marxist thought.

To Marx, at any historical time, people have a certain level of productive capacity. This capacity depends on the technology available to them (machines, tools, etc.), the natural environment (fertile or infertile land, water, etc.), and their own knowledge and skills. These Marx calls the "material forces of production." Marx believed that the material forces of production determine how people survive economically (e.g., in nomadic food gathering or industrial production). And, Marx thought, *the material forces of production determine how people relate to one another socially in the process of producing and exchanging things and ideas* (e.g., as master and slave, as capitalist and worker). Marx called these production and exchange relationships the "social relations of production."

Together, the material forces of production and the social relations of production (the economic base of society) mold what Marx called the "superstructure": the way people think, their legal systems, their political and religious institutions, and their worldviews. In brief, Marx held that the dominant ideas and institutions of any society are determined by people's material being.

THE INFORMATIONAL MODE OF DEVELOPMENT

According to urban theorist Manuel Castells (1989), two key factors—the restructuring of capitalism, started more than a generation ago in the 1970s and 1980s, plus a technological revolution—are transforming the cities and regions of the world. The main process in this transition is not, he thought, the shift from manufactured goods to services but the "emergence of information processing as the core, fundamental activity," which conditions the production, distribution, management, and consumption processes. Indeed, Castells argued that "our economies should be characterized as information economies, rather than as service economies" (167).

How are these changes affecting cities and regions? Castells said that one result is this: High-level decision making is increasingly centralized in global cities such as New York, and organizational management is decentralized within major metropolitan areas.

Not all theorists agreed (or agree) with Castells (and Mandel). For example, many conservative and liberal thinkers do not make such necessary and inevitable links between economics and social–political life.

Yet most social scientists—whatever their ideological perspective—agree that the way people organize

themselves economically and the productive forces available to them have a great impact on their lives. This applies to cities too. As two non-Marxist urbanists put it decades ago, "economic forces are prime determinants of the ecological and physical structures of cities. Directly or indirectly, these factors influence the pattern of living as well as the social and governmental institutions of metropolitan complexes" (Bollens and Schmandt, 1970:72).

A PARTICIPATORY BUDGET

In a few places around the world, governments encourage local groups to participate in the budget-making process. Perhaps the best known of these efforts takes place in Porto Alegre, Brazil, a city of over 1.3 million inhabitants.

Essentially, the participatory budgeting process in Porto Alegre, started in 1989, aims to redistribute city resources to the more vulnerable social groups via participatory democracy. This rather complex system is, according to U.S. and Portuguese scholar De Sousa Santos (1998), "a form of counter-hegemonic globalization" that tries to open up spaces for democratic participation—an alternative to the dominant forms of development.

Does it work? De Sousa Santos concludes that the participatory budget has been a "remarkable way of promoting the participation of the citizens in decisions concerning distributive justice, effectiveness of decisions, and accountability of the municipal executive and of the delegates elected by the communities" to various representative bodies. Over 80 Brazilian cities, the vast majority (90 percent) run by the Workers' Party, are adopting the system in some form. Its success has been noted internationally. But, he warns, we are living in a historical era of "structural pessimism" in which there is a tendency to be complacent toward what exists and "too suspicious" toward emergent, unfamiliar realities. Thus, in De Sousa Santos's (1998) view, participatory budgeting, which he calls a "rare bird of realistic utopia," can easily fail.

A NEWER VOCABULARY

RESTORATIVE ECONOMY AND SUSTAINABILITY

A generation ago, those preaching the end of industrialism were dubbed extremists. Years later, consumers were buying their books, if not all their ideas. Take, for example, Paul Hawken's books, some with coauthors: *The Ecology of Commerce* (1993), *Blessed Unrest: How the Largest Movement in the World Came into Being and Why No One Saw It Coming* (2007), and *Natural Capitalism* (2000) with Amory and Hunter Lovins. Hawken, an apostle of socially responsible capitalism, warned in *The Ecology of Commerce* that if we want to avert commercial and biological catastrophe, we must "end industrialism as we know it." How? Not by recycling burrito foil and tin cans. In his view, such measures do not go far enough; he warned that the planet's "carrying capacity" had already been surpassed—and he wrote that in 1993! Rather, he said, it is up to business to create a sustainable, restorative economy by ambitious measures that use market principles, not government mandates. These include creating incentives that will encourage businesses to make decisions on the basis of long-term ecological (and commercial) sustainability, not short-term (and short-sighted) gain. For example, he suggests that the price of a product should include the cost of cleaning up its wastes, such as plastic in automobiles.

In *Blessed Unrest: How the Largest Movement in the World Came into Being and Why No One Saw It Coming* (2007), entrepreneur–environmentalist Hawken changes his tune a bit but remains optimistic. He writes that a number of activist groups are changing the world, "working toward ecological sustainability and social justice." He says that these groups are not ideological or centralized but rather spontaneous, organic responses to the recognition that environmental problems are social-justice problems.

In *Natural Capitalism* ([2000] 2008)), Hawken et al. detail how some companies are practicing a new, more efficient and profitable type of industrialism, which not only saves the environment but also creates jobs. Calling their approach "natural capitalism," they argue that business can be good for the environment. For instance, Interface of Atlanta (Georgia) tripled profits and doubled jobs by creating an environmentally friendly system of recycling floor coverings for businesses.

Some voices are not so optimistic. For one, Paul Kennedy (2008), a historian at Yale, thinks that the environment and environmentalists are in for a very hard slog, given higher oil and food prices, which are likely "to erode even further many of the gains and assumptions held by the environmentalist movement." Intensified oil drilling, the return to nuclear power, the pressures upon forests, the favoring of corn-based ethanol, the increased possibility of a turn to genetically modified farming, and the boost to First-World agricultural protectionism, Kennedy thinks, must make for "glum reading" for environmentalists.

It is noteworthy that optimist Hawken (and his coauthors) published both *Natural Capitalism* and *Blessed Unrest* before the United Nations Intergovernmental Panel on Climate Change (IPCC), the Nobel prize–winning scientific group (see Introduction), warned of global warming's devastating global effects in its report. IPCC Chair Rajendra Pachauri said the November 2007 report implied a new moral imperative, calling for a "new ethic" whereby every person in the world realizes the climate challenge and starts to "take action through changes in lifestyle and attitude" (in Hood, 2007).

Not all agree, of course (see Introduction). The White House responded to the IPCC report, for example, with disapproval at what a Bush science advisor called its imprecise wording and scientific definition.

We might guess, correctly, that "ecological economists" would not agree with the IPCC's prescriptions either. These economists think that environmental degradation is rooted in economic failures. Starting with the assumption that what is important to people is not strictly analyzable by economics alone, they offer a *Blueprint for a Sustainable Economy* (Pearce and Barbier, 2000).

It should not come as a surprise that many economists disagree about what sustains an economy. For example, in the United States, Committee for Economic Development economists Ehrlich and Swartz (2004) credit—rather than blame—trade and foreign investment by contemporary private corporations as the ultimate hope for the environment and so-called developing nations.

Meantime, a new green movement has spread on U.S. college campuses. At the Oberlin (Ohio) campus, for one, there is a sustainability house—SEED (Student Experiment in Ecological Design)—where students seek to reduce their carbon footprints and convince administrators to do the same.

Poet William Blake knew that what is unimaginable today can become conventional wisdom tomorrow. A generation ago, a notion like a biologically sustainable economy that restores nature as it goes may have been considered unimaginable. No longer. Currently, at least to many worldwide, former gardening company executive Hawken looks more like a visionary than a kook (although he may be seen, post-IPCC report, as too timid). He is far from alone. Others, such as Australian scientist Tim Flannery (2006), are considered by many to be visionaries, arguing that global warming and the earth's carbon dioxide pollution can be ameliorated if we shift from our current global reliance on fossil fuels.

THE ECONOMY OF METROPOLITAN AREAS

CITIES AND MSAS IN THE NATIONAL AND GLOBAL ECONOMIES

"No city is an island." This truism can be illustrated at both the national and international levels.

First, the national level. The United States is one mass market for goods, information, and services. Despite some clarion calls to eat only food grown locally, corner bakeries no longer supply the bulk of bread for sandwiches in small towns throughout the United States, and local grocers do not supply the bulk of cold cuts for big-city consumers. Similarly, local authors do not publish the vast majority of high school textbooks; regional and national corporations do. Anyone, whether in Bangor or Bakersfield or Bangkok, can buy geegaws on eBay. Or gamble on Internet poker sites. Or access pornography from who knows where.

Second, the international level. To a significant degree, there is a world market and a system of cities. The globe is a single economic unit, not a collection of separate nations, let alone cities. As noted earlier, major corporations tend to be multinational and multilocational, producing and distributing their goods globally. Many "U.S." brand names—McDonald's, Levi's, and Coca-Cola, to name a few—are as familiar to people in Paris and Tokyo as to those in New York or Booneville (Figure 18.5). These MNCs salute

no particular flag; their workforces, materials, and profits are transnational. For example, in 2006, Coca-Cola's worldwide volume rose 5 percent; the company's smallest increases were in the United States and Europe (Bloomberg News, 2006). (By the early 1990s, 80 percent of Coca-Cola's operating profits came from outside the United States.) As the president of a major MNC put it (before it was acquired by AT&T, the world's largest telecommunications company): "We at NCR [National Cash Register] think of ourselves as a globally competitive company that happens to be headquartered in the United States" (in Uchitelle, 1989:A1).

Economist Nouriel Roubini said, in fall 2006, that the United States was likely to face enormous

Fig. 18.5 U.S.-IDENTIFIED BRAND NAMES. McDonald's, Coca-Cola, and Levi's are internationally known brand names of U.S.-identified MNCs. These golden arches are found in Kyoto, Japan. (Tim Teninty)

challenges, including a huge housing bust, an enormous credit crisis, an oil shock, and a deep recession. New York University professor Roubini, speaking before economists at the International Monetary Fund, painted a bleak scenario: homeowners defaulting on their mortgages, trillions of dollars of mortgage-backed securities unraveling worldwide, and the global financial system sputtering to a halt. These developments, he predicted, could cripple or destroy investment banks and other major financial institutions (e.g., Fannie Mae). After Roubini's talk, the moderator quipped, "I think perhaps we will need a stiff drink after that." The audience laughed (Mihm, 2008:11), but few were laughing a year later. (Some call Roubini "Dr. Doom.")

The international political economy—and the steps that governments take to shore it up (or not)—and national policies affect U.S. metropolitan economies in different ways. Here are a few examples:

1. *International recession and the strength of the dollar.* When tourism ebbs due to recession, it hurts Tahoe City, California, more than Indianapolis, Indiana. Ditto for global tourist draws, such as Kyoto and Cancun. If the dollar falls vis-à-vis the British pound or euro, fewer U.S. tourists may travel to Europe or the United Kingdom, affecting countless businesses there, including hotels, restaurants, and souvenir shops. Conversely, a weak dollar may draw more European tourists to the United States. When the dollar is weak—say, vis-à-vis the euro—U.S. exports typically increase. Thus, cities and metro areas that export goods and services to Europe gain.

   The international economy often has unintended consequences on U.S. cities. For example, many airlines cut flights under pressure of rising fuel costs in 2007 and beyond. This hurt secondary U.S. cities more than the largest cities. Airports in such places as Cincinnati, Honolulu, Oakland, and Las Vegas were expected to lose more than 10 percent of their scheduled service in 2008 as a result of airline service cutbacks (Koenig, 2008:16). Translated into dollar signs, this means that businesses such as parking, popcorn stands, and other concessions will have fewer customers and less profit.

2. *Global politics.* In the United States, the end of the cold war meant reductions in military contracts and personnel. These losses of funds and jobs adversely affected module production centers and innovation centers more than, say, retirement centers. Conversely, wars in Afghanistan and Iraq meant new jobs for U.S. module production centers and perhaps innovation centers but not retirement centers and leisure playgrounds.

3. *Immigration.* Cuban immigration helped to transform Miami from a sleepy community into an international boomtown and a supermarket for affluent Latin American tourists (Chapter 9). Today, debates over immigration rage, not only in the United States, particularly over its economic and social impacts.

4. *International pacts.* One impact of the North American Free Trade Agreement (NAFTA) has been new employment in some cities, increased unemployment in others. For example, *maquiladoras*, non-Mexican-owned plants located within 50 miles of the U.S. border, have transformed the Mexican landscape and society.

5. *Terrorist threats, war, and political–social instability.* Aside from drops in tourism, cities considered dangerous do not normally attract business investment. Thus, in recent times Kabul, Khartoum, and cities in southern Thailand (the scene of political massacres in the late 2000s) have not been magnets for overseas (or local) tourists or investors.

6. *Energy availability and costs.* As gas and other energy sources soar in price, cities in the United States and elsewhere are rethinking their public-transportation policies. Since 2000, for example, more than a dozen U.S. cities either restored existing streetcar lines, which run on overhead electrical wires, or introduced new ones. (Some cities, including San Francisco, never got rid of their streetcar systems.) By 2008, over 40 U.S. cities were looking into the possibility of bringing back streetcars, hoping to ease traffic congestion and lure people back from the suburbs. Further, energy costs may have significant impacts on cities and suburbs as those who work in cities seek to lower their

transport costs by moving back to the city. In addition, increased energy costs could lead to more telecommuting in some cases.

How much a particular metropolitan area suffers or benefits during times of international or national economic change depends on many factors. Some important factors are (1) the industry mix, (2) demographic and social factors, (3) geographic location, and (4) dependence on petroleum products and proximity to energy sources.

The Industry (or Productive) Mix

The degree to which a particular metropolitan area benefits or suffers from changes in the global and national economies depends partially on the mix of productive activities there. (*Note*: Economists use the term "industry mix," but, in my view, the term "productive mix" better captures the notion that services and information—not manufacturing—typify the U.S. economy today.)

If the U.S. economy expands and household incomes rise, consumers tend to spend their additional money on cars and luxury items, not suntan lotion or dish towels. Hence, metropolitan areas producing goods subject to elastic demand (cars, luxury items, durable goods) tend to benefit during times of national economic growth. But during hard economic times, when people make do by fixing up their old cars rather than purchasing new ones, these areas tend to suffer disproportionately. That is the meaning of the now, obsolete saying "Whenever the nation catches a cold, Detroit gets pneumonia."

Reflecting recent realities, my paraphrase seems more applicable: "When the Chinese economy catches a cold, the global economy gets pneumonia." (At this writing, Detroit is struggling to survive against double pneumonia; auto executives were slow to make smaller, less profitable cars, and international competition drove a better bargain.)

Metropolitan areas that produce junk food, computerized billing services, toilet paper, and other products with inelastic demand are not in favorable positions during growth periods. But they tend to suffer less during economic downturns or recessions. Why? Because people don't give up eating junk food

or drinking beer during hard times. Nor do they cancel insurance policies or stop renting movies. As one Associated Press headline put it, "Recession? Eat, Drink, Smoke and Be Merry" (Wardell, 2008).

Richmond, Virginia, is one city whose product mix cushions (or once did) the effects of economic downturns. Tom Robbins explained why in his novel *Even Cowgirls Get the Blues*:

> Richmond, Virginia, has been called a "depression-proof" city. That is because its economy has one leg in life insurance and the other in tobacco. During times of economic bellyache, tobacco sales climb even as other sales tumble.... Perhaps a cigarette gives an unemployed man something to do with his hands.... In times of depression, policy-holders somehow manage to keep up their life insurance premiums.... Perhaps they insist on dignity in death since they never had it in life....
>
> *(1976:38)*

Note, however, that electronic technologies, international shifts in production (e.g., outsourcing to cheaper labor markets), plus changing attitudes/laws can make cities and towns everywhere much less depression-proof. Take, for example, tobacco. Since Robbins published his novel in 1976, cigarettes have been outlawed in many restaurants and public buildings globally or highly regulated in many cities across the globe as a health hazard. Ad campaigns in some countries discourage young people from ever starting to smoke, thus cutting into future sales. In addition, towns once primarily dependent upon sales of nearby tobacco have been hard hit by competition and/or the end of government subsidies for tobacco. This is the case of some small towns in southwest France.

Note, also, that U.S. national politics and international events can affect a town's coffers. For example, if economic fortunes sink (as in many towns in the 2000s), immigration detention stands out as a rare growth industry. (The U.S. Congress doubled annual spending on it in the period 2004–2008.) Jails from New England to New Mexico, dominated by private industries that run them, made the immigration crackdown pay off. In a town with a very sizeable Latino community, such as Central Falls, Rhode Island, inmates nearly doubled in one year—to the delight of the city council president. His logic: The more detainees they have in jail, the more money the town gets.

Demographic and Social Factors

A metropolitan area's (and a nation's) ability to respond quickly to change such as technological innovation depends partly on its people. Cities with large proportions of unskilled, elderly, or narrowly trained people may suffer more in times of national economic slump than those with a highly adaptable labor force.

In addition, one-industry towns with highly specialized workers face economic disaster if new technology (or outsourcing) makes their functions obsolete. This is what happened to the railroaders in a town called Caliente. As the case study later in this chapter details, Caliente suffered (at least near) "Death by Dieselization."

In past decades, economic change shuttered many mill towns in the United States. But some are trying to reinvent themselves. For one, after losing thousands of jobs in the closed-down paper mills, Berlin, New Hampshire, is trying to spur growth with a combination of public goods, specifically, a new prison and privately owned tourism facilities (an all-terrain-vehicle park).

Women and girls in cities, particularly in countries that experience severe unemployment and deprivation such as Moldova and Cambodia, face a particularly grizzly fate: ending up as sex slaves. Many, if not most, have no clue (when they answer an ad in their local newspaper for a shop girl or maid) what their future holds: being trafficked, sold, and resold to pimps in a worldwide sex trade.

Geographic Location

Chicago is located midway between the New York Stock Exchange and the Western frontier. That is one way to explain Chicago's importance at the start of the past century. It was, as Carl Sandburg memorialized in his hymn to the city, "Hog Butcher for the World" and "The Nation's Freight Handler."

Today, Sandburg would have to revise his lines. The stockyards moved west years ago. But Chicago's transport function remains important, and the world's second busiest airport is located there. (Chicago, once the United States's "second city" in population terms [and original home to The Second City comedy improv troupe, including Bill Murray, Amy Sedaris,

Steve Carell, Alan Arkin, and the Belushi brothers, among others], is now third largest population-wise after New York City and Los Angeles. Chicago, once home to the world's busiest passenger airport, lost that title to Atlanta, Georgia, in about 2000. For other explanations of Chicago's importance between 1900 and 1920, see Chapter 1.)

With technological change, fast communications, changing national needs, new international competitors, changes in the price and supply of energy, and/or the discovery of some important natural resource, cities can gain or lose strategic importance. A generation ago, for instance, small towns like Rock Springs, Wyoming, grew quickly as energy sources were extracted from the earth around them. Just as quickly, they can lose their basic reason for existence and become ghost towns. Or some, like Central City, Colorado (a nineteenth-century gold mining center), and Cordes (created as a "bastide" or protected, market town in 1222, the first in a series of early urban resettlement projects in southwest France) return to life decades or centuries later as tourist draws.

Energy Needs

Availability of energy sources and easy access to transportation have played a major role in city growth for millennia. Early industrial firms, for instance, had to locate near available sources of energy, such as water power. Technological innovations—electricity, combustion engines, telephones, computers, e-mail, and the like—brought changes in industrial, services, information, and residential locations. In the process, some older urban-industrial areas in the United States became victims of change. However, other areas, including Silicon Valley, California, and Bengaluru, India, flourished.

Energy shortages and rising energy costs are bound to have widespread but uneven effects. Here are a few examples: (1) National governments in the oil-rich United Arab Emirates (UAE) have reinvested their profits in expanding cities, exploding with new businesses and structures. (2) Cities from Tours, France, to Dakar, Senegal, and beyond face possible nuclear leaks or expensive oil; they may face very hard times. (3) High prices for oil are fueling one of the largest-ever transfers of wealth in history. Specifically, consumers of oil paid $4–5 billion more for crude oil each day in 2007 than they did just 5 years earlier (Mufson, 2007: Al). This means that oil companies and oil-producing nations pumped more than $2 trillion into their coffers in 2007 alone. Understandably, this also means that some places that import oil will try to cut usage. Examples: Seoul, South Korea, sponsors a no-driving campaign, and Paris, France, makes it easier to ride a bike around the city via its successful rent-a-bike, Vélib, program. Meanwhile, others may spend their new oil wealth to buy weaponry. (4) Angry consumers may revolt against higher fuel prices. A *Washington Post* reporter says that 2007 demonstrations in cities in Burma (Myanmar) "were triggered by a government decision to raise fuel prices" (Mufson, 2007:A1), not the repression of civil rights. (Note, however, that global oil prices fell considerably during the economic recession in the late 2000s; some nations, including Russia and the UAE, may experience serious repercussions because they depended on high oil prices.)

Many effects of energy shortages and rising costs—as well as possible environmental dangers from the use and misuse of energy sources—are still unclear. Will cities located near important energy sources mushroom in population? Will suburbs far from city centers become ghost towns? Will technological and organizational innovations—perhaps long-charge hydrogen cells or electric cars and "smart" homes—allow growing numbers of working mothers, juggling home and work duties, to "compute" rather than commute to work?

Some think that the suburban landscape in the United States will change drastically with increasing gas prices; they toll the bell for the end of the suburbs as we have known them (e.g., Kunstler, 2006). Others point to increased public-transport use; in 2007, for example, use of busses increased 6 percent in Chicago (NBC5, 2008).

To conclude: Forces external to a city or metro area's control, such as the economic state of the nation and the world (or possible global warming), cannot be controlled by people in any one metropolis. But the effects of national or global economic change can be cushioned somewhat by local policy. A declining MSA dependent on a single industry might attempt to attract growth industries to its area. Or it might engage in massive retooling efforts for local workers. But no metropolitan area can change forces beyond its control.

Whether they like it or not, cities are economic creatures of the nation and, increasingly, of the world. This was brought home to workers and politicians from Shenzen, China, to Detroit, Michigan, during the global economic recession that started around 2007; this economic "downturn" meant, in part, that fewer buyers bought products manufactured in industrial cities everywhere and that, consequently, jobs were cut, housing prices dropped, and city coffers were less full or even nearly empty.

BASIC AND NONBASIC SECTORS

All productive activities that help residents of an urban area earn a living constitute that area's **economic base**. These activities include manufacturing, retail trade, sales, tourism, information and services, professional and managerial work, clerical and construction work, and transport.

Once again, the notion that cities can't exist if local residents merely take in each other's washing becomes crucial in understanding how local economies work. Interaction and exchange between the city or MSA and the world beyond its boundaries are essential for continued existence.

Economists draw a sharp distinction between two types of economic activity: basic and nonbasic. **Basic economic activities** are goods and services produced primarily for export out of the city or metropolitan area. Such goods and services constitute the export sector. Examples include TV productions and movies from the Los Angeles–Long Beach area or Bollywood in Mumbai, India; software designs from Seattle or Bengaluru; and refrigerators from Amana, Iowa. (Tourism counts as a basic activity, although its products—souvenir T-shirts, hotel rooms, restaurant meals, and so on—are bought or consumed on the spot, not literally exported.) **Nonbasic** goods and services are primarily produced for local consumption. Examples include beauty shops, restaurants, cleaners, gas stations, and dairies (Figure 18.6).

Most urban economists argue that a city's or an MSA's potential for economic growth depends on the

Fig. 18.6 NONBASIC SECTOR. Garage sales, gas stations, beauty shops, and cleaners are part of an urban area's nonbasic economic sector. (Brack Brown)

strength of its export or basic sector. The rationale is as follows: Export goods and services bring money in from outside the urban area, money that finances the importing of goods that the urban area doesn't produce for itself. In addition, the logic goes, nonbasic activity is largely dependent on basic activity. For example, if a chemical plant closes and the majority of a city's workers become unemployed, they will no longer patronize local retail or service establishments (e.g., restaurants, furniture stores, hair stylists) to the same extent, and eventually these operations will contract or fold.

Over a half-century ago, conventional wisdom about the importance of the basic sector to a local economy was challenged by planner Hans Blumenfeld (1955:131). He argued that a strong nonbasic sector is the key to a strong local economy, not the reverse.

In either case, both positions rest on an implicit assumption: Cities are like nations, self-sufficient in certain productive activities and dependent on the outside world for others. For this reason, economists use international trade terms when discussing basic and nonbasic sectors. Thus, an MSA is said to improve its *balance of payments* position if it can produce locally some product that it formerly imported. An MSA is said to enjoy a *comparative advantage* if it can produce a commodity more efficiently and more cheaply than another urban area.

THE UNDERGROUND ECONOMY

Some productive activities never get counted as part of the basic or nonbasic sector because they remain **underground** (off the books). Underground income is not reported for tax purposes. For instance, many household helpers, service personnel who receive tips, successful gamblers, garage-sale holders, and drug dealers do not declare their earnings (Figure 18.7).

The underground economy may play havoc with (1) statistics concerning income and jobs and (2) the amount of funds available for public projects. First, people listed as "unemployed" may earn significant amounts of money in off-the-books jobs. Second, unreported income may have impacts on a country's tax system. In the United States, the Internal Revenue Service estimates that the "the tax gap," that is, the difference between what taxpayers should have paid and what they actually paid on legal earnings on a timely basis, was $345 billion in tax year 2001 (Furman, 2006). (In some places, it is common for artisans to be paid off the books, saving both employer and employee significant taxes.) If people exchange services (e.g., babysitting for computer assistance), they do not typically report these exchanges as income; and thus, "exchangers" too become part of the underground economy. And so do **"freegans"** (the term blends "free" and "vegan"), eco-conscious, anticonsumerists who forage in urban dumpsters for free, nutritious food; they try to avoid the marketplace—and the taxes paid there—as a political statement.

IDENTIFYING BASIC SECTOR INDUSTRIES

How can the export or basic sector activity within a city or an MSA be identified? Mainstream econo-

Fig. 18.7 THE UNDERGROUND ECONOMY. Globally, unknowable amounts (guesstimated in the many billions of dollars) in the off-the-books economy go unreported and thus untaxed. Some think that one component of the underground economy, illicit drug-trade profits (typically "laundered" and invested in legal endeavors), account for more than 2 percent of the gross domestic product of the United States. (Lisa Siegel Sullivan)

mists use either (1) the employment base method or (2) input–output analysis.

Employment Base Method

The **employment base method** of identifying basic sector industries compares local and national employment patterns. Here is a hypothetical example. In your city, about 6 percent of the labor force works in the food and kindred products industry. If the national average is less than 2 percent, we can assume that your city exports food products. Similarly, if less than 1 percent of the local labor force produces nonelectrical machinery, while the national average is over 2 percent, we can assume that your city imports nonelectrical machinery.

The employment base method can be used for either specific industries or major sectors of the economy (e.g., public administration, durable goods manufacturing, and nondurable goods manufacturing). Using U.S. census data, the percentage of the

labor force employed in these sectors (and the national average for each sector) can be found. It is clear that a highly specialized area (like Silicon Valley for computers or Washington, D.C., for public administration) will show the greatest deviation from national employment patterns.

Input–Output Analysis

The employment base method gives a quick and rather simple view of a local economy's basic and nonbasic sectors. But it can't show the interconnections between local industries. Nor can it show how increases in one sector of the local economy will affect other sectors. For this kind of evaluation, an **input–output analysis** is needed.

Input–output analysis works on the following assumptions: Every good or output produced (financial services, cars, public administration, etc.) requires inputs (labor, raw materials, etc.). If expansion occurs in one industry, additional inputs will be needed; some will be obtained locally and others from outside the community, often across borders. Those added inputs from within the local community will stimulate other local activity. These effects snowball; more inputs stimulate more local purchases—at restaurants, by retail outlets from wholesalers, and so forth. Using input–output analysis, these interindustry relations can be detailed.

Economists have constructed more sophisticated models to describe and predict interindustry flows within a larger region. Yet such models have not been very helpful to decision makers. Problems of data collection, the complexity of real-world transactions (including global trade), and theoretical problems have so far limited the practical applications of input–output analyses (Figure 18.8).

CASE STUDY: CALIENTE

What happened to the town of Caliente illustrates many of the abstract notions just mentioned. As you read this case history, recall some of the factors that influence the state—if not the fate—of U.S. cities and MSAs: (1) the health of their labor market, their tax base, and the effectiveness of government-support programs; (2) the productive mix, demographic and social factors, geographic location, and energy needs;

MY, THIS IS IMPRESSIVE, HEAVY STUFF!

ACTUALLY, IT'S GIBBERISH

WHAT?

Fig. 18.8 GARBAGE IN, GARGAGE OUT (GIGO). Bad data are not improved by running them through a computer. (© 1976 Richard Hedman)

(3) the basic–nonbasic sector distinction; (4) changes in the national economy; and (5) the international political economy.

Over a half-century ago, in 1949, sociologist Fred Cottrell studied a small desert town in the United States. He called this town "Caliente" (which may or may not be its real name). Caliente had only one reason for existence: It serviced steam engines as they moved between Salt Lake City and Los Angeles.

When the diesel locomotive replaced the steam engine, Caliente's repair shops were no longer needed because diesel engines need less frequent servicing than steam engines. Geographically, Caliente was no longer strategic.

This technological switch from steam resulted in "Death by Dieselization" (1951). For a city so dependent on one industry—railroading—the closing of the railroad shops and the permanent loss of railroad jobs meant the collapse of Caliente's economic base.

After the initial shock of disbelief, Caliente's residents tried to find a new economic base. Cottrell (1972) said in his update on Caliente that several ventures were tried, including agriculture and tourism. Then fate took a strange turn. The federal government wanted to use land near Caliente to test atomic devices. At the time, the potential negative externalities of this project were largely unknown, and local

citizens didn't protest this land use, for atomic testing would bring jobs. (In fact, only a few jobs were created this way.) Then, during the Korean War, when the primary source of tungsten was cut off, the federal government paid for a mill near Caliente's profitable deposit. Over time, however, the tungsten mine closed down, and the nuclear test site workers moved to housing closer to their work. So, despite its effort to find a new economic base, the economic picture was bleak in the early 1970s (Cottrell, 1972:76).

Given this bleak picture, one might expect Caliente to become a ghost town. After all, it lost not only its economic base but also much of its tax base: "the railroad tore down, gave away or abandoned much of its fixed structure. In turn it demanded and got a reappraisal that reduced Caliente's tax revenue" (Cottrell, 1972:78). And many other towns in the region did become ghost towns when they stopped exporting ore and thus could not pay for imported goods.

But Caliente did not die. It survived. It didn't exactly prosper, but it did survive. How? Initially by attempting to rebuild its export sector. Then, by government support for various projects, including a mill for tungsten, a rare metal whose supply was interrupted by international politics. And then by providing services to residents—education, nursing, parks, and so forth. But how did residents pay for these services? In large measure through railroad retirement benefits, state pensions, Social Security payments, and other government support programs.

Cottrell (1972:84) concluded that the income of most Caliente residents did not come from exporting goods to the market. Instead, it came from sources outside the town "who pay Caliente people for doing things mostly for each other." In this sense, Caliente represents a national trend away from producing things and toward delivering consumer services.

In the long run, can Caliente survive with no export sector? A generation ago, Cottrell was dubious. But, judging from its Web site as of 2008, the town remains alive—if not exactly thriving. It boasts a grocery store, several motels, three auto repair shops, a service station, plus five restaurants for its approximately 1,000 residents (down from a previous high of 5,000 residents). Its Web site says this about the town's history:

> For more than 40 years, Caliente was one of the major division points on the railroad line. When steam engines were replaced by diesel locomotives in the 1940's, the division point moved to Las Vegas. Without the depot as a main railroad stop, the town's growth dwindled but not its spirit.
>
> *(LincolnCountyNevada.com, n.d.)*

Interestingly, the Web site hardly mentions that Caliente's fortunes have largely been determined by outsiders. (It does mention a gun battle between a local landowner and two major railroad companies in times gone by). This, of course, is not new for Caliente. Past decisions were also made by faraway decision makers: railroad managers and stockholders.

Caliente is far from a typical town. But its story, although several generations old, indicates how little control a one-industry (specialized function) town has over its own fate, particularly when technological change renders its specialized function obsolete. And it illustrates the importance of government support programs to improve the health of the town's tax base and labor market.

Outsiders have always determined Caliente's fate. In contemporary times, they are state voters and federal government decision makers instead of private railroad managers.

Cottrell stressed the ironies concerning the U.S. value of individualism and the belief in the market. The people of Caliente were rugged individualists, believers in the "American way" of the price system and progress.

Fiercely independent in an interdependent world, some Caliente people suffered more than others for their beliefs: "'good citizens' who assumed family and community responsibility are the greatest losers...those who were—by middle class norms—most moral were the most heavily penalized" (Cottrell, 1951:360, 1972:68). Those who could pick up and leave the community—who owned no property there and had not sunk deep roots—"the nomads," suffered least. The final irony is that for all their rugged frontier individualism, these people on the desert "must listen ever more closely to the beat of a distant drummer to whose cadence they must march" (1972:85).

The small town of Caliente was created by outsiders for technological reasons. The site happened to be located at a point on the transcontinental railroad where steam engines needed to be serviced. Technology and geography (lack of physical barriers) dictated Caliente's location.

Towns like Caliente that have a relatively undiversified economy (one that produces only a narrow range of goods and services) can also find themselves in a shaky economic position, without much warning, if technological change hits. The shutdown of a military base or a branch manufacturing plant of an MNC can spell economic disaster for local residents. Such decisions are made outside the local community—by outsiders. As the people of Caliente found out, local residents have little influence over location decisions that so vitally affect their lives and livelihoods.

To conclude: The case of Caliente's dependence on outsiders for its existence—both originally and years later—is extreme. The decision that originally created Caliente was not complicated. By contrast, business location decisions in the global economy are much more complex. Economically, producers of goods and services often maximize efficiency and profit by grouping or clustering together in dense settlements. Historically, this economic fact helps to explain the existence and development of cities. However, in a timeless and borderless economy, many functions can be—and are—decentralized across metropolitan and global landscapes.

Note: Not all U.S. desert towns share Caliente's history. For one, Rhyolite, Nevada, was founded in 1904 as a gold-rush town. In its heyday, it numbered 10,000 people and boasted 45 saloons, several dance halls, and 85 mining companies. But a few years after a national financial panic in 1907, the population fell below 1,000. By 1920, its number had shrunk to 14. By the mid-1980s, some entrepreneurs hoped for Rhyolite's transformation: They wanted to turn the ghost town into a homosexual community. It failed. The promoters raised only $100 of their $2.25 million asking price.

Another town not far from Rhyolite was doomed by forces beyond its control too. Located near a giant tungsten mine, Rovana, California, was created as a company town in the eastern Sierra Nevada Mountains before World War II. At its height, one of every 10 workers in its county (Inyo) worked for the mine. But decades later global economics spelled the end of mining there: It could not compete with China's tungsten. By the 2000s, the tungsten mine closed, leaving miners jobless. Many nearby businesses closed, and the town (and its local tax base) was ruined.

HOW GLOBALIZATION AFFECTS LOCAL FINANCE

Throughout this book, I insist on this notion: Cities exist within a complex, interdependent national and international system. This is important for understanding a variety of issues, including who gets what city services—and who finally pays for them.

Cities in many parts of the world can and have experienced severe financial woes, even bankruptcy. In the past generation, Philadelphia teetered on the brink of insolvency, and New York City faced a budget gap of more than $2 billion. Tokyo sold off plots of land when it was strapped for money in the late 1970s. By 2008, many U.S. cities faced decreasing tax coffers, due in part to the "subprime mortgage fallout" (and resulting drops in property tax payments) plus increasing costs for public services. Vallejo, California, for one, declared bankruptcy in May 2008, after suffering an over $16-million shortfall; some critics blamed

the Bay Area city's "overgenerous" labor contracts with police and firefighter unions for exacerbating its fiscal problems.

Vallejo's recent plight calls to mind an earlier bankruptcy, that of Bridgeport, Connecticut, in 1991. That was before the mortgage meltdown in the United States that started in 2006. Still, like Vallejo, Bridgeport's bankruptcy epitomized the struggle of many cities to balance revenues and expenditures inside both a fluid federalist system and a volatile global economy.

What public services urbanites get in Bridgeport (or Biloxi or Boston) and how much in taxes they pay for them depend substantially on two factors. Both are outside their control: (1) a volatile global economy and (2) changes in the federal system.

A VOLATILE GLOBAL ECONOMY

How does the global economy—far beyond the reach of local politicians and local control—affect cities? It all depends. At the international level, a massive U.S. trade deficit can lead to a decline in U.S. exports. This is what happened a generation ago. One result was increased urban unemployment, particularly in manufacturing. More urban unemployment, in turn, decreased the local tax base. Local tax bases can also be severely decreased if the price of homes (and thus their tax assessment base) drops significantly.

Other international events have local impacts too. Here are just a few examples: The dollar falls vis-à-vis the euro (a recent reality), which means, among other things, that U.S.-produced goods and services are cheaper for consumers using euros; this boosts U.S. exports. The European Union hits a downturn, resulting in lowered demand for U.S. goods. Chinese producers decide that their best markets lie in Europe, Africa, Asia, South America, and the Middle East, that is, everywhere *but* the United States (a reality for many manufacturers who fear U.S. growing protectionism and a weak dollar vis-à-vis the euro). Medium and highly skilled workers in India replace some U.S. workers (a reality in some fields, particularly customer services and computer analysis). Repercussions of any of these events will be felt from Keokuk, Boise, and beyond in terms of services and local taxes.

Next, at the national level, such events or processes as a mushrooming federal deficit, decreased federal aid to cities, changing types of federal aid, and recession can take a heavy toll on local finances. These happened to U.S. cities in the 1980s and beyond (and is happening at this writing).

U.S. cities have fewer options than the federal government. They cannot borrow to finance operating deficits. In recent years, many slashed services and deferred maintenance on roads and other facilities.

In 1993, over 50 percent of the cities participating in the annual National League of Cities' Fiscal Conditions Survey predicted that their spending would exceed their revenues. (A decade earlier, only one-fourth reported deficit spending.].) By 2006, the National League of Cities' Fiscal Conditions Survey showed that nearly two in three (65%) city finance officers reported that their cities were better able to meet financial needs than in the previous year, 2005. Indeed, their assessment of their cities' fiscal conditions in 2006 improved dramatically since 2003, the low point after a fiscal recession, when only 19 percent of city finance officers said their cities were better able to meet financial needs than in the previous year (Pagano and Hoene, 2006).

Yet, city finance officials know all too well that turnarounds can face both directions. Recessions (or worse) could figuratively sink their cities.

Time was when states in the United States often rescued their own creatures, the cities. However, by the early 1990s, over one-half of the states faced serious budget deficits and couldn't bail out local governments (Pammer, 1992:3). Indeed, the governor of California, the nation's largest state population-wise, turned the tables on local governments: He shifted some local taxes to the state level. By 2008, both the state of California and some of its cities were ailing financially.

How do cities and states cushion global and national impacts on tax capacity? Some develop a municipal or state foreign policy. For instance, San Francisco and San Jose, California, have sent mayors to Asia to drum up trade. The state of Iowa has a full-time staff to attract international business to the state, acting as its own department of commerce. Other places, both cities and counties, try to diversify their economic bases.

PAYING FOR LOCAL SERVICES

Each nation has its own system of collecting and distributing funds for local public services. Some have a variety of local taxes, including the habitation of a property, business inventory, and garbage pickup. In the case of France, cities also receive funds from the national government on the basis of a complex formula.

The total package of public services received by U.S. city residents comes from local, state, and federal sources. This complex, multi-tiered governmental system collects revenue, provides public services, and returns some money for local use.

At the local level, the main money-raiser in the United States is the *property tax* (an annual tax on land and buildings based on their assessed monetary value). But dependence on this tax is drawing ire from many sources and for many reasons. Here is one critique: In the *Des Moines Register*, Jason Clayworth (2006) claimed that Des Moines, Iowa's, "financial house teeters on a foundation that's become old, cracked and in need of repair." Des Moines was far from alone, Clayworth said. On the contrary, he argued that city officials and experts—like those in thousands of cities across the nation—base their spending plan "on an archaic system that relies largely on property taxes to pay for basic services such as police and fire protection."

Since Clayworth wrote that, the "mortgage meltdown crisis" further endangered thousands of cities' coffers. How? First, people who default on their home loans don't pay their property taxes. Second, with some lag time, the value of many houses drops due to a sagging real estate market; typically, lower assessments mean lower property taxes. Indeed, by late fall 2008, three U.S. cities—Philadelphia, Atlanta, and Phoenix—had requested a slice of the $700-billion bailout money from the federal government to assist in paying their bills. Others were considering requesting federal funds to help bail them out too (Dearen, 2008). Finally, given the aftershocks of the global financial crisis, business too can have its taxes reduced or refunded. For example, New York City was facing a budget shortfall (expected to climb to $4 billion by 2010) but gave back more than $800 million to companies which overpaid their taxes in 2008.

In recent years, taxpayers in many U.S. cities and towns have seen increases in property taxes and decreases in local services. This situation reflects higher home valuations plus local governments' struggle to cover such rising costs as pensions, health care, and utilities. In Massachusetts, for example, residential property taxes increased almost 50 percent from 2000 to 2007. (Many homes declined in value in 2006 and beyond after a subprime mortgage credit crisis in spring 2006, but their valuation was set before the housing market decline.)

Aside from the big gun of the property tax, other local money-raisers include the following: *user charges* (direct charges paid by users of publicly provided services such as bridge tolls); *sales and excise taxes* (paid at the time of purchase), *local income tax* (far from universal, paid by individuals or corporations to local government), and finally, *miscellaneous taxes* such as Las Vegas's gambling tax and San Francisco's hotel tax. (The biggest money-raiser in France, by comparison, is the TVA, a 19.6 percent [in 2008] value-added tax paid at the time of purchase. Like other sales taxes, it is regressive; that is, it hurts low-income people more than high-income people because the proportion of tax paid by a low-income person is greater than that paid by a higher-income person. When asked how socialists could continue such an unfair [to poorer taxpayers] tax, a prominent socialist shrugged and responded, "It's the only tax we can collect." [Martin Malvy, personal conversation, Limogne-en-Quercy, France, 1998].)

The mix of local government activities that gets funded via the incremental budgeting process is topped by educational expenditures. The remainder is divided among services ranging from sewage to administration. (For another way to determine parts of a city or local government budget, see earlier, "A Participatory Budget.")

Predictably, the single most important determinant of spending at the local level is the availability of money. But other factors, including political environment as well as income and age distributions of residents, for example, also help to explain differences in spending levels and service mixes among urban and suburban communities.

Ultimately, local public finance is tied to metropolitan, state, national, and global production/consumption as well as local value preferences. How much is produced in a city, state, nation, and the world affects the public services that citizens get.

The public goods and services that citizens want to consume reflect their values. How much is available for public allocation determines the limits of public spending.

One added factor is worth noting: Some people in the United States wish to opt out of many public services altogether. They prefer private solutions: hiring police, teachers, and other "public" servants—and paying for these services privately. Some folks in gated communities, for instance, pay private police to patrol their grounds, and they send their children to private schools.

Now we turn to other issues that affect local finance. First, impacts of location decisions. Then, a few trends with serious consequences.

In the postindustrial, energy- and climate change-conscious era, location decisions become very complex. Energy shortages and rising costs may force business firms and their workers to relocate. Manufacturing firms may move out of U.S. metropolitan areas altogether—into the urban areas of China, India, Mexico, or global technoburbs. At the same time, some businesses (e.g., Tesla Motors, which makes electric cars in California) decide to bypass the global supply line and save on transport costs by making parts nearby instead of outsourcing to cheaper-labor countries such as Thailand. Firms that depend on software and fax machines, rather than oil, may scatter to the rural countryside. Large numbers of professionals and white-collar workers may communicate rather than commute to work. All such phenomena are affecting both global business and residential location patterns—as well as tax revenues.

Without pretending to be clairvoyant, we can identify some trends that will affect the economic life of U.S. cities as well as cities everywhere. The few mentioned here are categorized as international, national, and regional; but it will become clear that these categories are often inseparable.

INTERNATIONAL TRENDS

In times of financial crises and corporate defaults, whole countries—such as Iceland in 2008—may consider bankruptcy. Wherever crises of credit and finance start, they now can quickly envelop cities and nations throughout the globe. Here are some other trends with international implications.

The political economy of energy, particularly oil (and efforts to reduce the world's dependence on oil), is affecting cities everywhere. Indeed, Michael Klare (2008) writes that there is a "new international energy order," a geopolitical development changing the international balance of power. Together with research results on alternative energies, private and public players (e.g., oil producers, governments) promote policies that have serious implications, albeit very different ones, for different cities.

The same might be said for water, a must-have component of so many agricultural and other products. *The ever-widening income gap between rich and poor nations* (and rich and poor people within postindustrial nations) has impacts on local governments as well as individuals. More U.S. firms will probably leave U.S. metropolitan areas for overseas locations, where labor is cheaper and unions are weak or banned. (However, rising transport costs due to soaring oil prices may cancel out cheaper labor costs.) The world's poor nations could boycott some U.S. products made in metropolitan areas, affecting the export sector of local economies. Or the dollar could become so cheap vis-à-vis other currencies—say, the euro—that North American products would become more attractive than, say, European products. And poor nations could band together and sharply increase the price of their raw materials, affecting cities in various ways, depending on the products they produce. Or poor nations could be more successful in getting richer nations to lift their agricultural subsidies, thus allowing farm products from poorer nations to better compete in the world marketplace.

Global criminal groups, particularly those adept at using the Internet, can wreak economic havoc. In 2008, for instance, a multinational identity-theft ring allegedly stole more than 41 million credit and debit card numbers and then, U.S. prosecutors charged, sold them on the black market. Businesses and their customers can lose time, energy, and lots of money. (If guilty, this ring symbolizes a different kind of crime syndicate from the hierarchical, blood-bound "family" portrayed in *The Godfather* movies.) Criminal groups know no borders now, and they have become sophisticated technologically.

The threat of global financial collapse. According to "the prophet of boom and doom," former Wall Street trader Nassim Nicholas Taleb (2008), globalization creates enormous fragility in the financial system. He thinks that this threatens global markets. In a nutshell, here is Taleb's reasoning: Due to mergers, there is a smaller number of very large, interrelated banks. This means that when one fails, they all fail. If a financial crisis happens, it will be bigger and more difficult than ever before. There may be fewer failures in this new, concentrated financial system, but—if and when they occur—they will be disastrous (Taleb, 2008). (Taleb was far from alone in his doomsaying. In fall 2006, "global nomad" and "Dr. Doom" Nouriel Roubini, a formerly obscure economics professor at New York University [a Farsi, Italian, Hebrew, and English speaker] warned that a crisis was brewing. According to Roubini, this could destroy investment banks and other financial institutions such as Fannie Mae and Freddie Mac: a housing bust, an oil shock, sharply declining consumer confidence and, finally, a deep recession [in Mihm, 2008:11].)

U.S. NATIONAL, REGIONAL, AND STATE TRENDS AND POLICIES

During the war in Iraq, one-time Republican strategist Kevin Phillips said that there was one reason the United States is interested in the Middle East: oil. Indeed, Phillips said, people who think that the United States is interested in the Middle East for any reason except oil are grossly misguided (2006). At the same time, U.S. President George W. Bush insisted that U.S. and allied troops invaded Iraq for several reasons, none of which included oil.

Kevin Phillips is not alone. Many observers, often on the left but not always, suspect that the official rationales for the war (e.g., overthrowing a tyrant, fighting terrorism, rebuilding a democratic country) were far from the only reasons for fighting in oil-rich Iraq. Indeed, one critic (Behan, 2006) heralded the "Triumph of the Petropublicans," claiming that "the invasions of both Afghanistan and Iraq were undertaken, respectively, to secure the pipeline route from the Caspian Basin and to guarantee access to the enormous inventories of Iraqi crude—in both cases to the colossal benefit of American and British oil companies—and that the 'Global War on Terror' is merely an elegant and fraudulent smokescreen." Another critic, John Judas (2006) of the *New Republic*, thinks that the choice for the United States is stark: war or energy conservation. Note that these critics have their critics too.

Other powerful voices doubt that oil is the only reason the United States and others sent troops to Iraq or the Middle East. For one, during the so-called First Gulf War in the early 1990s, then secretary of state James Baker was asked why U.S. troops were fighting in the oil-rich Persian Gulf. He replied simply, "Jobs."

National policymakers in the United States and elsewhere, notably the late Winston Churchill in England, predicted energy's all-important—perhaps primary—role in the future of the economy. Indeed, the Gulf Wars reminded global citizens of oil's importance to advanced industrialized or postindustrial countries and to those nations that aspire to that category.

People disagree on the underlying reasons for the war in Iraq. But one impact concerning oil and other sources of energy is clear: Energy crunches and national energy policies have different impacts on cities and regions. In the United States, for example, cities in the "energy corridor" between Houston and New Orleans are in a very different position from Frostbelt cities. In Mexico, the world's second biggest field by output, the Cantarell oil field, continues to deteriorate; its fast fade will batter the Mexican economy, particularly oil-dependent metropolitan areas. The falling output of Cantarell (in 2007 the field produced one of every 5 0 barrels of oil on the global market; by 2015 Mexico may have to import oil) also means that the United States is going to be even more dependent on Mideast oil (Luhnow, 2007:A1).

Several other trends or policies bear close watch, particularly the ever-increasing reach of MNCs, the level of government support programs, the increasing income gap between rich and poor within a nation and among nations, the commitment to conserve energy and/or to switch to nonpolluting alternative sources such as sun and wind, and the increasing use of the euro (rather than the dollar) as the preferred international currency. All of these affect the fate of cities in the United States

But the precise effects of these trends and policies remain debated—and debatable. Still, one thing is apparent: Individual cities, postsuburban areas, and MSAs have little ability to control their own fate.

ANOTHER LOOK

Theorists agree on the importance of economic factors to the fate of cities. But they disagree on how the economy today really works—and how it could work better.

The dean of free marketeers, the late Milton Friedman, looked to supply, demand, price, and the market mechanism to explain how the U.S. economic system should work. Generally, conservatives and libertarians base their economic views on a psychological assumption: that individuals and business firms are rational, self-interested profit maximizers. They see the workings of the marketplace as a technical issue, not a moral one.

Liberals like the late John Kenneth Galbraith pointed to the lack of equity in the conservative stance. For example, if the poor cannot afford heating fuel in times of skyrocketing prices, should the market dictate that they go cold while the rich don't? Liberals think not. Further, liberals tend to favor spending public money to retrain the U.S. labor force to meet the challenges of the world economy. For one, political economist Robert B. Reich, before serving in the Clinton cabinet, advocated retraining programs in his book *The Work of Nations: Preparing Ourselves for 21st Century Capitalism* (1991). Also, liberals point to the problems of social disorder and political instability that might follow from a pure market doctrine. Thousands of cold, angry people might not shiver alone but rather start burning down cities in frustration or out of a feeling of relative deprivation.

Marxists—joined by strange comrades such as Charles Lindblom—reject the notion of market sovereignty. In their view, giant corporations manipulate the market, removing uncertainties from the pursuit of profits. Radicals do not expect government at any level—federal, state, or local—to change what they perceive as a gross imbalance between corporate power and citizen subordination.

Meanwhile, many think that nations are becoming less important economically, even obsolete, in the global economy. Perhaps paradoxically, some theorists suggest that cities will become the basic unit for thinking about the production, consumption, and exchange of commodities as well as the generation of wealth and jobs. However, this stance remains very controversial.

Note that while theorists and politicians continue to debate economic issues, citizens in the United States and elsewhere are experiencing a growing sense of powerlessness over their collective economic fates. Some turn inward to find their own souls via a series of therapies. Some consume things and show off symbols. Others downscale. Some tune out by turning on. Still others turn to collective answers—single-interest groups, party politics, or private militia.

Finally, in the United States there seems to be an enormous gap between what *is* (giant private corporations and big government) and what many think *should be* (smaller government, individualism). This gap between "traditional" U.S. values and modern U.S. institutions is not easily reconcilable, at least not without dismantling major institutions. This suggests the following irony: In an era of worldwide economic interdependence, near-global economic recession, and U.S. federal government intervention in the marketplace (e.g., financial bailouts of private institutions such as financial institutions and car manufacturers), some voices cry out for more self-sufficiency and more local autonomy. Seeing how this contradiction works out in the political and economic spheres awaits us.

KEY TERMS

Basic and nonbasic economic activities (or sectors) The basic economic sector consists of goods and services produced primarily for export out of the community (exception: tourism-connected items such as hotel rooms). The nonbasic economic sector consists of those goods and services produced primarily for local consumption, such as garage sales and hair styling shops.

Capital A term with many denotations. To a non-Marxist, machines, factories and plants, and stores or stocks of finished and unfinished goods. To some Marxists, all of these and the way in which they are used (the social relationships of production). To Marxist economist Ernest Mandel ([1972] 1987:591), capital is "exchange-value which seeks a further accretion of value"; it first appears "in a society of petty commodity producers in the form of owners of money (merchants or usurers) who intervene in the market with the aim of buying goods in order to resell them at a profit."

Capitalism To a non-Marxist, an economic system in which capital or wealth is primarily the private property of capitalists (synonyms: *free enterprise system, profit system, price system*). To a Marxist, an economic–social–political system based on private property and the domination and exploitation by capitalists of nonpropertied workers.

Demand The degree to which consumers want and will pay for a product. Demand curves illustrate that the higher the price of a good, the fewer the people who will be willing to buy it.

Economic base In orthodox economics, all activities that produce income for members of a community. In Marxist social thought, the productive forces of society and the social relations of production.

Efficiency Measured (by economists) using a ratio of units of output to units of cost. The efficiency of a business firm is related to its profitability.

Employment base method A method for identifying basic sector activities by comparing local and national employment patterns.

Equity Fairness or justice in the distribution of something, such as benefits or burdens.

Externalities Spillover effects or indirect consequences—either positive or negative—to individuals or groups not directly involved in the action. Such spillovers occur outside the market so that those affected, for better or worse, neither pay nor receive payment for the activity. Externalities occur when private benefits or costs do not equal social benefits or costs.

Freegan The word, coined about 2003, is a blend of "free" and "vegan." The Freegan.info Web site says that it refers to an urban, eco-friendly, anticonsumerist who tries to engage in a total boycott of "an economic system where the profit motive has eclipsed ethical considerations and where massively complex systems of productions ensure that all the products we buy will have detrimental impacts most of which we may never even consider. Thus, instead of avoiding the purchase of products from one bad company only to support another, we avoid buying anything to the greatest degree we are able." Typically, freegans avoid the marketplace and forage in dumpsters for free, nutritious food that has not harmed the planet, people, or animals.

Input–output analysis A method of measuring the interconnections between industries in a city, MSA, or region. It attempts to show how the growth or decline in one basic sector industry will affect other sectors or industries.

Monopoly capitalism A late stage of capitalism (following the commercial and industrial stages) identified by Marxist theorists. Baran and Sweezy (1966) characterize this stage as one in which the typical economic unit is the giant corporation and the problem faced by such a corporation is absorption of the surplus.

Price To market theorists, the financial cost of a good or service determined by the market of supply and demand. Marxist theorists stress the degree to which prices are fixed by cartels or large corporations under monopoly capitalism.

Profit To market theorists, the net income of a business firm after all expenses of production have been paid. To Marxist theorists, one form of profit derives from surplus value.

Supply The quantity of a good provided to the market at a given price. Supply curves slope upward, indicating that the higher the price, the more of the good will be supplied to the market.

Surplus value A Marxist concept, key to Marx's analysis of capitalism. He reasoned that business profits are based in the production sphere. This means that, in Marx's view, one source of profit is the exploitation of labor; that is, human labor power becomes the source of value that goes unpaid by the capitalist employer. If, for instance, a worker spends 3 hours in "necessary labor" (necessary to subsist) and 3 hours in "surplus labor" (the time in which the worker produces exclusively for the employer), the surplus labor time is the source of surplus value.

Underground economy Unreported and thus untaxed income. Examples include money from unreported restaurant tips, drug deals, and babysitting. Synonyms: *off the books, under the table*.

PROJECTS

1. **Basic sector**. Using the employment base method, try to determine what goods and services your community exports. For the United States, helpful data sources are U.S. Bureau of the Census publications.

2. **Masters of their own fate?** Interview various members of your community (including presumed decision makers such as elected and appointed officials, the unemployed, members of different occupational groups, students, etc.). Pose the following questions: (a) What are five or six important decisions or events that have affected the economic life of this community in the past decade? (b) Who was responsible for these decisions? (Alternatively, what forces led to them?) Note the patterns of response. For instance, do interviewees tend to name local decision makers or events? Do they draw links between what happened nationally and internationally (e.g., oil policies, government support programs, new technologies) and local economic life?

3. **Content analysis of economics' texts**. Compare and contrast five college texts, looking at the way they explain "the market." What are the authors' attitudes toward the market? Are any ideas systematically excluded or denigrated?

4. **Energy's influence on policy**. Choose two countries with relatively high or growing energy needs—say, the United States and China or India. Investigate how their international relations might be influenced by energy needs. For example, explore the relationships between oil- or natural gas–rich nations (e.g., Uzbekistan) and the two countries. Do private companies play any role in determining policy? If so, is their role key? What do you conclude about the role of energy and energy-based companies in policymaking at the international level in each case? In your research,

did you find any evidence that governments below the national level (e.g., city or state governments) had any input into international energy policies?

SUGGESTIONS FOR FURTHER LEARNING

The first urban economics book published in the United States is Wilbur R. Thompson, *A Preface to Urban Economics* (Baltimore, Md.: Johns Hopkins University Press, 1965). Although a classic in the field, it is not recommended for beginners. For readable and iconoclastic interpretations, see Jane Jacobs's *The Economy of Cities* (New York: Vintage, 1976) and *Cities and the Wealth of Nations: Principles of Economic Life* (New York: Random House, 1984).

For an impassioned look at the link between climate change and global warming, see Australian mammalogist and paleontologist Tim Flannery's *The Weather Makers: How Man Is Changing the Climate and What It Means for Life on Earth* (New York: Atlantic Monthly Press, 2006). The title suggests how urgent Flannery believes the issue has become.

Published more than a generation ago, Richard J. Barnet and Ronald E. Muller's *Global Reach* (New York: Simon and Schuster, Touchstone, 1974) remains a valuable study about the power of MNCs. Chapter 2, "From Globaloney to the Global Shopping Center," shows how "industry has transcended geography." Barnet and John Cavanagh's update, *Global Dreams: Imperial Corporations and the New World Order* (New York: Simon and Schuster, 1994), paints a portrait of global corporations as they evolved from the 1970s through the early 1990s. They claim that MNCs have replaced national power and dominate the fate of the world's economy and people.

The late, distinguished French historian Fernand Braudel wrote a series of books about early capitalism, translated into English. According to a leading U.S. proponent of Braudel's ideas, sociologist Immanuel Wallerstein, Braudel disagreed with both Marx and classical liberals about the nature of capitalism. Wallerstein, for example, says that Braudel saw capitalism as the system of the *antimarket*, not the free market. See Wallerstein's review article, "Braudel on Capitalism, or Everything Upside Down" in the *Journal of Modern History* 63(June 1991):354–361.

John Kenneth Galbraith's important book *The New Industrial State*, first published in 1967, was republished in 2007 (Princeton, N.J.: Princeton University Press). It features a new introduction by Galbraith's economist son, James, a professor at the University of Texas at Austin and an iconoclast in his own right.

Charles E. Lindblom, professor emeritus of economics and political science at Yale University and author of the controversial *Politics and Markets* (1978) revisited the subject after the end of the so-called cold war. The result is *The Market System: What It Is, How It Works, and What to Make of It* (New Haven, Conn.: Yale University Press [2001] 2002).

For a brief description of the theory of the capitalist city, see "The City of Theory" by Sir Peter Hall in *Cities of Tomorrow* (Oxford: Blackwell, [1988] 1990). Hall is one of the leading urbanists of our time.

For a classic case study of a city and its relationship to its metropolitan region, see Edgar M. Hoover and Raymond Vernon, *Anatomy of a Metropolis* (New York: Doubleday, 1962). For a very different approach, see Barry Bluestone and Mary Huff Stevenson, *The Urban Experience: Economics, Society, and Public Policy* (New York: Oxford University Press, 2008), which addresses the changing function of U.S. metro areas in an age of global competition; it focuses on contemporary "problems" facing both cities and suburbs.

The pioneer in economic base studies, Charles M. Tiebout, described the nature and uses of input–output analysis. See his *The Community Economic Base Study* (New York: Committee for Economic Development, 1962).

One element in the nationalization of economic enterprise is the franchise. See Stan Luxenberg, *Roadside Empires: How the Chain Franchised America* (New York: Viking Penguin, 1985).

Numerous films deal with economic change and technology's impact on social life. Charlie Chaplin's *Modern Times* (1936) focuses on the Little Tramp's attempt to adjust to the machine age; it contains classic sequences on assembly line speed-ups and an automatic feeding machine. Michael Moore's *Roger and Me* (1989) and its sequel, *Pets or Meat?* (1992), are comic and tongue-in-cheek—but ultimately tragic and radical—looks at Flint, Michigan's, attempt to survive GM's auto plant closings and deindustrialization. Orson Welles's film *The Magnificent Ambersons* (1942) depicts the economic and social impact on a small town of industrialization.

The late Louis Malle's documentary *Phantom India* (1968) contains a section on Calcutta that suggests the interrelationship between that city's present poverty and past history (e.g., the separation of jute fields and jute factories when partition of Bengal took place in 1947).

For an exploration into the Internet's impact on the economy, business, and daily life, see Manuel Castells, *The Internet Galaxy: Reflections on the Internet, Business, and Society* (New York: Oxford University Press, 2003). Castells is a leading commentator on things urban as well as cyberspace.

In *Infotopia: How Many Minds Produce Knowledge* (New York: Oxford University Press [2006] 2008), law professor Cass Sunstein looks at how the efforts of many people online help to amass knowledge. He also discusses "prediction markets," such as the Iowa Electronic Market, designed to help companies make better decisions.

REFERENCES

Abrams, Neil. 2008. "A portrait of the world in 2018." TADOW! International Politics & Markets (October 24): http://tadow1.blogspot.com/

Baran, Paul A., and Paul M. Sweezy. 1966. *Monopoly Capital: An Essay on the American Economic and Social Order*. New York: Monthly Review Press.

Behan, Richard W. 2006. "George Bush's other civil war: Triumph of the petropublicans." *Counterpunch* (November 1): http://www.counterpunch.org/behan11012006.html

Bloomberg News. 2006. "Coca-Cola profit up 10% on strength in overseas markets." *New York Times* (April 30): http://www.nytimes.com/2006/04/20/business/20coke.html?scp=2&sq=Profits,%20worldwide,%20of%20Coke&st=cse

Blumenfeld, Hans. 1955. "The economic base of the metropolis: Critical remarks on the 'basic–nonbasic' concept." *Journal of the American Institute of Planners* 21:114–132.

Bollens, John C., and Henry J. Schmandt. 1970. *The Metropolis: Its People, Politics, Economic Life*, 2nd ed. New York: Harper & Row.

Bullard, Robert D., ed. 1994. *Unequal Protection: Environmental Justice and Communities of Color*. San Francisco: Sierra Club.

Castells, Manuel. 1989. *The Informational City: Information Technology, Economic Restructuring and the Urban-Regional Process*. Oxford: Blackwell.

Clayworth, Jason. 2006. "Des Moines finances need long-term solution." *Des Moines Register* (February 26): http://www.ncna.org/index.cfm?fuseaction=page.viewPage&pageID=661&nodeID=1

Cottrell, William Fred. 1951. "Death by dieselization: A case study in the reaction to technological change." *American Sociological Review* 16:358–385.

———. 1972. *Technology, Man, and Progress*. Columbus, Ohio: Merrill.

Coupland, Douglas. 1994. "Rem Koolhaas, post-nationalist architect." *New York Times* (national edition) (September 11):H45.

Dearen, Jason. 2008. "Cities wrestle with economic bailout request." (November 15): http://www.sfgate.com/cgi-bin/article.cgi?f=/n/a/2008/11/14/national/w080149S73.DTL&hw=Cities+request+bailout+funds&sn=001&sc=1000

De Sousa Santos, Bonaventura. 1998. "Participatory budgeting in Porto Alegre: Toward a redistributive democracy." *Politics & Society* 26(4):461–510.

Ehrlich, Everett M., and Elliot Schwartz. 2004. "Engaging the global enterprise to promote economic development." Pp. 3–27 in Ralph Christy, ed., *Achieving Sustainable Communities in a Global Economy: Alternative Private Strategies and Public Policies*. Singapore: World Scientific Publishing.

Flannery, Tim. 2006. *The Weather Makers: How Man Is Changing the Climate and What It Means for Life on Earth*. New York: Atlantic Monthly Press.

Fox, Matthew. 2006. *A New Reformation: Creation Spirituality and the Transformation of Christianity*. Rochester, Vt.: Inner Traditions.

Friedman, Milton. 1970. "Social responsibility of business is to increase its profits." *New York Times Magazine* (September 13):32+.

Furman, Jason. 2006. "Closing the tax gap." Center on Budget and Policy Priorities (April 10): http://www.cbpp.org/4-10-06tax3.htm

Galbraith, James. 2008. *The Predator State: How Conservatives Abandoned the Free Market and Why Liberals Should Too*. New York: Free Press.

Galbraith, John Kenneth. 1968. *The New Industrial State*. New York: Signet.

———. 1979. "Oil: A solution." *New York Review of Books* (September 27):3–6.

Gurley, John G. 1975. *Challengers to Capitalism: Marx, Lenin, and Mao*. San Francisco: San Francisco Book.

Hawken, Paul. 1993. *The Ecology of Commerce: A Declaration of Sustainability*. New York: HarperBusiness.

Hawken, Paul, Amory Lovins, and L. Hunter Lovins. [2000] 2008 *Natural Capitalism: Creating the Next Industrial Revolution.*Boston:Back Bay Books.

———. 2007. *Blessed Unrest: How the Largest Movement in the World Came into Being and Why No One Saw It Coming.* New York: Viking.

Heilbroner, Robert, and Lester Thurow. 1994. *Economics Explained: Everything You Need to Know About How the Economy Works and Where It's Going,* rev. and updated ed. New York: Simon and Schuster, Touchstone.

Hood, Marlowe. 2007. "UN chief demands climate 'breakthrough' after key report." *Yahoo News* (November 17): http://news.yahoo.com/s/afp/20071117/sc_afp/unclimatewarmingipccban

Jacobs, Jane. 1984. *Cities and the Wealth of Nations: Principles of Economic Life.* New York: Random House.

Judas, John. 2006. Interview on NPR's *Marketplace.* (May 25) KQED radio.

Kennedy, Paul. 2008. "An environmentalist's nightmare." *International Herald Tribune* (July 11): http://www.iht.com/articles/2008/07/11/opinion/edkennedy.php?page=2. Klare, Michael T. 2008. *Rising Powers, Shrinking Planet: The New Geopolitics of Energy.* New York: Metropolitan Books.

Koenig, David. 2008. "Flight cuts pinching U.S. airports." *International Herald Tribune* (August 12):16.

Kotz, David M., Terrence McDonough, and Michael Reich, eds. 1994. *Social Structures of Accumulation: The Political Economy of Growth and Crisis.* Cambridge: Cambridge University Press.

Kunstler, James Howard. 2006. *The Long Emergency: Surviving the End of Oil, Climate Change, and Other Converging Catastrophes of the Twenty-First Century.* New York: Grove Press.

Leibenstein, Harvey. 1976. *Beyond Economic Man: A New Framework for Microeconomics.* Cambridge, Mass.: Harvard University Press.

Levitt, Steven D., and Stephen J. Dubner. 2005. *Freakonomics: A Rogue Economist Explores the Hidden Side of Everything.* New York: HarperCollins.

LincolnCounty Nevada.com. n.d. "The town of Caliente." http://www.lincolncountynevada.com/caliente.html

Lindblom, Charles E. 1978. *Politics and Markets.* New York: Basic Books.

Luhnow, David. 2007. "Mexico tries to save a big, fading oil field." *Wall Street Journal* (April 5):A1+.

Mandel, Ernest. [1972] 1987. *Late Capitalism.* Trans. Joris De Bres. London: Verso.

McLeod, Christopher, director. 2001. *Hopi Land* (Film, 29 minutes). Reading, Pa.: Bullfrog Films (for Earth Island Institute).

Mihm, Stephen. 2008. "The seer who saw the storm coming." *International Herald Tribune* (August 16–17):11.

Mufson, Steven. 2007. "Oil price rise causes global shift in wealth: Iran, Russia and Venezuela feel the benefits." *Washington Post* (November 10):A1.

NBC5. 2008. "NBC5's 8 pm news update. msg." (July 11): http://video.nbc5.com/player/?id=274617

Pagano, Michael A., and Christopher W. Hoene. 2006. "City fiscal conditions in 2006." *Research Brief on America's Cities.* National League of Cities. Issue 2006–3.

Pearce, David, and Edward B. Barbier, 2000. *Blueprint for a Sustainable Economy.* London: Earthscan.

Phillips, Kevin. 2006. Talk at the First Congregational Church, Berkeley, CA, sponsored by Cody's Books.

Reich, Robert B. 1991. *The Work of Nations: Preparing Ourselves for 21st Century Capitalism.* New York: Knopf.

Robbins, Tom. 1976. *Even Cowgirls Get the Blues.* Boston: Houghton Mifflin.

Samuelson, Paul A. 1964. *Economics* 6th ed. New York: McGraw-Hill.

Samuelson, Paul A.and William D. Nordhaus. 1992. *Economics,* 14th ed. New York: McGraw-Hill.

Smith, Adam. [1776] 1970. *The Wealth of Nations.* New York: Penguin.

Starhawk. 2005. *The Earth Path: Grounding Your Spirit in the Rhythms of Nature.* New York: HarperOne.

Taleb, Nassim Nicholas. 2008. Interview with Paul Salmon, PBS, *The Newshour* (October 21).

Uchitelle, Louis. 1989. "Spread of US plants abroad is slowing exports." *New York Times* (national edition) (March 26):A1+

Wardell, Jane. 2008. "Recession? Eat, drink, smoke and be merry" (August 12): http://seattlepi.nwsource.com/business/1310ap_recession_party.html

Martin Gorosh

CHAPTER 19

BLUE-COLLAR, WHITE-COLLAR, NO-COLLAR, SHIRTLESS

When discussing work, the Chinese curse seems especially applicable: "May you live in interesting times." Globally, we all live in interesting—and stressful—times. People in postindustrial nations are adjusting to new working conditions, or joblessness. Some, particularly those in the financial or high-tech sector, have moved from richer to poorer nations in search of new employment (e.g., from New York City to Bengaluru). Millions of others are moving in another direction: from farmwork to urban industry—or joblessness. In the United States, many white- and blue-collar workers, young and old, high-tech and low-tech, are not able to fulfill the "American dream" (Greenhouse, 2008).

Years ago sociologist Herbert Gans suggested that people in postindustrial nations were headed for a "postwork society." There (or here), "the full-time job is no longer the basic source of people's income, status, and self-respect" (1993:B3). With a different spin, some call this a "gig economy," where people do two or more "gigs" (part-time jobs, typically without benefits) in order to make ends meet.

This chapter is about jobs and joblessness. It traces the great historical changes in the nature and meaning of work. First, it peeks at the so-called postwork society. Then, it looks backward: to preindustrial and early industrial times in Europe and North America. Next, it returns to modern times, investigating worker alienation and dissatisfaction. It also examines differing occupational structures of some contemporary U.S. cities, probing what the changing of types and locations of jobs implies for cities and city dwellers. Finally, it looks at those within Metropolitan Statistical Areas (MSAs) who are unemployed and underemployed or who are employed full-time but can't make it economically: the metropolitan poor.

THE POSTWORK SOCIETY

"What do you want to do when you grow up?" A first-grade teacher in Houston got the following answers from her 6-year-old students: airline pilot, soldier, rock star, police officer, U.S. president, teacher, and doctor. Interestingly, not one said she or he wanted to collect bugs, travel to foreign lands, chat online all day, or hike in the woods. All answered by naming work-related roles. Why? Because in the United States, people's identity has been tied traditionally to their work.

Apparently, these first-graders had already absorbed the message: In the United States, to a significant degree, *you are what you do*. (*Note*: Neilsen Claritas heralds another notion: You are where you live. See Chapter 8.)

This situation of work-related roles and status in the United States is changing for a number of reasons—structural, social, psychological, and moral. On the one hand, those who create new Internet identities or avatars might say that *you become whom you claim to be*. On the other hand, structural change can change people's options: As the United States moved from an industrial to a postindustrial society, more people had less work, at least paid work, to do. By the time they grow up, these first-graders may find that technology and globalization have changed the nature of much of the work they actually end up doing, giving them a great deal of time for leisure, unpaid work, or low-wage labor.

Indeed, we could hypothesize that in postindustrial societies, such as the United States, the key question for a substantial portion of the population is no longer "What do you do?" (the question typical in *Gesellschaft* societies) but rather "What are you into?" That is, many are defining themselves in terms of their leisure interests, whether it be surfing at the ocean or on a computer, singing in a church choir, creating alternative identities via the Internet, or collecting vintage beer cans.

Moreover, in postindustrial societies, many are finding that they *have* to define themselves in terms of their leisure activities if they wish to retain their dignity. Why? Not everyone trained in a trade or an occupation is able to practice it. This phenomenon is rooted in structural and technological factors. For example, due to the new international division of labor, many U.S. industrial and service jobs (e.g., customer service call center assistants) moved "offshore." Increasingly, U.S. higher-paid managers are also finding that they can be replaced by lower-paid managers offshore too. Other jobs, such as dictation secretary, have been made nearly obsolete by technological change. Others, such as computer analyst, often attract too many prospective workers, causing a structural mismatch between jobs and people. So, it's no surprise when a house painter turns out to have a Ph.D. in religious studies.

Still, some innovative, knowledge workers—"no-collars" as sociologist Andrew Ross calls them ([2003] 2004)—have more than 40-hour-per-week work in the new digital economy. Working late in informal, open settings (perhaps with dogs snoring at their feet), the no- or low-heeled, jeans-adorned, no-collars share a nonconformist spirit at work and live in upscale suburbs or trendy urban neighborhoods like SER 04 Young Digerati. What a contrast with the blue-collar, assembly–line workers, who may share parking lots at work but not residential neighborhoods with the no-collars. Instead, Ross ([2003]2004) says, in some communities assembly-line workers are segregated in shabby bantustans.

THE HUMAN DIMENSION: WORK AND THE INDIVIDUAL

Traveling back a few hundred years in time and space to seventeenth-century London, we find the following situation: bakers requesting an increase in the price of bread. The bakers supported their request with the following information about their work setting and weekly costs:

> Thirteen people there were in such an establishment: the baker and his wife, four paid employees who were called journeymen, two maidservants, two apprentices, and the baker's three children. Food cost more than anything else, more than raw materials and nearly four times as much as wages. Clothing was charged up, too, not only for man, wife, and children but for the apprentices as well. Even school fees were included in the cost of baking bread.
>
> *(Laslett, [1965] 1971:1)*

This image—a world without complex machines or complex organizations—provides a striking contrast to that of a modern factory or office. In preindustrial England, workers produced their bread and clothing without electricity or layers of bosses. They worked by hand, creating a finished product with coworkers who were family members or with whom personal ties were established.

The bakers' small-scale, technologically simple world of work is a world we have lost. Before mourning its passing, however, recall its less romantic aspects. Work was hard and long. Children often started productive activity at age 3 or 4, and women played a subordinate role. There was no worker's compensation or unemployment insurance and few occupational standards for health or safety. People died young.

First in England and then in continental Europe, the passing of the world of preindustrial work brought sweeping changes. Urbanization and industrialization changed where people lived, how they worked, how they related to one another, and how they related to the products of their labor.

LOWELL, MASSACHUSETTS: WORKING CONDITIONS OF AMERICA'S FIRST FEMALE LABOR FORCE

Now, let's return to one of the grand designer's cities, Lowell, Massachusetts (Chapter 17), to examine some characteristics of early industrial society. Lowell illustrates what happened in the beginning phases of the industrialization and urbanization processes in the United States: (1) the rural–urban shift, (2) the increase scale and organization of work, and (3) the changing conditions and psychological meaning of work.

Lowell was one of the United States's first mill towns, named after the designer of a version of a power loom, Francis Cabot Lowell. (Lowell devised a mill system in which raw fiber was manufactured into cloth under a single roof.) Incorporated in the 1820s, the town of Lowell drew unmarried young women, daughters of Yankee farmers, to its mill jobs.

Contrary to popular belief, it was young women—not men—who first worked in manufacturing; they pioneered in the textile mills. Why? As Howe (1978:9) comments, "men's work" in the fields was considered more valuable and irreplaceable. Young women came from the countryside and moved into company-owned boarding houses within walking distance of the mills. These women workers were kept under strict supervision by house mothers in their living quarters and by mill managers in their workplaces. Church attendance was compulsory, and an early curfew was enforced. Hence, the mill women—America's first female industrial labor force—exchanged countryside for city, family for house mothers and mill managers, and family concern for tight social control.

The mill women also exchanged self-paced work for labor discipline and small-scale work for large-scale industrial organization. No longer did they do chores with their family unit. Now they labored side by side with hundreds of strangers from other rural communities, each one doing a small part of the whole production process.

Writings by the mill workers themselves reveal mill working conditions: poor lighting, little ventilation, noise, overcrowding, long hours (80 hours a week), and low wages. One anonymous worker describes the rhythm of her workday: "Up before day, at the clang of the bell—and out of the mill by the clang of the bell—into the mill and at work, in obedience to that ding-dong of a bell—just as though we were so many living machines" (in Eisler, 1977:161).

NEW ENGLAND TO THE NEW SOUTH TO OFFSHORE: MORE HARD TIMES IN THE MILL

Factory conditions in the United States have changed a great deal since those early days in Lowell, Massachusetts. Ironically, however, textile manufacturing represents an important exception.

Hard times in the mill for men and women (and children) have been the norm, not the exception, since the first textile mill in the United States was established in 1791 in Pawtucket, Rhode Island. The textile industry has had a long, unhappy history: low wages, long hours, child labor, speed-up, company-dominated mill towns, chronic unemployment, and instability (see Fowke and Glazer, 1961:523).

In the late nineteenth century, New England cotton mills started moving south to take advantage of cheaper labor. These textile mills helped to build the "New South." People from the backwoods flocked into the mill towns of North Carolina and other southern states, attracted by the promise of a few dollars in their pocket every week. But soon the glamour wore thin, and local folk began singing the "Winnsboro Cotton-mill Blues":

> When I die don't bury me at all
> Just hang me up on the spool room wall,
> Place a knotter in my hand,
> So I can spool my way to the Promised Land
> I got the blues, got them Winnsboro cotton-mill
> blues...

By the mid-1920s, the Piedmont (a region from southern Virginia through the central Carolinas and into northern Georgia and Alabama) had eclipsed New England as the world's primary producer of cloth and yarn. Still, wages stayed low. But the prices of shoes and food went up. When white workers followed organizers and joined unions, they were blacklisted. African Americans had no chance to join unions; the vast majority were excluded from textile jobs.

After World War II, more mills moved to the South. Northern industrialists were attracted mainly by a cheap, unorganized labor pool, tax breaks, and

cut-rate utilities provided by local communities and private business to sweeten the pot.

Not much had changed by the 1980s. In *Hard Times, Cotton Mill Girls*, Victoria Byerly (1986:4) gives this personal memoir of mill work in her hometown of Thomasville, North Carolina:

> My work in the mill was turning the cuffs down on little girls' socks. It was the next person's job to pack them in plastic. I had to turn thousands of socks a day before I could make the production quota. Any less and I would be out of a job. Everyone arrived a few minutes early in the morning and cut lunch a few minutes short to be ready to go when the whistle blew. At the sound of the whistle it was a race with the clock as I stood using every part of my body to move rhythmically back and forth to keep the pace required for production.

Byerly's account of southern mill rhythms echoes the Lowell women workers' sentiments of much earlier decades.

One mill worker interviewed by Byerly, Johnny Mae Fields, expressed her feelings of being exploited and dehumanized in Kannapolis, a mill town where she worked: "Everyone is upset all the time, you know, weeping and gnashing teeth....[The mill owner] is a businessman from the top of his head to his toes, and I don't think he cares what color you are, he just doesn't regard mill workers as human beings..." (1986:6).

Norma Rae (1979), portrayed by Sally Field, told the story of the struggle to unionize a southern textile town in the 1970s. As the Oscar-winning film showed, hard times in the mill were not gone and long forgotten.

In the late 1970s, textile manufacturing was the only major U.S. industry not significantly unionized, and it was the South's dominant industry. It accounted for about one-fifth of all jobs and $1.8 billion in annual sales.

No longer. Now southern cotton mills are becoming history—literally (and figuratively). In 2004, standing in front of the Cannon #1 plant in Kannapolis, North Carolina, a grassroots coalition of cotton mill historians and museums announced a textile heritage initiative (Southwide Textile Heritage Initiative, 2004) (http://www.textileheritage.org/news/pr01.htm). This was 1 year after the Pillowtex Corporation announced the state's biggest-ever industrial shutdown.

Pillowtex was not the first southern textile company to close, nor would it be the last. Indeed, by the 2000s cut-and-sew apparel manufacturing was the category that topped declining employment in the United States, followed by four other textile mill occupations (U.S. Census Bureau, 2007:395). By 2014, the U.S. Bureau of Labor Statistics (2007) estimates that there will be almost 50 percent fewer machine operators like Norma Rae at work in U.S. textile mills.

Since Norma Rae's struggle and Johnny Mae Fields's interview in Kannapolis, major changes in many southern mill towns made hard times even harder. Some shops that moved south after the unionization of northern mills moved again, this time to non-union locations offshore in East Asia and the Pacific Islands. (By 2005, raising broiler chickens brought South Carolina more money and jobs than cotton. Broilers brought in 31 percent of the state's total farm receipts, and cotton brought in only 4.8 percent [U.S. Department of Agriculture, 2007]).

Competition from offshore mills drove down wages even more. For example, in Kannapolis, the town where Johnny Mae Fields had worked, mill workers were laid off and later rehired—at lower wages—to do one job: sew "Made in the USA" labels over Taiwanese labels (Byerly, 1986:7). Ironically, many "Made in the USA" labels were attached to garments made in foreign-owned factories in places like Saipan, the Northern Marianas, by foreign workers. (Until the Multifiber Agreement [MFA] was rescinded, workers—contracted mainly from China, the Philippines, and other Asian countries—earned about half of the U.S. federal minimum wage and typically lived eight to a room in barracks' conditions much more cramped than those of the nineteenth-century mill women in Lowell, Massachusetts.) In the early 1990s, *New York Times* reporter Philip Shenon wrote that workers in Saipan complained they lived in "virtual captivity" (1993:A6). In a nutshell, as the *New York Times* headlined its news story, "Saipan Sweatshops Are No American Dream." (*Sidenote*: Jack Abramoff, later convicted of federal felonies, lobbied

successfully to keep Congress from imposing minimum wage standards in Saipan.)

Most North Americans may be unfamiliar with working conditions in Saipan, called "indentured servitude" or "slavery" by some observers (Shenon, 1993:A6). But anyone who visits a shopping mall will be familiar with the labels they make (or made): Arrow, Liz Claiborne, The Gap, Geoffrey Beene, Eddie Bauer, and Levi's have all made clothes on Saipan, an island that is part of the American commonwealth in the western Pacific. This was no mom-and-pop operation either: In one year, about $279 million worth of wholesale clothing, "virtually all of it made by foreign labor," was shipped from Saipan to the United States.

What a difference a shift in global trade policy can make. In January 2005, a 30-year-old international trade pact, the MFA, ended. (The MFA had imposed global quotas on textile and apparel production, thus limiting the output of manufacturing giants such as China.) While in force, the MFA allowed, even promoted, clothing industries to develop in small countries and parts of the U.S. commonwealth, such as the Northern Marianas, which would not have been able to compete otherwise. Thus, low-paid work in sweatshops—as well as exploitative sex work—sprung up in Saipan and other places.

When the MFA ended in 2005, all the Abramoff lobbying could not help the Saipan sweatshop owners and workers, both mainly Chinese. (At least 12 garment factories closed by 2007. Even though they were paid low wages, underwent forced abortions, and had to pay off huge debts in many cases to come to Saipan, garment workers in Saipan staged demonstrations to protest the closing of their factories and consequent joblessness, not their inability to affect global trade policy.)

Global and regional economic associations can also have enormous impacts on work and workers. Take, for example, Romania's entrance into the European Union (EU) in 2007. To deal with chronic labor shortages, Romanian textile factories imported workers from China because, as the Romanian manager of a Swiss-owned apparel factory in Bacau, Romania, put it, "We don't have any Romanian workers because they have all left to work in [western]

Fig. 19.2 THE MOBILITY OF CAPITAL. Money is homeless. Investment capital salutes no national, state, or local flag. All other things being equal, a mill, software development company, or other enterprise will pick up stakes and relocate "offshore" if it can make products or provide services more profitably. Some contrast the mobility of capital to the relative immobility of labor. (Richard Hedman)

Europe" (Nicolescu in Brunwasser, 2007). Romania's low wages and increased freedom of movement around Europe, facilitated by its entrance into the EU, had led to foreign investment and emigration of workers. (*Note*: The global recession that started in the late 2000s can play havoc with industrial policies everywhere, including EU member states Romania and Latvia.)

MODERN TIMES

The United States, like other postindustrial societies, has fewer and fewer people working in mills and factories. By 1970, about 50 percent of all job holders in the United States were working in the service-information sector. By 2007, less than 10 percent of the U.S. labor force was employed in manufacturing. Such bland statistics, of course, hide the shattered lives and rusted dreams of individuals who once worked in mills and factories.

Sweatshops, Electronic or Machine-Driven

In postindustrial society (*Techno$chaft*), more and more people work in fast-food franchises and offices, many of them factory-like in the sense that they are highly mechanized (Mills, 1951:chapter 9). Indeed, much modern work—at McDonald's or the office—has been termed the "electronic sweatshop": Clerks are automated, and professionals are turned into clerks.

Whether office or factory, some significant similarities between work now and in earlier times still exist. Few people, then or now, produce things with their own tools; most workers do only a small part of the entire production process, and most work in hierarchically structured organizations.

Of course, there is great variety in the working conditions of people in the United States today. On the one hand, there is the skilled craftsperson who sees a job through from start to finish and the researcher who sifts data alone at her or his computer (See Chapter Opener photo.) On the other hand, there is the autoworker who only attaches left-rear bumpers the customer-service clerk whose calls are monitored electronically by managers, and the McJobs waitress who takes orders from everybody.

Are people unhappy attaching left-rear bumpers or taking orders? If employed, do they feel lucky to have work, no matter how boring? Does the assembly line inevitably lead to meaninglessness because it breaks up jobs into tiny pieces? Is high-tech office work dehumanizing? We now turn to such questions, noting how the structure and organization of work affect the individual's feeling about his or her work.

ALIENATION

As societies shift from economies based on agriculture and small-scale cottage industries to relatively simple industrial economies (symbolized by Lowell, Massachusetts) or to more complex industrial organization, many changes take place in the nature of work.

Usually, the location, scale, type, and nature of work are transformed. First, the location of work (and residence) changes. In preindustrial economies, much work must take place on or near agricultural land. Without machine-powered transport and other advanced technology, people extract a living from their natural environment and live near it. Productive activities do not cluster in cities; they are decentralized in villages and small towns. Indeed, big cities were the exception in preindustrial Europe and North America. In contrast, work activities in industrial societies arise in and cluster in urban areas. Raw materials, labor to transform them into a finished product, and transport to move them become concentrated in cities.

Note: Some predict that much work will again become decentralized in postindustrial society. They argue that fast transport and communications technologies will permit many people to work and live in small towns and rural places. Others hope this will happen as more people eat what's grown locally; "sustainable food" activists, who present a withering critique of industrially produced food, are among these hopefuls.

Second, the type of work changes. In preindustrial societies, the majority of people are engaged in primary-sector activities—farming, mining, fishing, and other extractive activities. In industrial economies, secondary-sector activities—transforming raw materials into manufactured products—dominate.

In postindustrial economies, tertiary-sector activities—services and information—dominate. That the United States has been a postindustrial society for some time is indicated by a few statistics. Over a generation ago, American Telephone & Telegraph (AT&T), an information-based company, became the first U.S. company in the nation's history to have assets of over $100 billion. It also employed almost 1 million people, more than the nation's largest industrial firm at the time, General Motors.

Third, the scale of work changes. The family farm or the 13-person bakery is no longer the typical production unit. Even the textile mills of Lowell are small by the standards of today's auto assembly plant.

Finally, the nature of work changes. In preindustrial societies, people do not have much mastery over nature, but they do exercise some control over their work process. In handicraft and cottage industries, for instance, artisans own the tools of their trade, have a tradition of craftsmanship, work at their own pace, and introduce some variation into their products. Compare that situation with modern industry, exemplified by the assembly line. The left-rear bumper attacher has no discretion over how or where to place the bumper on the car; the pace of work and the product are standardized, and workers don't own the machinery they use.

In brief, then, in modern industry, the worker has little control over the work process at any level—from macro decisions about what product will be made or how much it will cost down to decisions concerning the pace of work, the arrangement of work space, or what tools are used. These conditions of industrial labor produce standardized products efficiently. And according to many observers, they also produce alienated human beings, powerless people who feel estranged from their work and themselves.

Karl Marx was the first theorist to focus on alienating work. In the *Economic and Philosophic Manuscripts of 1844*, Marx began to investigate the concept of **alienation**, and his ideas have exerted a powerful influence ever since on Marxists and non-Marxists alike (Figure 19.3). In fact, the term "alienation" has entered the social scientist's general vocabulary, regardless of discipline or ideological bent. However, not all theorists agree with Marx on its definition or causes. According to Marx, alienation is not part of industrial production per se. It is inevitable *only* under a certain kind of social organization of industrial work—capitalist production.

Here is how Marx (1972) came to this conclusion. To Marx, human history proceeds in developmental stages: from primitive communities to slave states to feudalism and then to capitalist systems. Under European feudalism (the productive system preceding capitalism), serfs' labor was not seen as a commodity to be bought and sold in the marketplace; a paternalistic relationship operated between manor lord and serfs, with obligations recognized on both sides. Goods and services in the feudal system were produced mainly for personal use and local markets.

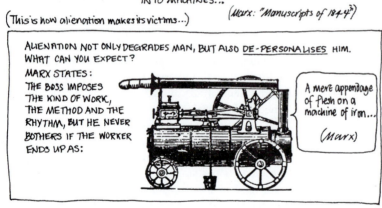

Fig. 19.3 ALIENATION À LA MARX. (Rius, *Marx for Beginners* [New York: Pantheon, 1978], p. 79. English translation © 1976 by Richard Appignanesi. Originally published in English in Great Britain by Writers and Readers Publishing Cooperative. Reprinted by permission of Pantheon Books, a division of Random House, Inc.)

Then, during the sixteenth century, a new mode of production began to undermine serfdom and the rural manor system of European feudalism: commercial capitalism. As the new class of merchant capitalists grew, so did trade, market exchanges, and towns. Over the course of several hundred years, commercial (or mercantile) capitalism developed into industrial capitalism. By the mid-nineteenth century, the transformation to industrial capitalism was complete.

In Marx's view, it was this mode of production, capitalism, that inevitably led to the workers' alienation. *For the first time in human history, people became wage laborers, selling their labor on the open market just like any other commodity.* According to Marx, this transformed people into commodities, dehumanizing and depersonalizing them.

To illustrate how Marx viewed the process of alienation, let's return to the example of Lowell,

Massachusetts. Marx would have viewed it something like this: Mr. Lowell buys the labor of young women, puts it to work, and treats it like any other tool of production (e.g., a machine). This labor force—or human labor power—then becomes a source of value to Mr. Lowell, just like any other machine. How? By producing surplus value. Workers in Lowell's mill put in a 13-hour day. But they produce enough to pay for their own food, shelter, and other needs in only 4 or 5 hours; this is necessary work time. During the remaining working hours, the worker produces a surplus product, over and above what she or he requires to meet personal needs. This *surplus product is pure profit* for the employer.

To Marx, *private ownership of the means of production is the highest form of alienation*. Marx reasoned as follows: Private ownership of the factories and other means of production results in the labor of the many being transformed into the capital of the few. It means that the very essence of human beings (*Homo faber*, people as producers)—the creative act of work—is transformed into a possession of someone else, the capitalist employer. In this way, *what formerly belonged to human beings (the products of their labor) is taken away and "alienated" from them*, the rightful owners. This leaves workers dispossessed. They own nothing—neither the tools of their trade nor the finished product. In the end, people become alienated not only from their own products but also from themselves. It is this process of capitalist industrial production that degrades and depersonalizes humans.

How can nonalienated work be established? According to Marx, only capitalism's replacement by a new mode of production, socialism, can establish an unalienated relationship between workers and work.

Non-Marxists as well as those calling themselves Marxists have quarreled with Marx's interpretation of the causes of alienation as well as its potential cure. Most notably, sociologist Max Weber (in Gerth and Mills [1922]1958) argued that the mode of production in modern society has little impact on alienation. In his view, bureaucracy, the state, and large-scale industrial organization are inherently alienating, whether capitalist or socialist. Following Weber, others argue that Chinese workers assembling autos or pushing pens in factory-like offices will become just as alienated from work and themselves as their counterparts in Lordstown or L'vov. Given this premise—that *bureaucracy and hierarchy are the real culprits, no matter who owns the means of production*—the cures offered to end alienation range from ending hierarchy to living in voluntary simplicity within smaller, more self-sufficient communities to building networks of worker-owned and -operated businesses.

Much research shows that inherently alienating tendencies do exist in the techniques of modern manufacturing and bureaucratic organization. For instance, a now classic sociological study of textile work, auto assembly, print shops, and chemical plants by Robert Blauner (1964) contended that alienation is built into industrial work. Yet, Blauner argued, the organization of work can mitigate some of technology's effects. Technological imperatives of the auto industry may dictate a certain kind of work—fast and fragmented—but the reorganization of work (e.g., job rotation) may minimize some alienating features.

At the same time, a series of studies claim that modern work is *not* the outcome of autonomous technical processes. Such studies argue that, formerly, large business corporations depended on hierarchical control over workers in a system of delegated authority, which made first-line supervisors (foremen) into petty tyrants over workers. To curb the first-line supervisor's power, employers turned to another form of control: technical control, embedded in the design of production itself. Instead of obeying first-line supervisors, workers obeyed the dictates of the assembly-line process itself. In other words, *the specific design of machines prestructured the work*. First-line supervisors thus became mere enforcers of prestructured work.

Now, most industrial workers globally may still work under the system of technical control. However, modern companies, like IBM, use a more subtle system of control: *bureaucratic control*. Here, domination is also hidden; it is not in the machines. Instead, both supervisors and workers alike become subject to the dictates of "company policy."

Many think that modern work has been systematically degraded. This degradation, it is claimed, goes past the assembly line to clerical work, retail jobs, and the service trades.

If modern work has become less fulfilling and more alienating, can the situation be turned around? Many think that job enrichment and flex-time can make a difference. Whether such programs actually humanize work or offer workers the mere illusion of control is much debated. (The sense of being in control, illusory or not, is apparently good for morale as well as one's health [Marmot, 2005].)

Workers' cooperatives may serve to lessen alienation. Perhaps the best-known workers' co-op is located in and around Mondragon in Spain's Basque region. It consists of a network of more than 160 worker-owned and -operated cooperatives involving 23,000 member owners in the city or environs of Mondragon. Essentially, Mondragon is an experiment in social reconstruction through cooperative community based on cooperative entrepreneurship. It puts nonalienating work above money, and it runs on principles of democracy and self-management, including one member, one vote and the pursuit of *equilibrio* or "balance." Started in 1956, it had become one of Spain's 12 largest companies by 1996, and it has spawned co-op communities elsewhere, including Africa, Japan, India, and the Americas (e.g., on the Pine Ridge Reservation of the Oglala Lakota, discussed in Chapter 9). Outside of Spain, participants are often poor people of color.

Fig. 19.4 THE CHEESEBOARD, A WORKERS' COOPERATIVE. Started in the 1960s by owner-workers, this bread and cheese shop in Berkeley, California, is still going strong. It offers age-based discounts, with consumers 100 years old getting free cheese. According to Steve Sucher, one of the owner-workers, "We pride ourselves on being the only bakery to close on May Day." Some joke that they serve a body politic divided into radical minds and bourgeois stomachs. (Barbara Cohen)

In the United States, a spate of workers' co-ops appeared in the 1960s and 1970s as part of larger social movements. A few remain, including The Cheese Board in Berkeley, California (Figure 19.4). What keeps them going? Ethnographer Ann Arnett Ferguson (1991:112) concluded that the members of the collective shared two basic organizational principles: worker control and a minimal division of labor.

This brings us back to familiar challenges, encountered by the ancient Greeks as well as present-day societies: Can there be experts without gross social inequalities? Is it possible to have both extreme task specialization and democracy? Is most work doomed to be alienating and meaningless in the complex division of labor? The nineteenth-century French sociologist Emile Durkheim wrote about these issues from a different angle from his German contemporary Marx.

THE ANOMIC DIVISION OF LABOR

Sociologist Emile Durkheim ([1893] 1966) theorized that, under normal conditions in organically solid society, the complex division of labor would bring people together in a way that would make them feel interdependent (Chapter 6). However, Durkheim warned that under abnormal conditions an **anomic division of labor** could occur, disrupting social solidarity.

If extreme specialization of function goes hand in hand with a decrease in communication between people doing different specialized tasks, then an anomic division of labor results. In this situation, individuals become isolated from each other, separated by lack of understanding. In turn, this lack of communication leads to a lack of rules that define and regulate relationships among individuals, each performing a specialized job.

Durkheim's example of the anomic division of labor was the conflict between management and labor during the early stages of industrialization. At that time there were few agreed-on rules governing their relationship. We might extend Durkheim's concept and apply it to other aspects of contemporary work. For instance, many workers now feel that their work is not only boring but meaningless. They don't see how their specialized task matters to the rest of society. Like characters in Charlie Chaplin's film *Modern Times*

(1936), they feel like so many cogs in a machine. A bank clerk turned firefighter put it like this:

> [T]he firemen, you actually see them produce. You see them put out a fire. You see them come out with babies in their hands. You see them give mouth-to-mouth when a guy's dying. . . . That's real. To me that's what I want to be. I worked in a bank. You know, it's just paper. It's not real. You're lookin' at numbers. But I can look back and say, "I helped put out a fire. I helped save somebody." It shows something I did on this earth.
>
> *(Terkel, 1975:589)*

The anomic division of labor may be hastened in post-industrial society. The gaps between expert groups and lay publics are growing wider. Communities with common values and common goals are based increasingly on occupation. In addition, people in the United States (and other postindustrial societies) tend to live—and work—apart from people unlike themselves in terms of education, status, and tastes (Chapter 7), thereby further widening the communications gap between various groups.

Occupationally based communities—academics, doctors, race-car drivers, and so on—often discourage communication with outsiders by speaking and writing in esoteric jargon and monopolizing their expertise instead of sharing it widely. This trend does not bode well for a democratic society. Nor does it encourage a sense of mutual interdependence.

To conclude: Industrial work, for disputed reasons, can lead to alienation from self, others, and the products of one's labor. Under certain conditions, industrial organization can also lead to an anomic division of labor in which people lack a feeling of mutual interdependence and believe that their work lacks social meaning.

In the United States, traditionally alienating work such as auto assembly and textile manufacturing has been fading away, eliminated by technological change and global competition. This means that, if they find jobs, more and more people are doing service and white-collar work, producing paper, ideas, and services instead of manufactured goods.

Does it follow, then, that *most* work is becoming more satisfying in the postindustrial economy? Probably not, as Max Weber might have predicted.

For Weber, Marx was right about the wage worker being separated from the products of his or her labor, but Marx did not go far enough. Weber thought that wage workers represented only one case of a universal trend toward bureaucratization. In other words, when white-collar workers function in a bureaucratic system, they encounter a machine "as soulless as... machines made of iron and steel" (Simone Weil in W. E. Upjohn Institute, 1973:39). Already, many white-collar workers in lower-echelon jobs complain of white-collar woes: boring, dull, routine jobs. Those with a college education and high expectations for self-fulfillment through work are particularly prone to high turnover and subtle forms of sabotage. And those not in charge suffer higher rates of stress (and illness) than their bosses (see Marmot, 2005).

Yet, many of the most unhappy workers (and their families), such as ex-autoworkers in Detroit, prefer work to no work. No matter how alienating work is, it is work. And it pays the bills.

WORKER SATISFACTION, OVERWORK, AND STRESS

Today's stressed administrative assistants, hoping they will not come down with carpal tunnel syndrome from word processing 8 hours a day, are not in the same position as characters in a Charles Dickens novel who toiled from dawn to dusk for starvation wages. Nor are Internet-based customer-service clerks of the 2000s like the Lowell mill women of the 1840s, closely supervised by their bosses at home as well as in the workplace. Still, worker dissatisfaction remains widespread.

A generation ago, the *majority* of American workers reported that they were not satisfied with their work. Taking a look at *Work in America* (W. E. Upjohn Institute, 1973:16), a task force found that 43 percent of **white-collar** workers—and only 23 percent of **blue-collar** workers—would choose to do similar work again (16). (The study's authors reported that whether a worker would again choose the same work is the best single indicator of job satisfaction.)

Around that time, Garson (1973: 173) found that 0 percent of U.S. autoworkers would choose the same work again. Now, many of those desperately dissatisfied workers no longer have the option of doing the same work: Hundreds of thousands of autoworkers,

the most dissatisfied group, lost jobs during U.S. deindustrialization. If they can find a job at all, it is likely to be just as unsatisfying—and to pay less.

Update: *The New American Workplace* (Lawler and O'Toole, 2006) is a follow-up to the 1973 study *Work in America*. It explores how work has changed in the intervening 35 years. Among the authors' conclusions: health care, pay incentives, opportunities for training—all considered "normal" perks in earlier decades—are now being eroded by a combination of factors related to the global economy, including outsourcing, productivity pressures, and decreased job security. While job satisfaction is down, stress and overwork are up.

In general, job satisfaction is linked to type of work and occupational status. Specifically, mental laborers (like Reich's "symbolic analysts") are more satisfied than manual laborers. Further, job satisfaction is linked to social status; the higher the status of an occupation, the more satisfied are its practitioners (and, according to Dr. Michael Marmot's *The Status Syndrome* [2005], they suffer fewer health concerns). A U.S. government study based on 2004–2006 data, for example, found that the most depressing jobs in the United States—that is, jobs where full-time workers aged 18–64 reported the highest rates of depression—were personal care and service, such as changing diapers of the elderly (10.8 percent depressed), and food preparers and servers, such as hamburger-flippers (10.3 percent) (in Associated Press, 2007).

High pay and high job satisfaction also tend to go together. However, this relationship is unclear because most highly paid jobs also rank high in other characteristics valued by workers (e.g., social esteem, job autonomy, challenge of the work itself).

Yet, job satisfaction is not necessarily linked to pay or high status. Take, for example, nonelite daily journalists (reporters and editors working for nonprestigious media). As a group, these journalists are far from highly paid, but a generation ago they were among the most satisfied of any occupational group in the United States. Why? One study (Phillips, 1975) suggested that they feel autonomous and mentally challenged by nonroutine work. And, importantly, they felt that they contributed to society, all factors contributing to their job satisfaction. (*Update*:According to many news reports, technological changes and workforce cuts have lowered morale among many still-working journalists as they wonder whether or not they will keep their jobs.)

Is it any surprise that, at least in one survey, mathematician is rated the "best" job in the United States? An in-depth look at 200 jobs by CareerCast.com (reported by the American Sociological Association (2009)found that—in terms of job security, stress, hiring, basic physical safety, income, and job environment—the most appealing job opportunities were as follows: (1) mathematician, (2) actuary, (3) statistician, (4) biologist, (5) software engineer, (6) computer systems analyst, (7) historian, and (8) sociologist. The worst jobs were as follows: (1) lumberjack, (2) dairy farmer, (3) taxi driver, (4)seaman, (5) emergency medical technician, (6) roofer, (7) garbage collector, and (8) welder.

This leads us to wonder about "dirty" work as several of the worst jobs can be considered "dirty," particularly collecting garbage. A generation ago, a highly paid steel worker in Illinois said that "it's hard to take pride in a bridge you're never gonna cross, in a door you're never gonna open." For him, the problem wasn't the fact that his work is dirty but that he felt no sense of contributing to society, no sense of achievement (in Terkel, 1975:2). The steel worker's comment suggests that *the social meaning of work*—not necessarily the work itself—is important for individuals. (Now, decades later, that worker would probably be jobless; there are few steelworkers left in the area due to plant shutdowns.)

No work—even society's dirtiest work, the collection of garbage, for example—is inherently alienating. At least that is what some studies show (e.g., Perry, 1978). Apparently, lack of control over work and/or lack of ownership seem to be some roots of alienation today.

Yet, few answers to the issue of job alienation are evident, although the number of thinkers about work (and the leisure time to think about it) has never been greater. Radical intellectuals, particularly Marxists, are going through a profound crisis of thought, reconsidering the question of whether or not bureaucracy is inherently alienating. Ultraconservatives in Europe and the Middle East are returning to ideas best suited to a preindustrial, aristocratic or tribal community.

Conservatives tend to believe that most people need close supervision and hierarchical control; this is what organization theorist Douglas McGregor (in Bennis, 1970) called the "theory X" of human behavior. In contrast, liberals tend to subscribe to what McGregor called the "theory Y" of human behavior: that work is natural and that most people will work hard if they have a chance to fulfill their human potential.

And yes, there is a "theory Z." This theory focuses on Japanese workers, commonly referred to as "salarymen." Very popular for a brief moment in the United States, theory Z refers to a participative management style once common in Japan. It suggests that humane working conditions increase not only productivity and profits to the company but also the self-esteem of employees (Ouchi, [1981] 1982:165). In the United States, theory Z was criticized by radicals as a company-oriented philosophy masquerading as workplace democracy, inspiring employee loyalty without giving workers any real control.

Theory Z is not much talked about today because, most importantly, conditions in Japan have changed. As reporter Martin Fackler (2008) put it, "Japan's salarymen, famous for their work ethic and their corporate loyalty, fueled [Japan's] rise. But more recently, they have borne the brunt of its economic decline, enduring lower wages, job insecurity and long hours of unpaid overtime." Slowly, and reluctantly, salarymen are standing up for their rights by suing employers and thus rewriting the social contract that once bound workers to companies with "near feudal bonds of loyalty" (Fackler, 2008) as Japan becomes a post-industrial economy. Further, suicide in Japan has claimed many of the salarymen's lives. Of a recent epidemic of suicides, over 70 percent were males 40 or over and 57 percent were jobless. For unemployed former salarymen, suicide can be a "rational decision," according to sociologist Masahiro Yamada in Tokyo (in Wiseman, 2008:1) because when a Japanese breadwinner commits suicide, the family can collect his life insurance. In addition, insurers pay off a home mortgage.

Japanese employees once knew they had lifetime, secure jobs. Economic downtowns, among other factors, changed that. In early 2009, for example, in an attempt to cut costs in the wake of evaporating demand, Japanese electronics giant Panasonic announced a mass layoff.

To conclude: What doomed theory Z as a management ideology was structural change: the linchpin of Japan's system of employer–employee loyalty— lifetime employment—started to fall victim to corporate layoffs, plant closings, and competition in the global economy. Shades of Durkheim's notion of convergence!

WORKER UNDERWORK—AND STRESS

In times of economic downtown, recession, or fullblown depression, overwork is not the key issue. On the contrary. As a *New York Times* reporter put it in 2008,

> Throughout the United States, businesses grappling with declining fortunes are cutting hours for those on their payrolls. Self-employed people are suffering a drop in demand for their services, like music lessons, catering and management consulting. Growing numbers of people are settling for part-time work out of a failure to secure a full-time position.
>
> *(Goodman, 2008a)*

While much attention in U.S. media focused on job loss during the 2008 presidential campaign, lowered pay for millions of workers (due to shrinking hours during an economic downturn) did not capture headlines. If collected, no data were released to the public that revealed if less pay, tighter belts, and stress over personal and collective economic fortunes were affecting individual and family behavior as well as economic and political decision making. (This remains the case as of this writing.)

LOCAL OCCUPATIONAL STRUCTURES

Let's shift now from the impact of work on the individual to its impact on an entire community. This means looking at the occupational structures of individual cities, suburbs, and postsuburban areas.

THE RELATIONSHIP OF JOBS TO SOCIAL CLIMATE AND GOVERNANCE

A community's occupational profile—that is, a snapshot of its employment mix—gives clues to its social character, its economic vitality, and even its recreational facilities. This kind of information is useful to scholars, policymakers, and potential investors.

Understanding a community's occupational profile can also be helpful in our everyday lives. For instance, suppose you find yourself in the enviable position of being able to choose from among five equally attractive job offers in as many communities. How will you choose? For the sake of argument, let's say that you don't care about the city's physical climate, but you do care about its cultural–aesthetic facilities. The cultural climate you prefer, of course, depends on your personal tastes and background. But whatever scenes you favor (country music bars, soul food restaurants, body-building gyms, mega-malls, coffee houses, union meetings, bowling alleys, etc.), you can get some idea if they exist by examining a community's occupational profile. (You won't be able to get a total picture without sorting through additional data, but we'll return to that later.)

If one industry dominates a community—say, textiles or software design—it will be reflected in that area's social climate. But, remember, no table of census data can reveal the relationship between what a city or postsuburban area produces and how that place looks and feels: Only a thorough grounding in economic and cultural history can provide such insight (e.g., the textile industry's resistance to unionization, the computer professionals' preference for bicycling over bowling, and the lack of attention to city beautification in older auto-plant towns).

Also, the composition of a community's labor force has some bearing on its governmental structure. In the United States, city council–manager government appears more often in white-collar than in blue-collar towns. The employment mix also has some bearing on informal power structures. More specifically, we can expect different patterns of influence in Springdale, Arkansas (the chicken capital of the United States), and high-technology, professional Menlo Park, California.

Returning to Logan and Molotch's typology of U.S. cities outlined in Chapter 5, we can see that the occupational mix of a city has important, sometimes grave, implications for an urban area's vitality. For instance, without a massive conversion from war preparation to peacetime uses, an "innovation center" such as Silicon Valley in northern California suffers a much more severe economic downturn from the drying up of defense contracts than, say, a retirement center.

CHANGING U.S. EMPLOYMENT PATTERNS

In the 1950s, for the first time in human history, more people in a single nation were thinking about things, managing things, and communicating about things than actually producing things. Most, but not all, theorists agree that this momentous shift, made possible by advanced technology, signaled the emergence of postindustrial society.

As detailed elsewhere in this book, the transformation to postindustrialism in the United States led to many changes. Here are some: regional shifts (from Frostbelt to Sunbelt), intrametropolitan shifts (from central city to outside central city), and shifts from primary-sector economic activities (which provide the basic raw materials for existence, such as agriculture, fishing, mining, and forestry) and secondary-sector activities (which transform primary raw materials into finished goods) to tertiary-sector activities (consisting of services, wholesale and retail trade, information processing, communication, utilities, finance, insurance, public services and government, real estate, and transportation).

Some effects of postindustrialism, combined with impacts of global restructuring, can sometimes be seen with the naked eye, notably abandoned factories dotting the inner-city landscape (or formerly abandoned factories transformed into lofts, restaurants, and condos). But other impacts are invisible or harder to see; these include the decline in union membership. Here, let's examine two of these hard-to-see phenomena: (1) temporary or contingent work and (2) dual cities.

CONTINGENT OR TEMPORARY WORK

Years ago, Apple Computer was praised by organizational theorists as a management model of caring and sharing. In Cupertino, California, its Silicon Valley headquarters, Apple provided on-site child care, a generous profit-sharing plan, and many other employee perks. By 1993, however, the company was paring down, cutting down on full-time employees in a shaky economy. Over 20 percent of Apple's workforce were

temporaries or, in Appletalk, members of the "ring"— employees on short-term contracts without health or other benefits—not the "core." Even after Apple rebounded with the success of their iPhone, iPod, and music-related products, they continue to depend on contract employees. (Just how many is pure speculation; the company seems not to say publicly. However, in one location, Boise, Idaho, 3,000 "permtemps" workers were employed in 2005.)

The day of the 40-hour week with benefits has vanished for millions of people in the United States and elsewhere. Replacing full-time workers are consultants, strategists, flexible workers, temps, independent contractors, contingent workers, disposables, or throwaway workers.

Whatever they're called, including workers in the "gig economy," they're everywhere—from the university classroom and the health clinic to the factory and office. And their numbers are increasing: In 1982, about 75 percent of the jobs people found were neither part-time nor temporary; by 2005, persons working full-time in nonfarm jobs had declined to just about 43 percent. (U.S. Bureau of the Census 2007:table 588). Some may prefer part-time or temporary work. For most, however, it is involuntary.

The United States holds the world's record for multiple job holders. In 2005, over 7.5 million held multiple jobs. Some labor economists suggest why: Wages from one job are insufficient.

Few new temporary jobs pay as well as full-time jobs. Nor do they come with regular benefits. Indeed, some in the United States fear—while others praise— the rise of a new class of cheaper, temporary workers. From the corporate point of view, the creation of a two-tier wage system (where temps get no health benefits and earn $2 to $3 less per hour than permanent employees who work alongside them) is a boon to U.S. manufacturers.

Some jobs are easier to outsource than others. Customer-service reps can be outsourced from the United States after retraining employees to speak with a U.S. accent. So-called professionals, including university teachers, once believed that they were less vulnerable; but they too may be partially resourced via Internet courses and teleconferencing. In addition, many full-time, tenure-track teachers have been replaced by part-timers who earn little, forego health benefits, commute far and wide to several sites, and enjoy little influence in the school's governance.

Economists say that economic recessions speed the shift to temporary or contingent work. Most think that the shift, started in the 1990s, is permanent. Indeed, some say that if and when the U.S. economy improves, it will not bring a return to permanent work.

The shift to temporary work (what some are calling increasingly normal work in the "gig economy") brings up a host of political questions as well as psychological, sociological, and economic ones. For instance, will core employees parallel core countries in Wallerstein's world system; that is, will they try to control their rings (periphery) in a colonial manner? Will U.S. labor unions, already severely weakened by global restructuring and deindustrialization, lose more clout? How do workers adjust to much more uncertainty and instability in their work lives? How does insecurity at work affect parenting and political participation? The answers are still unclear.

THE DUAL CITY

The term "**dual city**" comes from John Mollenkopf and Manuel Castells's 1991 book of the same name. But the concept is much older. In the Western world, it dates at least to Plato's *Republic*. Plato held that any city—however small—is divided into two: one the city of the poor, the other of the rich. The upshot, according to the philosopher, is that these two cities are at war with one another

In modern times, the most famous visual restatement of this notion of a dual city is Fritz Lang's classic film *Metropolis* (1927). In Lang's metropolis, the poor lived underground and the wealthy aboveground.

Mollenkopf and Castells say that New York is such a dual city. In their view, it is "a paradoxical mix of splendor and decay"—a city composed of two separate and unequal cities where slums flourish, homelessness increases, and ethnic hostility is rife amid sumptuous office blocks with a core of mainly white male professionals and managers.

New York City prospered during the 1980s, but not all residents shared the wealth. Instead, the authors claim, residents experienced increased income inequality.

Who won and who lost the most in this transformation? In the 1977–1986 decade, Mollenkopf and Castells state that "the higher the income of a stratum, the faster its income grew" (1991:400). In contrast, the real income of the bottom 10 percent decreased by nearly 11 percent. As a result, the poverty rate in New York City jumped from 19 percent to 23 percent between 1977 and 1986.

Mollenkopf and Castells conclude that New York City experienced "social polarization," not just inequality: "the rich are becoming richer and the poor are becoming poorer in absolute terms" (401). Today, anyone looking for an apartment in Manhattan or other boroughs of New York City realizes that "social polarization" continues.

Nevertheless, Mollenkopf and Castells say, New York's social structure is so complex that it should *not* be reduced to a dichotomy between rich and poor. Instead, they note that two opposing forces dominate New York City's social structure: *corporate upper professionals*, who "constitute a coherent social network" and whose interests are directly linked to the development of the city's corporate economy, versus *the remaining social strata* (e.g., an army of clerical workers; low-skilled workers; immigrant manual workers, particularly Dominicans and Chinese; a middle class based in the public sector; those outside the formal labor force). They conclude that economic, cultural, and political polarization in New York City "takes the form of a contrast between a comparatively cohesive core of professionals in the advanced corporate services and a disorganized periphery fragmented by race, ethnicity, gender, occupational and industrial location" (Mollenkopf and Castells, 1991:402).

Does the dual city typify postindustrial cities? Yes, suggest Mollenkopf and Castells. Further, they tie together the social, economic, spatial, and technological aspects of postindustrial society: "The dual city is the social expression of the emerging spatial form of postindustrial society, while the global city is its economic expression, and the informational city its technological expression" (1991:415).

What class, then, dominates New York City and other dual cities? In the postindustrial era generally, they say, it is "the managerial technocracy allied to the global financial elite." This class has a key resource: "exclusive access to the most important information" (415).

Update: "Social polarization" and income inequality in New York City have increased since Mollenkopf and Castells published *Dual City: Restructuring New York* in 1991. According to American studies professor and sociologist Andrew Ross ([2003]2004:57), New York City in the 1980s was still the nation's largest manufacturing town "with 36,000 factories producing 10 percent of all American goods and employing 50 percent of the city's workers." Then, manufacturing was slashed—to 7 percent of the city's jobs. By the year 2000, Manhattan was the "alpha domain of Reich's symbolic analysts—managers, consultants, designers, and financiers—attended by armies of immigrant workers who supported the FIRE [finance, insurance, and real estate] industries...." Ross concludes that "No other great city in history has seen its economy and the essence of its social character transformed so fundamentally in such a short period of time." (After big shifts in the U.S. finance industry in 2008, we can expect more changes in New York and other global cities.)

Cantor and Mason (2007:1) of the Working Families Party think that New York City continued to grow larger than ever after suffering fiscal crisis because its "strategic role as a financial hub and as a continued attraction to immigrants gave it a unique resilience." In addition, they say, a very professional and competent city government under Mayor Bloomberg added to the revitalized city. Indeed, they claim, "The quintessential businessman mayor [Bloomberg] has turned out to be a uniquely pro-government mayor" (4). Cantor and Mason also credit successful coalitions of unions and community groups for turning New York City into "an arena for progressive policy-making."

Cantor and Mason conclude that New York has a special opportunity to address the vast inequality that characterizes most U.S. cities. In large measure, they say, this is due to two factors: its favorable electoral environment (e.g., an unusual "fusion" law allowing candidates to run on multiple party lines) in combination with increasingly powerful community groups.

To conclude: According to Mollenkopf and Castells, the dual city is based on the dichotomy between the "organized center" and the "disorganized peripheries."

Once again, we have a core and ring, this time Big Apple style. Interestingly, world-systems theory, Appletalk, and the dual city concept share an image: a dichotomy between core and periphery (ring) that describes polarization and inequality.

Some elected officials admit that their cities have pockets of gross inequality with problems similar to those in poor countries. Particularly after economic shocks, rising energy prices, and mortgage foreclosures, local public officials seem stymied in efforts to decrease polarization and inequality.

Yet, some, including Cantor and Mason (2007), think it may be possible to have a less unequal, less "Third-World" city via strong community and labor voices. But their "solution" to gross inequality in New York—a move from opposition to governance by labor and community groups—is a vision undoubtedly not shared by conservatives, libertarians, and most liberals. (Let us recall that a disparate lot of "goo-goos," including businesspersons and professionals, led the fight to reform U.S. city politics about a century ago after the exposure of corruption, graft, and other vices by administrations dominated by white ethnic groups and labor, among others.)

THE DUAL NATION

The United States is showing the same two-tier pattern as New York City. By 2005, U.S. income inequality had vastly increased from earlier times: The top 1 percent of people in the United States (those with incomes that year of more than $348,000) received their largest share of national income since 1928. The top 10 percent (roughly those earning more than $100,000) also reached a level of income share not seen since before the Great Depression in 1929. Meantime, average incomes for those in the bottom 90 percent dipped slightly (0.6 percent) compared to the previous year. Gains went largely to the top 1 percent, whose incomes rose an average of more than $1.1 million each (Johnston, 2007).

Typically, wealth or net worth is more concentrated than income. (The *net worth* of a household is what it owns, including real estate, stocks, savings accounts, and so on, minus what it owes, such as home mortgage, credit card debt, and loans.) Some groups in the United States, including most African Americans, have less net worth than whites and, thus, have less to pass on to their children.

By 1995, the United States was the most economically unequal industrial or postindustrial nation. It has retained that dubious distinction as of 2007—and beyond.

POVERTY IN U.S. METROPOLITAN AREAS

Poverty and unemployment dominate the life situation of many in the "disorganized peripheries." And as big corporate employers in the United States continue to downsize or outsource, employees of all collars or "no collar" in the core are not immune to pink slips and long-term joblessness.

Now let's take a closer look at the **unemployed**, the **underemployed**, and the full-time **employed** who still can't survive economically in the U.S. MSAs: the metropolitan poor. We begin by defining "poverty."

DEFINING POVERTY

Being poor in the United States is largely a question of definition—official government definition. That is, if the federal government's threshold for poverty changes, millions of people can be thrown out of poverty—or into poverty—on paper. For example, the U.S. Census Bureau's statistics for 2004 show an overall poverty rate (2007) of 17.3 percent (up from 12.8 percent in 1989). But the former chair of a congressional committee on hunger says that the threshold should be raised to include destitute people. If this were done, millions more would be considered poor.

Similarly, some think that today's poverty threshold is ridiculously low because it neglects common needs, such as child-care expenses (see Chapter 2). This view is buoyed by U.S. Agriculture Department studies on hunger in the United States: In 2005, about 35.1 million people said that they had gone hungry for at least some period during the year. In 2006, this number increased to about 35.5 million people or about 12.1 percent of the population in the United States, not counting homeless people (in Yen, 2007:A5).

The current federal definition of **poverty** is based on a Social Security Administration (SSA) index. This measurement system, which originated in the work of SSA employee Mollie Orshansky, was established in 1964. It has been revised slightly over the years and is adjusted annually for inflation. It uses money income before taxes; it does not include capital gains or non-cash benefits (e.g., public housing, Medicaid, and food stamps).

Currently, most analysts in the United States use the SSA poverty definition, an absolute standard of money income. Essentially, the SSA poverty threshold is calculated by determining subsistence food costs and multiplying that figure by the number of people in the household. Households with an income below the threshold are classified as poor.

Poverty thresholds do not vary from place to place within the United States. They are the same in California and Alabama and on farms and nonfarms (Formerly, the U.S. Census Bureau made a distinction between farm and nonfarm.) Consider these numbers: In the United States, in 2008, one person living alone, 65 or younger, was considered poor if earning $11,201 or less. A family of four (with two children under 18) was considered poor with an annual income of $21,834 or less (U.S. Census,2008?). (In 1977, the threshold for a nonfarm individual under 65 was $3,267 [all data in this paragraph from U.S. Census Bureau, 2008]).

Some people think that the SSA definition, which does not count nonmonetary benefits as income, *overestimates* the extent of poverty in the United States. These critics point out that the SSA definition does not include unreported income from the underground economy.

However, other critics say that the threshold is too low. The low threshold remains, critics claim, largely because no administration gains public-relations points from an increase in national poverty.

Some radical critics of government poverty measures maintain that the standard should be based on *relative* rather than *absolute* guidelines. These critics argue that being poor in America can be measured only in comparison with being rich.

Some liberal critics say that the assumptions of the SSA are outdated. Because families today spend much more for housing, the formula should be based on housing, not food. Doing so would raise the poverty threshold about 50 percent.

Other critics think that nondollar measures should be included in measuring poverty. The National

Academy of Sciences, for one, recommends that poverty be based on "disposable income" (the cash and noncash benefits left after a family pays essential expenses and taxes) and that geographical location should be taken into account (e.g., it costs less to live in small-town Mississippi than New York City).

What difference does it make if non-SSA definitions of poverty are used? A great difference! Using the National Academy's measure, there would be higher poverty rates for families lacking health insurance but lower rates for families receiving public assistance. Using the Children's Defense Fund measure (which includes infant mortality rates and the incidence of malnutrition), we would find that the percentage of malnourished children is higher in the United States than in some poor countries, like Somalia, where U.S. troops were dispatched under President Bill Clinton to bring food to the starving.

Using the official yardstick, the SSA income threshold, how many Americans are poor? An increasing number. The nationwide total in 1978 was 24.5 million (11.4 percent of the population). By 2004, the number (and the percentage) had climbed: Almost 37 million (12.7 percent) were living below the poverty line (U.S. Census 2007, Table 692). If the National Academy of Sciences' alternative definition had been used, about 2.5 million more would have been considered poor.

Using the SSA threshold, here are a few breakdowns by age and race/ethnicity for one year, 2004: 17.3 percent of all children in the United States were considered poor; over one-third (33.3%)of all African American children, 28.6 percent of Hispanic children, 9.5 percent of Asian/Pacific Islander children, and 14.2 percent of white children fell below the poverty line. The breakdown for those 65 and older living below the poverty line was this: 23.9 percent of African Americans, 13.2 percent of Asians, 18.7 percent of Hispanics, and 8.3 percent of whites (*Statistical Abstract of the United States*, 2007:Tables 693, 694).

To conclude: How U.S. poverty is defined and measured has serious consequences. If, for example, poverty statistics reflected cost-of-living differences among geographical areas, the flow of federal funds would increase to higher-cost areas, such as New York City, and decrease to lower-cost areas, such as Mississippi. Indeed, poverty statistics affect how billions of federal dollars are distributed for a variety of local programs, including child nutrition.

WHO ARE THE U.S. METROPOLITAN POOR?

As of 2005, about 45 percent of all poor in the United States were white. But African Americans, Hispanics, and Native Americans were disproportionately poor.

Where do the poor live? In 2005, for the first time in U.S. history, more poor people in the United States lived in suburbs of big cities (31 percent) than inside big cities (30 percent). (Still, there were more poor people in cities [18.4 percent] than in their close-in suburbs [9.4 percent] due to the cities' larger populations. Residents of large U.S. cities in the 2000s were twice as likely to be poor than suburbanites.)

Between 1991 and 2005, there was a geographical shift of the poor in the United States. Many poor people moved from cities to mainly inner suburbs.

Where in the United States are the disparities greater between suburbs and cities? In the Northeast and Midwest. According to Alan Berube of the Brookings Institution (2006), these differences are the results of historical patterns of segregation and the policies that insured them.

Who are the poor families of the United States? In 2004, they were disproportionately headed by female householders without a spouse present (28.4 percent of all households). They were also disproportionately African American (almost 23 percent) and young (30.3 percent between 15 and 24).

Which ethnic groups topped the poverty list? By the turn of the twenty-first century, Southeast Asians—primarily Vietnamese, Lao, Hmong, and Cambodian immigrants—continued as they had in the 1990s to have the highest rate of dependence on public welfare of any racial or ethnic group (Tang, 2000). However, that changed soon after. And not because the Southeast Asians "made it" out of poverty. Rather because national welfare policy changed: Five years after President Clinton signed the Personal Responsibility and Work Opportunity Reconciliation Act (PRWORA) in 1996, federal cash assistance programs, namely Aid to Families with Dependent Children (AFDC), were eliminated for citizens and immigrants.

The "end of welfare as we know it," the promise of the Clinton PRWORA bill, did indeed get 9 million

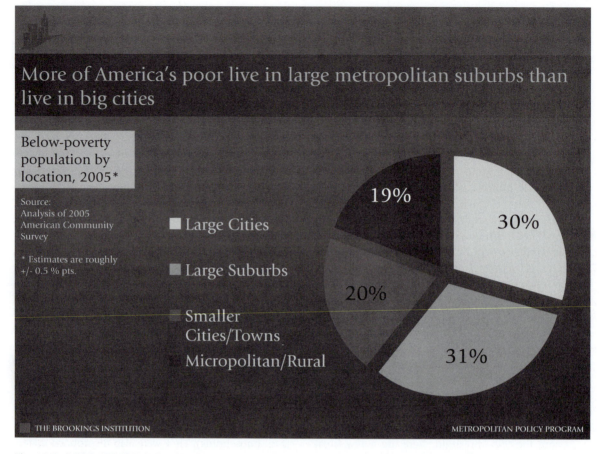

Fig. 19.5   WHO ARE THE U.S. METROPOLITAN POOR? *Source:* Alan Berube, Brookings Institution, 2006, "Metropolitan Poverty in the United States," p. 10 (http://www.brookings.edu/metro/speeches/20060928_metropoverty.pdf)

off the welfare rolls. However, according to *New York Times* reporter Jason DeParle ([2004] 2005:2+), many of those millions went from welfare to low-wage workfare, thereby swelling the ranks of the working poor. Furthermore, the PRWORA bill works best when the economy is booming, not during an economic downturn. Thus, according to another *New York Times* reporter, "forcing families to rely on work instead of government money went well [in the United States] from 1996 to 2000, when the economy was booming and paychecks were plentiful, economists say. Since then, however, job creation has slowed and poverty has risen" (Goodman, 2008b).

How many worked full-time but still fell below the poverty line? In 2000, before PRWORA fully kicked in,

there were about 6.4 million full-time, working poor in the United States. By 2003, the number had climbed to 7.4 million. (Note, however, that these numbers are disputed as much too low. Some suggest that a more accurate number would be 30+ million persons.)

By some reports, unknown numbers of formerly unpoor, middle-class families have become increasingly strapped after energy costs soared and house payments became unaffordable in the 2000s. By 2008, many were living in their cars to save money—and maintain transport to their jobs. Whatever the official definition of poverty may be, such downwardly mobile people may well define themselves as poor.

Before continuing, let's recall a few caveats about poverty statistics. First, some people never get into any statistical database. As noted earlier, there is an active off-the-books or underground economy in the United States (and elsewhere). This means that people—who knows how many—earn cash but don't report it for income tax purposes. Others may trade services—say, babysitting—and bypass the cash economy. The implication is that many classified as unemployed and/or poor may not be.

Second, census takers tend to undercount the urban poor and homeless. This has serious results for cities, particularly for the distribution of federal funds based on the number of persons below the poverty line.

Finally, the method of measuring employment and unemployment probably needs revision. The late Sar Levitan, onetime chair of a national commission on employment statistics, said years ago that unemployment numbers "come close to being straight random numbers" at the local level (in Shabecoff, 1978:19). Since this is the level at which federal public employment funds are allocated, the numbers game is crucial to cities. Further, Levitan questioned whether 16- and 17-year-olds who are full-time students (and who look for a job for a few hours per week) should really be counted as part of the labor force, which they still are. Meanwhile, the plaque on Levitan's office wall provided the proper cautionary note: "Statistics Are No Substitute for Good Judgment."

To conclude: By the mid-2000s, the metropolitan poor in the United States were disproportionately female, African American, Southeast Asian, and Latino. For the first time ever, suburbs near large U.S. cities had higher percentages of residents below the poverty line than the cities they ringed.

If alternative definitions of income are used, millions more are thrown into poverty. Two alternative definitions, noted by the U.S. Census Bureau, put either 19.4 percent or 12.9 percent of all people in the United States below the poverty line in 2004 (U.S. Bureau of the Census, 2007:Table 698, notes 2, 3).

More and more U.S. children, in both cities and suburbs, are living in poverty. As of 2005, almost one-third of all poor Americans were children, under age 18.

The increasingly high rates of children in poverty, in both suburbs and cities, are related to the transformation of the American economy, declining real wages for most workers, and nonaffluent families' moving in relatively large numbers from central cities to suburbs. In *Growing Up Empty: The Hunger Epidemic in America* (2002), journalist Loretta Schwartz-Nobel claims that there are more children without homes and living in poverty than in the years of the Great Depression in the United States, the 1930s.

WHY ARE THEY POOR?

Why did 37 million people in the United States fall below the official poverty line in 2005? Was it mainly bad luck? Bad families? Horrible housing? Poor educations? Laziness or lack of smarts? World conditions?

It comes as no surprise that observers disagree on the causes and cures of poverty. Some believe that the poor shall be with us always. Some think that the poor are poor because they are oppressed, lazy, not too bright, or seduced by the welfare or "nanny" state. Or that they have too many babies and have them too soon. Or that they need tax relief and higher minimum wages. Or they need our help, or they need to help themselves. Or they need a kinder economic system.

In different eras, different notions dominate social thought. And some resurface, like old wines in new bottles. For instance, social Darwinism dominated poverty beliefs several generations ago.

Briefly, social Darwinism held (and still holds) that those who reach the top of the economic ladder are the fittest, surviving and winning the struggle for existence. By implication, the poor are unfit. This idea has resurfaced in recent years with a new twist: the claim that poverty is linked to genetic inheritance. Exhaustive social research shows that genes and IQ scores have relatively little effect on economic success. But whether social or biological, Darwinian theories of poverty die hard.

Another notion is rooted even more deeply in U.S. thought: Anyone who works hard can succeed. In this view, anyone who wants a job can get one, work hard, and make it. Thus, the poor are just lazy. The Horatio Alger stories in the period of rapid industrialization popularized this aspect of the American dream and strengthened the belief in the so-called Protestant work ethic. (In recent global recessions and technological shifts, this notion is coming under great pressure.)

Much social research shows that most poor people in the United States prefer to work, identifying their

Fig. 19.6 WHY DOES POVERTY EXIST? Theorists disagree. Radicals think that poverty is a structural feature of capitalism. Liberals think that poverty can be decreased within existing institutional structures. Conservatives hold that poverty stems from personal failure and/or lower-class attitudes. (Margaret Bourke-White, *Life* magazine. © 1937 Time, Inc.)

self-esteem with work as strongly as do the nonpoor. Many studies point to the problem of low-paying work that rarely provides economic independence.

But social science findings have done little to change firm beliefs or prejudices. No matter what social scientists find, some will continue to believe that poor people are lazy people.

Currently, several different notions about the causes of poverty dominate academic and/or policy-making circles. Here is a brief summary of competing notions:

1. *Poverty as personal failure.* In this view, poverty is largely the result of personal failure and

lower-class attitudes; certain psychological traits (e.g., present time orientation) prevent the poor from changing their status. In brief, it holds that lower-class people lack typically middle-class attitudes about planning ahead, saving for a rainy day, and pursuing an education. This view is associated with conservative political thought.

2. *Poverty as a culture, passed on from generation to generation.* This view, associated with the late anthropologist Oscar Lewis, holds that the poor are present time–oriented and lack planning ability. But the *reasons* the poor act

differently from the nonpoor have little to do with individual failure (as view 1 holds) and much to do with the class-stratified, capitalistic societies they live in. Based on fieldwork in Latin America and the United States, Lewis (1964) argued that the poor lack the means to break the cycle of poverty. So they adapt as best they can—in a subculture set apart from other subcultures in capitalist society. This subculture—the **culture of poverty**—is transmitted from one generation to the next, making it nearly impossible to break the chains that bind. Lewis's concept—the culture of poverty—remains much debated.

3. *Poverty as a lack of opportunity.* This view, associated with liberals, holds that the poor lack the skills and education to find employment in a high-tech society. Extending opportunities for the poor—without disturbing existing institutions—is the solution that follows from this stance, exemplified by the War on Poverty in the 1960s (and beyond) and programs such as affirmative action and so-called minority set-asides.

4. *Poverty as a result of racism or ethnic discrimination.* In this view, people of color are disproportionately poor because they have been systematically discriminated against in a variety of ways, both blatant and subtle, that limit opportunities. Being disadvantaged is expressed in myriad ways, from being turned down for a bank loan to being turned down for membership in exclusive clubs where business is done over dinner. Further, in this view, social isolation and/or residential segregation, faced by many African Americans and Latinos, cuts them off from job leads gained by weak ties. The solutions that follow from this position range from aggressive monitoring of institutions that discriminate (e.g., banks that redline) and enforcing antidiscrimination laws to changing the way localities fund public schools (to provide better education for children in racially isolated and poor areas) and holding "diversity" training sessions.

5. *Poverty as a result of structural shifts, most importantly, deindustrialization and technological change.*

In this view, associated with liberals such as Robert Reich, U.S. workers were thrown out of work as part of global shifts in production and new technologies. One solution that follows from this logic is worker retraining.

6. *Poverty as a structural feature of capitalism.* This view, held by Marxist-oriented scholars, holds that under capitalism some are poor because others are rich. In this view, the capitalist state helps capitalists to maintain power over wage workers and thus cannot be expected to intervene meaningfully to end poverty—for that would mean speeding capitalism's downfall.

Although it is possible to combine some of these views—say, poverty as lack of opportunity and racism—no synthesis of all these views is possible. They are too at odds with one another. But a study we've considered briefly before, *Tally's Corner* by Elliot Liebow (1967), does include aspects of both the structural and social psychological perspectives. Let us now return to this classic study.

TALLY'S CORNER

The New Deal Carry-out shop is on a corner in downtown Washington, D.C. It would be within easy walking distance of the White House…if anyone cared to walk there, but no one ever does.…One block south of the Carry-out is a broad avenue which serves roughly to divide the Carry-out neighborhood from the downtown business and shopping district.

(Liebow, 1967:17, 18)

It was here, in this zone-in-transition, African American ghetto neighborhood, that urban anthropologist Liebow did his participant-observation research. One of the first questions he asked was, "Why are these men hanging out on streetcorners?" Some might think there's a simple answer: They don't want to work. That's what a truck driver said when some of the men refused his offer of work: "These men wouldn't take a job if it were handed to them on a platter." Several street-corner men did fit the truck driver's stereotype. Leroy preferred playing pinball to working at parking lots, and Sea Cat, "an excellent story teller," walked out on his job. Arthur, age 28, didn't want to work. But Liebow found that most did work—at weekend or evening jobs—and thus they could hang out near the carry-out shop during the day. Some of the street-corner men were doing illegal work—hustling. Liebow thought that this made sense since the legal work available to them was low-paying, low-status, and dead-end.

Liebow disputed notions that the poor are present time–oriented and can't plan ahead (as Oscar Lewis thought). To the contrary, "when Richard squanders a week's pay in two days it is not because he is 'present-time oriented,' unaware or unconcerned with his future. He does so precisely because he is aware of the future and the hopelessness of it all" (Liebow, 1967:66). *Thus, what may seem to others as a present time orientation is interpreted by Liebow as a future time orientation.* The difference is that it is a future filled with trouble. He gives the following concrete example:

> One day, after Tally had gotten paid, he gave me four twenty-dollar bills and asked me to keep them for him. Three days later he asked me for the money. I returned it and asked why he did not put his money in a bank. He said that the banks close at two o'clock. I argued that there were four or more banks within a two-block radius of where he was working at the time and that he could easily get to any one of them on his lunch hour. "No, man," he said, "you don't understand. They close at two o'clock and they closed Saturday and Sunday. Suppose I get into trouble and I got to make it [leave]. Me get out of town, and everything I got in the world layin' up in that bank? No good! No good!" (69).

The result of their structural situation, Liebow said, was a constant awareness of a troubled future. This discouraged Tally and the other street-corner men from putting money in the bank, sinking roots, committing themselves to a family or friends, and devoting their energies to a job, for all these commitments could hold them hostage.

WHAT SHOULD BE DONE ABOUT POVERTY?

Some poor townsmen were sitting around discussing the vexing question of poverty. "Poverty is hell," one man said, "but I know how to remedy this evil. People should put all they own into a common pot so that there would be enough for everyone." Another man, Hershel by name, responded, "That is indeed a fine plan, but the question is how to carry it out. I suggest we divide the task. I'll get the endorsement of the poor. You can tackle the rich" (in Howe and Greenberg, 1954).

Folk tales, like this one from nineteenth-century Russia, often contain ideological visions. So do programs sponsored by government or private organizations that seek to end or hide poverty.

During the 1960s, federal, state, and local government responses to poverty were dominated by a liberal vision. This means that the policy thrust was toward increased funds for cities and programs aimed at widening economic opportunities. Such programmatic responses to poverty included Project Head Start and the War on Poverty's Community Action Program.

By the 1990s, homelessness and poverty in the United States had increased, not decreased. But by 2000 few seemed to be asking, "What is to be done?" Radical critics had long since dismissed liberal notions of equal opportunity and government programs, claiming that the big winners of most so-called antipoverty programs are not the poor but the affluent, including corporations that run work-training centers.

For different reasons, conservatives and libertarians also dismiss liberal solutions to poverty. Conservatives and neoconservatives think that big government can't solve the problem of poverty and shouldn't try. Their alternative: Let the market mechanism of supply and demand, not government, regulate social problems. They and libertarians tend to favor removing constraints on the market so that it can work "properly." Hence, they suggest repealing minimum wage laws, reasoning that without a minimum wage employers would hire more low-skilled people and unemployment would decrease. Libertarians and conservatives also press for laws favoring business expansion and tax reduction on the trickle-down premise: money poured in at the top will filter down to the poor. Yet, in the 2000s it was so-called conservatives in the Bush administration who proposed national government intervention in the market, leading to significant bailouts of U.S. financial institutions. In other words, hard-and-fast ideological lines can be quickly broken.

In the past, positions on "free trade" broke down on ideological lines, but here too the sands seem to be shifting a bit. For example, in the midst of a deepening recession, free-traders in the United Kingdom and other members of the EU seem to be undergoing a mood swing away from globalization and toward protectionism. Libertarians remain free-traders. They tend to prefer the unilateral elimination of commercial barriers (rather than free-trade pacts, which they feel are cumbersome).

But some liberals are rethinking their position. For decades, liberal economists opposed trade barriers, arguing that free trade would enrich the United States (and its trading partners), despite the harm it does to some U.S. workers. However, some liberals are changing their tune. Take, for example, Alan S. Blinder, once a Federal Reserve Board vice chair and longtime adviser to Democratic presidential wannabes. In 2001 Blinder said that "Like 99% of economists since the days of Adam Smith, I am a free trader down to my toes" (in Wessel and Davis, 2007:A1). By 2007, Blinder—still a free-trader—said that the new economy of communications technology could put as many as 40 million jobs at risk in the United States in coming years. Among his "solutions": a focus on person-to-person jobs, such as child day-care providers and doctors (jobs hard to outsource electronically).

Former labor secretary and current professor Robert Reich (2007) is also a liberal free-trader. To deal with the issue he calls job loss due to "software or elsewhere" (i.e., being replaced by technology or global workers), he calls for more skills training and a "reverse income tax" for those at the bottom of the income pyramid.

Radicals do not view retooling or other liberal responses to U.S. poverty as useful. Nor do they think that pouring money in at the top helps the poor. They claim that the economic pie may grow bigger, but the share for the poor remains the same or even decreases, as it has done since the 1980s. Indeed, radicals point out that since the 1980s the income distribution in the United States has been growing more and more unequal. (The opposite is true for Great Britain, previously much more inegalitarian than the United States.)

Radicals (as well as liberals and, recently, some conservatives) might point to ever-increasing inequality in the United States as troubling. By 1995, the richest 1 percent of the U.S. population held about 33 percent of all private wealth. The U.S. Census Bureau reported that the portion of national income earned by the top 20 percent of households grew to 50.4 percent in 2005 (in Parks, 2006), up from 45.6 percent in 1985. Meanwhile, the bottom 60 percent of U.S. households received 26.6 percent of the national income, down from 29.9 percent 20 years before. During the same year, 2005, the average head of a Standard & Poor's 500 (an index of stocks designed to be a leading indicator of U.S. equities) made $13.51 million in total compensation.

Radicals also point to the deceptive quality of government-sponsored antipoverty programs. They argue that job-retraining programs, for example, may convince the public that something is being done to end poverty but, in reality, they are only preserving a system of structured inequality: capitalism. In the radical view, the idea of equal opportunity for advancement is false. It is equivalent to comparing a lottery ticket to a savings bond that always pays off. In the words of Simone de Beauvoir (1953), "any ticket may be the winning one, but only a tiny percentage of them actually do win." To end poverty, radicals argue, the institutional and class structure that perpetuates it must be changed—not just around the edges, as liberals would have it, but at its core: capitalist productive relations.

ANOTHER LOOK

For individuals, on-the-job stress and meaninglessness remain serious issues. This holds true across occupational categories as well as national boundaries. For instance, in Japan, many suffer job stress and *karoshi*—death from overwork. In the United States, some surveys show that the majority are dissatisfied with their work. And, according to the United Nations International Labor Organization, job stress afflicts workers worldwide.

Meanwhile, neither widespread worker dissatisfaction nor job stress is high on the political agenda. Instead, the clarion call in the United States and Western Europe is *jobs, jobs, jobs*. Youth joblessness is up in many subcommunities. Public and private officials propose retraining programs for former manufacturing workers and "the outsourced" but fail to specify what kinds of jobs the displaced workers will be trained for. In this atmosphere, we cannot expect those with jobs to risk them by speaking out against on-the-job boredom, repression, stress, or low wages.

Unfortunately, there is little public debate concerning the probability that, along with a single-family home, work that is dignified, interesting, and well-paid is becoming an impossible dream for more and more persons in the United States. What this means for long-term living standards, poverty rates, and the quality of life is another difficult but undebated question. Instead of debate, potential voters are typically offered pat slogans and contentless hope.

A final thought on theory and practice: In 1837, an anonymous contributor to the *Edinburgh Review* commented that "newspapers are perhaps the best representative, at any given time, of the real moral and intellectual state of the greater part of a population" (Anonymous, 1837:197).

Today, we might substitute newer media—TV and blogs—for newspapers. Focusing here on TV, what stories does it tell us about the quality of work, the nature of poverty, and the route to success in metropolitan America? In numerous TV sitcoms and dramas—in hospitals and police stations, for example—work is challenging and family-like, even fun. People "make it" by luck and pluck, not government assistance. These TV stories that we tell and retell ourselves avoid stark realities: Work is not fun for most Americans; millions of people work full-time but remain poor, and many get government subsidies of some sort (e.g., money for not growing a particular crop, cheap grazing rights on federal land, bailouts for failed businesses).

As the era of postindustrialism progresses, it will be interesting to watch TV, blog, and vlog portrayals of work, leisure, self-fulfillment, and poverty. Will the stories change? Stay tuned.

KEY TERMS

Alienation A widely used concept in social science, philosophy, and the humanities with various meanings. As used by Marx, who focused on labor, alienation is the process by which the worker is dispossessed of his or her product by the capitalist mode of production. Other theorists center on varying aspects of alienation: self-estrangement, meaninglessness, and powerlessness.

Anomic division of labor According to Durkheim, an abnormal form of the division of labor that occurs when extreme specialization of tasks is coupled with a decrease in communication between individuals performing different specialized tasks. This leads to vague rules governing relationships between groups and lack of a sense of interdependence in organically solid society.

Blue-collar A category of workers (as opposed to white-collar and service workers) formerly used by the U.S. Census Bureau but still popularly used. It includes automobile mechanics, assembly-line workers, transport operators, and nonfarm laborers.

Culture of poverty Oscar Lewis's term, referring to his belief that the poor in capitalist societies possess and transmit to their children a distinct set of cultural–sociopsychological traits that sets them apart from the nonpoor. These characteristics, Lewis believed, are universal and include the inability to plan ahead, wife beating, and low levels of education and income.

Dual city Any city divided in two—one part poor, the other rich. The term dates at least to Plato's *Republic*. In John Hull Mollenkopf and Manuel Castells's view, it is the social expression of the spatial form of postindustrial society.

Employed As defined by the U.S. Census Bureau, an employed person is a civilian 16 years of age and over who (1) did any work as a paid employee or worked 15 or more hours as an unpaid worker on a family farm or in a family business or (2) had a job but did not work during the week that the census took a count due to illness, bad weather, vacation, industrial strikes, or personal reasons.

Poverty A controversial term referring most often to lack of money and material possessions; some analysts include lack of power over decision-making processes. Most U.S. analysts use the Social Security Administration's measure of poverty, which establishes a threshold by calculating the subsistence food costs for a family of more than three persons and multiplying that figure by 3. Critics of this absolute standard of poverty argue that poverty is relative to wealth; hence, a relative, not an absolute, standard should be used.

Underemployment Inadequate employment of three different types: (1) too few hours of work, (2) inadequate income level, and (3) mismatch of occupation and skills. Distinguished from *unemployment*.

Unemployed As defined by the U.S. Census Bureau, a civilian 16 years of age or older who was neither at work nor holding a job (but temporarily not working) or looking for work during the previous 4 weeks and available to accept a job.

White-collar A category of workers (as opposed to blue-collar and "no-collar" workers) formerly used by the U.S. Census Bureau but still used popularly. White-collar workers include professional and technical workers (e.g., teachers, lawyers, radio operators), nonfarm managers and administrators (e.g., business executives), sales workers (e.g., retail sales clerks), and clerical workers (e.g., typists).

PROJECTS

1. **Working: personal views**. How do people feel about the work they do? Interview people in your community who engage in different activities—professor, garbage collector, secretary, sales clerk, farm worker, doctor, and so forth. Try to find out if they would choose the same work again if they had a choice, what they like most about their jobs, what they would change about their working conditions, and what they dislike about their work. Do any patterns emerge?

2. **Slavery and involuntary servitude**. What jobs, in what communities worldwide, tend to be performed by desperately poor people who are virtual slaves or prisoners? Do any enterprises in or near your community employ such labor? If so, do owners allow access to their employees by reporters or union organizers? What laws or organizations work to protect these workers? What rationales do governments or private employers use for perpetuating these working conditions? *Note*: Before setting out on this research project, discuss it with local contacts who might assess any possible risks.

3. **Are you what you do?** When attending social gatherings, note how guests describe themselves. If most are students, what information do they share? If most are not students, do they tell you—within the first 5 minutes—about the work they do? Where they went to school? What status markers do they mention? (Note that in some countries, notably France, you can spend an evening with people and never know about their work or their educational background.) What do you conclude from this cursory, anecdotal study about the importance of work to identity in the United States?

SUGGESTIONS FOR FURTHER LEARNING

Changes in work, workplaces, and wage structures in the United States, including the decline in relatively high-paid, semiskilled work and the decline in unionization, are the subject of many studies. See, for example, a provocative study, *Who's Not Working and Why: Employment, Cognitive Skills, Wages, and the Changing U.S. Labor Market* (New York: Cambridge University Press, 2000) by economists Frederic L. Pryor and David L. Schaffer.

How people feel about their work is the subject of a number of personal statements. *Roger and Me* and *Pets or Meat?*, Michael Moore's films about his hometown, Flint, Michigan, are Swiftian satires on work (and nonwork) at GM's Flint plant. Although a generation old, one oral history is a stand-out: Studs Terkel's *Working* (New York: Avon, 1975); it presents dozens of people speaking about their work.

Some of the United States's most renowned literature focuses on work and its alienating effects. Most notable is Arthur Miller's haunting indictment of the economic system that results in alienation *Death of a Salesman*, in *Collected Plays* (New York: Viking, 1957).

Work is the focus of a subfield of sociology: the sociology of occupations and professions. Within this subfield, there has been an outpouring of gender-based research since the mid-1960s. One groundbreaking study compares working men's and women's relative contributions to housework and child care: Arlie Hochschild with Anne Machung, *The Second Shift* (New York: Avon, 1989). It reveals that in about 80 percent of the two-career families studied, the majority of women accept the inequity of their doing the housework but tend to suffer frequent illness and exhaustion. In *Small, Foreign, and Female* (Berkeley: University of California Press, forthcoming), Karen Hossfeld looks at the interplay of race, class, and gender and the life chances of immigrant women working in Silicon Valley.

Peter Laslett's *The World We Have Lost* (New York: Scribner, [1965] 1971) is a sociological history of preindustrial England. Lloyd Bonfield, Richard Smith, and Keith Wrightson, eds., *The World We Have Gained* (Oxford: Blackwell, 1986), is a collection of essays published by Laslett's students and colleagues. The essay topics range across western Europe from the thirteenth to the nineteenth centuries and deal with such topics as marriage, courtship, and occupational structures in late medieval and early modern times.

For a sociological analysis of management ideologies in the course of industrialization, see Reinhard Bendix, *Work and Authority in Industry* (New York: Harper Torchbooks, [1956] 1963). The book "deals with ideologies of management which seek to justify the subordination of large masses of men [and women] to the discipline of factory work and to the authority of employers."

How were the old mills as workplaces? Anthropologist Anthony F. C. Wallace examines old mills and tenements south of Philadelphia in his brilliant account *Rockdale: The Growth of an American Village in the Early Industrial Revolution* (New York: Knopf, 1978).

Theories on the relationship of work and welfare from a radical perspective are presented by Frances Fox Piven and Richard Cloward, *Regulating the Poor* (New York: Vintage, 1971). In this now classic work, they argue that welfare regulates both the poor and members of the labor force.

A very different view of work and poverty is contained in Edward Banfield, *The Unheavenly City Revisited* (Boston: Little, Brown, 1974), now considered a classic statement of the conservative (or neoconservative) position.

Films dealing with work, welfare, and poverty include Charlie Chaplin's classic *Modern Times* (1936) and Paul Schrader's *Blue Collar* (1978). Frederick Wiseman's documentary *Welfare* (1975) attacks the red tape and callousness of the welfare system, showing its effects on those who work in it as well as those who depend on it. For a portrayal of the rhythm of factory life in the late nineteenth century, see the opening scenes of *The Organizer* (1964), which creates the mood of modern industrial life as workers pour into the factory to the purr of machines. Barbara Kopple's

award-winning film *Harlan County, U.S.A.* (1976) shows the rhythm of work in the coal mines, as well as management–labor struggles and union problems in "bloody Harlan" County, Kentucky. The feature film *Salt of the Earth* (1954) intertwines three themes of exploitation from a radical perspective: management versus labor, Anglo versus Latino miners, and women's oppression by men. The film's director, Herbert J. Biberman, was one of the Hollywood Ten, blacklisted during the McCarthy era.

Sebastião Salgado celebrates the heroism and dignity of anonymous working women and men, from coal miners in India to steel workers in France. One of his photo exhibits, "Workers: An Archeology of the Industrial Age," toured the United States during the 1990s.

An unusual monument to working-class heroes, mainly teenagers who lost their lives on whaling boats in far-flung places, can be found in New Bedford, Massachusetts's Seamen's Bethel. The walls are lined with marble tablets marking their contributions.

Sudhir Alladi Venkatesh's *Off the Books: The Underground Economy of the Urban Poor* (Cambridge, Mass.: Harvard University Press, 2006) examines the underground economy of a poor Chicago neighborhood. The Columbia sociology professor finds a thriving system of legal and illegal exchanges.

An older novel *Kanikosen (A Crab Factory Ship)*, written in 1929 by Takiji Kobayashi, was a best-seller in Japan in 2008, selling an estimated 300,000 copies. This Japanese Marxist novel has regained popularity, some Japanese professors think, because it reflects current anxieties about job security, growing wage gaps, growing costs of pensions, and the plight of low-paid part-time workers; with the end of lifetime employment and high economic growth, insecurity has set in among Japan's younger and older workers. An excerpt from the book, in English, is available in Donald Keene, *Modern Japanese Literature: From 1868 to the Present Day* (New York: Grove Press, 1994). A movie *Kanikozen* (1953), in Japanese, was made from the book; it may be available at rental stores specializing in foreign films.

Work is also an enduring theme in folk music. The song "John Henry" immortalizes the competition between human and machine that (apparently) took place in West Virginia; a statue in Summers County immortalizes the miner, not the machine. For an introduction to labor songs, listen to John Greenway, *American Industrial Folksongs* (Riverside 12–607) and *American History in Ballad and Song* (Folkways FH 5801), as well as a number of songs sung and played by Pete Seeger, especially *American Industrial Ballads* (Folkways FH 5251).

For views on the shift from the world of preindustrial to industrial work in Europe, see E. P. Thompson, *The Making of the English Working Class* (New York: Vintage, 1963), a classic work of scholarship sympathetic to the workers' struggle to nourish the tree of liberty. Herbert Gutman attempts to do for the U.S. working class what Thompson did for the first working class (in England) in his collection of essays *Work, Culture, and Society in Industrializing America, 1815–1919* (New York: Knopf, 1976). This book has already been influential in giving a new interpretation of American labor history.

Charlie Chaplin is not the only artist to envision people as cogs in a machine. Many painters reflect this vision, including Ferdinand Leger. Some see the architecture of the Bauhaus school, which is rational, efficient, and unadorned, as another response to technological advance. Ludwig Mies van der Rohe's glass apartment building at 880 Lake Shore Drive in Chicago is one example of Bauhaus style.

A classic work on race, poverty, and social policy is Kenneth B. Clark, *Dark Ghetto* (New York: Harper Torchbooks, 1965). For a "searing expose" of urban U.S. schools, see Kozol's book on public school resegregation, *The Shame of the Nation: The Restoration of Apartheid Schooling in America* (New York: Three Rivers Press, 2006).

REFERENCES

American Sociological Association. 2009. *Member News & Notes* (January): http://www.asanet.org/cs/topnav/members/membernewsand_notesjanuary2009

Anonymous. 1837. *Edinburgh Review* 65:197.

Associated Press. 2007. "Depressed workers personal care, food workers most depressed." USAToday.com (October 23): http://jobs.aol.com/article/_a/depressed-workers/20071017115909990001

Bennis, Warren. 1970. *American Bureaucracy*. Chicago: Aldine.

Berube, Alan. 2006. "Metropolitan poverty in the United States." Poverty & Place Workshop, Cambridge, UK (September 28): http://www.brookings.edu/metro/speeches/20060928_metropoverty.pdf

Blauner, Robert. 1964. *Alienation and Freedom: The Factory Worker and His Industry*. Chicago: University of Chicago Press.

Brunwasser, Matthew. 2007. "Romania's economy threatened by worker shortage." *International Herald Tribune* (April 10): http://www.iht.com/articles/2007/04/10/news/factory.php

Bureau of Labor Statistics, U.S. Department of Labor. 2007. *Career Guide to Industries, 2006–07 Edition, Textile, Textile Product, and Apparel Manufacturing* (April 10): http://www.bls.gov/oco/cg/cgs015.htm

Byerly, Victoria. 1986. *Hard Times, Cotton Mill Girls: Personal Histories of Womanhood and Poverty in the South*. Ithaca, N.Y.: ILR Press.

Cantor, Dan, and J. W. Mason. 2007. "Paradox and the city: Why the working class has political power." *Footnotes* 35(4):A1+.

de Beauvoir, Simone. 1953. *America Day by Day*. New York: Grove Press.

———. [2004] 2005. *American Dream: Three Women, Ten Kids, and a Nation's Drive to End Welfare*. New York: Penguin.

De Parle, Jason [2004] 2005. *American Dream: Three Women, Ten Kids and a Nation's Drive to End Welfare*. New York: Penguin.

Durkheim, Emile. [1893] 1966. *The Division of Labor in Society*. New York: Free Press.

Eisler, Benita. 1977. *The Lowell Offering: Writings by New England Mill Women (1840–1945)*. Philadelphia: Lippincott.

Fackler, Martin. 2008. "Japanese salarymen fight back." *International Herald Tribune* (June 12): http://www.iht.com/articles/2008/06/11/business/11suits.php?WT.mc_id=newsalert

Ferguson, Ann Arnett. 1991. "Managing without managers: Crisis and resolution in a collective bakery." Pp. 108–132 in Michael Burawoy et al., eds., *Ethnography Unbound: Power and Resistance in the Modern Metropolis*. Berkeley: University of California Press.

Fowke, Edith, and Joe Glazer, eds., [1960] 1961. *Songs of Work and Freedom*. Garden City: N.Y.:Doubleday, Dolphin.

Gans, Herbert J. 1993. "Scholars' role in planning a 'post-work society'." *Chronicle of Higher Education* (June 9):B3.

Garson, G. David. 1973. "Automobile workers and the radical dream." *Politics and Society* 3:163–177.

Goodman, Peter S. 2008a. "Workers get fewer hours, deepening the downturn." *New York Times* (April 18): http://www.nytimes.com/2008/04/18/business/18hours.html?_r=1&th&emc=th&oref=slogin

———. 2008b. "From welfare shift in '96, a reminder for Clinton." *New York Times* (April 11): http://www.nytimes.com/2008/04/11/us/politics/11welfare.html?_r=1&oref=slogin

Greenhouse, Stephen. 2008. *The Big Squeeze: Tough Times for the American Worker*. New York City: Alfred Knopf.

Howe, Louise Kapp. 1978. *Pink Collar Workers: Inside the World of Women's Work*. New York: Avon.

Howe, Irving, and Eliezer Greenberg, eds. 1954. New York: Viking A Treasury of *Yiddish Stories*.

Johnston, David Cay. 2007. "Income gap is widening, data shows." *New York Times* (March 29):C1.

Laslett, Peter. [1965] 1971. *The World We Have Lost*. New York: Scribner.

Lawler, Edward E., and James O' Toole, eds.2006. *America at Work: Choices and Challenges*.New York: Palgrave Macmillan.

Lewis, Oscar. 1964. "The culture of poverty." Pp. 149–174 in J. J. TePaske and S. N. Fisher, eds., *Explosive Forces in Latin America*. Columbus: Ohio State University Press.

Liebow, Elliot. 1967. *Tally's Corner: A Study of Negro Streetcorner Men*. Boston: Little, Brown.

Marmot, Michael. 2005. *The Status Syndrome: How Social Standing Affects Our Health and Longevity*. New York: Owl Books.

Marx, Karl. 1972. *Karl Marx: The Essential Writings*. Ed. Frederic L. Bender. New York: Harper & Row.

Mills, C. Wright. 1951. *White Collar*. New York: Oxford University Press.

Mollenkopf, John Hull, and Manuel Castells, eds. 1991. *Dual City: Restructuring New York*. New York: Russell Sage Foundation.

Noble, David F. 1977. *America by Design*. New York: Knopf.

Ouchi, William G. [1981] 1982. *Theory Z: How American Business Can Meet the Japanese Challenge*. New York: Avon.

Parks, James. 2006. "America worries as income gap widens." (December 14): http://blog.aflcio.org/2006/12/14/america-worries-as-income-gap-widens/

Perry, Stewart E. 1978. *San Francisco Scavengers*. Berkeley: University of California Press.

Phillips, E. Barbara. 1975. "The artists of everyday life: Journalists, their craft, and their consciousness." Ph.D. diss., Syracuse University.

Reich, Robert. 2007. *KALW News*. KALW-radio, San Francisco (April 18):7:00–7:30 p.m.

Ross, Andrew. [2003]2004. *No Collar: The Humane Workplace and Its Hidden Costs*. Philadelphia, PA: Temple University Press.

Schwartz-nobel, Loretta. 2002. *Growing Up Empty: The Hunger Epidemic in America*. New York: HarperCollins.

Shabecoff, Philip. 1978. "Overhaul is urged in jobless figures." *New York Times* (July 16):19.

Shenon, Philip. 1993. "Saipan sweatshops are no American dream." *New York Times* (national edition) (July 18):A1+.

Southwide Textile Heritage Initiative. 2004: http://www.textileheritage.org/news/pr01.htm

Statistical Abstract of the United States. 2007.

Tang, Eric. 2000. "Collateral damage: Southeast Asian poverty in the United States." *Social Text* 18.1:55–57

Terkel, Studs. 1975. *Working*. New York: Avon.

U.S. Bureau of the Census.2007. *Statistical Abstract of the United States*. Washington, D.C.: Government Printing Office.

———. 2008 "Poverty." http://www.census.gov/hhes/www/poverty/threshld/thresh08.html

U.S. Department of Agriculture. 2007. "State fact sheets: South Carolina (March 26): http://www.ers.usda.gov/StateFacts/SC.htm

Weber, Max. [1922] 1958. Pp. 180–195 in Hans H. Gerth and C. Wright Mills, eds., and trans. *From Max Weber: Essays in Sociology*. New York: Oxford University Press.

Wessel, David, and Bob Davis. 2007. "Pain from free trade spurs second thoughts." *Wall Street Journal* (March 28):A1+.

W. E. Upjohn Institute for Employment Research. 1973. *Work in America: Report of a Special Task Force to the Secretary of Health, Education, and Welfare*. Cambridge, Mass.: MIT Press.

Wiseman, Paul. 2008. "Japanese suicide rate soaring." *USA Today* (July 21):1.

Wolff, Edward N. 2002. *Top Heavy: The Increasing Inequality of Wealth in America and What Can Be Done About It*, 2nd ed. New York: New Press.

Richard Hedman

FINALE
TO BE CONTINUED

Imagine a huge blank wall.

"How boring is a blank wall," sigh the city council members. Moving quickly against boredom (and graffiti), they vote funds for 500 paintbrushes and truckloads of nonspray paint. Then they invite men, women, and children from each block to transform a blank wall in the central business district into a giant mural about city life.

The idea spread. Soon "muralmania" gripped the nation's cities and suburbs. People everywhere were painting scenes on blank walls. "Cities and suburbs grow curiouser and curiouser," sniffed urbanists. "This muralmania deserves our undivided attention," they decided. So, grant proposals were written—and funded.

Social scientists swung into action. An economist collected data on the time spent painting instead of working at paid employment and the consequent rise or fall in the gross national product. Teams of participant-observers joined paint crews in 21 cities and 32 suburbs. A political scientist studied the relationships that developed between city hall flaks and neighborhood block groups. A geographer charted the location of blank walls in small, medium-sized, and large cities and suburbs. A sociologist gathered data on the social backgrounds of those who sketched skyscrapers versus those who painted playgrounds. A mass communications researcher examined the impact of muralmania on Internet use. And on and on...

One year passed. Conferences on muralmania were held globally. Scholars presented learned papers, including "Ethnic Styles of Depicting City Hall," "The Spatial Relation of City Murals to Transport Nodes," "How Paint Crews Handle Conflict on Scaffolds," "Globalization of Culture: The Case of Muralmania," and "A Cost–Benefit Analysis of Muralmania with Emphasis on Changes in Consumer Buying Patterns."

Meanwhile, political commentators reflected on the deeper meanings of muralmania. According to a radical pundit, "Muralmania presents a strong case against capitalism. We have nonalienated labor, working collectively in their own interest, to creatively humanize the cities. The lesson is clear: We can end alienation if we end capitalism." A liberal drew a different lesson: "Muralmania presents a strong case for equal opportunity. Given an equal chance to express themselves and a little on-the-scaffold training, all people in the United States—regardless of social background, color, or creed—can rise to the top rungs of the ladder." A conservative columnist disagreed, writing that "muralmania presents a strong case for letting the free market work without government interference. Well, mostly—if conditions do not equal a financial tsunami."

The conservative continued, "The market provided gallons of paint at cheaper prices and employed some jobless in paint factories. The message is self-evident: Keep the government out of running and regulating our lives, and the nation will prosper." Other voices are raised. A decentralist commented, "How beautiful is smallness. Muralmania presents a strong case for local community action. Just imagine what energy would be released through neighborhood government." A centralist, on the other hand, argued that "muralmania presents a strong case for central coordination and economies of scale. Without regional paint buying and the vast administrative effort that went into organizing paint crews, muralmania would have fizzled out."

Clearly, muralmania had captured the nation's imagination. And way beyond. Amid the talk shows, online comments, newspaper editorials, parades, and block parties, social scientists continued their analysis. One team of content analysts carefully examined photos of all city scenes painted by all the people on all the cities' walls. Grounded—rather, flooded—in data, they constructed a typology to make sense out of the infinite variety of urban images painted on once-blank walls. Seventy-five categories of images were devised. Here are just a few:

1. Types of people depicted by occupation (several thousand subcategories, taken from the U.S. Department of Labor's job title dictionary).

2. Types of people depicted by race (25 subcategories, taken from the 1990 U.S. census).
3. Types of technology depicted by energy source (17 subcategories, including feet and hands, electronic, and appropriate).
4. Types of ideas expressed by symbols (10 subcategories, including religious, political, and economic).

After constructing this typology of urban images painted during muralmania, the social scientists looked at data about the muralists themselves. Then, as is their bent, they constructed numerous hypotheses. Here's one about differential perceptions of urban life: Big-city radicals tend to paint public buildings, while small-town conservatives tend to paint private homes and small businesses. During a coffee, tea, or yoghurt break, the urbanists sat around and waxed poetic. "Isn't it amazing," said one, "that each city speaks with a distinctive voice. Take Los Angeles and San Francisco, for example. Their murals have very different images. Concerning suburbanites' images, they are very diverse. Frankly, I have never felt comfortable in the L.A. region."

A colleague chided, "Really, you are so Bostonian! I bet you feel right at home in San Francisco. After all, it's an eastern look-alike. Its personality was created by enterprising Easterners bitten by the gold bug and out to strike it rich. It just doesn't feel like L.A., that space-age autopia, that western surfurbia."

"Good grief," moaned an older urban theorist. "Your discussion of San Francisco and Los Angeles is disturbing. All my scholarly life, I've been searching for the fundamental forces that govern modern urban life. I have tried to discover the structures and institutions that underlie modern cities everywhere. Now you remind me of the vast differences between two cities, both located in postindustrial society. Is there no hope of constructing a theory that can explain urban life and behavior in Los Angeles, San Francisco, Boston, Moscow, Beijing, and Keokuk, Iowa?"

Others chimed in. One said, "An international team of hundreds of scientists discovered the top quark some time ago. [The quark is the last of 12 subatomic building blocks now thought to constitute the material world.] This finding is central to understanding the nature of time, matter, and the universe. But for us to search for the fundamental components of urban life—city quarks—seems less fruitful. In my view, no one element can possibly explain how all cities work at any historical point in time. Neither can any one theory."

Another added, "I agree. First off, what we label a 'city' is not a single beast. The name 'city' covers administrative capitals, commercial-trade centers, military garrisons, religious shrine settlements, and rather small trading posts. How can any single theory explain urban existence in these various kinds of cities? Clearly, being an urbanite in New York City and in Crescent City, California, is a qualitatively different experience. Furthermore, cities aren't single units. Take a big city like Chicago. It's got diverse neighborhoods. It's got urban villages and cosmopolitan corners. It's got bread makers in small shops and computer programmers in tall buildings. It's got folks like my grandparents, who came to the city from a Mississippi farm, and it's got my kids, who think that chocolate milk comes from chocolate-colored cows."

A political sociologist entered the discussion. "Yes, yes, Even so, some key concepts can help us to understand how cities work. These concepts concern underlying structures and institutions, whether they're experienced in people's heads or not. My candidates for key concepts include economic and social interdependence, specialization, and differentiation."

An anthropologist suggested that "population size and growth and population density could be added to the list. She noted that theorists since the ancient Greeks have pointed to the importance of population size and density for human relations. "Now," she commented, "some anthropologists claim that there are 'magic numbers' that influence, even determine, human behavior. Some even claim they have the exact number. For instance, the magic number for hunter–gatherer bands is 25; over that, people risk conflict and fighting. In early villages, the magic number is 100; over that, villagers tend to split into two villages. And so on."

"Hmm," a skeptic wondered aloud. "This magic number business is a bit too deterministic for my taste." "Well," said the anthropologist, "I can show you evidence from 102 societies—including baboons and Bushmen—where the numbers work." The skeptic

responded, "You can show me all the evidence you want. My intuition tells me it's nonsense."

The discussion heated up. At this point, one urbanist tried to lower the temperature level: "Colleagues, let us give our imagination free play. How might you explain how cities work to a person who had never seen or lived in one—say, an Aché tribesperson in Venezuela today or the proverbial person on Mars?"

The first scholar answered, "I would use the analogy of the human body. Each organ of the body performs a particular function. The heart, for instance, pumps the blood through the human system, and the brain coordinates motor activity. Each organ is useless on its own. Organs function together in harmony, and together they form a living, organic system. This living system can't be described merely by talking about each separate organ because the body is more than the sum of its parts. It is the same with cities. The lifeblood of cities—goods, services, ideas—is circulated throughout the metropolitan system by networks of transport and communication. Managers and administrators, like the human brain, coordinate human activity. And just like the human body, the city is more than the sum of its parts. In addition, just as the body grows and becomes differentiated into specific organs and systems, cities grow more complex and become differentiated internally."

The second scholar responded, "Your analogy is elegant and easy to understand. That is why it is so seductive. Yet, it doesn't convey the possibilities for randomness, change and conflict. Someone once said that cities are places where unexpected things happen. Your metropolitan system-as-human-body metaphor neglects this sense of spontaneity. Also, human bodies have boundaries that everyone can see. Cities don't. Where, for instance, do the boundaries of New York City begin and end? On a map, the political boundaries are clear. But the eyes and ears of the Big Apple stretch across the globe. In addition, the whole idea of a metropolitan system may be passé in postsuburban America. No, your metaphor is misleading. The metaphor of the city as a machine—with meshing gears and parts all working in harmony—suffers from similar shortcomings, in my opinion."

The third scholar answered, "Let me offer another metaphor from the world of biology. This is only fair, since Charles Darwin took his idea of the survival of the fittest from Herbert Spencer, a sociologist (who, incidentally, gave us the metaphor of society as a human body). I think the city is most like a single cell. Just as it is in the nature of cells in the body to pool their resources and to fuse when possible, I think it is in the nature of urban life for people to come together and join with each other in common activity whenever possible."

"Colleagues," a fourth interjected, "I prefer to return to our empirical evidence for our metaphor. Murals all over show the city to be a swirl of nonagricultural activities. So I offer this image: the city as collage."

Another urbanist spoke up: "This discussion reminds me of elephant stories. One person looks at the city and sees bodies and systems. Another sees single cells trying to fuse together. Still another sees a collage or a mosaic. Similarly, one searches for underlying structures and institutions. Another focuses on subjective meanings of city life. Still another seeks fundamental elements of city life everywhere. And some stick to the available evidence, while others depend on intuition. Each approach has its merits—and limits. The trouble is, they don't seem to lend themselves to synthesis. So, what is to be done?"

"No doubt some of us will continue to dissect small pieces of the urban scene," answered a plumber-turned-theoretician. She continues, "Some will focus on substantive issues—urban transport, terrorism, pollution, and so on. Some will explore particular parts of urban culture. Others will try to make connections between the small pieces and theoretical issues. Still others will try to merge theory and practice, applying their knowledge to improve the quality of urban life. Whatever we do, I hope we remember former high-level civil servant John Gardner's admonition: 'We must have respect for both our plumbers and our philosophers, or neither our pipes nor our theories will hold water.'"

Hopefully, all of us will continue the long search for knowledge by sharing our evidence and insights and by asking better questions. That is why I cannot say "The End." That is why I say instead, "To Be Continued..."

BRIEF BIOGRAPHIES

Any list of notables is bound to dissatisfy some and to offend or outrage others. This relatively short list reflects my judgment of persons whose ideas, research, and/or actions have significantly contributed to urban theory or practice, either directly or indirectly. Thus, I include Max Weber, Emile Durkheim, Karl Marx, and other macro-level social theorists because their conceptual frameworks have had an important impact on urban studies. Others, including Robert Moses and Frederick Law Olmsted, are known primarily as doers rather than thinkers, and their doings influenced the shape of modern urban America. Still others, such as the late Milton Friedman and John Kenneth Galbraith, are included because they represent points of view to be reckoned with.

Who is systematically underrepresented or excluded from this list? There are few behind-the-scenes urban policymakers. Were there more space, I would have liked to include Abraham Levitt and sons of Levittown, David Rockefeller of the Chase Manhattan Bank, and others whose decisions (e.g., suburban development, redlining of urban areas) have had enormous impact on U.S cities, suburbs, and postsuburban areas. I would have liked to include an entire section on city biographies, but that is a list in itself. Also, there are few poets, artists, or writers of the city; a more complete listing would include many people from the United States (e.g., Georgia O'Keefe, Woody Allen, Tom Wolfe, John Ashbery, Walt Whitman, Saul Bellow, Thomas Wolfe, Finley Peter Dunne, Frank

Norris) and beyond. Thus, this list is necessarily incomplete. It is merely a list of some notable contributors to the study or practice of things urban.

Jane Addams (1860–1935) College-educated, well-traveled social reformer. Founder of Chicago's Hull House in 1889, first president of the Women's International League for Peace and Freedom, and cowinner of the Nobel Peace Prize for 1931, Jane Addams started at Hull House and moved into a wider political arena of social reform. She helped to promote labor legislation, set up juvenile courts, sponsored municipal government reform, and agitated for women's suffrage.

Edward C. Banfield (1916–1999) Neoconservative urbanist best known for his controversial book, *The Unheavenly City* (1968), which drew a storm of criticism from liberals and radicals for its gloomy view of human nature and government's ability to do much about urban problems. Earlier works include coauthorship of classic studies of city decision making: *Politics, Planning, and the Public Interest* (1955) and *City Politics* (1963). Political scientist Banfield was a Professor of Government and Urban Government at Harvard University.

Pierre Bourdieu (1930–2002) Not considered an urbanist. French sociologist and activist, his key concepts include "cultural capital" and "habitus." A lover of intellectual combat, he considered himself "to the left of the left." He fought against neoliberalism and for the rights of workers and undocumented immigrants.

Ernest W. Burgess (1886–1966) Formulator of the Burgess hypothesis. Burgess hypothesized that U.S. industrial cities are structured in concentric zones. Burgess was a principal figure in the University of Chicago's school of sociology and urban theory. *The City* (1925), coauthored with Robert E. Park and Roderick D. McKenzie, exerted a powerful influence on urban sociologists, geographers, economists, and other students of the city.

Daniel Burnham (1846–1912) Architect, city planner, and highly skilled propagandist for his own ideas, Burnham is best remembered for building according to a preestablished plan. Influenced by Baron Haussmann's plan and redo of Paris in the nineteenth century, he was the inspiration behind the Columbian Exposition Fairgrounds, called the White City, at the Chicago World's Fair of 1893. Later he devised the Chicago Plan of 1909, gaining business support for his notion of the City Beautiful. He has been called the predecessor of New York City's Robert Moses because of his obsession with highways and his policies, which led to the eviction of poor people in order to widen Chicago's thoroughfares. Burnham's vision is revealed in his quip: "Make no little plans. They have no magic to stir men's blood."

Manuel Castells (b. 1942) Spanish-born, French-trained, multidisciplinary urban theorist. Castells, who taught for many years at the University of California at Berkeley and at various universities throughout the world, is one of the leading contemporary analysts of the city. Influenced by Marx and twentieth-century French structural neo-Marxists, he attempts to link types of urban organization to forms of capitalism.

V. Gordon Childe (1892–1957) Australian–British archeologist whose thesis stressed the importance of environment (capable of producing an agricultural surplus), larger population, technology, and social structure (emergence of a governing elite) to the origin of cities in ancient Mesopotamia. He was Professor of Prehistoric Archeology at the University of Edinburgh.

Walter Christaller (1893–1969) The developer of central place theory, Christaller published a seminal book, *Central Places in Southern Germany* (1933), describing the size, spacing, and number of so-called central places in a region.

Robert Dahl (b. 1915) Author of the influential study of urban decision making *Who Governs?* (1961), which presents a pluralist view of community power structure. A prolific writer, Dahl, now professor emeritus of political science at Yale University, joined the Democratic Socialist Organizing Committee in the late 1970s.

Richard J. Daley (1902–1976) Chicago's late mayor (1955–1976) and boss of the Cook County Democratic Party machine, often considered to be the last surviving old-style city machine in U.S. politics. Daley was a second-generation Irish American and self-made man who never moved from his small neighborhood house or lost his working-class accent and malapropisms. He was undisputed master of ethnic politics in Chicago during his tenure as mayor. However his various policies are interpreted, observers agree that Daley had political clout.

Richard M. Daley (b. 1942) Voted the best mayor of the United States's largest five cities by *Time* magazine, "Son of Boss" (Richard J. Daley) has been elected Chicago's mayor six times as of this writing.

Mike Davis (b. 1946) Former truck driver and meat-cutter, Davis is a professor in the University of California system, a MacArthur (Genius) Fellowship winner, and urban theorist who is straightforwardly Marxist and almost always refreshingly contrarian. Born in southern California, he has written extensively about Los Angeles, including *City of Quartz* (1990). He is not known for being Pollyannaish. Some of his books focus on disasters and urban challenges, including *Planet of Slums* (2006).

Emile Durkheim (1858–1917) Eminent French sociologist who asked a key question: How do individuals make up a stable, cohesive society? In his first book, *The Division of Labor in Society* (1893), Durkheim addressed this question by examining two forms of social solidarity: mechanical and organic. He theorized that in modern (organically solid) societies, social cohesion results from, or is expressed by, social differentiation (division of labor).

Milton Friedman (1912–2006) Arguably one of the two most influential economic theorists of the twentieth century (the other being John Maynard Keynes). A public intellectual and the leading spokesperson for U.S. economic conservatives (and, later, libertarians) for decades. A pure market theorist, Friedman proposed market solutions to national and urban problems. His most famous quip: "There is no such thing as a free lunch." He taught at the University of Chicago before he joined the Hoover Institution at Stanford. Although he never held any government post, he and his free-market ideas influenced the economic policies of many countries, including the United States, England, and Chile.

John Kenneth Galbraith (1908–2006) A self-proclaimed "abiding liberal," Canadian-born Galbraith long served as a member of Harvard University's economics department. He produced numerous books, including *The New Industrial State* ([1967] 1971), and played political roles, including ambassador to India during the 1960s. (Ironically, his ideological opponent, Daniel Patrick Moynihan, followed him at the New Delhi Embassy several years later.)

Herbert Gans (b. 1927) Author of *The Urban Villagers* (1962), *The Levittowners* (1967), and many studies about ethnicity in the United States. Eminent sociologist and city planner, Gans disputes Wirth's notion that urbanism is a way of life.

Erving Goffman (1922–1982) Called "the Kafka of our time" for his vision of routine encounters, Canadian-born sociologist Goffman was known for his dramaturgical model of social interaction: People present themselves or perform in various masks, depending on the audience and the impression they wish to manage. To Goffman, social interaction in public and semipublic places is guided by unspoken rules (norms) that help maintain public order.

David Harvey (b. 1935) A leading and influential urban analyst, influenced by Marx's writings, concerned with the relationship of the built environment and the spread of industrial capitalism. He taught at Johns Hopkins for many years before becoming the Halford Mackinder Professor of Geography at Oxford University. Recently, he has been Distinguished Professor of Anthropology at the Graduate Center of the City University of New York.

Baron Georges-Eugène Haussmann (1809–1891) French public official and city planner who planned and oversaw bold changes in Paris's layout, including razing hundreds of dwellings, under Napoleon III in the nineteenth century. Even today, Paris reflects his aesthetic of radiating boulevards dotted with monuments and points of interests. The reasons he and Napoleon III undertook the remake are disputed (e.g., was it purely for beautification? And/or the improved health of the residents via better sewage and water facilities? And/ or easier crowd control?). One grand boulevard he created in Paris is named after him. His ideas were influential outside France. For one, Daniel Burnham in Chicago was a keen admirer.

Floyd Hunter (1912–1992) Author of *Community Power Structure: A Study of Decision Makers* ([1953] 1963), a classic statement of the elitist model of community power, and an update, *Atlanta's Policymakers Revisited* (1979).

Jane Jacobs (1916–2006) Popularizer of unconventional ideas about cities and city planning. As a journalist and later editor of *Architectural Forum*, Jacobs grew increasingly critical of planning that destroyed communities, separated land uses, and rebuilt sterile areas. Her best-selling book *The Death and Life of Great American Cities* (1961) presents an alternative view in which planners should protect neighborhoods, mix land uses, and pay attention to design details that matter to people. In *The Economy of Cities* (1970), she argued that the first cities led to agriculture, not vice versa.

Henri Lefebvre (1901–1991) French seminal thinker whose original work is wide-ranging, from urbanism and architecture to the production of space and dialectical logic. His writings influenced a generation of younger urbanists who brought space back into social theory.

Elliot Liebow (1925–1994) Author of the classic *Tally's Corner* (1967), a study of black street-corner men in Washington, D.C. Anthropologist Liebow hung out with the unskilled urban men and, based on his firsthand observation, drew a portrait of their social and work situations, linking their way of life to macro-level social forces. In 1993, he published a study of homeless women in suburban Washington, D.C. Between books, he worked as a U.S. government bureaucrat.

Kevin Lynch (1918–1984) A key figure in urban design, Lynch invented a vocabulary that still dominates urban design. He was concerned with making cities more imageable so that their residents find them understandable and reassuring. After an apprenticeship with Frank Lloyd Wright, Lynch turned to teaching. His best-known work is *The Image of the City* (1960). He taught in the Department of Urban Studies and Planning at the Massachusetts Institute of Technology.

Malcolm X (1925–1965) Second in command of the Black Muslim movement in the United States during the early 1960s, he left the party after a policy disagreement with party leader Elijah Muhammad. He was believed to have been forming a new movement when he was assassinated in 1965.

Karl Marx (1818–1883) Revered by many, feared by some, and loathed by others, Marx's ideas are inescapable. Although his ideas have not been widely popular in the United States, he was known to Americans in the nineteenth century through his articles for the *New York Daily Tribune* between 1852 and 1862. Further, Marxian concepts, particularly alienation, have become part of the working vocabulary of social scientists, whatever their attitude toward Marx's work. Marx's major writings include the early *The German Ideology* (1846) and the three-volume, magisterial *Capital* (1867, 1885, 1894).

Robert Moses (1888–1981) Master builder of U.S. cities, Moses used his base as head of public authorities in New York City to establish a new kind of political machine, lubricated by money but rooted in bureaucratic power instead of ward-level politics. He mobilized banks, contractors, labor unions, the mass media, insurance companies, and churches to shape the physical structure of New York City and social policies. He has been called the single most powerful man in New York City and the chief influence on U.S. cities in the twentieth century.

Daniel Patrick Moynihan (1927–2003) Democratic senator from New York and spokesperson for neoconservatives, Moynihan served as U.S. ambassador to India, urbanist at the Joint Center for Urban Studies at MIT and Harvard University, Nixon's policy advisor, and U.S. ambassador to the United Nations. A prolific writer, Moynihan was the author or coauthor of numerous urban studies, including *Beyond the Melting Pot* (1963), a study of five ethnic groups in New York City. His longtime interest in ethnicity extended to the international scene; in his book *Pandaemonium* (1993), polymath Moynihan revealed the qualities for which he is known: forthrightness, wit, and phrase-making ability ("benign neglect" was his term—his policy advice to the Nixon administration for certain social issues).

Lewis Mumford (1895–1990) A charter member of the Regional Planning Association of America in 1923 (whose studies influenced the eventual building of Radburn, New Jersey, and other greenbelt towns). With the publication of *The Culture of Cities* (1938), Mumford gained a worldwide reputation. In the course of writing more than 20 books, he came to represent a particular view of urban life and urban "solutions." In his own words, "the city should be an organ of love; and the best economy of cities is the care and culture of men.... Otherwise the sterile gods of power, unrestrained by organic limits or human goals, will remake man in their own faceless image and bring human history to an end."

Frederick Law Olmsted (1822–1903) Pioneer U.S. landscape architect. Olmsted was the moving force behind many projects to make the natural environment accessible to urbanites, including Central Park in New York City, before the era of Boss Tweed. Olmsted left his mark on countless U.S. parks, waterfronts, and civic areas.

Robert E. Park (1864–1944) Member of the Chicago school of sociology and collaborator with Ernest W. Burgess in developing the ecological perspective on urban phenomena, Park was a news reporter and social reformer turned sociologist. He taught sociology at the University of Chicago from 1914 to 1933.

Pericles (ca. 490–429 BCE) Led citizens of the Athenian polis to overthrow a ruling oligarchy in about 463 BCE. Under his democratic leadership, Greek culture flourished, producing what is often called the Golden Age of Pericles. His most famous speech, the "Funeral Oration," was given on the occasion of a funeral for soldiers who had died in the war between Athens and Sparta.

Henri Pirenne (1862–1935) Belgian economic historian who advanced a thesis tracing medieval European cities to the revival of commerce in the twelfth century.

George Washington Plunkitt (1842–1924) A crackerbarrel philosopher of machine politics. A lifelong Tammany Hall politician in New York City from the days of Boss Tweed until his death, Plunkitt gave a classic description and defense of the city machine, including "honest graft."

Carl Sandburg (1878–1967) Born in Galesburg, Illinois, to Swedish immigrants, Sandburg was a poet, Lincoln scholar, humanitarian, and newspaper writer. *The People, Yes* (1936) is often considered to be his epic. Sandburg's bold images of industrial cities are double-edged, noting both the promise and the problems they portend. But in general, he celebrated urban industrial society and the countless Americans who created it.

Adam Smith (1723–1790) Known primarily for *An Inquiry into the Nature and Causes of the Wealth of Nations* (1776), considered the first comprehensive system of political economy. A professor at the University of Glasgow, he used the concept of the invisible hand, whereby the individual seeks personal gain and thus promotes the public interest. Smith viewed the world as a well-ordered, harmonious mechanism. His ideas lie at the base of laissez-faire economics.

Robert Sommer (b. 1929) He observes how people actually use airports, classrooms, convalescent homes, and other spaces in order to provide guidance to architects and other design professionals. His study *Personal Space* (1969) is a seminal work on the way in which people relate to their immediate space. He has been a Distinguished Professor of Psychology emeritus at the University of California–Davis since 2003.

Lincoln Steffens (1866–1936) A muckraking journalist and antimachine crusader, Steffens authored a series of magazine articles in 1903 exposing *The Shame of the Cities*. He concluded that "the source and sustenance of bad government [are] not the bribe taker, but the bribe giver, the man we are so proud of, our successful businessman." Later in life, Steffens studied, wrote, and lectured in defense of the Russian Revolution. His autobiography is a notable literary contribution.

W. I. Thomas (1863–1947) Contributed the concept of "the definition of the situation" to social psychology. His best-known book (with Florian Znaniecki), *The Polish Peasant in Europe and America* (1918), details the connections between the individual's definition of the situation and his or her family and community background. For Thomas, the interrelationship of individual personality and social order was a key concern.

Ferdinand Tönnies (1855–1936) German sociologist who identified two contrasting types of society and mentality: *Gemeinschaft* (community) and *Gesellschaft* (society). Tönnies, like Marx, traced social development as an evolutionary transition from primitive communism and village–town individualism to capitalistic urban individualism and, in the future, to state socialism. Tönnies's concepts, although not original, have influenced generations of scholars.

William Marcy Tweed (1823–1878) Boss of the New York City Tweed Ring from 1866 to 1871 and the symbol of a corrupt machine politician. Originally a chair maker and voluntary fireman, Tweed became an alderman (1852–1853), sat in Congress (1853–1855), and was repeatedly elected to the New York State Senate. In 1870, he was made commissioner of public works for the city. But his real power came informally as the Grand Sachem (head) of Tammany Hall, New York City's Democratic Party machine. He was criminally and civilly indicted for various frauds and eventually jailed. After a brief escape to Cuba and Spain (1875–1876), he was recaptured and died in a New York jail while suits were pending against him for recovery of $6 million.

Edward L. Ullman (1912–1976) Together with Chauncy Harris (1914–2003), Ullman developed the multiple nuclei model of internal city structure, which holds that city space is organized around a number of independent centers of commercial, manufacturing, and residential activity. He taught geography at various universities.

Samuel Bass Warner, Jr. (b. 1928) U.S. urban historian whose particular fascination is the interplay between social history and physical space. Among his books are *The Private City* (1968), which examines Philadelphia's society and physical form in the late eighteenth, mid-nineteenth, and early twentieth centuries, and *Streetcar Suburbs* (1962), which describes the social and physical dynamics of Boston's preautomobile suburbs at the end of the nineteenth century.

W. Lloyd Warner (1898–1970) With his research associates, U.S. social anthropologist Warner set the pattern of research for future generations with the *Yankee City* series, studies of urban social stratification. Warner developed two techniques for studying what he called social class, but he actually measured social status, not class. In general, Warner found that U.S. cities have a "system of open classes" (i.e., status groups).

Max Weber (1864–1920) A classic figure in the European liberal tradition whose sociological work ranged from the theory of bureaucracy and authority to the methodology of social science. His works *The Protestant Ethic and the Spirit of Capitalism* (1904–1905), *The City* (1921), and "Status, Class, Party" (1922) continue to stimulate debate even today. Rationalization of modern life was a theme in Weber's political sociology. He envisioned the dawn of an age in which bureaucracy would be like an "iron cage," reducing the individual's role within an ever-expanding network of management and control.

William H. Whyte (1917–1999) A U.S. social scientist by avocation, not vocation. He observed social behavior in public urban spaces, particularly streets. He advised bottom–up planning, and his views influenced city planners. He was also the author of *The Organization Man* (1956), an influential study of the ethics, ideology, and lifestyle of the "new middle class" that ran big business and public organizations. In the section on the organization man at home in the suburbs, Whyte detailed his fear that the norms of the suburb, like those of the corporation, violate the spirit of individualism.

Louis Wirth (1897–1952) Member of the Chicago school of sociology and disciple of Robert E. Park. He is best remembered for his classic essay, "Urbanism as a Way of Life" (1938), in which he argues that large size, heterogeneity, and high density in the city lead to a particularly urban way of life.

INDEX

2